The Sourcebook of Local Court and County Record Retrievers

Third Edition

The Definitive Guide to Searching for Public Record
Information at the State Level

Public Record Research Library

©1997 By BRB Publications, Inc.
4653 South Lakeshore Drive, Suite 3
Tempe, AZ 85282
(800) 929-3811
www.brbpub.com

Public Record Research Library

The Sourcebook of Local Court and County Record Retrievers

The National Guide to Information Retrievers who Search Indexes and obtain Documents from Federal, State and Local Courts, and from County Agencies

©1997 By BRB Publications, Inc.
4653 South Lakeshore Drive, Suite 3
Tempe, AZ 85282
(800) 929-3811

ISBN 1-879792-37-0

Edited by Michael L. Sankey & Carl R. Ernst.   Cover Design by Robin Fox & Associates

Cataloging-in-Publication Data

025.5	**Ernst, Carl R., 1942 Mar 19-**
ERN	The sourcebook of local court and county record retrievers : the national guide to information retrievers who pull files and documents from US, state and local courts, and from county agencies / Carl R. Ernst, editor-in-chief : Michael L. Sankey, publisher. - 1997 ed. Tempe, Ariz : BRB Publications, Inc., ©1997.

      560 p. ; 8.5 x 11 in.   (the Public record research library)
includes index.

      Summary: A County-by-vounty directory to researchers who visit and pull documents at courthouses and county recorder's offices.

      ISBN 1-879792-37-0

      1. Court records - Research - United States - Directories 2. Public records - Research - United States - Directories 3. Legal research - United States - Directories I. Sankey, Michael L. II. BRB Publications III . Title IV. Title: Local court and county record retrievers

    KF8700.A19S66 1997   025.5'24'02573-dc20

Provided in cooperation with Unique Books, Inc.

Acknowledgments

We wish to extend a special *thank you* and appreciation to—

All the Owners, Administrators and Personnel of the firms profiled herein.

We enjoyed talking to all of you and learning about your businesses and your approaches to the public record industry. This is the third time around for many of you—we have seen your businesses grow. For those 300+ retrievers profiled for the first time, we hope the coming year is successful. The accuracy of this edition is a direct reflection of all of you having the interest and taking the time to help us assemble the leading publication of its kind for your industry. Our sincere thanks, to you, from all of us at BRB Publications, Inc.

Dave Johnson, Roshelle McMullen, Dan Smith, Annette Talley, Carl R. Ernst, and Michael L. Sankey
January 2, 1997

Table of Contents

Before You Start...

All of the information contained in this *Sourcebook* is based upon the responses to surveys conducted by our staff. The geographic coverage and profile information listed for each retriever is based upon their own responses to our survey. We have tried to reflect these responses accurately, but we are not responsible for the answers.

The retriever entries in **Section One-County Index** are based solely on regular, physical, hands-on retrieval of records at the county court house or recorder's office. This retrieval is performed by either:

- The individual listed; or

- People working exclusively for the retriever as employees (not as independent contractors or correspondents who may also work for other search firms).

We do recognize the importance of independent contractors and correspondents. Many of the retrievers listed in this book utilize such people. This is duly noted in **Section Two-Retriever Profiles**.

The Code of Professional Conduct, as committed to by the more than 400 members of the Public Record Retriever Network, is printed on page xvii. This code does not apply to the other 1,962 retrievers in this Sourcebook . However, we hope they all do (or will) pattern their business practices after these guidelines. Also, please note the Retriever Satisfaction Survey included as a separate sheet with you book. We would like to hear from you concerning your experiences with public record retrievers.

Finally, any company or individual wishing to appear in future editions of *The Sourcebook of Local Court and County Record Retrievers* is encouraged to obtain a questionnaire by contacting BRB Publications:

4653 South Lakeshore Drive, Suite 3
Tempe, AZ 85282
800-929-3811
fax: 800-929-3810

Introduction-

Obtaining Public Record Data

Acquiring Public Record Information

There are two ways to obtain a piece of information- whether the information is public record or not:
1. Look it up yourself, or
2. Have someone else look it up for you.

In the world of public records, you may be able to look it up (or "do the search") yourself under two circumstances:
1. The information is available on-line so you can dial it up, or
2. The information is available in your own geographic area.

If you wish to retrieve the information on-line, you need to be comfortable with the on-line search logic and/or with the type of information you seek, especially before trying to obtain it yourself. If the information is local to you, you need to understand how the office and its records are organized. If you are not able to look it up yourself, to whom do you go?

Two Categories of Public Record Professionals
We distinguish Public Record Retrievers from Public Record Providers as follows:
- **Providers-** Companies which furnish search and retrieval services through a network of sources, including their own employees, correspondents and on-line databases.
- **Retrievers-** Companies and individuals which directly access sources (repositories) of information.

In other words, a Retriever or his/her personnel goes directly to the agency to look up the information, just like you might have done yourself. On the following page you will find **Chart I- Provider or Retriever**. This chart will help you determine whether you need to use a Retriever or Provider.

Another Difference Between Retrievers and Providers
A practical distinction of importance to our readers is that a Retriever may be relied upon for strong knowledge in a local area, whereas a Provider has a breadth of knowledge and experience in a wider geographic range.

Many Do Both
Remember that many companies act as both Retriever and Providers. They retrieve records in the areas surrounding their offices and use correspondents for other areas and they may access on-line systems, locally and nationally. Also many Providers, like many Retrievers, are specialists in a specific type of public record, such as court records or UCC records. For more information regarding companies that provide on-line search and access to proprietary databases, see our publication, *The Sourcebook of Online Public Record Experts*.

Chart I—Provider or Retriever

Here is a handy chart to help you decide whether to use a Retriever or a Provider to perform your public record search project:

Date: _____ Project: _____		HIGH	MODERATE	LOW
1.	What is my level of expertise in the type of information I need?	HIGH	MODERATE	LOW
2.	Do I know where the information is located?	YES	NOT SURE	NO
3.	Do I know how to search for the information?	YES	NOT SURE	NO
4.	Can I obtain the information directly?	YES	DON'T KNOW	NO
5.	What is the age of the information that is accessible?	KNOW	DON'T KNOW	
6.	Does the information in its final form need interpretation?	YES	DON'T KNOW	NO
7.	What is my budget to obtain the information?	LOW	MEDIUM	HIGH

	↓	↓	↓
If you circled a preponderance of answers in one column, you should—	Call a Retriever	Consider a Provider	Call a Provider

If you decide a Provider is right for your project, our companion publication, *The Sourcebook of Public Record Experts*, may be helpful.

Introduction-

How to use this Sourcebook

The Sourcebook of Local Court and County Record Retrievers is divided into two sections:

Section One- County Index

Each of the 3,140 counties, parishes, independent cities and equivalent jurisdictions in the United States is listed here by state. Each heading indicated the types of records available in that jurisdiction. The Summary of Codes Table, illustrated on page xiii, explains the meaning of each heading abbreviation. For your convenience, this table is repeated at times throughout the Sourcebook.

Retrievers Shown County by County

Each retriever who accesses government offices in a jurisdiction is listed under that jurisdiction's heading. Entries have been added in this edition for Canada (page 3) and the Virgin Islands. The bullets beside each retriever indicate the specific types of information accessed. A profile of each retriever is found in Section Two. Public Record Retriever Network members (see page xvi) are designated with their logo like this:

Find a Retriever Fast

The telephone number along with the company name is given in the County Index. The 800 number is given if the retriever provided one.

Coverage Claimed

Entries in this publication are based upon the response of each retrieval firm. There are firms whose people access every county in a state either because of their resources or because of the nature of the geography, but in some cases it may be that the claim was possibly overstated. For example, if is not useful to our readers to have a small firm located in New York City listed as handling Erie County, 500 miles away.

Therefore, we try to hold the number of counties covered by any one firm to ten, unless the firm gives us compelling evidence that it covers more than ten counties within the turnaround time frame indicated in the company profile. However, some firms may still have overstated their territory.

All firms are listed under the counties they indicate they serve. You should never incur a "correspondent fee" from a retrieval firm for a listed county. However, mileage or some similar fee may be charged for remote counties. We would appreciate your reporting to us any instances where a retriever did use a correspondent or where excessive charges were incurred.

State Capitals

The county containing state offices within a state is designated by the word "Capital" after the county name.

How to use this Sourcebook *cont...*

Section Two- Retriever Profiles

Information about each of the 2,400+ Retrievers in this Sourcebook is included in this section. Retrievers are listed in alphabetical order. Individual names are alphabetized by last name first, unless they appear as part of a company name. If the word "The" appears to be a connected part of the company name, you will find that company in the "T" section.

Each Profile contains:

- Retriever name
- Address
- Telephone number, including 800 number if available
- Fax number, including 800 number if available
- Local retrieval area- a list of counties served
- Billing and payment terms
- Project turnaround times
- Other geographic areas serviced through correspondents
- Special expertise

Although we indicate the usual billing practices used by each of the retrieval companies, we continue not to include any information about actual fees because fees depend upon the type of project requested and are subject to change.

Branch offices of larger retriever firms are listed individually with the branch's corresponding retrieval area. Compare the county to the coverage area in the profiles to determine which branch serves that county. PRRN members are designated with the logo.

Note: Federal Court Searching

Federal courts are designated within those jurisdictions where courts that maintain records are located. The number of locations are-

- 243 US District Courts (DT), and
- 170 US Bankruptcy Courts (BK)

For more complete information about the federal court system, see our publication, *The Sourcebook of Federal Courts.*

SUMMARY OF CODES

COURT RECORDS

CODE	GOVERNMENT AGENCY	TYPE OF INFORMATION
DT	US District Court	Federal civil and criminal cases
BK	Bankruptcy Court	United States bankruptcy cases
CV	Civil Court	Municipal, county and state level civil cases
CR	Criminal Court	Municipal, county and state level criminal cases
PR	Probate Court	Wills and estate cases

COUNTY RECORDS

CODE	GOVERNMENT AGENCY	TYPE OF INFORMATION
UC	UCC Filing Office	Uniform Commercial Code and other personal property liens
RE	Recorder of Deeds	Real property transactions and liens
TX	Tax Assessor	Real property tax information
VS	Vital Records Office	Vital statistics—birth, death, marriage, divorce, etc.
VR	Voter Registration Office	Voter registration and campaign contribution information

- "CODE" designates the agency and type of information obtainable in each county from a retriever.
- The time zone for each county is abbreviated as follows: EST—Eastern Standard Time; CST—Central; MST—Mountain; PST—Pacific; AK—Alaska; HT—Hawaii.
- ▥—This symbol designates a Public Record Retriever Network member.
- "(SOP)" after the retriever name designates **Service of Process**.
- Individual retrievers without a company name are listed in order of their last name.
- US District and Bankruptcy courts are indicated only in the counties where courts are located.

Introduction-

How to Choose a Competent Retriever

The four significant attributes of the kind of Retriever you want on your side are:

1. **Local Experience and Expertise**
   - Knows exactly where to go to obtain the information you need
   - Knows personally the people who work at the government agency
   - Knows exactly what the records look like and what the contents mean
2. **Searching Time Frame**
   - Knows just how long the project will take
   - Knows whether it is possible to expedite the project
   - Completes the project as promised
3. **Delivery of Document**
   - Can deliver the document when and where as required
   - Can guarantee the search will be legal
   - Knows and explains the possible problems involved in obtaining the information you need
4. **Cost**
   - Knows the basis for the costs (copy fee, cert fee, search fee, etc.) that will be incurred
   - Can estimate the total fee

When You Call

Chart II- Eleven Questions to Ask a Retriever, on the following page, is a hands-on guide to finding the right Retriever for your project or public record need. The chart illustrates the kinds of questions you want answered before committing your project to a Retriever. Retrievers who are experienced and who do the searches themselves, (as is frequently the case in court records and real estate searching), are often more complete and accurate than the jurisdiction itself would be. In fact, many jurisdictions will not perform a search and require the use of an outside retriever or researcher.

Other Research Tools

Having some knowledge about a jurisdiction's record keeping policies and retrieval procedures is always a plus when hiring a retriever. For example, if you know records are indexed by only defendant or are accessibly on a public access terminal, you can tell if the retriever really does know the nuances of a particular courthouse. For those who need to access county/court records frequently, we recommend the *Sourcebook of County Court Records* and the *Sourcebook of County Asset/Lien Records*. These publications profile in depth more than 10,000 physical locations of county level public records.

Chart II—ELEVEN QUESTIONS TO ASK A RETRIEVER

Once you know if you want to use a Retriever, use these questions, addressed to the Retriever, to determine if the Retriever you call is right for your project. The questions are also generally applicable to choosing a Provider.

Date: _____ Project: _____ Retriever: _____ Telephone: _____ Contact Name:			
1a.	What is your expertise in the type of information I need?	HIGH	MEDIUM	LOW
1b.	What is your expertise in dealing with the agency where the information is stored?	HIGH	MEDIUM	LOW
2a.	How frequently do you access the agency where the information I need is stored?	DAILY	WEEKLY	OTHER
2b.	How frequently do you access the specific information I need?	DAILY	WEEKLY	OTHER
3.	Are the original documents stored at this agency?	YES	NO	DON'T KNOW
4.	Do you access the information yourself or through a third party?	SELF		THIRD PARTY
5.	Who does the actual search for the information?	WE DO	AGENCY	
6.	How long before some results are known?	1-2 DAYS	LESS THAN A WEEK	OTHER
7.	In what form will I receive the information?	AS YOU WISH	VERBAL	DOCS ONLY
8.	Will you interpret the information for me?	YES	NO	
9.	Will my search be legal and remain confidential?	YES		DON'T KNOW
10.	What are all the costs I will (may) incur to obtain the information?	EXPLAINED	NOT FULLY EXPLAINED	DON'T KNOW
11.	Do you serve other clients who have needs like mine and may I talk to a few of them?	YES		NO
		↓	↓	↓
		Consider This Retriever	Consider Other Retrievers	Do Not Use This Retriever

If you circled a preponderance of answers in one column, you should—

The Public Record Retriever Network

Public Record Retriever Network (PRRN)

The purpose of PRRN, established in 1995, is to promote the establishment of standards in the public record retrieval industry so that you, our readers, can have more confidence in the results you obtain from using public record retrievers like those profiled in this publication. PRRN is directed by the principals of BRB Publications, Carl R. Ernst and Michael Sankey, who together have a total of 26 years experience in the field.

Code of Professional Conduct

Each member of PRRN commits to the Code of Professional Conduct shown on the next page. Each member receives a certificate that defines the ten guidelines that comprise the Code. Any retriever that you use, whether a member of PRRN or not, should follow these guidelines in order to perform public record retrieval to your satisfaction.

Listing in the County Index

PRRN members retrieve public records in 1,961 counties (62% of all counties in the US) in 50 states, including state capitals where they also search and file documents with the various state agencies that maintain public records. PRRN members are listed in the County Index under each county and are designated by the logo as follows:

 BRB Publications Inc.......800-929-3811

Retriever Satisfaction Survey

We are especially interested in knowing whether each member of PRRN is living up to the commitment represented by the Code of Professional Conduct. Therefore, we have included a separate survey form with this publication for you to communicate your experience, both positive and negative, with public record retrievers to us.

Negative comments will be held in confidence by us. Based on your input, we reserve the right to exclude any firms from this publication that particularly fail to maintain a standard of professional conduct acceptable to our readers.

 # Code of Professional Conduct

The Public Record Retriever Network (PRRN) Code consists of ten guidelines according to which each member of the Network conducts its business.

Competency Guidelines

The Competency Guidelines refer to each of the types of records a PRRN member is proficient in retrieving, as specified in *The Sourcebook of Local Court and County Record Retrievers.*

1. We know where each type of local public record is maintained.
2. We access these agencies regularly.
3. We understand the contents of the documents we retrieve.
4. We search records ourselves in those agencies that do not conduct searches for the public.
5. We maintain good relationships with agency personnel.

Client Service Guidelines

The Client Service Guidelines refer to the way in which each member of PRRN is expected to serve its clients.

1. We return calls promptly.
2. We complete projects as promised.
3. We explain our charges in advance.
4. We will expedite results, on request.
5. We will explain how agencies maintain their records, on request.

Section One

County Index

SUMMARY OF CODES

COURT RECORDS

CODE	GOVERNMENT AGENCY	TYPE OF INFORMATION
DT	US District Court	Federal civil and criminal cases
BK	Bankruptcy Court	United States bankruptcy cases
CV	Civil Court	Municipal, county and state level civil cases
CR	Criminal Court	Municipal, county and state level criminal cases
PR	Probate Court	Wills and estate cases

COUNTY RECORDS

CODE	GOVERNMENT AGENCY	TYPE OF INFORMATION
UC	UCC Filing Office	Uniform Commercial Code and other personal property liens
RE	Recorder of Deeds	Real property transactions and liens
TX	Tax Assessor	Real property tax information
VS	Vital Records Office	Vital statistics—birth, death, marriage, divorce, etc.
VR	Voter Registration Office	Voter registration and campaign contribution information

- "CODE" designates the agency and type of information obtainable in each county from a retriever.
- The time zone for each county is abbreviated as follows: EST—Eastern Standard Time; CST—Central; MST—Mountain; PST—Pacific; AK—Alaska; HT—Hawaii.
- ▥—This symbol designates a Public Record Retriever Network member.
- "(SOP)" after the retriever name designates Service of Process.
- Individual retrievers without a company name are listed in order of their last name.
- US District and Bankruptcy courts are indicated only in the counties where courts are located.

CANADA

	CV	CR	PR	CANADA	UC	RE	TX	VS	VR
	•	•	•	🏛 Idealogic (SOP) (Ontario) 800-265-0361	•	•	•	•	
	•	•	•	🏛 Mercury Service Inc (British Columbia) 604-228-9993	•	•			

ALABAMA

	CV	CR	PR	AUTAUGA (CST)	UC	RE	TX	VS	VR
			•	Advantage Title Co 334-244-9992	•	•	•		
	•	•		🏛 Alpha Research LLC (SOP) 205-755-7008			•		
			•	Autauga Abstract 334-361-0606	•	•	•		
	•	•	•	Fidelity Legal Investigation Inc (SOP) 205-988-8644	•	•	•	•	
	•	•	•	🏛 Hollingsworth Court Reporting Inc 504-769-3386	•	•	•	•	

	CV	CR	PR	BALDWIN (CST)	UC	RE	TX	VS	VR
	•	•	•	Aalpha Omega Investigations Inc (SOP) 904-433-7016	•	•	•	•	
	•	•		🏛 Alpha Research LLC (SOP) 205-755-7008			•		
	•	•	•	🏛 Brabston Legal Investigations Inc (SOP) 334-666-5666	•	•	•		
	•	•	•	🏛 Hollingsworth Court Reporting Inc 504-769-3386	•	•	•	•	

	CV	CR	PR	BARBOUR (CST)	UC	RE	TX	VS	VR
	•	•		🏛 Alpha Research LLC (SOP) 205-755-7008			•		
	•	•	•	🏛 Hollingsworth Court Reporting Inc 504-769-3386	•	•	•	•	
	•	•	•	McNeal Investigations (SOP) 601-826-5104	•	•	•	•	•
			•	🏛 V & A Research Etc 334-774-7092	•	•	•	•	

	CV	CR	PR	BIBB (CST)	UC	RE	TX	VS	VR
	•	•		🏛 Alpha Research LLC (SOP) 205-755-7008			•		
			•	Capstone Title Services 205-759-1105	•	•	•		
	•	•	•	🏛 Hollingsworth Court Reporting Inc 504-769-3386	•	•	•	•	

	CV	CR	PR	BLOUNT (CST)	UC	RE	TX	VS	VR
	•	•	•	🏛 Charles F Edgar & Associates (SOP) 205-539-7761	•	•	•		
				Facts Title Service 205-593-8308	•	•	•	•	
	•	•	•	🏛 Hollingsworth Court Reporting Inc 504-769-3386	•	•	•	•	

	CV	CR	PR	BULLOCK (CST)	UC	RE	TX	VS	VR
	•	•		🏛 Alpha Research LLC (SOP) 205-755-7008			•		
	•	•	•	🏛 Hollingsworth Court Reporting Inc 504-769-3386	•	•	•	•	
	•	•	•	McNeal Investigations (SOP) 601-826-5104	•	•	•	•	•

	CV	CR	PR	BUTLER (CST)	UC	RE	TX	VS	VR
	•	•	•	🏛 Hollingsworth Court Reporting Inc 504-769-3386	•	•	•	•	
	•	•	•	McNeal Investigations (SOP) 601-826-5104	•	•	•	•	•
	•		•	🏛 Morris, Melissa F 334-222-1986	•	•	•		

BK	CV	CR	PR	CALHOUN (CST)	UC	RE	TX	VS	VR
•		•		🏛 ADM & Associates Inc 800-242-5999					
•	•	•		🏛 Alpha Research LLC (SOP) 205-755-7008			•		
•	•	•	•	🏛 Charles F Edgar & Associates (SOP) 205-539-7761	•	•	•		
•	•	•		ESP Technology Inc (SOP) 800-942-8801	•	•	•	•	•
				Facts Title Service 205-593-8308	•	•	•	•	
•	•	•	•	🏛 Hollingsworth Court Reporting Inc 504-769-3386	•	•	•	•	

CHAMBERS (CST)

CV	CR	PR	Listing	Phone	UC	RE	TX	VS	VR
•	•	•	🏛 Hollingsworth Court Reporting Inc	504-769-3386	•	•	•	•	

CHEROKEE (CST)

CV	CR	PR	Listing	Phone	UC	RE	TX	VS	VR
•	•	•	🏛 Charles F Edgar & Associates (SOP)	205-539-7761	•	•	•		
			Facts Title Service	205-593-8308	•	•	•	•	
•	•	•	🏛 Hollingsworth Court Reporting Inc	504-769-3386	•	•	•	•	
•		•	Title Guaranty & Trust of Chattanooga	615-266-5751	•	•	•		

CHILTON (CST)

CV	CR	PR	Listing	Phone	UC	RE	TX	VS	VR
		•	Advantage Title Co	334-244-9992	•	•	•		
•	•		🏛 Alpha Research LLC (SOP)	205-755-7008			•		
•		•	🏛 Hollingsworth Court Reporting Inc	504-769-3386	•	•	•		

CHOCTAW (CST)

CV	CR	PR	Listing	Phone	UC	RE	TX	VS	VR
		•	Chambless, Linda	205-846-3697	•	•	•		
•	•	•	🏛 Hollingsworth Court Reporting Inc	504-769-3386	•	•	•	•	
•	•	•	McNeal Investigations (SOP)	601-826-5104	•	•	•	•	•

CLARKE (CST)

CV	CR	PR	Listing	Phone	UC	RE	TX	VS	VR
•	•	•	🏛 Brabston Legal Investigations Inc (SOP)	334-666-5666	•	•	•		
		•	Chambless, Linda	205-846-3697	•	•	•		
•	•	•	🏛 Hollingsworth Court Reporting Inc	504-769-3386	•	•	•	•	
•	•	•	McNeal Investigations (SOP)	601-826-5104	•	•	•	•	•

CLAY (CST)

CV	CR	PR	Listing	Phone	UC	RE	TX	VS	VR
•	•	•	🏛 Hollingsworth Court Reporting Inc	504-769-3386	•	•	•	•	

CLEBURNE (CST)

CV	CR	PR	Listing	Phone	UC	RE	TX	VS	VR
•	•	•	🏛 Hollingsworth Court Reporting Inc	504-769-3386	•	•	•	•	

COFFEE (CST)

CV	CR	PR	Listing	Phone	UC	RE	TX	VS	VR
•	•	•	🏛 Hollingsworth Court Reporting Inc	504-769-3386	•	•	•	•	
•	•	•	McNeal Investigations (SOP)	601-826-5104	•	•	•	•	•
		•	🏛 V & A Research Etc	334-774-7092	•	•	•	•	

COLBERT (CST)

CV	CR	PR	Listing	Phone	UC	RE	TX	VS	VR
•		•	🏛 Blackwell Land & Title Research	205-533-2439	•	•	•		
•	•	•	🏛 Charles F Edgar & Associates (SOP)	205-539-7761	•	•	•		
•	•	•	🏛 Hollingsworth Court Reporting Inc	504-769-3386	•	•	•	•	

CONECUH (CST)

CV	CR	PR	Listing	Phone	UC	RE	TX	VS	VR
•	•	•	🏛 Hollingsworth Court Reporting Inc	504-769-3386	•	•	•	•	
•	•	•	McNeal Investigations (SOP)	601-826-5104	•	•	•	•	•
•		•	🏛 Morris, Melissa F	334-222-1986	•	•	•		
		•	Presley, Deloris	334-867-2968	•	•	•		

COOSA (CST)

CV	CR	PR	Listing	Phone	UC	RE	TX	VS	VR
•	•	•	🏛 Hollingsworth Court Reporting Inc	504-769-3386	•	•	•	•	

COVINGTON (CST)

CV	CR	PR	Listing	Phone	UC	RE	TX	VS	VR
•	•	•	🏛 Hollingsworth Court Reporting Inc	504-769-3386	•	•	•	•	
•	•	•	McNeal Investigations (SOP)	601-826-5104	•	•	•	•	•
•		•	🏛 Morris, Melissa F	334-222-1986	•	•	•		
		•	Presley, Deloris	334-867-2968	•	•	•		

CRENSHAW (CST)

CV	CR	PR	Listing	Phone	UC	RE	TX	VS	VR
•	•	•	🏛 Hollingsworth Court Reporting Inc	504-769-3386	•	•	•	•	
•	•	•	McNeal Investigations (SOP)	601-826-5104	•	•	•	•	•
•	•	•	🏛 Morris, Melissa F	334-222-1986	•	•	•	•	

CULLMAN (CST)

CV	CR	PR	Listing	Phone	UC	RE	TX	VS	VR
•		•	🏛 Blackwell Land & Title Research	205-533-2439	•	•	•		

					UC	RE	TX	VS	VR
•	•	•	🏛 Charles F Edgar & Associates (SOP) 205-539-7761		•	•	•		
			Facts Title Service 205-593-8308		•	•	•	•	
•	•	•	Fidelity Legal Investigation Inc (SOP) 205-988-8644		•	•	•	•	
•	•	•	🏛 Hollingsworth Court Reporting Inc 504-769-3386		•	•	•	•	

CV	CR	PR	DALE (CST)	UC	RE	TX	VS	VR
•	•	•	🏛 Hollingsworth Court Reporting Inc 504-769-3386	•	•	•	•	
•	•	•	McNeal Investigations (SOP) 601-826-5104	•	•	•	•	•
		•	🏛 V & A Research Etc 334-774-7092	•	•	•	•	

CV	CR	PR	DALLAS (CST)	UC	RE	TX	VS	VR
		•	Capstone Title Services 205-759-1105	•	•	•		
•	•	•	🏛 Hollingsworth Court Reporting Inc 504-769-3386	•	•	•	•	
•	•	•	McNeal Investigations (SOP) 601-826-5104	•	•	•	•	•

CV	CR	PR	DE KALB (CST)	UC	RE	TX	VS	VR
•	•	•	B & B Reporting Inc (SOP) 205-574-2524	•	•	•	•	
•		•	🏛 Blackwell Land & Title Research 205-533-2439	•	•	•		
•	•	•	🏛 Charles F Edgar & Associates (SOP) 205-539-7761	•	•	•		
		•	Facts Title Service 205-593-8308	•	•	•	•	
•	•	•	🏛 Hollingsworth Court Reporting Inc 504-769-3386	•	•	•	•	
•		•	Title Guaranty & Trust of Chattanooga 615-266-5751	•	•	•		

CV	CR	PR	ELMORE (CST)	UC	RE	TX	VS	VR
		•	Advantage Title Co 334-244-9992	•	•	•		
		•	Autauga Abstract 334-361-0606	•	•	•		
•	•	•	🏛 Hollingsworth Court Reporting Inc 504-769-3386	•	•	•	•	

CV	CR	PR	ESCAMBIA (CST)	UC	RE	TX	VS	VR
•	•	•	🏛 Hollingsworth Court Reporting Inc 504-769-3386	•	•	•	•	
•	•	•	McNeal Investigations (SOP) 601-826-5104	•	•	•	•	•
•		•	🏛 Morris, Melissa F 334-222-1986	•	•	•		
		•	Presley, Deloris 334-867-2968	•	•	•		

CV	CR	PR	ETOWAH (CST)	UC	RE	TX	VS	VR
	•		🏛 ADM & Associates Inc 800-242-5999					
•	•		🏛 Alpha Research LLC (SOP) 205-755-7008			•		
•		•	🏛 Blackwell Land & Title Research 205-533-2439	•	•	•		
•	•	•	🏛 Charles F Edgar & Associates (SOP) 205-539-7761	•	•	•		
			Facts Title Service 205-593-8308	•	•	•	•	
•	•	•	🏛 Hollingsworth Court Reporting Inc 504-769-3386	•	•	•	•	

CV	CR	PR	FAYETTE (CST)	UC	RE	TX	VS	VR
		•	Capstone Title Services 205-759-1105	•	•	•		
•	•	•	🏛 Hollingsworth Court Reporting Inc 504-769-3386	•	•	•	•	

CV	CR	PR	FRANKLIN (CST)	UC	RE	TX	VS	VR
•	•	•	🏛 Charles F Edgar & Associates (SOP) 205-539-7761	•	•	•		
•	•	•	🏛 Hollingsworth Court Reporting Inc 504-769-3386	•	•	•	•	

CV	CR	PR	GENEVA (CST)	UC	RE	TX	VS	VR
•	•	•	🏛 Hollingsworth Court Reporting Inc 504-769-3386	•	•	•	•	
•	•	•	McNeal Investigations (SOP) 601-826-5104	•	•	•	•	•
		•	🏛 V & A Research Etc 334-774-7092	•	•	•		
		•	Willingham, Jeanette 334-898-7625	•	•	•		

CV	CR	PR	GREENE (CST)	UC	RE	TX	VS	VR
		•	Capstone Title Services 205-759-1105	•	•	•		
•	•	•	🏛 Hollingsworth Court Reporting Inc 504-769-3386	•	•	•	•	

CV	CR	PR	HALE (CST)	UC	RE	TX	VS	VR
		•	Capstone Title Services 205-759-1105	•	•	•		
•	•	•	🏛 Hollingsworth Court Reporting Inc 504-769-3386	•	•	•	•	

CV	CR	PR	HENRY (CST)		UC	RE	TX	VS	VR
•	•	•	🏛 Hollingsworth Court Reporting Inc 504-769-3386		•	•	•	•	
•	•	•	McNeal Investigations (SOP) 601-826-5104		•	•	•	•	•
		•	🏛 V & A Research Etc 334-774-7092		•	•	•	•	

CV	CR	PR	HOUSTON (CST)		UC	RE	TX	VS	VR
	•		🏛 ADM & Associates Inc 800-242-5999						
•	•		🏛 Alpha Research LLC (SOP) 205-755-7008				•		
•	•	•	🏛 Hollingsworth Court Reporting Inc 504-769-3386		•	•	•	•	
•	•	•	McNeal Investigations (SOP) 601-826-5104		•	•	•	•	•
•			Title Guaranty & Trust of Chattanooga 615-266-5751		•	•	•		
		•	🏛 V & A Research Etc 334-774-7092		•	•	•	•	

CV	CR	PR	JACKSON (CST)		UC	RE	TX	VS	VR
•	•	•	B & B Reporting Inc (SOP) 205-574-2524		•	•	•	•	
•		•	🏛 Blackwell Land & Title Research 205-533-2439		•	•	•		
•	•	•	🏛 Charles F Edgar & Associates (SOP) 205-539-7761		•	•	•		
			Facts Title Service 205-593-8308		•	•	•	•	
•	•	•	🏛 Hollingsworth Court Reporting Inc 504-769-3386		•	•	•	•	

DT	BK	CV	CR	PR	JEFFERSON (CST)		UC	RE	TX	VS	VR
•	•		•		🏛 ADM & Associates Inc 800-242-5999						
•	•	•	•		🏛 Alpha Research LLC (SOP) 205-755-7008			•			
•	•	•	•	•	Bankruptcy Services Inc 214-424-6500						
				•	🏛 Blakney, Betty 205-325-5112		•	•	•		•
•	•	•	•	•	🏛 Charles F Edgar & Associates (SOP) 205-539-7761		•	•	•		
•	•	•	•	•	Fidelity Legal Investigation Inc (SOP) 205-988-8644		•	•	•	•	
•	•	•	•	•	🏛 Hollingsworth Court Reporting Inc 504-769-3386		•	•	•	•	
•	•	•	•	•	🏛 Mid-South Legal Services (SOP) 205-326-0900		•	•	•	•	
•	•	•		•	Solons Legal Documents Svc Center 800-732-0175						

CV	CR	PR	LAMAR (CST)		UC	RE	TX	VS	VR
•	•	•	🏛 Hollingsworth Court Reporting Inc 504-769-3386		•	•	•	•	

DT	CV	CR	PR	LAUDERDALE (CST)		UC	RE	TX	VS	VR
•	•	•		🏛 Alpha Research LLC (SOP) 205-755-7008				•		
•	•		•	🏛 Blackwell Land & Title Research 205-533-2439		•	•	•		
•	•	•	•	🏛 Charles F Edgar & Associates (SOP) 205-539-7761		•	•	•		
•	•	•	•	🏛 Hollingsworth Court Reporting Inc 504-769-3386		•	•	•	•	

CV	CR	PR	LAWRENCE (CST)		UC	RE	TX	VS	VR
		•	🏛 Blackwell Land & Title Research 205-533-2439		•	•	•		
•	•	•	🏛 Charles F Edgar & Associates (SOP) 205-539-7761		•	•	•		
•	•	•	🏛 Hollingsworth Court Reporting Inc 504-769-3386		•	•	•	•	

CV	CR	PR	LEE (CST)		UC	RE	TX	VS	VR
	•		🏛 ADM & Associates Inc 800-242-5999						
•	•		🏛 Alpha Research LLC (SOP) 205-755-7008				•		
•	•	•	🏛 Attorney & Court Service of Georgia (SOP) 706-322-3554		•	•	•	•	•
•	•	•	🏛 Hollingsworth Court Reporting Inc 504-769-3386		•	•	•	•	

CV	CR	PR	LIMESTONE (CST)		UC	RE	TX	VS	VR
		•	🏛 Blackwell Land & Title Research 205-533-2439		•	•	•		
•	•	•	🏛 Charles F Edgar & Associates (SOP) 205-539-7761		•	•	•		
•	•	•	🏛 Hollingsworth Court Reporting Inc 504-769-3386		•	•	•	•	

CV	CR	PR	LOWNDES (CST)		UC	RE	TX	VS	VR
		•	Advantage Title Co 334-244-9992		•	•	•		
•	•	•	🏛 Hollingsworth Court Reporting Inc 504-769-3386		•	•	•	•	
•	•	•	McNeal Investigations (SOP) 601-826-5104		•	•	•	•	•

CV	CR	PR	MACON (CST)		UC	RE	TX	VS	VR
		•	Advantage Title Co 334-244-9992		•	•	•		

DT	BK	CV	CR	PR	Company	Phone	UC	RE	TX	VS	VR
		•	•	•	🏛 Hollingsworth Court Reporting Inc	504-769-3386	•	•	•	•	

MADISON (CST)

DT	CV	CR	PR	Company	Phone	UC	RE	TX	VS	VR
•		•		🏛 ADM & Associates Inc	800-242-5999					
•		•		🏛 Alpha Research LLC (SOP)	205-755-7008			•		
	•	•	•	B & B Reporting Inc (SOP)	205-574-2524	•	•	•	•	
•	•	•		🏛 Blackwell Land & Title Research	205-533-2439	•	•	•		
				Facts Title Service	205-593-8308	•	•	•	•	
•	•	•	•	🏛 Hollingsworth Court Reporting Inc	504-769-3386	•	•	•	•	

MARENGO (CST)

CV	CR	PR	Company	Phone	UC	RE	TX	VS	VR
•	•	•	🏛 Hollingsworth Court Reporting Inc	504-769-3386	•	•	•	•	
•	•	•	McNeal Investigations (SOP)	601-826-5104	•	•	•	•	•

MARION (CST)

CV	CR	PR	Company	Phone	UC	RE	TX	VS	VR
•	•	•	🏛 Charles F Edgar & Associates (SOP)	205-539-7761	•	•	•		
•	•	•	🏛 Hollingsworth Court Reporting Inc	504-769-3386	•	•	•	•	

MARSHALL (CST)

CV	CR	PR	Company	Phone	UC	RE	TX	VS	VR
•	•	•	B & B Reporting Inc (SOP)	205-574-2524	•	•	•	•	
•		•	🏛 Blackwell Land & Title Research	205-533-2439	•	•	•		
•	•	•	🏛 Charles F Edgar & Associates (SOP)	205-539-7761	•	•	•		
			Facts Title Service	205-593-8308	•	•	•	•	
•	•	•	🏛 Hollingsworth Court Reporting Inc	504-769-3386	•	•	•	•	

MOBILE (CST)

DT	BK	CV	CR	PR	Company	Phone	UC	RE	TX	VS	VR
•	•		•		🏛 ADM & Associates Inc	800-242-5999					
•	•	•	•		🏛 Alpha Research LLC (SOP)	205-755-7008			•		
•	•	•	•	•	🏛 Brabston Legal Investigations Inc (SOP)	334-666-5666	•	•	•		
•	•	•	•	•	🏛 Hollingsworth Court Reporting Inc	504-769-3386	•	•	•	•	
•	•	•	•	•	McNeal Investigations (SOP)	601-826-5104	•	•	•	•	•

MONROE (CST)

CV	CR	PR	Company	Phone	UC	RE	TX	VS	VR
		•	Chambless, Linda	205-846-3697	•	•	•		
•	•	•	🏛 Hollingsworth Court Reporting Inc	504-769-3386	•	•	•	•	
•	•	•	McNeal Investigations (SOP)	601-826-5104	•	•	•	•	•
		•	Presley, Deloris	334-867-2968	•	•	•		

MONTGOMERY (CAPITAL) (CST)

DT	BK	CV	CR	PR	Company	Phone	UC	RE	TX	VS	VR
•			•		🏛 ADM & Associates Inc	800-242-5999					
					Advantage Title Co	334-244-9992	•	•	•		
•	•	•	•		🏛 Alpha Research LLC (SOP)	205-755-7008			•		
•	•	•	•	•	🏛 Hollingsworth Court Reporting Inc	504-769-3386	•	•	•	•	
•	•	•	•	•	McNeal Investigations (SOP)	601-826-5104	•	•	•	•	•
•	•		•	•	Solons Legal Documents Svc Center	800-732-0175					

MORGAN (CST)

BK	CV	CR	PR	Company	Phone	UC	RE	TX	VS	VR
•	•		•	🏛 Blackwell Land & Title Research	205-533-2439	•	•	•		
•	•	•	•	🏛 Hollingsworth Court Reporting Inc	504-769-3386	•	•	•		

PERRY (CST)

CV	CR	PR	Company	Phone	UC	RE	TX	VS	VR
•	•	•	Barnes Jr, James M (SOP)	334-683-6060	•	•	•	•	
•	•	•	🏛 Hollingsworth Court Reporting Inc	504-769-3386	•	•	•	•	

PICKENS (CST)

CV	CR	PR	Company	Phone	UC	RE	TX	VS	VR
		•	Capstone Title Services	205-759-1105	•	•	•		
•	•	•	🏛 Hollingsworth Court Reporting Inc	504-769-3386	•	•	•	•	

PIKE (CST)

CV	CR	PR	Company	Phone	UC	RE	TX	VS	VR
•	•		🏛 Alpha Research LLC (SOP)	205-755-7008			•		
•	•	•	🏛 Hollingsworth Court Reporting Inc	504-769-3386	•	•	•	•	
•	•	•	McNeal Investigations (SOP)	601-826-5104	•	•	•	•	•
		•	🏛 V & A Research Etc	334-774-7092	•	•	•	•	

RANDOLPH (CST)

CV	CR	PR			UC	RE	TX	VS	VR
•	•	•	Hollingsworth Court Reporting Inc	504-769-3386	•	•	•	•	

RUSSELL (CST)

CV	CR	PR			UC	RE	TX	VS	VR
•	•		Alpha Research LLC (SOP)	205-755-7008			•		
•	•	•	Attorney & Court Service of Georgia (SOP)	706-322-3554	•	•	•	•	•
•	•	•	Hollingsworth Court Reporting Inc	504-769-3386	•	•	•	•	

SHELBY (CST)

CV	CR	PR			UC	RE	TX	VS	VR
•	•		Alpha Research LLC (SOP)	205-755-7008			•		
•	•	•	Fidelity Legal Investigation Inc (SOP)	205-988-8644	•	•	•	•	
•	•	•	Hollingsworth Court Reporting Inc	504-769-3386	•	•	•	•	
•	•	•	Mid-South Legal Services (SOP)	205-326-0900	•	•	•	•	

ST. CLAIR (CST)

CV	CR	PR			UC	RE	TX	VS	VR
•	•	•	Charles F Edgar & Associates (SOP)	205-539-7761	•	•	•		
			Facts Title Service	205-593-8308	•	•	•	•	
		•	Fidelity Legal Investigation Inc (SOP)	205-988-8644	•	•	•	•	
•	•	•	Hollingsworth Court Reporting Inc	504-769-3386	•	•	•	•	
•	•	•	Mid-South Legal Services (SOP)	205-326-0900	•	•	•	•	

SUMTER (CST)

CV	CR	PR			UC	RE	TX	VS	VR
•	•	•	Hollingsworth Court Reporting Inc	504-769-3386	•	•	•	•	

TALLADEGA (CST)

CV	CR	PR			UC	RE	TX	VS	VR
	•		ADM & Associates Inc	800-242-5999					
•	•		Alpha Research LLC (SOP)	205-755-7008			•		
•	•	•	Charles F Edgar & Associates (SOP)	205-539-7761	•	•	•		
			Facts Title Service	205-593-8308	•	•	•	•	
•	•	•	Hollingsworth Court Reporting Inc	504-769-3386	•	•	•	•	
•	•	•	Mid-South Legal Services (SOP)	205-326-0900	•	•	•	•	

TALLAPOOSA (CST)

CV	CR	PR			UC	RE	TX	VS	VR
•	•	•	Hollingsworth Court Reporting Inc	504-769-3386	•	•	•	•	

TUSCALOOSA (CST)

BK	CV	CR	PR			UC	RE	TX	VS	VR
•		•		ADM & Associates Inc	800-242-5999					
•	•	•		Alpha Research LLC (SOP)	205-755-7008			•		
			•	Capstone Title Services	205-759-1105	•	•	•		
•	•	•	•	Hollingsworth Court Reporting Inc	504-769-3386	•	•	•	•	
•	•	•	•	Mid-South Legal Services (SOP)	205-326-0900	•	•	•	•	
•		•	•	Solons Legal Documents Svc Center	800-732-0175					

WALKER (CST)

CV	CR	PR			UC	RE	TX	VS	VR
		•	Capstone Title Services	205-759-1105	•	•	•		
•	•	•	Charles F Edgar & Associates (SOP)	205-539-7761	•	•	•		
•	•	•	Hollingsworth Court Reporting Inc	504-769-3386	•	•	•	•	
•	•	•	Mid-South Legal Services (SOP)	205-326-0900	•	•	•	•	

WASHINGTON (CST)

CV	CR	PR			UC	RE	TX	VS	VR
		•	Chambless, Linda	205-846-3697	•	•	•		
•	•	•	Hollingsworth Court Reporting Inc	504-769-3386	•	•	•	•	
•	•	•	McNeal Investigations (SOP)	601-826-5104	•	•	•	•	•

WILCOX (CST)

CV	CR	PR			UC	RE	TX	VS	VR
•	•	•	Hollingsworth Court Reporting Inc	504-769-3386	•	•	•	•	
•	•	•	McNeal Investigations (SOP)	601-826-5104	•	•	•	•	•

WINSTON (CST)

CV	CR	PR			UC	RE	TX	VS	VR
•	•	•	Charles F Edgar & Associates (SOP)	205-539-7761	•	•	•		
•	•	•	Hollingsworth Court Reporting Inc	504-769-3386	•	•	•	•	

ALASKA

| | | CV | CR | PR | ALEUTIAN ISLANDS, EAST (AK) | UC | RE | TX | VS | VR |

See adjoining counties for retrievers ....

| | | CV | CR | PR | ALEUTIAN ISLANDS, WEST (AK) | UC | RE | TX | VS | VR |

See adjoining counties for retrievers ....

DT BK CV CR PR — ANCHORAGE BOROUGH (CAPITAL) (AK) — UC RE TX VS VR

DT	BK	CV	CR	PR	Retriever	UC	RE	TX	VS	VR
•	•	•	•	•	Alaska Litigation Services 907-258-7400	•	•	•	•	•
•	•	•	•	•	🏛 Alaska Records 800-808-5105	•	•	•	•	
•	•	•	•	•	Anchorage and Matsu Process Service (SOP) ... 907-258-3211	•	•	•	•	
•	•	•	•	•	CT Corporation System 800-874-8820	•	•	•	•	
•	•	•	•	•	Freelance Legal Secretary 907-278-8855	•	•	•		
•	•				🏛 Hogan Information Services 405-278-6954					
•	•		•	•	Informa Alaska Inc 907-563-4375	•	•	•		
•	•		•	•	Information Services of Anchorage 907-272-4688	•	•			•
•	•	•	•	•	Legal Search 907-258-4752	•	•	•		
•	•	•	•	•	Paladin Legal Services (SOP) 907-694-5222	•	•	•	•	

		CV	CR	PR	BARROW DISTRICT (AK)	UC	RE	TX	VS	VR
		•		•	Fairbanks Title Agency 907-456-6626	•	•	•		

| | | CV | CR | PR | BETHEL (AK) | UC | RE | TX | VS | VR |

See adjoining counties for retrievers ....

| | | CV | CR | PR | BRISTOL BAY BOROUGH (AK) | UC | RE | TX | VS | VR |

See adjoining counties for retrievers ....

		CV	CR	PR	CAPE NOME DISTRICT (AK)	UC	RE	TX	VS	VR
		•		•	Fairbanks Title Agency 907-456-6626	•	•	•		

DT CV CR PR — FAIRBANKS NORTH STAR BOROUGH (AK) — UC RE TX VS VR

DT	CV	CR	PR	Retriever	UC	RE	TX	VS	VR
•	•	•	•	Alaska Litigation Services 907-258-7400	•	•	•	•	•
•	•	•	•	🏛 Alaska Records 800-808-5105	•	•	•		•
•	•	•	•	Fairbanks Courier Service (SOP)................... 907-452-4292	•	•	•		
•	•	•	•	Fairbanks Process Service (SOP) 907-456-3023	•	•	•	•	
•	•		•	Fairbanks Title Agency 907-456-6626	•	•	•		
•	•	•	•	🏛 Fort Enterprises Process Srv & Inv (SOP) 907-488-7766	•	•	•		

		CV	CR	PR	FORT GIBBON DISTRICT (AK)	UC	RE	TX	VS	VR
		•		•	Fairbanks Title Agency 907-456-6626	•	•	•		

| | | CV | CR | PR | HAINES BOROUGH (AK) | UC | RE | TX | VS | VR |

See adjoining counties for retrievers ....

		CV	CR	PR	HOMER DISTRICT (AK)	UC	RE	TX	VS	VR
		•	•	•	Freelance Legal Secretary 907-278-8855	•	•	•	•	

DT CV CR PR — JUNEAU BOROUGH (AK) — UC RE TX VS VR

DT	CV	CR	PR	Retriever	UC	RE	TX	VS	VR
•	•	•	•	Alaska Litigation Services 907-258-7400	•	•	•	•	•
•	•	•	•	🏛 Alaska Records 800-808-5105	•	•	•		•
•	•	•	•	Complete Corporate Services of Alaska 907-790-4956	•	•	•		

		CV	CR	PR	KENAI PENINSULA BOROUGH (AK)	UC	RE	TX	VS	VR
		•	•	•	Alaska Litigation Services 907-258-7400	•	•	•	•	•
		•	•	•	🏛 Alaska Records 800-808-5105	•	•	•		•
		•	•	•	Freelance Legal Secretary 907-278-8855	•	•	•		

| DT | | CV | CR | PR | KETCHIKAN GATEWAY BOROUGH (AK) | UC | RE | TX | VS | VR |

See adjoining counties for retrievers ....

		CV	CR	PR	KODIAK ISLAND BOROUGH (AK)	UC	RE	TX	VS	VR
		•	•	•	Freelance Legal Secretary 907-278-8855	•	•	•	•	

		CV	CR	PR	KOTZEBUE DISTRICT (AK)	UC	RE	TX	VS	VR
		•		•	Fairbanks Title Agency 907-456-6626	•	•	•		

		CV	CR	PR	MANLEY HOT SPRINGS DISTRICT (AK)	UC	RE	TX	VS	VR
		•		•	Fairbanks Title Agency 907-456-6626	•	•	•		

		CV	CR	PR	MATANUSKA-SUSITNA BOROUGH (AK)	UC	RE	TX	VS	VR
		•	•	•	Alaska Litigation Services 907-258-7400	•	•	•	•	•
		•	•	•	Legal Search 907-258-4752	•	•	•	•	
		•	•	•	Paladin Legal Services (SOP) 907-694-5222	•	•	•	•	

		CV	CR	PR	MOUNT McKINLEY DISTRICT (AK)	UC	RE	TX	VS	VR
		•		•	Fairbanks Title Agency 907-456-6626	•	•	•		

		CV	CR	PR	NENANA DISTRICT (AK)	UC	RE	TX	VS	VR
		•		•	Fairbanks Title Agency 907-456-6626	•	•	•		

DT		CV	CR	PR	NOME (AK)	UC	RE	TX	VS	VR
					See adjoining counties for retrievers					

		CV	CR	PR	NORTH SLOPE BOROUGH (AK)	UC	RE	TX	VS	VR
					See adjoining counties for retrievers					

		CV	CR	PR	NORTHWEST ARCTIC BOROUGH (AK)	UC	RE	TX	VS	VR
					See adjoining counties for retrievers					

		CV	CR	PR	NULATO DISTRICT (AK)	UC	RE	TX	VS	VR
		•		•	Fairbanks Title Agency 907-456-6626	•	•	•		

		CV	CR	PR	PALMER DISTRICT (AK)	UC	RE	TX	VS	VR
		•	•	•	🏛 Alaska Records 800-808-5105	•	•	•		•
		•	•	•	Anchorage and Matsu Process Service (SOP) 907-258-3211	•	•	•	•	
		•	•	•	Freelance Legal Secretary 907-278-8855	•	•	•	•	

		CV	CR	PR	PRINCE OF WALES-OUTER KETCHIKAN (AK)	UC	RE	TX	VS	VR
					See adjoining counties for retrievers					

		CV	CR	PR	RAMPART DISTRICT (AK)	UC	RE	TX	VS	VR
		•		•	Fairbanks Title Agency 907-456-6626	•	•	•		

		CV	CR	PR	SITKA BOROUGH (AK)	UC	RE	TX	VS	VR
					See adjoining counties for retrievers					

		CV	CR	PR	SKAGWAY-HOONAH-ANGOON (AK)	UC	RE	TX	VS	VR
					See adjoining counties for retrievers					

		CV	CR	PR	SOUTHEAST FAIRBANKS (AK)	UC	RE	TX	VS	VR
					See adjoining counties for retrievers					

		CV	CR	PR	VALDEZ DISTRICT (AK)	UC	RE	TX	VS	VR
		•	•	•	🏛 Alaska Records 800-808-5105	•	•	•		•

		CV	CR	PR	VALDEZ-CORDOVA (AK)	UC	RE	TX	VS	VR
		•	•	•	Alaska Litigation Services 907-258-7400	•	•	•	•	•
		•	•	•	Freelance Legal Secretary 907-278-8855	•	•	•	•	

		CV	CR	PR	WADE HAMPTON (AK)	UC	RE	TX	VS	VR
					See adjoining counties for retrievers					

		CV	CR	PR	WRANGELL-PETERSBURG (AK)	UC	RE	TX	VS	VR
					See adjoining counties for retrievers					

		CV	CR	PR	YUKON-KOYUKUK (AK)	UC	RE	TX	VS	VR
					See adjoining counties for retrievers					

ARIZONA

APACHE (MST)

CV	CR	PR		UC	RE	TX	VS	VR
•	•	•	Hollingsworth Court Reporting Inc 504-769-3386	•	•	•	•	

COCHISE (MST)

CV	CR	PR		UC	RE	TX	VS	VR
•	•	•	Arizona Search 520-294-8350	•	•	•	•	
•	•	•	E-Z Messenger Attorney Service Inc (SOP) 520-623-8436	•	•	•		
•	•	•	Hollingsworth Court Reporting Inc 504-769-3386	•	•	•	•	
•	•	•	Impact Invesigations (SOP) 800-447-3174	•	•	•	•	•
•	•	•	MacIntire & Associates (SOP) 800-641-2737	•	•	•		•
•	•		Personnel Information Plus (SOP) 520-320-0611		•	•		•

COCONINO (MST)

CV	CR	PR		UC	RE	TX	VS	VR
•	•	•	Fleming Attorney Service (SOP) 800-776-3301	•	•	•	•	•
•	•	•	Hollingsworth Court Reporting Inc 504-769-3386	•	•	•	•	
•	•	•	Northern Arizona Investigations (SOP) 800-657-2747	•	•	•		
•	•	•	The Information Super Store 800-774-6585	•	•	•	•	•

GILA (MST)

CV	CR	PR		UC	RE	TX	VS	VR
•	•	•	Hollingsworth Court Reporting Inc 504-769-3386	•	•	•	•	

GRAHAM (MST)

CV	CR	PR		UC	RE	TX	VS	VR
•	•	•	Hollingsworth Court Reporting Inc 504-769-3386	•	•	•	•	
•	•	•	MacIntire & Associates (SOP) 800-641-2737	•	•	•		•

GREENLEE (MST)

CV	CR	PR		UC	RE	TX	VS	VR
•	•	•	Hollingsworth Court Reporting Inc 504-769-3386	•	•	•	•	
•	•	•	MacIntire & Associates (SOP) 800-641-2737	•	•	•		•

LA PAZ (MST)

CV	CR	PR		UC	RE	TX	VS	VR
•	•	•	Desert Investigations 602-726-4398	•	•	•	•	
•	•	•	Hollingsworth Court Reporting Inc 504-769-3386	•	•	•	•	

MARICOPA (CAPITAL) (MST)

DT	BK	CV	CR	PR		UC	RE	TX	VS	VR
•	•	•	•	•	AccuSearch 800-962-7019	•	•	•		•
•	•	•	•	•	Arizona Express Attorney Services (SOP) 602-604-8248	•	•	•	•	•
•	•	•	•	•	Beacom-Sauter Attorney Services 800-380-8081	•	•	•		
•	•	•	•	•	CSC 602-234-9600	•	•	•		
•	•	•	•	•	Capitol Document Services Inc 800-255-4052	•		•		
•	•	•	•	•	Cobra Company of Arizona 602-978-6010	•	•	•		•
•	•	•	•	•	DL Express Inc (SOP) 602-285-9901	•	•	•	•	•
•	•	•	•	•	Delta Investigations & Intelligence Agency (SOP) 602-945-6169	•	•	•	•	•
•	•	•	•	•	Fleming Attorney Service (SOP) 800-776-3301	•	•	•	•	•
•	•	•	•	•	Hawkins and Campbell Inc (SOP) 602-254-6147	•	•	•	•	•
•	•				Hogan Information Services 405-278-6954					
•	•	•	•	•	Hollingsworth Court Reporting Inc 504-769-3386	•	•	•	•	
•	•	•	•	•	Impact Invesigations (SOP) 800-447-3174	•	•	•	•	•
•					Lambert Research Services 602-433-7677					
•	•	•	•	•	MacIntire & Associates (SOP) 800-641-2737	•	•	•		•
•	•	•	•	•	MarTech Inc (SOP) 800-346-0189	•	•	•		•
•	•	•	•	•	NDR (National Document Retrieval) 800-829-5578	•	•	•		•
•	•	•	•	•	Personnel Information Plus (SOP) 520-320-0611		•	•		•
•	•	•	•	•	Phelps & Phelps Investigations 800-347-9918	•	•	•	•	•
•	•				Records Research & Retrieval 800-944-5211		•	•		•
•	•	•	•	•	Security Source Nationwide (SOP) 303-628-3973	•	•	•		•
•	•	•	•	•	Slover Investigations 602-917-3708	•	•	•		•
•	•	•	•	•	The Information Super Store 800-774-6585	•	•	•	•	•
•	•	•	•	•	Track Down Inc (SOP) 888-252-8521	•	•	•		•
•	•	•	•	•	Win With Information (WWI Assoc) 602-661-9628	•	•	•	•	•

MOHAVE (MST)

CV	CR	PR		UC	RE	TX	VS	VR
•	•	•	Hollingsworth Court Reporting Inc 504-769-3386	•	•	•	•	

		•	•	•	🏛 MHR and Associates (SOP) 520-753-4777	•	•	•	•	•
		•	•	•	The Information Super Store 800-774-6585	•	•	•	•	•

		CV	CR	PR	NAVAJO (MST)	UC	RE	TX	VS	VR
		•	•	•	🏛 Hollingsworth Court Reporting Inc 504-769-3386	•	•	•	•	
		•	•	•	🏛 Northern Arizona Investigations (SOP) 800-657-2747	•	•	•	•	•

DT	BK	CV	CR	PR	PIMA (MST)	UC	RE	TX	VS	VR
•	•	•	•	•	🏛 Arizona Search 520-294-8350	•	•	•	•	
•	•	•	•	•	🏛 Capitol Document Services Inc 800-255-4052	•		•	•	
•	•	•	•	•	Cobra Company of Arizona 602-978-6010	•		•	•	•
•	•	•	•	•	🏛 DL Express Inc (SOP) 602-285-9901	•		•	•	•
•	•	•	•	•	E-Z Messenger Attorney Service Inc (SOP) 520-623-8436	•		•	•	
•	•	•	•	•	Fleming Attorney Service (SOP) 800-776-3301	•		•	•	
•	•	•	•	•	Gonzales, Linda 520-622-1729	•		•	•	•
•	•	•	•	•	🏛 Hawkins and Campbell Tucson Inc (SOP) 520-628-9737	•		•	•	•
•	•	•	•		🏛 Hogan Information Services 405-278-6954					
•	•	•	•	•	🏛 Hollingsworth Court Reporting Inc 504-769-3386	•	•	•	•	
•	•	•	•		🏛 InfoCheck 520-577-8987	•		•		
•	•	•	•	•	🏛 Information Search Associates 888-448-4477	•		•	•	
•	•	•	•	•	🏛 Kroes Detective Agency (SOP) 800-249-0694	•		•		•
		•			🏛 Lambert Research Services 602-433-7677			•		
•	•	•	•	•	🏛 MacIntire & Associates (SOP) 800-641-2737	•		•		•
•	•	•	•	•	MarTech Inc (SOP) 800-346-0189	•		•	•	•
•	•	•	•	•	NDR (National Document Retrieval) 800-829-5578	•		•	•	•
•	•	•	•		🏛 Personnel Information Plus (SOP) 520-320-0611			•	•	•
•	•	•	•	•	🏛 Phelps & Phelps Investigations 800-347-9918			•	•	•
•	•	•	•	•	The Information Super Store 800-774-6585	•	•	•	•	•
•	•	•	•	•	🏛 Trace Unlimited (SOP) 520-299-0015	•	•	•	•	•

		CV	CR	PR	PINAL (MST)	UC	RE	TX	VS	VR
		•	•	•	🏛 Arizona Search 520-294-8350	•	•	•	•	
		•	•	•	Cobra Company of Arizona 602-978-6010	•	•	•	•	•
		•	•	•	Fleming Attorney Service (SOP) 800-776-3301	•	•	•	•	•
		•	•	•	🏛 Hollingsworth Court Reporting Inc 504-769-3386	•	•	•	•	
		•	•	•	Impact Invesigations (SOP) 800-447-3174	•	•	•	•	•
		•			🏛 Lambert Research Services 602-433-7677			•	•	
		•	•	•	NDR (National Document Retrieval) 800-829-5578	•	•	•	•	•

		CV	CR	PR	SANTA CRUZ (MST)	UC	RE	TX	VS	VR
		•	•	•	E-Z Messenger Attorney Service Inc (SOP) 520-623-8436	•	•	•		
		•	•	•	🏛 Hollingsworth Court Reporting Inc 504-769-3386	•	•	•	•	
		•	•	•	🏛 MacIntire & Associates (SOP) 800-641-2737	•	•	•		•

		CV	CR	PR	YAVAPAI (MST)	UC	RE	TX	VS	VR
		•	•	•	Fleming Attorney Service (SOP) 800-776-3301	•	•	•	•	•
		•	•	•	🏛 Hollingsworth Court Reporting Inc 504-769-3386	•	•	•	•	
		•	•	•	🏛 Palmer Investigative Services (SOP) 800-280-2951	•	•	•		•

	BK	CV	CR	PR	YUMA (MST)	UC	RE	TX	VS	VR
	•	•	•		🏛 AWS Investigations Inc (SOP) 800-429-1099			•	•	
	•	•	•	•	Desert Investigations 602-726-4398	•	•	•	•	
	•				🏛 Hogan Information Services 405-278-6954					
	•	•	•	•	🏛 Hollingsworth Court Reporting Inc 504-769-3386	•	•	•	•	
	•	•	•		Wallace Document Retrieval 520-726-5055	•	•	•	•	

ARKANSAS

CV	CR	PR	ARKANSAS (CST)	UC	RE	TX	VS	VR
•	•	•	Arkansas Corp Research & Service Co 501-374-3843	•	•	•	•	•
			Arkansas County Title Co Inc 501-673-3981	•	•	•		
•	•	•	⛫ Hollingsworth Court Reporting Inc 504-769-3386	•	•	•		
•	•	•	Quest Research Inc 501-374-4712	•	•	•		
•	•	•	Wilson & Associates 501-534-1200	•	•	•	•	•

CV	CR	PR	ASHLEY (CST)	UC	RE	TX	VS	VR
•	•	•	Arkansas Corp Research & Service Co 501-374-3843	•	•	•	•	•
•	•	•	⛫ Hollingsworth Court Reporting Inc 504-769-3386	•	•	•		
•	•	•	Quest Research Inc 501-374-4712	•	•	•		
•	•	•	Wilson & Associates 501-534-1200	•	•	•	•	•

CV	CR	PR	BAXTER (CST)	UC	RE	TX	VS	VR
•	•	•	Arkansas Corp Research & Service Co 501-374-3843	•	•	•	•	•
•		•	Baxter County Abstract Co 501-425-8989	•	•	•		
•	•	•	⛫ Hollingsworth Court Reporting Inc 504-769-3386	•	•	•		
•		•	Ozark Title & Guaranty Co 501-743-3333	•	•	•		
•	•	•	Quest Research Inc 501-374-4712	•	•	•		

CV	CR	PR	BENTON (CST)	UC	RE	TX	VS	VR
•	•		⛫ Alpha Research LLC (SOP) 205-755-7008			•		
•	•	•	Arkansas Corp Research & Service Co 501-374-3843	•	•	•	•	•
•	•	•	⛫ Hollingsworth Court Reporting Inc 504-769-3386	•	•	•	•	
•	•	•	North Winds Investigations Inc (SOP) 800-530-4514	•	•	•	•	•
•	•	•	Quest Research Inc 501-374-4712	•	•	•		
•		•	Tucker Abstract Co 501-273-2111	•	•	•		

CV	CR	PR	BOONE (CST)	UC	RE	TX	VS	VR
•	•	•	Arkansas Corp Research & Service Co 501-374-3843	•	•	•	•	•
•	•	•	⛫ Hollingsworth Court Reporting Inc 504-769-3386	•	•	•	•	
•		•	Ozark Title & Guaranty Co 501-743-3333	•	•	•		
•		•	Quest Research Inc 501-374-4712	•	•	•		
•		•	Wilson & Associates 501-375-1820	•	•	•		

CV	CR	PR	BRADLEY (CST)	UC	RE	TX	VS	VR
•	•	•	Arkansas Corp Research & Service Co 501-374-3843	•	•	•	•	•
•	•	•	⛫ Hollingsworth Court Reporting Inc 504-769-3386	•	•	•	•	
•	•	•	Martin Abstract Co 501-226-7487	•	•	•		
•	•	•	Quest Research Inc 501-374-4712	•	•	•		
•	•	•	Wilson & Associates 501-534-1200	•	•	•	•	•

CV	CR	PR	CALHOUN (CST)	UC	RE	TX	VS	VR
•	•	•	Arkansas Corp Research & Service Co 501-374-3843	•	•	•	•	•
•	•	•	⛫ Hollingsworth Court Reporting Inc 504-769-3386	•	•	•	•	
•	•	•	Lyon Abstract Company (SOP) 501-836-8084	•	•	•		
•	•	•	Quest Research Inc 501-374-4712	•	•	•		
•		•	Wilson & Associates 501-375-1820	•	•	•		

CV	CR	PR	CARROLL (CST)	UC	RE	TX	VS	VR
•	•	•	Arkansas Corp Research & Service Co 501-374-3843	•	•	•	•	•
•		•	Berryville Abstract and Title Co 501-423-2535	•	•	•		
•		•	⛫ Hollingsworth Court Reporting Inc 504-769-3386	•	•	•		
•			Jackson Abstract Inc 501-423-2285	•	•	•		
•		•	Ozark Title & Guaranty Co 501-743-3333	•	•	•		
•	•	•	Quest Research Inc 501-374-4712	•	•	•		

CV	CR	PR	CHICOT (CST)	UC	RE	TX	VS	VR
•	•	•	Arkansas Corp Research & Service Co 501-374-3843	•	•	•	•	•
•	•	•	⛫ Hollingsworth Court Reporting Inc 504-769-3386	•	•	•		
•	•	•	Quest Research Inc 501-374-4712	•	•	•		

					UC	RE	TX	VS	VR
•	•	•	Wilson & Associates	501-534-1200	•	•	•	•	•

CV	CR	PR		CLARK (CST)	UC	RE	TX	VS	VR
•	•	•	Arkansas Corp Research & Service Co	501-374-3843	•	•	•	•	•
•	•	•	Clark County Abstract Co	501-246-2821	•	•	•		
•	•	•	🏛 Hollingsworth Court Reporting Inc	504-769-3386	•	•	•	•	
•	•	•	Quest Research Inc	501-374-4712	•	•	•		
•		•	Wilson & Associates	501-375-1820	•	•	•		

CV	CR	PR		CLAY (CST)	UC	RE	TX	VS	VR
•	•	•	Arkansas Corp Research & Service Co	501-374-3843	•	•	•	•	•
•	•	•	🏛 Hollingsworth Court Reporting Inc	504-769-3386	•	•	•	•	
•	•	•	Quest Research Inc	501-374-4712	•	•	•		
•		•	Wilson & Associates	501-375-1820	•	•	•		

CV	CR	PR		CLEBURNE (CST)	UC	RE	TX	VS	VR
•	•	•	Arkansas Corp Research & Service Co	501-374-3843	•	•	•	•	•
•	•	•	🏛 Hollingsworth Court Reporting Inc	504-769-3386	•	•	•	•	
•	•	•	Professional Title & Abstract Co	501-362-3136	•	•	•	•	
•	•	•	Quest Research Inc	501-374-4712	•	•	•		
•		•	Wilson & Associates	501-375-1820	•	•	•		

CV	CR	PR		CLEVELAND (CST)	UC	RE	TX	VS	VR
•	•	•	Arkansas Corp Research & Service Co	501-374-3843	•	•	•	•	•
•	•	•	🏛 Hollingsworth Court Reporting Inc	504-769-3386	•	•	•	•	
•	•	•	Martin Abstract Co	501-226-7487	•	•	•		
•	•	•	Quest Research Inc	501-374-4712	•	•	•		
•	•	•	Tinnon Beshear Abstract Co	501-325-6832	•	•	•	•	
•	•	•	Wilson & Associates	501-534-1200	•	•	•	•	•

CV	CR	PR		COLUMBIA (CST)	UC	RE	TX	VS	VR
•	•		🏛 Alpha Research LLC (SOP)	205-755-7008			•		
•	•	•	Arkansas Corp Research & Service Co	501-374-3843	•	•	•	•	
•			Dauzat, Sandra	501-772-7110	•		•		
•		•	DeSoto Abstract	318-798-1198	•	•	•		
•	•	•	Gillenwater, Joe (SOP)	800-962-9453	•	•	•	•	
•	•	•	🏛 Hollingsworth Court Reporting Inc	504-769-3386	•	•	•	•	
•	•	•	Lyon Abstract Company (SOP)	501-836-8084	•	•	•		
•	•	•	Quest Research Inc	501-374-4712	•	•	•		
•	•	•	Security Abstract Co	501-234-5990	•	•	•		
•	•	•	Wilson & Associates	501-375-1820	•	•	•		

CV	CR	PR		CONWAY (CST)	UC	RE	TX	VS	VR
•	•	•	Arkansas Corp Research & Service Co	501-374-3843	•	•	•	•	•
•	•	•	🏛 Hollingsworth Court Reporting Inc	504-769-3386	•	•	•	•	
•	•	•	Morrilton Abstract Co	501-354-2611	•	•	•		
•	•	•	Quest Research Inc	501-374-4712	•	•	•		
•	•	•	Wilson & Associates	501-375-1820	•	•	•		

DT	CV	CR	PR		CRAIGHEAD (CST)	UC	RE	TX	VS	VR
•	•	•		🏛 Alpha Research LLC (SOP)	205-755-7008			•		
•	•	•	•	Arkansas Corp Research & Service Co	501-374-3843	•	•	•	•	•
•	•	•	•	Craighead County Abstract	501-935-9900	•	•	•		
•	•	•	•	Easy Way	501-239-2760	•	•	•		
•	•	•	•	🏛 Hollingsworth Court Reporting Inc	504-769-3386	•	•	•		
•	•	•	•	Markle Northeast Title Co	501-935-7410		•	•		
•	•	•	•	Quest Research Inc	501-374-4712	•	•	•		
•	•		•	Wilson & Associates	501-375-1820	•	•	•		

CV	CR	PR		CRAWFORD (CST)	UC	RE	TX	VS	VR
•	•		🏛 Alpha Research LLC (SOP)	205-755-7008			•		
•	•	•	Arkansas Corp Research & Service Co	501-374-3843	•	•	•	•	•
•	•	•	Crawford County Abstract Co	501-474-2711	•	•	•		

• • •	Deister Ward & Witcher of Arkansas	501-782-7448	• • • •
• •	Hebert Land Services	918-647-9524	• • • •
• • •	🏛 Hollingsworth Court Reporting Inc	504-769-3386	• • • • •
• • •	Mac Abstract & Title Insurance Co	501-782-3053	• • •
• • •	North Winds Investigations Inc (SOP)	800-530-4514	• • • •
• • •	Quest Research Inc	501-374-4712	• • •
• •	Wilson & Associates	501-375-1820	• • •

CV	CR	PR	CRITTENDEN (CST)	UC	RE	TX	VS	VR
•	•		🏛 Alpha Research LLC (SOP) 205-755-7008			•		
•	•	•	Arkansas Corp Research & Service Co 501-374-3843	•	•	•	•	•
•	•	•	🏛 Cheslock Investigations (SOP) 901-681-9663	•	•	•	•	•
•	•	•	🏛 Hollingsworth Court Reporting Inc 504-769-3386	•	•	•	•	
•	•	•	Quest Research Inc 501-374-4712	•	•	•		
•	•	•	RecordServe/John Kelley Enterprises 901-853-5320	•	•	•	•	
•	•	•	Schaeffer Papers (SOP) 800-848-6119		•			
•		•	Wilson & Associates 501-375-1820	•	•	•		

CV	CR	PR	CROSS (CST)	UC	RE	TX	VS	VR
•	•		🏛 Alpha Research LLC (SOP) 205-755-7008			•		
•	•	•	Arkansas Corp Research & Service Co 501-374-3843	•	•	•	•	•
•	•	•	🏛 Hollingsworth Court Reporting Inc 504-769-3386	•	•	•	•	
•	•	•	Quest Research Inc 501-374-4712	•	•	•		
•		•	Wilson & Associates 501-375-1820	•	•	•		

CV	CR	PR	DALLAS (CST)	UC	RE	TX	VS	VR
•	•	•	Arkansas Corp Research & Service Co 501-374-3843	•	•	•	•	•
•	•	•	🏛 Hollingsworth Court Reporting Inc 504-769-3386	•	•	•	•	
•	•	•	Lyon Abstract Company (SOP) 501-836-8084	•	•	•	•	
•	•	•	Quest Research Inc 501-374-4712	•	•	•		
•	•	•	Wilson & Associates 501-534-1200	•	•	•	•	•

CV	CR	PR	DESHA (CST)	UC	RE	TX	VS	VR
•	•	•	Arkansas Corp Research & Service Co 501-374-3843	•	•	•	•	•
•	•	•	🏛 Hollingsworth Court Reporting Inc 504-769-3386	•	•	•	•	
•	•	•	Quest Research Inc 501-374-4712	•	•	•		
•		•	Smith Abstract Co Inc 501-222-5001		•	•		
•	•	•	Wilson & Associates 501-534-1200	•	•	•	•	•

CV	CR	PR	DREW (CST)	UC	RE	TX	VS	VR
•	•	•	Arkansas Corp Research & Service Co 501-374-3843	•	•	•	•	•
•	•	•	Drew County Abstract & Title Co 501-367-6607	•	•	•	•	
•	•	•	🏛 Hollingsworth Court Reporting Inc 504-769-3386	•	•	•	•	
•	•	•	Quest Research Inc 501-374-4712	•	•	•		
•	•	•	Wilson & Associates 501-534-1200	•	•	•	•	•

CV	CR	PR	FAULKNER (CST)	UC	RE	TX	VS	VR
•	•		🏛 Alpha Research LLC (SOP) 205-755-7008			•		
•	•	•	Arkansas Corp Research & Service Co 501-374-3843	•	•	•	•	•
•	•	•	🏛 Hollingsworth Court Reporting Inc 504-769-3386	•	•	•	•	
•	•	•	🏛 Pro Facto Inc 501-988-5340	•	•	•	•	•
•	•	•	Quest Research Inc 501-374-4712	•	•	•		
•		•	Wilson & Associates 501-375-1820	•	•	•		

CV	CR	PR	FRANKLIN (CST)	UC	RE	TX	VS	VR
•	•	•	Arkansas Corp Research & Service Co 501-374-3843	•	•	•	•	•
•	•	•	Deister Ward & Witcher of Arkansas 501-782-7448	•	•	•	•	
•		•	Hebert Land Services 918-647-9524	•	•	•	•	•
•	•	•	🏛 Hollingsworth Court Reporting Inc 504-769-3386	•	•	•	•	
•	•	•	Quest Research Inc 501-374-4712	•	•	•		
•		•	Wilson & Associates 501-375-1820	•	•	•		

FULTON (CST)

CV	CR	PR	Provider	Phone	UC	RE	TX	VS	VR
•	•	•	Arkansas Corp Research & Service Co	501-374-3843	•	•	•	•	•
•	•	•	Hollingsworth Court Reporting Inc	504-769-3386	•	•	•	•	
•	•	•	Quest Research Inc	501-374-4712	•	•	•		
•		•	Wilson & Associates	501-375-1820	•	•	•		

GARLAND (CST)

DT	CV	CR	PR	Provider	Phone	UC	RE	TX	VS	VR
•	•	•		Alpha Research LLC (SOP)	205-755-7008			•		
•	•	•	•	Arkansas Corp Research & Service Co	501-374-3843	•	•	•	•	•
			•	Guaranty Title Co	501-321-2856	•	•	•		
•	•	•	•	Hollingsworth Court Reporting Inc	504-769-3386	•	•	•	•	
	•	•	•	Hot Spring County Title Services Inc	501-332-3770	•	•	•	•	
•	•	•	•	Quest Research Inc	501-374-4712	•	•	•		
•	•		•	Wilson & Associates	501-375-1820	•	•	•		

GRANT (CST)

CV	CR	PR	Provider	Phone	UC	RE	TX	VS	VR
•	•	•	Arkansas Corp Research & Service Co	501-374-3843	•	•	•	•	•
•	•	•	Hollingsworth Court Reporting Inc	504-769-3386	•	•	•	•	
•	•	•	Hot Spring County Title Services Inc	501-332-3770	•	•	•	•	
•	•	•	Quest Research Inc	501-374-4712	•	•	•		
•	•	•	Wilson & Associates	501-534-1200	•	•	•	•	•

GREENE (CST)

CV	CR	PR	Provider	Phone	UC	RE	TX	VS	VR
•	•		Alpha Research LLC (SOP)	205-755-7008			•		
•	•	•	Arkansas Corp Research & Service Co	501-374-3843	•	•	•	•	•
•	•	•	Easy Way	501-239-2760	•	•	•		
•	•	•	Hollingsworth Court Reporting Inc	504-769-3386	•	•	•	•	
•	•	•	Quest Research Inc	501-374-4712	•	•	•		
•		•	Wilson & Associates	501-375-1820	•	•	•		

HEMPSTEAD (CST)

CV	CR	PR	Provider	Phone	UC	RE	TX	VS	VR
•	•	•	Arkansas Corp Research & Service Co	501-374-3843	•	•	•	•	•
•			Dauzat, Sandra	501-772-7110	•				
•	•	•	Gillenwater, Joe (SOP)	800-962-9453	•	•		•	
•	•	•	Hempstead County Abstract and Title	501-777-2351	•	•	•		
•	•	•	Hollingsworth Court Reporting Inc	504-769-3386	•	•	•		
•	•	•	Quest Research Inc	501-374-4712	•	•	•		
	•	•	Wilson & Associates	501-375-1820	•	•	•		

HOT SPRING (CST)

CV	CR	PR	Provider	Phone	UC	RE	TX	VS	VR
•	•	•	Arkansas Corp Research & Service Co	501-374-3843	•	•	•	•	•
•	•	•	Hollingsworth Court Reporting Inc	504-769-3386	•	•	•	•	
•	•	•	Hot Spring County Title Services Inc	501-332-3770	•	•	•	•	
•	•	•	Quest Research Inc	501-374-4712	•	•	•		
•		•	Wilson & Associates	501-375-1820	•	•	•		

HOWARD (CST)

CV	CR	PR	Provider	Phone	UC	RE	TX	VS	VR
•	•	•	Arkansas Corp Research & Service Co	501-374-3843	•	•	•	•	•
•			Dauzat, Sandra	501-772-7110	•		•		
•	•	•	Gillenwater, Joe (SOP)	800-962-9453	•	•		•	•
•	•	•	Hollingsworth Court Reporting Inc	504-769-3386	•	•	•	•	
•	•	•	Quest Research Inc	501-374-4712	•	•	•		
		•	Wilson & Associates	501-375-1820	•	•	•		

INDEPENDENCE (CST)

CV	CR	PR	Provider	Phone	UC	RE	TX	VS	VR
•	•		Alpha Research LLC (SOP)	205-755-7008			•		
•	•	•	Arkansas Corp Research & Service Co	501-374-3843	•	•	•	•	•
•	•	•	Hollingsworth Court Reporting Inc	504-769-3386	•	•	•	•	
•	•	•	Independence County Abstract Co	501-793-3333	•	•	•		
•	•	•	Quest Research Inc	501-374-4712	•	•	•		
		•	Wilson & Associates	501-375-1820	•	•	•		

IZARD (CST)

CV	CR	PR			UC	RE	TX	VS	VR
•	•	•	Arkansas Corp Research & Service Co	501-374-3843	•	•	•	•	•
•	•	•	🏛 Hollingsworth Court Reporting Inc	504-769-3386	•	•	•	•	
•	•	•	Izard County Abstract Co	501-368-4818	•	•	•		
•	•		Quest Research Inc	501-374-4712	•	•	•		
•		•	Wilson & Associates	501-375-1820	•	•	•		

JACKSON (CST)

CV	CR	PR			UC	RE	TX	VS	VR
•	•		🏛 Alpha Research LLC (SOP)	205-755-7008			•		
•	•	•	Arkansas Corp Research & Service Co	501-374-3843	•	•	•	•	•
•	•	•	🏛 Hollingsworth Court Reporting Inc	504-769-3386	•	•	•	•	
•		•	Miller Newell Abstract	501-523-8976	•	•	•		
•	•	•	Quest Research Inc	501-374-4712	•	•	•		
•		•	Wilson & Associates	501-375-1820	•	•	•		

JEFFERSON (CST)

DT	CV	CR	PR			UC	RE	TX	VS	VR
	•	•		🏛 Alpha Research LLC (SOP)	205-755-7008			•		
•	•	•	•	Arkansas Corp Research & Service Co	501-374-3843	•	•	•	•	•
•	•	•	•	🏛 Hollingsworth Court Reporting Inc	504-769-3386	•	•	•	•	
•	•	•	•	🏛 Pro Facto Inc	501-988-5340	•	•	•	•	•
•	•	•	•	Quest Research Inc	501-374-4712	•	•	•	•	•
•	•	•	•	Wilson & Associates	501-534-1200	•	•	•	•	•

JOHNSON (CST)

CV	CR	PR			UC	RE	TX	VS	VR
•	•	•	Arkansas Corp Research & Service Co	501-374-3843	•	•	•	•	•
•	•	•	Deister Ward & Witcher of Arkansas	501-782-7448	•	•	•	•	
•	•	•	🏛 Hollingsworth Court Reporting Inc	504-769-3386	•	•	•	•	
•	•	•	Quest Research Inc	501-374-4712	•	•	•		

LAFAYETTE (CST)

CV	CR	PR			UC	RE	TX	VS	VR
•	•	•	Arkansas Corp Research & Service Co	501-374-3843	•	•	•	•	•
•			Dauzat, Sandra	501-772-7110	•		•		
		•	DeSoto Abstract	318-798-1198	•	•	•		
•	•	•	Gillenwater, Joe (SOP)	800-962-9453	•		•	•	•
•	•	•	🏛 Hollingsworth Court Reporting Inc	504-769-3386	•	•	•	•	
•	•	•	Lyon Abstract Company (SOP)	501-836-8084	•	•	•	•	
•	•	•	Patton Abstract and Title Inc	501-921-4263	•	•	•	•	
•	•	•	Quest Research Inc	501-374-4712	•	•	•		
•		•	Wilson & Associates	501-375-1820	•	•	•		

LAWRENCE (CST)

CV	CR	PR			UC	RE	TX	VS	VR
•	•	•	Arkansas Corp Research & Service Co	501-374-3843	•	•	•	•	•
•	•	•	🏛 Hollingsworth Court Reporting Inc	504-769-3386	•	•	•	•	
•	•	•	Mullen Abstract Co	501-886-2452	•	•	•		
•	•	•	Quest Research Inc	501-374-4712	•	•	•		
•	•	•	Wilson & Associates	501-375-1820	•	•	•		

LEE (CST)

CV	CR	PR			UC	RE	TX	VS	VR
•	•		🏛 Alpha Research LLC (SOP)	205-755-7008			•		
•	•	•	Arkansas Corp Research & Service Co	501-374-3843	•	•	•	•	•
•		•	Daggett Abstract Co	501-295-3434	•	•	•		
•	•	•	🏛 Hollingsworth Court Reporting Inc	504-769-3386	•	•	•	•	
•	•	•	Quest Research Inc	501-374-4712	•	•	•		
•		•	Wilson & Associates	501-375-1820	•	•	•		

LINCOLN (CST)

CV	CR	PR			UC	RE	TX	VS	VR
•	•	•	Arkansas Corp Research & Service Co	501-374-3843	•	•	•	•	•
•	•	•	🏛 Hollingsworth Court Reporting Inc	504-769-3386	•	•	•	•	
•	•	•	Lincoln Abstract Co	501-628-3144	•	•	•		
•	•	•	Quest Research Inc	501-374-4712	•	•	•		
•	•	•	Wilson & Associates	501-534-1200	•	•	•	•	•

CV	CR	PR	LITTLE RIVER (CST)		UC	RE	TX	VS	VR
●	●	●	Arkansas Corp Research & Service Co 501-374-3843		●	●	●	●	●
●	●	●	Gillenwater, Joe (SOP) 800-962-9453		●	●	●	●	●
●	●	●	🏛 Hollingsworth Court Reporting Inc 504-769-3386		●	●	●		
●	●	●	McIver Abstract & Insurance Co 501-898-3502		●	●			
●	●	●	Quest Research Inc 501-374-4712		●	●	●		
●		●	Wilson & Associates 501-375-1820		●	●	●		

CV	CR	PR	LOGAN (CST)		UC	RE	TX	VS	VR
●	●	●	Arkansas Corp Research & Service Co 501-374-3843		●	●	●	●	●
●	●	●	Deister Ward & Witcher of Arkansas 501-782-7448		●	●	●	●	
●		●	Hebert Land Services 918-647-9524		●	●	●	●	
●	●	●	🏛 Hollingsworth Court Reporting Inc 504-769-3386		●	●	●		
●	●	●	Quest Research Inc 501-374-4712		●	●	●		
●		●	Wilson & Associates 501-375-1820		●	●	●		

CV	CR	PR	LONOKE (CST)		UC	RE	TX	VS	VR
●	●		🏛 Alpha Research LLC (SOP) 205-755-7008				●		
●		●	Arkansas Corp Research & Service Co 501-374-3843		●	●	●		●
●	●	●	First State Abstract 501-676-2486		●	●	●		
●	●	●	🏛 Hollingsworth Court Reporting Inc 504-769-3386		●	●	●		
●	●	●	🏛 James, Cristina R 501-843-5025		●	●	●	●	●
●	●	●	Quest Research Inc 501-374-4712		●	●	●		
●		●	Wilson & Associates 501-375-1820		●	●	●		

CV	CR	PR	MADISON (CST)		UC	RE	TX	VS	VR
●	●	●	Arkansas Corp Research & Service Co 501-374-3843		●	●	●	●	●
●	●	●	🏛 Hollingsworth Court Reporting Inc 504-769-3386		●	●	●	●	
●	●	●	Quest Research Inc 501-374-4712		●	●	●		
●	●	●	Town & Country Abstract Co 501-738-2055		●	●	●		

CV	CR	PR	MARION (CST)		UC	RE	TX	VS	VR
●	●	●	Arkansas Corp Research & Service Co 501-374-3843		●	●	●	●	●
●	●	●	🏛 Hollingsworth Court Reporting Inc 504-769-3386		●	●	●	●	
●		●	Ozark Title & Guaranty Co 501-743-3333		●	●	●		
●	●	●	Quest Research Inc 501-374-4712		●	●	●		
●		●	Wilson & Associates 501-375-1820		●	●	●		

DT	CV	CR	PR	MILLER (CST)		UC	RE	TX	VS	VR
●	●	●		🏛 Alpha Research LLC (SOP) 205-755-7008				●		
●	●	●	●	Arkansas Corp Research & Service Co 501-374-3843		●	●	●		
	●			Dauzat, Sandra 501-772-7110		●				
●	●	●	●	Gillenwater, Joe (SOP) 800-962-9453		●		●		●
●	●	●	●	🏛 Hollingsworth Court Reporting Inc 504-769-3386		●	●	●		
	●	●	●	Marion County Abstract Co 501-449-4218		●	●	●		
●	●	●	●	Quest Research Inc 501-374-4712		●	●	●		
●	●		●	Wilson & Associates 501-375-1820		●	●	●		

CV	CR	PR	MISSISSIPPI (CST)		UC	RE	TX	VS	VR
●	●	●	Arkansas Corp Research & Service Co 501-374-3843		●	●	●	●	●
●	●	●	🏛 Hollingsworth Court Reporting Inc 504-769-3386		●	●	●	●	
●		●	Prewitt-Rogers Abstract Co 501-563-2137		●	●	●		
●	●	●	Quest Research Inc 501-374-4712		●	●	●		
●		●	Wilson & Associates 501-375-1820		●	●	●		

CV	CR	PR	MONROE (CST)		UC	RE	TX	VS	VR
●	●	●	Arkansas Corp Research & Service Co 501-374-3843		●	●	●	●	●
●	●	●	🏛 Hollingsworth Court Reporting Inc 504-769-3386		●	●	●	●	
●	●	●	Menard Title & Abstract Co Inc 501-747-3712			●	●	●	
●	●	●	Quest Research Inc 501-374-4712		●	●	●		
●		●	Wilson & Associates 501-375-1820		●	●	●		

CV	CR	PR	MONTGOMERY (CST)		UC	RE	TX	VS	VR
•	•	•	Arkansas Corp Research & Service Co 501-374-3843		•	•	•	•	•
•	•	•	Deister Ward & Witcher of Arkansas 501-782-7448		•	•	•	•	
•	•	•	🏛 Hollingsworth Court Reporting Inc 504-769-3386		•	•	•	•	
•	•	•	Quest Research Inc 501-374-4712		•	•	•		
•		•	Wilson & Associates 501-375-1820		•	•	•		

CV	CR	PR	NEVADA (CST)		UC	RE	TX	VS	VR
•	•	•	Arkansas Corp Research & Service Co 501-374-3843		•	•	•	•	•
•			Dauzat, Sandra 501-772-7110		•		•		
•	•	•	Gillenwater, Joe (SOP) 800-962-9453		•		•		•
•	•	•	🏛 Hollingsworth Court Reporting Inc 504-769-3386		•	•	•	•	
•	•	•	Quest Research Inc 501-374-4712		•	•	•		
•		•	Wilson & Associates 501-375-1820		•	•	•		

CV	CR	PR	NEWTON (CST)		UC	RE	TX	VS	VR
•	•	•	Arkansas Corp Research & Service Co 501-374-3843		•	•	•	•	•
•	•	•	🏛 Hollingsworth Court Reporting Inc 504-769-3386		•	•	•	•	
•		•	Ozark Title & Guaranty Co 501-743-3333		•	•	•		
•	•	•	Quest Research Inc 501-374-4712		•	•	•		
•		•	Wilson & Associates 501-375-1820		•	•	•		

CV	CR	PR	OUACHITA (CST)		UC	RE	TX	VS	VR
•	•		🏛 Alpha Research LLC (SOP) 205-755-7008				•		
•	•	•	Arkansas Corp Research & Service Co 501-374-3843		•	•	•	•	•
•		•	DeSoto Abstract 318-798-1198		•	•	•		
•	•	•	🏛 Hollingsworth Court Reporting Inc 504-769-3386		•	•	•	•	
•	•	•	Lyon Abstract Company (SOP) 501-836-8084		•	•	•	•	
•	•	•	Quest Research Inc 501-374-4712		•	•	•		
•		•	Wilson & Associates 501-375-1820		•	•	•		

CV	CR	PR	PERRY (CST)		UC	RE	TX	VS	VR
•	•	•	Arkansas Corp Research & Service Co 501-374-3843		•	•	•	•	•
•	•	•	Deister Ward & Witcher of Arkansas 501-782-7448		•	•	•	•	
•	•	•	🏛 Hollingsworth Court Reporting Inc 504-769-3386		•	•	•	•	
•	•	•	Quest Research Inc 501-374-4712		•	•	•		
•		•	Wilson & Associates 501-375-1820		•	•	•		

CV	CR	PR	PHILLIPS (CST)		UC	RE	TX	VS	VR
•	•	•	Arkansas Corp Research & Service Co 501-374-3843		•	•	•	•	•
•	•	•	🏛 Hollingsworth Court Reporting Inc 504-769-3386		•	•	•	•	
•		•	🏛 Hornor-Morris Abstract Co 501-338-8306		•	•	•		
•	•	•	Quest Research Inc 501-374-4712		•	•	•		
•		•	Tappan Abstract 501-338-3311		•	•	•		
•		•	Wilson & Associates 501-375-1820		•	•	•		

CV	CR	PR	PIKE (CST)		UC	RE	TX	VS	VR
•	•	•	Arkansas Corp Research & Service Co 501-374-3843		•	•	•	•	•
•	•	•	Deister Ward & Witcher of Arkansas 501-782-7448		•	•	•	•	
•	•	•	🏛 Hollingsworth Court Reporting Inc 504-769-3386		•	•	•	•	
•	•	•	Quest Research Inc 501-374-4712		•	•	•		
•		•	Wilson & Associates 501-375-1820		•	•	•		

CV	CR	PR	POINSETT (CST)		UC	RE	TX	VS	VR
•	•		🏛 Alpha Research LLC (SOP) 205-755-7008				•		
•	•	•	Arkansas Corp Research & Service Co 501-374-3843		•	•	•	•	•
•	•	•	🏛 Hollingsworth Court Reporting Inc 504-769-3386		•	•	•	•	
•	•	•	Poinsett County Abstract Co 501-578-5914		•	•	•		
•	•	•	Quest Research Inc 501-374-4712		•	•	•		
•		•	Wilson & Associates 501-375-1820		•	•	•		

CV	CR	PR	POLK (CST)		UC	RE	TX	VS	VR
•	•	•	Arkansas Corp Research & Service Co 501-374-3843		•	•	•	•	•

DT	BK	CV	CR	PR			UC	RE	TX	VS	VR
		•	•	•	Deister Ward & Witcher of Arkansas 501-782-7448		•	•	•	•	
		•	•	•	🏛 Hollingsworth Court Reporting Inc 504-769-3386		•	•	•	•	
		•	•	•	Martin Abstract Co 501-394-1963		•	•	•		
		•	•	•	Quest Research Inc 501-374-4712		•	•	•		
		•		•	Wilson & Associates 501-375-1820		•	•	•		

		CV	CR	PR	POPE (CST)		UC	RE	TX	VS	VR
		•		•	Arkansas Corp Research & Service Co 501-374-3843		•	•	•	•	•
		•			Hebert Land Services 918-647-9524		•	•	•	•	•
		•	•	•	🏛 Hollingsworth Court Reporting Inc 504-769-3386		•	•	•	•	
		•	•	•	Quest Research Inc 501-374-4712		•	•	•		
		•		•	Wilson & Associates 501-375-1820		•	•	•		

		CV	CR	PR	PRAIRIE (CST)		UC	RE	TX	VS	VR
		•	•	•	Arkansas Corp Research & Service Co 501-374-3843		•	•	•	•	•
		•	•	•	🏛 Hollingsworth Court Reporting Inc 504-769-3386		•	•	•	•	
		•	•	•	Moody Abstract Co 501-998-7531		•	•	•	•	
		•	•	•	Quest Research Inc 501-374-4712		•	•	•		
		•		•	Wilson & Associates 501-375-1820		•	•	•		

DT	BK	CV	CR	PR	PULASKI (CAPITAL) (CST)		UC	RE	TX	VS	VR
•	•	•	•		🏛 Alpha Research LLC (SOP)....................................... 205-755-7008			•			
•	•	•	•	•	Arkansas Corp Research & Service Co 501-374-3843		•				
•	•	•	•	•	Bankruptcy Services Inc 214-424-6500						
•	•				🏛 Hogan Information Services 405-278-6954						
•	•	•	•	•	🏛 Hollingsworth Court Reporting Inc 504-769-3386		•	•	•	•	
•	•	•	•	•	🏛 James, Cristina R 501-843-5025		•	•	•	•	•
•	•	•	•	•	North Winds Investigations Inc (SOP) 800-530-4514		•	•	•	•	•
•	•	•	•	•	🏛 Pro Facto Inc 501-988-5340		•	•	•	•	•
•	•	•	•	•	Quest Research Inc 501-374-4712		•	•	•		
•	•	•		•	Wilson & Associates 501-375-1820		•	•	•		

		CV	CR	PR	RANDOLPH (CST)		UC	RE	TX	VS	VR
		•	•	•	Arkansas Corp Research & Service Co 501-374-3843		•	•	•	•	•
		•	•	•	🏛 Hollingsworth Court Reporting Inc 504-769-3386		•	•	•	•	
		•	•	•	Quest Research Inc 501-374-4712		•	•	•		
		•	•	•	Service Abstract Company (SOP).................................. 501-892-4538		•	•	•		
		•		•	Wilson & Associates 501-375-1820		•	•	•		

		CV	CR	PR	SALINE (CST)		UC	RE	TX	VS	VR
		•	•	•	Arkansas Corp Research & Service Co 501-374-3843		•	•	•	•	•
		•	•	•	🏛 Hollingsworth Court Reporting Inc 504-769-3386		•	•	•	•	
		•	•	•	🏛 Pro Facto Inc 501-988-5340		•	•	•		•
		•	•	•	Quest Research Inc 501-374-4712		•	•	•		
		•	•	•	Saline County Abstract 501-778-2471		•	•	•	•	
		•		•	Wilson & Associates 501-375-1820		•	•	•		

		CV	CR	PR	SCOTT (CST)		UC	RE	TX	VS	VR
		•	•	•	Arkansas Corp Research & Service Co 501-374-3843		•	•	•	•	•
		•	•	•	Deister Ward & Witcher of Arkansas 501-782-7448		•	•	•	•	
		•			Hebert Land Services 918-647-9524		•	•	•	•	•
		•	•	•	🏛 Hollingsworth Court Reporting Inc 504-769-3386		•	•	•	•	
		•	•	•	Quest Research Inc 501-374-4712		•	•	•		
		•		•	Wilson & Associates 501-375-1820		•	•	•		

		CV	CR	PR	SEARCY (CST)		UC	RE	TX	VS	VR
		•	•	•	Arkansas Corp Research & Service Co 501-374-3843		•	•	•	•	•
		•	•	•	🏛 Hollingsworth Court Reporting Inc 504-769-3386		•	•	•	•	
		•		•	Ozark Title & Guaranty Co 501-743-3333		•	•	•		
		•	•	•	Quest Research Inc 501-374-4712		•	•	•		
		•		•	Wilson & Associates 501-375-1820		•	•	•		

SEBASTIAN (CST)

DT	CV	CR	PR	Company	Phone	UC	RE	TX	VS	VR
•	•	•		Alpha Research LLC (SOP)	205-755-7008			•		
•	•	•	•	Arkansas Corp Research & Service Co	501-374-3843	•	•	•	•	•
	•	•	•	Deister Ward & Witcher of Arkansas	501-782-7448	•	•	•	•	•
	•		•	Hebert Land Services	918-647-9524	•	•	•	•	•
•	•	•	•	Hollingsworth Court Reporting Inc	504-769-3386	•	•	•	•	
•	•		•	Mac Abstract & Title Insurance Co	501-782-3053	•	•			
•		•	•	Mosley Abstract Co	501-782-3053	•	•			
•	•	•	•	North Winds Investigations Inc (SOP)	800-530-4514	•	•	•	•	•
•	•	•	•	Quest Research Inc	501-374-4712	•	•	•		

SEVIER (CST)

CV	CR	PR	Company	Phone	UC	RE	TX	VS	VR
•	•	•	Arkansas Corp Research & Service Co	501-374-3843	•	•	•	•	•
•			Dauzat, Sandra	501-772-7110	•				
•	•	•	Gillenwater, Joe (SOP)	800-962-9453	•	•	•	•	•
•	•	•	Hollingsworth Court Reporting Inc	504-769-3386	•	•	•	•	
•	•	•	Quest Research Inc	501-374-4712	•	•	•		
•		•	Wilson & Associates	501-375-1820	•	•	•		

SHARP (CST)

CV	CR	PR	Company	Phone	UC	RE	TX	VS	VR
•	•		Alpha Research LLC (SOP)	205-755-7008			•		
•	•	•	Arkansas Corp Research & Service Co	501-374-3843	•	•	•	•	•
•	•	•	Hollingsworth Court Reporting Inc	504-769-3386	•	•	•	•	
•	•	•	Quest Research Inc	501-374-4712	•	•	•		
•	•	•	Sharp County Abstract Co Inc	501-994-7314	•	•	•		
•		•	Wilson & Associates	501-375-1820	•	•	•		

ST. FRANCIS (CST)

CV	CR	PR	Company	Phone	UC	RE	TX	VS	VR
•	•		Alpha Research LLC (SOP)	205-755-7008			•		
•	•	•	Arkansas Corp Research & Service Co	501-374-3843	•	•	•	•	•
•	•	•	Hollingsworth Court Reporting Inc	504-769-3386	•	•	•	•	
•	•	•	Quest Research Inc	501-374-4712	•	•	•		
•		•	Wilson & Associates	501-375-1820	•	•	•		

STONE (CST)

CV	CR	PR	Company	Phone	UC	RE	TX	VS	VR
•	•	•	Arkansas Corp Research & Service Co	501-374-3843	•	•	•	•	•
•	•	•	Hollingsworth Court Reporting Inc	504-769-3386	•	•	•	•	
•	•	•	Mountain View Abstract Co	501-269-8410	•	•	•		
•	•	•	Quest Research Inc	501-374-4712	•	•	•		
•		•	Wilson & Associates	501-375-1820	•	•	•		

UNION (CST)

DT	CV	CR	PR	Company	Phone	UC	RE	TX	VS	VR
•	•	•		Alpha Research LLC (SOP)	205-755-7008			•		
•	•	•	•	Arkansas Corp Research & Service Co	501-374-3843	•	•	•	•	•
			•	DeSoto Abstract	318-798-1198	•	•	•		
•	•	•	•	Hollingsworth Court Reporting Inc	504-769-3386	•	•	•	•	
•	•	•	•	Lyon Abstract Company (SOP)	501-836-8084	•	•	•	•	
•	•	•	•	Quest Research Inc	501-374-4712	•	•	•		
			•	Union Abstract Co	501-863-6053	•	•	•		
•	•	•	•	Wilson & Associates	501-534-1200	•	•	•	•	•

VAN BUREN (CST)

CV	CR	PR	Company	Phone	UC	RE	TX	VS	VR
•	•	•	Arkansas Corp Research & Service Co	501-374-3843	•	•	•	•	•
•	•	•	Hollingsworth Court Reporting Inc	504-769-3386	•	•	•	•	
•	•	•	Quest Research Inc	501-374-4712	•	•	•		
•		•	Wilson & Associates	501-375-1820	•	•	•		

WASHINGTON (CST)

DT	BK	CV	CR	PR	Company	Phone	UC	RE	TX	VS	VR
•	•	•	•		Alpha Research LLC (SOP)	205-755-7008			•		
•	•	•	•	•	Arkansas Corp Research & Service Co	501-374-3843	•	•	•	•	•
•				•	Bronson Abstract Co	501-521-4100	•	•			
•	•	•	•	•	Hollingsworth Court Reporting Inc	504-769-3386	•	•	•	•	

	CV	CR	PR	WHITE (CST)	UC	RE	TX	VS	VR
	•	•		🏛 Alpha Research LLC (SOP) 205-755-7008			•		
	•	•	•	Arkansas Corp Research & Service Co 501-374-3843	•	•	•	•	•
	•	•	•	Citizen's Abstract Co 501-268-5571	•	•	•		
	•	•	•	🏛 Hollingsworth Court Reporting Inc 504-769-3386	•	•	•	•	
	•	•	•	Quest Research Inc 501-374-4712	•	•	•		
	•		•	Strother-Wilbourn Land Title Co 501-268-8273	•	•	•		
	•		•	Wilson & Associates 501-375-1820	•	•	•		

	CV	CR	PR	WOODRUFF (CST)	UC	RE	TX	VS	VR
	•	•		🏛 Alpha Research LLC (SOP) 205-755-7008			•		
	•	•	•	Arkansas Corp Research & Service Co 501-374-3843	•	•	•	•	•
	•	•	•	Eldridge III, John D 501-347-2521	•	•	•	•	
	•	•	•	🏛 Hollingsworth Court Reporting Inc 504-769-3386	•	•	•	•	
	•	•	•	Quest Research Inc 501-374-4712	•	•	•		
	•	•	•	Wilson & Associates 501-375-1820	•	•	•		

	CV	CR	PR	YELL (CST)	UC	RE	TX	VS	VR
	•	•	•	Arkansas Corp Research & Service Co 501-374-3843	•	•	•	•	•
	•	•	•	Deister Ward & Witcher of Arkansas 501-782-7448	•	•	•	•	
	•		•	Hebert Land Services 918-647-9524	•	•	•	•	•
	•	•	•	🏛 Hollingsworth Court Reporting Inc 504-769-3386	•	•	•	•	
	•	•	•	Quest Research Inc 501-374-4712	•	•	•		
	•	•	•	Wilson & Associates 501-375-1820	•	•	•		

Above the tables:

• • • • •	North Winds Investigations Inc (SOP) 800-530-4514	• • • • •
• • • • •	Quest Research Inc 501-374-4712	• • •

CALIFORNIA

BK	CV	CR	PR	ALAMEDA (PST)	UC	RE	TX	VS	VR
	•	•		A Fast Copy Inc (SOP) 510-462-9191		•	•		
•	•	•	•	ACE Legal Assistance (SOP) 415-864-2020		•		•	
	•	•	•	AD Services (SOP) 800-827-9101		•	•	•	
	•	•		Accelerated Legal Services (ALS) 510-417-1854					
•	•	•	•	Adila-Gray Process Servers (SOP) 510-582-8812	•	•	•	•	
•	•	•	•	Attorney's Diversified Services 510-835-9176	•	•	•	•	
•	•	•	•	Attorney's Messenger Service 510-937-4581		•	•	•	
•	•	•	•	Attorneys' Service Limited (SOP) 408-293-9111	•	•	•	•	
•				Bankruptcy Bulletin Weekly Inc 409-854-2777					
•	•	•	•	Bankruptcy Services Inc 405-232-1748					
•	•	•	•	Bay Cities Attorney Services (SOP) 510-444-4800		•	•	•	•
•	•	•	•	CAR-Computer Assisted Research (SOP) 888-223-3456	•	•	•	•	
•	•	•	•	CT Corporation System 800-874-8820	•	•	•	•	
•	•	•	•	Court Record Consultants (SOP) 818-366-1906	•	•	•	•	
•	•	•		Cross, Laura 415-239-8950	•	•	•	•	•
•	•	•		Dee Moody Investigations 415-571-8598	•	•			
•	•	•		▥ FYP Inc 800-569-7143					
•	•	•	•	Fax & File Legal Services Inc (SOP) 415-491-0606	•	•	•	•	
•				▥ Hogan Information Services 405-278-6954					
•	•	•		▥ Infonet 800-849-6207	•	•	•	•	
•	•	•	•	Johnston, John Thomas 415-885-6211	•	•	•	•	•
•	•	•		Lecat, Michel B 415-925-9090	•	•	•	•	
•	•	•	•	Lone Star Legal 415-255-8550	•	•	•	•	
•	•	•	•	Marco & Company (SOP) 707-747-1802	•	•	•	•	
•	•	•	•	Michael Ramey & Associates Inc 510-820-8900	•	•	•	•	
•	•	•	•	▥ PFC Information Services 510-653-0666	•	•	•	•	•
•	•	•	•	Pacific Corporate & Title Services 800-266-9469	•	•	•	•	
•	•	•	•	Pacific Corporate & Title Services 800-230-4988	•	•	•	•	
•	•	•	•	▥ Patten Investigations (SOP) 800-291-1922	•	•	•	•	
•	•	•	•	▥ Pernell & Sons Investigations 510-436-4688	•	•	•	•	
•	•	•	•	▥ Probus Research (SOP) 888-934-3848	•	•	•	•	•
•	•	•	•	▥ Rafael Jorge Investigations 800-344-3754	•	•	•	•	
•	•	•	•	▥ Rapid Research 510-883-1602				•	•
	•	•	•	▥ Records Search 408-399-4747					
•	•	•	•	Research Information Services 800-766-3320	•	•	•	•	
•	•	•	•	Researchers 415-543-9555	•				
•	•	•	•	Ross Legal Services 415-485-0736					
•	•	•	•	St Ives (SOP) 800-995-9443					
•	•	•	•	The Amherst Group 800-521-0237	•	•	•	•	•
•	•	•	•	▥ The August Professional Group (SOP) 415-441-9627	•	•	•	•	
•	•	•	•	Wakeman Microfilm Service 510-886-7667		•	•		
•	•	•	•	Western Attorney Services 415-487-4140	•	•	•	•	

CV	CR	PR	ALPINE (PST)	UC	RE	TX	VS	VR
•	•	•	Amador/Calaveras County Attorneys Svc (SOP) 800-399-9365	•	•	•	•	•
•	•		▥ Infonet 800-849-6207	•	•	•	•	

CV	CR	PR	AMADOR (PST)	UC	RE	TX	VS	VR
•	•	•	Amador/Calaveras County Attorneys Svc (SOP) 800-399-9365	•	•	•	•	•
•	•		▥ Infonet 800-849-6207	•	•	•	•	
•	•	•	▥ M L Cozart Copy Service 209-334-2171	•	•	•	•	•
•	•	•	▥ Rafael Jorge Investigations 800-344-3754	•	•	•	•	
•	•	•	Valley Copy Service Inc (SOP) 209-524-0223	•	•	•	•	•
•	•	•	Vigil Enterprises (SOP) 800-541-3220	•	•	•	•	

CV	CR	PR	BUTTE (PST)	UC	RE	TX	VS	VR
•	•	•	Attorney's Diversified Services (SOP) 916-241-1228	•	•	•	•	•
•	•	•	California Search Services 800-333-3391	•	•	•	•	
•	•	•	Fred Waters Investigations (SOP) 800-506-5060		•	•	•	

CV	CR	PR			UC	RE	TX	VS	VR
•	•		🏛 Infonet 800-849-6207		•	•	•	•	
•	•	•	North State Process (SOP) 916-241-2228		•	•	•	•	
•	•	•	RCC & Associates (SOP)......................... 916-533-7944		•	•	•	•	•
•	•	•	St Ives (SOP) 800-995-9443						
•			The Legal Source 800-786-8163						

CV	CR	PR	CALAVERAS (PST)	UC	RE	TX	VS	VR
•	•	•	Amador/Calaveras County Attorneys Svc (SOP) 800-399-9365	•	•	•	•	
•	•	•	Attorney's Diversified Services 209-948-6110	•	•	•	•	
•	•		🏛 Infonet 800-849-6207	•	•	•	•	
•	•	•	🏛 M L Cozart Copy Service 209-334-2171	•	•	•	•	•
•	•	•	Pergerson & Associates 209-474-3020	•	•	•	•	•
•	•	•	🏛 Rafael Jorge Investigations 800-344-3754	•	•	•	•	

CV	CR	PR	COLUSA (PST)	UC	RE	TX	VS	VR
•	•		🏛 Infonet 800-849-6207	•	•	•	•	
•	•	•	Kern Attorney Service Inc (SOP) 213-483-4900		•	•	•	
•	•	•	RCC & Associates (SOP)......................... 916-533-7944	•	•	•	•	•
•	•	•	St Ives (SOP) 800-995-9443					
•			The Legal Source 800-786-8163					

CV	CR	PR	CONTRA COSTA (PST)	UC	RE	TX	VS	VR
•	•		A Fast Copy Inc (SOP) 510-462-9191		•	•		
•	•	•	ACE Legal Assistance (SOP)...................... 415-864-2020		•		•	
•	•	•	AD Services (SOP) 800-827-9101		•	•	•	
•	•		Accelerated Legal Services (ALS) 510-417-1854					
•	•	•	Adila-Gray Process Servers (SOP) 510-582-8812	•	•	•	•	
•	•	•	Attorney's Diversified Services 510-835-9176	•	•	•	•	
•	•	•	Attorney's Messenger Service 510-937-4581		•			
•	•	•	Bay Cities Attorney Services (SOP) 510-444-4800		•	•	•	•
•	•	•	CT Corporation System 800-874-8820	•	•	•	•	
•	•	•	Court Record Consultants (SOP) 818-366-1906	•	•	•	•	
•	•		Cross, Laura 415-239-8950	•	•	•	•	•
•	•	•	Fax & File Legal Services Inc (SOP)............ 415-491-0606	•	•	•	•	
•	•		🏛 Infonet 800-849-6207	•	•	•	•	
•	•		Lecat, Michel B 415-925-9090	•	•	•	•	
•	•	•	Lone Star Legal 415-255-8550	•	•	•	•	
•	•	•	Pacific Corporate & Title Services 800-266-9469	•	•	•	•	•
•	•	•	🏛 Patten Investigations (SOP) 800-291-1922	•	•	•	•	
•	•	•	🏛 Pernell & Sons Investigations 510-436-4688	•	•	•	•	•
•	•	•	🏛 Probus Research (SOP)........................ 888-934-3848	•	•	•	•	•
•	•	•	🏛 Rafael Jorge Investigations 800-344-3754	•	•	•	•	
•	•	•	🏛 Records Search 408-399-4747					
•	•	•	Research Information Services 800-766-3320	•	•	•	•	
•	•	•	Researchers 415-543-9555	•				
•	•	•	Ross Legal Services 415-485-0736					
•	•	•	St Ives (SOP) 800-995-9443					
•	•	•	The Amherst Group 800-521-0237	•	•	•	•	•
•	•	•	🏛 The August Professional Group (SOP) 415-441-9627	•	•	•	•	
•	•	•	Wakeman Microfilm Service 510-886-7667		•	•	•	
•	•	•	🏛 West Coast MCI (SOP)........................ 510-372-8909	•	•	•	•	
•	•	•	Western Attorney Services 415-487-4140	•	•	•	•	

CV	CR	PR	DEL NORTE (PST)	UC	RE	TX	VS	VR
•	•		🏛 Infonet 800-849-6207	•	•	•	•	
•	•	•	Research and Investigative Associates (SOP)..................... 707-444-8767	•	•	•	•	

CV	CR	PR	EL DORADO (PST)	UC	RE	TX	VS	VR
•	•	•	🏛 All American Information Services 916-632-2149	•	•	•	•	•
•	•	•	Amador/Calaveras County Attorneys Service (SOP).......... 916-672-9330	•	•	•	•	•
•	•	•	Attorney's Diversified Services (SOP)............. 916-441-4396	•	•	•	•	
•	•	•	CAR-Computer Assisted Research (SOP) 888-223-3456	•	•	•	•	

DT	BK	CV	CR	PR			UC	RE	TX	VS	VR
		•	•	•	CSC (SOP) 800-222-2122		•	•	•	•	
		•	•	•	Cal Title/Sacramento Attorneys' Svc 800-952-5650		•	•	•	•	
		•	•	•	Capitol Legal Service Inc 916-443-7112						
		•	•	•	DataSearch Inc 800-452-3282		•	•	•	•	•
		•	•	•	Document Resources 800-344-2382		•	•	•	•	
		•	•		🏛 EIS 916-933-9858						
		•	•	•	El Dorado Co Attorney Service (SOP) 916-672-0433						
		•	•	•	🏛 Infonet 800-849-6207		•	•	•		
	•	•	•	•	🏛 Legalese (SOP) 888-300-3579		•	•	•	•	
	•	•	•	•	🏛 Lubey, Rita L (SOP) 916-722-2568		•	•	•	•	
	•	•	•	•	🏛 M L Cozart Copy Service 209-334-2171		•	•	•	•	
	•	•	•	•	🏛 Norcal Public Records Service 800-252-0910		•	•	•	•	•
		•	•	•	Pacific Corporate & Title Services 800-266-9469		•	•	•	•	•
		•	•	•	Pergerson & Associates 209-474-3020		•	•	•	•	
		•	•	•	Quality Business Information 916-684-5860		•	•	•	•	
		•	•	•	🏛 Rafael Jorge Investigations 800-344-3754		•	•	•	•	
		•	•	•	Researchers 415-543-9555		•				
		•	•	•	Sierra Legal Services (SOP) 916-878-2203		•				
		•	•	•	St Ives (SOP) 800-995-9443						
		•	•		🏛 Unisource Screening & Information (SOP) 909-783-0909						
		•	•	•	Vigil Enterprises (SOP) 800-541-3220		•	•	•	•	
		•	•	•	William Olmsted Investigations 916-646-3443		•	•	•	•	

DT	BK	CV	CR	PR	FRESNO (PST)		UC	RE	TX	VS	VR
•	•	•	•	•	Accessible Paralegal Services (SOP) 209-264-3412		•	•	•	•	•
•	•	•	•	•	Action Legal Support Services (SOP) 209-432-3337		•	•	•	•	•
•	•	•	•	•	Arval Legal Services (SOP) 209-924-1404		•		•	•	•
•	•	•	•	•	Attorney Service of Merced (SOP) 209-383-3233		•	•	•		
•	•	•	•	•	Attorney's Diversified Services 209-233-1475		•	•	•		
•					Bankruptcy Bulletin Weekly Inc 409-854-2777						
•	•	•	•	•	Bankruptcy Services Inc 405-232-1748						
•	•	•	•	•	CT Corporation System 800-874-8820		•	•	•	•	
•	•	•	•	•	Central Valley Records Service 209-525-8786		•		•	•	•
•	•	•	•	•	Court Record Consultants (SOP) 818-366-1906		•	•	•	•	
•	•				🏛 Hogan Information Services 405-278-6954						
•	•		•		🏛 Infonet 800-849-6207		•	•	•	•	
•	•	•	•	•	Loss Protection & Investigations Inc 800-268-7472			•	•	•	•
	•	•	•		Mike Moore Private Investigations (SOP) 800-993-3832		•	•	•	•	
•	•	•	•	•	🏛 Norcal Public Records Service 800-252-0910		•	•	•	•	•
•	•	•	•	•	Orum, Dora 209-251-5193		•	•	•	•	•
•	•	•	•	•	🏛 Rafael Jorge Investigations 800-344-3754		•	•	•	•	
•	•	•	•	•	Research Information Services 800-766-3320		•	•	•	•	
•	•	•	•	•	Valley Copy Service Inc (SOP) 209-524-0223		•	•	•	•	•
•	•	•	•		Wilson Enterprises 209-437-9602						

CV	CR	PR	GLENN (PST)		UC	RE	TX	VS	VR
•	•	•	California Search Services 800-333-3391		•	•	•	•	
•	•		🏛 Infonet 800-849-6207		•	•	•	•	
•	•	•	RCC & Associates (SOP) 916-533-7944		•	•	•	•	•
•			The Legal Source 800-786-8163						

CV	CR	PR	HUMBOLDT (PST)		UC	RE	TX	VS	VR
•	•	•	Attorney's Diversified Services (SOP) 916-241-1228		•	•	•	•	•
•	•		🏛 Infonet 800-849-6207		•	•	•	•	
•	•	•	North State Process (SOP) 916-241-2228		•	•	•	•	
•	•	•	Research and Investigative Associates (SOP) 707-444-8767		•	•	•	•	

CV	CR	PR	IMPERIAL (PST)		UC	RE	TX	VS	VR
•	•	•	🏛 Action Court Services Inc 800-227-1174		•			•	
•	•	•	🏛 Britton, Frank (SOP) 800-343-4429		•	•	•	•	•
•	•	•	Desert Investigations 602-726-4398		•	•	•	•	
•	•	•	Hughes/AMS Attorney Service (SOP) 619-683-2000		•	•	•	•	•

CV	CR	PR		UC	RE	TX	VS	VR
•	•	•	🏛 ID-Check Records 800-340-4473	•	•	•	•	
•	•		🏛 Infonet 800-849-6207	•	•	•	•	
•	•	•	🏛 Rafael Jorge Investigations 800-344-3754	•	•	•	•	
•	•	•	The Amherst Group 800-521-0237	•	•	•	•	•
•	•		🏛 Unisource Screening & Information (SOP) 909-783-0909					

CV	CR	PR	INYO (PST)	UC	RE	TX	VS	VR
•	•	•	Andrews, Sharron 619-878-2038	•	•	•	•	•
•	•		🏛 Infonet 800-849-6207	•	•	•	•	
•	•	•	🏛 Rafael Jorge Investigations 800-344-3754	•	•	•	•	
•	•	•	Sierra Attorney Service (SOP) 619-872-1208		•	•	•	

CV	CR	PR	KERN (PST)	UC	RE	TX	VS	VR
•	•	•	🏛 APSCREEN Inc (SOP) 800-327-8732	•	•	•	•	•
•	•	•	All-American Attorney Services (SOP) 800-838-9044	•	•	•	•	•
•	•	•	Attorney's Diverisified Services (SOP) 805-323-2377	•	•	•		
•	•	•	Court Record Consultants (SOP) 818-366-1906	•				
•	•	•	🏛 File Finders 619-474-7667					
•	•		🏛 Infonet 800-849-6207	•		•	•	
•	•	•	Kern Public Research 805-636-6397	•		•	•	
•	•		Mike Moore Private Investigations (SOP) 800-993-3832	•		•	•	
•	•	•	🏛 Rafael Jorge Investigations 800-344-3754	•		•	•	
•	•		Research Information Services 800-766-3320	•		•	•	
•	•		The Daily Report 805-322-3226	•	•	•	•	
•	•		🏛 Unisource Screening & Information (SOP) 909-783-0909					

CV	CR	PR	KINGS (PST)	UC	RE	TX	VS	VR
•	•	•	Accessible Paralegal Services (SOP) 209-264-3412	•	•	•	•	•
•	•	•	Arval Legal Services (SOP) 209-924-1404	•	•	•	•	•
•	•	•	Attorney's Diversified Services 209-233-1475	•	•	•	•	
•	•		🏛 Infonet 800-849-6207	•	•	•	•	
•	•		Mike Moore Private Investigations (SOP) 800-993-3832	•	•	•	•	
•	•	•	🏛 Rafael Jorge Investigations 800-344-3754	•	•	•	•	

CV	CR	PR	LAKE (PST)	UC	RE	TX	VS	VR
•	•	•	Attorney's Diversified Services 707-545-5455	•	•	•	•	
•	•		🏛 Infonet 800-849-6207	•	•	•	•	
•	•	•	Mendo-Lake Paralegals (SOP) 707-263-8755	•	•	•		

CV	CR	PR	LASSEN (PST)	UC	RE	TX	VS	VR
•	•	•	Attorney's Diversified Services (SOP) 916-241-1228	•	•	•	•	•
•	•		🏛 Infonet 800-849-6207	•	•	•	•	
•	•	•	North State Process (SOP) 916-241-2228	•	•	•	•	
•	•	•	RCC & Associates (SOP) 916-533-7944	•	•	•	•	•
•			The Legal Source 800-786-8163					

DT	BK	CV	CR	PR	LOS ANGELES (PST)	UC	RE	TX	VS	VR
•	•	•	•	•	A & M Attorney Services Inc (SOP) 310-426-8306		•		•	
•	•	•	•	•	A California Process and Attorney Svc (SOP) 909-381-5185	•	•	•	•	
•	•	•	•		ABI Attorney Service (SOP) 800-266-0613		•		•	
•	•	•	•		🏛 APSCREEN Inc (SOP) 800-327-8732	•	•	•	•	•
•	•	•	•		🏛 Aaron Anderson Agency (SOP) 800-408-5350	•		•		
•	•	•	•		🏛 Access Research 800-456-9613		•	•		
•	•	•	•	•	🏛 Action Court Services Inc 800-227-1174	•		•		
•	•	•	•	•	All-American Attorney Services (SOP) 800-838-9044	•	•	•	•	•
•	•	•	•		🏛 AmeriSearch (SOP) 888-462-1600	•		•		•
•	•	•	•	•	American Attorney Service (SOP) 714-374-4886		•		•	•
•	•	•	•	•	BG's Process Serving (SOP) 800-491-2477		•		•	
	•				Bankruptcy Bulletin Weekly Inc 409-854-2777					
	•				Bankruptcy Services Inc 405-232-1748					
•	•	•	•	•	Barristers Attorney Service (SOP) 213-747-3322	•	•	•	•	•
•	•	•	•	•	Bollinger Attorney Service (SOP) 818-902-6009		•	•	•	•
•	•	•	•		CSC 800-458-0700	•		•		

•	•	•	•	•	CT Corporation System	800-874-8820	•	•	•	•	
•	•	•	•	•	California Law Retrieval Serv (Cal Info)	213-957-5035	•	•	•		
•	•	•	•	•	Capitol City Network	916-395-2917	•	•	•		
•	•	•	•	•	Confidential Information Search	818-377-5789	•	•	•	•	•
•	•	•	•	•	Copy Central	213-687-3900	•	•	•		
•					Court Copies & Images Inc	619-696-9650					
•	•	•	•	•	Court Record Consultants (SOP)	818-366-1906	•	•	•		
•	•	•	•		Crutchfield Investigators Inc (SOP)	310-559-3371	•	•			
•	•	•	•	•	DDS Legal Support Systems (SOP)	714-662-5555		•	•		
•	•	•	•	•	DDS Legal Support Systems (SOP)	213-482-5555		•	•		
•	•	•	•	•	Daily Journal Corporation	800-952-5232	•	•	•	•	
•	•	•	•	•	Dante's Attorney Service (SOP)	213-613-1417	•	•	•		
•	•	•	•	•	EAGLE i communications (SOP)	310-280-0106	•	•	•	•	•
•	•	•	•	•	Equity Title Search (SOP)	800-683-0214	•	•	•	•	•
•	•	•	•	•	Executive Attorney Service Inc (SOP)	213-482-6680	•	•	•		
•	•	•	•	•	Fax & File Legal Services Inc (SOP)	415-491-0606	•	•	•		
•	•	•	•	•	🗑 File Finders	619-474-7667					
•	•				General Services	310-859-1122					
•					Glass, Howard	310-827-8473					
•	•	•	•		Global Projects Ltd (SOP)	800-859-8109	•	•	•	•	
•	•	•	•		Gumshoe Investigations Agency (SOP)	800-476-7660	•	•	•	•	
•	•				🗑 Hogan Information Services	405-278-6954					
•	•	•	•		🗑 ID-Check Records	800-340-4473	•	•	•	•	
•	•	•	•		🗑 Infonet	800-849-6207	•	•	•		
	•	•			Information Direct	800-700-0440					
•	•	•	•	•	Kern Attorney Service Inc (SOP)	213-483-4900		•	•		
•	•	•	•	•	LegalNet Inc	310-530-2200	•	•	•	•	
•	•	•	•	•	Los Angeles Legal Service (SOP)	213-259-9499		•			
		•			🗑 Luther, Eleda	805-250-8254					
•	•				🗑 Nerio, Joe Y	909-824-9358		•		•	
•	•	•	•	•	Pacific Corporate & Title Services	800-266-9469	•	•	•	•	•
•	•	•	•	•	Pacific Corporate & Title Services	800-230-4988	•	•	•	•	•
•	•	•	•	•	Parasec	800-603-5868	•	•	•	•	
•	•	•	•	•	Prompt Legal Services (SOP)	310-838-9000	•	•	•	•	•
•	•	•	•	•	🗑 RAM Services (SOP)	714-441-0230	•	•	•	•	
•	•	•	•	•	🗑 Rafael Jorge Investigations	800-344-3754	•	•	•	•	
•	•	•	•	•	Research Information Services	800-766-3320	•	•	•	•	
•	•	•	•	•	Research and Retrieval	800-707-8771	•	•	•	•	
•	•	•	•	•	S & J Attorney Service (SOP)	310-558-8088	•	•	•	•	•
•	•	•	•	•	🗑 Specialized Investigations (SOP)	800-714-3728	•	•	•	•	
•	•	•	•	•	The Amherst Group	800-521-0237	•	•	•	•	•
•	•	•	•		🗑 The Knowledge Bank	818-224-5235	•	•	•		
	•	•			🗑 Unisource Screening & Information (SOP)	909-783-0909					

CV	CR	PR	MADERA (PST)	Phone	UC	RE	TX	VS	VR
•	•	•	Accessible Paralegal Services (SOP)	209-264-3412	•	•	•	•	•
•	•	•	Attorney Service of Merced (SOP)	209-383-3233	•	•	•	•	
•	•	•	Attorney's Diversified Services	209-233-1475	•	•	•	•	
•	•	•	Central Valley Records Service	209-525-8786	•		•	•	•
	•		🗑 Infonet	800-849-6207	•	•	•	•	
•	•	•	🗑 Rafael Jorge Investigations	800-344-3754	•	•	•	•	

CV	CR	PR	MARIN (PST)	Phone	UC	RE	TX	VS	VR
•	•	•	ACE Legal Assistance (SOP)	415-864-2020		•		•	
•	•	•	Attorney's Diversified Services	707-545-5455	•	•	•	•	
•	•	•	Bay Cities Attorney Services (SOP)	510-444-4800		•	•	•	•
•	•	•	CT Corporation System	800-874-8820	•	•	•	•	
•	•	•	Capitol City Network	916-395-2917	•	•	•	•	•
•		•	Cross, Laura	415-239-8950	•	•	•	•	•
	•		🗑 FYP Inc	800-569-7143					
•	•	•	Fax & File Legal Services Inc (SOP)	415-491-0606	•	•	•	•	
•	•	•	🗑 Groves Associates	800-447-6837	•	•	•	•	

CV	CR	PR			UC	RE	TX	VS	VR
•	•		🏛 Infonet	800-849-6207	•	•	•	•	
•	•		Lecat, Michel B	415-925-9090	•	•	•	•	
•	•	•	Lone Star Legal	415-255-8550	•	•	•	•	
•	•	•	Marco & Company (SOP)	707-747-1802	•	•	•	•	
•	•	•	Michael Ramey & Associates Inc	510-820-8900	•	•	•	•	
•	•	•	Pacific Corporate & Title Services	800-266-9469	•	•	•	•	•
•	•	•	🏛 Pernell & Sons Investigations	510-436-4688	•	•	•	•	•
•	•	•	🏛 Probus Research (SOP)	888-934-3848	•	•	•	•	•
•	•	•	🏛 Rafael Jorge Investigations	800-344-3754	•	•	•	•	
•	•	•	Randall, Jean (SOP)	415-897-2361	•	•	•	•	
•	•	•	Research Information Services	800-766-3320	•	•	•		
•	•	•	Researchers	415-543-9555	•				
•	•	•	Ross Legal Services	415-485-0736					
•	•	•	St Ives (SOP)	800-995-9443					
•	•	•	The Amherst Group	800-521-0237	•	•	•	•	•
•	•	•	🏛 The August Professional Group (SOP)	415-441-9627	•	•	•	•	
•	•	•	Wakeman Microfilm Service	510-886-7667		•	•	•	
•	•	•	Western Attorney Services	415-487-4140	•	•	•	•	

CV	CR	PR	MARIPOSA (PST)		UC	RE	TX	VS	VR
•	•	•	Attorney Service of Merced (SOP)	209-383-3233	•	•	•	•	
•	•	•	Attorney's Diversified Services	209-576-0273	•	•	•	•	
•	•		🏛 Infonet	800-849-6207	•	•	•	•	
•	•	•	🏛 Rafael Jorge Investigations	800-344-3754	•	•	•	•	

CV	CR	PR	MENDOCINO (PST)		UC	RE	TX	VS	VR
•	•	•	Attorney's Diversified Services	707-545-5455	•	•	•	•	
•	•	•	Frazier & Associates (SOP)	707-463-1297	•	•	•	•	
•	•		🏛 Infonet	800-849-6207	•	•	•	•	
•	•	•	Research Information Services	800-766-3320	•	•	•	•	
•	•	•	Research and Investigative Associates (SOP)	707-444-8767	•	•	•	•	

CV	CR	PR	MERCED (PST)		UC	RE	TX	VS	VR
•	•	•	Attorney Service of Merced (SOP)	209-383-3233	•	•	•	•	
•	•	•	Attorney's Diversified Services	209-576-0273	•	•	•	•	
•	•	•	Central Valley Records Service	209-525-8786	•		•	•	•
•	•		🏛 Infonet	800-849-6207	•	•	•	•	
•	•	•	LEGWORK (SOP)	209-577-3053	•	•	•	•	•
•	•	•	Pergerson & Associates	209-474-3020	•	•	•	•	
•	•	•	🏛 Rafael Jorge Investigations	800-344-3754	•	•	•	•	•
•	•	•	Valley Copy Service Inc (SOP)	209-524-0223	•	•	•	•	•

CV	CR	PR	MODOC (PST)		UC	RE	TX	VS	VR
•	•		🏛 Infonet	800-849-6207	•	•	•	•	

CV	CR	PR	MONO (PST)		UC	RE	TX	VS	VR
•	•		🏛 Infonet	800-849-6207	•	•	•	•	
•	•	•	🏛 Rafael Jorge Investigations	800-344-3754	•	•	•	•	

CV	CR	PR	MONTEREY (PST)		UC	RE	TX	VS	VR
•	•	•	Attorney Service of California (SOP)	408-688-6066	•	•	•	•	
			Attorney Service of California-Monterey	408-375-4009					
•	•	•	Attorney Service of California-Salinas	408-633-6247	•	•	•	•	
•	•		🏛 Charpontier, Alvin W	408-292-2822	•		•	•	
•	•		🏛 Infonet	800-849-6207	•	•	•	•	
•	•	•	🏛 Pacific Coast Legal Services (SOP)	800-845-8821	•	•	•	•	
•	•	•	Pacific Corporate & Title Services	800-266-9469	•	•	•	•	•
•	•	•	🏛 Probus Research (SOP)	888-934-3848	•	•	•	•	•
•	•	•	🏛 Rafael Jorge Investigations	800-344-3754	•	•	•	•	
•	•	•	Research Information Services	800-766-3320	•	•	•	•	
•	•	•	Researchers	415-543-9555	•				
•	•	•	🏛 SuperBureau Inc	800-541-6821	•	•	•	•	
•	•	•	Tri County Process Service (SOP)	800-757-7623					

CV	CR	PR		UC	RE	TX	VS	VR
•	•	•	Western Attorney Services ... 415-487-4140	•	•	•	•	

CV	CR	PR	NAPA (PST)	UC	RE	TX	VS	VR
•	•	•	Bay Cities Attorney Services (SOP) 510-444-4800		•	•	•	•
•	•		Groves Associates 800-447-6837	•	•	•	•	
•	•		Infonet 800-849-6207	•	•	•	•	
•	•		Lecat, Michel B 415-925-9090	•	•	•	•	
•	•	•	Lone Star Legal 415-255-8550	•	•	•	•	
•	•	•	M L Cozart Copy Service 209-334-2171	•	•	•	•	•
•	•	•	Pacific Corporate & Title Services 800-266-9469	•	•	•	•	•
•	•	•	Patten Investigations (SOP) 800-291-1922	•	•	•	•	
•	•	•	Probus Research (SOP) 888-934-3848	•	•	•	•	•
•	•	•	Rafael Jorge Investigations 800-344-3754	•	•	•	•	
•	•	•	St Ives (SOP) 800-995-9443					
•	•	•	The Amherst Group 800-521-0237	•	•	•	•	•

CV	CR	PR	NEVADA (PST)	UC	RE	TX	VS	VR
•	•	•	Attorney's Diversified Services (SOP) 916-441-4396	•	•	•	•	
•	•	•	CAR-Computer Assisted Research (SOP) 888-223-3456	•	•	•	•	
•	•	•	Capitol Legal Service Inc 916-443-7112					
•	•		Infonet 800-849-6207	•	•	•	•	
•	•		Norcal Public Records Service 800-252-0910	•	•	•	•	•
•	•		RCC & Associates (SOP) 916-533-7944	•	•	•	•	
•	•		Researchers 415-543-9555	•				
•	•	•	Sierra Legal Services (SOP) 916-878-2203	•	•	•	•	•
•			The Legal Source 800-786-8163					
•	•	•	Vigil Enterprises (SOP) 800-541-3220	•	•	•	•	

DT	BK	CV	CR	PR	ORANGE (PST)	UC	RE	TX	VS	VR
•	•	•	•	•	A & M Attorney Services Inc (SOP) 310-426-8306		•	•		
•	•	•	•	•	A California Process and Attorney Svc (SOP) 909-381-5185	•	•	•		
•	•	•	•		ABI Attorney Service (SOP) 800-266-0613		•	•		
•	•	•	•		APSCREEN Inc (SOP) 800-327-8732	•		•		
•	•	•	•		Aaron Anderson Agency (SOP) 800-408-5350			•		
•	•	•	•		Access Research 800-456-9613		•	•		
•	•	•	•	•	Action Court Services Inc 800-227-1174	•				
•	•	•	•	•	All Counties Attorney Service 714-558-1403		•	•		
•	•	•	•	•	All-American Attorney Services (SOP) 800-838-9044		•	•	•	•
•	•	•	•		AmeriSearch (SOP) 888-462-1600	•				•
•	•	•	•		American Attorney Service (SOP) 714-374-4886		•	•		
•	•	•	•	•	BG's Process Serving (SOP) 800-491-2477		•	•		
	•				Bankruptcy Bulletin Weekly Inc 409-854-2777					
•	•	•	•		Bankruptcy Services Inc 405-232-1748					
•	•	•	•	•	Barristers Attorney Service (SOP) 213-747-3322	•	•	•	•	•
•	•	•	•	•	Bollinger Attorney Service (SOP) 818-902-6009		•	•	•	•
•	•	•	•	•	Bosic and Bosic (SOP) 909-788-1988		•	•	•	•
•	•	•	•		CSC 800-458-0700	•		•		
•	•	•	•	•	CT Corporation System 800-874-8820	•		•		
•	•	•	•	•	California Law Retrieval Serv (Cal Info) 213-957-5035	•	•	•		
•	•	•	•	•	Court Record Consultants (SOP) 818-366-1906	•	•	•		
•	•	•	•	•	Crutchfield Investigators Inc (SOP) 310-559-3371	•	•	•		
•	•	•	•	•	DDS Legal Support Systems (SOP) 714-662-5555		•	•		
•	•	•	•	•	DDS Legal Support Systems (SOP) 213-482-5555		•	•		
•	•	•	•	•	Daily Journal Corporation 800-952-5232	•	•	•		
•	•	•	•	•	Dante's Attorney Service (SOP) 213-613-1417		•	•		
•	•	•	•	•	Equity Title Search (SOP) 800-683-0214		•	•		•
•	•	•	•	•	Executive Attorney Service Inc (SOP) 213-482-6680	•	•	•		
•	•	•	•	•	Fax & File Legal Services Inc (SOP) 415-491-0606	•	•	•		
•	•	•	•		General Services 310-859-1122					
•	•	•	•		Glass, Howard 310-827-8473					
•	•	•	•	•	Global Projects Ltd (SOP) 800-859-8109	•	•	•		•
•	•	•	•	•	Gumshoe Investigations Agency (SOP) 800-476-7660	•	•	•	•	

							UC	RE	TX	VS	VR
•	•				Hogan Information Services 405-278-6954						
•	•	•	•	•	ID-Check Records 800-340-4473		•	•	•	•	
		•	•	•	IPSA/Background Plus (SOP) 800-631-1700		•	•	•	•	•
•	•	•	•		Infonet 800-849-6207		•	•	•	•	
		•	•		Information Direct 800-700-0440						
•	•	•	•	•	Kern Attorney Service Inc (SOP) 213-483-4900			•	•	•	•
		•	•	•	Klendshoj, Ole 714-998-1218		•	•	•	•	•
•	•	•	•	•	LegalNet Inc 310-530-2200		•	•	•	•	
•	•	•	•		Nerio, Joe Y 909-824-9358			•	•	•	
•	•				One Hour Court Services 714-558-1403						
•	•	•	•	•	Pacific Corporate & Title Services 800-266-9469		•	•	•	•	•
•	•	•	•	•	Pacific Corporate & Title Services 800-230-4988		•	•	•	•	•
•	•	•	•	•	RAM Services (SOP) 714-441-0230		•	•	•	•	
•	•	•	•	•	Rafael Jorge Investigations 800-344-3754		•	•	•	•	
•	•	•	•	•	Research Information Services 800-766-3320		•	•	•	•	
•	•	•	•	•	Research and Retrieval 800-707-8771		•	•	•	•	
•	•	•	•	•	S & J Attorney Service (SOP) 310-558-8088		•	•	•	•	•
•	•	•	•	•	Specialized Investigations (SOP) 800-714-3728		•	•	•	•	
•	•	•	•	•	The Amherst Group 800-521-0237		•	•	•	•	•
		•	•		Unisource Screening & Information (SOP) 909-783-0909		•	•	•	•	

CV	CR	PR	PLACER (PST)	UC	RE	TX	VS	VR
•	•	•	All American Information Services 916-632-2149	•	•	•	•	•
•	•	•	Attorney's Diversified Services (SOP) 916-441-4396	•	•	•	•	
•	•	•	CAR-Computer Assisted Research (SOP) 888-223-3456	•	•	•	•	
•	•	•	CSC (SOP) 800-222-2122	•	•	•	•	
•	•	•	Cal Title/Sacramento Attorneys' Svc 800-952-5650	•	•	•	•	
•	•	•	Capitol City Network 916-395-2917	•	•	•	•	•
•	•	•	Capitol Legal Service Inc 916-443-7112					
•	•	•	Document Resources 800-344-2382	•	•	•	•	
•	•		EIS 916-933-9858					
•	•	•	El Dorado Co Attorney Service (SOP) 916-672-0433					
•	•	•	Fax & File Legal Services Inc (SOP) 415-491-0606	•	•	•	•	
•	•		Infonet 800-849-6207	•	•	•	•	
•	•	•	LEGWORK (SOP) 916-944-0581	•	•	•	•	•
•	•	•	Legalese (SOP) 888-300-3579	•	•	•	•	
•	•	•	Lubey, Rita L (SOP) 916-722-2568	•	•	•	•	
•	•	•	M L Cozart Copy Service 209-334-2171	•	•	•	•	•
•	•	•	McCoy Investigations 800-287-6789			•	•	
•	•	•	Norcal Public Records Service 800-252-0910	•	•	•	•	
•	•	•	Pacific Corporate & Title Services 800-266-9469	•	•	•	•	
•	•	•	Pergerson & Associates 209-474-3020	•	•	•	•	•
•	•	•	Quality Business Information 916-684-5860	•	•	•	•	•
•	•	•	Rafael Jorge Investigations 800-344-3754	•	•	•	•	
•	•	•	Research Information Services 800-766-3320	•	•	•	•	
•	•	•	Researchers 415-543-9555	•				
•	•	•	Sierra Legal Services (SOP) 916-878-2203	•	•	•	•	•
•	•	•	St Ives (SOP) 800-995-9443					
•	•	•	United Attorneys' Services 916-457-3000	•	•	•	•	•
•	•	•	Vigil Enterprises (SOP) 800-541-3220	•	•	•	•	
•	•	•	William Olmsted Investigations 916-646-3443	•	•	•	•	

CV	CR	PR	PLUMAS (PST)	UC	RE	TX	VS	VR
•	•	•	Attorney's Diversified Services (SOP) 916-241-1228	•	•	•	•	•
•	•		Infonet 800-849-6207	•	•	•	•	
•	•	•	RCC & Associates (SOP) 916-533-7944	•	•	•	•	•
•			The Legal Source 800-786-8163					

DT	CV	CR	PR	RIVERSIDE (PST)	UC	RE	TX	VS	VR
•	•	•	•	A California Process and Attorney Svc (SOP) 909-381-5185	•	•	•	•	•
•	•	•	•	APSCREEN Inc (SOP) 800-327-8732	•	•	•	•	•
•	•	•		Aaron Anderson Agency (SOP) 800-408-5350	•		•		

•	•	•			🏛 Access Research 800-456-9613			•	•
•	•	•	•		🏛 Action Court Services Inc 800-227-1174	•		•	•
•	•	•	•		All-American Attorney Services (SOP) 800-838-9044	•	•	•	•	•
•	•	•	•		American Legal Services (SOP) 619-323-5445				
•	•	•	•		Bollinger Attorney Service (SOP) 818-902-6009		•	•	•
•	•	•	•		Bosic and Bosic (SOP)...................................... 909-788-1988		•	•	•	•
•	•	•	•		CT Corporation System 800-874-8820	•	•	•	•
•		•	•		Court Record Consultants (SOP) 818-366-1906	•	•	•	•
	•	•	•		Crystal Clear Copy Service (SOP) 619-947-5699		•	•	•
•	•	•	•		DDS Legal Support Systems (SOP)................ 714-662-5555		•	•	•
•	•	•	•		DDS Legal Support Systems (SOP)................ 213-482-5555		•	•	•
•	•	•	•		Daily Journal Corporation 800-952-5232	•	•	•	•
•	•	•	•		Dante's Attorney Service (SOP)..................... 213-613-1417		•	•	•
•	•	•	•		Equity Title Search (SOP) 800-683-0214		•	•	•
•	•	•	•		Executive Attorney Service Inc (SOP) 213-482-6680	•	•	•	•	•
•		•			Glass, Howard 310-827-8473				
•	•	•	•		Global Projects Ltd (SOP) 800-859-8109	•	•	•	•
	•	•	•		Green, Richard J (SOP).................................. 619-770-4702				
•	•	•	•		Gumshoe Investigations Agency (SOP)......... 800-476-7660	•	•	•	•	•
•		•	•		🏛 Infonet 800-849-6207	•	•	•	•
•	•	•			Information Direct 800-700-0440				
•	•	•	•		Kern Attorney Service Inc (SOP) 213-483-4900		•	•	•
•	•		•		🏛 Nerio, Joe Y 909-824-9358		•	•	•
•		•	•		Pacific Corporate & Title Services 800-266-9469	•	•	•	•	•
•		•	•		Pacific Corporate & Title Services 800-230-4988	•	•	•	•	•
•	•	•	•		RASCAL (SOP)... 909-693-0165		•	•	
•	•	•	•		🏛 Rafael Jorge Investigations 800-344-3754	•	•	•	•
•	•	•	•		Research Information Services 800-766-3320	•	•	•	•
•	•	•	•		🏛 Specialized Investigations (SOP) 800-714-3728	•	•	•	•
•	•	•	•		The Amherst Group 800-521-0237	•	•	•	•	•
		•	•		🏛 Unisource Screening & Information (SOP) 909-783-0909				

DT	BK	CV	CR	PR	SACRAMENTO (CAPITAL) (PST)	UC	RE	TX	VS	VR
•	•	•	•	•	Attorney's Aid Inc of Sacramento (SOP) 916-443-3915	•				
•	•	•	•	•	Attorney's Diversified Services (SOP).................................. 916-441-4396	•	•	•	•	
	•				Bankruptcy Bulletin Weekly Inc 409-854-2777					
•		•		•	Bankruptcy Services Inc 405-232-1748					
•		•		•	CAR-Computer Assisted Research (SOP) 888-223-3456	•	•	•	•	
•	•	•	•	•	CSC (SOP).. 800-222-2122	•	•	•	•	
•	•	•	•	•	CT Corporation System 800-874-8820	•	•	•	•	
•	•	•	•	•	Cal Title/Sacramento Attorneys' Svc 800-952-5650	•	•	•	•	
					California Drivers Records 800-852-6219	•	•	•	
•	•	•	•	•	California Search Services 800-333-3391	•	•	•	•
•	•	•	•	•	Capitol City Network 916-395-2917	•	•	•	•	•
•	•	•	•	•	Capitol Legal Service Inc 916-443-7112					
					Capitol Services 916-443-0657	•				
•	•	•	•	•	Confi-Chek 800-821-7404	•	•	•	•
•	•	•	•	•	Court Record Consultants (SOP) 818-366-1906	•	•	•	•
•	•	•	•	•	DataSearch Inc 800-452-3282	•	•	•	•	•
•	•	•	•	•	Document Resources 800-344-2382	•	•	•	•
					🏛 EIS 916-933-9858					
	•	•	•	•	El Dorado Co Attorney Service (SOP) 916-672-0433				
•					🏛 FYP Inc 800-569-7143					
•	•	•	•	•	Fax & File Legal Services Inc (SOP).................................... 415-491-0606	•	•	•	•
•	•	•	•	•	Fred Waters Investigations (SOP)....................................... 800-506-5060		•	•	•
•	•	•	•	•	🏛 Infonet 800-849-6207	•	•	•	•
	•	•	•	•	🏛 Investigative Services 916-394-1897				
•	•	•	•	•	LEGWORK (SOP)... 916-944-0581	•	•	•	•	•
•	•	•	•	•	🏛 Legalese (SOP) 888-300-3579	•	•	•	•
•	•	•	•	•	🏛 Logan Registration Service Inc 800-524-4111	•				
•	•	•	•	•	🏛 Lubey, Rita L (SOP) 916-722-2568	•	•	•	
•	•	•	•	•	🏛 M L Cozart Copy Service 209-334-2171	•	•	•	•	•

						UC	RE	TX	VS	VR
●	●	●	●	●	McCoy Investigations 800-287-6789				●	●
●	●	●	●	●	🏛 Norcal Public Records Service 800-252-0910	●	●	●	●	●
●	●	●	●	●	Pacific Corporate & Title Services 800-266-9469	●	●	●	●	●
●	●	●	●	●	Pacific Corporate & Title Services 800-230-4988	●	●	●	●	●
●	●	●	●	●	Parasec 800-603-5868	●	●	●	●	●
●	●	●	●	●	Pergerson & Associates 209-474-3020	●	●	●	●	●
●	●	●	●	●	Quality Business Information 916-684-5860	●	●	●	●	
●	●	●	●	●	🏛 Rafael Jorge Investigations 800-344-3754	●	●	●	●	
●	●	●	●	●	Research Information Services 800-766-3320	●	●	●	●	
●	●	●	●	●	Research and Retrieval 800-707-8771	●	●	●	●	
●	●	●	●	●	Researchers 415-543-9555	●				
					Searching Registration Service 800-488-0238	●	●		●	
●	●	●	●		Seyfried Support Services 916-366-9136					
	●	●		●	Sierra Legal Services (SOP) 916-878-2203	●	●		●	●
●	●	●	●	●	St Ives (SOP) 800-995-9443					
●	●	●	●	●	The Amherst Group 800-521-0237	●	●		●	●
●	●	●	●	●	Unisearch Inc 800-769-1864	●		●	●	
	●	●	●		🏛 Unisource Screening & Information (SOP) 909-783-0909					
●	●	●	●	●	United Attorneys' Services 916-457-3000	●	●	●	●	●
●	●	●	●	●	Valley Copy Service Inc (SOP) 209-524-0223	●	●	●	●	●
●	●	●	●	●	Vigil Enterprises (SOP) 800-541-3220	●	●	●	●	
●	●	●	●	●	William Olmsted Investigations 916-646-3443	●	●	●	●	

	CV	CR	PR	SAN BENITO (PST)	UC	RE	TX	VS	VR
	●	●	●	Attorney Service of California (SOP) 408-688-6066	●	●	●	●	
	●	●		🏛 Charpontier, Alvin W 408-292-2822	●		●	●	
	●	●		🏛 Infonet 800-849-6207	●		●	●	
	●	●	●	🏛 Rafael Jorge Investigations 800-344-3754	●		●	●	
				Tri County Process Service (SOP) 800-757-7623					

BK	CV	CR	PR	SAN BERNARDINO (PST)	UC	RE	TX	VS	VR
●	●	●	●	A California Process and Attorney Svc (SOP) 909-381-5185	●	●	●	●	●
●	●	●	●	ABI Attorney Service (SOP) 800-266-0613		●			
●	●	●	●	🏛 APSCREEN Inc (SOP) 800-327-8732	●	●	●	●	●
●	●	●		🏛 Aaron Anderson Agency (SOP) 800-408-5350	●		●	●	
●	●	●		🏛 Access Research 800-456-9613		●		●	
●	●	●	●	🏛 Action Court Services Inc 800-227-1174	●		●	●	
●	●	●	●	All-American Attorney Services (SOP) 800-838-9044	●	●	●	●	●
●	●	●	●	American Attorney Service (SOP) 714-374-4886		●	●	●	●
●	●	●	●	American Legal Services (SOP) 619-323-5445					
●				Bankruptcy Bulletin Weekly Inc 409-854-2777					
●	●	●	●	Bankruptcy Services Inc 405-232-1748					
●	●	●	●	Bollinger Attorney Service (SOP) 818-902-6009		●	●	●	●
●	●	●	●	Bosic and Bosic (SOP) 909-788-1988		●	●	●	●
●	●	●	●	CT Corporation System 800-874-8820	●	●	●	●	
●	●	●	●	Court Record Consultants (SOP) 818-366-1906	●	●	●	●	
●	●	●		Crutchfield Investigators Inc (SOP) 310-559-3371	●	●	●		
●	●	●	●	Crystal Clear Copy Service (SOP) 619-947-5699				●	
●	●	●	●	DDS Legal Support Systems (SOP) 714-662-5555		●	●	●	
●	●	●	●	DDS Legal Support Systems (SOP) 213-482-5555		●	●	●	
●	●	●	●	Daily Journal Corporation 800-952-5232	●	●	●	●	
●	●	●	●	Dante's Attorney Service (SOP) 213-613-1417		●	●	●	
●	●	●	●	Executive Attorney Service Inc (SOP) 213-482-6680	●	●	●	●	
●		●		Glass, Howard 310-827-8473					
●	●	●	●	Global Projects Ltd (SOP) 800-859-8109	●	●	●	●	●
	●	●	●	🏛 Grissom & Associates (SOP) 800-861-6483	●	●	●	●	
●	●	●	●	Gumshoe Investigations Agency (SOP) 800-476-7660	●	●	●	●	●
●				🏛 Hogan Information Services 405-278-6954					
●	●	●	●	🏛 ID-Check Records 800-340-4473	●	●	●	●	
●	●	●		🏛 Infonet 800-849-6207	●		●	●	
	●	●		Information Direct 800-700-0440					
●	●	●		🏛 Nerio, Joe Y 909-824-9358		●		●	

DT	BK	CV	CR	PR		UC	RE	TX	VS	VR
•	•	•	•		Pacific Corporate & Title Services 800-266-9469	•	•	•	•	•
•	•		•		Pacific Corporate & Title Services 800-230-4988	•	•	•	•	
•	•	•	•		🏛 Rafael Jorge Investigations 800-344-3754	•	•	•	•	
•	•	•	•		Research Information Services 800-766-3320	•	•	•	•	
•	•	•	•		🏛 Specialized Investigations (SOP) 800-714-3728	•	•	•	•	
•	•	•	•		The Amherst Group 800-521-0237	•	•	•	•	•
	•	•			🏛 Unisource Screening & Information (SOP) 909-783-0909					

DT	BK	CV	CR	PR	SAN DIEGO (PST)	UC	RE	TX	VS	VR
•	•	•	•	•	🏛 APSCREEN Inc (SOP) 800-327-8732	•	•	•	•	•
•	•	•	•		🏛 Aaron Anderson Agency (SOP) 800-408-5350	•		•		
•	•	•	•		🏛 Access Research 800-456-9613			•	•	
•	•	•		•	Accu-Tech Professional Services (SOP) 800-275-7189	•		•		
•	•	•	•	•	🏛 Action Court Services Inc 800-227-1174	•		•		
•	•	•	•		All-American Attorney Services (SOP) 800-838-9044	•		•	•	•
•	•	•	•	•	Alpha Attorney Service (SOP) 619-235-8008	•		•	•	
•	•	•	•	•	American Attorney Service (SOP) 714-374-4886	•		•	•	•
•					Bankruptcy Bulletin Weekly Inc 409-854-2777					
•	•	•	•	•	Bankruptcy Services Inc 405-232-1748					
•	•	•	•	•	CT Corporation System 800-874-8820	•	•	•	•	
•	•	•	•	•	Campanella Attorney Services Inc (SOP) 619-696-8131	•	•	•		
•	•	•	•		Court Copies & Images Inc 619-696-9650					
•	•	•	•	•	Court Record Consultants (SOP) 818-366-1906	•	•	•		
•	•	•	•		Crutchfield Investigators Inc (SOP) 310-559-3371	•	•	•		
•	•	•	•	•	DDS Legal Support Systems (SOP) 714-662-5555		•		•	
•	•	•	•	•	DDS Legal Support Systems (SOP) 213-482-5555		•		•	
•	•	•	•	•	Daily Journal Corporation 800-952-5232	•	•	•	•	
•	•	•	•	•	DataFile 800-843-6688	•	•	•	•	
•	•	•	•	•	DataSearch Inc 800-452-3282	•	•	•	•	•
•	•	•	•	•	🏛 File Finders 619-474-7667					
•	•	•	•	•	Gumshoe Investigations Agency (SOP) 800-476-7660	•	•	•	•	
•	•	•	•		🏛 Hogan Information Services 405-278-6954					
•	•	•	•	•	Hughes/AMS Attorney Service (SOP) 619-683-2000	•	•	•	•	•
•	•	•	•	•	🏛 ID-Check Records 800-340-4473	•	•	•	•	
•	•	•	•	•	🏛 Infonet 800-849-6207	•	•	•	•	
•	•	•	•		Information Direct 800-700-0440					
•	•	•	•	•	Kern Attorney Service Inc (SOP) 213-483-4900		•	•	•	
•	•	•	•	•	🏛 Krotzer Legal Service (SOP) 619-232-1291	•	•	•	•	
•	•	•	•	•	🏛 L & J Research 619-575-2205	•	•	•		
•	•	•	•	•	🏛 Owens & Associates Investigations (SOP) 800-297-1343	•	•	•	•	
•	•	•	•	•	Pacific Corporate & Title Services 800-266-9469	•	•	•	•	•
•	•	•	•	•	Parasec 800-603-5868	•	•	•	•	
		•	•	•	RASCAL (SOP) 909-693-0165		•	•		
•	•	•	•	•	🏛 Rafael Jorge Investigations 800-344-3754	•	•	•	•	
•	•	•	•	•	Research Information Services 800-766-3320	•	•	•	•	
•	•	•	•	•	Research and Retrieval 800-707-8771	•	•	•	•	
•	•	•	•	•	San Diego Attorney Service Inc 619-236-9585					
•	•	•	•	•	🏛 Specialized Investigations (SOP) 800-714-3728	•	•	•	•	
			•	•	State Court Retrievers 619-687-3897		•			
•	•	•	•	•	The Amherst Group 800-521-0237	•	•	•	•	•
	•	•	•		🏛 Unisource Screening & Information (SOP) 909-783-0909					
•	•	•	•	•	🏛 WE Investigate Inc (SOP) 619-672-1664	•	•	•	•	

	BK	CV	CR	PR	SAN FRANCISCO (PST)	UC	RE	TX	VS	VR
	•	•	•	•	A & A Legal Services (SOP) 415-697-9431	•	•	•	•	
	•	•	•	•	ACE Legal Assistance (SOP) 415-864-2020		•		•	
		•	•		Accelerated Legal Services (ALS) 510-417-1854					
	•	•	•	•	Attorney's Diversified Services 800-775-3455	•	•	•	•	
	•	•	•	•	Attorney's Messenger Service 510-937-4581		•		•	
	•	•	•	•	Attorneys' Service Limited (SOP) 408-293-9111	•	•	•	•	
	•				Bankruptcy Bulletin Weekly Inc 409-854-2777					
	•	•	•	•	Bankruptcy Services Inc 405-232-1748					

	CV	CR	PR		UC	RE	TX	VS	VR
	•	•	•	🏛 Baxter, Timothy & Sara 415-333-6247	•	•	•	•	
•	•	•	•	Bay Cities Attorney Services (SOP) 510-444-4800	•	•	•	•	•
•	•	•	•	CAR-Computer Assisted Research (SOP) 888-223-3456	•	•	•	•	
•	•	•	•	CT Corporation System 800-874-8820	•	•	•	•	
•	•	•	•	Capitol City Network 916-395-2917	•	•	•	•	•
	•	•	•	🏛 Charpontier, Alvin W 408-292-2822	•	•	•	•	
•	•	•	•	Court Record Consultants (SOP) 818-366-1906	•	•	•	•	
	•	•	•	Dee Moody Investigations 415-571-8598	•	•			
			•	🏛 FYP Inc 800-569-7143					
•	•	•	•	Fax & File Legal Services Inc (SOP) 415-491-0606	•	•	•	•	
			•	🏛 Hogan Information Services 405-278-6954					
•	•	•	•	🏛 Incognito Services (SOP) 800-782-7672	•	•	•	•	•
•	•	•	•	InfoHawks 415-666-3914	•	•	•	•	•
	•	•	•	🏛 Infonet 800-849-6207	•	•	•	•	
•	•	•	•	🏛 Inquiry Services Inc (SOP) 888-444-4033	•	•	•	•	
	•	•	•	Johnston, John Thomas 415-885-6211	•	•	•	•	•
	•	•	•	Lecat, Michel B 415-925-9090	•	•	•	•	
•	•	•	•	Lone Star Legal 415-255-8550	•	•	•	•	
•	•	•	•	Marco & Company (SOP) 707-747-1802	•	•	•	•	
•	•	•	•	Michael Ramey & Associates Inc 510-820-8900	•	•	•	•	
		•	•	P.R.I.D.E. Enterprises 800-465-7743					
	•	•	•	🏛 PFC Information Services 510-653-0666	•	•	•	•	•
•	•	•	•	Pacific Corporate & Title Services 800-266-9469	•	•	•	•	•
	•	•	•	Pacific Corporate & Title Services 800-230-4988	•	•	•	•	•
•	•	•	•	🏛 Pernell & Sons Investigations 510-436-4688	•	•	•	•	
•	•	•	•	🏛 Probus Research (SOP) 888-934-3848	•	•	•	•	•
•	•	•	•	🏛 Rafael Jorge Investigations 800-344-3754	•	•	•	•	
•	•	•	•	🏛 Rapid Research 510-883-1602				•	•
•	•	•	•	🏛 Records Search 408-399-4747					
•	•	•	•	Research Information Services 800-766-3320	•	•	•	•	
•	•	•	•	Research and Retrieval 800-707-8771	•	•	•		
•	•	•	•	Researchers 415-543-9555	•				
•	•	•	•	Ross Legal Services 415-485-0736					
•	•	•	•	St Ives (SOP) 800-995-9443					
•	•	•	•	The Amherst Group 800-521-0237	•	•	•	•	•
•	•	•	•	🏛 The August Professional Group (SOP) 415-441-9627	•	•	•	•	
	•	•	•	🏛 Triad Consultants Ltd (SOP) 415-994-6600		•		•	•
•	•	•	•	Wakeman Microfilm Service 510-886-7667		•	•		
•	•	•	•	Western Attorney Services 415-487-4140	•		•		

CV	CR	PR	SAN JOAQUIN (PST)	UC	RE	TX	VS	VR
•	•	•	Attorney Service of Merced (SOP) 209-383-3233	•	•	•	•	
•	•	•	Attorney's Aid Inc of Modesto 209-522-9901					
•	•	•	Attorney's Diversified Services 209-948-6110	•	•	•	•	
•	•	•	CAR-Computer Assisted Research (SOP) 888-223-3456	•	•	•	•	
•	•	•	CT Corporation System 800-874-8820	•	•	•	•	
•	•	•	Cal Title/Sacramento Attorneys' Svc 800-952-5650	•	•	•	•	
•	•	•	Capitol City Network 916-395-2917	•	•	•	•	•
•	•	•	Central Valley Records Service 209-525-8786	•		•		•
•	•	•	Document Resources 800-344-2382	•	•	•	•	
•	•	•	🏛 Infonet 800-849-6207	•	•	•	•	
•	•	•	🏛 Legalese (SOP) 888-300-3579	•	•	•	•	
•	•	•	🏛 M L Cozart Copy Service 209-334-2171	•	•	•	•	•
•	•	•	Pacific Corporate & Title Services 800-266-9469	•	•	•	•	•
•	•	•	Pacific Corporate & Title Services 800-230-4988	•	•	•	•	•
•	•	•	Pergerson & Associates 209-474-3020	•	•	•	•	•
•	•	•	🏛 Rafael Jorge Investigations 800-344-3754	•	•	•	•	
•	•	•	Research Information Services 800-766-3320	•	•	•	•	
•	•	•	St Ives (SOP) 800-995-9443					
•	•	•	United Attorneys' Services 916-457-3000	•	•	•	•	•
•	•	•	Valley Copy Service Inc (SOP) 209-524-0223	•	•	•	•	•
•	•	•	William Olmsted Investigations 916-646-3443	•	•	•	•	

San Luis Obispo (PST)

CV	CR	PR	Service	Phone	UC	RE	TX	VS	VR
•	•	•	Attorney's Diversified Services	805-543-1458	•	•	•	•	
•	•		Infonet	800-849-6207	•	•	•	•	
•	•	•	Rafael Jorge Investigations	800-344-3754	•	•	•	•	
•	•	•	Research Information Services	800-766-3320	•	•	•	•	

San Mateo (PST)

CV	CR	PR	Service	Phone	UC	RE	TX	VS	VR
•	•	•	A & A Legal Services (SOP)	415-697-9431	•	•	•	•	
•	•	•	Attorneys' Service Limited (SOP)	408-293-9111	•	•	•	•	
•	•		Baxter, Timothy & Sara	415-333-6247	•	•	•		
•	•	•	Bay Cities Attorney Services (SOP)	510-444-4800		•	•	•	•
•	•	•	Better Process	408-292-2360		•		•	
•	•		Charpontier, Alvin W	408-292-2822	•		•	•	
•	•		Dee Moody Investigations	415-571-8598	•	•			
			FYP Inc	800-569-7143					
•	•	•	Fax & File Legal Services Inc (SOP)	415-491-0606	•		•	•	
•	•	•	Incognito Services (SOP)	800-782-7672	•	•	•	•	•
•	•	•	Infonet	800-849-6207	•	•	•	•	
•	•	•	Inquiry Services Inc (SOP)	888-444-4033	•	•	•	•	
•	•		Lecat, Michel B	415-925-9090	•	•	•	•	
•	•		Lone Star Legal	415-255-8550	•	•	•	•	
•	•	•	Marco & Company (SOP)	707-747-1802	•	•	•	•	
	•		P.R.I.D.E. Enterprises	800-465-7743					
•		•	Pacific Corporate & Title Services	800-266-9469	•	•	•	•	•
•		•	Pacific Corporate & Title Services	800-230-4988	•	•	•	•	•
•	•	•	Pernell & Sons Investigations	510-436-4688	•	•	•	•	
•	•	•	Probus Research (SOP)	888-934-3848	•	•	•	•	
•	•	•	Rafael Jorge Investigations	800-344-3754	•	•	•	•	
•	•	•	Rapid Research	510-883-1602				•	•
•	•	•	Records Search	408-399-4747					
•	•	•	Research Information Services	800-766-3320	•	•	•	•	
•	•	•	Researchers	415-543-9555	•				
•	•	•	Ross Legal Services	415-485-0736					
•	•	•	The August Professional Group (SOP)	415-441-9627	•	•	•	•	
•	•		Triad Consultants Ltd (SOP)	415-994-6600		•		•	•
•	•	•	Wakeman Microfilm Service	510-886-7667		•	•	•	
•	•	•	Western Attorney Services	415-487-4140	•	•	•	•	

Santa Barbara (PST)

BK	CV	CR	PR	Service	Phone	UC	RE	TX	VS	VR
•	•	•	•	All-American Attorney Services (SOP)	800-838-9044	•	•	•	•	•
•	•	•	•	Associated Attorney Services (SOP)	805-898-0022	•	•	•	•	
•				Bankruptcy Bulletin Weekly Inc	409-854-2777					
•	•	•	•	Bankruptcy Services Inc	405-232-1748					
•	•	•	•	Commercial Process Servicing Inc (SOP)	800-382-0088		•	•	•	
•	•	•	•	Court Record Consultants (SOP)	818-366-1906	•	•	•		
•	•	•	•	Express Network Inc	805-650-6666	•	•	•		
•	•	•	•	Gumshoe Investigations Agency (SOP)	800-476-7660	•	•	•	•	•
	•	•	•	Infonet	800-849-6207	•	•	•	•	
	•	•		Information Direct	800-700-0440					
•	•	•	•	LEGWORK (SOP)	805-965-3908	•	•	•	•	•
•	•	•	•	Rafael Jorge Investigations	800-344-3754	•	•	•	•	
•	•	•	•	Research Information Services	800-766-3320	•	•	•	•	
•	•	•	•	Services for Attorneys (SOP)	805-564-4107		•	•	•	
•	•	•	•	Specialized Investigations (SOP)	800-714-3728	•	•	•	•	
•	•	•	•	The Amherst Group	800-521-0237	•	•	•	•	•
•	•	•	•	Title Runners	805-685-5576	•	•	•	•	
	•	•		Unisource Screening & Information (SOP)	909-783-0909					

Santa Clara (PST)

DT	BK	CV	CR	PR	Service	Phone	UC	RE	TX	VS	VR
•	•	•	•	•	ACE Legal Assistance (SOP)	415-864-2020		•		•	
		•	•	•	AD Services (SOP)	800-827-9101		•	•	•	

CV	CR	PR				UC	RE	TX	VS	VR
•	•	•	•	•	Attorneys' Service Limited (SOP) 408-293-9111	•	•	•	•	
					Bankruptcy Bulletin Weekly Inc 409-854-2777					
•	•	•	•	•	Bankruptcy Services Inc 405-232-1748					
•	•	•	•	•	Bay Cities Attorney Services (SOP) 510-444-4800		•	•	•	•
•	•	•	•	•	Better Process 408-292-2360		•	•	•	
•	•	•	•	•	CT Corporation System 800-874-8820	•	•	•	•	
•	•	•	•	•	Capitol City Network 916-395-2917	•	•	•	•	•
•	•	•	•		Charpontier, Alvin W 408-292-2822	•	•	•	•	
•	•	•	•	•	Court Record Consultants (SOP) 818-366-1906	•	•	•	•	
•	•	•	•		Dee Moody Investigations 415-571-8598	•	•			
•	•	•	•		FYP Inc 800-569-7143					
•	•	•	•	•	Fax & File Legal Services Inc (SOP) 415-491-0606	•				
•	•	•	•	•	Haber Investigations (SOP) 800-382-6333	•	•	•	•	•
•	•	•	•		Hogan Information Services 405-278-6954					
•	•	•	•		Infonet 800-849-6207	•	•	•	•	
•	•	•	•		Justifacts Credential Verification Inc 800-356-6885					
•	•	•	•		Lecat, Michel B 415-925-9090	•				
•	•	•	•	•	Lone Star Legal 415-255-8550	•	•	•		
•	•	•	•	•	Marco & Company (SOP) 707-747-1802	•	•	•	•	
•	•	•	•		P.R.I.D.E. Enterprises 800-465-7743	•				
•	•	•	•	•	Pacific Coast Legal Services (SOP) 800-845-8821	•	•	•	•	
•	•	•	•		Pacific Corporate & Title Services 800-266-9469	•	•	•		•
•	•	•	•		Pacific Corporate & Title Services 800-230-4988	•	•	•	•	
•	•	•	•	•	Pernell & Sons Investigations 510-436-4688	•	•	•	•	•
•	•	•	•	•	Probus Research (SOP) 888-934-3848	•	•	•	•	•
•	•	•	•	•	Rafael Jorge Investigations 800-344-3754	•	•	•	•	
	•	•	•	•	Records Search 408-399-4747					
•	•	•	•	•	Research Information Services 800-766-3320	•	•	•	•	
•	•	•	•	•	Researchers 415-543-9555	•				
•	•	•	•	•	The Amherst Group 800-521-0237	•	•	•	•	•
•	•	•	•	•	Wakeman Microfilm Service 510-886-7667	•	•	•	•	
•	•	•	•	•	Western Attorney Services 415-487-4140	•	•	•	•	

CV	CR	PR		SANTA CRUZ (PST)		UC	RE	TX	VS	VR
•	•	•		Attorney Service of California (SOP) 408-688-6066		•	•	•	•	
•	•			Charpontier, Alvin W 408-292-2822		•	•	•	•	
	•	•		Infonet 800-849-6207		•	•	•	•	
•	•	•		Pacific Coast Legal Services (SOP) 800-845-8821		•	•	•	•	
•	•	•		Pacific Corporate & Title Services 800-266-9469		•	•	•	•	•
•	•	•		Probus Research (SOP) 888-934-3848		•	•	•	•	•
•	•	•		Rafael Jorge Investigations 800-344-3754		•	•	•	•	
•	•	•		Records Search 408-399-4747					
•	•	•		Research Information Services 800-766-3320		•	•	•	•	
•	•	•		Researchers 415-543-9555		•			
				Tri County Process Service (SOP) 800-757-7623					

CV	CR	PR		SHASTA (PST)		UC	RE	TX	VS	VR
•	•	•		Attorney's Diversified Services (SOP) 916-241-1228		•	•	•	•	•
•	•	•		California Search Services 800-333-3391		•	•	•	•	
•	•	•		Fred Waters Investigations (SOP) 800-506-5060		•	•	•	
•	•			Infonet 800-849-6207		•	•	•	•	
•	•	•		North State Process (SOP) 916-241-2228		•	•	•	•	
•	•	•		RCC & Associates (SOP) 916-533-7944		•	•	•	•	•
•				The Legal Source 800-786-8163					

CV	CR	PR		SIERRA (PST)		UC	RE	TX	VS	VR
•	•			Infonet 800-849-6207		•	•	•	•	

CV	CR	PR		SISKIYOU (PST)		UC	RE	TX	VS	VR
•	•	•		Attorney's Diversified Services (SOP) 916-241-1228		•	•	•	•	•
•	•	•		Cleveland Investigations (SOP) 800-888-6629		•	•	•	•	•
•	•	•		Hanlon, E J (SOP) 916-842-3588		•	•	•	•	•

CV	CR	PR			UC	RE	TX	VS	VR
•	•		🏛 Infonet 800-849-6207		•	•	•	•	
•	•	•	North State Process (SOP) 916-241-2228		•	•	•	•	
•	•	•	RCC & Associates (SOP) 916-533-7944		•	•	•	•	•

CV	CR	PR	SOLANO (PST)		UC	RE	TX	VS	VR
•	•	•	Attorney's Diversified Services 510-835-9176		•	•	•	•	
•	•	•	Attorney's Diversified Services (SOP) 916-441-4396		•	•	•	•	
•	•	•	Bay Cities Attorney Services (SOP) 510-444-4800			•	•	•	•
•	•	•	Cal Title/Sacramento Attorneys' Svc 800-952-5650		•	•	•	•	
•	•	•	Capitol Legal Service Inc 916-443-7112						
•	•	•	Document Resources 800-344-2382		•	•	•	•	
•	•	•	Fax & File Legal Services Inc (SOP) 415-491-0606		•	•	•	•	
•	•	•	🏛 Groves Associates 800-447-6837		•	•	•	•	
•	•	•	🏛 Infonet 800-849-6207		•	•	•	•	
•	•	•	🏛 Lubey, Rita L (SOP) 916-722-2568		•	•	•	•	
•	•	•	🏛 M L Cozart Copy Service 209-334-2171		•	•	•	•	•
•	•	•	Marco & Company (SOP) 707-747-1802		•	•	•	•	
•	•	•	🏛 Norcal Public Records Service 800-252-0910		•	•	•	•	•
•	•	•	Pacific Corporate & Title Services 800-266-9469		•	•	•	•	•
•	•	•	🏛 Patten Investigations (SOP) 800-291-1922		•	•	•	•	
•	•	•	Pergerson & Associates 209-474-3020		•	•	•	•	•
•	•	•	🏛 Probus Research (SOP) 888-934-3848		•	•	•	•	•
•	•	•	🏛 Rafael Jorge Investigations 800-344-3754		•	•	•	•	
•	•	•	Research Information Services 800-766-3320		•	•	•	•	
•	•	•	Researchers 415-543-9555		•				
•	•	•	St Ives (SOP) 800-995-9443						
•	•	•	Wakeman Microfilm Service 510-886-7667			•	•	•	
•	•	•	🏛 West Coast MCI (SOP) 510-372-8909		•	•	•	•	
•	•	•	Western Attorney Services 415-487-4140		•	•	•	•	

BK	CV	CR	PR	SONOMA (PST)		UC	RE	TX	VS	VR
•	•	•	•	🏛 Action Court Services Inc 800-227-1174		•		•		
•	•	•	•	Attorney's Diversified Services 707-545-5455		•	•	•	•	
•				Bankruptcy Bulletin Weekly Inc 409-854-2777						
•			•	Bankruptcy Services Inc 405-232-1748						
•	•	•	•	Bay Cities Attorney Services (SOP) 510-444-4800			•	•	•	•
•	•	•	•	CT Corporation System 800-874-8820		•	•	•	•	
•	•	•	•	Capitol City Network 916-395-2917		•	•	•	•	•
•	•	•	•	Fax & File Legal Services Inc (SOP) 415-491-0606		•	•	•	•	
•	•	•	•	🏛 Groves Associates 800-447-6837		•	•	•	•	
•				🏛 Hogan Information Services 405-278-6954						
•	•	•		🏛 Infonet 800-849-6207		•	•	•	•	
•	•	•		Lecat, Michel B 415-925-9090		•	•	•	•	
•	•	•	•	Lone Star Legal 415-255-8550		•	•	•	•	
•	•	•	•	🏛 Norcal Public Records Service 800-252-0910		•	•	•	•	•
•	•	•	•	Pacific Corporate & Title Services 800-266-9469		•	•	•	•	•
•	•	•	•	🏛 Rafael Jorge Investigations 800-344-3754		•	•	•	•	
•	•	•	•	Research Information Services 800-766-3320		•	•	•	•	
•	•	•		Researchers 415-543-9555		•				
•	•	•	•	Ross Legal Services 415-485-0736		•	•	•	•	
•	•	•	•	SRS Private Investigations Inc (SOP) 707-537-1091		•	•	•	•	
•	•	•	•	The Amherst Group 800-521-0237		•	•	•	•	•
•	•	•	•	Western Attorney Services 415-487-4140		•	•	•	•	

BK	CV	CR	PR	STANISLAUS (PST)		UC	RE	TX	VS	VR
	•	•	•	Attorney Service of Merced (SOP) 209-383-3233		•	•	•	•	
	•	•	•	Attorney's Aid Inc of Modesto 209-522-9901						
	•	•	•	Attorney's Diversified Services 209-576-0273		•		•	•	
•				Bankruptcy Bulletin Weekly Inc 409-854-2777						
•		•	•	Bankruptcy Services Inc 405-232-1748						
•	•	•	•	Capitol City Network 916-395-2917		•	•	•	•	•
•	•	•	•	Central Valley Records Service 209-525-8786		•		•	•	•

•			🏛 Hogan Information Services 405-278-6954		
•	•	•	🏛 Infonet 800-849-6207	• • • •
•	•	•	•	LEGWORK (SOP)... 209-577-3053	• • • • •
•	•	•	•	🏛 M L Cozart Copy Service 209-334-2171	• • • • •
•	•	•	•	Pacific Corporate & Title Services 800-266-9469	• • • • •
•	•	•	•	Pergerson & Associates 209-474-3020	• • • •
•	•	•	•	🏛 Rafael Jorge Investigations 800-344-3754	• • •
•	•	•	•	Researchers 415-543-9555	•
•	•	•	•	Valley Copy Service Inc (SOP) 209-524-0223	• • • •

CV	CR	PR	SUTTER (PST)	UC	RE	TX	VS	VR
•	•	•	Attorney's Diversified Services (SOP)..................... 916-441-4396	•	•	•	•	
•	•	•	Capitol Legal Service Inc 916-443-7112		•	•	•	
•	•	•	Document Resources 800-344-2382	•	•	•	•	
•	•	•	Fred Waters Investigations (SOP)...................... 800-506-5060		•	•	•	
•	•		🏛 Infonet 800-849-6207	•	•	•	•	
•	•	•	🏛 Legalese (SOP) 888-300-3579	•	•	•	•	
•	•	•	🏛 Norcal Public Records Service 800-252-0910	•	•	•	•	•
•	•	•	RCC & Associates (SOP)................................. 916-533-7944	•	•	•	•	•
•	•	•	🏛 Rafael Jorge Investigations 800-344-3754	•	•	•	•	
•	•	•	Researchers 415-543-9555	•				
•			The Legal Source 800-786-8163					
•	•	•	William Olmsted Investigations 916-646-3443	•		•	•	

CV	CR	PR	TEHAMA (PST)	UC	RE	TX	VS	VR
•	•	•	Attorney's Diversified Services (SOP)..................... 916-241-1228	•	•	•	•	•
•	•	•	California Search Services 800-333-3391	•	•	•	•	
•	•		🏛 Infonet 800-849-6207	•	•	•	•	
•	•	•	North State Process (SOP) 916-241-2228	•	•	•	•	
•	•	•	RCC & Associates (SOP)................................. 916-533-7944	•	•	•	•	•
•			The Legal Source 800-786-8163					
•	•	•	Valley Copy Service Inc (SOP) 209-524-0223	•	•	•	•	•

CV	CR	PR	TRINITY (PST)	UC	RE	TX	VS	VR
•	•	•	Attorney's Diversified Services (SOP)..................... 916-241-1228	•	•	•	•	•
•	•		🏛 Infonet 800-849-6207	•	•	•	•	
•	•	•	North State Process (SOP) 916-241-2228	•	•	•	•	
•	•	•	RCC & Associates (SOP)................................. 916-533-7944	•	•	•	•	
•	•	•	Research and Investigative Associates (SOP)..................... 707-444-8767	•	•	•	•	

CV	CR	PR	TULARE (PST)	UC	RE	TX	VS	VR
•	•	•	Accessible Paralegal Services (SOP)..................... 209-264-3412	•	•	•	•	
•	•	•	Arval Legal Services (SOP)............................... 209-924-1404	•		•	•	
•	•	•	Attorney's Diversified Services 209-233-1475	•	•	•	•	
•	•		🏛 Infonet 800-849-6207	•	•	•	•	
•	•		Mike Moore Private Investigations (SOP)..................... 800-993-3832	•	•	•	•	
•	•	•	🏛 Rafael Jorge Investigations 800-344-3754	•	•	•	•	
•	•	•	Valley Copy Service Inc (SOP) 209-524-0223	•	•	•	•	•

CV	CR	PR	TUOLUMNE (PST)	UC	RE	TX	VS	VR
•	•	•	Attorney's Diversified Services 209-576-0273	•	•	•	•	
•	•	•	Central Valley Records Service 209-525-8786	•		•	•	•
•	•		🏛 Infonet 800-849-6207	•	•	•	•	
•	•	•	🏛 Rafael Jorge Investigations 800-344-3754	•	•	•	•	

CV	CR	PR	VENTURA (PST)	UC	RE	TX	VS	VR
•	•	•	🏛 APSCREEN Inc (SOP)................................. 800-327-8732	•	•	•	•	•
•	•	•	🏛 Action Court Services Inc 800-227-1174	•			•	•
•	•	•	All-American Attorney Services (SOP)..................... 800-838-9044		•	•	•	•
•	•	•	Bollinger Attorney Service (SOP)...................... 818-902-6009		•	•	•	•
•	•	•	Commercial Process Servicing Inc (SOP)..................... 800-382-0088		•	•	•	•
•	•	•	Court Record Consultants (SOP)........................ 818-366-1906	•	•	•	•	
•	•		Crutchfield Investigators Inc (SOP)..................... 310-559-3371	•	•	•		

CV	CR	PR		UC	RE	TX	VS	VR
•	•	•	DDS Legal Support Systems (SOP) 714-662-5555		•		•	
•	•	•	DDS Legal Support Systems (SOP) 213-482-5555		•		•	
•	•	•	Daily Journal Corporation 800-952-5232	•	•	•	•	
•	•	•	Dante's Attorney Service (SOP).....................213-613-1417		•	•	•	
•	•	•	Executive Attorney Service Inc (SOP) 213-482-6680	•	•	•	•	
•	•	•	Express Network Inc 805-650-6666	•	•		•	
•	•	•	File Finders 619-474-7667					
•			Glass, Howard 310-827-8473					
•	•	•	Global Projects Ltd (SOP) 800-859-8109	•	•	•	•	•
•	•	•	Gumshoe Investigations Agency (SOP)..........800-476-7660	•	•	•	•	•
•	•	•	ID-Check Records 800-340-4473	•	•	•	•	
•	•		Infonet 800-849-6207	•	•	•	•	
•	•		Information Direct 800-700-0440	•	•	•	•	
•	•	•	Kern Attorney Service Inc (SOP) 213-483-4900		•	•	•	
•	•	•	LEGWORK (SOP).......................................805-965-3908	•	•	•	•	•
•	•	•	Legal Eye & Legal Judgment Services 800-985-1409	•	•	•	•	•
•	•	•	Rafael Jorge Investigations 800-344-3754	•	•	•	•	
•	•	•	Research Information Services 800-766-3320	•	•	•	•	
•	•	•	S & J Attorney Service (SOP).......................310-558-8088	•	•	•		•
•	•	•	The Amherst Group 800-521-0237	•	•	•	•	
•	•		The Knowledge Bank 818-224-5235	•	•	•	•	
•	•	•	Title Runners 805-685-5576	•	•	•	•	
•	•		Unisource Screening & Information (SOP) 909-783-0909					

CV	CR	PR	YOLO (PST)	UC	RE	TX	VS	VR
•	•	•	Attorney's Diversified Services (SOP)...............916-441-4396	•	•	•	•	
•	•	•	CAR-Computer Assisted Research (SOP) 888-223-3456	•	•	•	•	
•	•	•	Cal Title/Sacramento Attorneys' Svc 800-952-5650	•	•	•	•	
•	•	•	Capitol Legal Service Inc 916-443-7112					
•	•	•	Document Resources 800-344-2382	•	•	•	•	
•	•	•	Fred Waters Investigations (SOP)....................800-506-5060		•	•	•	
•	•		Infonet 800-849-6207	•	•	•	•	
•		•	LEGWORK (SOP).......................................916-944-0581	•	•	•		•
•		•	Legalese (SOP) 888-300-3579	•	•			
•		•	Lubey, Rita L (SOP) 916-722-2568	•	•			
•		•	M L Cozart Copy Service 209-334-2171	•	•	•	•	•
•	•	•	McCoy Investigations 800-287-6789				•	•
•	•	•	Norcal Public Records Service 800-252-0910	•	•	•	•	•
•	•	•	Pergerson & Associates 209-474-3020	•	•			
•	•	•	Quality Business Information 916-684-5860	•	•	•	•	•
•	•	•	Researchers 415-543-9555	•				
•	•	•	St Ives (SOP) 800-995-9443					
•	•	•	United Attorneys' Services 916-457-3000	•	•	•	•	•
•	•	•	Vigil Enterprises (SOP) 800-541-3220	•	•	•	•	
•	•	•	William Olmsted Investigations 916-646-3443	•	•	•	•	

CV	CR	PR	YUBA (PST)	UC	RE	TX	VS	VR
•	•	•	Attorney's Diversified Services (SOP)...............916-441-4396	•	•	•	•	
•	•	•	Document Resources 800-344-2382	•	•	•	•	
•	•	•	Fred Waters Investigations (SOP)....................800-506-5060		•	•	•	
•	•		Infonet 800-849-6207	•	•	•	•	
•	•	•	Legalese (SOP) 888-300-3579	•	•	•	•	
•	•	•	Norcal Public Records Service 800-252-0910	•	•	•	•	•
•	•	•	Pergerson & Associates 209-474-3020	•	•	•	•	•
•	•	•	RCC & Associates (SOP)..............................916-533-7944	•	•	•	•	
•	•	•	Rafael Jorge Investigations 800-344-3754	•	•	•	•	
•	•	•	Researchers 415-543-9555	•				
•	•	•	St Ives (SOP) 800-995-9443					
•			The Legal Source 800-786-8163					
•	•	•	William Olmsted Investigations 916-646-3443	•	•	•	•	

COLORADO

CV	CR	PR	ADAMS (MST)		UC	RE	TX	VS	VR
•	•		A & A Background Screening	303-457-9223					•
•	•	•	AAA Process Servers Inc (SOP)	800-293-6098	•	•			
•	•		APSSI/Colorado Research	800-552-4065	•	•	•		
•	•	•	CSC	800-423-7398	•	•	•	•	
•	•	•	Centennial Coverages Inc	800-338-8221	•	•	•	•	•
•	•	•	Chris Wright & Associates	303-776-0291	•	•	•	•	
•	•	•	Colorado Records Search Inc	303-972-3424	•	•	•	•	
•	•	•	Deister Ward & Witcher Inc	303-790-8426	•	•	•	•	
•	•	•	Etzold, Steve	800-455-3768	•	•	•	•	•
	•		HR Plus	800-332-7587					
		•	🏛 Henritze, Barbara K	303-499-3750		•	•	•	•
			Home Title (SOP)	303-758-4300		•	•		
•	•	•	Interwest Investigations	303-223-2212	•	•	•	•	
•	•	•	🏛 National Business Information Service	303-680-2712	•	•	•	•	•
•	•	•	Peregrine Investigation & Research (SOP)	303-441-7442	•	•	•	•	
•	•	•	R A Heales & Associates Ltd	303-671-8700	•	•	•	•	
•	•	•	🏛 Search Company International	800-727-2120	•	•	•	•	•
•	•	•	🏛 Security Source Nationwide (SOP)	303-628-3973	•	•	•	•	•

CV	CR	PR	ALAMOSA (MST)		UC	RE	TX	VS	VR

See adjoining counties for retrievers ....

CV	CR	PR	ARAPAHOE (MST)		UC	RE	TX	VS	VR
•	•		A & A Background Screening	303-457-9223					•
•	•	•	AAA Process Servers Inc (SOP)	800-293-6098	•	•			
•	•		APSSI/Colorado Research	800-552-4065	•	•	•		
•	•	•	Access Information	800-827-7607	•	•	•	•	
•	•	•	CSC	800-423-7398	•	•	•	•	
•	•	•	Centennial Coverages Inc	800-338-8221	•	•	•	•	•
•	•	•	Chris Wright & Associates	303-776-0291	•	•	•	•	
•	•	•	Colorado Records Search Inc	303-972-3424	•	•	•	•	
•	•	•	Deister Ward & Witcher Inc	303-790-8426	•	•	•	•	
•	•	•	Etzold, Steve	800-455-3768	•	•	•	•	•
•	•		🏛 Financial Investigations Inc (SOP)	303-469-3831	•	•	•	•	
	•		HR Plus	800-332-7587					
		•	🏛 Henritze, Barbara K	303-499-3750		•	•	•	•
			Home Title (SOP)	303-758-4300		•	•		
•	•	•	Interwest Investigations	303-223-2212	•	•	•	•	
•	•	•	🏛 National Business Information Service	303-680-2712	•	•	•	•	•
•	•	•	Peregrine Investigation & Research (SOP)	303-441-7442	•	•	•	•	•
•	•	•	R A Heales & Associates Ltd	303-671-8700	•	•	•	•	
•	•	•	🏛 Search Company International	800-727-2120	•	•	•	•	•
•	•	•	🏛 Security Source Nationwide (SOP)	303-628-3973	•	•	•	•	•

CV	CR	PR	ARCHULETA (MST)		UC	RE	TX	VS	VR
			Colorado Land Title	303-264-4178	•	•	•		
•	•	•	Pagosa Springs Title Co	303-264-4141	•	•	•		

CV	CR	PR	BACA (MST)		UC	RE	TX	VS	VR

See adjoining counties for retrievers ....

CV	CR	PR	BENT (MST)		UC	RE	TX	VS	VR
			Bent County Abstract Co	719-456-0381	•	•	•		

CV	CR	PR	BOULDER (MST)		UC	RE	TX	VS	VR
•	•	•	AAA Process Servers Inc (SOP)	800-293-6098	•	•			
•	•		APSSI/Colorado Research	800-552-4065	•	•	•		
•	•	•	Access Information	800-827-7607	•	•	•	•	
•	•		Background Information Services	303-442-3960	•				

CV	CR	PR		UC	RE	TX	VS	VR
●	●	●	CSC 800-423-7398	●	●	●	●	
●	●	●	Centennial Coverages Inc 800-338-8221	●	●	●	●	●
●	●	●	Chris Wright & Associates 303-776-0291	●	●	●	●	
●	●	●	Colorado Records Search Inc 303-972-3424	●	●	●	●	
●	●	●	Etzold, Steve 800-455-3768	●	●	●	●	●
●	●		🏛 Financial Investigations Inc (SOP) 303-469-3831	●	●	●	●	
	●		HR Plus 800-332-7587					
●		●	🏛 Henritze, Barbara K 303-499-3750		●		●	
			Home Title (SOP) 303-758-4300		●		●	
●	●	●	Interwest Investigations 303-223-2212	●		●	●	
●	●	●	Peregrine Investigation & Research (SOP) 303-441-7442	●	●	●	●	●
●	●	●	R A Heales & Associates Ltd 303-671-8700	●	●	●	●	
●	●	●	🏛 Search Company International 800-727-2120	●	●	●	●	●
●	●	●	🏛 Security Source Nationwide (SOP) 303-628-3973	●	●	●	●	●
●	●	●	Special Service Investigations (SOP) 970-490-5200	●	●	●	●	

CV	CR	PR	CHAFFEE (MST)	UC	RE	TX	VS	VR
			Chaffee Title-Abstract Co 719-539-2215	●	●	●		

CV	CR	PR	CHEYENNE (MST)	UC	RE	TX	VS	VR
	●		Cheyenne County Abstract Co 719-767-5585	●	●	●		
●	●	●	Deister Ward & Witcher Inc 303-790-8426	●	●	●	●	

CV	CR	PR	CLEAR CREEK (MST)	UC	RE	TX	VS	VR
●	●	●	Clear Creek-Gelpin Abstract & Title Corp 303-569-2391	●	●	●	●	

CV	CR	PR	CONEJOS (MST)	UC	RE	TX	VS	VR
			See adjoining counties for retrievers					

CV	CR	PR	COSTILLA (MST)	UC	RE	TX	VS	VR
			See adjoining counties for retrievers					

CV	CR	PR	CROWLEY (MST)	UC	RE	TX	VS	VR
			Crowley County Insurance & Title 719-267-4778	●	●	●		
●	●	●	Deister Ward & Witcher Inc 303-790-8426	●	●	●	●	

CV	CR	PR	CUSTER (MST)	UC	RE	TX	VS	VR
●		●	Fremont/Custer County Abstract Co 719-275-4141	●	●	●	●	

CV	CR	PR	DELTA (MST)	UC	RE	TX	VS	VR
			Western Title Insurance Agency Inc 303-874-8286	●	●	●		

DT	BK	CV	CR	PR	DENVER (CAPITAL) (MST)	UC	RE	TX	VS	VR
●	●	●	●		A & A Background Screening 303-457-9223					●
●	●	●	●	●	AAA Process Servers Inc (SOP) 800-293-6098	●	●			
●	●	●	●		APSSI/Colorado Research 800-552-4065	●	●	●		
●	●	●	●	●	Access Information 800-827-7607	●	●	●	●	
●	●	●	●	●	CSC 800-423-7398	●	●	●	●	
●	●	●	●		Centennial Coverages Inc 800-338-8221	●	●	●	●	●
●	●	●	●		Chris Wright & Associates 303-776-0291	●	●	●	●	
●	●	●	●	●	Colorado Records Search Inc 303-972-3424	●	●	●	●	
●	●	●	●	●	Etzold, Steve 800-455-3768	●	●	●	●	●
●	●	●	●		🏛 Financial Investigations Inc (SOP) 303-469-3831	●	●	●		
●	●				HR Plus 800-332-7587					
●		●	●	●	🏛 Henritze, Barbara K 303-499-3750		●		●	●
●	●				🏛 Hogan Information Services 405-278-6954					
					Home Title (SOP) 303-758-4300		●		●	
●	●	●	●		Interwest Investigations 303-223-2212	●	●	●	●	
	●				NACM/Rocky Mountain Affiliate 303-837-1280					
●	●	●	●	●	🏛 National Business Information Service 303-680-2712	●	●		●	
	●			●	PCS Inc (SOP) 800-792-2108		●	●	●	
●	●	●	●	●	Peregrine Investigation & Research (SOP) 303-441-7442	●	●	●	●	●
●	●	●	●	●	R A Heales & Associates Ltd 303-671-8700	●	●	●	●	

					Search Company International	800-727-2120					
•	•	•	•	•	🏛 Search Company International	800-727-2120	•	•	•	•	•
•	•	•	•	•	🏛 Security Source Nationwide (SOP)	303-628-3973	•	•	•	•	•

CV	CR	PR	DOLORES (MST)		UC	RE	TX	VS	VR
			Montezuma-Dolores Title Co — 970-565-8491		•	•	•		

CV	CR	PR	DOUGLAS (MST)		UC	RE	TX	VS	VR
•	•		A & A Background Screening — 303-457-9223						•
•	•	•	AAA Process Servers Inc (SOP) — 800-293-6098		•	•			
•	•		APSSI/Colorado Research — 800-552-4065		•	•	•		
•	•	•	CSC — 800-423-7398		•	•	•	•	
•	•	•	Centennial Coverages Inc — 800-338-8221		•	•	•	•	•
•	•	•	Colorado Records Search Inc — 303-972-3424		•	•	•	•	
•	•	•	Deister Ward & Witcher Inc — 303-790-8426		•	•	•	•	
•	•	•	Etzold, Steve — 800-455-3768		•	•	•	•	•
			Home Title (SOP) — 303-758-4300			•	•		
•	•	•	🏛 National Business Information Service — 303-680-2712		•	•	•	•	•
•	•	•	Peregrine Investigation & Research (SOP) — 303-441-7442		•	•	•	•	•
•	•	•	R A Heales & Associates Ltd — 303-671-8700		•	•	•	•	
•	•	•	🏛 Search Company International — 800-727-2120		•	•	•	•	•

CV	CR	PR	EAGLE (MST)		UC	RE	TX	VS	VR
			Home Title (SOP) — 303-758-4300			•	•		

CV	CR	PR	EL PASO (MST)		UC	RE	TX	VS	VR
•	•		APSSI/Colorado Research — 800-552-4065		•	•	•		
•	•	•	🏛 Applied Professional Research (APRO) — 888-686-0701		•	•	•	•	•
•	•	•	Colorado Records Search Inc — 303-972-3424		•	•	•	•	
•	•		🏛 Financial Investigations Inc (SOP) — 303-469-3831		•	•	•		
	•		HR Plus — 800-332-7587						
			Home Title (SOP) — 303-758-4300			•	•		
•	•	•	Legal Express — 719-578-0407		•				
	•		🏛 PreSearch Background Services — 800-562-8077						
•	•	•	R A Heales & Associates Ltd — 303-671-8700		•	•	•	•	
•	•	•	🏛 Search Company International — 800-727-2120		•	•	•	•	•

CV	CR	PR	ELBERT (MST)		UC	RE	TX	VS	VR
•	•	•	Deister Ward & Witcher Inc — 303-790-8426		•	•	•	•	

CV	CR	PR	FREMONT (MST)		UC	RE	TX	VS	VR
•		•	Fremont/Custer County Abstract Co — 719-275-4141		•	•	•	•	
•	•	•	🏛 Search Company International — 800-727-2120		•	•	•	•	•

CV	CR	PR	GARFIELD (MST)		UC	RE	TX	VS	VR
•	•	•	Deister Ward & Witcher Inc — 303-790-8426		•	•	•	•	

CV	CR	PR	GILPIN (MST)		UC	RE	TX	VS	VR
•	•	•	Clear Creek-Gelpin Abstract & Title Corp — 303-569-2391		•	•	•	•	
•	•	•	Colorado Records Search Inc — 303-972-3424		•	•	•	•	

CV	CR	PR	GRAND (MST)		UC	RE	TX	VS	VR
			Home Title (SOP) — 303-758-4300			•	•		

CV	CR	PR	GUNNISON (MST)		UC	RE	TX	VS	VR
•	•	•	Deister Ward & Witcher Inc — 303-790-8426		•	•	•	•	

CV	CR	PR	HINSDALE (MST)		UC	RE	TX	VS	VR
•	•	•	Hinsdale County Title Co — 303-944-2614		•	•	•	•	

CV	CR	PR	HUERFANO (MST)		UC	RE	TX	VS	VR
			Dotter Abstract & Associates — 719-738-1730		•	•	•	•	

CV	CR	PR	JACKSON (MST)		UC	RE	TX	VS	VR
			See adjoining counties for retrievers						

CV	CR	PR	JEFFERSON (MST)		UC	RE	TX	VS	VR
●	●		A & A Background Screening 303-457-9223						●
●	●	●	AAA Process Servers Inc (SOP)...................... 800-293-6098		●	●			
●	●		APSSI/Colorado Research 800-552-4065		●	●	●		
●	●	●	Access Information 800-827-7607		●	●	●	●	
●	●	●	CSC 800-423-7398		●	●	●	●	
●	●	●	Centennial Coverages Inc 800-338-8221		●	●	●	●	
●	●	●	Chris Wright & Associates 303-776-0291		●	●	●	●	●
●	●	●	Colorado Records Search Inc 303-972-3424		●	●	●	●	
●	●	●	Etzold, Steve 800-455-3768		●	●	●	●	●
	●		HR Plus 800-332-7587						
		●	⑯ Henritze, Barbara K 303-499-3750			●	●	●	●
			Home Title (SOP) 303-758-4300			●	●		
●	●	●	Interwest Investigations 303-223-2212		●	●	●	●	
●	●	●	⑯ National Business Information Service 303-680-2712		●	●	●	●	
●	●	●	Peregrine Investigation & Research (SOP)...... 303-441-7442		●	●	●	●	●
●	●	●	R A Heales & Associates Ltd 303-671-8700		●	●	●	●	
●	●	●	⑯ Search Company International 800-727-2120		●	●	●	●	●
●	●	●	⑯ Security Source Nationwide (SOP)............ 303-628-3973		●	●	●	●	●

CV	CR	PR	KIOWA (MST)		UC	RE	TX	VS	VR
●	●	●	Deister Ward & Witcher Inc 303-790-8426		●	●	●	●	
			Kiowa County Abstract Co 719-438-5811		●	●			

CV	CR	PR	KIT CARSON (MST)		UC	RE	TX	VS	VR
●	●	●	Deister Ward & Witcher Inc 303-790-8426		●	●	●	●	

CV	CR	PR	LA PLATA (MST)		UC	RE	TX	VS	VR
			La Plata Abstract Co 303-247-5464		●	●	●		

CV	CR	PR	LAKE (MST)		UC	RE	TX	VS	VR
●	●	●	Lake County Abstract Co 719-486-2688		●	●	●	●	

CV	CR	PR	LARIMER (MST)		UC	RE	TX	VS	VR
●	●	●	Chris Wright & Associates 303-776-0291		●	●	●	●	
●	●	●	Colorado Records Search Inc 303-972-3424		●	●	●	●	
	●		HR Plus 800-332-7587						
●	●	●	Interwest Investigations 303-223-2212		●	●	●	●	
●	●	●	Pro-Serve Investigative Services (SOP)........... 970-407-0813		●	●	●	●	●
●	●	●	⑯ Search Company International 800-727-2120		●	●	●	●	●
●	●	●	Special Service Investigations (SOP)............... 970-490-5200		●	●	●	●	●

CV	CR	PR	LAS ANIMAS (MST)		UC	RE	TX	VS	VR
●		●	Southern Colorado Title Co 719-846-4944		●	●	●	●	

CV	CR	PR	LINCOLN (MST)		UC	RE	TX	VS	VR
●	●	●	Deister Ward & Witcher Inc 303-790-8426		●	●	●	●	
			Home Title (SOP) 303-758-4300			●	●		

CV	CR	PR	LOGAN (MST)		UC	RE	TX	VS	VR
●	●	●	Deister Ward & Witcher Inc 303-790-8426		●	●	●	●	

CV	CR	PR	MESA (MST)		UC	RE	TX	VS	VR
			Abstract & Title Co of Mesa County Inc 303-242-8234			●	●	●	
●	●	●	Deister Ward & Witcher Inc 303-790-8426		●	●	●	●	

CV	CR	PR	MINERAL (MST)		UC	RE	TX	VS	VR
			Rio Grande Mineral Abstract 719-657-3366		●	●	●		

CV	CR	PR	MOFFAT (MST)		UC	RE	TX	VS	VR
			See adjoining counties for retrievers						

CV	CR	PR	MONTEZUMA (MST)	UC	RE	TX	VS	VR
			Montezuma-Dolores Title Co 970-565-8491	●	●	●		

CV	CR	PR	MONTROSE (MST)	UC	RE	TX	VS	VR
●	●	●	Deister Ward & Witcher Inc 303-790-8426	●	●	●	●	
			Western Title Insurance Agency Inc 303-249-7944	●	●	●		

CV	CR	PR	MORGAN (MST)	UC	RE	TX	VS	VR
			Home Title (SOP) 303-758-4300		●	●		

CV	CR	PR	OTERO (MST)	UC	RE	TX	VS	VR
●	●	●	Deister Ward & Witcher Inc 303-790-8426	●	●	●	●	

CV	CR	PR	OURAY (MST)	UC	RE	TX	VS	VR
●	●	●	Attorneys' Title Agency Inc 303-325-4911	●	●	●		
			Western Title Insurance Agency Inc 303-249-7944	●	●	●		

CV	CR	PR	PARK (MST)	UC	RE	TX	VS	VR
●	●	●	Deister Ward & Witcher Inc 303-790-8426	●	●	●	●	

CV	CR	PR	PHILLIPS (MST)	UC	RE	TX	VS	VR
●	●	●	Deister Ward & Witcher Inc 303-790-8426	●	●	●	●	

CV	CR	PR	PITKIN (MST)	UC	RE	TX	VS	VR
●	●	●	Deister Ward & Witcher Inc 303-790-8426	●	●	●	●	

CV	CR	PR	PROWERS (MST)	UC	RE	TX	VS	VR
●	●	●	Guaranty Abstract Co 719-336-3261	●	●	●		

CV	CR	PR	PUEBLO (MST)	UC	RE	TX	VS	VR
●	●	●	Colorado Records Search Inc 303-972-3424	●	●	●	●	
●	●	●	🏛 Search Company International 800-727-2120	●	●	●	●	●

CV	CR	PR	RIO BLANCO (MST)	UC	RE	TX	VS	VR
●	●	●	Deister Ward & Witcher Inc 303-790-8426	●	●	●	●	

CV	CR	PR	RIO GRANDE (MST)	UC	RE	TX	VS	VR
			Rio Grande Mineral Abstract 719-657-3366	●	●	●		

CV	CR	PR	ROUTT (MST)	UC	RE	TX	VS	VR
●	●	●	Teresa D Havens & Associates (SOP) 970-638-0455	●	●	●	●	●

CV	CR	PR	SAGUACHE (MST)	UC	RE	TX	VS	VR
●	●	●	Saguache County Abstract & Investment 719-655-2611	●	●	●	●	●

CV	CR	PR	SAN JUAN (MST)	UC	RE	TX	VS	VR
●	●	●	Attorneys' Title Agency Inc 303-325-4911	●	●	●		

CV	CR	PR	SAN MIGUEL (MST)	UC	RE	TX	VS	VR
●	●	●	Attorneys' Title Agency Inc 303-325-4911	●	●	●		

CV	CR	PR	SEDGWICK (MST)	UC	RE	TX	VS	VR
●	●	●	Deister Ward & Witcher Inc 303-790-8426	●	●	●	●	

CV	CR	PR	SUMMIT (MST)	UC	RE	TX	VS	VR
●	●	●	Deister Ward & Witcher Inc 303-790-8426	●	●	●	●	
			Home Title (SOP) 303-758-4300		●	●		
●	●	●	McCormick Detective Agency (SOP) 970-453-6378	●	●	●	●	●

CV	CR	PR	TELLER (MST)	UC	RE	TX	VS	VR
●	●	●	🏛 Applied Professional Research (APRO) 888-686-0701	●	●	●	●	●
			Home Title (SOP) 303-758-4300		●	●		
●	●	●	Legal Express 719-578-0407	●	●	●		
●	●	●	🏛 Search Company International 800-727-2120	●	●	●	●	●

CV	CR	PR	WASHINGTON (MST)		UC	RE	TX	VS	VR
			Washington County Title Company 303-345-2256		•	•	•		

CV	CR	PR	WELD (MST)		UC	RE	TX	VS	VR
•	•	•	Centennial Coverages Inc 800-338-8221		•	•	•	•	•
•	•	•	Chris Wright & Associates 303-776-0291		•	•	•	•	
•	•	•	Colorado Records Search Inc 303-972-3424		•	•	•	•	
•	•	•	Deister Ward & Witcher Inc 303-790-8426		•	•	•	•	
•	•	•	Interwest Investigations 303-223-2212		•	•	•	•	
•	•	•	Pro-Serve Investigative Services (SOP)..................... 970-407-0813		•	•	•	•	•
•	•		Research & Revisions Etc 303-351-6276		•	•	•	•	
•	•	•	🏛 Search Company International 800-727-2120		•	•	•	•	•
•	•	•	Special Service Investigations (SOP)........................ 970-490-5200		•	•	•	•	•

CV	CR	PR	YUMA (MST)		UC	RE	TX	VS	VR
			Duke, Frank (SOP) 303-332-4042						

SUMMARY OF CODES

COURT RECORDS

CODE	GOVERNMENT AGENCY	TYPE OF INFORMATION
DT	US District Court	Federal civil and criminal cases
BK	Bankruptcy Court	United States bankruptcy cases
CV	Civil Court	Municipal, county and state level civil cases
CR	Criminal Court	Municipal, county and state level criminal cases
PR	Probate Court	Wills and estate cases

COUNTY RECORDS

CODE	GOVERNMENT AGENCY	TYPE OF INFORMATION
UC	UCC Filing Office	Uniform Commercial Code and other personal property liens
RE	Recorder of Deeds	Real property transactions and liens
TX	Tax Assessor	Real property tax information
VS	Vital Records Office	Vital statistics—birth, death, marriage, divorce, etc.
VR	Voter Registration Office	Voter registration and campaign contribution information

- "CODE" designates the agency and type of information obtainable in each county from a retriever.
- The time zone for each county is abbreviated as follows: EST—Eastern Standard Time; CST—Central; MST—Mountain; PST—Pacific; AK—Alaska; HT—Hawaii.
- 🏛—This symbol designates a Public Record Retriever Network member.
- "(SOP)" after the retriever name designates Service of Process.
- Individual retrievers without a company name are listed in order of their last name.
- US District and Bankruptcy courts are indicated only in the counties where courts are located.

CONNECTICUT

DT	BK	CV	CR	PR	FAIRFIELD (EST)		UC	RE	TX	VS	VR
•	•	•		•	Austin & Associates Inc	914-968-3700	•	•	•		•
•	•	•		•	CW Credit Abstract Co	718-423-9430	•	•	•		
•	•		•	•	Data Reporting Corp	203-287-1294	•	•	•		
•	•	•	•	•	Information Management Systems Inc (SOP)	860-229-1119	•	•	•	•	•
•	•	•	•	•	NEWSI (SOP)	800-517-4636	•	•	•	•	•
•	•	•		•	Nationwide Information Services (SOP)	800-227-0575	•	•	•	•	
•	•	•	•	•	North East Court Services Inc (SOP)	800-235-0794	•	•			
•	•	•	•	•	Pro Search Inc	203-348-6994	•	•	•	•	
•	•	•	•	•	TJM & Associates	800-749-4254	•	•	•	•	•

DT	BK	CV	CR	PR	HARTFORD (CAPITAL) (EST)		UC	RE	TX	VS	VR
•	•	•	•	•	Applied Investigative Group (SOP)	860-895-8590	•	•	•	•	
•	•	•		•	CSC	860-724-1228	•	•	•	•	
•	•	•		•	CW Credit Abstract Co	718-423-9430	•	•	•		
•	•		•	•	Data Reporting Corp	203-287-1294	•	•	•		
•	•	•	•	•	First Security Service Corp	617-568-8845	•	•	•	•	
•	•	•	•	•	Information Management Systems Inc (SOP)	860-229-1119	•	•	•	•	•
•	•	•	•	•	NEWSI (SOP)	800-517-4636	•	•	•	•	•
•	•	•		•	Nationwide Information Services (SOP)	800-227-0575	•	•	•	•	
•	•	•	•	•	TJM & Associates	800-749-4254	•	•	•	•	•

CV	CR	PR	LITCHFIELD (EST)		UC	RE	TX	VS	VR
•		•	CW Credit Abstract Co	718-423-9430	•	•	•		
	•	•	Data Reporting Corp	203-287-1294	•	•	•		
•	•	•	Information Management Systems Inc (SOP)	860-229-1119	•	•	•	•	•
•	•	•	NEWSI (SOP)	800-517-4636	•	•	•	•	•
•			Nationwide Information Services (SOP)	800-227-0575	•	•	•	•	

CV	CR	PR	MIDDLESEX (EST)		UC	RE	TX	VS	VR
•		•	CW Credit Abstract Co	718-423-9430	•	•	•		
	•	•	Data Reporting Corp	203-287-1294	•	•	•		
•	•	•	Information Management Systems Inc (SOP)	860-229-1119	•	•	•	•	•
•	•	•	NEWSI (SOP)	800-517-4636	•	•	•	•	•
•			Nationwide Information Services (SOP)	800-227-0575	•	•	•	•	
•			Shickel, Valerie	860-767-2269	•	•	•	•	•
•	•	•	TJM & Associates	800-749-4254	•	•	•	•	•

DT	CV	CR	PR	NEW HAVEN (EST)		UC	RE	TX	VS	VR
•	•		•	CW Credit Abstract Co	718-423-9430	•	•	•		
•		•	•	Data Reporting Corp	203-287-1294	•	•	•		
•	•	•	•	Information Management Systems Inc (SOP)	860-229-1119	•	•	•	•	•
•	•	•	•	NEWSI (SOP)	800-517-4636	•	•	•	•	•
•	•			Nationwide Information Services (SOP)	800-227-0575	•	•	•	•	
	•		•	Shickel, Valerie	860-767-2269	•	•	•	•	•
			•	Strickland, Joan	203-488-6251	•	•	•		
•	•	•	•	TJM & Associates	800-749-4254	•	•	•	•	•

CV	CR	PR	NEW LONDON (EST)		UC	RE	TX	VS	VR
		•	Arnold, Platt	203-691-1125	•	•	•		
•		•	CW Credit Abstract Co	718-423-9430	•	•	•		
	•	•	Data Reporting Corp	203-287-1294	•	•	•		
•	•	•	Information Management Systems Inc (SOP)	860-229-1119	•	•	•	•	
•			Nationwide Information Services (SOP)	800-227-0575	•	•	•	•	
•		•	Shickel, Valerie	860-767-2269	•	•	•	•	•

CV	CR	PR	TOLLAND (EST)		UC	RE	TX	VS	VR
•		•	Applied Investigative Group (SOP)	860-895-8590	•	•	•		
•		•	CW Credit Abstract Co	718-423-9430	•	•	•		
	•	•	Data Reporting Corp	203-287-1294	•	•	•		

CV	CR	PR		UC	RE	TX	VS	VR

| | | | 🏛 Information Management Systems Inc (SOP)................ 860-229-1119 | | | | | |
| | | | Nationwide Information Services (SOP)............................ 800-227-0575 | | | | | |

CV	CR	PR	WINDHAM (EST)	UC	RE	TX	VS	VR

			CW Credit Abstract Co 718-423-9430					
			Data Reporting Corp 203-287-1294					
			🏛 Information Management Systems Inc (SOP)................ 860-229-1119					
			Nationwide Information Services (SOP)............................ 800-227-0575					

SUMMARY OF CODES

COURT RECORDS

CODE	GOVERNMENT AGENCY	TYPE OF INFORMATION
DT	US District Court	Federal civil and criminal cases
BK	Bankruptcy Court	United States bankruptcy cases
CV	Civil Court	Municipal, county and state level civil cases
CR	Criminal Court	Municipal, county and state level criminal cases
PR	Probate Court	Wills and estate cases

COUNTY RECORDS

CODE	GOVERNMENT AGENCY	TYPE OF INFORMATION
UC	UCC Filing Office	Uniform Commercial Code and other personal property liens
RE	Recorder of Deeds	Real property transactions and liens
TX	Tax Assessor	Real property tax information
VS	Vital Records Office	Vital statistics—birth, death, marriage, divorce, etc.
VR	Voter Registration Office	Voter registration and campaign contribution information

- "CODE" designates the agency and type of information obtainable in each county from a retriever.
- The time zone for each county is abbreviated as follows: EST—Eastern Standard Time; CST—Central; MST—Mountain; PST—Pacific; AK—Alaska; HT—Hawaii.
- 🏛—This symbol designates a Public Record Retriever Network member.
- "(SOP)" after the retriever name designates Service of Process.
- Individual retrievers without a company name are listed in order of their last name.
- US District and Bankruptcy courts are indicated only in the counties where courts are located.

DELAWARE

CV	CR	PR	KENT (CAPITAL) (EST)		UC	RE	TX	VS	VR
●	●		Accu-Fax Employment Screening Svcs	215-234-0700	●	●	●	●	●
●		●	Atlantic Title & Abstract Co	302-658-2102	●	●	●	●	
●	●	●	🏛 CSC	800-927-9800	●	●	●	●	
			CSC (SOP)	302-674-1221	●		●		
●	●	●	🏛 CorpAmerica Inc	888-736-4300	●	●	●		
●	●	●	🏛 DDR (Delaware Document Retrieval) (SOP)	800-343-1742	●	●	●		
●	●		Delaware Attorney Services (SOP)	302-429-0657	●	●	●	●	
●	●	●	Delmarva Abstractors (SOP)	410-228-6044	●	●	●		
●	●		Incorporating Services Ltd	800-346-4646	●	●	●	●	
	●		🏛 Infomation Retrieval Services	302-337-0548				●	●
●	●		Interstate Abstract Inc	609-795-4000	●	●	●	●	
●	●	●	🏛 Kutlus & Company (SOP)	888-726-5335	●	●	●		
●	●		🏛 National Background Investigations Inc	800-798-0079	●	●	●		
●			National Corporate Research Inc	800-483-1140	●	●	●		
●	●		National Legal Process (SOP)	302-429-0652	●	●	●	●	
●	●	●	Research Information Services	800-685-3320	●	●	●	●	

DT	BK	CV	CR	PR	NEW CASTLE (EST)		UC	RE	TX	VS	VR
●	●	●	●		Accu-Fax Employment Screening Svcs	215-234-0700	●	●	●	●	●
		●		●	Atlantic Title & Abstract Co	302-658-2102	●	●	●	●	
●	●	●	●	●	🏛 CSC	800-927-9800	●	●	●	●	
●	●	●	●	●	🏛 CorpAmerica Inc	888-736-4300	●	●	●		
●	●	●	●	●	🏛 DDR (Delaware Document Retrieval) (SOP)	800-343-1742	●	●	●		
●	●	●	●		Delaware Attorney Services (SOP)	302-429-0657	●	●	●	●	
●	●	●	●		Incorporating Services Ltd	800-346-4646	●	●	●	●	
			●		🏛 Infomation Retrieval Services	302-337-0548				●	●
●	●	●	●		Interstate Abstract Inc	609-795-4000	●	●	●	●	
●	●	●	●	●	🏛 Kutlus & Company (SOP)	888-726-5335	●	●	●		
●	●	●	●	●	Legal Beagles Inc (SOP)	800-743-9897	●	●	●	●	
			●	●	🏛 National Background Investigations Inc	800-798-0079					
●	●	●	●		National Legal Process (SOP)	302-429-0652	●	●	●	●	
●	●	●	●	●	Research Information Services	800-685-3320	●	●	●	●	

CV	CR	PR	SUSSEX (EST)		UC	RE	TX	VS	VR
●	●		Accu-Fax Employment Screening Svcs	215-234-0700	●	●	●	●	●
●		●	Atlantic Title & Abstract Co	302-658-2102	●	●	●	●	
●	●	●	🏛 CSC	800-927-9800	●	●	●	●	
●	●	●	🏛 CorpAmerica Inc	888-736-4300	●	●	●		
●	●	●	🏛 DDR (Delaware Document Retrieval) (SOP)	800-343-1742	●	●	●		
●	●		Delaware Attorney Services (SOP)	302-429-0657	●	●	●	●	
●	●	●	Delmarva Abstractors (SOP)	410-228-6044	●	●	●		
●	●		Incorporating Services Ltd	800-346-4646	●	●	●	●	
	●		🏛 Infomation Retrieval Services	302-337-0548				●	●
●	●		Interstate Abstract Inc	609-795-4000	●	●	●	●	
●	●	●	🏛 Kutlus & Company (SOP)	888-726-5335	●	●	●		
●	●		🏛 National Background Investigations Inc	800-798-0079	●	●	●		
●	●		National Legal Process (SOP)	302-429-0652	●	●	●	●	
●	●	●	Research Information Services	800-685-3320	●	●	●	●	
●	●	●	Researchers Ltd	302-856-7442	●	●	●		

DISTRICT OF COLUMBIA

DT	BK	CV	CR	PR	DISTRICT OF COLUMBIA (EST)	UC	RE	TX	VS	VR
•	•	•	•	•	ABIS Inc 800-669-2247	•	•	•		•
•	•	•		•	Accurate Legal Service (SOP) 800-236-9853		•			
•	•	•	•		🗑 Alpha Research LLC (SOP) 205-755-7008			•		
•	•	•	•	•	Barrett You & Associates Inc (SOP) 800-944-6607	•	•	•	•	
•	•	•	•	•	CSC 800-241-6518	•	•	•	•	
•	•	•	•	•	🗑 CorpAssist - DC Office (SOP) 800-438-2996	•	•	•	•	•
		•	•		Davis Detective Agency (Data Search Int'l) (SOP) 800-782-0445	•	•	•	•	
•	•	•	•	•	Document Resources (SOP) 800-945-7339	•	•	•	•	•
•	•	•			Douglas Investigations Ltd 800-747-0820					
•	•	•	•	•	Enterprise Title Company Inc 703-538-2470	•	•	•	•	•
•	•	•	•	•	Estate Title and Escrow Inc 703-385-5850	•	•			
•	•	•	•	•	FDR Info Centers 800-874-4337	•	•	•		
•	•				Government Liaison Services Inc 800-642-6564					
•	•	•	•	•	Instant Information Systems 703-281-9312	•	•	•	•	
•	•	•	•	•	🗑 Investigative Consultants Inc 202-562-1500	•	•	•	•	•
•	•	•	•	•	M & M Search Service Inc 202-393-3144	•	•	•	•	
•	•	•	•	•	🗑 Mohr Information Services 800-799-4363	•	•	•		•
•	•	•	•	•	🗑 Reveal Inc (SOP) 800-276-4826	•	•	•	•	•
•	•	•	•	•	🗑 Security Consultants Inc (SOP) 202-686-3953	•	•	•	•	•
•	•	•	•	•	The Seto Company 202-416-1898	•	•	•	•	•
•	•	•	•	•	🗑 Torri's Legal Services (SOP) 800-990-7378	•	•	•	•	
•	•	•	•	•	🗑 University Process Service (SOP) 301-681-7206	•	•	•		
•	•	•	•	•	W A Haag & Associates Inc (SOP) 703-765-2138	•	•	•	•	•
•	•	•	•	•	Washington Document Service 800-728-5201	•	•	•	•	

FLORIDA

DT	CV	CR	PR	ALACHUA (EST)		UC	RE	TX	VS	VR
•	•	•		Alpha Research LLC (SOP) 205-755-7008				•		
•	•	•	•	Hollingsworth Court Reporting Inc 504-769-3386		•	•	•	•	
•	•	•	•	Pacific Photocopy & Research 800-934-6999		•	•	•	•	
•	•	•	•	RSI 800-881-5993		•		•		•
•	•	•	•	SIC Inc (SOP) 305-751-0015		•	•			
•	•	•	•	SingleSource Services Corp 800-713-3412		•		•	•	•

CV	CR	PR	BAKER (EST)		UC	RE	TX	VS	VR
•	•		Alpha Research LLC (SOP) 205-755-7008				•		
•	•	•	Hollingsworth Court Reporting Inc 504-769-3386		•	•	•	•	
•	•	•	Pacific Photocopy & Research 904-355-1062		•	•	•	•	
•	•	•	SingleSource Services Corp 800-713-3412		•		•	•	•
•		•	Tri-County Title Services 904-755-5566		•	•	•		

CV	CR	PR	BAY (CST)		UC	RE	TX	VS	VR
•	•		Alpha Research LLC (SOP) 205-755-7008				•		
•	•	•	Corporate Access Inc (SOP) 800-969-1666		•	•	•	•	•
•	•	•	Hollingsworth Court Reporting Inc 504-769-3386		•	•	•	•	
•	•	•	Pacific Photocopy & Research 800-934-6999		•	•	•	•	
•	•	•	Pacific Photocopy & Research Services 904-435-3183		•	•	•	•	
•	•	•	Research Express 904-421-0387		•	•	•	•	
•	•	•	SingleSource Services Corp 800-713-3412		•		•	•	•

CV	CR	PR	BRADFORD (EST)		UC	RE	TX	VS	VR
•	•		Alpha Research LLC (SOP) 205-755-7008				•		
•		•	Bradford Title Service 904-964-4747		•	•	•		
•	•	•	Hollingsworth Court Reporting Inc 504-769-3386		•	•	•	•	
•	•	•	Pacific Photocopy & Research 904-355-1062		•	•	•	•	
•	•	•	SingleSource Services Corp 800-713-3412		•		•	•	•

CV	CR	PR	BREVARD (EST)		UC	RE	TX	VS	VR
•	•	•	A Very Private Eye Inc (SOP) 800-277-7095		•	•	•	•	•
•	•		Alpha Research LLC (SOP) 205-755-7008				•		
•	•	•	Andrews Agency Inc (SOP) 407-649-2085		•	•	•	•	
•	•	•	Crummey Investigations Inc (SOP) 407-724-0518		•	•	•	•	
•	•	•	Fidelity Title and Guaranty Company 407-740-7131		•	•	•	•	
•	•	•	Hollingsworth Court Reporting Inc 504-769-3386		•	•	•	•	
•			ICDI Inc 407-299-6300		•	•	•		
•	•	•	Independent Research Assoc 407-277-0076		•	•	•	•	
•	•	•	Pacific Photocopy & Research 407-425-7234		•	•	•	•	•
•	•	•	SingleSource Services Corp 800-713-3412		•		•	•	•
•	•	•	World Class Investigations (SOP) 407-728-0641			•	•		

DT	CV	CR	PR	BROWARD (EST)		UC	RE	TX	VS	VR
•	•	•	•	ATT Investigations Inc 800-733-4405		•	•	•	•	
•	•	•		Access Research Center Inc 305-771-0499		•	•	•		•
		•		Accu-Screen Inc 800-689-2228		•				
	•	•		Alpha Research LLC (SOP) 205-755-7008				•		
•	•	•	•	Bill Greenberg Special Services Inc (SOP) 800-654-0002		•	•	•	•	•
•	•	•	•	Compass Investigations (SOP) 954-527-5722		•	•	•	•	•
		•		Computer Assisted Research On-Line 800-329-6397		•				
	•			Deception Control Inc 800-776-1660			•	•	•	•
•	•	•	•	Esquire Express Inc (SOP) 305-530-9580		•	•	•	•	•
•	•	•	•	FLA Search Company 561-969-6594		•	•	•	•	•
	•			Factual Business Information 305-592-7600		•	•	•		
•	•	•	•	Ft Lauderdale-Miami Courthouse Rsrch 954-434-6819		•		•	•	•
•	•	•	•	High-Tech Investigations Inc 888-881-7441		•		•	•	•
		•		Hogan Information Services 405-278-6954		•	•	•		
•	•	•	•	Hollingsworth Court Reporting Inc 504-769-3386		•	•	•	•	

CV	CR	PR		UC	RE	TX	VS	VR
•	•	•	•	📖 Investigative Services International (SOP) 305-868-7775	•	•	•	•	•
•	•	•	•	📖 JM Search Services Inc 800-393-7563	•	•	•	•	•
•	•	•	•	📖 Judicial Research & Retrieval Services 800-529-6226	•	•	•	•	•
•	•	•	•	Pacific Photocopy & Research 305-764-5646	•	•	•	•	•
•	•	•	•	📖 Patrick Investigative Services Inc 800-700-2958	•	•	•	•	•
•	•	•	•	📖 RSI 800-881-5993	•	•	•	•	•
•	•	•	•	📖 Raven International Investigations Inc 800-719-1626	•	•	•	•	•
•	•	•	•	SIC Inc (SOP) 305-751-0015	•	•	•	•	•
•	•	•	•	Search/America 800-572-8815	•	•	•	•	•
•	•	•	•	📖 SingleSource Services Corp 800-713-3412	•	•	•	•	•
•	•	•	•	📖 The Records Reviewer Inc 954-947-1186	•	•	•	•	•
•	•	•	•	Verbatim Investigative Services Inc (SOP) 800-750-4231	•	•	•	•	•

CV	CR	PR	CALHOUN (CST)	UC	RE	TX	VS	VR
•	•		CSC 800-342-8086	•	•			
•	•	•	Calhoun-Liberty Abstract Co 904-674-8311	•	•			
•	•	•	Corporate Access Inc (SOP) 800-969-1666	•	•		•	•
•	•	•	📖 Hollingsworth Court Reporting Inc 504-769-3386	•	•	•		
•	•	•	📖 Research Express 904-421-0387	•	•	•		
•	•	•	📖 SingleSource Services Corp 800-713-3412	•	•	•		•
•			Sunstate Research Associates Inc 800-621-7234	•	•			
•	•	•	UCC Filing & Search Services 800-822-5436	•	•	•	•	

CV	CR	PR	CHARLOTTE (EST)	UC	RE	TX	VS	VR
•	•		📖 Alpha Research LLC (SOP) 205-755-7008		•			
•		•	📖 Guzman Enterprises 941-743-3690	•	•	•		
•	•	•	📖 Hollingsworth Court Reporting Inc 504-769-3386	•	•	•		
•	•	•	McCormack, Trisha A & Thomas 941-955-9998	•	•	•	•	
•	•	•	Pacific Photocopy & Research 813-885-3854	•	•	•	•	
•	•	•	📖 SingleSource Services Corp 800-713-3412	•		•	•	•
•	•	•	Youngblood Process Service (SOP) 813-743-4952	•	•	•	•	

CV	CR	PR	CITRUS (EST)	UC	RE	TX	VS	VR
•	•		📖 Alpha Research LLC (SOP) 205-755-7008		•			
•	•	•	Brainard Research and Reporting Service 813-931-8370					
•	•	•	📖 Hollingsworth Court Reporting Inc 504-769-3386	•	•	•		
•	•	•	Pacific Photocopy & Research 904-355-1062	•	•	•		
•	•	•	📖 Records Research 352-544-5997	•	•	•		•
•	•	•	📖 SingleSource Services Corp 800-713-3412	•		•	•	

CV	CR	PR	CLAY (EST)	UC	RE	TX	VS	VR
•	•		📖 Alpha Research LLC (SOP) 205-755-7008		•			
•	•	•	📖 First Coast Investigations Inc (SOP) 904-398-4076	•	•	•	•	
•	•		📖 G & L Research Associates 904-743-4116	•	•			
•	•	•	📖 Hollingsworth Court Reporting Inc 504-769-3386	•	•	•		
•	•	•	Pacific Photocopy & Research 904-355-1062	•	•	•		
•	•	•	📖 SingleSource Services Corp 800-713-3412	•		•	•	•

CV	CR	PR	COLLIER (EST)	UC	RE	TX	VS	VR
	•		Accu-Screen Inc 800-689-2228					
•	•		📖 Alpha Research LLC (SOP) 205-755-7008		•			
•	•	•	📖 Hollingsworth Court Reporting Inc 504-769-3386	•	•	•	•	
•	•	•	Lawyers' Abstract Service Inc 941-774-2627	•	•	•	•	
•	•	•	Pacific Photocopy & Research 813-885-3854	•	•	•	•	
•	•	•	SIC Inc (SOP) 305-751-0015	•	•	•	•	
•	•	•	Search/America 800-572-8815	•	•	•	•	•
•	•	•	📖 SingleSource Services Corp 800-713-3412	•		•	•	•

CV	CR	PR	COLUMBIA (EST)	UC	RE	TX	VS	VR
•	•	•	📖 Hollingsworth Court Reporting Inc 504-769-3386	•	•	•	•	
•	•	•	Pacific Photocopy & Research 904-355-1062	•	•	•	•	
•	•	•	Pacific Photocopy & Research 800-934-6999	•				
•	•	•	📖 SingleSource Services Corp 800-713-3412	•		•	•	•

							UC	RE	TX	VS	VR
		•		•	Tri-County Title Services	904-755-5566	•	•	•		

DT	BK	CV	CR	PR	DADE (EST)		UC	RE	TX	VS	VR
•	•	•	•	•	ATT Investigations Inc	800-733-4405	•	•	•	•	
•	•	•	•		Alpha Research LLC (SOP)	205-755-7008			•		
•	•	•	•	•	Bill Greenberg Special Services Inc (SOP)	800-654-0002	•	•	•	•	•
•	•	•	•	•	Compass Investigations (SOP)	954-527-5722	•	•	•	•	•
				•	Computer Assisted Research On-Line	800-329-6397	•	•			
		•	•		Deception Control Inc	800-776-1660		•	•	•	•
•	•	•	•	•	Esquire Express Inc (SOP)	305-530-9580	•	•	•		
•	•	•	•	•	FLA Search Company	561-969-6594	•	•	•	•	•
		•	•		Factual Business Information	305-592-7600	•	•	•		
•	•	•	•	•	Ft Lauderdale-Miami Courthouse Rsrch	954-434-6819	•	•	•		
•	•	•	•	•	High-Tech Investigations Inc	888-881-7441	•	•	•	•	•
•	•	•	•	•	Hollingsworth Court Reporting Inc	504-769-3386	•	•			
•	•	•	•	•	Inquiry Services Inc (SOP)	888-444-4033					
•	•	•	•	•	Investigative Services International (SOP)	305-868-7775	•	•	•	•	•
•	•	•	•	•	JM Search Services Inc	800-393-7563	•	•	•		•
•	•	•	•	•	Judicial Research & Retrieval Services	800-529-6226	•	•	•	•	
•	•	•			Legal Records Research	800-721-0524	•	•	•		
•	•	•	•	•	Pacific Photocopy & Research	305-371-7330	•	•	•		
•	•	•	•	•	Patrick Investigative Services Inc	800-700-2958	•	•	•	•	•
•	•	•	•	•	RSI	800-881-5993	•	•	•	•	•
•	•	•	•	•	Raven International Investigations Inc	800-719-1626	•	•	•		
•	•	•	•	•	SIC Inc (SOP)	305-751-0015	•	•	•	•	
•	•	•	•	•	Search/America	800-572-8815	•	•	•	•	•
•	•	•	•	•	SingleSource Services Corp	800-713-3412	•	•	•	•	•
•	•	•	•	•	The Records Reviewer Inc	954-947-1186	•	•	•	•	
•	•	•	•	•	Verbatim Investigative Services Inc (SOP)	800-750-4231	•	•	•	•	•
•	•	•	•	•	Vollrath, Robert (SOP)	305-829-5559	•	•	•	•	

		CV	CR	PR	DE SOTO (EST)		UC	RE	TX	VS	VR
		•	•		Alpha Research LLC (SOP)	205-755-7008			•		
		•	•	•	Chambers Investigations	800-792-1107	•	•	•	•	
		•	•	•	DeSoto Abstract Co	941-494-3656	•	•	•	•	
		•		•	Guzman Enterprises	941-743-3690	•	•	•	•	
		•	•	•	Hollingsworth Court Reporting Inc	504-769-3386	•	•	•		
		•	•	•	Pacific Photocopy & Research	813-885-3854	•	•	•		
		•	•	•	SingleSource Services Corp	800-713-3412	•		•	•	•

		CV	CR	PR	DIXIE (EST)		UC	RE	TX	VS	VR
		•	•		Alpha Research LLC (SOP)	205-755-7008			•		
		•	•	•	Gilchrist Title Services Inc	352-463-6403	•	•	•	•	
		•	•	•	Hollingsworth Court Reporting Inc	504-769-3386	•	•	•		
		•	•	•	Pacific Photocopy & Research	800-934-6999	•	•	•	•	
		•	•	•	Research Express	904-421-0387	•	•	•	•	
		•	•	•	SingleSource Services Corp	800-713-3412	•		•	•	•
		•		•	Suwanne Title and Abstract Inc	352-493-2564	•	•	•		
			•	•	Tri-County Title Services	904-755-5566	•	•	•		

DT	BK	CV	CR	PR	DUVAL (EST)		UC	RE	TX	VS	VR
•	•	•	•		Alpha Research LLC (SOP)	205-755-7008			•		
		•	•	•	Collins Title & Abstract Co Inc	904-829-6600	•	•	•	•	
		•	•	•	Fidelity Title and Guaranty Company	407-740-7131	•	•	•	•	
•		•	•	•	First Coast Investigations Inc (SOP)	904-398-4076	•	•	•	•	
•		•	•	•	G & L Research Associates	904-743-4116	•	•	•	•	
•	•	•	•	•	Hollingsworth Court Reporting Inc	504-769-3386	•	•	•		
•		•	•	•	Judicial Research & Retrieval Services	800-529-6226	•	•	•	•	
•	•	•	•	•	Pacific Photocopy & Research	904-355-1062	•	•	•		
•	•	•	•	•	RSI	800-881-5993	•	•	•	•	•
•	•	•	•	•	SIC Inc (SOP)	305-751-0015	•	•	•	•	
•	•	•	•	•	SingleSource Services Corp	800-713-3412	•		•	•	•

DT	BK	CV	CR	PR	ESCAMBIA (CST)	UC	RE	TX	VS	VR
•	•	•	•	•	Aalpha Omega Investigations Inc (SOP) ... 904-433-7016	•	•	•	•	
•	•	•			🏛 Alpha Research LLC (SOP) ... 205-755-7008			•		
•	•	•	•	•	Carol Ann Bailey CLA Inc ... 904-623-9431	•	•			•
•	•	•	•	•	🏛 Hollingsworth Court Reporting Inc ... 504-769-3386	•	•			
•	•	•	•	•	🏛 Judicial Research & Retrieval Services ... 800-529-6226	•	•			
•	•	•	•	•	Pacific Photocopy & Research Services ... 904-435-3183	•				
		•			Prime Time Process Service (SOP) ... 904-457-1021					
		•	•	•	🏛 Research Express ... 904-421-0387	•	•	•	•	
•	•	•	•	•	🏛 SingleSource Services Corp ... 800-713-3412	•		•	•	•

CV	CR	PR	FLAGLER (EST)	UC	RE	TX	VS	VR
•	•	•	Collins Title & Abstract Co Inc ... 904-829-6600	•	•	•	•	
•	•	•	Fidelity Title and Guaranty Company ... 407-740-7131	•	•	•	•	
•		•	Flagler County Abstract Co ... 904-437-4151	•	•	•	•	
•	•	•	🏛 Hollingsworth Court Reporting Inc ... 504-769-3386	•	•			
•	•	•	Pacific Photocopy & Research ... 904-355-1062	•	•	•	•	
•	•	•	🏛 SingleSource Services Corp ... 800-713-3412	•		•	•	•

CV	CR	PR	FRANKLIN (EST)	UC	RE	TX	VS	VR
•	•	•	Acumen Investigations (SOP) ... 904-668-0824	•	•	•	•	•
•	•	•	Advanced Investigations Inc (SOP) ... 904-222-1998	•	•	•	•	
•	•		🏛 Alpha Research LLC (SOP) ... 205-755-7008			•		
•			CSC ... 800-342-8086	•				
•	•	•	Corporate Access Inc (SOP) ... 800-969-1666	•	•	•	•	•
•	•	•	🏛 Hollingsworth Court Reporting Inc ... 504-769-3386	•	•		•	
•	•	•	Pacific Photocopy & Research ... 800-934-6999	•	•	•	•	
•	•	•	🏛 Research Express ... 904-421-0387	•	•	•	•	

CV	CR	PR	GADSDEN (EST)	UC	RE	TX	VS	VR
•	•	•	Acumen Investigations (SOP) ... 904-668-0824	•	•	•	•	•
•	•	•	Advanced Investigations Inc (SOP) ... 904-222-1998	•	•	•	•	
•	•		🏛 Alpha Research LLC (SOP) ... 205-755-7008			•		
•	•		CSC ... 800-342-8086	•		•		
			Capitol Services ... 904-878-4734					
•	•	•	Corporate Access Inc (SOP) ... 800-969-1666	•	•	•	•	•
•		•	Gadsden Abstract Co ... 904-627-6811	•	•		•	
•	•	•	🏛 Hollingsworth Court Reporting Inc ... 504-769-3386	•	•		•	
•	•	•	🏛 Judicial Research & Retrieval Services ... 800-529-6226	•	•		•	
•	•	•	Pacific Photocopy & Research ... 800-934-6999	•	•		•	
•	•	•	🏛 Research Express ... 904-421-0387	•	•	•	•	
•	•	•	🏛 SingleSource Services Corp ... 800-713-3412	•	•	•		•
•	•	•	🏛 State Information Bureau ... 800-881-1742	•	•	•	•	•
•			Sunstate Research Associates Inc ... 800-621-7234	•		•		
•	•	•	UCC Filing & Search Services ... 800-822-5436	•	•	•	•	

CV	CR	PR	GILCHRIST (EST)	UC	RE	TX	VS	VR
•	•		🏛 Alpha Research LLC (SOP) ... 205-755-7008			•		
•	•	•	Gilchrist Title Services Inc ... 352-463-6403	•	•	•	•	
•	•	•	🏛 Hollingsworth Court Reporting Inc ... 504-769-3386	•	•		•	
•	•	•	Pacific Photocopy & Research ... 800-934-6999	•		•	•	
•	•	•	🏛 Research Express ... 904-421-0387	•	•	•	•	
•		•	Suwanne Title and Abstract Inc ... 352-493-2564	•	•	•		
		•	Tri-County Title Services ... 904-755-5566	•	•	•		

CV	CR	PR	GLADES (EST)	UC	RE	TX	VS	VR
•	•		🏛 Alpha Research LLC (SOP) ... 205-755-7008			•		
•	•	•	🏛 Hollingsworth Court Reporting Inc ... 504-769-3386	•	•		•	
•	•	•	Okeechobee Abstract and Title Ins Inc ... 813-763-3710	•	•	•		
•	•	•	Pacific Photocopy & Research ... 813-885-3854	•		•	•	

	CV	CR	PR	GULF (CST)	UC	RE	TX	VS	VR
Alpha Research LLC (SOP) ... 205-755-7008	•	•					•		
Corporate Access Inc (SOP) ... 800-969-1666	•	•	•		•	•	•	•	•
Hollingsworth Court Reporting Inc ... 504-769-3386	•	•	•		•	•	•	•	
Pacific Photocopy & Research ... 800-934-6999	•	•	•		•		•	•	

	CV	CR	PR	HAMILTON (EST)	UC	RE	TX	VS	VR
Alpha Research LLC (SOP) ... 205-755-7008	•	•					•		
Hollingsworth Court Reporting Inc ... 504-769-3386	•	•	•		•	•	•	•	
Pacific Photocopy & Research ... 904-355-1062	•	•	•		•	•	•	•	
Pacific Photocopy & Research ... 800-934-6999	•	•	•		•		•	•	
Research Express ... 904-421-0387	•	•	•		•		•	•	
SingleSource Services Corp ... 800-713-3412	•	•	•		•		•	•	•
Tri-County Title Services ... 904-755-5566	•		•		•	•	•		

	CV	CR	PR	HARDEE (EST)	UC	RE	TX	VS	VR
Alpha Research LLC (SOP) ... 205-755-7008	•	•					•		
Hollingsworth Court Reporting Inc ... 504-769-3386	•	•	•		•	•	•	•	
Pacific Photocopy & Research ... 813-885-3854	•	•	•		•	•	•	•	
SingleSource Services Corp ... 800-713-3412	•	•	•		•		•	•	•

	CV	CR	PR	HENDRY (EST)	UC	RE	TX	VS	VR
Hollingsworth Court Reporting Inc ... 504-769-3386	•	•	•		•	•	•	•	
Pacific Photocopy & Research ... 813-885-3854	•	•	•		•	•	•	•	
Palm Title Inc ... 813-675-4545	•	•	•		•	•	•	•	

	CV	CR	PR	HERNANDO (EST)	UC	RE	TX	VS	VR
Brainard Research and Reporting Service ... 813-931-8370	•	•	•						
Hollingsworth Court Reporting Inc ... 504-769-3386	•	•	•		•	•	•	•	
Pacific Photocopy & Research ... 813-885-3854	•	•	•		•	•	•	•	
Records Research ... 352-544-5997	•	•	•		•	•	•		•
SingleSource Services Corp ... 800-713-3412	•	•	•		•		•	•	•

	CV	CR	PR	HIGHLANDS (EST)	UC	RE	TX	VS	VR
Alpha Research LLC (SOP) ... 205-755-7008	•	•					•		
Highlands Abstract and Title Co ... 941-385-0340	•		•		•	•	•		
Hollingsworth Court Reporting Inc ... 504-769-3386	•	•	•		•	•	•	•	
Pacific Photocopy & Research ... 305-371-7330	•	•	•		•	•	•	•	
SingleSource Services Corp ... 800-713-3412	•	•	•		•		•	•	•
South Ridge Abstract and Title Co ... 941-385-2521	•	•	•		•	•	•	•	
Sunshine State Abstract & Title ... 941-382-9797	•	•	•		•	•	•	•	

DT	BK	CV	CR	PR	HILLSBOROUGH (EST)	UC	RE	TX	VS	VR
•	•	•	•	•	ADREM Profiles Inc ... 800-483-9929	•		•	•	•
•	•	•			Accu-Screen Inc ... 800-689-2228					
•	•	•	•	•	All Phase Reports (SOP) ... 813-885-9822	•		•	•	•
•	•	•	•		Alpha Research LLC (SOP) ... 205-755-7008			•		
•	•	•	•	•	Bay Area Search Inc ... 800-478-4618	•	•	•		
•		•	•	•	Brainard Research and Reporting Service ... 813-931-8370					
•	•	•	•	•	EX-CEL Investigations (SOP) ... 813-527-5440	•	•	•	•	•
•		•	•	•	Gietzen & Associates Inc (SOP) ... 813-254-4383					
•					Hogan Information Services ... 405-278-6954	•				
•	•	•	•	•	Hollingsworth Court Reporting Inc ... 504-769-3386	•	•	•	•	
•	•	•	•	•	I.G.B. Associates Inc ... 813-226-8810	•	•	•		•
•	•	•	•	•	Intelligence Network Inc ... 813-449-0072	•	•	•	•	
•	•	•	•	•	Judicial Research & Retrieval Services ... 800-529-6226	•	•	•	•	
•	•	•	•	•	North American Investigations (SOP) ... 800-270-2628	•	•	•	•	•
•		•	•	•	Pacific Photocopy & Research ... 813-885-3854	•	•	•	•	
•	•	•	•	•	RSI ... 800-881-5993	•	•	•	•	•
•	•	•	•	•	Search/America ... 800-572-8815	•	•	•	•	•
•	•	•	•	•	SingleSource Services Corp ... 800-713-3412	•		•	•	•
•	•	•	•	•	T L Dearth Records Research & Recovery ... 813-671-2140	•	•	•	•	

HOLMES (CST)

CV	CR	PR	Provider	Phone	UC	RE	TX	VS	VR
•	•		Alpha Research LLC (SOP)	205-755-7008			•		
•	•	•	Hollingsworth Court Reporting Inc	504-769-3386	•	•	•	•	
•			Sunstate Research Associates Inc	800-621-7234	•		•		

INDIAN RIVER (EST)

CV	CR	PR	Provider	Phone	UC	RE	TX	VS	VR
•	•	•	Crummey Investigations Inc (SOP)	407-724-0518	•	•	•	•	•
•	•	•	Hollingsworth Court Reporting Inc	504-769-3386	•	•	•	•	
•	•	•	Pacific Photocopy & Research	305-371-7330	•	•	•	•	
•	•		Reliable Research	407-334-5854	•	•			
•	•	•	SingleSource Services Corp	800-713-3412	•	•	•	•	
		•	Treasure Coast Abstract & Title Ins Co	561-461-7190	•	•	•		
•	•	•	World Class Investigations (SOP)	407-728-0641	•	•	•		

JACKSON (CST)

CV	CR	PR	Provider	Phone	UC	RE	TX	VS	VR
•	•	•	Hollingsworth Court Reporting Inc	504-769-3386	•	•	•	•	
•	•	•	Pacific Photocopy & Research	800-934-6999	•	•	•		
•	•	•	Research Express	904-421-0387	•	•	•		
•	•	•	SingleSource Services Corp	800-713-3412	•	•	•		•
•			Sunstate Research Associates Inc	800-621-7234	•				
•	•	•	UCC Filing & Search Services	800-822-5436	•	•	•	•	

JEFFERSON (EST)

CV	CR	PR	Provider	Phone	UC	RE	TX	VS	VR
•	•	•	Acumen Investigations (SOP)	904-668-0824	•	•	•	•	•
•	•	•	Advanced Investigations Inc (SOP)	904-222-1998	•	•	•	•	
•	•		CSC	800-342-8086	•		•		
•	•	•	Corporate Access Inc (SOP)	800-969-1666	•	•	•		•
•	•	•	Hollingsworth Court Reporting Inc	504-769-3386	•	•	•	•	
•	•	•	North Florida Abstract & Title Company	904-997-2670	•	•	•		
•	•	•	Pacific Photocopy & Research	800-934-6999	•	•	•		
•	•	•	R.E.M. Resources Inc	800-737-0736	•	•	•		•
•	•	•	Research Express	904-421-0387	•	•	•		
•	•	•	SingleSource Services Corp	800-713-3412	•	•	•	•	•
•	•	•	State Information Bureau	800-881-1742		•		•	•
•			Sunstate Research Associates Inc	800-621-7234	•		•		
•	•	•	UCC Filing & Search Services	800-822-5436	•	•	•	•	

LAFAYETTE (EST)

CV	CR	PR	Provider	Phone	UC	RE	TX	VS	VR
•	•		CSC	800-342-8086	•		•		
•	•	•	Hollingsworth Court Reporting Inc	504-769-3386	•	•	•	•	
•	•	•	Pacific Photocopy & Research	800-934-6999	•		•	•	
•	•	•	Research Express	904-421-0387	•	•	•	•	
•		•	Tri-County Title Services	904-755-5566	•	•	•		

LAKE (EST)

CV	CR	PR	Provider	Phone	UC	RE	TX	VS	VR
•	•	•	A Very Private Eye Inc (SOP)	800-277-7095	•	•	•	•	•
•	•	•	Andrews Agency Inc (SOP)	407-649-2085	•	•	•	•	
•	•	•	Fidelity Title and Guaranty Company	407-740-7131	•	•	•	•	
•	•	•	Hollingsworth Court Reporting Inc	504-769-3386	•	•	•	•	
•	•	•	Pacific Photocopy & Research	407-425-7234	•	•	•		
•	•	•	SingleSource Services Corp	800-713-3412	•		•	•	•

LEE (EST)

DT	CV	CR	PR	Provider	Phone	UC	RE	TX	VS	VR
•	•	•		Alpha Research LLC (SOP)	205-755-7008			•		
•	•		•	Guzman Enterprises	941-743-3690	•	•	•		
•	•	•	•	Hollingsworth Court Reporting Inc	504-769-3386	•	•	•	•	
•	•	•	•	Pacific Photocopy & Research	813-885-3854	•	•	•	•	
•	•	•	•	Search/America	800-572-8815	•	•	•	•	•
•	•	•	•	SingleSource Services Corp	800-713-3412	•		•	•	•

LEON (CAPITAL) (EST)

DT	BK	CV	CR	PR	Provider	Phone	UC	RE	TX	VS	VR
•	•	•	•	•	Acumen Investigations (SOP)	904-668-0824	•	•	•	•	•

							UC	RE	TX	VS	VR
•	•	•	•	•	Advanced Investigations Inc (SOP)	904-222-1998	•	•	•	•	
•	•	•	•		CSC	800-342-8086	•		•		
•	•				Capitol Services	904-878-4734					
•	•	•	•	•	Corporate Access Inc (SOP)	800-969-1666	•	•	•	•	•
•	•	•	•	•	Florida Information Associates	904-878-0188	•	•	•	•	
•	•	•	•	•	Hollingsworth Court Reporting Inc	504-769-3386	•	•	•	•	
•	•	•	•	•	International Research Bureau Inc (IRB)	800-814-7714	•	•	•	•	•
•	•	•	•	•	Judicial Research & Retrieval Services	800-529-6226	•	•	•	•	
•	•	•	•	•	Pacific Photocopy & Research	800-934-6999	•		•	•	
•	•	•	•	•	R.E.M. Resources Inc	800-737-0736	•	•	•	•	•
•	•	•	•	•	RSI	800-881-5993	•	•	•	•	
			•	•	Research Express	904-421-0387	•	•	•		
			•	•	SingleSource Services Corp	800-713-3412	•		•	•	•
•	•	•	•	•	State Information Bureau	800-881-1742	•	•	•	•	
•	•	•			Sunstate Research Associates Inc	800-621-7234	•		•		
•	•	•	•	•	UCC Filing & Search Services	800-822-5436	•	•	•	•	

CV	CR	PR	LEVY (EST)		UC	RE	TX	VS	VR
•	•		Alpha Research LLC (SOP)	205-755-7008			•		
•	•	•	Gilchrist Title Services Inc	352-463-6403	•	•	•		
•	•	•	Hollingsworth Court Reporting Inc	504-769-3386	•	•	•		
•	•	•	Pacific Photocopy & Research	800-934-6999	•	•	•		
•	•	•	Research Express	904-421-0387	•	•	•		
•	•	•	SingleSource Services Corp	800-713-3412	•		•	•	•
•		•	Suwanne Title and Abstract Inc	352-493-2564	•	•	•		

CV	CR	PR	LIBERTY (EST)		UC	RE	TX	VS	VR
•	•	•	Acumen Investigations (SOP)	904-668-0824	•	•	•	•	•
•	•	•	Advanced Investigations Inc (SOP)	904-222-1998	•	•	•	•	
•	•		Alpha Research LLC (SOP)	205-755-7008			•		
•	•		CSC	800-342-8086	•		•		
•	•	•	Calhoun-Liberty Abstract Co	904-674-8311	•	•	•		
•	•	•	Corporate Access Inc (SOP)	800-969-1666	•	•	•	•	•
•	•	•	Hollingsworth Court Reporting Inc	504-769-3386	•	•	•		
•	•	•	Pacific Photocopy & Research	800-934-6999	•		•	•	
•	•	•	Research Express	904-421-0387	•	•	•	•	
•	•	•	SingleSource Services Corp	800-713-3412	•		•	•	•
•			Sunstate Research Associates Inc	800-621-7234	•		•		
•	•	•	UCC Filing & Search Services	800-822-5436	•	•	•	•	

CV	CR	PR	MADISON (EST)		UC	RE	TX	VS	VR
•	•		Alpha Research LLC (SOP)	205-755-7008			•		
•	•		CSC	800-342-8086	•		•		
•	•	•	Hollingsworth Court Reporting Inc	504-769-3386	•	•	•	•	
•	•	•	Pacific Photocopy & Research	800-934-6999	•		•	•	
•	•	•	Research Express	904-421-0387	•	•	•	•	
•	•	•	SingleSource Services Corp	800-713-3412	•		•	•	•
•			Sunstate Research Associates Inc	800-621-7234	•		•		
•	•	•	UCC Filing & Search Services	800-822-5436	•	•	•	•	

CV	CR	PR	MANATEE (EST)		UC	RE	TX	VS	VR
•	•	•	Accurate Legal Services (SOP)	941-365-3335	•	•	•		•
•	•		Alpha Research LLC (SOP)	205-755-7008			•		
•	•	•	Brainard Research and Reporting Service	813-931-8370					
•	•		Chambers Investigations	800-792-1107	•	•	•		
•	•	•	Guzman Enterprises	941-743-3690	•	•	•		
•	•	•	Hollingsworth Court Reporting Inc	504-769-3386	•	•	•		
•	•	•	McCormack, Trisha A & Thomas	941-955-9998	•	•	•		•
•	•	•	Pacific Photocopy & Research	813-885-3854	•	•	•	•	
•	•	•	Search/America	800-572-8815	•	•	•	•	•
•	•	•	SingleSource Services Corp	800-713-3412	•	•	•	•	•
•	•	•	Steele Investigation Agency (SOP)	813-758-5890	•	•	•	•	•

CV	CR	PR	MARION (EST)	UC	RE	TX	VS	VR
•	•	•	Fidelity Title and Guaranty Company 407-740-7131	•	•	•	•	
•	•	•	Hollingsworth Court Reporting Inc 504-769-3386	•	•	•	•	•
•	•	•	Pacific Photocopy & Research 904-355-1062	•	•	•	•	
•	•	•	SingleSource Services Corp 800-713-3412	•		•	•	•

CV	CR	PR	MARTIN (EST)	UC	RE	TX	VS	VR
•	•		Alpha Research LLC (SOP) 205-755-7008			•		
•	•	•	FLA Search Company 561-969-6594	•	•	•	•	
•	•	•	Hollingsworth Court Reporting Inc 504-769-3386	•	•	•	•	
•	•	•	Information Search Inc 561-624-5115	•	•	•	•	•
•		•	Okeechobee Abstract and Title Ins Inc 813-763-3710	•	•	•		
•	•	•	Pacific Photocopy & Research 305-371-7330	•	•	•	•	
•	•		Reliable Research 407-334-5854	•	•	•		
•	•	•	SingleSource Services Corp 800-713-3412	•		•	•	•
		•	Treasure Coast Abstract & Title Ins Co 561-461-7190	•	•	•		

CV	CR	PR	MONROE (EST)	UC	RE	TX	VS	VR
•	•		Factual Business Information 305-592-7600	•	•	•	•	
•	•	•	Hollingsworth Court Reporting Inc 504-769-3386	•	•	•	•	
•	•	•	Independent Abstract & Title 305-294-5105	•	•	•	•	
•	•		Office Services of the Keys 305-853-1155	•	•	•	•	•
•	•	•	Pacific Photocopy & Research 305-371-7330	•	•	•	•	
•	•	•	Raven International Investigations Inc 800-719-1626	•	•	•	•	
•	•	•	SIC Inc (SOP) 305-751-0015	•	•	•	•	

CV	CR	PR	NASSAU (EST)	UC	RE	TX	VS	VR
•	•		Alpha Research LLC (SOP) 205-755-7008			•		
•	•	•	First Coast Investigations Inc (SOP) 904-398-4076	•	•	•		
•	•		G & L Research Associates 904-743-4116	•		•		
•	•	•	Hollingsworth Court Reporting Inc 504-769-3386	•	•	•		
•	•	•	Pacific Photocopy & Research 904-355-1062	•	•	•		
•	•	•	SingleSource Services Corp 800-713-3412	•		•	•	•

CV	CR	PR	OKALOOSA (CST)	UC	RE	TX	VS	VR
•	•	•	Aalpha Omega Investigations Inc (SOP) 904-433-7016	•	•	•	•	
•	•	•	Hollingsworth Court Reporting Inc 504-769-3386	•	•	•	•	
•	•	•	Pacific Photocopy & Research Services 904-435-3183	•	•	•	•	
•	•	•	Research Express 904-421-0387	•	•	•	•	
•	•	•	SingleSource Services Corp 800-713-3412	•		•	•	•

CV	CR	PR	OKEECHOBEE (EST)	UC	RE	TX	VS	VR
•	•	•	Hollingsworth Court Reporting Inc 504-769-3386	•	•	•	•	
•	•	•	Okeechobee Abstract and Title Ins Inc 813-763-3710	•	•	•		
•	•	•	Pacific Photocopy & Research 305-371-7330	•	•	•	•	
•	•	•	SingleSource Services Corp 800-713-3412	•		•	•	•
		•	Treasure Coast Abstract & Title Ins Co 561-461-7190	•	•	•		

DT	BK	CV	CR	PR	ORANGE (EST)	UC	RE	TX	VS	VR
•	•	•	•	•	A Very Private Eye Inc (SOP) 800-277-7095	•	•	•	•	•
•		•			Accu-Screen Inc 800-689-2228					
•		•	•		Alpha Research LLC (SOP) 205-755-7008			•		
•		•	•	•	Andrews Agency Inc (SOP) 407-649-2085	•	•	•		
•	•	•	•	•	Fidelity Title and Guaranty Company 407-740-7131	•	•	•		
•		•			Hogan Information Services 405-278-6954					
•	•	•	•	•	Hollingsworth Court Reporting Inc 504-769-3386	•	•	•		
•	•	•	•	•	ICDI Inc 407-299-6300	•	•	•		
•	•	•	•	•	Independent Research Assoc 407-277-0076	•	•	•		
•	•	•	•	•	Investigative Legal Services Inc (SOP) 407-426-7433	•	•	•		
•	•	•	•	•	Judicial Research & Retrieval Services 800-529-6226	•	•	•		
•	•	•	•	•	Merlin Information 888-434-6337	•	•	•	•	•
•	•	•	•	•	Pacific Photocopy & Research 407-425-7234	•	•	•	•	

					Provider	Phone	UC	RE	TX	VS	VR
•	•	•	•	•	RSI	800-881-5993	•	•	•	•	•
•	•	•	•	•	SIC Inc (SOP)	305-751-0015	•	•	•	•	
•	•	•	•	•	SingleSource Services Corp	800-713-3412	•		•	•	•

CV	CR	PR	OSCEOLA (EST)	Phone	UC	RE	TX	VS	VR
•	•	•	A Very Private Eye Inc (SOP)	800-277-7095	•	•	•		
•	•		Alpha Research LLC (SOP)	205-755-7008			•		
•	•		Andrews Agency Inc (SOP)	407-649-2085					
•	•	•	Fidelity Title and Guaranty Company	407-740-7131	•	•	•		
•	•	•	Hollingsworth Court Reporting Inc	504-769-3386	•	•	•		
•	•	•	Independent Research Assoc	407-277-0076	•	•			
•	•	•	Investigative Legal Services Inc (SOP)	407-426-7433	•	•	•		
•	•	•	Merlin Information	888-434-6337	•	•	•	•	
•	•	•	Pacific Photocopy & Research	407-425-7234	•	•	•		
•	•	•	SingleSource Services Corp	800-713-3412	•		•	•	•

DT	CV	CR	PR	PALM BEACH (EST)	Phone	UC	RE	TX	VS	VR
•	•	•	•	ATT Investigations Inc	800-733-4405	•	•	•	•	
•	•	•		Alpha Research LLC (SOP)	205-755-7008			•		
•	•	•	•	Barnett Title Services Inc	407-833-0824	•	•	•		•
•	•	•	•	Bill Greenberg Special Services Inc (SOP)	800-654-0002	•	•	•	•	•
•	•	•	•	Compass Investigations (SOP)	954-527-5722	•	•	•	•	•
			•	Computer Assisted Research On-Line	800-329-6397	•				
	•			Deception Control Inc	800-776-1660			•	•	•
•	•	•	•	Esquire Express Inc (SOP)	305-530-9580	•	•	•		
•	•	•	•	FLA Search Company	561-969-6594	•	•	•	•	•
	•	•		Factual Business Information	305-592-7600		•	•	•	
•	•	•	•	Gateway USA	800-727-7772	•	•	•	•	•
•	•	•	•	High-Tech Investigations Inc	888-881-7441	•	•	•	•	•
•	•	•	•	Hollingsworth Court Reporting Inc	504-769-3386	•	•	•		
•	•	•	•	Information Search Inc	561-624-5115	•	•	•	•	•
•	•	•	•	Investigative Services International (SOP)	305-868-7775	•	•	•	•	•
•	•	•	•	JM Search Services Inc	800-393-7563	•	•	•		•
•	•	•	•	Judicial Research & Retrieval Services	800-529-6226	•	•	•		
•	•	•	•	Mulberry, David (SOP)	800-704-1287	•	•	•	•	
•	•	•	•	NIA Academy of Public Records Rsrch	561-624-5100	•	•	•		
•	•	•	•	Pacific Photocopy & Research	561-832-3878	•	•	•		
•	•	•	•	Paralegal Field Research Service (SOP)	800-256-7459	•	•	•	•	
•	•	•	•	RSI	800-881-5993	•	•	•	•	
•	•	•	•	Raven International Investigations Inc	800-719-1626	•	•	•	•	
•	•	•	•	SIC Inc (SOP)	305-751-0015	•	•	•		
•	•	•	•	Scholtes Investigation & Attorney Svcs (SOP)	407-683-4174		•	•		
•	•	•	•	Search/America	800-572-8815	•	•	•	•	
•	•	•	•	SingleSource Services Corp	800-713-3412	•		•	•	•
•	•	•	•	The Records Reviewer Inc	954-947-1186	•	•	•		
•	•	•	•	Verbatim Investigative Services Inc (SOP)	800-750-4231	•	•	•	•	•

CV	CR	PR	PASCO (EST)	Phone	UC	RE	TX	VS	VR
•	•	•	ADREM Profiles Inc	800-483-9929	•		•	•	•
	•		Accu-Screen Inc	800-689-2228					
•	•	•	All Phase Reports (SOP)	813-885-9822	•	•	•	•	•
•	•		Alpha Research LLC (SOP)	205-755-7008			•		
•	•		Brainard Research and Reporting Service	813-931-8370					
•	•	•	Gietzen & Associates Inc (SOP)	813-254-4383		•			
•	•	•	Hollingsworth Court Reporting Inc	504-769-3386	•	•	•		
•	•	•	Pacific Photocopy & Research	813-885-3854	•	•	•		
•	•	•	Search/America	800-572-8815	•	•	•		•
•	•	•	SingleSource Services Corp	800-713-3412	•		•	•	
•	•	•	T L Dearth Records Research & Recovery	813-671-2140	•	•	•	•	

CV	CR	PR	PINELLAS (EST)	Phone	UC	RE	TX	VS	VR
•	•	•	ADREM Profiles Inc	800-483-9929	•		•	•	•

CV	CR	PR	Provider	Phone	UC	RE	TX	VS	VR
•			Accu-Screen Inc	800-689-2228					
•	•	•	🏛 All Phase Reports (SOP)	813-885-9822	•	•	•	•	•
•	•		🏛 Alpha Research LLC (SOP)	205-755-7008		•			
•			Applicant Insight Ltd	813-934-0042		•			
•	•	•	🏛 Bay Area Search Inc	800-478-4618	•	•	•	•	
•	•	•	Brainard Research and Reporting Service	813-931-8370					
•	•	•	🏛 EX-CEL Investigations (SOP)	813-527-5440	•	•	•	•	
•	•	•	Gietzen & Associates Inc (SOP)	813-254-4383		•	•		
•	•	•	🏛 Hollingsworth Court Reporting Inc	504-769-3386	•	•	•	•	
•	•	•	🏛 I.G.B. Associates Inc	813-226-8810	•	•	•	•	
•	•	•	Intelligence Network Inc	813-449-0072	•	•	•	•	
•	•	•	🏛 Judicial Research & Retrieval Services	800-529-6226	•	•	•	•	
•	•	•	🏛 North American Investigations (SOP)	800-270-2628	•	•	•	•	•
•	•	•	Pacific Photocopy & Research	813-885-3854	•	•	•	•	
•	•	•	🏛 RSI	800-881-5993	•	•	•	•	•
•	•	•	SIC Inc (SOP)	305-751-0015	•	•	•	•	•
•	•	•	Search/America	800-572-8815	•	•	•	•	•
•	•	•	🏛 SingleSource Services Corp	800-713-3412	•	•	•	•	•
•	•	•	T L Dearth Records Research & Recovery	813-671-2140	•	•	•	•	

CV	CR	PR	**POLK (EST)**		UC	RE	TX	VS	VR
•	•	•	🏛 A Very Private Eye Inc (SOP)	800-277-7095	•	•	•	•	•
•	•	•	🏛 All Phase Reports (SOP)	813-885-9822	•	•	•	•	•
•	•	•	🏛 Alpha Research LLC (SOP)	205-755-7008		•			
•	•	•	🏛 Bay Area Search Inc	800-478-4618	•	•	•	•	
•	•	•	Brainard Research and Reporting Service	813-931-8370					
•		•	Fidelity Title and Guaranty Company	407-740-7131	•	•	•	•	
•	•	•	Gietzen & Associates Inc (SOP)	813-254-4383		•	•		
•	•	•	🏛 Hollingsworth Court Reporting Inc	504-769-3386	•	•	•	•	
•	•	•	Pacific Photocopy & Research	813-885-3854	•	•	•	•	
•	•	•	🏛 SingleSource Services Corp	800-713-3412	•		•	•	•
•	•	•	T L Dearth Records Research & Recovery	813-671-2140	•	•	•	•	

CV	CR	PR	**PUTNAM (EST)**		UC	RE	TX	VS	VR
•	•		🏛 Alpha Research LLC (SOP)	205-755-7008		•			
•	•	•	Collins Title & Abstract Co Inc	904-829-6600	•	•	•	•	
•	•	•	🏛 Hollingsworth Court Reporting Inc	504-769-3386	•	•	•	•	
•	•	•	Pacific Photocopy & Research	904-355-1062	•	•	•	•	
•	•	•	🏛 SingleSource Services Corp	800-713-3412	•		•	•	•

CV	CR	PR	**SANTA ROSA (CST)**		UC	RE	TX	VS	VR
•	•	•	Aalpha Omega Investigations Inc (SOP)	904-433-7016	•	•	•	•	
•	•	•	Carol Ann Bailey CLA Inc	904-623-9431	•	•	•	•	•
•	•	•	🏛 Hollingsworth Court Reporting Inc	504-769-3386	•	•	•	•	
•	•	•	Pacific Photocopy & Research Services	904-435-3183	•	•	•	•	
•	•	•	🏛 Research Express	904-421-0387	•	•	•	•	
•	•	•	🏛 SingleSource Services Corp	800-713-3412	•		•	•	•

CV	CR	PR	**SARASOTA (EST)**		UC	RE	TX	VS	VR
•	•	•	Accurate Legal Services (SOP)	941-365-3335	•	•		•	
•	•		🏛 Alpha Research LLC (SOP)	205-755-7008		•			
•	•	•	Brainard Research and Reporting Service	813-931-8370					
•		•	Chambers Investigations	800-792-1107	•	•	•	•	
•		•	🏛 Guzman Enterprises	941-743-3690	•	•	•		
•	•	•	🏛 Hollingsworth Court Reporting Inc	504-769-3386	•	•	•	•	
•	•	•	McCormack, Trisha A & Thomas	941-955-9998	•	•	•	•	•
•	•	•	Pacific Photocopy & Research	813-885-3854	•	•	•	•	
•	•	•	Search/America	800-572-8815	•	•	•	•	•
•	•	•	🏛 SingleSource Services Corp	800-713-3412	•		•	•	•
•	•	•	🏛 Steele Investigation Agency (SOP)	813-758-5890	•	•	•	•	•

CV	CR	PR	SEMINOLE (EST)		UC	RE	TX	VS	VR
•	•	•	A Very Private Eye Inc (SOP)	800-277-7095	•	•	•	•	•
•	•		Alpha Research LLC (SOP)	205-755-7008			•		
•	•	•	Andrews Agency Inc (SOP)	407-649-2085	•	•	•	•	
•	•	•	Fidelity Title and Guaranty Company	407-740-7131	•	•	•	•	
•	•	•	Hollingsworth Court Reporting Inc	504-769-3386	•	•	•	•	
•	•	•	ICDI Inc	407-299-6300	•	•	•		
•	•	•	Independent Research Assoc	407-277-0076	•	•	•		
•	•	•	Investigative Legal Services Inc (SOP)	407-426-7433	•	•	•	•	
•	•	•	Merlin Information	888-434-6337	•	•	•	•	•
•	•	•	Pacific Photocopy & Research	407-425-7234	•	•	•	•	
•	•	•	SingleSource Services Corp	800-713-3412	•		•	•	•

CV	CR	PR	ST. JOHNS (EST)		UC	RE	TX	VS	VR
•	•		Alpha Research LLC (SOP)	205-755-7008			•		
•	•	•	Collins Title & Abstract Co Inc	904-829-6600	•	•	•	•	
•	•		G & L Research Associates	904-743-4116	•		•		
•	•	•	Hollingsworth Court Reporting Inc	504-769-3386	•	•	•	•	
•	•	•	Pacific Photocopy & Research	904-355-1062	•	•	•	•	
•	•	•	SingleSource Services Corp	800-713-3412	•		•	•	•

CV	CR	PR	ST. LUCIE (EST)		UC	RE	TX	VS	VR
•	•	•	FLA Search Company	561-969-6594	•	•	•	•	•
•	•	•	Hollingsworth Court Reporting Inc	504-769-3386	•	•	•	•	
•	•	•	Pacific Photocopy & Research	305-371-7330	•	•	•	•	
•		•	Reliable Research	407-334-5854	•	•	•		
•	•	•	SingleSource Services Corp	800-713-3412	•		•	•	•
•			Treasure Coast Abstract & Title Ins Co	561-461-7190	•	•	•		

CV	CR	PR	SUMTER (EST)		UC	RE	TX	VS	VR
•	•		Alpha Research LLC (SOP)	205-755-7008			•		
•	•	•	Hollingsworth Court Reporting Inc	504-769-3386	•	•	•	•	
•	•	•	Pacific Photocopy & Research	904-355-1062	•	•	•	•	
•	•	•	Records Research	352-544-5997	•	•	•		•
•	•	•	SingleSource Services Corp	800-713-3412	•		•	•	•

CV	CR	PR	SUWANNEE (EST)		UC	RE	TX	VS	VR
•	•		Alpha Research LLC (SOP)	205-755-7008			•		
•	•		CSC	800-342-8086	•		•		
•	•	•	Hollingsworth Court Reporting Inc	504-769-3386	•	•	•	•	
•	•	•	Pacific Photocopy & Research	904-355-1062	•		•	•	
•	•	•	Pacific Photocopy & Research	800-934-6999	•		•	•	
•	•	•	Research Express	904-421-0387	•		•	•	
•	•	•	SingleSource Services Corp	800-713-3412	•		•	•	•
•		•	Tri-County Title Services	904-755-5566	•	•	•		

CV	CR	PR	TAYLOR (EST)		UC	RE	TX	VS	VR
•	•		Alpha Research LLC (SOP)	205-755-7008			•		
•	•		CSC	800-342-8086	•		•		
•			Capitol Services	904-878-4734					
•	•	•	Hollingsworth Court Reporting Inc	504-769-3386	•	•	•	•	
•	•	•	Pacific Photocopy & Research	800-934-6999	•		•	•	
•	•	•	Research Express	904-421-0387	•	•	•	•	
•	•	•	UCC Filing & Search Services	800-822-5436	•	•	•	•	

CV	CR	PR	UNION (EST)		UC	RE	TX	VS	VR
•	•		Alpha Research LLC (SOP)	205-755-7008			•		
•	•	•	Hollingsworth Court Reporting Inc	504-769-3386	•	•	•	•	
•	•	•	Pacific Photocopy & Research	904-355-1062	•	•	•	•	
•	•	•	SingleSource Services Corp	800-713-3412	•		•	•	•
•		•	Tri-County Title Services	904-755-5566	•	•	•		

CV	CR	PR	VOLUSIA (EST)		UC	RE	TX	VS	VR
•	•		🏛 Alpha Research LLC (SOP) 205-755-7008				•		
•	•	•	Andrews Agency Inc (SOP) 407-649-2085		•	•	•	•	
•	•	•	Fidelity Title and Guaranty Company 407-740-7131		•	•	•	•	
•	•	•	🏛 Hollingsworth Court Reporting Inc 504-769-3386		•	•	•	•	
•		•	ICDI Inc 407-299-6300		•	•	•		
•	•	•	🏛 Independent Research Assoc 407-277-0076		•	•	•		
•	•	•	🏛 Merlin Information 888-434-6337		•	•	•	•	•
•	•	•	Pacific Photocopy & Research 407-425-7234		•	•	•	•	•
•	•	•	🏛 RSI 800-881-5993		•	•	•	•	•
•	•	•	SIC Inc (SOP) 305-751-0015		•	•	•	•	•
•	•	•	🏛 SingleSource Services Corp 800-713-3412		•		•	•	•
•	•	•	Volusia Legal Services (SOP) 904-822-9067						

CV	CR	PR	WAKULLA (EST)		UC	RE	TX	VS	VR
•	•	•	Acumen Investigations (SOP) 904-668-0824		•	•	•	•	•
•	•	•	Advanced Investigations Inc (SOP) 904-222-1998		•	•	•	•	
•	•		🏛 Alpha Research LLC (SOP) 205-755-7008				•		
•	•		CSC 800-342-8086		•		•		
			Capitol Services 904-878-4734						
•	•	•	Corporate Access Inc (SOP) 800-969-1666		•	•	•	•	•
•	•	•	🏛 Hollingsworth Court Reporting Inc 504-769-3386		•	•	•	•	
•	•	•	Pacific Photocopy & Research 800-934-6999		•		•	•	
•	•	•	🏛 Research Express 904-421-0387		•	•	•	•	
•	•	•	🏛 SingleSource Services Corp 800-713-3412		•		•	•	•
•	•	•	🏛 State Information Bureau 800-881-1742		•	•	•	•	
•			Sunstate Research Associates Inc 800-621-7234		•		•		
•	•	•	UCC Filing & Search Services 800-822-5436		•	•	•	•	

CV	CR	PR	WALTON (CST)		UC	RE	TX	VS	VR
•	•	•	Aalpha Omega Investigations Inc (SOP) 904-433-7016		•	•	•	•	
•	•		🏛 Alpha Research LLC (SOP) 205-755-7008				•		
•	•	•	🏛 Hollingsworth Court Reporting Inc 504-769-3386		•	•	•	•	
•	•	•	Pacific Photocopy & Research Services 904-435-3183		•	•	•	•	
•	•	•	🏛 Research Express 904-421-0387		•	•	•	•	

CV	CR	PR	WASHINGTON (CST)		UC	RE	TX	VS	VR
•	•	•	🏛 Hollingsworth Court Reporting Inc 504-769-3386		•	•	•	•	
•	•	•	Pacific Photocopy & Research 800-934-6999		•		•	•	
•	•	•	Pacific Photocopy & Research Services 904-435-3183		•	•	•	•	
•	•	•	🏛 Research Express 904-421-0387		•	•	•	•	
•			Sunstate Research Associates Inc 800-621-7234		•		•		

GEORGIA

CV	CR	PR	APPLING (EST)		UC	RE	TX	VS	VR
•	•	•	Liberty Corporate Services Inc 800-334-2735		•	•	•	•	
•	•	•	🏛 Rowell, Betty M 912-449-0849		•	•	•	•	

CV	CR	PR	ATKINSON (EST)		UC	RE	TX	VS	VR
•	•	•	Liberty Corporate Services Inc 800-334-2735		•	•	•	•	
•	•	•	Roberts Abstracting Inc 912-532-5105		•	•	•		

CV	CR	PR	BACON (EST)		UC	RE	TX	VS	VR
•	•	•	Liberty Corporate Services Inc 800-334-2735		•	•	•	•	
•	•	•	🏛 Rowell, Betty M 912-449-0849		•	•	•	•	

CV	CR	PR	BAKER (EST)		UC	RE	TX	VS	VR
•		•	Dougherty Abstract & Title Service Inc 912-888-9035			•	•		
•	•	•	Liberty Corporate Services Inc 800-334-2735		•	•	•	•	
•	•		Thurman Investigative Services Inc 912-759-1700						

CV	CR	PR	BALDWIN (EST)		UC	RE	TX	VS	VR
•	•	•	Liberty Corporate Services Inc 800-334-2735		•	•	•	•	
•		•	Pro Title Inc 912-781-9344		•	•	•		

CV	CR	PR	BANKS (EST)		UC	RE	TX	VS	VR
•	•		🏛 Alpha Research LLC (SOP) 205-755-7008				•		
•	•	•	🏛 Dargason Information Services 770-418-9256		•	•	•	•	•
•	•	•	EL-RU Inc (SOP) 404-963-8023		•	•	•	•	•
•	•	•	🏛 Hollingsworth Court Reporting Inc 504-769-3386		•	•	•	•	
•	•	•	Liberty Corporate Services Inc 800-334-2735		•	•	•	•	
•	•	•	Wilmot, Sally 800-282-2686		•	•	•	•	

CV	CR	PR	BARROW (EST)		UC	RE	TX	VS	VR
•	•	•	🏛 Dargason Information Services 770-418-9256		•	•	•	•	•
•	•	•	EL-RU Inc (SOP) 404-963-8023		•	•	•	•	•
•	•	•	🏛 Ed Knight Information Service 800-282-6418		•	•	•		
•	•	•	🏛 Hollingsworth Court Reporting Inc 504-769-3386		•	•	•	•	
•	•	•	Liberty Corporate Services Inc 800-334-2735		•	•	•	•	
•	•	•	🏛 MLQ Attorney Services (SOP) 800-446-8794		•	•	•	•	
•	•	•	Wilmot, Sally 800-282-2686		•	•	•	•	

CV	CR	PR	BARTOW (EST)		UC	RE	TX	VS	VR
•	•	•	🏛 Atlanta Attorney Services (SOP) 800-804-4078		•	•	•	•	•
•	•	•	🏛 Ed Knight Information Service 800-282-6418		•	•	•		
•	•	•	🏛 FACFIND Network Inc 800-343-6641		•	•	•	•	
•	•	•	Holcomb, David M (SOP) 770-388-3712		•	•	•	•	•
•	•	•	🏛 Hollingsworth Court Reporting Inc 504-769-3386		•	•	•	•	
•	•	•	Liberty Corporate Services Inc 800-334-2735		•	•	•	•	
•	•	•	🏛 MLQ Attorney Services (SOP) 800-446-8794		•	•	•	•	
•	•	•	🏛 Specialty Services (SOP) 770-942-8264		•	•	•	•	•

CV	CR	PR	BEN HILL (EST)		UC	RE	TX	VS	VR
•	•	•	Liberty Corporate Services Inc 800-334-2735		•	•	•	•	
•	•	•	🏛 Specialty Services (SOP) 770-942-8264		•	•	•	•	•

CV	CR	PR	BERRIEN (EST)		UC	RE	TX	VS	VR
•	•	•	Liberty Corporate Services Inc 800-334-2735		•	•	•	•	
•	•	•	Roberts Abstracting Inc 912-532-5105		•	•	•		
•	•	•	🏛 Specialty Services (SOP) 770-942-8264		•	•	•		•

DT	BK	CV	CR	PR	BIBB (EST)		UC	RE	TX	VS	VR
•	•	•	•		🏛 Alpha Research LLC (SOP) 205-755-7008				•		
•	•	•	•	•	🏛 FACFIND Network Inc 800-343-6641		•	•	•	•	
•	•	•	•	•	Graystone Investigations Inc (SOP) 912-743-5551		•	•	•	•	

							UC	RE	TX	VS	VR
•	•	•	•	•	Liberty Corporate Services Inc 800-334-2735		•	•	•	•	
				•	Pro Title Inc 912-781-9344		•	•	•		
•	•	•	•	•	🏛 Specialty Services (SOP) 770-942-8264		•	•	•	•	•

CV	CR	PR	BLECKLEY (EST)	UC	RE	TX	VS	VR
•	•	•	Liberty Corporate Services Inc 800-334-2735	•	•	•	•	
•		•	Pro Title Inc 912-781-9344	•	•	•		

CV	CR	PR	BRANTLEY (EST)	UC	RE	TX	VS	VR
•	•	•	Liberty Corporate Services Inc 800-334-2735	•	•	•	•	
•	•	•	🏛 Rowell, Betty M 912-449-0849	•	•	•	•	

CV	CR	PR	BROOKS (EST)	UC	RE	TX	VS	VR
•	•		🏛 Alpha Research LLC (SOP) 205-755-7008			•		
•	•	•	Liberty Corporate Services Inc 800-334-2735	•	•	•	•	
•			Sunstate Research Associates Inc 800-621-7234	•		•		

CV	CR	PR	BRYAN (EST)	UC	RE	TX	VS	VR
•	•	•	Josey, Cheryl S 912-653-2707	•	•	•	•	
•	•	•	Liberty Corporate Services Inc 800-334-2735	•	•	•	•	
•	•	•	🏛 Specialty Services (SOP) 770-942-8264	•	•	•	•	•

CV	CR	PR	BULLOCH (EST)	UC	RE	TX	VS	VR
•	•	•	Cooper Research Inc (SOP) 912-897-9028	•	•	•	•	•
•	•	•	Josey, Cheryl S 912-653-2707	•	•	•	•	
•	•	•	Liberty Corporate Services Inc 800-334-2735	•	•	•	•	
•	•	•	🏛 Specialty Services (SOP) 770-942-8264	•	•	•	•	•

CV	CR	PR	BURKE (EST)	UC	RE	TX	VS	VR
•	•	•	Liberty Corporate Services Inc 800-334-2735	•	•	•	•	
•	•	•	Weber, Attorney David V 706-860-8160	•	•	•	•	

CV	CR	PR	BUTTS (EST)	UC	RE	TX	VS	VR
•	•		🏛 Alpha Research LLC (SOP) 205-755-7008			•		
•	•	•	🏛 Ed Knight Information Service 800-282-6418	•	•	•		
•	•	•	🏛 FACFIND Network Inc 800-343-6641	•	•	•	•	
•	•	•	🏛 Hollingsworth Court Reporting Inc 504-769-3386	•	•	•	•	
•	•	•	Law Office of Roger Gladden (SOP) 404-550-0749	•	•	•		
•	•	•	Liberty Corporate Services Inc 800-334-2735	•	•	•	•	
•	•	•	Pro Title Inc 912-781-9344	•	•	•		
•	•	•	🏛 Specialty Services (SOP) 770-942-8264	•	•	•	•	•

CV	CR	PR	CALHOUN (EST)	UC	RE	TX	VS	VR
•		•	Dougherty Abstract & Title Service Inc 912-888-9035		•	•		
•	•	•	Liberty Corporate Services Inc 800-334-2735	•	•	•	•	
•	•		Thurman Investigative Services Inc 912-759-1700					

CV	CR	PR	CAMDEN (EST)	UC	RE	TX	VS	VR
•	•	•	Liberty Corporate Services Inc 800-334-2735	•	•	•	•	

CV	CR	PR	CANDLER (EST)	UC	RE	TX	VS	VR
•	•	•	Liberty Corporate Services Inc 800-334-2735	•	•	•	•	

CV	CR	PR	CARROLL (EST)	UC	RE	TX	VS	VR
•	•	•	🏛 Ed Knight Information Service 800-282-6418	•	•	•		
•	•	•	🏛 FACFIND Network Inc 800-343-6641	•	•	•	•	
•	•	•	🏛 Glass & Carson Investigation Svcs (SOP) 770-603-2887	•	•	•	•	•
•	•	•	Liberty Corporate Services Inc 800-334-2735	•	•	•	•	
•	•	•	🏛 Specialty Services (SOP) 770-942-8264	•	•	•	•	•

CV	CR	PR	CATOOSA (EST)	UC	RE	TX	VS	VR
	•		Bell, Jan 706-278-7216	•	•	•		
•	•	•	🏛 Hollingsworth Court Reporting Inc 504-769-3386	•	•	•		
•	•	•	Liberty Corporate Services Inc 800-334-2735	•	•	•	•	

CV	CR	PR		UC	RE	TX	VS	VR
•	•	•	Specialty Services (SOP) 770-942-8264	•	•	•	•	•
•		•	Title Guaranty & Trust of Chattanooga 615-266-5751	•	•	•		

		CV	CR	PR	CHARLTON (EST)	UC	RE	TX	VS	VR
		•	•		Frederick, June 912-496-2354	•	•	•		
		•	•	•	Liberty Corporate Services Inc 800-334-2735	•	•	•	•	
		•	•	•	Rowell, Betty M 912-449-0849	•	•	•	•	

DT	BK	CV	CR	PR	CHATHAM (EST)	UC	RE	TX	VS	VR
•	•	•	•		Alpha Research LLC (SOP).................205-755-7008			•		
•	•	•	•	•	Cooper Research Inc (SOP) 912-897-9028	•	•	•	•	•
		•	•	•	Josey, Cheryl S 912-653-2707	•	•	•	•	•
•	•	•	•	•	Liberty Corporate Services Inc 800-334-2735	•	•	•	•	•
•	•	•	•	•	Specialty Services (SOP) 770-942-8264	•	•	•	•	•

CV	CR	PR	CHATTAHOOCHEE (EST)	UC	RE	TX	VS	VR
•	•	•	Attorney & Court Service of Georgia (SOP) 706-322-3554	•	•	•	•	•
•	•	•	Liberty Corporate Services Inc 800-334-2735	•	•	•	•	

CV	CR	PR	CHATTOOGA (EST)	UC	RE	TX	VS	VR
•	•	•	Liberty Corporate Services Inc 800-334-2735	•	•	•	•	
•	•	•	Specialty Services (SOP) 770-942-8264	•	•	•	•	•
•		•	Title Guaranty & Trust of Chattanooga 615-266-5751	•	•	•		

CV	CR	PR	CHEROKEE (EST)	UC	RE	TX	VS	VR
•	•		Alpha Research LLC (SOP).........................205-755-7008			•		
•	•	•	Atlanta Attorney Services (SOP) 800-804-4078	•	•	•	•	•
•	•	•	Dargason Information Services 770-418-9256	•	•	•	•	•
•	•	•	EL-RU Inc (SOP).................................404-963-8023	•	•	•	•	•
•	•	•	Ed Knight Information Service 800-282-6418	•	•	•		
•	•	•	FACFIND Network Inc 800-343-6641	•	•	•	•	
•	•	•	Glass & Carson Investigation Svcs (SOP) 770-603-2887	•	•	•	•	•
•	•	•	Holcomb, David M (SOP) 770-388-3712	•	•	•	•	•
•	•	•	Hollingsworth Court Reporting Inc 504-769-3386	•	•	•	•	
•	•	•	Liberty Corporate Services Inc 800-334-2735	•	•	•	•	
•	•	•	MLQ Attorney Services (SOP) 800-446-8794	•	•	•	•	
•	•	•	Specialty Services (SOP) 770-942-8264	•	•	•	•	•

CV	CR	PR	CLARKE (EST)	UC	RE	TX	VS	VR
•	•		Alpha Research LLC (SOP).........................205-755-7008			•		
•	•	•	EL-RU Inc (SOP).................................404-963-8023	•	•	•	•	•
•	•	•	Liberty Corporate Services Inc 800-334-2735	•	•	•	•	
•	•	•	Specialty Services (SOP) 770-942-8264	•	•	•	•	•
•	•	•	Wilmot, Sally 800-282-2686	•	•	•	•	

CV	CR	PR	CLAY (EST)	UC	RE	TX	VS	VR
•	•	•	Liberty Corporate Services Inc 800-334-2735	•	•	•	•	
•	•		Thurman Investigative Services Inc 912-759-1700					

CV	CR	PR	CLAYTON (EST)	UC	RE	TX	VS	VR
•	•	•	APS Attorney Service (SOP) 800-245-0122	•	•	•	•	•
•	•		Alpha Research LLC (SOP).........................205-755-7008			•		
•	•	•	Atlanta Attorney Services (SOP) 800-804-4078	•	•	•	•	•
•	•	•	Attorneys' Personal Services (SOP)...............800-245-0122	•	•	•	•	•
•		•	Direct Corporate Services Inc 800-783-7904	•	•	•	•	•
•		•	Document Resources 800-532-9876	•	•	•	•	•
•	•	•	EL-RU Inc (SOP).................................404-963-8023	•	•	•	•	•
•	•	•	Ed Knight Information Service 800-282-6418	•	•	•		
•		•	Elliott, Schuyler 404-373-0886	•	•	•	•	•
•	•	•	Glass & Carson Investigation Svcs (SOP) 770-603-2887	•	•	•	•	•
•	•	•	Holcomb, David M (SOP) 770-388-3712	•	•	•	•	•
•	•	•	Hollingsworth Court Reporting Inc 504-769-3386	•	•	•	•	
•	•	•	John Roberson Investigations (SOP) 800-325-0914	•	•	•	•	

CV	CR	PR	Provider	Phone	UC	RE	TX	VS	VR
•	•	•	Liberty Corporate Services Inc	800-334-2735	•	•	•	•	
•	•	•	MGC Courier Inc	800-822-1084	•	•			
•	•	•	🏛 MLQ Attorney Services (SOP)	800-446-8794	•	•	•	•	
•	•		Slueth Research	404-288-4598	•	•			
•	•	•	🏛 Specialty Services (SOP)	770-942-8264	•	•	•	•	•

CLINCH (EST)

CV	CR	PR	Provider	Phone	UC	RE	TX	VS	VR
•	•	•	Liberty Corporate Services Inc	800-334-2735	•	•	•	•	

COBB (EST)

CV	CR	PR	Provider	Phone	UC	RE	TX	VS	VR
•	•	•	🏛 APS Attorney Service (SOP)	800-245-0122	•	•	•	•	•
•	•		ASAP Legal Documents	404-241-8130		•		•	
•	•		🏛 Alpha Research LLC (SOP)	205-755-7008			•		
•	•	•	🏛 Atlanta Attorney Services (SOP)	800-804-4078	•	•	•	•	
•	•	•	Attorneys' Personal Services (SOP)	800-245-0122	•	•	•	•	•
•	•	•	🏛 Charley's Legal Angels (SOP)	770-419-0259	•	•	•	•	•
•	•		Direct Corporate Services Inc	800-783-7904	•	•	•		
•	•		Document Resources	800-532-9876	•	•	•	•	•
•	•	•	EL-RU Inc (SOP)	404-963-8023	•	•	•	•	•
•	•		🏛 Ed Knight Information Service	800-282-6418	•	•	•		
•	•	•	Elliott, Schuyler	404-373-0886	•	•	•	•	
•	•	•	🏛 FACFIND Network Inc	800-343-6641	•	•	•		
•	•	•	🏛 Glass & Carson Investigation Svcs (SOP)	770-603-2887	•	•	•		•
•	•		Holcomb, David M (SOP)	770-388-3712	•	•	•		•
•	•	•	🏛 Hollingsworth Court Reporting Inc	504-769-3386	•	•	•	•	
•	•	•	🏛 John Roberson Investigations (SOP)	800-325-0914	•	•	•	•	
•	•	•	Liberty Corporate Services Inc	800-334-2735	•	•	•	•	
•	•	•	MGC Courier Inc	800-822-1084	•	•			
•	•	•	🏛 MLQ Attorney Services (SOP)	800-446-8794	•	•	•	•	
•	•		Phoenix Investigations (SOP)	800-999-4701	•	•	•	•	
•	•		Slueth Research	404-288-4598	•	•	•		
•	•	•	🏛 Specialty Services (SOP)	770-942-8264	•	•	•	•	•

COFFEE (EST)

CV	CR	PR	Provider	Phone	UC	RE	TX	VS	VR
•	•	•	Liberty Corporate Services Inc	800-334-2735	•	•	•	•	

COLQUITT (EST)

CV	CR	PR	Provider	Phone	UC	RE	TX	VS	VR
•	•	•	Liberty Corporate Services Inc	800-334-2735	•	•	•	•	
•	•	•	🏛 Specialty Services (SOP)	770-942-8264	•	•	•	•	•
•			Sunstate Research Associates Inc	800-621-7234	•	•			

COLUMBIA (EST)

CV	CR	PR	Provider	Phone	UC	RE	TX	VS	VR
•	•		🏛 Alpha Research LLC (SOP)	205-755-7008			•		
•	•		🏛 FACFIND Network Inc	800-343-6641	•	•	•		
•	•	•	Liberty Corporate Services Inc	800-334-2735	•	•	•		
•	•	•	🏛 Specialty Services (SOP)	770-942-8264	•	•	•	•	•
•	•	•	Weber, Attorney David V	706-860-8160	•	•	•	•	

COOK (EST)

CV	CR	PR	Provider	Phone	UC	RE	TX	VS	VR
•	•		🏛 Alpha Research LLC (SOP)	205-755-7008			•		
•	•	•	Liberty Corporate Services Inc	800-334-2735	•	•	•	•	
•	•	•	Roberts Abstracting Inc	912-532-5105	•	•	•		
•	•	•	🏛 Specialty Services (SOP)	770-942-8264	•	•	•	•	•
•			Sunstate Research Associates Inc	800-621-7234	•	•			

COWETA (EST)

DT	BK	CV	CR	PR	Provider	Phone	UC	RE	TX	VS	VR
•	•	•	•	•	🏛 Atlanta Attorney Services (SOP)	800-804-4078	•	•	•	•	•
•	•	•	•	•	🏛 Ed Knight Information Service	800-282-6418	•	•	•		
•	•	•	•	•	Elliott, Schuyler	404-373-0886	•	•	•		
•	•	•	•	•	🏛 FACFIND Network Inc	800-343-6641	•	•	•		
•	•	•	•	•	🏛 Hogan Information Services	405-278-6954					
•	•	•	•	•	🏛 Hollingsworth Court Reporting Inc	504-769-3386	•	•	•	•	
•	•	•	•	•	🏛 John Roberson Investigations (SOP)	800-325-0914	•	•	•	•	

						Company	Phone					
•	•	•	•	•		Liberty Corporate Services Inc	800-334-2735	•	•	•	•	
•	•	•	•	•		🏛 MLQ Attorney Services (SOP)	800-446-8794	•	•	•	•	
•	•	•	•	•		🏛 Specialty Services (SOP)	770-942-8264	•	•	•	•	•

	CV	CR	PR	CRAWFORD (EST)	UC	RE	TX	VS	VR
	•	•	•	Graystone Investigations Inc (SOP) ... 912-743-5551	•	•	•	•	•
	•	•	•	Liberty Corporate Services Inc ... 800-334-2735	•	•	•	•	
	•		•	Pro Title Inc ... 912-781-9344	•	•	•		

	CV	CR	PR	CRISP (EST)	UC	RE	TX	VS	VR
	•	•	•	Liberty Corporate Services Inc ... 800-334-2735	•	•	•	•	
				South Georgia Title ... 912-273-1977		•			
	•	•		Thurman Investigative Services Inc ... 912-759-1700					

	CV	CR	PR	DADE (EST)	UC	RE	TX	VS	VR
	•	•	•	🏛 Hollingsworth Court Reporting Inc ... 504-769-3386	•	•	•	•	
	•	•	•	Liberty Corporate Services Inc ... 800-334-2735	•	•	•	•	
	•	•	•	🏛 Specialty Services (SOP) ... 770-942-8264	•	•	•	•	•
	•		•	Title Guaranty & Trust of Chattanooga ... 615-266-5751	•	•	•		

	CV	CR	PR	DAWSON (EST)	UC	RE	TX	VS	VR
	•	•	•	🏛 Dargason Information Services ... 770-418-9256	•	•	•	•	•
	•	•	•	EL-RU Inc (SOP) ... 404-963-8023	•	•	•	•	•
	•	•	•	Liberty Corporate Services Inc ... 800-334-2735	•	•	•	•	

	CV	CR	PR	DE KALB (EST)	UC	RE	TX	VS	VR
	•	•	•	🏛 APS Attorney Service (SOP) ... 800-245-0122	•	•	•	•	•
	•	•		ASAP Legal Documents ... 404-241-8130		•		•	
	•	•		🏛 Alpha Research LLC (SOP) ... 205-755-7008		•			
	•	•	•	🏛 Atlanta Attorney Services (SOP) ... 800-804-4078	•	•	•	•	•
	•	•	•	Attorneys' Personal Services (SOP) ... 800-245-0122	•	•	•	•	•
	•	•	•	🏛 Charley's Legal Angels (SOP) ... 770-419-0259	•	•	•	•	•
	•	•	•	Direct Corporate Services Inc ... 800-783-7904	•	•	•		
	•	•	•	Document Resources ... 800-532-9876	•	•	•	•	
	•	•	•	EL-RU Inc (SOP) ... 404-963-8023	•	•	•	•	•
	•	•	•	🏛 Ed Knight Information Service ... 800-282-6418	•	•	•		
	•	•	•	Elliott, Schuyler ... 404-373-0886	•	•	•		
	•	•	•	🏛 FACFIND Network Inc ... 800-343-6641	•	•	•		
	•	•	•	🏛 Glass & Carson Investigation Svcs (SOP) ... 770-603-2887	•	•	•		•
	•	•	•	Holcomb, David M (SOP) ... 770-388-3712	•	•	•		•
	•	•	•	🏛 Hollingsworth Court Reporting Inc ... 504-769-3386	•	•	•		
	•	•	•	🏛 John Roberson Investigations (SOP) ... 800-325-0914	•	•	•		
	•	•	•	Liberty Corporate Services Inc ... 800-334-2735	•	•	•	•	
	•	•	•	MGC Courier Inc ... 800-822-1084	•	•			
	•	•	•	🏛 MLQ Attorney Services (SOP) ... 800-446-8794	•	•	•	•	
	•	•	•	Phoenix Investigations (SOP) ... 800-999-4701	•	•	•	•	
	•	•		Slueth Research ... 404-288-4598	•	•	•		
	•	•	•	🏛 Specialty Services (SOP) ... 770-942-8264	•	•	•	•	•

	CV	CR	PR	DECATUR (EST)	UC	RE	TX	VS	VR
	•	•		🏛 Alpha Research LLC (SOP) ... 205-755-7008		•			
	•	•		CSC ... 800-342-8086	•	•			
	•	•	•	Liberty Corporate Services Inc ... 800-334-2735	•	•	•	•	
	•			Sunstate Research Associates Inc ... 800-621-7234	•	•			
	•	•		Thurman Investigative Services Inc ... 912-759-1700					

	CV	CR	PR	DODGE (EST)	UC	RE	TX	VS	VR
	•	•	•	Liberty Corporate Services Inc ... 800-334-2735	•	•	•	•	
	•		•	Pro Title Inc ... 912-781-9344	•	•	•		

	CV	CR	PR	DOOLY (EST)	UC	RE	TX	VS	VR
	•	•	•	Liberty Corporate Services Inc ... 800-334-2735	•	•	•	•	
	•		•	Pro Title Inc ... 912-781-9344	•	•	•		

DOUGHERTY (EST)

DT	CV	CR	PR	Provider	Phone	UC	RE	TX	VS	VR
•	•	•		Alpha Research LLC (SOP)	205-755-7008			•		
			•	Dougherty Abstract & Title Service Inc	912-888-9035		•	•		
•	•	•	•	Liberty Corporate Services Inc	800-334-2735	•	•	•	•	
•	•	•	•	Specialty Services (SOP)	770-942-8264	•	•	•	•	•
	•	•		Thurman Investigative Services Inc	912-759-1700					

DOUGLAS (EST)

CV	CR	PR	Provider	Phone	UC	RE	TX	VS	VR
•	•		Alpha Research LLC (SOP)	205-755-7008			•		
•	•	•	Atlanta Attorney Services (SOP)	800-804-4078	•	•	•		•
•	•	•	Ed Knight Information Service	800-282-6418	•	•	•		
•	•	•	FACFIND Network Inc	800-343-6641	•	•	•		
•	•	•	Glass & Carson Investigation Svcs (SOP)	770-603-2887	•	•	•	•	
•	•	•	Holcomb, David M (SOP)	770-388-3712	•	•	•	•	•
•	•	•	Hollingsworth Court Reporting Inc	504-769-3386	•	•	•		
•	•	•	Liberty Corporate Services Inc	800-334-2735	•	•	•		
•	•	•	MLQ Attorney Services (SOP)	800-446-8794	•	•	•		
•	•		Slueth Research	404-288-4598	•	•	•		
•	•	•	Specialty Services (SOP)	770-942-8264	•	•	•	•	•

EARLY (EST)

CV	CR	PR	Provider	Phone	UC	RE	TX	VS	VR
•	•	•	Liberty Corporate Services Inc	800-334-2735	•	•	•	•	
•	•		Thurman Investigative Services Inc	912-759-1700					

ECHOLS (EST)

CV	CR	PR	Provider	Phone	UC	RE	TX	VS	VR
•	•	•	Liberty Corporate Services Inc	800-334-2735	•	•	•	•	

EFFINGHAM (EST)

CV	CR	PR	Provider	Phone	UC	RE	TX	VS	VR
•	•	•	Liberty Corporate Services Inc	800-334-2735	•	•	•	•	
•	•	•	Specialty Services (SOP)	770-942-8264	•	•	•	•	•

ELBERT (EST)

CV	CR	PR	Provider	Phone	UC	RE	TX	VS	VR
•	•	•	Liberty Corporate Services Inc	800-334-2735	•	•	•	•	
•	•	•	Wilmot, Sally	800-282-2686	•	•	•	•	

EMANUEL (EST)

CV	CR	PR	Provider	Phone	UC	RE	TX	VS	VR
•	•	•	Liberty Corporate Services Inc	800-334-2735	•	•	•	•	

EVANS (EST)

CV	CR	PR	Provider	Phone	UC	RE	TX	VS	VR
•	•	•	Josey, Cheryl S	912-653-2707	•	•	•	•	
•	•	•	Liberty Corporate Services Inc	800-334-2735	•	•	•	•	

FANNIN (EST)

CV	CR	PR	Provider	Phone	UC	RE	TX	VS	VR
•	•	•	Dargason Information Services	770-418-9256	•	•	•	•	•
•	•	•	Hollingsworth Court Reporting Inc	504-769-3386	•	•	•	•	
•	•	•	Liberty Corporate Services Inc	800-334-2735	•	•	•	•	
•		•	Title Guaranty & Trust of Chattanooga	615-266-5751	•	•	•		

FAYETTE (EST)

CV	CR	PR	Provider	Phone	UC	RE	TX	VS	VR
•	•		Alpha Research LLC (SOP)	205-755-7008			•		
•	•	•	Ed Knight Information Service	800-282-6418	•	•	•		
•	•	•	FACFIND Network Inc	800-343-6641	•	•	•	•	
•	•	•	Glass & Carson Investigation Svcs (SOP)	770-603-2887	•	•	•	•	•
•	•	•	John Roberson Investigations (SOP)	800-325-0914	•	•	•	•	
•	•	•	Liberty Corporate Services Inc	800-334-2735	•	•	•	•	
•	•	•	MLQ Attorney Services (SOP)	800-446-8794	•	•	•	•	
•	•	•	Specialty Services (SOP)	770-942-8264	•	•	•	•	•

FLOYD (EST)

DT	BK	CV	CR	PR	Provider	Phone	UC	RE	TX	VS	VR
•	•	•	•		Alpha Research LLC (SOP)	205-755-7008			•		
		•	•		Broom's Appraisals & Research	706-290-1000	•	•	•		
•		•	•	•	FACFIND Network Inc	800-343-6641	•	•	•	•	
•	•				Hogan Information Services	405-278-6954					

DT	BK	CV	CR	PR			UC	RE	TX	VS	VR
•	•	•	•	•	Liberty Corporate Services Inc	800-334-2735	•	•	•	•	
•	•	•	•	•	🏛 Specialty Services (SOP)	770-942-8264	•	•	•	•	•

	CV	CR	PR	FORSYTH (EST)		UC	RE	TX	VS	VR
	•	•		🏛 Alpha Research LLC (SOP)	205-755-7008			•		
	•	•	•	🏛 Atlanta Attorney Services (SOP)	800-804-4078	•	•	•	•	•
	•	•	•	🏛 Dargason Information Services	770-418-9256	•	•	•	•	•
	•	•	•	EL-RU Inc (SOP)	404-963-8023	•	•	•	•	•
	•	•	•	🏛 Ed Knight Information Service	800-282-6418	•	•	•	•	•
	•	•	•	Graystone Investigations Inc (SOP)	912-743-5551	•	•	•	•	•
	•	•	•	Holcomb, David M (SOP)	770-388-3712	•	•	•	•	•
	•	•	•	🏛 Hollingsworth Court Reporting Inc	504-769-3386	•	•	•	•	•
	•	•	•	Liberty Corporate Services Inc	800-334-2735	•	•	•	•	•
	•	•	•	🏛 MLQ Attorney Services (SOP)	800-446-8794	•	•	•	•	•
	•	•	•	🏛 Specialty Services (SOP)	770-942-8264	•	•	•	•	•

	CV	CR	PR	FRANKLIN (EST)		UC	RE	TX	VS	VR
	•	•		🏛 Alpha Research LLC (SOP)	205-755-7008			•		
	•	•	•	Liberty Corporate Services Inc	800-334-2735	•	•	•	•	

DT	BK	CV	CR	PR	FULTON (CAPITAL) (EST)		UC	RE	TX	VS	VR
•	•	•	•	•	🏛 APS Attorney Service (SOP)	800-245-0122	•	•	•	•	•
•	•	•	•		🏛 Alpha Research LLC (SOP)	205-755-7008			•		
•	•	•	•	•	🏛 Atlanta Attorney Services (SOP)	800-804-4078	•	•	•	•	•
•	•	•	•	•	Attorneys' Personal Services (SOP)	800-245-0122	•	•	•	•	•
•	•	•	•	•	CSC	800-241-5834	•	•	•	•	•
•	•	•	•	•	🏛 Charley's Legal Angels (SOP)	770-419-0259	•	•	•	•	•
•	•	•	•	•	Direct Corporate Services Inc	800-783-7904	•	•	•	•	•
•	•	•	•	•	Document Resources	800-532-9876	•	•	•	•	•
•	•	•	•	•	EL-RU Inc (SOP)	404-963-8023	•	•	•	•	•
•	•	•	•	•	🏛 Ed Knight Information Service	800-282-6418	•	•	•	•	•
•	•	•	•		Elliott, Schuyler	404-373-0886	•	•	•	•	
•	•	•	•	•	🏛 FACFIND Network Inc	800-343-6641	•	•	•	•	
•	•	•	•	•	🏛 Glass & Carson Investigation Svcs (SOP)	770-603-2887	•	•	•		•
•	•				🏛 Hogan Information Services	405-278-6954	•				
•	•	•	•	•	Holcomb, David M (SOP)	770-388-3712	•	•	•	•	•
•	•	•	•	•	🏛 Hollingsworth Court Reporting Inc	504-769-3386	•	•	•	•	
•	•	•	•	•	🏛 John Roberson Investigations (SOP)	800-325-0914	•	•	•	•	
•	•	•	•		Liberty Corporate Services Inc	800-334-2735	•	•	•	•	
			•	•	MGC Courier Inc	800-822-1084	•	•	•		
•	•	•	•	•	🏛 MLQ Attorney Services (SOP)	800-446-8794	•	•	•	•	
•	•	•	•	•	Phoenix Investigations (SOP)	800-999-4701	•	•	•	•	
•	•	•	•		Slueth Research	404-288-4598	•	•	•		
•	•	•	•	•	🏛 Specialty Services (SOP)	770-942-8264	•	•	•	•	•

	CV	CR	PR	GILMER (EST)		UC	RE	TX	VS	VR
		•		Bell, Jan	706-278-7216	•	•	•	•	
	•	•	•	🏛 Dargason Information Services	770-418-9256	•	•	•	•	•
	•	•	•	🏛 Hollingsworth Court Reporting Inc	504-769-3386	•	•	•	•	
	•	•	•	Liberty Corporate Services Inc	800-334-2735	•	•	•	•	
	•		•	Title Guaranty & Trust of Chattanooga	615-266-5751	•	•	•		

	CV	CR	PR	GLASCOCK (EST)		UC	RE	TX	VS	VR
	•	•	•	Liberty Corporate Services Inc	800-334-2735	•	•	•	•	

DT		CV	CR	PR	GLYNN (EST)		UC	RE	TX	VS	VR
		•	•	•	Josey, Cheryl S	912-653-2707	•	•	•	•	
•		•	•	•	Liberty Corporate Services Inc	800-334-2735	•	•	•	•	
•		•	•	•	🏛 Specialty Services (SOP)	770-942-8264	•	•	•	•	•

	CV	CR	PR	GORDON (EST)		UC	RE	TX	VS	VR
	•	•		🏛 Alpha Research LLC (SOP)	205-755-7008			•		
		•		Bell, Jan	706-278-7216	•	•	•		

CV	CR	PR			UC	RE	TX	VS	VR
•	•		Broom's Appraisals & Research 706-290-1000		•	•	•		
•	•	•	Liberty Corporate Services Inc 800-334-2735		•	•	•	•	
•	•	•	🏛 Specialty Services (SOP) 770-942-8264		•	•	•	•	•
•		•	Title Guaranty & Trust of Chattanooga 615-266-5751		•	•	•		

CV	CR	PR	GRADY (EST)		UC	RE	TX	VS	VR
•	•		🏛 Alpha Research LLC (SOP) 205-755-7008				•		
•	•		CSC 800-342-8086		•		•		
•	•	•	Liberty Corporate Services Inc 800-334-2735		•	•	•	•	
•			Sunstate Research Associates Inc 800-621-7234		•		•		

CV	CR	PR	GREENE (EST)		UC	RE	TX	VS	VR
•	•	•	Liberty Corporate Services Inc 800-334-2735		•	•	•	•	
•	•	•	Merritt Jr, Charles W 706-342-9668		•	•	•	•	

CV	CR	PR	GWINNETT (EST)		UC	RE	TX	VS	VR
•	•	•	🏛 APS Attorney Service (SOP) 800-245-0122		•	•	•	•	•
•	•		ASAP Legal Documents 404-241-8130		•		•		
•	•		🏛 Alpha Research LLC (SOP) 205-755-7008				•		
•	•	•	🏛 Atlanta Attorney Services (SOP) 800-804-4078		•	•	•	•	•
•	•	•	Attorneys' Personal Services (SOP) 800-245-0122		•	•	•	•	•
•	•	•	🏛 Charley's Legal Angels (SOP) 770-419-0259		•	•	•	•	•
•	•	•	🏛 Dargason Information Services 770-418-9256		•	•	•	•	•
•		•	Direct Corporate Services Inc 800-783-7904		•	•	•	•	
•		•	Document Resources 800-532-9876		•	•	•	•	•
•	•	•	EL-RU Inc (SOP) 404-963-8023		•	•	•	•	•
•	•	•	🏛 Ed Knight Information Service 800-282-6418		•	•	•	•	
•		•	Elliott, Schuyler 404-373-0886		•	•	•	•	
•	•	•	🏛 Glass & Carson Investigation Svcs (SOP) 770-603-2887		•	•	•	•	
•		•	Holcomb, David M (SOP) 770-388-3712		•	•	•	•	
•	•	•	🏛 Hollingsworth Court Reporting Inc 504-769-3386		•	•	•	•	
•	•	•	🏛 John Roberson Investigations (SOP) 800-325-0914		•	•	•	•	
•	•	•	Liberty Corporate Services Inc 800-334-2735		•	•	•	•	
•	•	•	MGC Courier Inc 800-822-1084		•	•			
•	•	•	🏛 MLQ Attorney Services (SOP) 800-446-8794		•	•	•	•	
•	•	•	Phoenix Investigations (SOP) 800-999-4701		•	•	•	•	
•	•		Slueth Research 404-288-4598		•	•	•		
•	•	•	🏛 Specialty Services (SOP) 770-942-8264		•	•	•	•	•
•	•	•	Wilmot, Sally 800-282-2686		•	•	•	•	

CV	CR	PR	HABERSHAM (EST)		UC	RE	TX	VS	VR
•	•		🏛 Alpha Research LLC (SOP) 205-755-7008				•		
•	•	•	🏛 Dargason Information Services 770-418-9256		•	•	•	•	•
•	•	•	🏛 Hollingsworth Court Reporting Inc 504-769-3386		•	•	•	•	
•	•	•	Liberty Corporate Services Inc 800-334-2735		•	•	•	•	

DT	BK	CV	CR	PR	HALL (EST)		UC	RE	TX	VS	VR
•	•	•	•		🏛 Alpha Research LLC (SOP) 205-755-7008				•		
•	•	•	•	•	🏛 Atlanta Attorney Services (SOP) 800-804-4078		•	•	•	•	•
•	•	•	•	•	🏛 Dargason Information Services 770-418-9256		•	•	•	•	•
•	•	•	•	•	EL-RU Inc (SOP) 404-963-8023		•	•	•	•	•
•	•				🏛 Hogan Information Services 405-278-6954						
•		•	•	•	Liberty Corporate Services Inc 800-334-2735		•	•	•	•	
•	•	•	•	•	🏛 MLQ Attorney Services (SOP) 800-446-8794		•	•	•	•	
•	•	•	•	•	🏛 Specialty Services (SOP) 770-942-8264		•	•	•	•	•
		•	•	•	Wilmot, Sally 800-282-2686		•	•	•	•	

CV	CR	PR	HANCOCK (EST)		UC	RE	TX	VS	VR
•	•	•	Liberty Corporate Services Inc 800-334-2735		•	•	•	•	
•		•	Pro Title Inc 912-781-9344		•	•	•		

CV	CR	PR	HARALSON (EST)		UC	RE	TX	VS	VR
•	•	•	🏛 FACFIND Network Inc 800-343-6641		•	•	•	•	

CV	CR	PR			UC	RE	TX	VS	VR
•	•	•	🏛 Hollingsworth Court Reporting Inc 504-769-3386		•	•	•	•	
•	•	•	Liberty Corporate Services Inc 800-334-2735		•	•	•	•	
•	•	•	🏛 Specialty Services (SOP) 770-942-8264		•	•	•	•	•

CV	CR	PR	HARRIS (EST)	UC	RE	TX	VS	VR
•	•	•	🏛 Attorney & Court Service of Georgia (SOP) 706-322-3554	•	•	•	•	•
•	•	•	Liberty Corporate Services Inc 800-334-2735	•	•	•	•	

CV	CR	PR	HART (EST)	UC	RE	TX	VS	VR
•	•	•	Liberty Corporate Services Inc 800-334-2735	•	•	•	•	

CV	CR	PR	HEARD (EST)	UC	RE	TX	VS	VR
•	•	•	🏛 FACFIND Network Inc 800-343-6641	•	•	•	•	
•	•	•	Liberty Corporate Services Inc 800-334-2735	•	•	•	•	

CV	CR	PR	HENRY (EST)	UC	RE	TX	VS	VR
•	•		🏛 Alpha Research LLC (SOP) 205-755-7008			•		
•	•	•	🏛 Atlanta Attorney Services (SOP) 800-804-4078	•	•	•	•	•
•	•	•	EL-RU Inc (SOP) 404-963-8023	•	•	•	•	•
•	•	•	🏛 Ed Knight Information Service 800-282-6418	•	•	•	•	
•	•	•	🏛 FACFIND Network Inc 800-343-6641	•	•	•	•	
•	•	•	🏛 Hollingsworth Court Reporting Inc 504-769-3386	•	•	•	•	
•	•	•	🏛 John Roberson Investigations (SOP) 800-325-0914	•	•	•	•	
•	•	•	Liberty Corporate Services Inc 800-334-2735	•	•	•	•	
•	•	•	MGC Courier Inc 800-822-1084	•	•			
•	•	•	🏛 MLQ Attorney Services (SOP) 800-446-8794	•	•	•		
•	•		Slueth Research 404-288-4598	•	•	•		
•	•	•	🏛 Specialty Services (SOP) 770-942-8264	•	•	•	•	•

CV	CR	PR	HOUSTON (EST)	UC	RE	TX	VS	VR
•	•		🏛 Alpha Research LLC (SOP) 205-755-7008			•		
•	•	•	🏛 FACFIND Network Inc 800-343-6641	•	•	•	•	
•	•	•	Graystone Investigations Inc (SOP) 912-743-5551	•	•	•	•	•
•	•	•	Liberty Corporate Services Inc 800-334-2735	•	•	•	•	

CV	CR	PR	IRWIN (EST)	UC	RE	TX	VS	VR
•	•	•	Liberty Corporate Services Inc 800-334-2735	•	•	•	•	
•	•	•	🏛 Specialty Services (SOP) 770-942-8264	•	•	•	•	•

CV	CR	PR	JACKSON (EST)	UC	RE	TX	VS	VR
•	•	•	EL-RU Inc (SOP) 404-963-8023	•	•	•	•	•
•	•	•	🏛 Hollingsworth Court Reporting Inc 504-769-3386	•	•	•	•	
•	•	•	Liberty Corporate Services Inc 800-334-2735	•	•	•	•	
•	•	•	Wilmot, Sally 800-282-2686	•	•	•	•	

CV	CR	PR	JASPER (EST)	UC	RE	TX	VS	VR
•	•	•	🏛 FACFIND Network Inc 800-343-6641	•	•	•	•	
•	•	•	🏛 Hollingsworth Court Reporting Inc 504-769-3386	•	•	•	•	
•	•	•	Liberty Corporate Services Inc 800-334-2735	•	•	•	•	
•	•	•	Merritt Jr, Charles W 706-342-9668	•	•	•	•	
•		•	Pro Title Inc 912-781-9344	•	•	•		

CV	CR	PR	JEFF DAVIS (EST)	UC	RE	TX	VS	VR
•	•	•	Liberty Corporate Services Inc 800-334-2735	•	•	•	•	

CV	CR	PR	JEFFERSON (EST)	UC	RE	TX	VS	VR
•	•	•	Liberty Corporate Services Inc 800-334-2735	•	•	•	•	

CV	CR	PR	JENKINS (EST)	UC	RE	TX	VS	VR
•	•	•	Liberty Corporate Services Inc 800-334-2735	•	•	•	•	

CV	CR	PR	JOHNSON (EST)	UC	RE	TX	VS	VR
•	•	•	Liberty Corporate Services Inc 800-334-2735	•	•	•	•	
•		•	Pro Title Inc 912-781-9344	•	•	•		

	CV	CR	PR	JONES (EST)		UC	RE	TX	VS	VR
	•	•	•	🏛 FACFIND Network Inc 800-343-6641		•	•	•	•	
	•	•	•	Graystone Investigations Inc (SOP) 912-743-5551		•	•	•	•	•
	•	•	•	Liberty Corporate Services Inc 800-334-2735		•	•	•	•	
	•		•	Pro Title Inc 912-781-9344		•	•	•		
	•	•	•	🏛 Specialty Services (SOP) 770-942-8264		•	•	•	•	•

	CV	CR	PR	LAMAR (EST)		UC	RE	TX	VS	VR
	•	•	•	🏛 FACFIND Network Inc 800-343-6641		•	•	•	•	
	•	•	•	🏛 Hollingsworth Court Reporting Inc 504-769-3386		•	•	•	•	
	•	•	•	Liberty Corporate Services Inc 800-334-2735		•	•	•	•	
	•		•	Pro Title Inc 912-781-9344		•	•	•		

	CV	CR	PR	LANIER (EST)		UC	RE	TX	VS	VR
	•	•	•	Liberty Corporate Services Inc 800-334-2735		•	•	•	•	
	•	•	•	Roberts Abstracting Inc 912-532-5105		•	•	•		

	CV	CR	PR	LAURENS (EST)		UC	RE	TX	VS	VR
	•	•	•	Liberty Corporate Services Inc 800-334-2735		•	•	•	•	
	•		•	Pro Title Inc 912-781-9344		•	•	•		

	CV	CR	PR	LEE (EST)		UC	RE	TX	VS	VR
	•	•		🏛 Alpha Research LLC (SOP) 205-755-7008			•			
	•		•	Dougherty Abstract & Title Service Inc 912-888-9035			•	•		
	•	•	•	Liberty Corporate Services Inc 800-334-2735		•	•	•	•	
	•	•	•	🏛 Specialty Services (SOP) 770-942-8264		•	•	•	•	•
	•	•		Thurman Investigative Services Inc 912-759-1700						

	CV	CR	PR	LIBERTY (EST)		UC	RE	TX	VS	VR
	•	•		🏛 Alpha Research LLC (SOP) 205-755-7008			•			
	•	•	•	Josey, Cheryl S 912-653-2707		•	•	•	•	
	•	•	•	Liberty Corporate Services Inc 800-334-2735		•	•	•	•	
	•	•	•	🏛 Specialty Services (SOP) 770-942-8264		•	•	•	•	•

	CV	CR	PR	LINCOLN (EST)		UC	RE	TX	VS	VR
	•	•	•	Liberty Corporate Services Inc 800-334-2735		•	•	•	•	

	CV	CR	PR	LONG (EST)		UC	RE	TX	VS	VR
	•	•	•	Josey, Cheryl S 912-653-2707		•	•	•	•	
	•	•	•	Liberty Corporate Services Inc 800-334-2735		•	•	•	•	

DT	CV	CR	PR	LOWNDES (EST)		UC	RE	TX	VS	VR
•	•	•	•	🏛 Alpha Research LLC (SOP) 205-755-7008			•			
•	•	•	•	CSC 800-342-8086		•	•			
•	•	•	•	Liberty Corporate Services Inc 800-334-2735		•	•	•	•	
•	•	•	•	Roberts Abstracting Inc 912-532-5105		•	•	•		
•	•	•	•	🏛 Specialty Services (SOP) 770-942-8264		•	•	•	•	•
•	•	•		Sunstate Research Associates Inc 800-621-7234		•	•			

	CV	CR	PR	LUMPKIN (EST)		UC	RE	TX	VS	VR
	•	•		🏛 Alpha Research LLC (SOP) 205-755-7008			•			
	•	•	•	EL-RU Inc (SOP) 404-963-8023		•	•	•	•	•
	•	•	•	Liberty Corporate Services Inc 800-334-2735		•	•	•	•	

	CV	CR	PR	MACON (EST)		UC	RE	TX	VS	VR
	•	•		🏛 Alpha Research LLC (SOP) 205-755-7008			•			
	•	•	•	Liberty Corporate Services Inc 800-334-2735		•	•	•	•	
	•		•	Pro Title Inc 912-781-9344		•	•	•		

	CV	CR	PR	MADISON (EST)		UC	RE	TX	VS	VR
	•	•	•	Liberty Corporate Services Inc 800-334-2735		•	•	•	•	
	•	•	•	🏛 Specialty Services (SOP) 770-942-8264		•	•	•	•	•
	•	•	•	Wilmot, Sally 800-282-2686		•	•	•	•	

CV	CR	PR	MARION (EST)	UC	RE	TX	VS	VR
•	•	•	Attorney & Court Service of Georgia (SOP) 706-322-3554	•	•	•	•	•
•	•	•	Liberty Corporate Services Inc 800-334-2735	•	•	•	•	

CV	CR	PR	MCDUFFIE (EST)	UC	RE	TX	VS	VR
•	•	•	Liberty Corporate Services Inc 800-334-2735	•	•	•	•	

CV	CR	PR	MCINTOSH (EST)	UC	RE	TX	VS	VR
•		•	Liberty Corporate Services Inc 800-334-2735	•	•	•	•	

CV	CR	PR	MERIWETHER (EST)	UC	RE	TX	VS	VR
•	•	•	FACFIND Network Inc 800-343-6641	•	•	•	•	
•	•	•	Liberty Corporate Services Inc 800-334-2735	•	•	•	•	

CV	CR	PR	MILLER (EST)	UC	RE	TX	VS	VR
•	•	•	Liberty Corporate Services Inc 800-334-2735	•	•	•	•	
•			Sunstate Research Associates Inc 800-621-7234	•		•		

CV	CR	PR	MITCHELL (EST)	UC	RE	TX	VS	VR
•		•	Dougherty Abstract & Title Service Inc 912-888-9035		•	•		
•	•	•	Liberty Corporate Services Inc 800-334-2735	•	•		•	
•			Sunstate Research Associates Inc 800-621-7234	•		•		
•	•		Thurman Investigative Services Inc 912-759-1700					

CV	CR	PR	MONROE (EST)	UC	RE	TX	VS	VR
•	•	•	Graystone Investigations Inc (SOP) 912-743-5551	•	•	•	•	•
•	•	•	Liberty Corporate Services Inc 800-334-2735	•	•	•	•	
•		•	Pro Title Inc 912-781-9344	•	•	•		
•	•	•	Specialty Services (SOP) 770-942-8264	•	•	•	•	•

CV	CR	PR	MONTGOMERY (EST)	UC	RE	TX	VS	VR
•	•	•	Liberty Corporate Services Inc 800-334-2735	•	•	•	•	

CV	CR	PR	MORGAN (EST)	UC	RE	TX	VS	VR
•	•	•	Hollingsworth Court Reporting Inc 504-769-3386	•	•	•	•	
•	•	•	Liberty Corporate Services Inc 800-334-2735	•	•	•	•	
•	•	•	Merritt Jr, Charles W 706-342-9668	•	•	•	•	

CV	CR	PR	MURRAY (EST)	UC	RE	TX	VS	VR
•	•		Alpha Research LLC (SOP) 205-755-7008			•		
	•		Bell, Jan 706-278-7216	•	•	•		
•	•	•	Hollingsworth Court Reporting Inc 504-769-3386	•	•	•	•	
•	•	•	Liberty Corporate Services Inc 800-334-2735	•	•		•	
•	•	•	Specialty Services (SOP) 770-942-8264	•	•	•	•	•
•		•	Title Guaranty & Trust of Chattanooga 615-266-5751	•	•	•		

DT	BK	CV	CR	PR	MUSCOGEE (EST)	UC	RE	TX	VS	VR
•	•	•	•		Alpha Research LLC (SOP) 205-755-7008			•		
•	•	•	•	•	Attorney & Court Service of Georgia (SOP) 706-322-3554	•	•	•	•	•
•	•	•	•	•	Glass & Carson Investigation Svcs (SOP) 770-603-2887	•	•	•		•
•	•	•	•	•	Liberty Corporate Services Inc 800-334-2735	•	•	•	•	
•	•	•	•	•	Specialty Services (SOP) 770-942-8264	•	•	•	•	•

CV	CR	PR	NEWTON (EST)	UC	RE	TX	VS	VR
•	•		Alpha Research LLC (SOP) 205-755-7008			•		
•	•	•	Atlanta Attorney Services (SOP) 800-804-4078	•	•	•	•	•
•	•	•	EL-RU Inc (SOP) 404-963-8023	•	•	•	•	•
•	•	•	Ed Knight Information Service 800-282-6418	•	•	•	•	
•	•	•	Hollingsworth Court Reporting Inc 504-769-3386	•	•	•	•	
•	•	•	Law Office of Roger Gladden (SOP) 404-550-0749	•	•	•	•	
•	•	•	Liberty Corporate Services Inc 800-334-2735	•	•	•	•	
•	•	•	MLQ Attorney Services (SOP) 800-446-8794	•	•	•	•	
•	•		Slueth Research 404-288-4598	•	•	•		

CV	CR	PR			UC	RE	TX	VS	VR
•	•	•	🏛 Specialty Services (SOP) 770-942-8264		•	•	•	•	•

OCONEE (EST)

CV	CR	PR			UC	RE	TX	VS	VR
•	•		🏛 Alpha Research LLC (SOP) 205-755-7008				•		
•	•	•	EL-RU Inc (SOP) 404-963-8023		•	•	•	•	•
•	•	•	Liberty Corporate Services Inc 800-334-2735		•	•	•	•	
•	•	•	Merritt Jr, Charles W 706-342-9668		•	•	•	•	
•	•	•	🏛 Specialty Services (SOP) 770-942-8264		•	•	•	•	•
•	•	•	Wilmot, Sally 800-282-2686		•	•	•	•	

OGLETHORPE (EST)

CV	CR	PR			UC	RE	TX	VS	VR
•	•	•	EL-RU Inc (SOP) 404-963-8023		•	•	•	•	•
•	•	•	Liberty Corporate Services Inc 800-334-2735		•	•	•	•	
•	•	•	🏛 Specialty Services (SOP) 770-942-8264		•	•	•	•	•
•	•	•	Wilmot, Sally 800-282-2686		•	•	•	•	

PAULDING (EST)

CV	CR	PR			UC	RE	TX	VS	VR
•	•	•	🏛 Atlanta Attorney Services (SOP) 800-804-4078		•	•	•	•	•
•	•	•	🏛 Ed Knight Information Service 800-282-6418		•	•	•		
•	•	•	🏛 FACFIND Network Inc 800-343-6641		•	•	•		
•	•	•	🏛 Hollingsworth Court Reporting Inc 504-769-3386		•	•	•		
•	•	•	Liberty Corporate Services Inc 800-334-2735		•	•	•		
•	•	•	🏛 MLQ Attorney Services (SOP) 800-446-8794		•	•	•		
•	•	•	🏛 Specialty Services (SOP) 770-942-8264		•	•	•	•	•

PEACH (EST)

CV	CR	PR			UC	RE	TX	VS	VR
•	•		🏛 Alpha Research LLC (SOP) 205-755-7008				•		
•	•	•	Graystone Investigations Inc (SOP) 912-743-5551		•	•	•	•	•
•	•	•	Liberty Corporate Services Inc 800-334-2735		•	•	•		
•		•	Pro Title Inc 912-781-9344		•	•	•		

PICKENS (EST)

CV	CR	PR			UC	RE	TX	VS	VR
•	•	•	🏛 Dargason Information Services 770-418-9256		•	•	•	•	•
•	•	•	EL-RU Inc (SOP) 404-963-8023		•	•	•	•	•
•	•	•	Holcomb, David M (SOP) 770-388-3712		•	•	•	•	•
•	•	•	🏛 Hollingsworth Court Reporting Inc 504-769-3386		•	•	•	•	
•	•	•	Liberty Corporate Services Inc 800-334-2735		•	•	•	•	

PIERCE (EST)

CV	CR	PR			UC	RE	TX	VS	VR
•	•		🏛 Alpha Research LLC (SOP) 205-755-7008				•		
•	•	•	Liberty Corporate Services Inc 800-334-2735		•	•	•	•	
•	•	•	🏛 Rowell, Betty M 912-449-0849		•	•	•	•	

PIKE (EST)

CV	CR	PR			UC	RE	TX	VS	VR
•	•	•	🏛 Ed Knight Information Service 800-282-6418		•	•	•		
•	•	•	🏛 FACFIND Network Inc 800-343-6641		•	•	•	•	
•	•	•	🏛 Hollingsworth Court Reporting Inc 504-769-3386		•	•	•	•	
•	•	•	Liberty Corporate Services Inc 800-334-2735		•	•	•	•	
•		•	Pro Title Inc 912-781-9344		•	•	•		

POLK (EST)

CV	CR	PR			UC	RE	TX	VS	VR
•	•	•	🏛 FACFIND Network Inc 800-343-6641		•	•	•	•	
•	•	•	Liberty Corporate Services Inc 800-334-2735		•	•	•	•	
•	•	•	🏛 Specialty Services (SOP) 770-942-8264		•	•	•	•	•

PULASKI (EST)

CV	CR	PR			UC	RE	TX	VS	VR
•	•	•	Liberty Corporate Services Inc 800-334-2735		•	•	•	•	
•		•	Pro Title Inc 912-781-9344		•	•	•		

PUTNAM (EST)

CV	CR	PR			UC	RE	TX	VS	VR
•	•	•	🏛 Hollingsworth Court Reporting Inc 504-769-3386		•	•	•	•	
•	•	•	Liberty Corporate Services Inc 800-334-2735		•	•	•	•	
•	•	•	Merritt Jr, Charles W 706-342-9668		•	•	•	•	

| | | | Pro Title Inc .... 912-781-9344 | • | • | • | | |

CV	CR	PR	**QUITMAN (EST)**	UC	RE	TX	VS	VR
•	•	•	Liberty Corporate Services Inc 800-334-2735	•	•	•	•	

CV	CR	PR	**RABUN (EST)**	UC	RE	TX	VS	VR
•	•	•	🏛 Dargason Information Services 770-418-9256	•	•	•	•	•
•	•	•	🏛 Hollingsworth Court Reporting Inc 504-769-3386	•	•	•	•	
•	•	•	Liberty Corporate Services Inc 800-334-2735	•	•	•	•	

CV	CR	PR	**RANDOLPH (EST)**	UC	RE	TX	VS	VR
•	•	•	Liberty Corporate Services Inc 800-334-2735	•	•	•	•	

DT	BK	CV	CR	PR	**RICHMOND (EST)**	UC	RE	TX	VS	VR
•	•	•	•		🏛 Alpha Research LLC (SOP) 205-755-7008			•		
•	•	•	•	•	🏛 FACFIND Network Inc 800-343-6641	•	•	•	•	
•	•	•	•	•	Liberty Corporate Services Inc 800-334-2735	•	•	•	•	
•	•	•	•	•	🏛 Specialty Services (SOP) 770-942-8264	•	•	•	•	•
•	•	•	•	•	Weber, Attorney David V 706-860-8160	•	•	•	•	

CV	CR	PR	**ROCKDALE (EST)**	UC	RE	TX	VS	VR
•	•		🏛 Alpha Research LLC (SOP) 205-755-7008			•		
•	•	•	Atlanta Attorney Services (SOP) 800-804-4078	•	•	•	•	•
•	•	•	EL-RU Inc (SOP) 404-963-8023	•	•	•	•	•
•	•	•	🏛 Ed Knight Information Service 800-282-6418	•	•	•		
•	•	•	Elliott, Schuyler 404-373-0886	•	•	•	•	
•	•	•	🏛 Hollingsworth Court Reporting Inc 504-769-3386	•	•	•	•	
•	•	•	Law Office of Roger Gladden (SOP) 404-550-0749	•	•	•		
•	•	•	Liberty Corporate Services Inc 800-334-2735	•	•	•	•	
•	•	•	MGC Courier Inc 800-822-1084	•				
•	•	•	🏛 MLQ Attorney Services (SOP) 800-446-8794	•	•	•	•	
•	•		Slueth Research 404-288-4598	•	•	•		
•	•	•	🏛 Specialty Services (SOP) 770-942-8264	•	•	•	•	•

CV	CR	PR	**SCHLEY (EST)**	UC	RE	TX	VS	VR
•	•	•	Liberty Corporate Services Inc 800-334-2735	•	•	•	•	

CV	CR	PR	**SCREVEN (EST)**	UC	RE	TX	VS	VR
•	•	•	Liberty Corporate Services Inc 800-334-2735	•	•	•	•	

CV	CR	PR	**SEMINOLE (EST)**	UC	RE	TX	VS	VR
•	•	•	Liberty Corporate Services Inc 800-334-2735	•	•	•	•	
•			Sunstate Research Associates Inc 800-621-7234	•		•		
•	•		Thurman Investigative Services Inc 912-759-1700					

CV	CR	PR	**SPALDING (EST)**	UC	RE	TX	VS	VR
•	•		🏛 Alpha Research LLC (SOP) 205-755-7008			•		
•	•	•	🏛 Ed Knight Information Service 800-282-6418	•	•	•		
•	•	•	🏛 Hollingsworth Court Reporting Inc 504-769-3386	•	•	•	•	
•	•	•	🏛 John Roberson Investigations (SOP) 800-325-0914	•	•	•	•	
•	•	•	Liberty Corporate Services Inc 800-334-2735	•	•	•	•	
•	•	•	🏛 MLQ Attorney Services (SOP) 800-446-8794	•	•	•	•	

CV	CR	PR	**STEPHENS (EST)**	UC	RE	TX	VS	VR
•	•	•	🏛 Dargason Information Services 770-418-9256	•	•	•	•	•
•	•	•	🏛 Hollingsworth Court Reporting Inc 504-769-3386	•	•	•	•	
•	•	•	Liberty Corporate Services Inc 800-334-2735	•	•	•	•	

CV	CR	PR	**STEWART (EST)**	UC	RE	TX	VS	VR
•	•	•	Liberty Corporate Services Inc 800-334-2735	•	•	•	•	

CV	CR	PR	**SUMTER (EST)**	UC	RE	TX	VS	VR
•	•		🏛 Alpha Research LLC (SOP) 205-755-7008			•		
•	•	•	Liberty Corporate Services Inc 800-334-2735	•	•	•	•	

CV	CR	PR			UC	RE	TX	VS	VR
•	•	•	🏛 Specialty Services (SOP) 770-942-8264		•	•	•	•	•
•	•		Thurman Investigative Services Inc 912-759-1700						

CV	CR	PR	TALBOT (EST)		UC	RE	TX	VS	VR
•	•	•	🏛 Attorney & Court Service of Georgia (SOP) 706-322-3554		•	•	•	•	•
•	•	•	Liberty Corporate Services Inc 800-334-2735		•	•	•	•	

CV	CR	PR	TALIAFERRO (EST)		UC	RE	TX	VS	VR
•	•	•	Liberty Corporate Services Inc 800-334-2735		•	•	•	•	

CV	CR	PR	TATTNALL (EST)		UC	RE	TX	VS	VR
•	•	•	Josey, Cheryl S 912-653-2707		•	•	•	•	
•	•	•	Liberty Corporate Services Inc 800-334-2735		•	•	•	•	

CV	CR	PR	TAYLOR (EST)		UC	RE	TX	VS	VR
•	•	•	🏛 Attorney & Court Service of Georgia (SOP) 706-322-3554		•	•	•	•	•
•	•	•	Liberty Corporate Services Inc 800-334-2735		•	•	•	•	
•		•	Pro Title Inc 912-781-9344		•	•	•		

CV	CR	PR	TELFAIR (EST)		UC	RE	TX	VS	VR
•	•	•	Liberty Corporate Services Inc 800-334-2735		•	•	•		
•		•	Pro Title Inc 912-781-9344		•	•	•		

CV	CR	PR	TERRELL (EST)		UC	RE	TX	VS	VR
•		•	Dougherty Abstract & Title Service Inc 912-888-9035			•	•		
•	•	•	Liberty Corporate Services Inc 800-334-2735		•	•	•	•	

CV	CR	PR	THOMAS (EST)		UC	RE	TX	VS	VR
•	•		🏛 Alpha Research LLC (SOP) 205-755-7008			•			
•	•		CSC 800-342-8086		•	•			
•	•	•	Corporate Access Inc (SOP) 800-969-1666		•	•	•	•	•
•	•	•	Liberty Corporate Services Inc 800-334-2735		•	•	•	•	
•			Sunstate Research Associates Inc 800-621-7234		•		•		
•	•		Thurman Investigative Services Inc 912-759-1700						

CV	CR	PR	TIFT (EST)		UC	RE	TX	VS	VR
•	•	•	Liberty Corporate Services Inc 800-334-2735		•	•	•	•	
•	•	•	Roberts Abstracting Inc 912-532-5105		•	•	•		
•	•	•	🏛 Specialty Services (SOP) 770-942-8264		•	•	•	•	•

CV	CR	PR	TOOMBS (EST)		UC	RE	TX	VS	VR
•	•	•	Liberty Corporate Services Inc 800-334-2735		•	•	•	•	

CV	CR	PR	TOWNS (EST)		UC	RE	TX	VS	VR
•	•	•	🏛 Dargason Information Services 770-418-9256		•	•	•	•	•
•	•	•	Liberty Corporate Services Inc 800-334-2735		•	•	•	•	

CV	CR	PR	TREUTLEN (EST)		UC	RE	TX	VS	VR
•	•	•	Liberty Corporate Services Inc 800-334-2735		•	•	•	•	
•		•	Pro Title Inc 912-781-9344		•	•	•		

CV	CR	PR	TROUP (EST)		UC	RE	TX	VS	VR
•	•	•	🏛 FACFIND Network Inc 800-343-6641		•	•	•	•	
•	•	•	Liberty Corporate Services Inc 800-334-2735		•	•	•	•	

CV	CR	PR	TURNER (EST)		UC	RE	TX	VS	VR
•	•	•	Liberty Corporate Services Inc 800-334-2735		•	•	•	•	
•	•	•	🏛 Specialty Services (SOP) 770-942-8264		•	•	•	•	•

CV	CR	PR	TWIGGS (EST)		UC	RE	TX	VS	VR
•	•	•	Liberty Corporate Services Inc 800-334-2735		•	•	•	•	
•		•	Pro Title Inc 912-781-9344		•	•	•		

CV	CR	PR	UNION (EST)		UC	RE	TX	VS	VR
•	•	•	🏛 Dargason Information Services 770-418-9256		•	•	•	•	•
•	•	•	Liberty Corporate Services Inc 800-334-2735		•	•	•	•	

CV	CR	PR	UPSON (EST)		UC	RE	TX	VS	VR
•	•	•	Liberty Corporate Services Inc 800-334-2735		•	•	•	•	
•		•	Pro Title Inc 912-781-9344		•	•	•		

CV	CR	PR	WALKER (EST)		UC	RE	TX	VS	VR
•	•		🏛 Alpha Research LLC (SOP).......... 205-755-7008				•		
•	•	•	🏛 Hollingsworth Court Reporting Inc 504-769-3386		•	•	•	•	
•	•	•	Liberty Corporate Services Inc 800-334-2735		•	•	•	•	
•	•	•	🏛 Specialty Services (SOP) 770-942-8264		•	•	•	•	•
•		•	Title Guaranty & Trust of Chattanooga 615-266-5751		•	•	•		

CV	CR	PR	WALTON (EST)		UC	RE	TX	VS	VR
•	•		🏛 Alpha Research LLC (SOP).......... 205-755-7008				•		
•	•	•	EL-RU Inc (SOP).......... 404-963-8023		•	•	•	•	•
•	•	•	🏛 Ed Knight Information Service 800-282-6418		•	•	•		
•		•	Elliott, Schuyler 404-373-0886		•	•	•	•	
•	•	•	🏛 FACFIND Network Inc 800-343-6641		•	•	•	•	
•	•	•	🏛 Hollingsworth Court Reporting Inc 504-769-3386		•	•	•	•	
•	•	•	Law Office of Roger Gladden (SOP) 404-550-0749		•	•	•	•	
•	•	•	Liberty Corporate Services Inc 800-334-2735		•	•	•	•	
•	•	•	🏛 MLQ Attorney Services (SOP) 800-446-8794		•	•	•	•	
•	•	•	Merritt Jr, Charles W 706-342-9668		•	•	•	•	
•	•	•	Wilmot, Sally 800-282-2686		•	•	•	•	

CV	CR	PR	WARE (EST)		UC	RE	TX	VS	VR
•	•	•	Liberty Corporate Services Inc 800-334-2735		•	•	•	•	
•	•	•	🏛 Rowell, Betty M 912-449-0849		•	•	•	•	

CV	CR	PR	WARREN (EST)		UC	RE	TX	VS	VR
•	•	•	Liberty Corporate Services Inc 800-334-2735		•	•	•	•	

CV	CR	PR	WASHINGTON (EST)		UC	RE	TX	VS	VR
•	•	•	Liberty Corporate Services Inc 800-334-2735		•	•	•	•	
•		•	Pro Title Inc 912-781-9344		•	•	•		

CV	CR	PR	WAYNE (EST)		UC	RE	TX	VS	VR
•	•	•	Liberty Corporate Services Inc 800-334-2735		•	•	•	•	
•	•	•	🏛 Rowell, Betty M 912-449-0849		•	•	•	•	
•	•	•	🏛 Specialty Services (SOP) 770-942-8264		•	•	•	•	•

CV	CR	PR	WEBSTER (EST)		UC	RE	TX	VS	VR
•	•	•	Liberty Corporate Services Inc 800-334-2735		•	•	•	•	

CV	CR	PR	WHEELER (EST)		UC	RE	TX	VS	VR
•	•	•	Liberty Corporate Services Inc 800-334-2735		•	•	•	•	
•		•	Pro Title Inc 912-781-9344		•	•	•		

CV	CR	PR	WHITE (EST)		UC	RE	TX	VS	VR
•	•		🏛 Alpha Research LLC (SOP).......... 205-755-7008				•		
•	•	•	🏛 Dargason Information Services 770-418-9256		•	•	•	•	•
•	•	•	EL-RU Inc (SOP).......... 404-963-8023		•	•	•	•	•
•	•	•	Liberty Corporate Services Inc 800-334-2735		•	•	•	•	

CV	CR	PR	WHITFIELD (EST)		UC	RE	TX	VS	VR
•	•		🏛 Alpha Research LLC (SOP).......... 205-755-7008				•		
	•		Bell, Jan 706-278-7216		•	•	•		
•	•	•	🏛 Hollingsworth Court Reporting Inc 504-769-3386		•	•	•	•	
•	•	•	Liberty Corporate Services Inc 800-334-2735		•	•	•	•	
•	•	•	🏛 Specialty Services (SOP) 770-942-8264		•	•	•	•	•

			Title Guaranty & Trust of Chattanooga 615-266-5751	•	•	•		

CV	CR	PR	WILCOX (EST)	UC	RE	TX	VS	VR
•	•	•	Liberty Corporate Services Inc 800-334-2735	•	•	•	•	

CV	CR	PR	WILKES (EST)	UC	RE	TX	VS	VR
•	•	•	Liberty Corporate Services Inc 800-334-2735	•	•	•	•	

CV	CR	PR	WILKINSON (EST)	UC	RE	TX	VS	VR
•	•	•	Liberty Corporate Services Inc 800-334-2735	•	•	•	•	
•		•	Pro Title Inc 912-781-9344	•	•	•		

CV	CR	PR	WORTH (EST)	UC	RE	TX	VS	VR
•		•	Dougherty Abstract & Title Service Inc 912-888-9035		•	•		
•	•	•	Liberty Corporate Services Inc 800-334-2735	•	•	•	•	
•	•	•	🏛 Specialty Services (SOP) 770-942-8264	•	•	•	•	•

SUMMARY OF CODES

COURT RECORDS

CODE	GOVERNMENT AGENCY	TYPE OF INFORMATION
DT	US District Court	Federal civil and criminal cases
BK	Bankruptcy Court	United States bankruptcy cases
CV	Civil Court	Municipal, county and state level civil cases
CR	Criminal Court	Municipal, county and state level criminal cases
PR	Probate Court	Wills and estate cases

COUNTY RECORDS

CODE	GOVERNMENT AGENCY	TYPE OF INFORMATION
UC	UCC Filing Office	Uniform Commercial Code and other personal property liens
RE	Recorder of Deeds	Real property transactions and liens
TX	Tax Assessor	Real property tax information
VS	Vital Records Office	Vital statistics—birth, death, marriage, divorce, etc.
VR	Voter Registration Office	Voter registration and campaign contribution information

- "CODE" designates the agency and type of information obtainable in each county from a retriever.
- The time zone for each county is abbreviated as follows: EST—Eastern Standard Time; CST—Central; MST—Mountain; PST—Pacific; AK—Alaska; HT—Hawaii.
- 🏛—This symbol designates a Public Record Retriever Network member.
- "(SOP)" after the retriever name designates Service of Process.
- Individual retrievers without a company name are listed in order of their last name.
- US District and Bankruptcy courts are indicated only in the counties where courts are located.

HAWAII

	CV	CR	PR	HAWAII (HT)		UC	RE	TX	VS	VR
	•	•	•	Doc-U-Search Hawaii 808-523-1200		•	•	•	•	
	•	•	•	Fitzgerald, Judith A 808-263-2120		•	•	•	•	•
	•	•	•	🏛 Honolulu Information Service (SOP)................ 808-732-8778		•	•	•	•	
	•	•	•	Wood & Tait Inc 800-774-8585		•				

DT	BK	CV	CR	PR	HONOLULU (CAPITAL) (HT)		UC	RE	TX	VS	VR
•	•	•	•	•	Doc-U-Search Hawaii 808-523-1200		•	•	•	•	
•	•	•	•	•	Fitzgerald, Judith A 808-263-2120		•	•	•	•	
•	•				🏛 Hogan Information Services 405-278-6954						
•	•	•	•	•	🏛 Honolulu Information Service (SOP)................ 808-732-8778		•	•	•	•	•
•	•	•	•	•	The Niles Agency (SOP)................................ 808-591-7707		•	•	•		
•	•	•	•	•	Wood & Tait Inc 800-774-8585		•				

	CV	CR	PR	KALAWAO (HT)		UC	RE	TX	VS	VR
	•	•	•	Doc-U-Search Hawaii 808-523-1200		•	•	•	•	

	CV	CR	PR	KAUAI (HT)		UC	RE	TX	VS	VR
	•	•	•	Fitzgerald, Judith A 808-263-2120		•	•	•	•	
	•	•	•	🏛 Honolulu Information Service (SOP)................ 808-732-8778		•	•	•	•	•
	•	•	•	Wood & Tait Inc 800-774-8585		•				

	CV	CR	PR	MAUI (HT)		UC	RE	TX	VS	VR
	•	•	•	Doc-U-Search Hawaii 808-523-1200		•	•	•	•	
	•	•	•	Fitzgerald, Judith A 808-263-2120		•	•	•	•	
	•	•	•	🏛 Honolulu Information Service (SOP)................ 808-732-8778		•	•	•	•	•
	•	•	•	Wood & Tait Inc 800-774-8585		•				

IDAHO

DT	BK	CV	CR	PR	ADA (CAPITAL) (MST)		UC	RE	TX	VS	VR
•	•	•	•	•	Burr Investigation (SOP) 800-582-5441		•	•	•	•	
•	•	•	•	•	🏛 C & D Enterprises (SOP) 208-466-2555		•	•	•	•	•
•	•	•	•	•	CT Corporation System 800-874-8820		•	•	•	•	
•	•	•	•	•	D & D Research & Info Co (SOP) 888-327-8860		•	•	•	•	•
•	•	•	•	•	Drake Detective Agency 208-377-3463		•	•	•	•	
•	•				🏛 Hogan Information Services 405-278-6954						
•		•	•	•	Lord and Associates (SOP) 208-939-8258		•	•	•		
•	•	•	•	•	🏛 Record Search and Information Svcs 800-366-1906		•	•	•	•	•
•	•	•	•	•	Tri-County Process Serving (SOP) 800-473-3454		•	•	•	•	•

		CV	CR	PR	ADAMS (MST)		UC	RE	TX	VS	VR
		•	•	•	Burr Investigation (SOP) 800-582-5441		•	•	•	•	
		•	•	•	🏛 C & D Enterprises (SOP) 208-466-2555		•	•	•	•	•
		•	•	•	🏛 Record Search and Information Svcs 800-366-1906		•	•	•	•	•

	BK	CV	CR	PR	BANNOCK (MST)		UC	RE	TX	VS	VR
	•	•	•	•	Carter Investigations 800-449-2920		•	•	•	•	
	•	•	•	•	🏛 Record Search and Information Svcs 800-366-1906		•	•	•	•	•

		CV	CR	PR	BEAR LAKE (MST)		UC	RE	TX	VS	VR
		•	•	•	First Idaho Title Co 208-847-1300		•	•	•		
		•	•	•	🏛 Record Search and Information Svcs 800-366-1906		•	•	•	•	•

		CV	CR	PR	BENEWAH (PST)		UC	RE	TX	VS	VR
		•	•	•	Action Agency (SOP) 208-263-9586		•	•	•	•	
		•	•	•	Gem State Investigations (SOP) 208-746-4152		•	•	•		
		•	•	•	🏛 Record Search and Information Svcs 800-366-1906		•	•	•	•	•

		CV	CR	PR	BINGHAM (MST)		UC	RE	TX	VS	VR
		•	•	•	Carter Investigations 800-449-2920		•	•	•	•	
		•	•	•	🏛 Record Search and Information Svcs 800-366-1906		•	•	•	•	•

		CV	CR	PR	BLAINE (MST)		UC	RE	TX	VS	VR
		•	•	•	🏛 American Eagle Invest & Pers Security 208-788-9527		•	•	•	•	
		•	•	•	Burr Investigation (SOP) 800-582-5441		•	•	•	•	
		•	•	•	🏛 Record Search and Information Svcs 800-366-1906		•	•	•	•	•

		CV	CR	PR	BOISE (MST)		UC	RE	TX	VS	VR
		•	•	•	Burr Investigation (SOP) 800-582-5441		•	•	•	•	
		•	•	•	🏛 C & D Enterprises (SOP) 208-466-2555		•	•	•	•	•
		•	•	•	Drake Detective Agency 208-377-3463		•	•	•	•	
		•	•	•	Lord and Associates (SOP) 208-939-8258		•	•	•		
		•	•	•	🏛 Record Search and Information Svcs 800-366-1906		•	•	•	•	•
		•	•	•	Tri-County Process Serving (SOP) 800-473-3454		•	•	•	•	•

		CV	CR	PR	BONNER (PST)		UC	RE	TX	VS	VR
		•	•	•	Action Agency (SOP) 208-263-9586		•	•	•	•	
		•	•	•	🏛 Record Search and Information Svcs 800-366-1906		•	•	•	•	•
		•	•	•	🏛 Reed, Linda V 208-266-1373		•		•		

		CV	CR	PR	BONNEVILLE (MST)		UC	RE	TX	VS	VR
		•	•	•	🏛 Record Search and Information Svcs 800-366-1906		•	•	•	•	•

		CV	CR	PR	BOUNDARY (PST)		UC	RE	TX	VS	VR
		•	•	•	Action Agency (SOP) 208-263-9586		•	•	•	•	
		•	•	•	🏛 Record Search and Information Svcs 800-366-1906		•	•	•	•	•

		CV	CR	PR	BUTTE (MST)		UC	RE	TX	VS	VR
					Idaho Title & Trust Co 208-527-8517		•	•	•		
		•	•	•	🏛 Record Search and Information Svcs 800-366-1906		•	•	•	•	•

CV	CR	PR	CAMAS (MST)		UC	RE	TX	VS	VR
•	•	•	🏛 American Eagle Invest & Pers Security 208-788-9527		•	•	•	•	
•	•	•	🏛 Record Search and Information Svcs 800-366-1906		•	•	•	•	•

CV	CR	PR	CANYON (MST)		UC	RE	TX	VS	VR
•	•	•	Burr Investigation (SOP) 800-582-5441		•	•	•	•	
•	•	•	🏛 C & D Enterprises (SOP) 208-466-2555		•	•	•	•	•
•	•	•	Drake Detective Agency 208-377-3463		•	•	•	•	
•	•	•	Lord and Associates (SOP) 208-939-8258		•	•	•		
•	•	•	🏛 Record Search and Information Svcs 800-366-1906		•	•	•	•	•
•	•	•	Tri-County Process Serving (SOP) 800-473-3454		•	•	•	•	•

CV	CR	PR	CARIBOU (MST)		UC	RE	TX	VS	VR
•	•	•	Carter Investigations 800-449-2920		•	•	•	•	
•	•	•	🏛 Record Search and Information Svcs 800-366-1906		•	•	•	•	•

CV	CR	PR	CASSIA (MST)		UC	RE	TX	VS	VR
•	•	•	Burr Investigation (SOP) 800-582-5441		•	•	•	•	
		•	Cassia County Abstract Co 208-678-8347		•	•	•		
•	•	•	🏛 Record Search and Information Svcs 800-366-1906		•	•	•	•	•

CV	CR	PR	CLARK (MST)		UC	RE	TX	VS	VR
•	•	•	🏛 Record Search and Information Svcs 800-366-1906		•	•	•	•	•

CV	CR	PR	CLEARWATER (PST)		UC	RE	TX	VS	VR
•	•	•	Gem State Investigations (SOP) 208-746-4152		•	•	•	•	
•	•	•	🏛 Record Search and Information Svcs 800-366-1906		•	•	•	•	•

CV	CR	PR	CUSTER (MST)		UC	RE	TX	VS	VR
•	•	•	Carter Investigations 800-449-2920		•	•	•	•	
•	•	•	🏛 Record Search and Information Svcs 800-366-1906		•	•	•	•	•

CV	CR	PR	ELMORE (MST)		UC	RE	TX	VS	VR
•	•	•	Burr Investigation (SOP) 800-582-5441		•	•	•	•	
•	•	•	🏛 C & D Enterprises (SOP) 208-466-2555		•	•	•	•	•
•	•	•	Lord and Associates (SOP) 208-939-8258		•	•	•		
•	•	•	🏛 Record Search and Information Svcs 800-366-1906		•	•	•	•	•
•	•	•	Tri-County Process Serving (SOP) 800-473-3454		•	•	•	•	•

CV	CR	PR	FRANKLIN (MST)		UC	RE	TX	VS	VR
•	•	•	Preston Land Title Co 800-365-7720		•	•	•	•	
•	•	•	🏛 Record Search and Information Svcs 800-366-1906		•	•	•	•	•

CV	CR	PR	FREMONT (MST)		UC	RE	TX	VS	VR
•	•	•	🏛 Record Search and Information Svcs 800-366-1906		•	•	•	•	•

CV	CR	PR	GEM (MST)		UC	RE	TX	VS	VR
•	•	•	Burr Investigation (SOP) 800-582-5441		•	•	•	•	
•	•	•	🏛 C & D Enterprises (SOP) 208-466-2555		•	•	•	•	•
•	•	•	Lord and Associates (SOP) 208-939-8258		•	•	•		
•	•	•	🏛 Record Search and Information Svcs 800-366-1906		•	•	•	•	•
•	•	•	Tri-County Process Serving (SOP) 800-473-3454		•	•	•	•	•

CV	CR	PR	GOODING (MST)		UC	RE	TX	VS	VR
•	•	•	🏛 American Eagle Invest & Pers Security 208-788-9527		•	•	•	•	
•	•	•	Burr Investigation (SOP) 800-582-5441		•	•	•	•	
•	•	•	🏛 Record Search and Information Svcs 800-366-1906		•	•	•	•	•

CV	CR	PR	IDAHO (PST)		UC	RE	TX	VS	VR
			Anderson, Edith L 208-983-2754		•	•	•		
•	•	•	Gem State Investigations (SOP) 208-746-4152		•	•	•	•	
•	•	•	🏛 Record Search and Information Svcs 800-366-1906		•	•	•	•	•

BK	CV	CR	PR	JEFFERSON (MST)	UC	RE	TX	VS	VR
	•	•	•	🏛 Record Search and Information Svcs 800-366-1906	•	•	•	•	•

BK	CV	CR	PR	JEROME (MST)	UC	RE	TX	VS	VR
	•	•	•	🏛 American Eagle Invest & Pers Security 208-788-9527	•	•	•	•	
	•	•	•	🏛 Record Search and Information Svcs 800-366-1906	•	•	•	•	

BK	CV	CR	PR	KOOTENAI (PST)	UC	RE	TX	VS	VR
	•	•	•	Action Agency (SOP) 208-263-9586	•	•	•	•	
•	•	•	•	🏛 Record Search and Information Svcs 800-366-1906	•	•	•	•	•

BK	CV	CR	PR	LATAH (PST)	UC	RE	TX	VS	VR
	•	•	•	Action Agency (SOP) 208-263-9586	•	•	•	•	
•	•	•	•	Gem State Investigations (SOP)..................................... 208-746-4152	•	•	•	•	
	•	•	•	Pullman Process Service (SOP) 509-332-8310					
•	•	•	•	🏛 Record Search and Information Svcs 800-366-1906	•	•	•	•	•

	CV	CR	PR	LEMHI (MST)	UC	RE	TX	VS	VR
	•	•	•	Lemhi Title Co 208-756-2977	•	•	•	•	
	•	•	•	🏛 Record Search and Information Svcs 800-366-1906	•	•	•	•	•

	CV	CR	PR	LEWIS (PST)	UC	RE	TX	VS	VR
	•	•	•	Gem State Investigations (SOP)..................................... 208-746-4152	•	•	•	•	
	•	•	•	Lewis County Abstract 208-937-2621		•	•		
	•	•	•	🏛 Record Search and Information Svcs 800-366-1906	•	•	•	•	•

	CV	CR	PR	LINCOLN (MST)	UC	RE	TX	VS	VR
	•	•	•	🏛 American Eagle Invest & Pers Security 208-788-9527	•	•	•	•	
	•	•	•	🏛 Record Search and Information Svcs 800-366-1906	•	•	•	•	•

	CV	CR	PR	MADISON (MST)	UC	RE	TX	VS	VR
	•	•	•	🏛 Record Search and Information Svcs 800-366-1906	•	•	•	•	•

	CV	CR	PR	MINIDOKA (MST)	UC	RE	TX	VS	VR
	•	•	•	Burr Investigation (SOP) 800-582-5441	•	•	•	•	
	•	•	•	🏛 Record Search and Information Svcs 800-366-1906	•	•	•	•	•

	CV	CR	PR	NEZ PERCE (PST)	UC	RE	TX	VS	VR
	•	•	•	Action Agency (SOP) 208-263-9586	•	•	•	•	
	•	•	•	Gem State Investigations (SOP)..................................... 208-746-4152	•	•	•	•	
	•	•	•	🏛 Record Search and Information Svcs 800-366-1906	•	•	•	•	•

	CV	CR	PR	ONEIDA (MST)	UC	RE	TX	VS	VR
	•	•	•	Carter Investigations 800-449-2920	•	•	•	•	
	•	•	•	🏛 Record Search and Information Svcs 800-366-1906	•	•	•	•	•

	CV	CR	PR	OWYHEE (MST)	UC	RE	TX	VS	VR
	•	•	•	Burr Investigation (SOP) 800-582-5441	•	•	•	•	
	•	•	•	🏛 C & D Enterprises (SOP)... 208-466-2555	•	•	•	•	
	•	•	•	Lord and Associates (SOP) 208-939-8258	•	•	•		
	•	•	•	🏛 Record Search and Information Svcs 800-366-1906	•	•	•	•	•

	CV	CR	PR	PAYETTE (MST)	UC	RE	TX	VS	VR
	•	•	•	🏛 C & D Enterprises (SOP)... 208-466-2555	•	•	•	•	•
	•	•	•	Lord and Associates (SOP) 208-939-8258	•	•	•		
	•	•	•	🏛 Record Search and Information Svcs 800-366-1906	•	•	•	•	•
	•	•	•	Tri-County Process Serving (SOP) 800-473-3454	•	•	•	•	

	CV	CR	PR	POWER (MST)	UC	RE	TX	VS	VR
	•	•	•	Carter Investigations 800-449-2920	•	•	•	•	
	•	•	•	🏛 Record Search and Information Svcs 800-366-1906	•	•	•	•	•

	CV	CR	PR	SHOSHONE (PST)	UC	RE	TX	VS	VR
	•	•	•	Action Agency (SOP) 208-263-9586	•	•	•	•	

CV	CR	PR		UC	RE	TX	VS	VR
•	•	•	🏛 Record Search and Information Svcs 800-366-1906	•	•	•	•	•

CV	CR	PR	**TETON (MST)**	UC	RE	TX	VS	VR
			Alliance Title and Escrow Corp 800-214-1418	•	•	•		
			First American Title 208-354-2771		•	•		
•	•	•	🏛 Record Search and Information Svcs 800-366-1906	•	•	•	•	•

CV	CR	PR	**TWIN FALLS (MST)**	UC	RE	TX	VS	VR
•	•	•	🏛 American Eagle Invest & Pers Security 208-788-9527	•	•	•	•	
•	•	•	Burr Investigation (SOP) 800-582-5441	•	•	•	•	
•	•	•	🏛 Record Search and Information Svcs 800-366-1906	•	•	•	•	•

CV	CR	PR	**VALLEY (MST)**	UC	RE	TX	VS	VR
•	•	•	Burr Investigation (SOP) 800-582-5441	•	•	•	•	
•	•	•	🏛 C & D Enterprises (SOP) 208-466-2555	•	•	•	•	•
•	•	•	Drake Detective Agency 208-377-3463	•	•	•	•	
•	•	•	Lord and Associates (SOP) 208-939-8258	•	•	•		
•	•	•	🏛 Record Search and Information Svcs 800-366-1906	•	•	•	•	•
•	•	•	Tri-County Process Serving (SOP) 800-473-3454	•	•	•	•	•

CV	CR	PR	**WASHINGTON (MST)**	UC	RE	TX	VS	VR
•	•	•	🏛 C & D Enterprises (SOP) 208-466-2555	•	•	•	•	•
•	•	•	Lord and Associates (SOP) 208-939-8258	•	•	•		
•	•	•	🏛 Record Search and Information Svcs 800-366-1906	•	•	•	•	•

ILLINOIS

	CV	CR	PR	ADAMS (CST)		UC	RE	TX	VS	VR
	•		•	Marion County Abstract Co (SOP) 800-952-5314		•	•	•	•	
	•	•		T.G.I.F. 217-223-4186		•	•	•	•	•

	CV	CR	PR	ALEXANDER (CST)		UC	RE	TX	VS	VR
				See adjoining counties for retrievers						

	CV	CR	PR	BOND (CST)		UC	RE	TX	VS	VR
				See adjoining counties for retrievers						

	CV	CR	PR	BOONE (CST)		UC	RE	TX	VS	VR
	•	•	•	🏛 Chattel Mortgage Reporter Inc 847-234-8805		•	•	•	•	
	•	•		🏛 Cobra Security and Investigations (SOP) 847-622-8946						
	•		•	Hubly Adj Inc (SOP) 815-877-3053				•		
	•		•	Northwestern Illinois Title 815-235-1477		•	•	•		
	•	•	•	Stewart and Associates Inc (SOP) 815-235-3807		•	•	•	•	•
	•	•	•	🏛 Thomas, Julie L (SOP) 815-234-2261		•	•	•	•	•

	CV	CR	PR	BROWN (CST)		UC	RE	TX	VS	VR
				See adjoining counties for retrievers						

	CV	CR	PR	BUREAU (CST)		UC	RE	TX	VS	VR
	•	•	•	🏛 Associated Title Co 800-713-4224		•	•	•	•	
	•		•	Northwestern Illinois Title 815-235-1477		•	•	•		

	CV	CR	PR	CALHOUN (CST)		UC	RE	TX	VS	VR
	•	•	•	Moses, Ralph J 618-576-2632		•	•	•	•	

	CV	CR	PR	CARROLL (CST)		UC	RE	TX	VS	VR
	•		•	Northwestern Illinois Title 815-235-1477		•	•	•		
	•	•	•	Stewart and Associates Inc (SOP) 815-235-3807		•	•	•	•	•

	CV	CR	PR	CASS (CST)		UC	RE	TX	VS	VR
	•	•	•	Document Resources 800-292-9493		•	•	•	•	

	CV	CR	PR	CHAMPAIGN (CST)		UC	RE	TX	VS	VR
	•	•	•	CPD Inc (SOP) 217-429-2711		•	•	•	•	
	•	•	•	McGough & Associates (SOP) 800-543-1316			•	•	•	•

	CV	CR	PR	CHRISTIAN (CST)		UC	RE	TX	VS	VR
	•	•	•	Document Resources 800-292-9493		•	•	•	•	
	•	•	•	🏛 Faxxon Legal Information Services Inc 800-932-9966		•	•	•	•	•

	CV	CR	PR	CLARK (CST)		UC	RE	TX	VS	VR
	•		•	Everhart and Everhart Abstractors 217-849-2671		•	•	•	•	

	CV	CR	PR	CLAY (CST)		UC	RE	TX	VS	VR
				See adjoining counties for retrievers						

	CV	CR	PR	CLINTON (CST)		UC	RE	TX	VS	VR
	•	•	•	D & L Investigations (SOP) 618-236-2232		•	•	•	•	

	CV	CR	PR	COLES (CST)		UC	RE	TX	VS	VR
	•	•	•	CPD Inc (SOP) 217-429-2711		•	•	•	•	
	•		•	🏛 Folks Finders Ltd 800-277-3318					•	•

DT	BK	CV	CR	PR	COOK (CST)		UC	RE	TX	VS	VR
•	•	•	•	•	🏛 AM Legal Service Inc 800-203-4160		•		•	•	
•	•	•			Accu-Screen Inc 800-689-2228						
•	•	•	•		Accurate Research Inc 800-628-0303				•	•	•
•	•	•	•		🏛 Alpha Research LLC (SOP) 205-755-7008				•		
•	•	•	•	•	🏛 Atkinson & Haworth Inc (SOP) 312-915-0211		•	•	•	•	•

●	●	●	●	●	CSC 800-621-6526	●		●		
●	●	●	●	●	Centennial Coverages Inc 800-338-8221	●	●	●	●	●
●	●	●	●	●	🏛 Centennial Coverages Inc 800-995-6041	●	●	●	●	●
			●	●	🏛 Cobra Security and Investigations (SOP)...... 847-622-8946					
●	●	●	●	●	Condor International Inc (SOP) 630-357-0090	●	●	●	●	●
●	●	●	●	●	🏛 Datasource Reports 888-986-0101	●	●	●	●	●
●	●	●	●	●	Document Resources 800-292-9493	●	●	●	●	
●	●	●	●		🏛 Infotrack Information Services Inc 800-275-5594		●			
●	●	●	●	●	LaSalle Process Servers (SOP) 312-263-0620	●		●	●	●
●	●	●	●	●	🏛 Law Bulletin Publishing Co 312-644-7800	●		●		
●	●	●	●	●	Legal Data Resources (SOP)....................... 800-735-9207	●		●	●	
			●	●	McGough & Associates (SOP) 800-543-1316	●		●	●	
●	●	●	●	●	Metro Clerking Inc 312-263-2977	●		●	●	
			●	●	Northwest Corporate Protection Inc (SOP)...... 630-876-7991	●		●	●	
●	●	●	●	●	🏛 Paul J Ciolino & Associates (SOP) 312-226-6300	●		●		●
			●	●	Record Information Services 630-365-6490	●		●	●	
●	●	●	●	●	🏛 Security Source Nationwide (SOP)............. 303-628-3973	●		●	●	
●	●	●	●	●	🏛 Spyglass Pre-Employment Specialist (SOP)... 800-555-4018	●		●	●	
●	●	●	●	●	🏛 Tyler-McLennon Inc-Illinois 847-297-4460	●		●		●
●	●	●	●	●	Unisearch Inc 800-215-5168	●		●	●	
●	●	●	●	●	VTS Inc (SOP).. 800-538-4464	●		●	●	●

	CV	CR	PR	CRAWFORD (CST)	UC	RE	TX	VS	VR
	●	●	●	Lawrence County Title 618-943-4464	●	●	●		

	CV	CR	PR	CUMBERLAND (CST)	UC	RE	TX	VS	VR
	●		●	Everhart and Everhart Abstractors 217-849-2671	●	●	●	●	
	●		●	🏛 Folks Finders Ltd 800-277-3318				●	●

	CV	CR	PR	DE KALB (CST)	UC	RE	TX	VS	VR
	●		●	🏛 AM Legal Service Inc 800-203-4160	●	●	●	●	
	●		●	🏛 Chattel Mortgage Reporter Inc 847-234-8805	●	●	●	●	
	●		●	🏛 Cobra Security and Investigations (SOP)........... 847-622-8946					
	●			🏛 Infotrack Information Services Inc 800-275-5594		●			
	●		●	🏛 Law Bulletin Publishing Co 312-644-7800	●		●		
	●		●	McGough & Associates (SOP) 800-543-1316			●	●	●
	●			Midwest Applicant Screen Service (SOP) 847-516-3340	●		●		
	●		●	Northwestern Illinois Title 815-235-1477	●	●	●		
	●			Record Information Services 630-365-6490	●	●	●		
	●		●	Stewart and Associates Inc (SOP)................... 815-235-3807	●	●	●		●
	●		●	🏛 Tyler-McLennon Inc-Illinois 847-297-4460	●	●	●		●
	●		●	VTS Inc (SOP)... 800-538-4464	●	●	●	●	●

	CV	CR	PR	DE WITT (CST)	UC	RE	TX	VS	VR
	●	●	●	CPD Inc (SOP)... 217-429-2711	●	●	●	●	

	CV	CR	PR	DOUGLAS (CST)	UC	RE	TX	VS	VR
	●	●	●	Douglas County Abstract Co Inc 217-253-3214	●	●	●	●	

	CV	CR	PR	DU PAGE (CST)	UC	RE	TX	VS	VR
	●	●	●	🏛 AM Legal Service Inc 800-203-4160	●	●	●	●	
			●	Accu-Screen Inc 800-689-2228					
	●	●	●	Accurate Research Inc 800-628-0303			●	●	●
	●	●		🏛 Alpha Research LLC (SOP) 205-755-7008			●		
	●	●	●	🏛 Atkinson & Haworth Inc (SOP)..................... 312-915-0211	●	●	●	●	●
	●	●	●	🏛 Centennial Coverages Inc 800-995-6041	●	●	●	●	●
	●	●	●	Centennial Coverages Inc 800-338-8221	●	●	●	●	●
	●	●	●	🏛 Chattel Mortgage Reporter Inc 847-234-8805	●	●	●		
	●	●	●	🏛 Cobra Security and Investigations (SOP)........... 847-622-8946					
	●	●	●	Condor International Inc (SOP) 630-357-0090	●	●	●	●	●
	●	●	●	🏛 Datasource Reports 888-986-0101	●	●	●	●	●
	●	●	●	Document Resources 800-292-9493	●	●	●	●	
	●	●		🏛 Infotrack Information Services Inc 800-275-5594		●			

• • •	🏛 Law Bulletin Publishing Co 312-644-7800	•		•		
• • •	Legal Data Resources (SOP)........................... 800-735-9207	•	•	•	•	•
• • •	McGough & Associates (SOP) 800-543-1316		•	•	•	•
• • •	Metro Clerking Inc 312-263-2977	•	•	•		•
• •	Midwest Applicant Screen Service (SOP) 847-516-3340	•				
• •	Northwest Corporate Protection Inc (SOP)...... 630-876-7991	•	•	•	•	•
• • •	🏛 Paul J Ciolino & Associates (SOP).............. 312-226-6300	•	•	•		•
• •	Record Information Services 630-365-6490	•	•	•	•	
• • •	🏛 Spyglass Pre-Employment Specialist (SOP)....... 800-555-4018	•	•	•		
• • •	🏛 Tyler-McLennon Inc-Illinois 847-297-4460	•	•	•		•
• • •	Unisearch Inc 800-215-5168	•	•	•	•	
• • •	VTS Inc (SOP)... 800-538-4464	•	•	•	•	•

CV CR PR	EDGAR (CST)	UC RE TX VS VR
• • •	Edgar County Title Co 217-465-5821	• • • •

CV CR PR	EDWARDS (CST)	UC RE TX VS VR
	See adjoining counties for retrievers	

CV CR PR	EFFINGHAM (CST)	UC RE TX VS VR
• •	Everhart and Everhart Abstractors 217-849-2671	• • • •
• •	🏛 Folks Finders Ltd 800-277-3318	• •

CV CR PR	FAYETTE (CST)	UC RE TX VS VR
	See adjoining counties for retrievers	

CV CR PR	FORD (CST)	UC RE TX VS VR
• • •	CPD Inc (SOP)... 217-429-2711	• • • •
• • •	McGough & Associates (SOP) 800-543-1316	• • • •

DT BK CV CR PR	FRANKLIN (CST)	UC RE TX VS VR
• • • • •	Heartland Investigations (SOP) 618-687-4900	• • • • •
• •	🏛 Hogan Information Services 405-278-6954	
• •	Kotner, Jeff 618-273-7611	• • •
• • •	Palmer and Murrie Abstract Co Inc 618-993-3866	• • • •
• •	Real Estate Data Inc 618-964-1907	• • •
• • • • • •	Terry Sharp Law Office 618-242-0246	• • • •

CV CR PR	FULTON (CST)	UC RE TX VS VR
	Security Services Inc (SSI) (SOP) 800-383-4312	• •
• • •	Wilson Abstract Co 309-833-2049	• • • •

CV CR PR	GALLATIN (CST)	UC RE TX VS VR
• •	Kotner, Jeff 618-273-7611	• • •

CV CR PR	GREENE (CST)	UC RE TX VS VR
• • •	Falcon Investigations 217-742-5796	• • • • •
• •	O H Vivell Title Co 217-942-3733	• •

CV CR PR	GRUNDY (CST)	UC RE TX VS VR
• •	🏛 Infotrack Information Services Inc 800-275-5594	•
• • •	🏛 Paul J Ciolino & Associates (SOP)............... 312-226-6300	• • • •

CV CR PR	HAMILTON (CST)	UC RE TX VS VR
• •	Kotner, Jeff 618-273-7611	• • •

CV CR PR	HANCOCK (CST)	UC RE TX VS VR
• •	Marion County Abstract Co (SOP)..................... 800-952-5314	• • • •
• • •	Wilson Abstract Co 309-833-2049	• • • •

CV CR PR	HARDIN (CST)	UC RE TX VS VR
• •	Hardin County Abstract Company 618-287-7944	• • • •
• •	Kotner, Jeff 618-273-7611	• • •

CV	CR	PR	HENDERSON (CST)		UC	RE	TX	VS	VR
•	•	•	Wilson Abstract Co 309-833-2049		•	•	•	•	

CV	CR	PR	HENRY (CST)		UC	RE	TX	VS	VR
•	•	•	J M White Investigations (SOP) 309-794-1499		•	•	•	•	•
•		•	Northwestern Illinois Title 815-235-1477		•	•	•		

CV	CR	PR	IROQUOIS (CST)		UC	RE	TX	VS	VR
•	•	•	Skimerhorn Investigations (SOP) 815-933-0843		•	•	•	•	•

CV	CR	PR	JACKSON (CST)		UC	RE	TX	VS	VR
•	•	•	Heartland Investigations (SOP) 618-687-4900		•	•	•	•	•
•		•	Kotner, Jeff 618-273-7611		•	•	•		
•		•	Real Estate Data Inc 618-964-1907		•	•	•		

CV	CR	PR	JASPER (CST)		UC	RE	TX	VS	VR
•	•	•	Eaton Abstract Company 618-783-8474		•	•	•		

CV	CR	PR	JEFFERSON (CST)		UC	RE	TX	VS	VR
•	•	•	Heartland Investigations (SOP) 618-687-4900		•	•	•	•	•
•	•	•	Terry Sharp Law Office 618-242-0246		•	•	•	•	

CV	CR	PR	JERSEY (CST)		UC	RE	TX	VS	VR
•	•	•	Compu-Fact Research Inc 314-291-3308		•	•	•		

CV	CR	PR	JO DAVIESS (CST)		UC	RE	TX	VS	VR
•		•	Northwestern Illinois Title 815-235-1477		•	•	•		
•	•	•	Stewart and Associates Inc (SOP) 815-235-3807		•	•	•	•	•

CV	CR	PR	JOHNSON (CST)		UC	RE	TX	VS	VR
•	•		🏛 Alpha Research LLC (SOP) 205-755-7008			•			
•		•	Johnson County Abstract 618-658-3721		•	•	•		
•		•	Kotner, Jeff 618-273-7611		•	•	•		
•	•	•	Palmer and Murrie Abstract Co Inc 618-993-3866		•	•	•	•	
•		•	Real Estate Data Inc 618-964-1907		•	•	•		

CV	CR	PR	KANE (CST)		UC	RE	TX	VS	VR
•	•	•	🏛 AM Legal Service Inc 800-203-4160		•	•	•	•	
•	•	•	Accurate Research Inc 800-628-0303				•	•	•
•	•	•	🏛 Atkinson & Haworth Inc (SOP)..................... 312-915-0211		•	•	•	•	•
•	•	•	🏛 Centennial Coverages Inc 800-995-6041		•	•	•	•	•
•	•	•	Centennial Coverages Inc 800-338-8221		•	•	•	•	•
•	•	•	🏛 Chattel Mortgage Reporter Inc 847-234-8805		•	•	•	•	
•	•	•	🏛 Cobra Security and Investigations (SOP)....... 847-622-8946				•	•	•
•	•	•	Condor International Inc (SOP) 630-357-0090			•	•	•	•
•	•	•	🏛 Datasource Reports 888-986-0101		•	•	•	•	•
•	•		🏛 Infotrack Information Services Inc 800-275-5594			•			
•	•	•	🏛 Law Bulletin Publishing Co 312-644-7800		•		•		
•	•	•	McGough & Associates (SOP) 800-543-1316				•	•	
•	•	•	Metro Clerking Inc 312-263-2977		•	•	•	•	•
•	•		Midwest Applicant Screen Service (SOP) 847-516-3340		•		•		
•	•	•	Northwest Corporate Protection Inc (SOP)........... 630-876-7991		•	•	•	•	•
•	•		Record Information Services 630-365-6490		•	•	•	•	
•	•	•	🏛 Spyglass Pre-Employment Specialist (SOP)..... 800-555-4018		•	•	•	•	
•	•	•	🏛 Tyler-McLennon Inc-Illinois 847-297-4460		•	•	•		•
•	•	•	VTS Inc (SOP)... 800-538-4464		•	•	•	•	•

CV	CR	PR	KANKAKEE (CST)		UC	RE	TX	VS	VR
•	•	•	🏛 Chattel Mortgage Reporter Inc 847-234-8805		•	•	•	•	
•	•		🏛 Infotrack Information Services Inc 800-275-5594			•			
•	•	•	Skimerhorn Investigations (SOP) 815-933-0843		•	•	•	•	•

KENDALL (CST)

CV	CR	PR	Retriever	Phone	UC	RE	TX	VS	VR
•	•	•	🗑 AM Legal Service Inc	800-203-4160	•	•	•	•	
•	•	•	🗑 Chattel Mortgage Reporter Inc	847-234-8805	•	•	•	•	
•	•		🗑 Cobra Security and Investigations (SOP)	847-622-8946					
•	•	•	🗑 Law Bulletin Publishing Co	312-644-7800	•		•		
•	•		McGough & Associates (SOP)	800-543-1316		•	•		•
•	•		Midwest Applicant Screen Service (SOP)	847-516-3340	•				
•	•	•	Northwest Corporate Protection Inc (SOP)	630-876-7991	•	•	•		•
•	•		Record Information Services	630-365-6490	•	•	•	•	
•	•	•	VTS Inc (SOP)	800-538-4464	•	•	•	•	•

KNOX (CST)

CV	CR	PR	Retriever	Phone	UC	RE	TX	VS	VR
			Security Services Inc (SSI) (SOP)	800-383-4312	•	•			

LA SALLE (CST)

CV	CR	PR	Retriever	Phone	UC	RE	TX	VS	VR
•	•	•	🗑 Chattel Mortgage Reporter Inc	847-234-8805	•	•	•	•	
•		•	Northwestern Illinois Title	815-235-1477	•	•	•		

LAKE (CST)

CV	CR	PR	Retriever	Phone	UC	RE	TX	VS	VR
•	•	•	🗑 AM Legal Service Inc	800-203-4160	•	•	•	•	
•	•	•	Accurate Research Inc	800-628-0303		•	•	•	•
•	•	•	Centennial Coverages Inc	800-338-8221	•	•	•	•	•
•	•	•	🗑 Chattel Mortgage Reporter Inc	847-234-8805	•	•	•	•	
•	•		🗑 Cobra Security and Investigations (SOP)	847-622-8946					
•	•	•	Condor International Inc (SOP)	630-357-0090	•	•	•	•	•
•	•	•	🗑 Datasource Reports	888-986-0101	•	•	•	•	•
•	•		🗑 Infotrack Information Services Inc	800-275-5594		•			
•	•	•	🗑 Law Bulletin Publishing Co	312-644-7800	•		•		
•	•	•	Legal Data Resources (SOP)	800-735-9207	•	•	•	•	•
•	•	•	McGough & Associates (SOP)	800-543-1316		•	•	•	•
•	•		Metro Clerking Inc	312-263-2977	•	•	•	•	•
•	•		Midwest Applicant Screen Service (SOP)	847-516-3340	•	•	•		
•	•	•	Northwest Corporate Protection Inc (SOP)	630-876-7991	•	•	•		•
•	•	•	🗑 Paul J Ciolino & Associates (SOP)	312-226-6300	•	•	•		•
•	•		Record Information Services	630-365-6490	•	•	•	•	
•	•	•	🗑 Spyglass Pre-Employment Specialist (SOP)	800-555-4018	•	•	•	•	
•	•	•	🗑 Tyler-McLennon Inc-Illinois	847-297-4460	•	•	•	•	
•	•	•	VTS Inc (SOP)	800-538-4464	•	•	•	•	•

LAWRENCE (CST)

CV	CR	PR	Retriever	Phone	UC	RE	TX	VS	VR
•		•	Lawrence County Title	618-943-4464	•	•	•		

LEE (CST)

CV	CR	PR	Retriever	Phone	UC	RE	TX	VS	VR
•	•	•	🗑 Chattel Mortgage Reporter Inc	847-234-8805	•	•	•	•	
•		•	Northwestern Illinois Title	815-235-1477	•	•	•		
•	•	•	Stewart and Associates Inc (SOP)	815-235-3807	•	•	•	•	•

LIVINGSTON (CST)

CV	CR	PR	Retriever	Phone	UC	RE	TX	VS	VR
			See adjoining counties for retrievers						

LOGAN (CST)

CV	CR	PR	Retriever	Phone	UC	RE	TX	VS	VR
•	•	•	CPD Inc (SOP)	217-429-2711	•	•	•	•	
•	•	•	Document Resources	800-292-9493	•	•	•	•	
•	•	•	🗑 Faxxon Legal Information Services Inc	800-932-9966	•	•	•	•	•

MACON (CST)

CV	CR	PR	Retriever	Phone	UC	RE	TX	VS	VR
•	•	•	CPD Inc (SOP)	217-429-2711	•	•	•	•	
•	•	•	Document Resources	800-292-9493	•	•	•	•	
•	•	•	🗑 Faxxon Legal Information Services Inc	800-932-9966	•	•	•	•	•

MACOUPIN (CST)

CV	CR	PR	Retriever	Phone	UC	RE	TX	VS	VR
•	•	•	Barker, Jess	800-666-0036	•	•	•	•	•
•	•	•	CPD Inc (SOP)	217-429-2711	•	•	•	•	

CV	CR	PR	MADISON (CST)	UC	RE	TX	VS	VR
•	•	•	Barker, Jess 800-666-0036	•	•	•	•	•
•	•	•	Compu-Fact Research Inc 314-291-3308	•	•	•		
•	•	•	D & L Investigations (SOP) 618-236-2232	•	•	•		
•	•	•	Easterling & Steinmetz Inc (SOP) 800-467-4480	•	•	•	•	•
			🏛 Gleem Credit Services 314-521-1300					
		•	St Vrain Resources (SOP) 314-821-9029	•	•	•		•
•	•	•	🏛 Tyler-McLennon Inc-Illinois 847-297-4460	•	•	•		•

CV	CR	PR	MARION (CST)	UC	RE	TX	VS	VR
•	•	•	Terry Sharp Law Office 618-242-0246	•	•	•	•	

CV	CR	PR	MARSHALL (CST)	UC	RE	TX	VS	VR
•		•	Northwestern Illinois Title 815-235-1477	•	•	•		
			Security Services Inc (SSI) (SOP) 800-383-4312	•	•			

CV	CR	PR	MASON (CST)	UC	RE	TX	VS	VR
			See adjoining counties for retrievers					

CV	CR	PR	MASSAC (CST)	UC	RE	TX	VS	VR
•	•	•	Heartland Investigations (SOP) 618-687-4900	•	•	•	•	•

CV	CR	PR	MCDONOUGH (CST)	UC	RE	TX	VS	VR
•	•	•	Wilson Abstract Co 309-833-2049	•	•	•		

CV	CR	PR	MCHENRY (CST)	UC	RE	TX	VS	VR
•	•	•	🏛 AM Legal Service Inc 800-203-4160	•	•	•	•	
•	•	•	Accurate Research Inc 800-628-0303			•	•	•
•	•	•	🏛 Chattel Mortgage Reporter Inc 847-234-8805	•	•	•		
•	•		🏛 Cobra Security and Investigations (SOP) 847-622-8946					
•	•	•	Condor International Inc (SOP) 630-357-0090	•		•	•	
•	•	•	🏛 Datasource Reports 888-986-0101	•	•	•	•	
•	•		🏛 Infotrack Information Services Inc 800-275-5594	•		•		
•	•		🏛 Law Bulletin Publishing Co 312-644-7800	•		•		
•	•	•	McGough & Associates (SOP) 800-543-1316	•		•	•	
•	•	•	Metro Clerking Inc 312-263-2977	•		•		
•	•		Midwest Applicant Screen Service (SOP) 847-516-3340	•		•		
•	•	•	Northwest Corporate Protection Inc (SOP) 630-876-7991	•		•	•	
•	•	•	Northwestern Illinois Title 815-235-1477	•	•	•		
•	•	•	🏛 Paul J Ciolino & Associates (SOP) 312-226-6300	•	•	•	•	•
•	•	•	Record Information Services 630-365-6490	•	•	•	•	
•	•	•	🏛 Tyler-McLennon Inc-Illinois 847-297-4460	•	•	•		•
•	•	•	VTS Inc (SOP) 800-538-4464	•	•	•	•	
•	•	•	🏛 Vanagas, Melissa 815-338-9234	•	•	•	•	•

CV	CR	PR	MCLEAN (CST)	UC	RE	TX	VS	VR
•	•	•	CPD Inc (SOP) 217-429-2711	•	•	•	•	
			Security Services Inc (SSI) (SOP) 800-383-4312	•	•			

CV	CR	PR	MENARD (CST)	UC	RE	TX	VS	VR
•	•	•	Document Resources 800-292-9493	•	•	•	•	

CV	CR	PR	MERCER (CST)	UC	RE	TX	VS	VR
•	•	•	J M White Investigations (SOP) 309-794-1499	•	•	•	•	•

CV	CR	PR	MONROE (CST)	UC	RE	TX	VS	VR
•	•	•	Compu-Fact Research Inc 314-291-3308	•	•	•		
•	•	•	D & L Investigations (SOP) 618-236-2232	•	•	•	•	
•	•	•	Monroe County Title Co 618-939-8292	•	•	•	•	
•	•	•	🏛 Tyler-McLennon Inc-Illinois 847-297-4460	•	•	•		•

CV	CR	PR	MONTGOMERY (CST)	UC	RE	TX	VS	VR
•	•	•	Barker, Jess 800-666-0036	•	•	•	•	•

			•	•	•	CPD Inc (SOP)..217-429-2711	•	•	•	•	

	CV	CR	PR	MORGAN (CST)	UC	RE	TX	VS	VR
	•	•	•	Document Resources 800-292-9493	•	•	•	•	
	•	•	•	Falcon Investigations 217-742-5796	•	•	•	•	•
	•	•	•	🏛 Faxxon Legal Information Services Inc 800-932-9966	•	•	•	•	•

	CV	CR	PR	MOULTRIE (CST)	UC	RE	TX	VS	VR
	•	•	•	CPD Inc (SOP)..217-429-2711	•	•	•	•	
	•		•	Citzen Abstract Co 217-728-7132	•	•	•	•	

	CV	CR	PR	OGLE (CST)	UC	RE	TX	VS	VR
	•	•	•	🏛 Chattel Mortgage Reporter Inc 847-234-8805	•	•	•	•	
	•		•	Northwestern Illinois Title 815-235-1477	•	•	•		
	•	•	•	Stewart and Associates Inc (SOP)................815-235-3807	•	•	•	•	•
	•	•	•	🏛 Thomas, Julie L (SOP)...............................815-234-2261	•	•	•	•	

DT	BK	CV	CR	PR	PEORIA (CST)	UC	RE	TX	VS	VR
•	•	•	•	•	Accurate Research Inc 800-628-0303			•	•	•
•	•				🏛 Hogan Information Services 405-278-6954					
•	•	•	•	•	J M White Investigations (SOP) 309-794-1499	•	•	•	•	•
•	•				Security Services Inc (SSI) (SOP) 800-383-4312	•	•			

	CV	CR	PR	PERRY (CST)	UC	RE	TX	VS	VR
				See adjoining counties for retrievers					

	CV	CR	PR	PIATT (CST)	UC	RE	TX	VS	VR
	•	•	•	CPD Inc (SOP)..217-429-2711	•	•	•	•	

	CV	CR	PR	PIKE (CST)	UC	RE	TX	VS	VR
	•	•	•	Falcon Investigations 217-742-5796	•	•	•	•	•
	•		•	Marion County Abstract Co (SOP)................800-952-5314	•	•	•		

	CV	CR	PR	POPE (CST)	UC	RE	TX	VS	VR
	•		•	Kotner, Jeff 618-273-7611	•	•	•		

	CV	CR	PR	PULASKI (CST)	UC	RE	TX	VS	VR
	•		•	Pulaski County Abstract Company 618-748-9233	•	•	•	•	

	CV	CR	PR	PUTNAM (CST)	UC	RE	TX	VS	VR
	•	•	•	🏛 Associated Title Co 800-713-4224	•	•	•	•	
	•		•	Northwestern Illinois Title 815-235-1477	•	•	•		

	CV	CR	PR	RANDOLPH (CST)	UC	RE	TX	VS	VR
	•	•	•	Compu-Fact Research Inc 314-291-3308	•	•	•		
	•	•	•	Heartland Investigations (SOP) 618-687-4900	•	•	•	•	•

	CV	CR	PR	RICHLAND (CST)	UC	RE	TX	VS	VR
	•	•	•	Lawrence County Title 618-943-4464	•	•	•		

DT		CV	CR	PR	ROCK ISLAND (CST)	UC	RE	TX	VS	VR
•		•	•	•	J M White Investigations (SOP) 309-794-1499	•	•	•	•	•
•		•	•	•	J.R. Investigations (SOP)..............................515-965-2637	•	•	•	•	•
•		•		•	Northwestern Illinois Title 815-235-1477	•	•	•		

	CV	CR	PR	SALINE (CST)	UC	RE	TX	VS	VR
	•	•	•	Heartland Investigations (SOP) 618-687-4900	•	•	•	•	•
	•		•	Kotner, Jeff 618-273-7611	•	•	•		
	•	•	•	Palmer and Murrie Abstract Co Inc 618-993-3866	•	•	•		
	•		•	Real Estate Data Inc 618-964-1907	•	•	•		

DT	BK	CV	CR	PR	SANGAMON (CAPITAL) (CST)	UC	RE	TX	VS	VR
•	•	•	•	•	Barker, Jess 800-666-0036	•	•	•	•	•
•	•	•	•	•	CPD Inc (SOP)..217-429-2711	•	•	•	•	

DT	BK	CV	CR	PR			UC	RE	TX	VS	VR
•	•	•	•	•	CSC (SOP)	800-877-2556	•	•	•	•	
•	•	•	•	•	Document Resources	800-292-9493	•	•	•	•	
•	•	•	•	•	🏛 Faxxon Legal Information Services Inc	800-932-9966	•	•	•	•	•
•	•				🏛 Hogan Information Services	405-278-6954					
•	•	•	•	•	🏛 Tenant Registry Inc	217-793-8146	•		•	•	•

		CV	CR	PR	SCHUYLER (CST)		UC	RE	TX	VS	VR
		•	•	•	Wilson Abstract Co	309-833-2049	•	•	•	•	

		CV	CR	PR	SCOTT (CST)		UC	RE	TX	VS	VR
		•	•	•	Falcon Investigations	217-742-5796	•	•	•	•	•

		CV	CR	PR	SHELBY (CST)		UC	RE	TX	VS	VR
		•		•	🏛 Folks Finders Ltd	800-277-3318				•	•
		•		•	Shelby County Land Title Corp	217-774-2623	•	•	•	•	

DT	BK	CV	CR	PR	ST. CLAIR (CST)		UC	RE	TX	VS	VR
•	•	•	•	•	Bankruptcy Services Inc	214-424-6500					
				•	Barker, Jess	800-666-0036	•	•	•	•	•
				•	Compu-Fact Research Inc	314-291-3308	•	•	•	•	
•	•	•	•	•	D & L Investigations (SOP)	618-236-2232	•	•	•	•	
•	•	•	•	•	Easterling & Steinmetz Inc (SOP)	800-467-4480	•	•	•	•	•
				•	🏛 Gleem Credit Services	314-521-1300					
•		•	•	•	St Vrain Resources (SOP)	314-821-9029	•	•	•		•
•	•	•	•	•	🏛 Tyler-McLennon Inc-Illinois	847-297-4460	•	•	•		•

		CV	CR	PR	STARK (CST)		UC	RE	TX	VS	VR
		•	•	•	J M White Investigations (SOP)	309-794-1499	•	•	•	•	•
					Security Services Inc (SSI) (SOP)	800-383-4312	•	•			

		CV	CR	PR	STEPHENSON (CST)		UC	RE	TX	VS	VR
		•		•	Hubly Adj Inc (SOP)	815-877-3053			•		
		•		•	Northwestern Illinois Title	815-235-1477	•	•	•		
		•	•	•	Stewart and Associates Inc (SOP)	815-235-3807	•	•	•	•	•
		•	•	•	🏛 Thomas, Julie L (SOP)	815-234-2261	•	•	•	•	•

		CV	CR	PR	TAZEWELL (CST)		UC	RE	TX	VS	VR
		•	•	•	J M White Investigations (SOP)	309-794-1499	•	•	•	•	•
		•		•	🏛 Secretarial Outsource Services	309-347-3736					
					Security Services Inc (SSI) (SOP)	800-383-4312	•	•			

		CV	CR	PR	UNION (CST)		UC	RE	TX	VS	VR
		•	•	•	Heartland Investigations (SOP)	618-687-4900	•	•	•	•	•
		•		•	Real Estate Data Inc	618-964-1907	•	•	•		

DT	BK	CV	CR	PR	VERMILION (CST)		UC	RE	TX	VS	VR
•	•				🏛 Hogan Information Services	405-278-6954					

		CV	CR	PR	WABASH (CST)		UC	RE	TX	VS	VR
		•	•	•	Lawrence County Title	618-943-4464	•	•	•		

		CV	CR	PR	WARREN (CST)		UC	RE	TX	VS	VR
		•	•	•	Wilson Abstract Co	309-833-2049	•	•	•	•	

		CV	CR	PR	WASHINGTON (CST)		UC	RE	TX	VS	VR
					See adjoining counties for retrievers						

		CV	CR	PR	WAYNE (CST)		UC	RE	TX	VS	VR
		•	•	•	Heartland Investigations (SOP)	618-687-4900	•	•	•	•	•

		CV	CR	PR	WHITE (CST)		UC	RE	TX	VS	VR
		•	•	•	Heartland Investigations (SOP)	618-687-4900	•	•	•	•	•
		•		•	Kotner, Jeff	618-273-7611	•	•	•		

WHITESIDE (CST)

CV	CR	PR		UC	RE	TX	VS	VR
•		•	Northwestern Illinois Title 815-235-1477	•	•	•		
•	•	•	Stewart and Associates Inc (SOP) 815-235-3807	•	•	•	•	•

WILL (CST)

CV	CR	PR		UC	RE	TX	VS	VR
•	•	•	Accurate Research Inc 800-628-0303			•	•	•
•	•	•	Chattel Mortgage Reporter Inc 847-234-8805	•	•	•	•	
•	•	•	Condor International Inc (SOP) 630-357-0090	•	•	•	•	
•	•	•	Datasource Reports 888-986-0101	•	•	•	•	•
•	•	•	Infotrack Information Services Inc 800-275-5594		•			
•	•	•	Law Bulletin Publishing Co 312-644-7800	•		•		
•	•	•	Legal Data Resources (SOP) 800-735-9207	•	•	•	•	•
•	•	•	McGough & Associates (SOP) 800-543-1316	•	•	•	•	
•	•	•	Metro Clerking Inc 312-263-2977	•				
•	•	•	Northwest Corporate Protection Inc (SOP) 630-876-7991	•	•	•	•	
•	•	•	Paul J Ciolino & Associates (SOP) 312-226-6300	•	•	•	•	
•	•		Record Information Services 630-365-6490	•	•	•	•	
•	•	•	Skimerhorn Investigations (SOP) 815-933-0843	•	•	•	•	•
•	•	•	Spyglass Pre-Employment Specialist (SOP) 800-555-4018	•	•	•	•	
•	•	•	Tyler-McLennon Inc-Illinois 847-297-4460	•	•	•		•

WILLIAMSON (CST)

CV	CR	PR		UC	RE	TX	VS	VR
•	•	•	Heartland Investigations (SOP) 618-687-4900	•	•	•	•	•
•		•	Kotner, Jeff 618-273-7611	•	•	•		
•	•	•	Palmer and Murrie Abstract Co Inc 618-993-3866	•	•	•		
•		•	Real Estate Data Inc 618-964-1907	•	•	•		
•	•	•	Terry Sharp Law Office 618-242-0246	•	•	•	•	

WINNEBAGO (CST)

DT	BK	CV	CR	PR		UC	RE	TX	VS	VR
		•	•	•	Chattel Mortgage Reporter Inc 847-234-8805	•	•	•	•	
		•	•		Cobra Security and Investigations (SOP) 847-622-8946					
•	•	•	•	•	Gregg Investigations Inc of Janesville (SOP) 800-866-1976	•	•	•	•	
•	•	•	•	•	Gregg Investigations Inc of Madison (SOP) 800-866-1976	•	•	•	•	•
•	•				Hogan Information Services 405-278-6954					
•	•	•	•	•	Hubly Adj Inc (SOP) 815-877-3053		•			
•	•	•	•	•	Infotrack Information Services Inc 800-275-5594		•			
•	•	•	•	•	Law Bulletin Publishing Co 312-644-7800	•	•			
				•	Northwestern Illinois Title 815-235-1477	•	•	•		
•		•	•		Record Information Services 630-365-6490	•	•	•	•	
•	•	•	•	•	Stewart and Associates Inc (SOP) 815-235-3807	•	•	•	•	•
•	•	•	•	•	Thomas, Julie L (SOP) 815-234-2261	•	•	•	•	•
•	•	•	•	•	Tyler-McLennon Inc-Illinois 847-297-4460	•	•	•		•

WOODFORD (CST)

CV	CR	PR		UC	RE	TX	VS	VR
			Security Services Inc (SSI) (SOP) 800-383-4312	•	•			

INDIANA

	CV	CR	PR	ADAMS (EST)	UC	RE	TX	VS	VR
	●	●	●	Tri-County Land Title 219-589-3139	●	●	●	●	

DT	BK	CV	CR	PR	ALLEN (EST)	UC	RE	TX	VS	VR
●	●	●	●	●	Express Process Service/Investigations (SOP).......... 800-899-1872	●	●	●	●	●
●	●				🏛 Hogan Information Services 405-278-6954					
●	●	●	●	●	J-C Investigations (SOP)........................ 219-262-2832	●	●	●	●	●

	CV	CR	PR	BARTHOLOMEW (EST)	UC	RE	TX	VS	VR
	●	●		McGinley Paralegal & Search Services (SOP) 317-630-9721	●	●	●		
	●	●	●	🏛 Myers Investigations Inc (SOP)................ 800-788-8018	●	●	●	●	●

	CV	CR	PR	BENTON (EST)	UC	RE	TX	VS	VR
	●		●	Benton County Abstract & Title 317-884-1140	●	●	●		
	●	●	●	Tippecanoe Title Services Inc 317-423-2457	●	●	●		

	CV	CR	PR	BLACKFORD (EST)	UC	RE	TX	VS	VR
	●	●	●	Tri-County Land Title 219-589-3139	●	●	●	●	

	CV	CR	PR	BOONE (EST)	UC	RE	TX	VS	VR
	●		●	🏛 Central Indiana Paralegal Svc 317-636-1311	●		●		
	●	●	●	Express Process Service/Investigations (SOP).......... 800-899-1872	●	●	●	●	●
	●	●	●	🏛 International Investigators Inc (SOP)........... 317-925-1496	●	●	●	●	
	●	●		McGinley Paralegal & Search Services (SOP) 317-630-9721	●	●	●		
	●			Royal Title Services 800-773-7279	●	●	●	●	
	●		●	Three Rivers Title Co 219-424-2929	●	●	●	●	
	●	●	●	USA Inc - Private Investigators (SOP) 317-254-8721	●	●	●	●	●

	CV	CR	PR	BROWN (EST)	UC	RE	TX	VS	VR
	●	●		McGinley Paralegal & Search Services (SOP) 317-630-9721	●	●	●		
	●	●	●	🏛 Trace Investigations (SOP) 800-310-8857	●	●	●	●	●
	●	●	●	USA Inc - Private Investigators (SOP) 317-254-8721	●	●	●	●	●

	CV	CR	PR	CARROLL (EST)	UC	RE	TX	VS	VR
	●	●	●	Tippecanoe Title Services Inc 317-423-2457	●	●	●		

	CV	CR	PR	CASS (EST)	UC	RE	TX	VS	VR
	●	●	●	Tippecanoe Title Services Inc 317-423-2457	●	●	●		

	CV	CR	PR	CLARK (EST)	UC	RE	TX	VS	VR
	●	●	●	Eagle Investigations Inc (SOP)............... 800-344-2454	●	●	●	●	
	●		●	Salem Title Corporation 812-883-5806	●	●	●	●	
	●		●	Southern Indiana Abstract & Title Co 812-944-4931	●	●	●	●	
	●	●	●	🏛 Steve Knight Services (SOP)................ 812-288-8528	●	●	●	●	●

	CV	CR	PR	CLAY (EST)	UC	RE	TX	VS	VR
	●	●		McGinley Paralegal & Search Services (SOP) 317-630-9721	●	●	●		
	●	●	●	Moomaw Abstract Corp 812-384-4702	●	●	●		

	CV	CR	PR	CLINTON (EST)	UC	RE	TX	VS	VR
	●	●		McGinley Paralegal & Search Services (SOP) 317-630-9721	●	●	●		
	●	●	●	Tippecanoe Title Services Inc 317-423-2457	●	●	●		

	CV	CR	PR	CRAWFORD (EST)	UC	RE	TX	VS	VR
	●		●	Salem Title Corporation 812-883-5806	●	●	●	●	

	CV	CR	PR	DAVIESS (EST)	UC	RE	TX	VS	VR
	●		●	James F Havill Attorney at Law PC 812-254-0050	●	●	●	●	
	●	●		McGinley Paralegal & Search Services (SOP) 317-630-9721	●	●	●		
	●	●	●	Moomaw Abstract Corp 812-384-4702	●	●	●		

CV	CR	PR	DeKalb (EST)	UC	RE	TX	VS	VR
•	•	•	TWT Title 800-742-9362	•	•	•		
•		•	Three Rivers Title Co 219-424-2929	•	•	•	•	

CV	CR	PR	Dearborn (EST)	UC	RE	TX	VS	VR
•	•		🗑 AM Search & Retrieve 812-438-4166	•	•	•	•	•
•	•	•	All State Investigations (SOP) 800-741-4711	•	•	•	•	•

CV	CR	PR	Decatur (EST)	UC	RE	TX	VS	VR
•		•	Ford Abstract Corp 812-663-2190	•	•	•		
•	•		McGinley Paralegal & Search Services (SOP) 317-630-9721	•	•	•		

CV	CR	PR	Delaware (EST)	UC	RE	TX	VS	VR
•		•	Kings Title & Abstract Co 800-288-1642	•	•	•		
•	•		McGinley Paralegal & Search Services (SOP) 317-630-9721	•	•	•		

CV	CR	PR	Dubois (EST)	UC	RE	TX	VS	VR
			See adjoining counties for retrievers					

CV	CR	PR	Elkhart (EST)	UC	RE	TX	VS	VR
•	•	•	Baker, Jami Christensen 800-403-5207	•	•	•		
•	•	•	Bennett, Barbara A 219-262-9345	•	•	•		
•	•	•	J-C Investigations (SOP) 219-262-2832	•	•	•	•	•
•		•	Land Grant Title Group Inc 219-295-1620	•	•	•		
•	•	•	Main Street Title Corp 219-533-3774	•	•	•	•	
•		•	McKesson Title Corp 800-261-8437	•	•	•		

CV	CR	PR	Fayette (EST)	UC	RE	TX	VS	VR
•	•		McGinley Paralegal & Search Services (SOP) 317-630-9721	•	•	•		

DT	BK	CV	CR	PR	Floyd (EST)	UC	RE	TX	VS	VR
•	•	•	•	•	Eagle Investigations Inc (SOP) 800-344-2454	•	•	•	•	
•	•				🗑 Hogan Information Services 405-278-6954					
		•		•	Salem Title Corporation 812-883-5806	•	•	•		
		•		•	Southern Indiana Abstract & Title Co 812-944-4931	•	•	•		
•	•	•	•	•	🗑 Steve Knight Services (SOP) 812-288-8528	•	•	•	•	•

CV	CR	PR	Fountain (EST)	UC	RE	TX	VS	VR
•		•	Massey Abstract and Real Estate 317-793-4547	•	•	•		
•	•		McGinley Paralegal & Search Services (SOP) 317-630-9721	•	•	•		
•	•	•	Tippecanoe Title Services Inc 317-423-2457	•	•	•		

CV	CR	PR	Franklin (EST)	UC	RE	TX	VS	VR
•	•		🗑 AM Search & Retrieve 812-438-4166	•	•	•		•
•		•	Kings Title & Abstract Co 800-860-2990	•	•	•		

CV	CR	PR	Fulton (EST)	UC	RE	TX	VS	VR
•	•	•	Baker, Jami Christensen 800-403-5207	•	•	•		
•	•	•	Deamer & Deamer 219-223-3129	•	•	•	•	
•	•		McGinley Paralegal & Search Services (SOP) 317-630-9721	•	•	•		
•		•	McKesson Title Corp 800-261-8437	•	•	•		

CV	CR	PR	Gibson (CST)	UC	RE	TX	VS	VR
•		•	Druley, Ray M 812-753-4975	•	•	•		
•	•	•	Fidelity Search Inc 812-479-8704	•	•	•	•	

CV	CR	PR	Grant (EST)	UC	RE	TX	VS	VR
•	•	•	Grant County Abstract Co 317-664-7371	•	•	•		
•		•	Kings Title & Abstract Co 800-662-1299	•	•	•		

CV	CR	PR	Greene (EST)	UC	RE	TX	VS	VR
•	•		McGinley Paralegal & Search Services (SOP) 317-630-9721	•	•	•		
•	•	•	Moomaw Abstract Corp 812-384-4702	•	•	•		

CV	CR	PR	HAMILTON (EST)		UC	RE	TX	VS	VR
•		•	Central Indiana Paralegal Svc	317-636-1311	•		•		
•	•	•	Express Process Service/Investigations (SOP)	800-899-1872	•	•	•	•	•
•	•	•	International Investigators Inc (SOP)	317-925-1496	•	•	•	•	
•	•		McGinley Paralegal & Search Services (SOP)	317-630-9721	•	•			
•		•	Three Rivers Title Co	219-424-2929	•	•	•		
•	•	•	USA Inc - Private Investigators (SOP)	317-254-8721	•	•	•	•	•

CV	CR	PR	HANCOCK (EST)		UC	RE	TX	VS	VR
		•	Genealogically Yours	317-987-8820				•	
•	•	•	International Investigators Inc (SOP)	317-925-1496	•	•	•		
•	•		McGinley Paralegal & Search Services (SOP)	317-630-9721	•	•	•		
•	•	•	Myers Investigations Inc (SOP)	800-788-8018	•	•	•		•

CV	CR	PR	HARRISON (EST)		UC	RE	TX	VS	VR
•		•	Salem Title Corporation	812-883-5806	•	•	•	•	
•		•	Southern Indiana Abstract & Title Co	812-944-4931	•	•	•	•	

CV	CR	PR	HENDRICKS (EST)		UC	RE	TX	VS	VR
•		•	Central Indiana Paralegal Svc	317-636-1311	•		•		
•	•	•	Express Process Service/Investigations (SOP)	800-899-1872	•	•	•	•	•
•	•	•	International Investigators Inc (SOP)	317-925-1496	•	•	•	•	
•	•		McGinley Paralegal & Search Services (SOP)	317-630-9721	•	•	•		
•	•	•	USA Inc - Private Investigators (SOP)	317-254-8721	•	•	•	•	•

CV	CR	PR	HENRY (EST)		UC	RE	TX	VS	VR
		•	Genealogically Yours	317-987-8820				•	
•		•	Henry County Abstract Co	317-529-0302	•	•	•		
•		•	Kings Title & Abstract Co	800-860-2990	•	•	•		
•	•		McGinley Paralegal & Search Services (SOP)	317-630-9721	•	•	•		

CV	CR	PR	HOWARD (EST)		UC	RE	TX	VS	VR
•		•	Anderson Land Title Co	317-459-3183	•	•	•	•	
•	•		McGinley Paralegal & Search Services (SOP)	317-630-9721	•	•	•		

CV	CR	PR	HUNTINGTON (EST)		UC	RE	TX	VS	VR
•		•	Jones Abstract & Title Co Inc	219-356-2122	•	•	•		
•		•	Three Rivers Title Co	219-424-2929	•	•	•	•	

CV	CR	PR	JACKSON (EST)		UC	RE	TX	VS	VR
•	•		McGinley Paralegal & Search Services (SOP)	317-630-9721	•	•	•		
•	•	•	Myers Investigations Inc (SOP)	800-788-8018	•	•	•	•	•
•		•	Nierman & Nierman Title Co	812-358-4766	•	•	•		
•		•	North Vernon Abstract Co Inc	812-346-2259	•	•	•		
•		•	Salem Title Corporation	812-883-5806	•	•	•	•	

CV	CR	PR	JASPER (CST)		UC	RE	TX	VS	VR
•	•	•	Tippecanoe Title Services Inc	317-423-2457	•	•	•		

CV	CR	PR	JAY (EST)		UC	RE	TX	VS	VR
•		•	Jay County Abstract Company Inc	219-726-4303	•	•	•	•	
•		•	Jay Portland Abstract Inc Co	219-726-6466	•	•	•	•	
•	•	•	Tri-County Land Title	219-589-3139	•	•	•	•	

CV	CR	PR	JEFFERSON (EST)		UC	RE	TX	VS	VR
•		•	North Vernon Abstract Co Inc	812-346-2259	•	•	•		

CV	CR	PR	JENNINGS (EST)		UC	RE	TX	VS	VR
•		•	North Vernon Abstract Co Inc	812-346-2259	•	•	•		

CV	CR	PR	JOHNSON (EST)		UC	RE	TX	VS	VR
•		•	Central Indiana Paralegal Svc	317-636-1311	•		•		
•	•	•	Express Process Service/Investigations (SOP)	800-899-1872	•	•	•	•	•

CV	CR	PR		UC	RE	TX	VS	VR
•	•	•	🏛 International Investigators Inc (SOP) 317-925-1496	•	•	•	•	
•	•	•	McGinley Paralegal & Search Services (SOP) 317-630-9721	•	•	•		
•	•	•	🏛 Myers Investigations Inc (SOP) 800-788-8018	•	•	•	•	•
•	•	•	USA Inc - Private Investigators (SOP) 317-254-8721	•	•	•	•	•

CV	CR	PR	KNOX (EST)	UC	RE	TX	VS	VR
•		•	L Fay Hedden Abstract Office Inc 812-882-5273	•	•	•	•	
•	•		McGinley Paralegal & Search Services (SOP) 317-630-9721	•	•			

CV	CR	PR	KOSCIUSKO (EST)	UC	RE	TX	VS	VR
•	•	•	Baker, Jami Christensen 800-403-5207	•	•	•		
•	•	•	Bodkin Abstract Company Inc 219-267-7021	•	•	•	•	
•	•	•	J-C Investigations (SOP) 219-262-2832	•	•	•	•	•
•		•	McKesson Title Corp 800-261-8437	•	•	•		
•		•	Three Rivers Title Co 219-424-2929	•	•	•	•	

CV	CR	PR	LA PORTE (CST)	UC	RE	TX	VS	VR
•	•	•	J-C Investigations (SOP) 219-262-2832	•	•	•	•	•
•	•	•	🏛 M.J.T. Research 800-297-8406	•	•	•	•	•
•		•	McKesson Title Corp 800-261-8437	•	•	•		

CV	CR	PR	LAGRANGE (EST)	UC	RE	TX	VS	VR
•	•	•	Baker, Jami Christensen 800-403-5207	•	•	•		
•	•	•	J-C Investigations (SOP) 219-262-2832	•	•	•	•	•
•		•	LaGrange Title Company 219-463-3232	•	•	•		
•	•	•	TWT Title 800-742-9362	•	•	•		
•		•	Three Rivers Title Co 219-424-2929	•	•	•		

DT	BK	CV	CR	PR	LAKE (CST)	UC	RE	TX	VS	VR
•	•	•	•	•	Accurate Research Inc 800-628-0303			•	•	•
•	•	•	•	•	Express Process Service/Investigations (SOP) 800-899-1872	•	•	•	•	•
•	•				🏛 Hogan Information Services 405-278-6954					
		•		•	Land Grant Title Group Inc 219-295-1620	•	•	•		

CV	CR	PR	LAWRENCE (EST)	UC	RE	TX	VS	VR
•	•		McGinley Paralegal & Search Services (SOP) 317-630-9721	•	•	•		
•		•	Salem Title Corporation 812-883-5806	•	•	•	•	

CV	CR	PR	MADISON (EST)	UC	RE	TX	VS	VR
•		•	Kings Title & Abstract Co 800-317-1515	•	•	•		
•	•		McGinley Paralegal & Search Services (SOP) 317-630-9721	•	•	•		

DT	BK	CV	CR	PR	MARION (CAPITAL) (EST)	UC	RE	TX	VS	VR
				•	🏛 Central Indiana Paralegal Svc 317-636-1311	•		•		
•	•	•	•	•	Express Process Service/Investigations (SOP) 800-899-1872	•	•	•	•	•
				•	Genealogically Yours 317-987-8820				•	
•	•				🏛 Hogan Information Services 405-278-6954					
•	•	•	•	•	🏛 International Investigators Inc (SOP) 317-925-1496	•	•	•		
		•	•	•	McGinley Paralegal & Search Services (SOP) 317-630-9721	•	•	•		
•	•	•	•	•	🏛 Myers Investigations Inc (SOP) 800-788-8018	•	•	•		•
•	•	•			National Service Information Inc 317-266-0040	•		•	•	
				•	The Dataprompt Corporation 800-577-8157		•			
•	•	•	•	•	USA Inc - Private Investigators (SOP) 317-254-8721	•	•	•	•	•

CV	CR	PR	MARSHALL (EST)	UC	RE	TX	VS	VR
•	•	•	Baker, Jami Christensen 800-403-5207	•	•	•		
•	•	•	J-C Investigations (SOP) 219-262-2832	•	•	•	•	•
•		•	McKesson Title Corp 800-261-8437	•	•	•		

CV	CR	PR	MARTIN (EST)	UC	RE	TX	VS	VR
•	•		McGinley Paralegal & Search Services (SOP) 317-630-9721	•	•	•		

CV	CR	PR	MIAMI (EST)	UC	RE	TX	VS	VR
•		•	Wabash Valley Abstract Co Inc 317-472-4351	•	•	•		

CV	CR	PR	MONROE (EST)	UC	RE	TX	VS	VR
•	•	•	Bloomington Abstract Co 812-336-0121	•	•	•	•	
•	•	•	Express Process Service/Investigations (SOP)............ 800-899-1872	•	•	•	•	•
•	•		McGinley Paralegal & Search Services (SOP) 317-630-9721	•	•	•		
•	•	•	🏛 Myers Investigations Inc (SOP)........ 800-788-8018	•	•	•	•	•
•	•	•	🏛 Trace Investigations (SOP) 800-310-8857	•	•	•	•	•
•	•	•	USA Inc - Private Investigators (SOP) 317-254-8721	•	•	•	•	•

CV	CR	PR	MONTGOMERY (EST)	UC	RE	TX	VS	VR
•	•		McGinley Paralegal & Search Services (SOP) 317-630-9721	•	•	•		
•	•	•	Tippecanoe Title Services Inc 317-423-2457	•	•	•		

CV	CR	PR	MORGAN (EST)	UC	RE	TX	VS	VR
•		•	🏛 Central Indiana Paralegal Svc 317-636-1311	•		•		
•	•		McGinley Paralegal & Search Services (SOP) 317-630-9721	•		•		
•	•	•	🏛 Trace Investigations (SOP) 800-310-8857	•	•	•	•	•
•	•	•	USA Inc - Private Investigators (SOP) 317-254-8721	•	•	•	•	•

CV	CR	PR	NEWTON (CST)	UC	RE	TX	VS	VR
			See adjoining counties for retrievers					

CV	CR	PR	NOBLE (EST)	UC	RE	TX	VS	VR
•	•	•	Baker, Jami Christensen 800-403-5207	•	•	•		
•	•	•	Bodkin Abstract Company Inc 219-267-7021	•	•	•	•	
•	•	•	TWT Title 800-742-9362	•	•	•		
•		•	Three Rivers Title Co 219-424-2929	•	•	•	•	

CV	CR	PR	OHIO (EST)	UC	RE	TX	VS	VR
•	•		🏛 AM Search & Retrieve 812-438-4166	•	•	•		•

CV	CR	PR	ORANGE (EST)	UC	RE	TX	VS	VR
•		•	Orange County Abstract and Title Co Inc 812-723-3044	•	•	•	•	
•		•	Salem Title Corporation 812-883-5806	•	•	•	•	

CV	CR	PR	OWEN (EST)	UC	RE	TX	VS	VR
•	•		McGinley Paralegal & Search Services (SOP) 317-630-9721	•	•	•		

CV	CR	PR	PARKE (EST)	UC	RE	TX	VS	VR
•	•		McGinley Paralegal & Search Services (SOP) 317-630-9721	•	•	•		

CV	CR	PR	PERRY (EST)	UC	RE	TX	VS	VR
•	•		🏛 Summit Documents 502-281-5406	•	•	•	•	

CV	CR	PR	PIKE (EST)	UC	RE	TX	VS	VR
			See adjoining counties for retrievers					

CV	CR	PR	PORTER (CST)	UC	RE	TX	VS	VR
•	•	•	🏛 M.J.T. Research 800-297-8406	•	•	•	•	•

CV	CR	PR	POSEY (CST)	UC	RE	TX	VS	VR
•	•	•	Fidelity Search Inc 812-479-8704	•	•	•	•	•

CV	CR	PR	PULASKI (EST)	UC	RE	TX	VS	VR
•		•	McKesson Title Corp 800-261-8437	•	•	•		

CV	CR	PR	PUTNAM (EST)	UC	RE	TX	VS	VR
•	•		McGinley Paralegal & Search Services (SOP) 317-630-9721	•	•	•		

CV	CR	PR	RANDOLPH (EST)	UC	RE	TX	VS	VR
•		•	Kings Abstract Company 800-280-6323	•	•	•		

CV	CR	PR	RIPLEY (EST)	UC	RE	TX	VS	VR
•	•		🏛 AM Search & Retrieve 812-438-4166	•	•	•		•
•	•		McGinley Paralegal & Search Services (SOP) 317-630-9721	•	•	•		

CV	CR	PR			UC	RE	TX	VS	VR
•		•	North Vernon Abstract Co Inc 812-346-2259		•	•	•		

CV	CR	PR	RUSH (EST)		UC	RE	TX	VS	VR
•		•	Kings Title & Abstract Co 317-932-5757		•	•	•		
•	•		McGinley Paralegal & Search Services (SOP) 317-630-9721		•	•	•		

CV	CR	PR	SCOTT (EST)		UC	RE	TX	VS	VR
•		•	Salem Title Corporation 812-883-5806		•	•	•	•	

CV	CR	PR	SHELBY (EST)		UC	RE	TX	VS	VR
•		•	🗑 Central Indiana Paralegal Svc 317-636-1311		•		•		
•	•	•	🗑 International Investigators Inc (SOP) 317-925-1496		•	•	•	•	
•		•	Kings Title & Abstract Co 800-798-4545		•	•	•		
•	•		McGinley Paralegal & Search Services (SOP) 317-630-9721		•	•	•		

CV	CR	PR	SPENCER (CST)		UC	RE	TX	VS	VR
•	•		🗑 Summit Documents 502-281-5406		•	•	•	•	
•	•	•	Wetherill, Richard 812-649-2221		•	•	•	•	

DT	BK	CV	CR	PR	ST. JOSEPH (EST)		UC	RE	TX	VS	VR
		•	•	•	Baker, Jami Christensen 800-403-5207		•	•	•		
•	•	•	•	•	🗑 Case Services Inc (SOP) 219-291-0480		•	•	•	•	•
•	•				🗑 Hogan Information Services 405-278-6954						
•		•	•	•	J-C Investigations (SOP) 219-262-2832		•	•	•	•	•
•	•	•	•	•	🗑 M.J.T. Research 800-297-8406		•	•	•	•	•
		•		•	McKesson Title Corp 800-261-8437		•	•	•		

CV	CR	PR	STARKE (CST)		UC	RE	TX	VS	VR
•	•	•	Baker, Jami Christensen 800-403-5207		•	•	•		
•		•	McKesson Title Corp 800-261-8437		•	•	•		
•	•	•	Starke County Abstract Title & Guar 219-772-3733		•	•	•	•	

CV	CR	PR	STEUBEN (EST)		UC	RE	TX	VS	VR
•	•	•	Baker, Jami Christensen 800-403-5207		•	•	•		
•	•	•	TWT Title 800-742-9362		•	•	•		
•		•	Three Rivers Title Co 219-424-2929		•	•	•	•	

CV	CR	PR	SULLIVAN (EST)		UC	RE	TX	VS	VR
•	•		McGinley Paralegal & Search Services (SOP) 317-630-9721		•	•	•		
•		•	Moomaw Abstract Corp 812-384-4702		•	•	•		
•	•	•	Sullivan County Abstract Inc 812-268-4242		•	•	•		

CV	CR	PR	SWITZERLAND (EST)		UC	RE	TX	VS	VR
			See adjoining counties for retrievers						

DT		CV	CR	PR	TIPPECANOE (EST)		UC	RE	TX	VS	VR
•		•	•	•	Express Process Service/Investigations (SOP) 800-899-1872		•	•	•	•	•
•					🗑 Hogan Information Services 405-278-6954						
•		•	•		McGinley Paralegal & Search Services (SOP) 317-630-9721		•	•	•		
•		•	•		🗑 Smith, Pat 317-447-1684						
		•	•	•	Tippecanoe Title Services Inc 317-423-2457		•	•	•		

CV	CR	PR	TIPTON (EST)		UC	RE	TX	VS	VR
•		•	Anderson Land Title Co 317-459-3183		•	•	•	•	
•	•		McGinley Paralegal & Search Services (SOP) 317-630-9721		•	•	•		

CV	CR	PR	UNION (EST)		UC	RE	TX	VS	VR
			See adjoining counties for retrievers						

DT	BK	CV	CR	PR	VANDERBURGH (CST)		UC	RE	TX	VS	VR
•	•	•	•	•	Express Process Service/Investigations (SOP) 800-899-1872		•	•	•	•	•
•	•	•	•	•	Fidelity Search Inc 812-479-8704		•	•	•	•	•
•	•				🗑 Hogan Information Services 405-278-6954						
•		•	•	•	🗑 Summit Documents 502-281-5406		•	•	•	•	

CV	CR	PR	VERMILLION (EST)	UC	RE	TX	VS	VR
•		•	Massey Abstract and Real Estate 317-793-4547	•	•	•		
•	•		McGinley Paralegal & Search Services (SOP) 317-630-9721	•	•	•		

DT	BK	CV	CR	PR	VIGO (EST)	UC	RE	TX	VS	VR
•	•				🏛 Hogan Information Services 405-278-6954					
•		•	•		McGinley Paralegal & Search Services (SOP) 317-630-9721	•	•	•		

CV	CR	PR	WABASH (EST)	UC	RE	TX	VS	VR
•		•	Three Rivers Title Co 219-424-2929	•	•	•	•	

CV	CR	PR	WARREN (EST)	UC	RE	TX	VS	VR
•	•	•	Held Abstract Co Inc 317-762-2457	•	•	•		
•		•	Massey Abstract and Real Estate 317-793-4547	•	•	•		
•	•	•	Tippecanoe Title Services Inc 317-423-2457	•	•	•		

CV	CR	PR	WARRICK (CST)	UC	RE	TX	VS	VR
•	•	•	Fidelity Search Inc 812-479-8704	•	•	•	•	•
•	•		🏛 Summit Documents 502-281-5406	•	•	•	•	

CV	CR	PR	WASHINGTON (EST)	UC	RE	TX	VS	VR
•		•	Salem Title Corporation 812-883-5806	•	•	•	•	

CV	CR	PR	WAYNE (EST)	UC	RE	TX	VS	VR
•		•	Kings Abstract Company Inc 800-757-7762	•	•	•		
•	•		McGinley Paralegal & Search Services (SOP) 317-630-9721	•	•	•		

CV	CR	PR	WELLS (EST)	UC	RE	TX	VS	VR
•		•	Three Rivers Title Co 219-424-2929	•	•	•	•	
•	•	•	Tri-County Land Title 219-589-3139	•	•	•	•	

CV	CR	PR	WHITE (EST)	UC	RE	TX	VS	VR
•	•	•	Tippecanoe Title Services Inc 317-423-2457	•	•	•		

CV	CR	PR	WHITLEY (EST)	UC	RE	TX	VS	VR
•	•	•	Baker, Jami Christensen 800-403-5207	•	•	•		
•	•	•	Gates Land Title Corp 219-244-5127	•	•	•	•	
•	•	•	J-C Investigations (SOP).. 219-262-2832	•	•	•	•	•
•		•	Three Rivers Title Co 219-424-2929	•	•	•	•	

IOWA

	CV	CR	PR	ADAIR (CST)		UC	RE	TX	VS	VR
	•		•	Adair County Abstract 800-798-6129		•	•	•		
	•	•	•	J.R. Investigations (SOP) 515-965-2637		•	•	•	•	•
	•	•	•	Williamson Abstract Co 515-743-2175		•	•	•	•	

	CV	CR	PR	ADAMS (CST)		UC	RE	TX	VS	VR
	•	•	•	J.R. Investigations (SOP) 515-965-2637		•	•	•	•	•
	•	•	•	Nevius, Jean 515-322-3671		•	•	•		

	CV	CR	PR	ALLAMAKEE (CST)		UC	RE	TX	VS	VR
	•	•	•	J.R. Investigations (SOP) 515-965-2637		•	•	•	•	•
	•	•	•	Palmer Abstract Inc 319-568-3488		•	•	•	•	

	CV	CR	PR	APPANOOSE (CST)		UC	RE	TX	VS	VR
	•	•	•	Drake & Jay 515-437-1890		•	•	•	•	
	•	•	•	J.R. Investigations (SOP) 515-965-2637		•	•	•	•	•

	CV	CR	PR	AUDUBON (CST)		UC	RE	TX	VS	VR
	•	•	•	J.R. Investigations (SOP) 515-965-2637		•	•	•	•	•
	•	•	•	Wakelin, Diane K 712-243-2189		•	•	•	•	•

	CV	CR	PR	BENTON (CST)		UC	RE	TX	VS	VR
	•	•	•	Benton County Title Co 319-472-2369		•	•	•	•	
	•	•	•	🏛 Starr Investigations & Security (SOP) 319-393-1007		•	•	•	•	•

	CV	CR	PR	BLACK HAWK (CST)		UC	RE	TX	VS	VR
	•	•	•	Black Hawk Abstract Co 319-291-4000		•	•	•	•	
	•	•	•	🏛 Bob Prins Associates 319-232-4752		•	•	•	•	
	•	•	•	J.R. Investigations (SOP) 515-965-2637		•	•	•	•	•

	CV	CR	PR	BOONE (CST)		UC	RE	TX	VS	VR
	•	•	•	Boone County Abstract Co 515-432-3633		•	•	•	•	
	•	•	•	J.R. Investigations (SOP) 515-965-2637		•	•	•	•	•

	CV	CR	PR	BREMER (CST)		UC	RE	TX	VS	VR
	•	•	•	Bremer County Abstract Co 319-352-2710		•	•	•	•	

	CV	CR	PR	BUCHANAN (CST)		UC	RE	TX	VS	VR
				See adjoining counties for retrievers						

	CV	CR	PR	BUENA VISTA (CST)		UC	RE	TX	VS	VR
	•	•	•	Fritcher Abstract Co 712-732-2732		•	•	•	•	

	CV	CR	PR	BUTLER (CST)		UC	RE	TX	VS	VR
				See adjoining counties for retrievers						

	CV	CR	PR	CALHOUN (CST)		UC	RE	TX	VS	VR
	•	•	•	J.R. Investigations (SOP) 515-965-2637		•	•	•	•	•

	CV	CR	PR	CARROLL (CST)		UC	RE	TX	VS	VR
	•	•	•	J.R. Investigations (SOP) 515-965-2637		•	•	•	•	•

	CV	CR	PR	CASS (CST)		UC	RE	TX	VS	VR
	•	•	•	Cass County Abstract Co 712-243-2136		•	•	•	•	
	•	•	•	J.R. Investigations (SOP) 515-965-2637		•	•	•	•	•
	•	•	•	Wakelin, Diane K 712-243-2189		•	•	•	•	•

	CV	CR	PR	CEDAR (CST)		UC	RE	TX	VS	VR
	•	•	•	J.R. Investigations (SOP) 515-965-2637		•	•	•	•	•
	•	•	•	Land Title Corp 319-886-6915		•	•	•	•	
	•	•	•	🏛 Starr Investigations & Security (SOP) 319-393-1007		•	•	•	•	•

CV	CR	PR	CERRO GORDO (CST)		UC	RE	TX	VS	VR
•	•	•	Cerro Gordo Abstract Co 515-423-1145		•	•	•	•	
•	•	•	Intra-Lex Investigations Inc (SOP) 712-233-1639		•	•	•	•	
•	•	•	J.R. Investigations (SOP) 515-965-2637		•	•	•	•	•

CV	CR	PR	CHEROKEE (CST)		UC	RE	TX	VS	VR
•	•	•	First Abstract and Loan Co 712-225-3612		•	•	•		
•	•	•	Intra-Lex Investigations Inc (SOP) 712-233-1639		•	•	•	•	

CV	CR	PR	CHICKASAW (CST)		UC	RE	TX	VS	VR
•	•	•	G T Murphy Abstractor 515-394-4291		•	•	•	•	
•	•	•	J.R. Investigations (SOP) 515-965-2637		•	•	•	•	•

CV	CR	PR	CLARKE (CST)		UC	RE	TX	VS	VR
•	•	•	Banta Abstract Co 515-342-2029		•	•	•	•	
•	•	•	J.R. Investigations (SOP) 515-965-2637		•	•	•	•	•

CV	CR	PR	CLAY (CST)		UC	RE	TX	VS	VR
•	•		Fransen, Barbara 515-749-2761						
•	•	•	Intra-Lex Investigations Inc (SOP) 712-233-1639		•	•	•	•	
•	•	•	J.R. Investigations (SOP) 515-965-2637		•	•	•	•	•
•	•	•	Security Land Title Co 712-262-1074		•	•	•		

CV	CR	PR	CLAYTON (CST)		UC	RE	TX	VS	VR
•	•	•	Clayton County Abstract Co 319-245-1430		•	•	•	•	

CV	CR	PR	CLINTON (CST)		UC	RE	TX	VS	VR
•		•	Abstract & Title Guaranty Co 800-483-2842		•	•	•	•	
•	•	•	J.R. Investigations (SOP) 515-965-2637		•	•	•	•	•

CV	CR	PR	CRAWFORD (CST)		UC	RE	TX	VS	VR
•		•	Crawford County Abstract Co 712-263-5626			•	•	•	
•	•	•	J.R. Investigations (SOP) 515-965-2637		•	•	•	•	•

CV	CR	PR	DALLAS (CST)		UC	RE	TX	VS	VR
•	•	•	J.R. Investigations (SOP) 515-965-2637		•	•	•	•	•

CV	CR	PR	DAVIS (CST)		UC	RE	TX	VS	VR
•	•	•	Ball Abstracting 515-664-3188			•	•	•	
•	•	•	J.R. Investigations (SOP) 515-965-2637		•	•	•	•	•

CV	CR	PR	DECATUR (CST)		UC	RE	TX	VS	VR
•	•	•	Elson & Fulton Abstractors 515-446-4621		•	•	•	•	
•	•	•	J.R. Investigations (SOP) 515-965-2637		•	•	•	•	•

CV	CR	PR	DELAWARE (CST)		UC	RE	TX	VS	VR
•	•	•	Delaware County Abstract Co 319-927-4858		•	•	•	•	

CV	CR	PR	DES MOINES (CST)		UC	RE	TX	VS	VR
•	•	•	J.R. Investigations (SOP) 515-965-2637		•	•	•	•	•

CV	CR	PR	DICKINSON (CST)		UC	RE	TX	VS	VR
•	•	•	Cornell Abstract Co 712-336-3845		•	•	•	•	
•	•	•	Intra-Lex Investigations Inc (SOP) 712-233-1639		•	•	•	•	

CV	CR	PR	DUBUQUE (CST)		UC	RE	TX	VS	VR
•		•	Abeln Abstract Co 319-582-7148		•	•	•	•	
•	•	•	J.R. Investigations (SOP) 515-965-2637		•	•	•	•	•

CV	CR	PR	EMMET (CST)		UC	RE	TX	VS	VR
•	•	•	Estherville Abstract Co 712-362-3148		•	•	•	•	

CV	CR	PR	FAYETTE (CST)		UC	RE	TX	VS	VR

See adjoining counties for retrievers ....

CV	CR	PR	FLOYD (CST)		UC	RE	TX	VS	VR
•	•	•	Iowa Title & Realty Co 515-228-1515		•	•	•	•	
•	•	•	J.R. Investigations (SOP).......... 515-965-2637		•	•	•	•	•

CV	CR	PR	FRANKLIN (CST)		UC	RE	TX	VS	VR
•	•	•	Franklin County Abstract Co 515-456-4551		•	•	•	•	

CV	CR	PR	FREMONT (CST)		UC	RE	TX	VS	VR
•	•	•	J.R. Investigations (SOP).......... 515-965-2637		•	•	•	•	•
•	•	•	Larock, Kris 712-374-3019		•	•	•	•	•

CV	CR	PR	GREENE (CST)		UC	RE	TX	VS	VR
•	•	•	Greene County Abstract Company Inc 515-386-2191		•	•	•	•	
•	•	•	J.R. Investigations (SOP).......... 515-965-2637		•	•	•	•	•

CV	CR	PR	GRUNDY (CST)		UC	RE	TX	VS	VR
•	•	•	Community Title Co 319-824-3123		•	•	•	•	

CV	CR	PR	GUTHRIE (CST)		UC	RE	TX	VS	VR
•		•	Guthrie County Abstract 515-747-3705		•	•	•	•	

CV	CR	PR	HAMILTON (CST)		UC	RE	TX	VS	VR
•	•	•	J.R. Investigations (SOP).......... 515-965-2637		•	•	•	•	•
•	•	•	Neuroth, Tim 515-832-3156		•	•	•	•	

CV	CR	PR	HANCOCK (CST)		UC	RE	TX	VS	VR
•	•	•	Hancock County Abstract Co 515-923-2454		•	•	•		
•	•	•	Intra-Lex Investigations Inc (SOP).......... 712-233-1639		•	•	•	•	
•	•	•	J.R. Investigations (SOP).......... 515-965-2637		•	•	•	•	•

CV	CR	PR	HARDIN (CST)		UC	RE	TX	VS	VR
•	•	•	Munsigner, Maxine 515-858-3585		•	•	•		

CV	CR	PR	HARRISON (CST)		UC	RE	TX	VS	VR
•	•	•	Coit Enterprises 402-451-0462		•	•	•	•	•
•	•	•	Harrison County Title and Guaranty 712-644-2703			•	•		
•	•	•	PROTEC Systems Inc 800-691-0919			•	•	•	
•	•	•	🏛 Thomas, Donna 402-339-7291			•	•	•	

CV	CR	PR	HENRY (CST)		UC	RE	TX	VS	VR
•	•	•	Henry County Abstract Co 319-385-9017		•	•	•	•	

CV	CR	PR	HOWARD (CST)		UC	RE	TX	VS	VR
•	•	•	Howard County Abstract & Title Co 319-547-4944		•	•	•	•	

CV	CR	PR	HUMBOLDT (CST)		UC	RE	TX	VS	VR
•	•	•	Olson Humboldt County Abstract 515-332-2353		•	•	•	•	

CV	CR	PR	IDA (CST)		UC	RE	TX	VS	VR
•	•	•	Ida County Abstract Co 712-364-2287		•	•	•	•	
•	•	•	Intra-Lex Investigations Inc (SOP).......... 712-233-1639		•	•	•	•	

CV	CR	PR	IOWA (CST)		UC	RE	TX	VS	VR
•	•	•	Iowa County Abstract Company 319-642-7321		•	•	•		
•	•	•	🏛 Starr Investigations & Security (SOP) 319-393-1007		•	•	•	•	•

CV	CR	PR	JACKSON (CST)		UC	RE	TX	VS	VR
•	•	•	Iowa Title & Guaranty Co 319-652-6081		•	•	•	•	
•	•	•	J.R. Investigations (SOP).......... 515-965-2637		•	•	•	•	•

CV	CR	PR	JASPER (CST)		UC	RE	TX	VS	VR
•	•	•	J.R. Investigations (SOP).......... 515-965-2637		•	•	•	•	•

		CV	CR	PR	JEFFERSON (CST)	UC	RE	TX	VS	VR
		•	•	•	🏛 Jefferson County Abstract 515-472-5052	•	•	•		

		CV	CR	PR	JOHNSON (CST)	UC	RE	TX	VS	VR
		•	•	•	J.R. Investigations (SOP)................. 515-965-2637	•	•	•	•	•
		•	•	•	Reliance Title Services 319-354-6505	•	•	•	•	
		•	•	•	🏛 Starr Investigations & Security (SOP) 319-393-1007	•	•	•		•

		CV	CR	PR	JONES (CST)	UC	RE	TX	VS	VR
		•	•	•	Abstract & Title Services Inc 319-462-4828	•	•	•	•	
		•	•	•	J.R. Investigations (SOP)................. 515-965-2637	•	•	•	•	•
		•	•	•	🏛 Starr Investigations & Security (SOP) 319-393-1007	•	•	•	•	•

		CV	CR	PR	KEOKUK (CST)	UC	RE	TX	VS	VR
		•	•	•	Daniels, Mabel 515-673-6507	•	•	•	•	
		•	•	•	J.R. Investigations (SOP)................. 515-965-2637	•	•	•	•	•

		CV	CR	PR	KOSSUTH (CST)	UC	RE	TX	VS	VR
		•	•	•	Buchanan Abstract Co 515-295-3745		•	•		
		•	•	•	J.R. Investigations (SOP)................. 515-965-2637	•	•	•		•

		CV	CR	PR	LEE (CST)	UC	RE	TX	VS	VR
		•		•	American Abstract and Title 319-372-8110	•	•	•	•	

DT	BK	CV	CR	PR	LINN (CST)	UC	RE	TX	VS	VR
•	•	•	•	•	J.R. Investigations (SOP)................. 515-965-2637	•	•	•	•	•
•	•	•	•	•	🏛 Starr Investigations & Security (SOP) 319-393-1007	•	•	•	•	•
•	•	•	•	•	United Title Services Inc 319-365-1478	•	•	•	•	

		CV	CR	PR	LOUISA (CST)	UC	RE	TX	VS	VR
		•	•	•	J.R. Investigations (SOP)................. 515-965-2637	•	•	•	•	•
		•	•	•	Street, Keith 319-523-8164		•		•	

		CV	CR	PR	LUCAS (CST)	UC	RE	TX	VS	VR
		•	•	•	Chariton Abstract Co 515-774-2677	•	•	•	•	
		•	•	•	J.R. Investigations (SOP)................. 515-965-2637	•	•	•	•	•

		CV	CR	PR	LYON (CST)	UC	RE	TX	VS	VR
		•	•	•	Dirks, Lewis 605-331-6022	•	•	•	•	
		•	•	•	Lyon County Title 712-472-3758	•	•	•	•	

		CV	CR	PR	MADISON (CST)	UC	RE	TX	VS	VR
		•	•	•	J.R. Investigations (SOP)................. 515-965-2637	•	•	•	•	•
		•	•	•	Security Abstract and Title Inc 515-462-1691	•	•	•	•	•

		CV	CR	PR	MAHASKA (CST)	UC	RE	TX	VS	VR
		•	•	•	Daniels, Mabel 515-673-6507	•	•	•	•	
		•	•	•	J.R. Investigations (SOP)................. 515-965-2637	•	•	•	•	•
		•	•	•	Mahaska Title - Johnson Abstract Co 515-673-5666	•	•	•	•	

		CV	CR	PR	MARION (CST)	UC	RE	TX	VS	VR
		•	•	•	J.R. Investigations (SOP)................. 515-965-2637	•	•	•	•	•
		•	•	•	Marion County Abstract Co 515-842-3518	•	•	•	•	

		CV	CR	PR	MARSHALL (CST)	UC	RE	TX	VS	VR
		•	•	•	J.R. Investigations (SOP)................. 515-965-2637	•	•	•	•	•
		•	•	•	Marshall County Abstract Company 515-752-5358	•	•	•	•	

		CV	CR	PR	MILLS (CST)	UC	RE	TX	VS	VR
		•	•	•	Coit Enterprises 402-451-0462	•	•	•	•	•
		•	•	•	PROTEC Systems Inc 800-691-0919		•	•	•	
		•	•	•	🏛 Thomas, Donna 402-339-7291	•	•	•	•	

CV	CR	PR	MITCHELL (CST)	UC	RE	TX	VS	VR
•	•	•	Mitchell County Abstract Co 515-732-4571	•	•	•		

CV	CR	PR	MONONA (CST)	UC	RE	TX	VS	VR
•	•	•	Cutler, Sue 712-452-2021	•	•	•	•	
•	•	•	Intra-Lex Investigations Inc (SOP) 712-233-1639	•	•	•	•	

CV	CR	PR	MONROE (CST)	UC	RE	TX	VS	VR
•	•	•	Graham Abstract Co 515-932-7156	•	•	•	•	
•	•	•	J.R. Investigations (SOP) 515-965-2637	•	•	•	•	•

CV	CR	PR	MONTGOMERY (CST)	UC	RE	TX	VS	VR
•	•	•	J.R. Investigations (SOP) 515-965-2637	•	•	•	•	•
•	•	•	🗑 Young, Beth 712-767-2510	•	•	•	•	•

CV	CR	PR	MUSCATINE (CST)	UC	RE	TX	VS	VR
•	•	•	J.R. Investigations (SOP) 515-965-2637	•	•	•	•	•
•	•	•	Legal Abstract Co 319-263-3171	•	•	•	•	

CV	CR	PR	O'BRIEN (CST)	UC	RE	TX	VS	VR
			See adjoining counties for retrievers					

CV	CR	PR	OSCEOLA (CST)	UC	RE	TX	VS	VR
•	•	•	Dirks, Lewis 605-331-6022	•	•	•	•	
•	•	•	The Title Co Inc 712-754-2284	•	•	•	•	

CV	CR	PR	PAGE (CST)	UC	RE	TX	VS	VR
•	•	•	Page County Abstract and Title Company 712-542-3613	•	•	•		
•	•	•	🗑 Young, Beth 712-767-2510	•	•	•	•	•

CV	CR	PR	PALO ALTO (CST)	UC	RE	TX	VS	VR
•	•	•	Palo Alto County Abstract Co 712-852-4313	•	•	•	•	

CV	CR	PR	PLYMOUTH (CST)	UC	RE	TX	VS	VR
•	•	•	Intra-Lex Investigations Inc (SOP) 712-233-1639	•	•	•	•	
		•	Plymouth County Abstract 712-546-4564	•	•	•		

CV	CR	PR	POCAHONTAS (CST)	UC	RE	TX	VS	VR
•	•	•	J.R. Investigations (SOP) 515-965-2637	•	•	•	•	•
•	•	•	Peduska, Paul 712-335-4257	•	•	•	•	

DT	BK	CV	CR	PR	POLK (CAPITAL) (CST)	UC	RE	TX	VS	VR
•	•				🗑 Hogan Information Services 405-278-6954					
•	•	•	•	•	J.R. Investigations (SOP) 515-965-2637	•	•	•	•	•
•	•	•	•	•	Process Associates 515-244-2488	•	•	•	•	
•	•	•	•	•	🗑 Search Network Ltd 800-383-5050	•		•		

DT		CV	CR	PR	POTTAWATTAMIE (CST)	UC	RE	TX	VS	VR
•		•	•	•	Coit Enterprises 402-451-0462	•	•	•	•	•
•		•	•	•	J.R. Investigations (SOP) 515-965-2637	•	•	•	•	•
		•	•	•	PROTEC Systems Inc 800-691-0919		•	•	•	
•		•	•	•	🗑 Thomas, Donna 402-339-7291	•	•	•	•	

CV	CR	PR	POWESHIEK (CST)	UC	RE	TX	VS	VR
	•		Pittman, Julie 515-644-5114		•	•		

CV	CR	PR	RINGGOLD (CST)	UC	RE	TX	VS	VR
•	•	•	J.R. Investigations (SOP) 515-965-2637	•	•	•	•	•
•	•	•	Ringgold County Abstract Co Inc 515-464-3902	•	•	•	•	

CV	CR	PR	SAC (CST)	UC	RE	TX	VS	VR
•	•	•	J.R. Investigations (SOP) 515-965-2637	•	•	•	•	•
•	•	•	Sac County Abstract Co 712-662-7317	•	•	•	•	

SCOTT (CST)

DT	CV	CR	PR		UC	RE	TX	VS	VR
	•	•	•	Bettendorf Abstract Co ... 319-359-3646		•	•	•	
•	•	•	•	J M White Investigations (SOP) ... 309-794-1499	•	•	•	•	•
•	•	•	•	J.R. Investigations (SOP) ... 515-965-2637	•	•	•	•	•

SHELBY (CST)

CV	CR	PR		UC	RE	TX	VS	VR
•	•	•	J.R. Investigations (SOP) ... 515-965-2637	•	•	•	•	•
•	•	•	Ouren Title Inc ... 712-755-2174	•	•	•		

SIOUX (CST)

CV	CR	PR		UC	RE	TX	VS	VR
•	•	•	Dirks, Lewis ... 605-331-6022	•	•	•	•	
•	•	•	Intra-Lex Investigations Inc (SOP) ... 712-233-1639	•	•	•	•	
•	•	•	J.R. Investigations (SOP) ... 515-965-2637	•	•	•	•	•

STORY (CST)

CV	CR	PR		UC	RE	TX	VS	VR
•	•	•	Batman-Sayers Abstract & Title Co ... 515-382-4127	•	•	•	•	
•	•	•	J.R. Investigations (SOP) ... 515-965-2637	•	•	•	•	

TAMA (CST)

CV	CR	PR		UC	RE	TX	VS	VR
•	•	•	J.R. Investigations (SOP) ... 515-965-2637	•	•	•	•	•
•	•	•	Tama County Abstract ... 515-484-4386	•	•	•	•	

TAYLOR (CST)

CV	CR	PR		UC	RE	TX	VS	VR
•	•	•	J.R. Investigations (SOP) ... 515-965-2637	•	•	•	•	•
•	•	•	Park, June ... 712-523-3490	•	•	•	•	

UNION (CST)

CV	CR	PR		UC	RE	TX	VS	VR
•	•	•	J.R. Investigations (SOP) ... 515-965-2637	•	•	•	•	•

VAN BUREN (CST)

CV	CR	PR		UC	RE	TX	VS	VR
•	•	•	Van Buren Abstract Association ... 319-293-3783	•	•	•	•	

WAPELLO (CST)

CV	CR	PR		UC	RE	TX	VS	VR
•	•	•	Box & Box ... 515-682-4512	•	•	•		
•	•	•	J.R. Investigations (SOP) ... 515-965-2637	•	•	•	•	•

WARREN (CST)

CV	CR	PR		UC	RE	TX	VS	VR
•	•	•	J.R. Investigations (SOP) ... 515-965-2637	•	•	•	•	•
•	•	•	Warren County Abstract Company ... 515-961-7479	•	•	•	•	

WASHINGTON (CST)

CV	CR	PR		UC	RE	TX	VS	VR
			See adjoining counties for retrievers ...					

WAYNE (CST)

CV	CR	PR		UC	RE	TX	VS	VR
•	•	•	J.R. Investigations (SOP) ... 515-965-2637	•	•	•	•	•
•	•	•	John H Rider Abstract & Real Estate ... 515-872-1966	•	•	•		

WEBSTER (CST)

CV	CR	PR		UC	RE	TX	VS	VR
•	•	•	J.R. Investigations (SOP) ... 515-965-2637	•	•	•	•	•
•	•	•	Webster County-Butler & Rhodes Abstract ... 515-573-3341	•	•	•	•	

WINNEBAGO (CST)

CV	CR	PR		UC	RE	TX	VS	VR
•	•	•	Intra-Lex Investigations Inc (SOP) ... 712-233-1639	•	•	•	•	
•	•	•	J.R. Investigations (SOP) ... 515-965-2637	•	•	•	•	•
•	•	•	Winnebago County Abstract ... 515-582-3101	•	•	•		

WINNESHIEK (CST)

CV	CR	PR		UC	RE	TX	VS	VR
•	•	•	J.R. Investigations (SOP) ... 515-965-2637	•	•	•	•	•

WOODBURY (CST)

DT	CV	CR	PR		UC	RE	TX	VS	VR
	•	•	•	Intra-Lex Investigations Inc (SOP) ... 712-233-1639	•	•	•	•	
•	•	•	•	J.R. Investigations (SOP) ... 515-965-2637	•	•	•	•	•

CV CR PR	WORTH (CST)	UC RE TX VS VR
● ● ●	Intra-Lex Investigations Inc (SOP) 712-233-1639	● ● ● ●
● ● ●	Worth County Abstract Co Inc 515-324-1761	● ● ●

CV CR PR	WRIGHT (CST)	UC RE TX VS VR
● ● ●	Wright County Land Title Co 800-532-2259	● ● ● ●

SUMMARY OF CODES

COURT RECORDS

CODE	GOVERNMENT AGENCY	TYPE OF INFORMATION
DT	US District Court	Federal civil and criminal cases
BK	Bankruptcy Court	United States bankruptcy cases
CV	Civil Court	Municipal, county and state level civil cases
CR	Criminal Court	Municipal, county and state level criminal cases
PR	Probate Court	Wills and estate cases

COUNTY RECORDS

CODE	GOVERNMENT AGENCY	TYPE OF INFORMATION
UC	UCC Filing Office	Uniform Commercial Code and other personal property liens
RE	Recorder of Deeds	Real property transactions and liens
TX	Tax Assessor	Real property tax information
VS	Vital Records Office	Vital statistics—birth, death, marriage, divorce, etc.
VR	Voter Registration Office	Voter registration and campaign contribution information

- "CODE" designates the agency and type of information obtainable in each county from a retriever.
- The time zone for each county is abbreviated as follows: EST—Eastern Standard Time; CST—Central; MST—Mountain; PST—Pacific; AK—Alaska; HT—Hawaii.
- ▥—This symbol designates a Public Record Retriever Network member.
- "(SOP)" after the retriever name designates Service of Process.
- Individual retrievers without a company name are listed in order of their last name.
- US District and Bankruptcy courts are indicated only in the counties where courts are located.

KANSAS

CV	CR	PR	ALLEN (CST)	UC	RE	TX	VS	VR
•	•		🏛 Research Information Services Inc 800-522-3884	•	•	•		
•	•	•	Street Abstract Co 316-625-2421	•	•	•	•	

CV	CR	PR	ANDERSON (CST)	UC	RE	TX	VS	VR
•	•		🏛 Research Information Services Inc 800-522-3884	•	•	•		

CV	CR	PR	ATCHISON (CST)	UC	RE	TX	VS	VR
•	•		🏛 Research Information Services Inc 800-522-3884	•	•	•		

CV	CR	PR	BARBER (CST)	UC	RE	TX	VS	VR
•	•		🏛 Research Information Services Inc 800-522-3884	•	•	•		
•		•	Slamal & Swayden Inc 316-886-5141	•	•	•	•	

CV	CR	PR	BARTON (CST)	UC	RE	TX	VS	VR
•		•	Barton County Abstract and Title Co 316-793-3781	•	•	•		
•	•	•	Kansas Investigative Services Inc (SOP) 316-267-1356	•	•	•	•	•
•	•		🏛 Research Information Services Inc 800-522-3884	•	•	•		

CV	CR	PR	BOURBON (CST)	UC	RE	TX	VS	VR
•	•	•	Linn County Abstract Co 888-795-2949	•	•	•		
•	•		🏛 Research Information Services Inc 800-522-3884	•	•	•		

CV	CR	PR	BROWN (CST)	UC	RE	TX	VS	VR
•	•	•	Brown County Title Co 913-742-7103	•	•	•		
•	•		🏛 Research Information Services Inc 800-522-3884	•	•	•		

CV	CR	PR	BUTLER (CST)	UC	RE	TX	VS	VR
•	•	•	Allen Abstract Co 316-321-2410	•	•	•	•	
•	•	•	I Information Services (SOP) 800-658-1688	•	•	•	•	•
•	•	•	Investigations LLC (SOP) 800-658-1688	•	•	•	•	•
•	•	•	Kansas Investigative Services Inc (SOP) 316-267-1356	•	•	•	•	•
•	•		🏛 Research Information Services Inc 800-522-3884	•	•	•		

CV	CR	PR	CHASE (CST)	UC	RE	TX	VS	VR
•	•	•	Moon Abstract Co 316-342-1917	•	•	•	•	
•	•		🏛 Research Information Services Inc 800-522-3884	•	•	•		

CV	CR	PR	CHAUTAUQUA (CST)	UC	RE	TX	VS	VR
•	•	•	Chautauqua County Abstract Co Inc 316-725-3215	•	•	•	•	
•	•		🏛 Research Information Services Inc 800-522-3884	•	•	•		

CV	CR	PR	CHEROKEE (CST)	UC	RE	TX	VS	VR
•	•	•	Barrett Title Co 316-856-2355	•	•	•	•	
•	•	•	🏛 Kunkel, Joan & Kelli (SOP) 417-358-6494	•	•	•	•	•
•	•	•	NDXR Inc 800-687-5080	•	•	•	•	
•	•		🏛 Research Information Services Inc 800-522-3884	•	•	•		

CV	CR	PR	CHEYENNE (CST)	UC	RE	TX	VS	VR
•	•		🏛 Research Information Services Inc 800-522-3884	•	•	•		
•	•	•	The R M Jaqua Abstract Co 913-332-3041	•	•	•		

CV	CR	PR	CLARK (CST)	UC	RE	TX	VS	VR
•		•	Ashland Abstract & Title Co 316-635-2716	•	•	•	•	
•	•	•	Credit Bureau Services Inc (SOP) 316-275-6500	•	•	•	•	
•	•		🏛 Research Information Services Inc 800-522-3884	•	•	•		

CV	CR	PR	CLAY (CST)	UC	RE	TX	VS	VR
•	•	•	Attorney's Title Co 913-243-1357	•	•	•	•	
•	•	•	Eric H Swenson Co Abstracters 913-632-2535	•	•	•	•	
•	•		🏛 Research Information Services Inc 800-522-3884	•	•	•		

CV	CR	PR	CLOUD (CST)	UC	RE	TX	VS	VR
•	•	•	Attorney's Title Co 913-243-1357	•	•	•	•	
•	•		🏛 Research Information Services Inc 800-522-3884	•	•	•		

CV	CR	PR	COFFEY (CST)	UC	RE	TX	VS	VR
•	•	•	Moon Abstract Co 316-342-1917	•	•	•	•	
•	•		🏛 Research Information Services Inc 800-522-3884	•	•	•		
•	•	•	Street Abstract Co 316-625-2421	•	•	•	•	

CV	CR	PR	COMANCHE (CST)	UC	RE	TX	VS	VR
•		•	Comanche Abstract and Title Co 316-582-2125	•	•	•		
•	•		🏛 Research Information Services Inc 800-522-3884	•	•	•		

CV	CR	PR	COWLEY (CST)	UC	RE	TX	VS	VR
•	•	•	Barbour Title Co 316-221-0430	•	•	•	•	
•	•	•	Kansas Investigative Services Inc (SOP) 316-267-1356	•	•	•	•	•
•	•		🏛 Research Information Services Inc 800-522-3884	•	•	•		

CV	CR	PR	CRAWFORD (CST)	UC	RE	TX	VS	VR
•	•	•	🏛 Kunkel, Joan & Kelli (SOP) 417-358-6494	•	•	•	•	•
•	•	•	NDXR Inc 800-687-5080	•	•	•	•	
•	•		🏛 Research Information Services Inc 800-522-3884	•	•	•		

CV	CR	PR	DECATUR (CST)	UC	RE	TX	VS	VR
•	•	•	🏛 Farmers Title and Abstract Co 913-475-2381	•	•	•		
•	•	•	First Insurance Agency of Hoxie Inc 913-675-3252	•	•	•		
•	•		🏛 Research Information Services Inc 800-522-3884	•	•	•		

CV	CR	PR	DICKINSON (CST)	UC	RE	TX	VS	VR
•	•		🏛 Research Information Services Inc 800-522-3884	•	•	•		
•		•	Wyatt Land Title Services Inc 913-263-7722	•	•	•		

CV	CR	PR	DONIPHAN (CST)	UC	RE	TX	VS	VR
•	•	•	Guier Abstract & Title Co 913-985-3562	•	•	•	•	
•	•		🏛 Research Information Services Inc 800-522-3884	•	•	•		

CV	CR	PR	DOUGLAS (CST)	UC	RE	TX	VS	VR
•	•		🏛 Future Security Concepts 800-398-3051				•	
•	•	•	🏛 Hicks Information (SOP) 913-749-1898	•	•	•	•	•
•	•	•	Mercury Messengers Inc (SOP) 913-357-0078	•	•	•	•	
•	•		🏛 Research Information Services Inc 800-522-3884	•	•	•		

CV	CR	PR	EDWARDS (CST)	UC	RE	TX	VS	VR
•	•		🏛 Research Information Services Inc 800-522-3884	•	•	•		
•		•	Richardson Abstract Co Inc 316-659-2592	•	•	•		

CV	CR	PR	ELK (CST)	UC	RE	TX	VS	VR
•	•	•	Elk County Abstract & Title Co 316-374-2500	•	•	•	•	
•	•		🏛 Research Information Services Inc 800-522-3884	•	•	•		

CV	CR	PR	ELLIS (CST)	UC	RE	TX	VS	VR
•	•	•	Ellis County Abstract & Title Co 800-794-2690	•	•	•	•	
•	•	•	Kansas Investigative Services Inc (SOP) 316-267-1356	•	•	•	•	•
•	•		🏛 Research Information Services Inc 800-522-3884	•	•	•		

CV	CR	PR	ELLSWORTH (CST)	UC	RE	TX	VS	VR
•	•	•	G & H Abstract 800-640-7390	•	•	•	•	
•	•	•	Kansas Investigative Services Inc (SOP) 316-267-1356	•	•	•	•	•
•	•		🏛 Research Information Services Inc 800-522-3884	•	•	•		

CV	CR	PR	FINNEY (CST)	UC	RE	TX	VS	VR
•		•	Campbell Abstract Inc 316-275-7441	•	•	•		
•	•	•	Credit Bureau Services Inc (SOP) 316-275-6500	•	•	•	•	
•	•		🏛 Research Information Services Inc 800-522-3884	•	•	•		

CV	CR	PR	FORD (CST)		UC	RE	TX	VS	VR
•	•	•	Credit Bureau Services Inc (SOP)................316-275-6500		•	•	•	•	
•	•	•	Gray County Abstract Co Inc 316-855-3128		•	•	•		
•	•	•	Kansas Investigative Services Inc (SOP)................316-267-1356		•	•	•	•	•
•	•		🏛 Research Information Services Inc 800-522-3884		•	•	•		

CV	CR	PR	FRANKLIN (CST)		UC	RE	TX	VS	VR
•	•	•	Haley Abstract & Title Co 913-242-2457		•	•	•	•	
•	•	•	🏛 Hicks Information (SOP)................913-749-1898		•	•	•	•	•
•	•		🏛 Research Information Services Inc 800-522-3884		•	•	•		

CV	CR	PR	GEARY (CST)		UC	RE	TX	VS	VR
•	•		🏛 Information Retrieval Services 913-238-8753		•		•		
•	•		🏛 Research Information Services Inc 800-522-3884		•	•	•		

CV	CR	PR	GOVE (CST)		UC	RE	TX	VS	VR
•	•	•	First Insurance Agency of Hoxie Inc 913-675-3252		•	•	•		
•	•		🏛 Research Information Services Inc 800-522-3884		•	•	•		

CV	CR	PR	GRAHAM (CST)		UC	RE	TX	VS	VR
•	•	•	First Insurance Agency of Hoxie Inc 913-675-3252		•	•	•		
•	•		🏛 Research Information Services Inc 800-522-3884		•	•	•		

CV	CR	PR	GRANT (CST)		UC	RE	TX	VS	VR
•	•	•	American Title & Abstract Specialists 316-356-2100		•	•	•	•	
•	•	•	American Title & Abstract Specialists 316-624-9111		•	•	•	•	
•	•	•	PC Fraze Abstract Co 316-384-7828		•	•	•	•	
•	•		🏛 Research Information Services Inc 800-522-3884		•	•	•		

CV	CR	PR	GRAY (CST)		UC	RE	TX	VS	VR
•	•	•	Credit Bureau Services Inc (SOP)................316-275-6500		•	•	•	•	
•	•	•	Gray County Abstract Co Inc 316-855-3128		•	•	•		
•	•		🏛 Research Information Services Inc 800-522-3884		•	•	•		

CV	CR	PR	GREELEY (MST)		UC	RE	TX	VS	VR
•	•		🏛 Research Information Services Inc 800-522-3884		•	•	•		

CV	CR	PR	GREENWOOD (CST)		UC	RE	TX	VS	VR
•	•	•	Moon Abstract Co 316-342-1917		•	•	•		
•	•		🏛 Research Information Services Inc 800-522-3884		•	•	•		

CV	CR	PR	HAMILTON (MST)		UC	RE	TX	VS	VR
•	•	•	PC Fraze Abstract Co 316-384-7828		•	•	•	•	
•	•		🏛 Research Information Services Inc 800-522-3884		•	•	•		

CV	CR	PR	HARPER (CST)		UC	RE	TX	VS	VR
•	•		🏛 Research Information Services Inc 800-522-3884		•	•	•		

CV	CR	PR	HARVEY (CST)		UC	RE	TX	VS	VR
•	•	•	Hutchinson Title Co 316-669-8289		•	•	•	•	
•	•	•	I Information Services (SOP)................800-658-1688		•	•	•	•	•
•	•	•	Investigations LLC (SOP)................800-658-1688		•	•	•	•	•
•	•	•	Kansas Investigative Services Inc (SOP)................316-267-1356		•	•	•	•	•
•		•	Regier Agency Inc 316-283-2750		•	•	•		
•	•		🏛 Research Information Services Inc 800-522-3884		•	•	•		

CV	CR	PR	HASKELL (CST)		UC	RE	TX	VS	VR
•	•	•	Haskell County Abstract and Title 316-675-2322		•	•	•	•	
•	•		🏛 Research Information Services Inc 800-522-3884		•	•	•		

CV	CR	PR	HODGEMAN (CST)		UC	RE	TX	VS	VR
•	•	•	Hodgeman County Abstract & Title 316-357-8328		•	•	•	•	
•	•		🏛 Research Information Services Inc 800-522-3884		•	•	•		

CV	CR	PR	JACKSON (CST)	UC	RE	TX	VS	VR
•	•		🛆 Research Information Services Inc 800-522-3884	•	•	•		
•	•	•	🛆 Title Abstract Co 913-364-2040	•	•	•		

CV	CR	PR	JEFFERSON (CST)	UC	RE	TX	VS	VR
•	•	•	Finley Abstract & Title Co 913-863-2271	•	•	•	•	
•	•	•	🛆 Hicks Information (SOP) 913-749-1898	•	•	•	•	•
•	•		🛆 Research Information Services Inc 800-522-3884	•	•	•		

CV	CR	PR	JEWELL (CST)	UC	RE	TX	VS	VR
•	•	•	Miller, Gail L 913-378-3128	•	•	•		
•	•		🛆 Research Information Services Inc 800-522-3884	•	•	•		
•		•	Weltmer Law Office 913-378-3172	•	•	•	•	

CV	CR	PR	JOHNSON (CST)	UC	RE	TX	VS	VR
•	•		🛆 Clarence M Kelley and Associates (SOP) 816-756-2458					
•	•	•	Executive Investigative Services (SOP) 913-764-9484	•	•	•	•	•
•	•		🛆 Future Security Concepts 800-398-3051				•	
•	•		🛆 RSI 800-633-6125	•	•	•	•	
•	•		🛆 Research Information Services Inc 800-522-3884	•	•	•		
•	•	•	Silk Attorney Service 913-432-2755	•	•	•	•	

CV	CR	PR	KEARNY (CST)	UC	RE	TX	VS	VR
•	•	•	PC Fraze Abstract Co 316-384-7828	•	•	•	•	
•	•		🛆 Research Information Services Inc 800-522-3884	•	•	•		

CV	CR	PR	KINGMAN (CST)	UC	RE	TX	VS	VR
•	•	•	I Information Services (SOP) 800-658-1688	•	•	•	•	•
•	•	•	Investigations LLC (SOP) 800-658-1688	•	•	•	•	•
•		•	Kingman Abstract and Title Co Inc 316-532-2011	•	•	•		
•	•		🛆 Research Information Services Inc 800-522-3884	•	•	•		

CV	CR	PR	KIOWA (CST)	UC	RE	TX	VS	VR
•	•	•	Church & Grau 316-723-2552	•	•	•		
•	•		🛆 Research Information Services Inc 800-522-3884	•	•	•		

CV	CR	PR	LABETTE (CST)	UC	RE	TX	VS	VR
•	•	•	🛆 Kunkel, Joan & Kelli (SOP) 417-358-6494	•	•	•	•	•
•	•		🛆 Research Information Services Inc 800-522-3884	•	•	•		

CV	CR	PR	LANE (CST)	UC	RE	TX	VS	VR
•	•	•	Credit Bureau Services Inc (SOP) 316-275-6500	•	•	•	•	
•	•	•	Lane County Abstract Co Inc 316-397-5911	•	•	•		
•	•		🛆 Research Information Services Inc 800-522-3884	•	•	•		

CV	CR	PR	LEAVENWORTH (CST)	UC	RE	TX	VS	VR
•	•	•	🛆 Hicks Information (SOP) 913-749-1898	•	•	•	•	•
•	•		🛆 Research Information Services Inc 800-522-3884	•	•	•		
•	•	•	Silk Attorney Service 913-432-2755	•	•	•	•	

CV	CR	PR	LINCOLN (CST)	UC	RE	TX	VS	VR
•	•	•	Crawford Abstract & Real Estate Co 913-524-4228		•	•		
•	•	•	G & H Abstract 800-640-7390	•	•	•	•	
•	•		🛆 Research Information Services Inc 800-522-3884	•	•	•		

CV	CR	PR	LINN (CST)	UC	RE	TX	VS	VR
•	•	•	Linn County Abstract Co 888-795-2949	•	•	•		
•	•		🛆 Research Information Services Inc 800-522-3884	•	•	•		

CV	CR	PR	LOGAN (CST)	UC	RE	TX	VS	VR
•	•		🛆 Research Information Services Inc 800-522-3884	•	•	•		
•	•	•	The Gordon Company of Colby 913-462-7555	•	•	•		

CV	CR	PR	LYON (CST)	UC	RE	TX	VS	VR
•	•		Research Information Services Inc 800-522-3884	•	•	•		

CV	CR	PR	MARION (CST)	UC	RE	TX	VS	VR
•	•	•	Hannaford Abstract & Title Co 316-382-2130	•	•	•	•	
•	•		Research Information Services Inc 800-522-3884	•	•	•		

CV	CR	PR	MARSHALL (CST)	UC	RE	TX	VS	VR
•	•		Research Information Services Inc 800-522-3884	•	•	•		

CV	CR	PR	McPHERSON (CST)	UC	RE	TX	VS	VR
•	•	•	Hutchinson Title Co 316-669-8289	•	•	•	•	
•		•	McPherson County Abstract 316-241-1317	•	•	•		
•	•		Research Information Services Inc 800-522-3884	•	•	•		

CV	CR	PR	MEADE (CST)	UC	RE	TX	VS	VR
•	•	•	KOBS Abstracting 316-873-2421	•	•	•	•	
•	•		Research Information Services Inc 800-522-3884	•	•	•		

CV	CR	PR	MIAMI (CST)	UC	RE	TX	VS	VR
•	•		Research Information Services Inc 800-522-3884	•	•	•		
•	•	•	Winkler, Wendell D 913-294-2339	•	•	•		

CV	CR	PR	MITCHELL (CST)	UC	RE	TX	VS	VR
•	•	•	Attorney's Title Co 913-243-1357	•	•	•	•	
•	•		Research Information Services Inc 800-522-3884	•	•	•		

CV	CR	PR	MONTGOMERY (CST)	UC	RE	TX	VS	VR
•		•	Montgomery County Abstract Co 316-331-1440	•	•	•		
•	•		Research Information Services Inc 800-522-3884	•	•	•		

CV	CR	PR	MORRIS (CST)	UC	RE	TX	VS	VR
•	•	•	Moon Abstract Co 316-342-1917	•	•	•	•	
•	•		Research Information Services Inc 800-522-3884	•	•	•		

CV	CR	PR	MORTON (CST)	UC	RE	TX	VS	VR
•	•	•	American Title & Abstract Specialists 316-624-9111	•	•	•	•	
•	•	•	American Title & Abstract Specialists 316-356-2100	•	•	•	•	
•	•		Research Information Services Inc 800-522-3884	•	•	•		

CV	CR	PR	NEMAHA (CST)	UC	RE	TX	VS	VR
•	•	•	Nemaha County Abstract & Title Co 913-336-2137	•	•	•	•	
•	•		Research Information Services Inc 800-522-3884	•	•	•		

CV	CR	PR	NEOSHO (CST)	UC	RE	TX	VS	VR
•		•	Locke-Neosho Abstracts Inc 316-244-3641	•	•	•		
•	•		Research Information Services Inc 800-522-3884	•	•	•		

CV	CR	PR	NESS (CST)	UC	RE	TX	VS	VR
•	•	•	Credit Bureau Services Inc (SOP)................... 316-275-6500	•	•	•	•	
•	•		Research Information Services Inc 800-522-3884	•	•	•		

CV	CR	PR	NORTON (CST)	UC	RE	TX	VS	VR
•	•		Research Information Services Inc 800-522-3884	•	•	•		
•	•	•	Security Abstract Company 913-877-2141	•	•	•	•	

CV	CR	PR	OSAGE (CST)	UC	RE	TX	VS	VR
•	•	•	Hicks Information (SOP) 913-749-1898	•	•	•	•	•
•	•	•	Mercury Messengers Inc (SOP)....................... 913-357-0078	•	•	•	•	
•	•	•	Moon Abstract Co 316-342-1917	•	•	•	•	
•	•		Research Information Services Inc 800-522-3884	•	•	•		

CV	CR	PR	OSBORNE (CST)	UC	RE	TX	VS	VR
•	•	•	Gregory Abstract and Title Co Inc 913-346-5445	•	•	•	•	

					UC	RE	TX	VS	VR
•	•		🏛 Research Information Services Inc 800-522-3884		•	•	•		

CV	CR	PR	OTTAWA (CST)		UC	RE	TX	VS	VR
•	•		🏛 Research Information Services Inc 800-522-3884		•	•	•		

CV	CR	PR	PAWNEE (CST)		UC	RE	TX	VS	VR
•	•		🏛 Research Information Services Inc 800-522-3884		•	•	•		
•		•	Taylor Abstract Co 316-285-2026		•	•	•		

CV	CR	PR	PHILLIPS (CST)		UC	RE	TX	VS	VR
•	•	•	Keesee Abstracting Co 913-543-5115		•	•	•	•	
•	•		🏛 Research Information Services Inc 800-522-3884		•	•	•		

CV	CR	PR	POTTAWATOMIE (CST)		UC	RE	TX	VS	VR
•		•	Pottawatomie County Abstract Co 913-457-3441		•	•	•	•	
•	•		🏛 Research Information Services Inc 800-522-3884		•	•	•		

CV	CR	PR	PRATT (CST)		UC	RE	TX	VS	VR
•		•	Centennial Abstract of Pratt Inc 316-672-6889			•	•		
•	•		🏛 Research Information Services Inc 800-522-3884		•	•	•		

CV	CR	PR	RAWLINS (CST)		UC	RE	TX	VS	VR
•	•	•	Rawlins County Abstract and Title Co 913-626-3011		•	•	•	•	
•	•		🏛 Research Information Services Inc 800-522-3884		•	•	•		

CV	CR	PR	RENO (CST)		UC	RE	TX	VS	VR
•	•	•	Hutchinson Title Co 316-669-8289		•	•	•	•	
•	•	•	I Information Services (SOP) 800-658-1688		•	•	•	•	•
•	•	•	Investigations LLC (SOP) 800-658-1688		•	•	•	•	•
•	•	•	Kansas Investigative Services Inc (SOP) 316-267-1356		•	•	•	•	•
•	•		🏛 Research Information Services Inc 800-522-3884		•	•	•		

CV	CR	PR	REPUBLIC (CST)		UC	RE	TX	VS	VR
•	•	•	Attorney's Title Co 913-243-1357		•	•	•	•	
•	•		🏛 Research Information Services Inc 800-522-3884		•	•	•		

CV	CR	PR	RICE (CST)		UC	RE	TX	VS	VR
•	•	•	G & H Abstract 800-640-7390		•	•	•	•	
•	•		🏛 Research Information Services Inc 800-522-3884		•	•	•		

CV	CR	PR	RILEY (CST)		UC	RE	TX	VS	VR
•		•	Charlson & Wilson Bonded Abstracters 913-537-2900		•	•	•		
•	•		🏛 Research Information Services Inc 800-522-3884		•	•	•		

CV	CR	PR	ROOKS (CST)		UC	RE	TX	VS	VR
•	•	•	Ellis County Abstract & Title Co 800-794-2690		•	•	•	•	
•	•		🏛 Research Information Services Inc 800-522-3884		•	•	•		

CV	CR	PR	RUSH (CST)		UC	RE	TX	VS	VR
•		•	LaCrosse Abstract & Title 800-256-6911		•	•	•	•	
•	•		🏛 Research Information Services Inc 800-522-3884		•	•	•		

CV	CR	PR	RUSSELL (CST)		UC	RE	TX	VS	VR
•	•	•	G & H Abstract 800-640-7390		•	•	•	•	
•	•	•	Kansas Investigative Services Inc (SOP) 316-267-1356		•	•	•	•	•
•	•		🏛 Research Information Services Inc 800-522-3884		•	•	•		

CV	CR	PR	SALINE (CST)		UC	RE	TX	VS	VR
•		•	C W Lynn Abstract Co Inc 913-823-3706						
•	•		🏛 Research Information Services Inc 800-522-3884		•	•	•		

CV	CR	PR	SCOTT (CST)		UC	RE	TX	VS	VR
•	•	•	Credit Bureau Services Inc (SOP) 316-275-6500		•	•	•	•	
•	•		🏛 Research Information Services Inc 800-522-3884		•	•	•		

DT	BK	CV	CR	PR	Company	Phone	UC	RE	TX	VS	VR
		•		•	Scott County Abstract and Title Co Inc	316-872-3470	•	•	•		

SEDGWICK (CST)

DT	BK	CV	CR	PR	Company	Phone	UC	RE	TX	VS	VR
•	•	•	•		Clarence M Kelley and Associates (SOP)	816-756-2458					
		•		•	Columbian National Title Ins of Wichita	316-262-0387	•	•	•	•	
•	•	•	•		Future Security Concepts	800-398-3051				•	
•	•				Hogan Information Services	405-278-6954					
•	•	•	•	•	I Information Services (SOP)	800-658-1688	•	•	•		•
•	•	•	•	•	Investigations LLC (SOP)	800-658-1688	•	•	•	•	•
•	•	•	•	•	Kansas Investigative Services Inc (SOP)	316-267-1356	•	•	•	•	•
•	•	•	•		Research Information Services Inc	800-522-3884	•	•	•		

SEWARD (CST)

CV	CR	PR	Company	Phone	UC	RE	TX	VS	VR
•	•	•	American Title & Abstract Specialists	316-624-9111	•	•	•	•	
•	•	•	American Title & Abstract Specialists	316-356-2100	•	•	•	•	
•	•	•	Kansas Investigative Services Inc (SOP)	316-267-1356	•	•	•	•	•
•	•		Research Information Services Inc	800-522-3884	•	•	•		

SHAWNEE (CAPITAL) (CST)

DT	BK	CV	CR	PR	Company	Phone	UC	RE	TX	VS	VR
•	•	•	•		Clarence M Kelley and Associates (SOP)	816-756-2458					
•	•	•	•		Future Security Concepts	800-398-3051				•	
•	•				Hogan Information Services	405-278-6954					
•	•	•	•	•	Mercury Messengers Inc (SOP)	913-357-0078	•	•	•	•	
•	•	•	•		Research Information Services Inc	800-522-3884	•	•	•		
•	•	•	•		Search Network Ltd	800-338-3618	•		•		

SHERIDAN (CST)

CV	CR	PR	Company	Phone	UC	RE	TX	VS	VR
•	•	•	First Insurance Agency of Hoxie Inc	913-675-3252	•	•	•		
•	•		Research Information Services Inc	800-522-3884	•	•	•		
•	•	•	The Gordon Company of Colby	913-462-7555	•	•	•		

SHERMAN (MST)

CV	CR	PR	Company	Phone	UC	RE	TX	VS	VR
•	•		Research Information Services Inc	800-522-3884	•	•	•		
•		•	Teeters Abstract and Title Co	913-899-7138	•	•	•		
•	•	•	The Gordon Company of Colby	913-462-7555	•	•	•		

SMITH (CST)

CV	CR	PR	Company	Phone	UC	RE	TX	VS	VR
•		•	Collier Abstracts Inc	913-282-3351	•	•	•		
•	•		Research Information Services Inc	800-522-3884	•	•	•		

STAFFORD (CST)

CV	CR	PR	Company	Phone	UC	RE	TX	VS	VR
•	•		Research Information Services Inc	800-522-3884	•	•	•		
•		•	Stafford County Abstract & Title Co	316-549-3579	•	•	•	•	

STANTON (CST)

CV	CR	PR	Company	Phone	UC	RE	TX	VS	VR
•	•	•	American Title & Abstract Specialists	316-624-9111	•	•	•	•	
•	•	•	American Title & Abstract Specialists	316-356-2100	•	•	•	•	
•	•	•	PC Fraze Abstract Co	316-384-7828	•	•	•	•	
•	•		Research Information Services Inc	800-522-3884	•	•	•		

STEVENS (CST)

CV	CR	PR	Company	Phone	UC	RE	TX	VS	VR
•	•	•	American Title & Abstract Specialists	316-624-9111	•	•	•	•	
•	•	•	American Title & Abstract Specialists	316-356-2100	•	•	•	•	
•		•	McQueen Abstract Company	316-544-2311		•	•		
•	•		Research Information Services Inc	800-522-3884	•	•	•		

SUMNER (CST)

CV	CR	PR	Company	Phone	UC	RE	TX	VS	VR
•	•	•	I Information Services (SOP)	800-658-1688	•	•	•	•	•
•	•	•	Investigations LLC (SOP)	800-658-1688	•	•	•	•	•
•	•	•	Kansas Investigative Services Inc (SOP)	316-267-1356	•	•	•	•	•
•		•	Kansas Title Service	316-326-8508	•	•	•	•	
•	•		Research Information Services Inc	800-522-3884	•	•	•		

	CV	CR	PR	THOMAS (CST)	UC	RE	TX	VS	VR
	●	●	●	First Insurance Agency of Hoxie Inc 913-675-3252	●	●	●		
	●	●		🏛 Research Information Services Inc 800-522-3884	●	●	●		
	●	●	●	The Gordon Company of Colby 913-462-7555	●	●	●		

	CV	CR	PR	TREGO (CST)	UC	RE	TX	VS	VR
	●		●	Fowler Abstract & Title Inc 913-743-6422	●	●	●		
	●	●		🏛 Research Information Services Inc 800-522-3884	●	●	●		

	CV	CR	PR	WABAUNSEE (CST)	UC	RE	TX	VS	VR
	●	●	●	Moon Abstract Co 316-342-1917	●	●	●	●	
	●	●		🏛 Research Information Services Inc 800-522-3884	●	●	●		

	CV	CR	PR	WALLACE (MST)	UC	RE	TX	VS	VR
	●	●		🏛 Research Information Services Inc 800-522-3884	●	●	●		
	●		●	Teeters Abstract and Title Co 913-899-7138	●	●	●		

	CV	CR	PR	WASHINGTON (CST)	UC	RE	TX	VS	VR
	●	●	●	Attorney's Title Co 913-243-1357	●	●	●	●	
	●	●		🏛 Research Information Services Inc 800-522-3884	●	●	●		

	CV	CR	PR	WICHITA (CST)	UC	RE	TX	VS	VR
	●	●	●	Credit Bureau Services Inc (SOP)............316-275-6500	●	●	●	●	
	●	●		🏛 Research Information Services Inc 800-522-3884	●	●	●		
	●		●	Scott County Abstract and Title Co Inc 316-872-3470	●	●	●		

	CV	CR	PR	WILSON (CST)	UC	RE	TX	VS	VR
	●		●	Fink Abstract Co 316-378-2351	●	●	●	●	
	●	●		🏛 Research Information Services Inc 800-522-3884	●	●	●		

	CV	CR	PR	WOODSON (CST)	UC	RE	TX	VS	VR
	●	●		🏛 Research Information Services Inc 800-522-3884	●	●	●		
	●	●	●	Street Abstract Co 316-625-2421	●	●	●	●	

DT	BK	CV	CR	PR	WYANDOTTE (CST)	UC	RE	TX	VS	VR
●	●	●	●	●	Bankruptcy Services Inc 214-424-6500					
●	●	●	●		🏛 Clarence M Kelley and Associates (SOP)............816-756-2458					
●	●	●	●	●	Executive Investigative Services (SOP)............913-764-9484	●	●	●	●	●
●	●	●	●		🏛 Future Security Concepts 800-398-3051				●	
●	●	●	●		🏛 RSI 800-633-6125	●	●	●	●	
●	●	●	●		🏛 Research Information Services Inc 800-522-3884	●	●	●		
●	●	●	●	●	Silk Attorney Service 913-432-2755	●	●	●	●	

KENTUCKY

CV	CR	PR	ADAIR (CST)		UC	RE	TX	VS	VR
•	•	•	Harvey's Research 502-378-6452		•	•	•	•	
•	•	•	National Service Information Inc 800-235-0337		•		•	•	

CV	CR	PR	ALLEN (CST)		UC	RE	TX	VS	VR
•	•	•	Hollingsworth Court Reporting Inc 504-769-3386		•	•	•	•	
•	•	•	National Service Information Inc 800-235-0337		•		•	•	

CV	CR	PR	ANDERSON (EST)		UC	RE	TX	VS	VR
•	•	•	Equisearch 606-268-1206		•	•	•	•	
•	•	•	National Service Information Inc 800-235-0337		•		•	•	

CV	CR	PR	BALLARD (CST)		UC	RE	TX	VS	VR
•	•	•	National Service Information Inc 800-235-0337		•		•	•	

CV	CR	PR	BARREN (CST)		UC	RE	TX	VS	VR
•	•	•	Goodman & Nichols 502-524-9292		•	•	•	•	
•	•	•	Hollingsworth Court Reporting Inc 504-769-3386		•	•	•	•	
•	•	•	Moore Jr, Attorney Reed 502-487-6262		•	•	•		
•	•	•	National Service Information Inc 800-235-0337		•		•	•	

CV	CR	PR	BATH (EST)		UC	RE	TX	VS	VR
•	•	•	National Service Information Inc 800-235-0337		•		•	•	

CV	CR	PR	BELL (EST)		UC	RE	TX	VS	VR
•	•	•	National Service Information Inc 800-235-0337		•		•	•	
•	•	•	Weatherly Law Office 606-878-9661		•	•	•	•	

CV	CR	PR	BOONE (EST)		UC	RE	TX	VS	VR
•	•		AM Search & Retrieve 812-438-4166		•	•	•		•
•	•	•	Active Detective Bureau Inc (SOP) 513-541-6600		•	•	•	•	•
•	•	•	All State Investigations (SOP) 800-741-4711		•	•	•	•	•
•	•	•	District Security Inc 800-688-8721		•		•	•	
•	•	•	General Corporate Investigations (SOP) 800-735-7992		•	•	•	•	•
•	•	•	McKinley Paralegal Services 513-662-8106		•	•	•		
•	•	•	National Service Information Inc 800-235-0337		•		•	•	

CV	CR	PR	BOURBON (EST)		UC	RE	TX	VS	VR
•	•	•	Equisearch 606-268-1206		•	•	•	•	
•	•	•	National Service Information Inc 800-235-0337		•		•	•	

DT	CV	CR	PR	BOYD (EST)		UC	RE	TX	VS	VR
•	•	•	•	Daniel Agency 606-324-6029		•	•	•	•	•
•	•	•	•	Lew Davis Investigatons (SOP) 304-523-0055		•	•	•	•	•
		•	•	Liberty Record Search Inc 304-428-5126		•	•	•	•	
•	•	•	•	McBrayer McDennis Leslie & Kirkland 606-473-7303		•	•	•	•	•
•	•	•	•	National Service Information Inc 800-235-0337		•		•	•	

CV	CR	PR	BOYLE (EST)		UC	RE	TX	VS	VR
•	•	•	Equisearch 606-268-1206		•	•	•	•	
•	•	•	National Service Information Inc 800-235-0337		•		•	•	

CV	CR	PR	BRACKEN (EST)		UC	RE	TX	VS	VR
•	•	•	Clarke & Clarke 606-564-5527			•	•		
•	•	•	National Service Information Inc 800-235-0337		•		•	•	

CV	CR	PR	BREATHITT (EST)		UC	RE	TX	VS	VR
•	•		Feltner, Angela 606-436-5633		•	•	•		
•	•	•	Friend, Irene 606-464-2638		•	•	•	•	
•	•	•	Long, Gordon B 606-349-1558		•		•	•	
•	•	•	National Service Information Inc 800-235-0337		•		•	•	

CV	CR	PR	BRECKINRIDGE (CST)		UC	RE	TX	VS	VR
•	•	•	Eagle Investigations Inc (SOP) 800-344-2454		•	•	•	•	
•	•	•	McCarty, Attorney John 502-927-8800		•	•	•		
•	•	•	Mitchener, Kent D 502-422-2611		•	•	•	•	
•	•	•	National Service Information Inc 800-235-0337		•		•	•	

CV	CR	PR	BULLITT (EST)		UC	RE	TX	VS	VR
•	•	•	Attorney Services of Kentucky (SOP) 502-327-6677		•	•	•	•	•
•		•	🏛 Business Research International 502-348-6350		•	•	•	•	•
•	•	•	County Process Inc (SOP) 502-587-0051		•	•	•	•	
•	•		Data Search Kentucky 502-637-4658		•	•	•		
•	•	•	Eagle Investigations Inc (SOP) 800-344-2454		•	•		•	
•	•	•	National Service Information Inc 800-235-0337		•		•	•	

CV	CR	PR	BUTLER (CST)		UC	RE	TX	VS	VR
•	•	•	🏛 Hollingsworth Court Reporting Inc 504-769-3386		•	•	•	•	
•	•	•	National Service Information Inc 800-235-0337		•		•	•	

CV	CR	PR	CALDWELL (CST)		UC	RE	TX	VS	VR
•	•	•	🏛 Hollingsworth Court Reporting Inc 504-769-3386		•	•	•	•	
•	•	•	National Service Information Inc 800-235-0337		•		•	•	

CV	CR	PR	CALLOWAY (CST)		UC	RE	TX	VS	VR
			Lattus, Helen 901-885-0891		•	•	•		
•	•	•	National Service Information Inc 800-235-0337		•		•	•	

CV	CR	PR	CAMPBELL (EST)		UC	RE	TX	VS	VR
•	•	•	All State Investigations (SOP) 800-741-4711		•	•	•	•	•
•	•	•	District Security Inc 800-688-8721		•		•	•	
•	•	•	General Corporate Investigations (SOP) 800-735-7992		•	•	•	•	•
•	•	•	McKinley Paralegal Services 513-662-8106		•	•			
•	•	•	National Service Information Inc 800-235-0337		•		•	•	

CV	CR	PR	CARLISLE (CST)		UC	RE	TX	VS	VR
•	•	•	National Service Information Inc 800-235-0337		•		•	•	

CV	CR	PR	CARROLL (EST)		UC	RE	TX	VS	VR
			Berry & Floyd 502-845-2881		•	•	•		
•	•	•	National Service Information Inc 800-235-0337		•		•	•	

CV	CR	PR	CARTER (EST)		UC	RE	TX	VS	VR
			Albright, Gary 606-474-4253		•	•	•		
•	•	•	Daniel Agency 606-324-6029		•	•	•	•	•
•		•	🏛 Liberty Record Search Inc 304-428-5126		•	•	•		
•	•	•	McBrayer McDennis Leslie & Kirkland 606-473-7303		•	•	•	•	•
•	•	•	National Service Information Inc 800-235-0337		•		•	•	

CV	CR	PR	CASEY (EST)		UC	RE	TX	VS	VR
•	•	•	Equisearch 606-268-1206		•	•	•	•	
•	•	•	National Service Information Inc 800-235-0337		•		•	•	

CV	CR	PR	CHRISTIAN (CST)		UC	RE	TX	VS	VR
•	•		🏛 Alpha Research LLC (SOP) 205-755-7008				•		
•	•	•	🏛 Hollingsworth Court Reporting Inc 504-769-3386		•	•	•	•	
•	•	•	National Service Information Inc 800-235-0337		•		•	•	

CV	CR	PR	CLARK (EST)		UC	RE	TX	VS	VR
•	•	•	Equisearch 606-268-1206		•	•	•	•	
•	•	•	National Service Information Inc 800-235-0337		•		•	•	
•	•	•	Public Record Information Services 606-879-2141		•	•	•		

CV	CR	PR	CLAY (EST)		UC	RE	TX	VS	VR
•	•		Feltner, Angela 606-436-5633		•	•	•		

•	•	•	National Service Information Inc 800-235-0337	•		•	•	
•	•	•	Weatherly Law Office 606-878-9661	•	•	•	•	

	CV	CR	PR	CLINTON (CST)	UC	RE	TX	VS	VR
	•	•		🏛 Alpha Research LLC (SOP).......... 205-755-7008			•		
	•	•	•	National Service Information Inc 800-235-0337	•		•	•	

	CV	CR	PR	CRITTENDEN (CST)	UC	RE	TX	VS	VR
	•	•	•	National Service Information Inc 800-235-0337	•		•	•	

	CV	CR	PR	CUMBERLAND (CST)	UC	RE	TX	VS	VR
	•	•	•	🏛 Harvey's Research 502-378-6452	•	•	•	•	
	•	•	•	National Service Information Inc 800-235-0337	•		•	•	

DT	CV	CR	PR	DAVIESS (CST)	UC	RE	TX	VS	VR
•	•	•		🏛 Alpha Research LLC (SOP).......... 205-755-7008			•		
•	•	•	•	Equisearch 606-268-1206	•	•	•	•	
•	•	•	•	Fidelity Search Inc 812-479-8704	•	•	•	•	•
	•		•	Hicks III, Attorney John O 502-273-5749	•	•	•		
	•		•	McCarty, Attorney John 502-927-8800	•	•	•		
•	•	•	•	National Service Information Inc 800-235-0337	•		•	•	
	•	•		Stephen's Research 502-687-7329					
•	•	•		🏛 Summit Documents 502-281-5406	•	•	•	•	

	CV	CR	PR	EDMONSON (CST)	UC	RE	TX	VS	VR
	•	•	•	🏛 Hollingsworth Court Reporting Inc 504-769-3386	•	•	•	•	
	•	•	•	National Service Information Inc 800-235-0337	•		•	•	

	CV	CR	PR	ELLIOTT (EST)	UC	RE	TX	VS	VR
	•	•	•	Daniel Agency 606-324-6029	•	•	•	•	•
	•	•	•	National Service Information Inc 800-235-0337	•		•	•	

	CV	CR	PR	ESTILL (EST)	UC	RE	TX	VS	VR
	•	•	•	Friend, Irene 606-464-2638	•	•	•	•	
				Marcum, Hannah 606-723-4438	•	•	•		
	•	•	•	National Service Information Inc 800-235-0337	•		•	•	

DT	BK	CV	CR	PR	FAYETTE (EST)	UC	RE	TX	VS	VR
•	•	•	•		🏛 Alpha Research LLC (SOP).......... 205-755-7008			•		
•	•	•	•	•	Attorney Services of Kentucky (SOP).......... 502-327-6677	•	•	•	•	•
•	•	•	•	•	Bankruptcy Services Inc 214-424-6500					
•	•	•	•	•	County Process Inc (SOP) 502-587-0051	•	•	•		
•	•	•	•		Data Search Kentucky 502-637-4658	•	•	•		
•	•	•	•	•	Equisearch 606-268-1206	•	•	•	•	
•	•				🏛 Hogan Information Services 405-278-6954					
•	•	•	•	•	McBrayer McDennis Leslie & Kirkland 606-473-7303	•	•	•	•	•
•	•	•	•	•	National Service Information Inc 800-235-0337	•		•	•	
•	•	•	•	•	Public Record Information Services 606-879-2141	•	•	•		

	CV	CR	PR	FLEMING (EST)	UC	RE	TX	VS	VR
	•	•	•	Clarke & Clarke 606-564-5527		•	•		
	•	•	•	National Service Information Inc 800-235-0337	•		•	•	
	•	•	•	Suit McCartney Price 606-849-2338	•	•	•	•	

	CV	CR	PR	FLOYD (EST)	UC	RE	TX	VS	VR
	•	•	•	Combs and Combs PSC 606-437-6226	•	•			
	•	•	•	Daniel Agency 606-324-6029	•	•	•	•	•
	•		•	🏛 Liberty Record Search Inc 304-428-5126	•	•	•		
	•	•	•	National Service Information Inc 800-235-0337	•		•	•	

DT	CV	CR	PR	FRANKLIN (CAPITAL) (EST)	UC	RE	TX	VS	VR
•	•	•		🏛 Alpha Research LLC (SOP).......... 205-755-7008			•		
•	•	•	•	Attorney Services of Kentucky (SOP).......... 502-327-6677	•	•	•	•	•
•	•	•		Data Search Kentucky 502-637-4658	•	•	•		

CV CR PR				UC RE TX VS VR

• • • •	Equisearch	606-268-1206		• • • •
• • • •	McBrayer McDennis Leslie & Kirkland	606-473-7303		• • • • •
• • • •	National Service Information Inc	800-235-0337		• • • •
• • • •	Public Record Information Services	606-879-2141		• • •

CV CR PR	FULTON (CST)	UC RE TX VS VR
	Lattus, Helen 901-885-0891	• • •
• • •	National Service Information Inc 800-235-0337	• • •

CV CR PR	GALLATIN (EST)	UC RE TX VS VR
• • •	Huddleston & Huddleston Law Firm 606-567-2818	• • •
• • •	National Service Information Inc 800-235-0337	• • •

CV CR PR	GARRARD (EST)	UC RE TX VS VR
• • •	Equisearch 606-268-1206	• • • •
• • •	Layton, Attorney David K 606-792-4613	• • • •
• • •	National Service Information Inc 800-235-0337	• • •

CV CR PR	GRANT (EST)	UC RE TX VS VR
• • •	National Service Information Inc 800-235-0337	• • •

CV CR PR	GRAVES (CST)	UC RE TX VS VR
	Lattus, Helen 901-885-0891	• • •
• • •	National Service Information Inc 800-235-0337	• • •

CV CR PR	GRAYSON (CST)	UC RE TX VS VR
• • •	Guffey, Jerry 502-259-4828	• • • •
• • •	Mitchener, Kent D 502-422-2611	• • • •
• • •	National Service Information Inc 800-235-0337	• • •

CV CR PR	GREEN (EST)	UC RE TX VS VR
• • •	National Service Information Inc 800-235-0337	• • •

CV CR PR	GREENUP (EST)	UC RE TX VS VR
• • •	Daniel Agency 606-324-6029	• • • • •
•	🏛 Liberty Record Search Inc 304-428-5126	• • •
• • •	McBrayer McDennis Leslie & Kirkland 606-473-7303	• • • • •
• • •	National Service Information Inc 800-235-0337	• • •

CV CR PR	HANCOCK (CST)	UC RE TX VS VR
• • •	McCarty, Attorney John 502-927-8800	• • •
• • •	National Service Information Inc 800-235-0337	• • •
• •	🏛 Summit Documents 502-281-5406	• • •

CV CR PR	HARDIN (EST)	UC RE TX VS VR
• • •	Attorney Services of Kentucky (SOP) 502-327-6677	• • • • •
• •	Data Search Kentucky 502-637-4658	• • •
• • •	Eagle Investigations Inc (SOP) 800-344-2454	• • •
• •	Lincoln Trail Title Services Inc 502-765-5566	• • •
• • •	National Service Information Inc 800-235-0337	• • •

CV CR PR	HARLAN (EST)	UC RE TX VS VR
• • •	National Service Information Inc 800-235-0337	• • •

CV CR PR	HARRISON (EST)	UC RE TX VS VR
• • •	Equisearch 606-268-1206	• • • •
• • •	Hood & Whalen 606-234-4321	• • • •
• • •	National Service Information Inc 800-235-0337	• • •

CV CR PR	HART (CST)	UC RE TX VS VR
• • •	Goodman & Nichols 502-524-9292	• • • •
• • •	National Service Information Inc 800-235-0337	• • •

HENDERSON (CST)

CV	CR	PR			UC	RE	TX	VS	VR
•	•	•	Fidelity Search Inc	812-479-8704	•	•	•	•	•
•	•	•	National Service Information Inc	800-235-0337	•		•	•	
•	•		🏛 Summit Documents	502-281-5406	•	•	•	•	

HENRY (EST)

CV	CR	PR			UC	RE	TX	VS	VR
			Berry & Floyd	502-845-2881	•	•	•		
•	•	•	Eagle Investigations Inc (SOP)	800-344-2454	•	•	•	•	
•	•	•	Equisearch	606-268-1206	•	•	•	•	
•	•	•	Jeffries, Keith A	502-845-7603	•	•	•		
•	•	•	National Service Information Inc	800-235-0337	•		•	•	

HICKMAN (CST)

CV	CR	PR			UC	RE	TX	VS	VR
			Lattus, Helen	901-885-0891	•	•	•		
•	•	•	National Service Information Inc	800-235-0337	•		•	•	

HOPKINS (CST)

CV	CR	PR			UC	RE	TX	VS	VR
•	•		🏛 Alpha Research LLC (SOP)	205-755-7008			•		
•	•	•	🏛 Hollingsworth Court Reporting Inc	504-769-3386	•	•	•	•	
•	•	•	National Service Information Inc	800-235-0337	•		•	•	

JACKSON (EST)

CV	CR	PR			UC	RE	TX	VS	VR
•	•	•	National Service Information Inc	800-235-0337	•		•	•	

JEFFERSON (EST)

DT	BK	CV	CR	PR			UC	RE	TX	VS	VR
•	•	•	•		🏛 Alpha Research LLC (SOP)	205-755-7008			•		
•	•	•	•	•	Attorney Services of Kentucky (SOP)	502-327-6677	•	•	•	•	•
•	•	•	•	•	🏛 Business Research International	502-348-6350	•	•	•	•	•
•	•	•	•	•	County Process Inc (SOP)	502-587-0051	•	•	•		
•	•	•	•		Data Search Kentucky	502-637-4658	•	•	•		
•	•	•	•	•	Eagle Investigations Inc (SOP)	800-344-2454	•	•	•		
•	•				🏛 Hogan Information Services	405-278-6954					
•	•	•	•	•	National Service Information Inc	800-235-0337	•		•	•	
•	•	•	•		Steele Investigations & Info Svcs (SOP)	800-587-0965	•		•		
•	•	•	•	•	🏛 Steve Knight Services (SOP)	812-288-8528	•	•	•	•	•

JESSAMINE (EST)

CV	CR	PR			UC	RE	TX	VS	VR
•	•		🏛 Alpha Research LLC (SOP)	205-755-7008			•		
•	•	•	Equisearch	606-268-1206	•	•	•	•	
•	•	•	Layton, Attorney David K	606-792-4613	•	•	•	•	
•	•	•	National Service Information Inc	800-235-0337	•		•	•	

JOHNSON (EST)

CV	CR	PR			UC	RE	TX	VS	VR
•	•	•	Daniel Agency	606-324-6029	•	•	•	•	•
•		•	🏛 Liberty Record Search Inc	304-428-5126	•	•	•		
•	•	•	Long, Gordon B	606-349-1558	•	•	•		
•	•	•	National Service Information Inc	800-235-0337	•		•	•	

KENTON (EST)

DT	CV	CR	PR			UC	RE	TX	VS	VR
•	•	•	•	🏛 Active Detective Bureau Inc (SOP)	513-541-6600	•	•	•	•	•
•	•	•	•	All State Investigations (SOP)	800-741-4711	•	•	•	•	•
•	•	•	•	Attorney Services of Kentucky (SOP)	502-327-6677	•	•	•	•	•
•	•	•	•	District Security Inc	800-688-8721	•		•	•	
•	•	•	•	General Corporate Investigations (SOP)	800-735-7992	•	•	•	•	•
•	•	•	•	McKinley Paralegal Services	513-662-8106	•	•	•		
•	•	•	•	National Service Information Inc	800-235-0337	•		•	•	
•	•	•	•	🏛 Search International Inc	606-342-0456	•	•	•	•	•

KNOTT (EST)

CV	CR	PR			UC	RE	TX	VS	VR
•	•		Feltner, Angela	606-436-5633	•	•	•		
•	•	•	Long, Gordon B	606-349-1558	•	•	•		
•	•	•	National Service Information Inc	800-235-0337	•		•	•	

	CV	CR	PR	KNOX (EST)	UC	RE	TX	VS	VR
	•	•	•	National Service Information Inc 800-235-0337	•		•	•	
	•	•	•	Weatherly Law Office 606-878-9661	•	•	•	•	

	CV	CR	PR	LARUE (EST)	UC	RE	TX	VS	VR
	•	•	•	Goodman & Nichols 502-524-9292	•	•	•	•	
	•	•	•	National Service Information Inc 800-235-0337	•		•	•	

DT	CV	CR	PR	LAUREL (EST)	UC	RE	TX	VS	VR
•	•	•	•	National Service Information Inc 800-235-0337	•		•	•	
	•	•	•	Weatherly Law Office 606-878-9661	•	•	•	•	

	CV	CR	PR	LAWRENCE (EST)	UC	RE	TX	VS	VR
	•	•	•	Daniel Agency 606-324-6029	•	•	•	•	•
	•		•	🗑 Liberty Record Search Inc 304-428-5126	•	•	•		
	•	•	•	McBrayer McDennis Leslie & Kirkland 606-473-7303	•	•	•	•	•
	•	•	•	National Service Information Inc 800-235-0337	•		•	•	

	CV	CR	PR	LEE (EST)	UC	RE	TX	VS	VR
	•	•	•	Friend, Irene 606-464-2638	•	•	•	•	
	•	•	•	National Service Information Inc 800-235-0337	•		•	•	

	CV	CR	PR	LESLIE (EST)	UC	RE	TX	VS	VR
	•	•	•	Brashear, Attorney Leonard 606-672-3577	•	•	•		
	•	•		Feltner, Angela 606-436-5633	•	•	•		
	•	•	•	National Service Information Inc 800-235-0337	•		•	•	

	CV	CR	PR	LETCHER (EST)	UC	RE	TX	VS	VR
	•	•		Feltner, Angela 606-436-5633	•	•	•		
	•	•	•	National Service Information Inc 800-235-0337	•		•	•	

	CV	CR	PR	LEWIS (EST)	UC	RE	TX	VS	VR
	•		•	🗑 Liberty Record Search Inc 304-428-5126	•	•	•		
	•	•	•	McBrayer McDennis Leslie & Kirkland 606-473-7303	•	•	•	•	•
	•	•	•	National Service Information Inc 800-235-0337	•		•	•	

	CV	CR	PR	LINCOLN (EST)	UC	RE	TX	VS	VR
	•	•	•	Equisearch 606-268-1206	•	•	•	•	
	•	•	•	Layton, Attorney David K 606-792-4613	•	•	•	•	
	•	•	•	National Service Information Inc 800-235-0337	•		•	•	

	CV	CR	PR	LIVINGSTON (CST)	UC	RE	TX	VS	VR
	•	•	•	National Service Information Inc 800-235-0337	•		•	•	

	CV	CR	PR	LOGAN (CST)	UC	RE	TX	VS	VR
	•	•	•	🗑 Hollingsworth Court Reporting Inc 504-769-3386	•	•	•	•	
	•	•	•	National Service Information Inc 800-235-0337	•		•	•	

	CV	CR	PR	LYON (EST)	UC	RE	TX	VS	VR
	•	•	•	National Service Information Inc 800-235-0337	•		•	•	

	CV	CR	PR	MADISON (EST)	UC	RE	TX	VS	VR
	•	•		🗑 Alpha Research LLC (SOP) 205-755-7008			•		
	•	•	•	Equisearch 606-268-1206	•	•	•	•	
	•	•	•	National Service Information Inc 800-235-0337	•		•	•	

	CV	CR	PR	MAGOFFIN (EST)	UC	RE	TX	VS	VR
	•	•	•	Long, Gordon B 606-349-1558	•	•	•		
	•	•	•	National Service Information Inc 800-235-0337	•		•	•	

	CV	CR	PR	MARION (EST)	UC	RE	TX	VS	VR
	•	•	•	Avritt & Avritt 502-692-4270	•	•	•	•	
	•	•	•	National Service Information Inc 800-235-0337	•		•	•	

CV	CR	PR	MARSHALL (CST)		UC	RE	TX	VS	VR
•	•	•	National Service Information Inc	800-235-0337	•		•	•	

CV	CR	PR	MARTIN (EST)		UC	RE	TX	VS	VR
•	•	•	Daniel Agency	606-324-6029	•	•	•	•	•
•	•	•	National Service Information Inc	800-235-0337	•		•	•	

CV	CR	PR	MASON (EST)		UC	RE	TX	VS	VR
•	•	•	Clarke & Clarke	606-564-5527		•	•		
•	•	•	National Service Information Inc	800-235-0337	•		•	•	

DT	CV	CR	PR	MCCRACKEN (CST)		UC	RE	TX	VS	VR
				Lattus, Helen	901-885-0891	•	•	•		
•	•	•	•	National Service Information Inc	800-235-0337	•		•	•	

CV	CR	PR	MCCREARY (EST)		UC	RE	TX	VS	VR
•	•	•	King & King	606-354-2153	•	•	•		
•	•	•	National Service Information Inc	800-235-0337	•		•	•	

CV	CR	PR	MCLEAN (CST)		UC	RE	TX	VS	VR
•		•	Hicks III, Attorney John O	502-273-5749	•	•	•		
•	•	•	National Service Information Inc	800-235-0337	•		•	•	

CV	CR	PR	MEADE (EST)		UC	RE	TX	VS	VR
•	•	•	Attorney Services of Kentucky (SOP)	502-327-6677	•	•	•	•	•
•	•		Data Search Kentucky	502-637-4658	•	•	•		
•	•	•	Eagle Investigations Inc (SOP)	800-344-2454	•	•	•	•	
•	•	•	Mitchener, Kent D	502-422-2611	•	•	•	•	
•	•	•	National Service Information Inc	800-235-0337	•		•	•	

CV	CR	PR	MENIFEE (EST)		UC	RE	TX	VS	VR
•	•	•	National Service Information Inc	800-235-0337	•		•	•	

CV	CR	PR	MERCER (EST)		UC	RE	TX	VS	VR
•	•	•	Equisearch	606-268-1206	•	•	•	•	
•	•	•	National Service Information Inc	800-235-0337	•		•	•	

CV	CR	PR	METCALFE (CST)		UC	RE	TX	VS	VR
•	•	•	Harvey's Research	502-378-6452	•	•	•	•	
•	•	•	National Service Information Inc	800-235-0337	•		•	•	

CV	CR	PR	MONROE (CST)		UC	RE	TX	VS	VR
•	•	•	Moore Jr, Attorney Reed	502-487-6262	•	•	•		
•	•	•	National Service Information Inc	800-235-0337	•		•	•	

CV	CR	PR	MONTGOMERY (EST)		UC	RE	TX	VS	VR
•	•	•	Equisearch	606-268-1206	•	•	•	•	
•	•	•	National Service Information Inc	800-235-0337	•		•	•	

CV	CR	PR	MORGAN (EST)		UC	RE	TX	VS	VR
•	•	•	Daniel Agency	606-324-6029	•	•	•	•	•
•	•	•	National Service Information Inc	800-235-0337	•		•	•	

CV	CR	PR	MUHLENBERG (CST)		UC	RE	TX	VS	VR
•		•	Hicks III, Attorney John O	502-273-5749	•	•	•		
•	•	•	Hollingsworth Court Reporting Inc	504-769-3386	•	•	•	•	
•	•	•	National Service Information Inc	800-235-0337	•		•	•	

CV	CR	PR	NELSON (EST)		UC	RE	TX	VS	VR
•	•	•	Attorney Services of Kentucky (SOP)	502-327-6677	•	•	•	•	•
•		•	Business Research International	502-348-6350	•	•	•	•	•
•	•		Data Search Kentucky	502-637-4658	•	•	•		
•	•	•	Eagle Investigations Inc (SOP)	800-344-2454	•	•	•	•	
•	•	•	National Service Information Inc	800-235-0337	•		•	•	

CV	CR	PR	NICHOLAS (EST)		UC	RE	TX	VS	VR
•	•	•	National Service Information Inc	800-235-0337	•		•	•	

CV	CR	PR	OHIO (CST)		UC	RE	TX	VS	VR
•	•	•	Fidelity Search Inc	812-479-8704	•	•	•	•	•
•	•	•	McCarty, Attorney John	502-927-8800	•	•	•		
•	•	•	National Service Information Inc	800-235-0337	•		•	•	
•	•		🏛 Summit Documents	502-281-5406	•	•	•	•	

CV	CR	PR	OLDHAM (EST)		UC	RE	TX	VS	VR
•	•	•	Attorney Services of Kentucky (SOP)	502-327-6677	•	•	•	•	•
•			Berry & Floyd	502-845-2881	•	•	•		
•		•	🏛 Business Research International	502-348-6350	•	•	•		•
•	•	•	County Process Inc (SOP)	502-587-0051	•	•	•	•	
•	•		Data Search Kentucky	502-637-4658	•	•	•		
•	•	•	Eagle Investigations Inc (SOP)	800-344-2454	•	•	•	•	
•	•	•	Equisearch	606-268-1206	•	•	•	•	
•	•	•	National Service Information Inc	800-235-0337	•		•	•	

CV	CR	PR	OWEN (EST)		UC	RE	TX	VS	VR
•	•	•	National Service Information Inc	800-235-0337	•		•	•	

CV	CR	PR	OWSLEY (EST)		UC	RE	TX	VS	VR
•	•	•	Friend, Irene	606-464-2638	•	•	•	•	
•	•	•	National Service Information Inc	800-235-0337	•		•	•	

CV	CR	PR	PENDLETON (EST)		UC	RE	TX	VS	VR
•	•	•	National Service Information Inc	800-235-0337	•		•	•	

CV	CR	PR	PERRY (EST)		UC	RE	TX	VS	VR
•	•		Feltner, Angela	606-436-5633	•	•	•		
•	•	•	Friend, Irene	606-464-2638	•	•	•	•	
•	•	•	National Service Information Inc	800-235-0337	•		•	•	

DT	CV	CR	PR	PIKE (EST)		UC	RE	TX	VS	VR
•	•	•	•	Combs and Combs PSC	606-437-6226	•	•			
•	•	•	•	Daniel Agency	606-324-6029	•	•	•	•	•
			•	🏛 Liberty Record Search Inc	304-428-5126	•	•	•		
	•	•		Long, Gordon B	606-349-1558	•	•	•		
•	•	•	•	National Service Information Inc	800-235-0337	•		•	•	

CV	CR	PR	POWELL (EST)		UC	RE	TX	VS	VR
•	•	•	Friend, Irene	606-464-2638	•	•	•	•	
•	•	•	National Service Information Inc	800-235-0337	•		•	•	

CV	CR	PR	PULASKI (EST)		UC	RE	TX	VS	VR
•	•	•	King & King	606-354-2153	•	•	•		
•	•	•	National Service Information Inc	800-235-0337	•		•	•	
•	•	•	Weatherly Law Office	606-878-9661	•	•	•	•	

CV	CR	PR	ROBERTSON (EST)		UC	RE	TX	VS	VR
•	•	•	National Service Information Inc	800-235-0337	•		•	•	

CV	CR	PR	ROCKCASTLE (EST)		UC	RE	TX	VS	VR
•	•	•	National Service Information Inc	800-235-0337	•		•	•	
•	•	•	Weatherly Law Office	606-878-9661	•	•	•	•	

CV	CR	PR	ROWAN (EST)		UC	RE	TX	VS	VR
•	•	•	Daniel Agency	606-324-6029	•	•	•	•	•
	•	•	🏛 Liberty Record Search Inc	304-428-5126	•	•	•		
•	•	•	National Service Information Inc	800-235-0337	•		•	•	

	CV	CR	PR	RUSSELL (CST)		UC	RE	TX	VS	VR
	•	•	•	National Service Information Inc 800-235-0337		•		•	•	

	CV	CR	PR	SCOTT (EST)		UC	RE	TX	VS	VR
	•	•	•	Equisearch 606-268-1206		•	•	•	•	
	•	•	•	National Service Information Inc 800-235-0337		•		•	•	
	•	•	•	Public Record Information Services 606-879-2141		•	•	•		

	CV	CR	PR	SHELBY (EST)		UC	RE	TX	VS	VR
	•	•	•	Attorney Services of Kentucky (SOP) 502-327-6677		•	•	•	•	•
	•	•	•	County Process Inc (SOP) 502-587-0051		•	•	•	•	
	•	•		Data Search Kentucky 502-637-4658		•	•	•		
	•	•	•	Eagle Investigations Inc (SOP) 800-344-2454		•	•	•		
	•	•	•	Equisearch 606-268-1206		•	•	•		
	•	•	•	National Service Information Inc 800-235-0337		•		•	•	

	CV	CR	PR	SIMPSON (CST)		UC	RE	TX	VS	VR
	•	•	•	🏛 Hollingsworth Court Reporting Inc 504-769-3386		•	•	•	•	
	•	•	•	National Service Information Inc 800-235-0337		•		•	•	

	CV	CR	PR	SPENCER (EST)		UC	RE	TX	VS	VR
	•	•		Data Search Kentucky 502-637-4658		•	•	•		
	•	•	•	Eagle Investigations Inc (SOP) 800-344-2454		•	•	•		
	•	•	•	National Service Information Inc 800-235-0337		•		•	•	

	CV	CR	PR	TAYLOR (EST)		UC	RE	TX	VS	VR
	•	•	•	National Service Information Inc 800-235-0337		•		•	•	

	CV	CR	PR	TODD (CST)		UC	RE	TX	VS	VR
	•	•	•	🏛 Hollingsworth Court Reporting Inc 504-769-3386		•	•	•	•	
	•	•	•	National Service Information Inc 800-235-0337		•		•	•	

	CV	CR	PR	TRIGG (CST)		UC	RE	TX	VS	VR
	•	•	•	🏛 Hollingsworth Court Reporting Inc 504-769-3386		•	•	•	•	
	•	•	•	National Service Information Inc 800-235-0337		•		•	•	

	CV	CR	PR	TRIMBLE (EST)		UC	RE	TX	VS	VR
				Berry & Floyd 502-845-2881		•	•	•		
	•	•	•	Jeffries, Keith A 502-845-7603		•	•	•		
	•	•	•	National Service Information Inc 800-235-0337		•		•	•	

	CV	CR	PR	UNION (CST)		UC	RE	TX	VS	VR
	•	•	•	National Service Information Inc 800-235-0337		•		•	•	
	•	•		🏛 Summit Documents 502-281-5406		•	•	•	•	

DT	CV	CR	PR	WARREN (CST)		UC	RE	TX	VS	VR
•	•	•	•	🏛 Alpha Research LLC (SOP) 205-755-7008				•		
•	•	•	•	🏛 Hollingsworth Court Reporting Inc 504-769-3386		•	•	•	•	
•	•	•	•	National Service Information Inc 800-235-0337		•		•	•	
	•	•	•	Spidel, R Scott 502-782-8471		•		•		

	CV	CR	PR	WASHINGTON (EST)		UC	RE	TX	VS	VR
	•	•	•	National Service Information Inc 800-235-0337		•		•	•	

	CV	CR	PR	WAYNE (CST)		UC	RE	TX	VS	VR
	•	•	•	King & King 606-354-2153		•	•	•		
	•	•	•	National Service Information Inc 800-235-0337		•		•	•	

	CV	CR	PR	WEBSTER (CST)		UC	RE	TX	VS	VR
	•	•		🏛 Alpha Research LLC (SOP) 205-755-7008				•		
	•	•	•	National Service Information Inc 800-235-0337		•		•	•	
	•	•		🏛 Summit Documents 502-281-5406		•	•	•	•	

	CV	CR	PR	WHITLEY (EST)		UC	RE	TX	VS	VR
	•	•	•	King & King 606-354-2153		•	•	•		
	•	•	•	National Service Information Inc 800-235-0337		•		•	•	
	•	•	•	Weatherly Law Office 606-878-9661		•	•	•	•	

	CV	CR	PR	WOLFE (EST)		UC	RE	TX	VS	VR
	•	•	•	Friend, Irene 606-464-2638		•	•	•	•	
	•	•	•	Long, Gordon B 606-349-1558		•	•	•		
	•	•	•	National Service Information Inc 800-235-0337		•		•	•	

	CV	CR	PR	WOODFORD (EST)		UC	RE	TX	VS	VR
	•	•		🏛 Alpha Research LLC (SOP) 205-755-7008				•		
	•	•	•	Equisearch 606-268-1206		•	•	•	•	
	•	•	•	National Service Information Inc 800-235-0337		•		•	•	
	•	•	•	Public Record Information Services 606-879-2141		•	•	•		

SUMMARY OF CODES

COURT RECORDS

CODE	GOVERNMENT AGENCY	TYPE OF INFORMATION
DT	US District Court	Federal civil and criminal cases
BK	Bankruptcy Court	United States bankruptcy cases
CV	Civil Court	Municipal, county and state level civil cases
CR	Criminal Court	Municipal, county and state level criminal cases
PR	Probate Court	Wills and estate cases

COUNTY RECORDS

CODE	GOVERNMENT AGENCY	TYPE OF INFORMATION
UC	UCC Filing Office	Uniform Commercial Code and other personal property liens
RE	Recorder of Deeds	Real property transactions and liens
TX	Tax Assessor	Real property tax information
VS	Vital Records Office	Vital statistics—birth, death, marriage, divorce, etc.
VR	Voter Registration Office	Voter registration and campaign contribution information

- "CODE" designates the agency and type of information obtainable in each county from a retriever.
- The time zone for each county is abbreviated as follows: EST—Eastern Standard Time; CST—Central; MST—Mountain; PST—Pacific; AK—Alaska; HT—Hawaii.
- 🏛—This symbol designates a Public Record Retriever Network member.
- "(SOP)" after the retriever name designates Service of Process.
- Individual retrievers without a company name are listed in order of their last name.
- US District and Bankruptcy courts are indicated only in the counties where courts are located.

LOUISIANA

CV	CR	PR	ACADIA PARISH (CST)		UC	RE	TX	VS	VR
•	•	•	🏛 ABC Investigators Inc (SOP)..........................800-738-7300		•	•	•	•	
•		•	Access Louisiana Inc 800-489-5620		•	•	•		
•	•		🏛 Alpha Research LLC (SOP)................................205-755-7008				•		
•	•	•	Bayou Investigations Inc (SOP)........................800-256-9009		•	•	•	•	•
•	•	•	Forest & Forest 318-237-7651		•	•	•	•	•
•	•	•	🏛 Hollingsworth Court Reporting Inc 504-769-3386		•	•	•	•	
•	•	•	J L & A (SOP) 800-927-0251		•	•	•	•	
•		•	Pelican Land and Abstract Co Inc 318-436-3419		•	•	•		
•	•	•	🏛 Professional Services Bureau (SOP)..............800-960-2214		•	•	•	•	•

CV	CR	PR	ALLEN PARISH (CST)		UC	RE	TX	VS	VR
•	•	•	Abstracting and Legal Research Inc 318-473-9979		•	•	•	•	
•		•	Access Louisiana Inc 800-489-5620		•	•	•		
•	•		🏛 Alpha Research LLC (SOP)................................205-755-7008				•		
•	•		Helping Hand Services 318-463-2528		•				•
•	•	•	🏛 Hollingsworth Court Reporting Inc 504-769-3386		•	•	•	•	
•	•	•	J L & A (SOP) 800-927-0251		•	•	•	•	
•		•	Pelican Land and Abstract Co Inc 318-436-3419		•	•	•		
•	•	•	🏛 Professional Services Bureau (SOP)..............800-960-2214		•	•	•	•	•

CV	CR	PR	ASCENSION PARISH (CST)		UC	RE	TX	VS	VR
•	•	•	Abstracts by Godail 800-660-7318		•	•	•		
•		•	Access Louisiana Inc 800-489-5620		•	•	•		
•	•		🏛 Alpha Research LLC (SOP)................................205-755-7008				•		
•	•	•	Ascension Title Services Inc 504-677-8473		•	•	•		
•	•	•	Bombet & Associates (SOP)................................800-256-5333		•	•	•	•	•
•	•	•	🏛 Hollingsworth Court Reporting Inc 504-769-3386		•	•	•	•	
•	•	•	J L & A (SOP) 800-927-0251		•	•	•		
•	•	•	🏛 Professional Services Bureau (SOP)..............800-960-2214		•	•	•	•	•

CV	CR	PR	ASSUMPTION PARISH (CST)		UC	RE	TX	VS	VR
•	•	•	Abstracts by Godail 800-660-7318		•	•	•		
•		•	Access Louisiana Inc 800-489-5620		•	•	•		
•	•		🏛 Alpha Research LLC (SOP)................................205-755-7008				•		
•	•		Braud, Jerry M 504-447-1227		•	•	•		
•	•	•	🏛 Hollingsworth Court Reporting Inc 504-769-3386		•	•	•	•	
•	•	•	J L & A (SOP) 800-927-0251		•	•	•	•	
•	•	•	🏛 Professional Services Bureau (SOP)..............800-960-2214		•	•	•	•	•

CV	CR	PR	AVOYELLES PARISH (CST)		UC	RE	TX	VS	VR
•	•	•	Abstracting and Legal Research Inc 318-473-9979		•	•	•	•	
•		•	Access Louisiana Inc 800-489-5620		•	•	•		
•	•		🏛 Alpha Research LLC (SOP)................................205-755-7008				•		
•	•	•	🏛 Hollingsworth Court Reporting Inc 504-769-3386		•	•	•	•	
•	•	•	J L & A (SOP) 800-927-0251		•	•	•	•	
•	•	•	🏛 Professional Services Bureau (SOP)..............800-960-2214		•	•	•	•	•

CV	CR	PR	BEAUREGARD PARISH (CST)		UC	RE	TX	VS	VR
•		•	Access Louisiana Inc 800-489-5620		•	•	•		
•	•		🏛 Alpha Research LLC (SOP)................................205-755-7008				•		
•		•	Beauregard Abstract Co 318-463-7090		•	•	•		
•	•		Helping Hand Services 318-463-2528		•				•
•	•	•	🏛 Hollingsworth Court Reporting Inc 504-769-3386		•	•	•	•	
•	•	•	J L & A (SOP) 800-927-0251		•	•	•	•	
•		•	Pelican Land and Abstract Co Inc 318-436-3419		•	•	•		
•	•	•	🏛 Professional Services Bureau (SOP)..............800-960-2214		•	•	•	•	

CV	CR	PR	BIENVILLE PARISH (CST)		UC	RE	TX	VS	VR
•		•	Access Louisiana Inc 800-489-5620		•	•	•		

DT	BK	CV	CR	PR		UC	RE	TX	VS	VR
		•		•	Alpha Research LLC (SOP) 205-755-7008			•		
		•		•	DeSoto Abstract 318-798-1198	•	•	•		
		•	•	•	Hollingsworth Court Reporting Inc 504-769-3386	•	•	•	•	
		•	•	•	J L & A (SOP) 800-927-0251	•	•	•		
		•	•	•	North Louisiana Title Co Inc 800-515-7715	•	•	•		
		•	•	•	Professional Services Bureau (SOP) 800-960-2214	•	•	•	•	•

CV	CR	PR	**BOSSIER PARISH (CST)**	UC	RE	TX	VS	VR
•		•	Access Louisiana Inc 800-489-5620	•	•	•		
•	•		Alpha Research LLC (SOP) 205-755-7008			•		
•		•	DeSoto Abstract 318-798-1198	•	•	•		
•	•	•	Hollingsworth Court Reporting Inc 504-769-3386	•	•	•	•	
•		•	J L & A (SOP) 800-927-0251	•	•	•	•	
•		•	North Louisiana Title Co Inc 800-515-7715	•	•	•		
•	•	•	Professional Services Bureau (SOP) 800-960-2214	•	•	•	•	•
•	•	•	Southern Research Company (SOP) 888-772-6952	•	•	•	•	•
•		•	Taylor Title Inc 318-741-1373	•	•	•		

DT	BK	CV	CR	PR	**CADDO PARISH (CST)**	UC	RE	TX	VS	VR
•	•	•		•	Access Louisiana Inc 800-489-5620	•	•	•		
•	•	•	•		Alpha Research LLC (SOP) 205-755-7008			•		
•	•	•	•	•	Aymond Investigations Inc 318-797-4082	•	•	•	•	
		•		•	DeSoto Abstract 318-798-1198	•	•	•		
•	•	•	•	•	Hollingsworth Court Reporting Inc 504-769-3386	•	•	•	•	
•	•	•		•	J L & A (SOP) 800-927-0251	•	•	•	•	
•	•	•		•	North Louisiana Title Co Inc 800-515-7715	•	•	•		
•	•	•	•	•	Professional Services Bureau (SOP) 800-960-2214	•	•	•	•	•
•	•	•	•	•	Southern Research Company (SOP) 888-772-6952	•	•	•	•	•
		•		•	Taylor Title Inc 318-741-1373	•	•	•		

DT	CV	CR	PR	**CALCASIEU PARISH (CST)**	UC	RE	TX	VS	VR
•	•		•	Access Louisiana Inc 800-489-5620	•	•	•		
•	•	•		Alpha Research LLC (SOP) 205-755-7008			•		
•	•	•		Helping Hand Services 318-463-2528	•				•
•	•	•	•	Hollingsworth Court Reporting Inc 504-769-3386	•	•	•	•	
•	•	•	•	J L & A (SOP) 800-927-0251	•	•	•	•	
•	•	•		Pelican Land and Abstract Co Inc 318-436-3419	•	•	•	•	
•	•	•	•	Professional Services Bureau (SOP) 800-960-2214	•	•	•	•	•

CV	CR	PR	**CALDWELL PARISH (CST)**	UC	RE	TX	VS	VR
•		•	Access Louisiana Inc 800-489-5620	•	•	•		
•	•	•	Colvin, Melanie 318-396-6415	•	•	•	•	
•	•	•	Hollingsworth Court Reporting Inc 504-769-3386	•	•	•	•	
•	•	•	J L & A (SOP) 800-927-0251	•	•	•	•	
•	•	•	North Louisiana Title Co Inc 800-515-7715	•	•	•		
•	•	•	Professional Services Bureau (SOP) 800-960-2214	•	•	•	•	•

CV	CR	PR	**CAMERON PARISH (CST)**	UC	RE	TX	VS	VR
•		•	Access Louisiana Inc 800-489-5620	•	•	•		
•	•	•	Hollingsworth Court Reporting Inc 504-769-3386	•	•	•	•	
•	•	•	J L & A (SOP) 800-927-0251	•	•	•	•	
•		•	Pelican Land and Abstract Co Inc 318-436-3419	•	•	•		
•	•	•	Professional Services Bureau (SOP) 800-960-2214	•	•	•	•	•

CV	CR	PR	**CATAHOULA PARISH (CST)**	UC	RE	TX	VS	VR
•		•	Access Louisiana Inc 800-489-5620	•	•	•		
•	•	•	Hollingsworth Court Reporting Inc 504-769-3386	•	•	•	•	
•	•	•	J L & A (SOP) 800-927-0251	•	•	•	•	
•	•	•	North Louisiana Title Co Inc 800-515-7715	•	•	•		
•	•	•	Professional Services Bureau (SOP) 800-960-2214	•	•	•	•	•

CV	CR	PR	**CLAIBORNE PARISH (CST)**	UC	RE	TX	VS	VR
•		•	Access Louisiana Inc 800-489-5620	•	•	•		

							UC	RE	TX	VS	VR
	•	•		🏛 Alpha Research LLC (SOP)	205-755-7008				•		
	•	•	•	DeSoto Abstract	318-798-1198		•	•	•		
	•	•	•	🏛 Hollingsworth Court Reporting Inc	504-769-3386		•	•	•	•	
	•	•	•	J L & A (SOP)	800-927-0251		•	•	•	•	
	•	•	•	North Louisiana Title Co Inc	800-515-7715		•	•	•		
	•	•	•	🏛 Professional Services Bureau (SOP)	800-960-2214		•	•	•	•	•

CV	CR	PR	CONCORDIA PARISH (CST)		UC	RE	TX	VS	VR
•		•	Access Louisiana Inc	800-489-5620	•	•	•		
•	•		🏛 Alpha Research LLC (SOP)	205-755-7008			•		
•	•	•	🏛 Hollingsworth Court Reporting Inc	504-769-3386	•	•	•	•	
•	•	•	J L & A (SOP)	800-927-0251	•	•	•	•	
•	•	•	North Louisiana Title Co Inc	800-515-7715	•	•	•		
•	•	•	🏛 Professional Services Bureau (SOP)	800-960-2214	•	•	•	•	•

CV	CR	PR	DE SOTO PARISH (CST)		UC	RE	TX	VS	VR
•		•	Access Louisiana Inc	800-489-5620	•	•	•		
•	•		🏛 Alpha Research LLC (SOP)	205-755-7008			•		
•		•	DeSoto Abstract	318-798-1198	•	•	•		
•	•	•	🏛 Hollingsworth Court Reporting Inc	504-769-3386	•	•	•	•	
•	•	•	J L & A (SOP)	800-927-0251	•	•	•	•	
•	•	•	🏛 Professional Services Bureau (SOP)	800-960-2214	•	•	•	•	•

DT	BK	CV	CR	PR	EAST BATON ROUGE PARISH (CAPITAL) (CST)		UC	RE	TX	VS	VR
		•	•	•	Abstracts by Godail	800-660-7318	•	•	•		
•	•	•		•	Access Louisiana Inc	800-489-5620	•	•	•		
•	•	•	•	•	AccuScreen Systems (SOP)	800-383-6476	•		•		•
•	•	•	•		🏛 Alpha Research LLC (SOP)	205-755-7008			•		
•	•	•		•	Bombet & Associates (SOP)	800-256-5333	•	•	•	•	
•	•				🏛 Capitol Document Services Inc	800-408-1262	•		•		
•	•				🏛 Hogan Information Services	405-278-6954					
•	•	•	•	•	🏛 Hollingsworth Court Reporting Inc	504-769-3386	•	•	•	•	
•	•				Information Research	504-387-3878	•		•		
•	•	•	•	•	J L & A (SOP)	800-927-0251	•	•	•	•	
•	•	•	•	•	🏛 Professional Services Bureau (SOP)	800-960-2214	•	•	•	•	•

CV	CR	PR	EAST CARROLL PARISH (CST)		UC	RE	TX	VS	VR
•		•	Access Louisiana Inc	800-489-5620	•	•	•		
•	•	•	🏛 Hollingsworth Court Reporting Inc	504-769-3386	•	•	•	•	
•	•	•	J L & A (SOP)	800-927-0251	•	•	•	•	
•	•	•	North Louisiana Title Co Inc	800-515-7715	•	•	•		
•	•	•	🏛 Professional Services Bureau (SOP)	800-960-2214	•	•	•	•	•

CV	CR	PR	EAST FELICIANA PARISH (CST)		UC	RE	TX	VS	VR
•		•	Access Louisiana Inc	800-489-5620	•	•	•		
•	•	•	🏛 Hollingsworth Court Reporting Inc	504-769-3386	•	•	•	•	
•	•	•	J L & A (SOP)	800-927-0251	•	•	•	•	
•	•	•	🏛 Professional Services Bureau (SOP)	800-960-2214	•	•	•	•	•

CV	CR	PR	EVANGELINE PARISH (CST)		UC	RE	TX	VS	VR
•	•	•	Abstracting and Legal Research Inc	318-473-9979	•	•	•	•	
•		•	Access Louisiana Inc	800-489-5620	•	•	•		
•	•	•	Bayou Investigations Inc (SOP)	800-256-9009	•	•	•	•	•
•	•	•	🏛 Hollingsworth Court Reporting Inc	504-769-3386	•	•	•	•	
•	•	•	J L & A (SOP)	800-927-0251	•	•	•	•	
•	•	•	🏛 Professional Services Bureau (SOP)	800-960-2214	•	•	•	•	•

CV	CR	PR	FRANKLIN PARISH (CST)		UC	RE	TX	VS	VR
•		•	Access Louisiana Inc	800-489-5620	•	•	•		
•	•		🏛 Alpha Research LLC (SOP)	205-755-7008			•		
•	•	•	Colvin, Melanie	318-396-6415	•	•	•	•	
•	•	•	🏛 Hollingsworth Court Reporting Inc	504-769-3386	•	•	•	•	
•	•	•	J L & A (SOP)	800-927-0251	•	•	•	•	

CV	CR	PR		Phone	UC	RE	TX	VS	VR
•	•	•	North Louisiana Title Co Inc	800-515-7715	•	•	•		
•	•	•	🏛 Professional Services Bureau (SOP)	800-960-2214	•	•	•	•	•

CV	CR	PR	GRANT PARISH (CST)		UC	RE	TX	VS	VR
•	•	•	Abstracting and Legal Research Inc	318-473-9979	•	•	•	•	
•	•		Access Louisiana Inc	800-489-5620	•	•	•		
•	•		🏛 Alpha Research LLC (SOP)	205-755-7008			•		
•	•		🏛 Hollingsworth Court Reporting Inc	504-769-3386	•	•	•		
•	•	•	J L & A (SOP)	800-927-0251	•	•	•		
•	•	•	North Louisiana Title Co Inc	800-515-7715	•	•	•		
•	•	•	🏛 Professional Services Bureau (SOP)	800-960-2214	•	•	•	•	•

CV	CR	PR	IBERIA PARISH (CST)		UC	RE	TX	VS	VR
•		•	Access Louisiana Inc	800-489-5620	•	•	•		
•	•		🏛 Alpha Research LLC (SOP)	205-755-7008			•		
•	•	•	Bayou Investigations Inc (SOP)	800-256-9009	•	•	•	•	
•	•	•	🏛 Hollingsworth Court Reporting Inc	504-769-3386	•	•	•		
•	•	•	J L & A (SOP)	800-927-0251	•	•	•		
•	•	•	🏛 Professional Services Bureau (SOP)	800-960-2214	•	•	•	•	•

CV	CR	PR	IBERVILLE PARISH (CST)		UC	RE	TX	VS	VR
•		•	Access Louisiana Inc	800-489-5620	•	•	•		
•	•		🏛 Alpha Research LLC (SOP)	205-755-7008			•		
•	•	•	Ascension Title Services Inc	504-677-8473	•	•	•		
•	•	•	Bombet & Associates (SOP)	800-256-5333	•	•	•	•	
•	•	•	🏛 Hollingsworth Court Reporting Inc	504-769-3386	•	•	•		
•	•	•	J L & A (SOP)	800-927-0251	•	•	•	•	
•	•	•	🏛 Professional Services Bureau (SOP)	800-960-2214	•	•	•	•	•

CV	CR	PR	JACKSON PARISH (CST)		UC	RE	TX	VS	VR
•		•	Access Louisiana Inc	800-489-5620	•	•	•		
•	•	•	Colvin, Melanie	318-396-6415	•	•	•	•	
•	•	•	🏛 Hollingsworth Court Reporting Inc	504-769-3386	•	•	•	•	
•	•	•	J L & A (SOP)	800-927-0251	•	•	•	•	
•	•	•	North Louisiana Title Co Inc	800-515-7715	•	•	•		
•	•	•	🏛 Professional Services Bureau (SOP)	800-960-2214	•	•	•	•	•

CV	CR	PR	JEFFERSON PARISH (CST)		UC	RE	TX	VS	VR
•		•	Access Louisiana Inc	800-489-5620	•	•	•		
•	•		🏛 Alpha Research LLC (SOP)	205-755-7008			•		
•	•		Analytical Inspection Services	504-832-0869	•	•	•	•	•
•	•	•	Bombet & Associates (SOP)	800-256-5333	•	•	•	•	•
•	•	•	Braud, Jerry M	504-447-1227	•	•	•		
•	•	•	🏛 Hollingsworth Court Reporting Inc	504-769-3386	•	•	•		
•	•	•	J L & A (SOP)	800-927-0251	•	•	•		
•	•	•	LegalMedic Services Inc (SOP)	504-347-3408	•	•	•		•
•	•	•	Powell's Backtracking (SOP)	504-242-7700		•	•		
•	•	•	🏛 Professional Services Bureau (SOP)	800-960-2214	•	•	•		•
•	•	•	Vinson Detective Agency (SOP)	800-441-7899	•	•	•		

CV	CR	PR	JEFFERSON DAVIS PARISH (CST)		UC	RE	TX	VS	VR
•	•	•	🏛 ABC Investigators Inc (SOP)	800-738-7300	•	•	•		
•		•	Access Louisiana Inc	800-489-5620	•	•	•		
•	•		🏛 Alpha Research LLC (SOP)	205-755-7008			•		
•	•	•	Bayou Investigations Inc (SOP)	800-256-9009	•	•	•	•	
•	•	•	🏛 Hollingsworth Court Reporting Inc	504-769-3386	•	•	•		
•	•	•	J L & A (SOP)	800-927-0251	•	•	•		
		•	Pelican Land and Abstract Co Inc	318-436-3419	•	•	•		
•	•	•	🏛 Professional Services Bureau (SOP)	800-960-2214	•	•	•	•	

CV	CR	PR	LA SALLE PARISH (CST)		UC	RE	TX	VS	VR
•		•	Access Louisiana Inc	800-489-5620	•	•	•		
•	•	•	🏛 Hollingsworth Court Reporting Inc	504-769-3386	•	•	•		

•	•	•	J L & A (SOP) 800-927-0251	•	•	•	•	
•	•	•	North Louisiana Title Co Inc 800-515-7715	•	•	•		
•	•	•	🏛 Professional Services Bureau (SOP) 800-960-2214	•	•	•	•	•

DT	CV	CR	PR	**LAFAYETTE PARISH (CST)**	UC	RE	TX	VS	VR
•	•	•	•	🏛 ABC Investigators Inc (SOP) 800-738-7300	•	•	•	•	
•	•		•	Access Louisiana Inc 800-489-5620	•	•	•		
•	•		•	🏛 Alpha Research LLC (SOP) 205-755-7008			•		
•	•	•	•	Bayou Investigations Inc (SOP) 800-256-9009	•	•	•	•	•
•	•	•	•	Forest & Forest 318-237-7651	•	•	•	•	•
•	•	•	•	🏛 Hollingsworth Court Reporting Inc 504-769-3386	•	•	•	•	
•	•	•	•	J L & A (SOP) 800-927-0251	•	•	•	•	
•	•	•	•	🏛 Professional Services Bureau (SOP) 800-960-2214	•	•	•	•	•
•	•	•	•	🏛 Professional Services Bureau (SOP) 800-864-5154	•	•	•	•	

	CV	CR	PR	**LAFOURCHE PARISH (CST)**	UC	RE	TX	VS	VR
	•		•	Access Louisiana Inc 800-489-5620	•	•	•		
	•	•		🏛 Alpha Research LLC (SOP) 205-755-7008			•		
	•		•	Braud, Jerry M 504-447-1227	•	•	•		
	•	•	•	🏛 Hollingsworth Court Reporting Inc 504-769-3386	•	•	•	•	
	•	•	•	J L & A (SOP) 800-927-0251	•	•	•	•	
	•	•	•	🏛 Professional Services Bureau (SOP) 800-960-2214	•	•	•	•	•

	CV	CR	PR	**LINCOLN PARISH (CST)**	UC	RE	TX	VS	VR
	•		•	Access Louisiana Inc 800-489-5620	•	•	•		
	•	•		🏛 Alpha Research LLC (SOP) 205-755-7008			•		
	•		•	Colvin, Melanie 318-396-6415	•	•	•	•	
	•		•	DeSoto Abstract 318-798-1198	•	•	•		
	•	•	•	🏛 Hollingsworth Court Reporting Inc 504-769-3386	•	•	•	•	
	•	•	•	J L & A (SOP) 800-927-0251	•	•	•	•	
	•	•	•	North Louisiana Title Co Inc 800-515-7715	•	•	•		
	•	•	•	🏛 Professional Services Bureau (SOP) 800-960-2214	•	•	•	•	•

	CV	CR	PR	**LIVINGSTON PARISH (CST)**	UC	RE	TX	VS	VR
	•	•	•	Abstracts by Godail 800-660-7318	•	•	•		
	•		•	Access Louisiana Inc 800-489-5620	•	•	•		
	•	•		🏛 Alpha Research LLC (SOP) 205-755-7008			•		
	•	•	•	🏛 Hollingsworth Court Reporting Inc 504-769-3386	•	•	•	•	
	•	•	•	J L & A (SOP) 800-927-0251	•	•	•	•	
	•	•	•	Legal Resources 504-542-2199	•	•	•	•	
	•	•	•	🏛 Professional Services Bureau (SOP) 800-960-2214	•	•	•	•	•

	CV	CR	PR	**MADISON PARISH (CST)**	UC	RE	TX	VS	VR
	•		•	Access Louisiana Inc 800-489-5620	•	•	•		
	•	•	•	🏛 Hollingsworth Court Reporting Inc 504-769-3386	•	•	•	•	
	•	•	•	J L & A (SOP) 800-927-0251	•	•	•	•	
	•	•	•	North Louisiana Title Co Inc 800-515-7715	•	•	•		
	•	•	•	🏛 Professional Services Bureau (SOP) 800-960-2214	•	•	•	•	•

	CV	CR	PR	**MOREHOUSE PARISH (CST)**	UC	RE	TX	VS	VR
	•		•	Access Louisiana Inc 800-489-5620	•	•	•		
	•	•	•	Colvin, Melanie 318-396-6415	•	•	•	•	
	•	•	•	🏛 Hollingsworth Court Reporting Inc 504-769-3386	•	•	•	•	
	•	•	•	J L & A (SOP) 800-927-0251	•	•	•	•	
	•	•	•	North Louisiana Title Co Inc 800-515-7715	•	•	•		
	•	•	•	🏛 Professional Services Bureau (SOP) 800-960-2214	•	•	•	•	•

	CV	CR	PR	**NATCHITOCHES PARISH (CST)**	UC	RE	TX	VS	VR
	•	•	•	Abstracting and Legal Research Inc 318-473-9979	•	•	•	•	
	•		•	Access Louisiana Inc 800-489-5620	•	•	•		
	•	•		🏛 Alpha Research LLC (SOP) 205-755-7008			•		
	•	•	•	🏛 Hollingsworth Court Reporting Inc 504-769-3386	•	•	•	•	
	•	•	•	J L & A (SOP) 800-927-0251	•	•	•	•	

DT	BK	CV	CR	PR		UC	RE	TX	VS	VR
•	•	•			Professional Services Bureau (SOP) 800-960-2214	•	•	•	•	•

ORLEANS PARISH (CST)

DT	BK	CV	CR	PR		UC	RE	TX	VS	VR
•	•	•		•	Access Louisiana Inc 800-489-5620	•	•	•		
•	•	•	•		Alpha Research LLC (SOP) 205-755-7008			•		
•	•	•	•	•	Analytical Inspection Services 504-832-0869	•	•	•	•	•
•	•	•	•	•	Bankruptcy Services Inc 214-424-6500					
•	•	•	•	•	Bombet & Associates (SOP) 800-256-5333	•	•	•	•	•
•	•	•	•	•	Hollingsworth Court Reporting Inc 504-769-3386	•	•	•	•	
•	•	•	•	•	J L & A (SOP) 800-927-0251	•	•	•		
•	•	•	•	•	LegalMedic Services Inc (SOP) 504-347-3408	•	•	•	•	•
•	•	•	•	•	Powell's Backtracking (SOP) 504-242-7700			•	•	
•	•	•	•	•	Professional Services Bureau (SOP) 800-960-2214	•	•	•	•	•
•	•	•	•	•	Vinson Detective Agency (SOP) 800-441-7899	•	•	•		

OUACHITA PARISH (CST)

DT	CV	CR	PR		UC	RE	TX	VS	VR
•	•			Access Louisiana Inc 800-489-5620	•	•	•		
•		•		Alpha Research LLC (SOP) 205-755-7008			•		
	•	•	•	Colvin, Melanie 318-396-6415	•	•	•	•	
•	•	•	•	Hollingsworth Court Reporting Inc 504-769-3386	•	•	•	•	
•	•	•	•	J L & A (SOP) 800-927-0251	•	•	•	•	
•	•	•	•	North Louisiana Title Co Inc 800-515-7715	•	•	•		
•	•	•	•	Professional Services Bureau (SOP) 800-960-2214	•	•	•	•	•

PLAQUEMINES PARISH (CST)

CV	CR	PR		UC	RE	TX	VS	VR
•		•	Access Louisiana Inc 800-489-5620	•	•	•		
•	•		Alpha Research LLC (SOP) 205-755-7008			•		
•	•	•	Fleming, Glenn A 504-333-4331	•	•	•		
•	•	•	Hollingsworth Court Reporting Inc 504-769-3386	•	•	•	•	
•	•	•	J L & A (SOP) 800-927-0251	•	•	•	•	
•	•	•	Professional Services Bureau (SOP) 800-960-2214	•	•	•	•	•

POINTE COUPEE PARISH (CST)

CV	CR	PR		UC	RE	TX	VS	VR
•		•	Abstracts by Godail 800-660-7318	•	•	•		
•		•	Access Louisiana Inc 800-489-5620	•	•	•		
•	•		Alpha Research LLC (SOP) 205-755-7008			•		
•	•	•	Hollingsworth Court Reporting Inc 504-769-3386	•	•	•	•	
•	•	•	J L & A (SOP) 800-927-0251	•	•	•	•	
•	•	•	Professional Services Bureau (SOP) 800-960-2214	•	•	•	•	•

RAPIDES PARISH (CST)

DT	BK	CV	CR	PR		UC	RE	TX	VS	VR
		•	•	•	Abstracting and Legal Research Inc 318-473-9979	•	•	•	•	
		•	•	•	Abstracts by Godail 800-660-7318	•	•	•		
•		•		•	Access Louisiana Inc 800-489-5620	•	•	•		
•	•	•	•		Alpha Research LLC (SOP) 205-755-7008			•		
•	•	•	•	•	Hollingsworth Court Reporting Inc 504-769-3386	•	•	•	•	
•	•	•	•	•	J L & A (SOP) 800-927-0251	•	•	•	•	
•	•	•	•	•	North Louisiana Title Co Inc 800-515-7715	•	•	•		
•	•	•	•	•	Professional Services Bureau (SOP) 800-960-2214	•	•	•	•	•

RED RIVER PARISH (CST)

CV	CR	PR		UC	RE	TX	VS	VR
•		•	Access Louisiana Inc 800-489-5620	•	•	•		
•	•	•	Hollingsworth Court Reporting Inc 504-769-3386	•	•	•	•	
•	•	•	J L & A (SOP) 800-927-0251	•	•	•	•	
•	•	•	Professional Services Bureau (SOP) 800-960-2214	•	•	•	•	•

RICHLAND PARISH (CST)

CV	CR	PR		UC	RE	TX	VS	VR
•		•	Access Louisiana Inc 800-489-5620	•	•	•		
•	•	•	Colvin, Melanie 318-396-6415	•	•	•	•	
•	•	•	Hollingsworth Court Reporting Inc 504-769-3386	•	•	•	•	
•	•	•	J L & A (SOP) 800-927-0251	•	•	•	•	
•	•	•	North Louisiana Title Co Inc 800-515-7715	•	•	•		
•	•	•	Professional Services Bureau (SOP) 800-960-2214	•	•	•	•	•

	CV	CR	PR	SABINE PARISH (CST)		UC	RE	TX	VS	VR
	•	•	•	Abstracting and Legal Research Inc 318-473-9979		•	•	•	•	
	•		•	Access Louisiana Inc 800-489-5620		•	•	•		
	•	•		🏛 Alpha Research LLC (SOP) 205-755-7008				•		
	•	•		Helping Hand Services 318-463-2528		•				•
	•	•	•	🏛 Hollingsworth Court Reporting Inc 504-769-3386		•	•	•	•	
	•	•	•	J L & A (SOP) 800-927-0251		•	•	•	•	
	•	•	•	🏛 Professional Services Bureau (SOP) 800-960-2214		•	•	•	•	•

	CV	CR	PR	ST. BERNARD PARISH (CST)		UC	RE	TX	VS	VR
	•		•	Access Louisiana Inc 800-489-5620		•	•	•		
	•	•		🏛 Alpha Research LLC (SOP) 205-755-7008				•		
	•	•	•	🏛 Hollingsworth Court Reporting Inc 504-769-3386		•	•	•	•	
	•	•	•	J L & A (SOP) 800-927-0251		•	•	•	•	
	•	•	•	LegalMedic Services Inc (SOP) 504-347-3408		•	•	•	•	•
	•	•	•	Powell's Backtracking (SOP) 504-242-7700			•	•		
	•	•	•	🏛 Professional Services Bureau (SOP) 800-960-2214		•	•	•	•	•
	•	•	•	Vinson Detective Agency (SOP) 800-441-7899		•	•	•	•	

	CV	CR	PR	ST. CHARLES PARISH (CST)		UC	RE	TX	VS	VR
	•		•	Access Louisiana Inc 800-489-5620		•	•	•		
	•	•		🏛 Alpha Research LLC (SOP) 205-755-7008				•		
	•	•	•	Bombet & Associates (SOP) 800-256-5333		•	•	•		•
	•	•	•	Braud, Jerry M 504-447-1227		•	•	•	•	
	•	•	•	🏛 Hollingsworth Court Reporting Inc 504-769-3386		•	•	•	•	
	•	•	•	J L & A (SOP) 800-927-0251		•	•	•	•	
	•	•	•	🏛 Professional Services Bureau (SOP) 800-960-2214		•	•	•	•	•

	CV	CR	PR	ST. HELENA PARISH (CST)		UC	RE	TX	VS	VR
	•		•	Access Louisiana Inc 800-489-5620		•	•	•		
	•	•		🏛 Alpha Research LLC (SOP) 205-755-7008				•		
	•	•	•	🏛 Hollingsworth Court Reporting Inc 504-769-3386		•	•	•	•	
	•	•	•	J L & A (SOP) 800-927-0251		•	•	•	•	
	•	•	•	Legal Resources 504-542-2199		•	•	•	•	
	•	•	•	🏛 Professional Services Bureau (SOP) 800-960-2214		•	•	•	•	•

	CV	CR	PR	ST. JAMES PARISH (CST)		UC	RE	TX	VS	VR
	•		•	Access Louisiana Inc 800-489-5620		•	•	•		
	•	•	•	Ascension Title Services Inc 504-677-8473		•	•	•		
	•	•	•	🏛 Hollingsworth Court Reporting Inc 504-769-3386		•	•	•	•	
	•	•	•	J L & A (SOP) 800-927-0251		•	•	•	•	
	•	•	•	🏛 Professional Services Bureau (SOP) 800-960-2214		•	•	•	•	•

	CV	CR	PR	ST. JOHN THE BAPTIST PARISH (CST)		UC	RE	TX	VS	VR
	•		•	Access Louisiana Inc 800-489-5620		•	•	•		
	•	•		🏛 Alpha Research LLC (SOP) 205-755-7008				•		
	•	•	•	Bombet & Associates (SOP) 800-256-5333		•	•	•	•	•
	•	•	•	🏛 Hollingsworth Court Reporting Inc 504-769-3386		•	•	•	•	
	•	•	•	J L & A (SOP) 800-927-0251		•	•	•	•	
	•	•	•	🏛 Professional Services Bureau (SOP) 800-960-2214		•	•	•	•	•

BK	CV	CR	PR	ST. LANDRY PARISH (CST)		UC	RE	TX	VS	VR
•	•	•	•	🏛 ABC Investigators Inc (SOP) 800-738-7300		•	•	•	•	
•	•	•	•	Abstracting and Legal Research Inc 318-473-9979		•	•	•	•	
•	•	•	•	Abstracts by Godail 800-660-7318		•	•	•		
•	•		•	Access Louisiana Inc 800-489-5620		•	•	•		
•	•	•		🏛 Alpha Research LLC (SOP) 205-755-7008				•		
•	•	•	•	Bayou Investigations Inc (SOP) 800-256-9009		•	•	•	•	•
•	•	•	•	🏛 Hollingsworth Court Reporting Inc 504-769-3386		•	•	•	•	
•	•	•	•	J L & A (SOP) 800-927-0251		•	•	•	•	
•	•	•	•	🏛 Professional Services Bureau (SOP) 800-960-2214		•	•	•	•	•

ST. MARTIN PARISH (CST)

CV	CR	PR			UC	RE	TX	VS	VR
•		•	Access Louisiana Inc	800-489-5620	•	•	•		
•	•		🏛 Alpha Research LLC (SOP)	205-755-7008			•		
•	•	•	Bayou Investigations Inc (SOP)	800-256-9009	•	•	•	•	•
•	•	•	Forest & Forest	318-237-7651	•	•	•	•	•
•	•	•	🏛 Hollingsworth Court Reporting Inc	504-769-3386	•	•	•	•	
•	•	•	J L & A (SOP)	800-927-0251	•	•	•	•	
•	•	•	🏛 Professional Services Bureau (SOP)	800-960-2214	•	•	•	•	•

ST. MARY PARISH (CST)

CV	CR	PR			UC	RE	TX	VS	VR
•		•	Access Louisiana Inc	800-489-5620	•	•	•		
•	•		🏛 Alpha Research LLC (SOP)	205-755-7008			•		
•	•	•	Bayou Investigations Inc (SOP)	800-256-9009	•	•	•	•	•
•	•	•	🏛 Hollingsworth Court Reporting Inc	504-769-3386	•	•	•	•	
•	•	•	J L & A (SOP)	800-927-0251	•	•	•	•	
•	•	•	🏛 Professional Services Bureau (SOP)	800-960-2214	•	•	•	•	•

ST. TAMMANY PARISH (CST)

CV	CR	PR			UC	RE	TX	VS	VR
•		•	Access Louisiana Inc	800-489-5620	•	•	•		
•	•		🏛 Alpha Research LLC (SOP)	205-755-7008			•		
•	•	•	Bombet & Associates (SOP)	800-256-5333	•	•	•	•	•
•	•	•	🏛 Hollingsworth Court Reporting Inc	504-769-3386	•	•	•	•	
•	•	•	J L & A (SOP)	800-927-0251	•	•	•	•	
•	•	•	🏛 Legal Data Services	504-892-5194	•	•	•	•	
•	•	•	Legal Resources	504-542-2199	•	•	•	•	
•	•	•	LegalMedic Services Inc (SOP)	504-347-3408	•	•	•	•	•
•	•	•	Powell's Backtracking (SOP)	504-242-7700		•	•	•	
•	•	•	🏛 Professional Services Bureau (SOP)	800-960-2214	•	•	•	•	•

TANGIPAHOA PARISH (CST)

CV	CR	PR			UC	RE	TX	VS	VR
•		•	Access Louisiana Inc	800-489-5620	•	•	•		
•	•		🏛 Alpha Research LLC (SOP)	205-755-7008			•		
•	•	•	🏛 Hollingsworth Court Reporting Inc	504-769-3386	•	•	•	•	
•	•	•	J L & A (SOP)	800-927-0251	•	•	•	•	
•	•	•	Legal Resources	504-542-2199	•	•	•	•	
•	•	•	🏛 Professional Services Bureau (SOP)	800-960-2214	•	•	•	•	•

TENSAS PARISH (CST)

CV	CR	PR			UC	RE	TX	VS	VR
•		•	Access Louisiana Inc	800-489-5620	•	•	•		
•	•	•	Colvin, Melanie	318-396-6415	•	•	•	•	
•	•	•	🏛 Hollingsworth Court Reporting Inc	504-769-3386	•	•	•	•	
•	•	•	J L & A (SOP)	800-927-0251	•	•	•	•	
•	•	•	North Louisiana Title Co Inc	800-515-7715	•	•	•		
•	•	•	🏛 Professional Services Bureau (SOP)	800-960-2214	•	•	•	•	•

TERREBONNE PARISH (CST)

CV	CR	PR			UC	RE	TX	VS	VR
•		•	Access Louisiana Inc	800-489-5620	•	•	•		
•	•		🏛 Alpha Research LLC (SOP)	205-755-7008			•		
•	•	•	Braud, Jerry M	504-447-1227	•	•	•		
•	•	•	🏛 Hollingsworth Court Reporting Inc	504-769-3386	•	•	•	•	
•	•	•	J L & A (SOP)	800-927-0251	•	•	•	•	
•	•	•	🏛 Professional Services Bureau (SOP)	800-960-2214	•	•	•	•	•

UNION PARISH (CST)

CV	CR	PR			UC	RE	TX	VS	VR
•		•	Access Louisiana Inc	800-489-5620	•	•	•		
•	•	•	Colvin, Melanie	318-396-6415	•	•	•	•	
•	•	•	🏛 Hollingsworth Court Reporting Inc	504-769-3386	•	•	•	•	
•	•	•	J L & A (SOP)	800-927-0251	•	•	•	•	
•	•	•	North Louisiana Title Co Inc	800-515-7715	•	•	•		
•	•	•	🏛 Professional Services Bureau (SOP)	800-960-2214	•	•	•	•	•

CV	CR	PR	VERMILION PARISH (CST)		UC	RE	TX	VS	VR
•	•	•	🏛 ABC Investigators Inc (SOP).............................. 800-738-7300		•	•	•	•	
•		•	Access Louisiana Inc 800-489-5620		•	•	•		
•	•		🏛 Alpha Research LLC (SOP)............................... 205-755-7008				•		
•	•	•	Bayou Investigations Inc (SOP)........................... 800-256-9009		•	•	•	•	•
•	•	•	Forest & Forest 318-237-7651		•	•	•	•	•
•	•	•	🏛 Hollingsworth Court Reporting Inc 504-769-3386		•	•	•		
•	•	•	J L & A (SOP) 800-927-0251		•	•	•		
•	•	•	🏛 Professional Services Bureau (SOP)................... 800-960-2214		•	•	•	•	•

CV	CR	PR	VERNON PARISH (CST)		UC	RE	TX	VS	VR
•	•	•	Abstracting and Legal Research Inc 318-473-9979		•	•	•	•	
•		•	Access Louisiana Inc 800-489-5620		•	•	•		
•	•		🏛 Alpha Research LLC (SOP)............................... 205-755-7008				•		
•			Helping Hand Services 318-463-2528		•			•	
•	•	•	🏛 Hollingsworth Court Reporting Inc 504-769-3386		•	•	•		
•	•	•	J L & A (SOP) 800-927-0251		•	•	•		
•	•		Perry, Howard G 318-239-7044						
•	•	•	🏛 Professional Services Bureau (SOP)................... 800-960-2214		•	•	•	•	•

CV	CR	PR	WASHINGTON PARISH (CST)		UC	RE	TX	VS	VR
•		•	Access Louisiana Inc 800-489-5620		•	•	•		
•	•	•	🏛 Hollingsworth Court Reporting Inc 504-769-3386		•	•	•		
•	•	•	J L & A (SOP) 800-927-0251		•	•	•		
•	•	•	🏛 Legal Data Services 504-892-5194		•	•	•	•	
•	•	•	Legal Resources 504-542-2199		•	•	•	•	
•	•	•	🏛 Professional Services Bureau (SOP)................... 800-960-2214		•	•	•	•	•

CV	CR	PR	WEBSTER PARISH (CST)		UC	RE	TX	VS	VR
•		•	Access Louisiana Inc 800-489-5620		•	•	•		
•	•		🏛 Alpha Research LLC (SOP)............................... 205-755-7008				•		
•		•	DeSoto Abstract 318-798-1198		•	•	•		
•	•	•	🏛 Hollingsworth Court Reporting Inc 504-769-3386		•	•	•	•	
•	•	•	J L & A (SOP) 800-927-0251		•	•	•	•	
•	•	•	North Louisiana Title Co Inc 800-515-7715		•	•	•		
•	•	•	🏛 Professional Services Bureau (SOP)................... 800-960-2214		•	•	•	•	•

CV	CR	PR	WEST BATON ROUGE PARISH (CST)		UC	RE	TX	VS	VR
•	•	•	Abstracts by Godail 800-660-7318		•	•	•		
•		•	Access Louisiana Inc 800-489-5620		•	•	•		
•	•	•	AccuScreen Systems (SOP).................................. 800-383-6476		•		•		•
•	•		🏛 Alpha Research LLC (SOP)............................... 205-755-7008				•		
•	•	•	Bombet & Associates (SOP)................................ 800-256-5333		•	•	•	•	•
•	•	•	🏛 Hollingsworth Court Reporting Inc 504-769-3386		•	•	•	•	
•			Information Research 504-387-3878			•			
•	•	•	J L & A (SOP) 800-927-0251		•	•	•	•	
•	•	•	🏛 Professional Services Bureau (SOP)................... 800-960-2214		•	•	•	•	•

CV	CR	PR	WEST CARROLL PARISH (CST)		UC	RE	TX	VS	VR
•		•	Access Louisiana Inc 800-489-5620		•	•	•		
•	•	•	🏛 Hollingsworth Court Reporting Inc 504-769-3386		•	•	•	•	
•	•	•	J L & A (SOP) 800-927-0251		•	•	•	•	
•	•	•	North Louisiana Title Co Inc 800-515-7715		•	•	•		
•	•	•	🏛 Professional Services Bureau (SOP)................... 800-960-2214		•	•	•	•	•

CV	CR	PR	WEST FELICIANA PARISH (CST)		UC	RE	TX	VS	VR
•		•	Access Louisiana Inc 800-489-5620		•	•	•		
•	•	•	🏛 Hollingsworth Court Reporting Inc 504-769-3386		•	•	•	•	
•	•	•	J L & A (SOP) 800-927-0251		•	•	•	•	
•	•	•	🏛 Professional Services Bureau (SOP)................... 800-960-2214		•	•	•	•	•

	CV	CR	PR	WINN PARISH (CST)		UC	RE	TX	VS	VR
	•		•	Access Louisiana Inc 800-489-5620		•	•	•		
	•	•	•	Colvin, Melanie 318-396-6415		•	•	•	•	
	•	•	•	🏛 Hollingsworth Court Reporting Inc 504-769-3386		•	•	•	•	
	•	•	•	J L & A (SOP) 800-927-0251		•	•	•	•	
	•	•	•	North Louisiana Title Co Inc 800-515-7715		•	•	•	•	
	•	•	•	🏛 Professional Services Bureau (SOP) 800-960-2214		•	•	•	•	•

SUMMARY OF CODES

COURT RECORDS

CODE	GOVERNMENT AGENCY	TYPE OF INFORMATION
DT	US District Court	Federal civil and criminal cases
BK	Bankruptcy Court	United States bankruptcy cases
CV	Civil Court	Municipal, county and state level civil cases
CR	Criminal Court	Municipal, county and state level criminal cases
PR	Probate Court	Wills and estate cases

COUNTY RECORDS

CODE	GOVERNMENT AGENCY	TYPE OF INFORMATION
UC	UCC Filing Office	Uniform Commercial Code and other personal property liens
RE	Recorder of Deeds	Real property transactions and liens
TX	Tax Assessor	Real property tax information
VS	Vital Records Office	Vital statistics—birth, death, marriage, divorce, etc.
VR	Voter Registration Office	Voter registration and campaign contribution information

- "CODE" designates the agency and type of information obtainable in each county from a retriever.
- The time zone for each county is abbreviated as follows: EST—Eastern Standard Time; CST—Central; MST—Mountain; PST—Pacific; AK—Alaska; HT—Hawaii.
- 🏛—This symbol designates a Public Record Retriever Network member.
- "(SOP)" after the retriever name designates Service of Process.
- Individual retrievers without a company name are listed in order of their last name.
- US District and Bankruptcy courts are indicated only in the counties where courts are located.

MAINE

			CV	CR	PR	ANDROSCOGGIN (EST)		UC	RE	TX	VS	VR
			●	●	●	Public Information Resource 800-675-6350		●	●	●	●	

			CV	CR	PR	AROOSTOOK (EST)		UC	RE	TX	VS	VR
						See adjoining counties for retrievers						

DT	BK	CV	CR	PR	CUMBERLAND (EST)		UC	RE	TX	VS	VR
		●			Don E Leeman Enterprises 603-755-3030			●	●		
●	●	●	●		🏛 Maine Public Record Services 207-646-9065		●	●	●		
●	●	●	●	●	Public Information Resource 800-675-6350		●	●	●	●	

			CV	CR	PR	FRANKLIN (EST)		UC	RE	TX	VS	VR
			●	●	●	Public Information Resource 800-675-6350		●	●	●	●	

			CV	CR	PR	HANCOCK (EST)		UC	RE	TX	VS	VR
			●	●	●	Graham & Davis Abstracting 207-947-6344		●	●	●		
			●	●	●	Leighton Abstract 207-862-3512		●	●	●	●	

			CV	CR	PR	KENNEBEC (CAPITAL) (EST)		UC	RE	TX	VS	VR
			●	●	●	Facts Investigative Services 207-872-7505		●	●	●	●	
			●	●	●	Public Information Resource 800-675-6350		●	●	●	●	

			CV	CR	PR	KNOX (EST)		UC	RE	TX	VS	VR
			●	●		🏛 Maine Public Record Services 207-646-9065		●	●	●		
			●	●	●	Public Information Resource 800-675-6350		●	●	●	●	

			CV	CR	PR	LINCOLN (EST)		UC	RE	TX	VS	VR
			●	●		🏛 Maine Public Record Services 207-646-9065		●	●	●		
			●	●	●	Public Information Resource 800-675-6350		●	●	●	●	

			CV	CR	PR	OXFORD (EST)		UC	RE	TX	VS	VR
			●	●	●	Public Information Resource 800-675-6350		●	●	●	●	

DT	BK	CV	CR	PR	PENOBSCOT (EST)		UC	RE	TX	VS	VR
●	●	●	●	●	Graham & Davis Abstracting 207-947-6344		●	●	●		
●	●	●	●	●	Leighton Abstract 207-862-3512		●	●	●	●	

			CV	CR	PR	PISCATAQUIS (EST)		UC	RE	TX	VS	VR
			●	●	●	Graham & Davis Abstracting 207-947-6344		●	●	●		
			●	●	●	Leighton Abstract 207-862-3512		●	●	●	●	

			CV	CR	PR	SAGADAHOC (EST)		UC	RE	TX	VS	VR
			●	●		🏛 Maine Public Record Services 207-646-9065		●	●	●		
			●	●	●	Public Information Resource 800-675-6350		●	●	●	●	

			CV	CR	PR	SOMERSET (EST)		UC	RE	TX	VS	VR
			●	●	●	Facts Investigative Services 207-872-7505		●	●	●	●	
			●	●	●	Public Information Resource 800-675-6350		●	●	●	●	

			CV	CR	PR	WALDO (EST)		UC	RE	TX	VS	VR
			●	●	●	Graham & Davis Abstracting 207-947-6344		●	●	●		
			●	●	●	Leighton Abstract 207-862-3512		●	●	●	●	
			●	●		🏛 Maine Public Record Services 207-646-9065		●	●	●		

			CV	CR	PR	WASHINGTON (EST)		UC	RE	TX	VS	VR
						See adjoining counties for retrievers						

			CV	CR	PR	YORK (EST)		UC	RE	TX	VS	VR
			●			Don E Leeman Enterprises 603-755-3030			●	●		
			●	●		🏛 Maine Public Record Services 207-646-9065		●	●	●		

MARYLAND

	CV	CR	PR	ALLEGANY (EST)	UC	RE	TX	VS	VR
		•		Employment Screening Network 800-673-9089					
	•	•		🏛 National Background Investigations Inc 800-798-0079					

	CV	CR	PR	ANNE ARUNDEL (EST)	UC	RE	TX	VS	VR
	•	•	•	A P Legal Support Services 410-366-9109	•	•	•	•	
	•	•		🏛 Alpha Research LLC (SOP)........................ 205-755-7008			•		
	•	•	•	Barrett You & Associates Inc (SOP)........................ 800-944-6607	•	•	•	•	
	•	•	•	Chesapeake Services 800-834-7938	•	•	•	•	
	•	•		Davis Detective Agency (Data Search Int'l) (SOP)............. 800-782-0445	•	•	•	•	
	•	•	•	Dennis E Seymour & Associates (SOP) 410-269-5151	•	•	•	•	•
	•	•	•	Document Resources 800-777-8567	•	•	•	•	•
	•			Douglas Investigations Ltd 800-747-0820					
		•		Employment Screening Network 800-673-9089					
	•		•	Federal Research Corporation 202-783-2700	•	•	•		
	•		•	Harbor City Research Inc 800-445-6029	•	•	•		
	•	•	•	🏛 Hyland Information Services 888-449-5463	•	•	•	•	•
	•	•	•	🏛 Mohr Information Services 800-799-4363	•	•	•		•
	•	•		🏛 National Background Investigations Inc 800-798-0079					
	•	•	•	🏛 Security Consultants Inc (SOP) 202-686-3953	•	•	•	•	•
	•	•	•	🏛 University Process Service (SOP)........................ 301-681-7206	•	•	•		

DT	CV	CR	PR	BALTIMORE (CAPITAL) (EST)	UC	RE	TX	VS	VR
•	•	•	•	A P Legal Support Services 410-366-9109	•	•	•	•	
•	•	•	•	ABIS Inc 800-669-2247	•	•	•		•
•	•	•	•	Barrett You & Associates Inc (SOP)........................ 800-944-6607	•	•	•	•	
•	•	•	•	CSC 410-332-1540	•	•	•	•	
•	•	•	•	Dennis E Seymour & Associates (SOP) 410-269-5151	•	•	•	•	•
•	•	•	•	Document Resources 800-777-8567	•	•	•	•	•
	•			Employment Screening Network 800-673-9089					
•	•	•	•	Federal Research Corporation 202-783-2700	•	•	•		
•	•		•	Harbor City Research Inc 800-445-6029	•	•	•		
•				🏛 Hogan Information Services 405-278-6954					
•	•	•	•	🏛 Hyland Information Services 888-449-5463	•	•	•		•
•	•	•	•	M & M Search Service Inc 202-393-3144	•	•	•	•	
•	•		•	Maryland Research and Abstract Co 410-823-1944	•	•	•		
	•	•		🏛 National Background Investigations Inc 800-798-0079					
•	•	•	•	Process Service Unlimited Inc (SOP) 800-726-7068	•	•	•	•	•
•	•	•	•	🏛 Security Consultants Inc (SOP) 202-686-3953	•	•	•	•	•
•	•	•	•	🏛 University Process Service (SOP)........................ 301-681-7206	•	•	•		
•	•	•	•	W A Haag & Associates Inc (SOP) 703-765-2138	•	•	•	•	•

BK	CV	CR	PR	CITY OF BALTIMORE (CAPITAL) (EST)	UC	RE	TX	VS	VR
•	•	•	•	A P Legal Support Services 410-366-9109	•	•	•	•	
•	•	•	•	ABIS Inc 800-669-2247	•	•	•		•
•	•	•	•	CSC 410-332-1540	•	•	•	•	
•	•	•	•	Dennis E Seymour & Associates (SOP) 410-269-5151	•	•	•		•
•	•	•	•	Document Resources 800-777-8567	•	•	•	•	•
	•			Employment Screening Network 800-673-9089					
•	•	•	•	Federal Research Corporation 202-783-2700	•	•	•		
•	•		•	Harbor City Research Inc 800-445-6029	•	•	•		
•				🏛 Hogan Information Services 405-278-6954					
•	•	•	•	🏛 Hyland Information Services 888-449-5463	•	•	•	•	•
	•	•		🏛 National Background Investigations Inc 800-798-0079					
•	•	•	•	🏛 University Process Service (SOP)........................ 301-681-7206	•	•	•		
•	•	•	•	W A Haag & Associates Inc (SOP) 703-765-2138	•	•	•	•	•

	CV	CR	PR	CALVERT (EST)	UC	RE	TX	VS	VR
	•	•		Davis Detective Agency (Data Search Int'l) (SOP)............. 800-782-0445	•	•	•	•	
		•		Employment Screening Network 800-673-9089					

CV	CR	PR			UC	RE	TX	VS	VR
•	•		🏛 National Background Investigations Inc 800-798-0079						
•	•	•	W A Haag & Associates Inc (SOP) 703-765-2138		•	•	•	•	•

CV	CR	PR	CAROLINE (EST)	UC	RE	TX	VS	VR
•	•	•	Delmarva Abstractors (SOP)... 410-228-6044	•	•	•		
•	•	•	Dennis E Seymour & Associates (SOP) 410-269-5151	•	•	•	•	•
		•	Employment Screening Network 800-673-9089					
•		•	L and L Title Abstract Services 410-820-6566	•	•	•		
•	•		🏛 National Background Investigations Inc 800-798-0079					
•		•	Paralegal Services 410-820-8717	•	•	•	•	
•	•	•	Title Abstract Services 410-228-1188	•	•	•		

CV	CR	PR	CARROLL (EST)	UC	RE	TX	VS	VR
•	•	•	A P Legal Support Services 410-366-9109	•	•	•	•	
•	•	•	Document Resources 800-777-8567	•	•	•	•	•
		•	Employment Screening Network 800-673-9089					
•	•		🏛 National Background Investigations Inc 800-798-0079					
•	•	•	Process Service Unlimited Inc (SOP) 800-726-7068	•	•	•	•	•
•	•	•	🏛 University Process Service (SOP)................................. 301-681-7206	•	•	•		

CV	CR	PR	CECIL (EST)	UC	RE	TX	VS	VR
	•		Employment Screening Network 800-673-9089					
•	•		🏛 National Background Investigations Inc 800-798-0079					

CV	CR	PR	CHARLES (EST)	UC	RE	TX	VS	VR
•	•		Davis Detective Agency (Data Search Int'l) (SOP)............. 800-782-0445	•	•	•	•	
•	•	•	Document Resources 800-777-8567	•	•	•	•	•
		•	Employment Screening Network 800-673-9089					
•	•	•	M & M Search Service Inc 202-393-3144	•	•	•	•	
•	•		🏛 National Background Investigations Inc 800-798-0079					
•	•	•	🏛 University Process Service (SOP)................................. 301-681-7206	•	•	•		
•	•	•	W A Haag & Associates Inc (SOP) 703-765-2138	•	•	•	•	•

CV	CR	PR	DORCHESTER (EST)	UC	RE	TX	VS	VR
•	•	•	Delmarva Abstractors (SOP)... 410-228-6044	•	•	•		
	•		Employment Screening Network 800-673-9089					
		•	L and L Title Abstract Services 410-820-6566	•	•	•		
•	•		🏛 National Background Investigations Inc 800-798-0079					
•		•	Paralegal Services 410-820-8717	•	•	•	•	
•	•	•	Title Abstract Services 410-228-1188	•	•	•		

CV	CR	PR	FREDERICK (EST)	UC	RE	TX	VS	VR
•	•		🏛 Alpha Research LLC (SOP)... 205-755-7008			•		
•	•	•	Document Resources 800-777-8567	•	•	•	•	•
		•	Employment Screening Network 800-673-9089					
•	•	•	🏛 Mohr Information Services 800-799-4363	•	•	•		•
•	•		🏛 National Background Investigations Inc 800-798-0079					
•	•	•	Process Service Unlimited Inc (SOP) 800-726-7068	•	•	•	•	•
•	•	•	Quality Abstractors Inc 301-695-9329	•	•	•		
•	•	•	🏛 Security Consultants Inc (SOP) 202-686-3953	•	•	•	•	•
•	•	•	🏛 University Process Service (SOP)................................. 301-681-7206	•	•	•		

CV	CR	PR	GARRETT (EST)	UC	RE	TX	VS	VR
	•		Employment Screening Network 800-673-9089					
•	•		🏛 National Background Investigations Inc 800-798-0079					

CV	CR	PR	HARFORD (EST)	UC	RE	TX	VS	VR
•	•	•	A P Legal Support Services 410-366-9109	•	•	•	•	
•	•	•	Document Resources 800-777-8567	•	•	•	•	•
		•	Employment Screening Network 800-673-9089					
•	•	•	Federal Research Corporation 202-783-2700	•	•	•	•	
•		•	Harbor City Research Inc 800-445-6029	•	•	•		
•		•	Maryland Research and Abstract Co 410-823-1944	•	•	•		

•	•		🏛 National Background Investigations Inc 800-798-0079			
•	•	•	🏛 Orion Protective Services (SOP)................................. 800-705-7353	• • • • •

CV	CR	PR	HOWARD (EST)	UC	RE	TX	VS	VR
•	•	•	A P Legal Support Services 410-366-9109	•	•	•		
•	•		Davis Detective Agency (Data Search Int'l) (SOP)............ 800-782-0445	•	•	•		
•	•	•	Dennis E Seymour & Associates (SOP) 410-269-5151	•	•	•		•
•	•	•	Document Resources 800-777-8567	•	•	•		•
	•		Employment Screening Network 800-673-9089					
•	•		Federal Research Corporation 202-783-2700	•	•	•	•	
•		•	Harbor City Research Inc 800-445-6029	•	•	•		
•	•	•	🏛 Hyland Information Services 888-449-5463	•	•	•		•
•	•	•	🏛 Investigative Consultants Inc 202-562-1500	•	•	•	•	•
•	•		🏛 National Background Investigations Inc 800-798-0079					
•	•	•	Process Service Unlimited Inc (SOP) 800-726-7068	•	•	•	•	•
•	•	•	🏛 Security Consultants Inc (SOP) 202-686-3953	•	•	•	•	•
•	•	•	🏛 University Process Service (SOP)............................. 301-681-7206	•	•	•		

CV	CR	PR	KENT (EST)	UC	RE	TX	VS	VR
•	•	•	Dennis E Seymour & Associates (SOP) 410-269-5151	•	•	•	•	•
	•		Employment Screening Network 800-673-9089					
•	•		🏛 National Background Investigations Inc 800-798-0079					

BK	CV	CR	PR	MONTGOMERY (EST)	UC	RE	TX	VS	VR
•	•	•	•	ABIS Inc 800-669-2247	•	•	•		•
•	•		•	Accurate Legal Service (SOP) 800-236-9853	•				
•	•	•	•	🏛 Alpha Research LLC (SOP)................................... 205-755-7008			•		
•	•	•	•	Barrett You & Associates Inc (SOP)............................. 800-944-6607	•	•	•	•	
•	•	•	•	🏛 CorpAssist - DC Office (SOP)................................ 800-438-2996	•	•	•	•	•
•	•	•	•	Document Resources 800-777-8567	•	•	•	•	•
•	•			Douglas Investigations Ltd 800-747-0820					
	•		•	Elder Abstracts 301-762-3533	•				
		•		Employment Screening Network 800-673-9089					
•	•	•	•	FDR Info Centers 800-874-4337	•	•	•		
•	•	•	•	Harbor City Research Inc 800-445-6029	•	•	•		
•	•	•	•	Instant Information Systems 703-281-9312	•	•	•	•	
•	•	•	•	🏛 Investigative Consultants Inc 202-562-1500	•	•	•	•	•
•	•	•	•	🏛 Mohr Information Services 800-799-4363	•	•	•		•
	•			Montgomery Investigative Services (SOP)...................... 301-384-7777					•
•	•	•	•	🏛 National Background Investigations Inc 800-798-0079					
•	•	•	•	Process Service Unlimited Inc (SOP) 800-726-7068	•	•	•	•	•
•	•	•	•	Prudential Associates Inc (SOP)................................. 301-279-6700	•	•	•	•	•
•	•	•	•	🏛 Reveal Inc (SOP) 800-276-4826	•	•	•	•	•
•	•	•	•	🏛 Security Consultants Inc (SOP) 202-686-3953	•	•	•	•	•
•	•	•	•	The Seto Company 202-416-1898	•	•	•	•	•
•	•	•	•	🏛 University Process Service (SOP)............................. 301-681-7206	•	•	•	•	•
•	•	•	•	W A Haag & Associates Inc (SOP) 703-765-2138	•	•	•	•	•
•	•	•	•	Washington Document Service 800-728-5201	•	•	•	•	•

DT	CV	CR	PR	PRINCE GEORGE'S (EST)	UC	RE	TX	VS	VR
•		•	•	A P Legal Support Services 410-366-9109	•	•	•	•	
•	•	•	•	Accurate Legal Service (SOP) 800-236-9853	•				
•	•	•	•	🏛 Alpha Research LLC (SOP)................................... 205-755-7008			•		
•	•	•	•	Barrett You & Associates Inc (SOP)............................. 800-944-6607	•	•	•	•	
•	•	•	•	🏛 CorpAssist - DC Office (SOP)................................ 800-438-2996	•	•	•	•	•
	•	•	•	Davis Detective Agency (Data Search Int'l) (SOP)............ 800-782-0445	•	•	•	•	
•	•	•	•	Dennis E Seymour & Associates (SOP) 410-269-5151	•	•	•	•	•
•	•	•	•	Document Resources 800-777-8567	•	•	•	•	•
•	•			Douglas Investigations Ltd 800-747-0820					
	•		•	Elder Abstracts 301-762-3533	•				
		•		Employment Screening Network 800-673-9089					
•	•	•	•	FDR Info Centers 800-874-4337	•	•	•		

				Company	Phone	UC	RE	TX	VS	VR
•	•		•	Harbor City Research Inc	800-445-6029	•	•	•		
•	•	•	•	Instant Information Systems	703-281-9312	•	•	•	•	
•	•	•	•	🏛 Investigative Consultants Inc	202-562-1500	•	•	•	•	•
•	•	•	•	M & M Search Service Inc	202-393-3144	•	•	•	•	
•	•	•	•	🏛 Mohr Information Services	800-799-4363	•	•			•
•			•	Montgomery Investigative Services (SOP)	301-384-7777		•			•
•			•	🏛 National Background Investigations Inc	800-798-0079					
•			•	Process Service Unlimited Inc (SOP)	800-726-7068	•	•	•	•	
•	•	•	•	Prudential Associates Inc (SOP)	301-279-6700	•	•	•		
•	•	•	•	🏛 Reveal Inc (SOP)	800-276-4826	•	•	•	•	
•	•	•	•	🏛 Security Consultants Inc (SOP)	202-686-3953	•	•	•	•	
•	•	•	•	The Seto Company	202-416-1898	•	•	•	•	
•	•	•	•	🏛 University Process Service (SOP)	301-681-7206	•	•	•	•	
•	•	•	•	W A Haag & Associates Inc (SOP)	703-765-2138	•	•	•	•	•

CV	CR	PR	QUEEN ANNE'S (EST)		UC	RE	TX	VS	VR
•	•	•	Chesapeake Services	800-834-7938	•	•	•		
•	•	•	Dennis E Seymour & Associates (SOP)	410-269-5151	•	•	•	•	•
		•	Employment Screening Network	800-673-9089					
•	•		🏛 National Background Investigations Inc	800-798-0079					

CV	CR	PR	SOMERSET (EST)		UC	RE	TX	VS	VR
•	•	•	Ayres, Judith	757-336-5313	•	•	•	•	
	•		Employment Screening Network	800-673-9089					
•	•	•	🏛 MD Abstract & Survey Services	410-641-2298	•	•	•		
•	•		🏛 National Background Investigations Inc	800-798-0079					

CV	CR	PR	ST. MARY'S (EST)		UC	RE	TX	VS	VR
•	•		Davis Detective Agency (Data Search Int'l) (SOP)	800-782-0445	•	•	•	•	
•	•	•	Document Resources	800-777-8567	•	•	•	•	•
	•		Employment Screening Network	800-673-9089					
•	•		🏛 National Background Investigations Inc	800-798-0079					
•	•	•	Quality Abstractors Inc	301-695-9329	•	•	•		
•	•	•	W A Haag & Associates Inc (SOP)	703-765-2138	•	•	•	•	•

CV	CR	PR	TALBOT (EST)		UC	RE	TX	VS	VR
•	•	•	Accurate Abstracts Inc	410-819-0334	•	•	•	•	
•	•	•	Delmarva Abstractors (SOP)	410-228-6044	•	•	•		
•	•	•	Dennis E Seymour & Associates (SOP)	410-269-5151	•	•	•	•	•
		•	Employment Screening Network	800-673-9089					
•		•	L and L Title Abstract Services	410-820-6566	•	•	•		
•	•		🏛 National Background Investigations Inc	800-798-0079					
•		•	Paralegal Services	410-820-8717	•	•	•	•	
•	•	•	Title Abstract Services	410-228-1188	•	•	•		

CV	CR	PR	WASHINGTON (EST)		UC	RE	TX	VS	VR
•	•		🏛 Alpha Research LLC (SOP)	205-755-7008			•		
	•		Employment Screening Network	800-673-9089					
•	•	•	🏛 Mohr Information Services	800-799-4363	•	•	•		•
•	•		🏛 National Background Investigations Inc	800-798-0079					
•	•	•	Process Service Unlimited Inc (SOP)	800-726-7068	•	•	•	•	•
•	•	•	Prudential Associates Inc (SOP)	301-279-6700	•	•		•	
•	•	•	🏛 University Process Service (SOP)	301-681-7206	•	•	•		

CV	CR	PR	WICOMICO (EST)		UC	RE	TX	VS	VR
•	•	•	Ayres, Judith	757-336-5313	•	•	•	•	
•	•	•	Delmarva Abstractors (SOP)	410-228-6044	•	•	•		
		•	Employment Screening Network	800-673-9089					
•	•	•	🏛 MD Abstract & Survey Services	410-641-2298	•	•	•		
•	•		🏛 National Background Investigations Inc	800-798-0079					

CV	CR	PR	WORCESTER (EST)		UC	RE	TX	VS	VR
•	•	•	Ayres, Judith	757-336-5313	•	•	•	•	

- Employment Screening Network 800-673-9089
- ▥ MD Abstract & Survey Services 410-641-2298
- ▥ National Background Investigations Inc 800-798-0079

SUMMARY OF CODES

COURT RECORDS

CODE	GOVERNMENT AGENCY	TYPE OF INFORMATION
DT	US District Court	Federal civil and criminal cases
BK	Bankruptcy Court	United States bankruptcy cases
CV	Civil Court	Municipal, county and state level civil cases
CR	Criminal Court	Municipal, county and state level criminal cases
PR	Probate Court	Wills and estate cases

COUNTY RECORDS

CODE	GOVERNMENT AGENCY	TYPE OF INFORMATION
UC	UCC Filing Office	Uniform Commercial Code and other personal property liens
RE	Recorder of Deeds	Real property transactions and liens
TX	Tax Assessor	Real property tax information
VS	Vital Records Office	Vital statistics—birth, death, marriage, divorce, etc.
VR	Voter Registration Office	Voter registration and campaign contribution information

- "CODE" designates the agency and type of information obtainable in each county from a retriever.
- The time zone for each county is abbreviated as follows: EST—Eastern Standard Time; CST—Central; MST—Mountain; PST—Pacific; AK—Alaska; HT—Hawaii.
- ▥—This symbol designates a Public Record Retriever Network member.
- "(SOP)" after the retriever name designates Service of Process.
- Individual retrievers without a company name are listed in order of their last name.
- US District and Bankruptcy courts are indicated only in the counties where courts are located.

MASSACHUSETTS

	CV	CR	PR	BARNSTABLE (EST)		UC	RE	TX	VS	VR
	•	•	•	Barry Shuster & Associates 800-367-8227		•	•	•	•	•
	•	•	•	🏛 Essex County Paralegals Inc 800-922-4752		•	•	•		
	•	•	•	🏛 Simmons Agency Inc 800-237-8230		•	•		•	•

	CV	CR	PR	BERKSHIRE (EST)		UC	RE	TX	VS	VR
	•	•	•	Barry Shuster & Associates 800-367-8227		•	•	•	•	•
				Registry Research 413-528-3919		•	•		•	

	CV	CR	PR	BRISTOL (EST)		UC	RE	TX	VS	VR
	•	•	•	Barry Shuster & Associates 800-367-8227		•	•	•	•	•
	•	•	•	Bearak Reports 800-331-5677		•	•	•	•	•
	•	•	•	🏛 Essex County Paralegals Inc 800-922-4752		•	•	•		
	•	•	•	🏛 LegalTrieve Information Services 508-238-4227		•	•	•	•	
	•	•	•	Trax (SOP) 401-245-3004		•	•	•	•	•

	CV	CR	PR	DUKES (EST)		UC	RE	TX	VS	VR
	•	•	•	Barry Shuster & Associates 800-367-8227		•	•	•	•	•

	CV	CR	PR	ESSEX (EST)		UC	RE	TX	VS	VR
	•	•	•	🏛 A Scott Broadhurst Associates 617-536-3486		•	•	•		
	•	•	•	Barry Shuster & Associates 800-367-8227		•	•	•	•	•
	•	•	•	Bearak Reports 800-331-5677		•	•	•	•	•
	•	•	•	CSC (SOP) 800-225-6244		•	•	•	•	•
	•	•	•	DiNatale Detective Agency 617-227-4115		•	•	•	•	
	•	•	•	🏛 Essex County Paralegals Inc 800-922-4752		•	•	•		
	•	•	•	First Security Service Corp 617-568-8845		•	•	•	•	
	•	•	•	🏛 LegalTrieve Information Services 508-238-4227		•	•	•		•
	•	•	•	Northshore Paralegal Services 800-883-6020		•	•	•		•
	•	•	•	Paralegal Resource Center Inc 617-742-1939		•	•	•		
	•	•	•	Pickard & Associates Inc 508-468-4118		•	•	•		•
	•	•	•	🏛 Suburban Record Research 617-536-3486		•	•	•		

	CV	CR	PR	FRANKLIN (EST)		UC	RE	TX	VS	VR
	•	•	•	Barry Shuster & Associates 800-367-8227		•	•	•	•	•

DT	CV	CR	PR	HAMPDEN (EST)		UC	RE	TX	VS	VR
•	•	•	•	Barry Shuster & Associates 800-367-8227		•	•	•	•	•

	CV	CR	PR	HAMPSHIRE (EST)		UC	RE	TX	VS	VR
	•	•	•	Barry Shuster & Associates 800-367-8227		•	•	•	•	•

	CV	CR	PR	MIDDLESEX (EST)		UC	RE	TX	VS	VR
	•	•	•	🏛 A Scott Broadhurst Associates 617-536-3486		•	•	•		
	•	•	•	Barry Shuster & Associates 800-367-8227		•	•	•	•	•
	•	•	•	Bearak Reports 800-331-5677		•	•	•	•	•
	•	•	•	CSC (SOP) 800-225-6244		•	•	•	•	•
	•	•	•	DiNatale Detective Agency 617-227-4115		•	•	•	•	
	•			Don E Leeman Enterprises 603-755-3030			•	•		
	•	•	•	🏛 Essex County Paralegals Inc 800-922-4752		•	•	•		
	•	•	•	First Security Service Corp 617-568-8845		•	•	•	•	
	•	•	•	🏛 LegalTrieve Information Services 508-238-4227		•	•	•		•
	•	•	•	🏛 Michael B Fixman & Associates (SOP) 800-434-9626		•	•	•		•
	•	•	•	Northshore Paralegal Services 800-883-6020		•	•	•		•
	•	•		Pace, Walter J 617-389-6730			•	•		
	•	•	•	Paralegal Resource Center Inc 617-742-1939		•	•	•		
	•	•	•	Pickard & Associates Inc 508-468-4118		•	•	•		•
	•	•	•	Quirk Associates 617-326-1202		•	•		•	
	•	•	•	🏛 Simmons Agency Inc 800-237-8230		•	•		•	•
	•	•	•	🏛 Suburban Record Research 617-536-3486		•	•	•		

CV	CR	PR	NANTUCKET (EST)		UC	RE	TX	VS	VR
•	•	•	Barry Shuster & Associates 800-367-8227		•	•	•	•	•

CV	CR	PR	NORFOLK (EST)		UC	RE	TX	VS	VR
•	•	•	🏛 A Scott Broadhurst Associates 617-536-3486		•	•	•		
•	•	•	Barry Shuster & Associates 800-367-8227		•	•	•	•	•
•	•	•	Bearak Reports 800-331-5677		•	•	•	•	•
•	•	•	CSC (SOP) 800-225-6244		•	•	•	•	•
•	•	•	DiNatale Detective Agency 617-227-4115		•	•	•	•	
•			Don E Leeman Enterprises 603-755-3030			•	•		
•	•	•	🏛 Essex County Paralegals Inc 800-922-4752		•	•	•		
•	•		First Security Service Corp 617-568-8845		•	•	•	•	
•	•	•	🏛 LegalTrieve Information Services 508-238-4227		•	•	•		•
•	•	•	Northshore Paralegal Services 800-883-6020		•	•	•	•	•
•			Pace, Walter J 617-389-6730						
•	•	•	Paralegal Resource Center Inc 617-742-1939		•	•	•	•	
•	•	•	Quirk Associates 617-326-1202		•	•		•	
•	•	•	🏛 Simmons Agency Inc 800-237-8230		•	•	•	•	
•	•	•	🏛 Suburban Record Research 617-536-3486		•	•	•		

CV	CR	PR	PLYMOUTH (EST)		UC	RE	TX	VS	VR
•	•	•	Barry Shuster & Associates 800-367-8227		•	•	•	•	•
•	•	•	Bearak Reports 800-331-5677		•	•	•	•	•
•	•	•	DiNatale Detective Agency 617-227-4115		•	•	•	•	
•	•	•	🏛 Essex County Paralegals Inc 800-922-4752		•	•	•		
•	•	•	🏛 LegalTrieve Information Services 508-238-4227		•	•	•		•
•	•	•	Paralegal Resource Center Inc 617-742-1939		•	•	•	•	
•	•	•	Trax (SOP) 401-245-3004		•	•	•	•	•

DT	BK	CV	CR	PR	SUFFOLK (CAPITAL) (EST)		UC	RE	TX	VS	VR
•	•	•	•	•	🏛 A Scott Broadhurst Associates 617-536-3486		•	•	•		
•	•	•	•	•	Barry Shuster & Associates 800-367-8227		•	•	•	•	•
•	•	•	•	•	Bearak Reports 800-331-5677		•	•	•	•	•
•	•	•	•	•	CSC (SOP) 800-225-6244		•	•	•	•	•
•	•	•	•	•	DiNatale Detective Agency 617-227-4115		•	•	•	•	
•	•	•	•	•	🏛 Essex County Paralegals Inc 800-922-4752		•	•	•		
•	•	•	•	•	First Security Service Corp 617-568-8845		•	•	•	•	
•	•	•	•	•	🏛 LegalTrieve Information Services 508-238-4227		•	•	•		•
•	•	•	•	•	🏛 Michael B Fixman & Associates (SOP) 800-434-9626		•	•	•	•	•
•	•	•	•	•	Northshore Paralegal Services 800-883-6020		•	•	•	•	•
•	•	•			Pace, Walter J 617-389-6730						
•	•			•	Paralegal Resource Center Inc 617-742-1939		•	•	•	•	
•	•	•	•	•	Pickard & Associates Inc 508-468-4118		•	•	•	•	
		•	•	•	Quirk Associates 617-326-1202		•	•		•	
•	•	•	•	•	🏛 Simmons Agency Inc 800-237-8230		•	•	•	•	•
•	•	•	•	•	🏛 Suburban Record Research 617-536-3486		•	•	•		

DT	BK	CV	CR	PR	WORCESTER (EST)		UC	RE	TX	VS	VR
•	•	•	•	•	🏛 A Scott Broadhurst Associates 617-536-3486		•	•	•		
•	•	•	•	•	Barry Shuster & Associates 800-367-8227		•	•	•	•	•
•	•	•	•	•	Bearak Reports 800-331-5677		•	•	•	•	•
•	•	•	•	•	CSC (SOP) 800-225-6244		•	•	•	•	•
		•			Don E Leeman Enterprises 603-755-3030			•	•		
•	•	•	•	•	🏛 Essex County Paralegals Inc 800-922-4752		•	•	•		
		•	•	•	🏛 Gazoorian, Marcia A 508-754-9503			•	•	•	
•	•			•	Paralegal Resource Center Inc 617-742-1939		•	•	•	•	
		•	•	•	Quirk Associates 617-326-1202		•	•		•	
•	•	•	•	•	🏛 Suburban Record Research 617-536-3486		•	•	•		
•	•	•	•	•	🏛 Worcester Record Search (SOP) 508-842-7282		•	•	•		•

MICHIGAN

	CV	CR	PR	ALCONA (EST)		UC	RE	TX	VS	VR
	•	•	•	Landmark Title Corp 517-739-1471		•	•	•	•	
	•	•	•	Research North Inc of Alpena 616-347-7366		•	•	•	•	
	•	•	•	Research North Inc of Alpena (SOP).................... 517-356-4500		•	•	•	•	•

	CV	CR	PR	ALGER (EST)		UC	RE	TX	VS	VR
			•	Upper Penninsula Title and Abstract 800-743-2091		•	•	•		

	CV	CR	PR	ALLEGAN (EST)		UC	RE	TX	VS	VR
	•	•	•	🏛 FAR Retriever Bureau (SOP).................... 616-657-2166		•	•	•	•	•
	•	•		🏛 Independent Research Inc 616-429-9873		•	•	•	•	
			•	Lake Michigan Title Co 616-637-8595		•	•	•		
	•		•	🏛 Special Private Investigations Inc (SOP) 800-577-3783		•	•	•	•	

	CV	CR	PR	ALPENA (EST)		UC	RE	TX	VS	VR
	•	•	•	Huron Shores Abstract & Title 517-734-3344		•	•	•		
	•	•	•	Research North Inc of Alpena 616-347-7366		•	•	•	•	
	•	•	•	Research North Inc of Alpena (SOP).................... 517-356-4500		•	•	•	•	•

	CV	CR	PR	ANTRIM (EST)		UC	RE	TX	VS	VR
	•	•		🏛 Behind the Scene Investigations (SOP) 616-946-7198		•	•	•	•	•
	•	•	•	Research North Inc of Traverse City (SOP).................... 616-947-6300		•	•	•	•	•

	CV	CR	PR	ARENAC (EST)		UC	RE	TX	VS	VR
	•	•	•	Arenae Abstract & Title Co 517-846-6560		•	•	•	•	
	•		•	Bay County Abstract Co 800-321-0951		•	•	•		
	•	•	•	Ogeman Title Co 517-345-7240		•	•	•	•	

	CV	CR	PR	BARAGA (EST)		UC	RE	TX	VS	VR
	•	•	•	Copper Range Abstract & Title Co 906-482-7903		•	•	•	•	
	•	•	•	Research North Inc of Marquette (SOP).................... 906-225-1200		•	•	•	•	•

	CV	CR	PR	BARRY (EST)		UC	RE	TX	VS	VR
	•		•	Metropolitan Title Co 616-945-9447		•	•	•	•	
	•		•	🏛 Special Private Investigations Inc (SOP) 800-577-3783		•	•	•	•	
	•	•	•	The Fatman Intl Private Detective Svc (SOP).................... 616-964-2445		•	•	•	•	

DT	BK	CV	CR	PR	BAY (EST)		UC	RE	TX	VS	VR
•	•	•	•	•	🏛 A.S.K. Services Inc 313-416-1313		•	•	•	•	
		•		•	Bay County Abstract Co 800-321-0951		•	•	•		

	CV	CR	PR	BENZIE (EST)		UC	RE	TX	VS	VR
	•	•		🏛 Behind the Scene Investigations (SOP) 616-946-7198		•	•	•	•	•
			•	Benzie County Abstract & Title Co 616-882-9669		•	•	•		
	•	•	•	Research North Inc of Traverse City (SOP).................... 616-947-6300		•	•	•	•	•

	CV	CR	PR	BERRIEN (EST)		UC	RE	TX	VS	VR
	•	•	•	🏛 Case Services Inc (SOP).................... 219-291-0480		•	•	•	•	•
	•	•		🏛 Independent Research Inc 616-429-9873		•	•	•	•	

	CV	CR	PR	BRANCH (EST)		UC	RE	TX	VS	VR
	•		•	Branch County Abstract & Title Inc 517-278-7629		•	•	•	•	

	CV	CR	PR	CALHOUN (EST)		UC	RE	TX	VS	VR
	•	•	•	🏛 Philip Rosenberger Investigations (SOP).................... 800-468-9623		•	•	•	•	•
	•	•	•	Research North Inc of Lansing (SOP) 517-699-4100		•	•	•	•	•
	•	•	•	The Fatman Intl Private Detective Svc (SOP).................... 616-964-2445		•	•	•	•	

	CV	CR	PR	CASS (EST)		UC	RE	TX	VS	VR
	•	•	•	🏛 Case Services Inc (SOP) 219-291-0480		•	•	•	•	•
	•	•		🏛 Independent Research Inc 616-429-9873		•	•	•	•	

CV	CR	PR	Company	Phone	UC	RE	TX	VS	VR
•	•	•	St Joseph County Abstract Office Inc	616-467-6075	•	•	•	•	

CHARLEVOIX (EST)

CV	CR	PR	Company	Phone	UC	RE	TX	VS	VR
•	•	•	Research North Inc of Petoskey (SOP)	616-347-7366	•	•	•	•	•

CHEBOYGAN (EST)

CV	CR	PR	Company	Phone	UC	RE	TX	VS	VR
•	•	•	Cheboygan Straits Area Title	616-627-7181	•	•	•	•	
•	•	•	Research North Inc of Petoskey (SOP)	616-347-7366	•	•	•	•	•

CHIPPEWA (EST)

CV	CR	PR	Company	Phone	UC	RE	TX	VS	VR
•	•	•	Askwith, Elizabeth	906-632-6885	•	•	•		
		•	Chippewa Abstract and Title Co	906-632-0603		•	•		
		•	Mackinac Abstract and Title Co	906-643-7452	•	•	•		

CLARE (EST)

CV	CR	PR	Company	Phone	UC	RE	TX	VS	VR
			Great Lakes Title	616-775-0561	•	•	•		
		•	Houghton Lake Title & Escrow Co	517-366-5551	•	•	•	•	
•		•	Land Title & Abstract Inc	517-426-0011	•	•	•		
•		•	Mt Pleasant Abstract and Title Co	517-773-3651	•	•	•		

CLINTON (EST)

CV	CR	PR	Company	Phone	UC	RE	TX	VS	VR
•	•	•	Ingham County Sheriff's Dept-Civil Div (SOP)	517-393-1200	•	•	•		•
•	•	•	Internet Investigative Services Inc (SOP)	517-694-2879	•	•	•		•
•	•		🏛 Michigan Search Company	313-427-7224	•	•			
•	•	•	Research North Inc of Lansing (SOP)	517-699-4100	•	•	•	•	•

CRAWFORD (EST)

CV	CR	PR	Company	Phone	UC	RE	TX	VS	VR
		•	Alpine Title Co	517-732-7562		•	•		
•		•	AuSable Valley Abstract and Title Co	517-826-3385	•	•	•		
•	•	•	Crawford County Abstract & Title Co	517-348-9832	•	•	•	•	
		•	Houghton Lake Title & Escrow Co	517-366-5551	•	•	•	•	
		•	Main Abstract & Title Co	517-275-5600	•	•	•	•	

DELTA (EST)

CV	CR	PR	Company	Phone	UC	RE	TX	VS	VR
•	•	•	Research North Inc of Marquette (SOP)	906-225-1200	•	•	•	•	•
		•	Upper Penninsula Title and Abstract	800-743-2091	•	•	•		

DICKINSON (CST)

CV	CR	PR	Company	Phone	UC	RE	TX	VS	VR
•	•	•	Penninsula Title and Abstract Corp	906-875-6618	•	•	•		
•	•	•	Research North Inc of Marquette (SOP)	906-225-1200	•	•	•		•
		•	Superior Title and Abstract	906-774-9010		•	•		

EATON (EST)

CV	CR	PR	Company	Phone	UC	RE	TX	VS	VR
•	•	•	Ingham County Sheriff's Dept-Civil Div (SOP)	517-393-1200	•	•	•		•
•	•	•	Internet Investigative Services Inc (SOP)	517-694-2879	•	•	•		•
•	•	•	Research North Inc of Lansing (SOP)	517-699-4100	•	•	•	•	•

EMMET (EST)

CV	CR	PR	Company	Phone	UC	RE	TX	VS	VR
•	•	•	Research North Inc of Petoskey (SOP)	616-347-7366	•	•	•	•	•

GENESEE (EST)

DT	BK	CV	CR	PR	Company	Phone	UC	RE	TX	VS	VR
•	•	•	•	•	🏛 A.S.K. Services Inc	313-416-1313	•	•	•	•	
•		•	•		Abstractor Associates	810-778-7554	•	•	•		
•		•	•		Bureau of Confidential Information (SOP)	810-812-8782	•	•	•	•	•
				•	Centennial Title & Abstract Co	313-238-5100	•	•	•		
				•	Homestead Title	810-227-0140	•	•	•		
			•	•	Huffmaster Associates Inc (SOP)	800-446-1515	•	•	•		•
•		•			🏛 Independent Research Inc	616-429-9873	•	•	•		
•		•			🏛 Lynda Harris Document Search	800-621-4974	•	•	•		
•			•	•	Mallard Investigations	810-627-6605	•	•	•		
•	•	•		•	Metropolitan Title	313-234-4554	•	•	•		
•	•	•	•	•	🏛 SI Services Inc (SOP)	800-258-7604	•	•	•	•	•
•	•	•		•	Sargents Abstract & Title Co	313-767-2355	•	•	•		

	CV	CR	PR	GLADWIN (EST)		UC	RE	TX	VS	VR
			•	🏛 Gladwin County Abstract Company 517-426-7411		•	•	•		
			•	Gladwin Title Co 517-426-0011		•	•	•	•	
			•	Houghton Lake Title & Escrow Co 517-366-5551		•	•	•	•	
	•		•	Land Title & Abstract Inc 517-426-0011		•	•	•	•	

	CV	CR	PR	GOGEBIC (CST)		UC	RE	TX	VS	VR
	•		•	Iron Title & Abstract Co 715-561-3576		•	•	•		

	CV	CR	PR	GRAND TRAVERSE (EST)		UC	RE	TX	VS	VR
	•	•		🏛 Behind the Scene Investigations (SOP) 616-946-7198		•	•	•	•	•
				Benzie County Abstract & Title Co 616-882-9669		•	•	•		
			•	Grand Traverse Title Co 616-946-5686		•	•	•		
	•	•	•	Research North Inc of Traverse City (SOP) 616-947-6300		•	•	•	•	•

	CV	CR	PR	GRATIOT (EST)		UC	RE	TX	VS	VR
			•	Alma Abstract and Title Co 517-463-8325		•	•	•	•	

	CV	CR	PR	HILLSDALE (EST)		UC	RE	TX	VS	VR
			•	Hillsdale Title Company 517-437-7345			•	•	•	

	CV	CR	PR	HOUGHTON (EST)		UC	RE	TX	VS	VR
	•	•	•	Copper Range Abstract & Title Co 906-482-7903		•	•	•	•	
	•	•	•	Peninsula Title and Abstract Corp 906-875-6618		•	•	•		

	CV	CR	PR	HURON (EST)		UC	RE	TX	VS	VR
				See adjoining counties for retrievers						

DT	CV	CR	PR	INGHAM (CAPITAL) (EST)		UC	RE	TX	VS	VR
•	•	•	•	🏛 A.S.K. Services Inc 313-416-1313		•	•	•	•	
•	•	•	•	Document Resources 800-552-3453		•	•	•	•	•
•	•	•		🏛 Independent Research Inc 616-429-9873		•	•	•	•	
	•	•	•	Ingham County Sheriff's Dept-Civil Div (SOP) 517-393-1200		•	•	•		•
•	•	•	•	Internet Investigative Services Inc (SOP) 517-694-2879		•	•	•	•	•
•	•	•		🏛 Michigan Search Company 313-427-7224		•	•	•	•	
•	•	•	•	🏛 Philip Rosenberger Investigations (SOP) 800-468-9623		•	•	•	•	•
•	•	•	•	Research North Inc of Lansing (SOP) 517-699-4100		•	•	•	•	•
•	•	•	•	🏛 SI Services Inc (SOP) 800-258-7604		•	•	•	•	•

	CV	CR	PR	IONIA (EST)		UC	RE	TX	VS	VR
	•	•	•	Research North Inc of Lansing (SOP) 517-699-4100		•	•	•	•	•
	•		•	🏛 Special Private Investigations Inc (SOP) 800-577-3783		•	•	•	•	

	CV	CR	PR	IOSCO (EST)		UC	RE	TX	VS	VR
	•		•	Iosco County Abstract Office Ltd 517-362-3231		•	•	•	•	
	•	•	•	Landmark Title Corp 517-739-1471		•	•	•	•	

	CV	CR	PR	IRON (CST)		UC	RE	TX	VS	VR
	•	•	•	Peninsula Title and Abstract Corp 906-875-6618		•	•	•		

	CV	CR	PR	ISABELLA (EST)		UC	RE	TX	VS	VR
				Isabella County Abstract 517-773-3241			•	•	•	
	•		•	Midland Title Co 517-839-1003		•	•	•	•	
	•		•	Mt Pleasant Abstract and Title Co 517-773-3651		•	•	•		

	CV	CR	PR	JACKSON (EST)		UC	RE	TX	VS	VR
	•	•	•	🏛 Philip Rosenberger Investigations (SOP) 800-468-9623		•	•	•	•	•
	•	•	•	Research North Inc of Lansing (SOP) 517-699-4100		•	•	•	•	•

DT	CV	CR	PR	KALAMAZOO (EST)		UC	RE	TX	VS	VR
•	•	•	•	🏛 A.S.K. Services Inc 313-416-1313		•	•	•	•	
•	•	•	•	Abstractor Associates 810-778-7554		•	•	•		
•	•	•	•	🏛 FAR Retriever Bureau (SOP) 616-657-2166		•	•	•	•	•
•	•	•		🏛 Independent Research Inc 616-429-9873		•	•	•	•	

DT	BK	CV	CR	PR		Phone	UC	RE	TX	VS	VR
		•	•	•	Magic P I & Security Inc (SOP)	800-362-4388	•	•	•	•	

KALKASKA (EST)

		CV	CR	PR		Phone	UC	RE	TX	VS	VR
		•	•		Behind the Scene Investigations (SOP)	616-946-7198	•	•	•	•	•
		•	•	•	Research North Inc of Traverse City (SOP)	616-947-6300	•	•	•	•	•

KENT (EST)

DT	BK	CV	CR	PR		Phone	UC	RE	TX	VS	VR
•	•	•	•	•	A.S.K. Services Inc	313-416-1313	•	•	•		
•	•	•	•		Abstractor Associates	810-778-7554	•	•	•		
•	•	•	•		Independent Research Inc	616-429-9873	•	•	•		
•	•	•	•		Lynda Harris Document Search	800-621-4974	•	•	•		
•	•	•	•	•	Professional Courier Service	616-451-4445	•	•	•		
•	•	•	•	•	Special Private Investigations Inc (SOP)	800-577-3783	•	•	•		
•	•	•	•	•	The Fatman Intl Private Detective Svc (SOP)	616-964-2445	•	•	•		

KEWEENAW (EST)

		CV	CR	PR		Phone	UC	RE	TX	VS	VR
		•	•	•	Copper Range Abstract & Title Co	906-482-7903	•	•	•	•	

LAKE (EST)

		CV	CR	PR		Phone	UC	RE	TX	VS	VR
					Great Lakes Title	616-775-0561	•	•	•		
		•	•	•	Lake County Abstract Co Inc	616-745-3432	•	•	•	•	

LAPEER (EST)

		CV	CR	PR		Phone	UC	RE	TX	VS	VR
		•	•	•	Bureau of Confidential Information (SOP)	810-812-8782	•	•	•	•	•
		•	•	•	Homestead Title	810-227-0140	•	•	•	•	
		•	•	•	Huffmaster Associates Inc (SOP)	800-446-1515	•	•	•	•	•
		•	•	•	LaPeer County Abstract & Title Co Inc	313-664-9951	•	•	•	•	
		•	•	•	Mallard Investigations	810-627-6605	•	•	•	•	
		•	•	•	SI Services Inc (SOP)	800-258-7604	•	•	•	•	•

LEELANAU (EST)

		CV	CR	PR		Phone	UC	RE	TX	VS	VR
		•	•		Behind the Scene Investigations (SOP)	616-946-7198	•	•	•	•	•
				•	Leelanau Title Co	616-271-6191	•	•	•		

LENAWEE (EST)

		CV	CR	PR		Phone	UC	RE	TX	VS	VR
				•	American Title Company of Lenawee	517-263-4040	•	•	•	•	
		•	•	•	Bureau of Confidential Information (SOP)	810-812-8782	•	•	•	•	•
		•	•	•	Central Investigation (SOP)	800-281-8142	•	•	•	•	•
		•	•	•	Data Research Inc (SOP)	800-432-6607	•	•	•	•	•
		•	•	•	Research North Inc of Traverse City (SOP)	616-947-6300	•	•	•	•	•

LIVINGSTON (EST)

		CV	CR	PR		Phone	UC	RE	TX	VS	VR
		•	•	•	Abstractor Associates	810-778-7554	•	•	•		
		•	•	•	Homestead Title	810-227-0140	•	•	•		
		•	•	•	Huffmaster Associates Inc (SOP)	800-446-1515	•	•	•		•
		•	•	•	Landmark Title Service	810-227-1733	•	•	•		
		•	•	•	Legal Services (SOP)	810-353-0990	•	•	•		
		•	•	•	Research North Inc of Lansing (SOP)	517-699-4100	•	•	•	•	•
		•	•	•	SI Services Inc (SOP)	800-258-7604	•	•	•	•	•

LUCE (EST)

		CV	CR	PR		Phone	UC	RE	TX	VS	VR
				•	Mackinac Abstract and Title Co	906-643-7452	•	•	•		

MACKINAC (EST)

		CV	CR	PR		Phone	UC	RE	TX	VS	VR
				•	Chippewa Abstract and Title Co	906-632-0603		•	•		
				•	Mackinac Abstract and Title Co	906-643-7452	•	•	•		
		•	•	•	Research North Inc of Petoskey (SOP)	616-347-7366	•	•	•	•	•
				•	Whiteside Abstract and Title Insurance	906-643-9292	•	•	•		

MACOMB (EST)

		CV	CR	PR		Phone	UC	RE	TX	VS	VR
		•	•	•	A.S.K. Services Inc	313-416-1313	•	•	•	•	
		•	•	•	Abstractor Associates	810-778-7554	•	•	•		
		•	•	•	Bureau of Confidential Information (SOP)	810-812-8782	•	•	•	•	•
					Datatrace Information Services Inc	810-465-7020		•	•		

• • •	Finders Inc (SOP) 810-543-2405	•	• • • •
•	🏛 Franklin Court Research 810-356-4666		•
• • •	Huffmaster Associates Inc (SOP) 800-446-1515	•	• • •
• •	🏛 Independent Research Inc 616-429-9873	•	• • •
• • •	Legal Services (SOP) 810-353-0990	•	• • • •
• •	🏛 Lynda Harris Document Search 800-621-4974	•	• • •
• •	🏛 MGI (SOP) 800-929-1758	•	• • • •
• • •	Mallard Investigations 810-627-6605	•	• • •
• •	🏛 Michigan Search Company 313-427-7224	•	• • •
• • •	🏛 VISTA Inc 810-559-3500	•	• • •

CV	CR	PR	MANISTEE (EST)	UC	RE	TX	VS	VR
•	•	•	Manistee Abstract & Title Co 616-723-3397	•	•	•		
•	•	•	Research North Inc of Traverse City (SOP) 616-947-6300	•	•	•		•

DT	BK	CV	CR	PR	MARQUETTE (EST)	UC	RE	TX	VS	VR
				•	Great Northern Title & Abstract Inc 906-228-6100	•	•	•		
•	•	•	•	•	Research North Inc of Marquette (SOP) 906-225-1200	•	•	•	•	•
				•	Upper Penninsula Title and Abstract 800-743-2091	•	•	•		

CV	CR	PR	MASON (EST)	UC	RE	TX	VS	VR
			Mason County Abstract & Title Inc 800-305-6655	•	•	•		

CV	CR	PR	MECOSTA (EST)	UC	RE	TX	VS	VR
			Great Lakes Title 616-775-0561	•	•	•		

CV	CR	PR	MENOMINEE (CST)	UC	RE	TX	VS	VR
•	•	•	Associated Peninsula Title & Abstract Co 906-863-7871	•	•	•	•	
•	•	•	Research North Inc of Marquette (SOP) 906-225-1200	•	•	•	•	•
		•	Upper Penninsula Title and Abstract 800-743-2091	•	•	•		

CV	CR	PR	MIDLAND (EST)	UC	RE	TX	VS	VR
•		•	Midland Title Co 517-839-1003	•	•	•	•	

CV	CR	PR	MISSAUKEE (EST)	UC	RE	TX	VS	VR
		•	Houghton Lake Title & Escrow Co 517-366-5551	•	•	•	•	
•	•	•	Missaukee Title Co 616-839-4563	•	•	•	•	
•	•	•	Research North Inc of Traverse City (SOP) 616-947-6300	•	•	•		•

CV	CR	PR	MONROE (EST)	UC	RE	TX	VS	VR
•	•	•	Abstractor Associates 810-778-7554	•	•	•		
•	•	•	Central Investigation (SOP) 800-281-8142	•	•	•	•	•
•	•	•	Data Research Inc (SOP) 800-432-6607	•	•	•	•	•
•	•	•	Huffmaster Associates Inc (SOP) 800-446-1515	•	•	•	•	
•	•		🏛 Independent Research Inc 616-429-9873	•	•	•	•	
•	•	•	Legal Services (SOP) 810-353-0990	•	•	•	•	
•	•		🏛 Michigan Search Company 313-427-7224	•	•	•	•	
•	•	•	🏛 VISTA Inc 810-559-3500	•	•	•	•	

CV	CR	PR	MONTCALM (EST)	UC	RE	TX	VS	VR
			See adjoining counties for retrievers					

CV	CR	PR	MONTMORENCY (EST)	UC	RE	TX	VS	VR
•		•	Montmorency Abstract Inc 517-785-4889	•	•	•	•	
•	•	•	Research North Inc of Alpena 616-347-7366	•	•	•	•	
•	•	•	Research North Inc of Alpena (SOP) 517-356-4500	•	•	•	•	•

CV	CR	PR	MUSKEGON (EST)	UC	RE	TX	VS	VR
•	•	•	Duram, James C (SOP) 616-894-8325					
•	•		🏛 Independent Research Inc 616-429-9873	•	•	•	•	
•	•	•	Professional Courier Service 616-451-4445	•	•	•	•	
•		•	🏛 Special Private Investigations Inc (SOP) 800-577-3783	•	•	•	•	

NEWAYGO (EST)

CV	CR	PR		Phone	UC	RE	TX	VS	VR
•	•	•	Duram, James C (SOP)	616-894-8325					
•	•	•	Newaygo County Abstract and Title Co	800-536-5263	•	•	•	•	

OAKLAND (EST)

CV	CR	PR		Phone	UC	RE	TX	VS	VR
•	•	•	A.S.K. Services Inc	313-416-1313	•	•	•	•	
•	•	•	Abstractor Associates	810-778-7554	•	•	•		
•	•	•	Bureau of Confidential Information (SOP)	810-812-8782	•	•	•	•	•
			Datatrace Information Services Inc	810-465-7020		•	•		
•	•	•	Finders Inc (SOP)	810-543-2405	•	•	•	•	•
•			Franklin Court Research	810-356-4666			•		
•	•	•	Homestead Title	810-227-0140	•	•	•		
•	•	•	Huffmaster Associates Inc (SOP)	800-446-1515	•	•	•	•	•
•	•		Independent Research Inc	616-429-9873	•	•	•		
•		•	Landmark Title Service	810-227-1733	•	•	•		
•	•	•	Legal Services (SOP)	810-353-0990	•	•	•	•	•
•	•		Lynda Harris Document Search	800-621-4974	•	•	•		
•	•	•	MGI (SOP)	800-929-1758	•	•	•	•	•
•	•	•	Mallard Investigations	810-627-6605	•	•	•		
•	•		Michigan Search Company	313-427-7224	•	•	•		
•	•	•	SI Services Inc (SOP)	800-258-7604	•	•	•	•	•
•	•	•	VISTA Inc	810-559-3500	•	•	•	•	

OCEANA (EST)

CV	CR	PR		Phone	UC	RE	TX	VS	VR
•	•	•	Duram, James C (SOP)	616-894-8325					
•	•	•	Metropolitian Title Co	800-466-5263	•	•	•	•	

OGEMAW (EST)

CV	CR	PR		Phone	UC	RE	TX	VS	VR
•		•	AuSable Valley Abstract and Title Co	517-826-3385	•	•	•		
		•	Houghton Lake Title & Escrow Co	517-366-5551	•	•	•	•	
•	•	•	Landmark Title Corp	517-739-1471	•	•	•	•	
•	•	•	Ogeman Title Co	517-345-7240	•	•	•	•	
		•	Ogemaw County Abstract Co	517-345-0110	•	•	•		

ONTONAGON (EST)

CV	CR	PR		Phone	UC	RE	TX	VS	VR
•	•	•	Copper Range Abstract & Title Co	906-482-7903	•	•	•	•	

OSCEOLA (EST)

CV	CR	PR		Phone	UC	RE	TX	VS	VR
			Great Lakes Title	616-775-0561	•	•	•		
•	•	•	Lake County Abstract Co Inc	616-745-3432	•	•	•	•	

OSCODA (EST)

CV	CR	PR		Phone	UC	RE	TX	VS	VR
•		•	AuSable Valley Abstract and Title Co	517-826-3385	•	•	•		
•		•	Oscoda County Abstract Inc	517-826-5832	•	•	•		
•	•	•	Research North Inc of Alpena	616-347-7366	•	•	•	•	
•	•	•	Research North Inc of Alpena (SOP)	517-356-4500	•	•	•	•	•

OTSEGO (EST)

CV	CR	PR		Phone	UC	RE	TX	VS	VR
		•	Alpine Title Co	517-732-7562		•	•		
•	•	•	Otsego County Abstract Co	517-732-5765	•	•	•	•	
•	•	•	Research North Inc of Petoskey (SOP)	616-347-7366	•	•	•	•	•

OTTAWA (EST)

CV	CR	PR		Phone	UC	RE	TX	VS	VR
•	•	•	Duram, James C (SOP)	616-894-8325					
•	•		Independent Research Inc	616-429-9873	•	•	•	•	
•	•	•	Professional Courier Service	616-451-4445	•	•	•	•	
•		•	Special Private Investigations Inc (SOP)	800-577-3783	•	•	•	•	

PRESQUE ISLE (EST)

CV	CR	PR		Phone	UC	RE	TX	VS	VR
•	•	•	Huron Shores Abstract & Title	517-734-3344	•	•	•		
•		•	Presque Isle County Abstract	517-734-2816	•	•	•		
•	•	•	Research North Inc of Alpena	616-347-7366	•	•	•	•	
•	•	•	Research North Inc of Alpena (SOP)	517-356-4500	•	•	•	•	•

ROSCOMMON (EST)

CV	CR	PR	Firm	Phone	UC	RE	TX	VS	VR
		•	Houghton Lake Title & Escrow Co	517-366-5551	•	•	•	•	
		•	Main Abstract & Title Co	517-275-5600	•	•	•	•	

SAGINAW (EST)

CV	CR	PR	Firm	Phone	UC	RE	TX	VS	VR
•	•	•	🏛 A.S.K. Services Inc	313-416-1313	•	•	•	•	
•		•	Bay County Abstract Co	800-321-0951	•	•	•		
•	•	•	🏛 SI Services Inc (SOP)	800-258-7604	•	•	•	•	•

SANILAC (EST)

CV	CR	PR	Firm	Phone	UC	RE	TX	VS	VR
		•	Mid Michigan Title & Abstract Co Inc	313-648-4060	•	•	•	•	

SCHOOLCRAFT (EST)

CV	CR	PR	Firm	Phone	UC	RE	TX	VS	VR
•	•	•	Research North Inc of Marquette (SOP)	906-225-1200	•	•	•	•	•
		•	Upper Penninsula Title and Abstract	800-743-2091	•	•	•		

SHIAWASSEE (EST)

CV	CR	PR	Firm	Phone	UC	RE	TX	VS	VR
•	•	•	Homestead Title	810-227-0140	•	•	•	•	
•	•	•	🏛 Michigan Search Company	313-427-7224	•	•	•	•	
•	•	•	Research North Inc of Lansing (SOP)	517-699-4100	•	•	•	•	•
•	•	•	🏛 SI Services Inc (SOP)	800-258-7604	•	•	•	•	•

ST. CLAIR (EST)

CV	CR	PR	Firm	Phone	UC	RE	TX	VS	VR
•	•	•	Abstractor Associates	810-778-7554	•	•	•		
•	•	•	Huffmaster Associates Inc (SOP)	800-446-1515	•	•	•	•	•
•		•	Huron Title Co	313-987-2141	•	•	•		

ST. JOSEPH (EST)

CV	CR	PR	Firm	Phone	UC	RE	TX	VS	VR
•	•	•	St Joseph County Abstract Office Inc	616-467-6075	•	•	•	•	

TUSCOLA (EST)

CV	CR	PR	Firm	Phone	UC	RE	TX	VS	VR
•		•	Bay County Abstract Co	800-321-0951	•	•	•		
•	•	•	🏛 SI Services Inc (SOP)	800-258-7604	•	•	•	•	•

VAN BUREN (EST)

CV	CR	PR	Firm	Phone	UC	RE	TX	VS	VR
•	•	•	🏛 FAR Retriever Bureau (SOP)	616-657-2166	•	•	•	•	•
•	•		🏛 Independent Research Inc	616-429-9873	•	•	•	•	
		•	Lake Michigan Title Co	616-637-8595	•	•	•		
•	•	•	VanBuren County Abstract Office	616-657-4250	•	•	•	•	

WASHTENAW (EST)

DT	CV	CR	PR	Firm	Phone	UC	RE	TX	VS	VR
•	•	•	•	🏛 A.S.K. Services Inc	313-416-1313	•	•	•	•	
•	•	•	•	Abstractor Associates	810-778-7554	•	•	•		
•	•	•	•	Bureau of Confidential Information (SOP)	810-812-8782	•	•	•	•	•
•	•	•	•	Finders Inc (SOP)	810-543-2405	•	•	•	•	•
	•	•	•	Homestead Title	810-227-0140	•	•	•	•	
	•	•	•	Huffmaster Associates Inc (SOP)	800-446-1515	•	•	•	•	•
•	•	•		🏛 Independent Research Inc	616-429-9873	•	•	•	•	
	•		•	Landmark Title Service	810-227-1733	•	•	•	•	
•	•	•	•	Legal Services (SOP)	810-353-0990	•	•	•	•	•
•	•	•		🏛 Lynda Harris Document Search	800-621-4974	•	•	•	•	
•	•	•		🏛 Michigan Search Company	313-427-7224	•	•	•	•	
	•	•	•	Research North Inc of Lansing (SOP)	517-699-4100	•	•	•	•	•
•	•	•	•	🏛 VISTA Inc	810-559-3500	•	•	•	•	

WAYNE (EST)

DT	BK	CV	CR	PR	Firm	Phone	UC	RE	TX	VS	VR
•	•	•	•	•	🏛 A.S.K. Services Inc	313-416-1313	•	•	•	•	
•	•	•	•	•	Abstractor Associates	810-778-7554	•	•	•		
•	•	•	•	•	Bureau of Confidential Information (SOP)	810-812-8782	•	•	•	•	•
					🏛 Datatrace Information Services Inc	810-465-7020		•	•		
•		•	•	•	Finders Inc (SOP)	810-543-2405	•	•	•	•	•
		•	•		🏛 Franklin Court Research	810-356-4666			•		
		•	•	•	Huffmaster Associates Inc (SOP)	800-446-1515	•	•	•	•	•

•	•	•	•		🏛 Independent Research Inc 616-429-9873	•	•	•	•	
•	•	•	•	•	Legal Services (SOP)... 810-353-0990	•	•	•	•	•
•	•	•	•		🏛 Lynda Harris Document Search 800-621-4974	•	•	•	•	
•	•	•	•	•	🏛 MGI (SOP)... 800-929-1758	•	•	•	•	•
•	•	•	•	•	Mallard Investigations 810-627-6605	•	•	•	•	
•	•	•	•		🏛 Michigan Search Company 313-427-7224	•	•	•	•	
•	•	•	•	•	🏛 VISTA Inc 810-559-3500	•	•	•	•	

CV	CR	PR	WEXFORD (EST)	UC	RE	TX	VS	VR
•	•		🏛 Behind the Scene Investigations (SOP) 616-946-7198	•	•	•	•	•
			Great Lakes Title 616-775-0561	•	•	•		
•	•	•	Research North Inc of Traverse City (SOP)........................ 616-947-6300	•	•	•	•	•

SUMMARY OF CODES

COURT RECORDS

CODE	GOVERNMENT AGENCY	TYPE OF INFORMATION
DT	US District Court	Federal civil and criminal cases
BK	Bankruptcy Court	United States bankruptcy cases
CV	Civil Court	Municipal, county and state level civil cases
CR	Criminal Court	Municipal, county and state level criminal cases
PR	Probate Court	Wills and estate cases

COUNTY RECORDS

CODE	GOVERNMENT AGENCY	TYPE OF INFORMATION
UC	UCC Filing Office	Uniform Commercial Code and other personal property liens
RE	Recorder of Deeds	Real property transactions and liens
TX	Tax Assessor	Real property tax information
VS	Vital Records Office	Vital statistics—birth, death, marriage, divorce, etc.
VR	Voter Registration Office	Voter registration and campaign contribution information

- "CODE" designates the agency and type of information obtainable in each county from a retriever.
- The time zone for each county is abbreviated as follows: EST—Eastern Standard Time; CST—Central; MST—Mountain; PST—Pacific; AK—Alaska; HT—Hawaii.
- 🏛—This symbol designates a Public Record Retriever Network member.
- "(SOP)" after the retriever name designates Service of Process.
- Individual retrievers without a company name are listed in order of their last name.
- US District and Bankruptcy courts are indicated only in the counties where courts are located.

MINNESOTA

CV	CR	PR	AITKIN (CST)		UC	RE	TX	VS	VR
•			Aitkin County Abstract Co 218-927-3608			•	•		
•	•	•	🏛 Capitol Lien Records and Research 800-845-4077		•	•	•	•	•
•	•	•	Port-o-Wild's Security Services (SOP) 218-751-8200		•	•	•	•	

CV	CR	PR	ANOKA (CST)		UC	RE	TX	VS	VR
•	•	•	Accountable Process Servers (SOP) 612-427-0225		•	•	•	•	
•		•	Associated Abstracting Services of MN 612-861-7998		•	•	•		
•	•	•	🏛 Capitol Lien Records and Research 800-845-4077		•	•	•	•	•
•	•	•	Dovolos & Associates 612-321-0095		•	•	•	•	
	•		Empfacts 800-922-2702						
•		•	Heartland Corporate Services 800-327-8806		•	•	•	•	•
•	•	•	🏛 Heartland Information Services 800-967-1882		•	•	•	•	•
•	•	•	🏛 INPRO (SOP) 612-891-3617		•	•	•	•	•
•		•	Independent Abstracting Service Inc 612-789-8440		•	•	•	•	
•	•	•	🏛 Information Highway Inc 612-631-8131		•	•	•	•	
•	•	•	🏛 Information Reporting Services Inc 612-870-8770		•	•	•	•	•
•		•	Land Title Inc 612-638-1900		•	•	•	•	
•	•	•	Legal Courier Service (SOP) 612-332-7203		•	•	•	•	
•	•	•	Metro Legal Services 612-332-0202		•	•	•	•	
•	•	•	🏛 Professional Research Services Inc 612-941-9040		•	•	•	•	
•	•		🏛 Team Eagle 800-251-2540		•		•		
•		•	Twin City Abstract Corp 612-224-7072		•	•	•		
•	•	•	🏛 Verified Credentials 612-431-1811		•	•	•	•	

CV	CR	PR	BECKER (CST)		UC	RE	TX	VS	VR
•	•	•	🏛 Capitol Lien Records and Research 800-845-4077		•	•	•	•	•
	•		🏛 Horvath Enterprises 320-983-3253						
•	•	•	P.I. Services (SOP) 800-553-4842		•	•	•	•	
•	•	•	Port-o-Wild's Security Services (SOP) 218-751-8200		•	•	•	•	

CV	CR	PR	BELTRAMI (CST)		UC	RE	TX	VS	VR
•	•	•	ACME Research (SOP) 218-224-3239		•	•	•	•	
•	•	•	🏛 Capitol Lien Records and Research 800-845-4077		•	•	•	•	•
•		•	Complete Title Service of Walker Inc 800-837-2556		•	•	•		
•	•	•	Port-o-Wild's Security Services (SOP) 218-751-8200		•	•	•	•	
			Sathre Abstractors Inc 218-751-4565		•	•	•		

CV	CR	PR	BENTON (CST)		UC	RE	TX	VS	VR
•		•	Associated Abstracting Services of MN 612-861-7998		•	•	•		
•		•	Benton County Abstract Company 612-968-7278		•	•	•	•	
•	•	•	🏛 Capitol Lien Records and Research 800-845-4077		•	•	•	•	•
•		•	Heartland Title and Abstract Co 320-253-8860		•	•	•	•	
	•		🏛 Horvath Enterprises 320-983-3253						
•		•	Tri-County Abstract and Title Guaranty 800-892-2399		•	•	•		

CV	CR	PR	BIG STONE (CST)		UC	RE	TX	VS	VR
•	•	•	🏛 Capitol Lien Records and Research 800-845-4077		•	•	•	•	•

CV	CR	PR	BLUE EARTH (CST)		UC	RE	TX	VS	VR
•		•	Associated Abstracting Services of MN 612-861-7998		•	•	•		
•	•	•	🏛 Capitol Lien Records and Research 800-845-4077		•	•	•	•	•

CV	CR	PR	BROWN (CST)		UC	RE	TX	VS	VR
•		•	Associated Abstracting Services of MN 612-861-7998		•	•	•		
•	•	•	🏛 Capitol Lien Records and Research 800-845-4077		•	•	•	•	•
•			Minn*Dak Search Service 507-694-1168		•		•		
•	•	•	Skyline Consulting 507-359-1131		•	•	•	•	

CV	CR	PR	CARLTON (CST)		UC	RE	TX	VS	VR
•	•	•	Abstract and Title Services of Carlton Inc (SOP) 218-384-3450		•	•	•	•	

150

●	●	●	🏛 Capitol Lien Records and Research 800-845-4077	●	●	●	●	●

CV	CR	PR	CARVER (CST)	UC	RE	TX	VS	VR
●		●	Associated Abstracting Services of MN 612-861-7998	●	●	●		
●	●	●	🏛 Capitol Lien Records and Research 800-845-4077	●	●	●	●	●
	●		Empfacts 800-922-2702					
●		●	Heartland Corporate Services 800-327-8806	●	●	●	●	●
●	●	●	🏛 Heartland Information Services 800-967-1882	●	●	●	●	●
●	●	●	🏛 INPRO (SOP) 612-891-3617	●	●	●	●	●
●		●	Independent Abstracting Service Inc 612-789-8440	●	●	●	●	
●		●	🏛 Information Highway Inc 612-631-8131	●	●	●	●	
●	●	●	🏛 Information Reporting Services Inc 612-870-8770	●	●	●	●	●
●	●	●	Legal Courier Service (SOP) 612-332-7203	●	●	●	●	
●	●	●	Metro Legal Services 612-332-0202	●	●	●	●	
●	●	●	🏛 Professional Research Services Inc 612-941-9040	●	●	●	●	
●		●	🏛 Team Eagle 800-251-2540	●		●		
	●		Twin City Abstract Corp 612-224-7072	●	●	●		
●	●	●	🏛 Verified Credentials 612-431-1811	●	●	●	●	

CV	CR	PR	CASS (CST)	UC	RE	TX	VS	VR
●	●	●	ACME Research (SOP) 218-224-3239	●	●	●	●	
●	●	●	🏛 Capitol Lien Records and Research 800-845-4077	●	●	●	●	●
●		●	Complete Title Service of Walker Inc 800-837-2556	●	●	●		
	●	●	Cygneture Title Inc 218-828-0122	●	●	●		
●	●	●	Port-o-Wild's Security Services (SOP) 218-751-8200	●	●	●	●	
●		●	Tri-County Abstract and Title Guaranty 800-892-2399	●	●	●		

CV	CR	PR	CHIPPEWA (CST)	UC	RE	TX	VS	VR
●	●	●	🏛 Capitol Lien Records and Research 800-845-4077	●	●	●	●	●
●			Minn*Dak Search Service 507-694-1168	●		●		

CV	CR	PR	CHISAGO (CST)	UC	RE	TX	VS	VR
●		●	Associated Abstracting Services of MN 612-861-7998	●	●	●		
●	●	●	🏛 Capitol Lien Records and Research 800-845-4077	●	●	●	●	●
●		●	Independent Abstracting Service Inc 612-789-8440	●	●	●		
●		●	Land Title Inc 612-638-1900		●	●		
●	●	●	Peterson Abstract Co 612-257-4200	●	●	●		

CV	CR	PR	CLAY (CST)	UC	RE	TX	VS	VR
●	●	●	🏛 Capitol Lien Records and Research 800-845-4077	●	●	●	●	●
●		●	Cass County Abstract Co 701-232-3341	●	●	●		
●		●	Clay County Abstract Co 218-233-1358	●	●			
●	●	●	P.I. Services (SOP) 800-553-4842	●	●	●	●	
●	●		🏛 Team Eagle 800-251-2540	●		●		

CV	CR	PR	CLEARWATER (CST)	UC	RE	TX	VS	VR
●	●	●	🏛 Capitol Lien Records and Research 800-845-4077	●	●	●	●	●
●	●	●	Port-o-Wild's Security Services (SOP) 218-751-8200	●	●	●	●	

CV	CR	PR	COOK (CST)	UC	RE	TX	VS	VR
●	●	●	🏛 Capitol Lien Records and Research 800-845-4077	●	●	●	●	●

CV	CR	PR	COTTONWOOD (CST)	UC	RE	TX	VS	VR
●	●	●	🏛 Capitol Lien Records and Research 800-845-4077	●	●	●	●	●
●			Cottonwood County Abstract Company 507-831-1504		●	●		
●			Minn*Dak Search Service 507-694-1168	●		●		

CV	CR	PR	CROW WING (CST)	UC	RE	TX	VS	VR
●	●	●	🏛 Capitol Lien Records and Research 800-845-4077	●	●	●	●	●
●			Crow Wing County Abstract Co 218-829-7368	●	●	●		●
	●	●	Cygneture Title Inc 218-828-0122	●	●	●		
●	●	●	Port-o-Wild's Security Services (SOP) 218-751-8200	●	●	●		

CV	CR	PR	DAKOTA (CST)		UC	RE	TX	VS	VR
•	•		🏛 Alpha Court Records & Research	612-699-2222	•		•		
•		•	Associated Abstracting Services of MN	612-861-7998	•	•	•		
•	•	•	🏛 Capitol Lien Records and Research	800-845-4077	•	•	•	•	•
		•	Dakota County Abstract Co	320-437-5600	•	•	•		
•	•	•	Dovolos & Associates	612-321-0095	•	•	•	•	
	•		Empfacts	800-922-2702					
		•	Heartland Corporate Services	800-327-8806	•	•	•	•	•
•	•	•	🏛 INPRO (SOP)	612-891-3617	•	•	•	•	•
		•	Independent Abstracting Service Inc	612-789-8440	•	•	•		
•	•	•	🏛 Information Highway Inc	612-631-8131	•	•	•		
•	•	•	🏛 Information Reporting Services Inc	612-870-8770	•	•	•		•
		•	Land Title Inc	612-638-1900	•	•	•		
•	•	•	Legal Courier Service (SOP)	612-332-7203	•	•	•		
•	•	•	Metro Legal Services	612-332-0202	•	•	•		
•	•	•	Paragon Document Research Inc (SOP)	800-892-4235					•
•	•	•	🏛 Professional Research Services Inc	612-941-9040	•	•	•	•	
•		•	🏛 Team Eagle	800-251-2540	•		•		
•		•	Twin City Abstract Corp	612-224-7072		•			
•	•	•	🏛 Verified Credentials	612-431-1811	•	•	•	•	

CV	CR	PR	DODGE (CST)		UC	RE	TX	VS	VR
•	•	•	🏛 Capitol Lien Records and Research	800-845-4077	•	•	•	•	•

CV	CR	PR	DOUGLAS (CST)		UC	RE	TX	VS	VR
•	•	•	🏛 Capitol Lien Records and Research	800-845-4077	•	•	•	•	•
•		•	Douglas County Abstract Co	320-763-3426	•	•	•		

CV	CR	PR	FARIBAULT (CST)		UC	RE	TX	VS	VR
•	•	•	🏛 Capitol Lien Records and Research	800-845-4077	•	•	•	•	•
			Sharon K Hannaman Abstracter	507-526-5144		•	•		

CV	CR	PR	FILLMORE (CST)		UC	RE	TX	VS	VR
•	•	•	🏛 Capitol Lien Records and Research	800-845-4077	•	•	•	•	•

CV	CR	PR	FREEBORN (CST)		UC	RE	TX	VS	VR
•	•	•	Albert Lea Abstract Co	507-373-9001	•	•	•	•	
•		•	Associated Abstracting Services of MN	612-861-7998	•	•	•		
•	•	•	🏛 Capitol Lien Records and Research	800-845-4077	•	•	•		•

CV	CR	PR	GOODHUE (CST)		UC	RE	TX	VS	VR
•	•		Born, Shirley	612-388-6487	•		•	•	
•	•	•	🏛 Capitol Lien Records and Research	800-845-4077	•	•	•	•	•
•	•	•	🏛 Information Reporting Services Inc	612-870-8770	•	•	•	•	•

CV	CR	PR	GRANT (CST)		UC	RE	TX	VS	VR
•	•	•	🏛 Capitol Lien Records and Research	800-845-4077	•	•	•	•	•

DT	BK	CV	CR	PR	HENNEPIN (CAPITAL) (CST)		UC	RE	TX	VS	VR
		•	•		Accountable Process Servers (SOP)	612-427-0225	•	•	•	•	
		•	•		🏛 Alpha Court Records & Research	612-699-2222	•		•		
•	•	•		•	Associated Abstracting Services of MN	612-861-7998	•	•	•		
•	•	•	•	•	🏛 Capitol Lien Records and Research	800-845-4077	•	•	•	•	•
•	•	•	•	•	Dependable Legal Services (SOP)	888-945-9885		•	•		
•	•	•	•	•	Dovolos & Associates	612-321-0095	•	•	•	•	
			•		Empfacts	800-922-2702					
•	•	•		•	Heartland Corporate Services	800-327-8806	•	•	•	•	•
•	•	•	•	•	🏛 Heartland Information Services	800-967-1882	•	•	•	•	•
•	•	•	•	•	🏛 INPRO (SOP)	612-891-3617	•	•	•	•	•
				•	Independent Abstracting Service Inc	612-789-8440	•	•	•		
•	•	•	•	•	🏛 Information Highway Inc	612-631-8131	•	•	•		
•	•	•	•	•	🏛 Information Reporting Services Inc	612-870-8770	•	•	•	•	•
•	•	•		•	Land Title Inc	612-638-1900		•	•	•	

•	•	•	•	•	Legal Courier Service (SOP) 612-332-7203	•	•	•	•	
•	•	•	•	•	Metro Legal Services 612-332-0202	•	•	•	•	
•	•	•	•	•	Paragon Document Research Inc (SOP) 800-892-4235	•	•	•	•	•
•	•	•	•	•	🏛 Professional Research Services Inc 612-941-9040	•	•	•	•	
•	•	•	•		🏛 Team Eagle 800-251-2540	•	•	•		
•	•	•	•	•	Twin City Abstract Corp 612-224-7072	•	•	•		
•	•	•		•	Unisearch Inc 800-227-1256	•	•	•	•	
•	•	•	•	•	🏛 Verified Credentials 612-431-1811	•	•	•	•	

CV	CR	PR	HOUSTON (CST)	UC	RE	TX	VS	VR
•	•	•	🏛 Capitol Lien Records and Research 800-845-4077	•	•	•	•	•

CV	CR	PR	HUBBARD (CST)	UC	RE	TX	VS	VR
•	•	•	ACME Research (SOP) 218-224-3239	•	•	•	•	
•	•	•	🏛 Capitol Lien Records and Research 800-845-4077	•	•	•	•	•
•		•	Complete Title Service of Walker Inc 800-837-2556	•	•	•		
•	•	•	Port-o-Wild's Security Services (SOP) 218-751-8200	•	•	•	•	

CV	CR	PR	ISANTI (CST)	UC	RE	TX	VS	VR
•	•	•	Accountable Process Servers (SOP) 612-427-0225	•	•	•	•	
•		•	Associated Abstracting Services of MN 612-861-7998	•	•	•		
•	•	•	🏛 Capitol Lien Records and Research 800-845-4077	•	•	•	•	•
•		•	Independent Abstracting Service Inc 612-789-8440	•	•	•		

CV	CR	PR	ITASCA (CST)	UC	RE	TX	VS	VR
•	•	•	🏛 Capitol Lien Records and Research 800-845-4077	•	•	•	•	•
•	•	•	Itasca County Abstract Co 218-326-9601	•	•	•	•	•
•	•	•	Port-o-Wild's Security Services (SOP) 218-751-8200	•	•	•	•	

CV	CR	PR	JACKSON (CST)	UC	RE	TX	VS	VR
•	•	•	🏛 Capitol Lien Records and Research 800-845-4077	•	•	•	•	•
•			Minn*Dak Search Service 507-694-1168	•		•		

CV	CR	PR	KANABEC (CST)	UC	RE	TX	VS	VR
•	•	•	🏛 Capitol Lien Records and Research 800-845-4077	•	•	•	•	•
•		•	Tri-County Abstract and Title Guaranty 800-892-2399	•	•	•		

CV	CR	PR	KANDIYOHI (CST)	UC	RE	TX	VS	VR
•	•	•	🏛 Capitol Lien Records and Research 800-845-4077	•	•	•	•	•
•			Minn*Dak Search Service 507-694-1168	•		•		

CV	CR	PR	KITTSON (CST)	UC	RE	TX	VS	VR
•	•	•	🏛 Capitol Lien Records and Research 800-845-4077	•	•	•	•	•
•	•	•	Port-o-Wild's Security Services (SOP) 218-751-8200	•	•	•	•	

CV	CR	PR	KOOCHICHING (CST)	UC	RE	TX	VS	VR
•	•	•	🏛 Capitol Lien Records and Research 800-845-4077	•	•	•	•	•
•	•	•	Port-o-Wild's Security Services (SOP) 218-751-8200	•	•	•	•	

CV	CR	PR	LAC QUI PARLE (CST)	UC	RE	TX	VS	VR
•	•	•	🏛 Capitol Lien Records and Research 800-845-4077	•	•	•	•	•
•			Minn*Dak Search Service 507-694-1168	•		•		

CV	CR	PR	LAKE (CST)	UC	RE	TX	VS	VR
•	•	•	🏛 Capitol Lien Records and Research 800-845-4077	•	•	•	•	•

CV	CR	PR	LAKE OF THE WOODS (CST)	UC	RE	TX	VS	VR
•	•	•	🏛 Capitol Lien Records and Research 800-845-4077	•	•	•	•	•
•	•	•	Port-o-Wild's Security Services (SOP) 218-751-8200	•	•	•	•	
•	•	•	Raseau-Lake of the Woods Title & Abstract Co 218-634-2544	•	•	•	•	

CV	CR	PR	LE SUEUR (CST)	UC	RE	TX	VS	VR
•		•	Associated Abstracting Services of MN 612-861-7998	•	•	•		
•	•	•	🏛 Capitol Lien Records and Research 800-845-4077	•	•	•	•	•

CV	CR	PR		UC	RE	TX	VS	VR
•	•		🏛 Team Eagle 800-251-2540	•		•		

CV	CR	PR	LINCOLN (CST)	UC	RE	TX	VS	VR
•	•	•	🏛 Capitol Lien Records and Research 800-845-4077	•	•	•	•	•
•	•	•	Dirks, Lewis 605-331-6022	•	•	•	•	
•			Minn*Dak Search Service 507-694-1168	•		•		

CV	CR	PR	LYON (CST)	UC	RE	TX	VS	VR
•	•	•	🏛 Capitol Lien Records and Research 800-845-4077	•	•	•	•	•
•			Minn*Dak Search Service 507-694-1168	•		•		

CV	CR	PR	MAHNOMEN (CST)	UC	RE	TX	VS	VR
•	•	•	🏛 Capitol Lien Records and Research 800-845-4077	•	•	•	•	•
•		•	Mahnomen County Abstract Company 218-935-5227	•	•	•		
•	•	•	Port-o-Wild's Security Services (SOP) 218-751-8200	•	•	•	•	

CV	CR	PR	MARSHALL (CST)	UC	RE	TX	VS	VR
•	•	•	🏛 Capitol Lien Records and Research 800-845-4077	•	•	•	•	•
•	•	•	Port-o-Wild's Security Services (SOP) 218-751-8200	•	•	•	•	

CV	CR	PR	MARTIN (CST)	UC	RE	TX	VS	VR
•	•	•	🏛 Capitol Lien Records and Research 800-845-4077	•	•	•	•	•
•			Minn*Dak Search Service 507-694-1168	•		•		

CV	CR	PR	MCLEOD (CST)	UC	RE	TX	VS	VR
•		•	Associated Abstracting Services of MN 612-861-7998	•	•	•		
•	•	•	🏛 Capitol Lien Records and Research 800-845-4077	•	•	•	•	•
•	•		🏛 Team Eagle 800-251-2540	•		•		
•		•	Tri-County Abstract and Title Guaranty 800-892-2399	•	•	•		

CV	CR	PR	MEEKER (CST)	UC	RE	TX	VS	VR
•	•	•	🏛 Capitol Lien Records and Research 800-845-4077	•	•	•	•	•
•		•	Tri-County Abstract and Title Guaranty 800-892-2399	•	•	•		

CV	CR	PR	MILLE LACS (CST)	UC	RE	TX	VS	VR
•		•	Associated Abstracting Services of MN 612-861-7998	•	•	•		
•	•	•	🏛 Capitol Lien Records and Research 800-845-4077	•	•	•	•	•
•		•	🏛 Horvath Enterprises 320-983-3253					
•		•	Tri-County Abstract and Title Guaranty 800-892-2399	•	•	•		

CV	CR	PR	MORRISON (CST)	UC	RE	TX	VS	VR
•	•	•	🏛 Capitol Lien Records and Research 800-845-4077	•	•	•	•	•
	•	•	Cygneture Title Inc 218-828-0122	•	•	•	•	
		•	🏛 Horvath Enterprises 320-983-3253					
	•		Larson Abstract Co 320-632-5667	•	•	•	•	
•	•		Tri-County Abstract and Title Guaranty 800-892-2399	•	•	•		

CV	CR	PR	MOWER (CST)	UC	RE	TX	VS	VR
•		•	Associated Abstracting Services of MN 612-861-7998	•	•	•		
•	•	•	🏛 Capitol Lien Records and Research 800-845-4077	•	•	•	•	•

CV	CR	PR	MURRAY (CST)	UC	RE	TX	VS	VR
•	•	•	🏛 Capitol Lien Records and Research 800-845-4077	•	•	•	•	•
•	•	•	Dirks, Lewis 605-331-6022	•	•	•	•	
•			Minn*Dak Search Service 507-694-1168	•		•		

CV	CR	PR	NICOLLET (CST)	UC	RE	TX	VS	VR
•		•	Associated Abstracting Services of MN 612-861-7998	•	•	•		
•	•	•	🏛 Capitol Lien Records and Research 800-845-4077	•	•	•	•	•
•	•	•	🏛 Information Highway Inc 612-631-8131	•	•	•	•	

CV	CR	PR	NOBLES (CST)	UC	RE	TX	VS	VR
•	•	•	🏛 Capitol Lien Records and Research 800-845-4077	•	•	•	•	•
•	•	•	Dirks, Lewis 605-331-6022	•	•	•	•	

						UC	RE	TX	VS	VR
				Minn*Dak Search Service 507-694-1168		•		•		

		CV	CR	PR	NORMAN (CST)		UC	RE	TX	VS	VR
		•	•	•	🏛 Capitol Lien Records and Research 800-845-4077		•	•	•	•	•
		•	•	•	P.I. Services (SOP) 800-553-4842		•	•	•	•	
		•	•	•	Port-o-Wild's Security Services (SOP) 218-751-8200		•	•	•	•	

		CV	CR	PR	OLMSTED (CST)		UC	RE	TX	VS	VR
		•		•	Associated Abstracting Services of MN 612-861-7998		•	•	•		
		•	•	•	🏛 Capitol Lien Records and Research 800-845-4077		•	•	•	•	•
		•	•		🏛 Team Eagle 800-251-2540		•		•		

BK	CV	CR	PR	OTTER TAIL (CST)		UC	RE	TX	VS	VR
•	•	•	•	🏛 Capitol Lien Records and Research 800-845-4077		•	•	•	•	•
	•		•	N F Field Abstract Co 218-736-6844		•	•	•		
•	•	•	•	P.I. Services (SOP) 800-553-4842		•	•	•	•	
	•		•	West Central Abstracting Co 218-736-5685		•	•	•		

		CV	CR	PR	PENNINGTON (CST)		UC	RE	TX	VS	VR
		•	•	•	🏛 Capitol Lien Records and Research 800-845-4077		•	•	•	•	•
		•	•	•	Pennington County Abstract Co 218-681-2527			•	•	•	
		•	•	•	Port-o-Wild's Security Services (SOP) 218-751-8200		•	•	•	•	

		CV	CR	PR	PINE (CST)		UC	RE	TX	VS	VR
		•	•	•	🏛 Capitol Lien Records and Research 800-845-4077		•	•	•	•	•

		CV	CR	PR	PIPESTONE (CST)		UC	RE	TX	VS	VR
		•	•	•	🏛 Capitol Lien Records and Research 800-845-4077		•	•	•	•	•
		•	•	•	Dirks, Lewis 605-331-6022		•	•	•	•	
		•			Minn*Dak Search Service 507-694-1168		•		•		
					Pipestone County Abstract Co LLC 507-825-5519		•	•	•		

		CV	CR	PR	POLK (CST)		UC	RE	TX	VS	VR
		•	•	•	🏛 Capitol Lien Records and Research 800-845-4077		•	•	•	•	•
		•			Grand Forks Abstract Co 701-772-3484		•	•	•		
		•	•	•	Port-o-Wild's Security Services (SOP) 218-751-8200		•	•	•	•	
		•			Strander Abstract Inc 218-281-1191		•	•	•		

		CV	CR	PR	POPE (CST)		UC	RE	TX	VS	VR
		•	•	•	🏛 Capitol Lien Records and Research 800-845-4077		•	•	•	•	•
		•		•	Douglas County Abstract Co 320-763-3426		•	•	•		
		•			Minn*Dak Search Service 507-694-1168		•		•		

DT	BK	CV	CR	PR	RAMSEY (CST)		UC	RE	TX	VS	VR
•	•	•	•	•	Accountable Process Servers (SOP) 612-427-0225		•	•	•	•	
		•	•		🏛 Alpha Court Records & Research 612-699-2222		•		•		
•	•	•		•	Associated Abstracting Services of MN 612-861-7998		•	•	•		
•	•	•	•	•	🏛 Capitol Lien Records and Research 800-845-4077		•	•	•	•	•
•	•	•		•	Dependable Legal Services (SOP) 888-945-9885			•	•	•	
•	•	•	•	•	Dovolos & Associates 612-321-0095		•	•	•		
				•	Empfacts 800-922-2702						
•	•	•			Heartland Corporate Services 800-327-8806		•	•	•		•
•	•	•	•	•	🏛 Heartland Information Services 800-967-1882		•	•	•		•
•	•	•	•	•	🏛 INPRO (SOP) 612-891-3617		•	•	•		•
		•			Independent Abstracting Service Inc 612-789-8440		•	•	•		
•	•	•	•	•	🏛 Information Highway Inc 612-631-8131		•	•	•		
•	•	•	•	•	🏛 Information Reporting Services Inc 612-870-8770		•	•	•		•
•	•	•	•	•	Land Title Inc 612-638-1900			•	•		
•	•	•	•	•	Legal Courier Service (SOP) 612-332-7203		•	•	•		
•	•	•	•	•	Metro Legal Services 612-332-0202		•	•	•		
•	•	•	•	•	Paragon Document Research Inc (SOP) 800-892-4235		•	•	•		•
•	•	•	•	•	🏛 Professional Research Services Inc 612-941-9040		•	•	•	•	
•	•	•	•	•	🏛 Team Eagle 800-251-2540		•		•		

							UC	RE	TX	VS	VR
•	•	•		•	Twin City Abstract Corp 612-224-7072		•	•	•		
•	•	•	•	•	🏛 Verified Credentials 612-431-1811		•	•	•	•	

CV	CR	PR		RED LAKE (CST)		UC	RE	TX	VS	VR
•	•	•	🏛 Capitol Lien Records and Research 800-845-4077		•	•	•	•	•
•	•	•	Port-o-Wild's Security Services (SOP) 218-751-8200		•	•	•	•	

CV	CR	PR		REDWOOD (CST)		UC	RE	TX	VS	VR
•	•	•	🏛 Capitol Lien Records and Research 800-845-4077		•	•	•	•	•
•			Minn*Dak Search Service 507-694-1168		•	•			
	•	•	Renville County Abstract Co 320-523-5321		•	•			

CV	CR	PR		RENVILLE (CST)		UC	RE	TX	VS	VR
•	•	•	🏛 Capitol Lien Records and Research 800-845-4077		•	•	•	•	•
•			Minn*Dak Search Service 507-694-1168		•	•	•		
	•	•	Renville County Abstract Co 320-523-5321		•	•	•	•	

CV	CR	PR		RICE (CST)		UC	RE	TX	VS	VR
•		•	Associated Abstracting Services of MN 612-861-7998		•	•	•		
•	•	•	🏛 Capitol Lien Records and Research 800-845-4077		•	•	•	•	•
	•	•	Rice County Abstract & Title Co 507-332-2259		•	•	•	•	

CV	CR	PR		ROCK (CST)		UC	RE	TX	VS	VR
•	•	•	🏛 Capitol Lien Records and Research 800-845-4077		•	•	•		•
•	•	•	Dirks, Lewis 605-331-6022		•	•	•	•	
•			Minn*Dak Search Service 507-694-1168		•	•			

CV	CR	PR		ROSEAU (CST)		UC	RE	TX	VS	VR
•	•	•	🏛 Capitol Lien Records and Research 800-845-4077		•	•	•	•	•
•	•	•	Port-o-Wild's Security Services (SOP) 218-751-8200		•	•	•	•	
•	•	•	Roseau-Lake of the Woods Title 218-463-3313		•	•	•	•	

CV	CR	PR		SCOTT (CST)		UC	RE	TX	VS	VR
•		•	Associated Abstracting Services of MN 612-861-7998		•	•	•		
•	•	•	🏛 Capitol Lien Records and Research 800-845-4077		•	•	•	•	•
	•		Empfacts 800-922-2702						
•		•	Heartland Corporate Services 800-327-8806		•	•	•	•	
•	•	•	🏛 Heartland Information Services 800-967-1882		•	•	•	•	
•	•	•	🏛 INPRO (SOP) 612-891-3617		•	•	•	•	
•		•	Independent Abstracting Service Inc 612-789-8440		•	•	•	•	
•	•	•	🏛 Information Highway Inc 612-631-8131		•	•	•	•	
•	•	•	🏛 Information Reporting Services Inc 612-870-8770		•	•	•	•	
•	•	•	Legal Courier Service (SOP) 612-332-7203		•	•	•	•	
•	•	•	Metro Legal Services 612-332-0202		•	•	•	•	
•	•	•	🏛 Professional Research Services Inc 612-941-9040		•	•	•	•	
•	•		🏛 Team Eagle 800-251-2540		•		•		
•		•	Twin City Abstract Corp 612-224-7072		•	•	•		
•	•	•	🏛 Verified Credentials 612-431-1811		•	•	•	•	

CV	CR	PR		SHERBURNE (CST)		UC	RE	TX	VS	VR
•	•	•	Accountable Process Servers (SOP) 612-427-0225		•	•	•	•	
•		•	Associated Abstracting Services of MN 612-861-7998		•	•	•		
•	•	•	🏛 Capitol Lien Records and Research 800-845-4077		•	•	•	•	•
•	•	•	🏛 Heartland Information Services 800-967-1882		•	•	•	•	
•		•	Heartland Title and Abstract Co 320-253-8860		•	•	•	•	
•	•	•	🏛 INPRO (SOP) 612-891-3617		•	•	•	•	•
•		•	Independent Abstracting Service Inc 612-789-8440		•	•	•	•	
•	•	•	🏛 Information Highway Inc 612-631-8131		•	•	•	•	
•	•	•	Legal Courier Service (SOP) 612-332-7203		•	•	•	•	
•	•	•	Metro Legal Services 612-332-0202		•	•	•	•	
•	•		🏛 Team Eagle 800-251-2540		•		•		
•		•	Tri-County Abstract and Title Guaranty 800-892-2399		•	•	•		

		CV	CR	PR	SIBLEY (CST)		UC	RE	TX	VS	VR
		•		•	Associated Abstracting Services of MN 612-861-7998		•	•	•		
		•	•	•	🏛 Capitol Lien Records and Research 800-845-4077		•	•	•	•	•
		•	•		🏛 Team Eagle 800-251-2540		•		•		

DT	BK	CV	CR	PR	ST. LOUIS (CST)		UC	RE	TX	VS	VR
•	•	•	•	•	Abstract and Title Services of Carlton Inc (SOP) 218-384-3450		•	•	•	•	
•	•	•	•	•	🏛 Capitol Lien Records and Research 800-845-4077		•	•	•	•	•
•	•	•	•	•	🏛 Heartland Information Services 800-967-1882		•	•	•	•	•
•	•	•	•		🏛 Hogan Information Services 405-278-6954						
•	•	•	•		🏛 Team Eagle 800-251-2540		•		•		

		CV	CR	PR	STEARNS (CST)		UC	RE	TX	VS	VR
		•		•	Associated Abstracting Services of MN 612-861-7998		•	•	•		
		•	•	•	🏛 Capitol Lien Records and Research 800-845-4077		•	•	•	•	•
		•		•	Heartland Title and Abstract Co 320-253-8860		•	•	•	•	
			•		🏛 Horvath Enterprises 320-983-3253						
		•	•		🏛 Team Eagle 800-251-2540		•		•		
		•		•	Tri-County Abstract and Title Guaranty 800-892-2399		•	•	•		

		CV	CR	PR	STEELE (CST)		UC	RE	TX	VS	VR
		•		•	Associated Abstracting Services of MN 612-861-7998		•	•	•		
		•	•	•	🏛 Capitol Lien Records and Research 800-845-4077		•	•	•	•	•
		•	•	•	Steele County Abstract Co 507-451-6487		•	•	•		

		CV	CR	PR	STEVENS (CST)		UC	RE	TX	VS	VR
		•	•	•	🏛 Capitol Lien Records and Research 800-845-4077		•	•	•	•	•
		•			Minn*Dak Search Service 507-694-1168		•		•		

		CV	CR	PR	SWIFT (CST)		UC	RE	TX	VS	VR
		•	•	•	🏛 Capitol Lien Records and Research 800-845-4077		•	•	•	•	•
		•			Minn*Dak Search Service 507-694-1168		•		•		

		CV	CR	PR	TODD (CST)		UC	RE	TX	VS	VR
		•	•	•	🏛 Capitol Lien Records and Research 800-845-4077		•	•	•	•	•

		CV	CR	PR	TRAVERSE (CST)		UC	RE	TX	VS	VR
		•	•	•	🏛 Capitol Lien Records and Research 800-845-4077		•	•	•	•	•
		•			Minn*Dak Search Service 507-694-1168		•		•		

		CV	CR	PR	WABASHA (CST)		UC	RE	TX	VS	VR
		•	•		Born, Shirley 612-388-6487		•		•	•	
		•	•	•	🏛 Capitol Lien Records and Research 800-845-4077		•	•	•		•
		•		•	Wabasha County Abstract Co 612-565-3391		•	•	•	•	

		CV	CR	PR	WADENA (CST)		UC	RE	TX	VS	VR
		•	•	•	🏛 Capitol Lien Records and Research 800-845-4077		•	•	•	•	•

		CV	CR	PR	WASECA (CST)		UC	RE	TX	VS	VR
		•		•	Associated Abstracting Services of MN 612-861-7998		•	•	•		
		•	•	•	🏛 Capitol Lien Records and Research 800-845-4077		•	•	•	•	•

		CV	CR	PR	WASHINGTON (CST)		UC	RE	TX	VS	VR
		•	•		🏛 Alpha Court Records & Research 612-699-2222		•		•		
		•		•	Associated Abstracting Services of MN 612-861-7998		•	•	•		
		•	•	•	🏛 Capitol Lien Records and Research 800-845-4077		•	•	•	•	•
			•		Empfacts 800-922-2702						
		•		•	Heartland Corporate Services 800-327-8806		•	•	•	•	•
		•		•	🏛 Heartland Information Services 800-967-1882		•	•	•	•	•
		•	•	•	🏛 INPRO (SOP) 612-891-3617		•	•	•	•	•
		•		•	Independent Abstracting Service Inc 612-789-8440		•	•	•	•	•
		•	•	•	🏛 Information Highway Inc 612-631-8131		•	•	•	•	
		•	•	•	🏛 Information Reporting Services Inc 612-870-8770		•	•	•	•	•

•		•	Land Title Inc 612-638-1900			•	•	•	
•	•	•	Legal Courier Service (SOP) 612-332-7203	•		•	•	•	
•	•	•	Metro Legal Services 612-332-0202	•		•	•	•	
•	•	•	Paragon Document Research Inc (SOP) 800-892-4235	•		•	•		•
•	•	•	🏛 Professional Research Services Inc 612-941-9040	•		•	•	•	
•	•		🏛 Team Eagle 800-251-2540	•		•			
•		•	Twin City Abstract Corp 612-224-7072	•		•	•		
•	•	•	🏛 Verified Credentials 612-431-1811	•		•	•	•	

CV	CR	PR	WATONWAN (CST)	UC	RE	TX	VS	VR
•	•	•	🏛 Capitol Lien Records and Research 800-845-4077	•	•	•	•	•
•			Minn*Dak Search Service 507-694-1168	•		•		

CV	CR	PR	WILKIN (CST)	UC	RE	TX	VS	VR
•	•	•	🏛 Capitol Lien Records and Research 800-845-4077	•	•	•	•	•
•	•	•	P.I. Services (SOP) 800-553-4842	•	•	•	•	
•		•	Richland County Abstract Co 701-642-3781	•	•	•		
			Wilkin County Abstract 218-643-4002		•	•		

CV	CR	PR	WINONA (CST)	UC	RE	TX	VS	VR
•	•	•	🏛 Capitol Lien Records and Research 800-845-4077	•	•	•	•	•
•	•	•	🏛 Information Reporting Services Inc 612-870-8770	•	•	•	•	•

CV	CR	PR	WRIGHT (CST)	UC	RE	TX	VS	VR
•		•	Associated Abstracting Services of MN 612-861-7998	•	•	•		
•		•	🏛 Campbell Abstract Co 612-682-1252		•	•		
•	•	•	🏛 Capitol Lien Records and Research 800-845-4077	•	•	•	•	•
•		•	Heartland Corporate Services 800-327-8806	•	•	•	•	•
•		•	Independent Abstracting Service Inc 612-789-8440	•	•	•	•	
•	•	•	🏛 Information Highway Inc 612-631-8131	•	•	•	•	
•	•	•	🏛 Information Reporting Services Inc 612-870-8770	•	•	•	•	•
•	•	•	Legal Courier Service (SOP) 612-332-7203	•	•	•	•	
•	•	•	Metro Legal Services 612-332-0202	•	•	•	•	
•	•		🏛 Team Eagle 800-251-2540	•		•		
•		•	Tri-County Abstract and Title Guaranty 800-892-2399	•	•	•		

CV	CR	PR	YELLOW MEDICINE (CST)	UC	RE	TX	VS	VR
•	•	•	🏛 Capitol Lien Records and Research 800-845-4077	•	•	•	•	•
•			Minn*Dak Search Service 507-694-1168	•		•		

MISSISSIPPI

CV	CR	PR	ADAMS (CST)	UC	RE	TX	VS	VR
•	•		🏛 Alpha Research LLC (SOP) 205-755-7008			•		
•	•	•	Haynes, Brenette 601-843-2071	•	•	•		
•	•	•	🏛 Hollingsworth Court Reporting Inc 504-769-3386	•	•	•	•	
•	•	•	J L & A (SOP) 800-927-0251	•	•	•		
•	•	•	McNeal Investigations (SOP) 601-826-5104	•	•	•	•	•

CV	CR	PR	ALCORN (CST)	UC	RE	TX	VS	VR
•	•		🏛 Alpha Research LLC (SOP) 205-755-7008			•		
•	•	•	Hatcher, Attorney John A (SOP) 601-728-9444	•	•	•	•	
•	•	•	🏛 Hollingsworth Court Reporting Inc 504-769-3386	•	•	•		
•	•	•	J L & A (SOP) 800-927-0251	•	•	•		
•	•	•	Mitchell McNutt Threadgill et al 601-842-3871	•	•	•		

CV	CR	PR	AMITE (CST)	UC	RE	TX	VS	VR
•	•	•	Haynes, Brenette 601-843-2071	•	•	•		
•	•	•	🏛 Hollingsworth Court Reporting Inc 504-769-3386	•	•	•	•	
•	•	•	J L & A (SOP) 800-927-0251	•	•	•	•	
•	•	•	McNeal Investigations (SOP) 601-826-5104	•	•	•	•	•

CV	CR	PR	ATTALA (CST)	UC	RE	TX	VS	VR
•	•	•	🏛 Hollingsworth Court Reporting Inc 504-769-3386	•	•	•	•	
•	•	•	J L & A (SOP) 800-927-0251	•	•	•	•	
•	•	•	Shaw, John 601-289-3110	•	•	•		

CV	CR	PR	BENTON (CST)	UC	RE	TX	VS	VR
•	•	•	🏛 Hollingsworth Court Reporting Inc 504-769-3386	•	•	•	•	
•	•	•	J L & A (SOP) 800-927-0251	•	•	•	•	
•	•	•	🏛 Record-Check Services Inc 800-530-7226	•	•	•	•	•

CV	CR	PR	BOLIVAR (CST)	UC	RE	TX	VS	VR
•	•		🏛 Alpha Research LLC (SOP) 205-755-7008			•		
•	•	•	Haynes, Brenette 601-843-2071	•	•	•		
•	•	•	🏛 Hollingsworth Court Reporting Inc 504-769-3386	•	•	•	•	
•	•	•	J L & A (SOP) 800-927-0251	•	•	•	•	
•	•	•	Tweedle, Barbara 601-759-3762	•	•	•		

CV	CR	PR	CALHOUN (CST)	UC	RE	TX	VS	VR
•	•	•	🏛 Briley, Michael T (SOP) 601-983-2227	•	•	•	•	•
•	•	•	🏛 Hollingsworth Court Reporting Inc 504-769-3386	•	•	•	•	
•	•	•	J L & A (SOP) 800-927-0251	•	•	•	•	

CV	CR	PR	CARROLL (CST)	UC	RE	TX	VS	VR
•	•		🏛 Alpha Research LLC (SOP) 205-755-7008			•		
•	•	•	🏛 Hollingsworth Court Reporting Inc 504-769-3386	•	•	•	•	
•	•	•	J L & A (SOP) 800-927-0251	•	•	•	•	

CV	CR	PR	CHICKASAW (CST)	UC	RE	TX	VS	VR
•	•		🏛 Alpha Research LLC (SOP) 205-755-7008			•		
•	•	•	🏛 Hollingsworth Court Reporting Inc 504-769-3386	•	•	•	•	
•	•	•	J L & A (SOP) 800-927-0251	•	•	•	•	
•	•	•	Metz, George P 601-773-5804	•	•	•	•	•

CV	CR	PR	CHOCTAW (CST)	UC	RE	TX	VS	VR
•	•	•	Griffin, Joe C 601-285-6080	•	•	•	•	
•	•	•	🏛 Hollingsworth Court Reporting Inc 504-769-3386	•	•	•	•	
•	•	•	J L & A (SOP) 800-927-0251	•	•	•	•	
•	•	•	Shaw, John 601-289-3110	•	•	•		

CV	CR	PR	CLAIBORNE (CST)	UC	RE	TX	VS	VR
•	•	•	🏛 Hollingsworth Court Reporting Inc 504-769-3386	•	•	•	•	

•	•	•	J L & A (SOP) 800-927-0251	•	•	•	•	
•	•	•	McNeal Investigations (SOP) 601-826-5104	•	•	•	•	•

CV	CR	PR	CLARKE (CST)	UC	RE	TX	VS	VR
•	•		🏛 Alpha Research LLC (SOP).................................. 205-755-7008			•		
•	•	•	Brame Jr, Thomas Q (SOP) 601-764-4355	•	•	•	•	•
•	•	•	🏛 Hollingsworth Court Reporting Inc 504-769-3386	•	•	•	•	
•	•	•	J L & A (SOP) 800-927-0251	•	•	•	•	
•	•	•	McNeal Investigations (SOP) 601-826-5104	•	•	•	•	•
•	•	•	Williams, George 601-776-2111	•	•	•		

CV	CR	PR	CLAY (CST)	UC	RE	TX	VS	VR
•	•		🏛 Alpha Research LLC (SOP).................................. 205-755-7008			•		
•	•	•	🏛 Hollingsworth Court Reporting Inc 504-769-3386	•	•	•	•	
•	•	•	J L & A (SOP) 800-927-0251	•	•	•	•	
•	•	•	Metz, George P 601-773-5804	•	•	•	•	•

CV	CR	PR	COAHOMA (CST)	UC	RE	TX	VS	VR
•	•		🏛 Alpha Research LLC (SOP).................................. 205-755-7008			•		
•	•	•	🏛 Hollingsworth Court Reporting Inc 504-769-3386	•	•	•	•	
•	•	•	J L & A (SOP) 800-927-0251	•	•	•	•	

CV	CR	PR	COPIAH (CST)	UC	RE	TX	VS	VR
•	•	•	🏛 Hollingsworth Court Reporting Inc 504-769-3386	•	•	•	•	
•	•	•	J L & A (SOP) 800-927-0251	•	•	•	•	
•	•	•	McNeal Investigations (SOP) 601-826-5104	•	•	•	•	•
•	•	•	Varas, Jeffrey A 601-452-0360	•	•	•	•	

CV	CR	PR	COVINGTON (CST)	UC	RE	TX	VS	VR
•	•	•	🏛 Hollingsworth Court Reporting Inc 504-769-3386	•	•	•	•	
•	•	•	J L & A (SOP) 800-927-0251	•	•	•	•	
•	•	•	McNeal Investigations (SOP) 601-826-5104	•	•	•	•	•
•	•	•	Title Services Inc 800-736-9331	•	•	•		

CV	CR	PR	DE SOTO (CST)	UC	RE	TX	VS	VR
•	•		🏛 Alpha Research LLC (SOP).................................. 205-755-7008			•		
•	•	•	🏛 Cheslock Investigations (SOP) 901-681-9663	•	•	•	•	•
•	•	•	Cope Investigative Services LLC (SOP)............. 800-262-9301	•	•	•	•	•
•	•	•	🏛 Hollingsworth Court Reporting Inc 504-769-3386	•	•	•	•	
•	•	•	J L & A (SOP) 800-927-0251	•	•	•	•	
•	•	•	🏛 Lenow International Inc (SOP)......................... 901-726-0735	•	•	•	•	
•	•	•	🏛 Record-Check Services Inc 800-530-7226	•	•	•	•	•
•	•	•	RecordServe/John Kelley Enterprises 901-853-5320	•	•	•	•	
•	•	•	Schaeffer Papers (SOP)...................................... 800-848-6119		•			

DT	CV	CR	PR	FORREST (CST)	UC	RE	TX	VS	VR
•	•	•		🏛 Alpha Research LLC (SOP).................................. 205-755-7008			•		
•	•	•	•	🏛 Hollingsworth Court Reporting Inc 504-769-3386	•	•	•	•	
•	•	•	•	J L & A (SOP) 800-927-0251	•	•	•	•	
•	•	•	•	McNeal Investigations (SOP) 601-826-5104	•	•	•	•	•
	•	•	•	Title Services Inc 800-736-9331	•	•	•		

CV	CR	PR	FRANKLIN (CST)	UC	RE	TX	VS	VR
•	•	•	Graves Jr, K Maxwell 601-384-2733	•	•	•		
•	•	•	Haynes, Brenette 601-843-2071	•	•	•		
•	•	•	🏛 Hollingsworth Court Reporting Inc 504-769-3386	•	•	•	•	
•	•	•	J L & A (SOP) 800-927-0251	•	•	•	•	
•	•	•	McNeal Investigations (SOP) 601-826-5104	•	•	•	•	•

CV	CR	PR	GEORGE (CST)	UC	RE	TX	VS	VR
•	•	•	Dobbins, E Fred (SOP) 601-394-2301	•	•	•		
•	•	•	🏛 Hollingsworth Court Reporting Inc 504-769-3386	•	•	•	•	
•	•	•	J L & A (SOP) 800-927-0251	•	•	•	•	

CV	CR	PR			UC	RE	TX	VS	VR
•	•	•	McNeal Investigations (SOP)	601-826-5104	•	•	•	•	•

CV	CR	PR	GREENE (CST)		UC	RE	TX	VS	VR
•	•	•	Dobbins, E Fred (SOP)	601-394-2301	•	•	•		
•	•	•	🏛 Hollingsworth Court Reporting Inc	504-769-3386	•	•	•	•	
•	•	•	J L & A (SOP)	800-927-0251	•	•	•	•	
•	•	•	McNeal Investigations (SOP)	601-826-5104	•	•	•	•	•
•	•	•	Title Services Inc	800-736-9331	•	•	•		

CV	CR	PR	GRENADA (CST)		UC	RE	TX	VS	VR
•	•		🏛 Alpha Research LLC (SOP)	205-755-7008			•		
•	•	•	🏛 Hollingsworth Court Reporting Inc	504-769-3386	•	•	•	•	
•	•	•	J L & A (SOP)	800-927-0251	•	•	•	•	

CV	CR	PR	HANCOCK (CST)		UC	RE	TX	VS	VR
•	•		🏛 Alpha Research LLC (SOP)	205-755-7008			•		
•	•		🏛 Garrett, Francis A	601-798-4992	•				•
•	•	•	🏛 Hollingsworth Court Reporting Inc	504-769-3386	•	•	•	•	
•		•	Home Abstract & Title Co	601-863-4783	•	•	•		
•	•	•	J L & A (SOP)	800-927-0251	•	•	•		
•	•	•	McNeal Investigations (SOP)	601-826-5104	•	•	•	•	•

DT	BK	CV	CR	PR	HARRISON (CST)		UC	RE	TX	VS	VR
•	•	•	•		🏛 Alpha Research LLC (SOP)	205-755-7008			•		
•	•	•	•		🏛 Garrett, Francis A	601-798-4992	•				•
•	•				🏛 Hogan Information Services	405-278-6954					
•	•	•	•	•	🏛 Hollingsworth Court Reporting Inc	504-769-3386	•	•	•	•	
			•		Home Abstract & Title Co	601-863-4783	•	•	•		
•	•	•	•	•	J L & A (SOP)	800-927-0251	•	•	•	•	
•	•	•	•	•	McNeal Investigations (SOP)	601-826-5104	•	•	•	•	•

DT	BK	CV	CR	PR	HINDS (CAPITAL) (CST)		UC	RE	TX	VS	VR
•	•	•	•		🏛 Alpha Research LLC (SOP)	205-755-7008			•		
•	•	•	•	•	Brame Jr, Thomas Q (SOP)	601-764-4355	•	•	•	•	•
•	•	•	•	•	Cliff Childress Special Investigations	601-977-7484	•	•	•	•	•
•	•				🏛 Hogan Information Services	405-278-6954					
•	•	•	•	•	🏛 Hollingsworth Court Reporting Inc	504-769-3386	•	•	•	•	
•	•	•	•	•	J L & A (SOP)	800-927-0251	•	•	•	•	
•		•			🏛 Kirby-Muirhead, Chris	601-873-6308	•		•		
•	•			•	McAllister & Associates Inc (SOP)	601-977-0406	•	•	•		•
•	•	•	•	•	McNeal Investigations (SOP)	601-826-5104	•	•	•	•	•
		•	•	•	Varas, Jeffrey A	601-452-0360	•	•	•	•	

CV	CR	PR	HOLMES (CST)		UC	RE	TX	VS	VR
•	•	•	Gilmore, Billy J	601-834-2421	•	•	•		
•	•	•	🏛 Hollingsworth Court Reporting Inc	504-769-3386	•	•	•	•	
•	•	•	J L & A (SOP)	800-927-0251	•	•	•	•	
•	•	•	Shaw, John	601-289-3110	•	•	•		

CV	CR	PR	HUMPHREYS (CST)		UC	RE	TX	VS	VR
•	•	•	🏛 Hollingsworth Court Reporting Inc	504-769-3386	•	•	•	•	
•	•	•	J L & A (SOP)	800-927-0251	•	•	•	•	

CV	CR	PR	ISSAQUENA (CST)		UC	RE	TX	VS	VR
•	•	•	🏛 Hollingsworth Court Reporting Inc	504-769-3386	•	•	•	•	
•	•	•	J L & A (SOP)	800-927-0251	•	•	•	•	
•			🏛 Kirby-Muirhead, Chris	601-873-6308	•		•		
•		•	Wessinger, Charles Jr	601-873-6258	•	•	•		

CV	CR	PR	ITAWAMBA (CST)		UC	RE	TX	VS	VR
•	•		🏛 Alpha Research LLC (SOP)	205-755-7008			•		
•	•	•	Hatcher, Attorney John A (SOP)	601-728-9444	•	•	•	•	
•	•	•	🏛 Hollingsworth Court Reporting Inc	504-769-3386	•	•	•	•	

•	•	•	J L & A (SOP) 800-927-0251	•	•	•	•		
•	•	•	Richardson, Sharian 601-862-7879	•	•	•	•		

CV	CR	PR	JACKSON (CST)	UC	RE	TX	VS	VR
•	•		🏛 Alpha Research LLC (SOP)......................205-755-7008			•		
•	•		🏛 Garrett, Francis A 601-798-4992	•		•		•
•	•	•	🏛 Hollingsworth Court Reporting Inc 504-769-3386	•	•	•	•	
•		•	Home Abstract & Title Co 601-863-4783	•	•	•		
•	•	•	J L & A (SOP) 800-927-0251	•	•	•	•	
•	•	•	McNeal Investigations (SOP) 601-826-5104	•	•	•	•	•

CV	CR	PR	JASPER (CST)	UC	RE	TX	VS	VR
•	•		🏛 Alpha Research LLC (SOP)......................205-755-7008			•		
•	•	•	Brame Jr, Thomas Q (SOP) 601-764-4355	•	•	•	•	
•	•	•	🏛 Hollingsworth Court Reporting Inc 504-769-3386	•	•	•	•	
•	•	•	J L & A (SOP) 800-927-0251	•	•	•	•	
•	•	•	McNeal Investigations (SOP) 601-826-5104	•	•	•	•	

CV	CR	PR	JEFFERSON (CST)	UC	RE	TX	VS	VR
•	•	•	Haynes, Brenette 601-843-2071	•	•	•	•	
•	•	•	🏛 Hollingsworth Court Reporting Inc 504-769-3386	•	•	•	•	•
•	•	•	J L & A (SOP) 800-927-0251	•	•	•	•	
•	•	•	McNeal Investigations (SOP) 601-826-5104	•	•	•	•	

CV	CR	PR	JEFFERSON DAVIS (CST)	UC	RE	TX	VS	VR
•	•	•	🏛 Hollingsworth Court Reporting Inc 504-769-3386	•	•	•	•	
•	•	•	J L & A (SOP) 800-927-0251	•	•	•	•	
•	•	•	Title Services Inc 800-736-9331	•	•	•		

CV	CR	PR	JONES (CST)	UC	RE	TX	VS	VR
•	•		🏛 Alpha Research LLC (SOP)......................205-755-7008			•		
•	•	•	Brame Jr, Thomas Q (SOP) 601-764-4355	•	•	•	•	•
•	•	•	🏛 Hollingsworth Court Reporting Inc 504-769-3386	•	•	•	•	
•	•	•	J L & A (SOP) 800-927-0251	•	•	•	•	
•	•	•	McNeal Investigations (SOP) 601-826-5104	•	•	•	•	•
•	•	•	Title Services Inc 800-736-9331	•	•	•		

CV	CR	PR	KEMPER (CST)	UC	RE	TX	VS	VR
•	•	•	Briggs, Eddie J 601-743-5823	•	•	•	•	
•	•	•	🏛 Hollingsworth Court Reporting Inc 504-769-3386	•	•	•	•	
•	•	•	J L & A (SOP) 800-927-0251	•	•	•	•	
•	•	•	Metz, George P 601-773-5804	•	•	•	•	•

DT	CV	CR	PR	LAFAYETTE (CST)	UC	RE	TX	VS	VR
•	•	•	•	🏛 Alpha Research LLC (SOP)......................205-755-7008			•		
•	•	•	•	🏛 Briley, Michael T (SOP) 601-983-2227	•	•	•	•	•
•	•	•	•	🏛 Hollingsworth Court Reporting Inc 504-769-3386	•	•	•	•	
•	•	•	•	J L & A (SOP) 800-927-0251	•	•	•	•	

CV	CR	PR	LAMAR (CST)	UC	RE	TX	VS	VR
•	•		🏛 Alpha Research LLC (SOP)......................205-755-7008			•		
•	•	•	🏛 Hollingsworth Court Reporting Inc 504-769-3386	•	•	•	•	
•	•	•	J L & A (SOP) 800-927-0251	•	•	•	•	
•	•	•	McNeal Investigations (SOP) 601-826-5104	•	•	•	•	•
•	•	•	Title Services Inc 800-736-9331	•	•	•		

CV	CR	PR	LAUDERDALE (CST)	UC	RE	TX	VS	VR
•	•		🏛 Alpha Research LLC (SOP)......................205-755-7008			•		
•	•	•	Brame Jr, Thomas Q (SOP) 601-764-4355	•	•	•	•	•
•	•	•	🏛 Hollingsworth Court Reporting Inc 504-769-3386	•	•	•	•	
•	•	•	J L & A (SOP) 800-927-0251	•	•	•	•	
•	•	•	McAllister & Associates Inc (SOP) 601-977-0406	•	•	•	•	•
•	•	•	Metz, George P 601-773-5804	•	•	•	•	

CV	CR	PR	LAWRENCE (CST)	UC	RE	TX	VS	VR
•	•	•	🏛 Hollingsworth Court Reporting Inc 504-769-3386	•	•	•	•	
•	•	•	J L & A (SOP) 800-927-0251	•	•	•	•	
•	•	•	McNeal Investigations (SOP) 601-826-5104	•	•	•	•	•

CV	CR	PR	LEAKE (CST)	UC	RE	TX	VS	VR
•	•		🏛 Alpha Research LLC (SOP).............................. 205-755-7008			•		
•	•	•	Cliff Childress Special Investigations 601-977-7484	•	•	•	•	•
•	•	•	🏛 Hollingsworth Court Reporting Inc 504-769-3386	•	•	•	•	
•	•	•	J L & A (SOP) 800-927-0251	•	•	•	•	
•	•	•	Shaw, John 601-289-3110	•	•	•		

CV	CR	PR	LEE (CST)	UC	RE	TX	VS	VR
•	•		🏛 Alpha Research LLC (SOP).............................. 205-755-7008			•		
•	•	•	Hatcher, Attorney John A (SOP) 601-728-9444	•	•	•	•	
•	•	•	Hilkman Sumners Gozr and Gore 601-534-6326	•	•	•	•	
•	•	•	🏛 Hollingsworth Court Reporting Inc 504-769-3386	•	•	•	•	
•	•	•	J L & A (SOP) 800-927-0251	•	•	•	•	
•	•	•	Metz, George P 601-773-5804	•	•	•	•	•

CV	CR	PR	LEFLORE (CST)	UC	RE	TX	VS	VR
•	•		🏛 Alpha Research LLC (SOP).............................. 205-755-7008			•		
•	•	•	🏛 Hollingsworth Court Reporting Inc 504-769-3386	•	•	•	•	
•	•	•	J L & A (SOP) 800-927-0251	•	•	•	•	

CV	CR	PR	LINCOLN (CST)	UC	RE	TX	VS	VR
•	•		🏛 Alpha Research LLC (SOP).............................. 205-755-7008			•		
•	•	•	🏛 Hollingsworth Court Reporting Inc 504-769-3386	•	•	•	•	
•	•	•	J L & A (SOP) 800-927-0251	•	•	•	•	
•	•	•	Varas, Jeffrey A 601-452-0360	•	•	•	•	

CV	CR	PR	LOWNDES (CST)	UC	RE	TX	VS	VR
•	•		🏛 Alpha Research LLC (SOP).............................. 205-755-7008			•		
•	•	•	🏛 Hollingsworth Court Reporting Inc 504-769-3386	•	•	•	•	
•	•	•	J L & A (SOP) 800-927-0251	•	•	•	•	
•	•	•	Metz, George P 601-773-5804	•	•	•	•	•

CV	CR	PR	MADISON (CST)	UC	RE	TX	VS	VR
•	•		🏛 Alpha Research LLC (SOP).............................. 205-755-7008			•		
•	•	•	Cliff Childress Special Investigations 601-977-7484	•	•	•	•	•
•	•	•	🏛 Hollingsworth Court Reporting Inc 504-769-3386	•	•	•	•	
•	•	•	J L & A (SOP) 800-927-0251	•	•	•	•	
•			🏛 Kirby-Muirhead, Chris 601-873-6308	•		•		
•	•	•	McAllister & Associates Inc (SOP) 601-977-0406	•	•	•	•	•

CV	CR	PR	MARION (CST)	UC	RE	TX	VS	VR
•	•	•	🏛 Hollingsworth Court Reporting Inc 504-769-3386	•	•	•	•	
•	•	•	J L & A (SOP) 800-927-0251	•	•	•	•	
•	•	•	Title Services Inc 800-736-9331	•	•	•		

CV	CR	PR	MARSHALL (CST)	UC	RE	TX	VS	VR
•	•		🏛 Alpha Research LLC (SOP).............................. 205-755-7008			•		
•	•	•	🏛 Hollingsworth Court Reporting Inc 504-769-3386	•	•	•	•	
•	•	•	J L & A (SOP) 800-927-0251	•	•	•	•	
	•		L P Records 601-252-8960					
•	•	•	🏛 Record-Check Services Inc 800-530-7226	•	•	•	•	•
•	•	•	RecordServe/John Kelley Enterprises 901-853-5320	•	•	•	•	

DT	BK	CV	CR	PR	MONROE (CST)	UC	RE	TX	VS	VR
•	•	•	•		🏛 Alpha Research LLC (SOP).............................. 205-755-7008			•		
•	•	•	•	•	🏛 Hollingsworth Court Reporting Inc 504-769-3386	•	•	•	•	
•	•	•	•	•	J L & A (SOP) 800-927-0251	•	•	•	•	

CV	CR	PR	MONTGOMERY (CST)		UC	RE	TX	VS	VR
•	•	•	🏛 Hollingsworth Court Reporting Inc 504-769-3386		•	•	•	•	
•	•	•	J L & A (SOP) 800-927-0251		•	•	•	•	

CV	CR	PR	NESHOBA (CST)		UC	RE	TX	VS	VR
•	•	•	Cliff Childress Special Investigations 601-977-7484		•	•	•	•	•
•	•	•	🏛 Hollingsworth Court Reporting Inc 504-769-3386		•	•	•	•	
•	•	•	J L & A (SOP) 800-927-0251		•	•	•	•	
•	•	•	Metz, George P 601-773-5804		•	•	•	•	•

CV	CR	PR	NEWTON (CST)		UC	RE	TX	VS	VR
•	•	•	Brame Jr, Thomas Q (SOP) 601-764-4355		•	•	•	•	•
•	•	•	Clearman, Danny 601-635-3432		•	•	•	•	
•	•	•	🏛 Hollingsworth Court Reporting Inc 504-769-3386		•	•	•	•	
•	•	•	J L & A (SOP) 800-927-0251		•	•	•	•	

CV	CR	PR	NOXUBEE (CST)		UC	RE	TX	VS	VR
•	•	•	🏛 Hollingsworth Court Reporting Inc 504-769-3386		•	•	•	•	
•	•	•	J L & A (SOP) 800-927-0251		•	•	•	•	

CV	CR	PR	OKTIBBEHA (CST)		UC	RE	TX	VS	VR
•	•		🏛 Alpha Research LLC (SOP)............................. 205-755-7008				•		
•	•	•	🏛 Hollingsworth Court Reporting Inc 504-769-3386		•	•	•	•	
•	•	•	J L & A (SOP) 800-927-0251		•	•	•	•	

CV	CR	PR	PANOLA (CST)		UC	RE	TX	VS	VR
•	•		🏛 Alpha Research LLC (SOP)............................. 205-755-7008				•		
•	•	•	Baker, Gaines 601-563-9385		•	•	•	•	
•	•	•	🏛 Hollingsworth Court Reporting Inc 504-769-3386		•	•	•	•	
•	•	•	J L & A (SOP) 800-927-0251		•	•	•	•	

CV	CR	PR	PEARL RIVER (CST)		UC	RE	TX	VS	VR
•	•		🏛 Alpha Research LLC (SOP)............................. 205-755-7008				•		
•	•	•	🏛 Hollingsworth Court Reporting Inc 504-769-3386		•	•	•	•	
•	•	•	J L & A (SOP) 800-927-0251		•	•	•	•	
•	•	•	McNeal Investigations (SOP) 601-826-5104		•	•	•	•	•
•	•	•	Title Services Inc 800-736-9331		•	•	•		

CV	CR	PR	PERRY (CST)		UC	RE	TX	VS	VR
•	•	•	Dobbins, E Fred (SOP) 601-394-2301		•	•	•		
•	•	•	🏛 Hollingsworth Court Reporting Inc 504-769-3386		•	•	•	•	
•	•	•	J L & A (SOP) 800-927-0251		•	•	•	•	
•	•	•	McNeal Investigations (SOP) 601-826-5104		•	•	•	•	•
•	•	•	Title Services Inc 800-736-9331		•	•	•		

CV	CR	PR	PIKE (CST)		UC	RE	TX	VS	VR
•	•		🏛 Alpha Research LLC (SOP)............................. 205-755-7008				•		
•	•	•	🏛 Hollingsworth Court Reporting Inc 504-769-3386		•	•	•	•	
•	•	•	J L & A (SOP) 800-927-0251		•	•	•	•	
•	•	•	McNeal Investigations (SOP) 601-826-5104		•	•	•	•	•
•	•	•	Mord, Conrad 601-876-2611		•	•	•	•	
•	•	•	Regan, William Ben 601-783-2491		•	•	•	•	
•	•	•	Title Services Inc 800-736-9331		•	•	•		

CV	CR	PR	PONTOTOC (CST)		UC	RE	TX	VS	VR
•	•		🏛 Alpha Research LLC (SOP)............................. 205-755-7008				•		
•	•	•	Hilkman Sumners Gozr and Gore 601-534-6326		•	•	•	•	
•	•	•	🏛 Hollingsworth Court Reporting Inc 504-769-3386		•	•	•	•	
•	•	•	J L & A (SOP) 800-927-0251		•	•	•	•	

CV	CR	PR	PRENTISS (CST)		UC	RE	TX	VS	VR
•	•		🏛 Alpha Research LLC (SOP)............................. 205-755-7008				•		
•	•	•	Hatcher, Attorney John A (SOP) 601-728-9444		•	•	•	•	

•	•	•	🏛 Hollingsworth Court Reporting Inc 504-769-3386	•	•	•	•	
•	•	•	J L & A (SOP) 800-927-0251	•	•	•	•	

CV	CR	PR	QUITMAN (CST)	UC	RE	TX	VS	VR
•	•		🏛 Alpha Research LLC (SOP)...................................... 205-755-7008			•		
•	•	•	Baker, Gaines 601-563-9385	•	•	•	•	
•	•	•	🏛 Hollingsworth Court Reporting Inc 504-769-3386	•	•	•	•	
•	•	•	J L & A (SOP) 800-927-0251	•	•	•	•	

CV	CR	PR	RANKIN (CST)	UC	RE	TX	VS	VR
•	•		🏛 Alpha Research LLC (SOP)...................................... 205-755-7008			•		
•	•	•	Brame Jr, Thomas Q (SOP) 601-764-4355	•	•	•	•	•
•	•	•	Cliff Childress Special Investigations 601-977-7484	•	•	•	•	•
•	•	•	🏛 Hollingsworth Court Reporting Inc 504-769-3386	•	•	•	•	
•	•	•	J L & A (SOP) 800-927-0251	•	•	•	•	
•			🏛 Kirby-Muirhead, Chris 601-873-6308	•		•		
•		•	McAllister & Associates Inc (SOP) 601-977-0406	•	•	•	•	•
•	•	•	McNeal Investigations (SOP) 601-826-5104	•	•	•	•	•

CV	CR	PR	SCOTT (CST)	UC	RE	TX	VS	VR
•	•	•	Brame Jr, Thomas Q (SOP) 601-764-4355	•	•	•	•	•
•	•	•	Cliff Childress Special Investigations 601-977-7484	•	•	•	•	•
•	•	•	🏛 Hollingsworth Court Reporting Inc 504-769-3386	•	•	•	•	
•	•	•	J L & A (SOP) 800-927-0251	•	•	•	•	
•	•	•	Thompson & Hollingsworth PA 601-469-3411	•	•	•	•	

CV	CR	PR	SHARKEY (CST)	UC	RE	TX	VS	VR
•	•		🏛 Alpha Research LLC (SOP)...................................... 205-755-7008			•		
•	•	•	🏛 Hollingsworth Court Reporting Inc 504-769-3386	•	•	•	•	
•	•	•	J L & A (SOP) 800-927-0251	•	•	•	•	
•			🏛 Kirby-Muirhead, Chris 601-873-6308	•		•		
•	•	•	Wessinger, Charles Jr 601-873-6258	•	•	•	•	

CV	CR	PR	SIMPSON (CST)	UC	RE	TX	VS	VR
•	•	•	Brame Jr, Thomas Q (SOP) 601-764-4355	•	•	•	•	•
•	•	•	Buffington, B Scott 601-849-4267	•	•	•		
•	•	•	🏛 Hollingsworth Court Reporting Inc 504-769-3386	•	•	•	•	
•	•	•	J L & A (SOP) 800-927-0251	•	•	•	•	
•	•	•	McNeal Investigations (SOP) 601-826-5104	•	•	•	•	•
•	•	•	Title Services Inc 800-736-9331	•	•	•		

CV	CR	PR	SMITH (CST)	UC	RE	TX	VS	VR
•	•	•	Brame Jr, Thomas Q (SOP) 601-764-4355	•	•	•	•	•
•	•	•	🏛 Hollingsworth Court Reporting Inc 504-769-3386	•	•	•	•	
•	•	•	J L & A (SOP) 800-927-0251	•	•	•	•	
•	•	•	McNeal Investigations (SOP) 601-826-5104	•	•	•	•	•
•	•	•	Title Services Inc 800-736-9331	•	•	•		

CV	CR	PR	STONE (CST)	UC	RE	TX	VS	VR
•	•		🏛 Alpha Research LLC (SOP)...................................... 205-755-7008			•		
•	•	•	🏛 Hollingsworth Court Reporting Inc 504-769-3386	•	•	•	•	
•	•	•	J L & A (SOP) 800-927-0251	•	•	•	•	
•	•	•	McNeal Investigations (SOP) 601-826-5104	•	•	•	•	•
•	•	•	Title Services Inc 800-736-9331	•	•	•		

CV	CR	PR	SUNFLOWER (CST)	UC	RE	TX	VS	VR
•	•	•	🏛 Hollingsworth Court Reporting Inc 504-769-3386	•	•	•	•	
•	•	•	J L & A (SOP) 800-927-0251	•	•	•	•	

CV	CR	PR	TALLAHATCHIE (CST)	UC	RE	TX	VS	VR
•	•	•	Baker, Gaines 601-563-9385	•	•	•	•	
•	•	•	Cossar Jr, George P 601-647-5581	•	•	•	•	
•	•	•	🏛 Hollingsworth Court Reporting Inc 504-769-3386	•	•	•	•	

	CV	CR	PR		UC	RE	TX	VS	VR
	•	•	•	J L & A (SOP) 800-927-0251	•	•	•	•	

	CV	CR	PR	TATE (CST)	UC	RE	TX	VS	VR
	•	•		🏛 Alpha Research LLC (SOP)........................... 205-755-7008			•		
	•	•	•	Baker, Gaines 601-563-9385	•	•	•	•	
	•	•	•	Cope Investigative Services LLC (SOP).......... 800-262-9301	•	•	•	•	•
	•	•	•	🏛 Hollingsworth Court Reporting Inc 504-769-3386	•	•	•	•	
	•	•	•	J L & A (SOP) 800-927-0251	•	•	•	•	

	CV	CR	PR	TIPPAH (CST)	UC	RE	TX	VS	VR
	•	•		🏛 Alpha Research LLC (SOP)........................... 205-755-7008			•		
	•	•	•	Hatcher, Attorney John A (SOP) 601-728-9444	•	•	•	•	
	•	•	•	Hilkman Sumners Gozr and Gore 601-534-6326	•	•	•	•	
	•	•	•	🏛 Hollingsworth Court Reporting Inc 504-769-3386	•	•	•	•	
	•	•	•	J L & A (SOP) 800-927-0251	•	•	•	•	

	CV	CR	PR	TISHOMINGO (CST)	UC	RE	TX	VS	VR
	•	•		🏛 Alpha Research LLC (SOP)........................... 205-755-7008			•		
	•	•	•	Hatcher, Attorney John A (SOP) 601-728-9444	•	•	•	•	
	•	•	•	🏛 Hollingsworth Court Reporting Inc 504-769-3386	•	•	•	•	
	•	•	•	J L & A (SOP) 800-927-0251	•	•	•	•	
	•	•	•	Segars, Mark T 601-423-1006	•	•	•	•	

	CV	CR	PR	TUNICA (CST)	UC	RE	TX	VS	VR
	•	•		🏛 Alpha Research LLC (SOP)........................... 205-755-7008			•		
	•	•	•	🏛 Hollingsworth Court Reporting Inc 504-769-3386	•	•	•	•	
	•	•	•	J L & A (SOP) 800-927-0251	•	•	•	•	
	•	•	•	🏛 Record-Check Services Inc 800-530-7226	•	•	•	•	•

	CV	CR	PR	UNION (CST)	UC	RE	TX	VS	VR
	•	•		🏛 Alpha Research LLC (SOP)........................... 205-755-7008			•		
	•	•	•	Hatcher, Attorney John A (SOP) 601-728-9444	•	•	•	•	
	•	•	•	Hilkman Sumners Gozr and Gore 601-534-6326	•	•	•	•	
	•	•	•	🏛 Hollingsworth Court Reporting Inc 504-769-3386	•	•	•	•	
	•	•	•	J L & A (SOP) 800-927-0251	•	•	•	•	

	CV	CR	PR	WALTHALL (CST)	UC	RE	TX	VS	VR
	•	•	•	🏛 Hollingsworth Court Reporting Inc 504-769-3386	•	•	•	•	
	•	•	•	J L & A (SOP) 800-927-0251	•	•	•	•	
	•	•	•	McNeal Investigations (SOP) 601-826-5104	•	•	•	•	•
	•	•	•	Mord, Conrad 601-876-2611	•	•	•	•	
	•	•	•	Title Services Inc 800-736-9331	•	•	•		

	CV	CR	PR	WARREN (CST)	UC	RE	TX	VS	VR
	•	•		🏛 Alpha Research LLC (SOP)........................... 205-755-7008			•		
	•	•	•	Cliff Childress Special Investigations 601-977-7484	•	•	•	•	•
	•	•	•	🏛 Hollingsworth Court Reporting Inc 504-769-3386	•	•	•	•	
	•	•	•	J L & A (SOP) 800-927-0251	•	•	•	•	
	•			🏛 Kirby-Muirhead, Chris 601-873-6308	•				
	•	•	•	McAllister & Associates Inc (SOP) 601-977-0406	•	•	•	•	•

DT	CV	CR	PR	WASHINGTON (CST)	UC	RE	TX	VS	VR
•	•	•	•	🏛 Alpha Research LLC (SOP)........................... 205-755-7008			•		
	•		•	Evans, Robert D 601-378-2171	•	•	•		
•	•	•	•	🏛 Hollingsworth Court Reporting Inc 504-769-3386	•	•	•	•	
•	•	•	•	J L & A (SOP) 800-927-0251	•	•	•	•	
•	•			🏛 Kirby-Muirhead, Chris 601-873-6308	•		•		

	CV	CR	PR	WAYNE (CST)	UC	RE	TX	VS	VR
	•	•	•	🏛 Hollingsworth Court Reporting Inc 504-769-3386	•	•	•	•	
	•	•	•	J L & A (SOP) 800-927-0251	•	•	•	•	
	•	•	•	McNeal Investigations (SOP) 601-826-5104	•	•	•	•	•

MISSISSIPPI

CV	CR	PR	WEBSTER (CST)		UC	RE	TX	VS	VR
•	•	•	🗑 Hollingsworth Court Reporting Inc 504-769-3386		•	•	•	•	
•	•	•	J L & A (SOP) 800-927-0251		•	•	•	•	
•	•	•	Metz, George P 601-773-5804		•	•	•	•	•

CV	CR	PR	WILKINSON (CST)		UC	RE	TX	VS	VR
•	•	•	🗑 Hollingsworth Court Reporting Inc 504-769-3386		•	•	•	•	
•	•	•	J L & A (SOP) 800-927-0251		•	•	•	•	
•	•	•	McNeal Investigations (SOP) 601-826-5104		•	•	•	•	•

CV	CR	PR	WINSTON (CST)		UC	RE	TX	VS	VR
•	•	•	🗑 Hollingsworth Court Reporting Inc 504-769-3386		•	•	•	•	
•	•	•	J L & A (SOP) 800-927-0251		•	•	•	•	
•	•	•	Metz, George P 601-773-5804		•	•	•	•	•
•		•	Tucker, Taylor 601-773-9254		•	•	•	•	

CV	CR	PR	YALOBUSHA (CST)		UC	RE	TX	VS	VR
•	•	•	🗑 Hollingsworth Court Reporting Inc 504-769-3386		•	•	•	•	
•	•	•	J L & A (SOP) 800-927-0251		•	•	•	•	

CV	CR	PR	YAZOO (CST)		UC	RE	TX	VS	VR
•	•	•	🗑 Hollingsworth Court Reporting Inc 504-769-3386		•	•	•	•	
•	•	•	J L & A (SOP) 800-927-0251		•	•	•	•	
•			🗑 Kirby-Muirhead, Chris 601-873-6308		•		•		
•	•	•	McAllister & Associates Inc (SOP) 601-977-0406		•	•	•	•	•

MISSOURI

	CV	CR	PR	ADAIR (CST)	UC	RE	TX	VS	VR
	•		•	Real Data 573-893-4898	•	•	•		

	CV	CR	PR	ANDREW (CST)	UC	RE	TX	VS	VR
	•	•	•	🏛 Wilson & Associates (SOP) 816-233-6334	•	•	•	•	•

	CV	CR	PR	ATCHISON (CST)	UC	RE	TX	VS	VR
				See adjoining counties for retrievers					

	CV	CR	PR	AUDRAIN (CST)	UC	RE	TX	VS	VR
	•		•	Audrain County Abstract Co 573-581-5136	•	•	•		
	•		•	Real Data 573-893-4898	•	•	•		

	CV	CR	PR	BARRY (CST)	UC	RE	TX	VS	VR
	•	•	•	Barry County Abstract & Title 417-847-3224	•	•	•	•	
	•	•	•	National Investigative Services Inc 417-883-1213	•	•	•	•	

	CV	CR	PR	BARTON (CST)	UC	RE	TX	VS	VR
	•	•	•	Barton County Title Co 417-682-3100	•	•	•	•	
	•	•	•	🏛 Kunkel, Joan & Kelli (SOP) 417-358-6494	•	•	•	•	•
	•	•	•	National Investigative Services Inc 417-883-1213	•	•	•	•	

	CV	CR	PR	BATES (CST)	UC	RE	TX	VS	VR
				See adjoining counties for retrievers					

	CV	CR	PR	BENTON (CST)	UC	RE	TX	VS	VR
	•	•	•	Drake Land Title Co 816-438-5188	•	•	•		•
	•		•	Real Data 573-893-4898	•	•	•		

	CV	CR	PR	BOLLINGER (CST)	UC	RE	TX	VS	VR
	•	•	•	Bollinger County Abstract Co 573-238-2823	•	•	•		
	•	•		Interquest Information Services 800-455-1655	•	•	•	•	•

	CV	CR	PR	BOONE (CST)	UC	RE	TX	VS	VR
	•	•	•	🏛 Eagle & Associates LLC (SOP) 800-216-4860	•	•	•	•	•
	•		•	Guaranty Land Title 573-636-8388	•	•	•	•	
	•		•	Harmon Legal Process Service (SOP) 314-635-6690	•	•	•	•	
	•		•	Real Data 573-893-4898	•	•	•		

DT	CV	CR	PR	BUCHANAN (CST)	UC	RE	TX	VS	VR
•	•	•	•	🏛 Wilson & Associates (SOP) 816-233-6334	•	•	•	•	•

	CV	CR	PR	BUTLER (CST)	UC	RE	TX	VS	VR
	•		•	Butler County Abstract and Title Inc 573-686-1495	•	•	•		

	CV	CR	PR	CALDWELL (CST)	UC	RE	TX	VS	VR
				See adjoining counties for retrievers					

	CV	CR	PR	CALLAWAY (CST)	UC	RE	TX	VS	VR
	•		•	Guaranty Land Title 573-636-8388	•	•	•	•	
	•	•	•	Harmon Legal Process Service (SOP) 314-635-6690	•	•	•	•	
	•		•	Real Data 573-893-4898	•	•	•		

	CV	CR	PR	CAMDEN (CST)	UC	RE	TX	VS	VR
	•		•	Guaranty Land Title 573-636-8388	•	•	•	•	
	•		•	Real Data 573-893-4898	•	•	•		

DT	CV	CR	PR	CAPE GIRARDEAU (CST)	UC	RE	TX	VS	VR
	•		•	Cape Girardeau County Abstract and Title 573-335-5890		•	•	•	
•	•	•		Interquest Information Services 800-455-1655	•	•	•	•	•
			•	Preferred Land Title 573-756-6721	•	•	•		

	CV	CR	PR	CARROLL (CST)	UC	RE	TX	VS	VR
	•		•	Real Data 573-893-4898	•	•	•		

	CV	CR	PR	CARTER (CST)	UC	RE	TX	VS	VR
				See adjoining counties for retrievers					

	CV	CR	PR	CASS (CST)	UC	RE	TX	VS	VR
				See adjoining counties for retrievers					

	CV	CR	PR	CEDAR (CST)	UC	RE	TX	VS	VR
	•	•	•	National Investigative Services Inc 417-883-1213	•	•	•	•	

	CV	CR	PR	CHARITON (CST)	UC	RE	TX	VS	VR
	•	•	•	Chariton Abstract 816-288-3446	•	•	•	•	
	•		•	Real Data 573-893-4898	•	•	•		

	CV	CR	PR	CHRISTIAN (CST)	UC	RE	TX	VS	VR
	•	•	•	Evans Advanced Land and Title 417-581-8251	•	•	•		
	•		•	Hogan Land Title Co 417-869-6319		•	•		
	•	•	•	🏛 Kunkel, Joan & Kelli (SOP) 417-358-6494	•	•	•	•	•
	•	•	•	National Investigative Services Inc 417-883-1213	•	•	•	•	

	CV	CR	PR	CLARK (CST)	UC	RE	TX	VS	VR
	•		•	Real Data 573-893-4898	•	•	•		

	CV	CR	PR	CLAY (CST)	UC	RE	TX	VS	VR
	•	•		🏛 RSI 800-633-6125	•	•	•	•	
	•	•	•	Silk Attorney Service 913-432-2755	•	•	•	•	

	CV	CR	PR	CLINTON (CST)	UC	RE	TX	VS	VR
	•			Cameron Title Co Inc 800-530-5933		•	•		

DT	CV	CR	PR	COLE (CAPITAL) (CST)	UC	RE	TX	VS	VR
•	•			CSC 573-634-4363	•		•	•	
•	•	•	•	🏛 Eagle & Associates LLC (SOP) 800-216-4860	•	•	•	•	•
	•		•	Guaranty Land Title 573-636-8388	•	•	•	•	
•	•	•	•	Harmon Legal Process Service (SOP) 314-635-6690	•	•	•	•	
	•	•	•	Jeff City Filing 573-634-3894	•	•	•	•	
	•		•	Real Data 573-893-4898	•	•	•		

	CV	CR	PR	COOPER (CST)	UC	RE	TX	VS	VR
	•		•	Guaranty Land Title 573-636-8388	•	•	•	•	
	•		•	Real Data 573-893-4898	•	•	•		

	CV	CR	PR	CRAWFORD (CST)	UC	RE	TX	VS	VR
	•		•	Crawford County Title Co 573-885-6470	•	•	•	•	
	•		•	Real Data 573-893-4898	•	•	•		

	CV	CR	PR	DADE (CST)	UC	RE	TX	VS	VR
	•	•	•	National Investigative Services Inc 417-883-1213	•	•	•	•	
	•	•	•	Russel Abstract 417-637-2414	•	•	•		

	CV	CR	PR	DALLAS (CST)	UC	RE	TX	VS	VR
	•		•	Hogan Land Title Co 417-869-6319		•	•		
	•	•	•	National Investigative Services Inc 417-883-1213	•	•	•	•	

	CV	CR	PR	DAVIESS (CST)	UC	RE	TX	VS	VR
	•		•	Daviess County Abstracts 816-663-2155	•	•	•		

	CV	CR	PR	DE KALB (CST)	UC	RE	TX	VS	VR
	•			Cameron Title Co Inc 800-530-5933		•	•		

	CV	CR	PR	DENT (CST)	UC	RE	TX	VS	VR
	•		•	Real Data 573-893-4898	•	•	•		

	CV	CR	PR		UC	RE	TX	VS	VR
	•	•	•	Steelman Abstracting Co 573-729-6183	•	•	•		

DOUGLAS (CST)

CV	CR	PR		UC	RE	TX	VS	VR
•	•	•	Douglas County Abstract & Title Co 417-683-4701		•	•		
			Hiett Title Co 417-926-6163	•	•	•		
•	•	•	National Investigative Services Inc 417-883-1213	•	•	•	•	

DUNKLIN (CST)

CV	CR	PR		UC	RE	TX	VS	VR
			See adjoining counties for retrievers					

FRANKLIN (CST)

CV	CR	PR		UC	RE	TX	VS	VR
•	•	•	Compu-Fact Research Inc 314-291-3308	•	•	•		
•	•	•	Isador I Lamke PC 314-239-7808	•	•	•		

GASCONADE (CST)

CV	CR	PR		UC	RE	TX	VS	VR
•	•	•	Mundwiller, Donna 573-486-2925	•	•	•	•	
•		•	Real Data 573-893-4898	•	•	•		

GENTRY (CST)

CV	CR	PR		UC	RE	TX	VS	VR
•		•	Holden Abstract Co 816-726-3417	•	•	•		

GREENE (CST)

DT	CV	CR	PR		UC	RE	TX	VS	VR
	•	•	•	Compu-Fact Research Inc 314-291-3308	•	•	•		
	•			Hogan Land Title Co 417-869-6319		•	•		
•	•	•	•	Kunkel, Joan & Kelli (SOP) 417-358-6494	•	•	•	•	•
•	•	•	•	NDXR Inc 800-687-5080	•	•	•	•	
•	•	•	•	National Investigative Services Inc 417-883-1213	•	•	•	•	

GRUNDY (CST)

CV	CR	PR		UC	RE	TX	VS	VR
•	•	•	Best Abstract Title Co 816-359-2377	•	•	•	•	
•		•	Real Data 573-893-4898	•	•	•		

HARRISON (CST)

CV	CR	PR		UC	RE	TX	VS	VR
•		•	Harrison County Abstract Co Inc 816-425-3523	•	•	•		

HENRY (CST)

CV	CR	PR		UC	RE	TX	VS	VR
•		•	Henry County Abstract Co 800-748-7985	•	•	•		

HICKORY (CST)

CV	CR	PR		UC	RE	TX	VS	VR
•	•	•	Bentley Title Co 417-745-6626	•	•	•	•	
•	•	•	National Investigative Services Inc 417-883-1213	•	•	•	•	

HOLT (CST)

CV	CR	PR		UC	RE	TX	VS	VR
			See adjoining counties for retrievers					

HOWARD (CST)

CV	CR	PR		UC	RE	TX	VS	VR
•		•	Boggs, Karen V 816-848-2962		•		•	
		•	Forbes, Sylvia 816-248-3455		•	•	•	
•		•	Geo G Smith & Son Inc 816-248-2467	•	•	•	•	
		•	Guaranty Land Title 573-636-8388	•	•	•	•	
		•	Real Data 573-893-4898	•	•	•		

HOWELL (CST)

CV	CR	PR		UC	RE	TX	VS	VR
•		•	Ketlett-Landis-Brill Abstr & Land Title 417-256-2951	•	•	•		

IRON (CST)

CV	CR	PR		UC	RE	TX	VS	VR
•		•	American Heritage Abstract 573-431-1359	•	•	•		

JACKSON (CST)

DT	BK	CV	CR	PR		UC	RE	TX	VS	VR
•	•	•	•	•	Executive Investigative Services (SOP) 913-764-9484	•	•	•	•	•
•	•	•	•		RSI 800-633-6125	•	•	•	•	
•	•	•	•	•	Silk Attorney Service 913-432-2755	•	•	•	•	

JASPER (CST)

CV	CR	PR		UC	RE	TX	VS	VR
•	•	•	Kunkel, Joan & Kelli (SOP) 417-358-6494	•	•	•	•	•

CV	CR	PR			UC	RE	TX	VS	VR
•	•	•	NDXR Inc	800-687-5080	•	•	•	•	
•	•	•	National Investigative Services Inc	417-883-1213	•	•	•	•	

JEFFERSON (CST)

CV	CR	PR			UC	RE	TX	VS	VR
•	•	•	Compu-Fact Research Inc	314-291-3308	•	•	•		
•	•	•	Easterling & Steinmetz Inc (SOP)	800-467-4480	•	•	•	•	•
•	•	•	🏛 Tyler-McLennon Inc-Illinois	847-297-4460	•	•	•		•

JOHNSON (CST)

See adjoining counties for retrievers ....

KNOX (CST)

CV	CR	PR			UC	RE	TX	VS	VR
•		•	Real Data	573-893-4898	•	•	•		

LACLEDE (CST)

CV	CR	PR			UC	RE	TX	VS	VR
•	•	•	National Investigative Services Inc	417-883-1213	•	•	•	•	

LAFAYETTE (CST)

CV	CR	PR			UC	RE	TX	VS	VR
•	•	•	Lafayette County Land Title Company	816-259-4631	•	•	•	•	

LAWRENCE (CST)

CV	CR	PR			UC	RE	TX	VS	VR
•	•	•	🏛 Kunkel, Joan & Kelli (SOP)	417-358-6494	•	•	•	•	•
•	•	•	NDXR Inc	800-687-5080	•	•	•	•	
•	•	•	National Investigative Services Inc	417-883-1213	•	•	•	•	

LEWIS (CST)

CV	CR	PR			UC	RE	TX	VS	VR
•	•	•	Lewis County Abstract	573-767-5207	•	•	•		
•			Marion County Abstract Co (SOP)	800-952-5314	•	•	•	•	
•	•		Northeast Missouri Abstract Agency Inc	573-767-5430	•	•	•		
•		•	Real Data	573-893-4898	•	•	•		

LINCOLN (CST)

CV	CR	PR			UC	RE	TX	VS	VR
•	•	•	Assured Title Company	314-272-7511	•	•	•		
•	•	•	Easterling & Steinmetz Inc (SOP)	800-467-4480	•	•	•	•	•
		•	Griffith, Charlotte	573-242-3488		•	•		
•	•	•	Troy Title Co	314-528-2220	•	•	•		

LINN (CST)

CV	CR	PR			UC	RE	TX	VS	VR
•		•	Real Data	573-893-4898	•	•	•		

LIVINGSTON (CST)

CV	CR	PR			UC	RE	TX	VS	VR
•		•	Real Data	573-893-4898	•	•	•		
•		•	Staton Abstract & Title Co	816-646-1421	•	•	•	•	

MACON (CST)

CV	CR	PR			UC	RE	TX	VS	VR
•	•	•	A Verne Baker Abstract Co	816-385-6474	•	•	•	•	
•		•	Real Data	573-893-4898	•	•	•		
•	•	•	White Abstract Co	816-385-2515	•	•	•	•	

MADISON (CST)

CV	CR	PR			UC	RE	TX	VS	VR
•			American Heritage Abstract	573-431-1359	•	•	•		
		•	Preferred Land Title	573-756-6721	•	•	•		

MARIES (CST)

CV	CR	PR			UC	RE	TX	VS	VR
•	•	•	Hollenbeck Title Co	573-422-3633	•	•	•		
•		•	Real Data	573-893-4898	•	•	•		

MARION (CST)

CV	CR	PR			UC	RE	TX	VS	VR
•			Marion County Abstract Co (SOP)	800-952-5314	•	•	•	•	
•		•	Real Data	573-893-4898	•	•	•		
•		•	Wells Abstract Company	573-221-0644	•	•	•		

MCDONALD (CST)

CV	CR	PR			UC	RE	TX	VS	VR
•	•	•	🏛 Kunkel, Joan & Kelli (SOP)	417-358-6494	•	•	•	•	•

•	•	•	NDXR Inc 800-687-5080	•	•	•	•	
•	•	•	National Investigative Services Inc 417-883-1213	•	•	•	•	

CV	CR	PR	MERCER (CST)	UC	RE	TX	VS	VR
			Putnam County Abstract 816-947-3105	•	•	•		
•		•	Real Data 573-893-4898	•	•	•		

CV	CR	PR	MILLER (CST)	UC	RE	TX	VS	VR
•		•	Guaranty Land Title 573-636-8388	•	•	•	•	
•	•	•	Harmon Legal Process Service (SOP) 314-635-6690	•	•	•	•	
•	•	•	National Investigative Services Inc 417-883-1213	•	•	•	•	

CV	CR	PR	MISSISSIPPI (CST)	UC	RE	TX	VS	VR
•		•	Mississippi County Abstract & Loan Co 573-683-4671	•	•	•		

CV	CR	PR	MONITEAU (CST)	UC	RE	TX	VS	VR
•		•	Guaranty Land Title 573-636-8388	•	•	•	•	

CV	CR	PR	MONROE (CST)	UC	RE	TX	VS	VR
•		•	Marion County Abstract Co (SOP) 800-952-5314	•	•	•	•	
•	•	•	Monroe County Abstract and Title Co 816-327-4109	•	•	•		

CV	CR	PR	MONTGOMERY (CST)	UC	RE	TX	VS	VR
•	•	•	Assured Title Company 314-272-7511	•	•	•		
•	•	•	Montgomery County Abstract and Title Co 314-564-2298	•	•	•		

CV	CR	PR	MORGAN (CST)	UC	RE	TX	VS	VR
•		•	Guaranty Land Title 573-636-8388	•	•	•	•	
•	•	•	Harmon Legal Process Service (SOP) 314-635-6690	•	•	•	•	
•		•	Hubbard-Kavanaugh Abstract & Title 573-378-4411	•	•	•	•	
•		•	Real Data 573-893-4898	•	•	•		

CV	CR	PR	NEW MADRID (CST)	UC	RE	TX	VS	VR
•	•		Interquest Information Services 800-455-1655	•	•	•	•	•
•		•	Security Abstract Co 573-748-2372		•	•		

CV	CR	PR	NEWTON (CST)	UC	RE	TX	VS	VR
•	•	•	🏛 Kunkel, Joan & Kelli (SOP) 417-358-6494	•	•	•	•	•
•	•	•	NDXR Inc 800-687-5080	•	•	•	•	
•	•	•	National Investigative Services Inc 417-883-1213	•	•	•	•	

CV	CR	PR	NODAWAY (CST)	UC	RE	TX	VS	VR
•		•	Nodaway County Abstract Co 816-582-2332	•	•	•	•	

CV	CR	PR	OREGON (CST)	UC	RE	TX	VS	VR
			See adjoining counties for retrievers					

CV	CR	PR	OSAGE (CST)	UC	RE	TX	VS	VR
•		•	Guaranty Land Title 573-636-8388	•	•	•	•	
•	•	•	Harmon Legal Process Service (SOP) 314-635-6690	•	•	•	•	
•		•	Real Data 573-893-4898	•	•	•		

CV	CR	PR	OZARK (CST)	UC	RE	TX	VS	VR
•	•	•	National Investigative Services Inc 417-883-1213	•	•	•	•	

CV	CR	PR	PEMISCOT (CST)	UC	RE	TX	VS	VR
•		•	Pemiscot County Abstract & Investment Co 573-333-4666	•	•	•		

CV	CR	PR	PERRY (CST)	UC	RE	TX	VS	VR
•	•		Interquest Information Services 800-455-1655	•	•	•	•	•
•		•	Kiefer Title Co 314-547-7755	•	•	•		

CV	CR	PR	PETTIS (CST)	UC	RE	TX	VS	VR
•	•	•	Landmann Abstract & Title Co 816-826-0051	•	•	•	•	
•		•	Real Data 573-893-4898	•	•	•		

CV	CR	PR	PHELPS (CST)		UC	RE	TX	VS	VR
•	•	•	National Investigative Services Inc 417-883-1213		•	•	•	•	
•		•	Real Data 573-893-4898		•	•	•		

CV	CR	PR	PIKE (CST)		UC	RE	TX	VS	VR
		•	Griffith, Charlotte 573-242-3488			•	•		
		•	Henson, Anna Marie 573-324-2531			•	•	•	
•		•	Real Data 573-893-4898		•	•	•		
•		•	Sterne, Sarah 573-242-3240			•			

CV	CR	PR	PLATTE (CST)		UC	RE	TX	VS	VR
•	•		🏛 RSI 800-633-6125		•	•	•	•	
•	•	•	Silk Attorney Service 913-432-2755		•	•	•	•	

CV	CR	PR	POLK (CST)		UC	RE	TX	VS	VR
•	•	•	National Investigative Services Inc 417-883-1213		•	•	•	•	

CV	CR	PR	PULASKI (CST)		UC	RE	TX	VS	VR
	•	•	Ousley, Veda 573-736-5357		•	•	•	•	•
•		•	Real Data 573-893-4898		•	•	•		

CV	CR	PR	PUTNAM (CST)		UC	RE	TX	VS	VR
			Putnam County Abstract 816-947-3105		•	•	•		
•		•	Real Data 573-893-4898		•	•	•		

CV	CR	PR	RALLS (CST)		UC	RE	TX	VS	VR
•		•	Marion County Abstract Co (SOP) 800-952-5314		•	•	•	•	
•		•	Real Data 573-893-4898		•	•	•		
•		•	Wells Abstract Company 573-221-0644		•	•	•		

CV	CR	PR	RANDOLPH (CST)		UC	RE	TX	VS	VR
•		•	Real Data 573-893-4898		•	•	•		
•	•	•	Town and Country Abstract Co 816-277-3467		•	•	•		

CV	CR	PR	RAY (CST)		UC	RE	TX	VS	VR
			See adjoining counties for retrievers						

CV	CR	PR	REYNOLDS (CST)		UC	RE	TX	VS	VR
			See adjoining counties for retrievers						

CV	CR	PR	RIPLEY (CST)		UC	RE	TX	VS	VR
			See adjoining counties for retrievers						

CV	CR	PR	SALINE (CST)		UC	RE	TX	VS	VR
•		•	Real Data 573-893-4898		•	•	•		

CV	CR	PR	SCHUYLER (CST)		UC	RE	TX	VS	VR
			Putnam County Abstract 816-947-3105		•	•	•		
•		•	Real Data 573-893-4898		•	•	•		

CV	CR	PR	SCOTLAND (CST)		UC	RE	TX	VS	VR
•		•	Real Data 573-893-4898		•	•	•		
		•	Scotland County Abstract Inc 816-465-7052		•	•	•		

CV	CR	PR	SCOTT (CST)		UC	RE	TX	VS	VR
		•	Glastetter, Romana 573-264-2887			•	•	•	
•	•		Interquest Information Services 800-455-1655		•	•	•	•	•

CV	CR	PR	SHANNON (CST)		UC	RE	TX	VS	VR
•		•	Shannon County Abstract Co 573-226-3331		•	•	•		

CV	CR	PR	SHELBY (CST)		UC	RE	TX	VS	VR
•		•	Marion County Abstract Co (SOP) 800-952-5314		•	•	•	•	
•		•	Real Data 573-893-4898		•	•	•		

CV	CR	PR	ST. CHARLES (CST)	UC	RE	TX	VS	VR
•	•	•	Assured Title Company ... 314-272-7511	•	•	•		
•	•	•	Compu-Fact Research Inc ... 314-291-3308	•	•	•		
•	•	•	Easterling & Steinmetz Inc (SOP) ... 800-467-4480	•	•	•	•	•
•	•		🏛 Kyle, Michelle ... 314-544-3493	•	•	•		
•	•	•	🏛 PMDC Associates ... 314-583-1828	•	•	•	•	•
•	•	•	St Vrain Resources (SOP) ... 314-821-9029	•	•	•		•
•	•	•	🏛 Tyler-McLennon Inc-Illinois ... 847-297-4460	•	•	•		•

CV	CR	PR	ST. CLAIR (CST)	UC	RE	TX	VS	VR
			See adjoining counties for retrievers ...					

CV	CR	PR	ST. FRANCOIS (CST)	UC	RE	TX	VS	VR
•		•	American Heritage Abstract ... 573-431-1359	•	•	•		
•	•	•	Compu-Fact Research Inc ... 314-291-3308	•	•	•		
		•	Preferred Land Title ... 573-756-6721	•	•	•		

DT	BK	CV	CR	PR	ST. LOUIS (CST)	UC	RE	TX	VS	VR
•	•				Bankruptcy Services Inc ... 314-421-5749					
•		•	•	•	D & L Investigations (SOP) ... 618-236-2232	•	•	•	•	
•	•	•	•	•	Easterling & Steinmetz Inc (SOP) ... 800-467-4480	•	•	•		•
				•	🏛 Gleem Credit Services ... 314-521-1300					
		•	•		🏛 Kyle, Michelle ... 314-544-3493	•	•	•		
•		•	•	•	🏛 Lueken, Patricia O ... 314-631-5928	•	•	•		
•		•	•	•	🏛 PMDC Associates ... 314-583-1828	•	•	•	•	•
•		•	•	•	🏛 Tyler-McLennon Inc-Illinois ... 847-297-4460	•	•	•		•
		•			Worldwide Insurance Group ... 314-878-1800				•	

CV	CR	PR	CITY OF ST. LOUIS (CST)	UC	RE	TX	VS	VR
			Bankruptcy Services Inc ... 314-421-5749					
•	•	•	D & L Investigations (SOP) ... 618-236-2232	•	•	•	•	
•	•		🏛 Kyle, Michelle ... 314-544-3493	•	•	•		
•	•	•	🏛 Lueken, Patricia O ... 314-631-5928	•	•	•		
•	•	•	🏛 PMDC Associates ... 314-583-1828	•	•	•	•	•
•	•	•	St Vrain Resources (SOP) ... 314-821-9029	•	•	•		•
•	•	•	🏛 Tyler-McLennon Inc-Illinois ... 847-297-4460	•	•	•	•	•

CV	CR	PR	STE. GENEVIEVE (CST)	UC	RE	TX	VS	VR
•		•	American Heritage Abstract ... 573-431-1359	•	•	•		
		•	Preferred Land Title ... 573-756-6721	•	•	•		

CV	CR	PR	STODDARD (CST)	UC	RE	TX	VS	VR
•		•	County Wide Abstract and Title Co Inc ... 573-624-2436	•	•	•		
•	•		Interquest Information Services ... 800-455-1655	•	•	•	•	•

CV	CR	PR	STONE (CST)	UC	RE	TX	VS	VR
•		•	Hogan Land Title Co ... 417-869-6319		•	•		
•	•	•	National Investigative Services Inc ... 417-883-1213	•	•	•	•	

CV	CR	PR	SULLIVAN (CST)	UC	RE	TX	VS	VR
•		•	Real Data ... 573-893-4898	•	•	•		
•	•	•	Sullivan County Abstract Co ... 816-265-3744	•	•	•	•	

CV	CR	PR	TANEY (CST)	UC	RE	TX	VS	VR
•		•	Hogan Land Title Co ... 417-869-6319		•	•		
•	•	•	National Investigative Services Inc ... 417-883-1213	•	•	•	•	

CV	CR	PR	TEXAS (CST)	UC	RE	TX	VS	VR
•	•	•	Hiett Title Co ... 417-967-3660	•	•	•		

CV	CR	PR	VERNON (CST)	UC	RE	TX	VS	VR
•		•	Bowman's Vernon County Title Co ... 417-667-7565		•	•		
•	•	•	🏛 Kunkel, Joan & Kelli (SOP) ... 417-358-6494	•	•	•	•	•

●	●	●	NDXR Inc 800-687-5080	●	●	●	●	
●	●	●	National Investigative Services Inc 417-883-1213	●	●	●	●	

CV	CR	PR	WARREN (CST)	UC	RE	TX	VS	VR
●	●	●	Assured Title Company 314-272-7511	●	●	●		

CV	CR	PR	WASHINGTON (CST)	UC	RE	TX	VS	VR
●		●	American Heritage Abstract 573-431-1359	●	●	●		
		●	Preferred Land Title 573-756-6721	●	●	●		

CV	CR	PR	WAYNE (CST)	UC	RE	TX	VS	VR
			See adjoining counties for retrievers					

CV	CR	PR	WEBSTER (CST)	UC	RE	TX	VS	VR
●		●	D D Hamilton Abstract Co 417-859-2078	●	●	●		
●	●	●	National Investigative Services Inc 417-883-1213	●	●	●	●	

CV	CR	PR	WORTH (CST)	UC	RE	TX	VS	VR
●		●	Nodaway County Abstract Co 816-582-2332	●	●	●	●	

CV	CR	PR	WRIGHT (CST)	UC	RE	TX	VS	VR
			Hiett Title Co 417-926-6163	●	●	●		
●	●	●	Hiett Title Co 417-967-3660	●	●	●		
●	●	●	National Investigative Services Inc 417-883-1213	●	●	●	●	

MONTANA

	CV	CR	PR	BEAVERHEAD (MST)		UC	RE	TX	VS	VR
	●	●	●	Southern Mountain Abstract & Title 406-683-4445		●	●	●	●	

	CV	CR	PR	BIG HORN (MST)		UC	RE	TX	VS	VR
	●	●	●	Treasure State Title 406-665-3797		●	●	●	●	

	CV	CR	PR	BLAINE (MST)		UC	RE	TX	VS	VR
	●	●	●	Blaine County Title Co 406-357-3884		●	●	●	●	

	CV	CR	PR	BROADWATER (MST)		UC	RE	TX	VS	VR
	●	●	●	🏛 AEGIS Consulting & Investigations Inc 888-742-3447		●	●	●	●	●
			●	Meadowlark Search 406-449-5151		●	●	●	●	

	CV	CR	PR	CARBON (MST)		UC	RE	TX	VS	VR
	●	●	●	Carbon County Abstract & Title 406-446-1090		●	●	●	●	

	CV	CR	PR	CARTER (MST)		UC	RE	TX	VS	VR
	●	●	●	Mainstreet Business Services 406-232-6111		●	●	●	●	
	●		●	Security Abstract & Title Co 406-232-3415		●	●	●		

DT	CV	CR	PR	CASCADE (MST)		UC	RE	TX	VS	VR
●	●	●	●	First Montana Title Co of Great Falls 406-727-2600		●	●	●		
●	●	●	●	INFO/DATA 800-847-2716		●	●	●	●	●

	CV	CR	PR	CHOUTEAU (MST)		UC	RE	TX	VS	VR
	●	●	●	Chouteau County Abstract Co 406-622-3221		●	●	●		

	CV	CR	PR	CUSTER (MST)		UC	RE	TX	VS	VR
	●	●	●	Mainstreet Business Services 406-232-6111		●	●	●	●	
	●		●	Security Abstract & Title Co 406-232-3415		●	●	●		

	CV	CR	PR	DANIELS (MST)		UC	RE	TX	VS	VR
	●	●	●	Mainstreet Business Services 406-232-6111		●	●	●	●	
	●		●	Montana Abstract Co Inc 406-487-5961			●	●	●	
	●		●	Nichols, Jake 406-765-1651		●	●	●	●	

	CV	CR	PR	DAWSON (MST)		UC	RE	TX	VS	VR
	●		●	First American Title Co of Montana Inc 406-365-5482			●	●		
	●	●	●	Mainstreet Business Services 406-232-6111		●	●	●	●	

	CV	CR	PR	DEER LODGE (MST)		UC	RE	TX	VS	VR
	●	●	●	Montana Abstract & Title Co 406-723-6521		●	●	●	●	

	CV	CR	PR	FALLON (MST)		UC	RE	TX	VS	VR
	●	●	●	Mainstreet Business Services 406-232-6111		●	●	●	●	

	CV	CR	PR	FERGUS (MST)		UC	RE	TX	VS	VR
	●	●	●	Realty Title Co Inc 406-538-8176		●	●	●	●	

	CV	CR	PR	FLATHEAD (MST)		UC	RE	TX	VS	VR
	●	●	●	Flathead County Title Co 406-755-5028		●	●	●	●	

	CV	CR	PR	GALLATIN (MST)		UC	RE	TX	VS	VR
				See adjoining counties for retrievers						

	CV	CR	PR	GARFIELD (MST)		UC	RE	TX	VS	VR
	●	●	●	Mainstreet Business Services 406-232-6111		●	●	●	●	
	●		●	Security Abstract & Title Co 406-232-3415		●	●	●		

	CV	CR	PR	GLACIER (MST)		UC	RE	TX	VS	VR
				See adjoining counties for retrievers						

Court Records				Name	Phone	UC	RE	TX	VS	VR
	CV	CR	PR	**GOLDEN VALLEY (MST)**		UC	RE	TX	VS	VR
				Mid Montana Title Co	406-632-4145		•			
	CV	CR	PR	**GRANITE (MST)**		UC	RE	TX	VS	VR
	•	•	•	Montana Abstract & Title Co	406-723-6521	•	•	•	•	
	CV	CR	PR	**HILL (MST)**		UC	RE	TX	VS	VR
	•		•	Hill County Title Co	406-265-7624	•	•	•	•	
	CV	CR	PR	**JEFFERSON (MST)**		UC	RE	TX	VS	VR
	•		•	Meadowlark Search	406-449-5151	•	•	•	•	
	CV	CR	PR	**JUDITH BASIN (MST)**		UC	RE	TX	VS	VR
	•	•	•	INFO/DATA	800-847-2716	•	•	•	•	•
	•	•	•	Realty Title Co Inc	406-538-8176	•	•	•	•	
	CV	CR	PR	**LAKE (MST)**		UC	RE	TX	VS	VR
	•	•	•	First American Title & Escrow	800-331-2349	•	•	•	•	
	•		•	Lake County Abstract & Title Co	406-883-6226	•	•	•	•	
DT	CV	CR	PR	**LEWIS AND CLARK (CAPITAL) (MST)**		UC	RE	TX	VS	VR
•	•	•	•	🏛 AEGIS Consulting & Investigations Inc	888-742-3447	•	•	•	•	•
•	•		•	Helena Abstract & Title Co	406-442-5080	•	•	•	•	
•	•		•	INFO/DATA	800-847-2716	•	•	•	•	•
•	•		•	Meadowlark Search	406-449-5151	•	•	•	•	
	CV	CR	PR	**LIBERTY (MST)**		UC	RE	TX	VS	VR
	•		•	Marias Title Company	406-434-5156	•	•	•	•	
	CV	CR	PR	**LINCOLN (MST)**		UC	RE	TX	VS	VR
	•	•	•	Action Agency (SOP)	208-263-9586	•	•	•	•	
	•	•	•	First American Title & Escrow	406-293-3721	•	•	•	•	
	•	•	•	First American Title & Escrow	800-331-2349	•	•	•	•	
	CV	CR	PR	**MADISON (MST)**		UC	RE	TX	VS	VR
	•	•	•	Madison County Title Co	800-570-5337	•	•	•	•	
	CV	CR	PR	**MCCONE (MST)**		UC	RE	TX	VS	VR
	•		•	First American Title Co of Montana Inc	406-365-5482		•	•		
	•	•	•	Mainstreet Business Services	406-232-6111	•	•	•	•	
	CV	CR	PR	**MEAGHER (MST)**		UC	RE	TX	VS	VR
	•	•	•	INFO/DATA	800-847-2716	•	•	•	•	•
	•	•	•	Potter & Co	406-547-3355	•	•	•	•	
	CV	CR	PR	**MINERAL (MST)**		UC	RE	TX	VS	VR
	•	•	•	First American Title Co	406-822-3391	•	•	•	•	
DT	CV	CR	PR	**MISSOULA (MST)**		UC	RE	TX	VS	VR
•		•		Due Diligence Inc	800-644-0107					
	•	•	•	Insured Titles Inc	406-728-7900	•	•	•	•	
	CV	CR	PR	**MUSSELSHELL (MST)**		UC	RE	TX	VS	VR
				Musselshell County Title Inc	406-323-3165	•	•	•	•	
	CV	CR	PR	**PARK (MST)**		UC	RE	TX	VS	VR
	•	•	•	Security Title of Park County Inc	406-222-0362	•	•	•	•	
	CV	CR	PR	**PETROLEUM (MST)**		UC	RE	TX	VS	VR
	•	•	•	Realty Title Co Inc	406-538-8176	•	•	•	•	
	CV	CR	PR	**PHILLIPS (MST)**		UC	RE	TX	VS	VR
	•	•	•	Phillips County Abstract Co	406-654-1413	•	•	•	•	

CV	CR	PR	PONDERA (MST)		UC	RE	TX	VS	VR
•	•	•	INFO/DATA 800-847-2716		•	•	•	•	•
•	•	•	Pondera County Title Co 406-278-5823		•	•	•	•	

CV	CR	PR	POWDER RIVER (MST)		UC	RE	TX	VS	VR
•	•	•	Mainstreet Business Services 406-232-6111		•	•	•	•	

CV	CR	PR	POWELL (MST)		UC	RE	TX	VS	VR
•	•	•	Montana Abstract & Title Co 406-723-6521		•	•	•	•	

CV	CR	PR	PRAIRIE (MST)		UC	RE	TX	VS	VR
•	•	•	Mainstreet Business Services 406-232-6111		•	•	•	•	
•	•	•	Prairie Abstract & Title 406-637-5472		•	•	•	•	

CV	CR	PR	RAVALLI (MST)		UC	RE	TX	VS	VR
•		•	🏛 Bitterroot Research 406-363-4408		•	•	•	•	

CV	CR	PR	RICHLAND (MST)		UC	RE	TX	VS	VR
•	•	•	Mainstreet Business Services 406-232-6111		•	•	•	•	
•	•	•	Security Abstract Co 406-482-1010		•	•	•	•	

CV	CR	PR	ROOSEVELT (MST)		UC	RE	TX	VS	VR
•	•	•	Mainstreet Business Services 406-232-6111		•	•	•	•	
•		•	Nichols, Jake 406-765-1651		•	•	•	•	
•	•	•	Roosevelt County Abstract Co Inc 406-653-2800		•	•	•		

CV	CR	PR	ROSEBUD (MST)		UC	RE	TX	VS	VR
•	•	•	First Montana Title Co of Great Falls 406-727-2600		•	•	•		
•	•	•	Mainstreet Business Services 406-232-6111		•	•	•	•	

CV	CR	PR	SANDERS (MST)		UC	RE	TX	VS	VR
•	•	•	Action Agency (SOP) 208-263-9586		•	•	•	•	
•	•	•	First American Title Co 406-827-3591		•	•	•	•	

CV	CR	PR	SHERIDAN (MST)		UC	RE	TX	VS	VR
•	•	•	Mainstreet Business Services 406-232-6111		•	•	•	•	
•		•	Nichols, Jake 406-765-1651		•	•	•	•	

DT	BK	CV	CR	PR	SILVER BOW (MST)		UC	RE	TX	VS	VR
•	•	•		•	INFO/DATA 800-847-2716		•	•	•	•	•
•	•	•	•	•	Montana Abstract & Title Co 406-723-6521		•	•	•	•	

CV	CR	PR	STILLWATER (MST)		UC	RE	TX	VS	VR
•		•	Stillwater Abstract 406-322-5216		•	•	•		

CV	CR	PR	SWEET GRASS (MST)		UC	RE	TX	VS	VR
			Mid Montana Title Co 406-632-4145			•			

CV	CR	PR	TETON (MST)		UC	RE	TX	VS	VR
•	•	•	INFO/DATA 800-847-2716		•	•	•	•	•

CV	CR	PR	TOOLE (MST)		UC	RE	TX	VS	VR
•	•	•	INFO/DATA 800-847-2716		•	•	•	•	•
•	•	•	Marias Title Company 406-434-5156		•	•	•	•	

CV	CR	PR	TREASURE (MST)		UC	RE	TX	VS	VR
•	•	•	First Montana Title Co of Great Falls 406-727-2600		•	•	•		

CV	CR	PR	VALLEY (MST)		UC	RE	TX	VS	VR
•	•	•	Mainstreet Business Services 406-232-6111		•	•	•	•	
•	•	•	Valley County Abstract Company 406-228-2350		•	•	•	•	

CV	CR	PR	WHEATLAND (MST)		UC	RE	TX	VS	VR
			Mid Montana Title Co 406-632-4145			•			

					WIBAUX (MST)			UC	RE	TX	VS	VR
	CV	CR	PR									
	•	•	•	Mainstreet Business Services 406-232-6111			•	•	•	•	

					YELLOWSTONE (MST)			UC	RE	TX	VS	VR
DT	CV	CR	PR									
	•		•	Deister Ward & Witcher 800-443-7874			•	•	•	•	
•	•	•	•	First Montana Title Co of Great Falls 406-727-2600			•	•	•		

					YELLOWSTONE NATIONAL PARK (PART) (MST)			UC	RE	TX	VS	VR
	CV	CR	PR									

See adjoining counties for retrievers ....

SUMMARY OF CODES

COURT RECORDS

CODE	GOVERNMENT AGENCY	TYPE OF INFORMATION
DT	US District Court	Federal civil and criminal cases
BK	Bankruptcy Court	United States bankruptcy cases
CV	Civil Court	Municipal, county and state level civil cases
CR	Criminal Court	Municipal, county and state level criminal cases
PR	Probate Court	Wills and estate cases

COUNTY RECORDS

CODE	GOVERNMENT AGENCY	TYPE OF INFORMATION
UC	UCC Filing Office	Uniform Commercial Code and other personal property liens
RE	Recorder of Deeds	Real property transactions and liens
TX	Tax Assessor	Real property tax information
VS	Vital Records Office	Vital statistics—birth, death, marriage, divorce, etc.
VR	Voter Registration Office	Voter registration and campaign contribution information

- "CODE" designates the agency and type of information obtainable in each county from a retriever.
- The time zone for each county is abbreviated as follows: EST—Eastern Standard Time; CST—Central; MST—Mountain; PST—Pacific; AK—Alaska; HT—Hawaii.
- ▥—This symbol designates a Public Record Retriever Network member.
- "(SOP)" after the retriever name designates Service of Process.
- Individual retrievers without a company name are listed in order of their last name.
- US District and Bankruptcy courts are indicated only in the counties where courts are located.

NEBRASKA

CV	CR	PR	ADAMS (CST)		UC	RE	TX	VS	VR
•		•	Adams Land Title 402-463-4198		•	•	•		
•	•	•	Heritage Title Inc 402-463-6208		•	•	•	•	

CV	CR	PR	ANTELOPE (CST)		UC	RE	TX	VS	VR
•	•	•	Chilvers Abstract & Title Co 402-329-4525		•	•	•	•	

CV	CR	PR	ARTHUR (MST)		UC	RE	TX	VS	VR
•	•	•	Thalken Abstract & Title Co 308-284-3972		•	•	•	•	

CV	CR	PR	BANNER (MST)		UC	RE	TX	VS	VR
•	•	•	🏛 Taurus Data Search 308-436-3173		•	•	•	•	•
•	•	•	Thalken Abstract & Title Co 308-284-3972		•	•	•	•	

CV	CR	PR	BLAINE (CST)		UC	RE	TX	VS	VR
•	•	•	Russell Abstracting & Title 308-872-5938		•	•	•	•	

CV	CR	PR	BOONE (CST)		UC	RE	TX	VS	VR
			See adjoining counties for retrievers						

CV	CR	PR	BOX BUTTE (MST)		UC	RE	TX	VS	VR
•		•	Buchfinck Inc 308-762-4715		•	•	•	•	
•	•	•	Credit Bureau of Western Nebraska 308-632-2117		•	•	•	•	
•	•	•	Dawes County Abstract Co 308-432-4840		•	•	•		
•	•	•	🏛 Taurus Data Search 308-436-3173		•	•	•	•	•

CV	CR	PR	BOYD (CST)		UC	RE	TX	VS	VR
•	•	•	McCarthy Abstract Co 402-336-2860		•	•	•		

CV	CR	PR	BROWN (CST)		UC	RE	TX	VS	VR
	•		Brown County Abstract Co 402-387-2718		•	•	•		
•	•	•	Sandhills Title & Abstracting 402-376-2639		•	•	•	•	

CV	CR	PR	BUFFALO (CST)		UC	RE	TX	VS	VR
•	•	•	Adams Land Title 308-995-5615		•	•	•		
•		•	Adams Land Title 402-463-4198		•	•	•		
•		•	Barney Abstract & Title Co 308-234-5548		•	•	•		

CV	CR	PR	BURT (CST)		UC	RE	TX	VS	VR
•	•	•	Anderson Abstract Co 402-374-1476		•	•	•		

CV	CR	PR	BUTLER (CST)		UC	RE	TX	VS	VR
•	•	•	Beckner Title Company 402-747-2141		•	•	•	•	
•		•	Colfax County Title and Abstract Co 402-352-2027		•	•	•		
•		•	Mihulka, Elden 402-352-3053		•	•	•		

CV	CR	PR	CASS (CST)		UC	RE	TX	VS	VR
•	•	•	Coit Enterprises 402-451-0462		•	•	•	•	•
•	•	•	Otoe County Abstract Co 402-873-5511		•	•	•		
•	•	•	🏛 Thomas, Donna 402-339-7291		•	•	•	•	

CV	CR	PR	CEDAR (CST)		UC	RE	TX	VS	VR
•	•	•	Chilvers Abstract & Title Co 402-329-4525		•	•	•	•	
•	•	•	Intra-Lex Investigations Inc (SOP) 712-233-1639		•	•	•	•	
•	•	•	Merkel Abstract & Title 402-254-3547		•	•	•		

CV	CR	PR	CHASE (MST)		UC	RE	TX	VS	VR
•	•	•	Hines & Hines Lawyers 308-423-2611		•	•	•	•	
•	•	•	Thalken Abstract & Title Co 308-284-3972		•	•	•	•	

CV	CR	PR	CHERRY (MST)		UC	RE	TX	VS	VR
•	•	•	Sandhills Title & Abstracting 402-376-2639		•	•	•	•	

CHEYENNE (MST)

CV	CR	PR		UC	RE	TX	VS	VR
		•	Cheyenne County Abstract 308-254-5636	•	•	•		
•	•	•	Credit Bureau of Western Nebraska 308-632-2117	•	•	•	•	
•		•	Deuel County Abstract Co 308-874-2212	•	•	•		
•	•	•	🏛 Taurus Data Search 308-436-3173	•	•	•	•	•

CLAY (CST)

CV	CR	PR		UC	RE	TX	VS	VR
•		•	Adams Land Title 402-463-4198	•	•	•		
•	•	•	Clay County Abstract & Title 402-762-3645	•	•	•	•	

COLFAX (CST)

CV	CR	PR		UC	RE	TX	VS	VR
•		•	Colfax County Title and Abstract Co 402-352-2027	•	•	•		
•		•	Mihulka, Elden 402-352-3053	•	•	•		
•	•	•	Stanton Co Abstract 402-439-2142	•	•	•	•	

CUMING (CST)

CV	CR	PR		UC	RE	TX	VS	VR
•	•	•	Intra-Lex Investigations Inc (SOP) 712-233-1639	•	•	•	•	
•	•	•	Stanton Co Abstract 402-439-2142	•	•	•	•	

CUSTER (CST)

CV	CR	PR		UC	RE	TX	VS	VR
•	•	•	Russell Abstracting & Title 308-872-5938	•	•	•	•	

DAKOTA (CST)

CV	CR	PR		UC	RE	TX	VS	VR
•	•	•	Intra-Lex Investigations Inc (SOP) 712-233-1639	•	•	•	•	

DAWES (MST)

CV	CR	PR		UC	RE	TX	VS	VR
•	•	•	Credit Bureau of Western Nebraska 308-632-2117	•	•	•	•	
•	•	•	Dawes County Abstract Co 308-432-4840	•	•	•		

DAWSON (CST)

CV	CR	PR		UC	RE	TX	VS	VR
		•	The H O Smith Company 308-324-2216	•	•	•		

DEUEL (MST)

CV	CR	PR		UC	RE	TX	VS	VR
•		•	Deuel County Abstract Co 308-874-2212	•	•	•		
•	•	•	Thalken Abstract & Title Co 308-284-3972	•	•	•	•	

DIXON (CST)

CV	CR	PR		UC	RE	TX	VS	VR
•	•	•	Intra-Lex Investigations Inc (SOP) 712-233-1639	•	•	•	•	

DODGE (CST)

CV	CR	PR		UC	RE	TX	VS	VR
•	•	•	Coit Enterprises 402-451-0462	•	•	•	•	•
•	•	•	Intra-Lex Investigations Inc (SOP) 712-233-1639	•	•	•	•	

DOUGLAS (CST)

DT	BK	CV	CR	PR		UC	RE	TX	VS	VR
•	•	•	•	•	Coit Enterprises 402-451-0462	•	•	•	•	•
•	•				🏛 Hogan Information Services 405-278-6954					
		•	•	•	Intra-Lex Investigations Inc (SOP) 712-233-1639	•	•	•	•	
•	•	•	•	•	🏛 Thomas, Donna 402-339-7291	•	•	•	•	

DUNDY (MST)

CV	CR	PR		UC	RE	TX	VS	VR
•	•	•	Hines & Hines Lawyers 308-423-2611	•	•	•	•	

FILLMORE (CST)

CV	CR	PR		UC	RE	TX	VS	VR
•		•	Adams Land Title 402-463-4198	•	•	•		
•	•	•	Fillmore County Abstract Co 402-759-3413	•	•	•	•	

FRANKLIN (CST)

CV	CR	PR		UC	RE	TX	VS	VR
•	•	•	Adams Land Title 308-995-5615	•	•	•		
•	•	•	Franklin Abstracts & Land Title Inc 308-425-3654	•	•	•	•	

FRONTIER (CST)

CV	CR	PR		UC	RE	TX	VS	VR
•		•	McCook Abstract Company 308-345-5120	•	•	•		
•	•	•	Scott Abstract 308-532-8535	•	•	•	•	

CV	CR	PR	FURNAS (CST)		UC	RE	TX	VS	VR
•	•	•	Furnas County Title Co Inc 308-268-4005		•	•	•	•	

CV	CR	PR	GAGE (CST)		UC	RE	TX	VS	VR
•		•	Nebraska Title Company 402-228-2233		•	•	•		

CV	CR	PR	GARDEN (MST)		UC	RE	TX	VS	VR
•		•	Deuel County Abstract Co 308-874-2212		•	•	•		
•	•	•	Romig, Marvin T 308-772-4420		•	•	•		
•	•	•	Thalken Abstract & Title Co 308-284-3972		•	•	•	•	

CV	CR	PR	GARFIELD (CST)		UC	RE	TX	VS	VR
•	•	•	Crandall, Dale C 308-346-4284		•	•	•	•	

CV	CR	PR	GOSPER (CST)		UC	RE	TX	VS	VR
			See adjoining counties for retrievers						

CV	CR	PR	GRANT (MST)		UC	RE	TX	VS	VR
•	•	•	Thalken Abstract & Title Co 308-284-3972		•	•	•	•	

CV	CR	PR	GREELEY (CST)		UC	RE	TX	VS	VR
•	•	•	Janke Abstract Co 308-754-4251		•	•	•	•	

CV	CR	PR	HALL (CST)		UC	RE	TX	VS	VR
•		•	Adams Land Title 402-463-4198		•	•	•		

CV	CR	PR	HAMILTON (CST)		UC	RE	TX	VS	VR
•		•	Adams Land Title 402-463-4198		•	•	•		
•	•	•	First Securities Corp in Aurora 402-694-6926		•	•	•	•	

CV	CR	PR	HARLAN (CST)		UC	RE	TX	VS	VR
•	•	•	Adams Land Title 308-995-5615		•	•	•		
•	•	•	Franklin Abstracts & Land Title Inc 308-425-3654		•	•	•	•	
•	•	•	Furnas County Title Co Inc 308-268-4005		•	•	•	•	

CV	CR	PR	HAYES (CST)		UC	RE	TX	VS	VR
•		•	McCook Abstract Company 308-345-5120		•	•	•		
•	•	•	Scott Abstract 308-532-8535		•	•	•	•	

CV	CR	PR	HITCHCOCK (CST)		UC	RE	TX	VS	VR
•	•	•	Hines & Hines Lawyers 308-423-2611		•	•	•	•	
•		•	McCook Abstract Company 308-345-5120		•	•	•		

CV	CR	PR	HOLT (CST)		UC	RE	TX	VS	VR
•	•	•	McCarthy Abstract Co 402-336-2860		•	•	•		

CV	CR	PR	HOOKER (MST)		UC	RE	TX	VS	VR
•	•	•	Scott Abstract 308-532-8535		•	•	•	•	

CV	CR	PR	HOWARD (CST)		UC	RE	TX	VS	VR
•	•	•	Janke Abstract Co 308-754-4251		•	•	•	•	

CV	CR	PR	JEFFERSON (CST)		UC	RE	TX	VS	VR
•		•	Abstract and Title Inc 402-729-2771		•	•	•		

CV	CR	PR	JOHNSON (CST)		UC	RE	TX	VS	VR
•	•	•	Morrissey Morrissey & Dalluge 402-335-3344		•	•	•	•	

CV	CR	PR	KEARNEY (CST)		UC	RE	TX	VS	VR
•	•	•	Adams Land Title 308-995-5615		•	•	•		
•		•	Adams Land Title 402-463-4198		•	•	•		
		•	Miller Abstract and Title Co 308-832-0969		•	•	•		

			CV	CR	PR	KEITH (MST)	UC	RE	TX	VS	VR
			•		•	Deuel County Abstract Co 308-874-2212	•	•	•		
			•	•	•	Thalken Abstract & Title Co 308-284-3972	•	•	•	•	

			CV	CR	PR	KEYA PAHA (CST)	UC	RE	TX	VS	VR
				•		Brown County Abstract Co 402-387-2718	•	•	•		
			•	•	•	Sandhills Title & Abstracting 402-376-2639	•	•	•	•	

			CV	CR	PR	KIMBALL (MST)	UC	RE	TX	VS	VR
			•	•	•	Credit Bureau of Western Nebraska 308-632-2117	•	•	•	•	

			CV	CR	PR	KNOX (CST)	UC	RE	TX	VS	VR
			•	•	•	Chilvers Abstract & Title Co 402-329-4525	•	•	•	•	
			•	•	•	Intra-Lex Investigations Inc (SOP) 712-233-1639	•	•	•	•	

DT	BK	CV	CR	PR	LANCASTER (CAPITAL) (CST)	UC	RE	TX	VS	VR
•	•	•	•	•	Records Research Inc 402-476-3869	•	•	•	•	

			CV	CR	PR	LINCOLN (CST)	UC	RE	TX	VS	VR
			•	•	•	Scott Abstract 308-532-8535	•	•	•	•	

			CV	CR	PR	LOGAN (CST)	UC	RE	TX	VS	VR
			•	•	•	Scott Abstract 308-532-8535	•	•	•	•	

			CV	CR	PR	LOUP (CST)	UC	RE	TX	VS	VR
			•	•	•	Russell Abstracting & Title 308-872-5938	•	•	•	•	

			CV	CR	PR	MADISON (CST)	UC	RE	TX	VS	VR
			•	•	•	Northeast Nebraska Title & Escrow 800-870-2142	•	•	•	•	

			CV	CR	PR	McPHERSON (CST)	UC	RE	TX	VS	VR
			•	•	•	Scott Abstract 308-532-8535	•	•	•	•	

			CV	CR	PR	MERRICK (CST)	UC	RE	TX	VS	VR
			•	•	•	Beckner Title Company 402-747-2141	•	•	•	•	
			•	•	•	Janke Abstract Co 308-754-4251	•	•	•	•	

			CV	CR	PR	MORRILL (MST)	UC	RE	TX	VS	VR
			•	•	•	Credit Bureau of Western Nebraska 308-632-2117	•	•	•	•	
			•	•	•	🏛 Taurus Data Search 308-436-3173	•	•	•	•	•

			CV	CR	PR	NANCE (CST)	UC	RE	TX	VS	VR
			•	•	•	Janke Abstract Co 308-754-4251	•	•	•	•	

			CV	CR	PR	NEMAHA (CST)	UC	RE	TX	VS	VR
				•	•	Auburn Abstract and Title Company 402-274-4321	•	•	•		
			•	•	•	Morrissey Morrissey & Dalluge 402-335-3344	•	•	•	•	
			•	•	•	Otoe County Abstract Co 402-873-5511	•	•	•		

			CV	CR	PR	NUCKOLLS (CST)	UC	RE	TX	VS	VR
			•	•	•	Abstracts Inc 402-879-4341	•	•	•	•	
			•		•	Adams Land Title 402-463-4198	•	•	•		

			CV	CR	PR	OTOE (CST)	UC	RE	TX	VS	VR
			•	•	•	Morrissey Morrissey & Dalluge 402-335-3344	•	•	•	•	
			•	•	•	Otoe County Abstract Co 402-873-5511	•	•	•		

			CV	CR	PR	PAWNEE (CST)	UC	RE	TX	VS	VR
			•	•	•	Morrissey Morrissey & Dalluge 402-335-3344	•	•	•	•	
			•	•	•	Pawnee County Abstract Co 402-852-2577	•	•	•		
			•	•	•	Stehlik Law Office 402-852-2973	•	•	•		

			CV	CR	PR	PERKINS (MST)	UC	RE	TX	VS	VR
			•	•	•	Thalken Abstract & Title Co 308-284-3972	•	•	•	•	

CV	CR	PR	PHELPS (CST)		UC	RE	TX	VS	VR
•	•	•	Adams Land Title 308-995-5615		•	•	•		
•		•	Adams Land Title 402-463-4198		•	•	•		
		•	Dealey Abstract and Title Company 308-995-4622		•	•	•		

CV	CR	PR	PIERCE (CST)		UC	RE	TX	VS	VR
•	•	•	Chilvers Abstract & Title Co 402-329-4525		•	•	•	•	
•	•	•	Intra-Lex Investigations Inc (SOP) 712-233-1639		•	•	•	•	
•	•	•	Northeast Nebraska Title & Escrow 800-870-2142		•	•	•	•	

CV	CR	PR	PLATTE (CST)		UC	RE	TX	VS	VR
•	•	•	Platte County Title Co 402-563-4519		•	•	•	•	
•	•	•	Stanton Co Abstract 402-439-2142		•	•	•	•	

CV	CR	PR	POLK (CST)		UC	RE	TX	VS	VR
•	•	•	Beckner Title Company 402-747-2141		•	•	•	•	

CV	CR	PR	RED WILLOW (CST)		UC	RE	TX	VS	VR
•	•	•	Hines & Hines Lawyers 308-423-2611		•	•	•	•	
•		•	McCook Abstract Company 308-345-5120		•	•	•		

CV	CR	PR	RICHARDSON (CST)		UC	RE	TX	VS	VR
•	•	•	Morrissey Morrissey & Dalluge 402-335-3344		•	•	•	•	
•	•	•	Southeast Nebraska Abstract 402-245-4222		•	•	•		

CV	CR	PR	ROCK (CST)		UC	RE	TX	VS	VR
		•	Brown County Abstract Co 402-387-2718		•	•	•		

CV	CR	PR	SALINE (CST)		UC	RE	TX	VS	VR
•	•	•	Saline County Abstract 402-826-3312		•	•	•	•	

CV	CR	PR	SARPY (CST)		UC	RE	TX	VS	VR
•	•	•	Coit Enterprises 402-451-0462		•	•	•	•	•
•	•	•	Intra-Lex Investigations Inc (SOP) 712-233-1639		•	•	•	•	
•	•	•	PROTEC Systems Inc 800-691-0919			•	•	•	
•	•	•	🏛 Thomas, Donna 402-339-7291		•	•	•	•	

CV	CR	PR	SAUNDERS (CST)		UC	RE	TX	VS	VR
•	•	•	Coit Enterprises 402-451-0462		•	•	•	•	•
•	•	•	Hamilton & Johnson Abstract Inc 402-443-3081		•	•	•		

CV	CR	PR	SCOTTS BLUFF (MST)		UC	RE	TX	VS	VR
•	•	•	Credit Bureau of Western Nebraska 308-632-2117		•	•	•	•	
•	•	•	🏛 Taurus Data Search 308-436-3173		•	•	•	•	•

CV	CR	PR	SEWARD (CST)		UC	RE	TX	VS	VR
			See adjoining counties for retrievers						

CV	CR	PR	SHERIDAN (MST)		UC	RE	TX	VS	VR
•	•	•	Credit Bureau of Western Nebraska 308-632-2117		•	•	•	•	
•	•	•	Dawes County Abstract Co 308-432-4840		•	•	•		
•	•	•	Sandhills Abstracting 308-282-0715		•	•	•	•	

CV	CR	PR	SHERMAN (CST)		UC	RE	TX	VS	VR
•	•	•	Janke Abstract Co 308-754-4251		•	•	•	•	

CV	CR	PR	SIOUX (MST)		UC	RE	TX	VS	VR
•	•	•	Dawes County Abstract Co 308-432-4840		•	•	•		

CV	CR	PR	STANTON (CST)		UC	RE	TX	VS	VR
•	•	•	Intra-Lex Investigations Inc (SOP) 712-233-1639		•	•	•	•	
•	•	•	Stanton Co Abstract 402-439-2142		•	•	•	•	

NEBRASKA

CV	CR	PR	THAYER (CST)	UC	RE	TX	VS	VR
•		•	Thayer County Abstract Office Inc 402-768-6324	•	•	•		

CV	CR	PR	THOMAS (CST)	UC	RE	TX	VS	VR
•	•	•	Russell Abstracting & Title 308-872-5938	•	•	•	•	
•	•	•	Sandhills Title & Abstracting 402-376-2639	•	•	•	•	
•	•	•	Scott Abstract 308-532-8535	•	•	•	•	

CV	CR	PR	THURSTON (CST)	UC	RE	TX	VS	VR
•	•	•	Intra-Lex Investigations Inc (SOP)...................................... 712-233-1639	•	•	•	•	

CV	CR	PR	VALLEY (CST)	UC	RE	TX	VS	VR
			See adjoining counties for retrievers					

CV	CR	PR	WASHINGTON (CST)	UC	RE	TX	VS	VR
•	•	•	Coit Enterprises 402-451-0462	•	•	•	•	•
•	•	•	Intra-Lex Investigations Inc (SOP)...................................... 712-233-1639	•	•	•	•	
•	•	•	PROTEC Systems Inc 800-691-0919		•	•	•	
•	•	•	🏛 Thomas, Donna 402-339-7291	•	•	•	•	

CV	CR	PR	WAYNE (CST)	UC	RE	TX	VS	VR
•	•	•	Chilvers Abstract & Title Co 402-329-4525	•	•	•	•	
•	•	•	Intra-Lex Investigations Inc (SOP)...................................... 712-233-1639	•	•	•	•	

CV	CR	PR	WEBSTER (CST)	UC	RE	TX	VS	VR
•	•	•	Adams Land Title 308-995-5615	•	•	•		
•		•	Adams Land Title 402-463-4198	•	•	•		
•	•	•	Franklin Abstracts & Land Title Inc 308-425-3654	•	•	•	•	

CV	CR	PR	WHEELER (CST)	UC	RE	TX	VS	VR
•	•	•	McCarthy Abstract Co 402-336-2860	•	•	•		

CV	CR	PR	YORK (CST)	UC	RE	TX	VS	VR
•	•		York County Title Co 402-362-4405	•	•	•		

NEVADA

		CV	CR	PR	CARSON CITY (CAPITAL) (PST)	UC	RE	TX	VS	VR
		•		•	🏛 Capitol Document Services Inc 800-899-0490	•		•	•	•
		•	•	•	Reno/Carson Messenger Service Inc 800-222-4249	•	•	•	•	•

		CV	CR	PR	CHURCHILL (PST)	UC	RE	TX	VS	VR
					Nevada Land Services 800-233-4999	•	•	•		

DT	BK	CV	CR	PR	CLARK (PST)	UC	RE	TX	VS	VR
•	•	•	•	•	🏛 ADP Services (SOP) 702-798-8844	•	•	•	•	•
•	•	•	•	•	CSC (SOP) 702-882-3072	•	•	•	•	
•	•				🏛 Hogan Information Services 405-278-6954					
•	•	•	•	•	Las Vegas Legal Document 702-647-1627	•			•	
•	•	•	•		🏛 National Information Service 702-456-4583		•		•	
•	•	•	•	•	Pete Costanzo Private Investigations 702-868-4043	•	•		•	
•	•	•	•	•	🏛 Security Source Nationwide (SOP) 303-628-3973	•	•	•	•	•

		CV	CR	PR	DOUGLAS (PST)	UC	RE	TX	VS	VR
		•		•	🏛 Capitol Document Services Inc 800-899-0490	•		•	•	•
		•	•	•	Reno/Carson Messenger Service Inc 800-222-4249	•	•	•	•	•

		CV	CR	PR	ELKO (PST)	UC	RE	TX	VS	VR
					See adjoining counties for retrievers					

		CV	CR	PR	ESMERALDA (PST)	UC	RE	TX	VS	VR
					Nevada Land Services 800-233-4999	•	•	•		

		CV	CR	PR	EUREKA (PST)	UC	RE	TX	VS	VR
					Nevada Land Services 800-233-4999	•	•	•		

		CV	CR	PR	HUMBOLDT (PST)	UC	RE	TX	VS	VR
					Nevada Land Services 800-233-4999	•	•	•		

		CV	CR	PR	LANDER (PST)	UC	RE	TX	VS	VR
					Nevada Land Services 800-233-4999	•	•	•		

		CV	CR	PR	LINCOLN (PST)	UC	RE	TX	VS	VR
					Nevada Land Services 800-233-4999	•	•	•		

		CV	CR	PR	LYON (PST)	UC	RE	TX	VS	VR
					See adjoining counties for retrievers					

		CV	CR	PR	MINERAL (PST)	UC	RE	TX	VS	VR
					Nevada Land Services 800-233-4999	•	•	•		

		CV	CR	PR	NYE (PST)	UC	RE	TX	VS	VR
					Nevada Land Services 800-233-4999	•	•	•		

		CV	CR	PR	PERSHING (PST)	UC	RE	TX	VS	VR
					Nevada Land Services 800-233-4999	•	•	•		

		CV	CR	PR	STOREY (PST)	UC	RE	TX	VS	VR
		•		•	🏛 Capitol Document Services Inc 800-899-0490	•		•	•	•

DT	BK	CV	CR	PR	WASHOE (PST)	UC	RE	TX	VS	VR
•	•	•		•	🏛 Capitol Document Services Inc 800-899-0490	•		•	•	•
•	•	•	•	•	Reno/Carson Messenger Service Inc 800-222-4249	•	•	•	•	•
•	•	•	•	•	The Copy Store & More - Reno 702-329-0999	•	•	•	•	•

		CV	CR	PR	WHITE PINE (PST)	UC	RE	TX	VS	VR
					Nevada Land Services 800-233-4999	•	•	•		

NEW HAMPSHIRE

BELKNAP (EST)

CV	CR	PR			UC	RE	TX	VS	VR
•	•	•	Coast to Coast Research Network 800-933-5068		•	•	•	•	•
•	•	•	🏛 Doc*U*Search Inc 800-332-3034		•	•	•	•	
•			Don E Leeman Enterprises 603-755-3030			•	•		

CARROLL (EST)

CV	CR	PR			UC	RE	TX	VS	VR
•	•	•	Coast to Coast Research Network 800-933-5068		•	•	•	•	•
•	•	•	🏛 Doc*U*Search Inc 800-332-3034		•	•	•	•	
•			Don E Leeman Enterprises 603-755-3030			•	•		

CHESHIRE (EST)

CV	CR	PR			UC	RE	TX	VS	VR
•	•	•	Coast to Coast Research Network 800-933-5068		•	•	•	•	•
•	•	•	🏛 Doc*U*Search Inc 800-332-3034		•	•	•	•	

COOS (EST)

CV	CR	PR			UC	RE	TX	VS	VR
•	•	•	Coast to Coast Research Network 800-933-5068		•	•	•	•	•
•	•	•	🏛 Doc*U*Search Inc 800-332-3034		•	•	•	•	

GRAFTON (EST)

CV	CR	PR			UC	RE	TX	VS	VR
•	•	•	Coast to Coast Research Network 800-933-5068		•	•	•	•	•
•	•	•	🏛 Doc*U*Search Inc 800-332-3034		•	•	•	•	
•			Don E Leeman Enterprises 603-755-3030			•	•		

HILLSBOROUGH (EST)

BK	CV	CR	PR			UC	RE	TX	VS	VR
•	•	•	•	Coast to Coast Research Network 800-933-5068		•	•	•	•	•
•	•	•	•	🏛 Doc*U*Search Inc 800-332-3034		•	•	•	•	

MERRIMACK (CAPITAL) (EST)

DT	CV	CR	PR			UC	RE	TX	VS	VR
•	•	•	•	Coast to Coast Research Network 800-933-5068		•	•	•	•	•
•	•	•	•	🏛 Doc*U*Search Inc 800-332-3034		•	•	•	•	

ROCKINGHAM (EST)

CV	CR	PR			UC	RE	TX	VS	VR
•	•	•	Coast to Coast Research Network 800-933-5068		•	•	•	•	•
•	•	•	🏛 Doc*U*Search Inc 800-332-3034		•	•	•	•	
•			Don E Leeman Enterprises 603-755-3030			•	•		

STRAFFORD (EST)

CV	CR	PR			UC	RE	TX	VS	VR
•	•	•	Coast to Coast Research Network 800-933-5068		•	•	•	•	•
•	•	•	🏛 Doc*U*Search Inc 800-332-3034		•	•	•	•	
•			Don E Leeman Enterprises 603-755-3030			•	•		

SULLIVAN (EST)

CV	CR	PR			UC	RE	TX	VS	VR
•	•	•	Coast to Coast Research Network 800-933-5068		•	•	•	•	•
•	•	•	🏛 Doc*U*Search Inc 800-332-3034		•	•	•	•	

NEW JERSEY

CV	CR	PR	ATLANTIC (EST)		UC	RE	TX	VS	VR
•		•	CW Credit Abstract Co	718-423-9430	•	•	•		
•			Charles Jones Inc	800-792-8888	•	•			
•	•	•	Dennis Richman's Service (SOP)	215-977-9393	•	•	•	•	•
•	•	•	Fidelifacts	800-678-0007	•	•	•	•	•
•	•	•	Flink Findzum (SOP)	800-354-1215	•	•	•	•	
		•	Fuoti, Peg	609-625-9401					
•		•	Interstate Abstract Inc	609-795-4000	•	•	•	•	
•	•	•	Investech Inc (SOP)	800-392-7676	•	•	•	•	•
•	•	•	Kutlus & Company (SOP)	888-726-5335	•	•	•		
•	•		National Background Investigations Inc	800-798-0079					
•	•	•	North East Court Services Inc (SOP)	800-235-0794	•	•	•		
•	•	•	Searcher Girls Search & Abstract	800-292-2757	•	•	•	•	•
		•	Wortmann, Cheri	215-736-0486				•	

CV	CR	PR	BERGEN (EST)		UC	RE	TX	VS	VR
•		•	Austin & Associates Inc	914-968-3700	•	•	•		•
•	•	•	Biamonte, Joe	201-933-3590	•	•	•	•	
•		•	CW Credit Abstract Co	718-423-9430	•				
•		•	Callahan Lawyers Service (SOP)	201-489-2245	•	•	•		
•			Charles Jones Inc	800-792-8888	•				
•	•		Court Data Search	201-770-1170					
•	•	•	DLS (Demovsky Lawyer Service) (SOP)	800-443-1058	•				
•	•	•	Dennis Richman's Service (SOP)	215-977-9393	•	•	•	•	•
•	•	•	Dios, Dolores	800-763-2988	•	•	•		
•	•	•	Fidelifacts	800-678-0007	•	•	•	•	•
•		•	Gamma Investigative Research Inc (SOP)	800-878-9393	•				
•		•	Interstate Abstract Inc	609-795-4000	•	•	•	•	
•	•	•	Kutlus & Company (SOP)	888-726-5335	•	•	•		
•	•	•	Legal Wings Inc (SOP)	800-339-1286	•	•	•		•
•	•	•	Legal Wings Inc - Newark (SOP)	800-339-1286	•	•	•		
•	•	•	National Background Investigations Inc	800-798-0079					
•	•	•	North East Court Services Inc (SOP)	800-235-0794	•	•	•		
•	•	•	Orion Research Group	908-355-9337	•	•	•	•	•
•	•	•	Sarkisian, Michelle	201-342-7541	•	•	•		
•	•	•	Searcher Girls Search & Abstract	800-292-2757	•	•	•	•	•
		•	Wortmann, Cheri	215-736-0486				•	

CV	CR	PR	BURLINGTON (EST)		UC	RE	TX	VS	VR
•	•		Accu-Fax Employment Screening Svcs	215-234-0700	•	•	•	•	•
•	•		Best Legal Services Inc (SOP)	215-567-7777	•	•	•	•	
•		•	Burlington County Abstract Co	609-235-9435	•	•	•		
•		•	CW Credit Abstract Co	718-423-9430	•	•	•		
•			Charles Jones Inc	800-792-8888	•	•	•		
•	•	•	Craig, Nancy	609-261-5783	•	•	•	•	
•	•	•	Credit Lenders Service Agency Inc	609-751-7400	•	•	•		
•	•	•	Dennis Richman's Service (SOP)	215-977-9393	•	•	•	•	•
•	•	•	Fidelifacts	800-678-0007	•	•	•	•	•
•	•		Flink Findzum (SOP)	800-354-1215	•	•	•	•	
•		•	Interstate Abstract Inc	609-795-4000	•	•	•	•	
•	•	•	Kutlus & Company (SOP)	888-726-5335	•	•	•		
•	•	•	Legal Wings Inc (SOP)	800-339-1286	•	•	•	•	•
•	•	•	National Background Investigations Inc	800-798-0079	•	•	•		
•	•	•	North East Court Services Inc (SOP)	800-235-0794	•	•	•		
•	•	•	Searcher Girls Search & Abstract	800-292-2757	•	•	•	•	•
•	•		Talone and Associates	800-553-5189	•				
•	•	•	The Coynes (SOP)	215-945-6227	•	•	•	•	
		•	Wortmann, Cheri	215-736-0486				•	

CAMDEN (EST)

DT	BK	CV	CR	PR	Name	Phone	UC	RE	TX	VS	VR
•	•	•	•		Accu-Fax Employment Screening Svcs	215-234-0700	•	•	•	•	•
		•	•	•	Augatis, Eileen	609-853-9836	•	•	•	•	
•	•	•	•		Best Legal Services Inc (SOP)	215-567-7777	•	•	•		
•	•	•		•	CW Credit Abstract Co	718-423-9430	•	•	•		
•	•	•			Charles Jones Inc	800-792-8888	•	•	•		
		•		•	Cooper Abstract Co	609-667-4800	•	•	•		
		•	•	•	Credit Lenders Service Agency Inc	609-751-7400	•	•	•		
•	•	•	•	•	Dennis Richman's Service (SOP)	215-977-9393	•	•	•	•	•
•	•	•	•	•	🏛 Fidelifacts	800-678-0007	•	•	•	•	•
•	•	•	•	•	🏛 Flink Findzum (SOP)	800-354-1215	•		•	•	•
•	•	•	•		🏛 Hogan Information Services	405-278-6954					
•	•	•		•	Interstate Abstract Inc	609-795-4000	•	•	•	•	
•	•	•	•	•	🏛 Investech Inc (SOP)	800-392-7676	•	•	•	•	•
•	•	•	•	•	🏛 Kutlus & Company (SOP)	888-726-5335	•	•	•		
•	•	•	•	•	🏛 Legal Wings Inc (SOP)	800-339-1286	•	•	•	•	•
•	•	•	•		🏛 National Background Investigations Inc	800-798-0079					
•	•	•	•	•	🏛 North East Court Services Inc (SOP)	800-235-0794	•	•	•		
•	•	•	•	•	🏛 Searcher Girls Search & Abstract	800-292-2757	•	•	•	•	•
•	•	•	•		Talone and Associates	800-553-5189					
•	•	•	•	•	🏛 The Coynes (SOP)	215-945-6227	•	•	•	•	
				•	Wortmann, Cheri	215-736-0486			•		

CAPE MAY (EST)

CV	CR	PR	Name	Phone	UC	RE	TX	VS	VR
•		•	CW Credit Abstract Co	718-423-9430	•	•	•		
•			Charles Jones Inc	800-792-8888	•	•	•		
•	•	•	Dennis Richman's Service (SOP)	215-977-9393	•	•	•	•	•
•	•	•	🏛 Fidelifacts	800-678-0007	•	•	•	•	•
•	•		🏛 Flink Findzum (SOP)	800-354-1215	•	•	•		
•		•	Interstate Abstract Inc	609-795-4000	•	•	•	•	
•	•	•	🏛 Investech Inc (SOP)	800-392-7676	•	•	•	•	•
•	•	•	🏛 Kutlus & Company (SOP)	888-726-5335	•	•	•		
•	•		🏛 National Background Investigations Inc	800-798-0079					
•	•	•	🏛 North East Court Services Inc (SOP)	800-235-0794	•	•	•		
•	•	•	🏛 Searcher Girls Search & Abstract	800-292-2757	•	•	•	•	•
		•	Wortmann, Cheri	215-736-0486			•		

CUMBERLAND (EST)

CV	CR	PR	Name	Phone	UC	RE	TX	VS	VR
•		•	CW Credit Abstract Co	718-423-9430	•	•	•		
•			Charles Jones Inc	800-792-8888	•	•	•		
•	•	•	Dennis Richman's Service (SOP)	215-977-9393	•	•	•	•	•
•	•	•	🏛 Fidelifacts	800-678-0007	•	•	•	•	•
•	•		🏛 Flink Findzum (SOP)	800-354-1215	•	•	•		
•		•	Interstate Abstract Inc	609-795-4000	•	•	•		
•	•	•	🏛 Investech Inc (SOP)	800-392-7676	•	•	•		
•	•	•	🏛 Kutlus & Company (SOP)	888-726-5335	•	•	•		
•	•		🏛 National Background Investigations Inc	800-798-0079					
•	•	•	🏛 North East Court Services Inc (SOP)	800-235-0794	•	•	•		
•	•	•	🏛 Searcher Girls Search & Abstract	800-292-2757	•	•	•	•	•
		•	Wortmann, Cheri	215-736-0486			•		

ESSEX (EST)

DT	BK	CV	CR	PR	Name	Phone	UC	RE	TX	VS	VR
•	•	•		•	CW Credit Abstract Co	718-423-9430	•	•	•		
•	•	•			Charles Jones Inc	800-792-8888	•	•	•		
•	•	•	•		Court Data Search	201-770-1170					
•	•	•		•	DLS (Demovsky Lawyer Service) (SOP)	800-443-1058	•	•	•	•	•
•	•	•	•	•	Dennis Richman's Service (SOP)	215-977-9393	•	•	•	•	•
•	•	•		•	🏛 Dios, Dolores	800-763-2988	•	•	•		
•	•	•	•	•	🏛 Fidelifacts	800-678-0007	•	•	•	•	•
•	•	•	•		🏛 Hogan Information Services	405-278-6954					
•	•	•			Interstate Abstract Inc	609-795-4000	•	•	•		
•	•	•	•	•	🏛 Kutlus & Company (SOP)	888-726-5335	•	•	•		

						Name	Phone					
•	•	•	•	•	•	Legal Wings Inc (SOP)	800-339-1286	•	•	•	•	•
•	•	•	•	•		Legal Wings Inc - Newark (SOP)	800-339-1286	•	•	•	•	
				•		National Background Investigations Inc	800-798-0079					
	•	•	•	•		North East Court Services Inc (SOP)	800-235-0794	•	•	•		
•	•	•	•	•		Orion Research Group	908-355-9337	•	•	•	•	•
				•		Quest Abstract Inc	201-621-6558	•	•			
			•	•		Research Information Services	800-447-3320	•	•			
•	•	•	•	•		Searcher Girls Search & Abstract	800-292-2757	•	•	•	•	•
				•		Wortmann, Cheri	215-736-0486				•	

CV	CR	PR	GLOUCESTER (EST)	UC	RE	TX	VS	VR
•	•		Accu-Fax Employment Screening Svcs 215-234-0700	•	•	•	•	•
•	•	•	Augatis, Eileen 609-853-9836	•	•	•	•	
•	•		Best Legal Services Inc (SOP) 215-567-7777	•	•	•	•	
•		•	CW Credit Abstract Co 718-423-9430	•	•	•		
•			Charles Jones Inc 800-792-8888	•	•	•		
•	•	•	Dennis Richman's Service (SOP) 215-977-9393	•	•	•	•	•
		•	Derher, Linda 609-853-9836	•	•	•	•	
•	•		Fidelifacts 800-678-0007	•	•	•	•	•
•	•		Flink Findzum (SOP) 800-354-1215	•	•	•	•	
		•	Interstate Abstract Inc 609-795-4000	•	•	•		
•	•	•	Investech Inc (SOP) 800-392-7676	•	•	•	•	•
•	•	•	Kutlus & Company (SOP) 888-726-5335	•	•	•		
•			Lester, Bruce 609-853-9836		•			
•	•		National Background Investigations Inc 800-798-0079					
•	•	•	North East Court Services Inc (SOP) 800-235-0794	•	•	•		
•	•	•	Searcher Girls Search & Abstract 800-292-2757	•	•	•	•	•
•	•		Talone and Associates 800-553-5189					
		•	Wortmann, Cheri 215-736-0486				•	

CV	CR	PR	HUDSON (EST)	UC	RE	TX	VS	VR
•		•	CW Credit Abstract Co 718-423-9430	•	•	•		
•			Charles Jones Inc 800-792-8888	•	•	•		
•	•		Court Data Search 201-770-1170					
•	•	•	Dennis Richman's Service (SOP) 215-977-9393	•	•	•	•	•
•	•	•	Dios, Dolores 800-763-2988	•	•	•	•	
•	•	•	FDR Info Centers 212-742-1066	•	•	•	•	
•	•	•	Fidelifacts 800-678-0007	•	•	•	•	•
•	•		Gamma Investigative Research Inc (SOP) 800-878-9393	•	•	•		
•		•	Interstate Abstract Inc 609-795-4000	•	•	•		
•	•	•	Kutlus & Company (SOP) 888-726-5335	•	•	•		
•	•	•	Legal Wings Inc (SOP) 800-339-1286	•	•	•	•	•
•	•	•	Legal Wings Inc - Newark (SOP) 800-339-1286	•	•	•	•	
•	•	•	Metzler, Arthur 201-653-9676	•	•	•	•	
•	•		National Background Investigations Inc 800-798-0079					
•	•	•	North East Court Services Inc (SOP) 800-235-0794	•	•	•		
•	•	•	Research Information Services 800-447-3320	•	•	•		
•	•	•	Searcher Girls Search & Abstract 800-292-2757	•	•	•	•	•
•	•		Silver Eagle Services (SOP) 212-922-0223		•			
		•	Wortmann, Cheri 215-736-0486				•	

CV	CR	PR	HUNTERDON (EST)	UC	RE	TX	VS	VR
•		•	CW Credit Abstract Co 718-423-9430	•	•	•		
•			Charles Jones Inc 800-792-8888	•	•	•		
•	•	•	Dennis Richman's Service (SOP) 215-977-9393	•	•	•	•	•
•	•	•	Fidelifacts 800-678-0007	•	•	•	•	•
•		•	Interstate Abstract Inc 609-795-4000	•	•	•		
•	•	•	Kutlus & Company (SOP) 888-726-5335	•	•	•		
•	•	•	Legal Wings Inc (SOP) 800-339-1286	•	•	•	•	•
•	•		National Background Investigations Inc 800-798-0079					
•	•	•	North East Court Services Inc (SOP) 800-235-0794	•	•	•		
•	•	•	Searcher Girls Search & Abstract 800-292-2757	•	•	•	•	•

				•	Wortmann, Cheri	215-736-0486				•	

DT	BK	CV	CR	PR	MERCER (CAPITAL) (EST)		UC	RE	TX	VS	VR
•	•	•	•	•	CSC	800-631-2155	•	•	•	•	
•	•	•		•	CW Credit Abstract Co	718-423-9430	•	•	•		
•	•	•			Charles Jones Inc	800-792-8888	•	•	•		
			•	•	Credit Lenders Service Agency Inc	609-751-7400	•	•	•		
•	•	•	•	•	Dennis Richman's Service (SOP)	215-977-9393	•	•	•		•
•	•	•	•	•	Fidelifacts	800-678-0007	•	•	•	•	•
•	•	•			Flink Findzum (SOP)	800-354-1215	•	•	•	•	
•	•	•			Hogan Information Services	405-278-6954					
•	•	•		•	Interstate Abstract Inc	609-795-4000	•	•	•		
•	•	•	•	•	Kaufman Information Resources Inc	908-438-1967	•	•	•	•	
•	•	•	•	•	Kutlus & Company (SOP)	888-726-5335	•	•	•		
•	•	•	•	•	Legal Wings Inc (SOP)	800-339-1286	•	•	•	•	•
				•	Matejik, Stephen	609-394-9232	•	•			
		•	•		National Background Investigations Inc	800-798-0079					
•	•	•	•	•	North East Court Services Inc (SOP)	800-235-0794	•	•	•		
•	•	•	•	•	Orion Research Group	908-355-9337	•	•	•	•	•
•	•	•	•	•	Searcher Girls Search & Abstract	800-292-2757	•	•	•	•	•
•	•	•	•	•	Sikoral & Associates Investigations (SOP)	908-257-2550	•	•	•	•	•
•	•	•	•	•	The Coynes (SOP)	215-945-6227	•	•	•	•	
				•	Wortmann, Cheri	215-736-0486				•	
				•	Ziegler & Associates Inc	609-538-0508	•	•		•	•

CV	CR	PR	MIDDLESEX (EST)		UC	RE	TX	VS	VR
•	•	•	Axt, Erin	908-704-0087	•	•	•	•	
•		•	Belden, Bob	908-828-9765	•	•	•	•	
•		•	CW Credit Abstract Co	718-423-9430	•	•	•		
•			Charles Jones Inc	800-792-8888	•	•	•		
•	•		Commercial Investigation (SOP)	800-677-4190		•	•	•	•
•	•		Court Data Search	201-770-1170					
•	•	•	Dennis Richman's Service (SOP)	215-977-9393	•	•	•	•	•
•	•	•	Fidelifacts	800-678-0007	•	•	•	•	•
•		•	Interstate Abstract Inc	609-795-4000	•	•	•		
•	•	•	Kaufman Information Resources Inc	908-438-1967	•	•	•	•	
•	•	•	Kutlus & Company (SOP)	888-726-5335	•	•	•		
•	•	•	Legal Wings Inc (SOP)	800-339-1286	•	•	•		•
•	•		National Background Investigations Inc	800-798-0079					
•	•	•	North East Court Services Inc (SOP)	800-235-0794	•	•	•		
•	•	•	Orion Research Group	908-355-9337	•	•	•	•	•
•	•	•	Searcher Girls Search & Abstract	800-292-2757	•	•	•	•	•
•	•	•	Sikoral & Associates Investigations (SOP)	908-257-2550	•	•	•	•	•
		•	TABB Inc	800-887-8222					
			Wortmann, Cheri	215-736-0486				•	

CV	CR	PR	MONMOUTH (EST)		UC	RE	TX	VS	VR
•		•	CW Credit Abstract Co	718-423-9430	•	•	•		
•			Charles Jones Inc	800-792-8888	•	•	•		
•	•	•	Commercial DataBase Network	800-677-4190	•	•		•	•
•	•		Commercial Investigation (SOP)	800-677-4190		•	•	•	•
•	•	•	Dennis Richman's Service (SOP)	215-977-9393	•	•	•	•	•
•	•	•	Fidelifacts	800-678-0007	•	•	•	•	•
•	•		Flink Findzum (SOP)	800-354-1215	•	•	•	•	
		•	Forlenza, Janet C	908-303-1823	•	•	•		
•	•		G & O Abstracts Inc	908-577-0459	•	•	•	•	
•	•		Hetrich, Gilbert S	908-286-9233	•	•	•	•	
•		•	Interstate Abstract Inc	609-795-4000	•	•	•		
•	•	•	Kaufman Information Resources Inc	908-438-1967	•	•	•	•	
•	•	•	Kutlus & Company (SOP)	888-726-5335	•	•	•		
•	•	•	Legal Wings Inc (SOP)	800-339-1286	•	•	•		•
•	•		National Background Investigations Inc	800-798-0079					

CV	CR	PR			UC	RE	TX	VS	VR
•	•	•	North East Court Services Inc (SOP)	800-235-0794	•	•	•		
•	•	•	Searcher Girls Search & Abstract	800-292-2757	•	•	•	•	•
•	•	•	Sikoral & Associates Investigations (SOP)	908-257-2550	•	•	•	•	•
		•	Wortmann, Cheri	215-736-0486				•	

CV	CR	PR	MORRIS (EST)		UC	RE	TX	VS	VR
•	•	•	Axelrod, Ronald J	201-538-4606	•	•			
•		•	CW Credit Abstract Co	718-423-9430	•	•	•		
•			Charles Jones Inc	800-792-8888	•	•	•		
•	•		Court Data Search	201-770-1170					
•	•	•	Dennis Richman's Service (SOP)	215-977-9393	•	•	•	•	•
•	•	•	Dios, Dolores	800-763-2988	•	•	•	•	•
•	•	•	Fidelifacts	800-678-0007	•	•	•	•	•
•			Interstate Abstract Inc	609-795-4000	•	•	•		
•	•	•	Kutlus & Company (SOP)	888-726-5335	•	•	•		
•	•	•	Legal Wings Inc (SOP)	800-339-1286	•	•	•	•	•
•	•	•	Legal Wings Inc - Newark (SOP)	800-339-1286	•	•	•		
•		•	Liberty Record Search of NJ Inc	201-887-3854	•	•	•		
		•	Morris Hills Abstract Co	201-267-0450	•	•			
•	•		National Background Investigations Inc	800-798-0079					
•	•	•	North East Court Services Inc (SOP)	800-235-0794	•	•	•		
•	•	•	Orion Research Group	908-355-9337	•	•	•	•	•
•	•	•	Searcher Girls Search & Abstract	800-292-2757	•	•	•	•	•
•	•	•	Sikoral & Associates Investigations (SOP)	908-257-2550	•	•	•	•	•
	•	•	TABB Inc	800-887-8222					
•	•	•	Vogel, Fred & Margaret	201-539-5093	•	•	•	•	
		•	Wortmann, Cheri	215-736-0486				•	

CV	CR	PR	OCEAN (EST)		UC	RE	TX	VS	VR
•		•	CW Credit Abstract Co	718-423-9430	•	•	•		
•			Charles Jones Inc	800-792-8888	•	•	•		
•	•	•	Commercial Investigation (SOP)	800-677-4190	•	•	•	•	•
•	•	•	Dennis Richman's Service (SOP)	215-977-9393	•	•	•	•	•
•	•	•	Fidelifacts	800-678-0007	•	•	•	•	•
•	•	•	Flink Findzum (SOP)	800-354-1215	•	•	•		
•	•	•	Hetrich, Gilbert S	908-286-9233	•	•	•		
•			Interstate Abstract Inc	609-795-4000	•	•	•		
•	•	•	Investech Inc (SOP)	800-392-7676	•	•	•		•
•	•	•	Kutlus & Company (SOP)	888-726-5335	•	•	•		
•	•	•	Laratta, Margaret	908-349-1301	•	•	•		
•	•	•	Legal Wings Inc (SOP)	800-339-1286	•	•	•	•	•
•	•		National Background Investigations Inc	800-798-0079					
•	•	•	North East Court Services Inc (SOP)	800-235-0794	•	•	•		
•	•	•	Orion Research Group	908-355-9337	•	•	•	•	•
•	•	•	Searcher Girls Search & Abstract	800-292-2757	•	•	•	•	•
		•	Wortmann, Cheri	215-736-0486				•	
•	•	•	Yerks, Edna M	908-349-9747	•	•	•	•	

CV	CR	PR	PASSAIC (EST)		UC	RE	TX	VS	VR
•		•	CW Credit Abstract Co	718-423-9430	•	•	•		
•	•	•	Callahan Lawyers Service (SOP)	201-489-2245		•		•	•
•			Charles Jones Inc	800-792-8888	•	•	•		
•	•		Court Data Search	201-770-1170					
•	•	•	Dennis Richman's Service (SOP)	215-977-9393	•	•	•	•	•
•	•	•	Dios, Dolores	800-763-2988	•	•	•	•	•
•	•	•	Fidelifacts	800-678-0007	•	•	•	•	•
•		•	Gamma Investigative Research Inc (SOP)	800-878-9393	•	•	•		
•		•	Interstate Abstract Inc	609-795-4000	•	•	•		
•	•	•	Kutlus & Company (SOP)	888-726-5335	•	•	•		
•	•	•	Legal Wings Inc (SOP)	800-339-1286	•	•	•	•	•
•	•	•	Legal Wings Inc - Newark (SOP)	800-339-1286	•	•	•		
•		•	Liberty Record Search of NJ Inc	201-887-3854	•	•	•		

CV	CR	PR			UC	RE	TX	VS	VR
•	•		National Background Investigations Inc	800-798-0079					
•	•	•	North East Court Services Inc (SOP)	800-235-0794	•	•	•		
•	•	•	Searcher Girls Search & Abstract	800-292-2757	•	•	•	•	•
•	•	•	Wayne Professional Services (SOP)	201-696-7229		•	•	•	•
		•	Wortmann, Cheri	215-736-0486				•	

CV	CR	PR	SALEM (EST)		UC	RE	TX	VS	VR
•		•	CW Credit Abstract Co	718-423-9430	•	•	•		
•			Charles Jones Inc	800-792-8888	•	•	•		
•	•	•	Dennis Richman's Service (SOP)	215-977-9393	•	•	•	•	•
•	•	•	Fidelifacts	800-678-0007	•	•	•	•	•
•	•	•	Interstate Abstract Inc	609-795-4000	•	•	•	•	
•	•	•	Investech Inc (SOP)	800-392-7676	•	•	•	•	•
•	•	•	Kutlus & Company (SOP)	888-726-5335	•	•	•		
•			National Background Investigations Inc	800-798-0079					
•	•	•	North East Court Services Inc (SOP)	800-235-0794	•				
•	•	•	Searcher Girls Search & Abstract	800-292-2757	•	•	•	•	•
		•	Wortmann, Cheri	215-736-0486				•	

CV	CR	PR	SOMERSET (EST)		UC	RE	TX	VS	VR
•	•	•	Axt, Erin	908-704-0087	•	•	•	•	
	•	•	CMT Abstract	908-722-6565	•	•	•		
•		•	CW Credit Abstract Co	718-423-9430	•	•	•		
•			Charles Jones Inc	800-792-8888	•	•	•		
•	•	•	Dennis Richman's Service (SOP)	215-977-9393	•	•	•	•	•
•	•	•	Fidelifacts	800-678-0007	•	•	•	•	•
•			Interstate Abstract Inc	609-795-4000	•	•	•	•	
			KJK Abstract Co	908-725-6336	•	•	•		
•			Kaufman Information Resources Inc	908-438-1967	•	•	•	•	
•	•	•	Kutlus & Company (SOP)	888-726-5335	•	•	•		
•	•	•	Legal Wings Inc (SOP)	800-339-1286	•	•	•	•	•
•		•	Liberty Record Search of NJ Inc	201-887-3854	•	•	•		
•			National Background Investigations Inc	800-798-0079					
•	•	•	North East Court Services Inc (SOP)	800-235-0794	•				
•	•	•	Orion Research Group	908-355-9337	•	•	•	•	
•	•	•	Ronald J Axelrod and Associates	908-658-4606	•	•	•		
•	•	•	Searcher Girls Search & Abstract	800-292-2757	•	•	•	•	•
•	•	•	Sikoral & Associates Investigations (SOP)	908-257-2550	•	•	•	•	•
	•		TABB Inc	800-887-8222					
		•	Wortmann, Cheri	215-736-0486				•	

CV	CR	PR	SUSSEX (EST)		UC	RE	TX	VS	VR
•		•	CW Credit Abstract Co	718-423-9430	•	•	•		
•			Charles Jones Inc	800-792-8888	•	•	•		
•	•		Court Data Search	201-770-1170					
•	•	•	Dennis Richman's Service (SOP)	215-977-9393	•	•	•	•	•
•	•	•	Fidelifacts	800-678-0007	•	•	•	•	•
•	•	•	Gamma Investigative Research Inc (SOP)	800-878-9393	•	•	•		
•		•	Interstate Abstract Inc	609-795-4000	•	•	•		
•	•	•	Kutlus & Company (SOP)	888-726-5335	•	•	•		
•		•	Liberty Record Search of NJ Inc	201-887-3854	•				
•	•	•	Lora J Musilli & Associates	201-383-7763	•	•	•		
•			National Background Investigations Inc	800-798-0079					
•	•	•	North East Court Services Inc (SOP)	800-235-0794	•	•	•		
•	•	•	Searcher Girls Search & Abstract	800-292-2757	•	•	•	•	•
		•	Wortmann, Cheri	215-736-0486				•	

CV	CR	PR	UNION (EST)		UC	RE	TX	VS	VR
•		•	CW Credit Abstract Co	718-423-9430	•	•	•		
•			Charles Jones Inc	800-792-8888	•	•	•		
•	•		Court Data Search	201-770-1170					
•	•	•	Dennis Richman's Service (SOP)	215-977-9393	•	•	•	•	•

CV	CR	PR			UC	RE	TX	VS	VR
●	●	●	🏛 Dios, Dolores 800-763-2988		●	●	●		
●		●	Faithful Abstract 908-351-9398		●	●	●		
●	●	●	🏛 Fidelifacts 800-678-0007		●	●	●	●	●
●	●	●	Gamma Investigative Research Inc (SOP) 800-878-9393		●	●	●		
●	●	●	Interstate Abstract Inc 609-795-4000		●	●	●	●	
●	●	●	Kaufman Information Resources Inc 908-438-1967		●	●	●	●	
●	●	●	🏛 Kutlus & Company (SOP) 888-726-5335		●	●	●		
●	●	●	🏛 Legal Wings Inc (SOP) 800-339-1286		●	●	●	●	●
●	●	●	Legal Wings Inc - Newark (SOP) 800-339-1286		●	●	●	●	
●	●		🏛 National Background Investigations Inc 800-798-0079						
●	●	●	🏛 North East Court Services Inc (SOP) 800-235-0794		●	●	●		
●	●	●	Orion Research Group 908-355-9337		●	●	●	●	●
●			Quest Abstract Inc 201-621-6558		●	●	●		
●	●	●	🏛 Searcher Girls Search & Abstract 800-292-2757		●	●	●	●	●
●	●	●	Sikoral & Associates Investigations (SOP) 908-257-2550		●	●	●	●	●
●	●	●	Superior Subpoena Service 908-862-5660		●	●	●	●	
		●	Wortmann, Cheri 215-736-0486					●	

CV	CR	PR	WARREN (EST)	UC	RE	TX	VS	VR
●		●	CW Credit Abstract Co 718-423-9430	●	●	●		
●			Charles Jones Inc 800-792-8888	●	●	●		
●	●	●	Dennis Richman's Service (SOP) 215-977-9393	●	●	●	●	●
●	●	●	🏛 Fidelifacts 800-678-0007	●	●	●	●	●
●		●	Gamma Investigative Research Inc (SOP) 800-878-9393	●	●	●		
●		●	Interstate Abstract Inc 609-795-4000	●	●	●	●	
●			JAK Abstract 908-475-5007		●			
●		●	KCD Title 908-859-6524	●	●	●	●	
●	●	●	🏛 Kutlus & Company (SOP) 888-726-5335	●	●	●		
●	●		🏛 National Background Investigations Inc 800-798-0079					
●	●	●	🏛 North East Court Services Inc (SOP) 800-235-0794	●	●	●		
●	●	●	🏛 Searcher Girls Search & Abstract 800-292-2757	●	●	●	●	●
		●	Wortmann, Cheri 215-736-0486				●	

194

NEW MEXICO

DT	BK	CV	CR	PR	BERNALILLO (MST)	UC	RE	TX	VS	VR
•	•	•	•		Alpha Research LLC (SOP) 205-755-7008			•		
		•	•	•	Applied Professional Research (APRO) 888-686-0701	•	•	•	•	•
•	•	•			Capitol Document Services Inc 800-255-4381	•				
•	•	•			Casa De Search 800-757-0220	•		•		
•	•	•	•	•	Cobra Company 800-894-5825	•	•	•	•	•
•	•	•	•	•	Data Quest Inc 505-891-9326	•	•	•		
•	•				Hogan Information Services 405-278-6954					
		•	•	•	Lopez, Alfred (SOP) 505-239-6096	•	•	•		
		•	•	•	N.M. Factfinders Inc (SOP) 505-869-4829	•	•	•	•	•
•	•	•	•	•	Professional Services 505-823-2511	•	•	•	•	•
•	•	•	•	•	UCC Search Inc 800-453-9404	•	•	•		

CV	CR	PR	CATRON (MST)	UC	RE	TX	VS	VR
•			Casa De Search 800-757-0220	•		•		
•	•	•	County Abstract & Title Co 505-835-0573	•	•	•	•	

CV	CR	PR	CHAVES (MST)	UC	RE	TX	VS	VR
•			Casa De Search 800-757-0220	•		•		
•		•	Chaves County Abstract & Title Co 505-622-5340	•	•	•		

CV	CR	PR	CIBOLA (MST)	UC	RE	TX	VS	VR
•			Casa De Search 800-757-0220	•		•		
•	•	•	Lopez, Alfred (SOP) 505-239-6096	•	•	•	•	
•	•	•	N.M. Factfinders Inc (SOP) 505-869-4829	•	•	•	•	•

CV	CR	PR	COLFAX (MST)	UC	RE	TX	VS	VR
•			Casa De Search 800-757-0220	•		•		
•			Credit Bureau of Raton 505-445-2751	•		•		

CV	CR	PR	CURRY (MST)	UC	RE	TX	VS	VR
•			Casa De Search 800-757-0220	•		•		
•	•	•	Clovis Title and Abstract Company 505-762-4403	•	•	•	•	
•		•	Plains Title and Abstract Inc 505-762-4589	•	•	•		

CV	CR	PR	DE BACA (MST)	UC	RE	TX	VS	VR
•			Casa De Search 800-757-0220	•		•		

CV	CR	PR	DONA ANA (MST)	UC	RE	TX	VS	VR
•	•	•	AGO Investigations and Polygraph Ltd (SOP) 505-526-4303	•	•	•	•	•
•			Casa De Search 800-757-0220	•		•		
•	•	•	Legal Net Process Service (SOP) 915-532-7871	•	•	•	•	

CV	CR	PR	EDDY (MST)	UC	RE	TX	VS	VR
•		•	Caprock Title Co 915-687-3232	•	•	•		
•		•	Currier Abstract Company 505-746-9823	•	•	•		
•		•	Eddy County Abstract Co 505-887-2828	•	•	•	•	
•	•	•	Guaranty Title Co 505-887-3593	•	•	•		

CV	CR	PR	GRANT (MST)	UC	RE	TX	VS	VR
•	•	•	AGO Investigations and Polygraph Ltd (SOP) 505-526-4303	•	•	•	•	•
•			Casa De Search 800-757-0220	•		•		

CV	CR	PR	GUADALUPE (MST)	UC	RE	TX	VS	VR
•			Casa De Search 800-757-0220	•		•		
•	•	•	Territorial Title 505-425-3563	•	•	•	•	

CV	CR	PR	HARDING (MST)	UC	RE	TX	VS	VR
•			Casa De Search 800-757-0220	•		•		
•	•	•	Pritchett, Debbie 505-673-2301	•	•	•		•

CV	CR	PR	HIDALGO (MST)		UC	RE	TX	VS	VR
•			🏛 Casa De Search 800-757-0220		•		•		
•		•	Hidalgo County Abstract 505-542-9181		•	•	•	•	

CV	CR	PR	LEA (MST)		UC	RE	TX	VS	VR
•		•	Caprock Title Co 915-687-3232		•	•	•		
•			🏛 Casa De Search 800-757-0220		•		•		
•		•	Elliott & Waldron Title and Abstract 505-396-5846		•	•	•		

CV	CR	PR	LINCOLN (MST)		UC	RE	TX	VS	VR
•			🏛 Casa De Search 800-757-0220		•		•		
•		•	Lincoln County Abstract & Title Co 800-635-4692		•	•	•		

CV	CR	PR	LOS ALAMOS (MST)		UC	RE	TX	VS	VR
•			🏛 Casa De Search 800-757-0220		•		•		
•	•		UCC Search Inc 800-453-9404		•	•	•	•	

CV	CR	PR	LUNA (MST)		UC	RE	TX	VS	VR
•	•	•	AGO Investigations and Polygraph Ltd (SOP) 505-526-4303		•	•	•	•	•
•			🏛 Casa De Search 800-757-0220		•		•		
•	•	•	Mimbres Valley Abstract & Title Co 505-546-8896		•	•	•	•	

CV	CR	PR	McKINLEY (MST)		UC	RE	TX	VS	VR
•			🏛 Casa De Search 800-757-0220		•		•		
•	•	•	Lopez, Alfred (SOP) 505-239-6096		•	•	•		

CV	CR	PR	MORA (MST)		UC	RE	TX	VS	VR
•			🏛 Casa De Search 800-757-0220		•		•		
•	•	•	Territorial Title 505-425-3563		•	•	•		
•	•		UCC Search Inc 800-453-9404		•	•	•	•	

CV	CR	PR	OTERO (MST)		UC	RE	TX	VS	VR
•	•	•	Alamogordo Abstract & Title 505-437-2741		•	•	•	•	
•			🏛 Casa De Search 800-757-0220		•		•		

CV	CR	PR	QUAY (MST)		UC	RE	TX	VS	VR
•			🏛 Casa De Search 800-757-0220		•		•		

CV	CR	PR	RIO ARRIBA (MST)		UC	RE	TX	VS	VR
•			🏛 Casa De Search 800-757-0220		•		•		
•		•	Espanola Abstract Co 505-753-2248		•	•	•	•	
•	•		UCC Search Inc 800-453-9404		•	•	•	•	

CV	CR	PR	ROOSEVELT (MST)		UC	RE	TX	VS	VR
•			🏛 Casa De Search 800-757-0220		•		•		
•		•	Graham Abstract Co Inc 505-356-8505		•	•	•		

CV	CR	PR	SAN JUAN (MST)		UC	RE	TX	VS	VR
•			🏛 Casa De Search 800-757-0220		•		•		
•	•	•	San Juan County Abstract & Title 505-325-2808		•	•	•		

CV	CR	PR	SAN MIGUEL (MST)		UC	RE	TX	VS	VR
•			🏛 Casa De Search 800-757-0220		•		•		
•	•	•	Territorial Title 505-425-3563		•	•	•	•	
•	•		UCC Search Inc 800-453-9404		•	•	•	•	

CV	CR	PR	SANDOVAL (MST)		UC	RE	TX	VS	VR
•	•		🏛 Alpha Research LLC (SOP) 205-755-7008				•		
•			🏛 Capitol Document Services Inc 800-255-4381		•		•		
•			🏛 Casa De Search 800-757-0220		•		•		
•	•	•	🏛 Cobra Company 800-894-5825		•	•	•	•	•
•	•	•	Data Quest Inc 505-891-9326		•	•	•		
•	•	•	🏛 N.M. Factfinders Inc (SOP) 505-869-4829		•	•	•	•	•
•	•	•	🏛 Professional Services 505-823-2511		•	•	•	•	•

CV	CR	PR			UC	RE	TX	VS	VR
•	•		UCC Search Inc 800-453-9404		•	•	•	•	

CV	CR	PR	SANTA FE (CAPITAL) (MST)		UC	RE	TX	VS	VR
•			🏛 Capitol Document Services Inc 800-255-4381		•		•		
•			🏛 Casa De Search 800-757-0220		•		•		
•	•	•	🏛 N.M. Factfinders Inc (SOP) 505-869-4829		•	•	•	•	•
			New Mexico Records Search 505-986-0565		•				
•	•	•	🏛 Professional Services 505-823-2511		•	•	•	•	•
•	•		UCC Search Inc 800-453-9404		•	•	•	•	

CV	CR	PR	SIERRA (MST)		UC	RE	TX	VS	VR
•	•	•	AGO Investigations and Polygraph Ltd (SOP) 505-526-4303		•	•	•	•	•
•			🏛 Casa De Search 800-757-0220		•		•		

CV	CR	PR	SOCORRO (MST)		UC	RE	TX	VS	VR
•			🏛 Casa De Search 800-757-0220		•		•		
•	•	•	County Abstract & Title Co 505-835-0573		•	•	•	•	
•	•	•	🏛 N.M. Factfinders Inc (SOP) 505-869-4829		•	•	•		•

CV	CR	PR	TAOS (MST)		UC	RE	TX	VS	VR
•	•		UCC Search Inc 800-453-9404		•	•	•	•	

CV	CR	PR	TORRANCE (MST)		UC	RE	TX	VS	VR
•			🏛 Casa De Search 800-757-0220		•		•		
•	•	•	🏛 N.M. Factfinders Inc (SOP) 505-869-4829		•	•	•	•	•
•	•		UCC Search Inc 800-453-9404		•	•	•	•	

CV	CR	PR	UNION (MST)		UC	RE	TX	VS	VR
•			🏛 Casa De Search 800-757-0220		•		•		
•	•	•	Clayton Title Service Inc 505-374-9789		•	•	•	•	

CV	CR	PR	VALENCIA (MST)		UC	RE	TX	VS	VR
•	•		🏛 Alpha Research LLC (SOP) 205-755-7008				•		
•			🏛 Capitol Document Services Inc 800-255-4381		•		•		
•			🏛 Casa De Search 800-757-0220		•		•		
•	•	•	🏛 Cobra Company 800-894-5825		•	•	•	•	•
•	•	•	🏛 N.M. Factfinders Inc (SOP) 505-869-4829		•	•	•	•	•
•	•	•	🏛 Professional Services 505-823-2511		•	•	•	•	•
•	•		UCC Search Inc 800-453-9404		•	•	•	•	

NEW YORK

DT	BK	CV	CR	PR	ALBANY (CAPITAL) (EST)	UC	RE	TX	VS	VR
•	•	•	•		Access Information Services Inc (SOP) 800-388-1598	•	•	•		
•	•	•	•	•	Attorney's Process and Research Service (SOP) 518-465-8951	•	•	•	•	
•	•				Bankruptcy Reporter of Rochester 716-271-6000					
•	•	•	•	•	CMS (Consumer Marketing Services) 315-476-8414	•	•	•		
•	•	•	•	•	CSC (SOP) 800-833-9848	•	•	•	•	
•	•	•		•	CW Credit Abstract Co 718-423-9430	•	•	•		
•	•	•			Capitol Services Inc 800-662-0171	•		•	•	
•					Certified Document Retriever Bureau (SOP) 518-438-7956					
•	•	•	•		Corporate Service Bureau 518-463-8550	•		•	•	
•	•	•	•	•	DLS (Demovsky Lawyer Service) (SOP) 518-449-8411	•	•	•	•	
•	•	•	•	•	Document Resources 800-666-0061	•	•	•	•	•
				•	Four Corners Abstract 800-724-3668	•	•	•		
•	•	•			Intercounty Clearance Corporation (SOP) 800-229-4422	•	•	•		
•	•	•	•		Merola Services 315-652-5242		•			•
•	•				Monroe Title Insurance Corporation 800-966-6763	•	•	•		
•	•	•			National Corporate Research Ltd 800-828-0938	•	•	•		
•	•	•	•	•	Nationwide Information Services Inc 800-873-3482	•	•	•	•	•
•	•	•	•	•	New York Institute of Legal Research 914-245-8400	•	•	•	•	•
•	•	•	•	•	Relyea Services Inc (SOP) 800-854-4111	•	•	•		
•	•	•	•	•	Research Information Services 800-447-3320	•	•	•		
•	•				Ryco Information Services Inc 315-461-8308	•	•	•		
•	•	•	•	•	Smith Hicks, Susan 518-537-4103	•	•	•		
•	•	•	•	•	Tracers International (SOP) 800-872-2377	•	•	•	•	•
•	•	•	•	•	Zap! Courier Service 518-449-3361	•				

CV	CR	PR	ALLEGANY (EST)	UC	RE	TX	VS	VR
			Bankruptcy Reporter of Rochester 716-271-6000					
•	•	•	CMS (Consumer Marketing Services) 315-476-8414	•	•	•		
•		•	CW Credit Abstract Co 718-423-9430	•	•	•		
			Monroe Title Insurance Corporation 800-966-6763	•	•	•		
•	•	•	New York Institute of Legal Research 914-245-8400	•	•	•	•	•

CV	CR	PR	BRONX (EST)	UC	RE	TX	VS	VR
•	•	•	A.S.S.I.S.T. International 800-382-7747	•	•	•	•	•
•	•	•	APB Information Research Center Inc (SOP) 718-494-0750	•	•	•	•	
•	•	•	Alstate Process Service Inc (SOP) 516-667-1800	•	•	•	•	
•	•		Austin & Associates Inc 914-968-3700	•	•	•		•
•	•		Bridge Service Corp 800-225-2736	•	•	•	•	
•		•	CW Credit Abstract Co 718-423-9430	•	•	•		
•	•		Court Explorers LLC 212-945-6324	•	•	•		
•	•	•	DLS (Demovsky Lawyer Service) (SOP) 800-443-1058	•	•	•	•	•
•	•	•	FDR Info Centers 212-742-1066	•	•	•	•	
•	•	•	Fidelifacts 800-678-0007	•	•	•	•	
•			Intercounty Clearance Corporation (SOP) 800-229-4422	•	•	•		
•		•	Investigative Resources (SOP) 718-317-0043	•	•	•		•
•	•		LIDA Credit Agency Inc (SOP) 516-678-4600	•	•	•	•	•
•	•	•	LegalEase Inc (SOP) 800-393-1277	•	•	•	•	
•	•		Nationwide Court Services Inc (SOP) 516-981-4400	•	•	•	•	•
•	•	•	New York Institute of Legal Research 914-245-8400	•	•	•	•	•
•	•		North East Court Services Inc (SOP) 800-235-0794	•	•	•		
•	•		Pallorium Inc (SOP) 212-969-0286	•	•	•	•	•
•	•		Paper Chase Research 212-587-7071	•	•	•	•	•
•	•	•	Research Information Services 800-447-3320	•	•	•	•	
•	•	•	Search NY 718-854-1492	•	•	•	•	
•	•		Silver Eagle Services (SOP) 212-922-0223		•			
•	•	•	Washington Document Services 800-422-2776	•	•	•	•	
			Wilsearch Information Network 800-391-5502	•	•	•		

DT	CV	CR	PR	BROOME (EST)	UC	RE	TX	VS	VR
•				Bankruptcy Reporter of Rochester 716-271-6000					
•	•	•	•	🏛 CMS (Consumer Marketing Services) 315-476-8414	•	•	•		
•	•		•	CW Credit Abstract Co 718-423-9430	•	•	•		
•			•	Four Corners Abstract 800-724-3668	•	•	•		
•				Monroe Title Insurance Corporation 800-966-6763	•	•	•		
•	•	•	•	New York Institute of Legal Research 914-245-8400	•	•	•	•	•
				Ryco Information Services Inc 315-461-8308	•	•	•		

	CV	CR	PR	CATTARAUGUS (EST)	UC	RE	TX	VS	VR
				Bankruptcy Reporter of Rochester 716-271-6000					
	•	•	•	🏛 CMS (Consumer Marketing Services) 315-476-8414	•	•	•		
	•		•	CW Credit Abstract Co 718-423-9430	•	•	•		
	•		•	🏛 Cattaraugus Abstract Corp 800-559-1242	•	•	•		
				Monroe Title Insurance Corporation 800-966-6763	•	•	•		
	•	•	•	New York Institute of Legal Research 914-245-8400	•	•	•	•	•
				Ryco Information Services Inc 315-461-8308	•	•	•		

	CV	CR	PR	CAYUGA (EST)	UC	RE	TX	VS	VR
				Bankruptcy Reporter of Rochester 716-271-6000					
	•	•	•	🏛 CMS (Consumer Marketing Services) 315-476-8414	•	•	•		
	•		•	CW Credit Abstract Co 718-423-9430	•	•	•		
	•		•	Central New York Abstract Corporation 315-724-1614	•	•	•		
			•	Four Corners Abstract 800-724-3668	•	•	•		
				Monroe Title Insurance Corporation 800-966-6763	•	•	•		
	•	•	•	New York Institute of Legal Research 914-245-8400	•	•	•	•	•
	•	•	•	Northeast Investigations Inc (SOP)................ 800-484-5125	•	•	•	•	•

	CV	CR	PR	CHAUTAUQUA (EST)	UC	RE	TX	VS	VR
				Bankruptcy Reporter of Rochester 716-271-6000					
	•	•	•	🏛 CMS (Consumer Marketing Services) 315-476-8414	•	•	•		
	•		•	CW Credit Abstract Co 718-423-9430	•	•	•		
				Monroe Title Insurance Corporation 800-966-6763	•	•	•		
	•	•	•	New York Institute of Legal Research 914-245-8400	•	•	•	•	•
				Ryco Information Services Inc 315-461-8308	•	•	•		

	CV	CR	PR	CHEMUNG (EST)	UC	RE	TX	VS	VR
				Bankruptcy Reporter of Rochester 716-271-6000					
	•		•	🏛 CMS (Consumer Marketing Services) 315-476-8414	•	•	•		
	•		•	CW Credit Abstract Co 718-423-9430	•	•	•		
	•	•	•	🏛 Hurley, William 607-734-1743	•	•	•	•	•
				Monroe Title Insurance Corporation 800-966-6763	•	•	•		
	•	•	•	New York Institute of Legal Research 914-245-8400	•	•	•	•	

	CV	CR	PR	CHENANGO (EST)	UC	RE	TX	VS	VR
				Bankruptcy Reporter of Rochester 716-271-6000					
	•	•	•	🏛 CMS (Consumer Marketing Services) 315-476-8414	•	•	•		
	•		•	CW Credit Abstract Co 718-423-9430	•	•	•		
			•	Four Corners Abstract 800-724-3668	•	•	•		
				Monroe Title Insurance Corporation 800-966-6763	•	•	•		
	•	•	•	New York Institute of Legal Research 914-245-8400	•	•	•	•	•

	CV	CR	PR	CLINTON (EST)	UC	RE	TX	VS	VR
				Bankruptcy Reporter of Rochester 716-271-6000					
	•	•	•	🏛 CMS (Consumer Marketing Services) 315-476-8414	•	•	•		
	•		•	CW Credit Abstract Co 718-423-9430	•	•	•		
				Monroe Title Insurance Corporation 800-966-6763	•	•	•		
	•	•	•	New York Institute of Legal Research 914-245-8400	•	•	•	•	•

	CV	CR	PR	COLUMBIA (EST)	UC	RE	TX	VS	VR
	•	•	•	Attorney's Process and Research Service (SOP)................. 518-465-8951	•	•	•	•	
				Bankruptcy Reporter of Rochester 716-271-6000					

CV	CR	PR		UC	RE	TX	VS	VR
•	•	•	Bureau of Special Services (SOP) 800-772-7130	•	•	•	•	•
•	•	•	CMS (Consumer Marketing Services) 315-476-8414	•	•	•		
•		•	CW Credit Abstract Co 718-423-9430	•	•	•		
		•	Four Corners Abstract 800-724-3668	•	•	•		
			Monroe Title Insurance Corporation 800-966-6763	•	•			
•	•	•	New York Institute of Legal Research 914-245-8400	•	•	•	•	•
•	•	•	Onistagrawa Abstracting Corp 518-827-8088	•	•	•	•	
•	•	•	Smith Hicks, Susan 518-537-4103	•	•	•		

CV	CR	PR	CORTLAND (EST)	UC	RE	TX	VS	VR
			Bankruptcy Reporter of Rochester 716-271-6000					
•	•	•	CMS (Consumer Marketing Services) 315-476-8414	•	•	•		
•		•	CW Credit Abstract Co 718-423-9430	•	•	•		
			Monroe Title Insurance Corporation 800-966-6763	•	•	•		
•	•	•	New York Institute of Legal Research 914-245-8400	•	•	•	•	•

CV	CR	PR	DELAWARE (EST)	UC	RE	TX	VS	VR
			Bankruptcy Reporter of Rochester 716-271-6000					
•	•	•	CMS (Consumer Marketing Services) 315-476-8414	•	•	•		
•		•	CW Credit Abstract Co 718-423-9430	•	•	•		
		•	Four Corners Abstract 800-724-3668	•	•	•		
•		•	Harry W Hawley Inc 607-746-3860	•	•	•		
			Monroe Title Insurance Corporation 800-966-6763	•	•	•		
•	•	•	New York Institute of Legal Research 914-245-8400	•	•	•	•	•
•	•	•	Onistagrawa Abstracting Corp 518-827-8088	•	•	•	•	

BK	CV	CR	PR	DUTCHESS (EST)	UC	RE	TX	VS	VR
	•	•	•	American Legal Support Service Inc 914-473-5676	•	•	•	•	
•	•		•	Bureau of Special Services (SOP) 800-772-7130	•	•	•	•	•
•	•		•	CW Credit Abstract Co 718-423-9430	•	•	•		
•	•	•	•	Fidelifacts 800-678-0007	•	•	•	•	•
•	•		•	Fox Advertising 914-948-5200	•	•	•		
•	•	•	•	La Prade Services Inc (SOP) 914-473-0468	•	•	•	•	•
•	•	•	•	Metropolitan Delivery 914-463-0519	•	•	•	•	•
•	•	•	•	New York Institute of Legal Research 914-245-8400	•	•	•	•	•
•	•	•	•	Orange Abstractor Services Co (SOP) 914-294-3331	•	•	•		
•	•	•	•	Orange Paper Placers (SOP) 914-294-7810	•	•	•	•	
•	•	•	•	Paper Chase Research 212-587-7071	•	•	•		
•	•	•	•	Smith Hicks, Susan 518-537-4103	•	•	•		
•	•	•	•	Walsh Process & Legal Services (SOP) 888-438-9757	•	•	•	•	•
	•	•	•	Washington Document Services 800-422-2776					
•	•	•	•	Westchester Court Service (SOP) 914-948-5200	•	•	•	•	

DT	BK	CV	CR	PR	ERIE (EST)	UC	RE	TX	VS	VR
•	•	•	•	•	Action Process Service (SOP) 716-692-5032	•	•	•	•	
•	•				Bankruptcy Reporter of Rochester 716-271-6000					
•	•	•	•	•	CMS (Consumer Marketing Services) 315-476-8414	•	•	•		
•	•	•		•	CW Credit Abstract Co 718-423-9430	•	•	•		
•	•	•	•	•	Court House Research 716-873-8315	•	•	•		•
•	•	•	•	•	Ferrari 716-689-6577	•	•	•		
				•	Four Corners Abstract 800-724-3668	•	•	•		
	•	•	•	•	Juncewicz, Nina F (SOP) 716-873-8315	•	•	•		•
•	•				Monroe Title Insurance Corporation 800-966-6763	•	•	•		
•	•	•	•	•	New York Institute of Legal Research 914-245-8400	•	•	•	•	•
•	•	•	•	•	Paralegal Services of Buffalo 716-856-3818	•	•	•	•	•
					Ryco Information Services Inc 315-461-8308	•	•	•		

CV	CR	PR	ESSEX (EST)	UC	RE	TX	VS	VR
			Bankruptcy Reporter of Rochester 716-271-6000					
•	•	•	CMS (Consumer Marketing Services) 315-476-8414	•	•	•		
•		•	CW Credit Abstract Co 718-423-9430	•	•	•		
			Monroe Title Insurance Corporation 800-966-6763	•	•	•		

CV	CR	PR			UC	RE	TX	VS	VR
●	●	●	New York Institute of Legal Research	914-245-8400	●	●	●	●	●

CV	CR	PR	FRANKLIN (EST)		UC	RE	TX	VS	VR
			Bankruptcy Reporter of Rochester	716-271-6000					
●	●	●	🏛 CMS (Consumer Marketing Services)	315-476-8414	●	●	●		
●		●	CW Credit Abstract Co	718-423-9430	●	●	●		
●		●	Etna Abstract Corp	518-483-7204	●	●	●		
			Monroe Title Insurance Corporation	800-966-6763	●	●	●		
●	●	●	New York Institute of Legal Research	914-245-8400	●	●	●	●	●

CV	CR	PR	FULTON (EST)		UC	RE	TX	VS	VR
			Bankruptcy Reporter of Rochester	716-271-6000					
●	●	●	🏛 CMS (Consumer Marketing Services)	315-476-8414	●	●	●		
●		●	CW Credit Abstract Co	718-423-9430	●	●	●		
●		●	County Seat Abstract	518-762-3011	●	●	●		
		●	Four Corners Abstract	800-724-3668	●	●	●		
			Monroe Title Insurance Corporation	800-966-6763	●	●	●		
●	●	●	New York Institute of Legal Research	914-245-8400	●	●	●	●	●
●	●	●	Onistagrawa Abstracting Corp	518-827-8088	●	●	●	●	
		●	Sacandaga Abstract Corp	518-773-2828	●	●	●		

CV	CR	PR	GENESEE (EST)		UC	RE	TX	VS	VR
			Bankruptcy Reporter of Rochester	716-271-6000					
●	●	●	🏛 CMS (Consumer Marketing Services)	315-476-8414	●	●	●		
●		●	CW Credit Abstract Co	718-423-9430	●	●	●		
		●	Four Corners Abstract	800-724-3668	●	●	●		
			Monroe Title Insurance Corporation	800-966-6763	●	●	●		
●	●	●	New York Institute of Legal Research	914-245-8400	●	●	●	●	●

CV	CR	PR	GREENE (EST)		UC	RE	TX	VS	VR
●	●	●	Attorney's Process and Research Service (SOP)	518-465-8951	●	●	●	●	
			Bankruptcy Reporter of Rochester	716-271-6000					
●	●	●	Bureau of Special Services (SOP)	800-772-7130	●	●	●	●	●
●	●	●	🏛 CMS (Consumer Marketing Services)	315-476-8414	●	●	●		
●		●	CW Credit Abstract Co	718-423-9430	●	●	●		
		●	Four Corners Abstract	800-724-3668	●	●	●		
			Monroe Title Insurance Corporation	800-966-6763	●	●	●		
●	●	●	New York Institute of Legal Research	914-245-8400	●	●	●	●	●
●	●	●	Onistagrawa Abstracting Corp	518-827-8088	●	●	●	●	
●	●	●	🏛 Smith Hicks, Susan	518-537-4103	●	●			
●	●	●	Zap! Courier Service	518-449-3361	●		●	●	●

CV	CR	PR	HAMILTON (EST)		UC	RE	TX	VS	VR
			Bankruptcy Reporter of Rochester	716-271-6000					
●	●	●	🏛 CMS (Consumer Marketing Services)	315-476-8414	●	●	●		
●		●	CW Credit Abstract Co	718-423-9430	●	●	●		
●		●	County Seat Abstract	518-762-3011	●	●	●		
			Monroe Title Insurance Corporation	800-966-6763	●	●	●		
●	●	●	New York Institute of Legal Research	914-245-8400	●	●	●	●	●

CV	CR	PR	HERKIMER (EST)		UC	RE	TX	VS	VR
			Bankruptcy Reporter of Rochester	716-271-6000					
●	●	●	🏛 CMS (Consumer Marketing Services)	315-476-8414	●	●	●		
●		●	CW Credit Abstract Co	718-423-9430	●	●	●		
●		●	Central New York Abstract Corporation	315-724-1614	●	●	●		
		●	Four Corners Abstract	800-724-3668	●	●	●		
			Monroe Title Insurance Corporation	800-966-6763	●	●	●		
●	●	●	New York Institute of Legal Research	914-245-8400	●	●	●	●	●
●	●	●	Northeast Investigations Inc (SOP)	800-484-5125	●	●	●	●	●

CV	CR	PR	JEFFERSON (EST)		UC	RE	TX	VS	VR
			Bankruptcy Reporter of Rochester	716-271-6000					
●	●	●	🏛 CMS (Consumer Marketing Services)	315-476-8414	●	●	●		

DT	BK	CV	CR	PR		UC	RE	TX	VS	VR
			●	●	CW Credit Abstract Co 718-423-9430	●	●	●		
			●	●	Monroe Title Insurance Corporation 800-966-6763	●	●	●		
		●	●	●	New York Institute of Legal Research 914-245-8400	●	●	●	●	●
		●	●	●	Northeast Investigations Inc (SOP) 800-484-5125	●	●	●	●	●

DT	BK	CV	CR	PR	KINGS (EST)	UC	RE	TX	VS	VR
●	●	●	●	●	A.S.S.I.S.T. International 800-382-7747	●	●	●	●	●
●	●	●	●	●	APB Information Research Center Inc (SOP) 718-494-0750	●	●	●	●	
●	●	●	●	●	Alstate Process Service Inc (SOP) 516-667-1800	●	●	●	●	
●	●	●		●	Austin & Associates Inc 914-968-3700	●	●	●		●
●	●	●	●	●	Bridge Service Corp 800-225-2736	●	●	●	●	
●	●	●	●	●	CSC 800-221-0770	●	●	●		
●	●	●		●	CW Credit Abstract Co 718-423-9430	●	●	●		
●	●	●	●		Court Explorers LLC 212-945-6324	●	●			
●	●	●		●	DLS (Demovsky Lawyer Service) (SOP) 800-443-1058	●	●	●	●	●
●	●	●	●	●	Docutronics Information Services 800-227-5595	●				
●	●	●		●	FDR Info Centers 212-742-1066	●	●	●	●	
●	●	●	●	●	Fidelifacts 800-678-0007	●	●	●		●
●	●	●		●	Intercounty Clearance Corporation (SOP) 800-229-4422	●	●	●		
●	●	●			Investigative Resources (SOP) 718-317-0043	●	●	●	●	●
●	●	●		●	Keating & Walker (SOP) 800-797-6444	●	●	●	●	●
●	●	●		●	LIDA Credit Agency Inc (SOP) 516-678-4600	●	●	●	●	●
●	●	●		●	LegalEase Inc (SOP) 800-393-1277	●	●	●	●	
●	●	●			McLain Abstract 516-744-0064	●	●	●		
●	●	●	●	●	Nationwide Court Services Inc (SOP) 516-981-4400	●	●	●	●	●
●	●	●		●	New York Institute of Legal Research 914-245-8400	●	●	●	●	●
●	●	●	●	●	North East Court Services Inc (SOP) 800-235-0794	●	●	●		
●	●	●		●	Pallorium Inc (SOP) 212-969-0286	●	●	●	●	●
●	●	●	●	●	Paper Chase Research 212-587-7071	●	●	●	●	●
●	●	●		●	Research Information Services 800-447-3320	●	●	●	●	
●	●	●	●		Search NY 718-854-1492	●	●	●	●	
●	●	●	●		Silver Eagle Services (SOP) 212-922-0223		●			
●	●	●	●	●	Washington Document Services 800-422-2776					
					Wilsearch Information Network 800-391-5502	●	●	●		

CV	CR	PR	LEWIS (EST)	UC	RE	TX	VS	VR
			Bankruptcy Reporter of Rochester 716-271-6000					
●	●	●	CMS (Consumer Marketing Services) 315-476-8414	●	●	●		
●		●	CW Credit Abstract Co 718-423-9430	●	●	●		
			Monroe Title Insurance Corporation 800-966-6763	●	●	●		
●	●	●	National Abstract Corporation 800-535-3477	●	●	●		
●	●	●	New York Institute of Legal Research 914-245-8400	●	●	●	●	●

CV	CR	PR	LIVINGSTON (EST)	UC	RE	TX	VS	VR
			Bankruptcy Reporter of Rochester 716-271-6000					
●	●	●	CMS (Consumer Marketing Services) 315-476-8414	●	●	●		
●		●	CW Credit Abstract Co 718-423-9430	●	●	●		
		●	Four Corners Abstract 800-724-3668	●	●	●		
			Monroe Title Insurance Corporation 800-966-6763	●	●	●		
●	●	●	New York Institute of Legal Research 914-245-8400	●	●	●	●	●

CV	CR	PR	MADISON (EST)	UC	RE	TX	VS	VR
			Bankruptcy Reporter of Rochester 716-271-6000					
●	●	●	CMS (Consumer Marketing Services) 315-476-8414	●	●	●		
●		●	CW Credit Abstract Co 718-423-9430	●	●	●		
●		●	Central New York Abstract Corporation 315-724-1614	●	●	●		
		●	Four Corners Abstract 800-724-3668	●	●	●		
			Monroe Title Insurance Corporation 800-966-6763	●	●	●		
●	●	●	New York Institute of Legal Research 914-245-8400	●	●	●	●	●
●	●	●	Northeast Investigations Inc (SOP) 800-484-5125	●	●	●	●	●
●	●	●	Oneida Valley Abstract 315-363-1444	●	●	●		●
●			Services Rendered (SOP) 315-853-6327	●	●	●		●

DT	BK	CV	CR	PR	MONROE (EST)		UC	RE	TX	VS	VR
•	•	•			Balkin Library Management Services 716-482-1506			•			
•	•				Bankruptcy Reporter of Rochester 716-271-6000						
•	•	•	•	•	🏛 CMS (Consumer Marketing Services) 315-476-8414		•	•	•		
•	•	•		•	CW Credit Abstract Co 718-423-9430		•	•	•		
•	•	•	•	•	Executive Project Service (SOP) 716-377-5157		•	•	•	•	•
				•	Four Corners Abstract 800-724-3668		•	•	•		
•	•	•	•	•	Legal Recording of Rochester Inc 716-232-6710		•	•	•		
•	•				Monroe Title Insurance Corporation 800-966-6763		•	•	•		
•	•	•	•	•	New York Institute of Legal Research 914-245-8400		•	•	•	•	•
•	•	•	•	•	Northeast Investigations Inc (SOP)............... 800-484-5125		•	•	•	•	•
					Ryco Information Services Inc 315-461-8308		•	•	•		

		CV	CR	PR	MONTGOMERY (EST)		UC	RE	TX	VS	VR
					Bankruptcy Reporter of Rochester 716-271-6000						
		•	•	•	🏛 CMS (Consumer Marketing Services) 315-476-8414		•	•	•		
		•		•	CW Credit Abstract Co 718-423-9430		•	•	•		
		•	•	•	County Seat Abstract 518-762-3011		•	•	•		
				•	Four Corners Abstract 800-724-3668		•	•	•		
					Monroe Title Insurance Corporation 800-966-6763		•	•	•		
		•	•	•	New York Institute of Legal Research 914-245-8400		•	•	•	•	•
		•	•	•	Onistagrawa Abstracting Corp 518-827-8088		•	•	•		
				•	Sacandaga Abstract Corp 518-773-2828		•	•	•		

	BK	CV	CR	PR	NASSAU (EST)		UC	RE	TX	VS	VR
	•	•	•	•	APB Information Research Center Inc (SOP)....... 718-494-0750		•	•	•	•	
	•	•	•	•	Alstate Process Service Inc (SOP) 516-667-1800		•	•	•	•	
	•	•		•	🏛 Austin & Associates Inc 914-968-3700		•	•	•		•
	•	•		•	CW Credit Abstract Co 718-423-9430		•	•	•		
	•	•	•	•	DLS (Demovsky Lawyer Service) (SOP) 800-443-1058		•	•	•	•	•
	•	•	•	•	🏛 Fidelifacts 800-678-0007		•	•	•	•	•
	•	•	•	•	🏛 Gotcha Legal Process Service Inc (SOP) 516-751-1450		•	•	•	•	•
	•	•			🏛 Intercounty Clearance Corporation (SOP) 800-229-4422		•	•	•		
	•	•	•	•	Investigative Resources 718-317-0043		•	•	•	•	•
	•	•	•	•	J & J Associates (SOP) 800-850-5568		•	•	•	•	•
	•	•	•	•	🏛 Keating & Walker (SOP) 800-797-6444		•	•	•	•	•
	•	•	•	•	🏛 LIDA Credit Agency Inc (SOP)............... 516-678-4600		•	•	•	•	•
	•	•		•	🏛 LegalEase Inc (SOP) 800-393-1277		•	•	•	•	
	•	•		•	McLain Abstract 516-744-0064		•	•	•		
	•	•	•	•	🏛 Nationwide Court Services Inc (SOP) 516-981-4400		•	•	•	•	•
	•	•	•	•	New York Institute of Legal Research 914-245-8400		•	•	•	•	•
	•	•	•	•	Pallorium Inc (SOP)............... 212-969-0286		•	•	•	•	•
	•	•	•	•	🏛 Paper Chase Research 212-587-7071		•	•	•	•	•
	•	•		•	Reda's Attorney Service 516-821-6060		•	•	•		
	•	•	•	•	Research Information Services 800-447-3320		•	•	•		
	•	•	•	•	🏛 Search NY 718-854-1492		•	•	•		
	•	•	•	•	🏛 Security Enforcement Inc (SOP)............... 800-924-2896		•	•	•	•	•
	•	•			Silver Eagle Services (SOP) 212-922-0223			•			
	•	•	•	•	Washington Document Services 800-422-2776						
					🏛 Wilsearch Information Network 800-391-5502		•	•	•		

DT	BK	CV	CR	PR	NEW YORK (EST)		UC	RE	TX	VS	VR
•	•	•	•	•	A.S.S.I.S.T. International 800-382-7747		•	•	•	•	•
•	•	•	•	•	APB Information Research Center Inc (SOP)....... 718-494-0750		•	•	•	•	
•	•	•	•	•	Alstate Process Service Inc (SOP) 516-667-1800		•	•	•	•	
•	•	•	•	•	🏛 Austin & Associates Inc 914-968-3700		•	•	•		•
•	•	•	•	•	🏛 Bridge Service Corp 800-225-2736		•	•	•	•	
•	•	•	•	•	CSC 800-221-0770		•		•		
•	•	•	•	•	CW Credit Abstract Co 718-423-9430		•	•	•		
•	•	•	•	•	🏛 Court Explorers LLC 212-945-6324		•	•	•		
•	•	•	•	•	DLS (Demovsky Lawyer Service) (SOP) 800-443-1058		•	•	•	•	•
•	•	•	•	•	Document Resources 800-666-0061		•	•	•	•	•

•	•	•	•	•	Docutronics Information Services 800-227-5595	•				
•	•	•	•	•	FDR Info Centers 212-742-1066	•	•	•	•	
•	•	•	•	•	🛢 Fidelifacts 800-678-0007	•	•	•	•	•
•	•	•	•	•	General Information Services Inc 800-447-2080	•	•	•	•	•
•	•	•	•	•	🛢 Infoforum Inc 800-484-1301	•	•	•	•	
•	•	•			🛢 Intercounty Clearance Corporation (SOP) 800-229-4422	•				
•	•	•	•	•	Investigative Resources (SOP) 718-317-0043	•	•	•	•	•
•	•	•	•	•	J & J Associates (SOP) 800-850-5568	•				
•	•	•	•	•	🛢 Keating & Walker (SOP) 800-797-6444	•				
•	•	•	•	•	🛢 LIDA Credit Agency Inc (SOP) 516-678-4600	•	•	•	•	•
•	•	•	•	•	🛢 LegalEase Inc (SOP) 800-393-1277	•	•	•	•	•
•	•	•	•	•	🛢 Nationwide Court Services Inc (SOP) 516-981-4400	•	•	•	•	•
•	•	•	•	•	New York Institute of Legal Research 914-245-8400	•	•	•	•	•
•	•	•	•	•	🛢 North East Court Services Inc (SOP) 800-235-0794	•	•	•	•	•
•	•	•	•	•	Pallorium Inc (SOP) 212-969-0286	•	•	•	•	•
•	•	•	•	•	🛢 Paper Chase Research 212-587-7071	•	•	•	•	•
•	•	•	•	•	Research Information Services 800-447-3320	UC	•	•	•	•
•	•	•	•	•	🛢 Search NY 718-854-1492	•	•	•	•	
•	•	•	•		Silver Eagle Services (SOP) 212-922-0223	•				
					🛢 Wilsearch Information Network 800-391-5502	•	•	•		

	CV	CR	PR	NIAGARA (EST)	UC	RE	TX	VS	VR
	•	•	•	Action Process Service (SOP) 716-692-5032	•	•	•	•	
				Bankruptcy Reporter of Rochester 716-271-6000					
	•	•	•	🛢 CMS (Consumer Marketing Services) 315-476-8414	•	•	•		
	•		•	CW Credit Abstract Co 718-423-9430	•	•	•		
	•	•	•	🛢 Court House Research 716-873-8315	•	•	•	•	•
	•	•	•	Ferrari 716-689-6577	•	•	•	•	
			•	Four Corners Abstract 800-724-3668	•	•	•		
				Monroe Title Insurance Corporation 800-966-6763	•	•	•		
	•	•	•	New York Institute of Legal Research 914-245-8400	•	•	•	•	•
	•	•	•	🛢 Paralegal Services of Buffalo 716-856-3818	•	•	•	•	•
				Ryco Information Services Inc 315-461-8308	•	•	•		

DT	BK	CV	CR	PR	ONEIDA (EST)	UC	RE	TX	VS	VR
•	•				Bankruptcy Reporter of Rochester 716-271-6000					
•	•	•	•	•	🛢 CMS (Consumer Marketing Services) 315-476-8414	•	•	•		
•	•	•		•	CW Credit Abstract Co 718-423-9430	•	•	•		
		•		•	Central New York Abstract Corporation 315-724-1614	•	•	•		
				•	Four Corners Abstract 800-724-3668	•	•	•		
•	•	•	•	•	🛢 Midstate Legal Support Services (SOP) 315-797-8609	•	•	•		•
•	•				Monroe Title Insurance Corporation 800-966-6763	•	•	•		
•		•	•	•	New York Institute of Legal Research 914-245-8400	•	•	•	•	•
•		•	•	•	Northeast Investigations Inc (SOP) 800-484-5125	•	•	•	•	•
		•	•		Ryco Information Services Inc 315-461-8308	•	•	•		
•	•	•			🛢 Services Rendered (SOP) 315-853-6327	•	•	•		•

DT		CV	CR	PR	ONONDAGA (EST)	UC	RE	TX	VS	VR
•					Bankruptcy Reporter of Rochester 716-271-6000					
•			•	•	🛢 CMS (Consumer Marketing Services) 315-476-8414	•	•	•		
•			•		CW Credit Abstract Co 718-423-9430	•	•	•		
				•	Four Corners Abstract 800-724-3668	•	•	•		
•			•	•	🛢 Merola Services 315-652-5242		•			•
•					Monroe Title Insurance Corporation 800-966-6763	•	•	•		
•		•	•	•	New York Institute of Legal Research 914-245-8400	•	•	•	•	•
•		•	•	•	Northeast Investigations Inc (SOP) 800-484-5125	•	•	•	•	•
					Ryco Information Services Inc 315-461-8308	•	•	•		

	CV	CR	PR	ONTARIO (EST)	UC	RE	TX	VS	VR
				Bankruptcy Reporter of Rochester 716-271-6000					
	•	•	•	🛢 CMS (Consumer Marketing Services) 315-476-8414	•	•	•		
	•		•	CW Credit Abstract Co 718-423-9430	•	•	•		

CV	CR	PR	Company	Phone	UC	RE	TX	VS	VR
		•	Four Corners Abstract	800-724-3668	•	•	•		
			Monroe Title Insurance Corporation	800-966-6763	•	•	•		
•	•	•	New York Institute of Legal Research	914-245-8400	•	•	•	•	•

ORANGE (EST)

CV	CR	PR	Company	Phone	UC	RE	TX	VS	VR
•	•	•	A.S.S.I.S.T. International	800-382-7747	•	•	•	•	•
•	•	•	Attorney Service Bureau (SOP)	914-354-3357	•	•	•	•	•
•	•	•	Bureau of Special Services (SOP)	800-772-7130	•	•	•	•	•
		•	CW Credit Abstract Co	718-423-9430	•	•	•		
	•	•	Fidelifacts	800-678-0007	•	•	•		
		•	Hill-N-Dale Abstractors Inc	914-294-5110	•	•	•		
•		•	La Prade Services Inc (SOP)	914-473-0468	•	•	•	•	
•	•	•	Metropolitan Delivery	914-463-0519	•	•	•		•
			Monroe Title Insurance Corporation	800-966-6763	•	•	•		
•	•	•	New York Institute of Legal Research	914-245-8400	•	•	•		•
•	•	•	Orange Abstractor Services Co (SOP)	914-294-3331	•	•	•		
•	•	•	Orange Paper Placers (SOP)	914-294-7810	•	•	•	•	
•	•	•	Walsh Process & Legal Services (SOP)	888-438-9757	•	•	•	•	•
•	•	•	Westchester Court Service (SOP)	914-948-5200	•	•	•	•	

ORLEANS (EST)

CV	CR	PR	Company	Phone	UC	RE	TX	VS	VR
			Bankruptcy Reporter of Rochester	716-271-6000					
•	•	•	CMS (Consumer Marketing Services)	315-476-8414	•	•	•		
		•	CW Credit Abstract Co	718-423-9430	•	•	•		
		•	Four Corners Abstract	800-724-3668	•	•	•		
•	•	•	New York Institute of Legal Research	914-245-8400	•	•	•	•	•

OSWEGO (EST)

CV	CR	PR	Company	Phone	UC	RE	TX	VS	VR
			Bankruptcy Reporter of Rochester	716-271-6000					
•	•	•	CMS (Consumer Marketing Services)	315-476-8414	•	•	•		
		•	CW Credit Abstract Co	718-423-9430	•	•	•		
		•	Central New York Abstract Corporation	315-724-1614	•	•	•		
		•	Four Corners Abstract	800-724-3668	•	•	•		
			Monroe Title Insurance Corporation	800-966-6763	•	•	•		
•	•	•	New York Institute of Legal Research	914-245-8400	•	•	•	•	•
•	•	•	Northeast Investigations Inc (SOP)	800-484-5125	•	•	•	•	•

OTSEGO (EST)

CV	CR	PR	Company	Phone	UC	RE	TX	VS	VR
			Bankruptcy Reporter of Rochester	716-271-6000					
•	•	•	CMS (Consumer Marketing Services)	315-476-8414	•	•	•		
•		•	CW Credit Abstract Co	718-423-9430	•	•	•		
•		•	Central New York Abstract Corporation	315-724-1614	•	•	•		
			Monroe Title Insurance Corporation	800-966-6763	•	•	•		
•	•	•	New York Institute of Legal Research	914-245-8400	•	•	•	•	•
•	•	•	Onistagrawa Abstracting Corp	518-827-8088	•	•	•	•	

PUTNAM (EST)

CV	CR	PR	Company	Phone	UC	RE	TX	VS	VR
•	•	•	A.S.S.I.S.T. International	800-382-7747	•	•	•	•	•
•	•	•	Bureau of Special Services (SOP)	800-772-7130	•	•	•	•	•
•	•	•	CW Credit Abstract Co	718-423-9430	•	•	•		
•	•	•	Fidelifacts	800-678-0007	•	•	•	•	
•	•	•	Fox Advertising	914-948-5200	•	•	•		
•	•	•	La Prade Services Inc (SOP)	914-473-0468	•	•	•	•	
•	•	•	LegalEase Inc (SOP)	800-393-1277	•	•	•	•	
•	•	•	Metropolitan Delivery	914-463-0519	•	•	•		•
•	•	•	Nationwide Court Services Inc (SOP)	516-981-4400	•	•	•		•
•	•	•	New York Institute of Legal Research	914-245-8400	•	•	•		•
•	•	•	Orange Abstractor Services Co (SOP)	914-294-3331	•	•			
•	•	•	Orange Paper Placers (SOP)	914-294-7810	•	•			
•	•	•	Paper Chase Research	212-587-7071	•	•	•	•	
•	•	•	Walsh Process & Legal Services (SOP)	888-438-9757	•	•	•	•	•
•	•	•	Westchester Court Service (SOP)	914-948-5200	•	•	•	•	

CV	CR	PR	QUEENS (EST)		UC	RE	TX	VS	VR
●	●	●	A.S.S.I.S.T. International	800-382-7747	●	●	●	●	●
●	●	●	APB Information Research Center Inc (SOP)	718-494-0750	●	●	●	●	
●	●	●	Alstate Process Service Inc (SOP)	516-667-1800	●	●	●	●	
●		●	Austin & Associates Inc	914-968-3700	●	●	●		●
●	●	●	Bridge Service Corp	800-225-2736	●	●	●		
●	●	●	CSC	800-221-0770	●		●		
●		●	CW Credit Abstract Co	718-423-9430	●	●	●		
●	●		Court Explorers LLC	212-945-6324	●	●			
●	●	●	DLS (Demovsky Lawyer Service) (SOP)	800-443-1058	●	●	●	●	●
●	●	●	FDR Info Centers	212-742-1066	●	●	●	●	
●	●	●	Fidelifacts	800-678-0007	●	●	●		●
●			Intercounty Clearance Corporation (SOP)	800-229-4422	●	●	●		
●	●	●	Investigative Resources (SOP)	718-317-0043	●	●	●	●	●
●	●	●	Keating & Walker (SOP)	800-797-6444	●	●	●	●	
●	●	●	LIDA Credit Agency Inc (SOP)	516-678-4600	●	●	●	●	
●	●	●	LegalEase Inc (SOP)	800-393-1277	●	●	●	●	
●	●	●	McLain Abstract	516-744-0064	●	●	●		
●	●	●	Nationwide Court Services Inc (SOP)	516-981-4400	●	●	●		●
●	●	●	New York Institute of Legal Research	914-245-8400	●	●	●	●	●
●	●	●	North East Court Services Inc (SOP)	800-235-0794	●	●	●		
●	●	●	Pallorium Inc (SOP)	212-969-0286	●	●		●	●
●	●	●	Paper Chase Research	212-587-7071	●	●	●	●	●
●	●	●	Research Information Services	800-447-3320	●	●	●	●	
●	●	●	Search NY	718-854-1492	●	●	●	●	
●	●		Silver Eagle Services (SOP)	212-922-0223		●			
●	●	●	Washington Document Services	800-422-2776					
			Wilsearch Information Network	800-391-5502	●	●	●		

CV	CR	PR	RENSSELAER (EST)		UC	RE	TX	VS	VR
●	●		Access Information Services Inc (SOP)	800-388-1598	●	●	●		
●	●	●	Attorney's Process and Research Service (SOP)	518-465-8951	●	●	●	●	
			Bankruptcy Reporter of Rochester	716-271-6000					
●	●	●	CMS (Consumer Marketing Services)	315-476-8414	●	●	●		
●	●	●	CSC (SOP)	800-833-9848	●	●	●	●	
●		●	CW Credit Abstract Co	718-423-9430	●	●			
●			Capitol Services Inc	800-662-0171	●		●	●	
●	●		Corporate Service Bureau	518-463-8550	●		●	●	
●	●	●	DLS (Demovsky Lawyer Service) (SOP)	518-449-8411	●	●	●	●	
		●	Four Corners Abstract	800-724-3668	●	●	●		
●			Intercounty Clearance Corporation (SOP)	800-229-4422	●	●	●		
			Monroe Title Insurance Corporation	800-966-6763	●	●	●		
●	●	●	New York Institute of Legal Research	914-245-8400	●	●	●	●	●
●	●	●	Relyea Services Inc (SOP)	800-854-4111	●	●	●	●	
			Ryco Information Services Inc	315-461-8308	●	●	●		
●	●	●	Tracers International (SOP)	800-872-2377	●	●	●	●	●
●	●	●	Zap! Courier Service	518-449-3361	●		●	●	●

CV	CR	PR	RICHMOND (EST)		UC	RE	TX	VS	VR
●	●	●	A.S.S.I.S.T. International	800-382-7747	●	●	●	●	●
●	●	●	APB Information Research Center Inc (SOP)	718-494-0750	●	●	●	●	
●	●	●	Alstate Process Service Inc (SOP)	516-667-1800	●	●	●	●	
●	●	●	Bridge Service Corp	800-225-2736	●	●	●	●	
●		●	CW Credit Abstract Co	718-423-9430	●	●	●		
●	●	●	DLS (Demovsky Lawyer Service) (SOP)	800-443-1058	●	●	●	●	●
●	●	●	FDR Info Centers	212-742-1066	●	●	●	●	
●	●	●	Fidelifacts	800-678-0007	●	●	●	●	●
●	●	●	Investigative Resources (SOP)	718-317-0043	●	●	●	●	●
●	●	●	Keating & Walker (SOP)	800-797-6444	●	●	●	●	●
●	●	●	LIDA Credit Agency Inc (SOP)	516-678-4600	●	●	●	●	●
●		●	LegalEase Inc (SOP)	800-393-1277	●	●	●	●	

CV	CR	PR			UC	RE	TX	VS	VR
•	•	•	🏛 Nationwide Court Services Inc (SOP) 516-981-4400		•	•	•	•	•
•	•	•	New York Institute of Legal Research 914-245-8400		•	•	•	•	•
•	•	•	🏛 North East Court Services Inc (SOP) 800-235-0794		•	•	•		
•	•	•	Pallorium Inc (SOP) 212-969-0286		•	•	•	•	
•	•	•	🏛 Paper Chase Research 212-587-7071		•	•	•	•	
•	•	•	Research Information Services 800-447-3320		•	•	•	•	
•	•	•	🏛 Search NY 718-854-1492		•	•	•		
•	•	•	Silver Eagle Services (SOP) 212-922-0223		•				
•	•	•	Washington Document Services 800-422-2776						
			🏛 Wilsearch Information Network 800-391-5502		•	•	•		

CV	CR	PR	ROCKLAND (EST)		UC	RE	TX	VS	VR
•	•	•	A.S.S.I.S.T. International 800-382-7747		•	•	•	•	•
•	•	•	Attorney Service Bureau (SOP) 914-354-3357		•	•	•	•	•
•	•	•	Bureau of Special Services (SOP) 800-772-7130		•	•	•	•	•
•		•	CW Credit Abstract Co 718-423-9430		•	•	•		
•	•	•	DLS (Demovsky Lawyer Service) (SOP) 800-443-1058		•	•	•	•	
•	•	•	🏛 Fidelifacts 800-678-0007		•	•	•	•	
•		•	Fox Advertising 914-948-5200		•	•	•		
•	•	•	🏛 LegalEase Inc (SOP) 800-393-1277		•	•	•		
•	•	•	🏛 Nationwide Court Services Inc (SOP) 516-981-4400		•	•	•	•	•
•	•	•	New York Institute of Legal Research 914-245-8400		•	•	•	•	•
•	•	•	Orange Abstractor Services Co (SOP) 914-294-3331		•	•	•		
•	•	•	Orange Paper Placers (SOP) 914-294-7810		•	•			
•	•	•	Silver Eagle Services (SOP) 212-922-0223		•				
•	•	•	🏛 Walsh Process & Legal Services (SOP) 888-438-9757		•	•	•	•	•
•	•	•	Westchester Court Service (SOP) 914-948-5200		•	•	•	•	

CV	CR	PR	SARATOGA (EST)		UC	RE	TX	VS	VR
•	•		🏛 Access Information Services Inc (SOP) 800-388-1598		•	•	•		
•	•	•	Attorney's Process and Research Service (SOP) 518-465-8951		•	•	•	•	
			Bankruptcy Reporter of Rochester 716-271-6000						
•	•	•	🏛 CMS (Consumer Marketing Services) 315-476-8414		•	•	•		
•			CW Credit Abstract Co 718-423-9430		•	•	•		
		•	Four Corners Abstract 800-724-3668		•	•	•		
•			🏛 Intercounty Clearance Corporation (SOP) 800-229-4422		•	•	•		
			Monroe Title Insurance Corporation 800-966-6763		•	•	•		
•	•	•	New York Institute of Legal Research 914-245-8400		•	•	•	•	•
•	•	•	🏛 Relyea Services Inc (SOP) 800-854-4111		•	•	•	•	
			Ryco Information Services Inc 315-461-8308		•	•	•		
•	•	•	🏛 Tracers International (SOP) 800-872-2377		•	•	•	•	•
•	•	•	Zap! Courier Service 518-449-3361		•		•	•	•

CV	CR	PR	SCHENECTADY (EST)		UC	RE	TX	VS	VR
•	•		🏛 Access Information Services Inc (SOP) 800-388-1598		•	•	•		
•	•	•	Attorney's Process and Research Service (SOP) 518-465-8951		•	•	•	•	
			Bankruptcy Reporter of Rochester 716-271-6000						
•	•	•	🏛 CMS (Consumer Marketing Services) 315-476-8414		•	•	•		
•		•	CW Credit Abstract Co 718-423-9430		•	•	•		
•	•		Corporate Service Bureau 518-463-8550		•		•	•	
•	•	•	DLS (Demovsky Lawyer Service) (SOP) 518-449-8411		•	•	•	•	
		•	Four Corners Abstract 800-724-3668		•	•	•		
•	•	•	New York Institute of Legal Research 914-245-8400		•	•	•	•	•
•	•	•	Onistagrawa Abstracting Corp 518-827-8088		•	•	•	•	
•	•	•	🏛 Relyea Services Inc (SOP) 800-854-4111		•	•	•	•	
			Ryco Information Services Inc 315-461-8308		•	•	•		
•	•	•	🏛 Tracers International (SOP) 800-872-2377		•	•	•	•	•
•	•	•	Zap! Courier Service 518-449-3361		•		•	•	•

CV	CR	PR	SCHOHARIE (EST)		UC	RE	TX	VS	VR
			Bankruptcy Reporter of Rochester 716-271-6000						
•	•	•	🏛 CMS (Consumer Marketing Services) 315-476-8414		•	•	•		

		CW Credit Abstract Co 718-423-9430					
		Monroe Title Insurance Corporation 800-966-6763					
		New York Institute of Legal Research 914-245-8400					
		Onistagrawa Abstracting Corp 518-827-8088					
		🏛 Tracers International (SOP) 800-872-2377					

CV	CR	PR	SCHUYLER (EST)	UC	RE	TX	VS	VR
			Bankruptcy Reporter of Rochester 716-271-6000					
•	•	•	🏛 CMS (Consumer Marketing Services) 315-476-8414	•	•	•		
•		•	CW Credit Abstract Co 718-423-9430	•	•	•		
•	•	•	🏛 Hurley, William 607-734-1743	•	•	•	•	•
			Monroe Title Insurance Corporation 800-966-6763	•	•	•		
•	•	•	New York Institute of Legal Research 914-245-8400	•	•	•	•	•

CV	CR	PR	SENECA (EST)	UC	RE	TX	VS	VR
			Bankruptcy Reporter of Rochester 716-271-6000					
•	•	•	🏛 CMS (Consumer Marketing Services) 315-476-8414	•	•	•		
•		•	CW Credit Abstract Co 718-423-9430	•	•	•		
		•	Four Corners Abstract 800-724-3668	•	•	•		
			Monroe Title Insurance Corporation 800-966-6763	•	•	•		
•	•	•	New York Institute of Legal Research 914-245-8400	•	•	•	•	•

CV	CR	PR	ST. LAWRENCE (EST)	UC	RE	TX	VS	VR
			Bankruptcy Reporter of Rochester 716-271-6000					
•	•	•	🏛 CMS (Consumer Marketing Services) 315-476-8414	•	•	•		
•		•	CW Credit Abstract Co 718-423-9430	•				
•	•		J Tacchino Agency Private Investigators (SOP) 315-344-8828		•	•		
			Monroe Title Insurance Corporation 800-966-6763	•	•	•		
•	•	•	New York Institute of Legal Research 914-245-8400	•	•	•	•	•

CV	CR	PR	STEUBEN (EST)	UC	RE	TX	VS	VR
			Bankruptcy Reporter of Rochester 716-271-6000					
•	•	•	🏛 CMS (Consumer Marketing Services) 315-476-8414	•	•	•		
•		•	CW Credit Abstract Co 718-423-9430	•	•	•		
•	•	•	🏛 Hurley, William 607-734-1743	•	•	•	•	•
			Monroe Title Insurance Corporation 800-966-6763	•	•	•		
•	•	•	New York Institute of Legal Research 914-245-8400	•	•	•	•	•

DT	BK	CV	CR	PR	SUFFOLK (EST)	UC	RE	TX	VS	VR
•	•	•	•	•	A.S.S.I.S.T. International 800-382-7747	•	•	•	•	•
•	•	•	•	•	APB Information Research Center Inc (SOP) 718-494-0750	•	•	•	•	
•	•	•	•	•	Alstate Process Service Inc (SOP) 516-667-1800	•	•	•	•	
•	•	•	•	•	🏛 Austin & Associates Inc 914-968-3700	•	•	•		
•	•	•	•	•	CW Credit Abstract Co 718-423-9430	•	•	•		
•	•	•	•	•	🏛 Fidelifacts 800-678-0007	•	•	•	•	•
•	•	•	•	•	🏛 Gotcha Legal Process Service Inc (SOP) 516-751-1450	•	•	•		
•	•	•	•	•	🏛 Intercounty Clearance Corporation (SOP) 800-229-4422	•	•	•		
•	•	•	•	•	Investigative Resources 718-317-0043	•	•	•		
•	•	•	•	•	J & J Associates (SOP) 800-850-5568	•	•	•		
•	•	•	•	•	🏛 LIDA Credit Agency Inc (SOP) 516-678-4600	•	•	•		
•	•	•	•	•	McLain Abstract 516-744-0064	•	•	•		
•	•	•	•	•	🏛 Nationwide Court Services Inc (SOP) 516-981-4400	•	•	•	•	
•	•	•	•	•	New York Institute of Legal Research 914-245-8400	•	•	•	•	•
•	•	•	•	•	Pallorium Inc (SOP) 212-969-0286	•	•	•	•	
•	•	•	•	•	🏛 Paper Chase Research 212-587-7071	•	•	•	•	
•	•	•	•	•	Reda's Attorney Service 516-821-6060	•	•	•		
•	•	•	•	•	Research Information Services 800-447-3320	•	•	•		
•	•	•	•	•	🏛 Security Enforcement Inc (SOP) 800-924-2896	•	•	•	•	
•	•	•	•		Silver Eagle Services (SOP) 212-922-0223	•	•	•		
		•	•		🏛 Stovall, Donna (SOP) 516-744-5834	•	•			
•	•	•	•	•	Washington Document Services 800-422-2776					
					🏛 Wilsearch Information Network 800-391-5502	•	•	•		

CV	CR	PR	SULLIVAN (EST)	UC	RE	TX	VS	VR
•	•	•	Bureau of Special Services (SOP) 800-772-7130	•	•	•	•	•
•		•	CW Credit Abstract Co 718-423-9430	•	•	•		
•	•	•	Fox Advertising 914-948-5200	•	•	•		
•		•	Hill-N-Dale Abstractors Inc 914-294-5110	•	•	•		
•	•	•	Hudson Research Group Inc 914-747-1622	•	•	•		•
•	•	•	New York Institute of Legal Research 914-245-8400	•	•	•	•	•
•	•	•	Orange Abstractor Services Co (SOP) 914-294-3331	•	•	•		
•	•	•	Orange Paper Placers (SOP) 914-294-7810	•	•	•	•	
•	•	•	Westchester Court Service (SOP) 914-948-5200	•	•	•	•	

CV	CR	PR	TIOGA (EST)	UC	RE	TX	VS	VR
			Bankruptcy Reporter of Rochester 716-271-6000					
•	•	•	🏛 CMS (Consumer Marketing Services) 315-476-8414	•	•	•		
•		•	CW Credit Abstract Co 718-423-9430	•	•	•		
•		•	Four Corners Abstract 800-724-3668	•	•	•		
•	•	•	🏛 Hurley, William 607-734-1743	•	•	•	•	•
			Monroe Title Insurance Corporation 800-966-6763	•	•	•		
•		•	New York Institute of Legal Research 914-245-8400	•	•	•	•	•

CV	CR	PR	TOMPKINS (EST)	UC	RE	TX	VS	VR
			Bankruptcy Reporter of Rochester 716-271-6000					
•	•	•	🏛 CMS (Consumer Marketing Services) 315-476-8414	•	•	•		
•		•	CW Credit Abstract Co 718-423-9430	•	•	•		
•	•	•	🏛 Hurley, William 607-734-1743	•	•	•	•	•
			Monroe Title Insurance Corporation 800-966-6763	•	•	•		
•	•	•	New York Institute of Legal Research 914-245-8400	•	•	•	•	•
•		•	Tompkins and Watkins Abstract Corp 607-273-0884	•	•	•		

CV	CR	PR	ULSTER (EST)	UC	RE	TX	VS	VR
•	•	•	American Legal Support Service Inc 914-473-5676	•	•	•	•	
			Bankruptcy Reporter of Rochester 716-271-6000					
•		•	Bureau of Special Services (SOP) 800-772-7130	•	•	•		•
•		•	CW Credit Abstract Co 718-423-9430	•	•	•		
•	•	•	Fox Advertising 914-948-5200	•	•	•		
•		•	Hill-N-Dale Abstractors Inc 914-294-5110	•	•	•		
•	•	•	La Prade Services Inc (SOP) 914-473-0468	•	•	•	•	
•		•	New York Institute of Legal Research 914-245-8400	•	•	•	•	•
•	•	•	Orange Paper Placers (SOP) 914-294-7810	•	•	•	•	
•	•	•	Ranger Recovery (SOP) 914-679-2957	•	•	•	•	
•	•	•	🏛 Smith Hicks, Susan 518-537-4103	•	•	•		
•	•	•	🏛 Walsh Process & Legal Services (SOP) 888-438-9757	•	•	•		•
•	•	•	Westchester Court Service (SOP) 914-948-5200	•	•	•	•	

CV	CR	PR	WARREN (EST)	UC	RE	TX	VS	VR
			Bankruptcy Reporter of Rochester 716-271-6000					
•	•	•	🏛 CMS (Consumer Marketing Services) 315-476-8414	•	•	•		
•		•	CW Credit Abstract Co 718-423-9430	•	•	•		
			Monroe Title Insurance Corporation 800-966-6763	•	•	•		
•		•	New York Institute of Legal Research 914-245-8400	•	•	•	•	•

CV	CR	PR	WASHINGTON (EST)	UC	RE	TX	VS	VR
			Bankruptcy Reporter of Rochester 716-271-6000					
•	•	•	🏛 CMS (Consumer Marketing Services) 315-476-8414	•	•	•		
•		•	CW Credit Abstract Co 718-423-9430	•	•	•		
			Monroe Title Insurance Corporation 800-966-6763	•	•	•		
•		•	New York Institute of Legal Research 914-245-8400	•	•	•	•	•

CV	CR	PR	WAYNE (EST)	UC	RE	TX	VS	VR
			Bankruptcy Reporter of Rochester 716-271-6000					
•		•	🏛 CMS (Consumer Marketing Services) 315-476-8414	•	•	•		
•		•	CW Credit Abstract Co 718-423-9430	•	•	•		

DT	BK	CV	CR	PR		UC	RE	TX	VS	VR
				•	Four Corners Abstract 800-724-3668	•	•	•		
					Monroe Title Insurance Corporation 800-966-6763	•	•	•		
		•	•	•	New York Institute of Legal Research 914-245-8400	•	•	•	•	•
				•	Ryco Information Services Inc 315-461-8308	•	•	•		

DT	BK	CV	CR	PR	WESTCHESTER (EST)	UC	RE	TX	VS	VR
•	•	•	•	•	A.S.S.I.S.T. International 800-382-7747	•	•	•	•	•
		•		•	Allied Abstract Co 914-682-3433	•	•	•		
•	•	•	•	•	Attorney Service Bureau (SOP) 914-354-3357	•	•	•	•	•
•	•	•		•	🏛 Austin & Associates Inc 914-968-3700	•	•	•		•
•	•	•	•	•	Bureau of Special Services (SOP) 800-772-7130	•	•	•	•	•
•	•	•		•	CW Credit Abstract Co 718-423-9430	•	•	•		
•	•	•	•	•	DLS (Demovsky Lawyer Service) (SOP) 800-443-1058	•	•	•	•	
•	•	•	•	•	FDR Info Centers 212-742-1066	•	•	•		
•	•	•	•	•	🏛 Fidelifacts 800-678-0007	•	•	•	•	•
•	•	•		•	Fox Advertising 914-948-5200	•	•	•		
•	•	•	•	•	Gold Shield Private Investigators Inc (SOP) 914-997-0000	•	•	•		•
•	•	•	•	•	Hudson Research Group Inc 914-747-1622	•	•	•		
		•		•	🏛 Intercounty Clearance Corporation (SOP) 800-229-4422	•	•	•		
•	•	•	•	•	Investigative Resources 718-317-0043	•	•	•	•	•
•	•	•	•	•	🏛 Keating & Walker (SOP) 800-797-6444	•	•	•	•	•
•	•	•	•	•	🏛 LIDA Credit Agency Inc (SOP) 516-678-4600	•	•	•		
•	•	•	•	•	🏛 LegalEase Inc (SOP) 800-393-1277	•	•	•	•	•
•	•	•	•	•	🏛 Nationwide Court Services Inc (SOP) 516-981-4400	•	•	•	•	•
•	•	•	•	•	New York Institute of Legal Research 914-245-8400	•	•	•	•	•
•	•	•	•	•	Pallorium Inc (SOP) 212-969-0286	•	•			
•	•	•	•	•	🏛 Paper Chase Research 212-587-7071	•	•	•	•	•
•	•	•	•	•	Research Information Services 800-447-3320	•	•	•		
•	•	•	•	•	🏛 Search NY 718-854-1492	•	•	•	•	
•	•	•	•	•	Silver Eagle Services (SOP) 212-922-0223		•			
•	•	•	•	•	🏛 Walsh Process & Legal Services (SOP) 888-438-9757	•	•	•	•	•
•	•	•	•	•	Washington Document Services 800-422-2776					
•	•	•	•	•	Westchester Court Service (SOP) 914-948-5200	•	•	•	•	

CV	CR	PR	WYOMING (EST)	UC	RE	TX	VS	VR
			Bankruptcy Reporter of Rochester 716-271-6000					
•	•	•	🏛 CMS (Consumer Marketing Services) 315-476-8414	•	•	•		
•		•	CW Credit Abstract Co 718-423-9430	•	•	•		
			Monroe Title Insurance Corporation 800-966-6763	•	•	•		
•	•	•	New York Institute of Legal Research 914-245-8400	•	•	•	•	•

CV	CR	PR	YATES (EST)	UC	RE	TX	VS	VR
			Bankruptcy Reporter of Rochester 716-271-6000					
•	•	•	🏛 CMS (Consumer Marketing Services) 315-476-8414	•	•	•		
•		•	CW Credit Abstract Co 718-423-9430	•	•	•		
		•	Four Corners Abstract 800-724-3668	•	•	•		
•	•	•	🏛 Hurley, William 607-734-1743	•	•	•	•	•
			Monroe Title Insurance Corporation 800-966-6763	•	•	•		
•	•	•	New York Institute of Legal Research 914-245-8400	•	•	•	•	•

NORTH CAROLINA

CV	CR	PR	ALAMANCE (EST)	UC	RE	TX	VS	VR
•	•		🏛 Alpha Research LLC (SOP) 205-755-7008			•		
•	•		Greet America Public Record Svc Inc 214-320-9836					
•	•	•	🏛 NC Search Inc 910-273-4999	•	•	•		
•		•	Paralegal Services of North Carolina Inc (SOP) 919-821-7762	•	•	•	•	
•	•	•	🏛 SingleSource Services Corp 800-713-3412	•		•	•	•
•	•	•	Williams, Nancy 910-584-0450	•	•	•	•	

CV	CR	PR	ALEXANDER (EST)	UC	RE	TX	VS	VR
•	•		🏛 Alpha Research LLC (SOP) 205-755-7008			•		
•	•	•	🏛 Donna's Unlimited Searches 704-256-1418	•	•	•	•	
•	•		Greet America Public Record Svc Inc 214-320-9836					
•	•	•	🏛 NC Search Inc 910-273-4999	•	•	•		
•	•	•	🏛 SingleSource Services Corp 800-713-3412	•		•	•	•

CV	CR	PR	ALLEGHANY (EST)	UC	RE	TX	VS	VR
•	•		🏛 Alpha Research LLC (SOP) 205-755-7008			•		
•	•		Greet America Public Record Svc Inc 214-320-9836					
•	•	•	🏛 NC Search Inc 910-273-4999	•	•	•		
•	•	•	🏛 SingleSource Services Corp 800-713-3412	•		•	•	•

CV	CR	PR	ANSON (EST)	UC	RE	TX	VS	VR
•	•		🏛 Alpha Research LLC (SOP) 205-755-7008			•		
•	•		Greet America Public Record Svc Inc 214-320-9836					
•	•	•	🏛 NC Search Inc 910-273-4999	•	•	•		
•	•	•	🏛 SingleSource Services Corp 800-713-3412	•		•	•	•

CV	CR	PR	ASHE (EST)	UC	RE	TX	VS	VR
•	•		🏛 Alpha Research LLC (SOP) 205-755-7008			•		
•	•		Greet America Public Record Svc Inc 214-320-9836					
•	•	•	Miller & Mosley 704-264-1125	•	•	•	•	
•	•	•	🏛 NC Search Inc 910-273-4999	•	•	•		
•	•	•	🏛 SingleSource Services Corp 800-713-3412	•		•	•	•

CV	CR	PR	AVERY (EST)	UC	RE	TX	VS	VR
•	•		🏛 Alpha Research LLC (SOP) 205-755-7008			•		
•	•		Greet America Public Record Svc Inc 214-320-9836					
•	•	•	Miller & Mosley 704-264-1125	•	•	•	•	
•	•	•	🏛 NC Search Inc 910-273-4999	•	•	•		
•	•	•	🏛 SingleSource Services Corp 800-713-3412	•		•	•	•

CV	CR	PR	BEAUFORT (EST)	UC	RE	TX	VS	VR
•	•		🏛 Alpha Research LLC (SOP) 205-755-7008			•		
•	•	•	Coastal Investigative Services Inc (SOP) 919-355-0122	•	•	•	•	
•	•		Eastern North Carolina Invest & Process (SOP) 919-772-3346			•	•	
•	•		Greet America Public Record Svc Inc 214-320-9836					
•			Hamm, Sue P 919-322-5015	•	•	•	•	
•	•	•	🏛 NC Search Inc 910-273-4999	•	•	•		
•	•	•	🏛 SingleSource Services Corp 800-713-3412	•		•	•	•

CV	CR	PR	BERTIE (EST)	UC	RE	TX	VS	VR
•	•		🏛 Alpha Research LLC (SOP) 205-755-7008			•		
•	•		Greet America Public Record Svc Inc 214-320-9836					
•	•	•	🏛 NC Search Inc 910-273-4999	•	•	•		
•	•	•	🏛 SingleSource Services Corp 800-713-3412	•		•	•	•

CV	CR	PR	BLADEN (EST)	UC	RE	TX	VS	VR
•	•		🏛 Alpha Research LLC (SOP) 205-755-7008			•		
•	•		Eastern North Carolina Invest & Process (SOP) 919-772-3346			•	•	
•	•		Greet America Public Record Svc Inc 214-320-9836					
•	•	•	🏛 NC Search Inc 910-273-4999	•	•	•		

					UC	RE	TX	VS	VR
•	•	•	🏛 National Data Access Corp 800-390-2959		•	•	•	•	•
•	•	•	🏛 Paraprofessional Abstracts 800-522-5163		•	•	•		
•	•	•	🏛 SingleSource Services Corp 800-713-3412		•		•	•	•

	CV	CR	PR	BRUNSWICK (EST)	UC	RE	TX	VS	VR
	•	•		🏛 Alpha Research LLC (SOP) 205-755-7008			•		
	•	•		Greet America Public Record Svc Inc 214-320-9836					
	•	•	•	🏛 NC Search Inc 910-273-4999	•	•	•		
	•	•	•	🏛 National Data Access Corp 800-390-2959	•	•	•	•	•
	•	•	•	🏛 SingleSource Services Corp 800-713-3412	•		•	•	•

DT	CV	CR	PR	BUNCOMBE (EST)	UC	RE	TX	VS	VR
•	•	•		🏛 Alpha Research LLC (SOP) 205-755-7008			•		
•	•	•		Greet America Public Record Svc Inc 214-320-9836					
•	•	•	•	🏛 NC Search Inc 910-273-4999	•	•	•		
•	•	•	•	🏛 SingleSource Services Corp 800-713-3412	•		•	•	•
•	•	•	•	Watson, Kathi 704-648-5830	•	•	•	•	

	CV	CR	PR	BURKE (EST)	UC	RE	TX	VS	VR
	•	•		🏛 Alpha Research LLC (SOP) 205-755-7008			•		
	•	•	•	🏛 Donna's Unlimited Searches 704-256-1418	•	•	•	•	
	•	•		Greet America Public Record Svc Inc 214-320-9836					
	•	•	•	🏛 NC Search Inc 910-273-4999	•	•	•		
	•	•	•	🏛 SingleSource Services Corp 800-713-3412	•		•	•	•

	CV	CR	PR	CABARRUS (EST)	UC	RE	TX	VS	VR
	•	•		🏛 Alpha Research LLC (SOP) 205-755-7008			•		
	•	•	•	🏛 Asset Protection Associates Inc (SOP) 704-523-1651	•	•	•	•	•
	•	•		Greet America Public Record Svc Inc 214-320-9836					
	•	•		Haislip, Lisa 704-553-0974			•		
	•	•	•	🏛 NC Search Inc 910-273-4999	•	•	•		
	•	•	•	Professional Service of Process Inc (SOP) 704-532-6322	•	•	•	•	
	•	•	•	Sherrill, Victoria 704-938-9529	•	•	•		
	•	•	•	🏛 SingleSource Services Corp 800-713-3412	•		•	•	•

	CV	CR	PR	CALDWELL (EST)	UC	RE	TX	VS	VR
	•	•		🏛 Alpha Research LLC (SOP) 205-755-7008			•		
	•	•	•	🏛 Donna's Unlimited Searches 704-256-1418	•	•	•	•	
	•	•		Greet America Public Record Svc Inc 214-320-9836					
	•	•	•	🏛 NC Search Inc 910-273-4999	•	•	•		
	•	•	•	🏛 National Data Access Corp 800-390-2959	•	•	•	•	•
	•	•	•	🏛 SingleSource Services Corp 800-713-3412	•		•	•	•

	CV	CR	PR	CAMDEN (EST)	UC	RE	TX	VS	VR
	•	•		🏛 Alpha Research LLC (SOP) 205-755-7008			•		
	•	•		Greet America Public Record Svc Inc 214-320-9836					
	•	•	•	Hornthal Riley Ellis & Maland 919-335-0871	•	•	•	•	
	•	•	•	🏛 NC Search Inc 910-273-4999	•	•	•		
	•	•	•	🏛 National Data Access Corp 800-390-2959	•	•	•		•
	•	•	•	🏛 SingleSource Services Corp 800-713-3412	•		•	•	•

	CV	CR	PR	CARTERET (EST)	UC	RE	TX	VS	VR
	•	•		🏛 Alpha Research LLC (SOP) 205-755-7008			•		
	•	•		Greet America Public Record Svc Inc 214-320-9836					
	•	•	•	🏛 NC Search Inc 910-273-4999	•	•	•		
	•	•	•	🏛 National Data Access Corp 800-390-2959	•	•	•	•	•
	•	•	•	🏛 SingleSource Services Corp 800-713-3412	•		•	•	•

	CV	CR	PR	CASWELL (EST)	UC	RE	TX	VS	VR
	•	•		🏛 Alpha Research LLC (SOP) 205-755-7008			•		
	•	•		Greet America Public Record Svc Inc 214-320-9836					
	•	•	•	🏛 NC Search Inc 910-273-4999	•	•	•		
	•	•	•	🏛 SingleSource Services Corp 800-713-3412	•		•	•	•

CV	CR	PR			UC	RE	TX	VS	VR
•	•	•	Williams, Nancy 910-584-0450		•	•	•	•	

CV	CR	PR	CATAWBA (EST)		UC	RE	TX	VS	VR
•	•		Alpha Research LLC (SOP).................... 205-755-7008				•		
•	•	•	Donna's Unlimited Searches 704-256-1418		•	•	•	•	
•	•		Greet America Public Record Svc Inc 214-320-9836						
•	•		Haislip, Lisa 704-553-0974				•		
•	•	•	NC Search Inc 910-273-4999		•	•	•		
•	•	•	SingleSource Services Corp 800-713-3412		•		•	•	•

CV	CR	PR	CHATHAM (EST)		UC	RE	TX	VS	VR
•	•		Alpha Research LLC (SOP).................... 205-755-7008				•		
•	•		Eastern North Carolina Invest & Process (SOP).................... 919-772-3346				•	•	
•	•		Greet America Public Record Svc Inc 214-320-9836						
•	•	•	NC Search Inc 910-273-4999		•	•	•		
•	•	•	Paralegal Services of North Carolina Inc (SOP).................... 919-821-7762		•	•	•	•	
•	•	•	SingleSource Services Corp 800-713-3412		•		•	•	•

CV	CR	PR	CHEROKEE (EST)		UC	RE	TX	VS	VR
•	•		Alpha Research LLC (SOP).................... 205-755-7008				•		
•	•		Greet America Public Record Svc Inc 214-320-9836						
•	•	•	Lamancha Search Inc 704-837-7580		•	•	•	•	
•	•	•	NC Search Inc 910-273-4999		•	•	•		
•	•	•	SingleSource Services Corp 800-713-3412		•		•	•	•

CV	CR	PR	CHOWAN (EST)		UC	RE	TX	VS	VR
•	•		Alpha Research LLC (SOP).................... 205-755-7008				•		
•	•		Greet America Public Record Svc Inc 214-320-9836						
•	•	•	Hornthal Riley Ellis & Maland 919-335-0871		•	•	•	•	
•	•	•	NC Search Inc 910-273-4999		•	•	•		
•	•	•	National Data Access Corp 800-390-2959		•	•	•	•	•
•	•	•	SingleSource Services Corp 800-713-3412		•		•	•	•

CV	CR	PR	CLAY (EST)		UC	RE	TX	VS	VR
•	•		Alpha Research LLC (SOP).................... 205-755-7008				•		
•	•		Greet America Public Record Svc Inc 214-320-9836						
•	•	•	NC Search Inc 910-273-4999		•	•	•		
•	•	•	SingleSource Services Corp 800-713-3412		•		•	•	•

CV	CR	PR	CLEVELAND (EST)		UC	RE	TX	VS	VR
•	•	•	A-1 Hanline Investigations (SOP) 803-684-3200		•	•	•	•	•
•	•		Alpha Research LLC (SOP).................... 205-755-7008				•		
•	•		Greet America Public Record Svc Inc 214-320-9836						
•	•	•	NC Search Inc 910-273-4999		•	•	•		
•	•	•	Professional Service of Process Inc (SOP) 704-532-6322		•	•	•	•	
•	•	•	SingleSource Services Corp 800-713-3412		•		•	•	•

CV	CR	PR	COLUMBUS (EST)		UC	RE	TX	VS	VR
•	•		Alpha Research LLC (SOP).................... 205-755-7008				•		
•	•		Eastern North Carolina Invest & Process (SOP).................... 919-772-3346				•	•	
•	•		Greet America Public Record Svc Inc 214-320-9836						
•	•	•	NC Search Inc 910-273-4999		•	•	•		
•	•	•	National Data Access Corp 800-390-2959		•	•	•	•	•
•	•	•	SingleSource Services Corp 800-713-3412		•		•	•	•

CV	CR	PR	CRAVEN (EST)		UC	RE	TX	VS	VR
•	•		Alpha Research LLC (SOP).................... 205-755-7008				•		
•	•		Eastern North Carolina Invest & Process (SOP).................... 919-772-3346				•	•	
•	•		Greet America Public Record Svc Inc 214-320-9836						
•			Hamm, Sue P 919-322-5015		•	•	•		
•	•	•	NC Search Inc 910-273-4999		•	•	•		
•	•	•	National Data Access Corp 800-390-2959		•	•	•	•	•
•	•	•	SingleSource Services Corp 800-713-3412		•		•	•	•

•		Smith, Cheryl 919-633-3890	•	•	•

CV	CR	PR	CUMBERLAND (EST)	UC	RE	TX	VS	VR
•	•		🏛 Alpha Research LLC (SOP)............................205-755-7008			•		
•	•		Eastern North Carolina Invest & Process (SOP)...............919-772-3346			•	•	
•	•		Greet America Public Record Svc Inc 214-320-9836					
•	•	•	🏛 NC Search Inc 910-273-4999	•	•	•		
•		•	Paralegal Services of North Carolina Inc (SOP)..................919-821-7762	•	•	•		
•	•	•	🏛 Paraprofessional Abstracts 800-522-5163	•	•	•		
•	•	•	🏛 SingleSource Services Corp 800-713-3412	•		•	•	•

CV	CR	PR	CURRITUCK (EST)	UC	RE	TX	VS	VR
•	•		🏛 Alpha Research LLC (SOP)............................205-755-7008			•		
•	•	•	Coastal Investigative Services Inc (SOP)...........919-355-0122	•	•	•	•	
•	•		Greet America Public Record Svc Inc 214-320-9836					
•	•	•	🏛 NC Search Inc 910-273-4999	•	•	•		
•	•	•	🏛 National Data Access Corp 800-390-2959	•	•	•	•	•
•	•	•	🏛 SingleSource Services Corp 800-713-3412	•		•	•	•

CV	CR	PR	DARE (EST)	UC	RE	TX	VS	VR
•	•		🏛 Alpha Research LLC (SOP)............................205-755-7008			•		
•	•		Greet America Public Record Svc Inc 214-320-9836					
•	•	•	Hornthal Riley Ellis & Maland 919-335-0871	•	•	•	•	
•	•	•	🏛 NC Search Inc 910-273-4999	•	•	•		
•	•	•	🏛 National Data Access Corp 800-390-2959	•	•	•	•	•
•	•	•	🏛 SingleSource Services Corp 800-713-3412	•		•	•	•

CV	CR	PR	DAVIDSON (EST)	UC	RE	TX	VS	VR
•	•	•	Agency-One Investigations (SOP)....................800-468-7393	•	•	•		
•	•		🏛 Alpha Research LLC (SOP)............................205-755-7008			•		
•	•		Greet America Public Record Svc Inc 214-320-9836					
•	•	•	🏛 NC Search Inc 910-273-4999	•	•	•		
•	•	•	Professional Service of Process Inc (SOP) 704-532-6322	•	•	•	•	
•		•	Sherrill, Victoria 704-938-9529	•	•	•		
•	•	•	🏛 SingleSource Services Corp 800-713-3412	•		•	•	•

CV	CR	PR	DAVIE (EST)	UC	RE	TX	VS	VR
•	•		🏛 Alpha Research LLC (SOP)............................205-755-7008			•		
•	•		Greet America Public Record Svc Inc 214-320-9836					
•	•	•	🏛 NC Search Inc 910-273-4999	•	•	•		
•	•	•	🏛 SingleSource Services Corp 800-713-3412	•		•	•	•

CV	CR	PR	DUPLIN (EST)	UC	RE	TX	VS	VR
•	•		🏛 Alpha Research LLC (SOP)............................205-755-7008			•		
•	•		Eastern North Carolina Invest & Process (SOP).................919-772-3346			•	•	
•	•		Greet America Public Record Svc Inc 214-320-9836					
•	•	•	🏛 NC Search Inc 910-273-4999	•	•	•		
•	•	•	🏛 National Data Access Corp 800-390-2959	•	•	•	•	•
•	•	•	🏛 SingleSource Services Corp 800-713-3412	•		•	•	•

CV	CR	PR	DURHAM (EST)	UC	RE	TX	VS	VR
•	•		🏛 Alpha Research LLC (SOP)............................205-755-7008			•		
•	•		Eastern North Carolina Invest & Process (SOP).................919-772-3346			•	•	
•	•		Greet America Public Record Svc Inc 214-320-9836					
•	•	•	🏛 Lee Denney Private Investigations (SOP)........919-847-3344	•	•	•	•	•
•	•	•	🏛 NC Search Inc 910-273-4999	•	•	•		
•	•	•	🏛 National Data Access Corp 800-390-2959	•	•	•	•	•
•		•	Paralegal Services of North Carolina Inc (SOP)..................919-821-7762	•	•	•		
•	•	•	🏛 SingleSource Services Corp 800-713-3412	•		•	•	•

CV	CR	PR	EDGECOMBE (EST)	UC	RE	TX	VS	VR
•	•		🏛 Alpha Research LLC (SOP)............................205-755-7008			•		
•	•	•	Coastal Investigative Services Inc (SOP)...........919-355-0122	•	•	•	•	

BK	CV	CR	PR		UC	RE	TX	VS	VR
•	•			Eastern North Carolina Invest & Process (SOP).................919-772-3346				•	•
•	•			Greet America Public Record Svc Inc 214-320-9836					
•	•	•		🏛 NC Search Inc 910-273-4999	•	•	•		
•	•	•		🏛 SingleSource Services Corp 800-713-3412	•		•	•	•

BK	CV	CR	PR	FORSYTH (EST)	UC	RE	TX	VS	VR
•	•	•	•	Agency-One Investigations (SOP)......................................800-468-7393	•	•	•		
•	•	•		🏛 Alpha Research LLC (SOP)..205-755-7008			•		
•	•	•		Greet America Public Record Svc Inc 214-320-9836					
•	•	•	•	🏛 NC Search Inc 910-273-4999	•	•	•		
•	•	•	•	🏛 SingleSource Services Corp 800-713-3412	•		•	•	•
•	•	•	•	🏛 Turning Wheels Inc 910-621-9064	•	•	•	•	

CV	CR	PR	FRANKLIN (EST)	UC	RE	TX	VS	VR
•	•		🏛 Alpha Research LLC (SOP)..205-755-7008			•		
•	•		Eastern North Carolina Invest & Process (SOP).................919-772-3346				•	•
•	•		Greet America Public Record Svc Inc 214-320-9836					
•	•	•	🏛 NC Search Inc 910-273-4999	•	•	•		
•	•	•	🏛 National Data Access Corp 800-390-2959	•	•	•	•	
•	•	•	Paralegal Services of North Carolina Inc (SOP).................919-821-7762	•	•	•	•	
•	•	•	🏛 SingleSource Services Corp 800-713-3412	•		•	•	•

CV	CR	PR	GASTON (EST)	UC	RE	TX	VS	VR
•	•	•	A-1 Hanline Investigations (SOP) 803-684-3200	•	•	•	•	•
•	•		🏛 Alpha Research LLC (SOP)..205-755-7008			•		
•	•	•	🏛 Asset Protection Associates Inc (SOP) 704-523-1651	•	•	•	•	•
•	•	•	🏛 Barefoot Private Investigations (SOP)............................704-377-1000	•	•	•		•
•	•	•	Fewell Private Investigations (SOP)...................................803-327-7378	•	•	•	•	•
•	•		Greet America Public Record Svc Inc 214-320-9836					
•	•		Haislip, Lisa 704-553-0974			•		
•	•	•	🏛 NC Search Inc 910-273-4999	•	•	•		
•	•	•	Professional Service of Process Inc (SOP) 704-532-6322	•	•	•	•	
•	•	•	🏛 SingleSource Services Corp 800-713-3412	•		•	•	•

CV	CR	PR	GATES (EST)	UC	RE	TX	VS	VR
•	•		🏛 Alpha Research LLC (SOP)..205-755-7008			•		
•	•		Greet America Public Record Svc Inc 214-320-9836					
•	•	•	Hornthal Riley Ellis & Maland 919-335-0871	•	•	•	•	
•	•	•	🏛 NC Search Inc 910-273-4999	•	•	•		
•	•	•	🏛 National Data Access Corp 800-390-2959	•	•	•	•	
•	•	•	🏛 SingleSource Services Corp 800-713-3412	•		•	•	•

CV	CR	PR	GRAHAM (EST)	UC	RE	TX	VS	VR
•	•		🏛 Alpha Research LLC (SOP)..205-755-7008			•		
•	•		Greet America Public Record Svc Inc 214-320-9836					
•	•	•	🏛 NC Search Inc 910-273-4999	•	•	•		

CV	CR	PR	GRANVILLE (EST)	UC	RE	TX	VS	VR
•	•		🏛 Alpha Research LLC (SOP)..205-755-7008			•		
•	•		Eastern North Carolina Invest & Process (SOP).................919-772-3346				•	•
•	•		Greet America Public Record Svc Inc 214-320-9836					
•	•	•	🏛 NC Search Inc 910-273-4999	•	•	•		
•	•	•	🏛 National Data Access Corp 800-390-2959	•	•	•	•	
•	•	•	🏛 SingleSource Services Corp 800-713-3412	•		•	•	•

CV	CR	PR	GREENE (EST)	UC	RE	TX	VS	VR
•	•		🏛 Alpha Research LLC (SOP)..205-755-7008			•		
•	•		Greet America Public Record Svc Inc 214-320-9836					
•	•	•	🏛 NC Search Inc 910-273-4999	•	•	•		
•	•	•	🏛 National Data Access Corp 800-390-2959	•	•	•	•	•
•	•	•	Paralegal Enterprises Inc 919-758-6622	•	•	•	•	
•	•	•	🏛 SingleSource Services Corp 800-713-3412	•		•	•	•

GUILFORD (EST)

DT	BK	CV	CR	PR	Company	Phone	UC	RE	TX	VS	VR
•	•	•	•	•	Agency-One Investigations (SOP)	800-468-7393	•	•	•		
•	•	•	•		Alpha Research LLC (SOP)	205-755-7008			•		
•	•	•	•		Greet America Public Record Svc Inc	214-320-9836					
•	•	•	•	•	NC Search Inc	910-273-4999	•	•	•		
•	•	•	•	•	SingleSource Services Corp	800-713-3412	•		•	•	•
•	•	•	•	•	Turning Wheels Inc	910-621-9064	•	•	•	•	
		•	•	•	Williams, Nancy	910-584-0450	•	•	•	•	

HALIFAX (EST)

CV	CR	PR	Company	Phone	UC	RE	TX	VS	VR
•	•		Alpha Research LLC (SOP)	205-755-7008			•		
•	•		Eastern North Carolina Invest & Process (SOP)	919-772-3346			•	•	
•	•		Greet America Public Record Svc Inc	214-320-9836					
•	•	•	NC Search Inc	910-273-4999	•	•	•		
•	•	•	National Data Access Corp	800-390-2959	•	•	•	•	•
•	•	•	SingleSource Services Corp	800-713-3412	•		•	•	•

HARNETT (EST)

CV	CR	PR	Company	Phone	UC	RE	TX	VS	VR
•	•		Alpha Research LLC (SOP)	205-755-7008			•		
•	•		Eastern North Carolina Invest & Process (SOP)	919-772-3346			•	•	
•	•		Greet America Public Record Svc Inc	214-320-9836					
•	•	•	NC Search Inc	910-273-4999	•	•	•		
•	•	•	National Data Access Corp	800-390-2959	•	•	•		•
•	•		Paralegal Services of North Carolina Inc (SOP)	919-821-7762	•	•	•	•	
•	•	•	Paraprofessional Abstracts	800-522-5163	•	•	•		
•	•	•	SingleSource Services Corp	800-713-3412	•		•	•	•

HAYWOOD (EST)

CV	CR	PR	Company	Phone	UC	RE	TX	VS	VR
•	•		Alpha Research LLC (SOP)	205-755-7008			•		
•	•		Greet America Public Record Svc Inc	214-320-9836					
•	•	•	NC Search Inc	910-273-4999	•	•	•		
•	•	•	SingleSource Services Corp	800-713-3412	•		•	•	•
•		•	Watson, Kathi	704-648-5830	•	•	•	•	•

HENDERSON (EST)

CV	CR	PR	Company	Phone	UC	RE	TX	VS	VR
•	•		Alpha Research LLC (SOP)	205-755-7008			•		
•	•		Greet America Public Record Svc Inc	214-320-9836					
•	•	•	NC Search Inc	910-273-4999	•	•	•		
•	•	•	SingleSource Services Corp	800-713-3412	•		•	•	•

HERTFORD (EST)

CV	CR	PR	Company	Phone	UC	RE	TX	VS	VR
•	•		Alpha Research LLC (SOP)	205-755-7008			•		
•	•		Greet America Public Record Svc Inc	214-320-9836					
•	•	•	Hornthal Riley Ellis & Maland	919-335-0871	•	•	•	•	
•	•	•	NC Search Inc	910-273-4999	•	•	•		
•	•	•	National Data Access Corp	800-390-2959	•	•	•	•	•
•	•	•	SingleSource Services Corp	800-713-3412	•		•	•	•

HOKE (EST)

CV	CR	PR	Company	Phone	UC	RE	TX	VS	VR
•	•		Alpha Research LLC (SOP)	205-755-7008			•		
•	•		Eastern North Carolina Invest & Process (SOP)	919-772-3346			•	•	
•	•		Greet America Public Record Svc Inc	214-320-9836					
•	•	•	NC Search Inc	910-273-4999	•	•	•		
•	•	•	National Data Access Corp	800-390-2959	•	•	•	•	•
•	•	•	Paraprofessional Abstracts	800-522-5163	•	•	•		
•	•	•	SingleSource Services Corp	800-713-3412	•		•	•	•

HYDE (EST)

CV	CR	PR	Company	Phone	UC	RE	TX	VS	VR
•	•		Alpha Research LLC (SOP)	205-755-7008			•		
•	•		Greet America Public Record Svc Inc	214-320-9836					
•	•	•	NC Search Inc	910-273-4999	•	•	•		
•	•	•	SingleSource Services Corp	800-713-3412	•		•	•	•

DT	CV	CR	PR	IREDELL (EST)	UC	RE	TX	VS	VR
•	•	•		🏛 Alpha Research LLC (SOP) 205-755-7008			•		
•	•	•		Greet America Public Record Svc Inc 214-320-9836					
•	•	•	•	🏛 NC Search Inc 910-273-4999	•	•	•		
•	•	•	•	Professional Service of Process Inc (SOP) 704-532-6322	•	•	•	•	
		•	•	Sherrill, Victoria 704-938-9529	•	•	•		
•	•	•	•	🏛 SingleSource Services Corp 800-713-3412	•		•	•	•

	CV	CR	PR	JACKSON (EST)	UC	RE	TX	VS	VR
	•	•		🏛 Alpha Research LLC (SOP) 205-755-7008			•		
	•	•		Greet America Public Record Svc Inc 214-320-9836					
	•	•	•	🏛 NC Search Inc 910-273-4999	•	•	•		
	•	•	•	🏛 SingleSource Services Corp 800-713-3412	•		•	•	•
	•		•	Watson, Kathi 704-648-5830	•	•	•	•	

	CV	CR	PR	JOHNSTON (EST)	UC	RE	TX	VS	VR
	•	•		🏛 Alpha Research LLC (SOP) 205-755-7008			•		
	•	•		Eastern North Carolina Invest & Process (SOP) 919-772-3346			•	•	
	•	•		Greet America Public Record Svc Inc 214-320-9836					
	•	•	•	🏛 NC Search Inc 910-273-4999	•	•	•		
	•	•	•	🏛 National Data Access Corp 800-390-2959	•	•	•		•
	•		•	Paralegal Services of North Carolina Inc (SOP) 919-821-7762	•	•	•	•	
	•	•	•	🏛 SingleSource Services Corp 800-713-3412	•		•	•	•

	CV	CR	PR	JONES (EST)	UC	RE	TX	VS	VR
	•	•		🏛 Alpha Research LLC (SOP) 205-755-7008			•		
	•	•		Eastern North Carolina Invest & Process (SOP) 919-772-3346			•	•	
	•	•		Greet America Public Record Svc Inc 214-320-9836					
	•			Hamm, Sue P 919-322-5015	•	•	•		
	•	•	•	🏛 NC Search Inc 910-273-4999	•	•	•		
	•	•	•	🏛 National Data Access Corp 800-390-2959	•	•	•		•
	•	•	•	🏛 SingleSource Services Corp 800-713-3412	•		•	•	•
	•			Smith, Cheryl 919-633-3890	•	•	•		

	CV	CR	PR	LEE (EST)	UC	RE	TX	VS	VR
	•	•		🏛 Alpha Research LLC (SOP) 205-755-7008			•		
	•	•		Eastern North Carolina Invest & Process (SOP) 919-772-3346			•	•	
	•	•		Greet America Public Record Svc Inc 214-320-9836					
	•	•	•	🏛 NC Search Inc 910-273-4999	•	•	•		
	•	•	•	🏛 National Data Access Corp 800-390-2959	•	•	•	•	•
	•	•	•	🏛 SingleSource Services Corp 800-713-3412	•		•	•	•

	CV	CR	PR	LENOIR (EST)	UC	RE	TX	VS	VR
	•	•		🏛 Alpha Research LLC (SOP) 205-755-7008			•		
	•	•	•	Coastal Investigative Services Inc (SOP) 919-355-0122	•	•	•	•	
	•	•		Eastern North Carolina Invest & Process (SOP) 919-772-3346			•	•	
	•	•		Greet America Public Record Svc Inc 214-320-9836					
	•			Hamm, Sue P 919-322-5015	•	•	•		
	•	•	•	🏛 NC Search Inc 910-273-4999	•	•	•		
	•	•	•	🏛 National Data Access Corp 800-390-2959	•	•	•	•	•
	•	•	•	🏛 SingleSource Services Corp 800-713-3412	•		•	•	•

	CV	CR	PR	LINCOLN (EST)	UC	RE	TX	VS	VR
	•	•		🏛 Alpha Research LLC (SOP) 205-755-7008			•		
	•	•		Greet America Public Record Svc Inc 214-320-9836					
	•	•	•	🏛 NC Search Inc 910-273-4999	•	•	•		
	•	•	•	Professional Service of Process Inc (SOP) 704-532-6322	•	•	•	•	
	•	•	•	🏛 SingleSource Services Corp 800-713-3412	•		•	•	•

	CV	CR	PR	MACON (EST)	UC	RE	TX	VS	VR
	•	•		🏛 Alpha Research LLC (SOP) 205-755-7008			•		
	•	•		Greet America Public Record Svc Inc 214-320-9836					

CV	CR	PR	Provider	Phone	UC	RE	TX	VS	VR
•	•	•	🏛 NC Search Inc	910-273-4999	•	•	•		
•		•	Watson, Kathi	704-648-5830	•	•	•	•	

MADISON (EST)

CV	CR	PR	Provider	Phone	UC	RE	TX	VS	VR
•	•		🏛 Alpha Research LLC (SOP)	205-755-7008			•		
•	•		Greet America Public Record Svc Inc	214-320-9836					
•	•	•	🏛 NC Search Inc	910-273-4999	•	•	•		
•	•	•	🏛 SingleSource Services Corp	800-713-3412	•		•	•	•
•	•		Watson, Kathi	704-648-5830	•	•	•	•	

MARTIN (EST)

CV	CR	PR	Provider	Phone	UC	RE	TX	VS	VR
•	•		🏛 Alpha Research LLC (SOP)	205-755-7008			•		
•	•		Eastern North Carolina Invest & Process (SOP)	919-772-3346			•	•	
•	•		Greet America Public Record Svc Inc	214-320-9836					
•	•	•	🏛 NC Search Inc	910-273-4999	•	•	•		
•	•	•	🏛 SingleSource Services Corp	800-713-3412	•		•	•	•

McDOWELL (EST)

CV	CR	PR	Provider	Phone	UC	RE	TX	VS	VR
•	•		🏛 Alpha Research LLC (SOP)	205-755-7008			•		
•	•		Greet America Public Record Svc Inc	214-320-9836					
•	•	•	🏛 NC Search Inc	910-273-4999	•	•	•		
•	•	•	🏛 SingleSource Services Corp	800-713-3412	•		•	•	•

MECKLENBURG (EST)

DT	BK	CV	CR	PR	Provider	Phone	UC	RE	TX	VS	VR
•	•	•	•	•	A-1 Hanline Investigations (SOP)	803-684-3200	•	•	•	•	•
•	•	•	•		🏛 Alpha Research LLC (SOP)	205-755-7008			•		
•	•	•	•	•	🏛 Asset Protection Associates Inc (SOP)	704-523-1651	•	•	•	•	•
•	•	•	•	•	🏛 Barefoot Private Investigations (SOP)	704-377-1000	•	•	•	•	•
•	•	•	•	•	Fewell Private Investigations (SOP)	803-327-7378	•	•	•	•	•
•	•	•	•		Greet America Public Record Svc Inc	214-320-9836					
	•	•	•		Haislip, Lisa	704-553-0974			•		
•	•	•	•	•	🏛 NC Search Inc	910-273-4999	•	•	•		
•	•	•	•	•	Professional Service of Process Inc (SOP)	704-532-6322	•	•	•		
•	•	•	•	•	🏛 SingleSource Services Corp	800-713-3412	•		•	•	•

MITCHELL (EST)

CV	CR	PR	Provider	Phone	UC	RE	TX	VS	VR
•	•		🏛 Alpha Research LLC (SOP)	205-755-7008			•		
•	•		Greet America Public Record Svc Inc	214-320-9836					
•	•	•	🏛 NC Search Inc	910-273-4999	•	•	•		
•	•	•	🏛 SingleSource Services Corp	800-713-3412	•		•	•	•

MONTGOMERY (EST)

CV	CR	PR	Provider	Phone	UC	RE	TX	VS	VR
•	•		🏛 Alpha Research LLC (SOP)	205-755-7008			•		
•	•		Greet America Public Record Svc Inc	214-320-9836					
•	•	•	🏛 NC Search Inc	910-273-4999	•	•	•		
•	•	•	🏛 National Data Access Corp	800-390-2959	•	•	•	•	•
•	•	•	🏛 SingleSource Services Corp	800-713-3412	•		•	•	•

MOORE (EST)

CV	CR	PR	Provider	Phone	UC	RE	TX	VS	VR
•	•		🏛 Alpha Research LLC (SOP)	205-755-7008			•		
•	•		Eastern North Carolina Invest & Process (SOP)	919-772-3346			•	•	
•	•		Greet America Public Record Svc Inc	214-320-9836					
•	•	•	🏛 NC Search Inc	910-273-4999	•	•	•		
•	•	•	🏛 National Data Access Corp	800-390-2959	•	•	•	•	•
•	•	•	🏛 SingleSource Services Corp	800-713-3412	•		•	•	•

NASH (EST)

CV	CR	PR	Provider	Phone	UC	RE	TX	VS	VR
•	•		🏛 Alpha Research LLC (SOP)	205-755-7008			•		
•	•		Eastern North Carolina Invest & Process (SOP)	919-772-3346			•	•	
•	•		Greet America Public Record Svc Inc	214-320-9836					
•	•	•	🏛 NC Search Inc	910-273-4999	•	•	•		
•	•	•	🏛 National Data Access Corp	800-390-2959	•	•	•	•	•
•	•	•	🏛 SingleSource Services Corp	800-713-3412	•		•	•	•

DT	CV	CR	PR	NEW HANOVER (EST)	UC	RE	TX	VS	VR
•	•	•		🗑 Alpha Research LLC (SOP)..................................205-755-7008			•		
•	•	•		Eastern North Carolina Invest & Process (SOP).................919-772-3346			•	•	
•	•	•		Greet America Public Record Svc Inc 214-320-9836					
•	•	•	•	🗑 NC Search Inc 910-273-4999	•	•	•		
•	•	•	•	🗑 National Data Access Corp 800-390-2959	•	•	•	•	•
•	•	•	•	🗑 SingleSource Services Corp 800-713-3412	•		•	•	•

	CV	CR	PR	NORTHAMPTON (EST)	UC	RE	TX	VS	VR
	•	•		🗑 Alpha Research LLC (SOP)..................................205-755-7008			•		
	•	•		Eastern North Carolina Invest & Process (SOP).................919-772-3346			•	•	
	•	•		Greet America Public Record Svc Inc 214-320-9836					
	•	•	•	🗑 NC Search Inc 910-273-4999	•	•	•		
	•	•	•	🗑 National Data Access Corp 800-390-2959	•	•	•	•	•
	•	•	•	🗑 SingleSource Services Corp 800-713-3412	•		•	•	•

	CV	CR	PR	ONSLOW (EST)	UC	RE	TX	VS	VR
	•	•		🗑 Alpha Research LLC (SOP)..................................205-755-7008			•		
	•	•	•	Coastal Investigative Services Inc (SOP).......................919-355-0122	•	•	•		
	•	•		Eastern North Carolina Invest & Process (SOP).................919-772-3346			•	•	
	•	•		Greet America Public Record Svc Inc 214-320-9836					
	•	•	•	🗑 NC Search Inc 910-273-4999	•	•	•		
	•	•	•	🗑 National Data Access Corp 800-390-2959	•	•	•		•
	•	•	•	🗑 SingleSource Services Corp 800-713-3412	•	•	•	•	•
	•	•		🗑 Tarheel Paralegal Services 910-455-3178	•	•	•	•	•

	CV	CR	PR	ORANGE (EST)	UC	RE	TX	VS	VR
	•	•		🗑 Alpha Research LLC (SOP)..................................205-755-7008			•		
	•	•		Eastern North Carolina Invest & Process (SOP).................919-772-3346			•	•	
	•	•		Greet America Public Record Svc Inc 214-320-9836					
	•	•	•	🗑 NC Search Inc 910-273-4999	•	•	•		
	•	•	•	🗑 National Data Access Corp 800-390-2959	•	•	•		•
	•	•	•	Paralegal Services of North Carolina Inc (SOP)...............919-821-7762	•	•	•	•	
	•	•	•	🗑 SingleSource Services Corp 800-713-3412	•		•	•	•

	CV	CR	PR	PAMLICO (EST)	UC	RE	TX	VS	VR
	•	•		🗑 Alpha Research LLC (SOP)..................................205-755-7008			•		
	•	•		Greet America Public Record Svc Inc 214-320-9836					
	•			Hamm, Sue P 919-322-5015	•	•	•		
	•	•	•	🗑 NC Search Inc 910-273-4999	•	•	•		
	•	•	•	🗑 SingleSource Services Corp 800-713-3412	•	•	•	•	•
	•			Smith, Cheryl 919-633-3890	•	•	•		

	CV	CR	PR	PASQUOTANK (EST)	UC	RE	TX	VS	VR
	•	•		🗑 Alpha Research LLC (SOP)..................................205-755-7008			•		
	•	•		Greet America Public Record Svc Inc 214-320-9836					
	•	•	•	Hornthal Riley Ellis & Maland 919-335-0871	•	•	•	•	
	•	•	•	🗑 NC Search Inc 910-273-4999	•	•	•		
	•	•	•	🗑 National Data Access Corp 800-390-2959	•	•	•	•	
	•	•	•	🗑 SingleSource Services Corp 800-713-3412	•		•	•	•

	CV	CR	PR	PENDER (EST)	UC	RE	TX	VS	VR
	•	•		🗑 Alpha Research LLC (SOP)..................................205-755-7008			•		
	•	•		Eastern North Carolina Invest & Process (SOP).................919-772-3346			•	•	
	•	•		Greet America Public Record Svc Inc 214-320-9836					
	•	•	•	🗑 NC Search Inc 910-273-4999	•	•	•		
	•	•	•	🗑 National Data Access Corp 800-390-2959	•	•	•	•	•
	•	•	•	🗑 SingleSource Services Corp 800-713-3412	•		•	•	•

	CV	CR	PR	PERQUIMANS (EST)	UC	RE	TX	VS	VR
	•	•		🗑 Alpha Research LLC (SOP)..................................205-755-7008			•		
	•	•		Greet America Public Record Svc Inc 214-320-9836					

•	•	•	Hornthal Riley Ellis & Maland 919-335-0871	•	•	•	•	
•	•	•	🏛 NC Search Inc 910-273-4999	•	•	•		
•	•	•	🏛 National Data Access Corp 800-390-2959	•	•		•	•
•	•	•	🏛 SingleSource Services Corp 800-713-3412	•		•	•	•

CV	CR	PR	PERSON (EST)	UC	RE	TX	VS	VR
•	•		🏛 Alpha Research LLC (SOP)............................ 205-755-7008			•		
•	•		Greet America Public Record Svc Inc 214-320-9836					
•	•	•	🏛 NC Search Inc 910-273-4999	•	•			
•	•	•	🏛 National Data Access Corp 800-390-2959	•	•		•	•
•	•	•	🏛 SingleSource Services Corp 800-713-3412	•		•	•	•

DT	CV	CR	PR	PITT (EST)	UC	RE	TX	VS	VR
•	•	•		🏛 Alpha Research LLC (SOP)............................ 205-755-7008			•		
	•	•	•	Coastal Investigative Services Inc (SOP)............ 919-355-0122	•	•		•	
•	•	•		Eastern North Carolina Invest & Process (SOP)........ 919-772-3346			•	•	
•	•	•		Greet America Public Record Svc Inc 214-320-9836					
	•			Hamm, Sue P 919-322-5015	•	•		•	
•	•	•	•	🏛 NC Search Inc 910-273-4999	•	•			
•	•	•	•	Paralegal Enterprises Inc 919-758-6622	•	•		•	
•	•	•	•	🏛 SingleSource Services Corp 800-713-3412	•		•	•	•

CV	CR	PR	POLK (EST)	UC	RE	TX	VS	VR
•	•		🏛 Alpha Research LLC (SOP)............................ 205-755-7008			•		
•	•		Greet America Public Record Svc Inc 214-320-9836					
•	•	•	🏛 NC Search Inc 910-273-4999	•	•	•		
•	•	•	🏛 SingleSource Services Corp 800-713-3412	•		•	•	•

CV	CR	PR	RANDOLPH (EST)	UC	RE	TX	VS	VR
•	•		🏛 Alpha Research LLC (SOP)............................ 205-755-7008			•		
•	•		Eastern North Carolina Invest & Process (SOP)........ 919-772-3346			•	•	
•	•		Greet America Public Record Svc Inc 214-320-9836					
•	•	•	🏛 NC Search Inc 910-273-4999	•	•	•		
•	•	•	🏛 SingleSource Services Corp 800-713-3412	•		•	•	•

CV	CR	PR	RICHMOND (EST)	UC	RE	TX	VS	VR
•	•		🏛 Alpha Research LLC (SOP)............................ 205-755-7008			•		
•	•		Greet America Public Record Svc Inc 214-320-9836					
•	•	•	🏛 NC Search Inc 910-273-4999	•	•	•		
•	•	•	🏛 National Data Access Corp 800-390-2959	•	•		•	•
•	•	•	🏛 SingleSource Services Corp 800-713-3412	•		•	•	•

CV	CR	PR	ROBESON (EST)	UC	RE	TX	VS	VR
•	•		🏛 Alpha Research LLC (SOP)............................ 205-755-7008			•		
•	•		Eastern North Carolina Invest & Process (SOP)........ 919-772-3346			•	•	
•	•		Greet America Public Record Svc Inc 214-320-9836					
•	•	•	🏛 NC Search Inc 910-273-4999	•	•	•		
•	•	•	🏛 Paraprofessional Abstracts 800-522-5163	•	•	•		
•	•	•	🏛 SingleSource Services Corp 800-713-3412	•		•	•	•

CV	CR	PR	ROCKINGHAM (EST)	UC	RE	TX	VS	VR
•	•		🏛 Alpha Research LLC (SOP)............................ 205-755-7008			•		
•	•		Greet America Public Record Svc Inc 214-320-9836					
•	•	•	🏛 NC Search Inc 910-273-4999	•	•	•		
•	•	•	🏛 SingleSource Services Corp 800-713-3412	•		•	•	•
•	•	•	Williams, Nancy 910-584-0450	•	•	•		

CV	CR	PR	ROWAN (EST)	UC	RE	TX	VS	VR
•	•		🏛 Alpha Research LLC (SOP)............................ 205-755-7008			•		
•	•		Greet America Public Record Svc Inc 214-320-9836					
•	•	•	🏛 NC Search Inc 910-273-4999	•	•	•		
•	•	•	Professional Service of Process Inc (SOP) 704-532-6322	•	•	•	•	
•		•	Sherrill, Victoria 704-938-9529	•	•	•		

CV	CR	PR			UC	RE	TX	VS	VR
•	•	•	🏛 SingleSource Services Corp 800-713-3412		•		•	•	•

CV	CR	PR	RUTHERFORD (EST)	UC	RE	TX	VS	VR
•	•	•	A-1 Hanline Investigations (SOP) 803-684-3200	•	•	•	•	•
•	•		🏛 Alpha Research LLC (SOP) 205-755-7008			•		
•	•		Greet America Public Record Svc Inc 214-320-9836					
•	•	•	🏛 NC Search Inc 910-273-4999	•	•	•		
•	•	•	🏛 SingleSource Services Corp 800-713-3412	•		•	•	•

CV	CR	PR	SAMPSON (EST)	UC	RE	TX	VS	VR
•	•		🏛 Alpha Research LLC (SOP) 205-755-7008			•		
•	•		Eastern North Carolina Invest & Process (SOP) 919-772-3346			•	•	
•	•		Greet America Public Record Svc Inc 214-320-9836					
•	•	•	🏛 NC Search Inc 910-273-4999	•	•	•		
•	•	•	🏛 National Data Access Corp 800-390-2959	•	•	•	•	•
•	•	•	🏛 Paraprofessional Abstracts 800-522-5163	•	•	•		
•	•	•	🏛 SingleSource Services Corp 800-713-3412	•		•	•	•

CV	CR	PR	SCOTLAND (EST)	UC	RE	TX	VS	VR
•	•		🏛 Alpha Research LLC (SOP) 205-755-7008			•		
•	•		Greet America Public Record Svc Inc 214-320-9836					
•	•	•	🏛 NC Search Inc 910-273-4999	•	•	•		
•	•	•	🏛 National Data Access Corp 800-390-2959	•	•	•	•	•
•	•	•	🏛 Paraprofessional Abstracts 800-522-5163	•	•	•		
•	•	•	🏛 SingleSource Services Corp 800-713-3412	•		•	•	•

CV	CR	PR	STANLY (EST)	UC	RE	TX	VS	VR
•	•		🏛 Alpha Research LLC (SOP) 205-755-7008			•		
•	•		Greet America Public Record Svc Inc 214-320-9836					
•	•	•	🏛 NC Search Inc 910-273-4999	•	•	•		
•	•	•	🏛 National Data Access Corp 800-390-2959	•	•	•	•	•
•	•	•	Professional Service of Process Inc (SOP) 704-532-6322	•	•	•		
•		•	Sherrill, Victoria 704-938-9529	•	•	•		
•	•	•	🏛 SingleSource Services Corp 800-713-3412	•		•	•	•

CV	CR	PR	STOKES (EST)	UC	RE	TX	VS	VR
•	•	•	Agency-One Investigations (SOP) 800-468-7393	•	•	•		
•	•		🏛 Alpha Research LLC (SOP) 205-755-7008			•		
•	•		Greet America Public Record Svc Inc 214-320-9836					
•	•	•	🏛 NC Search Inc 910-273-4999	•	•	•		
•	•	•	🏛 SingleSource Services Corp 800-713-3412	•		•	•	•

CV	CR	PR	SURRY (EST)	UC	RE	TX	VS	VR
•	•		🏛 Alpha Research LLC (SOP) 205-755-7008			•		
•	•		Greet America Public Record Svc Inc 214-320-9836					
•	•	•	🏛 NC Search Inc 910-273-4999	•	•	•		
•	•	•	🏛 SingleSource Services Corp 800-713-3412	•		•	•	•

CV	CR	PR	SWAIN (EST)	UC	RE	TX	VS	VR
•	•		🏛 Alpha Research LLC (SOP) 205-755-7008			•		
•	•		Greet America Public Record Svc Inc 214-320-9836					
•	•	•	🏛 NC Search Inc 910-273-4999	•	•	•		
•	•	•	🏛 SingleSource Services Corp 800-713-3412	•		•	•	•
•		•	Watson, Kathi 704-648-5830	•	•	•	•	

CV	CR	PR	TRANSYLVANIA (EST)	UC	RE	TX	VS	VR
•	•		🏛 Alpha Research LLC (SOP) 205-755-7008			•		
•	•		Greet America Public Record Svc Inc 214-320-9836					
•	•	•	🏛 NC Search Inc 910-273-4999	•	•	•		
•	•	•	🏛 SingleSource Services Corp 800-713-3412	•		•	•	•

CV	CR	PR	TYRRELL (EST)	UC	RE	TX	VS	VR
•	•		🏛 Alpha Research LLC (SOP) 205-755-7008			•		

					UC	RE	TX	VS	VR
			Greet America Public Record Svc Inc 214-320-9836						
		•	Hornthal Riley Ellis & Maland 919-335-0871	•	•	•	•		
		•	🏛 NC Search Inc 910-273-4999	•	•	•			
		•	🏛 National Data Access Corp 800-390-2959	•	•	•	•	•	
		•	🏛 SingleSource Services Corp 800-713-3412	•	•	•	•	•	

CV	CR	PR	UNION (EST)		UC	RE	TX	VS	VR
•	•	•	A-1 Hanline Investigations (SOP) 803-684-3200	•	•	•	•	•	
•	•		🏛 Alpha Research LLC (SOP)...................................... 205-755-7008			•			
•	•	•	🏛 Asset Protection Associates Inc (SOP) 704-523-1651	•	•	•	•	•	
•	•	•	Fewell Private Investigations (SOP) 803-327-7378	•	•	•	•	•	
•	•		Greet America Public Record Svc Inc 214-320-9836						
•	•		Haislip, Lisa 704-553-0974		•				
•	•	•	🏛 NC Search Inc 910-273-4999	•	•	•			
•	•	•	🏛 SingleSource Services Corp 800-713-3412	•		•	•	•	

CV	CR	PR	VANCE (EST)		UC	RE	TX	VS	VR
•	•		🏛 Alpha Research LLC (SOP)...................................... 205-755-7008			•			
•	•		Eastern North Carolina Invest & Process (SOP)............ 919-772-3346			•	•		
•	•		Greet America Public Record Svc Inc 214-320-9836						
•	•	•	🏛 NC Search Inc 910-273-4999	•	•	•			
•	•	•	🏛 National Data Access Corp 800-390-2959	•	•	•	•	•	
•	•	•	🏛 SingleSource Services Corp 800-713-3412	•		•	•	•	

DT	BK	CV	CR	PR	WAKE (CAPITAL) (EST)		UC	RE	TX	VS	VR
•	•	•	•		🏛 Alpha Research LLC (SOP)...................................... 205-755-7008				•		
•	•	•	•		Eastern North Carolina Invest & Process (SOP)............ 919-772-3346				•	•	
•	•	•	•		Greet America Public Record Svc Inc 214-320-9836						
•	•	•	•	•	🏛 Lee Denney Private Investigations (SOP).................. 919-847-3344		•	•	•	•	•
•	•	•	•	•	🏛 NC Search Inc 910-273-4999		•	•	•		
•	•	•	•	•	🏛 National Data Access Corp 800-390-2959		•	•	•	•	•
•	•	•		•	Paralegal Services of North Carolina Inc (SOP)............ 919-821-7762		•	•	•	•	
•	•	•	•	•	🏛 SingleSource Services Corp 800-713-3412		•		•	•	•

CV	CR	PR	WARREN (EST)		UC	RE	TX	VS	VR
•	•		🏛 Alpha Research LLC (SOP)...................................... 205-755-7008			•			
•	•		Eastern North Carolina Invest & Process (SOP)............ 919-772-3346			•	•		
•	•		Greet America Public Record Svc Inc 214-320-9836						
•	•	•	🏛 NC Search Inc 910-273-4999	•	•	•			
•	•	•	🏛 National Data Access Corp 800-390-2959	•	•	•	•	•	
•	•	•	🏛 SingleSource Services Corp 800-713-3412	•		•	•	•	

CV	CR	PR	WASHINGTON (EST)		UC	RE	TX	VS	VR
•	•		🏛 Alpha Research LLC (SOP)...................................... 205-755-7008			•			
•	•		Greet America Public Record Svc Inc 214-320-9836						
•	•	•	Hornthal Riley Ellis & Maland 919-335-0871	•	•	•	•		
•	•	•	🏛 NC Search Inc 910-273-4999	•	•	•			
•	•	•	🏛 SingleSource Services Corp 800-713-3412	•		•	•	•	

CV	CR	PR	WATAUGA (EST)		UC	RE	TX	VS	VR
•	•		🏛 Alpha Research LLC (SOP)...................................... 205-755-7008			•			
•	•		Greet America Public Record Svc Inc 214-320-9836						
•	•	•	Miller & Mosley 704-264-1125	•	•	•	•		
•	•	•	🏛 NC Search Inc 910-273-4999	•	•	•			
•	•	•	🏛 SingleSource Services Corp 800-713-3412	•		•	•	•	

CV	CR	PR	WAYNE (EST)		UC	RE	TX	VS	VR
•	•		🏛 Alpha Research LLC (SOP)...................................... 205-755-7008			•			
•	•		Eastern North Carolina Invest & Process (SOP)............ 919-772-3346			•	•		
•	•		Greet America Public Record Svc Inc 214-320-9836						
•	•	•	🏛 NC Search Inc 910-273-4999	•	•	•	•		
•	•	•	🏛 National Data Access Corp 800-390-2959	•	•	•	•	•	
•		•	Paralegal Services of North Carolina Inc (SOP)............ 919-821-7762	•	•	•	•		

					UC	RE	TX	VS	VR
•	•	•		SingleSource Services Corp 800-713-3412	•		•	•	•

CV	CR	PR		**WILKES (EST)**	UC	RE	TX	VS	VR
•	•			Alpha Research LLC (SOP)...................... 205-755-7008			•		
•	•			Greet America Public Record Svc Inc 214-320-9836					
•	•	•		NC Search Inc 910-273-4999	•	•	•		
•	•	•		SingleSource Services Corp 800-713-3412	•		•	•	•

BK	CV	CR	PR	**WILSON (EST)**	UC	RE	TX	VS	VR
•	•	•		Alpha Research LLC (SOP)...................... 205-755-7008			•		
•	•	•		Eastern North Carolina Invest & Process (SOP)............ 919-772-3346			•	•	
•	•	•		Greet America Public Record Svc Inc 214-320-9836					
•	•	•	•	NC Search Inc 910-273-4999	•	•	•		
•	•	•	•	National Data Access Corp 800-390-2959	•	•	•	•	•
•	•	•	•	SingleSource Services Corp 800-713-3412	•		•	•	•

CV	CR	PR		**YADKIN (EST)**	UC	RE	TX	VS	VR
•	•	•		Agency-One Investigations (SOP)..................... 800-468-7393	•	•	•		
•	•			Alpha Research LLC (SOP)...................... 205-755-7008			•		
•	•			Greet America Public Record Svc Inc 214-320-9836					
•	•	•		NC Search Inc 910-273-4999	•	•	•		
•	•	•		SingleSource Services Corp 800-713-3412	•		•	•	•

CV	CR	PR		**YANCEY (EST)**	UC	RE	TX	VS	VR
•	•			Alpha Research LLC (SOP)...................... 205-755-7008			•		
•	•			Greet America Public Record Svc Inc 214-320-9836					
•	•	•		NC Search Inc 910-273-4999	•	•	•		
•	•	•		SingleSource Services Corp 800-713-3412	•		•	•	•

NORTH DAKOTA

	CV	CR	PR	ADAMS (MST)	UC	RE	TX	VS	VR
	●			Adams County Abstract Co 701-567-2224	●	●	●		
	●	●	●	Gion Law Office 701-563-4354	●	●	●	●	

	CV	CR	PR	BARNES (CST)	UC	RE	TX	VS	VR
	●	●	●	Credit Bureau of Valley City 701-845-3912	●	●	●	●	
	●	●	●	P.I. Services (SOP) 800-553-4842	●	●	●	●	

	CV	CR	PR	BENSON (CST)	UC	RE	TX	VS	VR
	●		●	Surety Title Co 701-947-2446	●	●	●		

	CV	CR	PR	BILLINGS (MST)	UC	RE	TX	VS	VR
	●			Dickinson Abstract Co 701-225-2271	●	●	●		

	CV	CR	PR	BOTTINEAU (CST)	UC	RE	TX	VS	VR
	●	●	●	Bottineau County Abtract Co 701-228-2215	●	●	●	●	

	CV	CR	PR	BOWMAN (MST)	UC	RE	TX	VS	VR
	●	●	●	Bowman & Slope County Abstract Co 701-523-5231	●	●	●	●	
	●	●	●	Gion Law Office 701-563-4354	●	●	●	●	

	CV	CR	PR	BURKE (CST)	UC	RE	TX	VS	VR
	●	●	●	Mountrail County Abstract and Title Co 701-628-2886	●	●	●		
	●	●	●	Wilkes Law Office 701-385-4082		●	●	●	

DT	CV	CR	PR	BURLEIGH (CAPITAL) (CST)	UC	RE	TX	VS	VR
	●		●	Bismarck Title Co 701-222-4247	●	●	●		
	●		●	Evans & Johnson Investigations Inc (SOP) 701-224-9743	●	●	●		
●	●	●	●	🏛 Search Company of North Dakota (SOP) 701-258-5375	●	●	●	●	●
●	●	●	●	The North Dakota Guaranty & Title Co 701-223-6835	●	●	●		
●	●	●	●	W T Butcher & Associates (SOP) 701-224-1541	●	●	●		

DT	BK	CV	CR	PR	CASS (CST)	UC	RE	TX	VS	VR
		●	●	●	Cass County Abstract Co 701-232-3341	●	●	●		
●	●				🏛 Hogan Information Services 405-278-6954					
●		●	●	●	P.I. Services (SOP) 800-553-4842	●	●	●	●	
●		●	●	●	🏛 Search Company of North Dakota (SOP) 701-258-5375	●	●	●	●	●
●		●	●	●	🏛 Team Eagle 800-251-2540	●		●		
●		●	●	●	W T Butcher & Associates (SOP) 701-224-1541	●	●	●	●	

	CV	CR	PR	CAVALIER (CST)	UC	RE	TX	VS	VR
	●			McHugh Abstract Co 701-256-2851	●	●	●	●	
	●	●	●	Welch & Ekman PC 701-284-7833	●	●	●	●	

	CV	CR	PR	DICKEY (CST)	UC	RE	TX	VS	VR
	●	●	●	Dickey County Abstract & Title 701-349-3450	●	●	●	●	

	CV	CR	PR	DIVIDE (CST)	UC	RE	TX	VS	VR
	●		●	Divide Abstract Co Inc 701-965-6352		●	●	●	

	CV	CR	PR	DUNN (MST)	UC	RE	TX	VS	VR
	●	●	●	Northwest Abstract and Title Inc 701-774-8829	●	●	●	●	

	CV	CR	PR	EDDY (CST)	UC	RE	TX	VS	VR
	●		●	Surety Title Co 701-947-2446	●	●	●		

	CV	CR	PR	EMMONS (CST)	UC	RE	TX	VS	VR
	●	●	●	Emmons County Abstract & Title 701-254-4261	●	●	●	●	

	CV	CR	PR	FOSTER (CST)	UC	RE	TX	VS	VR
	●	●	●	Foster County Abstract & Title 701-652-3164	●	●	●	●	

NORTH DAKOTA

CV	CR	PR	GOLDEN VALLEY (MST)	UC	RE	TX	VS	VR
•	•	•	The Abstract & Title Co 701-872-4531	•	•	•	•	

CV	CR	PR	GRAND FORKS (CST)	UC	RE	TX	VS	VR
•			Grand Forks Abstract Co 701-772-3484	•	•	•		

CV	CR	PR	GRANT (MST)	UC	RE	TX	VS	VR
•	•	•	Gion Law Office 701-563-4354	•	•	•	•	
•	•	•	Grant County Abstract Co 701-622-3556	•	•	•	•	

CV	CR	PR	GRIGGS (CST)	UC	RE	TX	VS	VR
•	•	•	Credit Bureau of Valley City 701-845-3912	•	•	•	•	
•		•	Surety Title Co 701-947-2446	•	•	•		

CV	CR	PR	HETTINGER (MST)	UC	RE	TX	VS	VR
•	•	•	Gion Law Office 701-563-4354	•	•	•	•	

CV	CR	PR	KIDDER (CST)	UC	RE	TX	VS	VR
•	•	•	Evans & Johnson Investigations Inc (SOP) 701-224-9743	•	•	•	•	

CV	CR	PR	LA MOURE (CST)	UC	RE	TX	VS	VR
•	•	•	Credit Bureau of Valley City 701-845-3912	•	•	•	•	
•	•	•	LaMoure County Abstract Co 701-883-4246	•	•	•	•	
•	•	•	Stutsman County Abstract 701-252-4870	•	•	•	•	

CV	CR	PR	LOGAN (CST)	UC	RE	TX	VS	VR
•			Logan County Abstract Co 701-754-2200	•	•	•		

CV	CR	PR	MCHENRY (CST)	UC	RE	TX	VS	VR
			See adjoining counties for retrievers					

CV	CR	PR	MCINTOSH (CST)	UC	RE	TX	VS	VR
			See adjoining counties for retrievers					

CV	CR	PR	MCKENZIE (CST)	UC	RE	TX	VS	VR
•		•	Abstract and Title Co 701-842-3366	•	•	•		
•	•	•	Mountrail County Abstract and Title Co 701-628-2886	•	•	•		

CV	CR	PR	MCLEAN (CST)	UC	RE	TX	VS	VR
•	•	•	Evans & Johnson Investigations Inc (SOP) 701-224-9743	•	•	•	•	
•	•	•	McLean County Abstract Inc 701-462-3244	•	•	•	•	
•	•	•	W T Butcher & Associates (SOP) 701-224-1541	•	•	•	•	

CV	CR	PR	MERCER (MST)	UC	RE	TX	VS	VR
•			Mercer County Abstract Co Inc 701-748-2190		•	•		

CV	CR	PR	MORTON (MST)	UC	RE	TX	VS	VR
•		•	Bismarck Title Co 701-222-4247	•	•	•		
•	•	•	Evans & Johnson Investigations Inc (SOP) 701-224-9743	•	•	•	•	
•	•	•	🏛 Search Company of North Dakota (SOP) 701-258-5375	•	•	•	•	•
•	•	•	W T Butcher & Associates (SOP) 701-224-1541	•	•	•	•	

CV	CR	PR	MOUNTRAIL (CST)	UC	RE	TX	VS	VR
•	•	•	Mountrail County Abstract and Title Co 701-628-2886	•	•	•		

CV	CR	PR	NELSON (CST)	UC	RE	TX	VS	VR
			See adjoining counties for retrievers					

CV	CR	PR	OLIVER (CST)	UC	RE	TX	VS	VR
•		•	Oliver County Abstract 701-794-3496	•	•	•		

CV	CR	PR	PEMBINA (CST)	UC	RE	TX	VS	VR
•		•	A Short Abstract Co 701-265-4176	•	•	•		

NORTH DAKOTA

CV	CR	PR	PIERCE (CST)		UC	RE	TX	VS	VR
•		•	Pierce County Abstract 701-776-6961		•	•	•		

CV	CR	PR	RAMSEY (CST)		UC	RE	TX	VS	VR
•	•	•	Credit Bureau of Devils Lake 701-662-6690		•	•	•	•	

CV	CR	PR	RANSOM (CST)		UC	RE	TX	VS	VR
•	•	•	Ransom County Title Co 701-683-5511		•	•	•	•	

CV	CR	PR	RENVILLE (CST)		UC	RE	TX	VS	VR
•		•	Renville Abstract Company Inc 701-756-6487		•	•	•	•	

CV	CR	PR	RICHLAND (CST)		UC	RE	TX	VS	VR
•	•	•	P.I. Services (SOP) 800-553-4842		•	•	•	•	
•		•	Richland County Abstract Co 701-642-3781		•	•	•		

CV	CR	PR	ROLETTE (CST)		UC	RE	TX	VS	VR
•	•	•	Rolette County Abstract Inc 701-477-3149		•	•	•	•	

CV	CR	PR	SARGENT (CST)		UC	RE	TX	VS	VR
•	•	•	Credit Bureau of Valley City 701-845-3912		•	•	•	•	
•		•	Richland County Abstract Co 701-642-3781		•	•	•		

CV	CR	PR	SHERIDAN (CST)		UC	RE	TX	VS	VR
•		•	Sheridan County Abstract Co 701-363-2285		•	•	•	•	

CV	CR	PR	SIOUX (MST)		UC	RE	TX	VS	VR
•	•	•	Evans & Johnson Investigations Inc (SOP) 701-224-9743		•	•	•	•	

CV	CR	PR	SLOPE (MST)		UC	RE	TX	VS	VR
•	•	•	Bowman & Slope County Abstract Co 701-523-5231		•	•	•	•	
•	•	•	Gion Law Office 701-563-4354		•	•	•	•	

CV	CR	PR	STARK (MST)		UC	RE	TX	VS	VR
•		•	Bismarck Title Co 701-222-4247		•	•	•		
•			Dickinson Abstract Co 701-225-2271		•	•	•		
•	•	•	Gion Law Office 701-563-4354		•	•	•	•	

CV	CR	PR	STEELE (CST)		UC	RE	TX	VS	VR
•			Cassell, M B 701-524-1961			•	•		
•	•	•	Credit Bureau of Valley City 701-845-3912		•	•	•	•	

CV	CR	PR	STUTSMAN (CST)		UC	RE	TX	VS	VR
•	•	•	P.I. Services (SOP) 800-553-4842		•	•	•	•	
•	•	•	Stutsman County Abstract 701-252-4870		•	•	•	•	

CV	CR	PR	TOWNER (CST)		UC	RE	TX	VS	VR
•		•	Towner County Abstract Co 701-968-3651		•	•	•		

CV	CR	PR	TRAILL (CST)		UC	RE	TX	VS	VR
•	•	•	P.I. Services (SOP) 800-553-4842		•	•	•	•	
•		•	Traill County Abstract Co 701-436-4880		•	•	•		

CV	CR	PR	WALSH (CST)		UC	RE	TX	VS	VR
•	•	•	Welch & Ekman PC 701-284-7833		•	•	•	•	

CV	CR	PR	WARD (CST)		UC	RE	TX	VS	VR
		•	J M Devine & Co Inc 701-852-6800		•	•	•		
•	•	•	Mountrail County Abstract and Title Co 701-628-2886		•	•	•		
•	•	•	W T Butcher & Associates (SOP) 701-224-1541		•	•	•	•	
•	•	•	Wilkes Law Office 701-385-4082			•	•	•	

CV	CR	PR	WELLS (CST)		UC	RE	TX	VS	VR
•	•	•	Wells County Abstract Co 701-547-3433		•	•	•	•	

CV	CR	PR	WILLIAMS (CST)	UC	RE	TX	VS	VR
•	•	•	Mountrail County Abstract and Title Co 701-628-2886	•	•	•		
•	•	•	Northwest Abstract and Title Inc 701-774-8829	•	•	•	•	

SUMMARY OF CODES

COURT RECORDS

CODE	GOVERNMENT AGENCY	TYPE OF INFORMATION
DT	US District Court	Federal civil and criminal cases
BK	Bankruptcy Court	United States bankruptcy cases
CV	Civil Court	Municipal, county and state level civil cases
CR	Criminal Court	Municipal, county and state level criminal cases
PR	Probate Court	Wills and estate cases

COUNTY RECORDS

CODE	GOVERNMENT AGENCY	TYPE OF INFORMATION
UC	UCC Filing Office	Uniform Commercial Code and other personal property liens
RE	Recorder of Deeds	Real property transactions and liens
TX	Tax Assessor	Real property tax information
VS	Vital Records Office	Vital statistics—birth, death, marriage, divorce, etc.
VR	Voter Registration Office	Voter registration and campaign contribution information

- "CODE" designates the agency and type of information obtainable in each county from a retriever.
- The time zone for each county is abbreviated as follows: EST—Eastern Standard Time; CST—Central; MST—Mountain; PST—Pacific; AK—Alaska; HT—Hawaii.
- ▥—This symbol designates a Public Record Retriever Network member.
- "(SOP)" after the retriever name designates Service of Process.
- Individual retrievers without a company name are listed in order of their last name.
- US District and Bankruptcy courts are indicated only in the counties where courts are located.

OHIO

	CV	CR	PR	ADAMS (EST)	UC	RE	TX	VS	VR
	●	●	●	Infinity Information Network Inc 614-261-1213	●	●	●	●	●
	●	●	●	National Service Information Inc 800-235-0337	●		●	●	
	●	●	●	Ohio Paralegal Services Inc 330-759-1430	●	●	●	●	●

	CV	CR	PR	ALLEN (EST)	UC	RE	TX	VS	VR
	●	●	●	Data-Quest Research and Recovery (SOP) 419-642-3031	●	●	●	●	●
	●	●	●	Infinity Information Network Inc 614-261-1213	●	●	●	●	●
	●	●	●	National Service Information Inc 800-235-0337	●		●	●	
	●	●		Oberdier, Cindy M 800-273-1858	●	●	●		
	●	●	●	Ohio Independent Title & Pub Rec Search (SOP) 419-447-7474	●	●	●		
	●	●	●	Ohio Paralegal Services Inc 330-759-1430	●	●	●	●	●

	CV	CR	PR	ASHLAND (EST)	UC	RE	TX	VS	VR
	●	●	●	Infinity Information Network Inc 614-261-1213	●	●	●	●	●
	●	●	●	🗑 Investigative Solutions 330-626-5655	●	●	●	●	●
	●	●	●	National Service Information Inc 800-235-0337	●		●	●	
	●	●	●	Ohio Paralegal Services Inc 330-759-1430	●	●	●	●	●
				Urban Title Search Services 419-289-0437	●	●	●		
	●	●	●	Wayne County Title Co 216-262-2916	●	●	●	●	

	CV	CR	PR	ASHTABULA (EST)	UC	RE	TX	VS	VR
	●	●	●	Akron/Canton/Cleveland Court Reporters (SOP) 330-376-8100	●	●	●	●	●
	●	●	●	Infinity Information Network Inc 614-261-1213	●	●	●	●	●
	●	●	●	🗑 Investigative Solutions 330-626-5655	●	●	●	●	●
	●	●	●	Management Information Services (SOP) 216-982-3959					
	●	●	●	National Service Information Inc 800-235-0337	●		●	●	
	●	●	●	Ohio Paralegal Services Inc 330-759-1430	●	●	●	●	●
	●		●	Trumbull County Abstract Co 330-399-1891	●	●	●		

	CV	CR	PR	ATHENS (EST)	UC	RE	TX	VS	VR
	●	●	●	Gable, Norma P 614-385-3201	●	●	●	●	
	●		●	Infinity Information Network Inc 614-261-1213	●	●	●		●
	●		●	🗑 Liberty Record Search Inc 304-428-5126	●	●	●		
	●	●	●	National Service Information Inc 800-235-0337	●	●	●		
	●	●	●	Ohio Paralegal Services Inc 330-759-1430	●	●	●	●	●
	●	●	●	West, Thomas 614-373-6688	●	●	●	●	

	CV	CR	PR	AUGLAIZE (EST)	UC	RE	TX	VS	VR
	●	●	●	Data-Quest Research and Recovery (SOP) 419-642-3031	●	●	●	●	●
	●	●	●	Infinity Information Network Inc 614-261-1213	●	●	●	●	●
	●	●	●	National Service Information Inc 800-235-0337	●		●	●	
	●	●	●	Ohio Paralegal Services Inc 330-759-1430	●	●	●	●	●

	CV	CR	PR	BELMONT (EST)	UC	RE	TX	VS	VR
	●	●	●	Claugus, Claudine 614-425-1831	●	●	●	●	●
	●	●	●	Doty, Dora 614-695-4917	●	●	●	●	
	●	●	●	Infinity Information Network Inc 614-261-1213	●	●	●	●	●
		●	●	🗑 Liberty Record Search Inc 304-428-5126	●	●	●		
	●	●	●	National Service Information Inc 800-235-0337	●		●	●	
	●	●	●	Ohio Paralegal Services Inc 330-759-1430	●	●	●	●	●
	●	●	●	Tomich, Vicki 304-845-7315	●	●	●	●	

	CV	CR	PR	BROWN (EST)	UC	RE	TX	VS	VR
	●	●	●	Infinity Information Network Inc 614-261-1213	●	●	●	●	●
	●	●	●	National Service Information Inc 800-235-0337	●		●	●	
	●	●	●	Ohio Paralegal Services Inc 330-759-1430	●	●	●	●	●

	CV	CR	PR	BUTLER (EST)	UC	RE	TX	VS	VR
	●	●	●	🗑 Active Detective Bureau Inc (SOP) 513-541-6600	●	●	●	●	●
	●	●	●	Advanced Background Check 513-254-9234	●	●	●		

						UC	RE	TX	VS	VR
•	•		🏛 Alpha Research LLC (SOP)	205-755-7008			•			
•	•	•	District Security Inc	800-688-8721	•		•	•	
•	•	•	General Corporate Investigations (SOP)	800-735-7992	•	•	•	•	•
•	•	•	Infinity Information Network Inc	614-261-1213	•	•	•	•	•
•			🏛 Kalyvas, Jim	614-759-7456	•	•	•		
•		•	McKinley Paralegal Services	513-662-8106	•	•	•		
			🏛 Midwest Investigative Services Inc (SOP)	800-227-9740			•	•	•
•			🏛 Miller, Cynthia H	513-474-6408	•	•	•		
•	•	•	National Service Information Inc	800-235-0337	•		•	•	
•	•	•	Ohio Paralegal Services Inc	330-759-1430	•	•	•	•	•
•	•	•	🏛 Tilton, Nellie	513-839-1176	•	•	•	•	

CV	CR	PR	CARROLL (EST)			UC	RE	TX	VS	VR
•	•	•	Akron/Canton/Cleveland Court Reporters (SOP)	330-376-8100	•	•	•	•	•
•	•	•	Infinity Information Network Inc	614-261-1213	•	•	•	•	•
•		•	🏛 Liberty Record Search Inc	304-428-5126	•	•	•		
•	•	•	National Service Information Inc	800-235-0337	•		•		
•	•	•	Ohio Paralegal Services Inc	330-759-1430	•	•	•	•	•
•	•	•	Rumancik, David M	330-837-7737	•	•	•	•	
•	•	•	Woodard and Bohse Law Office	330-343-8848	•	•	•	•	

CV	CR	PR	CHAMPAIGN (EST)			UC	RE	TX	VS	VR
•	•		🏛 Alpha Research LLC (SOP)	205-755-7008			•			
•		•	Blazinski, Al	513-698-7283	•	•	•	•	
•		•	Infinity Information Network Inc	614-261-1213	•	•	•	•	•
•	•	•	National Service Information Inc	800-235-0337	•		•	•	
•	•	•	Ohio Paralegal Services Inc	330-759-1430	•	•	•	•	•

CV	CR	PR	CLARK (EST)			UC	RE	TX	VS	VR
•	•	•	Advanced Background Check	513-254-9234	•	•	•		
•	•		🏛 Alpha Research LLC (SOP)	205-755-7008			•			
•	•	•	Blazinski, Al	513-698-7283	•	•	•		
•	•	•	🏛 Docutech Information Services	800-361-3310	•	•	•		
•	•	•	Infinity Information Network Inc	614-261-1213	•	•	•		•
	•		🏛 Midwest Investigative Services Inc (SOP)	800-227-9740		•		•	•
•	•	•	National Service Information Inc	800-235-0337	•		•	•	
•	•		Oberdier, Cindy M	800-273-1858	•	•	•		
•	•	•	Ohio Paralegal Services Inc	330-759-1430	•	•	•	•	•

CV	CR	PR	CLERMONT (EST)			UC	RE	TX	VS	VR
•	•	•	Advanced Background Check	513-254-9234	•	•	•		
•	•	•	District Security Inc	800-688-8721	•		•	•	
•	•	•	General Corporate Investigations (SOP)	800-735-7992	•	•	•	•	•
•	•	•	Infinity Information Network Inc	614-261-1213	•	•	•	•	•
•	•	•	McKinley Paralegal Services	513-662-8106	•	•	•		
•	•	•	🏛 Miller, Cynthia H	513-474-6408	•	•	•		•
•	•	•	National Service Information Inc	800-235-0337	•		•	•	
•	•	•	Ohio Paralegal Services Inc	330-759-1430	•	•	•	•	•

CV	CR	PR	CLINTON (EST)			UC	RE	TX	VS	VR
•	•		🏛 Alpha Research LLC (SOP)	205-755-7008			•			
•	•	•	Infinity Information Network Inc	614-261-1213	•	•	•	•	•
	•		🏛 Midwest Investigative Services Inc (SOP)	800-227-9740		•		•	•
•	•	•	National Service Information Inc	800-235-0337	•		•	•	
•	•	•	Ohio Paralegal Services Inc	330-759-1430	•	•	•	•	•

CV	CR	PR	COLUMBIANA (EST)			UC	RE	TX	VS	VR
•	•	•	Akron/Canton/Cleveland Court Reporters (SOP)	330-376-8100	•	•	•	•	•
•	•	•	Infinity Information Network Inc	614-261-1213	•	•	•	•	•
•	•	•	🏛 Investigative Solutions	330-626-5655	•	•	•	•	•
•	•	•	🏛 Liberty Record Search Inc	304-428-5126	•	•	•		
•	•	•	National Service Information Inc	800-235-0337	•		•		
•	•	•	Ohio Paralegal Services Inc	330-759-1430	•	•	•	•	•

	•			•	Trumbull County Abstract Co 330-399-1891		•	•	•		

CV	CR	PR	COSHOCTON (EST)	UC	RE	TX	VS	VR
•	•	•	Infinity Information Network Inc 614-261-1213	•	•	•	•	•
•	•	•	National Service Information Inc 800-235-0337	•		•	•	
•	•	•	Ohio Paralegal Services Inc 330-759-1430	•	•	•	•	•
•	•	•	Woodard and Bohse Law Office 330-343-8848	•	•	•	•	

CV	CR	PR	CRAWFORD (EST)	UC	RE	TX	VS	VR
•	•	•	Infinity Information Network Inc 614-261-1213	•	•	•	•	•
•	•	•	National Service Information Inc 800-235-0337	•		•	•	
•	•		Oberdier, Cindy M 800-273-1858	•	•	•		
•	•	•	Ohio Independent Title & Pub Rec Search (SOP) 419-447-7474	•	•			
•	•	•	Ohio Paralegal Services Inc 330-759-1430	•	•	•	•	•

DT	BK	CV	CR	PR	CUYAHOGA (EST)	UC	RE	TX	VS	VR
•	•	•	•	•	Akron/Canton/Cleveland Court Reporters (SOP) 330-376-8100	•	•	•	•	•
•	•	•	•	•	All Search & Service (SOP) 216-731-3794	•	•	•		
•	•	•	•	•	⊞ Allington International 800-747-5202	•		•	•	•
•	•	•	•		Attorney Services Inc (SOP) 216-431-7400		•	•		
•	•	•	•		Corporate Screening Services Inc 800-229-8606	•				
•	•	•	•	•	District Security Inc 800-688-8721	•		•		
•	•	•	•	•	⊞ Docutech Information Services 800-361-3310	•	•	•		
•	•	•	•	•	⊞ Eagle Communications (SOP) 216-646-9179	•	•	•		•
•	•	•	•	•	General Corporate Investigations (SOP) 800-735-7992	•	•	•	•	
•	•	•	•	•	IRS (Insight Research Systems) 216-663-5011	•	•	•	•	
•	•	•	•	•	Infinity Information Network Inc 614-261-1213	•	•	•	•	
		•	•		Infinity Infotrac 216-291-9696					
•	•	•	•	•	⊞ Investigative Solutions 330-626-5655	•	•	•	•	•
•	•	•	•		J H L Enterprises 216-845-2823	•		•		
•	•	•			⊞ Kalyvas, Jim 614-759-7456	•	•	•		
		•		•	Lorain County Title Co 800-624-5507	•	•	•	•	
•	•	•	•	•	⊞ Major Legal Services Inc (SOP) 216-579-9782	•	•	•	•	•
		•	•	•	Management Information Services (SOP) 216-982-3959					
•	•	•	•	•	National Service Information Inc 800-235-0337	•		•	•	
•	•	•	•	•	Ohio Paralegal Services Inc 330-759-1430	•	•	•	•	•
•	•	•	•	•	Records Deposition Service 614-365-9092	•	•	•		
•	•	•	•	•	The Pre-Check Company 216-226-7700					
•	•	•	•	•	Toni Rose Associates 800-848-0055	•	•	•	•	•

CV	CR	PR	DARKE (EST)	UC	RE	TX	VS	VR
•	•	•	Advanced Background Check 513-254-9234	•	•	•		
•	•	•	Blazinski, Al 513-698-7283	•	•	•	•	
•	•	•	Infinity Information Network Inc 614-261-1213	•	•	•	•	•
	•		⊞ Midwest Investigative Services Inc (SOP) 800-227-9740		•		•	•
•	•	•	National Service Information Inc 800-235-0337	•		•	•	
•	•	•	Ohio Paralegal Services Inc 330-759-1430	•	•	•	•	•
•	•	•	⊞ Tilton, Nellie 513-839-1176	•	•	•	•	

CV	CR	PR	DEFIANCE (EST)	UC	RE	TX	VS	VR
•	•	•	Central Investigation (SOP) 800-281-8142	•	•	•	•	•
•	•	•	Infinity Information Network Inc 614-261-1213	•	•	•	•	•
•	•		M & D Records Research (SOP) 419-693-5649	•		•		
•	•	•	National Service Information Inc 800-235-0337	•		•	•	
•	•	•	Ohio Paralegal Services Inc 330-759-1430	•	•	•	•	•

CV	CR	PR	DELAWARE (EST)	UC	RE	TX	VS	VR
•			Corporate Services of Ohio Inc 614-464-2400	•	•	•	•	
•	•	•	Document Resources 800-552-3453	•	•		•	•
•	•	•	⊞ Docutech Information Services 800-361-3310	•	•	•	•	
•	•	•	Infinity Information Network Inc 614-261-1213	•	•	•	•	•
•	•		⊞ Kalyvas, Jim 614-759-7456	•	•	•		
•	•	•	⊞ Miller, G Scott 614-363-1324	•	•	•	•	

	CV	CR	PR			UC	RE	TX	VS	VR
	•	•	•	National Service Information Inc 800-235-0337		•		•	•	
	•	•	•	Ohio Paralegal Services Inc 330-759-1430		•	•	•	•	•
	•		•	Q.S.I. (Quantum Software Inc) 614-224-9207		•	•	•		
	•	•	•	Records Deposition Service 614-365-9092		•	•	•	•	
	•	•	•	🏛 Resume Check/M. King & Associates (SOP) 800-932-4358		•	•	•	•	•

	CV	CR	PR	ERIE (EST)		UC	RE	TX	VS	VR
	•	•	•	Infinity Information Network Inc 614-261-1213		•	•	•	•	•
	•	•	•	🏛 Investigative Solutions 330-626-5655		•	•	•	•	•
	•		•	Lorain County Title Co 800-624-5507		•	•	•	•	•
	•	•	•	National Service Information Inc 800-235-0337		•		•	•	
	•	•	•	Ohio Independent Title & Pub Rec Search (SOP) 419-447-7474		•	•	•		
	•	•	•	Ohio Paralegal Services Inc 330-759-1430		•	•	•	•	•
	•	•	•	Toni Rose Associates 800-848-0055		•	•	•	•	•

	CV	CR	PR	FAIRFIELD (EST)		UC	RE	TX	VS	VR
	•			Corporate Services of Ohio Inc 614-464-2400		•	•	•	•	
	•	•	•	Document Resources 800-552-3453		•	•	•	•	•
	•	•	•	🏛 Docutech Information Services 800-361-3310		•	•	•	•	•
	•	•	•	Gable, Norma P 614-385-3201		•	•	•	•	•
	•	•	•	Infinity Information Network Inc 614-261-1213		•	•	•	•	•
	•			🏛 Kalyvas, Jim 614-759-7456		•	•	•		
	•	•	•	National Service Information Inc 800-235-0337		•		•	•	
	•	•	•	Ohio Paralegal Services Inc 330-759-1430		•	•	•	•	•
	•		•	Q.S.I. (Quantum Software Inc) 614-224-9207		•	•	•		
	•	•	•	🏛 Resume Check/M. King & Associates (SOP) 800-932-4358		•	•	•	•	•
	•	•		🏛 Six County Search (SOP) 614-962-3995		•	•	•		•

	CV	CR	PR	FAYETTE (EST)		UC	RE	TX	VS	VR
	•	•		🏛 Alpha Research LLC (SOP) 205-755-7008				•		
	•			Corporate Services of Ohio Inc 614-464-2400		•	•	•	•	
	•	•	•	Infinity Information Network Inc 614-261-1213		•	•	•	•	•
	•	•	•	National Service Information Inc 800-235-0337		•		•	•	
	•	•	•	Ohio Paralegal Services Inc 330-759-1430		•	•	•	•	•
	•		•	Q.S.I. (Quantum Software Inc) 614-224-9207		•	•	•		
	•	•		🏛 Six County Search (SOP) 614-962-3995		•	•	•		•

DT	BK	CV	CR	PR	FRANKLIN (CAPITAL) (EST)		UC	RE	TX	VS	VR
•	•	•	•	•	CSC (SOP) 800-688-9901		•	•	•	•	
•	•	•	•	•	🏛 Capital Retrieval Services (SOP) 614-344-1047		•	•	•	•	•
•	•	•	•	•	Confidential Services (SOP) 800-752-4581		•	•	•	•	
•	•	•	•		Corporate Services of Ohio Inc 614-464-2400		•	•	•	•	
•	•	•		•	District Security Inc 800-688-8721		•		•	•	
•	•	•	•	•	Document Resources 800-552-3453		•	•	•	•	•
•	•	•	•	•	🏛 Docutech Information Services 800-361-3310		•	•	•	•	
•	•				🏛 Hogan Information Services 405-278-6954						
•	•	•	•	•	Infinity Information Network Inc 614-261-1213		•	•	•	•	•
•	•	•			🏛 Kalyvas, Jim 614-759-7456		•	•	•		
		•	•	•	🏛 MBK Consulting 614-239-8977		•	•	•	•	•
•	•	•	•	•	National Service Information Inc 800-235-0337		•		•	•	
•	•	•	•		Oberdier, Cindy M 800-273-1858		•	•	•		
•	•	•	•	•	Ohio Paralegal Services Inc 330-759-1430		•	•	•	•	•
•	•	•		•	Q.S.I. (Quantum Software Inc) 614-224-9207		•	•	•		
•	•	•	•	•	Records Deposition Service 614-365-9092		•	•	•	•	
				•	🏛 RefCheck Information Services 614-777-8844						
•	•	•	•	•	🏛 Resume Check/M. King & Associates (SOP) 800-932-4358		•	•	•	•	•
•	•	•	•	•	The Pre-Check Company 216-226-7700						

	CV	CR	PR	FULTON (EST)		UC	RE	TX	VS	VR
	•	•	•	Central Investigation (SOP) 800-281-8142		•	•	•	•	•
	•	•	•	Data Research Inc (SOP) 800-432-6607		•	•	•	•	•
	•	•	•	Infinity Information Network Inc 614-261-1213		•	•	•	•	•

CV	CR	PR		UC	RE	TX	VS	VR
•	•		M & D Records Research (SOP) 419-693-5649	•		•		
•	•	•	National Service Information Inc 800-235-0337	•		•	•	
•	•	•	Ohio Paralegal Services Inc 330-759-1430	•	•	•	•	•

CV	CR	PR	GALLIA (EST)	UC	RE	TX	VS	VR
•	•	•	Infinity Information Network Inc 614-261-1213	•	•	•		
		•	🏛 Liberty Record Search Inc 304-428-5126	•	•	•		
•	•	•	National Service Information Inc 800-235-0337	•		•	•	
•	•	•	Ohio Paralegal Services Inc 330-759-1430	•	•	•	•	•

CV	CR	PR	GEAUGA (EST)	UC	RE	TX	VS	VR
•	•	•	Akron/Canton/Cleveland Court Reporters (SOP) 330-376-8100	•	•	•	•	•
•	•	•	🏛 Eagle Communications (SOP) 216-646-9179	•	•	•	•	•
•	•	•	Infinity Information Network Inc 614-261-1213	•	•	•	•	•
•	•	•	🏛 Investigative Solutions 330-626-5655	•	•	•	•	•
•	•	•	Management Information Services (SOP) 216-982-3959					
•	•	•	National Service Information Inc 800-235-0337	•		•	•	
•	•	•	Ohio Paralegal Services Inc 330-759-1430	•	•	•	•	•
•	•	•	Toni Rose Associates 800-848-0055	•	•	•	•	•
•		•	Trumbull County Abstract Co 330-399-1891	•	•	•		

CV	CR	PR	GREENE (EST)	UC	RE	TX	VS	VR
•	•	•	Advanced Background Check 513-254-9234	•	•	•		
•	•		🏛 Alpha Research LLC (SOP) 205-755-7008		•			
•	•	•	Blazinski, Al 513-698-7283	•	•	•	•	
•	•	•	Infinity Information Network Inc 614-261-1213	•	•	•	•	•
•	•	•	McKinley Paralegal Services 513-662-8106	•	•	•		
	•		🏛 Midwest Investigative Services Inc (SOP) 800-227-9740		•		•	•
•	•	•	National Service Information Inc 800-235-0337	•		•	•	
•	•		Oberdier, Cindy M 800-273-1858	•	•	•		
•	•	•	Ohio Paralegal Services Inc 330-759-1430	•	•	•	•	•

CV	CR	PR	GUERNSEY (EST)	UC	RE	TX	VS	VR
•	•	•	Doty, Dora 614-695-4917	•	•	•	•	
•	•	•	Infinity Information Network Inc 614-261-1213	•	•	•	•	•
•	•	•	National Service Information Inc 800-235-0337	•		•	•	
•	•	•	Ohio Paralegal Services Inc 330-759-1430	•	•	•	•	•
•	•	•	🏛 Six County Search (SOP) 614-962-3995	•	•	•	•	
•	•	•	Tomich, Vicki 304-845-7315	•	•	•	•	

DT	BK	CV	CR	PR	HAMILTON (EST)	UC	RE	TX	VS	VR
•	•	•	•	•	🏛 Active Detective Bureau Inc (SOP) 513-541-6600	•	•	•	•	•
•	•	•	•	•	Advanced Background Check 513-254-9234	•	•	•		
•	•	•	•	•	All State Investigations (SOP) 800-741-4711	•	•	•		
•	•	•	•	•	District Security Inc 800-688-8721	•		•	•	
•	•	•	•	•	🏛 Docutech Information Services 800-361-3310	•	•	•		
•	•	•	•	•	General Corporate Investigations (SOP) 800-735-7992	•	•	•	•	•
•				•	🏛 Hogan Information Services 405-278-6954	•		•		
•	•	•	•	•	Infinity Information Network Inc 614-261-1213	•	•	•	•	•
		•	•		🏛 Kalyvas, Jim 614-759-7456	•		•		
				•	McKinley Paralegal Services 513-662-8106	•	•	•		
•		•	•	•	Midwest Abstract Co 513-228-2292	•	•	•	•	
•		•	•	•	🏛 Miller, Cynthia H 513-474-6408	•	•	•		
•	•	•	•	•	National Service Information Inc 800-235-0337	•		•	•	
•	•	•	•	•	Ohio Paralegal Services Inc 330-759-1430	•	•	•	•	•
•	•	•	•	•	Q.S.I. (Quantum Software Inc) 614-224-9207	•	•	•	•	•
•		•	•	•	🏛 Queen City Paralegal 513-271-2766	•	•	•		
•	•	•	•	•	🏛 Search International Inc 606-342-0456	•	•	•	•	•

CV	CR	PR	HANCOCK (EST)	UC	RE	TX	VS	VR
•	•	•	Central Investigation (SOP) 800-281-8142	•	•	•	•	•
•	•	•	Data Research Inc (SOP) 800-432-6607	•	•	•	•	•
•	•	•	Infinity Information Network Inc 614-261-1213	•	•	•	•	•

CV	CR	PR		UC	RE	TX	VS	VR
•	•		M & D Records Research (SOP)................................419-693-5649	•		•		
•	•	•	National Service Information Inc 800-235-0337	•		•	•	
•	•		Oberdier, Cindy M 800-273-1858	•	•	•		
•	•	•	Ohio Independent Title & Pub Rec Search (SOP) 419-447-7474	•	•	•		
•	•	•	Ohio Paralegal Services Inc 330-759-1430	•	•	•	•	•

CV	CR	PR	HARDIN (EST)	UC	RE	TX	VS	VR
•	•	•	Data-Quest Research and Recovery (SOP).....................419-642-3031	•	•	•	•	•
•	•	•	Infinity Information Network Inc 614-261-1213	•	•	•	•	•
•	•	•	National Service Information Inc 800-235-0337	•		•	•	
•	•	•	Ohio Independent Title & Pub Rec Search (SOP) 419-447-7474	•	•	•		
•	•	•	Ohio Paralegal Services Inc 330-759-1430	•	•	•	•	•

CV	CR	PR	HARRISON (EST)	UC	RE	TX	VS	VR
•	•	•	Akron/Canton/Cleveland Court Reporters (SOP)..............330-376-8100	•	•	•	•	•
•	•	•	Claugus, Claudine 614-425-1831	•	•	•	•	•
•	•	•	Doty, Dora 614-695-4917	•	•	•	•	•
•	•	•	Infinity Information Network Inc 614-261-1213	•	•	•		•
•	•	•	National Service Information Inc 800-235-0337	•		•	•	
•	•	•	Ohio Paralegal Services Inc 330-759-1430	•	•	•	•	•
•	•	•	Tomich, Vicki 304-845-7315	•	•	•	•	
•	•	•	Woodard and Bohse Law Office 330-343-8848	•	•	•	•	

CV	CR	PR	HENRY (EST)	UC	RE	TX	VS	VR
•	•	•	Central Investigation (SOP)......................................800-281-8142	•	•	•	•	•
•	•	•	Infinity Information Network Inc 614-261-1213	•	•	•	•	•
•	•		M & D Records Research (SOP)................................419-693-5649	•		•		
•	•	•	National Service Information Inc 800-235-0337	•		•	•	
•	•	•	Ohio Paralegal Services Inc 330-759-1430	•	•	•	•	•

CV	CR	PR	HIGHLAND (EST)	UC	RE	TX	VS	VR
•	•	•	Infinity Information Network Inc 614-261-1213	•	•	•	•	•
•	•	•	National Service Information Inc 800-235-0337	•		•	•	
•	•	•	Ohio Paralegal Services Inc 330-759-1430	•	•	•	•	•

CV	CR	PR	HOCKING (EST)	UC	RE	TX	VS	VR
•	•	•	Clue Detective Agency 614-536-9600	•	•	•	•	•
•	•	•	Gable, Norma P 614-385-3201	•	•	•	•	•
•	•	•	Infinity Information Network Inc 614-261-1213	•	•	•	•	•
•	•	•	National Service Information Inc 800-235-0337	•		•	•	
•	•	•	Ohio Paralegal Services Inc 330-759-1430	•	•	•	•	•
•	•	•	West, Thomas 614-373-6688	•	•	•	•	

CV	CR	PR	HOLMES (EST)	UC	RE	TX	VS	VR
•	•	•	Akron/Canton/Cleveland Court Reporters (SOP)..............330-376-8100	•	•	•	•	•
•	•	•	Infinity Information Network Inc 614-261-1213	•	•	•	•	•
•	•	•	⛁ Investigative Solutions 330-626-5655	•	•	•	•	•
•	•	•	National Service Information Inc 800-235-0337	•		•	•	
•	•	•	Ohio Paralegal Services Inc 330-759-1430	•	•	•	•	•
•	•	•	Rumancik, David M 330-837-7737	•	•	•		
			Urban Title Search Services 419-289-0437	•	•			
•	•	•	Wayne County Title Co 216-262-2916	•	•	•	•	
•	•	•	Woodard and Bohse Law Office 330-343-8848	•	•	•	•	

CV	CR	PR	HURON (EST)	UC	RE	TX	VS	VR
•	•	•	Infinity Information Network Inc 614-261-1213	•	•	•	•	•
•	•	•	⛁ Investigative Solutions 330-626-5655	•	•	•	•	•
•	•	•	National Service Information Inc 800-235-0337	•		•	•	
•	•	•	Ohio Independent Title & Pub Rec Search (SOP) 419-447-7474	•	•	•		
•	•	•	Ohio Paralegal Services Inc 330-759-1430	•	•	•	•	•

CV	CR	PR	JACKSON (EST)	UC	RE	TX	VS	VR
•	•	•	Infinity Information Network Inc 614-261-1213	•	•	•	•	•

					UC	RE	TX	VS	VR
•	•	•	National Service Information Inc 800-235-0337		•		•	•	
•	•	•	Ohio Paralegal Services Inc 330-759-1430		•	•	•	•	•
•	•	•	Simmons & Grillo 614-596-5291		•	•	•	•	

CV	CR	PR	JEFFERSON (EST)	UC	RE	TX	VS	VR
•	•	•	Akron/Canton/Cleveland Court Reporters (SOP) 330-376-8100	•	•	•	•	•
•	•	•	Claugus, Claudine 614-425-1831	•	•	•	•	•
•	•	•	Doty, Dora 614-695-4917	•	•	•	•	•
•	•	•	Infinity Information Network Inc 614-261-1213	•	•	•	•	•
•		•	🏛 Liberty Record Search Inc 304-428-5126	•	•	•		
•	•	•	National Service Information Inc 800-235-0337	•		•	•	
•	•	•	Ohio Paralegal Services Inc 330-759-1430	•	•	•	•	•
•	•	•	Tomich, Vicki 304-845-7315	•	•	•		

CV	CR	PR	KNOX (EST)	UC	RE	TX	VS	VR
•	•	•	Infinity Information Network Inc 614-261-1213	•	•	•	•	•
•	•	•	National Service Information Inc 800-235-0337	•		•	•	
•	•	•	Ohio Paralegal Services Inc 330-759-1430	•	•	•	•	•

CV	CR	PR	LAKE (EST)	UC	RE	TX	VS	VR
•	•	•	Akron/Canton/Cleveland Court Reporters (SOP) 330-376-8100	•	•	•	•	•
•	•	•	🏛 Allington International 800-747-5202	•	•	•	•	•
•	•		Corporate Screening Services Inc 800-229-8606	•		•		
•	•	•	🏛 Eagle Communications (SOP) 216-646-9179	•		•	•	•
•	•	•	IRS (Insight Research Systems) 216-663-5011	•	•	•	•	•
•	•	•	Infinity Information Network Inc 614-261-1213	•	•	•	•	•
•	•		Infinity Infotrac 216-291-9696					
•	•	•	🏛 Investigative Solutions 330-626-5655	•	•	•	•	•
•	•	•	Management Information Services (SOP) 216-982-3959					
•	•	•	National Service Information Inc 800-235-0337	•		•	•	
•	•	•	Ohio Paralegal Services Inc 330-759-1430	•	•	•	•	•
•			Schneider, Tomma J 216-357-0280	•		•		
•	•	•	The Pre-Check Company 216-226-7700					
•	•	•	Toni Rose Associates 800-848-0055	•	•	•	•	•

CV	CR	PR	LAWRENCE (EST)	UC	RE	TX	VS	VR
•	•	•	Infinity Information Network Inc 614-261-1213	•	•	•	•	•
•	•	•	Lew Davis Investigatons (SOP) 304-523-0055	•	•	•	•	•
•		•	🏛 Liberty Record Search Inc 304-428-5126	•	•	•		
•	•	•	National Service Information Inc 800-235-0337	•		•	•	
•	•	•	Ohio Paralegal Services Inc 330-759-1430	•	•	•	•	•

CV	CR	PR	LICKING (EST)	UC	RE	TX	VS	VR
•	•	•	🏛 Capital Retrieval Services (SOP) 614-344-1047	•	•	•	•	•
•			Corporate Services of Ohio Inc 614-464-2400	•	•	•	•	
•		•	Document Resources 800-552-3453	•	•	•	•	
•	•	•	🏛 Docutech Information Services 800-361-3310	•	•	•		
•		•	Infinity Information Network Inc 614-261-1213	•	•	•	•	•
•		•	🏛 Kalyvas, Jim 614-759-7456	•	•	•		
•	•	•	National Service Information Inc 800-235-0337	•		•	•	
•	•		Oberdier, Cindy M 800-273-1858	•	•	•		
•	•	•	Ohio Paralegal Services Inc 330-759-1430	•	•	•	•	•
•	•	•	Q.S.I. (Quantum Software Inc) 614-224-9207	•	•	•		
•	•	•	🏛 Resume Check/M. King & Associates (SOP) 800-932-4358	•	•	•	•	•

CV	CR	PR	LOGAN (EST)	UC	RE	TX	VS	VR
•	•	•	Blazinski, Al 513-698-7283	•	•	•	•	
•	•	•	Infinity Information Network Inc 614-261-1213	•	•	•	•	•
•	•	•	National Service Information Inc 800-235-0337	•		•	•	
•	•	•	Ohio Paralegal Services Inc 330-759-1430	•	•	•	•	•

CV	CR	PR	LORAIN (EST)	UC	RE	TX	VS	VR
•	•	•	Akron/Canton/Cleveland Court Reporters (SOP) 330-376-8100	•	•	•	•	•

DT	BK	CV	CR	PR			UC	RE	TX	VS	VR
●	●	●			🏛 Allington International 800-747-5202		●	●	●	●	●
●	●				Corporate Screening Services Inc 800-229-8606		●		●		
●	●	●			🏛 Eagle Communications (SOP) 216-646-9179		●	●			
●	●	●			IRS (Insight Research Systems) 216-663-5011		●	●	●	●	
●	●	●			Infinity Information Network Inc 614-261-1213		●	●	●	●	●
●	●				Infinity Infotrac 216-291-9696						
●	●	●			🏛 Investigative Solutions 330-626-5655		●	●	●	●	●
●	●				Lorain County Title Co 800-624-5507		●	●			
●	●	●			Management Information Services (SOP) 216-982-3959						
●	●	●			National Service Information Inc 800-235-0337		●		●		
●	●	●			Ohio Paralegal Services Inc 330-759-1430		●		●		
●	●	●			The Pre-Check Company 216-226-7700						
●	●	●			Toni Rose Associates 800-848-0055		●	●	●	●	●

DT	BK	CV	CR	PR	LUCAS (EST)		UC	RE	TX	VS	VR
●	●	●	●	●	Central Investigation (SOP) 800-281-8142		●	●	●	●	●
●	●	●	●	●	Data Research Inc (SOP) 800-432-6607		●	●	●		
●	●				🏛 Hogan Information Services 405-278-6954						
●	●	●	●	●	Infinity Information Network Inc 614-261-1213		●	●	●	●	●
●	●	●			🏛 Kalyvas, Jim 614-759-7456		●	●			
●	●	●			M & D Records Research (SOP) 419-693-5649		●		●		
●	●	●	●		National Service Information Inc 800-235-0337		●		●	●	
●	●	●	●	●	Ohio Paralegal Services Inc 330-759-1430		●	●	●	●	●

CV	CR	PR	MADISON (EST)		UC	RE	TX	VS	VR
●	●		🏛 Alpha Research LLC (SOP) 205-755-7008				●		
●			Corporate Services of Ohio Inc 614-464-2400		●	●	●	●	
●	●	●	Document Resources 800-552-3453		●	●	●	●	●
●	●	●	Infinity Information Network Inc 614-261-1213		●	●	●	●	●
●	●	●	National Service Information Inc 800-235-0337		●		●	●	
●	●	●	Ohio Paralegal Services Inc 330-759-1430		●	●	●	●	●
●		●	Q.S.I. (Quantum Software Inc) 614-224-9207		●	●	●		

DT	BK	CV	CR	PR	MAHONING (EST)		UC	RE	TX	VS	VR
●	●	●	●	●	Akron/Canton/Cleveland Court Reporters (SOP) 330-376-8100		●	●	●	●	●
●	●				🏛 Hogan Information Services 405-278-6954						
●	●	●	●	●	Infinity Information Network Inc 614-261-1213		●	●	●	●	●
●	●	●	●	●	🏛 Investigative Solutions 330-626-5655		●	●	●	●	●
●	●	●	●		National Service Information Inc 800-235-0337		●		●	●	
●	●	●	●	●	Ohio Paralegal Services Inc 330-759-1430		●	●	●	●	●
●	●	●	●	●	Toni Rose Associates 800-848-0055		●	●	●	●	●
		●		●	Trumbull County Abstract Co 330-399-1891		●	●	●		

CV	CR	PR	MARION (EST)		UC	RE	TX	VS	VR
●			Corporate Services of Ohio Inc 614-464-2400		●	●	●	●	
●	●	●	Infinity Information Network Inc 614-261-1213		●	●	●	●	
●	●	●	National Service Information Inc 800-235-0337		●		●	●	
●	●	●	Oberdier, Cindy M 800-273-1858		●	●	●	●	
●	●	●	Ohio Paralegal Services Inc 330-759-1430		●	●	●	●	●

CV	CR	PR	MEDINA (EST)		UC	RE	TX	VS	VR
●	●	●	Akron/Canton/Cleveland Court Reporters (SOP) 330-376-8100		●	●	●	●	●
●	●	●	🏛 Allington International 800-747-5202		●	●	●	●	●
●			Corporate Screening Services Inc 800-229-8606		●				
●	●	●	Infinity Information Network Inc 614-261-1213		●	●	●	●	●
●	●		Infinity Infotrac 216-291-9696						
●	●	●	🏛 Investigative Solutions 330-626-5655		●	●	●	●	●
●	●		J H L Enterprises 216-845-2823		●		●		
●	●	●	Management Information Services (SOP) 216-982-3959						
●	●	●	National Service Information Inc 800-235-0337		●		●	●	
●	●	●	Oberdier, Cindy M 800-273-1858		●	●	●		
●	●	●	Ohio Paralegal Services Inc 330-759-1430		●	●	●	●	●

●	●	●	Olde Reserve Title Inc	330-273-3007	●	●	●	●		

CV	CR	PR	MEIGS (EST)		UC	RE	TX	VS	VR
●	●	●	Infinity Information Network Inc 614-261-1213		●	●	●	●	●
		●	🏛 Liberty Record Search Inc 304-428-5126		●	●	●		
●	●	●	National Service Information Inc 800-235-0337		●		●	●	
●	●	●	Ohio Paralegal Services Inc 330-759-1430		●	●	●	●	●
●	●	●	West, Thomas 614-373-6688		●	●	●	●	

CV	CR	PR	MERCER (EST)		UC	RE	TX	VS	VR
●	●	●	Data-Quest Research and Recovery (SOP) 419-642-3031		●	●	●	●	●
●	●	●	Hirschfeld Law Office 419-586-2323		●	●	●		
●	●	●	Infinity Information Network Inc 614-261-1213		●	●	●	●	●
●	●	●	🏛 Investigative Solutions 330-626-5655		●	●	●	●	●
●	●	●	National Service Information Inc 800-235-0337		●		●	●	
●	●	●	Ohio Paralegal Services Inc 330-759-1430		●	●	●	●	●

CV	CR	PR	MIAMI (EST)		UC	RE	TX	VS	VR
●	●	●	Advanced Background Check 513-254-9234		●	●	●		
●	●		🏛 Alpha Research LLC (SOP) 205-755-7008				●		
●	●	●	Blazinski, Al 513-698-7283		●	●		●	
●	●	●	Infinity Information Network Inc 614-261-1213		●	●	●	●	●
		●	🏛 Midwest Investigative Services Inc (SOP) 800-227-9740			●		●	●
●	●	●	National Service Information Inc 800-235-0337		●		●	●	
●	●	●	Ohio Paralegal Services Inc 330-759-1430		●	●	●	●	●
●	●	●	🏛 Tilton, Nellie 513-839-1176		●	●	●	●	

CV	CR	PR	MONROE (EST)		UC	RE	TX	VS	VR
●	●	●	Claugus, Claudine 614-425-1831		●	●	●	●	●
●	●	●	Doty, Dora 614-695-4917		●	●	●	●	
●	●	●	Infinity Information Network Inc 614-261-1213		●	●	●		●
●	●	●	National Service Information Inc 800-235-0337		●		●	●	
●	●	●	Ohio Paralegal Services Inc 330-759-1430		●	●	●	●	●
●	●	●	Tomich, Vicki 304-845-7315		●	●	●	●	

DT	BK	CV	CR	PR	MONTGOMERY (EST)		UC	RE	TX	VS	VR
●	●	●	●	●	A Higher Legal Process 800-528-9474		●	●	●	●	
●	●	●	●	●	Advanced Background Check 513-254-9234		●	●	●		
●	●	●			🏛 Alpha Research LLC (SOP) 205-755-7008				●		
		●	●	●	Blazinski, Al 513-698-7283		●	●		●	
●	●	●	●	●	District Security Inc 800-688-8721		●		●	●	
●	●	●	●	●	🏛 Docutech Information Services 800-361-3310		●		●	●	
●	●	●	●	●	Esprit de Corps Inc (SOP) 513-223-0700		●		●	●	●
●	●	●	●	●	General Corporate Investigations (SOP) 800-735-7992		●		●	●	●
●					🏛 Hogan Information Services 405-278-6954		●				
●	●	●	●	●	Infinity Information Network Inc 614-261-1213		●	●	●	●	●
●		●			🏛 Kalyvas, Jim 614-759-7456		●				
●	●	●		●	McKinley Paralegal Services 513-662-8106		●		●	●	
●	●	●	●		Midwest Abstract Co 513-228-2292		●	●	●	●	
●			●		🏛 Midwest Investigative Services Inc (SOP) 800-227-9740			●		●	●
●	●	●	●	●	National Service Information Inc 800-235-0337		●		●	●	
●		●			Oberdier, Cindy M 800-273-1858		●				
●	●	●	●	●	Ohio Paralegal Services Inc 330-759-1430		●	●	●	●	●
●		●	●	●	🏛 Tilton, Nellie 513-839-1176		●	●	●	●	

CV	CR	PR	MORGAN (EST)		UC	RE	TX	VS	VR
●	●	●	Infinity Information Network Inc 614-261-1213		●	●	●	●	●
●	●	●	National Service Information Inc 800-235-0337		●		●	●	
●	●	●	Ohio Paralegal Services Inc 330-759-1430		●		●	●	●
●	●	●	West, Thomas 614-373-6688		●	●	●	●	
●	●	●	Wilhelm, Shirley 614-374-8444		●	●	●	●	

MORROW (EST)

CV	CR	PR	Company	Phone	UC	RE	TX	VS	VR
•	•	•	Infinity Information Network Inc	614-261-1213	•	•	•	•	•
•	•	•	Linder, Tina	419-947-7240	•	•	•	•	
•	•	•	National Service Information Inc	800-235-0337	•		•	•	
•	•	•	Ohio Paralegal Services Inc	330-759-1430	•	•	•	•	•

MUSKINGUM (EST)

CV	CR	PR	Company	Phone	UC	RE	TX	VS	VR
•	•	•	Claugus, Claudine	614-425-1831	•	•	•	•	•
•	•	•	🏛 Docutech Information Services	800-361-3310	•	•	•	•	
•	•	•	Infinity Information Network Inc	614-261-1213	•	•	•	•	•
•	•	•	National Service Information Inc	800-235-0337	•		•	•	
•	•	•	Ohio Paralegal Services Inc	330-759-1430	•	•	•	•	•
•	•	•	🏛 Six County Search (SOP)	614-962-3995	•	•	•	•	•
•	•	•	West, Thomas	614-373-6688	•	•	•	•	

NOBLE (EST)

CV	CR	PR	Company	Phone	UC	RE	TX	VS	VR
•	•	•	Infinity Information Network Inc	614-261-1213	•	•	•	•	•
•	•	•	National Service Information Inc	800-235-0337	•		•	•	
•	•	•	Ohio Paralegal Services Inc	330-759-1430	•			•	
•	•	•	Tomich, Vicki	304-845-7315	•	•	•	•	
•	•	•	West, Thomas	614-373-6688	•	•	•	•	
•	•	•	Wilhelm, Shirley	614-374-8444	•	•	•	•	

OTTAWA (EST)

CV	CR	PR	Company	Phone	UC	RE	TX	VS	VR
•	•	•	Data Research Inc (SOP)	800-432-6607	•	•	•	•	•
•	•	•	Infinity Information Network Inc	614-261-1213	•	•	•	•	•
•	•	•	🏛 Investigative Solutions	330-626-5655	•	•	•	•	
•	•		M & D Records Research (SOP)	419-693-5649	•		•		
•	•	•	National Service Information Inc	800-235-0337	•		•	•	
•	•	•	Ohio Independent Title & Pub Rec Search (SOP)	419-447-7474	•	•	•		
•	•	•	Ohio Paralegal Services Inc	330-759-1430	•	•	•	•	•

PAULDING (EST)

CV	CR	PR	Company	Phone	UC	RE	TX	VS	VR
•	•	•	Infinity Information Network Inc	614-261-1213	•	•	•	•	•
•	•	•	National Service Information Inc	800-235-0337	•		•	•	
•	•	•	Ohio Paralegal Services Inc	330-759-1430	•	•	•	•	•

PERRY (EST)

CV	CR	PR	Company	Phone	UC	RE	TX	VS	VR
•	•	•	Clue Detective Agency	614-536-9600	•	•	•	•	
•	•	•	Gable, Norma P	614-385-3201	•	•	•	•	
•	•	•	Infinity Information Network Inc	614-261-1213	•	•	•		•
•	•	•	National Service Information Inc	800-235-0337	•		•	•	
•	•	•	Ohio Paralegal Services Inc	330-759-1430	•	•	•	•	•
•	•		🏛 Six County Search (SOP)	614-962-3995	•	•	•		•

PICKAWAY (EST)

CV	CR	PR	Company	Phone	UC	RE	TX	VS	VR
•			Corporate Services of Ohio Inc	614-464-2400	•	•	•	•	
•	•	•	Document Resources	800-552-3453	•	•	•		•
•	•	•	Infinity Information Network Inc	614-261-1213	•	•	•	•	•
•	•	•	National Service Information Inc	800-235-0337	•		•	•	
•	•	•	Ohio Paralegal Services Inc	330-759-1430	•	•	•	•	•
		•	Q.S.I. (Quantum Software Inc)	614-224-9207	•	•	•		
•	•	•	🏛 Resume Check/M. King & Associates (SOP)	800-932-4358	•	•	•		•
•	•		🏛 Six County Search (SOP)	614-962-3995	•	•	•		•

PIKE (EST)

CV	CR	PR	Company	Phone	UC	RE	TX	VS	VR
•	•	•	Infinity Information Network Inc	614-261-1213	•	•	•	•	•
•	•	•	National Service Information Inc	800-235-0337	•		•	•	
•	•	•	Ohio Paralegal Services Inc	330-759-1430	•	•	•	•	

PORTAGE (EST)

CV	CR	PR	Company	Phone	UC	RE	TX	VS	VR
•	•	•	Akron/Canton/Cleveland Court Reporters (SOP)	330-376-8100	•	•	•	•	•
•	•		Corporate Screening Services Inc	800-229-8606	•		•		

CV	CR	PR			UC	RE	TX	VS	VR
•	•	•	IRS (Insight Research Systems) 216-663-5011		•	•	•	•	•
•	•	•	Infinity Information Network Inc 614-261-1213		•	•	•	•	•
•	•		Infinity Infotrac 216-291-9696						
•		•	🏛 Investigative Solutions 330-626-5655		•	•		•	•
•	•		National Service Information Inc 800-235-0337		•		•	•	
•	•	•	Ohio Bar Title 330-297-7003		•	•	•	•	
•	•	•	Ohio Paralegal Services Inc 330-759-1430		•	•	•	•	•
•	•	•	🏛 Premier Research 330-297-1977		•	•	•		
•	•	•	Toni Rose Associates 800-848-0055		•	•	•	•	•
•	•	•	Trumbull County Abstract Co 330-399-1891		•	•	•		

CV	CR	PR	PREBLE (EST)		UC	RE	TX	VS	VR
•	•	•	Advanced Background Check 513-254-9234		•	•	•		
•	•	•	Blazinski, Al 513-698-7283		•	•	•	•	
•	•	•	Infinity Information Network Inc 614-261-1213		•	•	•	•	•
•	•	•	McKinley Paralegal Services 513-662-8106		•	•	•		
		•	🏛 Midwest Investigative Services Inc (SOP) ... 800-227-9740			•		•	•
•	•	•	National Service Information Inc 800-235-0337		•		•	•	
•	•	•	Ohio Paralegal Services Inc 330-759-1430		•	•	•	•	•
•	•	•	🏛 Tilton, Nellie 513-839-1176		•	•	•	•	

CV	CR	PR	PUTNAM (EST)		UC	RE	TX	VS	VR
•	•	•	Data-Quest Research and Recovery (SOP) 419-642-3031		•	•	•	•	•
•	•	•	Infinity Information Network Inc 614-261-1213		•	•	•	•	•
•	•	•	National Service Information Inc 800-235-0337		•		•	•	
•	•	•	Ohio Independent Title & Pub Rec Search (SOP) ... 419-447-7474		•	•	•		
•	•	•	Ohio Paralegal Services Inc 330-759-1430		•	•	•	•	•

CV	CR	PR	RICHLAND (EST)		UC	RE	TX	VS	VR
•	•	•	Infinity Information Network Inc 614-261-1213		•	•	•	•	•
•	•	•	National Service Information Inc 800-235-0337		•		•	•	
•	•	•	Ohio Paralegal Services Inc 330-759-1430		•	•	•	•	•
		•	Urban Title Search Services 419-289-0437		•	•			

CV	CR	PR	ROSS (EST)		UC	RE	TX	VS	VR
•	•	•	Infinity Information Network Inc 614-261-1213		•	•	•	•	•
•	•	•	National Service Information Inc 800-235-0337		•		•	•	
•	•	•	Ohio Paralegal Services Inc 330-759-1430		•	•	•	•	•
•		•	Q.S.I. (Quantum Software Inc) 614-224-9207		•	•	•		

CV	CR	PR	SANDUSKY (EST)		UC	RE	TX	VS	VR
•	•	•	Data Research Inc (SOP) 800-432-6607		•	•	•	•	•
•	•	•	Infinity Information Network Inc 614-261-1213		•	•	•	•	•
•	•	•	🏛 Investigative Solutions 330-626-5655		•	•		•	•
•	•		M & D Records Research (SOP) 419-693-5649		•		•		
•	•		National Service Information Inc 800-235-0337		•		•	•	
•	•	•	Ohio Independent Title & Pub Rec Search (SOP) ... 419-447-7474		•	•	•		
•	•	•	Ohio Paralegal Services Inc 330-759-1430		•	•	•	•	•
•	•	•	Research Associates 216-892-1000		•	•	•	•	

CV	CR	PR	SCIOTO (EST)		UC	RE	TX	VS	VR
•	•	•	Infinity Information Network Inc 614-261-1213		•	•	•	•	•
•	•	•	National Service Information Inc 800-235-0337		•		•	•	
•	•	•	Ohio Paralegal Services Inc 330-759-1430		•	•	•	•	•

CV	CR	PR	SENECA (EST)		UC	RE	TX	VS	VR
•	•	•	Infinity Information Network Inc 614-261-1213		•	•	•	•	•
•	•	•	National Service Information Inc 800-235-0337		•		•	•	
•	•	•	Ohio Independent Title & Pub Rec Search (SOP) ... 419-447-7474		•	•	•		
•	•	•	Ohio Paralegal Services Inc 330-759-1430		•	•	•	•	•

CV	CR	PR	SHELBY (EST)		UC	RE	TX	VS	VR
•	•	•	Blazinski, Al 513-698-7283		•	•	•	•	

BK	CV	CR	PR			UC	RE	TX	VS	VR
	•	•	•	Infinity Information Network Inc	614-261-1213	•	•	•	•	•
	•	•	•	National Service Information Inc	800-235-0337	•	•		•	•
	•	•	•	Ohio Paralegal Services Inc	330-759-1430	•	•	•	•	•

BK	CV	CR	PR	STARK (EST)		UC	RE	TX	VS	VR
•	•	•	•	Akron/Canton/Cleveland Court Reporters (SOP)	330-376-8100	•	•	•	•	•
	•	•		American Information Network Inc	330-484-6272					
	•	•		Corporate Screening Services Inc	800-229-8606	•		•		
•				Hogan Information Services	405-278-6954					
•	•	•	•	Infinity Information Network Inc	614-261-1213	•	•	•	•	•
•	•	•	•	Informed Directions	800-335-2889					
•	•	•	•	Investigative Solutions	330-626-5655	•	•	•	•	•
•	•	•	•	National Service Information Inc	800-235-0337	•		•		
•	•	•	•	Ohio Paralegal Services Inc	330-759-1430	•	•	•		•
•	•	•	•	Rumancik, David M	330-837-7737	•	•	•	•	

DT	BK	CV	CR	PR	SUMMIT (EST)		UC	RE	TX	VS	VR
•	•	•	•	•	Akron/Canton/Cleveland Court Reporters (SOP)	330-376-8100	•	•	•	•	•
•	•	•	•	•	All Search & Service (SOP)	216-731-3794	•	•	•		
•	•	•	•		Corporate Screening Services Inc	800-229-8606	•		•		
•	•	•	•	•	Docutech Information Services	800-361-3310	•	•	•		
•	•	•	•	•	Eagle Communications (SOP)	216-646-9179	•	•	•		•
•	•				Hogan Information Services	405-278-6954					
•	•	•	•	•	IRS (Insight Research Systems)	216-663-5011	•	•	•		•
•	•	•	•	•	Infinity Information Network Inc	614-261-1213	•	•	•	•	•
		•	•		Infinity Infotrac	216-291-9696					
•	•	•	•	•	Investigative Solutions	330-626-5655	•	•	•	•	•
•	•	•	•		Kalyvas, Jim	614-759-7456	•	•	•		
•	•	•	•	•	National Service Information Inc	800-235-0337	•		•	•	
•	•	•	•	•	Ohio Paralegal Services Inc	330-759-1430	•	•	•		•
•	•	•	•	•	Premier Research	330-297-1977	•	•			
•	•	•	•		Rumancik, David M	330-837-7737	•	•	•		
•	•	•	•	•	The Pre-Check Company	216-226-7700					

CV	CR	PR	TRUMBULL (EST)		UC	RE	TX	VS	VR
•	•	•	Akron/Canton/Cleveland Court Reporters (SOP)	330-376-8100	•	•	•	•	•
•	•	•	Infinity Information Network Inc	614-261-1213	•	•	•	•	•
•	•	•	Investigative Solutions	330-626-5655	•	•	•	•	•
•	•	•	National Service Information Inc	800-235-0337	•		•	•	
•	•	•	Ohio Paralegal Services Inc	330-759-1430	•	•	•		•
•	•	•	Rumancik, David M	330-837-7737	•	•	•	•	
•	•	•	Toni Rose Associates	800-848-0055	•	•	•	•	
•			Trumbull County Abstract Co	330-399-1891	•	•	•		

CV	CR	PR	TUSCARAWAS (EST)		UC	RE	TX	VS	VR
•	•	•	Akron/Canton/Cleveland Court Reporters (SOP)	330-376-8100	•	•	•	•	•
•	•	•	Claugus, Claudine	614-425-1831	•	•	•		•
•	•	•	Infinity Information Network Inc	614-261-1213	•	•	•	•	•
•	•	•	Investigative Solutions	330-626-5655	•	•	•	•	•
•	•	•	National Service Information Inc	800-235-0337	•		•	•	
•	•	•	Ohio Paralegal Services Inc	330-759-1430	•	•	•		•
•	•	•	Rumancik, David M	330-837-7737	•	•	•		
•	•	•	Woodard and Bohse Law Office	330-343-8848	•	•	•		

CV	CR	PR	UNION (EST)		UC	RE	TX	VS	VR
•			Corporate Services of Ohio Inc	614-464-2400	•	•	•		
•	•	•	Document Resources	800-552-3453	•	•	•	•	•
•	•	•	Infinity Information Network Inc	614-261-1213	•	•	•	•	•
•	•	•	Miller, G Scott	614-363-1324	•	•	•	•	
•	•	•	National Service Information Inc	800-235-0337	•		•	•	
•	•	•	Ohio Paralegal Services Inc	330-759-1430	•	•	•		•
•			Q.S.I. (Quantum Software Inc)	614-224-9207	•	•	•		

239

VAN WERT (EST)

CV	CR	PR			UC	RE	TX	VS	VR
•	•	•	Data-Quest Research and Recovery (SOP)	419-642-3031	•	•	•	•	•
•	•	•	Infinity Information Network Inc	614-261-1213	•	•	•	•	•
•	•	•	National Service Information Inc	800-235-0337	•		•	•	
•	•	•	Ohio Paralegal Services Inc	330-759-1430	•	•	•	•	•

VINTON (EST)

CV	CR	PR			UC	RE	TX	VS	VR
•	•	•	Gable, Norma P	614-385-3201	•	•	•	•	
•	•	•	Infinity Information Network Inc	614-261-1213	•	•	•	•	•
•	•	•	National Service Information Inc	800-235-0337	•		•	•	
•	•	•	Ohio Paralegal Services Inc	330-759-1430	•	•	•	•	•
•	•	•	Simmons & Grillo	614-596-5291	•	•	•	•	

WARREN (EST)

CV	CR	PR			UC	RE	TX	VS	VR
•	•	•	Advanced Background Check	513-254-9234	•	•	•		
•	•		🗑 Alpha Research LLC (SOP)	205-755-7008		•			
•		•	District Security Inc	800-688-8721	•		•	•	
•	•	•	General Corporate Investigations (SOP)	800-735-7992	•	•	•	•	•
•	•	•	Infinity Information Network Inc	614-261-1213	•	•	•	•	•
•	•	•	McKinley Paralegal Services	513-662-8106	•	•	•		
	•		🗑 Midwest Investigative Services Inc (SOP)	800-227-9740		•		•	•
•	•		🗑 Miller, Cynthia H	513-474-6408	•	•			•
•	•	•	National Service Information Inc	800-235-0337	•		•		
•	•	•	Ohio Paralegal Services Inc	330-759-1430	•	•	•	•	•

WASHINGTON (EST)

CV	CR	PR			UC	RE	TX	VS	VR
•	•	•	Infinity Information Network Inc	614-261-1213	•	•	•	•	•
		•	🗑 Liberty Record Search Inc	304-428-5126	•	•	•		
•	•	•	National Service Information Inc	800-235-0337	•		•	•	
•	•	•	Ohio Paralegal Services Inc	330-759-1430	•	•	•	•	•
•	•	•	West, Thomas	614-373-6688	•	•	•	•	
•	•	•	Wilhelm, Shirley	614-374-8444	•	•	•	•	

WAYNE (EST)

CV	CR	PR			UC	RE	TX	VS	VR
•	•	•	Akron/Canton/Cleveland Court Reporters (SOP)	330-376-8100	•	•	•	•	•
•	•	•	Infinity Information Network Inc	614-261-1213	•	•	•	•	•
•	•	•	🗑 Investigative Solutions	330-626-5655	•	•	•	•	•
•	•		J H L Enterprises	216-845-2823	•				
•	•	•	National Service Information Inc	800-235-0337	•				
•	•	•	Ohio Paralegal Services Inc	330-759-1430	•	•	•	•	•
•	•	•	Rumancik, David M	330-837-7737	•				
			Urban Title Search Services	419-289-0437	•	•	•		
•	•	•	Wayne County Title Co	216-262-2916	•	•	•	•	

WILLIAMS (EST)

CV	CR	PR			UC	RE	TX	VS	VR
•	•	•	Central Investigation (SOP)	800-281-8142	•	•	•	•	•
•	•	•	Data Research Inc (SOP)	800-432-6607	•	•	•	•	•
•	•	•	Infinity Information Network Inc	614-261-1213	•	•	•	•	•
•	•	•	M & D Records Research (SOP)	419-693-5649	•		•		
•	•	•	National Service Information Inc	800-235-0337	•	•	•	•	
•	•	•	Ohio Paralegal Services Inc	330-759-1430	•	•	•	•	•

WOOD (EST)

CV	CR	PR			UC	RE	TX	VS	VR
•	•	•	Central Investigation (SOP)	800-281-8142	•	•	•	•	•
•	•	•	Data Research Inc (SOP)	800-432-6607	•	•	•	•	•
•	•	•	Infinity Information Network Inc	614-261-1213	•	•	•	•	•
•	•	•	M & D Records Research (SOP)	419-693-5649	•		•		
•	•	•	National Service Information Inc	800-235-0337	•		•	•	
•	•	•	Ohio Independent Title & Pub Rec Search (SOP)	419-447-7474	•	•	•		
•	•	•	Ohio Paralegal Services Inc	330-759-1430	•	•	•	•	•

CV	CR	PR	WYANDOT (EST)	UC	RE	TX	VS	VR
•	•	•	Infinity Information Network Inc 614-261-1213	•	•	•	•	•
•	•	•	National Service Information Inc 800-235-0337	•		•	•	
•	•	•	Ohio Independent Title & Pub Rec Search (SOP) 419-447-7474	•	•	•		
•	•	•	Ohio Paralegal Services Inc 330-759-1430	•	•	•	•	•

SUMMARY OF CODES

COURT RECORDS

CODE	GOVERNMENT AGENCY	TYPE OF INFORMATION
DT	US District Court	Federal civil and criminal cases
BK	Bankruptcy Court	United States bankruptcy cases
CV	Civil Court	Municipal, county and state level civil cases
CR	Criminal Court	Municipal, county and state level criminal cases
PR	Probate Court	Wills and estate cases

COUNTY RECORDS

CODE	GOVERNMENT AGENCY	TYPE OF INFORMATION
UC	UCC Filing Office	Uniform Commercial Code and other personal property liens
RE	Recorder of Deeds	Real property transactions and liens
TX	Tax Assessor	Real property tax information
VS	Vital Records Office	Vital statistics—birth, death, marriage, divorce, etc.
VR	Voter Registration Office	Voter registration and campaign contribution information

- "CODE" designates the agency and type of information obtainable in each county from a retriever.
- The time zone for each county is abbreviated as follows: EST—Eastern Standard Time; CST—Central; MST—Mountain; PST—Pacific; AK—Alaska; HT—Hawaii.
- 🏛—This symbol designates a Public Record Retriever Network member.
- "(SOP)" after the retriever name designates Service of Process.
- Individual retrievers without a company name are listed in order of their last name.

US District and Bankruptcy courts are indicated only in the counties where courts are located.

OKLAHOMA

ADAIR (CST)

CV	CR	PR		Phone	UC	RE	TX	VS	VR
●	●	●	AAA Abstract Co Inc	918-696-2770	●	●	●	●	

ALFALFA (CST)

CV	CR	PR		Phone	UC	RE	TX	VS	VR
●		●	Alfalfa Guaranty Abstract Co	405-596-3394	●	●	●	●	
●	●	●	American Detective Agency (SOP)	888-657-4222	●	●	●	●	●
●	●	●	Territorial Title	505-425-3563	●	●	●	●	

ATOKA (CST)

CV	CR	PR		Phone	UC	RE	TX	VS	VR
●	●	●	Atoka Abstract Co Inc	405-889-7316	●	●	●	●	
●	●	●	Moore Mowdy & Youngblood	405-889-5656	●	●	●	●	

BEAVER (CST)

CV	CR	PR		Phone	UC	RE	TX	VS	VR
●		●	Beaver County Abstract Co	405-625-4423	●	●	●	●	

BECKHAM (CST)

CV	CR	PR		Phone	UC	RE	TX	VS	VR
●	●	●	Beckham County Abstract	405-928-3143	●	●	●	●	

BLAINE (CST)

CV	CR	PR		Phone	UC	RE	TX	VS	VR
●	●	●	American Detective Agency (SOP)	888-657-4222	●	●	●	●	●
●		●	Watonga Abstract Co	405-623-7248	●	●	●		

BRYAN (CST)

CV	CR	PR		Phone	UC	RE	TX	VS	VR
●	●	●	Marshall County Abstract Co	405-795-3212	●	●	●	●	
●	●	●	Moore Mowdy & Youngblood	405-889-5656	●	●	●	●	

CADDO (CST)

CV	CR	PR		Phone	UC	RE	TX	VS	VR
●	●	●	American Investigative & Security Svcs Inc (SOP)	800-219-9120	●	●	●	●	●
●	●	●	Lacey Pioneer Abstract Company Inc	405-247-5152	●	●	●	●	

CANADIAN (CST)

CV	CR	PR		Phone	UC	RE	TX	VS	VR
●	●	●	American Investigative & Security Svcs Inc (SOP)	800-219-9120	●	●	●	●	●
●			🗑 Document Retrieval Service	405-235-3653	●		●	●	●
●		●	Jayphil Investigations (SOP)	405-348-3410	●		●	●	●
●	●	●	Mid-West Investigations (SOP)	800-359-5410	●		●	●	●
		●	Redi-Info Information Services	800-349-7334					
●	●	●	Rus B Robison & Associates Inc (SOP)	800-827-7623	●	●	●	●	●
●	●	●	United Legal Services (SOP)	888-232-8432	●	●	●		

CARTER (CST)

CV	CR	PR		Phone	UC	RE	TX	VS	VR
●	●	●	Marshall County Abstract Co	405-795-3212	●	●	●	●	
●	●	●	Mid-West Investigations (SOP)	800-359-5410	●	●	●	●	●

CHEROKEE (CST)

CV	CR	PR		Phone	UC	RE	TX	VS	VR
●	●	●	Cherokee Capitol Abstract and Title	918-456-8851	●	●	●	●	

CHOCTAW (CST)

CV	CR	PR		Phone	UC	RE	TX	VS	VR
●		●	Choctaw County Abstract and Title	405-326-9616	●	●	●		

CIMARRON (CST)

See adjoining counties for retrievers ....

CLEVELAND (CST)

CV	CR	PR		Phone	UC	RE	TX	VS	VR
●		●	American First Abstract Co	405-321-7577	●	●	●		
●	●	●	American Investigative & Security Svcs Inc (SOP)	800-219-9120	●	●	●	●	●
●			🗑 Document Retrieval Service	405-235-3653	●		●	●	●
●	●	●	Jayphil Investigations (SOP)	405-348-3410	●		●	●	●
●	●	●	Mid-West Investigations (SOP)	800-359-5410	●		●	●	●
		●	Redi-Info Information Services	800-349-7334					
●	●	●	Rus B Robison & Associates Inc (SOP)	800-827-7623	●	●	●	●	●
●	●	●	United Legal Services (SOP)	888-232-8432	●	●	●		

CV	CR	PR	COAL (CST)	UC	RE	TX	VS	VR
•	•	•	Marshall County Abstract Co 405-795-3212	•	•	•	•	
•	•	•	Moore Mowdy & Youngblood 405-889-5656	•	•	•	•	

CV	CR	PR	COMANCHE (CST)	UC	RE	TX	VS	VR
•	•	•	▥ Anderson, H Ray 800-248-1900	•	•	•		•
	•		Redi-Info Information Services 800-349-7334					
•		•	Southwest Abstract Co 405-355-3680	•	•	•	•	

CV	CR	PR	COTTON (CST)	UC	RE	TX	VS	VR
•	•	•	▥ Anderson, H Ray 800-248-1900	•	•	•		•

CV	CR	PR	CRAIG (CST)	UC	RE	TX	VS	VR
•		•	Vinita Title Co 918-256-2617	•	•	•	•	

CV	CR	PR	CREEK (CST)	UC	RE	TX	VS	VR
•			▥ Document Retrieval Service 405-235-3653	•		•	•	•
•	•	•	Jones & Associates Inc (SOP) 918-583-4779	•	•	•	•	•
•	•	•	Rus B Robison & Associates Inc (SOP) 800-827-7623	•	•	•	•	•
•	•	•	SRT Investigations 800-800-7119	•	•	•	•	•
•		•	Union-Speer Abstract Co 918-224-4540	•	•	•		

CV	CR	PR	CUSTER (CST)	UC	RE	TX	VS	VR
•		•	Clinton Abstract Co Inc 405-323-3025	•	•	•		

CV	CR	PR	DELAWARE (CST)	UC	RE	TX	VS	VR
•		•	Delaware County Abstract Co 918-253-4425	•	•	•		
•	•	•	NDXR Inc 800-687-5080	•	•	•	•	

CV	CR	PR	DEWEY (CST)	UC	RE	TX	VS	VR
•	•	•	Dewey County Abstract Co 405-328-5556	•	•	•		

CV	CR	PR	ELLIS (CST)	UC	RE	TX	VS	VR
•		•	Woodward County Abstract Co 405-256-3344	•	•	•		

CV	CR	PR	GARFIELD (CST)	UC	RE	TX	VS	VR
•	•	•	American Detective Agency (SOP) 888-657-4222	•	•	•	•	•
•		•	J C Humphrey Abstract Co 405-237-3136	•	•	•		
	•		Redi-Info Information Services 800-349-7334					

CV	CR	PR	GARVIN (CST)	UC	RE	TX	VS	VR
•		•	MG Cox Abstract 405-238-2600		•	•	•	

CV	CR	PR	GRADY (CST)	UC	RE	TX	VS	VR
•	•	•	American Investigative & Security Svcs Inc (SOP) 800-219-9120	•	•	•	•	•
•			▥ Document Retrieval Service 405-235-3653	•		•	•	•
•	•	•	Mid-West Investigations (SOP) 800-359-5410	•	•	•	•	•
•	•	•	United Legal Services (SOP) 888-232-8432	•	•	•		
•		•	Washita Valley Abstract Co 405-224-6111	•	•	•		

CV	CR	PR	GRANT (CST)	UC	RE	TX	VS	VR
•	•	•	American Detective Agency (SOP) 888-657-4222	•	•	•	•	•
•		•	Grant County Abstract Co 405-395-2854	•	•	•		

CV	CR	PR	GREER (CST)	UC	RE	TX	VS	VR
•		•	Greer Guaranty Abstract Co 405-782-3121	•	•	•	•	

CV	CR	PR	HARMON (CST)	UC	RE	TX	VS	VR
•	•	•	Harmon County Abstract 405-688-9255	•	•	•	•	

CV	CR	PR	HARPER (CST)	UC	RE	TX	VS	VR
•		•	Woodward County Abstract Co 405-256-3344	•	•	•		

CV	CR	PR	HASKELL (CST)	UC	RE	TX	VS	VR
•		•	Guaranty Abstract Co 918-967-8876	•	•	•		
•		•	Hebert Land Services 918-647-9524	•	•	•	•	•
•	•	•	New Star Enterprises (SOP)................ 918-567-3241	•	•	•	•	•

CV	CR	PR	HUGHES (CST)	UC	RE	TX	VS	VR
•		•	Atlas Abstract Co 405-379-3311	•	•	•		

CV	CR	PR	JACKSON (CST)	UC	RE	TX	VS	VR
•		•	Jackson County Abstract Co 405-482-1235	•	•	•		

CV	CR	PR	JEFFERSON (CST)	UC	RE	TX	VS	VR
			See adjoining counties for retrievers					

CV	CR	PR	JOHNSTON (CST)	UC	RE	TX	VS	VR
•		•	Johnston County Abstract Co 405-371-9375	•	•	•		
•	•	•	Marshall County Abstract Co 405-795-3212	•	•	•	•	
•	•	•	Moore Mowdy & Youngblood 405-889-5656	•	•	•	•	

CV	CR	PR	KAY (CST)	UC	RE	TX	VS	VR
•		•	Albright Abstract & Title Guaranty 800-522-1251	•	•	•	•	
•	•	•	American Detective Agency (SOP) 888-657-4222	•	•	•	•	•

CV	CR	PR	KINGFISHER (CST)	UC	RE	TX	VS	VR
•	•	•	American Detective Agency (SOP) 888-657-4222	•	•	•	•	•
•			🏛 Document Retrieval Service 405-235-3653	•		•	•	•
•	•	•	Jayphil Investigations (SOP)................ 405-348-3410	•	•	•	•	•
•		•	Solomon Abstract Co Inc 405-375-4151	•	•	•		

CV	CR	PR	KIOWA (CST)	UC	RE	TX	VS	VR
•		•	Kiowa County Abstract Company 405-726-5283	•	•	•		

CV	CR	PR	LATIMER (CST)	UC	RE	TX	VS	VR
•		•	Hebert Land Services 918-647-9524	•	•	•	•	•
•		•	Latimer County Abstract Co 918-465-2131	•	•	•		
•	•	•	New Star Enterprises (SOP)................ 918-567-3241	•	•	•	•	•
•		•	Royce, Pat 918-465-3425	•	•	•	•	

CV	CR	PR	LE FLORE (CST)	UC	RE	TX	VS	VR
•		•	Hebert Land Services 918-647-9524	•	•	•	•	•
•	•	•	New Star Enterprises (SOP)................ 918-567-3241	•	•	•	•	•
•		•	Sooner Abstract & Title Co 918-647-3202	•	•	•	•	

CV	CR	PR	LINCOLN (CST)	UC	RE	TX	VS	VR
•		•	Abstract & Guarantee Co 405-258-1244	•	•	•		
•	•	•	American Investigative & Security Svcs Inc (SOP)........... 800-219-9120	•	•	•	•	•
•	•	•	Jayphil Investigations (SOP)................ 405-348-3410	•	•	•	•	•
•	•	•	United Legal Services (SOP) 888-232-8432	•	•	•		

CV	CR	PR	LOGAN (CST)	UC	RE	TX	VS	VR
•	•	•	American Investigative & Security Svcs Inc (SOP)........... 800-219-9120	•	•	•	•	•
•			🏛 Document Retrieval Service 405-235-3653	•		•	•	•
•	•	•	Jayphil Investigations (SOP)................ 405-348-3410	•	•	•	•	•
•	•	•	Mid-West Investigations (SOP) 800-359-5410	•	•	•	•	•
•	•	•	United Legal Services (SOP) 888-232-8432	•	•	•		

CV	CR	PR	LOVE (CST)	UC	RE	TX	VS	VR
			See adjoining counties for retrievers					

CV	CR	PR	MAJOR (CST)	UC	RE	TX	VS	VR
•	•	•	American Detective Agency (SOP) 888-657-4222	•	•	•	•	•
•	•	•	Fairview Abstract Co 405-227-4524	•	•	•	•	

MARSHALL (CST)

CV	CR	PR		UC	RE	TX	VS	VR
•	•	•	Marshall County Abstract Co 405-795-3212	•	•	•	•	

MAYES (CST)

CV	CR	PR		UC	RE	TX	VS	VR
•	•	•	Jones & Associates Inc (SOP) 918-583-4779	•	•	•	•	•
•		•	Mayes County Abstract 918-825-3074	•	•	•	•	

McCLAIN (CST)

CV	CR	PR		UC	RE	TX	VS	VR
•		•	American Abstract Company 405-527-7575	•	•	•		
•	•	•	American Investigative & Security Svcs Inc (SOP) 800-219-9120	•	•	•	•	•
•	•	•	Jayphil Investigations (SOP) 405-348-3410	•	•	•	•	•
•	•	•	Mid-West Investigations (SOP) 800-359-5410	•	•	•	•	•
•	•	•	United Legal Services (SOP) 888-232-8432	•	•	•		

McCURTAIN (CST)

CV	CR	PR		UC	RE	TX	VS	VR
•	•	•	New Star Enterprises (SOP) 918-567-3241	•	•	•	•	•
•		•	Southern Abstract & Title Co 405-286-2288	•	•	•	•	

McINTOSH (CST)

CV	CR	PR		UC	RE	TX	VS	VR
•		•	Eufaula Abstract & Title Co Inc 918-689-2241	•	•	•		

MURRAY (CST)

CV	CR	PR		UC	RE	TX	VS	VR
•	•	•	Marshall County Abstract Co 405-795-3212	•	•	•	•	
•		•	Murray County Abstract Inc 405-622-5294	•	•	•		

MUSKOGEE (CST)

DT		CV	CR	PR		UC	RE	TX	VS	VR
•		•			⊞ Document Retrieval Service 405-235-3653	•		•	•	•
•		•	•	•	SRT Investigations 800-800-7119	•	•	•	•	•

NOBLE (CST)

CV	CR	PR		UC	RE	TX	VS	VR
•	•	•	American Detective Agency (SOP) 888-657-4222	•	•	•	•	•
•	•	•	Powers Abstract Co Inc 405-336-4068	•	•	•		

NOWATA (CST)

CV	CR	PR		UC	RE	TX	VS	VR
•		•	Title Abstract Co 918-273-0225	•	•	•	•	

OKFUSKEE (CST)

CV	CR	PR		UC	RE	TX	VS	VR
•		•	Okfusee County Abstract Co 918-623-0565	•	•	•	•	

OKLAHOMA (CAPITAL) (CST)

DT	BK	CV	CR	PR		UC	RE	TX	VS	VR
•	•	•	•	•	American Investigative & Security Svcs Inc (SOP) 800-219-9120	•	•	•	•	•
•	•	•			⊞ Capitol Document Services Inc 800-432-0445	•				
•	•	•			⊞ Document Retrieval Service 405-235-3653	•		•	•	•
•	•				⊞ Hogan Information Services 405-278-6954					
•	•	•	•	•	Jayphil Investigations (SOP) 405-348-3410	•	•	•	•	•
•	•	•	•	•	Mid-West Investigations (SOP) 800-359-5410	•	•	•	•	•
		•			Redi-Info Information Services 800-349-7334					
•	•	•	•	•	Rus B Robison & Associates Inc (SOP) 800-827-7623	•		•	•	•
•	•	•	•	•	SRT Investigations 800-800-7119	•	•	•	•	•
•	•	•	•	•	United Legal Services (SOP) 888-232-8432	•	•	•		

OKMULGEE (CST)

BK	CV	CR	PR		UC	RE	TX	VS	VR
	•	•	•	ACB Credit Services 918-756-7741	•	•	•		
•	•	•	•	Jones & Associates Inc (SOP) 918-583-4779	•	•	•	•	•

OSAGE (CST)

CV	CR	PR		UC	RE	TX	VS	VR
•	•	•	American Detective Agency (SOP) 888-657-4222	•	•	•	•	•
•	•	•	Jones & Associates Inc (SOP) 918-583-4779	•	•	•	•	•

OTTAWA (CST)

CV	CR	PR		UC	RE	TX	VS	VR
•	•	•	⊞ Kunkel, Joan & Kelli (SOP) 417-358-6494	•	•	•	•	•
•	•	•	NDXR Inc 800-687-5080	•	•	•	•	
•	•	•	Photo Abstract Co 918-542-1871	•	•	•	•	

	CV	CR	PR	PAWNEE (CST)	UC	RE	TX	VS	VR
				See adjoining counties for retrievers					

	CV	CR	PR	PAYNE (CST)	UC	RE	TX	VS	VR
	●	●	●	American Detective Agency (SOP) 888-657-4222	●	●	●	●	●
	●			🛢 Document Retrieval Service 405-235-3653	●		●	●	●
	●	●	●	Mid-West Investigations (SOP) 800-359-5410	●	●	●	●	●
		●		Redi-Info Information Services 800-349-7334					

	CV	CR	PR	PITTSBURG (CST)	UC	RE	TX	VS	VR
	●		●	Hebert Land Services 918-647-9524	●	●	●	●	●
	●	●	●	New Star Enterprises (SOP) 918-567-3241	●	●	●	●	●
	●	●	●	Pioneer Abstract Co of McAlester Inc 918-423-0817	●	●	●	●	

	CV	CR	PR	PONTOTOC (CST)	UC	RE	TX	VS	VR
	●	●	●	Marshall County Abstract Co 405-795-3212	●	●	●	●	

	CV	CR	PR	POTTAWATOMIE (CST)	UC	RE	TX	VS	VR
	●	●	●	American Investigative & Security Svcs Inc (SOP)...... 800-219-9120	●	●	●	●	●
	●			🛢 Document Retrieval Service 405-235-3653	●		●	●	●
	●	●	●	Jayphil Investigations (SOP)....................... 405-348-3410	●	●	●	●	●
	●	●	●	Mid-West Investigations (SOP) 800-359-5410	●	●	●	●	●
	●	●	●	United Legal Services (SOP) 888-232-8432	●	●	●		

	CV	CR	PR	PUSHMATAHA (CST)	UC	RE	TX	VS	VR
	●	●	●	Moore Mowdy & Youngblood 405-889-5656	●	●	●	●	
	●	●	●	New Star Enterprises (SOP)....................... 918-567-3241	●	●	●	●	
	●		●	Pushmataha County Abstract Co 405-298-3189	●	●	●		

	CV	CR	PR	ROGER MILLS (CST)	UC	RE	TX	VS	VR
	●		●	Cheyenne Abstract Co Inc 405-497-3363	●	●	●		

	CV	CR	PR	ROGERS (CST)	UC	RE	TX	VS	VR
	●	●	●	Jones & Associates Inc (SOP)...................... 918-583-4779	●	●	●	●	●
	●	●	●	Rogers County Abstract Co 918-341-0525	●	●	●	●	
	●	●	●	Rus B Robison & Associates Inc (SOP) 800-827-7623	●	●	●	●	●

	CV	CR	PR	SEMINOLE (CST)	UC	RE	TX	VS	VR
	●	●	●	American Investigative & Security Svcs Inc (SOP)...... 800-219-9120	●	●	●	●	●
	●	●	●	Pioneer Abstract Co 405-257-3351	●	●	●	●	

	CV	CR	PR	SEQUOYAH (CST)	UC	RE	TX	VS	VR
	●		●	Hebert Land Services 918-647-9524	●	●	●	●	●
	●	●	●	Valley Land Title Co 918-775-4872	●	●	●	●	

	CV	CR	PR	STEPHENS (CST)	UC	RE	TX	VS	VR
	●		●	Stephens County Abstract Co 405-255-2525	●	●	●		

	CV	CR	PR	TEXAS (CST)	UC	RE	TX	VS	VR
	●		●	Guaranty Abstract & Title Co 405-338-3374	●	●	●		

	CV	CR	PR	TILLMAN (CST)	UC	RE	TX	VS	VR
				See adjoining counties for retrievers					

DT	BK	CV	CR	PR	TULSA (CST)	UC	RE	TX	VS	VR
●	●	●	●	●	🛢 Court Data Research Services 918-745-2231	●	●	●	●	●
			●		🛢 DAC Services 800-849-3019					
●	●	●			🛢 Document Retrieval Service 405-235-3653	●		●	●	●
●	●				🛢 Hogan Information Services 405-278-6954					
●	●	●	●	●	Jones & Associates Inc (SOP)....................... 918-583-4779	●	●	●	●	●
●	●	●	●	●	Mid-West Investigations (SOP) 800-359-5410	●	●	●	●	●
			●		Redi-Info Information Services 800-349-7334					
●	●	●	●	●	Rus B Robison & Associates Inc (SOP) 800-827-7623	●	●	●	●	●
●	●	●	●	●	SRT Investigations 800-800-7119	●	●	●	●	●

OKLAHOMA

CV	CR	PR	WAGONER (CST)	UC	RE	TX	VS	VR
•	•	•	Jones & Associates Inc (SOP)..918-583-4779	•	•	•	•	•
•	•	•	SRT Investigations 800-800-7119	•	•	•	•	•
•		•	Wagoner County Abstract Co 918-485-2215	•	•	•		

CV	CR	PR	WASHINGTON (CST)	UC	RE	TX	VS	VR
•	•	•	Jones & Associates Inc (SOP)..918-583-4779	•	•	•	•	•
•		•	Musselman Abstract Co 918-336-6410	•	•	•		

CV	CR	PR	WASHITA (CST)	UC	RE	TX	VS	VR
			See adjoining counties for retrievers					

CV	CR	PR	WOODS (CST)	UC	RE	TX	VS	VR
•	•	•	American Detective Agency (SOP) 888-657-4222	•	•	•	•	•
•	•	•	Woods County Abstract Corp 405-327-1746	•	•	•		

CV	CR	PR	WOODWARD (CST)	UC	RE	TX	VS	VR
•		•	Woodward County Abstract Co 405-256-3344	•	•	•		

SUMMARY OF CODES

COURT RECORDS

CODE	GOVERNMENT AGENCY	TYPE OF INFORMATION
DT	US District Court	Federal civil and criminal cases
BK	Bankruptcy Court	United States bankruptcy cases
CV	Civil Court	Municipal, county and state level civil cases
CR	Criminal Court	Municipal, county and state level criminal cases
PR	Probate Court	Wills and estate cases

COUNTY RECORDS

CODE	GOVERNMENT AGENCY	TYPE OF INFORMATION
UC	UCC Filing Office	Uniform Commercial Code and other personal property liens
RE	Recorder of Deeds	Real property transactions and liens
TX	Tax Assessor	Real property tax information
VS	Vital Records Office	Vital statistics—birth, death, marriage, divorce, etc.
VR	Voter Registration Office	Voter registration and campaign contribution information

- "CODE" designates the agency and type of information obtainable in each county from a retriever.
- The time zone for each county is abbreviated as follows: EST—Eastern Standard Time; CST—Central; MST—Mountain; PST—Pacific; AK—Alaska; HT—Hawaii.
- ⚏—This symbol designates a Public Record Retriever Network member.
- "(SOP)" after the retriever name designates Service of Process.
- Individual retrievers without a company name are listed in order of their last name.

US District and Bankruptcy courts are indicated only in the counties where courts are located.

OREGON

CV	CR	PR	BAKER (PST)		UC	RE	TX	VS	VR
●	●	●	M & M Legal Services (SOP) 503-963-9703			●	●	●	

CV	CR	PR	BENTON (PST)		UC	RE	TX	VS	VR
●	●	●	CT Corporation System 800-874-8820		●	●	●	●	
●	●	●	Cleveland Investigations (SOP) 800-888-6629		●	●	●	●	●
●	●	●	Data Research Inc 800-992-1983		●		●		
			Scrivelsby 800-484-2462			●	●		

CV	CR	PR	CLACKAMAS (PST)		UC	RE	TX	VS	VR
●	●		🏛 Background Investigations 800-955-1356		●		●		
●	●	●	Barrister Support Service (SOP) 503-246-8934		●	●		●	
●	●	●	CT Corporation System 800-874-8820		●	●	●	●	
●	●	●	Cleveland Investigations (SOP) 800-888-6629		●	●	●		●
●	●	●	Data Research Inc 800-992-1983		●		●		
●	●	●	Executive Messenger (SOP) 503-852-7222		●			●	
●	●	●	Fairchild Record Search Ltd 800-547-7007		●		●		
●	●	●	Lawyer's Legal Service (SOP) 800-224-7911		●	●	●		●
●	●		Marosi & Associates Inc (SOP) 800-858-3668		●	●			

CV	CR	PR	CLATSOP (PST)		UC	RE	TX	VS	VR
●	●	●	Data Research Inc 800-992-1983		●		●		
●	●	●	Lawyer's Legal Service (SOP) 800-224-7911		●	●	●		●

CV	CR	PR	COLUMBIA (PST)		UC	RE	TX	VS	VR
●	●	●	Cleveland Investigations (SOP) 800-888-6629		●	●	●	●	●
●	●	●	Data Research Inc 800-992-1983		●		●		
●	●	●	Lawyer's Legal Service (SOP) 800-224-7911		●	●	●		●

CV	CR	PR	COOS (PST)		UC	RE	TX	VS	VR
●	●	●	First American Title Insurance of Oregon 541-269-0119		●	●	●	●	
●	●	●	North Pacific Legal (SOP) 541-267-5118			●	●	●	

CV	CR	PR	CROOK (PST)		UC	RE	TX	VS	VR
●	●	●	Central Legal Service (SOP) 800-599-8133		●	●	●	●	
			Scrivelsby 800-484-2462			●	●		

CV	CR	PR	CURRY (PST)		UC	RE	TX	VS	VR
			Scrivelsby 800-484-2462			●	●		

CV	CR	PR	DESCHUTES (PST)		UC	RE	TX	VS	VR
●	●	●	CT Corporation System 800-874-8820		●	●	●	●	
●	●	●	Central Legal Service (SOP) 800-599-8133		●	●	●	●	

CV	CR	PR	DOUGLAS (PST)		UC	RE	TX	VS	VR
●			Douglas County Title Co 503-672-3388		●	●	●		
●	●	●	Key Title 541-673-1146		●	●	●		
			Scrivelsby 800-484-2462			●	●		

CV	CR	PR	GILLIAM (PST)		UC	RE	TX	VS	VR
			See adjoining counties for retrievers						

CV	CR	PR	GRANT (PST)		UC	RE	TX	VS	VR
			See adjoining counties for retrievers						

CV	CR	PR	HARNEY (PST)		UC	RE	TX	VS	VR
			See adjoining counties for retrievers						

CV	CR	PR	HOOD RIVER (PST)		UC	RE	TX	VS	VR
●	●	●	Lawyer's Legal Service (SOP) 800-224-7911		●	●	●		●

DT		CV	CR	PR	JACKSON (PST)	UC	RE	TX	VS	VR
•		•	•	•	CT Corporation System 800-874-8820	•	•	•	•	
•		•	•	•	Cleveland Investigations (SOP)........................... 800-888-6629	•	•	•	•	•
					Scrivelsby 800-484-2462		•	•		

		CV	CR	PR	JEFFERSON (PST)	UC	RE	TX	VS	VR
		•	•	•	Central Legal Service (SOP)............................. 800-599-8133	•	•	•	•	
					Scrivelsby 800-484-2462		•	•		

		CV	CR	PR	JOSEPHINE (PST)	UC	RE	TX	VS	VR
		•	•	•	Cleveland Investigations (SOP)........................... 800-888-6629	•	•	•	•	•
					Scrivelsby 800-484-2462		•	•		

		CV	CR	PR	KLAMATH (PST)	UC	RE	TX	VS	VR
		•	•	•	Cleveland Investigations (SOP)........................... 800-888-6629	•	•	•	•	•

		CV	CR	PR	LAKE (PST)	UC	RE	TX	VS	VR
					See adjoining counties for retrievers					

DT	BK	CV	CR	PR	LANE (PST)	UC	RE	TX	VS	VR
•	•	•	•	•	B & J/Barristers' Aide Inc (SOP)........................... 541-687-0747					
•	•	•	•	•	CT Corporation System 800-874-8820	•	•	•	•	
•	•	•	•	•	Cleveland Investigations (SOP)........................... 800-888-6629	•	•	•	•	•
•	•	•	•	•	Data Research Inc 800-992-1983	•		•		
•	•				🗑 Hogan Information Services 405-278-6954					
•	•	•	•	•	Oregon Process Service Inc (SOP)....................... 800-599-8133		•	•	•	
					Scrivelsby 800-484-2462		•	•		

		CV	CR	PR	LINCOLN (PST)	UC	RE	TX	VS	VR
		•	•	•	CT Corporation System 800-874-8820	•	•	•	•	
					Scrivelsby 800-484-2462		•	•		

		CV	CR	PR	LINN (PST)	UC	RE	TX	VS	VR
		•	•	•	Cleveland Investigations (SOP)........................... 800-888-6629	•	•	•	•	•
		•	•	•	Data Research Inc 800-992-1983	•		•		
					Scrivelsby 800-484-2462		•	•		

		CV	CR	PR	MALHEUR (MST)	UC	RE	TX	VS	VR
					See adjoining counties for retrievers					

		CV	CR	PR	MARION (CAPITAL) (PST)	UC	RE	TX	VS	VR
		•	•		🗑 Background Investigations 800-955-1356	•		•		
		•	•	•	CSC 503-589-1141	•		•		
		•	•	•	CT Corporation System 800-874-8820	•	•	•	•	
		•	•	•	Cleveland Investigations (SOP)........................... 800-888-6629	•	•	•	•	•
		•	•	•	Data Research Inc 800-992-1983	•		•		
		•	•	•	Executive Messenger (SOP) 503-852-7222	•			•	
		•	•	•	🗑 Inquiry Services Inc (SOP) 888-444-4033					
		•	•	•	Lawyer's Legal Service (SOP)............................. 800-224-7911	•	•	•		•
		•	•	•	Quik Check Records 503-373-3543	•	•	•		
					Scrivelsby 800-484-2462		•	•		
		•	•	•	Unisearch Inc 800-554-3113	•		•	•	

		CV	CR	PR	MORROW (PST)	UC	RE	TX	VS	VR
		•	•	•	CT Corporation System 800-874-8820	•	•	•	•	

DT	BK	CV	CR	PR	MULTNOMAH (PST)	UC	RE	TX	VS	VR
•	•	•	•		🗑 Background Investigations 800-955-1356	•		•		
•	•	•	•	•	Barrister Support Service (SOP)........................... 503-246-8934	•	•	•	•	
•	•	•	•	•	CT Corporation System 800-874-8820	•	•	•	•	
•	•	•	•	•	Cleveland Investigations (SOP)........................... 800-888-6629	•	•	•	•	•
•	•	•	•	•	Data Research Inc 800-992-1983	•		•		
•	•	•	•	•	Executive Messenger (SOP) 503-852-7222	•			•	

CV	CR	PR		Phone	UC	RE	TX	VS	VR
●	●	●	Fairchild Record Search Ltd	800-547-7007	●		●		
●	●	●	Lawyer's Legal Service (SOP)	800-224-7911	●	●	●		●
●	●	●	Marosi & Associates Inc (SOP)	800-858-3668	●	●			
●	●		⛁ Prospective Renters Verification Service	503-655-0888					

POLK (PST)

CV	CR	PR		Phone	UC	RE	TX	VS	VR
●	●	●	CT Corporation System	800-874-8820	●	●	●	●	
●	●	●	Cleveland Investigations (SOP)	800-888-6629	●	●	●	●	●
●	●	●	Data Research Inc	800-992-1983	●		●		

SHERMAN (PST)

See adjoining counties for retrievers ....

TILLAMOOK (PST)

See adjoining counties for retrievers ....

UMATILLA (PST)

CV	CR	PR		Phone	UC	RE	TX	VS	VR
●	●	●	M & M Legal Services (SOP)	503-963-9703		●	●	●	

UNION (PST)

CV	CR	PR		Phone	UC	RE	TX	VS	VR
●	●	●	Eastern Oregon Title	541-963-0514	●	●	●		
●	●	●	M & M Legal Services (SOP)	503-963-9703		●	●	●	

WALLOWA (PST)

CV	CR	PR		Phone	UC	RE	TX	VS	VR
●	●	●	M & M Legal Services (SOP)	503-963-9703		●	●	●	

WASCO (PST)

See adjoining counties for retrievers ....

WASHINGTON (PST)

CV	CR	PR		Phone	UC	RE	TX	VS	VR
●	●		⛁ Background Investigations	800-955-1356	●		●		
●	●	●	Barrister Support Service (SOP)	503-246-8934	●	●	●	●	
●	●	●	CT Corporation System	800-874-8820	●	●	●	●	
●	●	●	Cleveland Investigations (SOP)	800-888-6629	●	●	●	●	●
●	●	●	Data Research Inc	800-992-1983	●		●		
●	●	●	Executive Messenger (SOP)	503-852-7222	●			●	
●	●	●	Fairchild Record Search Ltd	800-547-7007	●		●		
●	●	●	Lawyer's Legal Service (SOP)	800-224-7911	●	●	●		●
●	●		Marosi & Associates Inc (SOP)	800-858-3668	●	●			
			Phillips, Devon L	503-693-8730		●	●		
			Scrivelsby	800-484-2462		●	●		

WHEELER (PST)

See adjoining counties for retrievers ....

YAMHILL (PST)

CV	CR	PR		Phone	UC	RE	TX	VS	VR
●	●	●	Cleveland Investigations (SOP)	800-888-6629	●	●	●	●	●
●	●	●	Data Research Inc	800-992-1983	●		●		
●	●	●	Executive Messenger (SOP)	503-852-7222	●			●	
●	●	●	Lawyer's Legal Service (SOP)	800-224-7911	●	●	●		●

PENNSYLVANIA

		CV	CR	PR	ADAMS (EST)	UC	RE	TX	VS	VR
		•	•	•	Abstract Land Associates Inc 717-763-1450	•	•	•	•	
		•	•	•	Abstract One Inc 717-854-3676	•	•	•		
		•	•	•	Colonial Valley Abstract Co 717-848-2871	•	•	•	•	
		•	•	•	Investigative Solutions of Pennsylvania 717-737-4324	•	•	•	•	•
		•	•	•	Pittsburgh Information and Research Co (SOP) 412-766-3832	•	•	•		

DT	BK	CV	CR	PR	ALLEGHENY (EST)	UC	RE	TX	VS	VR
•	•	•	•	•	🏛 Barrett Detective Bureau 412-521-2900	•	•	•	•	•
•	•	•		•	Bucci, Jerry J 412-833-9664	•	•			
		•			Coats, Janet 412-429-3427					
	•				Credit-facts of America 800-233-4747	•				
•		•	•		🏛 Justifacts Credential Verification Inc 800-356-6885					
•	•	•	•	•	Pittsburgh Information and Research Co (SOP) 412-766-3832	•	•	•		
•	•	•	•	•	🏛 Quest and Assoc Inc 412-563-1007	•	•	•	•	•
		•	•	•	Schillinger & Keith Abstracting Inc 800-275-2959	•	•	•		

		CV	CR	PR	ARMSTRONG (EST)	UC	RE	TX	VS	VR
		•	•	•	Falcon Abstract Co 800-828-4081	•	•	•	•	
		•	•	•	Lawyers' Abstract Co 412-283-3510	•	•	•		
		•	•	•	Pittsburgh Information and Research Co (SOP) 412-766-3832	•	•	•		
		•	•	•	Schillinger & Keith Abstracting Inc 800-275-2959	•	•	•	•	

		CV	CR	PR	BEAVER (EST)	UC	RE	TX	VS	VR
					Credit-facts of America 800-233-4747	•	•	•		
		•	•	•	Pittsburgh Information and Research Co (SOP) 412-766-3832	•	•	•		

		CV	CR	PR	BEDFORD (EST)	UC	RE	TX	VS	VR
		•	•		Bedford Credit Bureau 814-623-3213	•	•	•	•	
		•	•	•	Pittsburgh Information and Research Co (SOP) 412-766-3832	•	•	•		

BK	CV	CR	PR	BERKS (EST)	UC	RE	TX	VS	VR
•	•		•	ATACO Inc 800-220-2039	•	•	•		
•	•	•	•	Abstract Associates of Lancaster Inc (SOP) 717-291-5841	•	•	•	•	
•	•	•	•	Commonwealth Investigation Agency 610-433-2325	•	•	•	•	
•	•	•	•	🏛 Kutlus & Company (SOP) 888-726-5335	•	•	•		
•	•	•	•	Pellish and Pellish Attorneys at Law 717-622-2338	•	•	•		
•	•	•	•	Pittsburgh Information and Research Co (SOP) 412-766-3832	•	•	•		
•	•	•	•	Research Information Services 800-685-3320	•	•	•	•	
•	•	•	•	Strauss & Associates 610-378-9020	•	•	•	•	•
	•	•	•	William C Brown and Co 610-373-1516	•	•	•		

		CV	CR	PR	BLAIR (EST)	UC	RE	TX	VS	VR
		•	•		Bedford Credit Bureau 814-623-3213	•	•	•	•	
		•	•	•	🏛 Blair Abstracting Co 814-942-3701	•	•	•		
		•	•	•	Pittsburgh Information and Research Co (SOP) 412-766-3832	•	•	•		

		CV	CR	PR	BRADFORD (EST)	UC	RE	TX	VS	VR
		•	•	•	🏛 Hurley, William 607-734-1743	•	•	•	•	•
		•	•	•	Pittsburgh Information and Research Co (SOP) 412-766-3832	•	•	•		

		CV	CR	PR	BUCKS (EST)	UC	RE	TX	VS	VR
		•		•	ATACO Inc 800-220-2039	•	•	•		
		•	•		Accu-Fax Employment Screening Svcs 215-234-0700	•	•	•	•	•
		•	•	•	🏛 B & R Services for Professionals (SOP) 800-503-7400	•	•	•	•	
		•	•		Best Legal Services Inc (SOP) 215-567-7777	•	•	•	•	
		•	•	•	Commonwealth Investigation Agency 610-433-2325	•	•	•	•	
		•	•	•	Docutrans Inc (SOP) 215-751-9630	•	•	•		
		•	•	•	Interstate Abstract Inc 609-795-4000	•	•	•		
		•	•	•	🏛 Kutlus & Company (SOP) 888-726-5335	•	•	•		
		•	•	•	🏛 Legal Wings Inc (SOP) 800-339-1286	•	•	•	•	•

CV	CR	PR		Phone	UC	RE	TX	VS	VR
•	•	•	Pittsburgh Information and Research Co (SOP)	412-766-3832	•	•	•		
•	•	•	Research Information Services	800-685-3320	•	•	•	•	
•		•	Searchtec	800-762-5018	•	•	•	•	
•	•		Talone and Associates	800-553-5189					
•	•	•	The Coynes (SOP)	215-945-6227	•	•	•	•	

CV	CR	PR	BUTLER (EST)		UC	RE	TX	VS	VR
			Credit-facts of America	800-233-4747	•	•	•		
•	•	•	Lawyers' Abstract Co	412-283-3510	•	•	•		
•	•	•	Pittsburgh Information and Research Co (SOP)	412-766-3832	•	•	•		

DT	CV	CR	PR	CAMBRIA (EST)		UC	RE	TX	VS	VR
	•	•	•	B & G Ltd of Hollidaysburg	814-695-8414	•	•	•		
•	•	•	•	Bedford Credit Bureau	814-623-3213	•	•	•	•	
	•	•	•	Mainline Researchers	814-472-7913	•	•	•	•	
•	•	•	•	Pittsburgh Information and Research Co (SOP)	412-766-3832	•	•	•		
	•	•	•	Schillinger & Keith Abstracting Inc	800-275-2959	•	•	•	•	
	•			Somerset Abstract Co Ltd	814-445-9525	•	•	•		

CV	CR	PR	CAMERON (EST)		UC	RE	TX	VS	VR
•	•	•	Pittsburgh Information and Research Co (SOP)	412-766-3832	•	•			
•	•	•	Reed, David (SOP)	814-486-3349	•	•			•

CV	CR	PR	CARBON (EST)		UC	RE	TX	VS	VR
•	•	•	Commonwealth Investigation Agency	610-433-2325	•	•	•	•	
		•	Fidelity Home Abstract	800-224-5601	•	•	•		
	•	•	ILS Abstract (SOP)	717-454-5436	•	•	•	•	•
	•	•	Kutlus & Company (SOP)	888-726-5335	•	•	•		
	•	•	Pellish and Pellish Attorneys at Law	717-622-2338	•	•	•	•	
•	•	•	Pittsburgh Information and Research Co (SOP)	412-766-3832	•	•	•		
		•	Toma Abstract Inc	717-454-7899	•	•	•		

CV	CR	PR	CENTRE (EST)		UC	RE	TX	VS	VR
•	•	•	B & G Ltd of Hollidaysburg	814-695-8414	•	•	•		
•	•	•	Pittsburgh Information and Research Co (SOP)	412-766-3832	•	•	•		

CV	CR	PR	CHESTER (EST)		UC	RE	TX	VS	VR
•		•	ATACO Inc	800-220-2039	•	•	•	•	
•	•	•	Abstract Associates of Lancaster Inc (SOP)	717-291-5841	•	•	•	•	
•	•		Accu-Fax Employment Screening Svcs	215-234-0700	•	•	•		•
•	•		Best Legal Services Inc (SOP)	215-567-7777	•	•	•	•	
•		•	Interstate Abstract Inc	609-795-4000	•	•	•	•	
•	•	•	Kutlus & Company (SOP)	888-726-5335	•	•	•		
•	•	•	Legal Wings Inc (SOP)	800-339-1286	•	•	•	•	•
•	•		National Legal Process (SOP)	302-429-0652	•	•	•	•	
•	•	•	Pittsburgh Information and Research Co (SOP)	412-766-3832	•	•	•		
•		•	Searchtec	800-762-5018	•	•	•	•	
•	•		Talone and Associates	800-553-5189	•	•	•	•	
•	•	•	The Coynes (SOP)	215-945-6227	•	•	•	•	

CV	CR	PR	CLARION (EST)		UC	RE	TX	VS	VR
•	•	•	Falcon Abstract Co	800-828-4081	•	•	•	•	
•	•	•	Pittsburgh Information and Research Co (SOP)	412-766-3832	•	•	•		

CV	CR	PR	CLEARFIELD (EST)		UC	RE	TX	VS	VR
•	•	•	B & G Ltd of Hollidaysburg	814-695-8414	•	•	•		
•	•	•	Falcon Abstract Co	800-828-4081	•	•	•	•	
•	•	•	Pittsburgh Information and Research Co (SOP)	412-766-3832	•	•	•		

CV	CR	PR	CLINTON (EST)		UC	RE	TX	VS	VR
•	•	•	Pettengill, Sandra L	717-769-6070	•	•	•	•	
•	•	•	Pittsburgh Information and Research Co (SOP)	412-766-3832	•	•	•		

COLUMBIA (EST)

CV	CR	PR	Company	Phone	UC	RE	TX	VS	VR
•	•	•	American Abstract & Land Co	717-389-1174	•	•	•	•	
•	•	•	ILS Abstract (SOP)	717-454-5436	•	•	•	•	•
•	•	•	Pittsburgh Information and Research Co (SOP)	412-766-3832	•	•	•		
•		•	Toma Abstract Inc	717-454-7899	•	•	•		

CRAWFORD (EST)

CV	CR	PR	Company	Phone	UC	RE	TX	VS	VR
•	•	•	Pittsburgh Information and Research Co (SOP)	412-766-3832	•	•	•		
•			Realty Settlement Inc	814-336-1802	•	•	•		
•	•	•	Rumancik, David M	330-837-7737	•	•		•	

CUMBERLAND (EST)

CV	CR	PR	Company	Phone	UC	RE	TX	VS	VR
•	•	•	Abstract Land Associates Inc	717-763-1450	•	•	•	•	
•	•	•	Allmein, Christopher A	717-582-7743	•	•	•		
•	•	•	Credit Bureau of Greater Harrisburg	800-344-3125	•	•	•		
•	•	•	Investigative Solutions of Pennsylvania	717-737-4324	•	•	•	•	•
•	•	•	🏛 Kutlus & Company (SOP)	888-726-5335	•	•	•		
•	•	•	🏛 Nationwide Information Services Inc (SOP)	800-443-0824	•	•	•	•	•
•	•	•	Penncorp Service Group Inc	800-544-9050	•	•	•	•	
•	•	•	Pittsburgh Information and Research Co (SOP)	412-766-3832	•	•	•		
•	•		Priority One Attorney's Service (SOP)	800-444-1365	•	•	•		

DAUPHIN (CAPITAL) (EST)

DT	BK	CV	CR	PR	Company	Phone	UC	RE	TX	VS	VR
		•	•	•	Abstract Associates of Lancaster Inc (SOP)	717-291-5841	•	•	•	•	
		•	•	•	Abstract Land Associates Inc	717-763-1450	•	•	•	•	
•	•	•	•	•	CSC (SOP)	800-622-2300	•	•	•	•	
•	•	•	•	•	🏛 CSC	800-927-9800	•	•	•	•	
•	•	•	•	•	Commonwealth Investigation Agency	610-433-2325	•	•	•	•	
•	•	•	•	•	Credit Bureau of Greater Harrisburg	800-344-3125	•	•	•		
•	•	•	•	•	Document Resources	800-666-0061	•	•	•		•
•	•	•	•	•	Investigative Solutions of Pennsylvania	717-737-4324	•	•	•		•
•	•	•	•	•	🏛 Kutlus & Company (SOP)	888-726-5335	•	•	•		
•	•	•	•	•	🏛 Nationwide Information Services Inc (SOP)	800-443-0824	•	•	•	•	•
•	•	•	•	•	Penncorp Service Group Inc	800-544-9050	•	•	•	•	
•	•	•	•	•	Pittsburgh Information and Research Co (SOP)	412-766-3832	•	•	•		
•	•	•	•		Priority One Attorney's Service (SOP)	800-444-1365	•	•	•		

DELAWARE (EST)

CV	CR	PR	Company	Phone	UC	RE	TX	VS	VR
•		•	ATACO Inc	800-220-2039	•	•	•	•	
•	•	•	🏛 B & R Services for Professionals (SOP)	800-503-7400	•	•	•	•	
•	•		Best Legal Services Inc (SOP)	215-567-7777	•	•	•	•	
•	•	•	🏛 CSC	800-927-9800	•	•	•	•	
•		•	Docutrans Inc (SOP)	215-751-9630	•	•	•	•	
•		•	Interstate Abstract Inc	609-795-4000	•	•	•	•	
•	•	•	🏛 Kutlus & Company (SOP)	888-726-5335	•	•	•	•	
•	•	•	🏛 Legal Wings Inc (SOP)	800-339-1286	•	•	•	•	•
•	•		National Legal Process (SOP)	302-429-0652	•	•	•	•	
•		•	Pittsburgh Information and Research Co (SOP)	412-766-3832	•	•	•		
•		•	🏛 Searchtec	800-762-5018	•	•	•	•	
•	•		Talone and Associates	800-553-5189	•	•	•		
•	•	•	🏛 The Coynes (SOP)	215-945-6227	•	•	•	•	

ELK (EST)

CV	CR	PR	Company	Phone	UC	RE	TX	VS	VR
•	•	•	Falcon Abstract Co	800-828-4081	•	•	•	•	
•	•	•	Pittsburgh Information and Research Co (SOP)	412-766-3832	•	•	•		
•	•	•	Reed, David (SOP)	814-486-3349	•	•	•		•

ERIE (EST)

DT	BK	CV	CR	PR	Company	Phone	UC	RE	TX	VS	VR
		•	•	•	Chiota, Darlene	814-870-0064	•	•	•		
•	•	•	•	•	Pittsburgh Information and Research Co (SOP)	412-766-3832	•	•	•		

CV	CR	PR	FAYETTE (EST)	UC	RE	TX	VS	VR
•	•	•	Fayette Professional Services 412-439-1450	•	•	•	•	•
•	•	•	Pittsburgh Information and Research Co (SOP) 412-766-3832	•	•	•		

CV	CR	PR	FOREST (EST)	UC	RE	TX	VS	VR
•	•	•	Falcon Abstract Co 800-828-4081	•	•	•	•	
•	•	•	Pittsburgh Information and Research Co (SOP) 412-766-3832	•	•	•		

CV	CR	PR	FRANKLIN (EST)	UC	RE	TX	VS	VR
•	•	•	Abstract Land Associates Inc 717-763-1450	•	•	•	•	
•	•	•	Colonial Valley Abstract Co 717-848-2871	•	•	•	•	
•	•	•	Credit Bureau of Greater Harrisburg 800-344-3125	•	•	•		
•	•	•	Pittsburgh Information and Research Co (SOP) 412-766-3832	•	•	•		

CV	CR	PR	FULTON (EST)	UC	RE	TX	VS	VR
•	•		Bedford Credit Bureau 814-623-3213	•	•	•	•	
•	•	•	Pittsburgh Information and Research Co (SOP) 412-766-3832	•	•	•		

CV	CR	PR	GREENE (EST)	UC	RE	TX	VS	VR
•	•	•	Fayette Professional Services 412-439-1450	•	•	•	•	•
•	•	•	Pittsburgh Information and Research Co (SOP) 412-766-3832	•	•	•		

CV	CR	PR	HUNTINGDON (EST)	UC	RE	TX	VS	VR
•	•	•	B & G Ltd of Hollidaysburg 814-695-8414	•	•	•		
•	•		Bedford Credit Bureau 814-623-3213	•	•	•	•	
•	•	•	Pittsburgh Information and Research Co (SOP) 412-766-3832	•	•			

CV	CR	PR	INDIANA (EST)	UC	RE	TX	VS	VR
•	•	•	Pittsburgh Information and Research Co (SOP) 412-766-3832	•	•	•		
•	•	•	Schillinger & Keith Abstracting Inc 800-275-2959	•	•	•	•	

CV	CR	PR	JEFFERSON (EST)	UC	RE	TX	VS	VR
•	•	•	Brewer, Dorothy 814-849-8296	•	•	•		
•	•	•	Falcon Abstract Co 800-828-4081	•	•	•	•	
•	•	•	Pittsburgh Information and Research Co (SOP) 412-766-3832	•	•	•		
•	•	•	Schillinger & Keith Abstracting Inc 800-275-2959	•	•	•	•	

CV	CR	PR	JUNIATA (EST)	UC	RE	TX	VS	VR
•	•	•	Allmein, Christopher A 717-582-7743	•	•	•		
•	•	•	Credit Bureau of Greater Harrisburg 800-344-3125	•	•	•		
•	•	•	Pittsburgh Information and Research Co (SOP) 412-766-3832	•	•	•		
•	•	•	Rupert, Joyce 717-248-4649	•	•	•		

DT	CV	CR	PR	LACKAWANNA (EST)	UC	RE	TX	VS	VR
	•		•	Abstract Enterprises Inc 717-963-5290	•	•	•	•	
	•	•	•	All Pocono Abstract Inc 717-842-2753		•	•	•	
•	•	•	•	Commonwealth Investigation Agency 610-433-2325	•	•	•	•	
	•	•	•	JS Industries (SOP) 717-253-3136	•	•	•	•	•
•	•	•	•	🏛 Kutlus & Company (SOP) 888-726-5335	•	•	•	•	
•	•	•	•	Maximum Protection Inc (SOP) 717-655-3533	•	•	•	•	
•	•	•	•	Pittsburgh Information and Research Co (SOP) 412-766-3832	•	•	•		
•	•	•		Strein, Marg M 717-457-3939		•		•	•

CV	CR	PR	LANCASTER (EST)	UC	RE	TX	VS	VR
•	•	•	Abstract Associates of Lancaster Inc (SOP) 717-291-5841	•	•	•	•	
•	•	•	Abstract Land Associates Inc 717-763-1450	•	•	•	•	
•	•	•	Colonial Valley Abstract Co 717-848-2871	•	•	•	•	
•	•	•	Commonwealth Investigation Agency 610-433-2325	•	•	•	•	
•	•	•	Credit Bureau of Greater Harrisburg 800-344-3125	•	•	•		
•	•	•	Investigative Solutions of Pennsylvania 717-737-4324	•	•	•	•	•
•	•	•	🏛 Kutlus & Company (SOP) 888-726-5335	•	•	•		
•	•	•	🏛 Nationwide Information Services Inc (SOP) 800-443-0824	•	•	•	•	•
•	•	•	Penncorp Service Group Inc 800-544-9050	•	•	•	•	

CV	CR	PR		UC	RE	TX	VS	VR
•	•	•	Pittsburgh Information and Research Co (SOP) ... 412-766-3832	•	•	•		
•	•	•	Research Information Services ... 800-685-3320	•	•	•	•	

CV	CR	PR	LAWRENCE (EST)	UC	RE	TX	VS	VR
•	•	•	Pittsburgh Information and Research Co (SOP) ... 412-766-3832	•	•	•		
•	•	•	Turner, Helen ... 412-652-5402	•	•	•	•	

CV	CR	PR	LEBANON (EST)	UC	RE	TX	VS	VR
•	•	•	Abstract Associates of Lancaster Inc (SOP) ... 717-291-5841	•	•	•	•	
•	•	•	Abstract Land Associates Inc ... 717-763-1450	•	•	•	•	
•	•	•	Commonwealth Investigation Agency ... 610-433-2325	•	•	•		
•	•	•	Credit Bureau of Greater Harrisburg ... 800-344-3125	•	•	•		
•	•	•	🏛 Kutlus & Company (SOP) ... 888-726-5335	•	•	•		
•	•	•	🏛 Nationwide Information Services Inc (SOP) ... 800-443-0824	•	•	•	•	•
•	•	•	Pittsburgh Information and Research Co (SOP) ... 412-766-3832	•	•	•		

CV	CR	PR	LEHIGH (EST)	UC	RE	TX	VS	VR
•	•	•	Commonwealth Investigation Agency ... 610-433-2325	•	•	•	•	
•	•	•	Credit Bureau of Greater Harrisburg ... 800-344-3125	•	•	•		
•	•	•	🏛 Kutlus & Company (SOP) ... 888-726-5335	•	•	•		
•	•	•	Pittsburgh Information and Research Co (SOP) ... 412-766-3832	•	•	•		
		•	Zapf II, John A ... 610-868-5101	•	•	•		

BK	CV	CR	PR	LUZERNE (EST)	UC	RE	TX	VS	VR
			•	All Penn Abstract Co ... 717-823-5410	•	•	•		
•	•	•	•	ILS Abstract (SOP) ... 717-454-5436	•	•	•	•	•
•	•	•	•	🏛 Kutlus & Company (SOP) ... 888-726-5335	•	•	•		
•	•	•	•	Maximum Protection Inc (SOP) ... 717-655-3533	•	•	•	•	•
•	•	•	•	Pittsburgh Information and Research Co (SOP) ... 412-766-3832	•	•	•		
			•	Toma Abstract Inc ... 717-454-7899	•	•	•		

DT		CV	CR	PR	LYCOMING (EST)	UC	RE	TX	VS	VR
		•	•	•	Pettengill, Sandra L ... 717-769-6070	•	•	•	•	
•		•	•	•	Pittsburgh Information and Research Co (SOP) ... 412-766-3832	•	•	•		

CV	CR	PR	McKEAN (EST)	UC	RE	TX	VS	VR
•	•	•	Pittsburgh Information and Research Co (SOP) ... 412-766-3832	•	•	•		
•	•	•	Reed, David (SOP) ... 814-486-3349	•	•	•	•	•

CV	CR	PR	MERCER (EST)	UC	RE	TX	VS	VR
•	•	•	Pittsburgh Information and Research Co (SOP) ... 412-766-3832	•	•	•		
•			Realty Settlement Inc ... 814-336-1802	•	•			
•	•	•	Rumancik, David M ... 330-837-7737	•	•	•	•	

CV	CR	PR	MIFFLIN (EST)	UC	RE	TX	VS	VR
•	•	•	Credit Bureau of Greater Harrisburg ... 800-344-3125	•	•	•		
•	•	•	Kirk, Helen ... 717-248-4560	•	•	•		
•	•	•	Pittsburgh Information and Research Co (SOP) ... 412-766-3832	•	•	•		
•	•	•	Rupert, Joyce ... 717-248-4649	•	•	•		

CV	CR	PR	MONROE (EST)	UC	RE	TX	VS	VR
•	•	•	All Pocono Abstract Inc ... 717-842-2753		•	•	•	
•	•	•	Commonwealth Investigation Agency ... 610-433-2325	•	•	•	•	
		•	Fidelity Home Abstract ... 800-224-5601	•	•	•		
		•	🏛 Kutlus & Company (SOP) ... 888-726-5335	•	•	•		
•	•	•	Pittsburgh Information and Research Co (SOP) ... 412-766-3832	•	•	•		
•		•	Toma Abstract Inc ... 717-454-7899	•	•	•		

CV	CR	PR	MONTGOMERY (EST)	UC	RE	TX	VS	VR
•	•		Accu-Fax Employment Screening Svcs ... 215-234-0700	•	•	•	•	•
•	•	•	🏛 B & R Services for Professionals (SOP) ... 800-503-7400	•	•	•	•	
•	•		Best Legal Services Inc (SOP) ... 215-567-7777	•	•	•	•	
•	•	•	Docutrans Inc (SOP) ... 215-751-9630	•	•	•	•	

					UC	RE	TX	VS	VR
•		•	Interstate Abstract Inc 609-795-4000	•	•	•	•	
•	•	•	🏛 Kutlus & Company (SOP) 888-726-5335	•	•	•		
•	•	•	Pittsburgh Information and Research Co (SOP) 412-766-3832	•	•	•		
•		•	🏛 Searchtec 800-762-5018	•	•	•	•	
•	•		Talone and Associates 800-553-5189	•	•	•		
•	•	•	🏛 The Coynes (SOP) 215-945-6227	•	•	•	•	

CV	CR	PR	MONTOUR (EST)	UC	RE	TX	VS	VR
•	•	•	American Abstract & Land Co 717-389-1174	•	•	•	•	
•	•	•	Pittsburgh Information and Research Co (SOP) 412-766-3832	•	•	•		
•	•	•	S.A.F.E. 717-286-9831	•	•	•	•	
•		•	Toma Abstract Inc 717-454-7899	•	•	•		

CV	CR	PR	NORTHAMPTON (EST)	UC	RE	TX	VS	VR
•	•	•	Commonwealth Investigation Agency 610-433-2325	•	•	•	•	
•	•	•	Credit Bureau of Greater Harrisburg 800-344-3125	•	•	•		
•	•	•	Fidelity Home Abstract 800-224-5601	•	•	•		
•	•	•	🏛 Kutlus & Company (SOP) 888-726-5335	•	•	•		
•	•	•	Pittsburgh Information and Research Co (SOP) 412-766-3832	•	•	•		
•		•	Zapf II, John A 610-868-5101	•	•	•		

CV	CR	PR	NORTHUMBERLAND (EST)	UC	RE	TX	VS	VR
•	•	•	Pittsburgh Information and Research Co (SOP) 412-766-3832	•	•	•		
•	•	•	S.A.F.E. 717-286-9831	•	•	•	•	
•		•	Toma Abstract Inc 717-454-7899	•	•	•		

CV	CR	PR	PERRY (EST)	UC	RE	TX	VS	VR
•	•	•	Abstract Land Associates Inc 717-763-1450	•	•	•	•	
•	•	•	Allmein, Christopher A 717-582-7743	•	•	•		
•	•	•	Credit Bureau of Greater Harrisburg 800-344-3125	•	•	•		
•	•	•	Penncorp Service Group Inc 800-544-9050	•	•	•	•	
•	•	•	Pittsburgh Information and Research Co (SOP) 412-766-3832	•	•	•		

DT	BK	CV	CR	PR	PHILADELPHIA (EST)	UC	RE	TX	VS	VR
•	•	•	•		Accu-Fax Employment Screening Svcs 215-234-0700	•	•	•	•	•
•	•	•	•	•	🏛 B & R Services for Professionals (SOP) 800-503-7400	•	•	•		
•	•	•	•		Best Legal Services Inc (SOP) 215-567-7777	•	•	•		
•	•	•	•	•	🏛 CSC 800-927-9800	•	•	•		
•	•	•	•		Docutrans Inc (SOP) 215-751-9630	•	•	•		
•	•	•	•	•	Interstate Abstract Inc 609-795-4000	•	•	•		
•	•	•	•	•	🏛 Kutlus & Company (SOP) 888-726-5335	•	•	•		
•	•	•	•	•	🏛 Legal Wings Inc (SOP) 800-339-1286	•	•	•	•	•
•	•	•	•	•	Research Information Services 800-685-3320	•	•	•	•	
•	•	•	•	•	🏛 Searchtec 800-762-5018	•	•	•	•	
•	•	•	•		Talone and Associates 800-553-5189	•	•	•		
•	•	•	•	•	🏛 The Coynes (SOP) 215-945-6227	•	•	•	•	

CV	CR	PR	PIKE (EST)	UC	RE	TX	VS	VR
•		•	Able Abstract Co Inc 717-226-3358	•	•	•		
•	•	•	All Pocono Abstract Inc 717-842-2753		•	•	•	
•	•	•	Arbor Abstracting Co 717-253-0472	•	•	•	•	
•		•	Fidelity Home Abstract 800-224-5601	•	•	•		
•			Inter-County Abstract 717-253-4734		•			
•	•	•	Pittsburgh Information and Research Co (SOP) 412-766-3832	•	•	•		
•	•	•	Schroeder, Sharon 717-296-6604	•	•	•		•

CV	CR	PR	POTTER (EST)	UC	RE	TX	VS	VR
•	•	•	Pittsburgh Information and Research Co (SOP) 412-766-3832	•	•	•		
•	•	•	Reed, David (SOP) 814-486-3349	•	•	•		•

CV	CR	PR	SCHUYLKILL (EST)	UC	RE	TX	VS	VR
•		•	Assured Realty 717-622-1366	•	•	•		
•	•	•	Credit Bureau of Greater Harrisburg 800-344-3125	•	•	•		

●	●	●	ILS Abstract (SOP) 717-454-5436	●	●	●	●	●
●	●	●	🏛 Kutlus & Company (SOP) 888-726-5335	●	●	●	●	
●		●	O'Connor, Michael J 800-518-4529		●	●		
●		●	Pellish and Pellish Attorneys at Law 717-622-2338	●	●	●	●	
●	●	●	Pittsburgh Information and Research Co (SOP) 412-766-3832	●	●	●		
●		●	Toma Abstract Inc 717-454-7899	●	●	●		

CV	CR	PR	SNYDER (EST)	UC	RE	TX	VS	VR
●	●	●	Pittsburgh Information and Research Co (SOP) 412-766-3832	●	●	●		
●	●	●	S.A.F.E. 717-286-9831	●	●	●	●	

CV	CR	PR	SOMERSET (EST)	UC	RE	TX	VS	VR
●	●		Bedford Credit Bureau 814-623-3213	●	●	●	●	
●	●	●	Pittsburgh Information and Research Co (SOP) 412-766-3832	●	●	●		
●			Somerset Abstract Co Ltd 814-445-9525	●	●	●		

CV	CR	PR	SULLIVAN (EST)	UC	RE	TX	VS	VR
●	●	●	Pittsburgh Information and Research Co (SOP) 412-766-3832	●	●	●		

CV	CR	PR	SUSQUEHANNA (EST)	UC	RE	TX	VS	VR
●	●	●	Bartkis, Cindy 717-756-3093	●	●	●	●	
●	●	●	Pittsburgh Information and Research Co (SOP) 412-766-3832	●	●	●		

CV	CR	PR	TIOGA (EST)	UC	RE	TX	VS	VR
●	●	●	🏛 Hurley, William 607-734-1743	●	●	●	●	●
●	●	●	Pittsburgh Information and Research Co (SOP) 412-766-3832	●	●	●		

CV	CR	PR	UNION (EST)	UC	RE	TX	VS	VR
●	●	●	Pittsburgh Information and Research Co (SOP) 412-766-3832	●	●	●		
●	●	●	S.A.F.E. 717-286-9831	●	●	●	●	

CV	CR	PR	VENANGO (EST)	UC	RE	TX	VS	VR
●	●	●	Falcon Abstract Co 800-828-4081	●	●	●	●	
●	●	●	Pittsburgh Information and Research Co (SOP) 412-766-3832	●	●	●		
●			Realty Settlement Inc 814-336-1802	●	●	●		
●	●	●	Rumancik, David M 330-837-7737	●	●	●	●	

CV	CR	PR	WARREN (EST)	UC	RE	TX	VS	VR
●	●	●	Pittsburgh Information and Research Co (SOP) 412-766-3832	●	●	●		

CV	CR	PR	WASHINGTON (EST)	UC	RE	TX	VS	VR
			Credit-facts of America 800-233-4747	●	●	●		
●	●	●	Fayette Professional Services 412-439-1450	●	●	●	●	●
●	●		🏛 Justifacts Credential Verification Inc 800-356-6885					
●	●	●	Pittsburgh Information and Research Co (SOP) 412-766-3832	●	●	●		

CV	CR	PR	WAYNE (EST)	UC	RE	TX	VS	VR
●		●	Able Abstract Co Inc 717-226-3358	●	●	●		
●	●	●	All Pocono Abstract Inc 717-842-2753		●	●	●	
●	●	●	Arbor Abstracting Co 717-253-0472	●	●	●	●	
●		●	Fidelity Home Abstract 800-224-5601	●	●	●		
●			Inter-County Abstract 717-253-4734		●			
●	●	●	JS Industries (SOP) 717-253-3136	●	●	●	●	●
●	●	●	Pittsburgh Information and Research Co (SOP) 412-766-3832	●	●	●		
●	●	●	Schloesser, Kathleen 717-253-5368	●	●	●		

CV	CR	PR	WESTMORELAND (EST)	UC	RE	TX	VS	VR
			Credit-facts of America 800-233-4747	●	●	●		
●	●	●	Fayette Professional Services 412-439-1450	●	●	●	●	●
●	●		🏛 Justifacts Credential Verification Inc 800-356-6885					
●		●	Lawyers' Abstract Co 412-283-3510	●	●	●		
●	●	●	Pittsburgh Information and Research Co (SOP) 412-766-3832	●	●	●		
●	●	●	Schillinger & Keith Abstracting Inc 800-275-2959	●	●	●	●	

CV	CR	PR	WYOMING (EST)	UC	RE	TX	VS	VR
•	•	•	Garbus, Catherine J 717-836-6749	•	•	•	•	
•	•	•	Pittsburgh Information and Research Co (SOP) 412-766-3832	•	•	•		

CV	CR	PR	YORK (EST)	UC	RE	TX	VS	VR
•	•	•	Abstract Associates of Lancaster Inc (SOP) 717-291-5841	•	•	•	•	
•	•	•	Abstract One Inc 717-854-3676	•	•	•		
•	•	•	Campbell, Eugene R 717-846-5830	•	•	•		
•	•	•	Colonial Valley Abstract Co 717-848-2871	•	•	•	•	
•	•	•	Credit Bureau of Greater Harrisburg 800-344-3125	•	•	•		
•	•	•	Investigative Solutions of Pennsylvania 717-737-4324	•	•	•	•	•
•	•	•	🏛 Kutlus & Company (SOP) 888-726-5335	•	•	•		
•	•	•	Lamparski & Associates 717-235-1492	•	•	•	•	•
•	•	•	🏛 Nationwide Information Services Inc (SOP) 800-443-0824	•	•	•	•	•
•	•	•	Penncorp Service Group Inc 800-544-9050	•	•	•	•	
•	•	•	Pittsburgh Information and Research Co (SOP) 412-766-3832	•	•	•		
•	•		Priority One Attorney's Service (SOP) 800-444-1365	•	•	•		

RHODE ISLAND

CV	CR	PR	BRISTOL (EST)		UC	RE	TX	VS	VR
●	●	●	Barry Shuster & Associates	800-367-8227	●	●	●	●	●
●	●		🛢 Eyewitness Investigations	800-285-9690	●	●	●	●	●
●			🛢 McGuire Research Associates	401-647-7881	●	●	●		
●	●	●	Trax (SOP)	401-245-3004	●	●	●	●	●

CV	CR	PR	KENT (EST)		UC	RE	TX	VS	VR
●	●	●	Barry Shuster & Associates	800-367-8227	●	●	●	●	●
●	●		🛢 Eyewitness Investigations	800-285-9690	●	●	●	●	●
●			🛢 McGuire Research Associates	401-647-7881	●	●	●		
●	●	●	Trax (SOP)	401-245-3004	●	●	●	●	●

CV	CR	PR	NEWPORT (EST)		UC	RE	TX	VS	VR
●	●	●	Barry Shuster & Associates	800-367-8227	●	●	●	●	●
●	●		🛢 Eyewitness Investigations	800-285-9690	●	●	●	●	●
●			🛢 McGuire Research Associates	401-647-7881	●	●	●		
●	●	●	Trax (SOP)	401-245-3004	●	●	●	●	●

DT	BK	CV	CR	PR	PROVIDENCE (CAPITAL) (EST)		UC	RE	TX	VS	VR
●	●	●	●	●	Barry Shuster & Associates	800-367-8227	●	●	●	●	●
●	●	●	●		🛢 Eyewitness Investigations	800-285-9690	●	●	●	●	●
●	●	●			🛢 McGuire Research Associates	401-647-7881	●	●	●		
●	●	●	●	●	Trax (SOP)	401-245-3004	●	●	●	●	●

CV	CR	PR	WASHINGTON (EST)		UC	RE	TX	VS	VR
●	●	●	Barry Shuster & Associates	800-367-8227	●	●	●	●	●
●	●		🛢 Eyewitness Investigations	800-285-9690	●	●	●	●	●
●			🛢 McGuire Research Associates	401-647-7881	●	●	●		
●	●	●	Trax (SOP)	401-245-3004	●	●	●	●	●

SOUTH CAROLINA

	CV	CR	PR	ABBEVILLE (EST)		UC	RE	TX	VS	VR
	•	•		🏛 Alpha Research LLC (SOP) 205-755-7008				•		
	•	•		Greet America Public Record Svc Inc 214-320-9836						
	•	•	•	🏛 National Data Access Corp (SOP) 800-528-8790		•	•	•	•	•
	•	•	•	🏛 US Document Services Inc 800-796-0698		•	•	•	•	
	•	•	•	Upper State Title Corp 864-260-4649		•	•	•	•	
	•	•	•	🏛 Westwood Research 803-635-3716		•	•	•	•	

	CV	CR	PR	AIKEN (EST)		UC	RE	TX	VS	VR
	•	•		🏛 Alpha Research LLC (SOP) 205-755-7008				•		
	•		•	Garvin, Douglas G 803-649-6281		•				
	•	•		Greet America Public Record Svc Inc 214-320-9836						
	•	•	•	🏛 National Data Access Corp (SOP) 800-528-8790		•	•	•		•
	•	•	•	🏛 SingleSource Services Corp 800-713-3412		•		•	•	•
	•	•	•	🏛 US Document Services Inc 800-796-0698		•	•	•	•	
	•	•	•	🏛 Westwood Research 803-635-3716		•	•	•	•	

	CV	CR	PR	ALLENDALE (EST)		UC	RE	TX	VS	VR
	•	•		Greet America Public Record Svc Inc 214-320-9836						
	•	•	•	🏛 National Data Access Corp (SOP) 800-528-8790		•	•	•	•	•
	•	•	•	🏛 US Document Services Inc 800-796-0698		•	•	•	•	
	•	•	•	🏛 Westwood Research 803-635-3716		•	•	•	•	

	CV	CR	PR	ANDERSON (EST)		UC	RE	TX	VS	VR
	•	•		🏛 Alpha Research LLC (SOP) 205-755-7008				•		
	•	•	•	Cardinal & Coyne Agency (SOP) 864-680-8074		•	•	•	•	•
	•	•		Greet America Public Record Svc Inc 214-320-9836						
	•	•	•	🏛 National Data Access Corp (SOP) 800-528-8790		•	•	•	•	•
	•	•	•	Nolan & Associates 864-244-6593		•		•	•	
	•	•	•	🏛 US Document Services Inc 800-796-0698		•	•	•	•	
	•	•	•	Upper State Title Corp 864-260-4649		•	•	•	•	
	•	•	•	🏛 Westwood Research 803-635-3716		•	•	•	•	

	CV	CR	PR	BAMBERG (EST)		UC	RE	TX	VS	VR
	•	•	•	Collections 803-821-6485		•	•	•	•	•
	•	•		Greet America Public Record Svc Inc 214-320-9836						
	•		•	Horger Barnwell & Reid 803-531-3000		•		•	•	
	•	•	•	🏛 National Data Access Corp (SOP) 800-528-8790		•	•	•	•	•
	•	•	•	🏛 US Document Services Inc 800-796-0698		•	•	•	•	
	•	•	•	🏛 Westwood Research 803-635-3716		•	•	•	•	

	CV	CR	PR	BARNWELL (EST)		UC	RE	TX	VS	VR
	•	•		🏛 Alpha Research LLC (SOP) 205-755-7008				•		
	•	•	•	Collections 803-821-6485		•	•	•	•	•
	•	•		Greet America Public Record Svc Inc 214-320-9836						
	•	•	•	🏛 National Data Access Corp (SOP) 800-528-8790		•	•	•	•	•
	•	•	•	🏛 US Document Services Inc 800-796-0698		•	•	•	•	
	•	•	•	🏛 Westwood Research 803-635-3716		•	•	•	•	

	CV	CR	PR	BEAUFORT (EST)		UC	RE	TX	VS	VR
	•	•		🏛 Alpha Research LLC (SOP) 205-755-7008				•		
	•	•		Greet America Public Record Svc Inc 214-320-9836						
	•	•	•	🏛 NC Search Inc 910-273-4999		•	•	•		
	•	•	•	🏛 National Data Access Corp (SOP) 800-528-8790		•	•	•	•	•
	•	•	•	🏛 SingleSource Services Corp 800-713-3412		•		•	•	•
	•	•	•	The Bister Agency (SOP) 800-247-8375		•	•	•	•	
	•	•	•	🏛 US Document Services Inc 800-796-0698		•	•	•	•	
	•	•	•	🏛 Westwood Research 803-635-3716		•	•	•	•	

	CV	CR	PR	BERKELEY (EST)		UC	RE	TX	VS	VR
	•	•		🏛 Alpha Research LLC (SOP) 205-755-7008				•		
	•	•	•	Collections 803-821-6485		•	•	•	•	•
	•	•		Greet America Public Record Svc Inc 214-320-9836						
	•	•	•	🏛 National Data Access Corp (SOP) 800-528-8790		•	•	•	•	•
	•	•	•	Process Serving Unlimited (SOP) 803-728-2732		•		•		
	•	•	•	🏛 SingleSource Services Corp 800-713-3412		•		•	•	•
	•	•	•	🏛 US Document Services Inc 800-796-0698		•	•	•	•	
	•	•	•	🏛 Westwood Research 803-635-3716		•	•	•	•	

	CV	CR	PR	CALHOUN (EST)		UC	RE	TX	VS	VR
	•	•	•	Collections 803-821-6485		•	•	•	•	•
	•			Greet America Public Record Svc Inc 214-320-9836						
	•		•	Horger Barnwell & Reid 803-531-3000		•	•	•		
	•	•	•	🏛 NC Search Inc 910-273-4999		•	•	•		
	•	•	•	🏛 National Data Access Corp (SOP) 800-528-8790		•	•	•	•	•
	•	•	•	🏛 SingleSource Services Corp 800-713-3412		•		•	•	•
	•	•	•	🏛 US Document Services Inc 800-796-0698		•	•	•	•	
	•	•	•	🏛 Westwood Research 803-635-3716		•	•	•	•	

DT	CV	CR	PR	CHARLESTON (EST)		UC	RE	TX	VS	VR
•	•	•		🏛 Alpha Research LLC (SOP) 205-755-7008				•		
	•	•	•	Collections 803-821-6485		•	•	•	•	•
•	•	•		Greet America Public Record Svc Inc 214-320-9836						
•	•	•	•	🏛 NC Search Inc 910-273-4999		•	•	•		
•	•	•	•	🏛 National Data Access Corp (SOP) 800-528-8790		•	•	•		
•	•	•	•	Process Serving Unlimited (SOP) 803-728-2732		•		•		
•	•	•	•	🏛 SingleSource Services Corp 800-713-3412		•		•	•	•
•	•	•	•	🏛 US Document Services Inc 800-796-0698		•	•	•	•	
•	•	•	•	🏛 Westwood Research 803-635-3716		•	•	•	•	

	CV	CR	PR	CHEROKEE (EST)		UC	RE	TX	VS	VR
	•	•	•	A-1 Hanline Investigations (SOP) 803-684-3200		•	•	•	•	•
	•	•	•	Cardinal & Coyne Agency (SOP) 864-680-8074		•	•	•	•	•
	•	•	•	Fewell Private Investigations (SOP) 803-327-7378		•	•	•	•	•
	•	•		Greet America Public Record Svc Inc 214-320-9836						
	•	•	•	🏛 National Data Access Corp (SOP) 800-528-8790		•	•	•	•	•
	•	•	•	Nolan & Associates 864-244-6593		•		•	•	
	•	•	•	Professional Service of Process Inc (SOP) 704-532-6322		•		•	•	
	•	•	•	🏛 SingleSource Services Corp 800-713-3412		•		•	•	•
	•	•	•	🏛 US Document Services Inc 800-796-0698		•	•	•	•	
	•	•	•	🏛 Westwood Research 803-635-3716		•	•	•	•	

	CV	CR	PR	CHESTER (EST)		UC	RE	TX	VS	VR
	•	•	•	A-1 Hanline Investigations (SOP) 803-684-3200		•	•	•	•	•
	•	•	•	Cardinal & Coyne Agency (SOP) 864-680-8074		•	•	•	•	•
	•	•	•	Fewell Private Investigations (SOP) 803-327-7378		•	•	•	•	•
	•	•		Greet America Public Record Svc Inc 214-320-9836						
	•	•		Haislip, Lisa 704-553-0974				•		
	•	•	•	🏛 National Data Access Corp (SOP) 800-528-8790		•	•	•	•	•
	•	•	•	Polk Legal Service 803-366-9772		•	•	•		
	•	•	•	Professional Service of Process Inc (SOP) 704-532-6322		•	•	•	•	
	•	•	•	🏛 SingleSource Services Corp 800-713-3412		•	•	•	•	•
	•	•	•	🏛 US Document Services Inc 800-796-0698		•	•	•	•	
	•	•	•	🏛 Westwood Research 803-635-3716		•	•	•	•	

	CV	CR	PR	CHESTERFIELD (EST)		UC	RE	TX	VS	VR
	•	•		Greet America Public Record Svc Inc 214-320-9836						
	•	•	•	🏛 National Data Access Corp (SOP) 800-528-8790		•	•	•	•	•
	•	•	•	🏛 SingleSource Services Corp 800-713-3412		•		•	•	•
	•	•	•	🏛 US Document Services Inc 800-796-0698		•	•	•	•	
	•	•	•	🏛 Westwood Research 803-635-3716		•	•	•	•	

CV	CR	PR	CLARENDON (EST)		UC	RE	TX	VS	VR
•	•	•	Collections 803-821-6485		•	•	•	•	•
•	•	•	Cothran & Cothran 864-435-8495		•	•	•	•	
•	•		Greet America Public Record Svc Inc 214-320-9836						
•	•	•	🏛 National Data Access Corp (SOP) 800-528-8790		•	•		•	•
•	•	•	🏛 SingleSource Services Corp 800-713-3412		•		•	•	•
•	•	•	🏛 US Document Services Inc 800-796-0698		•	•	•	•	
•	•	•	🏛 Westwood Research 803-635-3716		•	•	•	•	

CV	CR	PR	COLLETON (EST)		UC	RE	TX	VS	VR
•	•	•	Collections 803-821-6485		•	•	•	•	•
•	•		Greet America Public Record Svc Inc 214-320-9836						
•	•	•	Low Country Abstractors (SOP) 803-538-5000		•	•		•	
•	•	•	🏛 National Data Access Corp (SOP) 800-528-8790		•	•	•	•	•
•	•	•	🏛 SingleSource Services Corp 800-713-3412		•		•	•	•
•	•	•	🏛 US Document Services Inc 800-796-0698		•	•	•	•	
•	•	•	🏛 Westwood Research 803-635-3716		•	•	•	•	

CV	CR	PR	DARLINGTON (EST)		UC	RE	TX	VS	VR
•	•		🏛 Alpha Research LLC (SOP) 205-755-7008				•		
•	•		Greet America Public Record Svc Inc 214-320-9836						
•	•	•	🏛 National Data Access Corp (SOP) 800-528-8790		•	•	•	•	•
•	•	•	🏛 SingleSource Services Corp 800-713-3412		•		•	•	•
•	•	•	🏛 US Document Services Inc 800-796-0698		•	•	•	•	
•	•	•	🏛 Westwood Research 803-635-3716		•	•	•	•	

CV	CR	PR	DILLON (EST)		UC	RE	TX	VS	VR
•	•		Greet America Public Record Svc Inc 214-320-9836						
•	•	•	🏛 National Data Access Corp (SOP) 800-528-8790		•	•	•	•	•
•	•	•	🏛 SingleSource Services Corp 800-713-3412		•		•	•	•
•	•	•	🏛 US Document Services Inc 800-796-0698		•	•	•	•	
•	•	•	🏛 Westwood Research 803-635-3716		•	•	•	•	

CV	CR	PR	DORCHESTER (EST)		UC	RE	TX	VS	VR
•	•		🏛 Alpha Research LLC (SOP) 205-755-7008				•		
•	•	•	Collections 803-821-6485		•	•	•	•	•
•	•		Greet America Public Record Svc Inc 214-320-9836						
•		•	Horger Barnwell & Reid 803-531-3000		•	•	•	•	
•	•	•	Low Country Abstractors (SOP) 803-538-5000		•	•	•	•	
•	•	•	🏛 National Data Access Corp (SOP) 800-528-8790		•	•	•	•	•
•	•	•	Process Serving Unlimited (SOP) 803-728-2732		•		•		
•	•	•	🏛 SingleSource Services Corp 800-713-3412		•		•	•	•
•	•	•	🏛 US Document Services Inc 800-796-0698		•	•	•	•	
•	•	•	🏛 Westwood Research 803-635-3716		•	•	•	•	

CV	CR	PR	EDGEFIELD (EST)		UC	RE	TX	VS	VR
•	•		Greet America Public Record Svc Inc 214-320-9836						
•		•	Hastings, Renee 803-637-5304		•	•	•		
•	•	•	🏛 National Data Access Corp (SOP) 800-528-8790		•	•	•		•
•	•	•	🏛 SingleSource Services Corp 800-713-3412		•		•	•	•
•	•	•	🏛 US Document Services Inc 800-796-0698		•	•	•	•	
•	•	•	🏛 Westwood Research 803-635-3716		•	•	•	•	

CV	CR	PR	FAIRFIELD (EST)		UC	RE	TX	VS	VR
•	•	•	Carolina Information Services Inc 803-786-8665		•	•	•	•	
•	•	•	Fewell Private Investigations (SOP) 803-327-7378		•	•	•	•	•
•	•		Greet America Public Record Svc Inc 214-320-9836						
•	•		Haislip, Lisa 704-553-0974				•		
•	•	•	🏛 NC Search Inc 910-273-4999		•	•	•		
•	•	•	🏛 National Data Access Corp (SOP) 800-528-8790		•	•	•	•	•
•	•	•	🏛 SingleSource Services Corp 800-713-3412		•		•	•	•
•	•	•	🏛 US Document Services Inc 800-796-0698		•	•	•	•	

DT	CV	CR	PR	Company	Phone	UC	RE	TX	VS	VR
	•	•		[icon] Westwood Research	803-635-3716	•	•	•	•	

FLORENCE (EST)

DT	CV	CR	PR	Company	Phone	UC	RE	TX	VS	VR
	•	•	•	A+ Abstracting	803-236-1072	•	•	•	•	
•	•	•		[icon] Alpha Research LLC (SOP)	205-755-7008			•		
•	•	•		Greet America Public Record Svc Inc	214-320-9836					
•	•	•	•	[icon] National Data Access Corp (SOP)	800-528-8790	•	•	•	•	•
•	•	•	•	[icon] SingleSource Services Corp	800-713-3412	•		•	•	•
•	•	•	•	[icon] US Document Services Inc	800-796-0698	•	•	•	•	
•	•	•	•	[icon] Westwood Research	803-635-3716	•	•	•	•	

GEORGETOWN (EST)

CV	CR	PR	Company	Phone	UC	RE	TX	VS	VR
•	•	•	A+ Abstracting	803-236-1072	•	•	•	•	
•	•		Greet America Public Record Svc Inc	214-320-9836					
•	•	•	[icon] Info Quest Inc	803-215-3463	•	•	•	•	•
•	•	•	[icon] National Data Access Corp (SOP)	800-528-8790	•	•	•	•	•
•	•	•	[icon] SingleSource Services Corp	800-713-3412	•		•	•	•
		•	Title Services Unlimited	803-527-6326	•	•	•	•	
•	•	•	[icon] Westwood Research	803-635-3716	•	•	•	•	

GREENVILLE (EST)

DT	CV	CR	PR	Company	Phone	UC	RE	TX	VS	VR
•	•	•		[icon] Alpha Research LLC (SOP)	205-755-7008			•		
•	•	•	•	Cardinal & Coyne Agency (SOP)	864-680-8074	•				•
•	•	•		Greet America Public Record Svc Inc	214-320-9836					
•	•	•	•	[icon] National Data Access Corp (SOP)	800-528-8790	•	•	•	•	•
•	•	•	•	Nolan & Associates	864-244-6593	•				
•	•	•	•	[icon] SingleSource Services Corp	800-713-3412	•		•	•	•
•	•	•	•	[icon] US Document Services Inc	800-796-0698	•	•	•	•	
			•	Upper State Title Corp	864-260-4649	•	•	•	•	
•	•	•	•	[icon] Westwood Research	803-635-3716	•	•	•	•	

GREENWOOD (EST)

CV	CR	PR	Company	Phone	UC	RE	TX	VS	VR
•	•		[icon] Alpha Research LLC (SOP)	205-755-7008			•		
•	•		Greet America Public Record Svc Inc	214-320-9836					
•	•	•	[icon] National Data Access Corp (SOP)	800-528-8790	•		•	•	•
•	•	•	[icon] SingleSource Services Corp	800-713-3412	•		•	•	•
•	•	•	[icon] US Document Services Inc	800-796-0698	•	•	•	•	
•	•	•	Upper State Title Corp	864-260-4649	•	•	•	•	
•	•	•	[icon] Westwood Research	803-635-3716	•	•	•	•	

HAMPTON (EST)

CV	CR	PR	Company	Phone	UC	RE	TX	VS	VR
•	•		[icon] Alpha Research LLC (SOP)	205-755-7008			•		
•	•		Greet America Public Record Svc Inc	214-320-9836					
•	•	•	Low Country Abstractors (SOP)	803-538-5000	•	•	•	•	•
•	•	•	[icon] National Data Access Corp (SOP)	800-528-8790	•	•	•	•	•
•	•	•	[icon] SingleSource Services Corp	800-713-3412	•		•	•	•
•	•	•	[icon] US Document Services Inc	800-796-0698	•	•	•	•	
•	•	•	[icon] Westwood Research	803-635-3716	•	•	•	•	

HORRY (EST)

CV	CR	PR	Company	Phone	UC	RE	TX	VS	VR
•	•	•	A+ Abstracting	803-236-1072	•	•	•	•	
•	•		[icon] Alpha Research LLC (SOP)	205-755-7008			•		
•	•		Greet America Public Record Svc Inc	214-320-9836					
•	•	•	[icon] Info Quest Inc	803-215-3463	•	•	•	•	•
•	•	•	[icon] National Data Access Corp (SOP)	800-528-8790	•	•	•	•	•
•	•	•	[icon] SingleSource Services Corp	800-713-3412	•	•	•	•	•
•	•	•	[icon] Westwood Research	803-635-3716	•	•	•	•	

JASPER (EST)

CV	CR	PR	Company	Phone	UC	RE	TX	VS	VR
•	•		[icon] Alpha Research LLC (SOP)	205-755-7008			•		
•	•		Greet America Public Record Svc Inc	214-320-9836					
•	•	•	[icon] National Data Access Corp (SOP)	800-528-8790	•	•	•	•	•
•	•	•	[icon] SingleSource Services Corp	800-713-3412	•		•	•	•

CV	CR	PR		UC	RE	TX	VS	VR
•	•	•	🏛 US Document Services Inc 800-796-0698	•	•	•	•	
•	•	•	🏛 Westwood Research 803-635-3716	•	•	•	•	

CV	CR	PR	KERSHAW (EST)	UC	RE	TX	VS	VR
•	•	•	Fewell Private Investigations (SOP) 803-327-7378	•	•	•	•	•
•	•		Greet America Public Record Svc Inc 214-320-9836					
•	•	•	🏛 NC Search Inc 910-273-4999	•	•	•		
•	•	•	🏛 National Data Access Corp (SOP) 800-528-8790	•	•	•	•	•
•	•	•	🏛 SingleSource Services Corp 800-713-3412	•		•	•	•
•	•	•	🏛 US Document Services Inc 800-796-0698	•	•	•	•	
•	•	•	🏛 Westwood Research 803-635-3716	•	•	•	•	

CV	CR	PR	LANCASTER (EST)	UC	RE	TX	VS	VR
•	•	•	A-1 Hanline Investigations (SOP) 803-684-3200	•	•	•	•	•
•	•	•	🏛 Asset Protection Associates Inc (SOP) 704-523-1651	•	•	•	•	•
•	•	•	Fewell Private Investigations (SOP) 803-327-7378	•	•	•	•	•
•	•		Greet America Public Record Svc Inc 214-320-9836					
•	•		Haislip, Lisa 704-553-0974			•		
•	•	•	🏛 National Data Access Corp (SOP) 800-528-8790	•	•	•	•	•
•	•	•	Polk Legal Service 803-366-9772	•	•	•	•	
•	•	•	🏛 SingleSource Services Corp 800-713-3412	•		•	•	•
•	•	•	🏛 US Document Services Inc 800-796-0698	•	•	•	•	
•	•	•	🏛 Westwood Research 803-635-3716	•	•	•	•	

CV	CR	PR	LAURENS (EST)	UC	RE	TX	VS	VR
•	•		🏛 Alpha Research LLC (SOP) 205-755-7008			•		
•	•	•	Cardinal & Coyne Agency (SOP) 864-680-8074	•	•	•	•	•
•	•		Greet America Public Record Svc Inc 214-320-9836					
•	•	•	🏛 National Data Access Corp (SOP) 800-528-8790	•	•	•	•	
•	•	•	Nolan & Associates 864-244-6593	•		•	•	
•	•	•	🏛 SingleSource Services Corp 800-713-3412	•		•	•	•
•	•	•	🏛 US Document Services Inc 800-796-0698	•	•	•	•	
•	•	•	Upper State Title Corp 864-260-4649	•	•	•	•	
•	•	•	🏛 Westwood Research 803-635-3716	•	•	•	•	

CV	CR	PR	LEE (EST)	UC	RE	TX	VS	VR
•	•	•	Cothran & Cothran 864-435-8495	•	•	•	•	
•	•		Greet America Public Record Svc Inc 214-320-9836					
•	•	•	🏛 National Data Access Corp (SOP) 800-528-8790	•	•	•		•
•	•	•	🏛 SingleSource Services Corp 800-713-3412	•		•	•	•
•	•	•	🏛 US Document Services Inc 800-796-0698	•	•	•	•	
•	•	•	🏛 Westwood Research 803-635-3716	•	•	•	•	

CV	CR	PR	LEXINGTON (EST)	UC	RE	TX	VS	VR
•	•		🏛 Alpha Research LLC (SOP) 205-755-7008			•		
•	•	•	Carolina Information Services Inc 803-786-8665	•	•	•	•	
•	•		Greet America Public Record Svc Inc 214-320-9836					
•		•	Lexington Title Corp 803-957-1243	•	•	•		
•	•	•	🏛 NC Search Inc 910-273-4999	•	•	•		
•	•	•	🏛 National Data Access Corp (SOP) 800-528-8790	•	•	•		•
•	•	•	Professional Service of Process Inc (SOP) 704-532-6322	•	•	•	•	•
•	•	•	🏛 SCC Information Services 803-957-1243	•	•	•		
•	•	•	🏛 SingleSource Services Corp 800-713-3412	•		•	•	•
•	•	•	🏛 US Document Services Inc 800-796-0698	•	•	•	•	
•	•	•	🏛 Westwood Research 803-635-3716	•	•	•	•	

CV	CR	PR	MARION (EST)	UC	RE	TX	VS	VR
•	•	•	A+ Abstracting 803-236-1072	•	•	•	•	
•	•		Greet America Public Record Svc Inc 214-320-9836					
•	•	•	K.R. 803-423-3041	•	•	•	•	
•	•	•	🏛 National Data Access Corp (SOP) 800-528-8790	•	•	•	•	•
•	•	•	🏛 SingleSource Services Corp 800-713-3412	•		•	•	•
•	•	•	🏛 US Document Services Inc 800-796-0698	•	•	•	•	

							UC	RE	TX	VS	VR
●	●	●		🏛 Westwood Research 803-635-3716			●	●	●	●	

	CV	CR	PR	MARLBORO (EST)			UC	RE	TX	VS	VR
	●	●		Greet America Public Record Svc Inc 214-320-9836							
	●	●	●	🏛 National Data Access Corp (SOP) 800-528-8790			●	●	●	●	●
	●	●	●	🏛 SingleSource Services Corp 800-713-3412			●		●	●	●
	●	●	●	🏛 US Document Services Inc 800-796-0698			●	●	●	●	
	●	●	●	🏛 Westwood Research 803-635-3716			●	●	●	●	

	CV	CR	PR	McCORMICK (EST)			UC	RE	TX	VS	VR
	●	●		🏛 Alpha Research LLC (SOP) 205-755-7008					●		
	●	●		Greet America Public Record Svc Inc 214-320-9836							
	●	●	●	🏛 National Data Access Corp (SOP) 800-528-8790			●	●	●	●	●
	●	●	●	🏛 SingleSource Services Corp 800-713-3412			●		●	●	●
	●	●	●	🏛 US Document Services Inc 800-796-0698			●	●	●	●	
	●	●	●	Upper State Title Corp 864-260-4649			●	●	●	●	
	●	●	●	🏛 Westwood Research 803-635-3716			●	●	●	●	

	CV	CR	PR	NEWBERRY (EST)			UC	RE	TX	VS	VR
	●	●		Greet America Public Record Svc Inc 214-320-9836							
	●	●	●	🏛 National Data Access Corp (SOP) 800-528-8790			●	●	●	●	●
	●	●	●	🏛 SingleSource Services Corp 800-713-3412			●		●	●	●
	●	●	●	🏛 US Document Services Inc 800-796-0698			●	●	●	●	
	●	●	●	🏛 Westwood Research 803-635-3716			●	●	●	●	

	CV	CR	PR	OCONEE (EST)			UC	RE	TX	VS	VR
	●	●	●	Bonham, Judy & Mark (SOP) 864-882-3761			●	●	●	●	
	●	●		Greet America Public Record Svc Inc 214-320-9836							
	●	●	●	🏛 National Data Access Corp (SOP) 800-528-8790			●	●	●	●	●
	●	●	●	🏛 SingleSource Services Corp 800-713-3412			●		●	●	●
	●	●	●	🏛 US Document Services Inc 800-796-0698			●	●	●	●	
	●	●	●	Upper State Title Corp 864-260-4649			●	●	●	●	
	●	●	●	🏛 Westwood Research 803-635-3716			●	●	●	●	

	CV	CR	PR	ORANGEBURG (EST)			UC	RE	TX	VS	VR
	●	●		🏛 Alpha Research LLC (SOP) 205-755-7008					●		
	●	●	●	Collections 803-821-6485			●	●	●	●	
	●	●	●	Cothran & Cothran 864-435-8495			●	●	●		
	●	●		Greet America Public Record Svc Inc 214-320-9836							
	●		●	Horger Barnwell & Reid 803-531-3000			●	●	●		
	●	●	●	🏛 National Data Access Corp (SOP) 800-528-8790			●	●	●	●	●
	●	●	●	🏛 SingleSource Services Corp 800-713-3412			●		●	●	●
	●	●	●	🏛 US Document Services Inc 800-796-0698			●	●	●	●	
	●	●	●	🏛 Westwood Research 803-635-3716			●	●	●	●	

	CV	CR	PR	PICKENS (EST)			UC	RE	TX	VS	VR
	●	●		🏛 Alpha Research LLC (SOP) 205-755-7008					●		
	●	●	●	Cardinal & Coyne Agency (SOP) 864-680-8074			●	●	●	●	●
	●	●		Greet America Public Record Svc Inc 214-320-9836							
	●	●	●	🏛 National Data Access Corp (SOP) 800-528-8790			●	●	●	●	●
	●	●	●	Nolan & Associates 864-244-6593			●		●	●	
	●	●	●	🏛 SingleSource Services Corp 800-713-3412			●		●	●	●
	●	●	●	Upper State Title Corp 864-260-4649			●	●	●	●	
	●	●	●	🏛 Westwood Research 803-635-3716			●	●	●	●	

DT	BK	CV	CR	PR	RICHLAND (CAPITAL) (EST)			UC	RE	TX	VS	VR
●	●	●	●		🏛 Alpha Research LLC (SOP) 205-755-7008					●		
●	●	●	●	●	Carolina Information Services Inc 803-786-8665			●	●	●	●	
●	●	●	●		Greet America Public Record Svc Inc 214-320-9836							
●	●	●	●	●	🏛 NC Search Inc 910-273-4999			●	●	●		
●	●	●	●	●	🏛 National Data Access Corp (SOP) 800-528-8790			●	●	●	●	●
●	●	●	●		Professional Service of Process Inc (SOP) 704-532-6322			●	●	●		
●	●	●	●	●	🏛 SingleSource Services Corp 800-713-3412			●		●	●	●

CV	CR	PR		Phone	UC	RE	TX	VS	VR
•	•	•	US Document Services Inc	800-796-0698	•	•	•	•	
•	•	•	Westwood Research	803-635-3716	•	•	•	•	

SALUDA (EST)

CV	CR	PR	Provider	Phone	UC	RE	TX	VS	VR
•	•		Greet America Public Record Svc Inc	214-320-9836					
•		•	Lexington Title Corp	803-957-1243	•	•	•		
•	•	•	National Data Access Corp (SOP)	800-528-8790	•	•	•	•	•
•	•	•	SCC Information Services	803-957-1243	•	•	•		
•	•	•	SingleSource Services Corp	800-713-3412	•		•	•	•
•	•	•	US Document Services Inc	800-796-0698	•	•	•	•	
•	•	•	Westwood Research	803-635-3716	•	•	•	•	

SPARTANBURG (EST)

CV	CR	PR	Provider	Phone	UC	RE	TX	VS	VR
•	•		Alpha Research LLC (SOP)	205-755-7008			•		
•	•	•	Cardinal & Coyne Agency (SOP)	864-680-8074	•	•	•	•	•
•	•		Greet America Public Record Svc Inc	214-320-9836					
•	•	•	NC Search Inc	910-273-4999	•	•	•		
•	•	•	National Data Access Corp (SOP)	800-528-8790	•	•	•		•
•	•	•	Nolan & Associates	864-244-6593	•				
•	•	•	SingleSource Services Corp	800-713-3412	•		•	•	•
•	•	•	US Document Services Inc	800-796-0698	•	•	•	•	
•	•	•	Upper State Title Corp	864-260-4649	•	•	•		
•	•	•	Westwood Research	803-635-3716	•	•	•	•	

SUMTER (EST)

CV	CR	PR	Provider	Phone	UC	RE	TX	VS	VR
•	•	•	Collections	803-821-6485	•	•	•	•	•
•	•	•	Cothran & Cothran	864-435-8495	•	•	•	•	
•	•		Greet America Public Record Svc Inc	214-320-9836					
•	•	•	National Data Access Corp (SOP)	800-528-8790	•		•	•	•
•	•	•	SingleSource Services Corp	800-713-3412	•		•	•	•
•	•	•	US Document Services Inc	800-796-0698	•	•	•	•	
•	•	•	Westwood Research	803-635-3716	•	•	•	•	

UNION (EST)

CV	CR	PR	Provider	Phone	UC	RE	TX	VS	VR
•	•	•	A-1 Hanline Investigations (SOP)	803-684-3200	•	•	•	•	•
•	•	•	Cardinal & Coyne Agency (SOP)	864-680-8074	•	•	•	•	•
•	•		Greet America Public Record Svc Inc	214-320-9836					
•	•	•	National Data Access Corp (SOP)	800-528-8790	•	•	•	•	•
•	•	•	SingleSource Services Corp	800-713-3412	•		•	•	•
•	•	•	US Document Services Inc	800-796-0698	•	•	•	•	
•	•	•	Westwood Research	803-635-3716	•	•	•	•	

WILLIAMSBURG (EST)

CV	CR	PR	Provider	Phone	UC	RE	TX	VS	VR
•	•	•	Cothran & Cothran	864-435-8495	•	•	•	•	
•	•		Greet America Public Record Svc Inc	214-320-9836					
•	•	•	National Data Access Corp (SOP)	800-528-8790	•		•	•	•
•	•	•	SingleSource Services Corp	800-713-3412	•		•	•	•
•	•	•	US Document Services Inc	800-796-0698	•	•	•	•	
•	•	•	Westwood Research	803-635-3716	•	•	•	•	

YORK (EST)

CV	CR	PR	Provider	Phone	UC	RE	TX	VS	VR
•	•	•	A-1 Hanline Investigations (SOP)	803-684-3200	•	•	•	•	•
•	•	•	Asset Protection Associates Inc (SOP)	704-523-1651	•	•	•	•	•
•	•	•	Cardinal & Coyne Agency (SOP)	864-680-8074	•	•	•	•	•
•	•	•	Fewell Private Investigations (SOP)	803-327-7378	•	•	•	•	•
•	•		Greet America Public Record Svc Inc	214-320-9836					
•			Haislip, Lisa	704-553-0974			•		
•	•	•	NC Search Inc	910-273-4999	•	•	•		
•	•	•	National Data Access Corp (SOP)	800-528-8790	•	•	•	•	•
•	•	•	Nolan & Associates	864-244-6593	•				
•	•	•	Polk Legal Service	803-366-9772	•	•	•		
•	•	•	Professional Service of Process Inc (SOP)	704-532-6322	•	•	•		
•	•	•	SingleSource Services Corp	800-713-3412	•		•	•	•
•	•	•	Westwood Research	803-635-3716	•	•	•	•	

SOUTH DAKOTA

CV	CR	PR	AURORA (CST)	UC	RE	TX	VS	VR
•	•	•	Aurora County Abstract 605-942-7770	•	•	•	•	
•	•		🏛 Research Information Services Inc 800-522-3884	•	•	•		

CV	CR	PR	BEADLE (CST)	UC	RE	TX	VS	VR
•		•	Huron Title Co 605-352-6157	•	•	•	•	
•			Minn*Dak Search Service 507-694-1168	•		•		
•	•		🏛 Research Information Services Inc 800-522-3884	•	•	•		

CV	CR	PR	BENNETT (MST)	UC	RE	TX	VS	VR
•	•	•	Home Abstract Co 605-685-6558	•	•	•	•	
•	•		🏛 Research Information Services Inc 800-522-3884	•	•	•		

CV	CR	PR	BON HOMME (CST)	UC	RE	TX	VS	VR
•	•	•	Christensen, Duane 605-364-7661	•	•	•	•	•
•	•	•	Intra-Lex Investigations Inc (SOP) 712-233-1639	•	•	•	•	
•	•		🏛 Research Information Services Inc 800-522-3884	•	•	•		

CV	CR	PR	BROOKINGS (CST)	UC	RE	TX	VS	VR
•	•	•	Dirks, Lewis 605-331-6022	•	•	•	•	
•			Minn*Dak Search Service 507-694-1168	•		•		
•	•		🏛 Research Information Services Inc 800-522-3884	•	•	•		

CV	CR	PR	BROWN (CST)	UC	RE	TX	VS	VR
•			Minn*Dak Search Service 507-694-1168	•		•		
•	•		🏛 Research Information Services Inc 800-522-3884	•	•	•		

CV	CR	PR	BRULE (CST)	UC	RE	TX	VS	VR
•	•	•	Brule County Abstract Co 605-734-4275		•	•		
•	•	•	Brule County Title and Insurance Co 605-734-5533	•	•	•	•	
•	•		🏛 Research Information Services Inc 800-522-3884	•	•	•		

CV	CR	PR	BUFFALO (CST)	UC	RE	TX	VS	VR
•	•	•	Brule County Title and Insurance Co 605-734-5533	•	•	•	•	
•	•		🏛 Research Information Services Inc 800-522-3884	•	•	•		

CV	CR	PR	BUTTE (MST)	UC	RE	TX	VS	VR
•	•	•	Frontier Cultural Service 605-673-2157	•	•	•	•	
•	•		🏛 Research Information Services Inc 800-522-3884	•	•	•		

CV	CR	PR	CAMPBELL (CST)	UC	RE	TX	VS	VR
•	•		🏛 Research Information Services Inc 800-522-3884	•	•	•		

CV	CR	PR	CHARLES MIX (CST)	UC	RE	TX	VS	VR
•	•		🏛 Research Information Services Inc 800-522-3884	•	•	•		

CV	CR	PR	CLARK (CST)	UC	RE	TX	VS	VR
•	•	•	Clark Abstract & Title Co 605-532-3812	•	•	•	•	
•			Minn*Dak Search Service 507-694-1168	•		•		
•	•		🏛 Research Information Services Inc 800-522-3884	•	•	•		

CV	CR	PR	CLAY (CST)	UC	RE	TX	VS	VR
•	•	•	Christensen, Duane 605-364-7661	•	•	•	•	•
•	•	•	Dirks, Lewis 605-331-6022	•	•	•	•	
•	•	•	Intra-Lex Investigations Inc (SOP) 712-233-1639	•	•	•	•	
•	•		🏛 Research Information Services Inc 800-522-3884	•	•	•		

CV	CR	PR	CODINGTON (CST)	UC	RE	TX	VS	VR
•			Minn*Dak Search Service 507-694-1168	•		•		
•	•		🏛 Research Information Services Inc 800-522-3884	•	•	•		
•	•	•	Watertown Title & Escrow Co 605-886-8406	•	•	•	•	

CORSON (MST)

CV	CR	PR	Provider	Phone	UC	RE	TX	VS	VR
•	•		🏛 Research Information Services Inc	800-522-3884	•	•	•		

CUSTER (MST)

CV	CR	PR	Provider	Phone	UC	RE	TX	VS	VR
•	•	•	Frontier Cultural Service	605-673-2157	•	•	•	•	
•	•		🏛 Research Information Services Inc	800-522-3884	•	•	•		

DAVISON (CST)

CV	CR	PR	Provider	Phone	UC	RE	TX	VS	VR
•			Minn*Dak Search Service	507-694-1168	•		•		
•	•		🏛 Research Information Services Inc	800-522-3884	•	•	•		

DAY (CST)

CV	CR	PR	Provider	Phone	UC	RE	TX	VS	VR
•		•	Grue Abstract Co	605-345-3891	•	•	•	•	
•			Minn*Dak Search Service	507-694-1168	•		•		
•	•		🏛 Research Information Services Inc	800-522-3884	•	•	•		

DEUEL (CST)

CV	CR	PR	Provider	Phone	UC	RE	TX	VS	VR
•	•	•	Deuel County Abstract Co	605-874-2381	•	•	•	•	
•			Minn*Dak Search Service	507-694-1168	•		•		
•	•		🏛 Research Information Services Inc	800-522-3884	•	•	•		

DEWEY (MST)

CV	CR	PR	Provider	Phone	UC	RE	TX	VS	VR
•	•		🏛 Research Information Services Inc	800-522-3884	•	•	•		
•	•	•	Titles of Dakota Inc	605-365-5247	•	•	•	•	

DOUGLAS (CST)

CV	CR	PR	Provider	Phone	UC	RE	TX	VS	VR
•	•	•	Douglas County Title Co	605-724-2235		•	•	•	
•	•		🏛 Research Information Services Inc	800-522-3884	•	•	•		

EDMUNDS (CST)

CV	CR	PR	Provider	Phone	UC	RE	TX	VS	VR
•	•		🏛 Research Information Services Inc	800-522-3884	•	•	•		

FALL RIVER (MST)

CV	CR	PR	Provider	Phone	UC	RE	TX	VS	VR
•	•	•	Frontier Cultural Service	605-673-2157	•	•	•	•	
•	•		🏛 Research Information Services Inc	800-522-3884	•	•	•		

FAULK (CST)

CV	CR	PR	Provider	Phone	UC	RE	TX	VS	VR
•	•		🏛 Research Information Services Inc	800-522-3884	•	•	•		

GRANT (CST)

CV	CR	PR	Provider	Phone	UC	RE	TX	VS	VR
•		•	Grant County Abstract & Title Co	605-432-5461	•	•	•		
•			Minn*Dak Search Service	507-694-1168	•		•		
•	•		🏛 Research Information Services Inc	800-522-3884	•	•	•		

GREGORY (CST)

CV	CR	PR	Provider	Phone	UC	RE	TX	VS	VR
•	•	•	Gregory County Abstract Co	605-775-2943	•	•	•		
•	•		🏛 Research Information Services Inc	800-522-3884	•	•	•		

HAAKON (MST)

CV	CR	PR	Provider	Phone	UC	RE	TX	VS	VR
•	•	•	Haakon County Abstract Co	605-859-2461	•	•	•		
•	•		🏛 Research Information Services Inc	800-522-3884	•	•	•		

HAMLIN (CST)

CV	CR	PR	Provider	Phone	UC	RE	TX	VS	VR
•	•	•	Dirks, Lewis	605-331-6022	•	•	•	•	
•			Minn*Dak Search Service	507-694-1168	•		•		
•	•		🏛 Research Information Services Inc	800-522-3884	•	•	•		

HAND (CST)

CV	CR	PR	Provider	Phone	UC	RE	TX	VS	VR
		•	Hand County Abstract & Title Co	605-853-2194	•	•	•	•	
•	•		🏛 Research Information Services Inc	800-522-3884	•	•	•		

HANSON (CST)

CV	CR	PR	Provider	Phone	UC	RE	TX	VS	VR
•	•	•	Hanson County Land & Abstract	605-239-4559	•	•	•	•	
•			Minn*Dak Search Service	507-694-1168	•		•		

				🏛 Research Information Services Inc 800-522-3884	● ● ●

		CV	CR	PR	**HARDING (MST)**	UC	RE	TX	VS	VR
		●	●	●	Harding County Abstract Co 605-375-3422	●	●	●	●	
		●	●		🏛 Research Information Services Inc 800-522-3884	●	●	●		

DT	BK	CV	CR	PR	**HUGHES (CAPITAL) (CST)**	UC	RE	TX	VS	VR
●	●				🏛 Hogan Information Services 405-278-6954					
●	●	●	●	●	Person, Marilyn 605-224-8168	●	●		●	
●	●	●	●		🏛 Research Information Services Inc 800-522-3884	●	●	●		

		CV	CR	PR	**HUTCHINSON (CST)**	UC	RE	TX	VS	VR
		●	●	●	Dirks, Lewis 605-331-6022	●	●	●	●	
		●	●	●	Oplinger Abstract & Title Inc 605-387-2335	●	●	●	●	
		●	●		🏛 Research Information Services Inc 800-522-3884	●	●	●		

		CV	CR	PR	**HYDE (CST)**	UC	RE	TX	VS	VR
		●	●		🏛 Research Information Services Inc 800-522-3884	●	●	●		

		CV	CR	PR	**JACKSON (MST)**	UC	RE	TX	VS	VR
		●	●	●	Brule County Abstract Co 605-734-4275		●	●		
		●	●	●	Frontier Cultural Service 605-673-2157	●	●	●	●	
		●	●	●	Jackson County Title Co 605-837-2286		●	●		
		●	●		🏛 Research Information Services Inc 800-522-3884	●	●	●		

		CV	CR	PR	**JERAULD (CST)**	UC	RE	TX	VS	VR
		●		●	Jerauld County Abstract Co Inc 605-539-1541	●	●	●	●	
		●	●		🏛 Research Information Services Inc 800-522-3884	●	●	●		

		CV	CR	PR	**JONES (CST)**	UC	RE	TX	VS	VR
		●	●	●	Jones County Abstract Co 605-669-2231	●	●	●	●	
		●	●		🏛 Research Information Services Inc 800-522-3884	●	●	●		

		CV	CR	PR	**KINGSBURY (CST)**	UC	RE	TX	VS	VR
		●	●	●	Dirks, Lewis 605-331-6022	●	●	●	●	
		●			Minn*Dak Search Service 507-694-1168	●		●		
		●	●		🏛 Research Information Services Inc 800-522-3884	●	●	●		

		CV	CR	PR	**LAKE (CST)**	UC	RE	TX	VS	VR
		●	●	●	Dirks, Lewis 605-331-6022	●	●	●	●	
		●			Minn*Dak Search Service 507-694-1168	●		●		
		●	●		🏛 Research Information Services Inc 800-522-3884	●	●	●		
		●		●	Weber Abstract Co 605-256-4640	●	●	●	●	

		CV	CR	PR	**LAWRENCE (MST)**	UC	RE	TX	VS	VR
		●	●	●	Frontier Cultural Service 605-673-2157	●	●	●	●	
		●	●	●	🏛 Legal Support Services - II 605-642-7146	●	●	●	●	●
		●	●		🏛 Research Information Services Inc 800-522-3884	●	●	●		

		CV	CR	PR	**LINCOLN (CST)**	UC	RE	TX	VS	VR
		●	●	●	Dirks, Lewis 605-331-6022	●	●	●	●	
		●	●	●	Intra-Lex Investigations Inc (SOP) 712-233-1639	●	●	●	●	
		●			Minn*Dak Search Service 507-694-1168	●		●		
		●	●		🏛 Research Information Services Inc 800-522-3884	●	●	●		

		CV	CR	PR	**LYMAN (CST)**	UC	RE	TX	VS	VR
		●	●	●	Brule County Abstract Co 605-734-4275		●	●		
		●	●	●	Lyman Title Co 605-869-2269		●	●		
		●	●		🏛 Research Information Services Inc 800-522-3884	●	●	●		

		CV	CR	PR	**MARSHALL (CST)**	UC	RE	TX	VS	VR
		●	●	●	Marshall Land & Title Co 605-448-5796	●	●	●	●	
		●			Minn*Dak Search Service 507-694-1168	●		●		
		●	●		🏛 Research Information Services Inc 800-522-3884	●	●	●		

		CV	CR	PR	MCCOOK (CST)		UC	RE	TX	VS	VR
		•	•	•	Dirks, Lewis 605-331-6022		•	•	•	•	
		•	•	•	McCook County Abstract & Title Ins 605-425-2612		•	•	•	•	
		•			Minn*Dak Search Service 507-694-1168		•		•		
		•	•		🏛 Research Information Services Inc 800-522-3884		•	•	•		

		CV	CR	PR	MCPHERSON (CST)		UC	RE	TX	VS	VR
				•	McPherson County Abstract Co 605-439-3614		•	•	•		
		•	•		🏛 Research Information Services Inc 800-522-3884		•	•	•		

		CV	CR	PR	MEADE (MST)		UC	RE	TX	VS	VR
		•	•	•	Frontier Cultural Service 605-673-2157		•	•	•	•	
		•	•		🏛 Research Information Services Inc 800-522-3884		•	•	•		
		•	•	•	Security Land & Abstract Co 605-347-3443		•	•	•	•	

		CV	CR	PR	MELLETTE (MST)		UC	RE	TX	VS	VR
		•	•	•	Mellette County Abstract Co 605-259-3181		•	•	•	•	
		•	•		🏛 Research Information Services Inc 800-522-3884		•	•	•		

		CV	CR	PR	MINER (CST)		UC	RE	TX	VS	VR
		•	•	•	Dirks, Lewis 605-331-6022		•	•	•	•	
		•	•	•	Fidelity Abstract & Title Co 605-772-5632		•	•	•	•	
		•			Minn*Dak Search Service 507-694-1168		•		•		
		•	•		🏛 Research Information Services Inc 800-522-3884		•	•	•		

DT	BK	CV	CR	PR	MINNEHAHA (CST)		UC	RE	TX	VS	VR
		•	•	•	Dirks, Lewis 605-331-6022		•	•	•	•	
•	•				🏛 Hogan Information Services 405-278-6954						
		•	•	•	Intra-Lex Investigations Inc (SOP) 712-233-1639		•	•	•	•	
•	•	•			Minn*Dak Search Service 507-694-1168		•		•		
•	•	•	•		🏛 Research Information Services Inc 800-522-3884		•	•	•		

		CV	CR	PR	MOODY (CST)		UC	RE	TX	VS	VR
		•	•	•	Dirks, Lewis 605-331-6022		•	•	•	•	
		•			Minn*Dak Search Service 507-694-1168		•		•		
		•		•	Moody County Abstract Co 605-997-3723		•	•	•		
		•	•		🏛 Research Information Services Inc 800-522-3884		•	•	•		

DT		CV	CR	PR	PENNINGTON (MST)		UC	RE	TX	VS	VR
•		•	•	•	Frontier Cultural Service 605-673-2157		•	•	•	•	
•		•	•	•	🏛 Legal Support Services - II 605-642-7146		•	•	•	•	•
•		•	•		🏛 Research Information Services Inc 800-522-3884		•	•	•		

		CV	CR	PR	PERKINS (MST)		UC	RE	TX	VS	VR
				•	Perkins County Abstract Co 605-244-5544		•	•	•	•	
		•	•		🏛 Research Information Services Inc 800-522-3884		•	•	•		

		CV	CR	PR	POTTER (CST)		UC	RE	TX	VS	VR
		•	•	•	Potter County Land & Abstract Inc 605-765-2858			•	•	•	
		•	•		🏛 Research Information Services Inc 800-522-3884		•	•	•		

		CV	CR	PR	ROBERTS (CST)		UC	RE	TX	VS	VR
		•			Minn*Dak Search Service 507-694-1168		•		•		
		•	•		🏛 Research Information Services Inc 800-522-3884		•	•	•		

		CV	CR	PR	SANBORN (CST)		UC	RE	TX	VS	VR
		•			Minn*Dak Search Service 507-694-1168		•		•		
		•	•		🏛 Research Information Services Inc 800-522-3884		•	•	•		
		•		•	Sanborn County Realty & Title 605-796-4417			•	•		

		CV	CR	PR	SHANNON (MST)		UC	RE	TX	VS	VR
		•	•		🏛 Research Information Services Inc 800-522-3884		•	•	•		

CV	CR	PR	SPINK (CST)	UC	RE	TX	VS	VR
•	•	•	Gillette Battey & McAreavey 605-472-1210	•	•	•	•	
•			Minn*Dak Search Service 507-694-1168	•		•		
•	•		🏛 Research Information Services Inc 800-522-3884	•	•	•		

CV	CR	PR	STANLEY (CST)	UC	RE	TX	VS	VR
•	•	•	Person, Marilyn 605-224-8168	•	•	•	•	
•	•		🏛 Research Information Services Inc 800-522-3884	•	•	•		
•	•	•	Titles of Dakota Inc 800-794-2725	•	•	•	•	

CV	CR	PR	SULLY (CST)	UC	RE	TX	VS	VR
•	•	•	Person, Marilyn 605-224-8168	•	•	•	•	
•	•		🏛 Research Information Services Inc 800-522-3884	•	•	•		
•	•	•	Titles of Dakota Inc 605-258-2291	•	•	•	•	

CV	CR	PR	TODD (MST)	UC	RE	TX	VS	VR
•	•		🏛 Research Information Services Inc 800-522-3884	•	•	•		
•		•	Tripp & Todd Title Company 605-842-0334	•	•	•	•	

CV	CR	PR	TRIPP (CST)	UC	RE	TX	VS	VR
•	•		🏛 Research Information Services Inc 800-522-3884	•	•	•		
•		•	Tripp & Todd Title Company 605-842-0334	•	•	•	•	

CV	CR	PR	TURNER (CST)	UC	RE	TX	VS	VR
•	•	•	Dirks, Lewis 605-331-6022	•	•	•	•	
•	•	•	Intra-Lex Investigations Inc (SOP) 712-233-1639	•	•	•	•	
•	•		🏛 Research Information Services Inc 800-522-3884	•	•	•		

CV	CR	PR	UNION (CST)	UC	RE	TX	VS	VR
•	•	•	Dirks, Lewis 605-331-6022	•	•	•	•	
•	•	•	Intra-Lex Investigations Inc (SOP) 712-233-1639	•	•	•	•	
•	•		🏛 Research Information Services Inc 800-522-3884	•	•	•		
•	•	•	Union County Abstract and Title Co 605-356-3180	•	•	•		

CV	CR	PR	WALWORTH (CST)	UC	RE	TX	VS	VR
•	•		🏛 Research Information Services Inc 800-522-3884	•	•	•		
•	•	•	Walworth County Abstract & Title 605-649-7772	•	•	•		

CV	CR	PR	YANKTON (CST)	UC	RE	TX	VS	VR
•	•	•	Christensen, Duane 605-364-7661	•	•	•	•	•
•	•	•	Dirks, Lewis 605-331-6022	•	•	•	•	
•	•	•	Intra-Lex Investigations Inc (SOP) 712-233-1639	•	•	•	•	
•	•		🏛 Research Information Services Inc 800-522-3884	•	•	•		

CV	CR	PR	ZIEBACH (MST)	UC	RE	TX	VS	VR
•	•		🏛 Research Information Services Inc 800-522-3884	•	•	•		
•	•	•	Titles of Dakota Inc 605-365-5247	•	•	•	•	

TENNESSEE

CV	CR	PR	ANDERSON (EST)	UC	RE	TX	VS	VR
•	•		🏛 Alpha Research LLC (SOP)............205-755-7008			•		
•	•	•	🏛 Business Research Services (SOP)..........800-608-4636	•	•	•	•	•
•	•	•	Greater Tennessee Title Co 423-482-1201	•	•	•	•	
•	•		Greet America Public Record Svc Inc 214-320-9836					
•	•	•	🏛 Hollingsworth Court Reporting Inc 504-769-3386	•	•	•	•	
•	•	•	🏛 Legal Investigations (SOP)............423-584-9700	•	•			
•	•		🏛 Records Research of Knoxville 423-524-2630	•		•		

CV	CR	PR	BEDFORD (CST)	UC	RE	TX	VS	VR
•	•		🏛 Alpha Research LLC (SOP)............205-755-7008			•		
•	•	•	🏛 Charles F Edgar & Associates (SOP)............205-539-7761	•	•	•		
•	•		Greet America Public Record Svc Inc 214-320-9836					
•	•	•	🏛 Hollingsworth Court Reporting Inc 504-769-3386	•	•	•	•	

CV	CR	PR	BENTON (CST)	UC	RE	TX	VS	VR
•	•	•	D K Abstract 901-662-7394	•	•	•		
•	•		Greet America Public Record Svc Inc 214-320-9836					
•	•	•	🏛 Hollingsworth Court Reporting Inc 504-769-3386	•	•	•	•	
			Lattus, Helen 901-885-0891	•	•	•		

CV	CR	PR	BLEDSOE (CST)	UC	RE	TX	VS	VR
•	•		🏛 Alpha Research LLC (SOP)............205-755-7008			•		
•	•		Greet America Public Record Svc Inc 214-320-9836					
•	•	•	🏛 Hollingsworth Court Reporting Inc 504-769-3386	•	•	•	•	
•		•	Real Estate Loan Services 423-855-0581	•	•	•		
•		•	Title Guaranty & Trust of Chattanooga 615-266-5751	•	•	•		

CV	CR	PR	BLOUNT (EST)	UC	RE	TX	VS	VR
•	•		🏛 Alpha Research LLC (SOP)............205-755-7008			•		
•	•	•	🏛 Business Research Services (SOP)..........800-608-4636	•	•	•	•	•
•	•	•	Greater Tennessee Title Co 423-482-1201	•	•	•	•	
•	•		Greet America Public Record Svc Inc 214-320-9836					
•	•	•	🏛 Hollingsworth Court Reporting Inc 504-769-3386	•	•	•	•	
•	•	•	🏛 Legal Investigations (SOP)............423-584-9700	•	•			
•	•		🏛 Records Research of Knoxville 423-524-2630	•		•		

CV	CR	PR	BRADLEY (EST)	UC	RE	TX	VS	VR
•	•		🏛 Alpha Research LLC (SOP)............205-755-7008			•		
•	•		Greet America Public Record Svc Inc 214-320-9836					
•	•	•	🏛 Hollingsworth Court Reporting Inc 504-769-3386	•	•	•	•	
•	•	•	🏛 Legal Investigations (SOP)............423-584-9700	•	•			
•		•	Real Estate Loan Services 423-855-0581	•	•	•		
•		•	Title Guaranty & Trust of Chattanooga 615-266-5751	•	•	•		

CV	CR	PR	CAMPBELL (EST)	UC	RE	TX	VS	VR
•	•		Greet America Public Record Svc Inc 214-320-9836					
•	•	•	🏛 Hollingsworth Court Reporting Inc 504-769-3386	•	•	•	•	
•	•	•	🏛 Legal Investigations (SOP)............423-584-9700	•	•			

CV	CR	PR	CANNON (CST)	UC	RE	TX	VS	VR
•	•		🏛 Alpha Research LLC (SOP)............205-755-7008			•		
•	•		Greet America Public Record Svc Inc 214-320-9836					
•	•	•	🏛 Hollingsworth Court Reporting Inc 504-769-3386	•	•	•	•	
•		•	SMS/Strategic Mortgage Services Inc 800-475-2334	•	•	•		

CV	CR	PR	CARROLL (CST)	UC	RE	TX	VS	VR
•	•	•	D K Abstract 901-662-7394	•	•	•		
•	•		Greet America Public Record Svc Inc 214-320-9836					
•	•	•	🏛 Hollingsworth Court Reporting Inc 504-769-3386	•	•	•	•	
			Lattus, Helen 901-885-0891	•	•	•		

	CV	CR	PR	CARTER (EST)		UC	RE	TX	VS	VR
	●	●		Greet America Public Record Svc Inc 214-320-9836						
	●	●	●	🏛 Hollingsworth Court Reporting Inc 504-769-3386		●	●	●	●	
	●	●	●	🏛 Legal Investigations (SOP) 423-584-9700		●	●			
	●	●	●	Simerly, Teresa 423-725-3901		●	●	●	●	

	CV	CR	PR	CHEATHAM (CST)		UC	RE	TX	VS	VR
	●	●		🏛 Alpha Research LLC (SOP) 205-755-7008				●		
	●	●	●	Capitol Filing Service Inc 615-646-1404		●	●	●		
	●	●		Greet America Public Record Svc Inc 214-320-9836						
	●	●	●	🏛 Hollingsworth Court Reporting Inc 504-769-3386		●	●	●	●	
				Laster, Brian 615-790-8252			●			
	●		●	SMS/Strategic Mortgage Services Inc 800-475-2334		●	●	●		

	CV	CR	PR	CHESTER (CST)		UC	RE	TX	VS	VR
	●	●		🏛 Alpha Research LLC (SOP) 205-755-7008				●		
	●	●	●	D K Abstract 901-662-7394		●	●	●		
	●		●	Douglas, Howard F 901-968-9381		●	●	●		
	●	●		Greet America Public Record Svc Inc 214-320-9836						
	●	●	●	🏛 Hollingsworth Court Reporting Inc 504-769-3386		●	●	●	●	

	CV	CR	PR	CLAIBORNE (EST)		UC	RE	TX	VS	VR
	●	●		Greet America Public Record Svc Inc 214-320-9836						
	●	●	●	🏛 Hollingsworth Court Reporting Inc 504-769-3386		●	●	●	●	
	●	●	●	🏛 Title Express Inc 423-587-9886		●	●	●		

	CV	CR	PR	CLAY (CST)		UC	RE	TX	VS	VR
	●	●		Greet America Public Record Svc Inc 214-320-9836						
	●	●	●	🏛 Hollingsworth Court Reporting Inc 504-769-3386		●	●	●	●	

	CV	CR	PR	COCKE (EST)		UC	RE	TX	VS	VR
	●	●	●	Greater Tennessee Title Co 423-482-1201		●	●	●		
	●	●		Greet America Public Record Svc Inc 214-320-9836						
			●	Harris, Eileen 423-397-7669		●	●	●		
	●	●	●	🏛 Hollingsworth Court Reporting Inc 504-769-3386		●	●	●	●	
	●	●	●	🏛 Legal Investigations (SOP) 423-584-9700		●	●			
	●	●	●	🏛 Title Express Inc 423-587-9886		●	●	●		

	CV	CR	PR	COFFEE (CST)		UC	RE	TX	VS	VR
	●	●		🏛 Alpha Research LLC (SOP) 205-755-7008				●		
	●	●	●	🏛 Charles F Edgar & Associates (SOP) 205-539-7761		●	●	●		
	●	●		Greet America Public Record Svc Inc 214-320-9836						
	●	●	●	🏛 Hollingsworth Court Reporting Inc 504-769-3386		●	●	●	●	
	●		●	Title Guaranty & Trust of Chattanooga 615-266-5751		●	●	●		

	CV	CR	PR	CROCKETT (CST)		UC	RE	TX	VS	VR
	●	●	●	D K Abstract 901-662-7394		●	●	●		
	●	●		Greet America Public Record Svc Inc 214-320-9836						
	●	●	●	🏛 Hollingsworth Court Reporting Inc 504-769-3386		●	●	●	●	
				Lattus, Helen 901-885-0891		●	●	●		

	CV	CR	PR	CUMBERLAND (CST)		UC	RE	TX	VS	VR
			●	🏛 Arms, Joan 615-879-2269		●	●	●	●	
	●	●		Greet America Public Record Svc Inc 214-320-9836						
	●	●	●	🏛 Hollingsworth Court Reporting Inc 504-769-3386		●	●	●	●	
	●	●	●	🏛 Legal Investigations (SOP) 423-584-9700		●	●			
	●		●	SMS/Strategic Mortgage Services Inc 800-475-2334		●	●	●		
	●		●	Source (SOP) 800-678-8774		●	●	●		●
	●	●	●	Warner, Larry M 615-484-1611		●	●	●	●	

DT	BK	CV	CR	PR	DAVIDSON (CAPITAL) (CST)		UC	RE	TX	VS	VR
●	●	●	●	●	🏛 Alpha Research LLC (SOP) 205-755-7008				●		

CV	CR	PR				Company	Phone	UC	RE	TX	VS	VR
●	●	●	●	●		Capitol Filing Service Inc	615-646-1404	●	●	●		
●	●	●	●	●		Contract Services Unlimited (SOP)	615-237-3142	●		●		●
●	●	●	●			Greet America Public Record Svc Inc	214-320-9836					
●	●					Hogan Information Services	405-278-6954					
●	●	●	●	●		Hollingsworth Court Reporting Inc	504-769-3386	●	●	●	●	
●	●	●	●	●		Information Retrieval Service	615-255-1708	●	●	●	●	
	●					Laster, Brian	615-790-8252		●			
●	●			●		Legal Eagles Attorney Services (SOP)	800-929-1285	●				
	●			●		Real Estate Loan Services	423-855-0581	●	●			
●	●	●		●		SMS/Strategic Mortgage Services Inc	800-475-2334	●	●			
●	●	●		●		The Search Is On	800-324-2050	●	●	●	●	●
	●					Wiley, Nancy	615-226-0792					

CV	CR	PR	DE KALB (CST)		UC	RE	TX	VS	VR
●	●		Alpha Research LLC (SOP)	205-755-7008			●		
●	●		Greet America Public Record Svc Inc	214-320-9836					
●	●	●	Hollingsworth Court Reporting Inc	504-769-3386	●	●	●	●	
●	●	●	SMS/Strategic Mortgage Services Inc	800-475-2334	●	●	●		
●	●	●	Source (SOP)	800-678-8774	●	●	●		●

CV	CR	PR	DECATUR (CST)		UC	RE	TX	VS	VR
●	●	●	D K Abstract	901-662-7394	●	●	●		
●		●	Douglas, Howard F	901-968-9381	●	●			
●	●		Greet America Public Record Svc Inc	214-320-9836					
●	●	●	Hollingsworth Court Reporting Inc	504-769-3386	●	●	●	●	

CV	CR	PR	DICKSON (CST)		UC	RE	TX	VS	VR
●	●		Alpha Research LLC (SOP)	205-755-7008			●		
●	●	●	Capitol Filing Service Inc	615-646-1404	●	●	●		
●	●		Eye Catcher Investigations	615-789-6165	●				●
●	●		Greet America Public Record Svc Inc	214-320-9836					
●	●	●	Hollingsworth Court Reporting Inc	504-769-3386	●	●	●	●	
●		●	SMS/Strategic Mortgage Services Inc	800-475-2334	●	●	●		

CV	CR	PR	DYER (CST)		UC	RE	TX	VS	VR
●	●		Alpha Research LLC (SOP)	205-755-7008			●		
●	●	●	D K Abstract	901-662-7394	●	●	●		
●	●		Greet America Public Record Svc Inc	214-320-9836					
●	●	●	Hollingsworth Court Reporting Inc	504-769-3386	●	●	●	●	
	●		Lattus, Helen	901-885-0891	●	●	●		

CV	CR	PR	FAYETTE (CST)		UC	RE	TX	VS	VR
●	●	●	Cope Investigative Services LLC (SOP)	800-262-9301	●	●	●	●	●
●	●	●	D K Abstract	901-662-7394	●	●	●		
		●	DJ Records	901-324-6209					
●	●		Greet America Public Record Svc Inc	214-320-9836					
●	●	●	Hollingsworth Court Reporting Inc	504-769-3386	●	●	●	●	
●	●	●	Record-Check Services Inc	800-530-7226	●	●	●	●	●
●	●	●	RecordServe/John Kelley Enterprises	901-853-5320	●	●	●		
●	●	●	Schaeffer Papers (SOP)	800-848-6119		●			

CV	CR	PR	FENTRESS (CST)		UC	RE	TX	VS	VR
		●	Arms, Joan	615-879-2269	●	●	●	●	
●	●		Greet America Public Record Svc Inc	214-320-9836					
●	●	●	Hollingsworth Court Reporting Inc	504-769-3386	●	●	●	●	
●	●	●	Legal Investigations (SOP)	423-584-9700	●	●			
●		●	SMS/Strategic Mortgage Services Inc	800-475-2334	●	●	●		

CV	CR	PR	FRANKLIN (CST)		UC	RE	TX	VS	VR
●	●		Alpha Research LLC (SOP)	205-755-7008			●		
●	●	●	Broadway, J Stephen	615-433-5979	●	●	●	●	
●	●	●	Charles F Edgar & Associates (SOP)	205-539-7761	●	●	●		
●	●		Greet America Public Record Svc Inc	214-320-9836					

CV	CR	PR		UC	RE	TX	VS	VR
•	•	•	Hollingsworth Court Reporting Inc ... 504-769-3386	•	•	•	•	
•		•	Title Guaranty & Trust of Chattanooga ... 615-266-5751	•	•	•		

CV	CR	PR	GIBSON (CST)	UC	RE	TX	VS	VR
•	•	•	D K Abstract ... 901-662-7394	•	•	•		
•	•		Greet America Public Record Svc Inc ... 214-320-9836					
•	•	•	Hollingsworth Court Reporting Inc ... 504-769-3386	•	•	•		•
•	•		Lattus, Helen ... 901-885-0891	•	•	•		

CV	CR	PR	GILES (CST)	UC	RE	TX	VS	VR
•	•		Alpha Research LLC (SOP) ... 205-755-7008			•		
•		•	Blackwell Land & Title Research ... 205-533-2439	•	•			
•	•	•	Broadway, J Stephen ... 615-433-5979	•	•	•	•	
•	•	•	Charles F Edgar & Associates (SOP) ... 205-539-7761	•	•			
•	•		Greet America Public Record Svc Inc ... 214-320-9836					
•	•	•	Hollingsworth Court Reporting Inc ... 504-769-3386	•	•	•		•
•		•	SMS/Strategic Mortgage Services Inc ... 800-475-2334	•	•			

CV	CR	PR	GRAINGER (EST)	UC	RE	TX	VS	VR
•	•		Greet America Public Record Svc Inc ... 214-320-9836					
		•	Harris, Eileen ... 423-397-7669	•	•	•		
•	•	•	Hollingsworth Court Reporting Inc ... 504-769-3386	•	•	•		•
•	•	•	Legal Investigations (SOP) ... 423-584-9700	•	•			
•	•	•	Title Express Inc ... 423-587-9886	•	•	•		

DT	CV	CR	PR	GREENE (EST)	UC	RE	TX	VS	VR
•	•	•		Greet America Public Record Svc Inc ... 214-320-9836					
		•	•	Harris, Eileen ... 423-397-7669	•	•	•		
•	•	•	•	Hollingsworth Court Reporting Inc ... 504-769-3386	•	•	•	•	
•	•	•	•	Legal Investigations (SOP) ... 423-584-9700	•	•			
	•	•	•	Title Express Inc ... 423-587-9886	•	•	•		

CV	CR	PR	GRUNDY (CST)	UC	RE	TX	VS	VR
•	•	•	Earlene Y Speer Law Offices ... 615-692-2368	•	•	•	•	•
•	•		Greet America Public Record Svc Inc ... 214-320-9836					
•	•	•	Hollingsworth Court Reporting Inc ... 504-769-3386	•	•	•		•
•	•	•	Title Guaranty & Trust of Chattanooga ... 615-266-5751	•	•	•		

CV	CR	PR	HAMBLEN (CST)	UC	RE	TX	VS	VR
•	•		Alpha Research LLC (SOP) ... 205-755-7008			•		
•	•		Greet America Public Record Svc Inc ... 214-320-9836					
		•	Harris, Eileen ... 423-397-7669	•	•	•		
•	•	•	Hollingsworth Court Reporting Inc ... 504-769-3386	•	•	•		•
•	•	•	Legal Investigations (SOP) ... 423-584-9700	•	•			
•	•	•	Title Express Inc ... 423-587-9886	•	•	•		

DT	BK	CV	CR	PR	HAMILTON (EST)	UC	RE	TX	VS	VR
•	•	•	•		Alpha Research LLC (SOP) ... 205-755-7008			•		
•	•	•	•		Greet America Public Record Svc Inc ... 214-320-9836					
•	•	•	•	•	Hollingsworth Court Reporting Inc ... 504-769-3386	•	•	•		•
•	•	•	•	•	Legal Investigations (SOP) ... 423-584-9700	•	•			
		•		•	Real Estate Loan Services ... 423-855-0581	•	•	•		
•	•	•		•	Title Guaranty & Trust of Chattanooga ... 615-266-5751	•	•	•		

CV	CR	PR	HANCOCK (EST)	UC	RE	TX	VS	VR
•	•		Greet America Public Record Svc Inc ... 214-320-9836					
•	•	•	Hollingsworth Court Reporting Inc ... 504-769-3386	•	•	•		•
•	•	•	Legal Investigations (SOP) ... 423-584-9700	•	•			
•	•	•	Title Express Inc ... 423-587-9886	•	•	•		

CV	CR	PR	HARDEMAN (CST)	UC	RE	TX	VS	VR
•	•	•	Cope Investigative Services LLC (SOP) ... 800-262-9301	•	•	•	•	•
•	•	•	D K Abstract ... 901-662-7394	•	•	•		

CV	CR	PR		UC	RE	TX	VS	VR
•	•		Greet America Public Record Svc Inc …… 214-320-9836					
•	•	•	🏛 Hollingsworth Court Reporting Inc …… 504-769-3386	•	•	•	•	
•	•	•	🏛 Record-Check Services Inc …… 800-530-7226	•	•	•	•	•

CV	CR	PR	HARDIN (CST)	UC	RE	TX	VS	VR
•	•	•	D K Abstract …… 901-662-7394	•	•	•		
•	•		Douglas, Howard F …… 901-968-9381	•	•	•		
•	•		Greet America Public Record Svc Inc …… 214-320-9836					
•	•	•	🏛 Hollingsworth Court Reporting Inc …… 504-769-3386	•	•	•	•	

CV	CR	PR	HAWKINS (EST)	UC	RE	TX	VS	VR
•	•		Greet America Public Record Svc Inc …… 214-320-9836					
	•		Harris, Eileen …… 423-397-7669	•	•	•		
•	•	•	🏛 Hollingsworth Court Reporting Inc …… 504-769-3386	•	•	•	•	
•	•	•	🏛 Title Express Inc …… 423-587-9886	•	•	•		

CV	CR	PR	HAYWOOD (CST)	UC	RE	TX	VS	VR
•	•	•	D K Abstract …… 901-662-7394	•	•	•		
•	•		Greet America Public Record Svc Inc …… 214-320-9836					
•	•	•	🏛 Hollingsworth Court Reporting Inc …… 504-769-3386	•	•	•	•	
•	•	•	🏛 Record-Check Services Inc …… 800-530-7226	•	•	•	•	•
•	•	•	Schaeffer Papers (SOP) …… 800-848-6119		•			

CV	CR	PR	HENDERSON (CST)	UC	RE	TX	VS	VR
•	•		🏛 Alpha Research LLC (SOP) …… 205-755-7008			•		
•	•	•	D K Abstract …… 901-662-7394	•	•	•		
•	•		Douglas, Howard F …… 901-968-9381	•	•	•		
•	•		Greet America Public Record Svc Inc …… 214-320-9836					
•	•	•	🏛 Hollingsworth Court Reporting Inc …… 504-769-3386	•	•	•	•	

CV	CR	PR	HENRY (CST)	UC	RE	TX	VS	VR
•	•	•	D K Abstract …… 901-662-7394	•	•	•		
•	•		Greet America Public Record Svc Inc …… 214-320-9836					
•	•	•	🏛 Hollingsworth Court Reporting Inc …… 504-769-3386	•	•	•	•	
			Lattus, Helen …… 901-885-0891	•	•	•		

CV	CR	PR	HICKMAN (CST)	UC	RE	TX	VS	VR
•	•	•	Capitol Filing Service Inc …… 615-646-1404	•	•	•		
•	•	•	D K Abstract …… 901-662-7394	•	•	•		
•	•		Greet America Public Record Svc Inc …… 214-320-9836					
•	•	•	🏛 Hollingsworth Court Reporting Inc …… 504-769-3386	•	•	•	•	
•	•	•	Larry R Dorning PC …… 615-796-5959	•	•	•		
•		•	SMS/Strategic Mortgage Services Inc …… 800-475-2334	•	•	•		

CV	CR	PR	HOUSTON (CST)	UC	RE	TX	VS	VR
•	•	•	D K Abstract …… 901-662-7394	•	•	•		
•	•		Greet America Public Record Svc Inc …… 214-320-9836					
•	•	•	🏛 Hollingsworth Court Reporting Inc …… 504-769-3386	•	•	•	•	
•		•	SMS/Strategic Mortgage Services Inc …… 800-475-2334	•	•	•		

CV	CR	PR	HUMPHREYS (CST)	UC	RE	TX	VS	VR
•	•	•	D K Abstract …… 901-662-7394	•	•	•		
•	•		Greet America Public Record Svc Inc …… 214-320-9836					
•	•	•	🏛 Hollingsworth Court Reporting Inc …… 504-769-3386	•	•	•	•	
•		•	SMS/Strategic Mortgage Services Inc …… 800-475-2334	•	•	•		

CV	CR	PR	JACKSON (CST)	UC	RE	TX	VS	VR
•	•		🏛 Alpha Research LLC (SOP) …… 205-755-7008			•		
•	•		Greet America Public Record Svc Inc …… 214-320-9836					
•	•	•	🏛 Hollingsworth Court Reporting Inc …… 504-769-3386	•	•	•	•	
•		•	SMS/Strategic Mortgage Services Inc …… 800-475-2334	•	•	•		
•	•	•	Source (SOP) …… 800-678-8774	•	•	•		•

	CV	CR	PR	JEFFERSON (EST)	UC	RE	TX	VS	VR
	●	●		Alpha Research LLC (SOP) 205-755-7008			●		
	●	●		Greet America Public Record Svc Inc ... 214-320-9836					
			●	Harris, Eileen 423-397-7669	●	●	●		
	●	●	●	Hollingsworth Court Reporting Inc ... 504-769-3386	●	●	●	●	
	●	●	●	Legal Investigations (SOP) ... 423-584-9700	●	●			
	●	●	●	Title Express Inc 423-587-9886	●	●	●		

	CV	CR	PR	JOHNSON (EST)	UC	RE	TX	VS	VR
	●	●		Greet America Public Record Svc Inc ... 214-320-9836					
	●	●	●	Hollingsworth Court Reporting Inc ... 504-769-3386	●	●	●	●	
	●	●	●	Legal Investigations (SOP) ... 423-584-9700	●	●			
	●	●	●	Simerly, Teresa 423-725-3901	●	●	●	●	

DT	BK	CV	CR	PR	KNOX (EST)	UC	RE	TX	VS	VR
●	●	●	●		Alpha Research LLC (SOP) ... 205-755-7008			●		
●	●	●	●	●	Business Research Services (SOP) ... 800-608-4636	●	●	●	●	●
		●	●	●	Greater Tennessee Title Co ... 423-482-1201	●	●	●	●	
●	●	●	●		Greet America Public Record Svc Inc ... 214-320-9836					
●	●	●	●	●	Hollingsworth Court Reporting Inc ... 504-769-3386	●	●	●	●	
●	●	●	●	●	Legal Investigations (SOP) ... 423-584-9700	●	●			
●	●	●	●		Records Research of Knoxville ... 423-524-2630	●		●		

	CV	CR	PR	LAKE (CST)	UC	RE	TX	VS	VR
	●	●	●	D K Abstract 901-662-7394	●	●	●		
	●	●		Greet America Public Record Svc Inc ... 214-320-9836					
	●	●	●	Hollingsworth Court Reporting Inc ... 504-769-3386	●	●	●	●	
				Lattus, Helen 901-885-0891	●	●	●		

	CV	CR	PR	LAUDERDALE (CST)	UC	RE	TX	VS	VR
	●	●	●	D K Abstract 901-662-7394	●		●		
	●	●		Greet America Public Record Svc Inc ... 214-320-9836					
	●	●	●	Hollingsworth Court Reporting Inc ... 504-769-3386	●	●		●	
	●	●	●	Record-Check Services Inc ... 800-530-7226	●	●	●	●	●

	CV	CR	PR	LAWRENCE (CST)	UC	RE	TX	VS	VR
	●		●	Blackwell Land & Title Research ... 205-533-2439	●	●	●		
	●		●	Broadway, J Stephen ... 615-433-5979	●	●	●	●	
	●		●	Charles F Edgar & Associates (SOP) ... 205-539-7761	●	●	●		
	●	●		Greet America Public Record Svc Inc ... 214-320-9836					
	●	●	●	Hollingsworth Court Reporting Inc ... 504-769-3386	●	●	●	●	
	●		●	Larry R Dorning PC ... 615-796-5959	●	●	●	●	
	●		●	SMS/Strategic Mortgage Services Inc ... 800-475-2334	●	●	●		

	CV	CR	PR	LEWIS (CST)	UC	RE	TX	VS	VR
	●	●		Greet America Public Record Svc Inc ... 214-320-9836					
	●	●	●	Hollingsworth Court Reporting Inc ... 504-769-3386	●	●	●	●	
	●		●	Larry R Dorning PC ... 615-796-5959	●	●	●	●	
	●		●	SMS/Strategic Mortgage Services Inc ... 800-475-2334	●	●	●		

	CV	CR	PR	LINCOLN (CST)	UC	RE	TX	VS	VR
	●	●		Alpha Research LLC (SOP) ... 205-755-7008			●		
	●		●	Blackwell Land & Title Research ... 205-533-2439	●	●	●		
	●		●	Broadway, J Stephen ... 615-433-5979	●	●	●	●	
	●		●	Charles F Edgar & Associates (SOP) ... 205-539-7761	●	●	●		
	●	●		Greet America Public Record Svc Inc ... 214-320-9836					
	●	●	●	Hollingsworth Court Reporting Inc ... 504-769-3386	●	●	●	●	

	CV	CR	PR	LOUDON (EST)	UC	RE	TX	VS	VR
	●	●	●	Business Research Services (SOP) ... 800-608-4636	●	●	●	●	●
	●	●	●	Greater Tennessee Title Co ... 423-482-1201	●	●	●	●	
	●	●		Greet America Public Record Svc Inc ... 214-320-9836					
	●	●	●	Hollingsworth Court Reporting Inc ... 504-769-3386	●	●	●	●	

			Legal Investigations (SOP) 423-584-9700			
•	•	•		•	•	
		•	Title Guaranty & Trust of Chattanooga 615-266-5751	•	•	•

CV	CR	PR	MACON (CST)	UC	RE	TX	VS	VR
•	•		Alpha Research LLC (SOP)................................205-755-7008			•		
•	•	•	Contract Services Unlimited (SOP) 615-237-3142	•		•		•
•	•		Greet America Public Record Svc Inc 214-320-9836					
•	•	•	Hollingsworth Court Reporting Inc 504-769-3386	•	•	•	•	
•		•	SMS/Strategic Mortgage Services Inc 800-475-2334	•	•	•		
•	•	•	Source (SOP) 800-678-8774	•	•	•		•

DT	BK	CV	CR	PR	MADISON (CST)	UC	RE	TX	VS	VR
•	•	•	•		Alpha Research LLC (SOP)................................205-755-7008			•		
•	•	•			D K Abstract 901-662-7394	•	•	•		
				•	Douglas, Howard F 901-968-9381	•	•	•		
•	•	•	•		Greet America Public Record Svc Inc 214-320-9836					
•	•	•	•	•	Hollingsworth Court Reporting Inc 504-769-3386	•	•	•	•	
					Lattus, Helen 901-885-0891	•	•	•		
•	•	•		•	Record-Check Services Inc 800-530-7226	•	•	•	•	•

CV	CR	PR	MARION (CST)	UC	RE	TX	VS	VR
•	•		Alpha Research LLC (SOP)................................205-755-7008			•		
•	•	•	Charles F Edgar & Associates (SOP)..................205-539-7761	•	•	•		
•	•		Greet America Public Record Svc Inc 214-320-9836					
•	•	•	Hollingsworth Court Reporting Inc 504-769-3386	•	•	•	•	
•		•	Real Estate Loan Services 423-855-0581	•	•	•		
•		•	Title Guaranty & Trust of Chattanooga 615-266-5751	•	•	•		

CV	CR	PR	MARSHALL (CST)	UC	RE	TX	VS	VR
•	•	•	Broadway, J Stephen 615-433-5979	•	•	•	•	
•	•		Greet America Public Record Svc Inc 214-320-9836					
•	•	•	Hollingsworth Court Reporting Inc 504-769-3386	•	•	•	•	
•		•	SMS/Strategic Mortgage Services Inc 800-475-2334	•	•	•		

CV	CR	PR	MAURY (CST)	UC	RE	TX	VS	VR
•	•	•	Capitol Filing Service Inc 615-646-1404	•	•	•		
•	•	•	Charles F Edgar & Associates (SOP)..................205-539-7761	•	•	•		
•	•		Greet America Public Record Svc Inc 214-320-9836					
•	•	•	Hollingsworth Court Reporting Inc 504-769-3386	•	•	•	•	
•	•	•	Larry R Dorning PC 615-796-5959	•	•	•	•	
			Laster, Brian 615-790-8252		•			
•		•	SMS/Strategic Mortgage Services Inc 800-475-2334	•	•	•		

CV	CR	PR	McMINN (EST)	UC	RE	TX	VS	VR
•	•		Alpha Research LLC (SOP)................................205-755-7008			•		
•	•		Greet America Public Record Svc Inc 214-320-9836					
•	•	•	Hollingsworth Court Reporting Inc 504-769-3386	•	•	•	•	
•	•	•	Legal Investigations (SOP) 423-584-9700	•	•			
•		•	Real Estate Loan Services 423-855-0581	•	•	•		
•		•	Title Guaranty & Trust of Chattanooga 615-266-5751	•	•	•		

CV	CR	PR	McNAIRY (CST)	UC	RE	TX	VS	VR
•	•	•	D K Abstract 901-662-7394	•	•	•		
•	•		Greet America Public Record Svc Inc 214-320-9836					
•	•	•	Hollingsworth Court Reporting Inc 504-769-3386	•	•	•	•	

CV	CR	PR	MEIGS (EST)	UC	RE	TX	VS	VR
•	•		Alpha Research LLC (SOP)................................205-755-7008			•		
•	•		Greet America Public Record Svc Inc 214-320-9836					
•	•	•	Hollingsworth Court Reporting Inc 504-769-3386	•	•	•	•	
•		•	Real Estate Loan Services 423-855-0581	•	•	•		
•		•	Title Guaranty & Trust of Chattanooga 615-266-5751	•	•	•		

CV	CR	PR	MONROE (EST)	UC	RE	TX	VS	VR
•	•		Greet America Public Record Svc Inc 214-320-9836					
•	•	•	🏛 Hollingsworth Court Reporting Inc 504-769-3386	•	•	•	•	
•	•	•	🏛 Legal Investigations (SOP) 423-584-9700	•	•			
•		•	Real Estate Loan Services 423-855-0581	•	•	•		
•		•	Title Guaranty & Trust of Chattanooga 615-266-5751	•	•	•		

CV	CR	PR	MONTGOMERY (CST)	UC	RE	TX	VS	VR
•	•		🏛 Alpha Research LLC (SOP)............ 205-755-7008		•			
•	•	•	Capitol Filing Service Inc 615-646-1404	•	•	•		
•	•		Eye Catcher Investigations 615-789-6165	•		•		•
•	•		Greet America Public Record Svc Inc 214-320-9836					
•	•	•	🏛 Hollingsworth Court Reporting Inc 504-769-3386	•	•	•	•	
			Laster, Brian 615-790-8252		•			
•		•	SMS/Strategic Mortgage Services Inc 800-475-2334	•	•	•		

CV	CR	PR	MOORE (CST)	UC	RE	TX	VS	VR
•	•	•	🏛 Charles F Edgar & Associates (SOP)............ 205-539-7761	•	•	•		
•	•		Greet America Public Record Svc Inc 214-320-9836					
•	•	•	🏛 Hollingsworth Court Reporting Inc 504-769-3386	•	•	•	•	

CV	CR	PR	MORGAN (EST)	UC	RE	TX	VS	VR
		•	🏛 Arms, Joan 615-879-2269	•	•	•	•	
•	•	•	Greater Tennessee Title Co 423-482-1201	•	•	•		
•	•		Greet America Public Record Svc Inc 214-320-9836					
•	•	•	🏛 Hollingsworth Court Reporting Inc 504-769-3386	•	•	•	•	
•	•	•	🏛 Legal Investigations (SOP) 423-584-9700	•	•			

CV	CR	PR	OBION (CST)	UC	RE	TX	VS	VR
•	•	•	D K Abstract 901-662-7394	•	•	•		
•	•		Greet America Public Record Svc Inc 214-320-9836					
•	•	•	🏛 Hollingsworth Court Reporting Inc 504-769-3386	•	•	•	•	
			Lattus, Helen 901-885-0891	•	•	•		

CV	CR	PR	OVERTON (CST)	UC	RE	TX	VS	VR
		•	🏛 Arms, Joan 615-879-2269	•	•	•	•	
•	•		Greet America Public Record Svc Inc 214-320-9836					
•	•	•	🏛 Hollingsworth Court Reporting Inc 504-769-3386	•	•	•	•	
•		•	SMS/Strategic Mortgage Services Inc 800-475-2334	•	•	•		
•	•	•	Source (SOP) 800-678-8774	•	•	•		•

CV	CR	PR	PERRY (CST)	UC	RE	TX	VS	VR
•	•	•	D K Abstract 901-662-7394	•	•	•		
•	•		Greet America Public Record Svc Inc 214-320-9836					
•	•	•	🏛 Hollingsworth Court Reporting Inc 504-769-3386	•	•	•	•	
•	•	•	Larry R Dorning PC 615-796-5959	•	•	•		
•		•	SMS/Strategic Mortgage Services Inc 800-475-2334	•	•	•		

CV	CR	PR	PICKETT (CST)	UC	RE	TX	VS	VR
		•	🏛 Arms, Joan 615-879-2269	•	•	•	•	
•	•		Greet America Public Record Svc Inc 214-320-9836					
•	•	•	🏛 Hollingsworth Court Reporting Inc 504-769-3386	•	•	•	•	
•		•	SMS/Strategic Mortgage Services Inc 800-475-2334	•	•	•		

CV	CR	PR	POLK (EST)	UC	RE	TX	VS	VR
•	•		🏛 Alpha Research LLC (SOP)............ 205-755-7008		•			
•	•		Greet America Public Record Svc Inc 214-320-9836					
•	•	•	🏛 Hollingsworth Court Reporting Inc 504-769-3386	•	•	•	•	
•		•	Real Estate Loan Services 423-855-0581	•	•	•		
•		•	Title Guaranty & Trust of Chattanooga 615-266-5751	•	•	•		

DT	CV	CR	PR	PUTNAM (CST)	UC	RE	TX	VS	VR
•	•	•		🏛 Alpha Research LLC (SOP)............ 205-755-7008		•			

•		🏛 Arms, Joan	615-879-2269	•	•	•	•
•	•	•	Greet America Public Record Svc Inc	214-320-9836	•	•	•
•	•	•	•	🏛 Hollingsworth Court Reporting Inc	504-769-3386	•	•	•
•	•	•	SMS/Strategic Mortgage Services Inc	800-475-2334	•	•	•
•	•	•	•	Source (SOP)	800-678-8774	•	•	•	•

CV	CR	PR	RHEA (EST)	UC	RE	TX	VS	VR
•	•		🏛 Alpha Research LLC (SOP)..................... 205-755-7008			•		
•	•		Greet America Public Record Svc Inc 214-320-9836					
•	•	•	🏛 Hollingsworth Court Reporting Inc 504-769-3386	•	•			
•	•	•	🏛 Legal Investigations (SOP) 423-584-9700	•	•			
•	•		Real Estate Loan Services 423-855-0581	•	•	•		
•	•		Title Guaranty & Trust of Chattanooga 615-266-5751	•	•	•		

CV	CR	PR	ROANE (EST)	UC	RE	TX	VS	VR
•	•	•	🏛 Business Research Services (SOP)............. 800-608-4636	•	•	•	•	•
•	•	•	Greater Tennessee Title Co 423-482-1201	•	•	•		
•	•	•	Greet America Public Record Svc Inc 214-320-9836					
•	•	•	🏛 Hollingsworth Court Reporting Inc 504-769-3386	•	•	•	•	
•	•	•	🏛 Legal Investigations (SOP) 423-584-9700	•	•			
•	•	•	Source (SOP) 800-678-8774	•	•	•		•

CV	CR	PR	ROBERTSON (CST)	UC	RE	TX	VS	VR
•	•		🏛 Alpha Research LLC (SOP)..................... 205-755-7008			•		
•	•	•	Capitol Filing Service Inc 615-646-1404	•	•	•		
•	•		Greet America Public Record Svc Inc 214-320-9836					
•	•	•	🏛 Hollingsworth Court Reporting Inc 504-769-3386	•	•	•	•	
			Laster, Brian 615-790-8252		•			
•		•	SMS/Strategic Mortgage Services Inc 800-475-2334	•	•	•		

CV	CR	PR	RUTHERFORD (CST)	UC	RE	TX	VS	VR
•	•		🏛 Alpha Research LLC (SOP)..................... 205-755-7008			•		
•	•	•	Capitol Filing Service Inc 615-646-1404	•	•	•		
•	•	•	Contract Services Unlimited (SOP) 615-237-3142	•		•		•
•	•		Greet America Public Record Svc Inc 214-320-9836					
•	•	•	🏛 Hollingsworth Court Reporting Inc 504-769-3386	•	•	•	•	
			Laster, Brian 615-790-8252		•			
•	•	•	Perry, Annie 615-459-9117	•	•	•		
•		•	SMS/Strategic Mortgage Services Inc 800-475-2334	•	•	•		

CV	CR	PR	SCOTT (EST)	UC	RE	TX	VS	VR
		•	🏛 Arms, Joan 615-879-2269	•	•	•	•	
•	•		Greet America Public Record Svc Inc 214-320-9836					
•	•	•	🏛 Hollingsworth Court Reporting Inc 504-769-3386	•	•	•	•	
•	•	•	🏛 Legal Investigations (SOP) 423-584-9700	•	•			

CV	CR	PR	SEQUATCHIE (CST)	UC	RE	TX	VS	VR
•	•		🏛 Alpha Research LLC (SOP)..................... 205-755-7008			•		
•	•		Greet America Public Record Svc Inc 214-320-9836					
•	•	•	🏛 Hollingsworth Court Reporting Inc 504-769-3386	•	•	•	•	
•		•	Real Estate Loan Services 423-855-0581	•	•	•		
•		•	Title Guaranty & Trust of Chattanooga 615-266-5751	•	•	•		

CV	CR	PR	SEVIER (EST)	UC	RE	TX	VS	VR
•	•	•	🏛 Business Research Services (SOP)............. 800-608-4636	•	•	•	•	•
•	•		Greet America Public Record Svc Inc 214-320-9836					
		•	Harris, Eileen 423-397-7669	•	•	•		
•	•	•	🏛 Hollingsworth Court Reporting Inc 504-769-3386	•	•	•	•	
•	•	•	🏛 Legal Investigations (SOP) 423-584-9700	•	•			
•	•	•	🏛 Title Express Inc 423-587-9886	•	•	•		

DT	BK	CV	CR	PR	SHELBY (CST)	UC	RE	TX	VS	VR
•	•	•	•		🏛 Alpha Research LLC (SOP)..................... 205-755-7008			•		

CV	CR	PR	Provider	Phone	UC	RE	TX	VS	VR
•	•	•	Cheslock Investigations (SOP)	901-681-9663	•	•	•	•	•
•	•	•	Cope Investigative Services LLC (SOP)	800-262-9301	•	•	•	•	•
		•	DJ Records	901-324-6209					
•	•	•	Greet America Public Record Svc Inc	214-320-9836					
•	•	•	Guardsmark	901-522-7800	•	•	•	•	
•	•	•	Hollingsworth Court Reporting Inc	504-769-3386	•	•	•	•	
•	•	•	Lenow International Inc (SOP)	901-726-0735	•	•	•	•	
•	•	•	National Background Reports Inc	800-526-4654	•	•	•		•
•	•	•	Record-Check Services Inc	800-530-7226	•	•	•		•
•	•	•	RecordServe/John Kelley Enterprises	901-853-5320	•	•			
•	•	•	Schaeffer Papers (SOP)	800-848-6119	•				

CV	CR	PR	SMITH (CST)		UC	RE	TX	VS	VR
•	•		Alpha Research LLC (SOP)	205-755-7008			•		
•	•	•	Contract Services Unlimited (SOP)	615-237-3142	•		•		•
•	•		Greet America Public Record Svc Inc	214-320-9836					
•	•	•	Hollingsworth Court Reporting Inc	504-769-3386	•	•	•		
		•	SMS/Strategic Mortgage Services Inc	800-475-2334	•	•	•		
•	•	•	Source (SOP)	800-678-8774	•	•	•		•

CV	CR	PR	STEWART (CST)		UC	RE	TX	VS	VR
•	•	•	D K Abstract	901-662-7394	•	•	•		
•	•		Greet America Public Record Svc Inc	214-320-9836					
•	•	•	Hollingsworth Court Reporting Inc	504-769-3386	•	•	•	•	
		•	SMS/Strategic Mortgage Services Inc	800-475-2334	•	•	•		

CV	CR	PR	SULLIVAN (EST)		UC	RE	TX	VS	VR
•	•		Alpha Research LLC (SOP)	205-755-7008			•		
•	•		Greet America Public Record Svc Inc	214-320-9836					
•	•	•	Hollingsworth Court Reporting Inc	504-769-3386	•	•	•	•	
•	•	•	Legal Investigations (SOP)	423-584-9700	•	•			
•	•	•	Simerly, Teresa	423-725-3901	•	•	•	•	

CV	CR	PR	SUMNER (CST)		UC	RE	TX	VS	VR
•	•		Alpha Research LLC (SOP)	205-755-7008			•		
•	•	•	Capitol Filing Service Inc	615-646-1404	•	•	•		
•	•	•	Contract Services Unlimited (SOP)	615-237-3142	•		•		•
•	•		Greet America Public Record Svc Inc	214-320-9836					
•	•	•	Hollingsworth Court Reporting Inc	504-769-3386	•	•	•	•	
			Laster, Brian	615-790-8252		•			
•		•	SMS/Strategic Mortgage Services Inc	800-475-2334	•	•	•		
•	•	•	The Search Is On	800-324-2050	•	•	•	•	•

CV	CR	PR	TIPTON (CST)		UC	RE	TX	VS	VR
•	•	•	Cope Investigative Services LLC (SOP)	800-262-9301	•	•	•	•	•
•	•	•	D K Abstract	901-662-7394	•	•	•		
•	•		Greet America Public Record Svc Inc	214-320-9836					
•	•	•	Hollingsworth Court Reporting Inc	504-769-3386	•	•	•	•	
•	•	•	Record-Check Services Inc	800-530-7226	•	•	•		•
•	•	•	RecordServe/John Kelley Enterprises	901-853-5320	•	•	•	•	
•	•	•	Schaeffer Papers (SOP)	800-848-6119	•				

CV	CR	PR	TROUSDALE (CST)		UC	RE	TX	VS	VR
•	•		Alpha Research LLC (SOP)	205-755-7008			•		
•	•	•	Capitol Filing Service Inc	615-646-1404	•	•	•		
•	•	•	Contract Services Unlimited (SOP)	615-237-3142	•		•		•
•	•		Greet America Public Record Svc Inc	214-320-9836					
•	•	•	Hollingsworth Court Reporting Inc	504-769-3386	•	•	•	•	
•		•	SMS/Strategic Mortgage Services Inc	800-475-2334	•	•	•		

CV	CR	PR	UNICOI (EST)		UC	RE	TX	VS	VR
•	•		Greet America Public Record Svc Inc	214-320-9836					
•	•	•	Hollingsworth Court Reporting Inc	504-769-3386	•	•	•	•	

•	•	•	Simerly, Teresa 423-725-3901	•	•	•	•	

CV	CR	PR	UNION (EST)	UC	RE	TX	VS	VR
•	•		Greet America Public Record Svc Inc 214-320-9836					
•	•	•	🏛 Hollingsworth Court Reporting Inc 504-769-3386	•	•	•	•	
•	•	•	🏛 Legal Investigations (SOP) 423-584-9700	•	•			

CV	CR	PR	VAN BUREN (CST)	UC	RE	TX	VS	VR
•	•		Greet America Public Record Svc Inc 214-320-9836					
•	•	•	🏛 Hollingsworth Court Reporting Inc 504-769-3386	•	•	•	•	
•		•	Title Guaranty & Trust of Chattanooga 615-266-5751	•	•	•		

CV	CR	PR	WARREN (CST)	UC	RE	TX	VS	VR
•	•		Greet America Public Record Svc Inc 214-320-9836					
•	•	•	🏛 Hollingsworth Court Reporting Inc 504-769-3386	•	•	•	•	

CV	CR	PR	WASHINGTON (EST)	UC	RE	TX	VS	VR
•	•		🏛 Alpha Research LLC (SOP).................... 205-755-7008			•		
•	•		Greet America Public Record Svc Inc 214-320-9836					
•	•	•	🏛 Hollingsworth Court Reporting Inc 504-769-3386	•	•	•	•	
•	•	•	🏛 Legal Investigations (SOP) 423-584-9700	•	•			
•	•	•	Simerly, Teresa 423-725-3901	•	•	•	•	

CV	CR	PR	WAYNE (CST)	UC	RE	TX	VS	VR
•	•	•	D K Abstract 901-662-7394	•	•	•		
•	•		Greet America Public Record Svc Inc 214-320-9836					
•	•	•	🏛 Hollingsworth Court Reporting Inc 504-769-3386	•	•	•	•	
•	•	•	Larry R Dorning PC 615-796-5959	•	•	•	•	
•		•	SMS/Strategic Mortgage Services Inc 800-475-2334	•	•	•		

CV	CR	PR	WEAKLEY (CST)	UC	RE	TX	VS	VR
•	•	•	D K Abstract 901-662-7394	•	•	•		
•	•		Greet America Public Record Svc Inc 214-320-9836					
•	•	•	🏛 Hollingsworth Court Reporting Inc 504-769-3386	•	•	•	•	
•			Lattus, Helen 901-885-0891	•	•	•		

CV	CR	PR	WHITE (CST)	UC	RE	TX	VS	VR
		•	🏛 Arms, Joan 615-879-2269	•	•	•	•	
•	•		Greet America Public Record Svc Inc 214-320-9836					
•	•	•	🏛 Hollingsworth Court Reporting Inc 504-769-3386	•	•	•	•	
•	•	•	SMS/Strategic Mortgage Services Inc 800-475-2334	•	•	•		
•	•	•	Source (SOP) 800-678-8774	•	•	•		•

CV	CR	PR	WILLIAMSON (CST)	UC	RE	TX	VS	VR
•	•		🏛 Alpha Research LLC (SOP).................... 205-755-7008			•		
•	•	•	Capitol Filing Service Inc 615-646-1404	•	•	•		
•	•	•	Contract Services Unlimited (SOP) 615-237-3142	•		•		•
•	•		Greet America Public Record Svc Inc 214-320-9836					
•	•	•	🏛 Hollingsworth Court Reporting Inc 504-769-3386	•	•	•	•	
			Laster, Brian 615-790-8252		•			
•		•	SMS/Strategic Mortgage Services Inc 800-475-2334	•	•	•		
•	•	•	The Search Is On 800-324-2050	•	•	•	•	•

CV	CR	PR	WILSON (CST)	UC	RE	TX	VS	VR
•	•		🏛 Alpha Research LLC (SOP).................... 205-755-7008			•		
•	•	•	Capitol Filing Service Inc 615-646-1404	•	•	•		
•	•	•	Contract Services Unlimited (SOP) 615-237-3142	•		•		•
•	•		Greet America Public Record Svc Inc 214-320-9836					
•	•	•	🏛 Hollingsworth Court Reporting Inc 504-769-3386	•	•	•	•	
			Laster, Brian 615-790-8252		•			
•		•	SMS/Strategic Mortgage Services Inc 800-475-2334	•	•	•		
•	•	•	The Search Is On 800-324-2050	•	•	•	•	•

TEXAS

CV	CR	PR	ANDERSON (CST)	UC	RE	TX	VS	VR
•	•		🏛 Alpha Research LLC (SOP) 205-755-7008			•		
•	•	•	Anderson County Abstract Co 903-729-5871	•	•	•	•	
•	•	•	Brubaker & Associates 903-595-4616	•	•	•	•	
•	•	•	Search Enterprises 817-752-2057	•	•	•	•	

CV	CR	PR	ANDREWS (CST)	UC	RE	TX	VS	VR
•	•	•	APROTEX 915-683-3518	•	•	•	•	
•	•		🏛 Alpha Research LLC (SOP) 205-755-7008			•		
•	•	•	🏛 Davick Services 800-658-6656	•	•	•	•	•

CV	CR	PR	ANGELINA (CST)	UC	RE	TX	VS	VR
•	•		🏛 Alpha Research LLC (SOP) 205-755-7008			•		
•	•	•	Lufkin Abstract 409-634-9611	•	•	•	•	

CV	CR	PR	ARANSAS (CST)	UC	RE	TX	VS	VR
•	•	•	Condor Investigations (SOP) 512-881-8977	•	•	•	•	•
•	•	•	🏛 Corpus Christi Court Services 512-887-8122	•	•	•	•	•
•	•	•	John Bullock & Co 512-992-3060	•	•	•	•	
•	•	•	Shawver and Associates (SOP) 800-364-2333	•	•	•	•	•
•	•	•	Texas Civil Process (SOP) 800-976-9595	•	•	•	•	
•	•	•	Texas Legal Support Service 512-883-2247	•	•	•	•	

CV	CR	PR	ARCHER (CST)	UC	RE	TX	VS	VR
			See adjoining counties for retrievers					

CV	CR	PR	ARMSTRONG (CST)	UC	RE	TX	VS	VR
•	•	•	Rollins, Jan 806-353-7886	•	•	•	•	
•	•	•	Security Abstract Co of Clarendon 806-874-3511	•	•	•	•	
•	•	•	Security Abstract Co of Claude 806-226-3621	•	•	•	•	
•	•	•	Security Abstract Co of Memphis 806-259-2931	•	•	•	•	

CV	CR	PR	ATASCOSA (CST)	UC	RE	TX	VS	VR
•	•	•	AKA Investigations & Process (SOP) 800-653-3817	•	•	•	•	•
•	•	•	Fred Meyers Company 210-349-8119	•	•	•	•	
•	•	•	Property Research & Documentation Service 800-520-7884	•	•	•	•	•
•	•	•	Property Research Associates Inc 888-523-1061	•	•	•	•	
•	•		Search Plus 800-465-1525				•	•

CV	CR	PR	AUSTIN (CST)	UC	RE	TX	VS	VR
•	•	•	Access Research Staff 512-321-1889	•	•	•	•	•
•	•		🏛 Alpha Research LLC (SOP) 205-755-7008			•		
•	•	•	🏛 Apex Information and Research Inc (A.I.R.) 800-330-4525	•	•	•	•	•
•	•	•	🏛 BAST Research Services Inc 713-777-8942	•	•	•		•
•	•		🏛 Business Information Service 409-865-2547	•	•	•	•	
•	•	•	🏛 The Research Staff Inc 800-822-3584	•	•	•		•

CV	CR	PR	BAILEY (CST)	UC	RE	TX	VS	VR
•	•	•	🏛 Davick Services 800-658-6656	•	•	•	•	•
•	•	•	Farwell Abstract Co Inc (SOP) 806-481-3361	•	•	•		

CV	CR	PR	BANDERA (CST)	UC	RE	TX	VS	VR
•	•	•	AKA Investigations & Process (SOP) 800-653-3817	•	•	•	•	•
•	•	•	Fred Meyers Company 210-349-8119	•	•	•	•	
•	•	•	🏛 Legal Records Investigations 210-675-6258	•	•	•	•	•
•	•	•	Property Research & Documentation Service 800-520-7884	•	•	•	•	•

CV	CR	PR	BASTROP (CST)	UC	RE	TX	VS	VR
•	•	•	AKA Investigations & Process of Austin (SOP) 800-933-8706	•	•	•	•	•
•	•	•	Access Research Staff 512-321-1889	•	•	•	•	•
•	•		🏛 Alpha Research LLC (SOP) 205-755-7008			•		

•	•	•	Assured Civil Process Agency (SOP).....................800-256-7160	•	•
•		•	Avian Corporate Records & Research (SOP) 512-326-3354	• • • • •	
•	•		CPS (Capital Process Service) 512-930-7378	•	
•	•	•	Capitol Commerce Reporter Inc 800-356-8282	• • • •	
•	•	•	🏛 John C Dunaway and Associates (SOP)...............512-835-5888	• • • • •	
•	•	•	Promesa Enterprises 800-474-4420	• • • • •	
•	•	•	🏛 Tyler-McLennon Inc 512-482-0808	• • • • •	

	CV	CR	PR	BAYLOR (CST)	UC	RE	TX	VS	VR
				See adjoining counties for retrievers					

	CV	CR	PR	BEE (CST)	UC	RE	TX	VS	VR
	•	•	•	Condor Investigations (SOP) 512-881-8977	•	•	•	•	•
	•	•	•	Shawver and Associates (SOP)..................800-364-2333	•	•	•	•	•
	•	•	•	Texas Civil Process (SOP)........................800-976-9595	•	•	•	•	

	CV	CR	PR	BELL (CST)	UC	RE	TX	VS	VR
	•	•		🏛 Alpha Research LLC (SOP).....................205-755-7008			•		
	•		•	American Abstract and Title Co Inc 817-526-9525	•	•	•	•	
	•	•		CPS (Capital Process Service) 512-930-7378			•		
	•	•	•	Document Resources 800-822-8084	•	•	•	•	
	•	•		🏛 Greenwood Research 800-771-0847	•	•	•		
	•	•	•	Search Enterprises 817-752-2057	•	•	•		
	•	•	•	🏛 Tyler-McLennon Inc 512-482-0808	•	•	•		•

DT	BK	CV	CR	PR	BEXAR (CST)	UC	RE	TX	VS	VR
•	•	•	•	•	AKA Investigations & Process (SOP) 800-653-3817	•	•	•	•	•
•	•	•	•	•	Access Research Staff 512-321-1889	•	•	•	•	•
•	•	•	•	•	🏛 Alpha Research LLC (SOP).........................205-755-7008			•		
•	•	•	•	•	🏛 Attorney's Service Bureau of Texas (SOP)...........214-522-5297	•	•	•		
•					Bankruptcy Bulletin Weekly Inc 409-854-2777					
•	•	•	•	•	Bankruptcy Services Inc 214-424-6500					
				•	Bexar Professional (SOP) 210-228-0083			•		•
•	•	•	•	•	🏛 Data Screen Inc 817-294-7671					
•	•	•	•	•	Document Resources 800-822-8084	•	•	•		
•	•	•	•	•	🏛 FYP Inc 800-569-7143	•	•	•	•	
•	•	•	•	•	Fred Meyers Company 210-349-8119	•	•	•	•	
•	•	•	•	•	Intranet Inc 903-593-9817	•	•	•	•	
•	•	•	•	•	🏛 Legal Records Investigations 210-675-6258	•	•	•		•
•	•	•	•	•	OTI Resources 800-728-2742	•		•		•
				•	🏛 Persona Data Corporation 800-735-9555					
•	•	•	•	•	Phoenix Information Services Inc (SOP)................800-918-8343	•	•	•	•	
•	•	•	•	•	🏛 Priority Information Services (SOP)..................210-699-9449	•	•	•	•	
•	•	•	•	•	Professional Civil Process (SOP).......................210-225-1239	•	•	•		
•	•	•	•	•	Professional Civil Process (SOP).......................800-950-7493	•	•	•		
•	•	•	•	•	Property Research & Documentation Service 800-520-7884	•	•	•	•	
•	•	•	•	•	Property Research Associates Inc 888-523-1061	•	•	•	•	
•	•	•	•	•	🏛 Quick Search 214-358-2840	•	•	•	•	
•		•			RJ Research 210-824-0037					
•	•	•			Search Plus 800-465-1525				•	•
•	•	•		•	Texas Abstract Services 800-484-5690		•			
•	•	•	•	•	Texas Industrial Security Inc 214-634-2791	•	•	•	•	
		•	•	•	The Cole Group 713-880-9494	•	•	•	•	
				•	The Dataprompt Corporation 800-577-8157		•			
•	•	•	•	•	🏛 The Electronic Detective 210-653-2110	•	•	•		•
•	•	•		•	TitleInfo 817-244-7757	•	•	•		
•	•	•	•	•	🏛 Tyler-McLennon Inc 512-482-0808	•	•	•		•

	CV	CR	PR	BLANCO (CST)	UC	RE	TX	VS	VR
	•	•	•	AKA Investigations & Process of Austin (SOP).................800-933-8706	•	•	•	•	•
	•	•	•	Capitol Commerce Reporter Inc 800-356-8282	•	•	•	•	
	•	•	•	Promesa Enterprises 800-474-4420	•	•	•	•	•

	CV	CR	PR	BORDEN (CST)	UC	RE	TX	VS	VR
	•	•	•	APROTEX 915-683-3518	•	•	•	•	
	•	•	•	🗑 Davick Services 800-658-6656	•	•	•	•	•

	CV	CR	PR	BOSQUE (CST)	UC	RE	TX	VS	VR
	•	•	•	Bosque Cen-Tex Title Inc 817-435-2722	•	•	•	•	
	•	•	•	Search Enterprises 817-752-2057	•	•	•	•	

DT	CV	CR	PR	BOWIE (CST)	UC	RE	TX	VS	VR
•	•	•		🗑 Alpha Research LLC (SOP) 205-755-7008			•		
•	•	•	•	Brubaker & Associates 903-595-4616	•	•	•	•	
•	•	•	•	Gillenwater, Joe (SOP) 800-962-9453	•		•	•	•
	•		•	Twin City Title Co Inc 903-793-7671	•	•	•		

	CV	CR	PR	BRAZORIA (CST)	UC	RE	TX	VS	VR
	•	•		🗑 Alpha Research LLC (SOP) 205-755-7008			•		
	•	•	•	🗑 Apex Information and Research Inc (A.I.R.) 800-330-4525	•	•	•	•	•
	•	•	•	🗑 BAST Research Services Inc 713-777-8942	•	•	•		•
	•	•	•	🗑 Court Record Research Inc 800-552-3353	•	•	•	•	•
	•	•		🗑 Data Screen Inc 817-294-7671	•	•	•		
				Fox Hunt 713-772-8018	•	•	•		•
	•	•	•	🗑 Houston Court Services Inc (SOP) 800-593-2023	•	•	•	•	•
	•	•		LawServ Inc (SOP) 713-228-1055	•	•	•	•	•
	•	•		Mesaa Unlimited (SOP) 713-759-7464	•	•	•	•	•
	•	•		Metropolitan Court Services (SOP) 713-616-6971	•	•	•	•	•
	•		•	Texas Abstract Services 800-484-5690		•			
	•	•	•	Texas Records Search (SOP) 800-869-1405	•	•	•	•	
	•	•	•	The Information Bank of Texas (SOP) 713-864-9122	•	•	•	•	•
	•	•	•	🗑 The Research Staff Inc 800-822-3584	•	•	•		•
	•	•	•	Walters & Associates (SOP) 281-242-2243	•	•	•	•	•

	CV	CR	PR	BRAZOS (CST)	UC	RE	TX	VS	VR
	•	•		🗑 Alpha Research LLC (SOP) 205-755-7008			•		
	•	•	•	🗑 BAST Research Services Inc 713-777-8942	•	•	•		•
	•	•	•	🗑 Houston Court Services Inc (SOP) 800-593-2023	•	•	•	•	•
	•	•	•	Search Enterprises 817-752-2057	•	•	•	•	
	•	•	•	The Court System Inc 800-856-0585	•	•	•	•	•
	•	•	•	🗑 The Research Staff Inc 800-822-3584	•	•	•		•

	CV	CR	PR	BREWSTER (CST)	UC	RE	TX	VS	VR
	•	•	•	Ellyson Abstract & Title Co of Brewster 915-837-5801	•	•	•	•	

	CV	CR	PR	BRISCOE (CST)	UC	RE	TX	VS	VR
	•	•	•	🗑 Davick Services 800-658-6656	•	•	•	•	•
	•	•	•	Guaranty Abstract Co 806-823-2354	•	•	•		

	CV	CR	PR	BROOKS (CST)	UC	RE	TX	VS	VR
				Border Abstract 210-791-5810	•	•	•		
	•	•	•	Condor Investigations (SOP) 512-881-8977	•	•	•	•	•
	•	•	•	Shawver and Associates (SOP) 800-364-2333	•	•	•	•	•
	•	•	•	Texas Civil Process (SOP) 800-976-9595	•	•	•	•	

	CV	CR	PR	BROWN (CST)	UC	RE	TX	VS	VR
	•	•	•	Adams, Tommy M 915-648-3024	•	•	•	•	
	•		•	Brown County Abstract Co 915-643-3631	•	•	•		
	•	•	•	Heartland Title Company 915-646-0509	•	•	•		

	CV	CR	PR	BURLESON (CST)	UC	RE	TX	VS	VR
	•	•	•	Botts Title Co 409-567-4602	•	•	•	•	

	CV	CR	PR	BURNET (CST)	UC	RE	TX	VS	VR
	•	•	•	AKA Investigations & Process of Austin (SOP) 800-933-8706	•	•	•	•	•
	•	•		🗑 Alpha Research LLC (SOP) 205-755-7008			•		

	CV	CR	PR			UC	RE	TX	VS	VR
	•	•	•	Assured Civil Process Agency (SOP) 800-256-7160			•			•
	•	•	•	Capitol Commerce Reporter Inc 800-356-8282		•	•	•	•	
	•	•	•	Promesa Enterprises 800-474-4420		•	•	•	•	•

	CV	CR	PR	CALDWELL (CST)	UC	RE	TX	VS	VR
	•	•	•	AKA Investigations & Process of Austin (SOP) 800-933-8706	•	•	•	•	•
	•	•	•	Access Research Staff 512-321-1889	•	•	•	•	•
	•	•	🏛 Alpha Research LLC (SOP) 205-755-7008			•		
	•		•	Assured Civil Process Agency (SOP) 800-256-7160		•			•
	•		•	Avian Corporate Records & Research (SOP) 512-326-3354	•	•	•	•	•
	•	•	•	Capitol Commerce Reporter Inc 800-356-8282	•	•	•	•	
	•	•	•	Promesa Enterprises 800-474-4420	•	•	•	•	
	•	•	•	Property Research Associates Inc 888-523-1061	•	•	•	•	
	•			Search Plus 800-465-1525				•	•
	•	•	•	🏛 Tyler-McLennon Inc 512-482-0808	•	•	•		•

	CV	CR	PR	CALHOUN (CST)	UC	RE	TX	VS	VR
	•	•		🏛 Alpha Research LLC (SOP) 205-755-7008			•		
	•		•	Bedgood Abstract & Title Co 512-552-6761	•	•	•		
	•	•	•	Condor Investigations (SOP) 512-881-8977	•	•	•	•	•

	CV	CR	PR	CALLAHAN (CST)	UC	RE	TX	VS	VR
	•	•	•	Russell-Surles Title Inc 915-854-1115	•	•	•		•

DT	CV	CR	PR	CAMERON (CST)	UC	RE	TX	VS	VR
•	•	•	•	🏛 Alpha Research LLC (SOP) 205-755-7008			•		
•	•	•	•	KJB Court Search (SOP) 210-971-8846	•	•	•	•	•
•	•	•	•	Professional Civil Process (SOP) 800-880-4223	•	•	•		
•	•	•	•	Professional Civil Process (SOP) 800-950-7493	•	•	•		
•	•	•	•	Shawver and Associates (SOP) 800-364-2333	•	•	•		•
•	•	•	•	🏛 Valley Court Services 210-412-2306	•	•	•	•	•

	CV	CR	PR	CAMP (CST)	UC	RE	TX	VS	VR
	•	•	•	Brubaker & Associates 903-595-4616	•	•	•	•	
	•		•	Camp County Land Abstract Co 903-856-3676	•	•	•		

	CV	CR	PR	CARSON (CST)	UC	RE	TX	VS	VR
	•	•	•	Credit Bureau Services of the Panhandle 806-669-3246	•	•	•	•	
	•	•	•	Rollins, Jan 806-353-7886	•	•	•	•	

	CV	CR	PR	CASS (CST)	UC	RE	TX	VS	VR
	•	•		🏛 Alpha Research LLC (SOP) 205-755-7008			•		
	•	•	•	Brubaker & Associates 903-595-4616	•	•	•	•	
	•		•	DeSoto Abstract 318-798-1198	•	•	•		
	•	•	•	Gillenwater, Joe (SOP) 800-962-9453	•		•	•	•

	CV	CR	PR	CASTRO (CST)	UC	RE	TX	VS	VR
	•	•	•	🏛 Davick Services 800-658-6656	•	•	•	•	•
	•	•	•	Rollins, Jan 806-353-7886	•	•	•	•	

	CV	CR	PR	CHAMBERS (CST)	UC	RE	TX	VS	VR
	•	•		🏛 Alpha Research LLC (SOP) 205-755-7008			•		
	•	•	•	🏛 BAST Research Services Inc 713-777-8942	•	•	•		•
	•	•		Caskey, Don W 713-422-7527	•		•		
	•	•	•	Texas Records Search (SOP) 800-869-1405	•	•	•	•	•
	•	•	•	🏛 The Research Staff Inc 800-822-3584	•	•	•		•

	CV	CR	PR	CHEROKEE (CST)	UC	RE	TX	VS	VR
	•	•		🏛 Alpha Research LLC (SOP) 205-755-7008			•		
	•	•	•	Brubaker & Associates 903-595-4616	•	•	•	•	

	CV	CR	PR	CHILDRESS (CST)	UC	RE	TX	VS	VR
	•		•	H S Black 817-937-3681	•	•	•	•	

	CV	CR	PR	CLAY (CST)	UC	RE	TX	VS	VR
				See adjoining counties for retrievers					

	CV	CR	PR	COCHRAN (CST)	UC	RE	TX	VS	VR
	•	•	•	Davick Services 800-658-6656	•	•	•	•	•

	CV	CR	PR	COKE (CST)	UC	RE	TX	VS	VR
	•	•	•	Coke County Abstract Co 915-453-2049	•	•	•	•	

	CV	CR	PR	COLEMAN (CST)	UC	RE	TX	VS	VR
	•	•	•	Coleman County Title Co 915-625-4628	•	•	•	•	

BK	CV	CR	PR	COLLIN (CST)	UC	RE	TX	VS	VR
•	•	•	•	AKA Investigations & Process of Dallas (SOP) 214-761-1174	•	•	•	•	
•	•	•		Accutrak 972-390-2195		•	•	•	
•	•	•		Alpha Research LLC (SOP) 205-755-7008			•		
•	•	•	•	Attorney Service Associates (SOP) 214-394-1175	•	•	•	•	•
•	•	•	•	Attorney's Service Bureau of Texas (SOP) 214-522-5297	•	•	•		
•				Background Research 817-926-5976					
•				Bankruptcy Bulletin Weekly Inc 409-854-2777					
•	•	•	•	Bankruptcy Services Inc 214-424-6500					
•	•	•	•	Brubaker & Associates 903-595-4616	•	•	•	•	
•	•	•	•	Charles L Layer Private Investigations (SOP) 800-771-4887	•	•	•	•	•
•	•	•		Courthouse Document Retrieval 972-644-4185	•	•	•		•
•	•	•		DFW Court Records (SOP) 800-436-0516		•	•		•
•	•	•		Data Screen Inc 817-294-7671					
•	•	•	•	Document Resources 800-822-8084	•	•	•	•	
•	•	•	•	Harold Eavenson & Associates (SOP) 972-771-5081	•	•	•	•	•
•	•	•	•	Intelnet Inc 888-636-3693	•	•	•	•	
•	•	•		National Crime Reporting Systems 800-687-0894					•
•	•	•	•	Nell Watkins & Assoc (SOP) 972-226-8811	•	•	•		•
•	•	•		OTI Resources 800-728-2742			•		•
•	•	•	•	PADIC Inc (SOP) 817-665-6130	•	•	•	•	•
				Police Report Acquisition Service 972-783-9505					
•	•	•	•	Quick Search 214-358-2840	•	•	•	•	•
	•	•		Record Retrieval Services 888-311-5001					
•				Ricochet (SOP) 214-855-0303		•			
•	•	•	•	Secrest Legal Services (SOP) 214-696-3959	•	•	•		
•	•	•	•	Security Information Service Inc (SOP) 800-525-5747	•	•	•		•
•	•	•	•	Stephens, Pat (SOP) 903-583-5215	•	•	•		•
•	•	•	•	Super Search 800-589-7029	•	•	•	•	
•	•	•	•	The Court System Inc 800-856-0585	•	•	•		•
		•		The Dataprompt Corporation 800-577-8157		•			
•	•		•	TitleInfo 817-244-7757	•	•	•		
•	•	•	•	Tyler-McLennon Inc 512-482-0808	•	•	•		•

	CV	CR	PR	COLLINGSWORTH (CST)	UC	RE	TX	VS	VR
				See adjoining counties for retrievers					

	CV	CR	PR	COLORADO (CST)	UC	RE	TX	VS	VR
	•	•	•	Apex Information and Research Inc (A.I.R.) 800-330-4525	•	•	•	•	•
	•	•	•	BAST Research Services Inc 713-777-8942	•	•	•		•
	•	•		Business Information Service 409-865-2547	•	•	•	•	
	•	•	•	Colorado County Abstract Co 409-732-6096	•	•	•	•	

	CV	CR	PR	COMAL (CST)	UC	RE	TX	VS	VR
	•	•	•	AKA Investigations & Process (SOP) 800-653-3817	•	•	•	•	•
	•	•	•	Access Research Staff 512-321-1889	•	•	•	•	•
	•	•		Alpha Research LLC (SOP) 205-755-7008			•		
	•		•	Bexar Professional (SOP) 210-228-0083	•	•	•	•	
	•	•	•	Bright Research Services 210-372-0170	•		•	•	
		•		FYP Inc 800-569-7143					

CV	CR	PR			UC	RE	TX	VS	VR
•	•	•	Fred Meyers Company	210-349-8119	•	•	•	•	
•	•	•	Priority Information Services (SOP)	210-699-9449	•	•	•	•	
•	•	•	Promesa Enterprises	800-474-4420	•	•	•	•	•
•	•	•	Property Research & Documentation Service	800-520-7884	•	•	•	•	•
•	•	•	Property Research Associates Inc	888-523-1061	•	•	•	•	
•	•		Search Plus	800-465-1525				•	•
•	•	•	Tyler-McLennon Inc	512-482-0808	•	•	•	•	

CV	CR	PR	COMANCHE (CST)		UC	RE	TX	VS	VR
•	•	•	Adams, Tommy M	915-648-3024	•	•	•	•	
•	•	•	Comanche County Abstract Co	915-356-2564	•	•	•	•	

CV	CR	PR	CONCHO (CST)		UC	RE	TX	VS	VR
•	•		Alpha Research LLC (SOP)	205-755-7008			•		
•	•	•	Surety Title Co of Eden	915-869-7081	•	•	•	•	

CV	CR	PR	COOKE (CST)		UC	RE	TX	VS	VR
•	•	•	PADIC Inc (SOP)	817-665-6130	•	•	•	•	•
•	•	•	Quick Search	214-358-2840	•	•	•	•	•

CV	CR	PR	CORYELL (CST)		UC	RE	TX	VS	VR
•		•	American Abstract and Title Co Inc	817-526-9525	•	•	•	•	
•	•	•	Search Enterprises	817-752-2057	•	•	•	•	

CV	CR	PR	COTTLE (CST)		UC	RE	TX	VS	VR
•		•	Jones & Renfrow Abstract Co	806-492-3573	•	•	•	•	

CV	CR	PR	CRANE (CST)		UC	RE	TX	VS	VR
•	•	•	APROTEX	915-683-3518	•	•	•	•	

CV	CR	PR	CROCKETT (CST)		UC	RE	TX	VS	VR
•	•	•	Crockett County Abstract Co	915-392-2232	•	•	•	•	

CV	CR	PR	CROSBY (CST)		UC	RE	TX	VS	VR
•	•	•	Davick Services	800-658-6656	•	•	•	•	•

CV	CR	PR	CULBERSON (CST)		UC	RE	TX	VS	VR
•		•	Advance Title Co	915-687-3355		•			

CV	CR	PR	DALLAM (CST)		UC	RE	TX	VS	VR
•	•	•	Hunter & Oelke	806-249-5632	•			•	
•	•	•	Lightspeed Couriers (SOP)	214-748-3340	•			•	

DT	BK	CV	CR	PR	DALLAS (CST)		UC	RE	TX	VS	VR
•	•	•	•	•	AKA Investigations & Process of Dallas (SOP)	214-761-1174	•	•	•	•	
		•			Accu-Source Inc	214-637-5006					
		•	•	•	Accutrak	972-390-2195		•	•	•	
•		•	•	•	Alpha Research LLC (SOP)	205-755-7008			•		
•		•	•	•	Attorney Service Associates (SOP)	214-394-1175	•	•	•	•	•
•		•	•	•	Attorney's Service Bureau of Texas (SOP)	214-522-5297	•	•			
•		•	•		Background Research	817-926-5976					
	•				Bankruptcy Bulletin Weekly Inc	409-854-2777					
•		•	•	•	Bankruptcy Services Inc	214-424-6500					
•	•	•	•	•	CSC (SOP)	800-654-3398	•		•		
•		•	•	•	Capitol Services Inc	800-345-4647	•		•		
•		•	•	•	Charles L Layer Private Investigations (SOP)	800-771-4887	•	•	•	•	•
•		•	•	•	Civil Process Service	800-866-2214	•	•	•		
•		•	•	•	Courthouse Document Retrieval	972-644-4185	•	•	•		•
•		•	•	•	DFW Court Records (SOP)	800-436-0516		•	•		•
•	•	•	•		Data Screen Inc	817-294-7671					
•		•	•	•	Document Resources	800-822-8084	•	•	•	•	
•		•	•		FYP Inc	800-569-7143					
•		•	•		Greet America Public Record Svc Inc	214-320-9836					
•	•	•	•	•	Harold Eavenson & Associates (SOP)	972-771-5081	•	•	•	•	•

CV	CR	PR			UC	RE	TX	VS	VR

• • • • •		Intelnet Inc	888-636-3693	• • • •					
• • • • •		Litigant Services Inc of Dallas	214-880-0070	• • • •					
• • • • •		National Crime Reporting Systems	800-687-0894					•	
• • • • •		🛍 Nell Watkins & Assoc (SOP)	972-226-8811	• • •				•	
• • • •		OTI Resources	800-728-2742	• • •				•	
• • • •		Osborn, Patricia J	214-349-3562	• •					
• • • • •		PADIC Inc (SOP)	817-665-6130	• • •				•	
• • • • •		Phoenix Information Services Inc (SOP)	800-918-8343	• • • •					
		Police Report Acquisition Service	972-783-9505						
• • • • •		Professional Civil Process (SOP)	800-950-7493	• • •				•	
• • • • •		🛍 Quick Search	214-358-2840	• • •				•	
• •		🛍 Record Retrieval Services	888-311-5001						
• • • • •		Reliable Courier (SOP)	214-823-5596			•	•		
• • • • •		🛍 Research Specialists Inc	214-263-0500	• •		•	•	•	
• •		Ricochet (SOP)	214-855-0303	•					
• • • • •		🛍 Secrest Legal Services (SOP)	214-696-3959	• •		•		•	
• • • • •		Security Information Service Inc (SOP)	800-525-5747	• • • •		•		•	
• • • • •		🛍 Super Search	800-589-7029	• • •		•		•	
• • • •		Texas Abstract Services	800-484-5690	• •		•		•	
• • • •		Texas Industrial Security Inc	214-634-2791	• • •		•		•	
• • • •		The Cole Group	713-880-9494	• • •		•		•	
• • • • •		The Court System Inc	800-856-0585	• • • •		•		•	
• •		The Dataprompt Corporation	800-577-8157					•	
• • • • •		The Information Bank of Texas (SOP)	713-864-9122	• • • •		•		•	
• • • •		TitleInfo	817-244-7757	• • •		•		•	
• • • • •		🛍 Tyler-McLennon Inc	512-482-0808	• • •		•		•	
• • • • •		Zumwalt Enterprises LLC	972-554-6968	• • • •		•		•	

CV	CR	PR	DAWSON (CST)		UC	RE	TX	VS	VR
• • •		APROTEX	915-683-3518	• •		•	•		
• • •		🛍 Davick Services	800-658-6656	• •		•	•	•	
		South Plain Abstract Co	806-872-3023	• •		•			

CV	CR	PR	DE WITT (CST)		UC	RE	TX	VS	VR
			See adjoining counties for retrievers						

CV	CR	PR	DEAF SMITH (CST)		UC	RE	TX	VS	VR
• • •		🛍 Davick Services	800-658-6656	• •		•	•	•	
• •		Rollins, Jan	806-353-7886	• •		•			

CV	CR	PR	DELTA (CST)		UC	RE	TX	VS	VR
• • •		Brubaker & Associates	903-595-4616	• •		•	•		
• • •		Delta County Title Co	903-395-4116	• •		•	•		
• • •		The Court System Inc	800-856-0585	• •		•	•	•	

CV	CR	PR	DENTON (CST)		UC	RE	TX	VS	VR
• • •		AKA Investigations & Process of Dallas (SOP)	214-761-1174	• •		•	•		
• •		🛍 Alpha Research LLC (SOP)	205-755-7008					•	
• • •		Attorney Service Associates (SOP)	214-394-1175	• •		•		•	
• • •		🛍 Attorney's Service Bureau of Texas (SOP)	214-522-5297	• •		•			
• •		Background Research	817-926-5976						
• • •		Charles L Layer Private Investigations (SOP)	800-771-4887	• •		•	•	•	
• •		DFW Court Records (SOP)	800-436-0516	• •		•		•	
• •		🛍 Data Screen Inc	817-294-7671					•	
• • •		Document Resources	800-822-8084	• •		•	•		
• • •		🛍 Harold Eavenson & Associates (SOP)	972-771-5081	• •		•	•	•	
• •		National Crime Reporting Systems	800-687-0894					•	
• •		OTI Resources	800-728-2742	• •		•		•	
• • •		PADIC Inc (SOP)	817-665-6130	• •		•		•	
		Police Report Acquisition Service	972-783-9505						
• • •		Professional Civil Process (SOP)	800-950-7493	• •		•	•	•	
• • •		Proffer, Janie	817-387-1214	• •		•	•	•	

• • •	🏛 Quick Search	214-358-2840	• • • • •
	Ricochet (SOP)	214-855-0303	•
• • •	Security Information Service Inc (SOP)	800-525-5747	• • • • •
• • •	🏛 Super Search	800-589-7029	• • • •
• • •	T D Disheroone Land Surveyor	800-645-0665	• • • •
•	The Court System Inc	800-856-0585	• • • • •
•	The Dataprompt Corporation	800-577-8157	•
• •	TitleInfo	817-244-7757	• • •
• • •	🏛 Tyler-McLennon Inc	512-482-0808	• • • •
• • •	Zumwalt Enterprises LLC	972-554-6968	• • • • •

CV	CR	PR	DICKENS (CST)	UC	RE	TX	VS	VR
•		•	Caprock Title Co 915-687-3232	•	•	•		
•	•	•	🏛 Davick Services 800-658-6656	•	•	•	•	•

CV	CR	PR	DIMMIT (CST)	UC	RE	TX	VS	VR
•	•	•	Elliott & Waldron Abstract Co of Dimmitt 210-876-2926	•	•	•	•	

CV	CR	PR	DONLEY (CST)	UC	RE	TX	VS	VR
•	•	•	Security Abstract Co of Clarendon 806-874-3511	•	•	•	•	
•	•	•	Security Abstract Co of Claude 806-226-3621	•	•	•	•	
•	•	•	Security Abstract Co of Memphis 806-259-2931	•	•	•	•	

CV	CR	PR	DUVAL (CST)	UC	RE	TX	VS	VR
•	•	•	Condor Investigations (SOP) 512-881-8977	•	•	•	•	•
•	•	•	🏛 Corpus Christi Court Services 512-887-8122	•	•	•	•	•
•	•	•	Shawver and Associates (SOP) 800-364-2333	•	•	•	•	•
•	•	•	Texas Civil Process (SOP) 800-976-9595	•	•	•	•	

CV	CR	PR	EASTLAND (CST)	UC	RE	TX	VS	VR
•	•	•	Eastland Title & Transfer Inc 817-629-2683	•	•	•		

CV	CR	PR	ECTOR (CST)	UC	RE	TX	VS	VR
•	•	•	APROTEX 915-683-3518	•	•	•	•	
•	•		🏛 Alpha Research LLC (SOP) 205-755-7008			•		
•	•		Basin Attorney Services 915-687-5346					
•	•	•	🏛 Davick Services 800-658-6656	•	•	•	•	•
•	•		Permian Court Reporters Inc 915-683-3032					
•	•	•	🏛 Tyler-McLennon Inc 512-482-0808	•	•	•		•

CV	CR	PR	EDWARDS (CST)	UC	RE	TX	VS	VR
•		•	Rocksprings Abstract and Title Co 210-683-2185	•	•	•	•	

DT	BK	CV	CR	PR	EL PASO (MST)	UC	RE	TX	VS	VR
•	•	•	•		🏛 Alpha Research LLC (SOP) 205-755-7008			•		
	•				Bankruptcy Bulletin Weekly Inc 409-854-2777					
•	•	•	•	•	Bankruptcy Services Inc 214-424-6500					
•	•	•	•		Greet America Public Record Svc Inc 214-320-9836					
•	•	•			🏛 Hogan Information Services 405-278-6954					
•	•	•	•	•	Legal Net Process Service (SOP) 915-532-7871	•		•	•	
•	•	•	•	•	Litigant Services Inc of El Paso 915-595-2309	•		•	•	
•	•	•	•		National Crime Reporting Systems 800-687-0894					•
•	•	•	•	•	Phoenix Information Services Inc (SOP) 800-918-8343	•		•	•	•
•	•	•	•	•	🏛 Quick Search 214-358-2840	•		•	•	•
•	•	•	•	•	🏛 Tyler-McLennon Inc 512-482-0808	•		•	•	•

CV	CR	PR	ELLIS (CST)	UC	RE	TX	VS	VR
•	•	•	Attorney Service Associates (SOP) 214-394-1175	•	•	•	•	•
•	•	•	Brubaker & Associates 903-595-4616	•	•	•	•	•
•	•	•	Charles L Layer Private Investigations (SOP) 800-771-4887	•	•	•	•	•
•	•		DFW Court Records (SOP) 800-436-0516	•	•			•
•	•	•	PADIC Inc (SOP) 817-665-6130	•	•	•	•	•
•	•	•	🏛 Quick Search 214-358-2840	•	•	•	•	•

●	●	●	Reliable Courier (SOP) 214-823-5596			●		●	
			Ricochet (SOP) 214-855-0303		●				
●	●	●	Search Enterprises 817-752-2057	●	●	●	●		
●	●	●	Security Information Service Inc (SOP) 800-525-5747	●	●	●	●	●	
●	●	●	🏛 Super Search 800-589-7029	●	●	●	●		
●	●	●	The Court System Inc 800-856-0585	●	●	●	●	●	
●	●	●	🏛 Tyler-McLennon Inc 512-482-0808	●	●	●		●	

CV	CR	PR	ERATH (CST)	UC	RE	TX	VS	VR
			See adjoining counties for retrievers					

CV	CR	PR	FALLS (CST)	UC	RE	TX	VS	VR
●	●	●	Falls County Abstract Co 817-883-2051	●	●	●	●	
		●	Falls County Title Co Inc 817-883-2112	●	●	●	●	
●	●	●	Search Enterprises 817-752-2057	●	●	●	●	

CV	CR	PR	FANNIN (CST)	UC	RE	TX	VS	VR
●	●	●	🏛 Quick Search 214-358-2840	●	●	●	●	●
●	●	●	Stephens, Pat (SOP) 903-583-5215	●	●	●		●

CV	CR	PR	FAYETTE (CST)	UC	RE	TX	VS	VR
●	●	●	Botts Title Co 409-567-4602	●	●	●	●	
●	●	●	Clear Title Co 409-968-5885	●	●	●	●	
●	●	●	Promesa Enterprises 800-474-4420	●	●	●	●	●

CV	CR	PR	FISHER (CST)	UC	RE	TX	VS	VR
●	●	●	🏛 Davick Services 800-658-6656	●	●	●	●	
●	●	●	Fisher County Abstract Co 915-776-2471	●	●	●	●	

CV	CR	PR	FLOYD (CST)	UC	RE	TX	VS	VR
●	●	●	🏛 Davick Services 800-658-6656	●	●	●	●	●

CV	CR	PR	FOARD (CST)	UC	RE	TX	VS	VR
●			Haynie, Leta Jo 817-684-1351				●	

CV	CR	PR	FORT BEND (CST)	UC	RE	TX	VS	VR
●	●		🏛 Alpha Research LLC (SOP) 205-755-7008			●		
●	●	●	🏛 Apex Information and Research Inc (A.I.R.) 800-330-4525	●	●	●	●	●
●	●	●	🏛 BAST Research Services Inc 713-777-8942	●	●	●		●
●	●	●	🏛 Court Record Research Inc 800-552-3353	●	●	●		●
●	●	●	🏛 Ervin Investigation & Research Svcs 888-203-6536	●	●	●		●
		●	🏛 FYP Inc 800-569-7143					
			Fox Hunt 713-772-8018	●		●		●
●	●	●	🏛 Houston Court Services Inc (SOP) 800-593-2023	●	●	●		●
●		●	LawServ Inc (SOP) 713-228-1055	●	●	●		
●		●	M.R.S. Datascope Inc (SOP) 800-899-3282			●		
●		●	Mesaa Unlimited (SOP) 713-759-7464	●		●		●
●		●	Metropolitan Court Services (SOP) 713-616-6971	●	●	●		●
			OTI Resources 800-728-2742		●			●
●	●	●	Professional Civil Process (SOP) 800-950-7493	●	●			
●	●	●	Southwest Patrol & Investigations 713-697-1577	●	●	●		●
●		●	Texas Abstract Services 800-484-5690		●			
●		●	Texas Records Search (SOP) 800-869-1405	●	●	●	●	●
●		●	The Information Bank of Texas (SOP) 713-864-9122	●	●	●	●	●
●	●	●	🏛 The Research Staff Inc 800-822-3584	●	●	●		●
●	●	●	🏛 Tyler-McLennon Inc 512-482-0808	●	●	●		●
●	●	●	Walters & Associates (SOP) 281-242-2243	●	●	●	●	●

CV	CR	PR	FRANKLIN (CST)	UC	RE	TX	VS	VR
●	●	●	Brubaker & Associates 903-595-4616	●	●	●	●	
●	●	●	Franklin County Abstract Co 903-537-4223	●	●	●	●	

FREESTONE (CST)

CV	CR	PR			UC	RE	TX	VS	VR
•	•	•	Search Enterprises	817-752-2057	•	•	•	•	

FRIO (CST)

See adjoining counties for retrievers ....

GAINES (CST)

CV	CR	PR			UC	RE	TX	VS	VR
•	•	•	Davick Services	800-658-6656	•	•	•	•	•
•		•	Gaines County Abstract Co	915-758-3351		•	•	•	

GALVESTON (CST)

DT	CV	CR	PR			UC	RE	TX	VS	VR
•	•	•		Alpha Research LLC (SOP)	205-755-7008			•		
•	•	•	•	Apex Information and Research Inc (A.I.R.)	800-330-4525	•	•	•	•	•
•	•	•	•	BAST Research Services Inc	713-777-8942	•	•	•		•
•	•	•	•	Court Record Research Inc	800-552-3353	•	•	•		•
•	•	•	•	Ervin Investigation & Research Svcs	888-203-6536	•	•	•	•	•
•	•	•	•	LawServ Inc (SOP)	713-228-1055	•	•	•		
•	•	•	•	M.R.S. Datascope Inc (SOP)	800-899-3282			•		
•	•	•	•	Mesaa Unlimited (SOP)	713-759-7464	•	•	•		•
•	•	•	•	Metropolitan Court Services (SOP)	713-616-6971	•	•	•	•	•
•	•	•		OTI Resources	800-728-2742	•		•		•
•	•		•	Texas Abstract Services	800-484-5690		•			
•	•	•	•	Texas Records Search (SOP)	800-869-1405	•	•	•		•
•	•	•	•	The Information Bank of Texas (SOP)	713-864-9122	•	•	•	•	•
•	•	•	•	The Research Staff Inc	800-822-3584	•	•	•		•
•	•	•	•	Tyler-McLennon Inc	512-482-0808	•	•	•		•
•	•	•	•	Walters & Associates (SOP)	281-242-2243	•	•	•	•	•

GARZA (CST)

CV	CR	PR			UC	RE	TX	VS	VR
•	•	•	Davick Services	800-658-6656	•	•	•	•	•
•	•	•	Pollard & Lott Inc	806-495-2989	•	•	•	•	

GILLESPIE (CST)

CV	CR	PR			UC	RE	TX	VS	VR
•		•	Fredericksburg Title Inc	210-997-3852	•	•	•		

GLASSCOCK (CST)

CV	CR	PR			UC	RE	TX	VS	VR
•	•	•	APROTEX	915-683-3518	•	•	•	•	
•		•	Elliott & Waldron Abstr Co of Glasscock	915-354-2231	•	•	•	•	

GOLIAD (CST)

CV	CR	PR			UC	RE	TX	VS	VR
•	•		Alpha Research LLC (SOP)	205-755-7008			•		
•		•	Bedgood Abstract & Title Co	512-645-3145	•	•	•		

GONZALES (CST)

CV	CR	PR			UC	RE	TX	VS	VR
•	•		Alpha Research LLC (SOP)	205-755-7008			•		
•	•	•	Bright Research Services	210-372-0170	•		•	•	
•	•		Search Plus	800-465-1525				•	•

GRAY (CST)

CV	CR	PR			UC	RE	TX	VS	VR
•	•	•	Caprock Land Title Company	800-253-3281	•	•	•	•	•
•	•	•	Credit Bureau Services of the Panhandle	806-669-3246	•	•	•	•	
•	•	•	Rollins, Jan	806-353-7886	•	•	•	•	

GRAYSON (CST)

DT	CV	CR	PR			UC	RE	TX	VS	VR
•	•	•		Alpha Research LLC (SOP)	205-755-7008			•		
•	•	•	•	Bankruptcy Services Inc	214-424-6500					
•	•	•	•	PADIC Inc (SOP)	817-665-6130	•	•	•	•	•
•	•	•	•	Quick Search	214-358-2840	•	•	•	•	
•	•	•	•	Stephens, Pat (SOP)	903-583-5215	•	•	•		•
•	•	•	•	The Court System Inc	800-856-0585	•	•	•	•	
•	•	•	•	Tyler-McLennon Inc	512-482-0808	•	•	•		•

	CV	CR	PR	GREGG (CST)	UC	RE	TX	VS	VR
	•	•		🏛 Alpha Research LLC (SOP) 205-755-7008			•		
	•	•	•	Brubaker & Associates 903-595-4616	•	•	•	•	
	•	•	•	Intelnet Inc 888-636-3693	•	•	•	•	

	CV	CR	PR	GRIMES (CST)	UC	RE	TX	VS	VR
	•	•	•	🏛 BAST Research Services Inc 713-777-8942	•	•	•		•
	•		•	Guaranty Title Co 409-873-2250	•	•	•		

	CV	CR	PR	GUADALUPE (CST)	UC	RE	TX	VS	VR
	•	•	•	AKA Investigations & Process (SOP) 800-653-3817	•	•	•	•	•
	•	•		🏛 Alpha Research LLC (SOP) 205-755-7008			•		
	•	•	•	🏛 Bright Research Services 210-372-0170	•		•	•	
	•	•	•	Fred Meyers Company 210-349-8119	•	•	•		
	•	•	•	🏛 Priority Information Services (SOP) 210-699-9449	•	•	•	•	
	•	•	•	Property Research & Documentation Service 800-520-7884	•	•	•	•	•
	•	•	•	Property Research Associates Inc 888-523-1061	•	•	•	•	
	•	•		Search Plus 800-465-1525			•	•	•

	CV	CR	PR	HALE (CST)	UC	RE	TX	VS	VR
	•	•	•	🏛 Davick Services 800-658-6656	•	•	•	•	•

	CV	CR	PR	HALL (CST)	UC	RE	TX	VS	VR
	•	•	•	Security Abstract Co of Clarendon 806-874-3511	•	•	•	•	
	•	•	•	Security Abstract Co of Claude 806-226-3621	•	•	•	•	
	•	•	•	Security Abstract Co of Memphis 806-259-2931	•	•	•	•	

	CV	CR	PR	HAMILTON (CST)	UC	RE	TX	VS	VR
	•	•	•	Adams, Tommy M 915-648-3024	•	•	•	•	

	CV	CR	PR	HANSFORD (CST)	UC	RE	TX	VS	VR
				See adjoining counties for retrievers					

	CV	CR	PR	HARDEMAN (CST)	UC	RE	TX	VS	VR
				See adjoining counties for retrievers					

	CV	CR	PR	HARDIN (CST)	UC	RE	TX	VS	VR
	•	•	•	🏛 BAST Research Services Inc 713-777-8942	•	•	•		•
	•		•	Hooks Title & Abstract 409-246-3447	•	•	•		
	•		•	🏛 The Research Staff Inc 800-822-3584	•	•	•		•

DT	BK	CV	CR	PR	HARRIS (CST)	UC	RE	TX	VS	VR
•	•	•	•	•	Access Research Staff 512-321-1889	•	•	•	•	•
•	•	•	•	•	🏛 Alpha Research LLC (SOP) 205-755-7008			•		
•	•	•	•	•	🏛 Apex Information and Research Inc (A.I.R.) 800-330-4525	•	•	•	•	•
•	•	•	•	•	🏛 Attorney's Service Bureau of Texas (SOP) 214-522-5297	•	•	•		
•	•	•	•	•	🏛 BAST Research Services Inc 713-777-8942	•	•	•		•
	•				Bankruptcy Bulletin Weekly Inc 409-854-2777					
•	•	•	•	•	Bankruptcy Services Inc 214-424-6500					
		•		•	CSC (SOP) 800-243-3779	•		•		
•		•		•	🏛 Capitol Services Inc 800-345-4647	•		•		
•	•	•	•	•	🏛 Court Record Research Inc 800-552-3353	•		•	•	•
•	•	•	•		🏛 Data Screen Inc 817-294-7671					
•		•	•	•	Document Resources 800-822-8084	•	•	•	•	
•	•	•	•	•	🏛 Ervin Investigation & Research Svcs 888-203-6536	•	•	•	•	•
•		•		•	🏛 FYP Inc 800-569-7143					
		•		•	Fox Hunt 713-772-8018	•	•	•		•
•	•				🏛 Hogan Information Services 405-278-6954					
•	•	•	•	•	🏛 Houston Court Services Inc (SOP) 800-593-2023	•	•	•		
		•		•	🏛 I.P.S. Inc 713-783-9996					
		•		•	🏛 Intellifacts Corporation 800-208-9422					
•	•	•	•	•	Intelnet Inc 888-636-3693	•	•	•	•	
•	•	•	•	•	Intranet Inc 903-593-9817	•	•	•	•	

					Company	Phone	UC	RE	TX	VS	VR
•	•	•	•	•	LawServ Inc (SOP)	713-228-1055	•	•	•	•	
•	•	•	•	•	M.R.S. Datascope Inc (SOP)	800-899-3282			•		
•	•	•	•	•	Mesaa Unlimited (SOP)	713-759-7464	•	•	•	•	•
•	•	•	•	•	Metropolitan Court Services (SOP)	713-616-6971	•	•	•	•	•
				•	OTI Resources	800-728-2742	•		•	•	
				•	🗑 Persona Data Corporation	800-735-9555					
•	•	•	•	•	Phoenix Information Services Inc (SOP)	800-918-8343	•	•	•	•	•
•	•	•	•	•	Professional Civil Process (SOP)	800-950-7493	•	•	•	•	
•	•	•	•	•	🗑 Quick Search	214-358-2840	•	•	•	•	•
•	•	•	•	•	Southwest Patrol & Investigations	713-697-1577	•	•	•		•
•	•	•	•		Texas Abstract Services	800-484-5690	•	•			
•	•	•	•	•	Texas Records Search (SOP)	800-869-1405	•	•	•	•	
	•	•	•		The Cole Group	713-880-9494	•				
			•		The Dataprompt Corporation	800-577-8157	•				
•	•	•	•	•	The Information Bank of Texas (SOP)	713-864-9122	•	•	•	•	•
•	•	•	•	•	🗑 The Research Staff Inc	800-822-3584	•	•	•		•
•	•	•	•	•	TitleInfo	817-244-7757	•	•	•	•	
•	•	•	•	•	🗑 Tyler-McLennon Inc	512-482-0808	•	•	•	•	•
•	•	•	•	•	Walters & Associates (SOP)	281-242-2243	•	•	•	•	•

DT	CV	CR	PR	HARRISON (CST)		UC	RE	TX	VS	VR
	•		•	DeSoto Abstract	318-798-1198	•	•	•		
•	•	•	•	The Court System Inc	800-856-0585	•	•	•	•	•

	CV	CR	PR	HARTLEY (CST)		UC	RE	TX	VS	VR
	•	•	•	Hunter & Oelke	806-249-5632	•		•		

	CV	CR	PR	HASKELL (CST)		UC	RE	TX	VS	VR
	•	•	•	Haskell Abstract & TItle Co	817-864-2604	•	•	•		

	CV	CR	PR	HAYS (CST)		UC	RE	TX	VS	VR
	•	•	•	AKA Investigations & Process of Austin (SOP)	800-933-8706	•	•	•	•	•
	•	•	•	Access Research Staff	512-321-1889	•	•	•	•	•
	•	•		🗑 Alpha Research LLC (SOP)	205-755-7008			•		
	•	•	•	Assured Civil Process Agency (SOP)	800-256-7160		•			•
	•		•	Avian Corporate Records & Research (SOP)	512-326-3354	•	•	•		•
	•	•	•	🗑 Bright Research Services	210-372-0170	•		•	•	
	•	•		CPS (Capital Process Service)	512-930-7378		•			
	•	•	•	Capitol Commerce Reporter Inc	800-356-8282	•	•	•		
	•	•		🗑 Capitol Services Inc	800-345-4647	•	•	•		
	•	•	•	Courthouse Services (SOP)	800-843-5725	•	•	•		•
	•	•		🗑 Data Screen Inc	817-294-7671		•			
	•	•	•	Document Resources	800-822-8084	•	•	•	•	
	•	•		🗑 FYP Inc	800-569-7143		•			
	•	•	•	🗑 John C Dunaway and Associates (SOP)	512-835-5888	•	•	•	•	•
	•	•	•	Promesa Enterprises	800-474-4420	•	•	•	•	
	•	•	•	Property Research & Documentation Service	800-520-7884	•	•	•	•	•
	•	•	•	Property Research Associates Inc	888-523-1061	•	•	•	•	
	•	•		Search Plus	800-465-1525		•			•
	•	•	•	🗑 Tyler-McLennon Inc	512-482-0808	•	•	•		•

	CV	CR	PR	HEMPHILL (CST)		UC	RE	TX	VS	VR
	•	•	•	Credit Bureau Services of the Panhandle	806-669-3246	•	•	•		

	CV	CR	PR	HENDERSON (CST)		UC	RE	TX	VS	VR
	•	•		🗑 Alpha Research LLC (SOP)	205-755-7008			•		
	•	•	•	Brubaker & Associates	903-595-4616	•	•	•	•	
	•		•	DeSoto Abstract	318-798-1198	•	•	•		
	•		•	Search Enterprises	817-752-2057	•	•	•		
	•	•	•	The Court System Inc	800-856-0585	•	•	•	•	•

DT	CV	CR	PR	HIDALGO (CST)		UC	RE	TX	VS	VR
•		•	•	🗑 Alpha Research LLC (SOP)	205-755-7008			•		

				KJB Court Search (SOP)..............................210-971-8846					
				Phoenix Information Services Inc (SOP)............800-918-8343					
				Professional Civil Process (SOP)....................800-880-4223					
				Professional Civil Process (SOP)....................800-950-7493					
				Shawver and Associates (SOP)......................800-364-2333					
				⛁ Valley Court Services 210-412-2306					

CV	CR	PR		HILL (CST)	UC	RE	TX	VS	VR
•	•		⛁ Alpha Research LLC (SOP)............205-755-7008				•		
•	•	•	Eastland Title Co 817-582-2762		•	•	•	•	
•	•	•	Search Enterprises 817-752-2057		•	•	•	•	

CV	CR	PR		HOCKLEY (CST)	UC	RE	TX	VS	VR
•	•	•	⛁ Davick Services 800-658-6656		•	•	•	•	•

CV	CR	PR		HOOD (CST)	UC	RE	TX	VS	VR
•	•		⛁ Alpha Research LLC (SOP)............205-755-7008				•		
•	•	•	⛁ Super Search 800-589-7029		•	•	•		
•	•	•	T D Disheroone Land Surveyor 800-645-0665		•	•	•		
•	•	•	⛁ Tyler-McLennon Inc 512-482-0808		•	•	•		•

CV	CR	PR		HOPKINS (CST)	UC	RE	TX	VS	VR
•	•	•	Brubaker & Associates 903-595-4616		•	•	•	•	
•	•	•	The Court System Inc 800-856-0585		•	•	•	•	•

CV	CR	PR		HOUSTON (CST)	UC	RE	TX	VS	VR
•		•	Aldrich Abstract Company 409-544-2013		•	•	•		
•	•	•	⛁ The Research Staff Inc 800-822-3584		•	•	•		•

CV	CR	PR		HOWARD (CST)	UC	RE	TX	VS	VR
•	•	•	APROTEX 915-683-3518		•	•	•	•	
	•	•	Big Spring Abstract & Title Co Inc 915-267-1604		•	•	•	•	
•	•	•	⛁ Davick Services 800-658-6656		•	•	•	•	•

CV	CR	PR		HUDSPETH (MST)	UC	RE	TX	VS	VR
•	•	•	Legal Net Process Service (SOP)........915-532-7871		•	•	•	•	

CV	CR	PR		HUNT (CST)	UC	RE	TX	VS	VR
•	•		Accutrak 972-390-2195			•	•	•	
•	•		⛁ Alpha Research LLC (SOP)............205-755-7008				•		
•	•	•	Brubaker & Associates 903-595-4616		•	•	•		
•	•	•	Charles L Layer Private Investigations (SOP)....800-771-4887		•	•	•	•	
•	•	•	⛁ Harold Eavenson & Associates (SOP)....972-771-5081		•	•	•	•	
•	•	•	⛁ Nell Watkins & Assoc (SOP)........972-226-8811		•	•	•	•	
•	•	•	⛁ Quick Search 214-358-2840		•	•	•	•	
•	•	•	Security Information Service Inc (SOP)....800-525-5747		•	•	•	•	
•	•	•	Stephens, Pat (SOP)..........................903-583-5215		•	•	•	•	
	•		The Dataprompt Corporation 800-577-8157		•				
•	•	•	⛁ Tyler-McLennon Inc 512-482-0808		•	•	•		•

CV	CR	PR		HUTCHINSON (CST)	UC	RE	TX	VS	VR
•	•	•	Rollins, Jan 806-353-7886		•	•	•	•	

CV	CR	PR		IRION (CST)	UC	RE	TX	VS	VR
			See adjoining counties for retrievers						

CV	CR	PR		JACK (CST)	UC	RE	TX	VS	VR
			Spiller Abstract 817-567-2271		•	•	•		

CV	CR	PR		JACKSON (CST)	UC	RE	TX	VS	VR
•	•	•	Guarantee Abstract 512-782-3591		•	•	•		

CV	CR	PR		JASPER (CST)	UC	RE	TX	VS	VR
•	•		⛁ Alpha Research LLC (SOP)............205-755-7008				•		

CV	CR	PR			UC	RE	TX	VS	VR
•	•	•	Garland Smith Abstract Co	409-384-2571	•	•	•	•	
•	•	•	🏛 The Research Staff Inc	800-822-3584	•	•	•		•

CV	CR	PR	JEFF DAVIS (CST)		UC	RE	TX	VS	VR
•		•	Jeff Davis County Abstract Co	915-426-3288	•	•	•		

DT	BK	CV	CR	PR	JEFFERSON (CST)		UC	RE	TX	VS	VR
•	•	•	•		🏛 Alpha Research LLC (SOP)	205-755-7008			•		
•	•	•	•	•	🏛 BAST Research Services Inc	713-777-8942	•	•	•		•
		•			Bankruptcy Bulletin Weekly Inc	409-854-2777					
•	•	•	•	•	Bankruptcy Services Inc	214-424-6500					
•	•				🏛 Hogan Information Services	405-278-6954					
•		•	•	•	Intranet Inc	903-593-9817	•	•	•	•	
•		•	•	•	LawServ Inc (SOP)	713-228-1055	•		•		
•		•	•	•	M.R.S. Datascope Inc (SOP)	800-899-3282			•		
•		•	•	•	Texas Records Search (SOP)	800-869-1405	•	•	•	•	•
•	•	•	•	•	🏛 The Research Staff Inc	800-822-3584	•	•	•		•
•	•	•	•	•	🏛 Tyler-McLennon Inc	512-482-0808	•	•	•		•

CV	CR	PR	JIM HOGG (CST)		UC	RE	TX	VS	VR
			Border Abstract	210-791-5810	•	•	•		

CV	CR	PR	JIM WELLS (CST)		UC	RE	TX	VS	VR
•	•	•	Condor Investigations (SOP)	512-881-8977	•	•	•	•	•
•	•	•	🏛 Corpus Christi Court Services	512-887-8122	•	•	•	•	•
•	•	•	Shawver and Associates (SOP)	800-364-2333	•	•	•	•	
•	•	•	Texas Civil Process (SOP)	800-976-9595	•	•	•	•	
•	•	•	Texas Legal Support Service	512-883-2247	•	•	•	•	

CV	CR	PR	JOHNSON (CST)		UC	RE	TX	VS	VR
•	•	•	🏛 Attorney's Service Bureau of Texas (SOP)	214-522-5297	•	•	•		
•	•	•	🏛 Quick Search	214-358-2840	•	•	•	•	•
•	•	•	Search Enterprises	817-752-2057	•	•	•	•	
•	•	•	Security Information Service Inc (SOP)	800-525-5747	•	•	•	•	•
•	•	•	🏛 Super Search	800-589-7029	•	•	•	•	
•	•	•	T D Disheroone Land Surveyor	800-645-0665	•	•	•	•	
•		•	TitleInfo	817-244-7757	•	•	•		

CV	CR	PR	JONES (CST)		UC	RE	TX	VS	VR
•	•	•	Jones County Abstract Co	915-823-3236	•	•	•	•	

CV	CR	PR	KARNES (CST)		UC	RE	TX	VS	VR
•		•	Karnes Land Title Co Inc	210-780-2221	•	•	•	•	

CV	CR	PR	KAUFMAN (CST)		UC	RE	TX	VS	VR
•	•	•	Charles L Layer Private Investigations (SOP)	800-771-4887	•	•	•	•	•
•	•	•	🏛 Harold Eavenson & Associates (SOP)	972-771-5081	•	•	•	•	•
•	•	•	🏛 Nell Watkins & Assoc (SOP)	972-226-8811	•	•	•	•	•
•	•	•	🏛 Quick Search	214-358-2840	•	•	•	•	•
•		•	Security Information Service Inc (SOP)	800-525-5747	•	•	•	•	•
•		•	The Court System Inc	800-856-0585	•	•	•	•	•
•	•	•	🏛 Tyler-McLennon Inc	512-482-0808	•	•	•	•	•

CV	CR	PR	KENDALL (CST)		UC	RE	TX	VS	VR
•	•	•	AKA Investigations & Process (SOP)	800-653-3817	•	•	•	•	•
	•	•	Bexar Professional (SOP)	210-228-0083	•	•	•	•	
•	•	•	Fred Meyers Company	210-349-8119	•	•	•	•	
•	•	•	🏛 Priority Information Services (SOP)	210-699-9449	•	•	•	•	
•	•	•	Property Research & Documentation Service	800-520-7884	•	•	•	•	•

CV	CR	PR	KENEDY (CST)		UC	RE	TX	VS	VR
•	•	•	John Bullock & Co	512-992-3060	•	•	•	•	
•	•	•	KJB Court Search (SOP)	210-971-8846	•	•	•	•	•

CV	CR	PR	KENT (CST)		UC	RE	TX	VS	VR
•		•	Caprock Title Co 915-687-3232		•	•	•		
•	•	•	🏛 Davick Services 800-658-6656		•	•	•	•	•

CV	CR	PR	KERR (CST)		UC	RE	TX	VS	VR
•	•		🏛 Alpha Research LLC (SOP)............................... 205-755-7008				•		
•	•	•	Property Research & Documentation Service 800-520-7884		•	•	•	•	•
•	•	•	Property Research Associates Inc 888-523-1061		•	•	•	•	

CV	CR	PR	KIMBLE (CST)		UC	RE	TX	VS	VR
•	•	•	Harrison, Lawrence 915-446-2317		•	•	•	•	

CV	CR	PR	KING (CST)		UC	RE	TX	VS	VR
•		•	Caprock Title Co 915-687-3232		•	•	•		
•	•	•	🏛 Davick Services 800-658-6656		•	•	•	•	•
•	•	•	Jones & Renfrow Abstract Co 806-492-3573		•	•	•	•	

CV	CR	PR	KINNEY (CST)		UC	RE	TX	VS	VR
			See adjoining counties for retrievers						

CV	CR	PR	KLEBERG (CST)		UC	RE	TX	VS	VR
•	•	•	Condor Investigations (SOP)............................... 512-881-8977		•	•	•	•	•
•	•	•	🏛 Corpus Christi Court Services 512-887-8122		•	•	•	•	•
•	•		🏛 I.P.S. Inc 713-783-9996						
•		•	John Bullock & Co 512-992-3060		•	•	•		
•	•	•	KJB Court Search (SOP)...................................... 210-971-8846		•	•	•	•	•
•	•	•	Shawver and Associates (SOP)............................ 800-364-2333		•	•	•	•	•
•	•	•	Texas Civil Process (SOP)................................... 800-976-9595		•	•	•	•	
•	•	•	Texas Legal Support Service 512-883-2247		•	•	•	•	

CV	CR	PR	KNOX (CST)		UC	RE	TX	VS	VR
			See adjoining counties for retrievers						

CV	CR	PR	LA SALLE (CST)		UC	RE	TX	VS	VR
			Border Abstract 210-791-5810		•	•	•		
•	•	•	LaSalle County Abstract Inc 210-879-3712		•	•	•	•	

CV	CR	PR	LAMAR (CST)		UC	RE	TX	VS	VR
•	•		🏛 Alpha Research LLC (SOP)............................... 205-755-7008				•		
•	•	•	Stephens, Pat (SOP)... 903-583-5215		•	•	•		•
•	•	•	The Court System Inc 800-856-0585		•	•	•	•	•

CV	CR	PR	LAMB (CST)		UC	RE	TX	VS	VR
•	•	•	🏛 Davick Services 800-658-6656		•	•	•	•	•

CV	CR	PR	LAMPASAS (CST)		UC	RE	TX	VS	VR
•	•	•	Adams, Tommy M 915-648-3024		•	•	•	•	
•	•		🏛 Alpha Research LLC (SOP)............................... 205-755-7008				•		
•	•		CPS (Capital Process Service) 512-930-7378				•		

CV	CR	PR	LAVACA (CST)		UC	RE	TX	VS	VR
•	•	•	Halletsville Abstract & Title Co 512-798-3291		•	•	•	•	

CV	CR	PR	LEE (CST)		UC	RE	TX	VS	VR
•	•	•	Access Research Staff 512-321-1889		•	•	•	•	•
•	•	•	Capitol Commerce Reporter Inc 800-356-8282		•	•	•	•	
•		•	Lee County Land & Abstract 409-542-3636		•	•	•	•	

CV	CR	PR	LEON (CST)		UC	RE	TX	VS	VR
•		•	Guaranty Title Co 903-536-2133		•	•	•	•	

CV	CR	PR	LIBERTY (CST)		UC	RE	TX	VS	VR
•	•		🏛 Alpha Research LLC (SOP)............................... 205-755-7008				•		
•	•	•	🏛 BAST Research Services Inc 713-777-8942		•	•	•		•

CV	CR	PR			UC	RE	TX	VS	VR
•	•		Caskey, Don W	713-422-7527	•		•		
•	•	•	Ervin Investigation & Research Svcs	888-203-6536	•	•	•	•	•
•	•	•	Texas Records Search (SOP)	800-869-1405	•	•	•	•	•
•	•	•	The Research Staff Inc	800-822-3584	•	•	•		•

CV	CR	PR	LIMESTONE (CST)		UC	RE	TX	VS	VR
•	•	•	Groesbeck Abstract & Title Co	817-729-3806	•	•	•	•	
•	•	•	Search Enterprises	817-752-2057	•	•	•	•	

CV	CR	PR	LIPSCOMB (CST)		UC	RE	TX	VS	VR
•	•	•	Credit Bureau Services of the Panhandle	806-669-3246	•	•	•	•	
		•	Lipscomb County Abstract Co	806-658-4525	•	•	•	•	
		•	Ochiltree County Abstract Company	806-435-4572	•	•	•		

CV	CR	PR	LIVE OAK (CST)		UC	RE	TX	VS	VR
•	•	•	Texas Civil Process (SOP)	800-976-9595	•	•	•	•	

CV	CR	PR	LLANO (CST)		UC	RE	TX	VS	VR
•	•	•	AKA Investigations & Process of Austin (SOP)	800-933-8706	•	•	•	•	•
•	•		Alpha Research LLC (SOP)	205-755-7008			•		
•	•		CPS (Capital Process Service)	512-930-7378			•		
•	•	•	Promesa Enterprises	800-474-4420	•	•	•	•	•

CV	CR	PR	LOVING (CST)		UC	RE	TX	VS	VR
•		•	Advance Title Co	915-687-3355		•			

DT	BK	CV	CR	PR	LUBBOCK (CST)		UC	RE	TX	VS	VR
•	•	•	•		Alpha Research LLC (SOP)	205-755-7008			•		
	•				Bankruptcy Bulletin Weekly Inc	409-854-2777					
•	•	•	•	•	Bankruptcy Services Inc	214-424-6500					
•	•	•	•	•	Davick Services	800-658-6656	•	•	•	•	•
•	•	•	•	•	Phoenix Information Services Inc (SOP)	800-918-8343	•	•	•	•	•
•	•	•	•	•	Rollins, Jan	806-353-7886	•	•	•		
•	•	•	•	•	Tyler-McLennon Inc	512-482-0808	•	•	•		•
		•	•	•	US Legal Support of Lubbock	806-747-8500	•	•	•	•	

CV	CR	PR	LYNN (CST)		UC	RE	TX	VS	VR
•	•	•	Davick Services	800-658-6656	•	•	•	•	•
•	•	•	Lynn County Abstract Co	806-998-4022	•	•	•		

CV	CR	PR	MADISON (CST)		UC	RE	TX	VS	VR
		•	Landmark Title Co of Madison County	409-348-5618	•	•	•		

CV	CR	PR	MARION (CST)		UC	RE	TX	VS	VR
•	•	•	Brubaker & Associates	903-595-4616	•	•	•	•	
		•	DeSoto Abstract	318-798-1198	•	•	•		

CV	CR	PR	MARTIN (CST)		UC	RE	TX	VS	VR
•		•	APROTEX	915-683-3518	•	•	•	•	
		•	Advance Title Co	915-687-3355			•		
•	•	•	Davick Services	800-658-6656	•	•	•	•	•

CV	CR	PR	MASON (CST)		UC	RE	TX	VS	VR
		•	First Mason Title Co	915-347-6388	•	•	•	•	

CV	CR	PR	MATAGORDA (CST)		UC	RE	TX	VS	VR
•	•		Alpha Research LLC (SOP)	205-755-7008			•		
•	•	•	Apex Information and Research Inc (A.I.R.)	800-330-4525	•	•	•	•	•
•	•	•	BAST Research Services Inc	713-777-8942	•	•			•
•	•		Bay City Abstract & Title	409-245-6321		•	•		
•	•	•	The Research Staff Inc	800-822-3584	•	•	•		•

CV	CR	PR	MAVERICK (CST)		UC	RE	TX	VS	VR
		•	Eagle Pass Title Co Inc	210-773-0555	•	•	•		

CV	CR	PR	McCULLOCH (CST)	UC	RE	TX	VS	VR
•	•	•	Jordan & McCulloch Abstracters Inc 915-597-2172	•	•	•		

DT	BK	CV	CR	PR	McLENNAN (CST)	UC	RE	TX	VS	VR
•	•	•	•		🏛 Alpha Research LLC (SOP)............ 205-755-7008		•			
•	•	•	•	•	Attorney Civil Process Service (SOP) 817-755-6447					
		•			Bankruptcy Bulletin Weekly Inc 409-854-2777					
•	•	•	•	•	Bankruptcy Services Inc 214-424-6500					
•	•	•	•		🏛 Greenwood Research 800-771-0847	•	•	•		
•	•				🏛 Hogan Information Services 405-278-6954					
•		•	•	•	Intelnet Inc 888-636-3693	•	•	•	•	
•	•	•	•	•	Search Enterprises 817-752-2057	•	•	•	•	
•	•	•	•	•	🏛 Tyler-McLennon Inc 512-482-0808	•	•	•		•

CV	CR	PR	McMULLEN (CST)	UC	RE	TX	VS	VR
•	•	•	McMullen County Title Co 512-274-3312	•	•	•	•	

CV	CR	PR	MEDINA (CST)	UC	RE	TX	VS	VR
•	•	•	AKA Investigations & Process (SOP) 800-653-3817	•	•	•	•	•
•	•		🏛 Alpha Research LLC (SOP) 205-755-7008		•			
•	•	•	Fred Meyers Company 210-349-8119	•	•	•		
•	•	•	🏛 Legal Records Investigations 210-675-6258	•	•	•	•	
•	•	•	Property Research & Documentation Service 800-520-7884	•	•	•	•	

CV	CR	PR	MENARD (CST)	UC	RE	TX	VS	VR
•	•	•	Neel, Ben 915-396-2351	•	•	•	•	

DT	BK	CV	CR	PR	MIDLAND (CST)	UC	RE	TX	VS	VR
•	•	•	•	•	APROTEX 915-683-3518	•	•	•	•	
•	•	•		•	Advance Title Co 915-687-3355		•			
•	•	•	•		🏛 Alpha Research LLC (SOP) 205-755-7008		•			
	•				Bankruptcy Bulletin Weekly Inc 409-854-2777					
•	•	•	•		Bankruptcy Services Inc 214-424-6500					
•	•	•	•		Basin Attorney Services 915-687-5346					
•	•	•	•	•	🏛 Davick Services 800-658-6656	•	•	•	•	•
•	•	•	•		Permian Court Reporters Inc 915-683-3032					
•	•	•	•	•	🏛 Tyler-McLennon Inc 512-482-0808	•	•	•		•

CV	CR	PR	MILAM (CST)	UC	RE	TX	VS	VR
•	•	•	Little River Land & Abstract 817-697-6962	•	•	•	•	•

CV	CR	PR	MILLS (CST)	UC	RE	TX	VS	VR
•	•	•	Adams, Tommy M 915-648-3024	•	•	•	•	

CV	CR	PR	MITCHELL (CST)	UC	RE	TX	VS	VR
•	•	•	APROTEX 915-683-3518	•	•	•	•	
•	•	•	Colorado City Abstract Co 915-728-3475	•	•	•		
•	•	•	🏛 Davick Services 800-658-6656	•	•	•	•	•

CV	CR	PR	MONTAGUE (CST)	UC	RE	TX	VS	VR
			See adjoining counties for retrievers					

CV	CR	PR	MONTGOMERY (CST)	UC	RE	TX	VS	VR
•	•		🏛 Alpha Research LLC (SOP)............ 205-755-7008		•			
•	•	•	🏛 Apex Information and Research Inc (A.I.R.) 800-330-4525	•	•	•	•	•
•	•	•	🏛 BAST Research Services Inc 713-777-8942	•	•	•	•	•
•	•	•	🏛 Court Record Research Inc 800-552-3353	•	•	•	•	•
•	•	•	🏛 Ervin Investigation & Research Svcs 888-203-6536	•	•	•	•	•
		•	🏛 FYP Inc 800-569-7143					
			Fox Hunt 713-772-8018	•	•	•	•	•
•	•	•	🏛 Houston Court Services Inc (SOP) 800-593-2023	•	•	•	•	•
•	•		🏛 I.P.S. Inc 713-783-9996					
•	•	•	LawServ Inc (SOP)............ 713-228-1055	•	•	•	•	

CV	CR	PR		Phone	UC	RE	TX	VS	VR
•	•	•	M.R.S. Datascope Inc (SOP)	800-899-3282					•
•	•	•	Metropolitan Court Services (SOP)	713-616-6971	•	•	•	•	•
•	•		National Crime Reporting Systems	800-687-0894					•
•	•	•	Southwest Patrol & Investigations	713-697-1577	•	•	•		•
•	•		Texas Abstract Services	800-484-5690		•			
•	•	•	Texas Records Search (SOP)	800-869-1405	•	•	•	•	•
•	•	•	The Cole Group	713-880-9494	•	•	•	•	
•	•	•	The Information Bank of Texas (SOP)	713-864-9122	•	•	•	•	•
•	•	•	The Research Staff Inc	800-822-3584	•	•	•		•
•	•	•	Tyler-McLennon Inc	512-482-0808	•	•	•		•

CV	CR	PR	MOORE (CST)		UC	RE	TX	VS	VR
•	•	•	Rollins, Jan	806-353-7886	•	•	•	•	

CV	CR	PR	MORRIS (CST)		UC	RE	TX	VS	VR
•	•	•	Brubaker & Associates	903-595-4616	•	•	•	•	

CV	CR	PR	MOTLEY (CST)		UC	RE	TX	VS	VR
•	•	•	Davick Services	800-658-6656	•	•	•	•	•

CV	CR	PR	NACOGDOCHES (CST)		UC	RE	TX	VS	VR
•	•		Alpha Research LLC (SOP)	205-755-7008			•		
•	•	•	Brubaker & Associates	903-595-4616	•	•	•	•	
•	•	•	East Texas Title & Abstract Co	409-560-1471	•	•	•		

CV	CR	PR	NAVARRO (CST)		UC	RE	TX	VS	VR
•	•		Alpha Research LLC (SOP)	205-755-7008			•		
		•	Navarro County Abstract Co	903-874-3768		•	•		
•	•	•	Search Enterprises	817-752-2057	•	•	•	•	

CV	CR	PR	NEWTON (CST)		UC	RE	TX	VS	VR
•	•	•	Garland Smith Abstract Co	409-384-2571	•	•	•	•	
•	•	•	The Research Staff Inc	800-822-3584	•	•	•		•

CV	CR	PR	NOLAN (CST)		UC	RE	TX	VS	VR
•		•	Beall Abstract and Title Co Inc	915-235-8646	•	•	•		
•	•	•	Davick Services	800-658-6656	•	•	•	•	•

DT	BK	CV	CR	PR	NUECES (CST)		UC	RE	TX	VS	VR
•	•	•	•		Alpha Research LLC (SOP)	205-755-7008			•		
	•				Bankruptcy Bulletin Weekly Inc	409-854-2777					
•	•	•	•	•	Bankruptcy Services Inc	214-424-6500					•
•	•	•	•	•	Brack Warren & Associates	512-884-8000	•	•	•	•	
•	•	•	•	•	Condor Investigations (SOP)	512-881-8977	•	•	•	•	•
•	•	•	•	•	Corpus Christi Court Services	512-887-8122	•	•	•		
•	•				Hogan Information Services	405-278-6954	•	•	•		
•	•	•	•	•	Intelnet Inc	888-636-3693	•	•	•	•	
•	•	•	•	•	John Bullock & Co	512-992-3060	•	•	•	•	
•	•	•	•	•	KJB Court Search (SOP)	210-971-8846	•	•	•	•	•
•	•				National Crime Reporting Systems	800-687-0894					•
•	•	•	•	•	Phoenix Information Services Inc (SOP)	800-918-8343	•	•	•	•	
•	•	•	•	•	Professional Civil Process (SOP)	800-950-7493	•	•	•	•	
•	•	•	•	•	Quick Search	214-358-2840	•	•	•	•	•
•	•				Ricochet (SOP)	214-855-0303		•			
•	•	•	•	•	Shawver and Associates (SOP)	800-364-2333	•	•	•	•	•
•	•	•	•	•	Texas Abstract Services	800-484-5690		•			
•	•	•	•	•	Texas Civil Process (SOP)	800-976-9595	•	•	•	•	
•	•	•	•	•	Texas Legal Support Service	512-883-2247	•	•	•	•	

CV	CR	PR	OCHILTREE (CST)		UC	RE	TX	VS	VR
•	•	•	Credit Bureau Services of the Panhandle	806-669-3246	•	•	•	•	
		•	Ochiltree County Abstract Company	806-435-4572	•	•	•		

	CV	CR	PR	OLDHAM (CST)	UC	RE	TX	VS	VR
				See adjoining counties for retrievers					

	CV	CR	PR	ORANGE (CST)	UC	RE	TX	VS	VR
	•	•		🏛 Alpha Research LLC (SOP)....................205-755-7008			•		
	•	•	•	🏛 BAST Research Services Inc 713-777-8942	•	•	•		•
	•	•	•	Texas Records Search (SOP) 800-869-1405	•	•	•	•	•
	•	•	•	🏛 The Research Staff Inc 800-822-3584	•	•	•		•

	CV	CR	PR	PALO PINTO (CST)	UC	RE	TX	VS	VR
	•		•	Elliott & Waldron Abstr Co of Palo Pinto 817-325-6564	•	•	•	•	

	CV	CR	PR	PANOLA (CST)	UC	RE	TX	VS	VR
	•	•	•	Brubaker & Associates 903-595-4616	•	•	•	•	
	•		•	DeSoto Abstract 318-798-1198	•	•	•		
	•		•	Panola County Abstract and Title Inc 903-693-3266	•	•	•		

	CV	CR	PR	PARKER (CST)	UC	RE	TX	VS	VR
	•	•	•	🏛 Attorney's Service Bureau of Texas (SOP)....214-522-5297	•	•	•		
	•	•	•	🏛 Super Search 800-589-7029	•	•	•	•	
	•	•	•	T D Disheroone Land Surveyor 800-645-0665	•	•	•	•	
	•		•	TitleInfo 817-244-7757	•	•	•		
	•		•	Weatherford-Parker County Abstract Co 817-594-4435	•	•	•		

	CV	CR	PR	PARMER (CST)	UC	RE	TX	VS	VR
	•	•	•	🏛 Davick Services 800-658-6656	•	•	•	•	•
	•	•	•	Farwell Abstract Co Inc (SOP) 806-481-3361	•	•	•		

	CV	CR	PR	PECOS (CST)	UC	RE	TX	VS	VR
	•		•	Elliott & Waldron Abstract Co of Pecos 915-336-5214	•	•	•	•	

	CV	CR	PR	POLK (CST)	UC	RE	TX	VS	VR
	•	•	•	🏛 BAST Research Services Inc 713-777-8942	•	•	•		•
	•	•	•	Bonds Process Service of East Texas (SOP)....409-377-4483	•	•	•	•	•
	•	•	•	🏛 The Research Staff Inc 800-822-3584	•	•	•		•

DT	BK	CV	CR	PR	POTTER (CST)	UC	RE	TX	VS	VR
•	•	•	•	•	🏛 Alpha Research LLC (SOP)....................205-755-7008			•		
	•				Bankruptcy Bulletin Weekly Inc 409-854-2777					
•	•	•			Bankruptcy Services Inc 214-424-6500					
•		•	•	•	🏛 Davick Services 800-658-6656	•	•	•	•	•
•		•	•	•	Garrison Legal Services 806-373-6204	•	•	•	•	
•		•	•	•	Mayfield, Billy 806-655-3878	•	•	•	•	•
•		•	•	•	Phoenix Information Services Inc (SOP)....800-918-8343	•	•	•	•	•
•		•	•	•	Rollins, Jan 806-353-7886	•	•	•	•	
•		•	•	•	🏛 Tyler-McLennon Inc 512-482-0808	•	•	•		•
•	•	•	•	•	US Legal Support (SOP)...........................806-374-2900		•			

	CV	CR	PR	PRESIDIO (CST)	UC	RE	TX	VS	VR
	•	•	•	Presidio County Abstract Co 915-729-4264	•	•	•		

	CV	CR	PR	RAINS (CST)	UC	RE	TX	VS	VR
	•	•	•	AAA Abstract Co Inc 903-473-2233	•	•	•	•	
	•	•	•	Brubaker & Associates 903-595-4616	•	•	•	•	

	CV	CR	PR	RANDALL (CST)	UC	RE	TX	VS	VR
	•	•		🏛 Alpha Research LLC (SOP)....................205-755-7008			•		
	•	•	•	🏛 Davick Services 800-658-6656	•	•	•	•	•
	•	•	•	Garrison Legal Services 806-373-6204	•	•	•	•	
	•	•	•	Mayfield, Billy 806-655-3878	•	•	•	•	•
	•	•	•	Rollins, Jan 806-353-7886	•	•	•	•	
	•	•	•	🏛 Tyler-McLennon Inc 512-482-0808	•	•	•		•
	•	•	•	US Legal Support (SOP)...........................806-374-2900		•			

CV	CR	PR	REAGAN (CST)	UC	RE	TX	VS	VR
•	•	•	APROTEX 915-683-3518	•	•	•	•	
•		•	Advance Title Co 915-687-3355		•			

CV	CR	PR	REAL (CST)	UC	RE	TX	VS	VR
•	•	•	Real County Title Co 210-232-5303	•	•	•		

CV	CR	PR	RED RIVER (CST)	UC	RE	TX	VS	VR
•	•	•	Brubaker & Associates 903-595-4616	•	•	•	•	
•		•	Gooding Title Co 903-427-3398	•	•	•		

DT	BK	CV	CR	PR	REEVES (CST)	UC	RE	TX	VS	VR
•	•	•		•	Advance Title Co 915-687-3355		•			
	•				Bankruptcy Bulletin Weekly Inc 409-854-2777					

CV	CR	PR	REFUGIO (CST)	UC	RE	TX	VS	VR
•	•	•	Condor Investigations (SOP) 512-881-8977	•	•	•	•	•
•	•	•	Shawver and Associates (SOP) 800-364-2333	•	•	•	•	•
•	•	•	Texas Civil Process (SOP) 800-976-9595	•	•	•	•	•

CV	CR	PR	ROBERTS (CST)	UC	RE	TX	VS	VR
•	•	•	Credit Bureau Services of the Panhandle 806-669-3246	•	•	•	•	

CV	CR	PR	ROBERTSON (CST)	UC	RE	TX	VS	VR
•		•	Guaranty Title Co 409-828-4688	•	•	•	•	
•	•	•	Search Enterprises 817-752-2057	•	•	•	•	

CV	CR	PR	ROCKWALL (CST)	UC	RE	TX	VS	VR
•	•		Accutrak 972-390-2195		•	•	•	
•	•		Alpha Research LLC (SOP) 205-755-7008			•		
•	•	•	Attorney Service Associates (SOP) 214-394-1175	•	•	•	•	•
•	•	•	Brubaker & Associates 903-595-4616	•	•	•		
•	•	•	Charles L Layer Private Investigations (SOP) 800-771-4887	•	•	•	•	•
•	•	•	Harold Eavenson & Associates (SOP) 972-771-5081	•	•	•	•	•
•	•	•	Nell Watkins & Assoc (SOP) 972-226-8811	•	•	•	•	•
•	•	•	Quick Search 214-358-2840	•	•	•	•	•
•	•	•	Security Information Service Inc (SOP) 800-525-5747	•	•	•	•	•
•	•	•	The Court System Inc 800-856-0585	•	•	•	•	
•	•	•	Tyler-McLennon Inc 512-482-0808	•	•	•		•

CV	CR	PR	RUNNELS (CST)	UC	RE	TX	VS	VR
•	•		Alpha Research LLC (SOP) 205-755-7008			•		
•	•	•	Surety Title Co of Ballenger 915-365-5713	•	•	•	•	

CV	CR	PR	RUSK (CST)	UC	RE	TX	VS	VR
•	•		Alpha Research LLC (SOP) 205-755-7008			•		
•	•	•	Brubaker & Associates 903-595-4616	•	•	•	•	
•		•	DeSoto Abstract 318-798-1198	•	•	•		

CV	CR	PR	SABINE (CST)	UC	RE	TX	VS	VR
•	•	•	East Texas Title & Abstract Co 409-787-2214	•	•	•	•	

CV	CR	PR	SAN AUGUSTINE (CST)	UC	RE	TX	VS	VR
•	•	•	Brubaker & Associates 903-595-4616	•	•	•	•	
•	•	•	East Texas Title & Abstract Co Inc 409-275-9786	•	•	•	•	

CV	CR	PR	SAN JACINTO (CST)	UC	RE	TX	VS	VR
•	•	•	BAST Research Services Inc 713-777-8942	•	•	•		•
•	•	•	Bonds Process Service of East Texas (SOP) 409-377-4483	•	•	•	•	•
•	•	•	The Research Staff Inc 800-822-3584	•	•	•		•

CV	CR	PR	SAN PATRICIO (CST)	UC	RE	TX	VS	VR
•	•		Alpha Research LLC (SOP) 205-755-7008			•		
•	•	•	Condor Investigations (SOP) 512-881-8977	•	•	•	•	•

CV	CR	PR			UC	RE	TX	VS	VR
•	•	•	Corpus Christi Court Services	512-887-8122	•	•	•	•	•
•	•	•	John Bullock & Co	512-992-3060	•	•	•	•	•
•	•	•	KJB Court Search (SOP)	210-971-8846	•	•	•	•	•
•	•	•	Shawver and Associates (SOP)	800-364-2333	•	•	•	•	•
•	•	•	Texas Civil Process (SOP)	800-976-9595	•	•	•	•	•
•	•	•	Texas Legal Support Service	512-883-2247	•	•	•	•	•

SAN SABA (CST)

CV	CR	PR			UC	RE	TX	VS	VR
•	•	•	Adams, Tommy M	915-648-3024	•	•	•	•	

SCHLEICHER (CST)

CV	CR	PR			UC	RE	TX	VS	VR
•	•	•	Benton Abstract & Title Co	915-853-2631	•	•	•		

SCURRY (CST)

CV	CR	PR			UC	RE	TX	VS	VR
•	•	•	Davick Services	800-658-6656	•	•	•	•	•
•	•	•	Scurry County Abstract Co	915-573-6339	•	•	•		

SHACKELFORD (CST)

CV	CR	PR			UC	RE	TX	VS	VR
•		•	Albany Abstract Co	915-762-3077	•	•	•	•	

SHELBY (CST)

CV	CR	PR			UC	RE	TX	VS	VR
•		•	DeSoto Abstract	318-798-1198	•	•	•		

SHERMAN (CST)

CV	CR	PR			UC	RE	TX	VS	VR
			See adjoining counties for retrievers						

SMITH (CST)

DT	BK	CV	CR	PR			UC	RE	TX	VS	VR
•	•	•	•		Alpha Research LLC (SOP)	205-755-7008			•		
	•				Bankruptcy Bulletin Weekly Inc	409-854-2777					
•	•	•	•	•	Bankruptcy Services Inc	214-424-6500					
		•	•	•	Brubaker & Associates	903-595-4616	•	•	•	•	
				•	DeSoto Abstract	318-798-1198	•	•	•	•	
•		•	•	•	Intranet Inc	903-593-9817	•	•	•	•	
				•	Smith County Abstract Co	903-597-7711	•	•	•		
•	•	•	•	•	The Court System Inc	800-856-0585	•	•	•	•	•
•	•	•	•	•	Tyler-McLennon Inc	512-482-0808	•	•	•		•

SOMERVELL (CST)

CV	CR	PR			UC	RE	TX	VS	VR
•	•	•	Super Search	800-589-7029	•	•	•	•	
•	•	•	Tyler-McLennon Inc	512-482-0808	•	•	•		•

STARR (CST)

CV	CR	PR			UC	RE	TX	VS	VR
•	•	•	KJB Court Search (SOP)	210-971-8846	•	•	•	•	•
•	•	•	Professional Civil Process (SOP)	800-880-4223	•	•	•	•	
•	•	•	Shawver and Associates (SOP)	800-364-2333	•	•	•	•	•

STEPHENS (CST)

CV	CR	PR			UC	RE	TX	VS	VR
			Stephens County Abstract	817-559-9089	•	•	•		

STERLING (CST)

CV	CR	PR			UC	RE	TX	VS	VR
•	•	•	APROTEX	915-683-3518	•	•	•	•	

STONEWALL (CST)

CV	CR	PR			UC	RE	TX	VS	VR
•		•	Caprock Title Co	915-687-3232	•	•	•		
•	•	•	Consolidated Abstract Co	817-989-3566	•	•	•	•	

SUTTON (CST)

CV	CR	PR			UC	RE	TX	VS	VR
•	•	•	Neel, Ben	915-396-2351	•	•	•	•	

SWISHER (CST)

CV	CR	PR			UC	RE	TX	VS	VR
•	•	•	Davick Services	800-658-6656	•	•	•	•	•
•	•	•	Rollins, Jan	806-353-7886	•	•	•	•	

DT	BK	CV	CR	PR	TARRANT (CST)	UC	RE	TX	VS	VR
•	•	•	•	•	AKA Investigations & Process of Dallas (SOP) 214-761-1174	•	•	•	•	
	•	•	•		Accutrak 972-390-2195		•	•	•	
•	•	•	•		🏛 Alpha Research LLC (SOP) 205-755-7008			•		
•	•	•	•	•	Attorney Service Associates (SOP) 214-394-1175	•	•	•	•	•
•	•	•	•	•	🏛 Attorney's Service Bureau of Texas (SOP) 214-522-5297	•	•	•		
•	•	•	•		Background Research 817-926-5976					
	•				Bankruptcy Bulletin Weekly Inc 409-854-2777					
•	•	•	•	•	Bankruptcy Services Inc 214-424-6500					
•	•	•	•	•	Charles L Layer Private Investigations (SOP) 800-771-4887	•	•	•	•	•
•	•	•	•	•	Civil Process Service 800-866-2214	•	•	•	•	
•	•	•	•	•	Courthouse Document Retrieval 972-644-4185	•	•	•	•	•
•	•	•	•		DFW Court Records (SOP) 800-436-0516		•	•		•
•	•	•	•		🏛 Data Screen Inc 817-294-7671					
•	•	•	•	•	Document Resources 800-822-8084	•	•	•	•	
•	•		•		🏛 FYP Inc 800-569-7143					
•	•	•	•	•	🏛 Harold Eavenson & Associates (SOP) 972-771-5081	•	•	•		
•	•				🏛 Hogan Information Services 405-278-6954					
•	•	•	•	•	Intelnet Inc 888-636-3693	•	•	•	•	
•	•	•	•	•	Intranet Inc 903-593-9817	•	•	•	•	
•	•	•	•	•	Lightspeed Couriers (SOP) 214-748-3340	•		•		
•	•		•		National Crime Reporting Systems 800-687-0894					•
•	•		•		OTI Resources 800-728-2742		•	•		•
•	•	•	•		Osborn, Patricia J 214-349-3562	•	•	•		•
•	•	•	•	•	PADIC Inc (SOP) 817-665-6130	•	•	•	•	•
•	•	•	•	•	Phoenix Information Services Inc (SOP) 800-918-8343	•	•	•	•	
					Police Report Acquisition Service 972-783-9505					
•	•	•	•	•	Professional Civil Process (SOP) 800-950-7493	•	•	•	•	
•	•	•	•	•	🏛 Quick Search 214-358-2840	•	•	•		
	•		•		🏛 Record Retrieval Services 888-311-5001					
•	•	•	•	•	Reliable Courier (SOP) 214-823-5596			•	•	
•	•	•	•	•	🏛 Research Specialists Inc 214-263-0500	•	•	•		
•	•				Ricochet (SOP) 214-855-0303			•		
•	•	•	•	•	Security Information Service Inc (SOP) 800-525-5747	•	•	•	•	•
•	•	•	•	•	🏛 Super Search 800-589-7029	•	•	•	•	•
•	•	•	•	•	T D Disheroone Land Surveyor 800-645-0665	•	•	•		
•	•	•	•	•	Texas Industrial Security Inc 214-634-2791	•	•	•		
		•		•	The Cole Group 713-880-9494	•	•	•		
•	•	•	•	•	The Court System Inc 800-856-0585	•	•	•	•	•
		•			The Dataprompt Corporation 800-577-8157					
•	•	•	•	•	The Information Bank of Texas (SOP) 713-864-9122	•	•	•		•
•	•	•		•	TitleInfo 817-244-7757	•	•			
•	•	•	•	•	🏛 Tyler-McLennon Inc 512-482-0808	•	•	•	•	•
•	•	•	•	•	Zumwalt Enterprises LLC 972-554-6968	•	•	•	•	•

DT		CV	CR	PR	TAYLOR (CST)	UC	RE	TX	VS	VR
		•	•	•	Alliance Title & Abstract Company 915-672-7021	•		•	•	
•		•	•		🏛 Alpha Research LLC (SOP) 205-755-7008			•		
		•	•	•	Russell-Surles Title Inc 915-854-1115	•	•	•		•

		CV	CR	PR	TERRELL (CST)	UC	RE	TX	VS	VR
					See adjoining counties for retrievers					

		CV	CR	PR	TERRY (CST)	UC	RE	TX	VS	VR
		•		•	Brownfield Abstract & Title Co 806-637-9595		•	•		
		•	•	•	🏛 Davick Services 800-658-6656	•	•	•	•	•

		CV	CR	PR	THROCKMORTON (CST)	UC	RE	TX	VS	VR
					See adjoining counties for retrievers					

		CV	CR	PR	TITUS (CST)	UC	RE	TX	VS	VR
		•	•	•	Brubaker & Associates 903-595-4616	•	•	•	•	

						UC	RE	TX	VS	VR
•		•		Titus County Title Company 903-577-0333		•	•	•	•	

DT		CV	CR	PR	**TOM GREEN (CST)**	UC	RE	TX	VS	VR
•		•	•		🏛 Alpha Research LLC (SOP).......... 205-755-7008			•		
		•	•	•	Surety Title Co of San Angelo 915-658-7588	•	•	•	•	

DT	BK	CV	CR	PR	**TRAVIS (CAPITAL) (CST)**	UC	RE	TX	VS	VR
•	•	•	•	•	AKA Investigations & Process of Austin (SOP).......... 800-933-8706	•	•	•	•	•
•	•	•	•	•	Access Research Staff 512-321-1889	•	•	•	•	•
•	•	•	•		🏛 Alpha Research LLC (SOP).......... 205-755-7008			•		
•	•	•	•	•	Assured Civil Process Agency (SOP).......... 800-256-7160		•			•
•	•	•	•	•	🏛 Attorney's Service Bureau of Texas (SOP).......... 214-522-5297	•	•	•		
•	•	•		•	Avian Corporate Records & Research (SOP) 512-326-3354	•	•	•	•	
	•				Bankruptcy Bulletin Weekly Inc 409-854-2777					
•	•	•	•	•	Bankruptcy Services Inc 214-424-6500					
•	•	•	•	•	Blumberg/Excelsior Corporate Svcs 512-478-6620	•	•	•	•	•
•	•	•	•		CPS (Capital Process Service) 512-930-7378			•		
•	•	•	•	•	CSC 800-532-4875	•	•	•	•	
•	•	•	•		Capitol Commerce Reporter Inc 800-356-8282	•	•	•	•	
•	•	•	•	•	🏛 Capitol Services Inc 800-345-4647	•	•	•		
•	•	•	•	•	Courthouse Services (SOP).......... 800-843-5725	•	•	•	•	•
•	•	•	•		🏛 Data Screen Inc 817-294-7671		•	•		
•	•	•	•	•	Document Resources 800-822-8084	•	•	•		
•	•	•	•		🏛 Ehrhardt, Sharon 512-331-6618	•		•		•
•	•		•		🏛 FYP Inc 800-569-7143					
•	•	•	•	•	Feaster & Associates (SOP).......... 512-459-1310	•	•	•	•	
•	•				🏛 Hogan Information Services 405-278-6954					
•	•	•	•	•	Intelnet Inc 888-636-3693	•	•	•	•	
•	•	•	•	•	Intranet Inc 903-593-9817	•	•	•	•	
•	•	•	•	•	🏛 John C Dunaway and Associates (SOP).......... 512-835-5888	•	•	•	•	•
•	•	•	•		National Crime Reporting Systems 800-687-0894					•
•	•	•	•		OTI Resources 800-728-2742	•		•		•
•	•	•	•	•	Phoenix Information Services Inc (SOP).......... 800-918-8343	•	•	•	•	•
•	•	•	•		🏛 Prime TEMPUS Inc 800-856-5600	•	•	•	•	•
•	•	•	•	•	Professional Civil Process (SOP).......... 800-950-7493	•	•	•	•	
•	•	•	•	•	Promesa Enterprises 800-474-4420	•	•	•	•	•
•	•	•	•	•	Property Research Associates Inc 888-523-1061	•	•	•		
•	•	•			RJ Research 210-824-0037					
•	•	•		•	Texas Abstract Services 800-484-5690		•			
		•			The Dataprompt Corporation 800-577-8157		•			
•	•	•	•	•	The Information Bank of Texas (SOP) 713-864-9122	•	•	•	•	•
•	•	•		•	TitleInfo 817-244-7757	•	•	•		
•	•	•	•	•	🏛 Tyler-McLennon Inc 512-482-0808	•	•	•		•

		CV	CR	PR	**TRINITY (CST)**	UC	RE	TX	VS	VR
		•	•	•	Bonds Process Service of East Texas (SOP).......... 409-377-4483	•	•	•	•	•
		•	•	•	🏛 The Research Staff Inc 800-822-3584	•	•	•		•
		•	•	•	Trinity County Abstract 409-642-1698	•	•	•	•	•

		CV	CR	PR	**TYLER (CST)**	UC	RE	TX	VS	VR
		•	•	•	🏛 BAST Research Services Inc 713-777-8942	•	•	•		•
		•	•	•	Search Enterprises 817-752-2057	•	•	•	•	

		CV	CR	PR	**UPSHUR (CST)**	UC	RE	TX	VS	VR
		•	•		🏛 Alpha Research LLC (SOP).......... 205-755-7008			•		
		•	•	•	Brubaker & Associates 903-595-4616	•	•	•	•	

		CV	CR	PR	**UPTON (CST)**	UC	RE	TX	VS	VR
		•	•	•	APROTEX 915-683-3518	•	•	•	•	
		•		•	Southwest Abstract & Title Co 915-693-2242	•	•	•		

		CV	CR	PR	**UVALDE (CST)**	UC	RE	TX	VS	VR
		•	•		🏛 Alpha Research LLC (SOP).......... 205-755-7008			•		

	•		•	Garner Abstracting & Land Inc 800-443-2065	•	•	•		

DT	CV	CR	PR	VAL VERDE (CST)	UC	RE	TX	VS	VR
				Bankruptcy Bulletin Weekly Inc 409-854-2777					
	•		•	Southwest Abstract Co Inc 210-775-8508	•	•	•	•	

	CV	CR	PR	VAN ZANDT (CST)	UC	RE	TX	VS	VR
	•	•		🏛 Alpha Research LLC (SOP) 205-755-7008			•		
	•	•	•	Brubaker & Associates 903-595-4616	•	•	•	•	
	•	•	•	Elliott & Waldron Abstr Co of Van Zandt 903-567-4127	•	•	•	•	
	•	•	•	🏛 Harold Eavenson & Associates (SOP) 972-771-5081	•	•	•	•	•
	•	•	•	The Court System Inc 800-856-0585	•	•	•	•	•

DT	CV	CR	PR	VICTORIA (CST)	UC	RE	TX	VS	VR
•	•	•		🏛 Alpha Research LLC (SOP) 205-755-7008			•		
	•		•	Bedgood Abstract & Title Co 512-573-1785	•	•			
•	•	•	•	Condor Investigations (SOP) 512-881-8977	•		•	•	
•	•	•		Search Plus 800-465-1525			•	•	
•	•	•	•	Shawver and Associates (SOP) 800-364-2333	•	•	•	•	
•	•	•	•	Texas Civil Process (SOP) 800-976-9595	•	•	•	•	
•	•	•	•	🏛 The Research Staff Inc 800-822-3584	•	•	•		•

	CV	CR	PR	WALKER (CST)	UC	RE	TX	VS	VR
	•	•		🏛 Alpha Research LLC (SOP) 205-755-7008			•		
	•	•	•	🏛 Apex Information and Research Inc (A.I.R.) 800-330-4525	•	•	•	•	•
	•	•	•	🏛 BAST Research Services Inc 713-777-8942	•	•	•	•	
	•	•	•	Bonds Process Service of East Texas (SOP) 409-377-4483	•	•	•	•	•
	•	•	•	🏛 The Research Staff Inc 800-822-3584	•	•	•		•

	CV	CR	PR	WALLER (CST)	UC	RE	TX	VS	VR
	•	•		🏛 Alpha Research LLC (SOP) 205-755-7008			•		
	•	•	•	🏛 Apex Information and Research Inc (A.I.R.) 800-330-4525	•	•	•	•	•
	•	•	•	🏛 BAST Research Services Inc 713-777-8942	•	•	•	•	•
	•	•		🏛 Business Information Service 409-865-2547	•	•	•	•	
	•	•		Spadachene, Tony 409-826-8610	•	•	•	•	
	•	•	•	🏛 The Research Staff Inc 800-822-3584	•	•	•		•
	•	•	•	Walters & Associates (SOP) 281-242-2243	•	•	•	•	•

	CV	CR	PR	WARD (CST)	UC	RE	TX	VS	VR
	•	•	•	APROTEX 915-683-3518	•	•	•	•	
	•		•	Pioneer-Ward County Abstract Co 915-943-5561	•	•	•		

	CV	CR	PR	WASHINGTON (CST)	UC	RE	TX	VS	VR
	•	•		🏛 Alpha Research LLC (SOP) 205-755-7008			•		
	•	•	•	🏛 BAST Research Services Inc 713-777-8942	•	•	•		•
	•	•	•	Botts Title Co 409-567-4602	•	•	•		
	•	•		🏛 Business Information Service 409-865-2547	•	•	•		

DT	CV	CR	PR	WEBB (CST)	UC	RE	TX	VS	VR
•	•	•		🏛 Alpha Research LLC (SOP) 205-755-7008			•		
				Border Abstract 210-791-5810	•	•	•		
•	•	•	•	Condor Investigations (SOP) 512-881-8977	•	•	•	•	•
•	•	•	•	Shawver and Associates (SOP) 800-364-2333	•	•	•	•	•

	CV	CR	PR	WHARTON (CST)	UC	RE	TX	VS	VR
	•	•		🏛 Alpha Research LLC (SOP) 205-755-7008			•		
	•	•	•	🏛 BAST Research Services Inc 713-777-8942	•	•	•		•
	•		•	Texas Abstract Services 800-484-5690		•			
	•	•	•	Walters & Associates (SOP) 281-242-2243	•	•	•	•	•

	CV	CR	PR	WHEELER (CST)	UC	RE	TX	VS	VR
	•	•	•	Credit Bureau Services of the Panhandle 806-669-3246	•	•	•	•	

DT	CV	CR	PR	WICHITA (CST)	UC	RE	TX	VS	VR
•	•	•		🏛 Alpha Research LLC (SOP)........................205-755-7008			•		
•	•	•	•	Professional Civil Process (SOP)..........................817-692-3011	•	•	•	•	•

	CV	CR	PR	WILBARGER (CST)	UC	RE	TX	VS	VR
	•	•		🏛 Alpha Research LLC (SOP)........................205-755-7008			•		
	•	•	•	VW Abstract 817-552-7712	•	•	•	•	•

	CV	CR	PR	WILLACY (CST)	UC	RE	TX	VS	VR
	•	•	•	KJB Court Search (SOP)...................................210-971-8846	•	•	•	•	•
	•	•	•	Professional Civil Process (SOP)..........................800-880-4223	•	•	•	•	•
	•	•	•	🏛 Valley Court Services 210-412-2306	•	•	•	•	•

	CV	CR	PR	WILLIAMSON (CST)	UC	RE	TX	VS	VR
	•	•	•	AKA Investigations & Process of Austin (SOP).................800-933-8706	•	•	•	•	•
	•	•		🏛 Alpha Research LLC (SOP)........................205-755-7008			•		
	•		•	American Abstract and Title Co 817-526-9525	•	•	•	•	
	•	•	•	Assured Civil Process Agency (SOP)........................800-256-7160		•			•
	•			Avian Corporate Records & Research (SOP) 512-326-3354	•	•	•	•	
	•	•		CPS (Capital Process Service) 512-930-7378		•			
	•	•	•	Capitol Commerce Reporter Inc 800-356-8282	•	•	•		
	•	•	•	🏛 Capitol Services Inc 800-345-4647	•		•		
	•	•	•	Courthouse Services (SOP)...............................800-843-5725	•	•	•		
	•	•	•	Document Resources 800-822-8084	•	•	•		
	•			🏛 Ehrhardt, Sharon 512-331-6618	•		•		•
	•			🏛 FYP Inc 800-569-7143					
	•	•	•	Feaster & Associates (SOP) 512-459-1310	•	•	•		
	•	•	•	🏛 John C Dunaway and Associates (SOP).................512-835-5888	•	•	•	•	•
	•	•		National Crime Reporting Systems 800-687-0894					•
	•		•	🏛 Prime TEMPUS Inc 800-856-5600	•	•	•		•
	•	•	•	Promesa Enterprises 800-474-4420	•	•	•	•	•
	•	•	•	Property Research Associates Inc 888-523-1061	•	•	•	•	
	•	•	•	🏛 Tyler-McLennon Inc 512-482-0808	•	•	•		•

	CV	CR	PR	WILSON (CST)	UC	RE	TX	VS	VR
	•	•	•	AKA Investigations & Process (SOP) 800-653-3817	•	•	•	•	•
	•	•		🏛 Alpha Research LLC (SOP)........................205-755-7008			•		
	•		•	Bexar Professional (SOP) 210-228-0083	•	•	•		
	•	•		National Crime Reporting Systems 800-687-0894					•
	•	•	•	Property Research Associates Inc 888-523-1061	•	•	•	•	
	•	•		Search Plus 800-465-1525				•	•

	CV	CR	PR	WINKLER (CST)	UC	RE	TX	VS	VR
	•		•	Advance Title Co 915-687-3355		•			

	CV	CR	PR	WISE (CST)	UC	RE	TX	VS	VR
	•	•		🏛 Alpha Research LLC (SOP)........................205-755-7008			•		
	•	•	•	🏛 Attorney's Service Bureau of Texas (SOP)..............214-522-5297	•	•	•		
	•	•	•	🏛 Quick Search 214-358-2840	•	•	•	•	•
	•	•	•	🏛 Super Search 800-589-7029	•	•	•	•	
	•	•	•	T D Disheroone Land Surveyor 800-645-0665	•	•	•	•	

	CV	CR	PR	WOOD (CST)	UC	RE	TX	VS	VR
	•	•		🏛 Alpha Research LLC (SOP)........................205-755-7008			•		
	•	•	•	Brubaker & Associates 903-595-4616	•	•	•	•	

	CV	CR	PR	YOAKUM (CST)	UC	RE	TX	VS	VR
	•	•	•	🏛 Davick Services 800-658-6656	•	•	•	•	•
	•	•	•	Yoakum County Abstract Co 806-456-2615		•	•		

	CV	CR	PR	YOUNG (CST)	UC	RE	TX	VS	VR
	•	•		🏛 Alpha Research LLC (SOP)........................205-755-7008			•		

CV CR PR	ZAPATA (CST)	UC RE TX VS VR
	Border Abstract 210-791-5810	● ● ●

CV CR PR	ZAVALA (CST)	UC RE TX VS VR
● ● ●	Zavala County Abstract Co Inc 210-374-3218	● ● ●

SUMMARY OF CODES

COURT RECORDS

CODE	GOVERNMENT AGENCY	TYPE OF INFORMATION
DT	US District Court	Federal civil and criminal cases
BK	Bankruptcy Court	United States bankruptcy cases
CV	Civil Court	Municipal, county and state level civil cases
CR	Criminal Court	Municipal, county and state level criminal cases
PR	Probate Court	Wills and estate cases

COUNTY RECORDS

CODE	GOVERNMENT AGENCY	TYPE OF INFORMATION
UC	UCC Filing Office	Uniform Commercial Code and other personal property liens
RE	Recorder of Deeds	Real property transactions and liens
TX	Tax Assessor	Real property tax information
VS	Vital Records Office	Vital statistics—birth, death, marriage, divorce, etc.
VR	Voter Registration Office	Voter registration and campaign contribution information

- "CODE" designates the agency and type of information obtainable in each county from a retriever.
- The time zone for each county is abbreviated as follows: EST—Eastern Standard Time; CST—Central; MST—Mountain; PST—Pacific; AK—Alaska; HT—Hawaii.
- ▥—This symbol designates a Public Record Retriever Network member.
- "(SOP)" after the retriever name designates Service of Process.
- Individual retrievers without a company name are listed in order of their last name.

US District and Bankruptcy courts are indicated only in the counties where courts are located.

UTAH

CV	CR	PR	BEAVER (MST)		UC	RE	TX	VS	VR
•	•	•	Cedar Land Title Inc 801-586-9984		•	•	•	•	
•		•	D W Moore and Assoc Inc 801-266-6585		•	•	•	•	
•		•	Security Title of Beaver County 801-438-2354		•	•	•		

CV	CR	PR	BOX ELDER (MST)		UC	RE	TX	VS	VR
•	•	•	🏛 All-Search 800-227-3152		•	•	•	•	•
•		•	D W Moore and Assoc Inc 801-266-6585		•	•	•	•	
•	•	•	Hillam Abstracting & Insurance Agency 801-723-5207		•	•	•		
•		•	The Home Abstract Co 800-669-7861		•	•	•		

CV	CR	PR	CACHE (MST)		UC	RE	TX	VS	VR
•		•	D W Moore and Assoc Inc 801-266-6585		•	•	•	•	
•	•	•	Hickman Land Title 800-365-7760		•	•	•	•	
•	•	•	Hillam Abstracting & Insurance Agency 801-723-5207		•	•	•		
•		•	The Home Abstract Co 800-669-7861		•	•	•		

CV	CR	PR	CARBON (MST)		UC	RE	TX	VS	VR
•		•	D W Moore and Assoc Inc 801-266-6585		•	•	•	•	
•	•	•	Deister Ward & Witcher of WY 800-829-8434		•	•	•	•	
•		•	Professional Title Services 801-637-2320		•	•			
•	•	•	Southeastern Utah Title 801-637-4455		•	•	•	•	
•	•	•	Sunrise Title Co 800-244-1644		•	•	•	•	

CV	CR	PR	DAGGETT (MST)		UC	RE	TX	VS	VR
•		•	D W Moore and Assoc Inc 801-266-6585		•	•	•	•	
•	•	•	Deister Ward & Witcher of WY 800-829-8434		•	•	•	•	
•	•	•	Sunrise Title Co 800-244-1644		•	•	•	•	

CV	CR	PR	DAVIS (MST)		UC	RE	TX	VS	VR
•	•	•	🏛 All-Search 800-227-3152		•	•	•	•	•
•		•	D W Moore and Assoc Inc 801-266-6585		•	•	•	•	
•	•	•	🏛 DataTrace Investigations Inc (SOP) 800-748-5335		•	•	•	•	•
•		•	The Home Abstract Co 800-669-7861		•	•	•		

CV	CR	PR	DUCHESNE (MST)		UC	RE	TX	VS	VR
•		•	D W Moore and Assoc Inc 801-266-6585		•	•	•	•	
•		•	Professional Title Services 801-637-2320		•	•	•		
•	•	•	Sunrise Title Co 800-244-1644		•	•	•	•	

CV	CR	PR	EMERY (MST)		UC	RE	TX	VS	VR
•		•	D W Moore and Assoc Inc 801-266-6585		•	•	•	•	
•		•	Professional Title Services 801-637-2320		•	•	•		
•	•	•	Southeastern Utah Title 801-637-4455		•	•	•	•	
•	•	•	Sunrise Title Co 800-244-1644		•	•	•	•	

CV	CR	PR	GARFIELD (MST)		UC	RE	TX	VS	VR
•	•	•	Cedar Land Title Inc 801-586-9984		•	•	•	•	
•		•	D W Moore and Assoc Inc 801-266-6585		•	•	•	•	
•	•	•	Security Title Co of Garfield County 801-676-8808		•	•	•	•	

CV	CR	PR	GRAND (MST)		UC	RE	TX	VS	VR
•		•	D W Moore and Assoc Inc 801-266-6585		•	•	•	•	
•	•	•	Southeastern Utah Title 801-637-4455		•	•	•	•	

CV	CR	PR	IRON (MST)		UC	RE	TX	VS	VR
•	•	•	Cedar Land Title Inc 801-586-9984		•	•	•	•	
•		•	D W Moore and Assoc Inc 801-266-6585		•	•	•	•	
•	•	•	Washington County Title Co 800-576-6770		•	•	•	•	

JUAB (MST)

CV	CR	PR	Company	Phone	UC	RE	TX	VS	VR
•		•	D W Moore and Assoc Inc	801-266-6585	•	•	•	•	
•	•	•	Juab Title & Abstract Co	601-623-0387	•	•	•		

KANE (MST)

CV	CR	PR	Company	Phone	UC	RE	TX	VS	VR
•	•	•	Cedar Land Title Inc	801-586-9984	•	•	•	•	
•		•	D W Moore and Assoc Inc	801-266-6585	•	•	•	•	
•	•	•	Southern Utah Title Co	801-644-5891	•	•	•	•	

MILLARD (MST)

CV	CR	PR	Company	Phone	UC	RE	TX	VS	VR
•		•	D W Moore and Assoc Inc	801-266-6585	•	•	•	•	
•	•	•	Juab Title & Abstract Co	601-623-0387	•	•	•		
•	•	•	Utah Title & Abstract	801-896-5429	•	•	•		

MORGAN (MST)

CV	CR	PR	Company	Phone	UC	RE	TX	VS	VR
•	•	•	🏛 All-Search	800-227-3152	•	•	•	•	•
•		•	D W Moore and Assoc Inc	801-266-6585	•	•	•	•	
•		•	The Home Abstract Co	800-669-7861	•	•	•		

PIUTE (MST)

CV	CR	PR	Company	Phone	UC	RE	TX	VS	VR
•		•	D W Moore and Assoc Inc	801-266-6585	•	•	•	•	
•	•	•	Security Title Co of Garfield County	801-676-8808	•	•	•	•	
•	•	•	Utah Title & Abstract	801-896-5429	•	•	•		

RICH (MST)

CV	CR	PR	Company	Phone	UC	RE	TX	VS	VR
•		•	D W Moore and Assoc Inc	801-266-6585	•	•	•	•	
•	•	•	Hickman Land Title	800-365-7760	•	•	•	•	

SALT LAKE (CAPITAL) (MST)

DT	BK	CV	CR	PR	Company	Phone	UC	RE	TX	VS	VR
•	•	•	•	•	🏛 All-Search	800-227-3152	•	•	•	•	•
•	•	•		•	D W Moore and Assoc Inc	801-266-6585	•	•	•	•	
•	•	•	•	•	🏛 DataTrace Investigations Inc (SOP)	800-748-5335	•	•	•	•	•

SAN JUAN (MST)

CV	CR	PR	Company	Phone	UC	RE	TX	VS	VR
•		•	D W Moore and Assoc Inc	801-266-6585	•	•	•	•	
•	•	•	Southeastern Utah Title	801-637-4455	•	•	•	•	

SANPETE (MST)

CV	CR	PR	Company	Phone	UC	RE	TX	VS	VR
•	•	•	Central Utah Title	801-835-1111	•	•	•	•	
•		•	D W Moore and Assoc Inc	801-266-6585	•	•	•	•	
•	•	•	Juab Title & Abstract Co	601-623-0387	•	•	•		

SEVIER (MST)

CV	CR	PR	Company	Phone	UC	RE	TX	VS	VR
•		•	D W Moore and Assoc Inc	801-266-6585	•	•	•	•	
•	•	•	Utah Title & Abstract	801-896-5429	•	•	•		

SUMMIT (MST)

CV	CR	PR	Company	Phone	UC	RE	TX	VS	VR
•	•	•	🏛 All-Search	800-227-3152	•	•	•	•	•
•		•	D W Moore and Assoc Inc	801-266-6585	•	•	•	•	
•	•	•	🏛 DataTrace Investigations Inc (SOP)	800-748-5335	•	•	•	•	•
•	•	•	Deister Ward & Witcher of WY	800-829-8434	•	•	•	•	
•		•	The Home Abstract Co	800-669-7861	•	•	•		

TOOELE (MST)

CV	CR	PR	Company	Phone	UC	RE	TX	VS	VR
•	•	•	🏛 All-Search	800-227-3152	•	•	•	•	•
•		•	D W Moore and Assoc Inc	801-266-6585	•	•	•	•	
•	•	•	Tooele Title Company	801-882-1120	•	•	•		

UINTAH (MST)

CV	CR	PR	Company	Phone	UC	RE	TX	VS	VR
•	•	•	🏛 All-Search	800-227-3152	•	•	•	•	•
•		•	D W Moore and Assoc Inc	801-266-6585	•	•	•	•	
•	•	•	Deister Ward & Witcher of WY	800-829-8434	•	•	•	•	
•	•	•	Sunrise Title Co	800-244-1644	•	•	•	•	

CV	CR	PR	UTAH (MST)		UC	RE	TX	VS	VR
•	•	•	🏛 All-Search 800-227-3152		•	•	•	•	•
•		•	D W Moore and Assoc Inc 801-266-6585		•	•	•	•	
•	•	•	🏛 DataTrace Investigations Inc (SOP)................... 800-748-5335		•	•	•	•	•

CV	CR	PR	WASATCH (MST)		UC	RE	TX	VS	VR
•	•	•	🏛 All-Search 800-227-3152		•	•	•	•	•
•		•	D W Moore and Assoc Inc 801-266-6585		•	•	•	•	
•	•	•	Deister Ward & Witcher of WY 800-829-8434		•	•	•	•	

CV	CR	PR	WASHINGTON (MST)		UC	RE	TX	VS	VR
•	•	•	🏛 All-Search 800-227-3152		•	•	•	•	•
•		•	D W Moore and Assoc Inc 801-266-6585		•	•	•	•	
•	•	•	Washington County Title Co 800-576-6770		•	•	•	•	

CV	CR	PR	WAYNE (MST)		UC	RE	TX	VS	VR
•		•	D W Moore and Assoc Inc 801-266-6585		•	•	•	•	
•	•	•	Utah Title & Abstract 801-896-5429		•	•	•		

CV	CR	PR	WEBER (MST)		UC	RE	TX	VS	VR
•	•	•	🏛 All-Search 800-227-3152		•	•	•	•	•
•		•	D W Moore and Assoc Inc 801-266-6585		•	•	•	•	
•	•	•	🏛 DataTrace Investigations Inc (SOP)................... 800-748-5335		•	•	•	•	•
•		•	The Home Abstract Co 800-669-7861		•	•	•		

VERMONT

VERMONT

		CV	CR	PR	ADDISON (EST)		UC	RE	TX	VS	VR
		•	•	•	New England Recovery Inc 802-433-6111		•	•	•	•	•

		CV	CR	PR	BENNINGTON (EST)		UC	RE	TX	VS	VR
		•	•	•	New England Recovery Inc 802-433-6111		•	•	•	•	•

		CV	CR	PR	CALEDONIA (EST)		UC	RE	TX	VS	VR
		•	•	•	New England Recovery Inc 802-433-6111		•	•	•	•	•

DT		CV	CR	PR	CHITTENDEN (EST)		UC	RE	TX	VS	VR
•		•	•	•	New England Recovery Inc 802-433-6111		•	•	•	•	•

		CV	CR	PR	ESSEX (EST)		UC	RE	TX	VS	VR
		•	•	•	New England Recovery Inc 802-433-6111		•	•	•	•	•

		CV	CR	PR	FRANKLIN (EST)		UC	RE	TX	VS	VR
		•	•	•	New England Recovery Inc 802-433-6111		•	•	•	•	•

		CV	CR	PR	GRAND ISLE (EST)		UC	RE	TX	VS	VR
		•	•	•	New England Recovery Inc 802-433-6111		•	•	•	•	•

		CV	CR	PR	LAMOILLE (EST)		UC	RE	TX	VS	VR
		•	•	•	New England Recovery Inc 802-433-6111		•	•	•	•	•

		CV	CR	PR	ORANGE (EST)		UC	RE	TX	VS	VR
		•	•	•	New England Recovery Inc 802-433-6111		•	•	•	•	•

		CV	CR	PR	ORLEANS (EST)		UC	RE	TX	VS	VR
		•	•	•	New England Recovery Inc 802-433-6111		•	•	•	•	•

DT	BK	CV	CR	PR	RUTLAND (EST)		UC	RE	TX	VS	VR
•	•	•	•	•	New England Recovery Inc 802-433-6111		•	•	•	•	•

		CV	CR	PR	WASHINGTON (CAPITAL) (EST)		UC	RE	TX	VS	VR
		•	•	•	New England Recovery Inc 802-433-6111		•	•	•	•	•

		CV	CR	PR	WINDHAM (EST)		UC	RE	TX	VS	VR
		•	•	•	New England Recovery Inc 802-433-6111		•	•	•	•	•

		CV	CR	PR	WINDSOR (EST)		UC	RE	TX	VS	VR
		•	•	•	New England Recovery Inc 802-433-6111		•	•	•	•	•

VIRGIN ISLANDS

VIRGIN ISLANDS

		CV	CR	PR	ST. CROIX (EST)		UC	RE	TX	VS	VR
		•	•	•	Dennis R Sheraw and Associates Inc (SOP) 809-773-3110		•	•	•	•	•

		CV	CR	PR	ST. JOHN (EST)		UC	RE	TX	VS	VR
		•	•	•	Dennis R Sheraw and Associates Inc (SOP) 809-773-3110		•	•	•	•	•

		CV	CR	PR	ST. THOMAS (EST)		UC	RE	TX	VS	VR
		•	•	•	Dennis R Sheraw and Associates Inc (SOP) 809-773-3110		•	•	•	•	•

VIRGINIA

ACCOMACK (EST)

CV	CR	PR			UC	RE	TX	VS	VR
●	●	●	Ayres, Judith	757-336-5313	●	●	●	●	
●	●	●	SingleSource Services Corp	800-713-3412	●		●	●	●

ALBEMARLE (EST)

DT	CV	CR	PR			UC	RE	TX	VS	VR
●	●	●	●	Ellerson, H Watkins	540-672-2109	●	●	●		
	●		●	Lawyer Title/Blue Ridge Agency Inc	804-295-7196	●	●	●		
●	●	●	●	SingleSource Services Corp	800-713-3412	●		●	●	●
●	●			UCC Retrievals	804-559-5919	●	●			

CITY OF ALEXANDRIA (EST)

DT	BK	CV	CR	PR			UC	RE	TX	VS	VR
●	●	●	●	●	ABIS Inc	800-669-2247	●	●	●		●
●	●	●	●		Alpha Research LLC (SOP)	205-755-7008			●		
●	●	●	●	●	CorpAssist - DC Office (SOP)	800-438-2996	●	●	●	●	●
●	●	●	●	●	Document Resources	800-468-4310	●	●	●	●	
●	●	●	●	●	Document Resources (SOP)	800-945-7339	●	●	●	●	●
●	●	●			Douglas Investigations Ltd	800-747-0820					
●	●	●	●	●	Enterprise Title Company Inc	703-538-2470	●	●	●	●	●
●	●	●	●	●	Estate Title and Escrow Inc	703-385-5850	●	●	●		
●	●	●	●	●	FDR Info Centers	800-874-4337	●	●	●		
●	●	●	●	●	Federal Research Corporation	202-783-2700	●	●	●		
●	●	●	●	●	Instant Information Systems	703-281-9312	●	●	●	●	
●	●	●	●	●	Mohr Information Services	800-799-4363	●	●	●		●
		●		●	National Background Investigations Inc	800-798-0079					
		●		●	Real Estate Information Service	800-924-1117	●	●	●		
●	●	●	●	●	Reveal Inc (SOP)	800-276-4826	●	●	●	●	●
●	●	●	●	●	Security Consultants Inc (SOP)	202-686-3953	●	●	●	●	●
●	●	●	●	●	SingleSource Services Corp	800-713-3412	●		●	●	●
●	●	●	●	●	The Seto Company	202-416-1898	●	●	●	●	●
●	●	●	●	●	University Process Service (SOP)	301-681-7206	●	●	●		
●	●	●	●	●	W A Haag & Associates Inc (SOP)	703-765-2138	●	●	●	●	●

ALLEGHANY (EST)

CV	CR	PR			UC	RE	TX	VS	VR
●	●	●	SingleSource Services Corp	800-713-3412	●		●	●	●
●	●	●	Singleton & Deeds	540-839-5009	●	●	●		

AMELIA (EST)

CV	CR	PR			UC	RE	TX	VS	VR
●	●	●	SingleSource Services Corp	800-713-3412	●		●	●	●
●			UCC Retrievals	804-559-5919	●	●			

AMHERST (EST)

CV	CR	PR			UC	RE	TX	VS	VR
●	●	●	Berry, William Thomas	804-263-4886	●	●	●	●	
●	●	●	SingleSource Services Corp	800-713-3412	●		●	●	●

APPOMATTOX (EST)

CV	CR	PR			UC	RE	TX	VS	VR
●	●	●	Brown-Browning, Gail	540-563-5699	●	●	●	●	
●	●	●	SingleSource Services Corp	800-713-3412	●		●	●	●

ARLINGTON (EST)

CV	CR	PR			UC	RE	TX	VS	VR
●	●	●	ABIS Inc	800-669-2247	●	●	●		●
●	●		Alpha Research LLC (SOP)	205-755-7008			●		
●	●	●	Barrett You & Associates Inc (SOP)	800-944-6607	●	●	●	●	
●	●	●	CorpAssist - DC Office (SOP)	800-438-2996	●	●	●		●
●	●	●	Document Resources	800-468-4310	●	●	●	●	
●	●	●	Document Resources (SOP)	800-945-7339	●	●	●	●	●
●	●		Douglas Investigations Ltd	800-747-0820					
●	●	●	Enterprise Title Company Inc	703-538-2470	●	●	●	●	●
●	●	●	Estate Title and Escrow Inc	703-385-5850	●	●	●		
●	●	●	Federal Research Corporation	202-783-2700	●	●	●	●	
●	●	●	Instant Information Systems	703-281-9312	●	●	●	●	

•	•	•	🏛 Investigative Consultants Inc 202-562-1500	•	•	•	•	•
•	•	•	Legal Courier Systems Inc (SOP) 800-869-8586		•	•	•	
•	•	•	🏛 Mohr Information Services 800-799-4363	•	•	•		•
•	•		🏛 National Background Investigations Inc 800-798-0079					
•		•	Real Estate Information Service 800-924-1117	•	•	•		
•	•	•	🏛 Reveal Inc (SOP) 800-276-4826	•	•	•	•	•
•	•	•	🏛 Security Consultants Inc (SOP) 202-686-3953	•	•	•	•	•
•	•	•	🏛 SingleSource Services Corp 800-713-3412	•	•	•	•	•
•	•	•	The Seto Company 202-416-1898	•	•	•	•	•
•	•	•	🏛 University Process Service (SOP) 301-681-7206	•	•	•		
•	•	•	W A Haag & Associates Inc (SOP) 703-765-2138	•	•	•	•	•
•	•	•	Washington Document Service 800-728-5201	•	•	•	•	

CV	CR	PR	AUGUSTA (EST)	UC	RE	TX	VS	VR
•	•	•	🏛 Data Abstract & Title Co Inc 540-949-6676	•	•	•		•
•		•	Lawyer Title/Blue Ridge Agency Inc 804-295-7196	•	•			
•	•	•	🏛 SingleSource Services Corp 800-713-3412	•		•	•	•

CV	CR	PR	BATH (EST)	UC	RE	TX	VS	VR
•	•	•	Singleton & Deeds 540-839-5009	•	•	•		

CV	CR	PR	BEDFORD (EST)	UC	RE	TX	VS	VR
•	•	•	🏛 Brown-Browning, Gail 540-563-5699	•	•	•	•	
•	•	•	🏛 SingleSource Services Corp 800-713-3412	•		•	•	•

CV	CR	PR	CITY OF BEDFORD (EST)	UC	RE	TX	VS	VR
•	•	•	🏛 Brown-Browning, Gail 540-563-5699	•	•	•	•	

CV	CR	PR	BLAND (EST)	UC	RE	TX	VS	VR
•	•		Fletcher, Jean R 540-763-2151	•	•	•		
•	•	•	🏛 SingleSource Services Corp 800-713-3412	•		•	•	•

CV	CR	PR	BOTETOURT (EST)	UC	RE	TX	VS	VR
•	•	•	Biesenbach, Betsy 703-982-7892	•	•	•		
•	•	•	🏛 Brown-Browning, Gail 540-563-5699	•	•	•	•	
•	•	•	🏛 SingleSource Services Corp 800-713-3412	•		•	•	•

CV	CR	PR	CITY OF BRISTOL (EST)	UC	RE	TX	VS	VR
•	•	•	🏛 SingleSource Services Corp 800-713-3412	•		•	•	•

CV	CR	PR	BRUNSWICK (EST)	UC	RE	TX	VS	VR
•	•	•	Allen III, William D 804-469-3977	•	•	•		
•	•	•	Hawthorne & Hawthorne PC 804-676-3275	•	•	•		
•	•	•	Sharrett, W Allan 804-634-2167	•	•	•		
•	•	•	🏛 SingleSource Services Corp 800-713-3412	•		•	•	•
•			UCC Retrievals 804-559-5919	•		•		

CV	CR	PR	BUCHANAN (EST)	UC	RE	TX	VS	VR
•	•	•	🏛 SingleSource Services Corp 800-713-3412	•		•	•	•

CV	CR	PR	BUCKINGHAM (EST)	UC	RE	TX	VS	VR
•	•	•	🏛 SingleSource Services Corp 800-713-3412	•		•	•	•
•			UCC Retrievals 804-559-5919	•		•		

CV	CR	PR	CITY OF BUENA VISTA (EST)	UC	RE	TX	VS	VR
•	•	•	🏛 Brown-Browning, Gail 540-563-5699	•	•	•	•	
•	•	•	🏛 SingleSource Services Corp 800-713-3412	•		•	•	•

CV	CR	PR	CAMPBELL (EST)	UC	RE	TX	VS	VR
•	•	•	🏛 Brown-Browning, Gail 540-563-5699	•	•	•	•	
•	•	•	🏛 SingleSource Services Corp 800-713-3412	•		•	•	•

CV	CR	PR	CAROLINE (EST)	UC	RE	TX	VS	VR
			Johnson, Lisa R 703-441-0099	•	•	•		

CV	CR	PR							
•	•	•	Libertino, Margene 540-785-9930	•	•	•			
•	•	•	🏛 SingleSource Services Corp 800-713-3412	•		•	•	•	
•	•	•	T D Title Services 804-633-6868	•		•	•		
•			UCC Retrievals 804-559-5919	•		•			

CV	CR	PR	CARROLL (EST)	UC	RE	TX	VS	VR
•	•		Fletcher, Jean R 540-763-2151	•	•	•		
•	•	•	🏛 SingleSource Services Corp 800-713-3412	•		•	•	•

CV	CR	PR	CHARLES CITY (EST)	UC	RE	TX	VS	VR
•	•	•	Hixson Enterprises 757-898-9865	•	•	•	•	•
•	•	•	🏛 SingleSource Services Corp 800-713-3412	•		•	•	•
•			UCC Retrievals 804-559-5919	•		•		

CV	CR	PR	CHARLOTTE (EST)	UC	RE	TX	VS	VR
•	•	•	🏛 Brown-Browning, Gail 540-563-5699	•	•	•		
•	•	•	Hawthorne & Hawthorne PC 804-676-3275	•	•	•		
•	•	•	🏛 SingleSource Services Corp 800-713-3412	•		•	•	•
•			UCC Retrievals 804-559-5919	•		•		

CV	CR	PR	CITY OF CHARLOTTESVILLE (EST)	UC	RE	TX	VS	VR
•	•	•	Ellerson, H Watkins 540-672-2109	•	•	•		
•		•	Lawyer Title/Blue Ridge Agency Inc 804-295-7196	•	•	•		
•			UCC Retrievals 804-559-5919	•		•		

CV	CR	PR	CITY OF CHESAPEAKE (EST)	UC	RE	TX	VS	VR
•	•		🏛 Alpha Research LLC (SOP) 205-755-7008			•		
•	•	•	🏛 Research & Retrieval Services (SOP) 757-463-0030	•	•	•		
•	•		🏛 Sherlock and Company 757-366-5142	•		•		
•	•	•	🏛 Title Search Services Inc 757-490-7009	•	•	•		
•	•		Vanderhoof, Linda 804-430-1316					

CV	CR	PR	CHESTERFIELD (EST)	UC	RE	TX	VS	VR
•	•	•	Allen III, William D 804-469-3977	•	•	•		
			CSC 800-237-1814	•	•	•		
•	•	•	Document Resources 800-468-4310	•	•	•	•	
•	•	•	Document Resources (SOP) 800-945-7339	•	•	•	•	•
•	•	•	🏛 SingleSource Services Corp 800-713-3412	•		•	•	•
•	•	•	The Marston Agency Inc (SOP) 800-308-7790	•	•	•	•	•
•	•	•	🏛 The Pettit Company 800-752-6158	•	•	•	•	
•			UCC Retrievals 804-559-5919	•		•		

CV	CR	PR	CLARKE (EST)	UC	RE	TX	VS	VR
•	•		🏛 Alpha Research LLC (SOP) 205-755-7008			•		
•	•	•	Estate Title and Escrow Inc 703-385-5850	•	•	•		
•	•	•	🏛 Mohr Information Services 800-799-4363	•	•	•		•
•	•	•	🏛 Reveal Inc (SOP) 800-276-4826	•	•	•	•	•
•	•	•	Shenandoah Title Services Inc 540-667-1393	•	•	•		
•	•	•	🏛 SingleSource Services Corp 800-713-3412	•		•	•	•

CV	CR	PR	CITY OF CLIFTON FORGE (EST)	UC	RE	TX	VS	VR
•	•	•	🏛 SingleSource Services Corp 800-713-3412	•		•	•	•
•	•	•	Singleton & Deeds 540-839-5009	•	•	•	•	

CV	CR	PR	CITY OF COLONIAL HEIGHTS (EST)	UC	RE	TX	VS	VR
•	•	•	Allen III, William D 804-469-3977	•	•	•		
•	•	•	🏛 SingleSource Services Corp 800-713-3412	•		•	•	•
•	•	•	🏛 The Pettit Company 800-752-6158	•	•	•	•	
•			UCC Retrievals 804-559-5919	•		•		

CV	CR	PR	CITY OF COVINGTON (EST)	UC	RE	TX	VS	VR
•	•	•	🏛 SingleSource Services Corp 800-713-3412	•		•	•	•
•	•	•	Singleton & Deeds 540-839-5009	•	•	•	•	

CRAIG (EST)

CV	CR	PR		Phone	UC	RE	TX	VS	VR
●	●		Fletcher, Jean R	540-763-2151	●	●	●		
●	●	●	🏛 SingleSource Services Corp	800-713-3412	●		●	●	●

CULPEPER (EST)

CV	CR	PR		Phone	UC	RE	TX	VS	VR
●	●	●	Ellerson, H Watkins	540-672-2109	●	●	●		
			Johnson, Lisa R	703-441-0099	●	●	●		
●	●	●	🏛 Reveal Inc (SOP)	800-276-4826	●	●	●	●	●
●	●	●	🏛 SingleSource Services Corp	800-713-3412	●		●	●	●

CUMBERLAND (EST)

CV	CR	PR		Phone	UC	RE	TX	VS	VR
●	●	●	🏛 SingleSource Services Corp	800-713-3412	●		●	●	●
●			UCC Retrievals	804-559-5919	●	●			

CITY OF DANVILLE (EST)

DT	CV	CR	PR		Phone	UC	RE	TX	VS	VR
●	●	●		Grant, Gary	804-799-3379	●	●	●		
●	●	●	●	🏛 SingleSource Services Corp	800-713-3412	●		●	●	●
●	●			UCC Retrievals	804-559-5919	●	●			

DICKENSON (EST)

CV	CR	PR		Phone	UC	RE	TX	VS	VR
●	●	●	🏛 SingleSource Services Corp	800-713-3412	●		●	●	●

DINWIDDIE (EST)

CV	CR	PR		Phone	UC	RE	TX	VS	VR
●	●	●	Allen III, William D	804-469-3977	●	●	●		
●	●	●	🏛 SingleSource Services Corp	800-713-3412	●		●	●	●
●	●	●	🏛 The Pettit Company	800-752-6158	●	●	●	●	
●			UCC Retrievals	804-559-5919	●	●			

CITY OF EMPORIA (EST)

CV	CR	PR		Phone	UC	RE	TX	VS	VR
●	●	●	🏛 Research & Retrieval Services (SOP)	757-463-0030	●	●	●		
●	●	●	Sharrett, W Allan	804-634-2167	●	●			
●	●	●	🏛 SingleSource Services Corp	800-713-3412	●		●	●	●

ESSEX (EST)

CV	CR	PR		Phone	UC	RE	TX	VS	VR
●	●	●	🏛 Investigative Consultants Inc	202-562-1500	●	●	●	●	●
●	●	●	McKerns & McKerns	804-580-8225	●	●	●		
●	●	●	🏛 SingleSource Services Corp	800-713-3412	●		●	●	●
●			UCC Retrievals	804-559-5919	●	●			

FAIRFAX (EST)

CV	CR	PR		Phone	UC	RE	TX	VS	VR
●	●	●	ABIS Inc	800-669-2247	●	●	●		●
●			Accurate Legal Service (SOP)	800-236-9853		●			
●	●	●	Barrett You & Associates Inc (SOP)	800-944-6607	●	●		●	
●	●	●	🏛 CorpAssist - DC Office (SOP)	800-438-2996	●	●		●	●
●	●	●	Document Resources	800-468-4310	●	●	●	●	
●	●	●	Document Resources (SOP)	800-945-7339	●	●	●	●	●
●	●	●	Enterprise Title Company Inc	703-538-2470	●	●	●	●	
●	●	●	Estate Title and Escrow Inc	703-385-5850	●	●			
●	●	●	FDR Info Centers	800-874-4337	●	●			
●	●	●	Federal Research Corporation	202-783-2700	●	●	●		
●			For The Record	703-323-9105		●			
●	●	●	Instant Information Systems	703-281-9312	●	●	●	●	
●	●	●	🏛 Investigative Consultants Inc	202-562-1500	●	●	●	●	●
●	●	●	Legal Courier Systems Inc (SOP)	800-869-8586		●	●	●	
●	●		🏛 Mohr Information Services	800-799-4363	●	●	●		●
●	●		🏛 National Background Investigations Inc	800-798-0079	●				
●			Real Estate Information Service	800-924-1117	●	●	●		
●	●	●	🏛 Reveal Inc (SOP)	800-276-4826	●	●	●	●	●
●	●	●	🏛 Security Consultants Inc (SOP)	202-686-3953	●	●	●	●	●
●	●	●	🏛 SingleSource Services Corp	800-713-3412	●		●	●	●
●	●	●	The Seto Company	202-416-1898	●	●	●	●	●
●	●	●	🏛 University Process Service (SOP)	301-681-7206	●	●	●	●	●
●	●	●	W A Haag & Associates Inc (SOP)	703-765-2138	●	●	●	●	●

| | | | Washington Document Service .... 800-728-5201 | • | • | • | • | |

CV	CR	PR	CITY OF FAIRFAX (EST)	UC	RE	TX	VS	VR
•	•		⛁ Alpha Research LLC (SOP)........................ 205-755-7008			•		
•	•	•	⛁ CorpAssist - DC Office (SOP)..................... 800-438-2996	•	•	•	•	•
•			Douglas Investigations Ltd 800-747-0820					
•	•	•	Instant Information Systems 703-281-9312	•	•	•	•	
•	•	•	⛁ Investigative Consultants Inc 202-562-1500	•	•	•	•	•
•	•	•	⛁ Mohr Information Services 800-799-4363	•	•	•		•
•	•		⛁ National Background Investigations Inc 800-798-0079	•				
•	•	•	⛁ Security Consultants Inc (SOP) 202-686-3953	•	•	•	•	•
•	•	•	W A Haag & Associates Inc (SOP) 703-765-2138	•	•	•	•	•

CV	CR	PR	CITY OF FALLS CHURCH (EST)	UC	RE	TX	VS	VR
•	•		⛁ National Background Investigations Inc 800-798-0079					
•	•	•	⛁ Reveal Inc (SOP) 800-276-4826	•	•	•	•	•
•	•	•	⛁ Security Consultants Inc (SOP) 202-686-3953	•	•	•	•	•

CV	CR	PR	FAUQUIER (EST)	UC	RE	TX	VS	VR
•	•		⛁ Alpha Research LLC (SOP)........................ 205-755-7008			•		
•	•	•	⛁ Battlefield Title (SOP)........................... 703-369-6900	•	•	•		
•	•	•	Estate Title and Escrow Inc 703-385-5850	•	•	•		
•	•	•	Legal Courier Systems Inc (SOP).................. 800-869-8586		•	•	•	
•	•	•	⛁ Mohr Information Services 800-799-4363	•	•	•		•
•	•	•	⛁ Reveal Inc (SOP) 800-276-4826	•	•	•	•	•
•	•	•	⛁ SingleSource Services Corp 800-713-3412	•		•	•	•

CV	CR	PR	FLOYD (EST)	UC	RE	TX	VS	VR
•	•	•	⛁ Brown-Browning, Gail 540-563-5699	•	•	•	•	
•	•		Fletcher, Jean R 540-763-2151	•	•	•		
•	•	•	⛁ SingleSource Services Corp 800-713-3412	•		•	•	•

CV	CR	PR	FLUVANNA (EST)	UC	RE	TX	VS	VR
•		•	Lawyer Title/Blue Ridge Agency Inc 804-295-7196	•	•	•		
•	•	•	⛁ SingleSource Services Corp 800-713-3412	•		•	•	•
•			UCC Retrievals 804-559-5919	•		•		

CV	CR	PR	FRANKLIN (EST)	UC	RE	TX	VS	VR
•	•	•	⛁ Brown-Browning, Gail 540-563-5699	•	•	•	•	
•	•		Fletcher, Jean R 540-763-2151	•	•	•		
•	•	•	⛁ SingleSource Services Corp 800-713-3412	•		•	•	•

CV	CR	PR	CITY OF FRANKLIN (EST)	UC	RE	TX	VS	VR
			See adjoining counties for retrievers					

CV	CR	PR	FREDERICK (EST)	UC	RE	TX	VS	VR
•	•		⛁ Alpha Research LLC (SOP)........................ 205-755-7008			•		
•	•	•	⛁ Investigative Consultants Inc 202-562-1500	•	•	•	•	•
•	•	•	⛁ Mohr Information Services 800-799-4363	•	•	•		•
•	•	•	⛁ Reveal Inc (SOP) 800-276-4826	•	•	•	•	•
•	•	•	Shenandoah Title Services Inc 540-667-1393	•	•	•		
•	•	•	⛁ SingleSource Services Corp 800-713-3412	•		•	•	•

CV	CR	PR	CITY OF FREDERICKSBURG (EST)	UC	RE	TX	VS	VR
•	•	•	Document Resources 800-468-4310	•	•	•	•	
•			Johnson, Lisa R 703-441-0099	•	•	•		
•			Libertino, Margene 540-785-9930	•	•	•		
•	•	•	⛁ Reveal Inc (SOP) 800-276-4826	•	•	•	•	•
•	•	•	⛁ SingleSource Services Corp 800-713-3412	•		•	•	•
•			UCC Retrievals 804-559-5919	•		•		

CV	CR	PR	CITY OF GALAX (EST)	UC	RE	TX	VS	VR
•	•		Fletcher, Jean R 540-763-2151	•	•	•		

					UC	RE	TX	VS	VR
•	•	•	🏛 SingleSource Services Corp 800-713-3412		•		•	•	•

CV	CR	PR	GILES (EST)	UC	RE	TX	VS	VR
•	•		Fletcher, Jean R 540-763-2151	•	•	•		
•	•	•	🏛 SingleSource Services Corp 800-713-3412	•		•	•	•

CV	CR	PR	GLOUCESTER (EST)	UC	RE	TX	VS	VR
•	•	•	Adkins, Charles E 804-843-4060	•	•	•		
•	•	•	Hixson Enterprises 757-898-9865	•	•	•	•	•
•	•	•	🏛 O'Connell, Nikki A 757-877-8469	•	•	•	•	•
•	•	•	🏛 SingleSource Services Corp 800-713-3412	•	•	•	•	•
•			UCC Retrievals 804-559-5919	•		•		

CV	CR	PR	GOOCHLAND (EST)	UC	RE	TX	VS	VR
•	•	•	Ellerson, H Watkins 540-672-2109	•	•	•		
•	•	•	🏛 SingleSource Services Corp 800-713-3412	•		•	•	•
•	•	•	The Marston Agency Inc (SOP) 800-308-7790	•	•	•	•	•
•	•	•	🏛 The Pettit Company 800-752-6158	•	•	•	•	•
•			UCC Retrievals 804-559-5919	•		•		

CV	CR	PR	GRAYSON (EST)	UC	RE	TX	VS	VR
•	•		Fletcher, Jean R 540-763-2151	•	•	•		
•	•	•	🏛 SingleSource Services Corp 800-713-3412	•		•	•	•

CV	CR	PR	GREENE (EST)	UC	RE	TX	VS	VR
•	•	•	Ellerson, H Watkins 540-672-2109	•	•	•		
•		•	Lawyer Title/Blue Ridge Agency Inc 804-295-7196	•	•	•		
•	•	•	🏛 SingleSource Services Corp 800-713-3412	•		•	•	•

CV	CR	PR	GREENSVILLE (EST)	UC	RE	TX	VS	VR
•	•	•	🏛 Research & Retrieval Services (SOP) 757-463-0030	•	•	•		
•	•	•	Sharrett, W Allan 804-634-2167	•	•	•		
•	•	•	🏛 SingleSource Services Corp 800-713-3412	•		•	•	•
•			UCC Retrievals 804-559-5919	•		•		

CV	CR	PR	HALIFAX (EST)	UC	RE	TX	VS	VR
•	•		Grant, Gary 804-799-3379	•	•	•		
•	•	•	Payne, Nita 804-476-2595	•	•	•	•	
•	•	•	🏛 SingleSource Services Corp 800-713-3412	•		•	•	•
•			UCC Retrievals 804-559-5919	•		•		

CV	CR	PR	CITY OF HAMPTON (EST)	UC	RE	TX	VS	VR
•	•		🏛 Faxalert Network 757-850-2870	•	•	•		•
•	•	•	🏛 O'Connell, Nikki A 757-877-8469	•	•	•	•	•
•	•	•	🏛 Research & Retrieval Services (SOP) 757-463-0030	•	•	•		
•	•		🏛 Sherlock and Company 757-366-5142	•	•			
•	•	•	🏛 SingleSource Services Corp 800-713-3412	•		•		
•	•		Vanderhoof, Linda 804-430-1316					

CV	CR	PR	HANOVER (EST)	UC	RE	TX	VS	VR
			CSC 800-237-1814	•	•	•		
•	•	•	🏛 SingleSource Services Corp 800-713-3412	•		•	•	•
•	•	•	The Marston Agency Inc (SOP) 800-308-7790	•	•	•	•	•
•	•	•	🏛 The Pettit Company 800-752-6158	•	•	•	•	
•			UCC Retrievals 804-559-5919	•		•		

DT	BK	CV	CR	PR	CITY OF HARRISONBURG (EST)	UC	RE	TX	VS	VR
•	•	•		•	Lawyers Title 540-433-8112	•	•	•		

DT		CV	CR	PR	HENRICO (EST)	UC	RE	TX	VS	VR
•					CSC 800-237-1814	•	•	•		
•		•	•	•	Document Resources 800-468-4310	•	•	•	•	
•		•	•	•	Document Resources (SOP) 800-945-7339	•	•	•	•	
•		•	•	•	Ellerson, H Watkins 540-672-2109	•	•	•		

CV	CR	PR		Phone	UC	RE	TX	VS	VR
•	•	•	SingleSource Services Corp	800-713-3412	•		•	•	•
•	•	•	The Marston Agency Inc (SOP)	800-308-7790	•	•	•	•	•
•	•	•	The Pettit Company	800-752-6158	•	•	•	•	
•	•		UCC Retrievals	804-559-5919	•		•		

CV	CR	PR	HENRY (EST)		UC	RE	TX	VS	VR
•	•	•	Brown-Browning, Gail	540-563-5699	•	•	•	•	
•	•		Grant, Gary	804-799-3379	•	•	•		
•	•	•	SingleSource Services Corp	800-713-3412	•		•	•	•
•			UCC Retrievals	804-559-5919	•		•		

CV	CR	PR	HIGHLAND (EST)		UC	RE	TX	VS	VR
•	•	•	Singleton & Deeds	540-839-5009	•	•	•	•	

CV	CR	PR	CITY OF HOPEWELL (EST)		UC	RE	TX	VS	VR
•	•	•	SingleSource Services Corp	800-713-3412	•		•	•	•
•	•	•	The Pettit Company	800-752-6158	•	•	•	•	
•			UCC Retrievals	804-559-5919	•		•		

CV	CR	PR	ISLE OF WIGHT (EST)		UC	RE	TX	VS	VR
•	•		Faxalert Network	757-850-2870	•	•	•		•
•	•	•	O'Connell, Nikki A	757-877-8469	•	•	•		•
•	•	•	Research & Retrieval Services (SOP)	757-463-0030	•	•	•		•
•	•	•	SingleSource Services Corp	800-713-3412	•		•	•	•

CV	CR	PR	JAMES CITY (EST)		UC	RE	TX	VS	VR
•	•		Faxalert Network	757-850-2870	•	•	•		•
•	•	•	Hixson Enterprises	757-898-9865	•	•	•	•	•
•	•	•	O'Connell, Nikki A	757-877-8469	•	•	•	•	•
•	•	•	Research & Retrieval Services (SOP)	757-463-0030	•	•	•	•	
•	•	•	SingleSource Services Corp	800-713-3412	•		•	•	•

CV	CR	PR	KING GEORGE (EST)		UC	RE	TX	VS	VR
			Johnson, Lisa R	703-441-0099	•	•	•		
			Libertino, Margene	540-785-9930	•	•	•		
•	•	•	SingleSource Services Corp	800-713-3412	•		•	•	•
•	•	•	T D Title Services	804-633-6868	•	•	•		
•			UCC Retrievals	804-559-5919	•		•		

CV	CR	PR	KING WILLIAM (EST)		UC	RE	TX	VS	VR
•	•	•	Adkins, Charles E	804-843-4060	•	•	•	•	
•	•	•	SingleSource Services Corp	800-713-3412	•		•	•	•
•			UCC Retrievals	804-559-5919	•		•		

CV	CR	PR	KING AND QUEEN (EST)		UC	RE	TX	VS	VR
•	•	•	Adkins, Charles E	804-843-4060	•	•	•	•	
•	•	•	Hixson Enterprises	757-898-9865	•	•	•	•	•
•	•	•	SingleSource Services Corp	800-713-3412	•		•	•	•
•	•	•	T D Title Services	804-633-6868	•	•	•		
•			UCC Retrievals	804-559-5919	•		•		

CV	CR	PR	LANCASTER (EST)		UC	RE	TX	VS	VR
•	•	•	McKerns & McKerns	804-580-8225	•	•	•		
•	•	•	SingleSource Services Corp	800-713-3412	•		•	•	•
•			UCC Retrievals	804-559-5919	•		•		

CV	CR	PR	LEE (EST)		UC	RE	TX	VS	VR
•	•	•	SingleSource Services Corp	800-713-3412	•		•	•	•

CV	CR	PR	CITY OF LEXINGTON (EST)		UC	RE	TX	VS	VR
•	•	•	Brown-Browning, Gail	540-563-5699	•	•	•	•	
•	•	•	SingleSource Services Corp	800-713-3412	•		•	•	•

	CV	CR	PR	LOUDOUN (EST)		UC	RE	TX	VS	VR
	•	•	•	ABIS Inc 800-669-2247		•	•	•		•
	•	•		🏛 Alpha Research LLC (SOP) 205-755-7008				•		
	•	•	•	🏛 CorpAssist - DC Office (SOP) 800-438-2996		•	•	•	•	•
	•	•	•	Enterprise Title Company Inc 703-538-2470		•	•	•	•	•
	•	•	•	Estate Title and Escrow Inc 703-385-5850		•	•	•		
	•	•	•	Federal Research Corporation 202-783-2700		•	•	•		
	•	•	•	Instant Information Systems 703-281-9312		•	•			
	•	•	•	Legal Courier Systems Inc (SOP) 800-869-8586		•	•	•	•	
	•	•	•	🏛 Mohr Information Services 800-799-4363		•	•	•		•
	•		•	Real Estate Information Service 800-924-1117		•	•	•		
	•	•	•	🏛 Reveal Inc (SOP) 800-276-4826		•	•	•	•	•
	•	•	•	🏛 Security Consultants Inc (SOP) 202-686-3953		•	•	•		
	•	•	•	Shenandoah Title Services Inc 540-667-1393		•	•	•		
	•	•	•	🏛 SingleSource Services Corp 800-713-3412		•		•	•	•
	•	•	•	W A Haag & Associates Inc (SOP) 703-765-2138		•	•	•	•	•

	CV	CR	PR	LOUISA (EST)		UC	RE	TX	VS	VR
	•	•	•	Ellerson, H Watkins 540-672-2109		•	•	•		
				Johnson, Lisa R 703-441-0099		•	•	•		
			•	Lawyer Title/Blue Ridge Agency Inc 804-295-7196		•	•			
	•	•	•	🏛 SingleSource Services Corp 800-713-3412		•		•	•	•
	•			UCC Retrievals 804-559-5919		•		•		

	CV	CR	PR	LUNENBURG (EST)		UC	RE	TX	VS	VR
	•	•	•	Hawthorne & Hawthorne PC 804-676-3275		•	•	•		
	•	•	•	🏛 SingleSource Services Corp 800-713-3412		•		•	•	•
	•			UCC Retrievals 804-559-5919		•		•		

DT	BK	CV	CR	PR	CITY OF LYNCHBURG (EST)		UC	RE	TX	VS	VR
•	•	•	•	•	🏛 Brown-Browning, Gail 540-563-5699		•	•	•	•	
•	•	•	•	•	🏛 SingleSource Services Corp 800-713-3412		•		•	•	•

	CV	CR	PR	MADISON (EST)		UC	RE	TX	VS	VR
	•	•	•	Ellerson, H Watkins 540-672-2109		•	•	•		
	•	•	•	🏛 Reveal Inc (SOP) 800-276-4826		•	•	•	•	•
	•	•	•	🏛 SingleSource Services Corp 800-713-3412		•		•	•	•

	CV	CR	PR	CITY OF MANASSAS (EST)		UC	RE	TX	VS	VR
	•	•	•	🏛 CorpAssist - DC Office (SOP) 800-438-2996		•	•	•	•	•
	•	•	•	🏛 Investigative Consultants Inc 202-562-1500		•	•	•	•	•
	•	•	•	🏛 Mohr Information Services 800-799-4363		•	•	•	•	•
	•	•	•	🏛 Reveal Inc (SOP) 800-276-4826		•	•	•	•	•

	CV	CR	PR	CITY OF MANASSAS PARK (EST)		UC	RE	TX	VS	VR
	•	•	•	🏛 Investigative Consultants Inc 202-562-1500		•	•	•	•	•

	CV	CR	PR	CITY OF MARTINSVILLE (EST)		UC	RE	TX	VS	VR
	•	•		Grant, Gary 804-799-3379		•	•	•		
	•	•	•	🏛 SingleSource Services Corp 800-713-3412		•		•	•	•

	CV	CR	PR	MATHEWS (EST)		UC	RE	TX	VS	VR
	•	•	•	Hixson Enterprises 757-898-9865		•	•	•	•	•
	•	•	•	🏛 SingleSource Services Corp 800-713-3412		•		•	•	•
	•			UCC Retrievals 804-559-5919		•		•		

	CV	CR	PR	MECKLENBURG (EST)		UC	RE	TX	VS	VR
	•	•	•	Hawthorne & Hawthorne PC 804-676-3275		•	•	•		
	•	•	•	Payne, Nita 804-476-2595		•	•	•	•	
	•	•	•	🏛 SingleSource Services Corp 800-713-3412		•		•	•	•
	•			UCC Retrievals 804-559-5919		•		•		

MIDDLESEX (EST)

CV	CR	PR		UC	RE	TX	VS	VR
•	•	•	Adkins, Charles E ... 804-843-4060	•	•	•	•	
•	•	•	🏛 SingleSource Services Corp ... 800-713-3412	•		•	•	•
•			UCC Retrievals ... 804-559-5919	•		•		

MONTGOMERY (EST)

CV	CR	PR		UC	RE	TX	VS	VR
•	•	•	🏛 Brown-Browning, Gail ... 540-563-5699	•	•	•	•	
•	•	•	Federal Research Corporation ... 202-783-2700	•	•	•	•	
•	•		Fletcher, Jean R ... 540-763-2151	•	•	•		
•	•	•	M & M Search Service Inc ... 202-393-3144	•	•	•	•	
•	•	•	🏛 SingleSource Services Corp ... 800-713-3412	•		•	•	•

NELSON (EST)

CV	CR	PR		UC	RE	TX	VS	VR
•	•	•	Berry, William Thomas ... 804-263-4886	•	•	•	•	
•		•	Lawyer Title/Blue Ridge Agency Inc ... 804-295-7196	•	•	•		
•	•	•	🏛 SingleSource Services Corp ... 800-713-3412	•		•	•	•

NEW KENT (EST)

CV	CR	PR		UC	RE	TX	VS	VR
•	•	•	Adkins, Charles E ... 804-843-4060	•	•	•	•	
•	•	•	🏛 SingleSource Services Corp ... 800-713-3412	•		•	•	•
•			UCC Retrievals ... 804-559-5919	•		•		

CITY OF NEWPORT NEWS (EST)

DT	BK	CV	CR	PR		UC	RE	TX	VS	VR
•	•	•	•		🏛 Faxalert Network ... 757-850-2870	•	•	•		•
•	•	•	•	•	🏛 O'Connell, Nikki A ... 757-877-8469	•	•	•	•	•
•	•	•	•	•	🏛 Research & Retrieval Services (SOP) ... 757-463-0030	•	•	•		
		•	•	•	🏛 Sherlock and Company ... 757-366-5142	•	•			
•	•	•	•	•	🏛 SingleSource Services Corp ... 800-713-3412	•		•	•	•
•	•	•	•		Vanderhoof, Linda ... 804-430-1316					

CITY OF NORFOLK (EST)

DT	BK	CV	CR	PR		UC	RE	TX	VS	VR
•	•	•	•		🏛 Alpha Research LLC (SOP) ... 205-755-7008			•		
•	•	•	•	•	🏛 Research & Retrieval Services (SOP) ... 757-463-0030	•	•	•		
•	•	•	•	•	🏛 Sherlock and Company ... 757-366-5142	•		•		
•	•	•	•	•	🏛 SingleSource Services Corp ... 800-713-3412	•		•	•	•
•	•	•	•	•	🏛 Title Search Services Inc ... 757-490-7009	•	•	•		
•	•	•	•		Vanderhoof, Linda ... 804-430-1316					

NORTHAMPTON (EST)

CV	CR	PR		UC	RE	TX	VS	VR
•	•	•	Ayres, Judith ... 757-336-5313	•	•	•	•	
•	•	•	🏛 SingleSource Services Corp ... 800-713-3412	•		•	•	•

NORTHUMBERLAND (EST)

CV	CR	PR		UC	RE	TX	VS	VR
•	•	•	McKerns & McKerns ... 804-580-8225	•	•	•		
•	•	•	🏛 SingleSource Services Corp ... 800-713-3412	•		•	•	•
•			UCC Retrievals ... 804-559-5919	•		•		

CITY OF NORTON (EST)

CV	CR	PR		UC	RE	TX	VS	VR
			See adjoining counties for retrievers ...					

NOTTOWAY (EST)

CV	CR	PR		UC	RE	TX	VS	VR
•	•	•	Allen III, William D ... 804-469-3977	•	•	•		
•	•	•	🏛 SingleSource Services Corp ... 800-713-3412	•		•	•	•
•			UCC Retrievals ... 804-559-5919	•		•		

ORANGE (EST)

CV	CR	PR		UC	RE	TX	VS	VR
•	•	•	Ellerson, H Watkins ... 540-672-2109	•	•	•		
•	•	•	Estate Title and Escrow Inc ... 703-385-5850	•	•	•		
•			Johnson, Lisa R ... 703-441-0099	•	•	•		
•		•	Lawyer Title/Blue Ridge Agency Inc ... 804-295-7196	•	•	•		
•	•	•	🏛 Reveal Inc (SOP) ... 800-276-4826	•	•	•	•	•
•	•	•	🏛 SingleSource Services Corp ... 800-713-3412	•		•	•	•

CV	CR	PR	PAGE (EST)	UC	RE	TX	VS	VR
•	•	•	🏛 Reveal Inc (SOP) 800-276-4826	•	•	•	•	•
•	•	•	Shenandoah Title Services Inc 540-667-1393	•	•	•		
•	•	•	🏛 SingleSource Services Corp 800-713-3412	•		•	•	•
•	•		🏛 Sprague, Sharry N 540-743-4874					

CV	CR	PR	PATRICK (EST)	UC	RE	TX	VS	VR
•	•		Fletcher, Jean R 540-763-2151	•	•	•		
•	•		Grant, Gary 804-799-3379	•	•	•		
•	•	•	🏛 SingleSource Services Corp 800-713-3412	•		•	•	•
•			UCC Retrievals 804-559-5919	•		•		

CV	CR	PR	CITY OF PETERSBURG (EST)	UC	RE	TX	VS	VR
•	•	•	Allen III, William D 804-469-3977	•	•	•		
•	•	•	🏛 SingleSource Services Corp 800-713-3412	•		•	•	•
•	•	•	The Marston Agency Inc (SOP) 800-308-7790	•	•	•	•	•
•	•	•	🏛 The Pettit Company 800-752-6158	•	•	•	•	
•			UCC Retrievals 804-559-5919	•		•		

CV	CR	PR	PITTSYLVANIA (EST)	UC	RE	TX	VS	VR
•	•	•	🏛 Brown-Browning, Gail 540-563-5699	•	•	•	•	
•	•		Grant, Gary 804-799-3379	•	•	•		
•	•	•	🏛 SingleSource Services Corp 800-713-3412	•		•	•	•
•			UCC Retrievals 804-559-5919	•		•		

CV	CR	PR	CITY OF POQUOSON (EST)	UC	RE	TX	VS	VR
•	•		🏛 Faxalert Network 757-850-2870	•	•	•		•
•	•	•	🏛 O'Connell, Nikki A 757-877-8469	•	•	•	•	•

CV	CR	PR	CITY OF PORTSMOUTH (EST)	UC	RE	TX	VS	VR
•	•	•	🏛 Research & Retrieval Services (SOP) 757-463-0030	•	•	•		
•	•		🏛 Sherlock and Company 757-366-5142	•		•		
•	•	•	🏛 SingleSource Services Corp 800-713-3412	•		•	•	•
•	•	•	🏛 Title Search Services Inc 757-490-7009	•	•	•		
•	•		Vanderhoof, Linda 804-430-1316					

CV	CR	PR	POWHATAN (EST)	UC	RE	TX	VS	VR
•	•	•	Document Resources 800-468-4310	•	•	•	•	
•	•	•	🏛 SingleSource Services Corp 800-713-3412	•		•	•	•
•	•	•	🏛 The Pettit Company 800-752-6158	•	•	•	•	
•			UCC Retrievals 804-559-5919	•		•		

CV	CR	PR	PRINCE EDWARD (EST)	UC	RE	TX	VS	VR
•	•	•	Hawthorne & Hawthorne PC 804-676-3275	•	•	•		
•	•	•	🏛 SingleSource Services Corp 800-713-3412	•		•	•	•
•			UCC Retrievals 804-559-5919	•		•		

CV	CR	PR	PRINCE GEORGE (EST)	UC	RE	TX	VS	VR
•	•	•	ABIS Inc 800-669-2247	•	•	•		•
•	•	•	Allen III, William D 804-469-3977	•	•	•		
•	•	•	Federal Research Corporation 202-783-2700	•	•	•	•	
•	•	•	🏛 SingleSource Services Corp 800-713-3412	•		•	•	•
•	•	•	🏛 The Pettit Company 800-752-6158	•	•	•	•	
•			UCC Retrievals 804-559-5919	•		•		

CV	CR	PR	PRINCE WILLIAM (EST)	UC	RE	TX	VS	VR
•	•	•	ABIS Inc 800-669-2247	•	•	•		•
•	•	•	🏛 Battlefield Title (SOP) 703-369-6900	•	•	•	•	•
•	•	•	🏛 CorpAssist - DC Office (SOP) 800-438-2996	•	•	•	•	•
•	•	•	Document Resources 800-468-4310	•	•	•	•	
•	•	•	Document Resources (SOP) 800-945-7339	•	•	•	•	•
•	•	•	Enterprise Title Company Inc 703-538-2470	•	•	•	•	•
•	•	•	Estate Title and Escrow Inc 703-385-5850	•	•	•		

			Federal Research Corporation 202-783-2700	•	•	•	•
•	•	•	Instant Information Systems 703-281-9312	•	•	•	•
•	•	•	🏛 Investigative Consultants Inc 202-562-1500	•	•	•	•	•
•	•	•	Legal Courier Systems Inc (SOP) 800-869-8586	•	•	•
•	•		🏛 Mohr Information Services 800-799-4363	•	•	•		•
•	•		🏛 National Background Investigations Inc 800-798-0079				
•	•	•	🏛 Reveal Inc (SOP) 800-276-4826	•	•	•	•
•	•	•	🏛 Security Consultants Inc (SOP) 202-686-3953	•	•		•
•	•	•	🏛 SingleSource Services Corp 800-713-3412	•		•	•	•
•	•	•	W A Haag & Associates Inc (SOP) 703-765-2138	•	•	•	•	•

CV	CR	PR	PULASKI (EST)	UC	RE	TX	VS	VR
•	•	•	🏛 Brown-Browning, Gail 540-563-5699	•	•	•	•
•	•		Fletcher, Jean R 540-763-2151	•	•	•
•	•	•	🏛 SingleSource Services Corp 800-713-3412	•		•	•	•

CV	CR	PR	CITY OF RADFORD (EST)	UC	RE	TX	VS	VR
•	•		Fletcher, Jean R 540-763-2151	•	•	•
•	•	•	🏛 SingleSource Services Corp 800-713-3412	•		•	•	•

CV	CR	PR	RAPPAHANNOCK (EST)	UC	RE	TX	VS	VR
•	•	•	🏛 Reveal Inc (SOP) 800-276-4826	•	•	•	•	•
•	•	•	🏛 SingleSource Services Corp 800-713-3412	•		•	•	•

CV	CR	PR	RICHMOND (EST)	UC	RE	TX	VS	VR
•	•	•	McKerns & McKerns 804-580-8225	•	•	•
•	•	•	🏛 SingleSource Services Corp 800-713-3412	•		•	•	•

BK	CV	CR	PR	CITY OF RICHMOND (CAPITAL) (EST)	UC	RE	TX	VS	VR
•				CSC 800-237-1814	•	•	•
•	•	•	•	Document Resources 800-468-4310	•	•	•	•
•	•	•	•	Federal Research Corporation 202-783-2700	•	•	•	•
•	•	•	•	🏛 SingleSource Services Corp 800-713-3412	•		•	•	•
•	•	•	•	The Marston Agency Inc (SOP)..................................... 800-308-7790	•	•	•	•
•	•	•	•	🏛 The Pettit Company 800-752-6158	•	•	•	•
•	•			UCC Retrievals 804-559-5919	•		•
•	•	•	•	Washington Document Service 800-728-5201	•	•	•	•

BK	CV	CR	PR	ROANOKE (EST)	UC	RE	TX	VS	VR
•	•	•	•	Biesenbach, Betsy 703-982-7892	•	•	•
•	•	•	•	🏛 Brown-Browning, Gail 540-563-5699	•	•	•	•
•	•	•		Fletcher, Jean R 540-763-2151	•	•	•
•	•	•	•	🏛 SingleSource Services Corp 800-713-3412	•		•	•	•

DT	CV	CR	PR	CITY OF ROANOKE (EST)	UC	RE	TX	VS	VR
•	•	•	•	Biesenbach, Betsy 703-982-7892	•	•	•
•	•	•	•	🏛 Brown-Browning, Gail 540-563-5699	•	•	•	•
•	•	•	•	🏛 SingleSource Services Corp 800-713-3412	•		•	•	•

CV	CR	PR	ROCKBRIDGE (EST)	UC	RE	TX	VS	VR
•	•	•	🏛 Brown-Browning, Gail 540-563-5699	•	•	•	•
•	•	•	🏛 SingleSource Services Corp 800-713-3412	•		•	•	•
•	•	•	Singleton & Deeds 540-839-5009	•	•	•

CV	CR	PR	ROCKINGHAM (EST)	UC	RE	TX	VS	VR
•	•	•	Blue Ridge Title & Abstract Co 540-432-0329	•	•	•	•
•		•	Lawyers Title 540-433-8112	•	•	•
•	•	•	🏛 SingleSource Services Corp 800-713-3412	•		•	•	•
•	•		🏛 Sprague, Sharry N 540-743-4874				

CV	CR	PR	RUSSELL (EST)	UC	RE	TX	VS	VR
•	•	•	🏛 SingleSource Services Corp 800-713-3412	•		•	•	•

CV	CR	PR	CITY OF SALEM (EST)		UC	RE	TX	VS	VR
•	•	•	Biesenbach, Betsy 703-982-7892		•	•	•		
•	•	•	🏛 Brown-Browning, Gail 540-563-5699		•	•	•	•	
•	•		Fletcher, Jean R 540-763-2151		•	•	•		
•	•	•	🏛 SingleSource Services Corp ... 800-713-3412		•		•	•	•

CV	CR	PR	SCOTT (EST)		UC	RE	TX	VS	VR
•	•		🏛 Alpha Research LLC (SOP).......... 205-755-7008				•		
•	•	•	🏛 SingleSource Services Corp ... 800-713-3412		•		•	•	•

CV	CR	PR	SHENANDOAH (EST)		UC	RE	TX	VS	VR
•	•	•	Shenandoah Title Services Inc 540-667-1393		•	•	•		
•	•	•	🏛 SingleSource Services Corp ... 800-713-3412		•		•	•	•
•	•		🏛 Sprague, Sharry N 540-743-4874						

CV	CR	PR	SMYTH (EST)		UC	RE	TX	VS	VR
•	•	•	🏛 SingleSource Services Corp ... 800-713-3412		•		•	•	•

CV	CR	PR	CITY OF SOUTH BOSTON (EST)		UC	RE	TX	VS	VR
•	•		Grant, Gary 804-799-3379		•	•	•		
•	•	•	Payne, Nita 804-476-2595		•	•	•	•	

CV	CR	PR	SOUTHAMPTON (EST)		UC	RE	TX	VS	VR
•	•	•	🏛 Research & Retrieval Services (SOP)........... 757-463-0030		•	•	•		
•	•	•	🏛 SingleSource Services Corp ... 800-713-3412		•		•	•	•
•			UCC Retrievals 804-559-5919		•		•		

CV	CR	PR	SPOTSYLVANIA (EST)		UC	RE	TX	VS	VR
•	•	•	Document Resources 800-468-4310		•	•	•	•	
•	•	•	Estate Title and Escrow Inc 703-385-5850		•	•	•		
•	•	•	Instant Information Systems 703-281-9312		•	•	•	•	
•			Johnson, Lisa R 703-441-0099		•	•	•		
•			Libertino, Margene 540-785-9930		•	•	•		
•	•	•	🏛 Reveal Inc (SOP) 800-276-4826		•	•	•	•	•
•	•	•	🏛 SingleSource Services Corp ... 800-713-3412		•		•	•	•
•			UCC Retrievals 804-559-5919		•		•		
•	•	•	W A Haag & Associates Inc (SOP) 703-765-2138		•	•	•	•	•

CV	CR	PR	STAFFORD (EST)		UC	RE	TX	VS	VR
•	•	•	🏛 Battlefield Title (SOP) 703-369-6900		•	•	•	•	
•	•	•	Estate Title and Escrow Inc 703-385-5850		•	•	•		
•	•	•	Instant Information Systems 703-281-9312		•	•	•	•	
•			Johnson, Lisa R 703-441-0099		•	•	•		
•	•	•	Legal Courier Systems Inc (SOP)..... 800-869-8586			•	•	•	
•			Libertino, Margene 540-785-9930		•	•	•		
•	•	•	🏛 Reveal Inc (SOP) 800-276-4826		•	•	•	•	•
•	•	•	🏛 SingleSource Services Corp ... 800-713-3412		•		•	•	•
•			UCC Retrievals 804-559-5919		•		•		
•	•	•	W A Haag & Associates Inc (SOP) 703-765-2138		•		•	•	

CV	CR	PR	CITY OF STAUNTON (EST)		UC	RE	TX	VS	VR
•	•	•	🏛 Data Abstract & Title Co Inc ... 540-949-6676		•	•	•		•
•	•	•	🏛 SingleSource Services Corp ... 800-713-3412		•		•	•	•

CV	CR	PR	CITY OF SUFFOLK (EST)		UC	RE	TX	VS	VR
•	•	•	🏛 Research & Retrieval Services (SOP)........... 757-463-0030		•	•	•		
•	•	•	🏛 SingleSource Services Corp ... 800-713-3412		•		•	•	•
•	•	•	🏛 Title Search Services Inc 757-490-7009		•	•	•		
•	•		Vanderhoof, Linda 804-430-1316						

CV	CR	PR	SURRY (EST)		UC	RE	TX	VS	VR
•	•	•	🏛 O'Connell, Nikki A 757-877-8469		•	•	•	•	•
•	•	•	🏛 SingleSource Services Corp ... 800-713-3412		•		•	•	•

	CV	CR	PR	SUSSEX (EST)	UC	RE	TX	VS	VR
	•	•	•	Allen III, William D 804-469-3977	•	•	•		
	•	•	•	🏛 SingleSource Services Corp 800-713-3412	•		•	•	•
	•			UCC Retrievals 804-559-5919	•		•		

	CV	CR	PR	TAZEWELL (EST)	UC	RE	TX	VS	VR
	•	•		Fletcher, Jean R 540-763-2151	•	•	•		
	•	•	•	🏛 SingleSource Services Corp 800-713-3412	•		•	•	•

	CV	CR	PR	CITY OF VIRGINIA BEACH (EST)	UC	RE	TX	VS	VR
	•	•		🏛 Alpha Research LLC (SOP) 205-755-7008			•		
	•	•	•	🏛 Research & Retrieval Services (SOP) 757-463-0030	•	•	•		
	•	•		🏛 Sherlock and Company 757-366-5142	•		•		
	•	•	•	🏛 SingleSource Services Corp 800-713-3412	•		•	•	•
	•	•	•	🏛 Title Search Services Inc 757-490-7009	•	•	•		
	•	•		Vanderhoof, Linda 804-430-1316					

	CV	CR	PR	WARREN (EST)	UC	RE	TX	VS	VR
	•	•		🏛 Alpha Research LLC (SOP) 205-755-7008			•		
	•	•	•	🏛 Mohr Information Services 800-799-4363	•	•	•		•
	•	•	•	🏛 Reveal Inc (SOP) 800-276-4826	•	•	•	•	•
	•	•	•	Shenandoah Title Services Inc 540-667-1393	•	•	•		
	•	•	•	🏛 SingleSource Services Corp 800-713-3412	•		•	•	•
	•	•		🏛 Sprague, Sharry N 540-743-4874					

DT	CV	CR	PR	WASHINGTON (EST)	UC	RE	TX	VS	VR
•	•	•		🏛 Alpha Research LLC (SOP) 205-755-7008			•		
•	•	•	•	🏛 SingleSource Services Corp 800-713-3412	•		•	•	•

	CV	CR	PR	CITY OF WAYNESBORO (EST)	UC	RE	TX	VS	VR
	•	•	•	🏛 Data Abstract & Title Co Inc 540-949-6676	•	•	•		•
	•	•	•	🏛 SingleSource Services Corp 800-713-3412	•		•	•	•

	CV	CR	PR	WESTMORELAND (EST)	UC	RE	TX	VS	VR
	•	•	•	McKerns & McKerns 804-580-8225	•	•	•		
	•	•	•	🏛 SingleSource Services Corp 800-713-3412	•		•	•	•
	•			UCC Retrievals 804-559-5919	•		•		

	CV	CR	PR	CITY OF WILLIAMSBURG (EST)	UC	RE	TX	VS	VR
	•	•	•	Hixson Enterprises 757-898-9865	•	•	•	•	•
	•	•	•	🏛 O'Connell, Nikki A 757-877-8469	•	•	•	•	•
	•	•	•	🏛 Research & Retrieval Services (SOP) 757-463-0030	•	•	•		
	•	•		Vanderhoof, Linda 804-430-1316					

	CV	CR	PR	CITY OF WINCHESTER (EST)	UC	RE	TX	VS	VR
	•	•		🏛 Alpha Research LLC (SOP) 205-755-7008			•		
	•	•	•	🏛 Mohr Information Services 800-799-4363	•	•	•		•
	•	•	•	🏛 Reveal Inc (SOP) 800-276-4826	•	•	•	•	•
	•	•	•	Shenandoah Title Services Inc 540-667-1393	•	•	•		
	•	•	•	🏛 SingleSource Services Corp 800-713-3412	•		•	•	•

DT	CV	CR	PR	WISE (EST)	UC	RE	TX	VS	VR
•	•	•	•	🏛 SingleSource Services Corp 800-713-3412	•		•	•	•

	CV	CR	PR	WYTHE (EST)	UC	RE	TX	VS	VR
	•	•		Fletcher, Jean R 540-763-2151	•	•	•		
	•	•	•	🏛 SingleSource Services Corp 800-713-3412	•		•	•	•

	CV	CR	PR	YORK (EST)	UC	RE	TX	VS	VR
	•	•		🏛 Faxalert Network 757-850-2870	•	•	•		•
	•	•	•	Hixson Enterprises 757-898-9865	•	•	•	•	•
	•	•	•	🏛 O'Connell, Nikki A 757-877-8469	•	•	•	•	•
	•	•	•	🏛 Research & Retrieval Services (SOP) 757-463-0030	•	•	•		
	•	•	•	🏛 SingleSource Services Corp 800-713-3412	•		•	•	•

WASHINGTON

CV	CR	PR	ADAMS (PST)		UC	RE	TX	VS	VR
•	•	•	🏛 AM-PM Services (SOP)................509-765-1776			•	•	•	•
•	•	•	ASAP Legal Messenger (SOP)........206-940-5347			•		•	•

CV	CR	PR	ASOTIN (PST)		UC	RE	TX	VS	VR
•	•	•	Gem State Investigations (SOP)........208-746-4152		•	•	•	•	
•	•	•	Pullman Process Service (SOP)........509-332-8310						

CV	CR	PR	BENTON (PST)		UC	RE	TX	VS	VR
•	•	•	CT Corporation System 800-874-8820		•	•	•	•	
•			Hawley, M M 509-547-6207		•	•	•		

CV	CR	PR	CHELAN (PST)		UC	RE	TX	VS	VR
•	•	•	🏛 AM-PM Services (SOP)................509-765-1776			•	•	•	•
•	•	•	ASAP Legal Messenger (SOP)........206-940-5347			•		•	•
•	•	•	Donald Jones Investigation/Process Svc (SOP)........509-662-7158		•	•	•	•	

CV	CR	PR	CLALLAM (PST)		UC	RE	TX	VS	VR
			See adjoining counties for retrievers						

CV	CR	PR	CLARK (PST)		UC	RE	TX	VS	VR
•	•	•	CT Corporation System 800-874-8820		•	•	•	•	
•	•	•	Fairchild Record Search Ltd 800-547-7007		•		•		
•	•	•	Lawyer's Legal Service (SOP) 800-224-7911		•	•	•		•
•	•		Marosi & Associates Inc (SOP) 800-858-3668		•	•			
•	•		🏛 Prospective Renters Verification Service 503-655-0888						

CV	CR	PR	COLUMBIA (PST)		UC	RE	TX	VS	VR
			See adjoining counties for retrievers						

CV	CR	PR	COWLITZ (PST)		UC	RE	TX	VS	VR
•	•		McGowan & Clark Investigations 206-828-3616		•		•		

CV	CR	PR	DOUGLAS (PST)		UC	RE	TX	VS	VR
•	•	•	🏛 AM-PM Services (SOP)................509-765-1776			•	•	•	•
•	•	•	ASAP Legal Messenger (SOP) 206-940-5347			•		•	•
•	•	•	Donald Jones Investigation/Process Svc (SOP)........509-662-7158		•	•	•	•	

CV	CR	PR	FERRY (PST)		UC	RE	TX	VS	VR
•	•	•	Ferry County Title & Escrow Co Inc 509-775-3119		•	•	•	•	

CV	CR	PR	FRANKLIN (PST)		UC	RE	TX	VS	VR
•	•	•	🏛 AM-PM Services (SOP)................509-765-1776			•	•	•	•
•			Hawley, M M 509-547-6207		•	•	•		

CV	CR	PR	GARFIELD (PST)		UC	RE	TX	VS	VR
•	•	•	Gem State Investigations (SOP)........208-746-4152		•	•	•	•	
•	•		McGowan & Clark Investigations 206-828-3616		•		•		
•	•	•	Pacific Process Service (SOP) 509-325-1371		•	•	•	•	•

CV	CR	PR	GRANT (PST)		UC	RE	TX	VS	VR
•	•	•	🏛 AM-PM Services (SOP)................509-765-1776			•	•	•	•
•	•	•	Donald Jones Investigation/Process Svc (SOP)........509-662-7158		•	•	•	•	

CV	CR	PR	GRAYS HARBOR (PST)		UC	RE	TX	VS	VR
•	•	•	🏛 ABC Legal Messenger (SOP) 206-682-1675		•	•	•	•	

CV	CR	PR	ISLAND (PST)		UC	RE	TX	VS	VR
•	•	•	🏛 ABC Legal Messenger (SOP) 206-682-1675		•	•	•	•	
•	•		🏛 Compass Solutions 800-814-8213						
•	•		McGowan & Clark Investigations 206-828-3616		•		•		

WASHINGTON

		CV	CR	PR	JEFFERSON (PST)	UC	RE	TX	VS	VR
		•		•	Charter Title Corp 800-401-1001	•	•	•		

DT	BK	CV	CR	PR	KING (PST)	UC	RE	TX	VS	VR
•	•	•	•	•	ABC Legal Messenger (SOP) 206-682-1675	•	•	•	•	
•	•	•	•	•	ASAP Legal Messenger (SOP) 206-940-5347		•		•	•
•	•	•	•	•	All Pro Info Search 206-583-1890	•	•	•		•
•	•	•	•	•	Attorney's Information Bureau Inc 206-622-1909	•	•	•	•	
•	•	•	•	•	CSC (SOP) 800-876-9436	•	•	•		
•	•	•	•	•	Commercial Information Services 800-308-2364	•	•	•	•	•
•	•	•	•		Compass Solutions 800-814-8213					
•	•	•	•	•	Fairchild Record Search Ltd 800-547-7007	•		•		
•	•				Hogan Information Services 405-278-6954					
•	•	•	•	•	Hoover Professional Investigative (SOP) ... 206-272-5090	•	•	•	•	
•	•	•	•	•	InfoSearch (SOP) 206-743-9407	•	•	•	•	•
•	•	•	•	•	Joden & Associates Inc (SOP) 206-441-5833	•	•	•		
•	•	•	•		Marosi & Associates Inc (SOP) 800-858-3668	•	•			
•	•	•	•		McGowan & Clark Investigations 206-828-3616	•		•		
		•	•		N W Legal Support Inc (SOP) 800-729-9426					
	•	•	•	•	On Point Investigations (SOP) 425-646-1143	•	•	•	•	•
•	•	•	•	•	Personal Background Investigations 800-949-9982	•	•	•	•	
•	•	•	•	•	Seattle Process Service Inc 800-842-8913					
•	•	•	•	•	Trident Investigative Service (SOP) 888-277-3238	•	•	•		•
•	•	•	•	•	Unisearch Inc 800-722-0708	•		•	•	

	CV	CR	PR	KITSAP (PST)	UC	RE	TX	VS	VR
	•	•	•	ABC Legal Messenger (SOP) 206-682-1675	•	•	•	•	
	•	•	•	ASAP Legal Messenger (SOP) 206-940-5347		•		•	•
	•	•	•	Attorney's Information Bureau Inc 206-622-1909	•	•	•	•	
	•	•	•	Commercial Information Services 800-308-2364	•	•	•	•	•
	•	•		Compass Solutions 800-814-8213					
	•	•	•	Fairchild Record Search Ltd 800-547-7007	•		•		
	•	•	•	Hoover Professional Investigative (SOP) ... 206-272-5090	•	•	•		
	•	•		N W Legal Support Inc (SOP) 800-729-9426					
	•	•	•	Personal Background Investigations 800-949-9982	•	•	•		

	CV	CR	PR	KITTITAS (PST)	UC	RE	TX	VS	VR
	•	•	•	AM-PM Services (SOP) 509-765-1776		•	•		•
	•	•	•	Attorney's Information Bureau Inc 206-622-1909	•	•	•	•	
	•	•	•	CT Corporation System 800-874-8820	•	•	•	•	

	CV	CR	PR	KLICKITAT (PST)	UC	RE	TX	VS	VR
				See adjoining counties for retrievers					

	CV	CR	PR	LEWIS (PST)	UC	RE	TX	VS	VR
	•	•	•	ABC Legal Messenger (SOP) 206-682-1675	•	•	•	•	

	CV	CR	PR	LINCOLN (PST)	UC	RE	TX	VS	VR
	•	•	•	AM-PM Services (SOP) 509-765-1776		•	•	•	•

	CV	CR	PR	MASON (PST)	UC	RE	TX	VS	VR
	•	•	•	ABC Legal Messenger (SOP) 206-682-1675	•	•	•	•	
	•	•	•	Hoover Professional Investigative (SOP) ... 206-272-5090	•	•	•	•	
	•	•	•	Unisearch Inc 800-722-0708	•		•	•	

	CV	CR	PR	OKANOGAN (PST)	UC	RE	TX	VS	VR
	•	•	•	Baines Title Company Inc 800-564-3420	•	•	•	•	

	CV	CR	PR	PACIFIC (PST)	UC	RE	TX	VS	VR
				See adjoining counties for retrievers					

	CV	CR	PR	PEND OREILLE (PST)	UC	RE	TX	VS	VR
	•	•	•	Action Agency (SOP) 208-263-9586	•	•	•	•	

DT	BK	CV	CR	PR		Phone	UC	RE	TX	VS	VR
		•	•	•	Pacific Process Service (SOP)	509-325-1371	•	•	•	•	•

DT	BK	CV	CR	PR	PIERCE (PST)	Phone	UC	RE	TX	VS	VR
•	•	•	•	•	🏛 ABC Legal Messenger (SOP)	206-682-1675	•	•	•	•	
•	•	•	•	•	ASAP Legal Messenger (SOP)	206-940-5347		•		•	•
•	•	•	•	•	All Pro Info Search	206-583-1890	•	•	•	•	•
•	•	•	•	•	🏛 Attorney's Information Bureau Inc	206-622-1909	•	•	•	•	
•	•	•	•	•	CSC (SOP)	800-876-9436	•	•	•		
•	•	•	•	•	🏛 Commercial Information Services	800-308-2364	•	•	•	•	•
•	•	•	•	•	🏛 Compass Solutions	800-814-8213					
•	•	•	•	•	Fairchild Record Search Ltd	800-547-7007	•		•		
•	•				🏛 Hogan Information Services	405-278-6954					
•	•	•	•	•	Hoover Professional Investigative (SOP)	206-272-5090	•	•	•	•	
•	•	•	•	•	McGowan & Clark Investigations	206-828-3616	•				
•	•	•	•	•	N W Legal Support Inc (SOP)	800-729-9426					
•	•	•	•	•	🏛 Personal Background Investigations	800-949-9982	•	•	•	•	
•	•	•	•	•	Seattle Process Service Inc	800-842-8913					
•	•	•	•	•	Unisearch Inc	800-722-0708	•		•	•	

CV	CR	PR	SAN JUAN (PST)	Phone	UC	RE	TX	VS	VR
•	•	•	Paper Chase (SOP)	360-378-3345	•	•	•	•	
•		•	San Juan County Title Co	360-376-4939	•	•	•	•	

CV	CR	PR	SKAGIT (PST)	Phone	UC	RE	TX	VS	VR
•	•	•	🏛 ABC Legal Messenger (SOP)	206-682-1675	•	•	•	•	
•	•	•	🏛 Commercial Information Services	800-308-2364	•	•	•	•	•
•	•		🏛 Compass Solutions	800-814-8213					
•	•	•	🏛 Fourth Corner Network Inc (SOP)	800-321-2455	•	•	•	•	•
•	•	•	🏛 Information Retrieval Services	800-769-3051	•	•	•	•	•
•	•	•	Unisearch Inc	800-722-0708	•		•	•	

CV	CR	PR	SKAMANIA (PST)		UC	RE	TX	VS	VR
			See adjoining counties for retrievers						

CV	CR	PR	SNOHOMISH (PST)	Phone	UC	RE	TX	VS	VR
•	•	•	🏛 ABC Legal Messenger (SOP)	206-682-1675	•	•	•	•	
•	•	•	ASAP Legal Messenger (SOP)	206-940-5347		•		•	•
•	•	•	All Pro Info Search	206-583-1890	•	•	•	•	•
•	•	•	🏛 Attorney's Information Bureau Inc	206-622-1909	•	•	•	•	
•	•	•	CSC (SOP)	800-876-9436	•	•	•	•	•
•	•	•	🏛 Commercial Information Services	800-308-2364	•	•	•	•	•
•	•		🏛 Compass Solutions	800-814-8213					
•	•	•	Fairchild Record Search Ltd	800-547-7007	•		•		
•	•	•	Hoover Professional Investigative (SOP)	206-272-5090	•	•	•	•	
•	•		InQuest Inc (SOP)	800-827-9182					
•	•	•	InfoSearch (SOP)	206-743-9407		•	•	•	
•	•	•	🏛 Information Retrieval Services	800-769-3051	•	•	•	•	•
•	•		McGowan & Clark Investigations	206-828-3616	•				
			N W Legal Support Inc (SOP)	800-729-9426					
•	•	•	🏛 Personal Background Investigations	800-949-9982	•	•	•	•	
•	•	•	Seattle Process Service Inc	800-842-8913					
•	•	•	Unisearch Inc	800-722-0708	•		•	•	

DT	BK	CV	CR	PR	SPOKANE (PST)	Phone	UC	RE	TX	VS	VR
•	•	•	•	•	A & A Attorney Services Inc	509-325-0001	•	•	•	•	
•	•	•	•		🏛 Compass Solutions	800-814-8213					
•	•				🏛 Hogan Information Services	405-278-6954					
•		•	•	•	McGowan & Clark Investigations	206-828-3616	•		•		
•	•	•	•	•	Pacific Process Service (SOP)	509-325-1371	•	•	•	•	•

CV	CR	PR	STEVENS (PST)	Phone	UC	RE	TX	VS	VR
•	•	•	Pacific Process Service (SOP)	509-325-1371	•	•	•	•	•
•	•	•	Stevens County Title	509-684-4589	•	•	•		

CV	CR	PR	THURSTON (CAPITAL) (PST)	UC	RE	TX	VS	VR
•	•	•	ABC Legal Messenger (SOP) 206-682-1675	•	•	•	•	
•	•	•	Attorney's Information Bureau Inc 206-622-1909	•	•	•	•	
•	•	•	CSC 360-754-9333	•		•		
•	•		Compass Solutions 800-814-8213					
•	•		McGowan & Clark Investigations 206-828-3616	•		•		
			N W Legal Support Inc (SOP) 800-729-9426					
•	•	•	Personal Background Investigations 800-949-9982	•	•	•	•	
•	•	•	Unisearch Inc 800-722-0708	•		•	•	

CV	CR	PR	WAHKIAKUM (PST)	UC	RE	TX	VS	VR
			See adjoining counties for retrievers					

CV	CR	PR	WALLA WALLA (PST)	UC	RE	TX	VS	VR
•		•	Walla Walla Title Co 509-525-8660	•	•	•	•	

CV	CR	PR	WHATCOM (PST)	UC	RE	TX	VS	VR
•	•	•	Commercial Information Services 800-308-2364	•	•	•	•	•
•	•		Compass Solutions 800-814-8213	•	•	•	•	•
•	•	•	Fourth Corner Network Inc (SOP) 800-321-2455	•	•	•	•	•

CV	CR	PR	WHITMAN (PST)	UC	RE	TX	VS	VR
•	•	•	Gem State Investigations (SOP) 208-746-4152	•	•	•	•	
•	•	•	Pacific Process Service (SOP) 509-325-1371	•	•	•	•	•
•	•	•	Pullman Process Service (SOP) 509-332-8310					

CV	CR	PR	YAKIMA (PST)	UC	RE	TX	VS	VR
•	•		Compass Solutions 800-814-8213					
•	•	•	Executive Process Service (SOP) 509-453-8307	•	•	•	•	
•	•	•	Legal Couriers Inc (SOP) 509-453-1134	•	•	•	•	
•	•		McGowan & Clark Investigations 206-828-3616	•		•		

WEST VIRGINIA

	CV	CR	PR	BARBOUR (EST)	UC	RE	TX	VS	VR
	•		•	🗑 Liberty Record Search Inc 304-428-5126	•	•	•		
	•	•	•	RLS Inc (SOP) 304-472-5555	•	•	•	•	•
	•	•	•	🗑 The Croson Agency 304-343-1564	•	•	•	•	•

DT	CV	CR	PR	BERKELEY (EST)	UC	RE	TX	VS	VR
•	•	•		🗑 Alpha Research LLC (SOP) 205-755-7008			•		
•	•	•	•	🗑 Mohr Information Services 800-799-4363	•	•	•		•
	•		•	Schramm, Susan Bailey 304-876-2750	•	•	•	•	
•	•	•	•	🗑 The Croson Agency 304-343-1564	•	•	•	•	•

	CV	CR	PR	BOONE (EST)	UC	RE	TX	VS	VR
	•	•	•	American Investigations 304-343-3346	•	•	•	•	
	•		•	🗑 Liberty Record Search Inc 304-428-5126	•	•	•		
	•	•	•	🗑 The Croson Agency 304-343-1564	•	•	•	•	•

	CV	CR	PR	BRAXTON (EST)	UC	RE	TX	VS	VR
	•		•	🗑 Liberty Record Search Inc 304-428-5126	•	•	•		
	•	•	•	RLS Inc (SOP) 304-472-5555	•	•	•	•	•
	•	•	•	🗑 The Croson Agency 304-343-1564	•	•	•	•	•

	CV	CR	PR	BROOKE (EST)	UC	RE	TX	VS	VR
	•	•	•	Claugus, Claudine 614-425-1831	•	•	•	•	•
	•	•	•	🗑 Liberty Record Search Inc 304-428-5126	•	•	•		
	•	•	•	🗑 The Croson Agency 304-343-1564	•	•	•		
	•	•	•	Tomich, Vicki 304-845-7315	•	•	•		

DT	CV	CR	PR	CABELL (EST)	UC	RE	TX	VS	VR
•	•	•	•	American Investigations 304-343-3346	•	•	•	•	
•	•	•	•	Lew Davis Investigatons (SOP) 304-523-0055	•	•	•	•	•
	•		•	🗑 Liberty Record Search Inc 304-428-5126	•	•	•		
•	•	•	•	🗑 The Croson Agency 304-343-1564	•	•	•	•	•

	CV	CR	PR	CALHOUN (EST)	UC	RE	TX	VS	VR
	•		•	🗑 Liberty Record Search Inc 304-428-5126	•	•	•		
	•	•	•	RLS Inc (SOP) 304-472-5555	•	•	•	•	•
	•	•	•	🗑 The Croson Agency 304-343-1564	•	•	•	•	•

	CV	CR	PR	CLAY (EST)	UC	RE	TX	VS	VR
	•		•	🗑 Liberty Record Search Inc 304-428-5126	•	•	•		
	•	•	•	🗑 The Croson Agency 304-343-1564	•	•	•	•	•

	CV	CR	PR	DODDRIDGE (EST)	UC	RE	TX	VS	VR
	•		•	🗑 Liberty Record Search Inc 304-428-5126	•	•	•		
	•	•	•	RLS Inc (SOP) 304-472-5555	•	•	•	•	•
	•	•	•	🗑 The Croson Agency 304-343-1564	•	•	•	•	•

	CV	CR	PR	FAYETTE (EST)	UC	RE	TX	VS	VR
	•	•	•	🗑 Dutton, Jacqueline E 304-658-4441	•	•	•	•	•
	•		•	🗑 Liberty Record Search Inc 304-428-5126	•	•	•		
	•	•	•	🗑 The Croson Agency 304-343-1564	•	•	•	•	•

	CV	CR	PR	GILMER (EST)	UC	RE	TX	VS	VR
	•		•	🗑 Liberty Record Search Inc 304-428-5126	•	•	•		
	•	•	•	RLS Inc (SOP) 304-472-5555	•	•	•	•	•
	•	•	•	🗑 The Croson Agency 304-343-1564	•	•	•	•	•

	CV	CR	PR	GRANT (EST)	UC	RE	TX	VS	VR
	•	•	•	Blue Ridge Title & Abstract Co 540-432-0329	•	•	•	•	
	•	•	•	Grant County Clerk's Office 304-257-4550	•	•	•	•	
	•		•	Paralegal Services 304-258-4287	•	•	•		

CV	CR	PR	Provider	Phone	UC	RE	TX	VS	VR
•	•	•	🏛 The Croson Agency	304-343-1564	•	•	•	•	•

GREENBRIER (EST)

CV	CR	PR	Provider	Phone	UC	RE	TX	VS	VR
•		•	🏛 Liberty Record Search Inc	304-428-5126	•	•	•		
•	•	•	🏛 The Croson Agency	304-343-1564	•	•	•	•	•

HAMPSHIRE (EST)

CV	CR	PR	Provider	Phone	UC	RE	TX	VS	VR
			Paralegal Services	304-258-4287	•	•	•		
•	•	•	🏛 The Croson Agency	304-343-1564	•	•	•	•	•

HANCOCK (EST)

CV	CR	PR	Provider	Phone	UC	RE	TX	VS	VR
•		•	🏛 Liberty Record Search Inc	304-428-5126	•	•	•		
•	•	•	🏛 The Croson Agency	304-343-1564	•	•	•	•	•
•	•	•	Tomich, Vicki	304-845-7315	•	•	•	•	

HARDY (EST)

CV	CR	PR	Provider	Phone	UC	RE	TX	VS	VR
			Paralegal Services	304-258-4287	•	•	•		
•	•	•	🏛 The Croson Agency	304-343-1564	•	•	•	•	•

HARRISON (EST)

DT	CV	CR	PR	Provider	Phone	UC	RE	TX	VS	VR
	•		•	🏛 Liberty Record Search Inc	304-428-5126	•	•	•		
	•	•	•	RLS Inc (SOP)	304-472-5555	•	•	•	•	•
•	•	•	•	🏛 The Croson Agency	304-343-1564	•	•	•	•	•

JACKSON (EST)

CV	CR	PR	Provider	Phone	UC	RE	TX	VS	VR
•	•	•	American Investigations	304-343-3346	•	•	•	•	
•		•	🏛 Liberty Record Search Inc	304-428-5126	•	•	•		
•	•	•	🏛 The Croson Agency	304-343-1564	•	•	•	•	•

JEFFERSON (EST)

CV	CR	PR	Provider	Phone	UC	RE	TX	VS	VR
•	•		🏛 Alpha Research LLC (SOP)	205-755-7008			•		
•	•	•	🏛 Mohr Information Services	800-799-4363	•	•	•		•
			Paralegal Services	304-258-4287	•	•	•		
•		•	Schramm, Susan Bailey	304-876-2750	•	•	•	•	
•	•	•	🏛 The Croson Agency	304-343-1564	•	•	•	•	•

KANAWHA (CAPITAL) (EST)

DT	BK	CV	CR	PR	Provider	Phone	UC	RE	TX	VS	VR
•	•			•	American Investigations	304-343-3346	•	•	•	•	
				•	🏛 Liberty Record Search Inc	304-428-5126	•	•	•		
•	•		•	•	🏛 The Croson Agency	304-343-1564	•	•	•		

LEWIS (EST)

CV	CR	PR	Provider	Phone	UC	RE	TX	VS	VR
•		•	🏛 Liberty Record Search Inc	304-428-5126	•	•	•		
•	•	•	RLS Inc (SOP)	304-472-5555	•	•	•	•	•
•	•	•	🏛 The Croson Agency	304-343-1564	•	•	•	•	•

LINCOLN (EST)

CV	CR	PR	Provider	Phone	UC	RE	TX	VS	VR
•	•	•	American Investigations	304-343-3346	•	•	•	•	
•		•	Lew Davis Investigatons (SOP)	304-523-0055	•	•	•		•
•		•	🏛 Liberty Record Search Inc	304-428-5126	•	•	•		
•	•	•	🏛 The Croson Agency	304-343-1564	•	•	•	•	•

LOGAN (EST)

CV	CR	PR	Provider	Phone	UC	RE	TX	VS	VR
•		•	🏛 Liberty Record Search Inc	304-428-5126	•	•	•		
•	•	•	RLS Inc (SOP)	304-472-5555	•	•	•	•	•
•	•	•	🏛 The Croson Agency	304-343-1564	•	•	•	•	•

MARION (EST)

CV	CR	PR	Provider	Phone	UC	RE	TX	VS	VR
•		•	🏛 Liberty Record Search Inc	304-428-5126	•	•	•		
•	•	•	RLS Inc (SOP)	304-472-5555	•	•	•	•	•
•	•	•	🏛 The Croson Agency	304-343-1564	•	•	•	•	•

MARSHALL (EST)

CV	CR	PR	Provider	Phone	UC	RE	TX	VS	VR
•	•	•	Claugus, Claudine	614-425-1831	•	•	•	•	•

•		•	🏛 Liberty Record Search Inc	304-428-5126	•	•	•		
•	•	•	🏛 The Croson Agency	304-343-1564	•	•	•	•	•
•	•	•	Tomich, Vicki	304-845-7315	•	•	•	•	

CV	CR	PR	**MASON (EST)**	UC	RE	TX	VS	VR
•	•	•	Lew Davis Investigatons (SOP)	304-523-0055	•	•	•		
•		•	🏛 Liberty Record Search Inc	304-428-5126	•	•	•		
•		•	Paralegal Services	304-675-1997	•	•	•		
•	•	•	🏛 The Croson Agency	304-343-1564	•	•	•		

CV	CR	PR	**McDOWELL (EST)**	UC	RE	TX	VS	VR
•		•	🏛 Liberty Record Search Inc	304-428-5126	•	•	•		
•	•	•	RLS Inc (SOP)	304-472-5555	•	•	•		
•	•	•	🏛 The Croson Agency	304-343-1564	•	•	•	•	•

DT	CV	CR	PR	**MERCER (EST)**	UC	RE	TX	VS	VR
	•		•	🏛 Liberty Record Search Inc	304-428-5126	•	•	•		
•	•	•	•	🏛 The Croson Agency	304-343-1564	•	•	•	•	•

CV	CR	PR	**MINERAL (EST)**	UC	RE	TX	VS	VR
•	•	•	🏛 The Croson Agency	304-343-1564	•	•	•	•	•

CV	CR	PR	**MINGO (EST)**	UC	RE	TX	VS	VR
•		•	🏛 Liberty Record Search Inc	304-428-5126	•	•	•		
•	•	•	🏛 The Croson Agency	304-343-1564	•	•	•		

CV	CR	PR	**MONONGALIA (EST)**	UC	RE	TX	VS	VR
•		•	🏛 Liberty Record Search Inc	304-428-5126	•	•	•		
•	•	•	RLS Inc (SOP)	304-472-5555	•	•	•		
•	•	•	🏛 The Croson Agency	304-343-1564	•	•	•		

CV	CR	PR	**MONROE (EST)**	UC	RE	TX	VS	VR
•		•	🏛 Liberty Record Search Inc	304-428-5126	•	•	•		
•	•	•	🏛 The Croson Agency	304-343-1564	•	•	•	•	•

CV	CR	PR	**MORGAN (EST)**	UC	RE	TX	VS	VR
			Paralegal Services	304-258-4287	•	•	•		
•		•	Schramm, Susan Bailey	304-876-2750	•	•	•	•	
•	•	•	🏛 The Croson Agency	304-343-1564	•	•	•	•	•

CV	CR	PR	**NICHOLAS (EST)**	UC	RE	TX	VS	VR
•	•	•	🏛 Dutton, Jacqueline E	304-658-4441	•	•	•	•	•
•		•	🏛 Liberty Record Search Inc	304-428-5126	•	•	•		
•	•	•	🏛 The Croson Agency	304-343-1564	•	•	•	•	•

DT	BK	CV	CR	PR	**OHIO (EST)**	UC	RE	TX	VS	VR
		•		•	🏛 Liberty Record Search Inc	304-428-5126	•	•	•		
•	•	•	•	•	🏛 The Croson Agency	304-343-1564	•	•	•	•	•
•	•	•	•	•	Tomich, Vicki	304-845-7315	•	•	•		

CV	CR	PR	**PENDLETON (EST)**	UC	RE	TX	VS	VR
•	•	•	Blue Ridge Title & Abstract Co	540-432-0329	•	•	•	•	
•	•	•	🏛 The Croson Agency	304-343-1564	•	•	•	•	

CV	CR	PR	**PLEASANTS (EST)**	UC	RE	TX	VS	VR
•		•	🏛 Liberty Record Search Inc	304-428-5126	•	•	•		
•	•	•	🏛 The Croson Agency	304-343-1564	•	•	•	•	•

CV	CR	PR	**POCAHONTAS (EST)**	UC	RE	TX	VS	VR
•		•	🏛 Liberty Record Search Inc	304-428-5126	•	•	•		
•	•	•	🏛 The Croson Agency	304-343-1564	•	•	•	•	

CV	CR	PR	**PRESTON (EST)**	UC	RE	TX	VS	VR
•		•	🏛 Liberty Record Search Inc	304-428-5126	•	•	•		

CV	CR	PR	Provider	Phone	UC	RE	TX	VS	VR
•	•	•	RLS Inc (SOP)	304-472-5555	•	•	•	•	•
•	•	•	🗑 The Croson Agency	304-343-1564	•	•	•	•	•

PUTNAM (EST)

CV	CR	PR	Provider	Phone	UC	RE	TX	VS	VR
•	•	•	American Investigations	304-343-3346	•	•			
•	•	•	Lew Davis Investigatons (SOP)	304-523-0055	•	•			•
•		•	🗑 Liberty Record Search Inc	304-428-5126	•	•	•		
•	•	•	🗑 The Croson Agency	304-343-1564	•	•	•	•	•

RALEIGH (EST)

DT	CV	CR	PR	Provider	Phone	UC	RE	TX	VS	VR
•	•	•	•	🗑 Dutton, Jacqueline E	304-658-4441	•	•	•	•	•
	•	•	•	🗑 Liberty Record Search Inc	304-428-5126	•	•	•		
•	•	•	•	🗑 The Croson Agency	304-343-1564	•	•	•	•	•

RANDOLPH (EST)

DT	CV	CR	PR	Provider	Phone	UC	RE	TX	VS	VR
	•		•	🗑 Liberty Record Search Inc	304-428-5126	•	•	•		
	•	•	•	RLS Inc (SOP)	304-472-5555	•	•	•	•	•
•	•	•	•	🗑 The Croson Agency	304-343-1564	•	•	•	•	•

RITCHIE (EST)

CV	CR	PR	Provider	Phone	UC	RE	TX	VS	VR
•		•	🗑 Liberty Record Search Inc	304-428-5126	•	•	•		
•	•	•	RLS Inc (SOP)	304-472-5555	•	•	•	•	•
•	•	•	🗑 The Croson Agency	304-343-1564	•	•	•	•	•
•	•	•	West, Thomas	614-373-6688	•	•	•	•	

ROANE (EST)

CV	CR	PR	Provider	Phone	UC	RE	TX	VS	VR
•		•	🗑 Liberty Record Search Inc	304-428-5126	•	•	•		
•	•	•	🗑 The Croson Agency	304-343-1564	•	•	•	•	•

SUMMERS (EST)

CV	CR	PR	Provider	Phone	UC	RE	TX	VS	VR
•		•	🗑 Liberty Record Search Inc	304-428-5126	•	•	•		
•	•	•	🗑 The Croson Agency	304-343-1564	•	•	•	•	•

TAYLOR (EST)

CV	CR	PR	Provider	Phone	UC	RE	TX	VS	VR
		•	Abruzzino, Patricia	304-265-1401	•	•	•	•	•
•		•	🗑 Liberty Record Search Inc	304-428-5126	•	•	•		
•	•	•	RLS Inc (SOP)	304-472-5555	•	•	•	•	•
•	•	•	🗑 The Croson Agency	304-343-1564	•	•	•	•	•

TUCKER (EST)

CV	CR	PR	Provider	Phone	UC	RE	TX	VS	VR
•	•	•	RLS Inc (SOP)	304-472-5555	•	•	•	•	•
•	•	•	🗑 The Croson Agency	304-343-1564	•	•	•	•	•

TYLER (EST)

CV	CR	PR	Provider	Phone	UC	RE	TX	VS	VR
•	•	•	Claugus, Claudine	614-425-1831	•	•	•	•	•
		•	🗑 Liberty Record Search Inc	304-428-5126	•	•	•	•	•
•	•	•	🗑 The Croson Agency	304-343-1564	•	•	•	•	•
•	•	•	West, Thomas	614-373-6688	•	•	•		

UPSHUR (EST)

CV	CR	PR	Provider	Phone	UC	RE	TX	VS	VR
		•	🗑 Liberty Record Search Inc	304-428-5126	•	•	•		
•	•	•	RLS Inc (SOP)	304-472-5555	•	•	•		•
•	•	•	🗑 The Croson Agency	304-343-1564	•	•	•	•	•

WAYNE (EST)

CV	CR	PR	Provider	Phone	UC	RE	TX	VS	VR
•	•	•	Lew Davis Investigatons (SOP)	304-523-0055	•	•	•	•	•
•	•	•	🗑 Liberty Record Search Inc	304-428-5126	•	•	•		
•	•	•	🗑 The Croson Agency	304-343-1564	•	•	•	•	•

WEBSTER (EST)

CV	CR	PR	Provider	Phone	UC	RE	TX	VS	VR
•	•	•	🗑 The Croson Agency	304-343-1564	•	•	•	•	•

WETZEL (EST)

CV	CR	PR	Provider	Phone	UC	RE	TX	VS	VR
•	•	•	Claugus, Claudine	614-425-1831	•	•	•	•	•

•		•	🏛 Liberty Record Search Inc 304-428-5126	•	•	•			
•	•	•	🏛 The Croson Agency 304-343-1564	•	•	•	•	•
•	•	•	Tomich, Vicki 304-845-7315	•	•	•	•
•	•	•	West, Thomas 614-373-6688	•	•	•	•

	CV	CR	PR	WIRT (EST)	UC	RE	TX	VS	VR
	•		•	🏛 Liberty Record Search Inc 304-428-5126	•	•	•	
	•	•	•	🏛 The Croson Agency 304-343-1564	•	•	•	•

DT	CV	CR	PR	WOOD (EST)	UC	RE	TX	VS	VR
	•	•	•	Claugus, Claudine 614-425-1831	•	•	•	•	•
	•		•	🏛 Liberty Record Search Inc 304-428-5126	•	•	•	
•	•	•	•	🏛 The Croson Agency 304-343-1564	•	•	•	•
	•	•	•	West, Thomas 614-373-6688	•	•	•	•

	CV	CR	PR	WYOMING (EST)	UC	RE	TX	VS	VR
	•		•	🏛 Liberty Record Search Inc 304-428-5126	•	•	•	
	•	•	•	🏛 The Croson Agency 304-343-1564	•	•	•	•

SUMMARY OF CODES

COURT RECORDS

CODE	GOVERNMENT AGENCY	TYPE OF INFORMATION
DT	US District Court	Federal civil and criminal cases
BK	Bankruptcy Court	United States bankruptcy cases
CV	Civil Court	Municipal, county and state level civil cases
CR	Criminal Court	Municipal, county and state level criminal cases
PR	Probate Court	Wills and estate cases

COUNTY RECORDS

CODE	GOVERNMENT AGENCY	TYPE OF INFORMATION
UC	UCC Filing Office	Uniform Commercial Code and other personal property liens
RE	Recorder of Deeds	Real property transactions and liens
TX	Tax Assessor	Real property tax information
VS	Vital Records Office	Vital statistics—birth, death, marriage, divorce, etc.
VR	Voter Registration Office	Voter registration and campaign contribution information

- "CODE" designates the agency and type of information obtainable in each county from a retriever.
- The time zone for each county is abbreviated as follows: EST—Eastern Standard Time; CST—Central; MST—Mountain; PST—Pacific; AK—Alaska; HT—Hawaii.
- 🏛—This symbol designates a Public Record Retriever Network member.
- "(SOP)" after the retriever name designates Service of Process.
- Individual retrievers without a company name are listed in order of their last name.

US District and Bankruptcy courts are indicated only in the counties where courts are located.

WISCONSIN

		CV	CR	PR	ADAMS (CST)		UC	RE	TX	VS	VR
		•		•	Adams County Land Titles 608-339-6634		•	•	•	•	
				•	Boles-Wallner Abstract and Title 715-423-6940		•	•	•		
		•	•	•	Marquette County Abstract 800-388-8485		•	•	•	•	
		•	•	•	Search Associates 414-325-9330		•	•	•		

		CV	CR	PR	ASHLAND (CST)		UC	RE	TX	VS	VR
		•		•	North Wisconsin Abstract Co 715-682-4234		•	•	•		
		•	•	•	Search Associates 414-325-9330		•	•	•		
		•	•	•	Surety Abstract & Title Company 715-339-2110		•	•	•	•	

		CV	CR	PR	BARRON (CST)		UC	RE	TX	VS	VR
		•		•	🗑 Barron County Title Services Inc 715-537-5633		•	•	•		
		•	•	•	Search Associates 414-325-9330		•	•	•		

		CV	CR	PR	BAYFIELD (CST)		UC	RE	TX	VS	VR
		•		•	North Wisconsin Abstract Co 715-682-4234		•	•	•		
		•	•	•	Search Associates 414-325-9330		•	•	•		

		CV	CR	PR	BROWN (CST)		UC	RE	TX	VS	VR
		•		•	Bay Title and Abstract Inc 414-431-6100		•	•	•		
		•	•		Interstate Reporting Co Inc (IRC) 800-837-6635		•		•		
		•	•	•	Search Associates 414-325-9330		•	•	•		

		CV	CR	PR	BUFFALO (CST)		UC	RE	TX	VS	VR
		•	•	•	Search Associates 414-325-9330		•	•	•		

		CV	CR	PR	BURNETT (CST)		UC	RE	TX	VS	VR
		•	•	•	Burnett County Abstract Co 715-349-2269		•	•	•		
		•	•	•	Search Associates 414-325-9330		•	•	•		

		CV	CR	PR	CALUMET (CST)		UC	RE	TX	VS	VR
		•		•	Bay Title and Abstract Inc 414-431-6100		•	•	•		
		•	•	•	Search Associates 414-325-9330		•	•	•		

		CV	CR	PR	CHIPPEWA (CST)		UC	RE	TX	VS	VR
		•	•	•	Search Associates 414-325-9330		•	•	•		
		•		•	The Title Co Inc 715-838-2800		•	•	•		

		CV	CR	PR	CLARK (CST)		UC	RE	TX	VS	VR
		•	•	•	🗑 Bill Bonham "The Investigator" (SOP) 715-842-1113		•	•	•	•	
				•	Boles-Wallner Abstract and Title 715-423-6940		•	•	•		
		•	•	•	Search Associates 414-325-9330		•	•	•		

		CV	CR	PR	COLUMBIA (CST)		UC	RE	TX	VS	VR
		•	•	•	Search Associates 414-325-9330		•	•	•		

		CV	CR	PR	CRAWFORD (CST)		UC	RE	TX	VS	VR
		•	•	•	Search Associates 414-325-9330		•	•	•		

DT	BK	CV	CR	PR	DANE (CAPITAL) (CST)		UC	RE	TX	VS	VR
		•		•	Bay Title and Abstract Inc 414-431-6100		•	•	•		
•	•	•	•		🗑 Dane County Legal Notice (SOP) 800-720-6871		•			•	
•	•	•	•	•	🗑 Gregg Investigations Inc of Janesville (SOP) 800-866-1976		•	•	•	•	
•	•	•	•	•	Gregg Investigations Inc of Madison (SOP) 800-866-1976		•	•	•	•	•
		•	•	•	Search Associates 414-325-9330		•	•	•		

		CV	CR	PR	DODGE (CST)		UC	RE	TX	VS	VR
		•	•	•	Search Associates 414-325-9330		•	•	•		

		CV	CR	PR	DOOR (CST)		UC	RE	TX	VS	VR
		•		•	Bay Title and Abstract Inc 414-431-6100		•	•	•		

CV	CR	PR			UC	RE	TX	VS	VR
•	•	•	Search Associates 414-325-9330		•	•	•		

CV	CR	PR	DOUGLAS (CST)		UC	RE	TX	VS	VR
•	•	•	Abstract and Title Services of Carlton Inc (SOP) 218-384-3450		•	•	•	•	
•	•	•	Search Associates 414-325-9330		•	•	•		

CV	CR	PR	DUNN (CST)		UC	RE	TX	VS	VR
			Dunn County Abstract & Title Inc 715-235-0875			•	•		
•	•	•	Search Associates 414-325-9330		•	•	•		
•		•	The Title Co Inc 715-838-2800		•	•	•		

BK	CV	CR	PR	EAU CLAIRE (CST)		UC	RE	TX	VS	VR
	•	•	•	Search Associates 414-325-9330		•	•	•		
	•		•	The Title Co Inc 715-838-2800		•	•	•		

CV	CR	PR	FLORENCE (CST)		UC	RE	TX	VS	VR
•		•	Florence County Abstract 715-528-3272		•	•	•	•	
•	•	•	Penninsula Title and Abstract Corp 906-875-6618		•	•	•		
•	•	•	Search Associates 414-325-9330		•	•	•		

CV	CR	PR	FOND DU LAC (CST)		UC	RE	TX	VS	VR
•		•	Bay Title and Abstract Inc 414-431-6100		•	•	•		
•	•	•	Search Associates 414-325-9330		•	•	•		
•	•	•	Wisconsin Title of Fond Du Lac 414-922-2200		•	•	•	•	

CV	CR	PR	FOREST (CST)		UC	RE	TX	VS	VR
•	•		Miller, Susan 715-478-3932				•		
•	•	•	Search Associates 414-325-9330		•	•	•		

CV	CR	PR	GRANT (CST)		UC	RE	TX	VS	VR
•	•	•	Grant County Abstract Co 608-723-4192		•	•	•	•	
•	•	•	Search Associates 414-325-9330		•	•	•		

CV	CR	PR	GREEN (CST)		UC	RE	TX	VS	VR
•	•	•	Ekum Abstract and Title 608-328-8221		•	•	•		
•	•	•	Search Associates 414-325-9330		•	•	•		

CV	CR	PR	GREEN LAKE (CST)		UC	RE	TX	VS	VR
•	•	•	Green Lake Title & Abstract Co 414-294-6070		•	•	•	•	
•	•	•	Marquette County Abstract 800-388-8485		•	•	•	•	
•	•	•	Search Associates 414-325-9330		•	•	•		

CV	CR	PR	IOWA (CST)		UC	RE	TX	VS	VR
•	•	•	Search Associates 414-325-9330		•	•	•		

CV	CR	PR	IRON (CST)		UC	RE	TX	VS	VR
•		•	Iron Title & Abstract Co 715-561-3576		•	•	•		
•	•	•	Search Associates 414-325-9330		•	•	•		

CV	CR	PR	JACKSON (CST)		UC	RE	TX	VS	VR
		•	Boles-Wallner Abstract and Title 715-423-6940		•	•	•		
•	•	•	Search Associates 414-325-9330		•	•	•		

CV	CR	PR	JEFFERSON (CST)		UC	RE	TX	VS	VR
•	•	•	Search Associates 414-325-9330		•	•	•		

CV	CR	PR	JUNEAU (CST)		UC	RE	TX	VS	VR
		•	Boles-Wallner Abstract and Title 715-423-6940		•	•	•		
•	•	•	Search Associates 414-325-9330		•	•	•		

CV	CR	PR	KENOSHA (CST)		UC	RE	TX	VS	VR
•	•	•	AGH Professional Investigations (SOP) 414-697-9933		•	•	•	•	•
•	•		Mueller, Aaron S 414-821-3405						
•	•	•	Process Associates/Milwaukee (SOP) 414-271-9574		•	•	•	•	•

			•	•	•	Search Associates 414-325-9330	•	•	•		
		CV	**CR**	**PR**		**KEWAUNEE (CST)**	**UC**	**RE**	**TX**	**VS**	**VR**
		•		•		Bay Title and Abstract Inc 414-431-6100	•	•	•		
		•	•	•		Search Associates 414-325-9330	•	•	•		
		CV	**CR**	**PR**		**LA CROSSE (CST)**	**UC**	**RE**	**TX**	**VS**	**VR**
		•	•	•		Search Associates 414-325-9330	•	•	•		
		CV	**CR**	**PR**		**LAFAYETTE (CST)**	**UC**	**RE**	**TX**	**VS**	**VR**
		•	•	•		Ekum Abstract and Title 608-328-8221	•	•	•		
		•		•		Lafayette County Abstract 608-776-3338	•	•	•		
		•	•	•		Search Associates 414-325-9330	•	•	•		
		CV	**CR**	**PR**		**LANGLADE (CST)**	**UC**	**RE**	**TX**	**VS**	**VR**
		•	•	•		🗑 Bill Bonham "The Investigator" (SOP).......................... 715-842-1113	•	•	•	•	
		•	•	•		Search Associates 414-325-9330	•	•	•		
		CV	**CR**	**PR**		**LINCOLN (CST)**	**UC**	**RE**	**TX**	**VS**	**VR**
		•	•	•		🗑 Bill Bonham "The Investigator" (SOP).......................... 715-842-1113	•	•	•	•	
		•	•	•		Search Associates 414-325-9330	•	•	•		
		CV	**CR**	**PR**		**MANITOWOC (CST)**	**UC**	**RE**	**TX**	**VS**	**VR**
		•		•		Bay Title and Abstract Inc 414-431-6100	•	•	•		
		•		•		First Abstract Title Co 414-684-1261	•	•	•	•	
		•	•	•		Search Associates 414-325-9330	•	•	•		
		CV	**CR**	**PR**		**MARATHON (CST)**	**UC**	**RE**	**TX**	**VS**	**VR**
		•	•	•		🗑 Bill Bonham "The Investigator" (SOP).......................... 715-842-1113	•	•	•	•	
		•		•		Boles-Wallner Abstract and Title 715-423-6940	•	•	•		
		•	•	•		Search Associates 414-325-9330	•	•	•		
		CV	**CR**	**PR**		**MARINETTE (CST)**	**UC**	**RE**	**TX**	**VS**	**VR**
		•		•		Bay Title and Abstract Inc 414-431-6100	•	•	•		
		•	•	•		Search Associates 414-325-9330	•	•	•		
		CV	**CR**	**PR**		**MARQUETTE (CST)**	**UC**	**RE**	**TX**	**VS**	**VR**
		•	•	•		Marquette County Abstract 800-388-8485	•	•	•	•	
		•	•	•		Search Associates 414-325-9330	•	•	•		
		CV	**CR**	**PR**		**MENOMINEE (CST)**	**UC**	**RE**	**TX**	**VS**	**VR**
		•		•		Bay Title and Abstract Inc 414-431-6100	•	•	•		
		•	•	•		Search Associates 414-325-9330	•	•	•		
		•	•	•		Wisconsin Title of Shawano Inc 715-524-2413	•	•	•		
DT	**BK**	**CV**	**CR**	**PR**		**MILWAUKEE (CST)**	**UC**	**RE**	**TX**	**VS**	**VR**
•	•	•	•	•		AGH Professional Investigations (SOP)............................ 414-697-9933	•	•	•	•	•
•	•					🗑 Hogan Information Services 405-278-6954					
•		•	•			Interstate Reporting Co Inc (IRC) 800-837-6635	•		•		
		•	•			Mueller, Aaron S 414-821-3405					
•		•	•	•		Process Associates/Milwaukee (SOP)............................ 414-271-9574	•	•	•	•	•
		•	•			Search Associates 414-325-9330	•	•	•		
•	•	•	•	•		🗑 The Todd Wiegele Research Co Inc 800-754-7800	•	•	•	•	
•	•	•	•	•		Townsend Detective & Security (SOP) 414-327-0221	•	•	•	•	
		CV	**CR**	**PR**		**MONROE (CST)**	**UC**	**RE**	**TX**	**VS**	**VR**
		•	•	•		Search Associates 414-325-9330	•	•	•		
		CV	**CR**	**PR**		**OCONTO (CST)**	**UC**	**RE**	**TX**	**VS**	**VR**
		•		•		Bay Title and Abstract Inc 414-431-6100	•	•	•		
		•	•	•		Search Associates 414-325-9330	•	•	•		
		CV	**CR**	**PR**		**ONEIDA (CST)**	**UC**	**RE**	**TX**	**VS**	**VR**
		•	•	•		Search Associates 414-325-9330	•	•	•		

CV	CR	PR	OUTAGAMIE (CST)		UC	RE	TX	VS	VR
•		•	B & H Abstract and Title	414-731-5494	•	•	•		
•		•	Bay Title and Abstract Inc	414-431-6100	•	•	•		
•	•	•	Search Associates	414-325-9330	•	•	•		

CV	CR	PR	OZAUKEE (CST)		UC	RE	TX	VS	VR
•	•		Interstate Reporting Co Inc (IRC)	800-837-6635	•		•		
•	•		Mueller, Aaron S	414-821-3405					
•	•	•	Process Associates/Milwaukee (SOP)	414-271-9574	•	•	•	•	•
•	•	•	Search Associates	414-325-9330	•	•	•		
•	•	•	🏛 The Todd Wiegele Research Co Inc	800-754-7800	•	•	•	•	

CV	CR	PR	PEPIN (CST)		UC	RE	TX	VS	VR
			Dunn County Abstract & Title Inc	715-235-0875		•	•		
•	•	•	Search Associates	414-325-9330	•	•	•		

CV	CR	PR	PIERCE (CST)		UC	RE	TX	VS	VR
•	•	•	Search Associates	414-325-9330	•	•	•		
•	•	•	St Croix Valley Title Services Inc	715-425-1519	•	•	•		

CV	CR	PR	POLK (CST)		UC	RE	TX	VS	VR
•	•	•	Oakey and Oakey Abstract Co	715-294-2624	•	•	•	•	
•	•	•	Search Associates	414-325-9330	•	•	•		

CV	CR	PR	PORTAGE (CST)		UC	RE	TX	VS	VR
•	•	•	🏛 Bill Bonham "The Investigator" (SOP)	715-842-1113	•	•	•	•	
	•		Boles-Wallner Abstract and Title	715-423-6940	•	•	•		
•	•	•	Search Associates	414-325-9330	•	•	•		

CV	CR	PR	PRICE (CST)		UC	RE	TX	VS	VR
•	•	•	Phillips Land Title Company	715-339-2230	•	•	•	•	
•	•	•	Search Associates	414-325-9330	•	•	•		

CV	CR	PR	RACINE (CST)		UC	RE	TX	VS	VR
•	•	•	AGH Professional Investigations (SOP)	414-697-9933	•	•	•	•	•
•	•		Mueller, Aaron S	414-821-3405					
•	•	•	Process Associates/Milwaukee (SOP)	414-271-9574	•	•	•	•	
•	•	•	Search Associates	414-325-9330	•	•	•		

CV	CR	PR	RICHLAND (CST)		UC	RE	TX	VS	VR
•	•	•	Search Associates	414-325-9330	•	•	•		
•	•	•	Wisconsin Title of Richland Center Inc	800-236-4596	•	•	•	•	

CV	CR	PR	ROCK (CST)		UC	RE	TX	VS	VR
•	•	•	🏛 Gregg Investigations Inc of Janesville (SOP)	800-866-1976	•	•	•	•	
•	•	•	Gregg Investigations Inc of Madison (SOP)	800-866-1976	•	•	•	•	•
•	•	•	Search Associates	414-325-9330	•	•	•		

CV	CR	PR	RUSK (CST)		UC	RE	TX	VS	VR
			Sawyer County Abstract	715-266-2312	•	•	•		
•	•	•	Search Associates	414-325-9330	•	•	•		

CV	CR	PR	SAUK (CST)		UC	RE	TX	VS	VR
•	•	•	Search Associates	414-325-9330	•	•	•		

CV	CR	PR	SAWYER (CST)		UC	RE	TX	VS	VR
			Sawyer County Abstract	715-266-2312	•	•	•		
•	•	•	Search Associates	414-325-9330	•	•	•		

CV	CR	PR	SHAWANO (CST)		UC	RE	TX	VS	VR
•		•	Bay Title and Abstract Inc	414-431-6100	•	•			
•	•	•	🏛 Bill Bonham "The Investigator" (SOP)	715-842-1113	•	•	•	•	
•	•	•	Search Associates	414-325-9330	•	•	•		
•	•	•	Wisconsin Title of Shawano Inc	715-524-2413		•	•		

CV	CR	PR	SHEBOYGAN (CST)		UC	RE	TX	VS	VR
•	•	•	Search Associates 414-325-9330		•	•	•		

CV	CR	PR	ST. CROIX (CST)		UC	RE	TX	VS	VR
•	•	•	🏛 Capitol Lien Records and Research 800-845-4077		•	•	•	•	•
•	•	•	Search Associates 414-325-9330		•	•	•		
•	•	•	St Croix Valley Title Services Inc 715-425-1519		•	•	•		

CV	CR	PR	TAYLOR (CST)		UC	RE	TX	VS	VR
•	•	•	🏛 Bill Bonham "The Investigator" (SOP)........................... 715-842-1113		•	•	•	•	
•	•	•	Search Associates 414-325-9330		•	•	•		

CV	CR	PR	TREMPEALEAU (CST)		UC	RE	TX	VS	VR
•	•	•	Search Associates 414-325-9330		•	•	•		

CV	CR	PR	VERNON (CST)		UC	RE	TX	VS	VR
•	•	•	Search Associates 414-325-9330		•	•	•		

CV	CR	PR	VILAS (CST)		UC	RE	TX	VS	VR
•		•	Northern Title of Vilas County 715-479-6459		•	•	•		
•	•	•	Search Associates 414-325-9330		•	•	•		

CV	CR	PR	WALWORTH (CST)		UC	RE	TX	VS	VR
•	•	•	Process Associates/Milwaukee (SOP)............................. 414-271-9574		•	•	•	•	•
•	•	•	Search Associates 414-325-9330		•	•	•		

CV	CR	PR	WASHBURN (CST)		UC	RE	TX	VS	VR
•	•	•	Search Associates 414-325-9330		•	•	•		

CV	CR	PR	WASHINGTON (CST)		UC	RE	TX	VS	VR
•	•	•	Process Associates/Milwaukee (SOP)............................. 414-271-9574		•	•	•	•	•
•	•	•	Search Associates 414-325-9330		•	•	•		
•	•	•	🏛 The Todd Wiegele Research Co Inc 800-754-7800		•	•	•	•	

CV	CR	PR	WAUKESHA (CST)		UC	RE	TX	VS	VR
•	•		Interstate Reporting Co Inc (IRC) 800-837-6635		•		•		
•	•		Mueller, Aaron S 414-821-3405						
•	•	•	Process Associates/Milwaukee (SOP)............................. 414-271-9574		•	•	•	•	•
•	•	•	Search Associates 414-325-9330		•	•	•		
•	•	•	🏛 The Todd Wiegele Research Co Inc 800-754-7800		•	•	•	•	

CV	CR	PR	WAUPACA (CST)		UC	RE	TX	VS	VR
•		•	Bay Title and Abstract Inc 414-431-6100		•	•	•		
•	•	•	🏛 Bill Bonham "The Investigator" (SOP)........................... 715-842-1113		•	•	•	•	
•	•	•	Search Associates 414-325-9330		•	•	•		

CV	CR	PR	WAUSHARA (CST)		UC	RE	TX	VS	VR
		•	Boles-Wallner Abstract and Title 715-423-6940		•	•	•		
•	•	•	Search Associates 414-325-9330		•	•	•		

CV	CR	PR	WINNEBAGO (CST)		UC	RE	TX	VS	VR
•		•	Bay Title and Abstract Inc 414-431-6100		•	•	•		
•	•	•	Search Associates 414-325-9330		•	•	•		

CV	CR	PR	WOOD (CST)		UC	RE	TX	VS	VR
•	•	•	🏛 Bill Bonham "The Investigator" (SOP)........................... 715-842-1113		•	•	•	•	
		•	Boles-Wallner Abstract and Title 715-423-6940		•	•			
•	•	•	Search Associates 414-325-9330		•	•	•		

WYOMING

	CV	CR	PR	ALBANY (MST)		UC	RE	TX	VS	VR
	●	●	●	Bontecou Investigative Services (SOP) 307-733-2637		●	●	●		●
	●	●	●	Deister Ward & Witcher of WY 800-829-8434		●	●	●	●	
	●	●	●	Executive Title Insurance Agency 307-638-4853		●	●	●		

	CV	CR	PR	BIG HORN (MST)		UC	RE	TX	VS	VR
	●	●	●	Deister Ward & Witcher of WY 800-829-8434		●	●	●	●	

	CV	CR	PR	CAMPBELL (MST)		UC	RE	TX	VS	VR
	●	●	●	Deister Ward & Witcher of WY 800-829-8434		●	●	●	●	
	●	●	●	Frontier Cultural Service 605-673-2157		●	●	●	●	

	CV	CR	PR	CARBON (MST)		UC	RE	TX	VS	VR
	●	●	●	Deister Ward & Witcher of WY 800-829-8434		●	●	●	●	

	CV	CR	PR	CONVERSE (MST)		UC	RE	TX	VS	VR
	●	●	●	Deister Ward & Witcher of WY 800-829-8434		●	●	●	●	
	●	●	●	NatCon Searches Inc 888-436-5576		●	●	●		

	CV	CR	PR	CROOK (MST)		UC	RE	TX	VS	VR
	●	●	●	Deister Ward & Witcher of WY 800-829-8434		●	●	●	●	
	●		●	First American Title Guaranty 307-283-1844		●	●	●		
	●	●	●	Frontier Cultural Service 605-673-2157		●	●	●	●	

	CV	CR	PR	FREMONT (MST)		UC	RE	TX	VS	VR
	●	●	●	Deister Ward & Witcher of WY 800-829-8434		●	●	●	●	

	CV	CR	PR	GOSHEN (MST)		UC	RE	TX	VS	VR
	●	●	●	Deister Ward & Witcher of WY 800-829-8434		●	●	●	●	
	●	●	●	Executive Title Insurance Agency 307-638-4853		●	●	●		

	CV	CR	PR	HOT SPRINGS (MST)		UC	RE	TX	VS	VR
	●	●	●	Deister Ward & Witcher of WY 800-829-8434		●	●	●	●	

	CV	CR	PR	JOHNSON (MST)		UC	RE	TX	VS	VR
	●	●	●	Deister Ward & Witcher of WY 800-829-8434		●	●	●	●	

DT	BK	CV	CR	PR	LARAMIE (CAPITAL) (MST)		UC	RE	TX	VS	VR
●	●	●	●	●	Bontecou Investigative Services (SOP) 307-733-2637		●	●	●		●
●	●	●	●	●	Deister Ward & Witcher of WY 800-829-8434		●	●	●	●	
●	●	●	●	●	Executive Title Insurance Agency 307-638-4853		●	●	●		
●	●				🏛 Hogan Information Services 405-278-6954						

	CV	CR	PR	LINCOLN (MST)		UC	RE	TX	VS	VR
	●	●	●	Deister Ward & Witcher of WY 800-829-8434		●	●	●	●	
	●	●	●	Land Title Co 800-365-7720		●	●	●	●	

	CV	CR	PR	NATRONA (MST)		UC	RE	TX	VS	VR
	●	●	●	Deister Ward & Witcher of WY 800-829-8434		●	●	●	●	
	●	●	●	NatCon Searches Inc 888-436-5576		●	●	●		
	●		●	Petroleum Title Service Inc 307-235-6237		●	●	●		

	CV	CR	PR	NIOBRARA (MST)		UC	RE	TX	VS	VR
	●	●	●	Deister Ward & Witcher of WY 800-829-8434		●	●	●	●	
	●	●	●	Frontier Cultural Service 605-673-2157		●	●	●	●	

	CV	CR	PR	PARK (MST)		UC	RE	TX	VS	VR
	●	●	●	Deister Ward & Witcher of WY 800-829-8434		●	●	●	●	

	CV	CR	PR	PLATTE (MST)		UC	RE	TX	VS	VR
	●	●	●	Deister Ward & Witcher of WY 800-829-8434		●	●	●	●	
	●	●	●	Executive Title Insurance Agency 307-638-4853		●	●	●		

CV	CR	PR	SHERIDAN (MST)		UC	RE	TX	VS	VR
•	•	•	Deister Ward & Witcher of WY 800-829-8434		•	•	•	•	

CV	CR	PR	SUBLETTE (MST)		UC	RE	TX	VS	VR
•	•	•	Deister Ward & Witcher of WY 800-829-8434		•	•	•	•	
•	•	•	Land Title Co 800-365-7720		•	•	•	•	

CV	CR	PR	SWEETWATER (MST)		UC	RE	TX	VS	VR
•	•	•	Deister Ward & Witcher of WY 800-829-8434		•	•	•	•	

CV	CR	PR	TETON (MST)		UC	RE	TX	VS	VR
•	•	•	Bontecou Investigative Services (SOP) 307-733-2637		•	•	•		•
•	•	•	Deister Ward & Witcher of WY 800-829-8434		•	•	•	•	
•	•	•	Land Title Co 800-365-7720		•	•	•	•	

CV	CR	PR	UINTA (MST)		UC	RE	TX	VS	VR
•	•	•	Deister Ward & Witcher of WY 800-829-8434		•	•	•	•	

CV	CR	PR	WASHAKIE (MST)		UC	RE	TX	VS	VR
•	•	•	Deister Ward & Witcher of WY 800-829-8434		•	•	•	•	

CV	CR	PR	WESTON (MST)		UC	RE	TX	VS	VR
•	•	•	Deister Ward & Witcher of WY 800-829-8434		•	•	•	•	
•	•	•	Frontier Cultural Service 605-673-2157		•	•	•	•	

Section Two

Retriever Profiles

A

A & A Attorney Services Inc

Phone: 509-325-0001
Fax: 509-328-3226

621 W Mallon Ave Suite 505
Spokane WA 99201-2181

Local Retrieval Area: WA-Spokane.

Normal turnaround time: 5 days. Projects are generally billed by the hour. The first project may require a prepayment.

Correspondent relationships: a network for the rest of Washington. They specialize in marriage/divorce and birth/death searches.

A & A Background Screening

Phone: 303-457-9223
Fax: 303-457-9223

11357 Fowler Dr
Northglenn CO 80233

Local Retrieval Area: CO-Adams, Arapahoe, Denver, Douglas, Jefferson.

Normal turnaround time: 11 day to 1 week. Projects are generally billed by the number of records located. The first project may require a prepayment. Terms are net 30 days upon approved credit. They specialize primarily in pre-employment background screening.

A & A Legal Services

Phone: 415-697-9431
Fax: 415-697-4640

849 Mitten Suite 10
Burlingame CA 94010

Local Retrieval and SOP Area: CA-San Francisco, San Mateo.

Normal turnaround time: a week to 10 days. However, rush service of 24-48 hours is also available. They charge by mile and/or per copy. The first project may require a prepayment.

A & M Attorney Services Inc

Phone: 310-426-8306
Fax: 310-426-6384

3831 Atlantic Ave
Long Beach CA 90807

Local Retrieval and SOP Area: CA-Los Angeles, Orange.

Normal turnaround time: 1-4 days. Projects are generally billed by the hour. Credit accounts are accepted.

A California Process & Atty Svc

Phone: 909-381-5185
Fax: 909-885-5199

206 S "D" St
San Bernardino CA 92401

Local Retrieval and SOP Area: CA-Los Angeles, Orange, Riverside, San Bernardino.

Normal turnaround time: 1-3 days. Projects are generally billed by the hour. The first project may require a prepayment.

Correspondent relationships: nationwide. They specialize in civil and real estate searches, process service and all attorney support services, including mobile photocopying and notary service.

A Fast Copy Inc

Phone: 510-462-9191
Fax: 510-846-6184

397 Ray St
Pleasanton CA 94566

Local Retrieval and SOP Area: CA-Alameda, Contra Costa.

Normal turnaround time: 15-30 days. Online computer ordering is also available. Projects are generally billed by the number of names searched or records located. Terms are net 30 days.

They specialize in microfilm, photocopy and reproduction of medical and legal records for personal injury or workers compensation claims and subpoena preparation and service.

A Higher Legal Process

Phone: 800-528-9474
513-222-6829
Fax: 513-222-4503

345 W 2nd St Suite 7
Dayton OH 45402

Local Retrieval Area: OH-Montgomery.

Normal turnaround time: varied depending on project. Projects are generally billed by the number of names searched or records located. The first project may require a prepayment.

Correspondent relationships: Greene, Darke, Preble, Miami, Clark, Warren and Butler.

A P Legal Support Services

Phone: 410-366-9109
Fax: 410-366-9403

2522 N Calvert St
Baltimore MD 21218

Local Retrieval Area: MD-Anne Arundel, Baltimore, City of Baltimore, Carroll, Harford, Howard, Prince George's.

Normal turnaround time: 24-48 hours. Expedited service available. Projects are generally billed by the hour. Credit accounts are accepted.

🏛 A Scott Broadhurst Associates

Phone: 617-536-3486
Fax: 508-785-2852

12 Main St
Dover MA 02030

Local Retrieval Area: MA-Essex, Middlesex, Norfolk, Suffolk, Worcester.

Normal turnaround time: 24-48 hours. A same day rush service is also available. Projects are generally billed by the number of names searched. Credit accounts are accepted.

They specialize in UCC, court record searches and real estate record searches.

A Short Abstract Co

Phone: 701-265-4176

PO Box 657
Cavalier ND 58220

Local Retrieval Area: ND-Pembina.

Normal turnaround time: 2 weeks. Fee basis will vary by type of project. Projects require prepayment.

They specialize in title searches and abstracts of title.

A Verne Baker Abstract Co

Phone: 816-385-6474
Fax: 816-385-6629

107 W Bourke St
Macon MO 63552

Local Retrieval Area: MO-Macon.

Normal turnaround time: next day. Projects are generally billed by the number of names searched. Credit accounts are accepted.

They specialize in title searches.

🏛 A Very Private Eye Inc

Phone: 800-277-7095
407-273-6646
Fax: 407-658-2555

4589 Southfield Ave
Orlando FL 32812

Local Retrieval and SOP Area: FL-Brevard, Lake, Orange, Osceola, Polk, Seminole.

Normal turnaround time: 24 hours. Online computer ordering is also available. Projects are generally billed by the hour. The first project may require a prepayment.

They specialize in electronic sweeps, backgrounds, intelligence, covert equipment, domestics, locates, formal government wiretapping export. They are 25 year law enforcement veterans. Cover all of Central FL, both civil and criminal investigations.

A+ Abstracting

Phone: 803-236-1072
Fax: 803-236-0806

PO Box 14261
Surfside Beach SC 29587

Local Retrieval Area: SC-Florence, Georgetown, Horry, Marion.

Normal turnaround time: 2 days. Fee basis varies by type of transaction. Credit accounts are accepted. Payment due upon receipt.

A-1 Hanline Investigations

Phone: 803-684-3200
Fax: 803-684-0600

67 N Congress Suite 200
York SC 29745

Local Retrieval and SOP Area: NC-Cleveland, Gaston, Mecklenburg, Rutherford, Union; SC-Cherokee, Chester, Lancaster, Union, York.

Normal turnaround time: 1 to 3 days. Online computer ordering is also available. Projects are generally billed by the hour. The first project may require a prepayment.

Correspondent relationships: Georgia. They perform pre-employment background checks, workers' compensation investigations, domestic surveillance as well as DMV, drivers license & vehicle registration information and asset searches.

▥ A.S.K. Services Inc

Phone: 313-416-1313
Fax: 313-416-9433

PO Box 87127
Canton MI 48187-0127

Local Retrieval Area: MI-Bay, Genesee, Ingham, Kalamazoo, Kent, Macomb, Oakland, Saginaw, Washtenaw, Wayne.

Normal turnaround time: 24-48 hours. Online computer ordering is also available. Projects are generally billed by the number of names searched. Credit accounts are accepted. Credit cards are accepted.

Correspondent relationships: Statewide contacts allow 24-48 hour service in all counties. They specialize in statewide civil, criminal, bankruptcy searches. UCC, tax lien searches and filings at all counties. They also do expedited real property/title searches.

A.S.S.I.S.T. International

Phone: 800-382-7747
212-244-2074
Fax: 212-563-1576

101 W 29th St
New York NY 10001

Local Retrieval Area: NY-Bronx, Kings, New York, Orange, Putnam, Queens, Richmond, Rockland, Suffolk, Westchester.

Normal turnaround time: immediate to 5 days. Projects are generally billed by the number of names searched. Credit accounts are accepted.

Correspondent relationships: nationwide. They are a full service investigation agency specializing in locates, investigations and surveillance. On-line computer searches are available.

AAA Abstract Co Inc

Phone: 918-696-2770
Fax: 918-696-5869

118 W Olive St
Stilwell OK 74960

Local Retrieval Area: OK-Adair.

Normal turnaround time: 1-10 days. Projects are generally billed by the number of records located. Projects require prepayment. Personal checks are accepted.

They specialize in abstracts by photocopies of actual documents, increasing accuracy of abstract and usefulness to examining attorney.

AAA Abstract Co Inc

Phone: 903-473-2233
Fax: 903-473-3069

PO Box 38 1 Planter St
Emory TX 75440

Local Retrieval Area: TX-Rains.

Normal turnaround time: 3-5 days. Fee basis varies by type of transaction. The first project may require a prepayment.

AAA Process Servers Inc

Phone: 800-293-6098
303-680-6874
Fax: 303-690-9951

PO Box 9114
Denver CO 80209

Local Retrieval and SOP Area: CO-Adams, Arapahoe, Boulder, Denver, Douglas, Jefferson.

Normal turnaround time: 24 hours to 1 week. Projects are generally billed by the hour. The first project may require a prepayment. Personal checks are accepted.

Correspondent relationships: El Paso and Pueblo. They specialize in process service, location of people and court retrieval.

Aalpha Omega Investigations Inc

Phone: 904-433-7016
Fax: 904-433-9689

221 E Garden St Suite 5E
Pensacola FL 32501

Local Retrieval and SOP Area: AL-Baldwin; FL-Escambia, Okaloosa, Santa Rosa, Walton.

Normal turnaround time: 24 hours for Escambia, 1 to 2 days for Santa Rosa, and 3 days for Okaloosa. Projects are generally billed by the number of names searched. The first project may require a prepayment. Credit cards are accepted.

They specialize in private investigations, bail bonds and certified process service.

▥ Aaron Anderson Agency

Phone: 800-408-5350
619-729-7293
Fax: 619-945-4157

785 Grand Ave Suite 100
Carlsbad CA 92008

Local Retrieval and SOP Area: CA-Los Angeles, Orange, Riverside, San Bernardino, San Diego.

Normal turnaround time: 2-3 days. Projects are generally billed by the number of names searched. Credit accounts are accepted. Monthly payment terms available.

Correspondent relationships: nationwide. They specialize in California workers' compensation information. All searches are "hands on". Owner is a retired US Probation/Parole Officer now licensed as a California Private Investigator.

▥ ABC Investigators Inc

Phone: 800-738-7300
318-783-6131
Fax: 318-783-7070

204 Winchester Suite 1A
Lafayette LA 70506

Local Retrieval and SOP Area: LA-Acadia Parish, Jefferson Davis Parish, Lafayette Parish, St. Landry Parish, Vermilion Parish.

Normal turnaround time: the same week. Projects are generally billed by the hour. Credit accounts are accepted.

Correspondent relationships: Acadia. They are a certified legal investigative firm.

▥ ABC Legal Messenger

910 5th Ave
Seattle WA 98104-1137

Phone: 206-682-1675
Fax: 206-624-4285

Local Retrieval and SOP Area: WA-Grays Harbor, Island, King, Kitsap, Lewis, Mason, Pierce, Skagit, Snohomish, Thurston.

Normal turnaround time: 1-2 days. Projects are generally billed by the number of names searched or records located. The first project may require a prepayment. Credit cards are accepted. They will also invoice. Personal checks are accepted.

Correspondent relationships: Whatcom, Clark, Cowlitz, WA; Washington, Multnomah and Clackama, OR. They are on-line with SCOMIS and Pacer, which allows them instant retrieval of court records.

Abeln Abstract Co

PO Box 92
Dubuque IA 52004

Phone: 319-582-7148
Fax: 319-582-5298

Local Retrieval Area: IA-Dubuque.

Normal turnaround time: 1 week. Projects are generally billed by the number of names searched. A charge for time is also included. Credit accounts are accepted.

They specialize in real estate and personal lien searches.

ABI Attorney Service

2038 W Park Ave
Redlands CA 92373

Phone: 800-266-0613
909-793-0613
Fax: 909-792-2590

Local Retrieval and SOP Area: CA-Los Angeles, Orange, San Bernardino.

Normal turnaround time: 10 days. Expedited service available. Projects are generally billed by the hour. Credit accounts are accepted.

They specialize in investigations, statements, court indexing and mobile photocopy. They serve all types of process, civil, family law and US District Courts.

ABIS Inc

PO Box 1150
Stephens City VA 22655-1150

Phone: 800-669-2247
540-687-3060
Fax: 540-687-3749

Local Retrieval Area: DC-District of Columbia; MD-Baltimore, City of Baltimore, Montgomery; VA-City of Alexandria, Arlington, Fairfax, Loudoun, Prince George, Prince William.

Normal turnaround time: 3-5 days. Online computer ordering is also available. Projects are generally billed by the number of names searched. Credit accounts are accepted.

Correspondent relationships: nationwide. They specialize in pre-employment screening.

Able Abstract Co Inc

300 Keystone St
Hawley PA 18428

Phone: 717-226-3358
Fax: 717-226-3473

Local Retrieval Area: PA-Pike, Wayne.

Normal turnaround time: 1-3 days for Wayne County, and 1-7 days for Pike County. Projects are generally billed by the hour. Credit accounts are accepted.

Patricia Abruzzino

Rt 4 Box 132A
Grafton WV 26354

Phone: 304-265-1401
Fax: 304-265-3016

Local Retrieval Area: WV-Taylor.

Normal turnaround time: 2-3 days. Projects are generally billed by the number of names searched. Credit accounts are accepted.

Abstract & Guarantee Co

812 Manuel Ave
Chandler OK 74834

Phone: 405-258-1244
Fax: 405-258-1657

Local Retrieval Area: OK-Lincoln.

Normal turnaround time: 48 hours. Fee basis will vary by the type of project. Credit accounts are accepted.

Abstract & Title Co of Mesa Co

PO Box 3738
Grand Junction CO 81502

Phone: 303-242-8234
Fax: 303-241-4925

Local Retrieval Area: CO-Mesa.

Normal turnaround time: 48 hours. Fee basis will vary by the type of project. Credit accounts are accepted.

They specialize in real estate title and escrow services.

Abstract & Title Guaranty Co

326 5th Ave S
Clinton IA 52732-4511

Phone: 800-483-2842
319-243-2027
Fax: 319-243-6108

Local Retrieval Area: IA-Clinton.

Normal turnaround time: 2-3 days. Expedited service available. Fee basis varies by type of transaction. Credit accounts are accepted.

Abstract & Title Services Inc

503 W Main PO Box 26
Anamosa IA 52205

Phone: 319-462-4828
Fax: 319-462-4958

Local Retrieval Area: IA-Jones.

Normal turnaround time: 1-5 days. Projects are generally billed by the number of names searched. Projects require prepayment.

Correspondent relationships: Linn and Scott Counties, Iowa and Rock Island, Illinois.

Abstract and Title Co

PO Box 720
Watford City ND 58854-0720

Phone: 701-842-3366
Fax: 701-842-2709

Local Retrieval Area: ND-McKenzie.

Normal turnaround time: varied depending on project. Projects are generally billed by the number of names searched. The first project may require a prepayment. Personal checks are accepted.

Abstract and Title Inc

413 D St PO Box 246
Fairbury NE 68352

Phone: 402-729-2771
Fax: 402-729-6366

Local Retrieval Area: NE-Jefferson.

Normal turnaround time: 24 hours. Projects are generally billed by the number of records located. Fee basis is per description of one ownership. The first project may require a prepayment.

Correspondent relationships: Gage, Saline and Thayer. They specialize in abstracting, title insurance, closing and research. They have been in business over 30 years and have a 100-year title plant.

Abstract and Title Services-Carlton

Phone: 218-384-3450
Fax: 218-384-3451

PO Box 556 210 3rd St
Carlton MN 55718

Local Retrieval and SOP Area: MN-Carlton, St. Louis; WI-Douglas.

Normal turnaround time: 24 hours, depending on travel time. Projects are generally billed by the hour. Credit accounts are accepted.

They specialize in real estate. However, they do searches for UCC filings, court judgments, tax liens, probate records and bankruptcy documents filed in the Recorder's office. They have access to the US Bankruptcy Court and judgment records in Duluth.

Abstract Associates of Lancaster

Phone: 717-291-5841
Fax: 717-291-4449

1903 Lititz Pike
Lancaster PA 17601-3805

Local Retrieval and SOP Area: PA-Berks, Chester, Dauphin, Lancaster, Lebanon, York.

Normal turnaround time: 1 week. Expedited service available. Fee basis will vary by the type of project. Credit accounts are accepted.

They specialize in lien searches, deed searches, financing statements, and document retrieval.

Abstract Enterprises Inc

Phone: 717-963-5290
Fax: 717-963-5291

628 Spruce St
Scranton PA 18503

Local Retrieval Area: PA-Lackawanna.

Normal turnaround time: 3 days. Fee basis will vary by the type of project. Credit accounts are accepted.

Abstract Land Associates Inc

Phone: 717-763-1450
Fax: 717-763-1664

3915 Market St
Camp Hill PA 17011

Local Retrieval Area: PA-Adams, Cumberland, Dauphin, Franklin, Lancaster, Lebanon, Perry.

Normal turnaround time: 3 days. Fee basis will vary by the type of project. The first project may require a prepayment.

They specialize in real estate.

Abstract One Inc

Phone: 717-854-3676
Fax: 717-845-1494

721 S George St
York PA 17403

Local Retrieval Area: PA-Adams, York.

Normal turnaround time: 24-48 hours. Fee basis will vary by the type of project. The first project may require a prepayment.

Correspondent relationships: Lancaster, Cumberland and Dauphin. They specialize in lien searches, criminal checks and UCC reports.

Abstracting and Legal Research

Phone: 318-473-9979
Fax: 318-449-9739

PO Box 127
Alexandria LA 71309-0127

Local Retrieval Area: LA-Allen Parish, Avoyelles Parish, Evangeline Parish, Grant Parish, Natchitoches Parish, Rapides Parish, Sabine Parish, St. Landry Parish, Vernon Parish.

Normal turnaround time: 48 hours for direct parishes and over 48 hours for the remainder of the state. Projects are generally billed by the number of names searched. The first project may require a prepayment.

Correspondent relationships: the remainder of the state. They specialize in parish records.

Abstractor Associates

Phone: 810-778-7554
Fax: 810-778-9730

17639 Woodland
Roseville MI 48066

Local Retrieval Area: MI-Genesee, Kalamazoo, Kent, Livingston, Macomb, Monroe, Oakland, St. Clair, Washtenaw, Wayne.

Normal turnaround time: 48 hours. Expedited service 24 hours. Projects are generally billed by the number of names searched. Credit accounts are accepted.

Correspondent relationships: Lenawee, Lapeer, Mason, Ingham, Tuscola, Huron, Bay, Saginaw, Berrien, Van Buren, Ottowa, Muskegon, Shiawasee. They specialize in asset/lien searches, litigation search and retrieval.

Abstracts by Godail

Phone: 800-660-7318
504-343-0351
Fax: 504-343-1341

251 Florida Blvd Suite 212
Baton Rouge LA 70801

Local Retrieval Area: LA-Ascension Parish, Assumption Parish, East Baton Rouge Parish, Livingston Parish, Pointe Coupee Parish, Rapides Parish, St. Landry Parish, West Baton Rouge Parish.

Normal turnaround time: 1-2 days. Projects are generally billed by the hour. The first project may require a prepayment.

They have been established for over 20 years.

Abstracts Inc

Phone: 402-879-4341
Fax: 402-879-4341

PO Box 465 306 N National
Superior NE 68978

Local Retrieval Area: NE-Nuckolls.

Normal turnaround time: 1 week. Fee basis varies by type of transaction. Credit accounts are accepted.

ACB Credit Services

Phone: 918-756-7741
Fax: 918-583-1001

PO Box 846
Okmulgee OK 74447

Local Retrieval Area: OK-Okmulgee.

Normal turnaround time: 2 days. Projects are generally billed by the number of names searched. The first project may require a prepayment. Credit cards are accepted.

Correspondent relationships: McIntosh and Okfuskie. They specialize in judgments and titles.

Accelerated Legal Services (ALS)

Phone: 510-417-1854
Fax: 510-886-9067

5052 Glenwood Ct Suite 10023
Pleasanton CA 94588-3715

Local Retrieval Area: CA-Alameda, Contra Costa, San Francisco.

Normal turnaround time: 48-72 hours. Expedited service available. Fee basis will vary by type of project. Credit accounts are accepted.

ALS has a second office: PO Box 1134, Sacramento, CA 95812.

Access Information

Phone: 800-827-7607
303-778-7677
Fax: 303-778-7691

900 E Louisiana Ave Suite 209
Denver CO 80210

Local Retrieval Area: CO-Arapahoe, Boulder, Denver, Jefferson.

Normal turnaround time: same or next day. Projects are generally billed by the hour. Credit accounts are accepted.

Correspondent relationships: most of Colorado and nationwide. They specialize in document research and retrieval.

Access Information Services Inc
Phone: 800-388-1598
518-452-1873
1773 Western Ave
Albany NY 12203
Fax: 800-388-1599
518-452-0822

Local Retrieval and SOP Area: NY-Albany, Rensselaer, Saratoga, Schenectady.

Normal turnaround time: 24-36 hours. Projects are generally billed by the number of names searched. The first project may require a prepayment.

Correspondent relationships: nationwide. They specialize in UCC preparation, filing and searching. Will search any public record nationwide.

Access Louisiana Inc
Phone: 800-489-5620
318-227-9730
400 Travis St Suite 1308
Shreveport LA 71101
Fax: 318-222-3053

Local Retrieval Area: LA-Acadia ParishAll Parishes.

Normal turnaround time: 72 hours. Projects are generally billed by the number of names searched. They offer a discount for volume. Credit accounts are accepted. Personal checks are accepted.

Correspondent relationships: Texas and Florida extensively and nationwide. They provide registered agent services for Louisiana & all corporate services & filings with the Secretary of State. They are on-line with the UCC system and corporate database with the Secretary of State.

Access Research
Phone: 800-456-9613
619-941-2887
1140 Prospect Place
Vista CA 92083
Fax: 619-941-2823

Local Retrieval Area: CA-Los Angeles, Orange, Riverside, San Bernardino, San Diego.

Normal turnaround time: 24-48 hours. Projects are generally billed by the number of names searched. Credit accounts are accepted.

Correspondent relationships: entire State of California. Also online with Colorado and Oklahoma civil and criminal databases. They specialize in criminal and civil searches throughout California. Also provide vital records, federal, bankruptcy and DMV records. Federal Records Center also accessed.

Access Research Center Inc
Phone: 305-771-0499
2761 NE 55th St
Fax: 305-772-9679
Fort Lauderdale FL 33308

Local Retrieval Area: FL-Broward.

Normal turnaround time: 24 hours. Projects are generally billed by the number of names searched. The first project may require a prepayment.

They specialize in document research and retrieval, county and state UCC searches, corporate, real estate, DMV and tax lien searches in Broward County.

Access Research Staff
Phone: 512-321-1889
1108 Chestnut St Suite A
Fax: 512-321-1889
Bastrop TX 78602

Local Retrieval Area: TX-Austin, Bastrop, Bexar, Caldwell, Comal, Harris, Hays, Lee, Travis.

Normal turnaround time: 24 hours. Projects are generally billed by the number of names searched. Also add trip charge. The first project may require a prepayment.

Correspondent relationships: all of Texas. They specialize in litigation support, oil and gas and title work.

Accessible Paralegal Services
Phone: 209-264-3412
532 N Fulton St
Fax: 209-264-0121
Fresno CA 93728-3402

Local Retrieval and SOP Area: CA-Fresno, Kings, Madera, Tulare.

Normal turnaround time: within 24 hour. Some courts records which have been archived take as long as 10 days depending on the county. Projects are generally billed by the number of names searched or records located. The first project may require a prepayment.

They specialize in all types of court records research and Workers' Compensation Appeal Board records.

Accountable Process Servers
Phone: 612-427-0225
222 E Main St Suite #110B
Fax: 612-427-2961
Anoka MN 55303

Local Retrieval and SOP Area: MN-Anoka, Hennepin, Isanti, Ramsey, Sherburne.

Normal turnaround time: 2 days. Projects are generally billed by the number of names searched. Credit accounts are accepted.

Correspondent relationships: the seven county metro area. They specialize in record retrieval and process serving.

Accu-Fax Employment Screening
Phone: 215-234-0700
1463D Gravel Pike PO Box 177
Fax: 215-234-0905
Perkiomenville PA 18074-0177

Local Retrieval Area: DE-Kent, New Castle, Sussex; NJ-Burlington, Camden, Gloucester; PA-Bucks, Chester, Montgomery, Philadelphia.

Normal turnaround time: 24-48 hours. Online computer ordering is also available. Projects are generally billed by the number of names searched. Fees are by county searched. The first project may require a prepayment.

Correspondent relationships: nationwide. They specialize in a full service program for all facets of employment screening. They also do motor vehicle records, UCC, civil litigation and property research.

Accu-Screen Inc
Phone: 800-689-2228
813-288-1920
PO Box 20767 5305 S MacDill Ave (33611)
Tampa FL 33622-0767
Fax: 813-288-1839

Local Retrieval Area: FL-Broward, Collier, Hillsborough, Orange, Pasco, Pinellas; IL-Cook, Du Page.

Normal turnaround time: 24-72 hours. Online computer ordering is also available. Projects are generally billed by the number of names searched. The first project may require a prepayment.

Correspondent relationships: nationwide. They specialize in county criminal records from over 3000 county courthouses throughout the United States.

Accu-Source Inc
Phone: 214-637-5006
8585 Stemmons Suite 1726
Fax: 214-637-1443
Dallas TX 75247

Local Retrieval Area: TX-Dallas.

Projects are generally billed by the number of names searched. Credit accounts are accepted. Terms are net 30 days.

Accu-Tech Professional Services

Phone: 800-275-7189
319 Elm St #101 PO Box 12037   619-232-9905
San Diego CA 92101   **Fax:** 619-232-5928
Local Retrieval and SOP Area: CA-San Diego.

Normal turnaround time: 4 days. Projects are generally billed by the number of names searched or records located. The first project may require a prepayment.

They specialize in court research and record retrieval.

Accurate Abstracts Inc

Phone: 410-819-0334
23651 Mt Pleasant Landing Circle   **Fax:** 410-745-9916
St Michaels MD 21663
Local Retrieval Area: MD-Talbot.

Normal turnaround time: 24 hours. Projects are generally billed by the number of names searched. Credit accounts are accepted.

Accurate Legal Service

Phone: 800-236-9853
331 8th St NE   202-547-5710
Washington DC 20002   **Fax:** 202-547-7836
Local Retrieval and SOP Area: DC-District of Columbia; MD-Montgomery, Prince George's; VA-Fairfax.

Normal turnaround time: 3-4 days. Projects are generally billed by the hour. The first project may require a prepayment.

Accurate Legal Services

Phone: 941-365-3335
PO Drawer 4635   **Fax:** 941-953-5616
Sarasota FL 34230
Local Retrieval and SOP Area: FL-Manatee, Sarasota.

Normal turnaround time: 2-4 business days. Online computer ordering is also available. Projects are generally billed by the hour. Travel expenses will be added to the fee for Manatee County (Bradenzon). Projects require prepayment. Visa is accepted.

They specialize in process service and database research including corporate, UCC, Department of Motor Vehicles, driver's license and social security number traces.

Accurate Research Inc

Phone: 800-628-0303
15028 S Cicero PO Box 465   708-535-0303
Oak Forest IL 60452   **Fax:** 708-535-2322
Local Retrieval Area: IL-Cook, Du Page, Kane, Lake, McHenry, Peoria, Will; IN-Lake.

Normal turnaround time: 48-72 hours. Projects are generally billed by the number of names searched. The first project may require a prepayment. Credit cards are accepted. Bi-monthly invoice available after first project prepayment.

Correspondent relationships: nationwide. They specialize in criminal and civil record searches. They also provide employment screening services.

AccuScreen Systems

Phone: 800-383-6476
717 Royal St   504-343-8378
Baton Rouge LA 70802   **Fax:** 504-343-8378
Local Retrieval and SOP Area: LA-East Baton Rouge Parish, West Baton Rouge Parish.

Normal turnaround time: 2 days. Projects are generally billed by the number of names searched. The first project may require a prepayment. Monthly billing available.

They specialize in criminal background checks, investigative services, pre-employment screening and drug testing.

🏛 AccuSearch

Phone: 800-962-7019
202 E McDowell Rd   602-252-8370
Phoenix AZ 85004   **Fax:** 800-632-2104
     602-252-8109
Local Retrieval Area: AZ-Maricopa.

Normal turnaround time: 24-48 hours. Online computer ordering is also available. Projects are generally billed by the number of names searched. Fee may also be based by index. Credit accounts are accepted.

Correspondent relationships: statewide. They specialize in multi-jurisdictional search and filing services including UCCs, liens, litigation, criminal, motor vehicle, real property and bankruptcy.

Accutrak

Phone: 972-390-2195
PO Box 260   **Fax:** 972-390-2195
Allen TX 75013
Local Retrieval Area: TX-Collin, Dallas, Hunt, Rockwall, Tarrant.

Normal turnaround time: 48 hours. Online computer ordering is also available. Projects are generally billed by the hour. Credit accounts are accepted. Payment due upon receipt.

Correspondent relationships: nationwide. They specialize in background investigations, missing persons, business competitive intelligence and asset searches.

ACE Legal Assistance

Phone: 415-864-2020
75 Lily Suite 202
San Francisco CA 94102
Local Retrieval and SOP Area: CA-Alameda, Contra Costa, Marin, San Francisco, Santa Clara.

Normal turnaround time: 3-5 days. They charge a flat rate per job. The first project may require a prepayment.

Correspondent relationships: Sonoma, San Mateo. They specialize in process serving, including summons and complaints, subpoenas, bank levy and wage attachments.

ACME Research

Phone: 218-224-3239
Rt 1 Box 91   **Fax:** 218-224-3239
Guthrie MN 56461-9728
Local Retrieval and SOP Area: MN-Beltrami, Cass, Hubbard.

Normal turnaround time: 72 hours. Online computer ordering is also available. Projects are generally billed by the hour. The first project may require a prepayment. Personal checks are accepted.

They specialize in personal injury investigation.

Action Agency

Phone: 208-263-9586
PO Box 704   **Fax:** 208-263-7032
Sandpoint ID 83864
Local Retrieval and SOP Area: ID-Benewah, Bonner, Boundary, Kootenai, Latah, Nez Perce, Shoshone; MT-Lincoln, Sanders; WA-Pend Oreille.

Normal turnaround time: 48 hours. Projects are generally billed by the hour. Credit accounts are accepted.

Correspondent relationships: nationwide. They specialize in locating missing persons.

Action Court Services Inc

Phone: 800-227-1174
15403 Grand Ave #2D PO Box 309 (92531-0309)
909-678-8259
Lake Elsinore CA 92530
Fax: 800-227-1109
909-678-5292

Local Retrieval Area: CA-Imperial, Los Angeles, Orange, Riverside, San Bernardino, San Diego, Sonoma, Ventura.

Normal turnaround time: 7-10 days. 1-2 days if rush job. Projects are generally billed by the number of records located. Credit accounts are accepted. Payment due upon receipt.

Correspondent relationships: nationwide.

Action Legal Support Services

Phone: 209-432-3337
5528 N Palm Suite 123
Fax: 209-432-1140
Fresno CA 93704

Local Retrieval and SOP Area: CA-Fresno.

Normal turnaround time: within 1 week. Projects are generally billed by the number of names searched or records located. The first project may require a prepayment.

Correspondent relationships: Tulare, Kings, Merced, Madera, Kern and Stanislaus, CA counties.

Action Process Service

Phone: 716-692-5032
PO Box 215
Fax: 716-692-5039
Buffalo NY 14215

Local Retrieval and SOP Area: NY-Erie, Niagara.

Normal turnaround time: varied depending on project. Projects are generally billed by the number of names searched. The first project may require a prepayment.

Correspondent relationships: the rest of New York.

Active Detective Bureau Inc

Phone: 513-541-6600
4239 Hamilton Ave
Fax: 513-541-4989
Cincinnati OH 45223-2033

Local Retrieval and SOP Area: KY-Boone, Kenton; OH-Butler, Hamilton.

Projects are generally billed by the hour. The first project may require a prepayment. Process service requires prepayment.

They are a full service investigative and process service company.

Acumen Investigations

Phone: 904-668-0824
1704 Thomasville Rd Box 214
Fax: 904-668-0824
Tallahassee FL 32303

Local Retrieval and SOP Area: FL-Franklin, Gadsden, Jefferson, Leon, Liberty, Wakulla.

Normal turnaround time: 1-3 days for Leon County. Projects are generally billed by the number of names searched. Credit accounts are accepted.

Correspondent relationships: the rest of Florida. They specialize in insurance defense/video surveillance, missing persons, process service, background investigations, matrimonial investigations, research and general investigations.

AD Services

Phone: 800-827-9101
39175 Liberty St Suite 215
510-795-1111
Fremont CA 94538
Fax: 510-793-2222

Local Retrieval and SOP Area: CA-Alameda, Contra Costa, Santa Clara.

Normal turnaround time: 2-5 days. Projects are generally billed by the hour. Credit accounts are accepted. All individuals must prepay, all companies are invoiced.

Adair County Abstract

Phone: 800-798-6129
230 Public Square
515-743-6129
Greenfield IA 50849

Local Retrieval Area: IA-Adair.

Normal turnaround time: 1-2 days. They charge a flat rate per project. Credit accounts are accepted.

Adams County Abstract Co

Phone: 701-567-2224
602 Adams Ave
Fax: 701-567-2910
Hettinger ND 58639

Local Retrieval Area: ND-Adams.

Normal turnaround time: 7-10 days. Fee basis will vary by the amount of time to perform the search. Projects require prepayment. They will also invoice.

They specialize in title and mineral searches.

Adams County Land Titles

Phone: 608-339-6634
PO Box 189
Fax: 608-339-9248
Friendship WI 53934

Local Retrieval Area: WI-Adams.

Normal turnaround time: 2-3 days. Fee basis varies by type of transaction. The first project may require a prepayment.

Adams Land Title

Phone: 402-463-4198
PO Box 1347
Fax: 402-463-6480
Hastings NE 68901

Local Retrieval Area: NE-Adams, Buffalo, Clay, Fillmore, Hall, Hamilton, Kearney, Nuckolls, Phelps, Webster.

Normal turnaround time: 2-3 days. Projects are generally billed by the number of records located. The first project may require a prepayment.

Correspondent relationships: the rest of Nebraska.

Adams Land Title

Phone: 308-995-5615
909 Tilden St
Holdrege NE 68949-1759

Local Retrieval Area: NE-Buffalo, Franklin, Harlan, Kearney, Phelps, Webster.

Normal turnaround time: 2-3 days..dd. Projects are generally billed by the number of records located. Credit accounts are accepted.

Correspondent relationships: Adams, Clay, Fillmore, Hall, Hamilton, and Nuckolls counties. They have a FAX number, but would prefer not to publish it.

Tommy M Adams

Phone: 915-648-3024
PO Box 782
Fax: 915-648-3067
Goldthwaite TX 76844

Local Retrieval Area: TX-Brown, Comanche, Hamilton, Lampasas, Mills, San Saba.

Normal turnaround time: 1-2 days. Projects are generally billed by the hour. The first project may require a prepayment.

He is an attorney in general practice.

Adila-Gray Process Servers

Phone: 510-582-8812
PO Box 2888
Fax: 510-582-6296
Castro Valley CA 94546

Local Retrieval and SOP Area: CA-Alameda, Contra Costa.

Normal turnaround time: 48 hours. Expedited service available. Projects are generally billed by the hour. The first project may require a prepayment.

Charles E Adkins

Phone: 804-843-4060
Fax: 804-843-9180

PO Box 112
West Point VA 23181

Local Retrieval Area: VA-Gloucester, King William, King and Queen, Middlesex, New Kent.

Normal turnaround time: up to a week. Projects are generally billed by the hour. The first project may require a prepayment.

☰ ADM & Associates Inc

Phone: 800-242-5999
205-525-5260
Fax: 205-525-4289

132 Windward Circle
Vincent AL 35178

Local Retrieval Area: AL-Calhoun, Etowah, Houston, Jefferson, Lee, Madison, Mobile, Montgomery, Talladega, Tuscaloosa.

Normal turnaround time: 24 hours. Projects are generally billed by the number of names searched. Credit accounts are accepted. Payable upon receipt of report unless other arrangements have been made.

They specialize in pre-employment screening reports. They also do criminal records, credit reports, MVR's, address traces, confirm education, professional licenses and/or previous employers.

☰ ADP Services

Phone: 702-798-8844
Fax: 702-798-8833

3975 W Quail Suite 4
Las Vegas NV 89118

Local Retrieval and SOP Area: NV-Clark.

Normal turnaround time: 24-36 hours. Rush service is also available. Projects are generally billed by the number of names searched. The first project may require a prepayment.

They specialize in private investigation (all phases), sub-rosa investigation (video surveillance), skip tracing, asset searches, on-site copying (doctors/hospitals/depositions) and statement taking. Licensed in Nevada, Arizona and California.

ADREM Profiles Inc

Phone: 800-483-9929
813-930-9025
Fax: 800-862-9520
813-932-7871

8910 N Dale Mabry Hwy Suite 30
Tampa FL 33614-1591

Local Retrieval Area: FL-Hillsborough, Pasco, Pinellas.

Normal turnaround time: 48 hours. Projects are generally billed by the number of names searched. The first project may require a prepayment. Credit cards are accepted.

Correspondent relationships: nationwide, Canada, France, England, Germany, Carribean and Central America. They are a full service public record research and retrieval firm. Their in-house staff includes law school graduates, investigators and other professional searchers.

Advance Title Co

Phone: 915-687-3355
Fax: 915-687-3358

206 N Main St
Midland TX 79701

Local Retrieval Area: TX-Culberson, Loving, Martin, Midland, Reagan, Reeves, Winkler.

Normal turnaround time: varied depending on project. Projects are generally billed by the number of names searched or records located. The first project may require a prepayment. They will also invoice. Personal checks are accepted.

They specialize in title examinations, mineral take off and name searches, abstracts and title insurance.

Advanced Background Check

Phone: 513-254-9234
Fax: 513-254-1171

259 Medford St
Dayton OH 45410

Local Retrieval Area: OH-Butler, Clark, Clermont, Darke, Greene, Hamilton, Miami, Montgomery, Preble, Warren.

Normal turnaround time: 24-48 hours. Projects are generally billed by the number of names searched or records located. The first project may require a prepayment. Invoicing is every 2-4 weeks.

Correspondent relationships: OH and parts of KY and IN. They have developed an experienced network statewide which can retrieve in 24-48 hours.

Advanced Investigations Inc

Phone: 904-222-1998
Fax: 904-222-6875

231 Lafayette Circle
Tallahassee FL 32303

Local Retrieval and SOP Area: FL-Franklin, Gadsden, Jefferson, Leon, Liberty, Wakulla.

Normal turnaround time: 2 working days. Corporate filings may be done the same day. Expedited service available. Projects are generally billed by the hour. Incurred expenses will be added to the fee. Credit accounts are accepted. They require a retainer until the client becomes established.

Correspondent relationships: Okaloosa County. They specialize in criminal and civil case work/investigations and process service.

Advantage Title Co

Phone: 334-244-9992
Fax: 334-272-4165

PO Box 83
Montgomery AL 36101-0083

Local Retrieval Area: AL-Autauga, Chilton, Elmore, Lowndes, Macon, Montgomery.

Normal turnaround time: 48 hours. Fee basis is per search. The first project may require a prepayment.

Correspondent relationships: Bullock, Butler, Creshaw, Pike, Dallas, Coosa, Tallapoosa, Lee, AL counties. They specialize in land title searches and title insurance for mortgage loans and land sales.

☰ AEGIS Consulting & Investigtns

Phone: 888-742-3447
406-449-3358
Fax: 406-449-4889

2400 Sunlight Circle, Suite 3 PO Box 9068
Helena MT 59601

Local Retrieval Area: MT-Broadwater, Lewis and Clark.

Normal turnaround time: 24 hours. Federal records take about 1 week. Projects are generally billed by the hour. The first project may require a prepayment. Please call to establish account.

Correspondent relationships: statewide. They specialize in fraud and private investigations, public records searches and retrieval, registered agent representation, public record filing, background and asset investigations and they are litigation support specialists.

Agency-One Investigations

Phone: 800-468-7393
919-760-4000
Fax: 919-760-4155

1332 Ashley Square
Winston-Salem NC 27103

Local Retrieval and SOP Area: NC-Davidson, Forsyth, Guilford, Stokes, Yadkin.

Normal turnaround time: 48 hours. Project billing methods vary. Projects require prepayment. They will also invoice.

They specialize in criminal, civil judgment, probate and property searches.

AGH Professional Investigations

Phone: 414-697-9933
Fax: 414-697-7983

9126 32nd Ave
Kenosha WI 53142

Local Retrieval and SOP Area: WI-Kenosha, Milwaukee, Racine.

Normal turnaround time: 48 hours. Projects are generally billed by the hour. The first project may require a prepayment.

They specialize in skip tracing and public records.

AGO Investigations and Polygraph

Phone: 505-526-4303

PO Box 16143
Las Cruces NM 88004

Local Retrieval and SOP Area: NM-Dona Ana, Grant, Luna, Sierra.

Normal turnaround time: 36-48 hours. Projects are generally billed by the hour. Credit accounts are accepted.

Correspondent relationships: El Paso, Texas and Bernallilo and Chavez. They specialize in asset checks.

Aitkin County Abstract Co

Phone: 218-927-3608
Fax: 218-927-6211

112 3rd St NW
Aitkin MN 56431

Local Retrieval Area: MN-Aitkin.

Normal turnaround time: 3-4 days. Projects are generally billed by the number of names searched. Projects require prepayment.

AKA Investigations & Process

Phone: 800-653-3817
210-224-4813
Fax: 210-224-5813

115 E Travis - The Milam Bldg Suite 1009
San Antonio TX 78205-1606

Local Retrieval and SOP Area: TX-Atascosa, Bandera, Bexar, Comal, Guadalupe, Kendall, Medina, Wilson.

Normal turnaround time: 24 hours. Project billing methods vary. Projects require prepayment. Credit cards are accepted.

Correspondent relationships: the rest of Texas. They specialize in investigations, service of process and document retrieval.

AKA Investigations & Process

Phone: 800-933-8706
512-476-7231
Fax: 512-476-4611

1300 Guadalupe Suite 207
Austin TX 78701

Local Retrieval and SOP Area: TX-Bastrop, Blanco, Burnet, Caldwell, Hays, Llano, Travis, Williamson.

Normal turnaround time: 24 hours. Project billing methods vary. The first project may require a prepayment. Credit cards are accepted.

Correspondent relationships: the rest of Texas. They specialize in investigations, process service and document retrieval.

AKA Investigations & Process

Phone: 214-761-1174
Fax: 214-653-2456

PO Box 224705
Dallas TX 75222-4705

Local Retrieval and SOP Area: TX-Collin, Dallas, Denton, Tarrant.

Normal turnaround time: 24 hours. Project billing methods vary. Credit accounts are accepted.

Correspondent relationships: the rest of Texas. They specialize in investigations, service of process and document retrieval.

Akron/Canton/Cleveland Court Rep

Phone: 330-376-8100
Fax: 330-376-0110

40 E Buchtel Ave
Akron OH 44308

Local Retrieval and SOP Area: OH-18 Counties.

Normal turnaround time: varied depending on project. Projects are generally billed by the hour. Credit accounts are accepted.

They specialize in accomplishing rush, priority, same day orders.

Alamogordo Abstract & Title

Phone: 505-437-2741
Fax: 505-437-3360

PO Box 76
Alamogordo NM 88311

Local Retrieval Area: NM-Otero.

Normal turnaround time: 1 week. Fee basis will vary by the type of project. The first project may require a prepayment.

They offer a full range of title functions.

Alaska Litigation Services

Phone: 907-258-7400
Fax: 907-258-7400

2006 Crataegus Circle
Anchorage AK 99508

Local Retrieval Area: AK-Anchorage Borough, Fairbanks North Star Borough, Juneau Borough, Kenai Peninsula Borough, Matanuska-Susitna Borough, Valdez-Cordova.

Normal turnaround time: 3 days. Expedited service available. Projects are generally billed by the hour. The first project may require a prepayment.

Correspondent relationships: Northern and Southeast Alaska. They specialize in locates, profiles, research, market data, labor relations, and other employment related investigations, and criminal and civil defense. Their office in Juneau covers that area of the state.

🏛 Alaska Records

Phone: 800-808-5105
907-333-5105
Fax: 907-333-5155

6648 E 16th Ave Suite B
Anchorage AK 99504

Local Retrieval Area: AK-Anchorage Borough, Fairbanks North Star Borough, Juneau Borough, Kenai Peninsula Borough, Palmer District, Valdez District.

Normal turnaround time: 24-48 hours. 3-5 days for outlying areas. Projects are generally billed by the number of names searched. Credit accounts are accepted.

Correspondent relationships: Fairbanks Northstar Borough. They specialize in UCC, asset/lien, litigations, real property, corporate/regestered agent, filing services, licensing/registrations. They cover all federal, state and county level agencies in Alaska. They are registered agents.

Albany Abstract Co

Phone: 915-762-3077

PO Box 817
Albany TX 76430

Local Retrieval Area: TX-Shackelford.

Normal turnaround time: up to a week. Fee basis will vary by the type of project. The first project may require a prepayment.

Albert Lea Abstract Co

Phone: 507-373-9001
Fax: 507-373-2528

205 S Washington Ave
Albert Lea MN 56007

Local Retrieval Area: MN-Freeborn.

Normal turnaround time: 1 day. Projects are generally billed by the number of names searched. Projects require prepayment.

They specialize in title searching.

Albright Abstract & Title Guaranty

Phone: 800-522-1251
405-362-2525

PO Box 467
Newkirk OK 74647   **Fax:** 405-362-3724

Local Retrieval Area: OK-Kay.

Normal turnaround time: 2-5 days. Fee is determined on a "per name plus time" basis. The first project may require a prepayment. Payment due upon delivery.

They specialize in title insurance, abstracts and lien reports.

Gary Albright

Phone: 606-474-4253

PO Box 1056
Grayson KY 41143

Local Retrieval Area: KY-Carter.

Normal turnaround time: 2 days. Fee basis will vary by the type of project. Projects require prepayment.

He specializes in real estate title matters.

Aldrich Abstract Company

Phone: 409-544-2013
Fax: 409-544-2411

513 E Houston
Crockett TX 75835

Local Retrieval Area: TX-Houston.

Normal turnaround time: 2-5 days. Projects are generally billed by the number of names searched. Credit accounts are accepted.

Alfalfa Guaranty Abstract Co

Phone: 405-596-3394
Fax: 405-596-3395

201 S Grand PO Box 224
Cherokee OK 73728

Local Retrieval Area: OK-Alfalfa.

Normal turnaround time: 1 to 2 days. Projects are generally billed by the hour. Credit accounts are accepted.

All American Information Svcs

Phone: 916-632-2149
Fax: 916-632-1845

6015 Rustic Hills Dr Suite 100
Rocklin CA 95677

Local Retrieval Area: CA-El Dorado, Placer.

Normal turnaround time: 24-48 hours. Online computer ordering is also available. Projects are generally billed by the number of names searched. Deposit and invoice for requested searches are final. The first project may require a prepayment.

Correspondent relationships: nationwide. The owner has an auditing background (inactive CPA)with 20 years experience, and as such has interest in business related research for businesses, attorneys and private investigators.

All Counties Attorney Service

Phone: 714-558-1403
Fax: 714-558-0261

1617 E 17th St Suite 2
Santa Ana CA 92701

Local Retrieval Area: CA-Orange.

Normal turnaround time: 1-2 days. Expedited service available. Projects are generally billed by the hour. Credit accounts are accepted.

All Penn Abstract Co

Phone: 717-823-5410
Fax: 717-822-2774

15 Public Square Suite 200
Wilkes-Barre PA 18701

Local Retrieval Area: PA-Luzerne.

Normal turnaround time: 1-2 weeks. They charge a flat rate per project. Credit accounts are accepted.

Correspondent relationships: Lackawanna. They specialize in real estate, closings and property searches.

All Phase Reports

Phone: 813-885-9822
Fax: 813-885-9822

11266 W Hillsborough Ave Suite 201
Tampa FL 33635-9762

Local Retrieval and SOP Area: FL-Hillsborough, Pasco, Pinellas, Polk.

Normal turnaround time: 24-48 hours. Expedited service available. Projects are generally billed by the hour. Fees are per name per court. Fees can be negotiated per project. Credit accounts are accepted. First 4 projects require prepayment.

Correspondent relationships: Broward, Dade, Orange and Osceola counties. A paralegal owned and operated company using expertise and technology searching both on-line and manual data. They also do process service.

All Pocono Abstract Inc

Phone: 717-842-2753
Fax: 717-842-8949

PO Box 396
Gouldsboro PA 18424

Local Retrieval Area: PA-Lackawanna, Monroe, Pike, Wayne.

Normal turnaround time: 1 week. Expedited service available. Fee basis will vary by the type of project. The first project may require a prepayment.

They specialize in real estate.

All Pro Info Search

Phone: 206-583-1890
Fax: 206-364-3984

PO Box 2663
Seattle WA 98111-2663

Local Retrieval Area: WA-King, Pierce, Snohomish.

Normal turnaround time: 48 hours. Expedited service available. Projects are generally billed by the number of names searched or records located. Fee basis will vary by the type of project. Credit accounts are accepted. Credit is accepted unless court file over 100 pages. They always discuss fee before completing order to "OK" with client.

They have the capability of accessing the whole state (excluding Garfield and Spokane cities), via computer, for criminal, civil, probate, divorce, judgments, state tax liens and guarduanship.

All Search & Service

Phone: 216-731-3794
Fax: 216-731-3794

2445 Lakeshore Blvd Suite 1523
Cleveland OH 44123

Local Retrieval and SOP Area: OH-Cuyahoga, Summit.

Normal turnaround time: 24 hours. Projects are generally billed by the number of names searched. Additional copy charges may apply. The first project may require a prepayment.

Correspondent relationships: Ohio, Indianna and Kentucky. They specialize in criminal and civil document retrieval. Designated special process server (domestic relations) in Cuyahoga and Summit counties.

All State Investigations

Phone: 800-741-4711
513-251-4000

1632 Gest St
Cincinnati OH 45204   **Fax:** 513-251-3890

Local Retrieval and SOP Area: IN-Dearborn; KY-Boone, Campbell, Kenton; OH-Hamilton.

Normal turnaround time: 1-5 business days. Fees are on a per search basis. The first project may require a prepayment. Credit cards are accepted.

Correspondent relationships: nationwide. They specialize in corporate investigation, insurance fraud and information services. They have a nationwide network of investigative specialists at their disposal.

All-American Attorney Services

Phone: 800-838-9044
10573 W Pico Blvd Suite 344   310-838-9000
Los Angeles CA 90064   **Fax:** 310-838-0855

Local Retrieval and SOP Area: CA-Kern, Los Angeles, Orange, Riverside, San Bernardino, San Diego, Santa Barbara, Ventura.

Normal turnaround time: 3-4 days. Projects are generally billed by the number of names searched. The first project may require a prepayment.

Correspondent relationships: nationwide. They specialize in hard-to serves, celebrity and other special circumstance services.

▥ All-Search

Phone: 800-227-3152
47 W 200 S Suite 104   801-532-7024
Salt Lake City UT 84101-1618   **Fax:** 801-532-7033

Local Retrieval Area: UT-11 Counties.

Normal turnaround time: 1-2 days for Utah and 1 to 4 days nationwide. Projects are generally billed by the number of names searched. Credit accounts are accepted.

Correspondent relationships: all counties nationwide and Canada. They specialize in corporate document retrieval and corporate filings. They also are a registered agent for Utah corporations.

Allen Abstract Co

Phone: 316-321-2410
PO Box 393   **Fax:** 316-321-2452
El Dorado KS 67042

Local Retrieval Area: KS-Butler.

Normal turnaround time: 2-4 days. Fee basis varies by type of transaction. Credit accounts are accepted.

William D Allen III

Phone: 804-469-3977
PO Box 366 13927 Boydton Plank Rd   **Fax:** 804-469-3977
Dinwiddie VA 23841

Local Retrieval Area: VA-Brunswick, Chesterfield, City of Colonial Heights, Dinwiddie, Nottoway, City of Petersburg, Prince George, Sussex.

Normal turnaround time: 1-2 days for Dinwiddie. Other counties could take up to 1 week. Projects are generally billed by the hour. The first project may require a prepayment.

He specializes in real estate and banking searches.

Alliance Title & Abstract Company

Phone: 915-672-7021
3402 N 1st St Suite 102   **Fax:** 915-676-7911
Abilene TX 79603

Local Retrieval Area: TX-Taylor.

Normal turnaround time: 2 days. Projects are generally billed by the number of names searched. The first project may require a prepayment.

They specialize in marriage/divorce and death searches.

Alliance Title and Escrow Corp

Phone: 800-214-1418
78 N Main PO Box 644   208-354-2285
Driggs ID 83422   **Fax:** 208-354-2285

Local Retrieval Area: ID-Teton.

Fees vary by type of project. Credit accounts are accepted.

American Land Title has 21 offices throughout Idaho.

Allied Abstract Co

Phone: 914-682-3433
PO Box 963   **Fax:** 914-682-3558
Mahopac NY 10541-0963

Local Retrieval Area: NY-Westchester.

Normal turnaround time: approximately 5 business days. A 24 hour special service arrangement can be made. Each project billed on a per case basis. Fee may also be based per abstract. Projects require prepayment.

They specialize in title examinations.

▥ Allington International

Phone: 800-747-5202
21400 Lorain Rd   216-333-0505
Cleveland OH 44126   **Fax:** 216-333-0506

Local Retrieval Area: OH-Cuyahoga, Lake, Lorain, Medina.

Normal turnaround time: 3 business days. Projects are generally billed by the number of names searched or records located. The first project may require a prepayment. Terms are net 15 days.

Correspondent relationships: nationwide. They specialize in employment screening programs, private investigations, drug testing, criminal and court record searches, motor vehicle information, workers' compensation claims, shopping services and security consulting.

Christopher A Allmein

Phone: 717-582-7743
Rd 3, Box 700A   **Fax:** 717-582-8015
Shermans Dale PA 17090

Local Retrieval Area: PA-Cumberland, Juniata, Perry.

Normal turnaround time: 24 hours for current owner information. Projects are generally billed by the number of names searched. The first project may require a prepayment.

Alma Abstract and Title Co

Phone: 517-463-8325
310 N State St   **Fax:** 517-463-2363
Alma MI 48801

Local Retrieval Area: MI-Gratiot.

Normal turnaround time: 1 week. Fee basis will vary by type of project. Credit accounts are accepted.

They specialize in real estate.

Alpha Attorney Service

Phone: 619-235-8008
655 Fourth Ave Suite 21   **Fax:** 619-231-9535
San Diego CA 92101

Local Retrieval and SOP Area: CA-San Diego.

Normal turnaround time: 2-7 days. Projects are generally billed by the hour. Credit accounts are accepted.

They specialize in process serving.

▥ Alpha Court Records & Rsrch

Phone: 612-699-2222
1326 Osceola Ave   **Fax:** 612-699-9004
St Paul MN 55105

Local Retrieval Area: MN-Dakota, Hennepin, Ramsey, Washington.

Normal turnaround time: same day or following day. Projects are generally billed by the number of names searched. Credit accounts are accepted. Terms are net 30 days.

They specialize in criminal background searches (felonies, misdemeanors and alcohol-related traffic). They also perform civil litigation and judgment searches, tax liens, UCC searches/filings and document retrieval.

Alpha Research LLC
Phone: 205-755-7008
1552 Tom Turner Rd
Fax: 205-755-6011
Billingsley AL 36006

Local Retrieval and SOP Area: Counties in 19 States.

Normal turnaround time: 48-72 hours. Projects are generally billed by the number of names searched. Credit accounts are accepted. Billing bi-monthly, net 10 days.

They specialize in criminal records retrieval by physical resources. Drug and alcohol testing available in several states.

Alpine Title Co
Phone: 517-732-7562
114 E Main
Fax: 517-732-6392
Gaylord MI 49735

Local Retrieval Area: MI-Crawford, Otsego.

Normal turnaround time: 3-5 business days. Projects are generally billed by the hour. The first project may require a prepayment.

They specialize in title insurance services.

Alstate Process Service Inc
Phone: 516-667-1800
1009 Grand Blvd
Fax: 516-667-0302
Deer Park NY 11729

Local Retrieval and SOP Area: NY-Bronx, Kings, Nassau, New York, Queens, Richmond, Suffolk.

Normal turnaround time: 48 hours. Fee basis will vary by the type of project. Credit accounts are accepted.

AM Legal Service Inc
Phone: 800-203-4160
79 W Monroe St Suite 621
312-782-7361
Chicago IL 60603
Fax: 312-782-2838

Local Retrieval Area: IL-Cook, De Kalb, Du Page, Kane, Kendall, Lake, McHenry.

Normal turnaround time: 24-48 hours. Projects are generally billed by the number of names searched. Credit accounts are accepted.

AM Search & Retrieve
Phone: 812-438-4166
4085 Salem Ridge Rd
Fax: 812-438-3175
Aurora IN 47001

Local Retrieval Area: IN-Dearborn, Franklin, Ohio, Ripley; KY-Boone.

Normal turnaround time: less than 48 hours. Projects are generally billed by the number of names searched. The first project may require a prepayment.

They specialize in consumer dispute verification, criminal background checks and UCC searhes.

AM-PM Services
Phone: 509-765-1776
PO Box 1776
Moses Lake WA 98837

Local Retrieval and SOP Area: WA-Adams, Chelan, Douglas, Franklin, Grant, Kittitas, Lincoln.

Normal turnaround time: 3 days or less. Projects are generally billed by the hour. 1 hour mimimum. Mileage at 35 cents per mile. The first project may require a prepayment. They accept money orders and cashier's checks.

They specialize in process serving and repos, and will go to the Canadian border.

Amador/Calaveras Co Atty Svc
Phone: 916-672-9330
1010 Camerado Dr Suite 100-A
Fax: 916-223-9404
Cameron Park CA 95682

Local Retrieval and SOP Area: CA-El Dorado.

Normal turnaround time: 1-3 days. Fee basis will vary by the type of project. The first project may require a prepayment.

They specialize in criminal defense investigations.

Amador/Calaveras Co Atty Svc
Phone: 800-399-9365
PO Box 773
209-223-3068
Jackson CA 95642
Fax: 209-223-9404

Local Retrieval and SOP Area: CA-Alpine, Amador, Calaveras.

Normal turnaround time: 1-3 days. Fee basis will vary by the type of project. The first project may require a prepayment.

They specialize in criminal defense investigation.

American Abstract & Land Co
Phone: 717-389-1174
6009 New Berwick Hwy
Fax: 717-387-0163
Bloomsburg PA 17815

Local Retrieval Area: PA-Columbia, Montour.

Normal turnaround time: 1-2 weeks. Expedited service available. They charge a flat rate per project. Credit accounts are accepted.

Correspondent relationships: Luzerne.

American Abstract and Title
Phone: 319-372-8110
617 8th St
Fax: 319-372-2628
Fort Madison IA 52627

Local Retrieval Area: IA-Lee.

Normal turnaround time: varies. Projects are generally billed by the number of names searched. Fee may be based per year searched. Credit accounts are accepted.

American Abstract and Title Co Inc
Phone: 817-526-9525
322 E Ave C
Fax: 817-526-9518
Killeen TX 76540

Local Retrieval Area: TX-Bell, Coryell, Williamson.

Normal turnaround time: 2 weeks. Fee basis will vary by the type of project. Projects require prepayment.

They specialize in closing loans including commercial and single family (1-4 family).

American Abstract Company
Phone: 405-527-7575
138 W Main PO Box 15565
Fax: 405-527-7574
Purcell OK 73080

Local Retrieval Area: OK-McClain.

Normal turnaround time: 1-2 days. Projects are generally billed by the number of names searched or records located. Credit accounts are accepted.

American Attorney Service
Phone: 714-374-4886
21851 Newland St Suite 285
Fax: 714-374-4886
Huntington Beach CA 92646-7638

Local Retrieval and SOP Area: CA-Los Angeles, Orange, San Bernardino, San Diego.

Normal turnaround time: 3 days. Expedited service available. They charge a flat fee per job. The first project may require a prepayment. Terms are net 15 days.

Correspondent relationships: nationwide.

American Detective Agency

PO Box 26
Enid OK 73701

Phone: 888-657-4222
405-237-4222
Fax: 405-632-7667

Local Retrieval and SOP Area: OK-11 Counties.

Normal turnaround time: less than 24 hours. Projects are generally billed by the number of names searched. The first project may require a prepayment. Credit cards are accepted.

Correspondent relationships: Texas, Missouri, Kansas, Arkansas and Colorado. They specialize in criminal and civil investigations.

American Eagle Investigation

PO Box 104
Sun Valley ID 83353

Phone: 208-788-9527
Fax: 208-788-9527

Local Retrieval Area: ID-Blaine, Camas, Gooding, Jerome, Lincoln, Twin Falls.

Normal turnaround time: 2 to 3 days. Projects are generally billed by the hour. The first project may require a prepayment.

American First Abstract Co

111 E Comanche
Norman OK 73069

Phone: 405-321-7577
Fax: 405-329-9795

Local Retrieval Area: OK-Cleveland.

Normal turnaround time: 3-5 days. Fee basis will vary by the type of project. The first project may require a prepayment.

They specialize in real estate title searches.

American Heritage Abstract

104A N Lincoln
Desloge MO 63601

Phone: 573-431-1359
Fax: 573-431-2137

Local Retrieval Area: MO-Iron, Madison, St. Francois, Ste. Genevieve, Washington.

Normal turnaround time: 1 week. Projects are generally billed by the number of names searched or records located. Credit accounts are accepted. Personal checks are accepted.

Correspondent relationships: Jefferson and St. Louis. They specialize in title insurance and land title searches.

American Information Network Inc

6919 Wren Ave NW
North Canton OH 44720

Phone: 330-484-6272
Fax: 330-484-1199

Local Retrieval Area: OH-Stark.

Normal turnaround time: 3 days. Online computer ordering is also available. Charges depend upon project. Projects require prepayment. Credit cards are accepted.

Correspondent relationships: nationwide. They specialize in locations, pre-employment screening, arrest records, asset search and MVR records.

American Investigations

1120 Main St
Charleston WV 25302-1108

Phone: 304-343-3346
Fax: 304-343-2211

Local Retrieval Area: WV-Boone, Cabell, Jackson, Kanawha, Lincoln, Putnam.

Normal turnaround time: 2 days. Projects are generally billed by the hour. Credit accounts are accepted.

American Investigative & Sec Svcs

5350 S Western Suite 307
Oklahoma City OK 73109

Phone: 800-219-9120
405-636-4222
Fax: 405-632-7667

Local Retrieval and SOP Area: OK-Caddo, Canadian, Cleveland, Grady, Lincoln, Logan, McClain, Oklahoma, Pottawatomie, Seminole.

Normal turnaround time: less than 24 hours. Projects are generally billed by the number of names searched. The first project may require a prepayment. Credit cards are accepted.

Correspondent relationships: TX, MO, KS, AR and CO. They specialize in criminal and civil investigations.

American Legal Services

225 S Civic Dr Suite 216
Palm Springs CA 92262

Phone: 619-323-5445
Fax: 619-323-5509

Local Retrieval and SOP Area: CA-Riverside, San Bernardino.

Normal turnaround time: 24-48 hours. Projects are generally billed by the number of names searched or records located. They also charge per page if they do any copies. The first project may require a prepayment.

Correspondent relationships: Los Angeles, Orange, San Diego, Imperial, San Francisco, and Sacramento counties. They specialize in record document photocopying and process serving.

American Legal Support Service

272 Mill St
Poughkeepsie NY 12601

Phone: 914-473-5676
Fax: 914-452-4731

Local Retrieval Area: NY-Dutchess, Ulster.

Normal turnaround time: 24-48 hours. Projects are generally billed by the hour. Credit accounts are accepted.

American Title & Abstract Speclsts

303 N Kansas Suite 103
Liberal KS 67901

Phone: 316-624-9111
Fax: 316-624-6610

Local Retrieval Area: KS-Grant, Morton, Seward, Stanton, Stevens.

Normal turnaround time: 1-3 days. Fee basis varies by type of transaction. The first project may require a prepayment.

American Title & Abstract Specialists

114 S Main Suite A
Ulysses KS 67880

Phone: 316-356-2100
Fax: 316-356-2161

Local Retrieval Area: KS-Grant, Morton, Seward, Stanton, Stevens.

Normal turnaround time: 3-5 days. Fee basis varies by type of transaction. The first project may require a prepayment.

American Title Company-Lenawee

237 N Main St
Adrian MI 49221

Phone: 517-263-4040
Fax: 517-265-2533

Local Retrieval Area: MI-Lenawee.

Normal turnaround time: 3 days. Fee basis will vary by type of project. Credit accounts are accepted.

They specialize in real estate.

⊞ AmeriSearch
12631 E Imperial Hwy Suite 217A
Santa Fe Springs CA 90670

Phone: 888-462-1600
310-462-1640
Fax: 888-462-1641
310-462-1641

Local Retrieval and SOP Area: CA-Los Angeles, Orange.

Normal turnaround time: same day in most cases. Projects are generally billed by the number of names searched. The first project may require a prepayment. Special discount prices for PRRN members.

Correspondent relationships: nationwide.

Analytical Inspection Services
720 Canton St
Jefferson LA 70121

Phone: 504-832-0869
Fax: 504-832-0869

Local Retrieval Area: LA-Jefferson Parish, Orleans Parish.

Normal turnaround time: 48 hours. Projects are generally billed by the number of names searched. The first project may require a prepayment.

Correspondent relationships: St Tammany Parish, St Charles Parish and St Bernard Parish. They specialize in criminal, misdemeanors and civil searches. They also do real estate.

Anchorage and Matsu Process Svc
PO Box 212041
Anchorage AK 99521

Phone: 907-258-3211
Fax: 907-333-3200

Local Retrieval and SOP Area: AK-Anchorage Borough, Palmer District.

Normal turnaround time: 2 days. Projects are generally billed by the hour. Credit accounts are accepted.

Correspondent relationships: most of Alaska. They specialize in process service.

Anderson Abstract Co
234 S 13th St Box 8
Tekamah NE 68061-0008

Phone: 402-374-1476
Fax: 402-374-1478

Local Retrieval Area: NE-Burt.

Normal turnaround time: 2 days. Projects are generally billed by the hour. Credit accounts are accepted.

Correspondent relationships: Washington, Thurston and Cuming Counties. They have provided record search, title insurance and abstracting services for over 90 years. In the Nebraska 402 area code, you may dial (800) 246-1476.

Anderson County Abstract Co
PO Box 847 519 N Church St
Palestine TX 75802

Phone: 903-729-5871
Fax: 903-729-1160

Local Retrieval Area: TX-Anderson.

Normal turnaround time: 1-2 days. Fee basis varies by type of transaction. The first project may require a prepayment.

They specialize in marriage/divorce and death searches.

Anderson Land Title Co
212 W Walnut St
Kokomo IN 46901

Phone: 317-459-3183
Fax: 317-459-3188

Local Retrieval Area: IN-Howard, Tipton.

Normal turnaround time: 2-3 days. Fee basis varies by type of transaction. Credit accounts are accepted.

Edith L Anderson
306 N Myrtle
Grangeville ID 83530

Phone: 208-983-2754

Local Retrieval Area: ID-Idaho.

Normal turnaround time: varied depending on job. Projects are generally billed by the number of names searched. Charges are varied depending on type of search. The first project may require a prepayment. There may be a minimum charge.

She specializes in real estate, mining records, lien, federal tax and state tax searches.

⊞ H Ray Anderson
618 F Ave
Lawton OK 73501

Phone: 800-248-1900
405-355-4450

Local Retrieval Area: OK-Comanche, Cotton.

Normal turnaround time: 24 hours. Projects are generally billed by the hour. Criminal searches are a flat rate. Credit accounts are accepted. Credit cards are accepted. Personal checks are accepted.

Correspondent relationships: Comanche, Cotton and other Southwestern OK areas. He specializes in workers' compenstion, defense, personal injuries, custody and asset searches.

Andrews Agency Inc
1422 W 29th St
Orlando FL 32805-6118

Phone: 407-649-2085
Fax: 407-649-3053

Local Retrieval and SOP Area: FL-Brevard, Lake, Orange, Osceola, Seminole, Volusia.

Normal turnaround time: 24 hours. Projects are generally billed by the hour. Credit accounts are accepted.

They specialize in process serving.

Sharron Andrews
Star Rte 1 Box 50
Independence CA 93526

Phone: 619-878-2038
Fax: 619-872-2712

Local Retrieval Area: CA-Inyo.

Normal turnaround time: 1-2 days. Projects are generally billed by the hour. The first project may require a prepayment. She will invoice companies.

APB Information Research Center
2047 Victory Blvd
Staten Island NY 10314

Phone: 718-494-0750
Fax: 718-494-0578

Local Retrieval and SOP Area: NY-Bronx, Kings, Nassau, New York, Queens, Richmond, Suffolk.

Normal turnaround time: 2 hours to 2 weeks. Projects are generally billed by the hour. The first project may require a prepayment. Payment due upon receipt of invoice.

Correspondent relationships: nationwide.

⊞ Apex Information & Rsrch (AIR)
16300 Katy Fwy Suite 190
Houston TX 77094-1600

Phone: 800-330-4525
281-398-6000
Fax: 281-398-6006

Local Retrieval Area: TX-Austin, Brazoria, Colorado, Fort Bend, Galveston, Harris, Matagorda, Montgomery, Walker, Waller.

Normal turnaround time: 24-48 hours. Online computer ordering is also available. Projects are generally billed by the number of names searched. Fees are per report. The first project may require a prepayment. Terms net 15 days.

Correspondent relationships: all of Texas. They specialize in forecolosure reports, ownership and lien reports, survey adjoiners, document retrieval, environmental 50 year title searches and background checks.

Applicant Insight Ltd

Phone: 813-934-0042
Fax: 813-938-7150

PO Box 1685
Tarpon Springs FL 34688-1685

Local Retrieval Area: FL-Pinellas.

Normal turnaround time: 3 business days. Projects are generally billed by the number of names searched. Credit accounts are accepted. Invoiced monthly.

Correspondent relationships: nationwide.

▥ Applied Investigative Group

Phone: 860-895-8590
Fax: 860-895-8593

8 N Main St Suite 144
West Hartford CT 06107

Local Retrieval and SOP Area: CT-Hartford, Tolland.

Normal turnaround time: 24-48 hours. Expedited service available. Projects are generally billed by the number of names searched. The first project may require a prepayment. Credit cards are accepted.

Correspondent relationships: the rest of the state. They specialize in record retrieval and asset location searches.

▥ Applied Professional Res(APRO)

Phone: 888-686-0701
719-686-0701
Fax: 719-686-0998

100 Stanford Pl
Woodland Park CO 80863

Local Retrieval Area: CO-El Paso, Teller; NM-Bernalillo.

Normal turnaround time: 1 to 3 days. Projects are generally billed by the number of names searched. The first project may require a prepayment. Personal checks accepted.

Correspondent relationships: Bernalillo County, NM. They specialize in background investigations and Colorado workers; compensation information. Searches are "hands on." Owner is a retired Police Lieutenant with extensive investigative court experience.

APROTEX

Phone: 915-683-3518
Fax: 915-570-0267

1011 W Washington
Midland TX 79701

Local Retrieval Area: TX-14 Counties.

Normal turnaround time: 1-2 days. Projects are generally billed by the hour. Expenses are also billed. Credit accounts are accepted.

They are a private investigation agency.

▥ APS Attorney Service

Phone: 800-245-0122
404-872-1200
Fax: 404-872-4578

1776 Peachtree Rd NW Suite 330 South
Atlanta GA 30309

Local Retrieval and SOP Area: GA-Clayton, Cobb, De Kalb, Fulton, Gwinnett.

Normal turnaround time: usually overnight if ordered by 2 pm. Rush service is also available. Projects are generally billed by the hour. The first project may require a prepayment.

Correspondent relationships: all counties in Georgia. They specialize in court filings, court research and service of process.

▥ APSCREEN Inc

Phone: 800-327-8732
714-646-4003
Fax: 714-646-5160

2043 Westcliff Dr Suite 300
Newport Beach CA 92660

Local Retrieval and SOP Area: CA-Kern, Los Angeles, Orange, Riverside, San Bernardino, San Diego, Ventura.

Normal turnaround time: 24-48 hours. Projects are generally billed by the number of names searched. Projects require prepayment. Credit cards are accepted.

Correspondent relationships: worldwide. They specialize in asset searches, document retrieval, research, fraud examinations, due diligence and permissible purpose credit reporting (licensed credit bureau).

APSSI/Colorado Research

Phone: 800-552-4065
303-930-9755
Fax: 303-930-9795

PO Box 24227
Denver CO 80224-0227

Local Retrieval Area: CO-Adams, Arapahoe, Boulder, Denver, Douglas, El Paso, Jefferson.

Normal turnaround time: 24-48 hours. Expedited service available. Projects are generally billed by the number of names searched. The first project may require a prepayment.

Correspondent relationships: nationwide. They specialize in public record research and document retrieval services.

Arbor Abstracting Co

Phone: 717-253-0472

109 9th St
Honesdale PA 18431

Local Retrieval Area: PA-Pike, Wayne.

Normal turnaround time: 24-48 hours. Rush service is also available. They charge a flat rate per project. Credit accounts are accepted. Payment expected upon presentation of file.

They specialize in real estate.

Arenae Abstract & Title Co

Phone: 517-846-6560
Fax: 517-846-6633

115 South Forest
Standish MI 48658

Local Retrieval Area: MI-Arenac.

Normal turnaround time: up to a week. Projects are generally billed by the hour. Projects require prepayment.

They specialize in title insurance.

▥ Arizona Express Attorney Svcs

Phone: 602-604-8248
Fax: 602-604-8248

3003 N Central Ave Suite 103-312
Phoenix AZ 85012

Local Retrieval and SOP Area: AZ-Maricopa.

Normal turnaround time: 24 hours. No project billing information was given. Credit accounts are accepted.

They specialize in service of process, asset searches, skip tracing, and court filings as well as public record retrieval. They also do investigations and video surveillance.

▥ Arizona Search

Phone: 520-294-8350
Fax: 520-294-8350

1440 W Irvington Rd Suite 5203
Tucson AZ 85746

Local Retrieval Area: AZ-Cochise, Pima, Pinal.

Normal turnaround time: 24 hours. Projects are generally billed by the number of names searched. The first project may require a prepayment.

Arkansas Corp Research & Svc

Phone: 501-374-3843
Fax: 501-374-3836

701 Green Mountain Dr Suite 703
Little Rock AR 72211

Local Retrieval Area: AR-All Counties.

Normal turnaround time: 1-3 days. Projects are generally billed by the number of names searched. The first project may require a prepayment.

They specialize in UCC searches.

Arkansas County Title Co Inc
Phone: 501-673-3981
Fax: 501-673-3981

PO Box 644
Stuttgart AR 72160

Local Retrieval Area: AR-Arkansas.

Normal turnaround time: up to 1 week. Projects are generally billed by the number of records located. Credit accounts are accepted. Out of town clients are charged a set up fee and must prepay.

They specialize in real estate abstracts.

🏛 Joan Arms
Phone: 615-879-2269
Fax: 615-879-2269

Box 96 Rock Creek Rt
Jamestown TN 38556

Local Retrieval Area: TN-Cumberland, Fentress, Morgan, Overton, Pickett, Putnam, Scott, White.

Normal turnaround time: 1-2 days. Projects are generally billed by the number of names searched. Fee basis is per search. Credit accounts are accepted. Payment due upon completion.

She specializes in real estate at the Register's office.

Platt Arnold
Phone: 203-691-1125

160 Upper Pattagansett Rd
East Lyme CT 06333

Local Retrieval Area: CT-New London.

Normal turnaround time: 48 hours for a rundown and 1 week for a full search. Fee basis will vary by the type of project. The first project may require a prepayment. Payment due upon receipt of report.

They specialize in land records, title searches, encumbances, taxes, flood, probate and foreclosure.

Arval Legal Services
Phone: 209-924-1404
Fax: 209-924-8378

PO Box 667
LeMoore CA 93245

Local Retrieval and SOP Area: CA-Fresno, Kings, Tulare.

Normal turnaround time: 1-3 days. Expedited service available. Projects are generally billed by the number of names searched. Credit accounts are accepted. Invoicing is upon completion or monthly invoicing.

Correspondent relationships: all California counties. They specialize in service of process and professional photocopying in their area.

ASAP Legal Documents
Phone: 404-241-8130

3829 Natalie Wy
Ellenwood GA 30049

Local Retrieval Area: GA-Cobb, De Kalb, Gwinnett.

Normal turnaround time: within hours. Fee basis will vary by type of project. Projects require prepayment.

ASAP Legal Messenger
Phone: 206-940-5347

6824 W 19th St Suite 215
Tacoma WA 98466

Local Retrieval and SOP Area: WA-Adams, Chelan, Douglas, King, Kitsap, Pierce, Snohomish.

Normal turnaround time: 3 days. Projects are generally billed by the number of names searched. The first project may require a prepayment.

Correspondent relationships: Washington and Oregon.

Ascension Title Services Inc
Phone: 504-677-8473
Fax: 504-677-8475

PO Box 117 16581 Airline Hwy
Gonzales LA 70707

Local Retrieval Area: LA-Ascension Parish, Iberville Parish, St. James Parish.

Normal turnaround time: 2-3 days. Fee basis varies by type of transaction. The first project may require a prepayment.

Ashland Abstract & Title Co
Phone: 316-635-2716

PO Box 888
Ashland KS 67831

Local Retrieval Area: KS-Clark.

Normal turnaround time: 2-3 days. Fee basis varies by type of transaction. The first project may require a prepayment.

Elizabeth Askwith
Phone: 906-632-6885
Fax: 906-632-6887

125 Arlington St
Sault Sainte Marie MI 49783

Local Retrieval Area: MI-Chippewa.

Normal turnaround time: 2-3 days. Expedited service available. Projects are generally billed by the number of names searched. The first project may require a prepayment. Prepayment required only for individuals. They will invoice companies.

She specializes in probate, real estate and commercial law.

🏛 Asset Protection Associates Inc
Phone: 704-523-1651
Fax: 704-525-5920

PO Box 11567
Charlotte NC 28220-1567

Local Retrieval and SOP Area: NC-Cabarrus, Gaston, Mecklenburg, Union; SC-Lancaster, York.

Normal turnaround time: 24-48 hours. Expedited service available at additional charge. Projects are generally billed by the number of names searched. The first project may require a prepayment.

They specialize in all types of information retrieval, employment screening, background information, locating people and businesses. They serve the business, legal and financial communities nationwide.

Associated Abstracting Services
Phone: 612-861-7998
Fax: 612-861-8076

PO Box 39047
Edina MN 55439

Local Retrieval Area: MN-26 Counties.

Normal turnaround time: 3 days. Projects are generally billed by the number of names searched. The first project may require a prepayment. Terms are net 30 days.

Orders must be received by 6 AM to be completed on same day.

Associated Attorney Services
Phone: 805-898-0022
Fax: 805-989-0012

123 W Padre St Suite 1
Santa Barbara CA 93105

Local Retrieval and SOP Area: CA-Santa Barbara.

Normal turnaround time: 24 hours. Projects are generally billed by the number of names searched or records located. The first project may require a prepayment.

Correspondent relationships: the state of California. They specialize in process service.

Associated Peninsula Title & Abstr
Phone: 906-863-7871
Fax: 906-863-1363

1112 10th St PO Box 516
Menominee MI 49858

Local Retrieval Area: MI-Menominee.

Normal turnaround time: 2-3 days. Projects are generally billed by the hour. $120.00 minimum for Title Insurance. $50.00 minimum for searches. The first project may require a prepayment. Terms are net 30 days.

They specialize in title insurance, title searches (letter reports), closings and escrows.

⌂ Associated Title Co
Phone: 800-713-4224
815-872-9601
Fax: 815-872-4701

717 S Main St
Princeton IL 61356

Local Retrieval Area: IL-Bureau, Putnam.

Normal turnaround time: 1 day for status checks of real estate records, 1-2 weeks for title insurance orders. Projects are generally billed by the number of names searched or records located. Credit accounts are accepted.

They specialize in title insurance, abstracts of title, title reports, lien searches and criminal searches.

Assured Civil Process Agency
Phone: 800-256-7160
512-477-2681
Fax: 512-477-6526

807 Nueces
Austin TX 78701

Local Retrieval and SOP Area: TX-Bastrop, Burnet, Caldwell, Hays, Travis, Williamson.

Normal turnaround time: 24-48 hours. Projects are generally billed by the hour. The first project may require a prepayment.

Correspondent relationships: Texas and the US. They specialize in process service and skip tracing.

Assured Realty
Phone: 717-622-1366
Fax: 717-622-4216

2nd & Norwegian St
Pottsville PA 17901

Local Retrieval Area: PA-Schuylkill.

Normal turnaround time: varied depending on search. Charges are varied depending on type of search. The first project may require a prepayment.

Assured Title Company
Phone: 314-272-7511
Fax: 314-441-3689

611 Westridge
O'Fallon MO 63366

Local Retrieval Area: MO-Lincoln, Montgomery, St. Charles, Warren.

Normal turnaround time: 5 working days. Projects are generally billed by the number of names searched. Credit accounts are accepted.

Correspondent relationships: St. Louis, Jefferson, Boone and Calloway. They specialize in record searching for title insurance and real estate closings.

ATACO Inc
Phone: 800-220-2039
610-436-6510
Fax: 610-436-8112

1324 W chester Pike Unit 101
West Chester PA 19382-6426

Local Retrieval Area: PA-Berks, Bucks, Chester, Delaware.

Normal turnaround time: 2-3 days for lien searches, up to 1 week for all other searches. Expedited service available. Fee basis will vary by the type of project. Credit accounts are accepted.

Correspondent relationships: all of Pennsylvania and Delaware. They specialize in real estate and abstracting.

⌂ Atkinson & Haworth Inc
Phone: 312-915-0211
Fax: 312-915-0255

750 N Franklin Suite 208
Chicago IL 60610

Local Retrieval and SOP Area: IL-Cook, Du Page, Kane.

Normal turnaround time: 24 hours or on rush basis. Projects are generally billed by the number of names searched or records located. Investigations are charges by the hour. The first project may require a prepayment. Terms are net 15 days.

Correspondent relationships: Madison, WI & Kane, IL counties. They specialize in workers' compensation, liability, locates, background, financial and asset, employee theft, criminal investigations and process service.

⌂ Atlanta Attorney Services
Phone: 800-804-4078
404-237-6407
Fax: 404-237-6409

2625 Piedmont Rd Suite 239
Atlanta GA 30324

Local Retrieval and SOP Area: GA-15 Counties.

Normal turnaround time: 48 hours. Expedited service available. Projects are generally billed by the number of names searched. The first project may require a prepayment.

Correspondent relationships: nationwide. They specialize in court searches, document retrieval, service of process, court filings and bankruptcy services.

Atlantic Title & Abstract Co
Phone: 302-658-2102
Fax: 302-658-7802

1220 Market St #201
Wilmington DE 19801

Local Retrieval Area: DE-Kent, New Castle, Sussex.

Normal turnaround time: 2-3 days for lien searches; up to 1 week for more extensive projects. Fee basis depends upon project. Credit accounts are accepted.

Atlas Abstract Co
Phone: 405-379-3311

125 W Broadway
Holdenville OK 74848

Local Retrieval Area: OK-Hughes.

Normal turnaround time: 1-2 weeks. Fee basis will vary by the type of project. The first project may require a prepayment. Payment due when abstract delivered.

Atoka Abstract Co Inc
Phone: 405-889-7316
Fax: 405-889-7317

308 E Court St
Atoka OK 74525

Local Retrieval Area: OK-Atoka.

Normal turnaround time: varied depending on project. Projects are generally billed by the hour. Credit accounts are accepted.

⌂ ATT Investigations Inc
Phone: 800-733-4405
954-733-4005
Fax: 954-677-0562

PO Box 25831
Fort Lauderdale FL 33320

Local Retrieval Area: FL-Broward, Dade, Palm Beach.

Normal turnaround time: 2-3 days. Projects are generally billed by the number of names searched or records located. The first project may require a prepayment.

Correspondent relationships: nationwide. They provide extensive public record retrieval in all courts and recorders offices.

🏛 Attorney & Court Service of GA

Phone: 706-322-3554
Fax: 706-322-2896

908 2nd Ave
Columbus GA 31901

Local Retrieval and SOP Area: AL-Lee, Russell; GA-Chattahoochee, Harris, Marion, Muscogee, Talbot, Taylor.

Projects are generally billed by the hour. Credit accounts are accepted.

Attorney Civil Process Service

Phone: 817-755-6447
Fax: 817-754-4050

620 Columbus Ave
Waco TX 76701

Local Retrieval and SOP Area: TX-McLennan.

Normal turnaround time: 2-3 days. Projects are generally billed by the number of names searched. Projects require prepayment.

They specialize in service of process, court records search, skip tracing and videotape depositions.

Attorney Service Associates

Phone: 214-394-1175
Fax: 214-492-4552

PO Box 116874
Carrollton TX 75011

Local Retrieval and SOP Area: TX-Collin, Dallas, Denton, Ellis, Rockwall, Tarrant.

Normal turnaround time: 24-48 hours. Expedited service available. Projects are generally billed by the number of names searched. The first project may require a prepayment. Terms are net 15 days, 5% late fee.

They specialize in investigations, process service, information retrieval and pre-employment screening.

Attorney Service Bureau

Phone: 914-354-3357
Fax: 914-358-4253

PO Box 382
Pomona NY 10970

Local Retrieval and SOP Area: NY-Orange, Rockland, Westchester.

Normal turnaround time: 7 working days. Expedited service available. Projects are generally billed by the number of names searched or records located. Projects require prepayment.

Correspondent relationships: New York and New Jersey. They specialize in process service and public record investigations.

Attorney Service of California

Phone: 408-688-6066
Fax: 408-688-6146

10096 Soquel Dr Suite 6
Aptos CA 95003

Local Retrieval and SOP Area: CA-Monterey, San Benito, Santa Cruz.

Normal turnaround time: 1-2 days. Expedited service available. Projects are generally billed by the number of names searched. The first project may require a prepayment.

They specialize in process service and investigations.

Attorney Service of California

Phone: 408-375-4009

270 El Dorado St
Monterey CA 93940

Local Retrieval Area: CA-Monterey.

Normal turnaround time: 1-2 days. Projects are generally billed by the number of names searched. The first project may require a prepayment.

Attorney Service of California

Phone: 408-633-6247

130 W Dabilan Suite 2
Salinas CA 93901

Local Retrieval Area: CA-Monterey.

Normal turnaround time: 1-2 days. Projects are generally billed by the number of names searched. The first project may require a prepayment.

Attorney Service of Merced

Phone: 209-383-3233
Fax: 209-383-0311

PO box 2351
Merced CA 95344

Local Retrieval and SOP Area: CA-Fresno, Madera, Mariposa, Merced, San Joaquin, Stanislaus.

Normal turnaround time: up to 3 days. Projects are generally billed by the number of names searched. The first project may require a prepayment.

They specialize in process serving and private investigative services.

Attorney Services Inc

Phone: 216-431-7400
Fax: 216-431-6149

3214 Prospect Ave E
Cleveland OH 44115-2600

Local Retrieval and SOP Area: OH-Cuyahoga.

Normal turnaround time: 3-7 days. Fee basis will vary by type of project. Credit accounts are accepted. Credit cards are accepted. Personal checks are accepted.

They specialize in subpeonas and summons.

Attorney Services of Kentucky

Phone: 502-327-6677
Fax: 502-327-8222

108 Daventry Ln Suite 100
Louisville KY 40223

Local Retrieval and SOP Area: KY-Bullitt, Fayette, Franklin, Hardin, Jefferson, Kenton, Meade, Nelson, Oldham, Shelby.

Normal turnaround time: 24 hours. Online computer ordering is also available. Projects are generally billed by the hour. The first project may require a prepayment.

Correspondent relationships: Clark, Floyd and Hancock, IN counties. They specialize in witness and defendant locates, asset searches, records research and driver's licenses.

Attorney's Aid Inc of Modesto

Phone: 209-522-9901
Fax: 209-522-3044

PO Box 912
Modesto CA 95353

Local Retrieval Area: CA-San Joaquin, Stanislaus.

Normal turnaround time: 2 days. Projects are generally billed by the hour. The first project may require a prepayment.

Attorney's Aid Inc of Sacramento

Phone: 916-443-3915
Fax: 916-325-2555

PO Box 1203
Sacramento CA 95812

Local Retrieval and SOP Area: CA-Sacramento.

Normal turnaround time: 2 days. Projects are generally billed by the hour. The first project may require a prepayment.

Attorney's Diverisfied Services

Phone: 805-323-2377
Fax: 805-323-3376

101 H St
Bakersfield CA 93304

Local Retrieval and SOP Area: CA-Kern.

Normal turnaround time: varied depending on project. Projects are generally billed by the number of names searched. Projects require prepayment. Credit cards are accepted.

They specialize in document management and litigation support.

Attorney's Diversified Services
741 N Fulton
Fresno CA 93728

Phone: 209-233-1475
Fax: 209-486-4119

Local Retrieval Area: CA-Fresno, Kings, Madera, Tulare.

Normal turnaround time: varied depending on project. Projects are generally billed by the number of names searched. Projects require prepayment.

They specialize in document management and litigation support.

Attorney's Diversified Services
342 Burney St
Modesto CA 95354

Phone: 209-576-0273
Fax: 209-576-0238

Local Retrieval Area: CA-Mariposa, Merced, Stanislaus, Tuolumne.

Normal turnaround time: varied depending on project. Projects are generally billed by the number of names searched. Projects require prepayment.

They specialize in document management and litigation support.

Attorney's Diversified Services
300 27th St
Oakland CA 94612

Phone: 510-835-9176
Fax: 510-835-0510

Local Retrieval Area: CA-Alameda, Contra Costa, Solano.

Normal turnaround time: varied depending on project. Projects are generally billed by the number of names searched. Projects require prepayment.

They specialize in document management and litigation support.

Attorney's Diversified Services
1957 Pine St
Redding CA 96001

Phone: 916-241-1228
Fax: 916-241-1508

Local Retrieval and SOP Area: CA-Butte, Humboldt, Lassen, Plumas, Shasta, Siskiyou, Tehama, Trinity.

Normal turnaround time: varied depending on project. Projects are generally billed by the hour. Projects require prepayment. Credit cards are accepted.

Correspondent relationships: nationwide. They specialize in document management and litigation support.

Attorney's Diversified Services
1424 21st St
Sacramento CA 95814

Phone: 916-441-4396
Fax: 916-443-1162

Local Retrieval and SOP Area: CA-El Dorado, Nevada, Placer, Sacramento, Solano, Sutter, Yolo, Yuba.

Normal turnaround time: varied depending on project. Projects are generally billed by the number of names searched. Projects require prepayment.

They specialize in document management and litigation support.

Attorney's Diversified Services
577 2nd St Suite 200
San Francisco CA 94107

Phone: 800-775-3455
415-882-1700
Fax: 415-882-1705

Local Retrieval Area: CA-San Francisco.

Normal turnaround time: varied depending on project. Projects are generally billed by the number of names searched. Projects require prepayment.

They specialize in document management and litigation support.

Attorney's Diversified Services
860 Walnut St
San Luis Obispo CA 93401

Phone: 805-543-1458
Fax: 805-541-4450

Local Retrieval Area: CA-San Luis Obispo.

Normal turnaround time: varied depending on project. Projects are generally billed by the number of names searched. Projects require prepayment.

They specialize in document management and litigation support.

Attorney's Diversified Services
2425 Cleveland Ave
Santa Rosa CA 95403

Phone: 707-545-5455
Fax: 707-545-5454

Local Retrieval Area: CA-Lake, Marin, Mendocino, Sonoma.

Normal turnaround time: varied depending on project. Projects are generally billed by the number of names searched. Projects require prepayment.

They specialize in document management and litigation support.

Attorney's Diversified Services
845 N California St
Stockton CA 95202

Phone: 209-948-6110
Fax: 209-948-0806

Local Retrieval Area: CA-Calaveras, San Joaquin.

Normal turnaround time: varied depending on project. Projects are generally billed by the number of names searched. Projects require prepayment.

They specialize in document management and litigation support.

🏛 Attorney's Information Bureau
C603 King County Courthouse
Seattle WA 98104

Phone: 206-622-1909
Fax: 206-622-2911

Local Retrieval Area: WA-King, Kitsap, Kittitas, Pierce, Snohomish, Thurston.

Normal turnaround time: 24 hours, same day is available for a higher fee. Fee basis varies by type of transaction. The first project may require a prepayment. Credit cards are accepted.

Correspondent relationships: Multnomah, OR county. They can search all of Washington county records through an on-line system.

Attorney's Messenger Service
1243 Alpine Rd Suite 106
Walnut Creek CA 94596

Phone: 510-937-4581
Fax: 510-935-7792

Local Retrieval Area: CA-Alameda, Contra Costa, San Francisco.

Normal turnaround time: 2 days. Expedited service available. Projects are generally billed by the number of names searched. Credit accounts are accepted.

Attorney's Process and Rsrch Svc
1 Columbia Pl
Albany NY 12207

Phone: 518-465-8951
Fax: 518-465-0449

Local Retrieval and SOP Area: NY-Albany, Columbia, Greene, Rensselaer, Saratoga, Schenectady.

Normal turnaround time: 4-5 days. Motor Vehicle Records may be retrieved immediately. Expedited service available. Online computer ordering is also available. Projects are generally billed by the hour. The first project may require a prepayment.

Attorney's Service Bureau of TX
Phone: 214-522-5297
Fax: 214-712-9215
PO Box 7120
Dallas TX 75209

Local Retrieval and SOP Area: TX-Bexar, Collin, Dallas, Denton, Harris, Johnson, Parker, Tarrant, Travis, Wise.

Normal turnaround time: 1-3 days. Expedited service available. Projects are generally billed by the number of names searched. The first project may require a prepayment. Credit cards are accepted. With established credit will invoice monthly.

Correspondent relationships: all of Texas and nationwide for courts and Federal Records Centers. They have extensive experience in all state & federal courts including Bankruptcy Courts, and all Secretary of State records, and have long term experience with Federal Records Centers & National Archives facilities.

Attorney's Title Co
Phone: 913-243-1357
Fax: 913-243-1359
PO Box 407
Concordia KS 66901-0407

Local Retrieval Area: KS-Clay, Cloud, Mitchell, Republic, Washington.

Normal turnaround time: 2-3 days. Projects are generally billed by the hour. The first project may require a prepayment.

Attorneys' Personal Services
Phone: 800-245-0122
404-872-1200
Fax: 404-872-4578
1776 Peachtree Rd NW Suite 330 S
Atlanta GA 30309-2344

Local Retrieval and SOP Area: GA-Clayton, Cobb, De Kalb, Fulton, Gwinnett.

Normal turnaround time: the same day. Projects are generally billed by the hour. A mileage fee is also added. The first project may require a prepayment.

Correspondent relationships: all counties in Georgia. They specialize in court research and process service. They also go to the Federal Records Center.

Attorneys' Service Limited
Phone: 408-293-9111
Fax: 408-293-9568
931 W Julian St
San Jose CA 95126

Local Retrieval and SOP Area: CA-Alameda, San Francisco, San Mateo, Santa Clara.

Normal turnaround time: 2 hours. Fees are based on a flat rate plus expenses. Credit accounts are accepted.

They specialize in researching fictitious business names.

Attorneys' Title Agency Inc
Phone: 303-325-4911
Fax: 303-325-7304
PO Box 517
Ouray CO 81427

Local Retrieval Area: CO-Ouray, San Juan, San Miguel.

Normal turnaround time: up to 1 week. Projects are generally billed by the hour. Credit accounts are accepted.

They specialize in real estate and title matters.

Auburn Abstract and Title Co
Phone: 402-274-4321
Fax: 402-274-4323
910 13th St
Auburn NE 68305

Local Retrieval Area: NE-Nemaha.

Normal turnaround time: 1-2 days. Projects are generally billed by the number of names searched. Projects require prepayment. They prefer prepay request, but will invoice. Personal checks are accepted.

Correspondent relationships: Richardson County.

Audrain County Abstract Co
Phone: 573-581-5136
Fax: 573-581-8752
PO Box 599
Mexico MO 65265

Local Retrieval Area: MO-Audrain.

Normal turnaround time: 2-3 days. Fee basis will vary by type of project. Credit accounts are accepted.

They specialize in real estate searches.

Eileen Augatis
Phone: 609-853-9836
731 Washington Ave
Woodbury NJ 08096

Local Retrieval Area: NJ-Camden, Gloucester.

Normal turnaround time: 24 hours. Fee basis will vary by the type of project. Credit accounts are accepted. Personal checks are accepted.

Aurora County Abstract
Phone: 605-942-7770
Fax: 605-942-7770
PO Box 367
Plankinton SD 57368

Local Retrieval Area: SD-Aurora.

Normal turnaround time: up to 3 weeks. Projects are generally billed by the number of names searched. Credit accounts are accepted.

AuSable Valley Abstract and Title
Phone: 517-826-3385
Fax: 517-826-3385
442 1/2 S Morenci PO Box 548
Mio MI 48647

Local Retrieval Area: MI-Crawford, Ogemaw, Oscoda.

Normal turnaround time: 5 working days. Projects are generally billed by the number of records located. Credit accounts are accepted. Some projects require prepayment.

Austin & Associates Inc
Phone: 914-968-3700
Fax: 914-968-3770
540 Nepperhan Ave Suite 200
Yonkers NY 10701

Local Retrieval Area: CT-Fairfield; NJ-Bergen; NY-Bronx, Kings, Nassau, New York, Queens, Suffolk, Westchester.

Normal turnaround time: 1-5 business days. Projects are generally billed by the number of names searched. The first project may require a prepayment.

Correspondent relationships: CT, MA and NJ. They specialize in asset and liability searches.

Autauga Abstract
Phone: 334-361-0606
Fax: 334-361-8402
PO Box 680399
Prattville AL 36068-0399

Local Retrieval Area: AL-Autauga, Elmore.

Normal turnaround time: 24-48 hours. Projects are generally billed by the hour. The first project may require a prepayment. Personal checks are accepted.

Avian Corporate Records & Rsrch
Phone: 512-326-3354
Fax: 512-326-3354
PO Box 161232
Austin TX 78716-1232

Local Retrieval and SOP Area: TX-Bastrop, Caldwell, Hays, Travis, Williamson.

Normal turnaround time: 24-36 hours or less. Expedited service available. Projects are generally billed by the number of names searched. The first project may require a prepayment.

They specialize in real property, appraisal district records, drivers records, foreclosure real estate, tax records, TX notary, court records filing and the Supreme Court of TX.

Avritt & Avritt

Phone: 502-692-4270
Fax: 502-692-3595

PO Box 671
Lebanon KY 40033

Local Retrieval Area: KY-Marion.

Normal turnaround time: 3-4 days. Projects are generally billed by the hour. The first project may require a prepayment.

⛬ AWS Investigations Inc

Phone: 800-429-1099
520-329-1099
Fax: 520-329-0058

PO Box 4574
Yuma AZ 85366-4574

Local Retrieval and SOP Area: AZ-Yuma.

Normal turnaround time: 3 working days. Projects are generally billed by the number of names searched or records located. The first project may require a prepayment.

⛬ Ronald J Axelrod

Phone: 201-538-4606
Fax: 201-267-4606

PO Box 275
Morris Plains NJ 07950

Local Retrieval Area: NJ-Morris.

Normal turnaround time: varies. Contact office to discuss your time frame. Projects are generally billed by the number of names searched. The first project may require a prepayment. Terms are net 30 days.

Correspondent relationships: Sussex, Bergen, Warren, Somerset and Hunterdon counties. They specialize in title searches and title abstracts, along with boundary/location deeds and filing of original documents.

Erin Axt

Phone: 908-704-0087
Fax: 908-322-8505

180 North Ave
Fanwood NJ 07023

Local Retrieval Area: NJ-Middlesex, Somerset.

Normal turnaround time: 24-48 hours. Fee basis will vary by the type of project. The first project may require a prepayment.

He specializes in credit checks and criminal searches.

Aymond Investigations Inc

Phone: 318-797-4082

PO Box 52004
Shreveport LA 71135

Local Retrieval Area: LA-Caddo Parish.

Normal turnaround time: 24-48 hours. Projects are generally billed by the hour. Credit accounts are accepted. They will accept prepay orders, personal checks or they will invoice.

Judith Ayres

Phone: 757-336-5313
Fax: 757-336-1357

3487 Accomack St
Chincoteague VA 23336

Local Retrieval Area: MD-Somerset, Wicomico, Worcester; VA-Accomack, Northampton.

Normal turnaround time: 24-48 hours. Rush service is also available. Fee basis will vary by type of project. Credit accounts are accepted.

Correspondent relationships: Norfolk and Virginia Beach, VA. She specializes in real estate, UCC searches, criminal and litigation. She also performs searches from the 1600's to the present.

B & B Reporting Inc

Phone: 205-574-2524
Fax: 205-259-4323

PO Box 191
Scottsboro AL 35768

Local Retrieval and SOP Area: AL-De Kalb, Jackson, Madison, Marshall.

Normal turnaround time: 1 day. Projects are generally billed by the number of names searched. The first project may require a prepayment. They will also invoice monthly.

Correspondent relationships: the rest of Alabama and nationwide. They specialize in state and federal court searches, and title and probate searches.

B & G Ltd of Hollidaysburg

Phone: 814-695-8414
Fax: 814-695-8496

516 Allegheny St Suite 1
Hollidaysburg PA 16648

Local Retrieval Area: PA-Cambria, Centre, Clearfield, Huntingdon.

Normal turnaround time: 24-48 hours. Projects are generally billed by the number of names searched. Credit accounts are accepted.

They specialize in real estate and abstracting.

B & H Abstract and Title

Phone: 414-731-5494
Fax: 414-731-5493

625 W Lawrence St
Appleton WI 54911

Local Retrieval Area: WI-Outagamie.

Normal turnaround time: 7-10 days. Projects are generally billed by the number of names searched or records located. The first project may require a prepayment. Personal checks are accepted.

They specialize in title insurance.

B & J/Barristers' Aide Inc

Phone: 541-687-0747
Fax: 541-687-0429

PO Box 88
Eugene OR 97440

Local Retrieval and SOP Area: OR-Lane.

Normal turnaround time: the next day. Projects are generally billed by the number of names searched. Charges will include costs. The first project may require a prepayment.

⛬ B & R Services for Professionals

Phone: 800-503-7400
215-546-7400
Fax: 215-985-0169

235 S 13th St
Philadelphia PA 19107

Local Retrieval and SOP Area: PA-Bucks, Delaware, Montgomery, Philadelphia.

Normal turnaround time: 24-48 hours. Projects are generally billed by the number of names searched or records located. The first project may require a prepayment.

Correspondent relationships: Dauphin. They specialize in court filings, record retrieval, process service, court reporting and private investigation.

Background Information Services

Phone: 303-442-3960
Fax: 303-442-1004

1800 30th St Suite 213
Boulder CO 80301

Local Retrieval Area: CO-Boulder.

Normal turnaround time: 1 day for MVR's. In state CBI is 5 days, and their database is immediate. Projects are generally billed by the number of names searched. Credit accounts are accepted. Terms are net 15 to 30 days.

Correspondent relationships: nationwide. They have their own database of civil, criminal, domestic relations, UCC, Secretary of State and Department of Revenue records. They also specialize in MVR's, credit checks, workers' compensation, pre-employment and tenant screening.

🏛 Background Investigations

Phone: 800-955-1356
503-639-6000
Fax: 800-955-1361
503-639-0160

PO Box 2228
Lake Oswego OR 97035

Local Retrieval Area: OR-Clackamas, Marion, Multnomah, Washington.

Normal turnaround time: 1-2 days. Projects are generally billed by the number of names searched. The first project may require a prepayment.

Correspondent relationships: natioinwide. They specialize in tenant screening, employment screening, criminal records, credit reports (national), SS# traces, US-driving records, OR-UCC, national address and phone number verification.

Background Research

Phone: 817-926-5976
Fax: 817-926-5977

2106 Wayside Circle
Fort Worth TX 76115

Local Retrieval Area: TX-Collin, Dallas, Denton, Tarrant.

Credit accounts are accepted.

Baines Title Company Inc

Phone: 800-564-3420
509-422-3420
Fax: 509-422-1901

PO Box 626 105 N 2nd St
Okanogan WA 98840

Local Retrieval Area: WA-Okanogan.

Normal turnaround time: 2 days. Fee basis varies by type of transaction. Credit accounts are accepted.

Gaines Baker

Phone: 601-563-9385
Fax: 601-561-0743

PO Box 1417
Batesville MS 38606

Local Retrieval Area: MS-Panola, Quitman, Tallahatchie, Tate.

Normal turnaround time: 1-2 days for Panola county and 2 days for the other counties. Projects are generally billed by the hour. The first project may require a prepayment.

He is an attorney in general practice.

Jami Christensen Baker

Phone: 800-403-5207
219-266-4652
Fax: 219-266-8399

28916 Kehres St
Elkhart IN 46514-9563

Local Retrieval Area: IN-Elkhart, Fulton, Kosciusko, LaGrange, Marshall, Noble, St. Joseph, Starke, Steuben, Whitley.

Normal turnaround time: no more than 48 hours. Projects are generally billed by the number of names searched. Credit accounts are accepted. Terms are net 10 days.

Correspondent relationships: De Kalb and Pulaski. She specializes in UCC, court record searching and real estate/ title searches.

Balkin Library Management Svcs

Phone: 716-482-1506
Fax: 716-654-5235

295 Hurstbourne Rd
Rochester NY 14609

Local Retrieval Area: NY-Monroe.

Normal turnaround time: 24 hours. Projects are generally billed by the hour. The first project may require a prepayment.

They specialize in small projects with a quick turnaround time.

Ball Abstracting

Phone: 515-664-3188
Fax: 515-664-3186

207 S Washington St
Bloomfield IA 52537

Local Retrieval Area: IA-Davis.

Normal turnaround time: 3-4 days. Fee basis will vary by the type of project. Credit accounts are accepted.

They specialize in title searches on real estate and personal lien searches in Davis County.

Bankruptcy Bulletin Weekly Inc

Phone: 409-854-2777
Fax: 409-854-2594

Rt 14 Box 7301
Nacogdoches TX 75964

Local Retrieval Area: CA-12 Counties; TX-16 Counties.

Normal turnaround time: 7 days behind court and 7 days file research. Online computer ordering is also available. Projects are generally billed by the number of names searched or records located. Fee basis also per extract. The first project may require a prepayment.

They specialize in collecting bankruptcy data for their on-line database.

Bankruptcy Reporter of Rochester

Phone: 716-271-6000
Fax: 716-381-1133

A Division of The Weller Corpanies 85 Kirk Dr
Rochester NY 14610-3523

Local Retrieval Area: NY-49 Counties.

Normal turnaround time: 3-5 business days. Fax orders are encouraged. The first project may require a prepayment. Flat fee charge plus copy cost and postage & handling. Commercial accounts are billed on net 10 day terms.

Correspondent relationships: nationwide for most bankruptcy courts. They specialize in the retrieval of bankruptcy information in all counties outside of the New York City Metropolitian area. Over 25 years of courthouse experience. Use extension 111 for 24 hour ordering service.

Bankruptcy Services Inc

Phone: 314-421-5749
Fax: 314-421-5046

211 N Broadway 7th Fl
St Louis MO 63102

Local Retrieval Area: MO-St. Louis, City of St. Louis.

Normal turnaround time: 1-3 days. Projects are generally billed by the number of names searched. The first project may require a prepayment.

Correspondent relationships: nationwide. They specialize in the retrieval of information from Bankruptcy and US District courts, nationwide.

Bankruptcy Services Inc

Phone: 405-232-1748
Fax: 405-232-9521

215 Dean A McGee Ave 1st Fl
Oklahoma City OK 73102

Local Retrieval Area: CA-12 Counties.

Normal turnaround time: same day for California, Missouri, Oklahoma and Texas. Other cities vary from the same day to 1 day. Projects are generally billed by the number of names searched. Credit accounts are accepted. Terms are net 30 days.

Correspondent relationships: nationwide including Puerto Rico and Hawaii. They specialize in the retrieval of information from US Bankruptcy and US District Courts, nationwide.

Bankruptcy Services Inc

Phone: 214-424-6500
Fax: 800-256-2800
214-424-1551

2000 N Central Expressway Suite 215
Plano TX 75074

Local Retrieval Area: AL-Jefferson; AR-Pulaski; IL-St. Clair; KS-Wyandotte; KY-Fayette; LA-Orleans Parish; TX-15 Counties.

Normal turnaround time: same day for California, Missouri, Oklahoma and Texas. Other places vary from the same day to 1 day. Online computer ordering is also available. Projects are generally billed by the number of names searched. The first project may require a prepayment. Terms are net 30 days.

Correspondent relationships: nationwide including Puerto Rico and Hawaii. They specialize in the retrieval of information from US Bankruptcy and US District Courts, nationwide.

Banta Abstract Co

Phone: 515-342-2029
Fax: 515-342-2029

108 E Washington St
Osceola IA 50213

Local Retrieval Area: IA-Clarke.

Normal turnaround time: 5 days. They charge a flat rate per project. The first project may require a prepayment.

They specialize in real estate title.

Barbour Title Co

Phone: 316-221-0430
Fax: 316-221-2839

216 E 9th Ave
Winfield KS 67156

Local Retrieval Area: KS-Cowley.

Normal turnaround time: 24-48 hours. Projects are generally billed by the number of names searched. The first project may require a prepayment.

🏛 Barefoot Private Investigations

Phone: 704-377-1000
Fax: 704-343-9226

227 W Trade St Suite 2110
Charlotte NC 28202

Local Retrieval and SOP Area: NC-Gaston, Mecklenburg.

Normal turnaround time: 48 hours. Projects are generally billed by the number of names searched or records located. The first project may require a prepayment. Credit cards are accepted.

They specialize in document retrieval and interviews.

Jess Barker

Phone: 800-666-0036
217-839-3219
Fax: 217-839-2901

400 Shelby
Gillespie IL 62033

Local Retrieval Area: IL-Macoupin, Madison, Montgomery, Sangamon, St. Clair.

Normal turnaround time: 48 hours. Expedited service available. Fees are per name per index searched. The first project may require a prepayment.

Correspondent relationships: California, Texas, Illinois, New York. He specializes in UCC, tax liens, judgments, pending suits and bankruptcy. He has a M.A. in Legal Studies focusing on law related research and writing.

James M Barnes Jr

Phone: 334-683-6060
Fax: 334-683-9242

PO Box 639
Marion AL 36756

Local Retrieval and SOP Area: AL-Perry.

Normal turnaround time: 3 days. Fee basis will vary by the type of the project. The first project may require a prepayment. Statements due within 30 days.

He is an attorney in general practice.

🏛 Barnett Title Services Inc

Phone: 407-833-0824
Fax: 407-833-2444

PO Box 334
West Palm Beach FL 33402

Local Retrieval Area: FL-Palm Beach.

Normal turnaround time: 48 hours. Projects are generally billed by the number of names searched or records located. The first project may require a prepayment.

Barney Abstract & Title Co

Phone: 308-234-5548
Fax: 308-236-9240

PO Box 546 2222 2nd Ave #100 (68847)
Kearney NE 68848

Local Retrieval Area: NE-Buffalo.

Normal turnaround time: up to two weeks. Fee basis varies by type of transaction. Credit accounts are accepted.

🏛 Barrett Detective Bureau

Phone: 412-521-2900
Fax: 412-521-2900

4652 Desdemona Ave
Pittsburgh PA 15217

Local Retrieval Area: PA-Allegheny.

Normal turnaround time: 24 hours for all Allegheny County records. Online computer ordering is also available. Projects are generally billed by the hour. Credit accounts are accepted. Credit cards are accepted.

Correspondent relationships: all counties in Pennsylvania. They specialize in criminal records. They also have nationwide telephone records (legal and confidential).

Barrett Title Co

Phone: 316-856-2355
Fax: 316-856-3408

PO Box 456
Baxter Springs KS 66713-0456

Local Retrieval Area: KS-Cherokee.

Normal turnaround time: 48-72 hours. Projects are generally billed by the number of names searched. Credit accounts are accepted.

Barrett You & Associates Inc

601 Indiana Ave NW Suite 620
Washington DC 20004

Phone: 800-944-6607
202-347-0101
Fax: 202-347-0102

Local Retrieval and SOP Area: DC-District of Columbia; MD-Anne Arundel, Baltimore, Montgomery, Prince George's; VA-Arlington, Fairfax.

Normal turnaround time: 2-48 hours. Projects are generally billed by the number of names searched. The first project may require a prepayment.

Correspondent relationships: nationwide. They specialize in research/retrieval of legal/financial documents at federal, state and local levels. Emphasis on federal courts and agencies. Also offer services at federal libraries (Library of Congress and National Library of Medicine).

Barrister Support Service

8700 SW 26th Suite L
Portland OR 97219

Phone: 503-246-8934
Fax: 503-246-0098

Local Retrieval and SOP Area: OR-Clackamas, Multnomah, Washington.

Normal turnaround time: 7-10 days. Expedited service available. Projects are generally billed by the hour. The first project may require a prepayment.

Correspondent relationships: Marion and Clark, WA counties. They specialize in service of process.

Barristers Attorney Service

850 Venice Blvd
Los Angeles CA 90015

Phone: 213-747-3322
Fax: 213-747-3303

Local Retrieval and SOP Area: CA-Los Angeles, Orange.

Normal turnaround time: 1-3 days. Same day rush service is also available. Projects are generally billed by the hour. The first project may require a prepayment. Credit cards are accepted.

Correspondent relationships: Ventura, Riverside and San Bernadino. They have over 20 years experience.

🏛 Barron County Title Services Inc

PO Box 129 135 S 3rd St
Barron WI 54812

Phone: 715-537-5633
Fax: 715-537-5634

Local Retrieval Area: WI-Barron.

Normal turnaround time: 24 hours. Projects are generally billed by the number of names searched or records located. The first project may require a prepayment. Personal checks accepted.

Correspondent relationships: Fond du Lac, Marathon, Door, Dodge and Green Lake, WI counties.

Barry County Abstract & Title

700 West St
Cassville MO 65625

Phone: 417-847-3224
Fax: 417-847-3118

Local Retrieval Area: MO-Barry.

Normal turnaround time: 5-10 days. Expedited service available. Projects are generally billed by the number of records located. The first project may require a prepayment.

Barry Shuster & Associates

PO Box 79578
North Dartmouth MA 02747

Phone: 800-367-8227
508-999-5436
Fax: 508-990-2655

Local Retrieval Area: MA-All Counties; RI-All Counties.

Normal turnaround time: the same day to 1 week. Fee basis will vary by jurisdiction. Credit accounts are accepted. Payment due upon receipt of completed work.

Correspondent relationships: nationwide. They specialize in UCC, state and federal tax liens, litigation and judgments. They also provide property, motor vehicle and pre-employment record retrieval.

Cindy Bartkis

RR 1 Box 137 H
Susquehanna PA 18847

Phone: 717-756-3093
Fax: 717-756-2560

Local Retrieval Area: PA-Susquehanna.

Normal turnaround time: 48 hours. Projects are generally billed by the number of names searched or records located. Credit accounts are accepted.

She specializes in real estate record searches.

Barton County Abstract and Title

2010 Forest
Great Bend KS 67530-4093

Phone: 316-793-3781
Fax: 316-793-5475

Local Retrieval Area: KS-Barton.

Normal turnaround time: 24-48 hours. Projects are generally billed by the hour. The first project may require a prepayment.

They specialize in title insurance and special ownership searches.

Barton County Title Co

122 W 10th St
Lamar MO 64759

Phone: 417-682-3100
Fax: 417-682-3100

Local Retrieval Area: MO-Barton.

Normal turnaround time: about one week. Fee basis will vary by the type of project. Credit accounts are accepted.

Basin Attorney Services

8502 FM 307
Midland TX 79701

Phone: 915-687-5346
Fax: 915-685-3260

Local Retrieval Area: TX-Ector, Midland.

Normal turnaround time: 24-48 hours. Projects are generally billed by the number of names searched. Credit accounts are accepted.

They specialize in bankruptcy.

🏛 BAST Research Services Inc

PO Box 740148
Houston TX 77274

Phone: 713-777-8942
Fax: 713-771-8236

Local Retrieval Area: TX-22 Counties.

Normal turnaround time: 1 to 5 days; 3-5 days for 50 year and asset searches. Rush service is available. Fees will vary by the type of search. The first project may require a prepayment.

Correspondent relationships: nationwide. They specialize document/courts research and retrieval, real estate title/lien reports including 50 year environmental searches and asset and liability searches.

Batman-Sayers Abstract & Title Co
Phone: 515-382-4127
1013 6th St
Fax: 515-382-4358
Nevada IA 50201

Local Retrieval Area: IA-Story.

Normal turnaround time: 3-5 days. Fee basis will vary by the type of project. Credit accounts are accepted.

They specialize in real estate title.

Battlefield Title
Phone: 703-369-6900
9246 Center St 2nd Fl
Manassas VA 22110

Local Retrieval and SOP Area: VA-Fauquier, Prince William, Stafford.

Normal turnaround time: 3 days. Projects are generally billed by the number of names searched. Fees are by hour for metes and bounds for real estate/commercial real estate 60 year. The first project may require a prepayment.

Correspondent relationships: Arlington, Alexandria, Loudoun, Warren and Culpepper, VA. They specialize in real estate title searches and looking for assets in real estate for judgment collections.

Baxter County Abstract Co
Phone: 501-425-8989
15 E 6th St
Fax: 501-425-9080
Mountain Home AR 72653

Local Retrieval Area: AR-Baxter.

Normal turnaround time: 5 days. Expedited service available. Fee basis will vary by type of project. Credit accounts are accepted.

They specialize in real estate.

Timothy & Sara Baxter
Phone: 415-333-6247
216 Onondaga Ave Suite 3
Fax: 415-333-6247
San Francisco CA 94112

Local Retrieval Area: CA-San Francisco, San Mateo.

Normal turnaround time: 1 day or less. Projects are generally billed by the number of names searched. Credit accounts are accepted. They bill bi-weekly or monthly with a net 30 days.

Correspondent relationships: Alameda, Contra Costa, Marin, Santa Clara, CA counties. They specialize in fast, accurate criminal background checks. They also handle a variety of other types of public record research and ducment retrieval.

Bay Area Search Inc
Phone: 800-478-4618
1550/F3 McMullen Booth Rd Box 212
813-724-5995
Clearwater FL 34619
Fax: 800-478-4619
813-724-8363

Local Retrieval Area: FL-Hillsborough, Pinellas, Polk.

Normal turnaround time: 24-48 hours for Hillsborough and Pinellas counties. All other counties are 2 to 3 days. Projects are generally billed by the number of names searched. The first project may require a prepayment.

They are proudly celebrating 10 years of service.

Bay Cities Attorney Services
Phone: 510-444-4800
1322 Webster St Suite 200
Fax: 510-419-0162
Oakland CA 94612-3232

Local Retrieval and SOP Area: CA-Alameda, Contra Costa, Marin, Napa, San Francisco, San Mateo, Santa Clara, Solano, Sonoma.

Normal turnaround time: the same day to 1 day. Projects are generally billed by the hour. The first project may require a prepayment.

Correspondent relationships: nationwide. They specialize in long distance rush court filings and research.

Bay City Abstract & Title
Phone: 409-245-6321
2228 Ave "G"
Fax: 409-245-1323
Bay City TX 77414

Local Retrieval Area: TX-Matagorda.

Normal turnaround time: 2-5 days. Projects are generally billed by the number of names searched. The first project may require a prepayment.

Bay County Abstract Co
Phone: 800-321-0951
406 7th St
517-895-9910
Bay City MI 48708
Fax: 517-895-5631

Local Retrieval Area: MI-Arenac, Bay, Saginaw, Tuscola.

Normal turnaround time: 3-4 days. Fee basis will vary by type of project. Credit accounts are accepted. They require out of town clients to prepay.

They specialize in real estate searches.

Bay Title and Abstract Inc
Phone: 414-431-6100
345 S Monroe Ave
Fax: 414-431-6101
Green Bay WI 54301

Local Retrieval Area: WI-14 Counties.

Normal turnaround time: 24 hours. Projects are generally billed by the number of names searched. Credit accounts are accepted. Personal checks are accepted.

Correspondent relationships: Manitowoc County.

Bayou Investigations Inc
Phone: 800-256-9009
PO Box 92825
318-235-2322
Lafayette LA 70509
Fax: 318-232-0365

Local Retrieval and SOP Area: LA-Acadia Parish, Evangeline Parish, Iberia Parish, Jefferson Davis Parish, Lafayette Parish, St. Landry Parish, St. Martin Parish, St. Mary Parish, Vermilion Parish.

Normal turnaround time: 72 hours. Projects are generally billed by the hour. Credit accounts are accepted.

Correspondent relationships: all of Louisiana. They specialize in research, investigations, surveillance, process service, video depositions and paralegal service.

Beacom-Sauter Attorney Services
Phone: 800-380-8081
45 W Jefferson Suite 700
602-258-8081
Phoenix AZ 85003
Fax: 602-258-8864

Local Retrieval Area: AZ-Maricopa.

Normal turnaround time: the same to the next day..dd. Projects are generally billed by the number of names searched. The first project may require a prepayment.

The company has more than 15 years experience in research of all courts and governmental agencies at the city, county, state and federal levels.

Beall Abstract and Title Co Inc

Phone: 915-235-8646
Fax: 915-235-5805

219 Oak St
Sweetwater TX 79556

Local Retrieval Area: TX-Nolan.

Normal turnaround time: 2-3 weeks. Project billing methods vary. Credit accounts are accepted. Personal checks are accepted.

Bearak Reports

Phone: 800-331-5677
508-620-0110
Fax: 508-620-0818

1101 Worcester Rd
Framingham MA 01701

Local Retrieval Area: MA-Bristol, Essex, Middlesex, Norfolk, Plymouth, Suffolk, Worcester.

Normal turnaround time: 1-5 business days. Online computer ordering is also available. Projects are generally billed by the number of names searched. The first project may require a prepayment. Credit cards are accepted. Terms are net 30 days with credit approval.

Correspondent relationships: nationwide. They specialize in nationwide asset searches and public document research and retrieval services.

Beauregard Abstract Co

Phone: 318-463-7090
Fax: 318-463-7094

104 W 2nd St PO Box 280
DeRidder LA 70634

Local Retrieval Area: LA-Beauregard Parish.

Normal turnaround time: 24 hours. Projects are generally billed by the number of names searched. The first project may require a prepayment. Terms are net 30 days.

They have tract index covering entire Beauregard Parish real estate, have all records on micro-film, have part on computer (last 10 years).

Beaver County Abstract Co

Phone: 405-625-4423
Fax: 405-625-3643

PO Box 928
Beaver OK 73932

Local Retrieval Area: OK-Beaver.

Normal turnaround time: 3-4 days. Projects are generally billed by the hour. Credit accounts are accepted.

Beckham County Abstract

Phone: 405-928-3143
Fax: 405-928-5000

PO Box 80
Sayre OK 73662

Local Retrieval Area: OK-Beckham.

Normal turnaround time: 1 week. Projects are generally billed by the number of records located. Credit accounts are accepted. Personal checks are accepted.

They specialize in situations affecting mineral or surface matters in Beckham County.

Beckner Title Company

Phone: 402-747-2141
Fax: 402-747-2151

258 N State St
Osceola NE 68651

Local Retrieval Area: NE-Butler, Merrick, Polk.

Normal turnaround time: 1 week. Fee basis varies by type of transaction. Credit accounts are accepted.

They specialize in title insurance searches.

Bedford Credit Bureau

Phone: 814-623-3213
Fax: 814-623-1602

130 W Penn St PO Box 126
Bedford PA 15522

Local Retrieval Area: PA-Bedford, Blair, Cambria, Fulton, Huntingdon, Somerset.

Normal turnaround time: 24 hours. Fees based on type of report. Credit accounts are accepted. Terms are net 30 days.

They specialize in property reports and current owner searches.

Bedgood Abstract & Title Co

Phone: 512-645-3145
Fax: 512-645-3265

PO Box 12
Goliad TX 77963

Local Retrieval Area: TX-Goliad.

Normal turnaround time: 1-2 days. Fee basis will vary by the type of project. The first project may require a prepayment.

Bedgood Abstract & Title Co

Phone: 512-552-6761
Fax: 512-552-7421

PO Box 143
Port Lavaca TX 77979

Local Retrieval Area: TX-Calhoun.

Normal turnaround time: 1-2 days. Fee basis will vary by the type of project. The first project may require a prepayment.

Bedgood Abstract & Title Co

Phone: 512-573-1785
Fax: 512-575-7581

PO Box 4807
Victoria TX 77903

Local Retrieval Area: TX-Victoria.

Normal turnaround time: 1-2 days. Fee basis will vary by the type of project. The first project may require a prepayment.

▥ Behind the Scene Investigations

Phone: 616-946-7198
Fax: 616-946-5735

PO Box 41
Traverse City MI 49685-0041

Local Retrieval and SOP Area: MI-Antrim, Benzie, Grand Traverse, Kalkaska, Leelanau, Wexford.

Normal turnaround time: a maximum of 5 days. Projects are generally billed by the hour. Credit accounts are accepted.

They specialize in locating people and workers' compensation investigation.

Bob Belden

Phone: 908-828-9765
Fax: 908-937-5844

PO Box 1234
New Brunswick NJ 08903

Local Retrieval Area: NJ-Middlesex.

Normal turnaround time: 24-48 hours. Projects are generally billed by the number of names searched. Credit accounts are accepted. Personal checks are accepted.

Jan Bell

Phone: 706-278-7216

124 Valley Dr
Dalton GA 30720-4101

Local Retrieval Area: GA-Catoosa, Gilmer, Gordon, Murray, Whitfield.

Normal turnaround time: 1-2 days. Expedited service available. Projects are generally billed by the number of names searched. Credit accounts are accepted.

She specializes in credit searches. She also searches open judgments, pending lawsuits, trade names, UCC financing statements and federal tax liens.

Barbara A Bennett
Phone: 219-262-9345
27469 Bittersweet Ln   **Fax:** 219-266-1845
Elkhart IN 46514

Local Retrieval Area: IN-Elkhart.

Normal turnaround time: no more that 48 hours. Projects are generally billed by the number of names searched. Fees are also invoiced by location. Credit accounts are accepted. Terms are net 10 days.

She specializes in UCC and court record searching, title searches and property reports.

Bent County Abstract Co
Phone: 719-456-0381
PO Box 183   **Fax:** 719-456-0381
Las Animas CO 81054

Local Retrieval Area: CO-Bent.

Normal turnaround time: 10 days. Fee basis will vary by the type of project. The first project may require a prepayment.

They specialize in title work.

Bentley Title Co
Phone: 417-745-6626
PO Box 104   **Fax:** 417-745-6160
Hermitage MO 65668

Local Retrieval Area: MO-Hickory.

Normal turnaround time: 1 week. Fee basis varies by type of transaction. Projects require prepayment.

Benton Abstract & Title Co
Phone: 915-853-2631
117 Main St   **Fax:** 915-853-2687
Eldorado TX 76936

Local Retrieval Area: TX-Schleicher.

Normal turnaround time: 1-2 days. Fee basis varies by type of transaction. The first project may require a prepayment.

Benton County Abstract & Title
Phone: 317-884-1140
PO Box 346   **Fax:** 317-884-1140
Fowler IN 47944

Local Retrieval Area: IN-Benton.

Normal turnaround time: 3-5 days. Fee basis will vary by the type of project. Credit accounts are accepted.

Benton County Abstract Company
Phone: 612-968-7278
481 Dewey St   **Fax:** 612-968-7278
Foley MN 56329-0128

Local Retrieval Area: MN-Benton.

Normal turnaround time: the same day. Projects are generally billed by the number of names searched or records located. Credit accounts are accepted. Personal checks are accepted.

Benton County Title Co
Phone: 319-472-2369
Box 839   **Fax:** 319-472-2360
Vinton IA 52349

Local Retrieval Area: IA-Benton.

Normal turnaround time: 2 days. Projects are generally billed by the number of names searched. The first project may require a prepayment.

Benzie County Abstract & Title Co
Phone: 616-882-9669
PO Box 27   **Fax:** 616-882-4363
Beulah MI 49617

Local Retrieval Area: MI-Benzie, Grand Traverse.

Normal turnaround time: 5 days. Projects are generally billed by the number of names searched. Projects require prepayment. They require clients requesting a title search to prepay, otherwise, they will invoice. Personal checks are accepted.

They also offer escrow service.

Berry & Floyd
Phone: 502-845-2881
19 N Main St   **Fax:** 502-845-4223
New Castle KY 40050

Local Retrieval Area: KY-Carroll, Henry, Oldham, Trimble.

Normal turnaround time: 3-4 days. Fee basis is "per job". The first project may require a prepayment.

William Thomas Berry
Phone: 804-263-4886
PO Box 354   **Fax:** 804-263-4285
Lovingston VA 22949

Local Retrieval Area: VA-Amherst, Nelson.

Normal turnaround time: 2 days. Projects are generally billed by the hour. The first project may require a prepayment.

Berryville Abstract and Title Co
Phone: 501-423-2535
406 Public Square   **Fax:** 501-423-6396
Berryville AR 72616

Local Retrieval Area: AR-Carroll.

Normal turnaround time: varied depending on project. Projects are generally billed by the number of names searched. Credit accounts are accepted.

They specialize in title insurance in the Eastern District of Carroll County.

Best Abstract Title Co
Phone: 816-359-2377
611 Main   **Fax:** 816-369-2377
Trenton MO 64683

Local Retrieval Area: MO-Grundy.

Normal turnaround time: 7 to 10 days. Fee basis varies by type of transaction. Credit accounts are accepted.

Best Legal Services Inc
Phone: 215-567-7777
1617 JFK Blvd Suite 230   **Fax:** 215-561-4546
Philadelphia PA 19103

Local Retrieval and SOP Area: NJ-Burlington, Camden, Gloucester; PA-Bucks, Chester, Delaware, Montgomery, Philadelphia.

Normal turnaround time: 2 days. Projects are generally billed by the number of names searched. The first project may require a prepayment.

Correspondent relationships: Lehigh, Allegheny, Lancaster, Dauphin, Luzerne and York. They specialize in serving legal papers.

Bettendorf Abstract Co
Phone: 319-359-3646
1987 Spruce Hills Dr   **Fax:** 319-359-3647
Bettendorf IA 52722

Local Retrieval Area: IA-Scott.

Normal turnaround time: up to 7 days. Projects are generally billed by the hour. The first project may require a prepayment.

They specialize in real estate and abstracting.

Better Process

Phone: 408-292-2360
Fax: 408-263-0768

1000 Ames Avemeda Suite D20
Milpitas CA 95035

Local Retrieval Area: CA-San Mateo, Santa Clara.

Normal turnaround time: 1-5 days. Expedited service available. Project billing methods vary. The first project may require a prepayment.

Correspondent relationships: Monterey, Marin, Contra Costa, Sonoma and Solano. They specialize in skip tracing and court records research.

Bexar Professional

Phone: 210-228-0083
Fax: 210-228-0066

104 Heinman Suite 200
San Antonio TX 78205

Local Retrieval and SOP Area: TX-Bexar, Comal, Kendall, Wilson.

Normal turnaround time: the same day to the next day. Projects are generally billed by the number of names searched or records located. The first project may require a prepayment.

Correspondent relationships: the state of Texas. They specialize in process service.

BG's Process Serving

Phone: 800-491-2477
714-526-0517
Fax: 714-447-0334

PO Box 7076
Fullerton CA 92834

Local Retrieval and SOP Area: CA-Los Angeles, Orange.

Projects are generally billed by the hour. The first project may require a prepayment.

Correspondent relationships: all of California. They specialize in rush assignments. They also can do court filings and process serving.

Joe Biamonte

Phone: 201-933-3590
Fax: 201-933-3590

49 Rose St
East Rutherford NJ 07073

Local Retrieval Area: NJ-Bergen.

Normal turnaround time: 24-48 hours. Projects are generally billed by the number of names searched. There is a minimum charge. Projects require prepayment.

Correspondent relationships: Essex county.

Betsy Biesenbach

Phone: 703-982-7892

1948 Belleville Rd SW
Roanoke VA 24015

Local Retrieval Area: VA-Botetourt, Roanoke, City of Roanoke, City of Salem.

Normal turnaround time: 24 hours for Roanoke City, Roanoke County and Salem City, and 48 hours for all others. Projects are generally billed by the number of names searched or records located. Credit accounts are accepted.

She specializes in UCC and criminal searches.

Big Spring Abstract & Title Co Inc

Phone: 915-267-1604
Fax: 915-267-1815

208 W 3rd St
Big Spring TX 79720

Local Retrieval Area: TX-Howard.

Normal turnaround time: 2-3 days. Fee basis will vary by the type of project. The first project may require a prepayment.

Bill Bonham "The Investigator"

Phone: 715-842-1113
Fax: 715-845-3340

1014 W Thomas St
Wausau WI 54401-5970

Local Retrieval and SOP Area: WI-Clark, Langlade, Lincoln, Marathon, Portage, Shawano, Taylor, Waupaca, Wood.

Normal turnaround time: 24 hours for Marathon County (criminal), up to 72 hours (civil), and 24-72 hours for the remaining counties served. Projects are generally billed by the hour. Charges are by name for searches performed in Marathon, Lincoln, Wood, Clark, Pontage, Langlade and Taylor counties. The first project may require a prepayment.

Correspondent relationships: Milwaukee and Green Bay. He is a criminal specialist and performs civil tort work.

Bill Greenberg Special Services

Phone: 800-654-0002
305-770-4438
Fax: 305-770-4458

19085 NE 3rd Ct
Miami FL 33179

Local Retrieval and SOP Area: FL-Broward, Dade, Palm Beach.

Normal turnaround time: 24 hours. Projects are generally billed by the number of names searched. Projects require prepayment. Credit cards are accepted. Monthly billing available.

Correspondent relationships: all counties in Florida. They specialize in process service.

Bismarck Title Co

Phone: 701-222-4247
Fax: 701-222-4413

PO Box 1811
Bismarck ND 58502

Local Retrieval Area: ND-Burleigh, Morton, Stark.

Normal turnaround time: 24 hours for verbal, 48 hours for paper. Fee basis are per base rate plus name. Credit accounts are accepted.

Correspondent relationships: abstract companies through the rest of the state.

Bitterroot Research

Phone: 406-363-4408
Fax: 406-363-4408

PO Box 1422
Hamilton MT 59840

Local Retrieval Area: MT-Ravalli.

Normal turnaround time: 1-5 days. Projects are generally billed by the hour. The first project may require a prepayment.

They specialize in water rights, mineral rights and easements.

Black Hawk Abstract Co

Phone: 319-291-4000
Fax: 319-291-3929

614 Sycamore St
Waterloo IA 50703

Local Retrieval Area: IA-Black Hawk.

Normal turnaround time: 24 hours. They charge a flat rate plus incurred costs. The first project may require a prepayment.

Blackwell Land & Title Research

Phone: 205-533-2439
Fax: 205-533-2439

1004 Longwood Dr
Huntsville AL 35801

Local Retrieval Area: AL-11 Counties; TN-Giles, Lawrence, Lincoln.

Normal turnaround time: 24-48 hours. Projects are generally billed by the number of names searched or records located. Credit accounts are accepted. Terms are net 30 days.

Correspondent relationships: Marshall county. They specialize in real estate searches, UCC searches, tax searches, enviromental searches and surrounding property owners.

Blaine County Title Co

Phone: 406-357-3884
Fax: 406-357-3114

PO Box 1328
Chinook MT 59523

Local Retrieval Area: MT-Blaine.

Normal turnaround time: 3 days. Projects are generally billed by the hour. The first project may require a prepayment.

Blair Abstracting Co

Phone: 814-942-3701
Fax: 814-944-4299

3615 Burgoon Rd
Altoona PA 16602

Local Retrieval Area: PA-Blair.

Normal turnaround time: 24 hours for current owner or lien searches, and 1 to 2 weeks for title searches. Projects are generally billed by the number of names searched or records located. Credit accounts are accepted.

They specialize in complete, 60-year title searches, and property or current owner searches.

Betty Blakney

Phone: 205-325-5112
Fax: 205-325-1437

1129 B 3rd St
Pleasant Grove AL 35127

Local Retrieval Area: AL-Jefferson.

Normal turnaround time: within 8 hours. Projects are generally billed by the number of names searched. Credit accounts are accepted. Payment due once statement is received.

She specializes in probate record searches and civil searches. She has 32 years experience in probate records.

Al Blazinski

Phone: 513-698-7283
Fax: 513-698-7283

36 Teri Drive
West Milton OH 45383

Local Retrieval Area: OH-Champaign, Clark, Darke, Greene, Logan, Miami, Montgomery, Preble, Shelby.

Normal turnaround time: 48-72 hours for real estate records and 72 hours for all other. Fee basis will vary by the type of project. Credit accounts are accepted.

He specializes in title work.

Bloomington Abstract Co

Phone: 812-336-0121
Fax: 812-336-6445

401 W 7th St
Bloomington IN 47404-3936

Local Retrieval Area: IN-Monroe.

Normal turnaround time: 3-5 days. Projects are generally billed by the number of names searched. Fee basis may include charge for length of search. Credit accounts are accepted.

They specialize in title searches and title insurance.

Blue Ridge Title & Abstract Co

Phone: 540-432-0329
Fax: 540-564-2734

PO Box 1203
Harrisonburg VA 22801

Local Retrieval Area: VA-Rockingham; WV-Grant, Pendleton.

Normal turnaround time: 2-4 days in Pendleton and Grant counties, 1-3 days in Rockingham County. Projects are generally billed by the number of names searched. Credit accounts are accepted. Payment due upon receipt.

They specialize in real estate.

Blumberg/Excelsior Corp Svcs

Phone: 512-478-6620
Fax: 512-478-0001

814 San Jacinto Blvd Suite 409
Austin TX 78701

Local Retrieval Area: TX-Travis.

Normal turnaround time: 24 hours. Projects are generally billed by the number of names searched or records located. Projects require prepayment. Credit cards are accepted.

Correspondent relationships: nationwide. They specialize in research, retrieval and file any type of public record.

Bob Prins Associates

Phone: 319-232-4752

401 Ardmore
Waterloo IA 50701

Local Retrieval Area: IA-Black Hawk.

Normal turnaround time: 2 days. Projects are generally billed by the number of names searched. They charge by the hour after 1 hour per name. Credit accounts are accepted. They request prepayment for copies only, and they will accept personal checks.

Bodkin Abstract Company Inc

Phone: 219-267-7021
Fax: 219-267-2502

122 W Main
Warsaw IN 46580

Local Retrieval Area: IN-Kosciusko, Noble.

Normal turnaround time: 1 week. They charge a flat rate per project. Credit accounts are accepted.

Karen V Boggs

Phone: 816-848-2962

3096 State Rd J
Franklin MO 65250

Local Retrieval Area: MO-Howard.

Normal turnaround time: varied depending on project. Projects are generally billed by the hour. Projects require prepayment.

She specializes in genealogy searches.

Boles-Wallner Abstract and Title

Phone: 715-423-6940
Fax: 715-423-6940

214 W Grand Ave
Wisconsin Rapids WI 54495-0575

Local Retrieval Area: WI-Adams, Clark, Jackson, Juneau, Marathon, Portage, Waushara, Wood.

Normal turnaround time: 48 hours. Projects are generally billed by the number of records located. The first project may require a prepayment.

Bollinger Attorney Service

Phone: 818-902-6009
Fax: 619-778-0610

PO Box 41885
Los Angeles CA 90041

Local Retrieval and SOP Area: CA-Los Angeles, Orange, Riverside, San Bernardino, Ventura.

Normal turnaround time: 24-36 hours. Rush (6-24 hours) and super rush (3-6 hours) service is also available. Projects are generally billed by the number of records located. The first project may require a prepayment.

Correspondent relationships: worldwide. They specialize in court filings, process serving, record searches from all agencies and paralegal services.

Bollinger County Abstract Co
Phone: 573-238-2823
Fax: 573-238-2823

PO Box 889 107 Walnut
Marble Hill MO 63764

Local Retrieval Area: MO-Bollinger.

Normal turnaround time: 7-10 days. Projects are generally billed by the hour. Credit accounts are accepted. Payment acceptance may vary.

They specialize in land title and geographic land locations.

Bombet & Associates
Phone: 800-256-5333
504-275-0796
Fax: 504-272-3631

12077 Old Hammond Hwy
Baton Rouge LA 70816

Local Retrieval and SOP Area: LA-Ascension Parish, East Baton Rouge Parish, Iberville Parish, Jefferson Parish, Orleans Parish, St. Charles Parish, St. John the Baptist Parish, St. Tammany Parish, West Baton Rouge Parish.

Normal turnaround time: 24-48 hours. Projects are generally billed by the hour. The first project may require a prepayment. Credit cards are accepted.

Correspondent relationships: nationwide and Republic of Panama. They specialize in general investigations, research and collections.

Bonds Process Service of East TX
Phone: 409-377-4483

PO Box 585
Pointblank TX 77364

Local Retrieval and SOP Area: TX-Polk, San Jacinto, Trinity, Walker.

Normal turnaround time: 1-2 days. Projects are generally billed by the hour. The first project may require a prepayment.

Correspondent relationships: Harris and Montgomery counties.

Judy & Mark Bonham
Phone: 864-882-3761

1509 Hiawassee Dr
Seneca SC 29672

Local Retrieval and SOP Area: SC-Oconee.

Normal turnaround time: varied depending on project. Projects are generally billed by the number of records located. Credit accounts are accepted.

She specializes in title searches.

Bontecou Investigative Services
Phone: 307-733-2637
Fax: 307-733-5258

350 E Broadway PO Box 2448
Jackson WY 83001

Local Retrieval and SOP Area: WY-Albany, Laramie, Teton.

Normal turnaround time: 3-5 business days. Projects are generally billed by the number of names searched. The first project may require a prepayment.

Correspondent relationships: Natrona, Sweetwater, Fremont, Park and Vinta. They specialize in background, civil litigation and investigations.

Boone County Abstract Co
Phone: 515-432-3633

814 8th St
Boone IA 50036

Local Retrieval Area: IA-Boone.

Normal turnaround time: up to 1 week. Projects are generally billed by the number of names searched. Credit accounts are accepted.

They specialize in real estate.

Border Abstract
Phone: 210-791-5810
Fax: 210-791-5555

5810 San Bernado Ave
Laredo TX 78041

Local Retrieval Area: TX-Brooks, Jim Hogg, La Salle, Webb, Zapata.

Normal turnaround time: 1-2 days. Fee basis varies according to the type of project. Projects require prepayment.

Shirley Born
Phone: 612-388-6487

1913 Perlich Ave Suite 104
Red Wing MN 55066

Local Retrieval Area: MN-Goodhue, Wabasha.

Normal turnaround time: 1 day. Projects are generally billed by the number of names searched. The first project may require a prepayment.

She specializes in criminal record searches.

Bosic and Bosic
Phone: 909-788-1988
Fax: 909-788-0634

PO Box 2005
Riverside CA 92516

Local Retrieval and SOP Area: CA-Orange, Riverside, San Bernardino.

Normal turnaround time: 1-2 days. Projects are generally billed by the hour. The first project may require a prepayment.

Correspondent relationships: primarily Los Angeles and San Diego Counties, but can retrieve records through most of the state.

Bosque Cen-Tex Title Inc
Phone: 817-435-2722
Fax: 817-435-2642

PO Box 899
Meridian TX 76665

Local Retrieval Area: TX-Bosque.

Normal turnaround time: 1-2 days. Fee basis will vary by the type of project. The first project may require a prepayment.

Bottineau County Abtract Co
Phone: 701-228-2215

PO Box 24
Bottineau ND 58318

Local Retrieval Area: ND-Bottineau.

Normal turnaround time: 3 days. Fee basis vary by the type of project. Credit accounts are accepted. Credit cards are accepted.

They specialize in oil and gas records.

Botts Title Co
Phone: 409-567-4602
Fax: 409-567-9358

PO Box 999
Caldwell TX 77836

Local Retrieval Area: TX-Burleson, Fayette, Washington.

Normal turnaround time: 1-2 days. Fee basis will vary by the type of project. Credit accounts are accepted.

Bowman & Slope County Abstract
Phone: 701-523-5231
Fax: 701-523-5231

PO Box 559
Bowman ND 58623

Local Retrieval Area: ND-Bowman, Slope.

Normal turnaround time: 1-3 days. Projects are generally billed by the hour. Credit accounts are accepted.

They specialize in title search.

Bowman's Vernon County Title Co
Phone: 417-667-7565
112 W Walnut   **Fax:** 417-667-7995
Nevada MO 64772

Local Retrieval Area: MO-Vernon.

Normal turnaround time: 5 days. Fee basis varies by type of transaction. Credit accounts are accepted. Out of state accounts must prepay.

Box & Box
Phone: 515-682-4512
304 N Court
Ottumwa IA 52501

Local Retrieval Area: IA-Wapello.

Normal turnaround time: 48 hours. They charge a flat rate per project. The first project may require a prepayment.

They specialize in real estate and abstracting.

▥ Brabston Legal Investigations
Phone: 334-666-5666
PO Box 91711   **Fax:** 334-661-8807
Mobile AL 36691-1711

Local Retrieval and SOP Area: AL-Baldwin, Clarke, Mobile.

Normal turnaround time: 2-3 days. Online computer ordering is also available. Projects are generally billed by the number of names searched. The first project may require a prepayment.

Correspondent relationships: the rest of Alabama. They are on-line with Alabama State Judicial Computer and Florida Department of Law Enforcement.

Brack Warren & Associates
Phone: 512-884-8000
PO Box 6497   **Fax:** 512-857-7007
Corpus Christi TX 78466

Local Retrieval Area: TX-Nueces.

Normal turnaround time: 1-2 days. Expedited service available. Projects are generally billed by the hour. Projects require prepayment.

Correspondent relationships: the rest of Texas, Mexico, Guatamala, and Chile. They specialize in investigative services.

Bradford Title Service
Phone: 904-964-4747
PO Box 208   **Fax:** 904-964-2304
Starke FL 32091

Local Retrieval Area: FL-Bradford.

Normal turnaround time: 2-3 days depending on the project. Projects are generally billed by the number of records located. Credit accounts are accepted. Payment due upon receipt of invoice.

Correspondent relationships: Union, Clay and Bradford, FL counties.

Brainard Research and Reporting
Phone: 813-931-8370
9806 Thornridge Rd   **Fax:** 813-931-7137
Tampa FL 33612

Local Retrieval Area: FL-Citrus, Hernando, Hillsborough, Manatee, Pasco, Pinellas, Polk, Sarasota.

Normal turnaround time: 48-72 hours. Expedited service available. No project billing information was given. The first project may require a prepayment. Terms are net 10 days.

Correspondent relationships: nationwide. They specialize in criminal record searches and legal research.

Thomas Q Brame Jr
Phone: 601-764-4355
PO Box 301 47A Hwy 15 S   **Fax:** 601-764-4356
Bay Springs MS 39422

Local Retrieval and SOP Area: MS-Clarke, Hinds, Jasper, Jones, Lauderdale, Newton, Rankin, Scott, Simpson, Smith.

Normal turnaround time: 1-3 days. Projects are generally billed by the hour. The first project may require a prepayment.

Correspondent relationships: Mississippi. He is in general practice.

Branch County Abstract & Title Inc
Phone: 517-278-7629
13 S Monroe Street   **Fax:** 517-279-7919
Coldwater MI 49036

Local Retrieval Area: MI-Branch.

Normal turnaround time: 3-5 days. Fee basis will vary by the type of project. Credit accounts are accepted.

They specialize in real estate transactions and title insurance.

Attorney Leonard Brashear
Phone: 606-672-3577
PO Box 677   **Fax:** 606-672-3627
Hyden KY 41749

Local Retrieval Area: KY-Leslie.

Normal turnaround time: up to 1 week. Projects are generally billed by the hour. Projects require prepayment.

Jerry M Braud
Phone: 504-447-1227
1312 Park Dr   **Fax:** 504-447-1227
Thibodaux LA 70301

Local Retrieval Area: LA-Assumption Parish, Jefferson Parish, Lafourche Parish, St. Charles Parish, Terrebonne Parish.

Normal turnaround time: 1-2 days. Projects are generally billed by the hour. The first project may require a prepayment.

She has been in business for over 40 years. She specializes in real estate, mineral and all public record searches.

Bremer County Abstract Co
Phone: 319-352-2710
218 E Bremer Ave   **Fax:** 319-352-0675
Waverly IA 50677

Local Retrieval Area: IA-Bremer.

Normal turnaround time: 3 days. Projects are generally billed by the number of names searched. Fee may also be based per claim. Projects require prepayment.

Dorothy Brewer
Phone: 814-849-8296
135 Roosevelt St
Brookville PA 15825

Local Retrieval Area: PA-Jefferson.

Normal turnaround time: 24 hours. Projects are generally billed by the number of names searched. Credit accounts are accepted.

She specializes in title searches.

▥ Bridge Service Corp
Phone: 800-225-2736
5 Beekman St Suite 925   212-267-8600
New York NY 10038   **Fax:** 888-267-8680
    212-267-8687

Local Retrieval Area: NY-Bronx, Kings, New York, Queens, Richmond.

Normal turnaround time: 2-3 days. Expedited service available. Projects are generally billed by the number of names searched or records located. The first project may require a prepayment.

Correspondent relationships: nationwide. They specialize in all filing and search services in the 5 counties which comprise New York City in all courts, agencies and offices.

Eddie J Briggs
Phone: 601-743-5823
Fax: 601-743-5824
PO Box 447 110 Hopper Ave
De Kalb MS 39328
Local Retrieval Area: MS-Kemper.

Normal turnaround time: 1-2 days. Projects are generally billed by the hour. The first project may require a prepayment.

▥ Bright Research Services
Phone: 210-372-0170
Fax: 210-372-2620
1411 Hummingbird
Seguin TX 78155
Local Retrieval Area: TX-Comal, Gonzales, Guadalupe, Hays.

Normal turnaround time: 24 hours. Expedited service available. Projects are generally billed by the number of names searched. Credit accounts are accepted. Monthly statement available.

▥ Michael T Briley
Phone: 601-983-2227
Fax: 601-983-2227
PO Box 2085
University MS 38677-2085
Local Retrieval and SOP Area: MS-Calhoun, Lafayette.

Normal turnaround time: 24 hours in Lafayette, 2-3 days in the other counties. Online computer ordering is also available. Projects are generally billed by the number of names searched. Fee basis varies by type of project. Credit accounts are accepted.

They specialize in criminal & civil searches, UCC, filing and real estate title searches.

▥ Frank Britton
Phone: 800-343-4429
619-357-6366
Fax: 619-357-2405
505 Emerson Ave, PO Box 1109
Calexico CA 92231
Local Retrieval and SOP Area: CA-Imperial.

Normal turnaround time: 48 hours. Projects are generally billed by the number of names searched. Minimum charge is $35.00. The first project may require a prepayment.

Correspondent relationships: repossessions and process serving in Mexico. He specializes in process service and skip tracing in Imperial County, CA and all of Mexico. He performs stake-outs, investigations to locate elusive victims, witnesses, etc. in Mexicali, Mexico and Imperial County.

J Stephen Broadway
Phone: 615-433-5979
Fax: 615-433-7297
310 Market St E
Fayetteville TN 37334-3024
Local Retrieval Area: TN-Franklin, Giles, Lawrence, Lincoln, Marshall.

Normal turnaround time: 2-3 days. Charges are varied depending on type of search. The first project may require a prepayment.

Bronson Abstract Co
Phone: 501-521-4100
Fax: 501-521-6452
PO Box 1149
Fayetteville AR 72702
Local Retrieval Area: AR-Washington.

Normal turnaround time: 2 days. Fee basis will vary by type of project. The first project may require a prepayment.
They specialize in real estate and public records.

Broom's Appraisals & Research
Phone: 706-290-1000
Fax: 706-290-1000
364 Kellett Rd
Rome GA 30165
Local Retrieval Area: GA-Floyd, Gordon.

Normal turnaround time: 3-5 days. Projects are generally billed by the number of names searched. The first project may require a prepayment.

Brown County Abstract Co
Phone: 402-387-2718
Fax: 402-387-2342
127 W 3rd St
Ainsworth NE 69210
Local Retrieval Area: NE-Brown, Keya Paha, Rock.

Normal turnaround time: 2-7 days. Fee basis includes a charge by the hour but there is a mimumim. Credit accounts are accepted. They specialize in title certificates.

Brown County Abstract Co
Phone: 915-643-3631
Fax: 915-643-5086
201 S Broadway St
Brownwood TX 76801
Local Retrieval Area: TX-Brown.

Normal turnaround time: 1-2 days. Projects are generally billed by the hour. The first project may require a prepayment. There is a possiblity of a retainer required.
They specialize in oil and gas searches.

Brown County Title Co
Phone: 913-742-7103
Fax: 913-742-7103
108 S 7th St
Hiawatha KS 66434
Local Retrieval Area: KS-Brown.

Normal turnaround time: 5-10 days. Projects are generally billed by the number of names searched. Credit accounts are accepted.

▥ Gail Brown-Browning
Phone: 540-563-5699
Fax: 540-362-7833
267 Preston Ave
Roanoke VA 24012
Local Retrieval Area: VA-19 Counties.

Normal turnaround time: 24-48 hours unless otherwise states. Projects are generally billed by the number of names searched. Credit accounts are accepted.

They specialize in title work, document retreival, UCC retrieval and tax liens.

Brownfield Abstract & Title Co
Phone: 806-637-9595
Fax: 806-637-7560
305B W Broadway
Brownfield TX 79316
Local Retrieval Area: TX-Terry.

Normal turnaround time: 2-3 days. It may average 1-2 weeks for difficult tracts. Project billing methods vary. Credit accounts are accepted. Personal checks are accepted.

Brubaker & Associates
Phone: 903-595-4616
PO Box 7334
Tyler TX 75711
Local Retrieval Area: TX-27 Counties.

Normal turnaround time: 1-2 days. Expedited service available. Projects are generally billed by the hour. Credit accounts are accepted.

Correspondent relationships: counties north of Angelina and east of Dallas.

Brule County Abstract Co
Phone: 605-734-4275
Fax: 605-734-4275
PO Box 378
Chamberlain SD 57325
Local Retrieval Area: SD-Brule, Jackson, Lyman.

Normal turnaround time: up to 2 weeks. Fee basis varies by type of transaction. Credit accounts are accepted.
They specialize in land records.

Brule County Title and Insurance

Phone: 605-734-5533
Fax: 605-734-5534

103 E Lawler
Chamberlain SD 57325

Local Retrieval Area: SD-Brule, Buffalo.

Normal turnaround time: varied depending on project. Projects are generally billed by the number of names searched. Credit accounts are accepted. Personal checks are accepted.

Jerry J Bucci

Phone: 412-833-9664
Fax: 412-833-9770

682 3rd St
Beaver PA 15009-2116

Local Retrieval Area: PA-Allegheny.

Normal turnaround time: 1-3 days depending on requirements. Projects are generally billed by the number of names searched. Credit accounts are accepted. Payable upon receipt.

He is an attorney who specializes in 2nd mortgage lien searches.

Buchanan Abstract Co

Phone: 515-295-3745
Fax: 515-295-7633

120 N Moore St
Algona IA 50511

Local Retrieval Area: IA-Kossuth.

Normal turnaround time: 2-3 days. Projects are generally billed by the number of names searched. Credit accounts are accepted.

Buchfinck Inc

Phone: 308-762-4715
Fax: 308-762-4716

PO Box 340
Alliance NE 69301

Local Retrieval Area: NE-Box Butte.

Normal turnaround time: the same day. They charge a flat rate per project. Credit accounts are accepted.

They specialize in title search and abstract.

B Scott Buffington

Phone: 601-849-4267

PO Box 745 115 Main St
Magee MS 39111

Local Retrieval Area: MS-Simpson.

Normal turnaround time: 1-2 days. Fee basis varies by type of transaction. The first project may require a prepayment.

He is in general practice.

Bureau of Confidential Information

Phone: 810-812-8782
Fax: 810-853-9483

PO Box 80726
Rochester MI 48308

Local Retrieval and SOP Area: MI-Genesee, Lapeer, Lenawee, Macomb, Oakland, Washtenaw, Wayne.

Normal turnaround time: 24-48 hours. Projects are generally billed by the hour. Mileage and other expenses may be charged. The first project may require a prepayment.

Correspondent relationships: Ohio, Indiana, Illinois and Wisconsin. They specialize in records research.

Bureau of Special Services

Phone: 800-772-7130
914-566-7600
Fax: 914-566-1050

84 Plattskill Tpke, Suite 115 PO Box 7160
Newburgh NY 12550

Local Retrieval and SOP Area: NY-Columbia, Dutchess, Greene, Orange, Putnam, Rockland, Sullivan, Ulster, Westchester.

Normal turnaround time: varied depending on project. Expedited service available. Online computer ordering is also available. Projects are generally billed by the hour. Some flat fees apply. The first project may require a prepayment.

Correspondent relationships: New York and New Jersey. They are a licensed and bonded investigative agency.

Burlington County Abstract Co

Phone: 609-235-9435
Fax: 609-235-9120

Tall Oaks Corporate Center 1000 Lenola Rd #203
Mapleshade NJ 08052

Local Retrieval Area: NJ-Burlington.

Normal turnaround time: 1-3 days. Fee basis will vary by the type of project. The first project may require a prepayment.

Correspondent relationships: the rest of New Jersey. They specialize in real estate.

Burnett County Abstract Co

Phone: 715-349-2269
Fax: 715-349-7604

24996 Hwy 35 N
Siren WI 54872

Local Retrieval Area: WI-Burnett.

Normal turnaround time: 3 days. Projects are generally billed by the number of names searched or records located. Credit accounts are accepted. Will invoice with a prepaid deposit.

They specialize in real estate title searches.

Burr Investigation

Phone: 800-582-5441
208-342-3463
Fax: 208-342-8097

PO Box 6486
Boise ID 83707

Local Retrieval and SOP Area: ID-13 Counties.

Normal turnaround time: several days. Projects are generally billed by the hour. Projects require prepayment.

Correspondent relationships: nationwide and international. They have 20 years combined law enforcement and investigative experience.

Business Information Service

Phone: 409-865-2547
Fax: 409-865-8918

531 S Holland
Bellville TX 77418

Local Retrieval Area: TX-Austin, Colorado, Waller, Washington.

Projects are generally billed by the number of names searched. Projects require prepayment.

Business Research International

Phone: 502-348-6350
Fax: 502-348-6350

2580 Nazareth Rd PO Box 2152
Bardstown KY 40004

Local Retrieval Area: KY-Bullitt, Jefferson, Nelson, Oldham.

Projects are generally billed by the number of names searched or records located. The first project may require a prepayment. They bill monthly.

Correspondent relationships: Floyd and Clark, IN counties. They specialize in heir tracing, genealogy research and public record searches and retrievals.

Business Research Services

Phone: 800-608-4636
423-691-8778
Fax: 423-690-8771

8720 Mill Run Dr
Knoxville TN 37922-6087

Local Retrieval and SOP Area: TN-Anderson, Blount, Knox, Loudon, Roane, Sevier.

Normal turnaround time: 1-3 days. Projects are generally billed by the number of names searched. Fee is per court. The first project may require a prepayment. Terms are net 15 days.

Correspondent relationships: nationwide. They specialize in civil and criminal record searches, secretary of state records, patent and trademark registrations, MVR records, UCC filings, real property records, aircraft title and pilot registration, consumer and business credit reports.

Butler County Abstract and Title

Phone: 573-686-1495
Fax: 573-686-3804

111 N Main
Poplar Bluff MO 63901

Local Retrieval Area: MO-Butler.

Normal turnaround time: 1-3 days. Projects are generally billed by the number of names searched or records located. The first project may require a prepayment. Personal checks are accepted.

C

C & D Enterprises

Phone: 208-466-2555
Fax: 208-466-2118

PO Box 11
Nampa ID 83653

Local Retrieval and SOP Area: ID-Ada, Adams, Boise, Canyon, Elmore, Gem, Owyhee, Payette, Valley, Washington.

Normal turnaround time: 24 to 48 hours. Projects are generally billed by the number of names searched. Fees vary by type of search required. Credit accounts are accepted. Monthly invoice or by prior agreement.

Correspondent relationships: Malheur County, OR. They specialize in the combined use of public records, computer databases, court record retrieval, UCC, searching and filing, bankruptcy and DMV.

C W Lynn Abstract Co Inc

Phone: 913-823-3706
Fax: 913-823-7922

121 N 7th St
Salina KS 67401

Local Retrieval Area: KS-Saline.

Normal turnaround time: 2-3 days. Charges vary by purchase price or mortgage amount. Credit accounts are accepted.

They specialize in title insurance.

Cal Title/Sacramento Attys' Svc

Phone: 800-952-5650
916-448-1397
Fax: 800-499-7599
916-448-1698

1005 12th St Suite E
Sacramento CA 95814

Local Retrieval Area: CA-El Dorado, Placer, Sacramento, San Joaquin, Solano, Yolo.

Normal turnaround time: 24 for state records, 2-3 days for county records. Projects are generally billed by the number of names searched. The first project may require a prepayment.

Correspondent relationships: nationwide.

Calhoun-Liberty Abstract Co

Phone: 904-674-8311
Fax: 904-674-3191

PO Box 216
Blountstown FL 32424

Local Retrieval Area: FL-Calhoun, Liberty.

Normal turnaround time: 3-5 days. Fee basis is per search. Projects require prepayment.

They specialize in title insurance.

California Drivers Records

Phone: 800-852-6219
916-456-4757
Fax: 800-488-0231
916-451-2351

PO Box 15314
Sacramento CA 95851-1314

Local Retrieval Area: CA-Sacramento.

Normal turnaround time: depends on requested information. Projects are generally billed by the number of names searched. Credit accounts are accepted. Terms are net 10 days.

California Law Rtrvl Svc (Cal Info)

Phone: 213-957-5035
Fax: 213-463-9889

6305 Yucca St Suite 603
Los Angeles CA 90028

Local Retrieval Area: CA-Los Angeles, Orange.

Normal turnaround time: the same day. Projects are generally billed by the hour. The first project may require a prepayment. Credit cards are accepted.

Correspondent relationships: San Diego, San Francisco, Sacramento and Orange. They can also run database searches through CDB-Infotek and OCLC.

California Search Services

Phone: 800-333-3391
916-527-6229
Fax: 916-529-2645

332 Pine St
Red Bluff CA 96080

Local Retrieval Area: CA-Butte, Glenn, Sacramento, Shasta, Tehama.

Normal turnaround time: 24-48 hours. Projects are generally billed by the number of names searched. Credit accounts are accepted. Credit cards are accepted. Terms are net 30 days.

Correspondent relationships: All of California except Humboldt. They specialize in deeds, property transfers, bankruptcies, liens, judgments and building permit searches.

Callahan Lawyers Service

Phone: 201-489-2245
Fax: 201-489-8093

50 Main St
Hackensack NJ 07602

Local Retrieval and SOP Area: NJ-Bergen, Passaic.

Normal turnaround time: 2-3 days. Same day rush service available. Fee basis is per job. The first project may require a prepayment. Credit cards are accepted.

Correspondent relationships: Morris and Hudson. They specialize in being a full service agency with secretaries, not machines. They complete jobs on time everytime.

Cameron Title Co Inc

Phone: 800-530-5933
816-632-6679
Fax: 816-632-1114

1317 N Walnut St
Cameron MO 64429

Local Retrieval Area: MO-Clinton, De Kalb.

Normal turnaround time: 2-5 days. Projects are generally billed by the number of names searched. Credit accounts are accepted.

They specialize in title insurance, abstracting, escrows and closing.

Camp County Land Abstract Co

Phone: 903-856-3676
Fax: 903-856-0470

PO Box 701
Pittsburg TX 75686

Local Retrieval Area: TX-Camp.

Normal turnaround time: 1-7 days. Fee basis will vary by the type of project. The first project may require a prepayment.

Campanella Attorney Services Inc

Phone: 619-696-8131
Fax: 619-696-1272

1357 7th Ave Suite C
San Diego CA 92101-4309

Local Retrieval and SOP Area: CA-San Diego.

Normal turnaround time: 1-3 days. Projects are generally billed by the number of records located. The first project may require a prepayment.

Correspondent relationships: nationwide. They specialize in civil court research, filing of court documents and service of process. They also deal with workers compensation, County Recorders and Court of Appeals and family law at Superior and Municipal Court levels.

Campbell Abstract Co

7 NW 2nd St PO Box 425
Buffalo MN 55313-0425

Phone: 612-682-1252
Fax: 612-682-5810

Local Retrieval Area: MN-Wright.

Normal turnaround time: 2-3 days. Projects are generally billed by the number of names searched or records located. The first project may require a prepayment. Terms are net 30 days.

They specialize in abstracts of title, owners and encumbrances and tract checks.

Campbell Abstract Inc

419 N 8th St
Garden City KS 67846

Phone: 316-275-7441
Fax: 316-275-8658

Local Retrieval Area: KS-Finney.

Normal turnaround time: 1-3 days. Projects are generally billed by the hour. The first project may require a prepayment.

Eugene R Campbell

18 S Goerge St Suite 203
York PA 17401

Phone: 717-846-5830
Fax: 717-852-7120

Local Retrieval Area: PA-York.

Normal turnaround time: 3 days. Projects are generally billed by the hour. Projects require prepayment.

Correspondent relationships: Lancaster. They specialize in real estate searches and criminal record searches.

Cape Girardeau County Abstract

400 Broadway Suite 101
Cape Girardeau MO 63701

Phone: 573-335-5890
Fax: 573-335-6381

Local Retrieval Area: MO-Cape Girardeau.

Normal turnaround time: 3 days. Projects are generally billed by the number of names searched or records located. Credit accounts are accepted.

They specialize in land title record searches.

Capital Retrieval Services

625 Country club Dr Suite A2
Newark OH 43055

Phone: 614-344-1047
Fax: 614-344-1047

Local Retrieval and SOP Area: OH-Franklin, Licking.

Projects are generally billed by the hour. The first project may require a prepayment. Terms are net 30 days.

Correspondent relationships: KY. They specialize in statewide document retrieval, dead beat dads and all electronic data. They do a no hit/no fee.

Capitol City Network

1347 F Florin Rd Suite 1877
Sacramento CA 95831

Phone: 916-395-2917
Fax: 916-429-2823

Local Retrieval Area: CA-Los Angeles, Marin, Placer, Sacramento, San Francisco, San Joaquin, Santa Clara, Sonoma, Stanislaus.

Normal turnaround time: 2-24 hours. Fee basis varies by type of transaction. The first project may require a prepayment.

Correspondent relationships: Texas, New Jersey, Nevada, Washington, DC. They specialize in legislative analysis and asset searches. They do all Secretary of State filings for California. They also do title searches throughout California.

Capitol Commerce Reporter Inc

PO Box 1572
Austin TX 78767

Phone: 800-356-8282
512-443-2992
Fax: 512-443-5565

Local Retrieval Area: TX-Bastrop, Blanco, Burnet, Caldwell, Hays, Lee, Travis, Williamson.

Normal turnaround time: 24 hours. Online computer ordering is also available. Projects are generally billed by the number of names searched. Credit accounts are accepted. Terms are net 30 days.

Correspondent relationships: nationwide..dd.

Capitol Document Services Inc

815 N 1st Ave Suite 4
Phoenix AZ 85003

Phone: 800-255-4052
602-254-4489
Fax: 602-258-5833

Local Retrieval Area: AZ-Maricopa, Pima.

Normal turnaround time: 24 hours in Maricopa, 24 hours in Pima, and 2 to 4 days in other Arizona counties. Projects are generally billed by the number of names searched. They sometimes charge by the hour depending on search. Credit accounts are accepted. Credit cards are accepted.

Correspondent relationships: the rest of Arizona and nationwide. They specialize in searching and filing services. They will search any public record at any level.

Capitol Document Services Inc

8550 United Plaza Blvd Bldg II, Suite 702
Baton Rouge LA 70809

Phone: 800-408-1262
504-922-4693
Fax: 504-922-4694

Local Retrieval Area: LA-East Baton Rouge Parish.

Normal turnaround time: within 24 hours. Projects are generally billed by the number of names searched. The first project may require a prepayment.

Correspondent relationships: nationwide. They specialize in UCC searches and filing, tax lien and judgment searches and corporation document filing and retrieval.

Capitol Document Services Inc

PO Box 1812
Albuquerque NM 87103

Phone: 800-255-4381
505-248-1612
Fax: 800-848-8511
505-248-1646

Local Retrieval Area: NM-Bernalillo, Sandoval, Santa Fe, Valencia.

Normal turnaround time: next day. Projects are generally billed by the number of names searched. Credit accounts are accepted. Credit cards are accepted.

Correspondent relationships: nationwide. They specialize in UCC searches and expedited filings. tax lien, judgment and pending litigation searches, corporation document filing and retrieval.

Capitol Document Services Inc

400 W King St Suite 302
Carson City NV 89703

Phone: 800-899-0490
702-884-0490
Fax: 702-884-0493

Local Retrieval Area: NV-Carson City, Douglas, Storey, Washoe.

Normal turnaround time: 1-2 days for the listed counties and 3-5 days for the network counties. The first project may require a prepayment. Credit cards are accepted.

Correspondent relationships: nationwide. They specialize in UCC searches and filings, Motor Vehicle Record searches and corporation document filings and retrieval.

🏛 Capitol Document Services Inc

Phone: 800-432-0445
405-232-0445

217 N Harvey Suite 213
Oklahoma City OK 73102   **Fax:** 405-232-0442

Local Retrieval Area: OK-Oklahoma.

Normal turnaround time: next day. Projects are generally billed by the number of names searched. The first project may require a prepayment. Credit cards are accepted.

They specialize in UCC searches and expedited filings, tax lien, judgment and pending litigation searches, corporation document filing and retrieval.

Capitol Filing Service Inc

Phone: 615-646-1404

7051 Highway 70 S Suite 333   **Fax:** 615-646-0810
Nashville TN 37221

Local Retrieval Area: TN-12 Counties.

Normal turnaround time: 1-3 days. Projects are generally billed by the number of names searched. Credit accounts are accepted.

Correspondent relationships: the rest of Tennessee. They specialize in corporate research and filing.

Capitol Legal Service Inc

Phone: 916-443-7112

PO Box 22605   **Fax:** 916-443-3131
Sacramento CA 95822-0605

Local Retrieval Area: CA-El Dorado, Nevada, Placer, Sacramento, Solano, Sutter, Yolo.

Normal turnaround time: 5 days. Expedited service available. Projects are generally billed by the hour. Credit accounts are accepted. Sometimes a set-up fee and prepayment is required.

They specialize in research and photocopying.

🏛 Capitol Lien Records & Rsrch

Phone: 800-845-4077
612-222-2500

PO Box 65727 768 Rice St (55117)
St Paul MN 55165   **Fax:** 800-845-4080
612-222-2110

Local Retrieval Area: MN-All Counties; WI-St. Croix.

Normal turnaround time: 1-3 days. Projects are generally billed by the number of names searched or records located. The first project may require a prepayment. Terms are net 30 days after first order. Personal checks are accepted.

Correspondent relationships: South Dakota, North Dakota, Montana, Wisconsin, Iowa and Colorado. They provide a weekly publication of all federal and state tax liens filed with the Secretary of State of Minnesota.

Capitol Services

Phone: 916-443-0657

926 J St Suite 919   **Fax:** 916-443-1908
Sacramento CA 95814

Local Retrieval Area: CA-Sacramento.

Normal turnaround time: 1 working day. Projects are generally billed by the number of records located. The first project may require a prepayment. Credit cards are accepted.

They provide document filing and retrieval at the California Secretary of State's office in Sacramento.

Capitol Services

Phone: 904-878-4734

1406 Hays St Suite 2   **Fax:** 800-226-7544
Tallahassee FL 32301   904-656-7543

Local Retrieval Area: FL-Gadsden, Leon, Taylor, Wakulla.

Normal turnaround time: 24 hours. Projects are generally billed by the number of names searched. If the search is extra long, they will charge by the hour. Credit accounts are accepted. They request prepayment if the charges are over $50. Personal checks are accepted.

Correspondent relationships: all counties in Florida. They specialize in state UCC's, preparing and filing corporations, motor vehicle record searches and county searches.

🏛 Capitol Services Inc

Phone: 800-662-0171
518-453-0171

40 Colvin Ave Suite 200
Albany NY 12206   **Fax:** 800-662-0275
518-453-0275

Local Retrieval Area: NY-Albany, Rensselaer.

Normal turnaround time: next day. Projects are generally billed by the number of names searched. Credit accounts are accepted. Credit cards are accepted.

Correspondent relationships: nationwide. They are a full service UCC and corporate search and filing branch of Capitol Services in Austin, TX, specializing in New York matters.

🏛 Capitol Services Inc

Phone: 800-345-4647
512-474-8377

1212 Guadalupe Suite 102
Austin TX 78701   **Fax:** 800-432-3622
512-476-3678

Local Retrieval Area: TX-Dallas, Harris, Hays, Travis, Williamson.

Normal turnaround time: the next day. Projects are generally billed by the number of names searched. The first project may require a prepayment. Credit cards are accepted.

Correspondent relationships: nationwide. They specialize in UCC, tax lien, judgment and sending litigation searches, expedited UCC filings and corporation document filing and retrieval.

Caprock Land Title Company

Phone: 800-253-3281
806-669-3281

PO Box 1418
Pampa TX 79066-1418   **Fax:** 806-669-3282

Local Retrieval Area: TX-Gray.

Normal turnaround time: the same day to several days depending on work load and searches requested. Projects are generally billed by the number of names searched or records located. Credit accounts are accepted. Personal checks are accepted.

Correspondent relationships: most Texas counties. They specialize in title insurance, escrow closings and abstracts of title.

Caprock Title Co

Phone: 915-687-3232

511 W Ohio Ave Suite 100   **Fax:** 915-687-3240
Midland TX 79701

Local Retrieval Area: NM-Eddy, Lea; TX-Dickens, Kent, King, Stonewall.

Normal turnaround time: up to a week. Fee basis will vary by the type of project. The first project may require a prepayment.

Correspondent relationships: West Texas, Southeast, New Mexico. They specialize in oil & gas, mineral interests and working interests.

Capstone Title Services

817 22nd Ave
Tuscaloosa AL 35401

Phone: 205-759-1105
Fax: 205-759-1106

Local Retrieval Area: AL-Bibb, Dallas, Fayette, Greene, Hale, Pickens, Tuscaloosa, Walker.

Normal turnaround time: 1-2 days. Projects are generally billed by the number of names searched. Fee basis may vary on length of search. Credit accounts are accepted. Personal checks are accepted. Credit accounts are not accepted.

They specialize in title insurance, limited title searches, UCC's, judgments, probate and loan closings.

CAR-Computer Assisted Research

7625 Sunrise Blvd Suite 201
Citrus Heights CA 95610

Phone: 888-223-3456
916-726-4841
Fax: 916-726-8884

Local Retrieval and SOP Area: CA-Alameda, El Dorado, Nevada, Placer, Sacramento, San Francisco, San Joaquin, Yolo.

Normal turnaround time: same day. Online computer ordering is also available. Projects are generally billed by the number of names searched or records located. The first project may require a prepayment. Credit cards are accepted.

Correspondent relationships: CA, AZ, NV, OR and UT. They specialize in retail loss control investigations, loss control consultant, surveillance, skip tracing, attorney and insurance investigations and locates and interviews.

Carbon County Abstract & Title

PO Box 787 105 N Broadway
Red Lodge MT 59068

Phone: 406-446-1090
Fax: 406-446-1091

Local Retrieval Area: MT-Carbon.

Normal turnaround time: 2-3 days. Fees vary by project. Credit accounts are accepted.

Cardinal & Coyne Agency

584 N Church St Suite 51
Spartanburg SC 29303

Phone: 864-680-8074
Fax: 864-583-4899

Local Retrieval and SOP Area: SC-Anderson, Cherokee, Chester, Greenville, Laurens, Pickens, Spartanburg, Union, York.

Normal turnaround time: 2 days. Expedited service available at no extra charge. Projects are generally billed by the number of names searched. Credit accounts are accepted. Open invoicing available.

Correspondent relationships: all other counties in South Carolina.

Carol Ann Bailey CLA Inc

8178 S Airport Rd
Milton FL 32583

Phone: 904-623-9431
Fax: 904-623-0104

Local Retrieval Area: FL-Escambia, Santa Rosa.

Normal turnaround time: 7-10 days. Extra charge for expedited services. Projects are generally billed by the hour. Credit accounts are accepted. They require a retainer. Personal checks are accepted.

Correspondent relationships: all other counties in Florida. She holds a specialty certification in civil litigation, criminal law and procedure, and Florida law. She is also licensed in Real Estate.

Carolina Information Services Inc

11071 Farrow Rd
Blythewood SC 29016

Phone: 803-786-8665
Fax: 803-735-0399

Local Retrieval Area: SC-Fairfield, Lexington, Richland.

Normal turnaround time: 3 days. Projects are generally billed by the number of names searched. Credit accounts are accepted.

Correspondent relationships: the rest of South Carolina.

Carter Investigations

PO Box 492
Pocatello ID 83204-0492

Phone: 800-449-2920
208-232-3592

Local Retrieval Area: ID-Bannock, Bingham, Caribou, Custer, Oneida, Power.

Normal turnaround time: 2 to 3 days. Projects are generally billed by the number of names searched. The first project may require a prepayment.

Correspondent relationships: northern Idaho. They specialize in child custody and domestic work.

Casa De Search

PO Box 1004
Pecos NM 87552

Phone: 800-757-0220
505-757-2147
Fax: 800-743-6217
505-757-2773

Local Retrieval Area: NM-31 Counties.

Normal turnaround time: 24-48 hours. Projects are generally billed by the number of names searched. Credit accounts are accepted.

Correspondent relationships: Eddy and Taos County, NM. They specialize in UCC (Chattel) searches, tax lien/judgment, civil/criminal, bankruptcy, DMV and UCC filing.

Case Services Inc

PO Box 2343
South Bend IN 46680

Phone: 219-291-0480
Fax: 219-291-0855

Local Retrieval and SOP Area: IN-St. Joseph; MI-Berrien, Cass.

Normal turnaround time: 48 hours. Most searches are a flat fee. The first project may require a prepayment.

They are a full line detective agency.

Don W Caskey

702 N Circle
Baytown TX 77520

Phone: 713-422-7527
Fax: 713-422-7527

Local Retrieval Area: TX-Chambers, Liberty.

Normal turnaround time: 2 days. Projects are generally billed by the number of names searched. Credit accounts are accepted. Bill monthly.

Cass County Abstract Co

518 Chestnut St
Atlantic IA 50022

Phone: 712-243-2136
Fax: 712-243-4360

Local Retrieval Area: IA-Cass.

Normal turnaround time: 1-14 days. Fee basis will vary by the type of project. Credit accounts are accepted.

Correspondent relationships: PA, NE, MN and CA.

Cass County Abstract Co

PO Box 826
Fargo ND 58107

Phone: 701-232-3341
Fax: 701-232-7851

Local Retrieval Area: MN-Clay; ND-Cass.

Normal turnaround time: 2 days. Fee basis will vary by type of search. Credit accounts are accepted.

They specialize in real estate.

M B Cassell

PO Box 235
Finley ND 58230-0235

Phone: 701-524-1961

Local Retrieval Area: ND-Steele.

Normal turnaround time: 1-3 days. Projects are generally billed by the number of names searched or records located. Credit accounts are accepted.

Cassia County Abstract Co

Phone: 208-678-8347
Fax: 208-678-8348

PO Box 548
Burley ID 83318

Local Retrieval Area: ID-Cassia.

Normal turnaround time: 10 days. Projects are generally billed by the hour. Projects require prepayment.

They specialize in real estate closing.

Cattaraugus Abstract Corp

Phone: 800-559-1242
716-938-9109
Fax: 716-938-6259

406 Erie St
Little Valley NY 14755

Local Retrieval Area: NY-Cattaraugus.

Normal turnaround time: 48 hours. Projects are generally billed by the number of names searched. The first project may require a prepayment.

Cedar Land Title Inc

Phone: 801-586-9984
Fax: 801-586-5095

PO Box 733
Cedar City UT 84721

Local Retrieval Area: UT-Beaver, Garfield, Iron, Kane.

Normal turnaround time: 3 days. Projects are generally billed by the hour. Credit accounts are accepted.

They specialize in title search and UCC.

Centennial Abstract of Pratt Inc

Phone: 316-672-6889
Fax: 316-672-6579

100 S Main
Pratt KS 67124

Local Retrieval Area: KS-Pratt.

Normal turnaround time: 3-5 days. Projects are generally billed by the number of names searched. The first project may require a prepayment.

Centennial Coverages Inc

Phone: 800-338-8221
303-699-0444
Fax: 800-995-6046
303-680-1808

15200 E Girard Ave Suite 4500
Aurora CO 80014

Local Retrieval Area: CO-Adams, Arapahoe, Boulder, Denver, Douglas, Jefferson, Weld; IL-Cook, Du Page, Kane, Lake.

Normal turnaround time: 2-10 days. Projects are generally billed by the number of names searched or records located. Fee is by the hour on chain-of-title. The first project may require a prepayment. Terms are net 10 days.

Correspondent relationships: nationwide. They specialize in real estate searches, UCC searches, skip tracing, civil and criminal court searches, asset investigations and real estate chain-of-title.

Centennial Coverages Inc

Phone: 800-995-6041
Fax: 800-995-6046

1527 colonial Pky Suite 300
Palatine IL 60067

Local Retrieval Area: IL-Cook, Du Page, Kane.

Normal turnaround time: 24-48 hours. Expedited service available. Projects are generally billed by the number of names searched or records located. The first project may require a prepayment. Terms are net 10 days.

Correspondent relationships: nationwide. They specialize in asset/lien searches, UCC administration and searches, real estate and mortgage searches, federal, state and county court searches, and skip tracing, all on a national basis.

Centennial Title & Abstract Co

Phone: 313-238-5100
Fax: 313-238-5270

G4137 Fenton Road
Burton MI 48529

Local Retrieval Area: MI-Genesee.

Normal turnaround time: 3-4 days. Fee basis will vary by the project. The first project may require a prepayment.

They specialize in real estate transactions.

Central Indiana Paralegal Svc

Phone: 317-636-1311
Fax: 317-636-1426

55 Monument Cir Suite 1424
Indianapolis IN 46204

Local Retrieval Area: IN-Boone, Hamilton, Hendricks, Johnson, Marion, Morgan, Shelby.

Normal turnaround time: 2-5 days. Projects are generally billed by the number of names searched. The first project may require a prepayment. Terms are net 30 days.

Correspondent relationships: all counties in Indiana. They specialize in legal research, document filing and retrieval at all government offices.

Central Investigation

Phone: 800-281-8142
419-474-5195
Fax: 419-474-5102

4841 Monroe St Suite 202
Toledo OH 43614

Local Retrieval and SOP Area: MI-Lenawee, Monroe; OH-Defiance, Fulton, Hancock, Henry, Lucas, Williams, Wood.

Normal turnaround time: 1 day. Fee basis is determined on each individual case. Projects require prepayment.

Correspondent relationships: northern Ohio.

Central Legal Service

Phone: 800-599-8133
541-389-8133
Fax: 541-382-7068

PO Box 409
Bend OR 97709

Local Retrieval and SOP Area: OR-Crook, Deschutes, Jefferson.

Normal turnaround time: 48 hours. Expedited service available. Projects are generally billed by the hour..dd. Credit accounts are accepted.

Central New York Abstract Corp

Phone: 315-724-1614
Fax: 315-724-0563

24 Elizabeth St, PO Box 268
Utica NY 13503

Local Retrieval Area: NY-Cayuga, Herkimer, Madison, Oneida, Oswego, Otsego.

Normal turnaround time: 1-2 days for reports and 1 to 2 weeks for abstracts. Projects are generally billed by the number of names searched or records located. Credit accounts are accepted.

Central Utah Title

Phone: 801-835-1111
Fax: 801-835-8824

140 N Main
Manti UT 84642

Local Retrieval Area: UT-Sanpete.

Normal turnaround time: 1 week. Projects are generally billed by the number of names searched. Credit accounts are accepted.

They specialize in escrow closings.

Central Valley Records Service

2101 Ottawa Ct
Modesto CA 95356

Phone: 209-525-8786
Fax: 209-525-8786

Local Retrieval Area: CA-Fresno, Madera, Merced, San Joaquin, Stanislaus, Tuolumne.

Normal turnaround time: 24 hours in Stanislaus; 24-48 hours in other counties. Projects are generally billed by the number of names searched. Credit accounts are accepted. Monthly billing available.

Correspondent relationships: Sacramento, Alameda, Santa Cruz, and Contra Costa counties, CA.

Cerro Gordo Abstract Co

10 N Washington Suite 300
Mason City IA 50401

Phone: 515-423-1145
Fax: 515-423-0289

Local Retrieval Area: IA-Cerro Gordo.

Normal turnaround time: 1-2 days. Projects are generally billed by the number of names searched. Fee basis may also be per description. Credit accounts are accepted.

They specialize in real estate.

Certified Document Retriever

PO Box 3150
Albany NY 12203-0150

Phone: 518-438-7956
Fax: 518-438-0502

Local Retrieval and SOP Area: NY-Albany.

Normal turnaround time: varies with type of document requested. Expedited service available. Projects are generally billed by the number of names searched or records located. The first project may require a prepayment. Terms are net 30 days.

They specialize in "certified" document retrieval for both corporate and motor vehicle records for New York State only.

Chaffee Title-Abstract Co

225 "G" St
Salida CO 81201

Phone: 719-539-2215
Fax: 719-539-2588

Local Retrieval Area: CO-Chaffee.

Normal turnaround time: 4-5 days. Fee basis will vary by the type of project. The first project may require a prepayment.

They specialize in real estate searching.

Chambers Investigations

520 12th St W
Bradenton FL 34205

Phone: 800-792-1107
941-747-7265
Fax: 941-747-0316

Local Retrieval Area: FL-De Soto, Manatee, Sarasota.

Normal turnaround time: 24 hours. Projects are generally billed by the hour. Projects require prepayment.

They specialize in private investigations.

Linda Chambless

PO Box 437
Millry AL 36558

Phone: 205-846-3697
Fax: 205-846-3697

Local Retrieval Area: AL-Choctaw, Clarke, Monroe, Washington.

Normal turnaround time: 48 hours. Projects are generally billed by the number of names searched. The first project may require a prepayment.

She specializes in real estate abstracts.

Chariton Abstract

300 S Walnut
Keytesville MO 65261

Phone: 816-288-3446
Fax: 816-288-3446

Local Retrieval Area: MO-Chariton.

Normal turnaround time: 3-4 days. Fee basis varies by type of transaction. Credit accounts are accepted.

Chariton Abstract Co

917 1/2 Braden
Chariton IA 50049

Phone: 515-774-2677

Local Retrieval Area: IA-Lucas.

Normal turnaround time: up to 2 weeks. Expedited service available. Fee basis will vary by the type of project. Credit accounts are accepted.

Charles F Edgar & Associates

2724 10th Ave SW
Huntsville AL 35805-4136

Phone: 205-539-7761
Fax: 205-539-7768

Local Retrieval and SOP Area: AL-19 Counties; TN-Bedford, Coffee, Franklin, Giles, Lawrence, Lincoln, Marion, Maury, Moore.

Normal turnaround time: 2-3 days. Projects are generally billed by the number of names searched. Credit accounts are accepted. Terms are net 30 days.

They specialize in corporation filings.

Charles Jones Inc

PO Box 8488
Trenton NJ 08650-8488

Phone: 800-792-8888
609-538-1000
Fax: 800-883-0677
609-883-0677

Local Retrieval Area: NJ-All Counties.

Normal turnaround time: 1-10 days. Online computer ordering is also available. Projects are generally billed by the number of names searched or records located. The first project may require a prepayment. Credit cards are accepted.

Correspondent relationships: mid-Atlantic and midwest states. They specialize in on-line searching and access, document filing and retrieval, list processing and bulk data sales and licensing.

Charles L Layer Private Investgtns

PO Box 608
Rockwall TX 75087

Phone: 800-771-4887
972-771-8685
Fax: 972-771-6705

Local Retrieval and SOP Area: TX-Collin, Dallas, Denton, Ellis, Hunt, Kaufman, Rockwall, Tarrant.

Normal turnaround time: 1 week. Projects are generally billed by the hour. Credit accounts are accepted. Terms are net 30 days after work completed.

Correspondent relationships: all of Texas. They specialize in insurance fraud investigations, surveillance and general investigations, including domestics.

Charley's Legal Angels

111 N Marietta Pky Suite B107
Marietta GA 30060

Phone: 770-419-0259
Fax: 770-419-0259

Local Retrieval and SOP Area: GA-Cobb, De Kalb, Fulton, Gwinnett.

Normal turnaround time: 24 hours for Gwinnett and Cobb counties, 48 hours for Fulton and DeKalb counties. Expedited service available. Projects are generally billed by the number of names searched. The first project may require a prepayment. Terms are net 30 days.

Correspondent relationships: Clayton, Cherokee, Douglas, Forsythe and Henry, GA counties. They specialize in criminal checks for pre-employment screening, process serving, criminal record checks, document retrieval, legal research, bankruptcy services and online research. Skip tracing and investigations services are also available.

Charlson & Wilson Bonded Abstr

111 N 4th St
Manhattan KS 66502

Phone: 913-537-2900
Fax: 913-537-2904

Local Retrieval Area: KS-Riley.

Normal turnaround time: 3-5 days. Projects are generally billed by the hour. Projects require prepayment.

Correspondent relationships: Pottawatomie. They specialize in any kind of title search.

Alvin W Charpontier

559 N 2nd St
San Jose CA 95112

Phone: 408-292-2822
Fax: 408-292-2822

Local Retrieval Area: CA-Monterey, San Benito, San Francisco, San Mateo, Santa Clara, Santa Cruz.

Normal turnaround time: 24 hours..dd. Projects are generally billed by the number of names searched. Credit accounts are accepted. Bill at the end of the month.

He specializes in criminal research for pre-employment screening.

Charter Title Corp

PO Box 598
Port Townsend WA 98368

Phone: 800-401-1001
360-385-1322
Fax: 360-385-1877

Local Retrieval Area: WA-Jefferson.

Normal turnaround time: 24 hours. Fees based on dollar value of transaction. The first project may require a prepayment.

They specialize in title insurance and escrow.

Chattel Mortgage Reporter Inc

582 N Oakwood Ave Suite 202
Lake Forest IL 60045

Phone: 847-234-8805
Fax: 847-234-8804

Local Retrieval Area: IL-13 Counties.

Normal turnaround time: 1-3 days. Projects are generally billed by the number of names searched or records located. Credit accounts are accepted. Personal checks are accepted.

Correspondent relationships: all of Illinois. They specialize in same day Cook County, IL UCC searches. They are known as the Cook County, IL (Chicago) UCC authority for 95 years. They have their own database for this county and microfilm dating back to 1973.

Chautauqua County Abstract Co

121 W Main St
Sedan KS 67361

Phone: 316-725-3215
Fax: 316-725-3215

Local Retrieval Area: KS-Chautauqua.

Normal turnaround time: 2-3 days. Fee basis varies by type of transaction. The first project may require a prepayment.

They specialize in abstract and title searching.

Chaves County Abstract & Title Co

PO Box 1476
Roswell NM 88202

Phone: 505-622-5340
Fax: 505-622-5346

Local Retrieval Area: NM-Chaves.

Normal turnaround time: varied depending on project. Fee basis vill vary by the type of project. The first project may require a prepayment.

Cheboygan Straits Area Title

PO Box 328
Cheboygan MI 49721

Phone: 616-627-7181
Fax: 616-627-6200

Local Retrieval Area: MI-Cheboygan.

Normal turnaround time: 2-5 days. Fee basis will vary by type of project. The first project may require a prepayment.

They specialize in land title searches.

Cherokee Capitol Abstract & Title

107 E Delaware St
Tahlequah OK 74464

Phone: 918-456-8851
Fax: 918-456-8322

Local Retrieval Area: OK-Cherokee.

Normal turnaround time: within the same day of request. Projects are generally billed by the number of records located. Credit accounts are accepted.

Chesapeake Services

PO Box 470
Chester MD 21619

Phone: 800-834-7938
410-643-3731
Fax: 410-643-4814

Local Retrieval Area: MD-Anne Arundel, Queen Anne's.

Normal turnaround time: 24-48 hours. Online computer ordering is also available. Projects are generally billed by the hour. The first project may require a prepayment.

An instate 800 number is available for established accounts. They have access to a statewide District Court computer system. They can communicate with accounts through Compu-Serve.

Cheslock Investigations

5657 S Rex Rd
Memphis TN 38119

Phone: 901-681-9663
Fax: 901-681-9413

Local Retrieval and SOP Area: AR-Crittenden; MS-De Soto; TN-Shelby.

Normal turnaround time: 24-48 hours, depending on volume. Projects are generally billed by the number of names searched. The first project may require a prepayment. Payment due upon receipt of information.

Correspondent relationships: nationwide.

Cheyenne Abstract Co Inc

PO Box 450
Cheyenne OK 73628

Phone: 405-497-3363

Local Retrieval Area: OK-Roger Mills.

Normal turnaround time: 2-3 days. Fee basis will vary by the type of project. Credit accounts are accepted.

Cheyenne County Abstract

Phone: 308-254-5636
Fax: 308-254-6159

1024 Jackson St
Sidney NE 69162

Local Retrieval Area: NE-Cheyenne.

Normal turnaround time: 3-5 days. Projects are generally billed by the number of records located. Credit accounts are accepted.

They specialize in oil record searches.

Cheyenne County Abstract Co

Phone: 719-767-5585
Fax: 719-767-5029

130 S 1st E
Cheyenne Wells CO 80810

Local Retrieval Area: CO-Cheyenne.

Normal turnaround time: up to 1 week. Projects are generally billed by the hour. Credit accounts are accepted.

They specialize in real estate title.

Chilvers Abstract & Title Co

Phone: 402-329-4525
Fax: 402-439-2145

101 E Main
Pierce NE 68767

Local Retrieval Area: NE-Antelope, Cedar, Knox, Pierce, Wayne.

Normal turnaround time: 1-3 days. Fee bases is a flat rate and per record. Credit accounts are accepted.

They specialize in title insurance.

Darlene Chiota

Phone: 814-870-0064

PO Box 1849
Erie PA 16507-0849

Local Retrieval Area: PA-Erie.

Normal turnaround time: 24-48 hours. Turnaround time is up to 1 week for title searches. Projects are generally billed by the number of names searched or records located. Credit accounts are accepted. She requests prepayment for copies, but will invoice for services.

She specializes in current owner searches.

Chippewa Abstract and Title Co

Phone: 906-632-0603
Fax: 906-632-6153

223 W Portage Suite 2
Sault Sainte Marie MI 49783

Local Retrieval Area: MI-Chippewa, Mackinac.

Normal turnaround time: 2-3 weeks in October through April and 5 to 6 weeks in May through September. Projects are generally billed by the hour. Projects require prepayment. Personal checks are accepted.

Correspondent relationships: the state of Michigan. They have been servicing Chippewa County for over 140 years.

Choctaw County Abstract and Title

Phone: 405-326-9616

PO Box 636
Hugo OK 74743

Local Retrieval Area: OK-Choctaw.

Normal turnaround time: 1 week. Fee basis will vary by the type of project. The first project may require a prepayment. Clients may make payments upon receipt.

Chouteau County Abstract Co

Phone: 406-622-3221

Box 578
Fort Benton MT 59442

Local Retrieval Area: MT-Chouteau.

Normal turnaround time: 2-4 days. Projects are generally billed by the hour. Credit accounts are accepted.

Chris Wright & Associates

Phone: 303-776-0291
Fax: 303-772-1861

PO Box 1034
Longmont CO 80502-1034

Local Retrieval Area: CO-Adams, Arapahoe, Boulder, Denver, Jefferson, Larimer, Weld.

Normal turnaround time: 1-3 days. Edpedited service available. Projects are generally billed by the hour. The first project may require a prepayment.

Correspondent relationships: the rest of the state.

Duane Christensen

Phone: 605-364-7661

RR 1 Box 42A
Utica SD 57067

Local Retrieval Area: SD-Bon Homme, Clay, Yankton.

Normal turnaround time: 24-48 hours. Projects are generally billed by the number of names searched. Credit accounts are accepted.

Church & Grau

Phone: 316-723-2552

109 W Florida Ave
Greensburg KS 67054

Local Retrieval Area: KS-Kiowa.

Normal turnaround time: 2-3 days. Fee basis varies by type of transaction. Credit accounts are accepted.

Citizen's Abstract Co

Phone: 501-268-5571
Fax: 501-268-7378

104 E Race Ave
Searcy AR 72143

Local Retrieval Area: AR-White.

Normal turnaround time: up to 1 week. Fee basis will vary by type of project. The first project may require a prepayment.

They specialize in land title and title insurance.

Citzen Abstract Co

Phone: 217-728-7132

11 W Harrison
Sullivan IL 61951

Local Retrieval Area: IL-Moultrie.

Normal turnaround time: 2 days. Fee basis varies by type of transaction. Credit accounts are accepted.

Civil Process Service

Phone: 800-866-2214
817-335-2446
Fax: 817-335-2445

512 Main St Suite 615
Fort Worth TX 76102

Local Retrieval Area: TX-Dallas, Tarrant.

Normal turnaround time: 24-48 hours. Projects are generally billed by the hour. Credit accounts are accepted.

Correspondent relationships: Northern Texas. They specialize in records research.

Clarence M Kelley and Assoc

Phone: 816-756-2458
Fax: 816-931-0795

3217 Broadway 4th Fl
Kansas City MO 64111

Local Retrieval and SOP Area: KS-Johnson, Sedgwick, Shawnee, Wyandotte.

Normal turnaround time: 1-3 days. Projects are generally billed by the number of names searched. The first project may require a prepayment. Credit cards are accepted.

Correspondent relationships: all of Missouri. They are a professional investigative and consulting firm with nationwide coverage. Services include surveillance, cause and origin investigation, undercovers, fraud and theft investigation, electronic countermeasures, and computer network security.

Clark Abstract & Title Co
Phone: 605-532-3812

PO Box 253
Clark SD 57225

Local Retrieval Area: SD-Clark.

Normal turnaround time: 2-3 days. Fee basis varies by type of transaction. Projects require prepayment.

Clark County Abstract Co
Phone: 501-246-2821
Fax: 501-246-2467

402 Clay St
Arkadelphia AR 71923

Local Retrieval Area: AR-Clark.

Normal turnaround time: 3 days. Expedited service available. Fee basis will vary by type of project. The first project may require a prepayment.

Clarke & Clarke
Phone: 606-564-5527
Fax: 606-564-4536

119 Sutton St
Maysville KY 41056

Local Retrieval Area: KY-Bracken, Fleming, Mason.

Normal turnaround time: up to 5 days. Fee basis varies by type of transaction. Credit accounts are accepted.

Claudine Claugus
Phone: 614-425-1831

34852 Hartshorne Ridge Rd
Graysville OH 45734

Local Retrieval Area: OH-Belmont, Harrison, Jefferson, Monroe, Muskingum, Tuscarawas; WV-Brooke, Marshall, Tyler, Wetzel, Wood.

Normal turnaround time: 24-72 hours. Fee basis is per piece. Credit accounts are accepted. Terms are net 30 days.

Correspondent relationships: Noble, Washington, Guernsey, Morgan counties. She specializes in UCC and title searches.

Clay County Abstract & Title
Phone: 402-762-3645
Fax: 402-762-3645

PO Box 38
Clay Center NE 68933

Local Retrieval Area: NE-Clay.

Normal turnaround time: 1-2 days. Fee basis varies by type of transaction. The first project may require a prepayment.

Clay County Abstract Co
Phone: 218-233-1358
Fax: 218-233-1359

113 S 12th St
Moorhead MN 56560

Local Retrieval Area: MN-Clay.

Normal turnaround time: 5-10 days. Online computer ordering is also available. Projects are generally billed by the number of names searched. Credit accounts are accepted. Personal checks are accepted.

Correspondent relationships: Becker, Otter Tail, Norman, Polk, Red Lake, Wilkin, Mahnomen, Marshall, Kittson and Roseau Counties.

Clayton County Abstract Co
Phone: 319-245-1430
Fax: 319-245-1430

126 S Main
Elkader IA 52043

Local Retrieval Area: IA-Clayton.

Normal turnaround time: 1 week. Fee basis will vary by the type of project. Credit accounts are accepted.

Clayton Title Service Inc
Phone: 505-374-9789
Fax: 505-374-8381

PO Box 327
Clayton NM 88415

Local Retrieval Area: NM-Union.

Normal turnaround time: 5-10 days. Fee basis will vary by the type of project. The first project may require a prepayment.

They specialize in abstracts, title insurance, oil and gas searches, mineral searches.

Clear Creek-Gelpin Abstract & Title
Phone: 303-569-2391
Fax: 303-569-2670

PO Box 545
Georgetown CO 80444

Local Retrieval Area: CO-Clear Creek, Gilpin.

Normal turnaround time: 3-5 days. Fee basis will vary by the type of project. The first project may require a prepayment.

They specialize in real estate and title matters.

Clear Title Co
Phone: 409-968-5885
Fax: 409-968-6082

140 S Washington St
La Grange TX 78945-2629

Local Retrieval Area: TX-Fayette.

Normal turnaround time: up to a week because the court is not computerized. Fee basis will vary by the type of project. The first project may require a prepayment.

Danny Clearman
Phone: 601-635-3432
Fax: 601-635-3432

PO Box 85 117 W Broad St
Decatur MS 39327

Local Retrieval Area: MS-Newton.

Normal turnaround time: 1-2 days. Projects are generally billed by the hour. The first project may require a prepayment.

He is in general practice. He specializes in marriage/divorce searches.

Cleveland Investigations
Phone: 800-888-6629
503-535-6005
Fax: 503-535-3411

6085 Waldlen
Talent OR 97540

Local Retrieval and SOP Area: CA-Siskiyou; OR-13 Counties.

Normal turnaround time: up to 3 days. Rush service is also available. Projects are generally billed by the number of names searched. The first project may require a prepayment. Will bill for established clients.

Correspondent relationships: Statewide and California.

Cliff Childress Special Investigtns
Phone: 601-977-7484
Fax: 601-353-6004

PO Box 5555
Jackson MS 39288-5555

Local Retrieval Area: MS-Hinds, Leake, Madison, Neshoba, Rankin, Scott, Warren.

Normal turnaround time: 24-48 hours. Expedited service available. Projects are generally billed by the hour. Flat rate may be arranged in some matters. The first project may require a prepayment. Partial prepayment required in some cases.

Correspondent relationships: Winston, Attala, Noxubee, Lowndes, Choctaw & Oktibbeha, MS counties. They specialize in legal and corporate investigations, including "paper-chase", fraud, conflict of interest, location of hidden assets, financial lifestyle, traffic and questionable death investigations.

Clinton Abstract Co Inc

Phone: 405-323-3025

519 Gary Blvd
Clinton OK 73601

Local Retrieval Area: OK-Custer.

Normal turnaround time: 2 days. Projects are generally billed by the number of names searched. Copy charges will be added to the fee. Credit accounts are accepted. Personal checks are accepted.

Clovis Title and Abstract Company

Phone: 505-762-4403
Fax: 505-762-4404

420 Mitchell St
Clovis NM 88101

Local Retrieval Area: NM-Curry.

Normal turnaround time: 2 days. Projects are generally billed by the number of records located. Credit accounts are accepted. Personal checks are accepted.

They specialize in title searches, abstracts of title, title insurance, lien searches and criminal searches.

Clue Detective Agency

Phone: 614-536-9600
Fax: 614-526-9600

PO Box 237
Rushville OH 43150-0237

Local Retrieval Area: OH-Hocking, Perry.

Normal turnaround time: 2-3 days. Projects are generally billed by the hour. Projects require prepayment. Credit cards are accepted.

They specialize in missing persons, adoptions search, skip-tracing, information services and general investigations.

CMS (Consumer Marketing Svc)

Phone: 315-476-8414
Fax: 315-476-8577

1201 E Fayette St
Syracuse NY 13210

Local Retrieval Area: NY-48 Counties.

Normal turnaround time: 24-48 hours. Expedited service available. Fees depend on type of search performed. The first project may require a prepayment. Terms are net 30 days.

Correspondent relationships: Pennsylvania, Ohio, West Virginia, New Jersey and Connecticut. They specialize in all functions of abstract/document retrieval within the county and state levels.

CMT Abstract

Phone: 908-722-6565
Fax: 908-722-5011

380 Catherine St
Somerville NJ 08876

Local Retrieval Area: NJ-Somerset.

Normal turnaround time: 24 hours. Fee basis will vary by type of project. Credit accounts are accepted.

They perform credit check searches, title searches and property searches at the county level.

Coast to Coast Research Network

Phone: 800-933-5068
603-783-0263
Fax: 800-933-7268
603-783-0263

PO Box 7018
Concord NH 03301-7001

Local Retrieval Area: NH-Belknap, Carroll, Cheshire, Coos, Grafton, Hillsborough, Merrimack, Rockingham, Strafford, Sullivan.

Normal turnaround time: 24-72 hours. Projects are generally billed by the number of names searched. They may also charge by place. Credit accounts are accepted. Terms are net 30 days.

Correspondent relationships: nationwide. They specialize in UCC, corporate searches, property title updates on current owner, tax liens, voter registration and real estate assessment records found in the individual towns or cities.

Coastal Investigative Services Inc

Phone: 919-355-0122
Fax: 919-355-1842

3219 Landmark St Bldg 5
Greenville NC 27834

Local Retrieval and SOP Area: NC-Beaufort, Currituck, Edgecombe, Lenoir, Onslow, Pitt.

Normal turnaround time: 24-72 hours. Online computer ordering is also available. Project billing methods vary. Copy costs will be added to the total. The first project may require a prepayment. Credit cards are accepted. They accept personal checks.

Janet Coats

Phone: 412-429-3427
Fax: 412-429-5884

133 Lee St Suite 403
Carnegie PA 15106-3150

Local Retrieval Area: PA-Allegheny.

Normal turnaround time: 24-48 hours. Fee basis varies by type of transaction. The first project may require a prepayment.

Cobra Company

Phone: 800-894-5825
505-275-5825
Fax: 505-292-7414

PO Box 30911
Albuquerque NM 87190-0911

Local Retrieval Area: NM-Bernalillo, Sandoval, Valencia.

Normal turnaround time: 24 hours. Projects are generally billed by the hour. The first project may require a prepayment. Established clientele terms are 2% 10 net 30.

They specialize in surveillance; exceptionally covert, dependable, 4 investigators in New Mexico. Each investigator must go through a 6 week intensive training program before coming on board with Cobra Company.

Cobra Company of Arizona

Phone: 602-978-6010
Fax: 602-938-1209

4410 W Union Hills Suite #7-223
Glendale AZ 85308

Local Retrieval Area: AZ-Maricopa, Pima, Pinal.

Normal turnaround time: 24 hours. Projects are generally billed by the hour. The first project may require a prepayment. Established clientele terms are 2% 10 net 30.

Correspondent relationships: Arizona. They specialize in surveillance: exceptionally covert, dependable with 6 investigators in Arizona. Each investigator must go through a 6 week intensive training period to come aboard with Cobra Company.

Cobra Security and Investigtns

Phone: 847-622-8946
Fax: 847-622-8042

164 Division St Suite 503
Elgin IL 60120

Local Retrieval and SOP Area: IL-Boone, Cook, De Kalb, Du Page, Kane, Kendall, Lake, McHenry, Winnebago.

Normal turnaround time: 1-3 business days. Projects are generally billed by the number of names searched. Projects require prepayment.

They specialize in full private investigative services.

Coit Enterprises

Phone: 402-451-0462
Fax: 402-451-3949

2560 Newport Ave Suite A
Omaha NE 68112-3326

Local Retrieval Area: IA-Harrison, Mills, Pottawattamie; NE-Cass, Dodge, Douglas, Sarpy, Saunders, Washington.

Normal turnaround time: 1 week. Expedited service available. Projects are generally billed by the number of names searched or records located. Projects require prepayment.

Coke County Abstract Co
3 E 6th
Robert Lee TX 76945

Phone: 915-453-2049
Fax: 915-453-2049

Local Retrieval Area: TX-Coke.

Normal turnaround time: 1-2 days. Fee basis will vary by the type of project. The first project may require a prepayment.

Coleman County Title Co
PO Box 865
Coleman TX 76834-0865

Phone: 915-625-4628
Fax: 915-625-4417

Local Retrieval Area: TX-Coleman.

Normal turnaround time: up to 5 days. Projects are generally billed by the hour. The first project may require a prepayment.

Colfax County Title and Abstract
1109 C St
Schuyler NE 68661

Phone: 402-352-2027
Fax: 402-352-2027

Local Retrieval Area: NE-Butler, Colfax.

Normal turnaround time: 1 week. Projects are generally billed by the hour. Credit accounts are accepted. Personal checks are accepted.

Correspondent relationships: nationwide.

Collections
PO Box 204
Summerville SC 29484

Phone: 803-821-6485
Fax: 803-873-6601

Local Retrieval Area: SC-Bamberg, Barnwell, Berkeley, Calhoun, Charleston, Clarendon, Colleton, Dorchester, Orangeburg, Sumter.

Normal turnaround time: 1-24 hours. Projects are generally billed by the number of names searched or records located. The first project may require a prepayment.

Correspondent relationships: Lee, Beauford and Florence, SC counties.

Collier Abstracts Inc
107 N Main St
Smith Center KS 66967-0254

Phone: 913-282-3351
Fax: 913-282-3351

Local Retrieval Area: KS-Smith.

Normal turnaround time: up to 1 week. Fee basis varies by type of transaction. Credit accounts are accepted. They request prepayment from out of state clients, but will invoice established customers.

Collins Title & Abstract Co Inc
139 King St
St Augustine FL 32084

Phone: 904-829-6600
Fax: 904-824-2870

Local Retrieval Area: FL-Duval, Flagler, Putnam, St. Johns.

Normal turnaround time: varied depending on project. Fee basis will vary by the type of project. Credit accounts are accepted.

They specialize in real estate title work.

Colonial Valley Abstract Co
216 E Market St
York PA 17403

Phone: 717-848-2871
Fax: 717-845-6161

Local Retrieval Area: PA-Adams, Franklin, Lancaster, York.

Normal turnaround time: 3 days. Fee basis will vary by the type of project. The first project may require a prepayment.

They specialize in real estate.

Colorado City Abstract Co
114 W 2nd St
Colorado City TX 79512

Phone: 915-728-3475
Fax: 915-728-8851

Local Retrieval Area: TX-Mitchell.

Normal turnaround time: 2-3 days. Fee basis will vary by the type of project. The first project may require a prepayment.

Colorado County Abstract Co
PO Box 428
Columbus TX 78934

Phone: 409-732-6096
Fax: 409-732-6096

Local Retrieval Area: TX-Colorado.

Normal turnaround time: 2-3 days. Fee basis will vary by the type of project. The first project may require a prepayment.

Colorado Land Title
PO Box 334
Pagosa Springs CO 81147

Phone: 303-264-4178
Fax: 303-264-4775

Local Retrieval Area: CO-Archuleta.

Normal turnaround time: up to 1 week. Fee basis is determined on a "flat rate" (plus costs). Projects require prepayment.

They specialize in real estate matters.

Colorado Records Search Inc
3066 W Prentice Ave Apt C
Littleton CO 80123-7725

Phone: 303-972-3424
Fax: 303-972-1068

Local Retrieval Area: CO-11 Counties.

Normal turnaround time: 24-48 hours. Projects are generally billed by the number of names searched or records located. Credit accounts are accepted.

Correspondent relationships: the rest of the state. They specialize in public record retrieval.

Columbian National Title Ins
216 W Murdock St
Wichita KS 67203-3870

Phone: 316-262-0387
Fax: 316-267-8427

Local Retrieval Area: KS-Sedgwick.

Normal turnaround time: 1-3 days. Fee basis varies by type of transaction. Credit accounts are accepted.

Melanie Colvin
116 LaSalle Circle
West Monroe LA 71291

Phone: 318-396-6415

Local Retrieval Area: LA-Caldwell Parish, Franklin Parish, Jackson Parish, Lincoln Parish, Morehouse Parish, Ouachita Parish, Richland Parish, Tensas Parish, Union Parish, Winn Parish.

Normal turnaround time: 24 hours within a 30 mile radius and 48 hours outside that radius. Projects are generally billed by the number of names searched. Credit accounts are accepted.

Correspondent relationships: West Carroll and East Carroll parishes.

Comanche Abstract and Title Co
120 E Main
Coldwater KS 67029

Phone: 316-582-2125
Fax: 316-582-2125

Local Retrieval Area: KS-Comanche.

Normal turnaround time: 7-10 days. Projects are generally billed by the number of names searched or records located. Credit accounts are accepted. Personal checks are accepted.

They specialize in title searches, ownership, mineral interest, leasehold, oil and gas searches, and certificates of title and abstracts.

Comanche County Abstract Co

Phone: 915-356-2564
Fax: 915-356-3066

PO Box 762
Comanche TX 76442

Local Retrieval Area: TX-Comanche.

Normal turnaround time: 2-5 days. Fee basis will vary by type of project. The first project may require a prepayment.

Combs and Combs PSC

Phone: 606-437-6226
Fax: 606-432-4414

411 Main St
Pikeville KY 41501

Local Retrieval Area: KY-Floyd, Pike.

Normal turnaround time: 1 week. Projects are generally billed by the hour. Projects require prepayment.

Correspondent relationships: Knott, Johnson and Martin.

Commercial DataBase Network

Phone: 800-677-4190
908-431-1406
Fax: 908-431-3680

30 South St
Freehold NJ 07728

Local Retrieval Area: NJ-Monmouth.

Normal turnaround time: 24-72 hours. Online computer ordering is also available. Projects are generally billed by the number of names searched or records located. The first project may require a prepayment. Credit cards are accepted. Monthly billing available.

Commercial Information Svcs

Phone: 800-308-2364
206-682-2306
Fax: 206-682-1074

PO Box 85105
Seattle WA 98145

Local Retrieval Area: WA-King, Kitsap, Pierce, Skagit, Snohomish, Whatcom.

Normal turnaround time: 24-48 hours. Projects are generally billed by the number of names searched. The first project may require a prepayment. Credit cards are accepted.

Correspondent relationships: the Northwest.

Commercial Investigation

Phone: 800-677-4190
908-431-3004
Fax: 908-431-3680

30 South St
Freehold NJ 07728

Local Retrieval and SOP Area: NJ-Middlesex, Monmouth, Ocean.

Normal turnaround time: varied depending on project. Online computer ordering is also available. Projects are generally billed by the hour. The first project may require a prepayment.

They specialize in on-line civil suit, judgments, liens, bankruptcy, landlord/tenant cases and pending litigation on individual or company names. They are on-line for property ownership & tax records in NJ, and motor vehicle records in NJ, NY, PA.

Commercial Process Servicing Inc

Phone: 800-382-0088
805-382-1036
Fax: 805-382-1037

1437 F S Victoria Ave Suite 350
Ventura CA 93003

Local Retrieval and SOP Area: CA-Santa Barbara, Ventura.

Normal turnaround time: varied depending on project. Projects are generally billed by the hour. Credit accounts are accepted. Personal checks are accepted.

Correspondent relationships: Los Angeles and Orange Counties. They specialize in court filings, process serving and deposition interpreting (English/Spanish).

Commonwealth Investigation Agcy

Phone: 610-433-2325

461 Linden St
Allentown PA 18102

Local Retrieval Area: PA-Berks, Bucks, Carbon, Dauphin, Lackawanna, Lancaster, Lebanon, Lehigh, Monroe, Northampton.

Normal turnaround time: 1-3 days. Projects are generally billed by the hour. Projects require prepayment.

Correspondent relationships: Luzerne, Lycoming, Montgomery, Philadelphia and Schuylkill. They are a full service private investigations firm.

Community Title Co

Phone: 319-824-3123
Fax: 319-824-6728

PO Box 188
Grundy Center IA 50638

Local Retrieval Area: IA-Grundy.

Normal turnaround time: 2-3 days. Fee basis varies by type of transaction. Credit accounts are accepted.

Compass Investigations

Phone: 954-527-5722
Fax: 954-527-4451

408 S Andrews Ave Suite 205
Ft Lauderdale FL 33301

Local Retrieval and SOP Area: FL-Broward, Dade, Palm Beach.

Normal turnaround time: the same day. Projects are generally billed by the hour. The first project may require a prepayment. Credit cards are accepted.

Correspondent relationships: all of Florida. They specialize in record research, surveillance and process service.

Compass Solutions

Phone: 800-814-8213
206-505-8213
Fax: 800-257-8893
206-505-7480

PO Box 2826
Seattle WA 98111

Local Retrieval Area: WA-Island, King, Kitsap, Pierce, Skagit, Snohomish, Spokane, Thurston, Whatcom, Yakima.

Normal turnaround time: 8 hours. Online computer ordering is also available. Projects are generally billed by the number of names searched. Credit accounts are accepted. Invoicing availalbe upon signing contract.

Correspondent relationships: nationwide. They specialize in criminal statewide record searches.

Complete Corporate Svcs of AK

Phone: 907-790-4956
Fax: 907-790-4954

PO Box 33735
Juneau AK 99803

Local Retrieval Area: AK-Juneau Borough.

Normal turnaround time: the same day. Fee basis will vary by the type of project. Projects require prepayment. They also will accept personal checks.

They specialize in searches at the State level.

Complete Title Service of Walker

Phone: 800-837-2556
218-547-2565
Fax: 218-547-2564

PO Box 966
Walker MN 56484

Local Retrieval Area: MN-Beltrami, Cass, Hubbard.

Normal turnaround time: 1-3 days. New abstracts average 10 to 14 days. Projects are generally billed by the number of names searched. Credit accounts are accepted. Personal checks are accepted.

They also provide closing and title insurance services.

Compu-Fact Research Inc

Phone: 314-291-3308
Fax: 314-939-1093

615 Mosport Dr
St Charles MO 63304-7925

Local Retrieval Area: IL-Jersey, Madison, Monroe, Randolph, St. Clair; MO-Franklin, Greene, Jefferson, St. Charles, St. Francois.

Normal turnaround time: 1 to 2 days. Projects are generally billed by the number of names searched. The first project may require a prepayment.

Correspondent relationships: MO, MI, Johnson, Sedgwick, Shawnee and Wyandotte, KS counties and Shelby, TN county. They specialize in public record retrieval.

Computer Assisted Rsrch On-Line

Phone: 800-329-6397
305-944-2111

1166 NE 182nd St
Miami FL 33162

Local Retrieval Area: FL-Broward, Dade, Palm Beach.

Normal turnaround time: 24 hours or less. Projects are generally billed by the number of names searched. The first project may require a prepayment. Credit cards are accepted.

Correspondent relationships: nationwide.

Condor International Inc

Phone: 630-357-0090
Fax: 630-293-5085

500 N Michigan Ave Suite 1920
Chicago IL 60611

Local Retrieval and SOP Area: IL-Cook, Du Page, Kane, Lake, McHenry, Will.

Normal turnaround time: 1-3 days. Projects are generally billed by the number of names searched. The first project may require a prepayment. Credit cards are accepted.

Correspondent relationships: nationwide. They specialize in skip tracing and locating of individuals for purpose of service of process, plus on-site Illinois vehicle registration records.

Condor Investigations

Phone: 512-881-8977
Fax: 512-884-1658

PO Box 181293
Corpus Christi TX 78480-1293

Local Retrieval and SOP Area: TX-12 Counties.

Normal turnaround time: 24-48 hours. Projects are generally billed by the hour. The first project may require a prepayment.

Correspondent relationships: Nueces, San Patricio, Aransas, Jim Wells, Duval and Kleberg. They specialize in service of civil process. They also have investigators available for background, surveillance, statements and skip tracing.

Confi-Chek

Phone: 800-821-7404
916-443-4822
Fax: 800-758-5859
916-443-7420

1507 24th St
Sacramento CA 95816

Local Retrieval Area: CA-Sacramento.

Online computer ordering is also available. Projects are generally billed by the number of names searched. The first project may require a prepayment. Credit cards are accepted.

They specialize in on-line services.

Confidential Information Search

Phone: 818-377-5789

20929-47 Ventura Blvd Suite 368
Woodland Hills CA 91364-2334

Local Retrieval Area: CA-Los Angeles.

Normal turnaround time: 48 hours to 5 days. Projects are generally billed by the number of names searched. Projects require prepayment. Non-refundable retainer required.

Correspondent relationships: OR, LA, TN and TX. They specialize in private investigations and executive personnel security. They have 15 years experience in high profile executive security. Parent company is Executive Security & Investigations.

Confidential Services

Phone: 800-752-4581
Fax: 614-338-1515

PO Box 091034
Columbus OH 43209

Local Retrieval and SOP Area: OH-Franklin.

Normal turnaround time: 24-72 hours. Projects are generally billed by the number of names searched or records located. The first project may require a prepayment. Credit cards are accepted.

Correspondent relationships: nationwide. They specialize in skip tracing.

Consolidated Abstract Co

Phone: 817-989-3566
Fax: 817-989-3566

PO Box 569
Aspermont TX 79502

Local Retrieval Area: TX-Stonewall.

Normal turnaround time: 1-2 days. Fee basis will vary by the type of project. The first project may require a prepayment.

Contract Services Unlimited

Phone: 615-237-3142
Fax: 615-237-9151

4019 Poplarhill Rd
Watertown TN 37184

Local Retrieval and SOP Area: TN-Davidson, Macon, Rutherford, Smith, Sumner, Trousdale, Williamson, Wilson.

Normal turnaround time: 24-48 hours. Projects are generally billed by the number of names searched. They bill by hour out of area. The first project may require a prepayment. 30 day billing cycle.

Correspondent relationships: Robertson, Williamson, DeKalb, Rutherford, Davidson, Jackson & Putman.

Cooper Abstract Co

Phone: 609-667-4800
Fax: 609-667-1642

401 Cooper Landing Rd Suite 6
Cherry Hill NJ 08002

Local Retrieval Area: NJ-Camden.

Normal turnaround time: 1 week. A rush service is also available. Fee basis will vary by the type of project. The first project may require a prepayment.

Correspondent relationships: Burlington & Glovcester, NJ counties. They specialize in title searches, title insurance and searches for missing heirs.

Cooper Research Inc

Phone: 912-897-9028
Fax: 912-897-6106

108 W Manta Cove
Savannah GA 31410

Local Retrieval and SOP Area: GA-Bulloch, Chatham.

Normal turnaround time: 48 hours. Online computer ordering is also available. Projects are generally billed by the hour. The first project may require a prepayment. Terms are net 30 days.

They specialize in all court house records, family records and newspaper microfilm of Georgia Historical Society.

Cope Investigative Services LLC

Phone: 800-262-9301
901-546-0611

2500 Mt Moriah Suite H-258

Memphis TN 38115-1523 **Fax:** 901-546-0614

Local Retrieval and SOP Area: MS-De Soto, Tate; TN-Fayette, Hardeman, Shelby, Tipton.

Normal turnaround time: 48 hours. Online computer ordering is also available. Projects are generally billed by the number of names searched or records located. The first project may require a prepayment.

Correspondent relationships: the states of AR, AL, CA, FL and TX. They specialize in service of process.

Copper Range Abstract & Title Co

Phone: 906-482-7903

707 Shelden Ave **Fax:** 906-482-7977

Houghton MI 49931

Local Retrieval Area: MI-Baraga, Houghton, Keweenaw, Ontonagon.

Normal turnaround time: 3 days. Fee basis will vary by type of project. Projects require prepayment.

They specialize in real estate.

Copy Central

Phone: 213-687-3900

255 S Grand Ave Suite 101 **Fax:** 213-687-7277

Los Angeles CA 90012

Local Retrieval Area: CA-Los Angeles.

Normal turnaround time: 12-24 hours. Expedited service available. Fee basis will vary with type of project. Credit accounts are accepted.

Cornell Abstract Co

Phone: 712-336-3845

1811 Hill Ave **Fax:** 712-336-1402

Spirit Lake IA 51360

Local Retrieval Area: IA-Dickinson.

Normal turnaround time: 2 days. Fee basis will vary by the type of project. Credit accounts are accepted.

They specialize in real estate.

CorpAmerica Inc

Phone: 888-736-4300
302-736-4300

30 Old Rudnick Ln

Dover DE 19901 **Fax:** 302-736-5620

Local Retrieval Area: DE-Kent, New Castle, Sussex.

Normal turnaround time: 1-2 days pending state systems time frame..dd. Projects are generally billed by the number of names searched. The first project may require a prepayment. Credit cards are accepted. Credit cards are subject to 5% rush fee.

Correspondent relationships: nationwide. They specialize in forming corporations and providing registered agent service in all 50 states and in retrieving Secretary of State records.

CorpAssist - DC Office

Phone: 800-438-2996
202-371-8090

1090 Vermont Ave NW Suite 910

Washington DC 20005 **Fax:** 202-371-1945

Local Retrieval and SOP Area: DC-District of Columbia; MD-Montgomery, Prince George's; VA-City of Alexandria, Arlington, Fairfax, City of Fairfax, Loudoun, City of Manassas, Prince William.

Normal turnaround time: 24-48 hours. Online computer ordering is also available. Projects are generally billed by the hour. The first project may require a prepayment. Terms are net 15 days for service companies.

Correspondent relationships: In every jurisdiction nationwide. They provide research services at all federal agencies and courts in addition to the traditional UCC's, tax liens, judgments, real estate, judgments, etc. They also offer national bank account searches.

Corporate Access Inc

Phone: 800-969-1666
904-222-2666

1116-D Thomasville Rd Mount Vernon Square

Tallahassee FL 32303 **Fax:** 904-222-1666

Local Retrieval and SOP Area: FL-Bay, Calhoun, Franklin, Gadsden, Gulf, Jefferson, Leon, Liberty, Wakulla; GA-Thomas.

Normal turnaround time: 24-48 hours. Projects are generally billed by the number of names searched. The first project may require a prepayment. Credit cards are accepted.

Correspondent relationships: nationwide.

Corporate Screening Services Inc

Phone: 800-229-8606
216-816-0500

16530 Commerce Court

Cleveland OH 44130-6305 **Fax:** 216-243-4204

Local Retrieval Area: OH-Cuyahoga, Lake, Lorain, Medina, Portage, Stark, Summit.

Normal turnaround time: 24-72 hours. Projects are generally billed by the number of names searched. Credit accounts are accepted.

Correspondent relationships: OH. They specialize in criminal and civil seaches at local county, State and Federal levels.

Corporate Service Bureau

Phone: 518-463-8550

283 Washington Ave **Fax:** 518-463-3752

Albany NY 12206

Local Retrieval Area: NY-Albany, Rensselaer, Schenectady.

Normal turnaround time: 1-5 business days. Projects are generally billed by the number of names searched. The first project may require a prepayment. Credit cards are accepted. They require prepayment for corporation filings.

Correspondent relationships: all of New York.

Corporate Services of Ohio Inc

Phone: 614-464-2400

50 W Broad St **Fax:** 614-464-1505

Columbus OH 43215

Local Retrieval Area: OH-Delaware, Fairfield, Fayette, Franklin, Licking, Madison, Marion, Pickaway, Union.

Normal turnaround time: 1-7 days. Projects are generally billed by the number of names searched. The first project may require a prepayment.

Correspondent relationships: Cuyahoga, Lucas, Hamilton, Summit, Butler, Clermont and Miami. (All Ohio counties with exception of extreme Southeast portion of State and Extreme Northeast portion of State. They specialize in corporate filings and retrieval of certified documents from the Secretary of State, all Franklin County Courts and all State agencies and departments.

🏛 Corpus Christi Court Services

Phone: 512-887-8122
Fax: 512-887-0335

PO Box 147
Corpus Christi TX 78403

Local Retrieval Area: TX-Aransas, Duval, Jim Wells, Kleberg, Nueces, San Patricio.

Normal turnaround time: the same day if order is received before 2:00PM. A 2 hour rush service is also available. Projects are generally billed by the number of names searched. The first project may require a prepayment.

Correspondent relationships: most counties in Texas and the United States. They specialize in bankruptcy.

George P Cossar Jr

Phone: 601-647-5581
Fax: 601-647-5434

PO Box 50
Charleston MS 38921

Local Retrieval Area: MS-Tallahatchie.

Normal turnaround time: 1-2 days. Projects are generally billed by the hour. The first project may require a prepayment.

He is an attorney working in real estate and estate planning.

Cothran & Cothran

Phone: 864-435-8495
Fax: 864-435-2653

PO Drawer 700
Manning SC 29102

Local Retrieval Area: SC-Clarendon, Lee, Orangeburg, Sumter, Williamsburg.

Normal turnaround time: 24-48 hours. Projects are generally billed by the number of records located. The first project may require a prepayment.

Correspondent relationships: the rest of the state.

Cottonwood County Abstract Co

Phone: 507-831-1504

900 3rd Ave PO Box 336 (56101-0336)
Windom MN 56101

Local Retrieval Area: MN-Cottonwood.

Normal turnaround time: varied depending on project. Expedited service available with additional charge. Projects are generally billed by the number of names searched or records located. Projects require prepayment. Personal checks are accepted.

They specialize in name searches, judgment searches, tax and bankruptcy searches.

County Abstract & Title Co

Phone: 505-835-0573
Fax: 505-835-3530

PO Box 614
Socorro NM 87801

Local Retrieval Area: NM-Catron, Socorro.

Normal turnaround time: 1-2 weeks. Projects are generally billed by the hour. Credit accounts are accepted.

They specialize in real estate and foreclosure searches.

County Process Inc

Phone: 502-587-0051
Fax: 502-585-3480

209 S 5th 2nd Floor
Louisville KY 40202

Local Retrieval and SOP Area: KY-Bullitt, Fayette, Jefferson, Oldham, Shelby.

Normal turnaround time: 2 days. Projects are generally billed by the hour. Projects require prepayment.

Correspondent relationships: New Orleans, LA; Atlanta, GA; Nashville, TN. They specialize in Kentucky motor vehicle information, Kentucky driver license information and legal process service.

County Seat Abstract

Phone: 518-762-3011

17 W Main St
Johnstown NY 12095

Local Retrieval Area: NY-Fulton, Hamilton, Montgomery.

Normal turnaround time: 3-5 days. Projects are generally billed by the hour. Credit accounts are accepted.

Correspondent relationships: all counties in New York. They specialize in title insurance searches.

County Wide Abstract and Title

Phone: 573-624-2436
Fax: 573-624-5376

4 S Elm St
Dexter MO 63841

Local Retrieval Area: MO-Stoddard.

Normal turnaround time: 2 days. Projects are generally billed by the number of names searched. The first project may require a prepayment.

Court Copies & Images Inc

Phone: 619-696-9650
Fax: 619-232-9998

325 W "F" St
San Diego CA 92101-6017

Local Retrieval Area: CA-Los Angeles, San Diego.

Normal turnaround time: 2 days. Online computer ordering is also available. No project billing information was given. Projects require prepayment. Credit cards are accepted.

They are contracted by federal courts to provide copy services to the public. Services, turnaround time and pricing vary by court.

🏛 Court Data Research Services

Phone: 918-745-2231
Fax: 918-745-2234

PO Box 1184
Tulsa OK 74101

Local Retrieval Area: OK-Tulsa.

Normal turnaround time: 24 hours. Projects are generally billed by the number of names searched. Flat rate available per court also. The first project may require a prepayment. Payment due upon receipt of invoice.

Correspondent relationships: Oklahoma, Cleveland, Ottawa and Wagoner. They specialize in court searches, title, criminal and bankruptcy searches.

Court Data Search

Phone: 201-770-1170
Fax: 201-770-1170

6 Sycamore Way
Mt Arlington NJ 07856

Local Retrieval Area: NJ-Bergen, Essex, Hudson, Middlesex, Morris, Passaic, Sussex, Union.

Normal turnaround time: 48 hours. Projects are generally billed by the number of names searched. Credit accounts are accepted.

They specialize in criminal and civil judgment checks.

🏛 Court Explorers LLC

Phone: 212-945-6324
Fax: 212-945-6325

300 Rector Place
New York NY 10280

Local Retrieval Area: NY-Bronx, Kings, New York, Queens.

Normal turnaround time: 1 to 3 days. Projects are generally billed by the number of names searched. The first project may require a prepayment. Credit cards are accepted.

Correspondent relationships: nationwide. They specialize in all public record filings and searches, locally and through nationwide correspondents.

🏛 Court House Research

299 Commonwealth Ave
Buffalo NY 14216

Phone: 716-873-8315
Fax: 716-873-2534

Local Retrieval Area: NY-Erie, Niagara.

Normal turnaround time: 24-48 hours. Projects are generally billed by the number of names searched. Credit accounts are accepted.

Correspondent relationships: New York, Colorado, Arizona and Massachusetts. They specialize in criminal searches, UCC searches, tax liens and probate record searches.

Court Record Consultants

17029 Devonshire Suite 166
Northridge CA 91325

Phone: 818-366-1906
Fax: 818-366-1985

Local Retrieval and SOP Area: CA-14 Counties.

Normal turnaround time: 1-2 days. Projects are generally billed by the number of names searched or records located. The first project may require a prepayment.

Correspondent relationships: the rest of the state. They specialize in pre-employment screening, private investigation and real estate research.

🏛 Court Record Research Inc

PO Box 3796
Houston TX 77253-3796

Phone: 800-552-3353
713-227-3353
Fax: 713-236-1970

Local Retrieval Area: TX-Brazoria, Fort Bend, Galveston, Harris, Montgomery.

Normal turnaround time: 2-3 days. Harris county same day service available. Rush service also available. Online computer ordering is also available. Projects are generally billed by the number of names searched. The first project may require a prepayment. Credit cards are accepted. Will also work on retainer.

Correspondent relationships: other counties in Texas. They specialize in obtaining copies of documents for pending and closed court cases from federal, state and local courts. They do asset searches and real estate oriented searches. They also now provide pre-employment screening searches.

Courthouse Document Retrieval

6610 Hilltop
Sachse TX 75048

Phone: 972-644-4185
Fax: 972-530-3305

Local Retrieval Area: TX-Collin, Dallas, Tarrant.

Normal turnaround time: 24 hours. Projects are generally billed by the number of names searched. Credit accounts are accepted. Terms are net 15 days.

Correspondent relationships: Harris, Travis and Bexar, TX counties. They cover the entire spectrum of document retrieval.

Courthouse Services

807 Brazos St Suite 316
Austin TX 78701-2508

Phone: 800-843-5725
512-477-6499
Fax: 512-327-5152

Local Retrieval and SOP Area: TX-Hays, Travis, Williamson.

Normal turnaround time: 24 hours. Online computer ordering is also available. Charges are by flat rate, case-by-case. The first project may require a prepayment.

Correspondent relationships: nationwide. They specialize in legal research, process service and document filing and retrieval.

CPD Inc

901 East Wood St
Decatur IL 62521

Phone: 217-429-2711
Fax: 217-429-2718

Local Retrieval and SOP Area: IL-12 Counties.

Normal turnaround time: 1-3 days. Projects are generally billed by the hour. The first project may require a prepayment.

Correspondent relationships: the rest of the state by ex-FBI agents. They specialize in forensic sciences, criminal and civil investigations and process service.

CPS (Capital Process Service)

404 W 9th Suite 101A
Georgetown TX 78626

Phone: 512-930-7378
Fax: 512-863-7574

Local Retrieval Area: TX-Bastrop, Bell, Hays, Lampasas, Llano, Travis, Williamson.

Normal turnaround time: 24 hours. Fees are charged by case. Credit accounts are accepted.

Correspondent relationships: the rest of Texas.

Nancy Craig

906 Russo Dr
Westhampton NJ 08060

Phone: 609-261-5783
Fax: 609-261-2531

Local Retrieval Area: NJ-Burlington.

Normal turnaround time: 24-48 hours. Projects are generally billed by the number of names searched. Credit accounts are accepted.

Craighead County Abstract

2207 Fowler Ave
Jonesboro AR 72401

Phone: 501-935-9900
Fax: 501-935-6548

Local Retrieval Area: AR-Craighead.

Normal turnaround time: up to 10 days. Expedited service available. Fee basis will vary by type of project. Credit accounts are accepted.

They specialize in real estate.

Dale C Crandall

PO Box 310
Burwell NE 68823

Phone: 308-346-4284
Fax: 308-346-5402

Local Retrieval Area: NE-Garfield.

Normal turnaround time: 1 week. Projects are generally billed by the number of records located. Credit accounts are accepted.

He is an attorney. He specializes in income tax, probate and general legal practice.

Crawford Abstract & Real Estate

PO Box 341
Lincoln KS 67455

Phone: 913-524-4228
Fax: 913-524-3042

Local Retrieval Area: KS-Lincoln.

Normal turnaround time: 2-3 days. Fee basis varies by type of transaction. The first project may require a prepayment.

Crawford County Abstract & Title

108 Burton Court
Grayling MI 49738

Phone: 517-348-9832
Fax: 517-348-7511

Local Retrieval Area: MI-Crawford.

Normal turnaround time: up to a week. Fee basis will vary by the type of project. Projects require prepayment. They require a prepayment for all out of area transactions.

They specialize in title insurance.

Crawford County Abstract Co
Phone: 501-474-2711
Fax: 501-474-2954
424 Main Street
Van Buren AR 72956

Local Retrieval Area: AR-Crawford.

Normal turnaround time: 2 days. Projects are generally billed by the number of names searched. Credit accounts are accepted.

They specialize in real estate.

Crawford County Abstract Co
Phone: 712-263-5626
Fax: 712-263-5627
PO Box 277 1211 Broadway
Denison IA 51442

Local Retrieval Area: IA-Crawford.

Normal turnaround time: 3 days. Projects are generally billed by the number of names searched or records located. Credit accounts are accepted.

Crawford County Title Co
Phone: 573-885-6470
Fax: 573-885-6472
600 W Washington St
Cuba MO 65453-1221

Local Retrieval Area: MO-Crawford.

Normal turnaround time: 1 week. Fee basis varies by type of transaction. Credit accounts are accepted.

Credit Bureau of Devils Lake
Phone: 701-662-6690
Fax: 701-662-6696
PO Box 792
Devils Lake ND 58301

Local Retrieval Area: ND-Ramsey.

Normal turnaround time: 3 days. Fee basis varies by type of transaction. Credit accounts are accepted.

They specialize in credit reporting and collections.

Credit Bureau Greater Harrisburg
Phone: 800-344-3125
717-236-8061
Fax: 800-526-8962
717-233-6116
2491 Baxton St PO Box 67533
Harrisburg PA 17106

Local Retrieval Area: PA-12 Counties.

Normal turnaround time: 48 hours. Expedited service available. Charges are by products ordered. Credit accounts are accepted. End of the month invoicing available.

Correspondent relationships: Pennsylvania and Maryland. They specialize in present owner searches, flood certificates, criminal checks, bankruptcy searches, county and state UCC searches, census tract and mortgage filings.

Credit Bureau of Raton
Phone: 505-445-2751
Fax: 505-445-2753
PO Box 938
Raton NM 87740

Local Retrieval Area: NM-Colfax.

Normal turnaround time: 2-4 days. Projects are generally billed by the number of names searched. Credit accounts are accepted.

They are a credit bureau who will pull paper records for customers.

Credit Bureau of Valley City
Phone: 701-845-3912
Fax: 701-845-0220
PO Box 912
Valley City ND 58072

Local Retrieval Area: ND-Barnes, Griggs, La Moure, Sargent, Steele.

Normal turnaround time: 2-3 days. Fee basis will vary by the type of project. Credit accounts are accepted. They request that all out of county clients prepay.

Credit Bureau of Western NE
Phone: 308-632-2117
Fax: 308-632-7135
PO Box 70
Scottsbluff NE 69363

Local Retrieval Area: NE-Box Butte, Cheyenne, Dawes, Kimball, Morrill, Scotts Bluff, Sheridan.

Normal turnaround time: 2-3 days. Projects are generally billed by the number of records located. Projects require prepayment.

They specialize in collections.

Credit Bureau Services Inc
Phone: 316-275-6500
Fax: 316-276-3744
1135 College Dr Suite # L1
Garden City KS 67846

Local Retrieval and SOP Area: KS-Clark, Finney, Ford, Gray, Lane, Ness, Scott, Wichita.

Normal turnaround time: up to one week. Fee basis varies by type of transaction. Credit accounts are accepted.

They are affiliated with TRW and will provide credit searches. They also publish a "Public Record Bulletin."

Credit Bureau Svcs of Panhandle
Phone: 806-669-3246
Fax: 806-669-6109
PO Box 2101
Pampa TX 79066-2101

Local Retrieval Area: TX-Carson, Gray, Hemphill, Lipscomb, Ochiltree, Roberts, Wheeler.

Normal turnaround time: 1-2 days. Expedited service available. Fee basis will vary by the type of project. Projects require prepayment. Terms are net 30 days.

They specialize in oil and gas records.

Credit Lenders Service Agency Inc
Phone: 609-751-7400
Fax: 800-648-0401
PO Box 508
Cherry Hill NJ 08003

Local Retrieval Area: NJ-Burlington, Camden, Mercer.

Normal turnaround time: 24 hours. Projects are generally billed by the number of names searched or records located. Credit accounts are accepted.

Credit-facts of America
Phone: 800-233-4747
412-232-3232
Fax: 800-332-2317
412-232-0903
530 William Penn Place Suite 120
Pittsburgh PA 15219

Local Retrieval Area: PA-Allegheny, Beaver, Butler, Washington, Westmoreland.

Normal turnaround time: 48-72 hours. Projects are generally billed by the number of names searched. Credit accounts are accepted. Terms are net 15 days.

Correspondent relationships: nationwide.

Crockett County Abstract Co
Phone: 915-392-2232
PO Drawer E
Ozona TX 76943

Local Retrieval Area: TX-Crockett.

Normal turnaround time: 2-3 days. Fee basis will vary by the type of project. The first project may require a prepayment.

Laura Cross
Phone: 415-239-8950
Fax: 415-337-0991
1381 Plymouth Ave
San Francisco CA 94112-1240

Local Retrieval Area: CA-Alameda, Contra Costa, Marin.

Normal turnaround time: 24 hours but often same day service. Projects are generally billed by the number of names searched or records located. The first project may require a prepayment. Terms are net 30 days.

Correspondent relationships: San Francisco, San Mateo and Santa Clara, CA counties.

Crow Wing County Abstract Co
Phone: 218-829-7368
Fax: 218-829-8586
PO Box 378
Brainerd MN 56401

Local Retrieval Area: MN-Crow Wing.

Normal turnaround time: 2-7 days. Projects are generally billed by the number of names searched. Credit accounts are accepted.

They specialize in land title.

Crowley County Insurance & Title
Phone: 719-267-4778
PO Box 398
Ordway CO 81063

Local Retrieval Area: CO-Crowley.

Normal turnaround time: up to 1 week. Fee basis will vary by the type of project. Credit accounts are accepted. Out of area clients must prepay.

They specialize in real estate title and abstract.

Crummey Investigations Inc
Phone: 407-724-0518
Fax: 407-728-0274
PO Box 510405
Melbourne Beach FL 32951-0405

Local Retrieval and SOP Area: FL-Brevard, Indian River.

Normal turnaround time: 24 hours. Online computer ordering is also available. Projects are generally billed by the hour. The first project may require a prepayment. Personal checks are accepted.

They specialize in missing persons.

Crutchfield Investigators Inc
Phone: 310-559-3371
501 S Beverly Dr 3rd Fl
Beverly Hills CA 90212

Local Retrieval and SOP Area: CA-Los Angeles, Orange, San Bernardino, San Diego, Ventura.

Normal turnaround time: 24 hours to 1 month depending on court. Projects are generally billed by the number of names searched. Fees depend on case file activity. The first project may require a prepayment.

Correspondent relationships: Nationwide, Mexico and Canada. They specialize in criminal background checks, driving records, credit checks with a signed release and asset searches.

Crystal Clear Copy Service
Phone: 619-947-5699
Fax: 619-949-1389
8479 9th Ave
Hesperia CA 92345

Local Retrieval and SOP Area: CA-Riverside, San Bernardino.

Normal turnaround time: 10 days. A 5 day rush service is also available. Fee basis will vary by the type of project. Credit accounts are accepted.

CSC
Phone: 602-234-9600
3636 N Central Ave Suite 970
Phoenix AZ 85012

Local Retrieval Area: .

Normal turnaround time: 1-2 days. Projects are generally billed by the number of names searched. The first project may require a prepayment.

Correspondent relationships: nationwide. They are part of the CSC Network of offices nationwide, specializing in UCC and corporate matters.

CSC
Phone: 800-458-0700
213-954-3854
Fax: 213-954-0871
5670 Wilshire Blvd Suite 750
Los Angeles CA 90036-5607

Local Retrieval Area: CA-Los Angeles, Orange.

Normal turnaround time: 1-2 days. Projects are generally billed by the number of names searched. Credit accounts are accepted. Credit cards are accepted.

Correspondent relationships: nationwide.

CSC
Phone: 800-222-2122
916-649-9916
Fax: 916-649-9933
2730 Gateway Oaks Dr Suite 100
Sacramento CA 95833-3503

Local Retrieval and SOP Area: CA-El Dorado, Placer, Sacramento.

Normal turnaround time: 1-2 days. Projects are generally billed by the number of names searched. The first project may require a prepayment. Credit cards are accepted.

Correspondent relationships: nationwide.

CSC
Phone: 800-423-7398
303-860-7052
Fax: 303-832-9050
1560 Broadway Suite 620
Denver CO 80202

Local Retrieval Area: CO-Adams, Arapahoe, Boulder, Denver, Douglas, Jefferson.

Normal turnaround time: 1-2 days. Projects are generally billed by the number of names searched. The first project may require a prepayment. Credit cards are accepted.

Correspondent relationships: nationwide.

CSC
Phone: 860-724-1228
30 High St
Hartford CT 06103

Local Retrieval Area: .

Normal turnaround time: 1-2 days. Projects are generally billed by the number of names searched. The first project may require a prepayment.

Correspondent relationships: nationwide. They are part of the CSC Network of offices nationwide, specializing in UCC and corporate matters.

CSC
Phone: 800-241-6518
202-408-3120
1090 Vermont Ave Suite 430
Washington DC 20005

Local Retrieval Area: .

Normal turnaround time: 1-2 days. Projects are generally billed by the number of names searched. The first project may require a prepayment.

Correspondent relationships: nationwide. They are part of the national network of CSC offices, specializing in UCC and corporate matters.

CSC
32 Loockerman Sq Suite 203
Dover DE 19904
Phone: 302-674-1221
Fax: 302-674-0266

Local Retrieval and SOP Area: DE-Kent.

Normal turnaround time: 1-2 days. Projects are generally billed by the number of names searched. Credit accounts are accepted. Credit cards are accepted.

Correspondent relationships: nationwide.

🏛 CSC
1013 Centre Rd
Wilmington DE 19805
Phone: 800-927-9800
302-998-0595
Fax: 302-998-7078

Local Retrieval Area: DE-Kent, New Castle, Sussex; PA-Dauphin, Delaware, Philadelphia.

Normal turnaround time: 24-48 hours. Online computer ordering is also available. Projects are generally billed by the number of names searched. They also charge by index. The first project may require a prepayment.

Correspondent relationships: a national network including rest of counties in Delaware and Pennsylvania. They have been doing business since 1899.

CSC
1201 Hays St
Tallahassee FL 32301-2607
Phone: 800-342-8086
904-222-9171
Fax: 904-222-0393

Local Retrieval Area: FL-11 Counties; GA-Decatur, Grady, Lowndes, Thomas.

Normal turnaround time: 1-2 days. Projects are generally billed by the number of names searched. The first project may require a prepayment. Credit cards are accepted.

Correspondent relationships: nationwide. They have the capacity to do searches nationwide.

CSC
100 Peachtree St Suite 660
Atlanta GA 30303
Phone: 800-241-5834
404-659-8831

Local Retrieval Area: .

Normal turnaround time: 1-2 days. Projects are generally billed by the number of names searched. The first project may require a prepayment.

Correspondent relationships: nationwide. They are part of the network of CSC offices nationwide, specializing in UCC and corporate matters.

CSC
33 N LaSalle St Suite 1925
Chicago IL 60602-2607
Phone: 800-621-6526
312-372-3332
Fax: 312-372-4996

Local Retrieval Area: IL-Cook.

Normal turnaround time: 1-3 days. Projects are generally billed by the number of names searched. The first project may require a prepayment. Credit cards are accepted.

Correspondent relationships: nationwide.

CSC
700 S 2nd St
Springfield IL 62704
Phone: 800-877-2556
217-522-1010
Fax: 217-544-4657

Local Retrieval and SOP Area: IL-Sangamon.

Normal turnaround time: 1-2 days. Projects are generally billed by the number of names searched. The first project may require a prepayment. Credit cards are accepted.

Correspondent relationships: nationwide. They have the capacity to do searches nationwide.

CSC
84 State St 5th Fl
Boston MA 02109-2202
Phone: 800-225-6244
617-227-9590
Fax: 617-523-3189

Local Retrieval and SOP Area: MA-Essex, Middlesex, Norfolk, Suffolk, Worcester.

Normal turnaround time: 1-2 days. Projects are generally billed by the number of names searched. The first project may require a prepayment. Credit cards are accepted.

Correspondent relationships: nationwide.

CSC
11 East Chase St Suite 4B
Baltimore MD 21202
Phone: 410-332-1540

Local Retrieval Area: .

Normal turnaround time: 1-2 days. Projects are generally billed by the number of names searched. The first project may require a prepayment.

Correspondent relationships: nationwide. They are part of the national CSC network of offices, specializing in UCC and corporate matters.

CSC
222 E Dunklin St
Jefferson City MO 65101-3127
Phone: 573-634-4363
Fax: 573-634-4266

Local Retrieval Area: MO-Cole.

Normal turnaround time: 1-2 days. Projects are generally billed by the number of names searched. Credit accounts are accepted.

Correspondent relationships: nationwide.

CSC
830 Bear Tavern Rd Suite 305
West Trenton NJ 08628-1020
Phone: 800-631-2155
609-771-1800
Fax: 609-530-0877

Local Retrieval Area: NJ-Mercer.

Normal turnaround time: 1-2 days. Projects are generally billed by the number of names searched. Credit accounts are accepted. Credit cards are accepted. Terms are net 30 days.

Correspondent relationships: nationwide.

CSC
502 E John St Room E
Carson City NV 89706-3078
Phone: 702-882-3072
Fax: 702-882-3354

Local Retrieval and SOP Area: NV-Clark.

Normal turnaround time: same day to 2 days. Projects are generally billed by the number of names searched. Credit accounts are accepted. Credit cards are accepted.

Correspondent relationships: nationwide. They specialize in public document retrieval, filing and research.

CSC
500 Central Ave
Albany NY 12206-2290
Phone: 800-833-9848
518-458-8111
Fax: 518-482-8864

Local Retrieval and SOP Area: NY-Albany, Rensselaer.

Normal turnaround time: 1-2 days. Projects are generally billed by the number of names searched. The first project may require a prepayment. Credit cards are accepted.

Correspondent relationships: nationwide.

CSC

375 Hudson St 11th FL
New York NY 10014-3658

Phone: 800-221-0770
212-463-2700
Fax: 212-807-9005

Local Retrieval Area: NY-Kings, New York, Queens.

Normal turnaround time: 2 days. Projects are generally billed by the number of names searched. Credit accounts are accepted. Credit cards are accepted.

Correspondent relationships: nationwide.

CSC

16 E Broad St Suite 610
Columbus OH 43215

Phone: 800-688-9901
614-463-9901

Local Retrieval and SOP Area: OH-Franklin.

Projects are generally billed by the number of names searched. They also charge by index. The first project may require a prepayment. Credit cards are accepted.

Correspondent relationships: nationwide.

CSC

285 Liberty St NE Suite 370
Salem OR 97301-3531

Phone: 503-589-1141
Fax: 503-589-1145

Local Retrieval Area: OR-Marion.

Normal turnaround time: 1-2 days. Projects are generally billed by the number of names searched. Credit accounts are accepted. Credit cards are accepted.

Correspondent relationships: nationwide.

CSC

319 Market St
Harrisburg PA 17101

Phone: 800-622-2300
717-234-9715
Fax: 717-234-9055

Local Retrieval and SOP Area: PA-Dauphin.

Normal turnaround time: 1-2 days. Projects are generally billed by the number of names searched. The first project may require a prepayment. Credit cards are accepted.

Correspondent relationships: nationwide. They have the capacity to do searches nationwide.

CSC

One Commodore Plaza 800 Brazos, Suite 330
Austin TX 78701

Phone: 800-532-4875
512-397-1550

Local Retrieval Area: .

Normal turnaround time: 1-2 days. Projects are generally billed by the number of names searched. The first project may require a prepayment.

Correspondent relationships: nationwide. They are part of the CSC network of offices, specializing in UCC and corporate matters.

CSC

400 N St Paul Suite 700
Dallas TX 75201

Phone: 800-654-3398
214-220-2061
Fax: 214-720-3872

Local Retrieval and SOP Area: TX-Dallas.

Normal turnaround time: 1-2 days. Projects are generally billed by the number of names searched. The first project may require a prepayment. Credit cards are accepted.

Correspondent relationships: nationwide.

CSC

600 Travis 18th Fl
Houston TX 77002-2912

Phone: 800-243-3779
713-228-9751
Fax: 713-228-9754

Local Retrieval and SOP Area: TX-Harris.

Projects are generally billed by the number of names searched. The first project may require a prepayment. Credit cards are accepted.

Correspondent relationships: nationwide.

CSC

11 S 12th St
Richmond VA 23219-4035

Phone: 800-237-1814
804-783-8208
Fax: 804-782-2275

Local Retrieval Area: VA-Chesterfield, Hanover, Henrico, City of Richmond.

Normal turnaround time: 1-3 days. Projects are generally billed by the number of names searched. Credit accounts are accepted. Credit cards are accepted.

Correspondent relationships: nationwide.

CSC

317 E 4th Ave Suite 310
Olympia WA 98501

Phone: 360-754-9333
Fax: 306-754-5781

Local Retrieval Area: WA-Thurston.

Normal turnaround time: 1-2 days. Projects are generally billed by the number of names searched. Credit accounts are accepted. Credit cards are accepted.

Correspondent relationships: nationwide.

CSC

520 Pike St Suite 1450
Seattle WA 98101

Phone: 800-876-9436
206-343-9436
Fax: 206-343-7318

Local Retrieval and SOP Area: WA-King, Pierce, Snohomish.

Normal turnaround time: 1-2 days. Projects are generally billed by the number of names searched. Credit accounts are accepted.

Correspondent relationships: nationwide.

CT Corporation System

49 Stevenson St Suite 300
San Francisco CA 94105

Phone: 800-874-8820
Fax: 800-828-3066

Local Retrieval Area: AK-Anchorage; CA-14 Counties; ID-Ada; OR-11 Counties; WA-3 Counties.

Normal turnaround time: a 2 day verbal response. Copies will follow. Projects are generally billed by the number of names searched or records located. Credit accounts are accepted.

Correspondent relationships: 95% of the counties nationwide. They specialize in UCC and litigation searches. They also handle filings in all jurisdictions.

Currier Abstract Company

PO Box 540
Artesia NM 88211-0540

Phone: 505-746-9823
Fax: 505-746-9661

Local Retrieval Area: NM-Eddy.

Normal turnaround time: 1 week. Fee basis will vary by the type of project. Credit accounts are accepted. Terms are net 30 days from invoice date.

The same family has been in business in Eddy County for over 50 years.

Sue Cutler
Phone: 712-452-2021

Box 41
Blencoe IA 51523-0041

Local Retrieval Area: IA-Monona.

Normal turnaround time: 3-5 days. Projects are generally billed by the number of names searched. The first project may require a prepayment. A per search minimum fee will be charged. Personal checks accepted.

CW Credit Abstract Co
Phone: 718-423-9430
Fax: 718-423-0027

214-20 41st Ave
Bayside NY 11361

Local Retrieval Area: CT-All Counties; NJ-All Counties; NY-All Counties.

Normal turnaround time: 3-5 days. Charges will vary by county and type of search. The first project may require a prepayment. Terms are net 30 days.

Correspondent relationships: Massachusetts, New Hampshire, Vermont, Rhode Island and Maine. They specialize in UCC searches and filings, property searches, real estate tax searches, deed chains, certificates of occupancy, flood searches and property appraisals.

Cygneture Title Inc
Phone: 218-828-0122
Fax: 218-828-0873

601 W Washington
Brainerd MN 56401

Local Retrieval Area: MN-Cass, Crow Wing, Morrison.

Normal turnaround time: 10 days. Fee basis will vary by type of project. Projects require prepayment. They will also invoice.

They specialize in real estate.

D

D & D Research & Info Co
Phone: 888-327-8860
208-322-9437
Fax: 208-327-8860

10378 Fairview Suite 132
Boise ID 83704

Local Retrieval and SOP Area: ID-Ada.

Normal turnaround time: 24-48 hours. Fees are by report. The first project may require a prepayment. Terms are net 30 days.

They specialize in skiptracing. Nationwide searches available. They also do Service of Process.

D & L Investigations
Phone: 618-236-2232
Fax: 618-236-7967

5610 W Main St
Belleville IL 62223

Local Retrieval and SOP Area: IL-Clinton, Madison, Monroe, St. Clair; MO-St. Louis, City of St. Louis.

Normal turnaround time: 48 hours. Projects are generally billed by the hour. The first project may require a prepayment.

They specialize in process serving.

D D Hamilton Abstract Co
Phone: 417-859-2078
Fax: 417-859-2020

PO Box 11
Marshfield MO 65706

Local Retrieval Area: MO-Webster.

Normal turnaround time: 48 hours. Projects are generally billed by the number of names searched or records located. Credit accounts are accepted.

They specialize in land title and civil judgments.

D K Abstract
Phone: 901-662-7394
Fax: 901-686-9373

Rt 1 Box 63
Atwood TN 38220

Local Retrieval Area: TN-26 Counties.

Normal turnaround time: 48 hours. Projects are generally billed by the number of names searched. Credit accounts are accepted. Personal checks are accepted.

D W Moore and Assoc Inc
Phone: 801-266-6585
Fax: 801-266-2031

203 E 6100 South
Murray UT 84107

Local Retrieval Area: UT-All Counties.

Normal turnaround time: 3-5 days. Projects are generally billed by the hour. Credit accounts are accepted.

They specialize in research and historical investigation, environmental review, and education services.

🏛 DAC Services
Phone: 800-849-3019
918-664-9991
Fax: 800-887-8994

4110 S 100th East Ave
Tulsa OK 74146-3639

Local Retrieval Area: OK-Tulsa.

Online computer ordering is also available. Projects are generally billed by the number of names searched. Credit accounts are accepted. Credit cards are accepted.

They specialize in pre-employment application screening and are one of the nation's leading providers of driving records to the insurance & trucking industries. They are online with 133 state and county repositories and courts to obtain criminal records.

Daggett Abstract Co
Phone: 501-295-3434
Fax: 501-295-3445

PO Box 646
Marianna AR 72360

Local Retrieval Area: AR-Lee.

Normal turnaround time: from 1 day to 1 week. Fee basis will vary by type of project. Projects require prepayment.

They specialize in title search and land ownership.

Daily Journal Corporation
Phone: 800-952-5232
Fax: 213-680-3682

915 E 1st St
Los Angeles CA 90012

Local Retrieval Area: CA-Los Angeles, Orange, Riverside, San Bernardino, San Diego, Ventura.

Normal turnaround time: 3-5 business days. Expedited service available. Projects are generally billed by the number of names searched. The first project may require a prepayment. Fees due upon receipt of invoice.

Correspondent relationships: all of California. They will record legal notices and coordinate publication of legal notices.

Dakota County Abstract Co
Phone: 320-437-5600
Fax: 320-437-8876

1250 Hwy 55
Hastings MN 55033

Local Retrieval Area: MN-Dakota.

Normal turnaround time: 5-10 days. Projects are generally billed by the number of names searched or records located. Projects require prepayment. They will also invoice.

Correspondent relationships: all counties in Minnesota. They specialize in title searches.

⊞ Dane County Legal Notice

Phone: 800-720-6871
608-251-1181
139 W Wilson St Suite 106
Madison WI 53703
Fax: 608-251-8999

Local Retrieval and SOP Area: WI-Dane.

Normal turnaround time: 24-48 hours. Projects are generally billed by the number of names searched. Credit accounts are accepted.

Daniel Agency

Phone: 606-324-6029
PO Box 342
Fax: 606-324-6029
Ashland KY 41105

Local Retrieval Area: KY-11 Counties.

Normal turnaround time: 2-3 days. Projects are generally billed by the hour. The first project may require a prepayment.

The company is a multifaceted real estate research and consulting firm providing abstracts of title, right-of-way & easement acquisition, appraisals, real estate & mineral acquisition and leasing and acquisition investigation. They are bonded.

Mabel Daniels

Phone: 515-673-6507
301 Sherman St
Beacon IA 52534-9711

Local Retrieval Area: IA-Keokuk, Mahaska.

Normal turnaround time: up to one week. Projects are generally billed by the hour. Credit accounts are accepted.

She specializes in genealogy searches.

Dante's Attorney Service

Phone: 213-613-1417
240 S Broadway Suite 200
Fax: 213-613-1501
Los Angeles CA 90012

Local Retrieval and SOP Area: CA-Los Angeles, Orange, Riverside, San Bernardino, Ventura.

Normal turnaround time: 1-3 days. Rush service is also available. Fee basis will vary with type of search. The first project may require a prepayment.

Correspondent relationships: San Diego and surrounding cities.

⊞ Dargason Information Services

Phone: 770-418-9256
1500 Pleasant Hill Rd Suite 107-103
Duluth GA 30136

Local Retrieval Area: GA-16 Counties.

Normal turnaround time: 24-48 hours. Billing method depends on type of project. The first project may require a prepayment.

Correspondent relationships: metropolitan Atlanta and other counties in Northern Georgia. The principal is a licensed private detective also capable of performing background and asset searches, surveillance, and witness location.

⊞ Data Abstract & Title Co Inc

Phone: 540-949-6676
437 Walnut Ave
Fax: 540-949-6678
Waynesboro VA 22980

Local Retrieval Area: VA-Augusta, City of Staunton, City of Waynesboro.

Normal turnaround time: 1-2 days. Projects are generally billed by the number of names searched. Fee basis is "per job". Credit accounts are accepted. Bill is sent with each completed order.

She specializes in real estate title abstracting.

Data Quest Inc

Phone: 505-891-9326
PO Box 15455
Fax: 505-891-9335
Rio Rancho NM 87174

Local Retrieval Area: NM-Bernalillo, Sandoval.

Normal turnaround time: 24-48 hours. Projects are generally billed by the number of names searched. Credit accounts are accepted.

They specialize in UCC records at all New Mexico county courts and Secretary of State's office.

Data Reporting Corp

Phone: 203-287-1294
Sturbridge Commons 250 State St Suite D-2
Fax: 203-281-1683
North Haven CT 06473

Local Retrieval Area: CT-All Counties.

Normal turnaround time: 3-5 working days. Projects are generally billed by the hour. Credit accounts are accepted.

Data Research Inc

Phone: 800-432-6607
911 Madison Ave
419-259-3656
Toledo OH 43624
Fax: 419-255-0519

Local Retrieval and SOP Area: MI-Lenawee, Monroe; OH-Fulton, Hancock, Lucas, Ottawa, Sandusky, Williams, Wood.

Normal turnaround time: 24-48 hours. Projects are generally billed by the number of names searched. Credit accounts are accepted. Will bill established accounts.

Correspondent relationships: nationwide. They specialize in pre-employment background searches and worker's comp fraud.

Data Research Inc

Phone: 800-992-1983
503-626-0594
4325 SW 94th Ave No 7
Portland OR 97225
Fax: 800-992-1984
503-526-9762

Local Retrieval Area: OR-11 Counties.

Normal turnaround time: 24-72 hours. Projects are generally billed by the number of names searched or records located. The first project may require a prepayment.

Correspondent relationships: the rest of the counties in Oregon. They specialize in all public records retrieved in State of Oregon.

⊞ Data Screen Inc

Phone: 817-294-7671
6813 Toledo Ct
Fax: 817-294-0773
Fort Worth TX 76133

Local Retrieval Area: TX-Bexar, Brazoria, Collin, Dallas, Denton, Harris, Hays, Tarrant, Travis.

Normal turnaround time: 24-48 hours. Projects are generally billed by the number of names searched. Credit accounts are accepted.

Correspondent relationships: TX. They specialize in criminal record checks and MVR's.

Data Search Kentucky

Phone: 502-637-4658
1374 Ouerbacker Ct
Fax: 502-637-4658
Louisville KY 40208

Local Retrieval Area: KY-Bullitt, Fayette, Franklin, Hardin, Jefferson, Meade, Nelson, Oldham, Shelby, Spencer.

Normal turnaround time: 48 hours. 24 hours for rush. Projects are generally billed by the number of names searched. Credit accounts are accepted. Terms are net 30 days.

Correspondent relationships: Grayson, Hart, LaRue, Washington, Marion and Breckinridge, KY counties. They specialize in Secretary of State searches, corporate records reseach and filing.

Data-Quest Research and Recvry

Phone: 419-642-3031
Fax: 419-642-2461

4200 W Lincoln Hwy
Gomer OH 45809

Local Retrieval and SOP Area: OH-Allen, Auglaize, Hardin, Mercer, Putnam, Van Wert.

Normal turnaround time: 2-3 days. Projects are generally billed by the number of names searched. Billing method depends on type of project. Projects require prepayment.

They specialize in debt collection, auto recoveries, information retrieval, and bail enforcement.

DataFile

Phone: 800-843-6688
Fax: 619-747-9013

PO Box 747
Escondido CA 92033

Local Retrieval Area: CA-San Diego.

Normal turnaround time: 24-48 hours. Projects are generally billed by the number of names searched. The first project may require a prepayment.

They specialize in retrieving records from the US District Court.

DataSearch Inc

Phone: 800-452-3282
916-925-3282
Fax: 916-922-5199

PO Box 15406
Sacramento CA 95851

Local Retrieval Area: CA-El Dorado, Sacramento, San Diego.

Normal turnaround time: 24-48 hours. Projects are generally billed by the number of names searched. Credit accounts are accepted. Credit cards are accepted.

Correspondent relationships: nationwide. They specialize in UCC, Corporate, LP, LLC and business name filing and search services. They also do searches to locate asset and address information. They have access to DMV and courthouse records.

▥ Datasource Reports

Phone: 888-986-0101
312-986-0101
Fax: 888-986-0396
312-986-0396

175 W Jackson Blvd Suite A-1810
Chicago IL 60604

Local Retrieval Area: IL-Cook, Du Page, Kane, Lake, McHenry, Will.

Normal turnaround time: 72 hours. Expedited service available. Projects are generally billed by the hour. The first project may require a prepayment.

Correspondent relationships: nationwide. They specialize in credit and background reports, insurance inspections and surveys to qualified clients.

▥ Datatrace Information Services

Phone: 810-465-7020
Fax: 810-465-0288

48 S Main St
Mt Clemens MI 48043

Local Retrieval Area: MI-Macomb, Oakland, Wayne.

Normal turnaround time: 3 days. The first project may require a prepayment. Net due upon receipt.

They specialize in posting automated title plants, title search reports (real estate) and document retrieval.

▥ DataTrace Investigations Inc

Phone: 800-748-5335
801-253-2400
Fax: 801-253-2478

1393 W 9000 S Suite 254
Salt Lake City UT 84088-9259

Local Retrieval and SOP Area: UT-Davis, Salt Lake, Summit, Utah, Weber.

Normal turnaround time: 24-48 hours. Expedited service available. Online computer ordering is also available. Projects are generally billed by the number of names searched. The first project may require a prepayment. Service agreement required for billing.

Correspondent relationships: nationwide. They specialize in asset and background investigations, skip tracing, locating hidden assets, criminal record checks and DMV and driving records.

Sandra Dauzat

Phone: 501-772-7110

Rt 7 Box 3080
Texarkana AR 75502

Local Retrieval Area: AR-Columbia, Hempstead, Howard, Lafayette, Miller, Nevada, Sevier.

Normal turnaround time: 12-72 hours. Projects are generally billed by the number of names searched. Credit accounts are accepted.

She specializes in UCC record searches.

▥ Davick Services

Phone: 800-658-6656
806-832-4349
Fax: 800-658-6656
806-832-4349

PO Box 1274
Shallowater TX 79363-1274

Local Retrieval Area: TX-35 Counties.

Normal turnaround time: 24-48 hours. Projects are generally billed by the number of names searched. The first project may require a prepayment. Personal checks are accepted.

They specialize in UCC, tax lien, judgments and property searches.

Daviess County Abstracts

Phone: 816-663-2155
Fax: 816-663-2156

106 N Market St
Gallatin MO 64640

Local Retrieval Area: MO-Daviess.

Normal turnaround time: 3 days. Projects are generally billed by the number of records located. Credit accounts are accepted.

They specialize in real estate searches.

Davis Detective Agency

Phone: 800-782-0445
301-843-7288
Fax: 301-932-4781

PO Box 102
Waldorf MD 20604-0102

Local Retrieval and SOP Area: DC-District of Columbia; MD-Anne Arundel, Calvert, Charles, Howard, Prince George's, St. Mary's.

Normal turnaround time: 3-5 days. Online computer ordering is also available. Projects are generally billed by the hour. The first project may require a prepayment. Personal checks are accepted.

They specialize in skips, locates, asset searches, court house searches, and court house records research in the Southern Maryland area and Washington, DC.

Dawes County Abstract Co

Phone: 308-432-4840
Fax: 308-432-2960

PO Box 1070
Chadron NE 69337

Local Retrieval Area: NE-Box Butte, Dawes, Sheridan, Sioux.

Normal turnaround time: 3 days. Projects are generally billed by the number of names searched. The first project may require a prepayment.

They specialize in title insurance and oil and gas reports.

DDR (Delaware Document Rtrvl)
Phone: 800-343-1742
917 King St PO Box 27
302-658-9911
Wilmington DE 19801
Fax: 302-658-9951
Local Retrieval and SOP Area: DE-Kent, New Castle, Sussex.

Normal turnaround time: same day. Projects are generally billed by the number of names searched. Credit accounts are accepted. Credit cards are accepted.

Correspondent relationships: Philadelphia, PA. They specialize in any type of search, document retrieval, filings, service of process and Secretary of State work.

DDS Legal Support Systems
Phone: 714-662-5555
2900 Bristol St Suite E-106
Fax: 714-662-3379
Costa Mesa CA 92626
Local Retrieval and SOP Area: CA-Los Angeles, Orange, Riverside, San Bernardino, San Diego, Ventura.

Normal turnaround time: 24 hours. Projects are generally billed by the hour. The first project may require a prepayment.

Correspondent relationships: throughout California. They specialize in document retrieval, court filing, process serving and skip tracing.

DDS Legal Support Systems
Phone: 213-482-5555
123 S Figueroa
Fax: 213-482-5006
Los Angeles CA 90012
Local Retrieval and SOP Area: CA-Los Angeles, Orange, Riverside, San Bernardino, San Diego, Ventura.

Normal turnaround time: 24 hours. Projects are generally billed by the hour. The first project may require a prepayment.

Correspondent relationships: throughout California. They specialize in document retrieval, court filing, process serving and skip tracing.

Dealey Abstract and Title Co
Phone: 308-995-4622
311 West Ave
Fax: 308-995-4622
Holdrege NE 68949
Local Retrieval Area: NE-Phelps.

Normal turnaround time: 24-48 hours. Fee basis will vary by type of project. Credit accounts are accepted.

Correspondent relationships: Buffalo, Kearney and Harlan counties.

Deamer & Deamer
Phone: 219-223-3129
109 E 9th St
Fax: 219-223-5001
Rochester IN 46975
Local Retrieval Area: IN-Fulton.

Normal turnaround time: 1 working week. Projects are generally billed by the number of records located. Credit accounts are accepted. Payment upon completion of work.

They specialize in title insurance.

Deception Control Inc
Phone: 800-776-1660
1885 W Commercial Blvd Suite 125
954-771-6900
Fort Lauderdale FL 33309
Fax: 954-776-7687
Local Retrieval Area: FL-Broward, Dade, Palm Beach.

Normal turnaround time: 48 hours. Online computer ordering is also available. Projects are generally billed by the number of names searched. The first project may require a prepayment.

Correspondent relationships: nationwide. They specialize in pre-employment screening of employees to include retrieval and application verification.

Dee Moody Investigations
Phone: 415-571-8598
999-C Edgewater Blvd Suite 330
Fax: 415-345-1362
Foster City CA 94404
Local Retrieval Area: CA-Alameda, San Francisco, San Mateo, Santa Clara.

Normal turnaround time: same day to 2-3 days. Projects are generally billed by the number of names searched. The first project may require a prepayment.

Correspondent relationships: nationwide.

Deister Ward & Witcher
Phone: 800-443-7874
2812 1st Ave N Suite 318
406-248-6481
Billings MT 59101
Fax: 406-248-6478
Local Retrieval Area: MT-Yellowstone.

Normal turnaround time: 2 days. Out of county can be done in 1 week. Projects are generally billed by the hour. Credit accounts are accepted.

They specialize in abstracts of title and mineral title research.

Deister Ward & Witcher Inc
Phone: 303-790-8426
13275 E Fremont Pl Suite 208
Fax: 303-790-7427
Englewood CO 80112-3917
Local Retrieval Area: CO-22 Counties.

Normal turnaround time: up to 1 week. Projects are generally billed by the hour. Credit accounts are accepted. They request prepayment from individuals, but will invoice attorneys and companies.

Correspondent relationships: nationwide. They specialize in real estate and title research.

Deister Ward & Witcher of AR
Phone: 501-782-7448
115 N 10th Suite A-107
Fax: 501-782-7448
Ft Smith AR 72901
Local Retrieval Area: AR-11 Counties.

Normal turnaround time: 2-3 days. Expedited service available. Fee basis will vary by the type of project. Credit accounts are accepted.

Deister Ward & Witcher of WY
Phone: 800-829-8434
PO Box 1846
Fax: 307-266-1823
Casper WY 82602
Local Retrieval Area: UT-Carbon, Daggett, Summit, Uintah, Wasatch; WY-23 Counties.

Normal turnaround time: varied depending on project. Fee basis will vary by the type of project. Credit accounts are accepted.

They specialize in oil and gas records.

Delaware Attorney Services
Phone: 302-429-0657
2000 Pennsylvaina Ave Suite 207
Fax: 302-429-0656
Wilmington DE 19806
Local Retrieval and SOP Area: DE-Kent, New Castle, Sussex.

Normal turnaround time: 2-5 days. Expedited service available. Projects are generally billed by the number of names searched. Credit accounts are accepted.

They specialize in skip tracing and process service.

Delaware County Abstract Co
Phone: 319-927-4858

304 E Main St
Manchester IA 52057

Local Retrieval Area: IA-Delaware.

Normal turnaround time: 1 day to 2 weeks. Projects are generally billed by the number of names searched. Credit accounts are accepted. They request prepayment from individuals, but will invoice businesses and established customers.

Delaware County Abstract Co
Phone: 918-253-4425

PO Box 930
Fax: 918-253-6224
Jay OK 74346

Local Retrieval Area: OK-Delaware.

Normal turnaround time: 2-3 days. Fee basis is determined per search. Credit accounts are accepted.

Delmarva Abstractors
Phone: 410-228-6044

4 Kiowa Rd PO Box 316
Fax: 410-228-1572
Cambridge MD 21613

Local Retrieval and SOP Area: DE-Kent, Sussex; MD-Caroline, Dorchester, Talbot, Wicomico.

Normal turnaround time: 24 to 48 hours. Credit accounts are accepted.

They specialize in title searches.

Delta County Title Co
Phone: 903-395-4116

PO Box 127
Fax: 903-395-2106
Cooper TX 75432

Local Retrieval Area: TX-Delta.

Normal turnaround time: varied depending on project. Projects are generally billed by the hour. Credit accounts are accepted.

Delta Investigations & Intelligence
Phone: 602-945-6169

3080 N Civic Center Plaza Suite 31
Fax: 602-970-6533
Scottsdale AZ 85251

Local Retrieval and SOP Area: AZ-Maricopa.

Normal turnaround time: 24-48 hours. Projects are generally billed by the hour. Projects require prepayment.

They specialize in asset research and background checks.

Dennis E Seymour & Associates
Phone: 410-269-5151

Box 3379
Fax: 410-268-5151
Annapolis MD 21403

Local Retrieval and SOP Area: MD-Anne Arundel, Baltimore, City of Baltimore, Caroline, Howard, Kent, Prince George's, Queen Anne's, Talbot.

Normal turnaround time: 3 working days. 1 day for MVA and Boat Registration. Online computer ordering is also available. Project billing methods vary. Database inquires are at fixed rate. Credit accounts are accepted. Credit cards are accepted.

Correspondent relationships: Washington, DC. They specialize in boat registrations, MVR's, circuit and district court criminal and civil record searching.

Dennis R Sheraw and Associates
Phone: 809-773-3110

2191 Church St Christiansted
Fax: 809-773-3113
St Croix VI 00820-4962

Local Retrieval and SOP Area: VI-St. Croix, St. John, St. Thomas.

Normal turnaround time: 1 week. Online computer ordering is also available. Projects are generally billed by the hour. The first project may require a prepayment.

Correspondent relationships: nationwide. Mr. Sheraw performs investigative services, excluding domestic relations.

Dennis Richman's Service
Phone: 215-977-9393

1601 Market St Suite 750
Fax: 215-977-9806
Philadelphia PA 19107

Local Retrieval and SOP Area: NJ-All Counties.

Normal turnaround time: same day to next day. Projects are generally billed by the number of names searched. Projects require prepayment.

Dependable Legal Services
Phone: 888-945-9885

920 Feltl Ct Suite 149
612-945-0349
Hopkins MN 55343
Fax: 612-945-5262

Local Retrieval and SOP Area: MN-Hennepin, Ramsey.

Normal turnaround time: 1-2 days. Projects are generally billed by the hour. Projects require prepayment.

Correspondent relationships: nationwide. They specialize in process serving and messenger service.

Linda Derher
Phone: 609-853-9836

204 Sycamore Ave
Fax: 609-853-9459
Sewell NJ 08080

Local Retrieval Area: NJ-Gloucester.

Normal turnaround time: 24-48 hours. Projects are generally billed by the number of names searched. The first project may require a prepayment. Personal checks are accepted.

Desert Investigations
Phone: 602-726-4398

905 E 26th Pl
Yuma AZ 85365

Local Retrieval Area: AZ-La Paz, Yuma; CA-Imperial.

Normal turnaround time: 24-48 hours. Projects are generally billed by the hour. Credit accounts are accepted.

They specialize in property inspections for mortgage companies.

DeSoto Abstract
Phone: 318-798-1198

2529 E 70th St Suite 110
Fax: 318-798-1210
Shreveport LA 71105-4044

Local Retrieval Area: AR-Columbia, Lafayette, Ouachita, Union; LA-Bienville Parish, Bossier Parish, Caddo Parish, Claiborne Parish, De Soto Parish, Lincoln Parish, Webster Parish; TX-Cass, Harrison, Henderson, Marion, Panola, Rusk, Shelby, Smith.

Normal turnaround time: varied depending on project. Projects are generally billed by the hour. The first project may require a prepayment.

Correspondent relationships: Southern Louisiana. They specialize in oil, gas and environmental assessment.

DeSoto Abstract Co

Phone: 941-494-3656
Fax: 941-494-3481

PO Drawer 31
Arcadia FL 33821

Local Retrieval Area: FL-De Soto.

Normal turnaround time: 3 days. Projects are generally billed by the number of records located. Credit accounts are accepted.

Correspondent relationships: Charlotte, Lee and Hardee Counties.

Deuel County Abstract Co

Phone: 308-874-2212
Fax: 308-874-3491

171 Vincent Ave
Chappell NE 69129

Local Retrieval Area: NE-Cheyenne, Deuel, Garden, Keith.

Normal turnaround time: 7-10 days. Credit accounts are accepted.

Deuel County Abstract Co

Phone: 605-874-2381
Fax: 605-874-2394

PO Box 737
Clear Lake SD 57226

Local Retrieval Area: SD-Deuel.

Normal turnaround time: 10 days. Fee basis will vary by the type of project. Projects require prepayment.

They specialize in title insurance.

Dewey County Abstract Co

Phone: 405-328-5556
Fax: 405-328-5484

PO Box 157
Taloga OK 73667

Local Retrieval Area: OK-Dewey.

Normal turnaround time: less than 1 week. Projects are generally billed by the number of names searched. Fee basis will vary by the type of project. Credit accounts are accepted.

DFW Court Records

Phone: 800-436-0516
Fax: 817-238-9765

PO Box 136721
Fort Worth TX 76136

Local Retrieval and SOP Area: TX-Collin, Dallas, Denton, Ellis, Tarrant.

Normal turnaround time: 24 hours for Tarrant and Dallas Counties, 48 to 72 hours for all other counties. Projects are generally billed by the number of names searched or records located. Credit accounts are accepted.

Correspondent relationships: Bexar and Harris Counties. They specialize in criminal, civil, bankruptcy and lien searches as well as document retrieval.

Dickey County Abstract & Title

Phone: 701-349-3450
Fax: 701-349-4850

PO Box 339
Ellendale ND 58436

Local Retrieval Area: ND-Dickey.

Normal turnaround time: varied depending on project. Fee basis will vary by the type of project. Credit accounts are accepted.

Dickinson Abstract Co

Phone: 701-225-2271
Fax: 701-225-4416

Para Sq Plza, 40 1st Ave W #203 PO Box 1243
Dickinson ND 58601

Local Retrieval Area: ND-Billings, Stark.

Normal turnaround time: 1 week. Projects are generally billed by the number of records located. Projects require prepayment.

DiNatale Detective Agency

Phone: 617-227-4115
Fax: 617-227-2587

45 Bowdoin St
Boston MA 02114

Local Retrieval Area: MA-Essex, Middlesex, Norfolk, Plymouth, Suffolk.

Normal turnaround time: 7-10 working days. Emergency requests can be taken. Online computer ordering is also available. Projects are generally billed by the hour. The first project may require a prepayment.

Correspondent relationships: Barnstable and Dukes. They specialize in civil and criminal pretrial investigations.

🏛 Dolores Dios

Phone: 800-763-2988
201-762-0194
Fax: 201-763-2988

25 Princeton St
Maplewood NJ 07040

Local Retrieval Area: NJ-Bergen, Essex, Hudson, Morris, Passaic, Union.

Normal turnaround time: 3 days. Projects are generally billed by the number of names searched or records located. Credit accounts are accepted. Payment due upon receipt.

She specializes in court record searches, real estate searches, foreclosures and tax sales.

Direct Corporate Services Inc

Phone: 800-783-7904
770-333-7205
Fax: 770-592-2274

PO Box 506
Snellville GA 30278

Local Retrieval Area: GA-Clayton, Cobb, De Kalb, Fulton, Gwinnett.

Normal turnaround time: 24-48 hours. Expedited service available. Projects are generally billed by the number of names searched. The first project may require a prepayment. Terms are net 30 days.

Correspondent relationships: Forsythe, Barrow and Cherokee, GA counties. They specialize in complete Metro Atlantic research for UCC, federal and state tax liens, judgments, litigation and title searches.

Lewis Dirks

Phone: 605-331-6022
Fax: 605-338-4837

PO Box 254
Sioux Falls SD 57101

Local Retrieval Area: IA-Lyon, Osceola, Sioux; MN-Lincoln, Murray, Nobles, Pipestone, Rock; SD-14 Counties.

Normal turnaround time: 2-3 days. Fee basis varies by type of transaction. The first project may require a prepayment.

He specializes in accident reconstruction and court investigations.

District Security Inc

Phone: 800-688-8721
513-731-6095
Fax: 513-731-6094

7374 Reading Rd Suite 117
Cincinnati OH 45237

Local Retrieval Area: KY-Boone, Campbell, Kenton; OH-Butler, Clermont, Cuyahoga, Franklin, Hamilton, Montgomery, Warren.

Normal turnaround time: 2 business days. Projects are generally billed by the number of names searched. Credit accounts are accepted. Terms are net 15 days.

Correspondent relationships: nationwide.

Divide Abstract Co Inc

Phone: 701-965-6352
Fax: 701-965-4243

PO Box 230
Crosby ND 58730

Local Retrieval Area: ND-Divide.

Normal turnaround time: varied depending on project. Projects are generally billed by the hour. Projects require prepayment. They will also invoice.

They specialize in oil title and mineral searches.

DJ Records

Phone: 901-324-6209
Fax: 901-323-5860

3532 Mayflower Ave
Memphis TN 38122

Local Retrieval Area: TN-Fayette, Shelby.

Normal turnaround time: 24 hours. Projects are generally billed by the number of names searched. Credit accounts are accepted. Will be billed once a month.

🏛 DL Express Inc

Phone: 602-285-9901
Fax: 602-285-0445

3507 N Central Suite 203
Phoenix AZ 85012

Local Retrieval and SOP Area: AZ-Maricopa, Pima.

Normal turnaround time: 24 hours. Projects are generally billed by the number of names searched or records located. The first project may require a prepayment. Payment due upon completion of work.

Correspondent relationships: Pinal, Pima and Coconino, AZ counties.

DLS (Demovsky Lawyer Service)

Phone: 518-449-8411
Fax: 518-449-2467

100 State St Suite 220
Albany NY 12207

Local Retrieval and SOP Area: NY-Albany, Rensselaer, Schenectady.

Normal turnaround time: 24 hours. Projects are generally billed by the hour. The first project may require a prepayment.

DLS (Demovsky Lawyer Service)

Phone: 800-443-1058
212-925-1220
Fax: 212-941-0235

401 Broadway Suite 510
New York NY 10013

Local Retrieval and SOP Area: NJ-Bergen, Essex; NY-Bronx, Kings, Nassau, New York, Queens, Richmond, Rockland, Westchester.

Normal turnaround time: 24 hours. Projects are generally billed by the hour. The first project may require a prepayment.

Correspondent relationships: New York, New Jersey and Connecticut. They specialize in detail oriented personal service.

E Fred Dobbins

Phone: 601-394-2301
Fax: 601-394-2778

PO Box 1090 St Francis & Lafayette St
Leakesville MS 39451

Local Retrieval and SOP Area: MS-George, Greene, Perry.

Normal turnaround time: 1 day. Projects are generally billed by the hour. The first project may require a prepayment.

He is an attorney specializing in property law.

🏛 Doc*U*Search Inc

Phone: 800-332-3034
603-224-2871
Fax: 603-224-2794

PO Box 777
Concord NH 03302-0777

Local Retrieval Area: NH-Belknap, Carroll, Cheshire, Coos, Grafton, Hillsborough, Merrimack, Rockingham, Strafford, Sullivan.

Normal turnaround time: varied depending on project. Fee basis will vary by type of search. The first project may require a prepayment. Terms are net 10 days.

Correspondent relationships: nationwide. They specialize in UCC searches.

Doc-U-Search Hawaii

Phone: 808-523-1200
Fax: 808-533-3686

1188 Bishop St Suite 2212
Honolulu HI 96813

Local Retrieval Area: HI-Hawaii, Honolulu, Kalawao, Maui.

Normal turnaround time: 2 days. Expedited service available. Projects are generally billed by the number of names searched or records located. The first project may require a prepayment.

Correspondent relationships: Maui, Kauai, Island of Hawaii.

Document Resources

Phone: 800-344-2382
Fax: 800-780-4795

1451 River Park Dr Suite 148
Sacramento CA 95815

Local Retrieval Area: CA-El Dorado, Placer, Sacramento, San Joaquin, Solano, Sutter, Yolo, Yuba.

Normal turnaround time: 1-3 days. Projects are generally billed by the number of names searched. Credit accounts are accepted.

Correspondent relationships: nationwide. They specialize in UCC, corporate and real property searches. They are associated with Information America, now an affiliate of West Publishing, a leading on-line public record provider.

Document Resources

Phone: 800-532-9876
Fax: 800-845-6319

600 W Peachtree St Suite 1200
Atlanta GA 30308

Local Retrieval Area: GA-Clayton, Cobb, De Kalb, Fulton, Gwinnett.

Normal turnaround time: 1-3 days. Projects are generally billed by the number of names searched. Credit accounts are accepted.

Correspondent relationships: nationwide. They specialize in UCC, corporate and real property searches. They are associated with Information America, now an affiliate of West Publishing, a leading on-line public record provider.

Document Resources

Phone: 800-292-9493
Fax: 800-437-3796

230 Broadway Suite 100
Springfield IL 62701

Local Retrieval Area: IL-Cass, Christian, Cook, Du Page, Logan, Macon, Menard, Morgan, Sangamon.

Normal turnaround time: 1-2 days. Projects are generally billed by the number of names searched. Credit accounts are accepted.

Correspondent relationships: nationwide. They specialize in UCC, corporate and real property searches. They are associated with Information America, now an affiliate of West Publishing, a leading on-line public record provider.

Document Resources

120 West Fayette St Suite 600
Baltimore MD 21201

Phone: 800-777-8567
410-659-2600
Fax: 800-778-2028
410-659-2625

Local Retrieval Area: MD-11 Counties.

Normal turnaround time: 1-3 days. Projects are generally billed by the number of names searched. Credit accounts are accepted.

Correspondent relationships: nationwide. They specialize in UCC, corporate and real property searches. They are associated with Information America, now an affiliate of West Publishing, a leading on-line public record provider.

Document Resources

35 E Gay St Suite 512
Columbus OH 43215

Phone: 800-552-3453
614-621-8880
Fax: 800-874-2727
614-621-8884

Local Retrieval Area: MI-Ingham; OH-Delaware, Fairfield, Franklin, Licking, Madison, Pickaway, Union.

Normal turnaround time: 1-3 days. Projects are generally billed by the number of names searched. Credit accounts are accepted. Terms are net 30 days.

Correspondent relationships: the rest of Ohio and nationwide. They specialize in UCC, corporate and real property searches. They are associated with Information America, now an affiliate of West Publishing, a leading on-line public record provider.

Document Resources

111 South St
Harrisburg PA 17101

Phone: 800-666-0061
Fax: 800-305-3318

Local Retrieval Area: NY-Albany, New York; PA-Dauphin.

Normal turnaround time: 1-3 days. Projects are generally billed by the number of names searched. Credit accounts are accepted.

Correspondent relationships: nationwide. They specialize in UCC, corporate and real property searches. They are associated with Information America, now an affiliate of West Publishing, a leading on-line public record provider.

Document Resources

PO Box 912
Austin TX 78767

Phone: 800-822-8084
512-480-0123
Fax: 800-554-2092
512-480-0147

Local Retrieval Area: TX-Bell, Bexar, Collin, Dallas, Denton, Harris, Hays, Tarrant, Travis, Williamson.

Normal turnaround time: 24-48 hours. Projects are generally billed by the number of names searched. Credit accounts are accepted.

Correspondent relationships: nationwide. They specialize in UCC, corporate and real property searches. They are associated with Information America, now an affiliate of West Publishing, a leading on-line public record provider.

Document Resources

1911 N Ft Myer Dr Suite 702
Arlington VA 22209

Phone: 800-945-7339
Fax: 202-347-0888

Local Retrieval and SOP Area: DC-District of Columbia; VA-City of Alexandria, Arlington, Chesterfield, Fairfax, Henrico, Prince William.

Normal turnaround time: 1-3 days. Projects are generally billed by the number of names searched. Credit accounts are accepted.

Correspondent relationships: nationwide. They specialize in UCC, corporate and real property searches. They are associated with Information America, now an affiliate of West Publishing, a leading on-line public record provider.

Document Resources

701 E Franklin St Suite 1412
Richmond VA 23219

Phone: 800-468-4310
804-644-0501
Fax: 800-448-5350

Local Retrieval Area: VA-City of Alexandria, Arlington, Chesterfield, Fairfax, City of Fredericksburg, Henrico, Powhatan, Prince William, City of Richmond, Spotsylvania.

Normal turnaround time: 1-3 days. Projects are generally billed by the number of names searched. Credit accounts are accepted.

Correspondent relationships: nationwide. They specialize in UCC, corporate and real property searches. They are associated with Information America, now an affiliate of West Publishing, a leading on-line public record provider.

⛁ Document Retrieval Service

PO Box 276
Oklahoma City OK 73101

Phone: 405-235-3653
Fax: 405-235-2691

Local Retrieval Area: OK-11 Counties.

Normal turnaround time: 24 hours Oklahoma County and Secretary of State, all other counties 48 hours or more. Projects are generally billed by the number of names searched. Credit accounts are accepted. Payment is due on receipt.

Correspondent relationships: the rest of Oklahoma. They specialize in Corporate retrieval and filings at the Secretary of State. They also search all (77) counties in Oklahoma for UCC filings, State and Federal tax liens and pending suits and judgments.

⛁ Docutech Information Services

529 E Town St
Columbus OH 43215

Phone: 800-361-3310
614-221-4625
Fax: 614-221-4658

Local Retrieval Area: OH-Clark, Cuyahoga, Delaware, Fairfield, Franklin, Hamilton, Licking, Montgomery, Muskingum, Summit.

Normal turnaround time: 24-48 hours. Expedited service available. Projects are generally billed by the number of names searched. Credit accounts are accepted. Payment due upon invoice.

Correspondent relationships: the rest of Ohio. They specialize in UCC searches, liens, suits, judgment searches, one owner property searches, asset searches, record retrieving, probate, domestic relations and bankruptcy.

Docutrans Inc

2207 Chestnut St 2nd Floor
Philadelphia PA 19103

Phone: 215-751-9630
Fax: 215-751-9631

Local Retrieval and SOP Area: PA-Bucks, Delaware, Montgomery, Philadelphia.

Normal turnaround time: 1-3 days. Rush service is also available. Fee basis will vary by the type of search. Credit accounts are accepted.

Docutronics Information Services

195 Broadway Suite 2004
New York NY 10007

Phone: 800-227-5595
212-233-7140
Fax: 212-233-7173

Local Retrieval Area: NY-Kings, New York.

Normal turnaround time: 4-24 hours. Projects are generally billed by the hour. Credit accounts are accepted. Credit cards are accepted. They accept personal checks. They accept American Express, Visa and MasterCard.

Correspondent relationships: nationwide.

Don E Leeman Enterprises

Phone: 603-755-3030

RR1 Box 3130 9 Karen Rd
Middleton NH 03887

Local Retrieval Area: MA-Middlesex, Norfolk, Worcester; ME-Cumberland, York; NH-Belknap, Carroll, Grafton, Rockingham, Strafford.

Normal turnaround time: depends on the job. Projects are generally billed by the number of names searched or records located. The first project may require a prepayment. Payment due upon delivery of records.

They specialize in current owner property searches, federal, state and local property tax liens and satisfactions of same. Also they do small claims and civil suits at the District Court level as well as criminal background checks at County Courthouse.

Donald Jones Investigation

Phone: 509-662-7158

PO Box 3243
Wenatchee WA 98807-3243

Local Retrieval and SOP Area: WA-Chelan, Douglas, Grant.

Normal turnaround time: 2-3 days. Projects are generally billed by the number of names searched. The first project may require a prepayment.

They specialize in investigation and information retrieval. A FAX is available for established customers.

Donna's Unlimited Searches

Phone: 704-256-1418
Fax: 704-256-1418

1859 Oleander Dr
Conover NC 28613

Local Retrieval Area: NC-Alexander, Burke, Caldwell, Catawba.

Normal turnaround time: 24-48 hours. Fee basis varies by type of transaction. The first project may require a prepayment.

Dotter Abstract & Associates

Phone: 719-738-1730
Fax: 719-738-1012

506 Main St
Walsenburg CO 81089

Local Retrieval Area: CO-Huerfano.

Normal turnaround time: 2-3 days. Fee basis will vary by the type of project. The first project may require a prepayment.

They specialize in real estate title and insurance.

Dora Doty

Phone: 614-695-4917

140 S Sugar St
St Clairsville OH 43950

Local Retrieval Area: OH-Belmont, Guernsey, Harrison, Jefferson, Monroe.

Normal turnaround time: 24 hours. Projects are generally billed by the number of names searched. Credit accounts are accepted.

She specializes in title and lien work.

Dougherty Abstract & Title Service

Phone: 912-888-9035

PO Box 841
Albany GA 31702

Local Retrieval Area: GA-Baker, Calhoun, Dougherty, Lee, Mitchell, Terrell, Worth.

Normal turnaround time: 48 hours. Fee basis will vary by the type of project. Credit accounts are accepted.

They specialize in real estate matters.

Douglas County Abstract & Title

Phone: 417-683-4701
Fax: 417-683-5980

113 E Public Square
Ava MO 65608

Local Retrieval Area: MO-Douglas.

Normal turnaround time: 5 working days. Fee basis will vary by type of project. Credit accounts are accepted.

Douglas County Abstract Co

Phone: 320-763-3426
Fax: 320-762-2455

616 Hawthrone St
Alexandria MN 56308

Local Retrieval Area: MN-Douglas, Pope.

Normal turnaround time: 1 week. Projects are generally billed by the number of names searched. Projects require prepayment. They also invoice.

Douglas County Abstract Co Inc

Phone: 217-253-3214
Fax: 217-253-3022

PO Box 167 110 E Sale St
Tuscola IL 61953

Local Retrieval Area: IL-Douglas.

Normal turnaround time: the same day. Projects are generally billed by the hour. Credit accounts are accepted.

Douglas County Title Co

Phone: 503-672-3388
Fax: 503-672-8110

629 SE Main St
Roseburg OR 97470

Local Retrieval Area: OR-Douglas.

Normal turnaround time: 2-3 days. Projects are generally billed by the hour. The first project may require a prepayment.

They specialize in real estate and escrow collections.

Douglas County Title Co

Phone: 605-724-2235

PO Box 366
Armour SD 57313

Local Retrieval Area: SD-Douglas.

Normal turnaround time: 4 days. Fee basis varies by type of transaction. Credit accounts are accepted.

Douglas Investigations Ltd

Phone: 800-747-0820
202-347-8840
Fax: 202-393-5657

431 N Lee St
Alexandria VA 22314-2301

Local Retrieval Area: DC-District of Columbia; MD-Anne Arundel, Montgomery, Prince George's; VA-City of Alexandria, Arlington, City of Fairfax.

Normal turnaround time: 1 week. Expedited service available. Projects are generally billed by the hour. Credit accounts are accepted. Personal checks are accepted.

Correspondent relationships: Maryland and Virginia. They are a licensed private investigative firm.

Howard F Douglas

Phone: 901-968-9381
Fax: 901-968-0261

PO Box 390
Lexington TN 38351

Local Retrieval Area: TN-Chester, Decatur, Hardin, Henderson, Madison.

Normal turnaround time: 24 hours. He charges a flat rate per search. Credit accounts are accepted.

He is an attorney and specializes in real estate record searches.

Dovolos & Associates
Phone: 612-321-0095
Fax: 612-333-2261
401 N 3rd St Suite 430
Minneapolis MN 55401

Local Retrieval Area: MN-Anoka, Dakota, Hennepin, Ramsey.

Normal turnaround time: same day if requested by 10AM, otherwise next day. Projects are generally billed by the number of names searched or records located. Credit accounts are accepted.

Drake & Jay
Phone: 515-437-1890
Fax: 515-437-1893
PO Box 367
Centerville IA 52544

Local Retrieval Area: IA-Appanoose.

Normal turnaround time: a couple of days. Fee basis will vary by the type of project, however, there is a minimum charge. Credit accounts are accepted. They will accept personal checks.

They do 10-year searches as a standard.

Drake Detective Agency
Phone: 208-377-3463
Fax: 208-377-2249
909 N Cole Rd
Boise ID 83704-8641

Local Retrieval Area: ID-Ada, Boise, Canyon, Valley.

Normal turnaround time: 24 to 48 hours. Projects are generally billed by the number of records located. Projects require prepayment.

They specialize in asset locations and fraud investigations.

Drake Land Title Co
Phone: 816-438-5188
Fax: 816-438-6644
167 W Main PO Box 998
Warsaw MO 65355-0998

Local Retrieval Area: MO-Benton.

Normal turnaround time: varied depending on project. Projects are generally billed by the number of names searched. The first project may require a prepayment.

They specialize in title insurance.

Drew County Abstract & Title Co
Phone: 501-367-6607
Fax: 501-367-6560
PO Box 533
Monticello AR 71655

Local Retrieval Area: AR-Drew.

Normal turnaround time: 2-3 days. Fee basis will vary by type of project. Projects require prepayment.

They specialize in title insurance.

Ray M Druley
Phone: 812-753-4975
Fax: 812-753-4612
PO Box 146
Ft Branch IN 47648

Local Retrieval Area: IN-Gibson.

Normal turnaround time: 5 days. Projects are generally billed by the number of names searched. Credit accounts are accepted.

He is an attorney.

Due Diligence Inc
Phone: 800-644-0107
406-728-0001
Fax: 406-728-0006
PO Box 8366
Missoula MT 59807

Local Retrieval Area: MT-Missoula.

Normal turnaround time: averages 36 hours. Online computer ordering is also available. Projects are generally billed by the number of names searched. Credit accounts are accepted.

They have direct correspondence with over 1,100 record retrievers.

Frank Duke
Phone: 303-332-4042
937 W 11th St
Wray CO 80758

Local Retrieval and SOP Area: CO-Yuma.

Normal turnaround time: 1 day depending on project. Fees are by type of service. Credit accounts are accepted. Terms are net 15 days.

He specializes in civil, citations, summons, interrogatories and garnishments.

Dunn County Abstract & Title Inc
Phone: 715-235-0875
Fax: 715-235-9690
815 7th St E
Menomonie WI 54751

Local Retrieval Area: WI-Dunn, Pepin.

Normal turnaround time: 1-2 days for Dunn county. For Pepin county up to 1 week. Fee basis varies by type of transaction. The first project may require a prepayment.

James C Duram
Phone: 616-894-8325
PO Box 43
Whitehall MI 49461-0043

Local Retrieval and SOP Area: MI-Muskegon, Newaygo, Oceana, Ottawa.

Normal turnaround time: 24 hours. Projects are generally billed by the hour. Projects require prepayment.

He specializes in serving of civil process.

�🏛 Jacqueline E Dutton
Phone: 304-658-4441
Fax: 304-658-3157
HC 66 Box 84A
Hico WV 25854

Local Retrieval Area: WV-Fayette, Nicholas, Raleigh.

Normal turnaround time: 24-48 hours. Projects are generally billed by the number of names searched. Credit accounts are accepted. Pay by check per once per month billing.

Correspondent relationships: Jackson County. She has been doing paralegal work for 4 years and received a degree from the College of West Virginia. Also does floor plan auditing.

E

E-Z Messenger Attorney Service
Phone: 520-623-8436
Fax: 520-624-1819
65 E Pennington
Tucson AZ 85701

Local Retrieval and SOP Area: AZ-Cochise, Pima, Santa Cruz.

Normal turnaround time: 24 hours. Projects are generally billed by the number of names searched. Projects require prepayment.

Correspondent relationships: the Phoenix metro area.

🏛 Eagle & Associates LLC
Phone: 800-216-4860
573-875-0438
Fax: 573-875-0533
2100 E Broadway Suite 323
Columbia MO 65201

Local Retrieval and SOP Area: MO-Boone, Cole.

Normal turnaround time: 24-48 hours. Projects are generally billed by the number of names searched or records located. The first project may require a prepayment.

Correspondent relationships: statewide. They specialize in criminal and civil records retrieval background records and searches.

🏛 Eagle Communications

Phone: 216-646-9179
Fax: 216-446-9181

Wings Information Network 6204 Westerham Rd
Cleveland OH 44124

Local Retrieval and SOP Area: OH-Cuyahoga, Geauga, Lake, Lorain, Summit.

Normal turnaround time: 24 to 72 hours. Projects are generally billed by the number of names searched. Billing dependent on type of search. Credit accounts are accepted.

Correspondent relationships: the US and Canada. They specialize in pre-employment screening, asset searches and business and individual background screenings.

EAGLE i communications

Phone: 310-280-0106
Fax: 310-280-0715

3318 Cattaraugus Ave
Culver City CA 90232

Local Retrieval and SOP Area: CA-Los Angeles.

Normal turnaround time: 24 to 72 hours. Projects are generally billed by the number of names searched. The first project may require a prepayment.

Correspondent relationships: the US and Canada. They specialize in asset searches and business and individual background screenings.

Eagle Investigations Inc

Phone: 800-344-2454
502-583-2453
Fax: 502-585-3480

200 S 7th St Suite 311
Louisville KY 40202

Local Retrieval and SOP Area: IN-Clark, Floyd; KY-Breckinridge, Bullitt, Hardin, Henry, Jefferson, Meade, Nelson, Oldham, Shelby, Spencer.

Normal turnaround time: 24-48 hours. Projects are generally billed by the number of names searched or records located. Projects require prepayment. They will also invoice.

They specialize in service of process, witness locates/statements and courthouse searches for records.

Eagle Pass Title Co Inc

Phone: 210-773-0555
Fax: 210-773-6886

PO Box 1316
Eagle Pass TX 78853

Local Retrieval Area: TX-Maverick.

Normal turnaround time: 1-2 days. Projects are generally billed by the number of names searched. Projects require prepayment.

Earlene Y Speer Law Offices

Phone: 615-692-2368
Fax: 615-692-2367

PO Box 310
Altamont TN 37301

Local Retrieval Area: TN-Grundy.

Normal turnaround time: 2 days. Projects are generally billed by the number of names searched. The first project may require a prepayment.

They specialize in title and UCC searches.

East Texas Title & Abstract Co

Phone: 409-787-2214
Fax: 409-787-2003

PO Box 1579
Hemphill TX 75948

Local Retrieval Area: TX-Sabine.

Normal turnaround time: up to a week. Projects are generally billed by the hour. The first project may require a prepayment.

East Texas Title & Abstract Co

Phone: 409-560-1471
Fax: 409-560-4771

112 S Pecan St
Nacogdoches TX 75961

Local Retrieval Area: TX-Nacogdoches.

Normal turnaround time: up to a week. Projects are generally billed by the hour. Credit accounts are accepted.

East Texas Title & Abstract Co Inc

Phone: 409-275-9786
Fax: 409-275-5069

PO Box 721
San Augustine TX 75972

Local Retrieval Area: TX-San Augustine.

Normal turnaround time: up to a week. Projects are generally billed by the hour. The first project may require a prepayment.

Easterling & Steinmetz Inc

Phone: 800-467-4480
314-725-4480
Fax: 314-725-9009

112 S Hanley Rd The Plaza in Clayton
St Louis MO 63105

Local Retrieval and SOP Area: IL-Madison, St. Clair; MO-Jefferson, Lincoln, St. Charles, St. Louis.

Normal turnaround time: 12-18 hours. Expedited service available. Online computer ordering is also available. Projects are generally billed by the number of names searched or records located. Flat rate special projects. Projects require prepayment. Credit cards are accepted. Terms are 30 day net to regular clients.

Correspondent relationships: global. They specialize in investigations, surveillance and specialized security matters.

Eastern North Carolina Investigtn

Phone: 919-772-3346
Fax: 919-772-3346

802 Vandora Ave
Garner NC 27529

Local Retrieval and SOP Area: NC-35 Counties.

Normal turnaround time: 1-3 days. Projects are generally billed by the hour. Credit accounts are accepted.

They also pull records from the Department of Corrections.

Eastern Oregon Title

Phone: 541-963-0514
Fax: 541-963-2391

PO Box 1084 1110 Spring Ave
La Grande OR 97850

Local Retrieval Area: OR-Union.

Normal turnaround time: 3 days. Project billing methods vary. Credit accounts are accepted.

Eastland Title & Transfer Inc

Phone: 817-629-2683
Fax: 817-629-2684

PO Box 855
Eastland TX 76448

Local Retrieval Area: TX-Eastland.

Normal turnaround time: 2-3 days. Fee basis will vary by the type of project. The first project may require a prepayment.

Eastland Title Co

Phone: 817-582-2762
Fax: 817-582-2760

PO Box 680
Hillsboro TX 76645

Local Retrieval Area: TX-Hill.

Normal turnaround time: up to a week. Fee basis will vary by the type of project. Credit accounts are accepted.

Easy Way

Phone: 501-239-2760
Fax: 501-236-7484

219 N Pruett
Paragould AR 72450

Local Retrieval Area: AR-Craighead, Greene.

Normal turnaround time: 2 days. Rush service is also available. Projects are generally billed by the hour. The first project may require a prepayment. Credit cards are accepted.

Correspondent relationships: Dunklin County, MO.

Eaton Abstract Company

Phone: 618-783-8474
Fax: 618-783-3199

122 S Van Buren St
Newton IL 62448

Local Retrieval Area: IL-Jasper.

Normal turnaround time: 24-48 hours. Projects are generally billed by the number of names searched or records located. Credit accounts are accepted.

They specialize in complete title service searches.

▥ Ed Knight Information Service

Phone: 800-282-6418
Fax: 800-282-6416

6651 Cameron Rd
Morrow GA 30260

Local Retrieval Area: GA-20 Counties.

Normal turnaround time: 1-2 days. Online computer ordering is also available. Projects are generally billed by the number of names searched. Credit accounts are accepted.

They specialize in lien searches in metropolitan Atlanta, but will drive to any county in Georgia for a reasonable fee.

Eddy County Abstract Co

Phone: 505-887-2828
Fax: 505-887-0824

116 N Canyon St
Carlsbad NM 88220

Local Retrieval Area: NM-Eddy.

Normal turnaround time: 12-24 hours. Projects are generally billed by the hour. The first project may require a prepayment.

They specialize in loan closing and mineral searches, and are fully computerized.

Edgar County Title Co

Phone: 217-465-5821
Fax: 217-463-7265

206 W Washington St
Paris IL 61944

Local Retrieval Area: IL-Edgar.

Normal turnaround time: 1-2 days. Projects are generally billed by the number of names searched. Credit accounts are accepted.

▥ Sharon Ehrhardt

Phone: 512-331-6618
Fax: 512-335-5353

604 Forest Trial
Cedar Park TX 78613

Local Retrieval Area: TX-Travis, Williamson.

Normal turnaround time: same day to 36 hours. Projects are generally billed by the number of names searched. Credit accounts are accepted. Will invoice once a month.

She specializes in criminal searches.

▥ EIS

Phone: 916-933-9858
Fax: 916-933-9592

2222 Francisco Blvd Suite 150-148
El Dorado Hills CA 95762

Local Retrieval Area: CA-El Dorado, Placer, Sacramento.

Normal turnaround time: 24-48 hours. Projects are generally billed by the number of names searched. Credit accounts are accepted. Due upon completion of job. Volume discounts.

They specialize in criminal and civil indexing.

Ekum Abstract and Title

Phone: 608-328-8221
Fax: 608-328-8223

912 17th Ave
Monroe WI 53566-0263

Local Retrieval Area: WI-Green, Lafayette.

Normal turnaround time: 1-2 days. Projects are generally billed by the number of names searched or records located. Credit accounts are accepted.

They specialize in real estate. They have their own in-house records of real estate. All other county records are 1 block away.

El Dorado Co Attorney Service

Phone: 916-672-0433
Fax: 916-676-2949

PO Box 1869
Shingle Springs CA 95682-1869

Local Retrieval and SOP Area: CA-El Dorado, Placer, Sacramento.

Normal turnaround time: 3-5 days. Expedited service available. Projects are generally billed by the hour. Projects require prepayment.

They specialize in process service and skip tracing.

EL-RU Inc

Phone: 404-963-8023
Fax: 404-682-1885

2061 Luke Edwards Rd
Dacula GA 30211

Local Retrieval and SOP Area: GA-22 Counties.

Normal turnaround time: 12-24 hours. Projects are generally billed by the number of names searched. Credit accounts are accepted.

Correspondent relationships: the rest of Georgia. They specialize in UCC searches and filing, tax liens, suits, judgments, employee background checks, motor vehicle checks, retrieval of court records and mortgage searches. They are also registered agents for corporations.

Elder Abstracts

Phone: 301-762-3533
Fax: 301-762-8479

350-A Hungerford Dr
Rockville MD 20850-4100

Local Retrieval Area: MD-Montgomery, Prince George's.

Normal turnaround time: 2-3 days. Fee basis will vary by type of project. Projects require prepayment.

They specialize in title abstracts and house location surveys.

John D Eldridge III

Phone: 501-347-2521
Fax: 501-347-5084

PO Box 479 128 1st St
Augusta AR 72006

Local Retrieval Area: AR-Woodruff.

Normal turnaround time: 1-2 days. Projects are generally billed by the hour. The first project may require a prepayment.

He specializes in general practice and marriage/divorcee searches.

Elk County Abstract & Title Co

Phone: 316-374-2500
Fax: 316-374-2500

PO Box 458
Howard KS 67349

Local Retrieval Area: KS-Elk.

Normal turnaround time: 1-2 days. Fee basis varies by type of transaction. Projects require prepayment.

H Watkins Ellerson

Phone: 540-672-2109
Fax: 540-672-2117

Attorney at Law PO Box 1080
Orange VA 22960

Local Retrieval Area: VA-Albemarle, City of Charlottesville, Culpeper, Goochland, Greene, Henrico, Louisa, Madison, Orange.

Normal turnaround time: 1 day for Orange, all others up to a week. Projects are generally billed by the hour. The first project may require a prepayment.

They specialize in tax, business and real estate searches.

Elliott & Waldron Abstr Glasscock

Phone: 915-354-2231
Fax: 915-354-2231

PO Box 156
Garden City TX 79739

Local Retrieval Area: TX-Glasscock.

Normal turnaround time: up to a week. Fee basis will vary by the type of project. The first project may require a prepayment.

Elliott & Waldron Abstr Palo Pinto

Phone: 817-325-6564
Fax: 817-325-1036

403 S Oak Ave
Mineral Wells TX 76067

Local Retrieval Area: TX-Palo Pinto.

Normal turnaround time: 2 days. Fee basis will vary by the type of project. The first project may require a prepayment.

Elliott & Waldron Abstr Van Zandt

Phone: 903-567-4127
Fax: 903-567-1757

305 E Tyler St
Canton TX 75103

Local Retrieval Area: TX-Van Zandt.

Normal turnaround time: 1-3 days. Fee basis will vary by the type of project. Credit accounts are accepted. Payment due upon completion.

Elliott & Waldron Abstract Dimmitt

Phone: 210-876-2926
Fax: 210-876-5077

PO Box 248
Carrizo Springs TX 78834

Local Retrieval Area: TX-Dimmit.

Normal turnaround time: 1-2 days. Fee basis will vary by the type of project. The first project may require a prepayment.

Elliott & Waldron Abstract Pecos

Phone: 915-336-5214
Fax: 915-336-7869

PO Box 1169
Fort Stockton TX 79735

Local Retrieval Area: TX-Pecos.

Normal turnaround time: up to a week. Fee basis will vary by the type of project. The first project may require a prepayment.

Elliott & Waldron Title & Abstract

Phone: 505-396-5846
Fax: 505-396-2490

PO Box 817
Lovington NM 88260

Local Retrieval Area: NM-Lea.

Normal turnaround time: varied depending on project. Fee basis will vary by type of project. Credit accounts are accepted.

Schuyler Elliott

Phone: 404-373-0886
Fax: 404-377-4847

PO Box 1181
Decatur GA 30031-1181

Local Retrieval Area: GA-Clayton, Cobb, Coweta, De Kalb, Fulton, Gwinnett, Rockdale, Walton.

Normal turnaround time: 24-48 hours for Fulton, Cobb, DeKalb, Gwinnett and Clayton counties. Projects are generally billed by the number of names searched or records located. They may give a discount for large orders. Credit accounts are accepted. Personal checks are accepted.

Correspondent relationships: most counties within 100 miles of Atlanta, Georgia.

Ellis County Abstract & Title Co

Phone: 800-794-2690
913-625-2316
Fax: 913-625-6349

110 E 12th St
Hays KS 67601

Local Retrieval Area: KS-Ellis, Rooks.

Normal turnaround time: 2-3 days. Projects are generally billed by the number of names searched. Credit accounts are accepted.

Ellyson Abstract & Title Brewster

Phone: 915-837-5801
Fax: 915-837-3509

PO Box 418
Alpine TX 79830

Local Retrieval Area: TX-Brewster.

Normal turnaround time: 2 days. Fee basis will vary by the type of project. The first project may require a prepayment.

Elson & Fulton Abstractors

Phone: 515-446-4621
Fax: 515-446-4888

203 NE Idaho
Leon IA 50144

Local Retrieval Area: IA-Decatur.

Normal turnaround time: 1-2 days. Fee basis varies by type of transaction. Credit accounts are accepted.

Emmons County Abstract & Title

Phone: 701-254-4261

PO Box 428
Linton ND 58552

Local Retrieval Area: ND-Emmons.

Normal turnaround time: 1-5 days. Fee basis will vary by the type of project. Credit accounts are accepted.

Empfacts

Phone: 800-922-2702
612-644-7808
Fax: 800-443-7875
612-644-7875

939 Hersey St
St Paul MN 55114

Local Retrieval Area: MN-Anoka, Carver, Dakota, Hennepin, Ramsey, Scott, Washington.

Normal turnaround time: 1-3 days. Projects are generally billed by the number of names searched. Credit accounts are accepted.

Employment Screening Network

Phone: 800-673-9089
Fax: 410-857-5105

4312 Black Rock Rd
Hampstead MD 21074

Local Retrieval Area: MD-All Counties.

Normal turnaround time: 24 hours in Maryland, other areas 3-5 days. Projects are generally billed by the number of names searched. Credit accounts are accepted. Credit cards are accepted.

Correspondent relationships: nationwide. They specialize in pre-employment background investigations, criminal records nationwide, driving records, credit inquiries, all phases of reference checking. They can offer Maryland statewide criminal records within 24 hours.

Enterprise Title Company Inc

Phone: 703-538-2470
Fax: 703-524-6149

5652 N 19th St
Arlington VA 22205

Local Retrieval Area: DC-District of Columbia; VA-City of Alexandria, Arlington, Fairfax, Loudoun, Prince William.

Projects are generally billed by the number of names searched. Charges depends on search. The first project may require a prepayment.

They also provide research in the federal agencies in Washington, DC, such as the Library of Congress, the Patent & Trademark Office, and the SEC and US Archives.

Equisearch

Phone: 606-268-1206
Fax: 606-268-1206

PO Box 21838
Lexington KY 40522-1838

Local Retrieval Area: KY-20 Counties.

Normal turnaround time: 24-48 hours. Fee basis will vary by type of project. The first project may require a prepayment.

Correspondent relationships: the rest of Kentucky.

Equity Title Search

Phone: 800-683-0214
213-965-0759
Fax: 213-965-1247

137 N Larchmont Blvd Suite 545
Los Angeles CA 90004

Local Retrieval and SOP Area: CA-Los Angeles, Orange, Riverside.

Normal turnaround time: 24 hours. They can expedite. Project billing methods vary. Fees vary by complexity of the project. The first project may require a prepayment.

Correspondent relationships: Florida, New Jersey, Illinois and Colorado. They specialize in locating people and assets.

Eric H Swenson Co Abstracters

Phone: 913-632-2535
Fax: 913-632-2255

707 5th St PO Box 92
Clay Center KS 67432

Local Retrieval Area: KS-Clay.

Normal turnaround time: 1-2 days. Projects are generally billed by the hour. The first project may require a prepayment. Personal checks are accepted.

Ervin Investigation & Research

Phone: 888-203-6536
713-362-7764
Fax: 713-362-7686

PO Box 368
Spring TX 77383

Local Retrieval Area: TX-Fort Bend, Galveston, Harris, Liberty, Montgomery.

Normal turnaround time: 24-48 hours. Online computer ordering is also available. Projects are generally billed by the number of names searched. Some credit accounts accepted. The first project may require a prepayment.

They specialize in legal and asset research and detailed background investigations. Their main clientele is law firms and insurance companies.

ESP Technology Inc

Phone: 800-942-8801
205-238-6377
Fax: 800-650-7276
205-238-6375

931 Noble St, AmSouth Bank Bldg Suite 600
Anniston AL 36201

Local Retrieval and SOP Area: AL-Calhoun.

Normal turnaround time: 24-48 hours. One hour average for statewide criminal, civil, domestic and traffic through SJIS. Projects are generally billed by the number of names searched. The first project may require a prepayment. Credit cards are accepted.

Correspondent relationships: all of Alabama. They specialize in corporate, legal & financial investigations, ligitation support, asset searches, locate service, process service, surveillance and video services, contract fraud, computer related crime and background investigations.

Espanola Abstract Co

Phone: 505-753-2248
Fax: 505-753-4392

PO Box 1282
Espanola NM 87532

Local Retrieval Area: NM-Rio Arriba.

Normal turnaround time: 10-14 days. Online computer ordering is also available. Projects are generally billed by the hour. Credit accounts are accepted. Payment is due upon delivery.

They are the only local title company with records dating back to county's inception.

Esprit de Corps Inc

Phone: 513-223-0700
Fax: 513-225-8866

130 W 2nd St Suite 1105
Dayton OH 45402

Local Retrieval and SOP Area: OH-Montgomery.

Normal turnaround time: 48 hours. Projects are generally billed by the number of names searched. The first project may require a prepayment. Credit cards are accepted.

Correspondent relationships: Preble, Clark, Greene, Warren, Butler and Hamilton. They are a licensed private investigations firm. They have access to Ohio vehicle registrations, auto titles and driving records. They also specialize in pre-employment screening and drug testing.

Esquire Express Inc

Phone: 305-530-9580
Fax: 305-530-8414

600 Brickell Ave Suite 203
Miami FL 33131

Local Retrieval and SOP Area: FL-Broward, Dade, Palm Beach.

Normal turnaround time: 24 hours. Same day service is available. Projects are generally billed by the hour. The first project may require a prepayment.

Correspondent relationships: Leon, Gadsden, Escumbia, Santa Rosa, Hillsborough and Pinellas. They specialize in civil, criminal, bankruptcy and public records retrieval throughout South Florida.

Essex County Paralegals Inc

Phone: 800-922-4752
508-921-5300
Fax: 508-921-5398

77 Bridge St
Beverly MA 01915

Local Retrieval Area: MA-Barnstable, Bristol, Essex, Middlesex, Norfolk, Plymouth, Suffolk, Worcester.

Normal turnaround time: 24-72 hours. Projects are generally billed by the number of names searched. Fees are per subject/jurisdiction. The first project may require a prepayment. Terms are net 30 days.

They specialize in UCC, tax liens, judgments and corporate document filing and retrieval. They also have microfiche Library of State UCC filings.

Estate Title and Escrow Inc

Phone: 703-385-5850
Fax: 703-385-1016

4041 University Dr Suite 302
Fairfax VA 22030

Local Retrieval Area: DC-District of Columbia; VA-City of Alexandria, Arlington, Clarke, Fairfax, Fauquier, Loudoun, Orange, Prince William, Spotsylvania, Stafford.

Normal turnaround time: 2-3 days. Projects are generally billed by the number of names searched. Credit accounts are accepted. Payment due upon reciept of invoice.

Correspondent relationships: the rest of Virginia and all of Maryland. They specialize in providing title evidence in real estate transactions, tax liens and other liens, UCC and court records. They are a full service title insurance company.

Estherville Abstract Co

Phone: 712-362-3148

121 N 6th St
Estherville IA 51334

Local Retrieval Area: IA-Emmet.

Normal turnaround time: 2 days. They charge a flat rate per search. Credit accounts are accepted.

Etna Abstract Corp

Phone: 518-483-7204
Fax: 518-483-7204

PO Box 462
Malone NY 12953

Local Retrieval Area: NY-Franklin.

Normal turnaround time: 1-2 weeks. Fee basis will vary per abstract. Credit accounts are accepted. Personal checks are accepted.

Steve Etzold

Phone: 800-455-3768
303-421-3768
Fax: 303-431-4535

6440 Wright St
Arvada CO 80004

Local Retrieval Area: CO-Adams, Arapahoe, Boulder, Denver, Douglas, Jefferson.

Normal turnaround time: 48 hours. Projects are generally billed by the hour. The first project may require a prepayment.

He specializes in all types of investigation, including insurance adjusting, photography, and credit checking.

Eufaula Abstract & Title Co Inc

Phone: 918-689-2241
Fax: 918-689-2248

PO BOX 548
Eufaula OK 74432

Local Retrieval Area: OK-McIntosh.

Normal turnaround time: 10 working days after receipt of order. Projects are generally billed by the hour. Credit accounts are accepted.

Evans & Johnson Investigations

Phone: 701-224-9743
Fax: 701-258-0049

2501 Lee Ave
Bismarck ND 58504

Local Retrieval and SOP Area: ND-Burleigh, Kidder, McLean, Morton, Sioux.

Normal turnaround time: 24 hours. Fee basis will vary by the type of project. The first project may require a prepayment.

Correspondent relationships: the entire state of North Dakota. They specialize in accident reconstruction, personal injury fraud, and workers' compensation investigations.

Evans Advanced Land and Title

Phone: 417-581-8251
Fax: 417-581-8280

203 N 2nd Ave PO Box 729
Ozark MO 65721

Local Retrieval Area: MO-Christian.

Normal turnaround time: 48 hours. Projects are generally billed by the number of names searched or records located. Credit accounts are accepted. They will accept cashiers checks.

Robert D Evans

Phone: 601-378-2171
Fax: 601-335-9049

PO Box 1498
Greenville MS 38702

Local Retrieval Area: MS-Washington.

Normal turnaround time: 1-2 days. Projects are generally billed by the hour. Projects require prepayment.

He is an attorney in general practice.

Everhart and Everhart Abstractors

Phone: 217-849-2671
Fax: 217-849-2671

PO Box 37
Toledo IL 62468

Local Retrieval Area: IL-Clark, Cumberland, Effingham.

Normal turnaround time: 3-4 days. Projects are generally billed by the number of names searched or records located. Credit accounts are accepted. Personal checks are accepted.

They specialize in title insurance and abstracts, and also perform judgment/lien, UCC and other record searches. There may be additional charges for Clark County searches due to distance from their home office.

🏛 EX-CEL Investigations

Phone: 813-527-5440
Fax: 813-573-4848

PO Box 22124
St Petersburg FL 33742

Local Retrieval and SOP Area: FL-Hillsborough, Pinellas.

Normal turnaround time: 48 hours. Projects are generally billed by the number of names searched. Copy expenses will be added to the fee. The first project may require a prepayment. Terms are net 15 days.

Correspondent relationships: Manatee, Sarasota and Pasco. They specialize in process service, background checks, locates and video surveillance. They also do traffic and boat record searches.

Executive Attorney Service Inc

Phone: 213-482-6680
Fax: 213-482-6688

201 N Figueroa St Suite 535
Los Angeles CA 90012

Local Retrieval and SOP Area: CA-Los Angeles, Orange, Riverside, San Bernardino, Ventura.

Normal turnaround time: varied depending on project. Projects are generally billed by the number of names searched. The first project may require a prepayment.

They specialize in service of writs.

Executive Investigative Services

Phone: 913-764-9484
Fax: 913-764-9484

PO Box 13308
Overland Park KS 66282-3308

Local Retrieval and SOP Area: KS-Johnson, Wyandotte; MO-Jackson.

Normal turnaround time: the same day. Projects are generally billed by the hour. Projects require prepayment.

Correspondent relationships: Miami, Douglas, Leavenworth counties in Kansas.

Executive Messenger

739 W Grant
Carlton OR 97111

Phone: 503-852-7222
Fax: 503-852-6897

Local Retrieval and SOP Area: OR-Clackamas, Marion, Multnomah, Washington, Yamhill.

Normal turnaround time: 36 hours. Projects are generally billed by the hour. The first project may require a prepayment.

Correspondent relationships: 15 counties in the surrounding area. They specialize in process serving.

Executive Process Service

PO Box 2886
Yakima WA 98907

Phone: 509-453-8307
Fax: 509-453-7396

Local Retrieval and SOP Area: WA-Yakima.

Normal turnaround time: same day or next day. Projects are generally billed by the hour. Fee basis varies by type of transaction. The first project may require a prepayment.

They specialize in process service.

Executive Project Service

144 Fairport Village Landing Suite 266
Fairport NY 14450

Phone: 716-377-5157
Fax: 716-377-1038

Local Retrieval and SOP Area: NY-Monroe.

Normal turnaround time: 1-2 days. Online computer ordering is also available. Projects are generally billed by the hour. The first project may require a prepayment.

Executive Title Insurance Agency

2123 Pioneer Ave
Cheyenne WY 82001

Phone: 307-638-4853
Fax: 307-634-0502

Local Retrieval Area: WY-Albany, Goshen, Laramie, Platte.

Normal turnaround time: 48 hours. Projects are generally billed by the number of names searched or records located. Credit accounts are accepted. Personal checks are accepted.

Their principals have 25 years experience in public records research, including certificates of ownership, encumbrance reports, and mineral certificates.

Express Network Inc

5450 Ralston St Suite 203
Ventura CA 93003

Phone: 805-650-6666

Local Retrieval Area: CA-Santa Barbara, Ventura.

Normal turnaround time: dependent on case. Charges are base rate plus per hour. The first project may require a prepayment. Credit cards are accepted.

Correspondent relationships: statewide.

Express Process Service/Invest

200 S Meridian St Suite 320
Indianapolis IN 46225-1076

Phone: 800-899-1872
317-639-4638
Fax: 317-266-1209

Local Retrieval and SOP Area: IN-Allen, Boone, Hamilton, Hendricks, Johnson, Lake, Marion, Monroe, Tippecanoe, Vanderburgh.

Normal turnaround time: 48 hours. Expedited service available. Projects are generally billed by the number of names searched. The first project may require a prepayment. Credit cards are accepted. Retrieval/copies of large documents may require prepayment.

Correspondent relationships: nationwide. They specialize in asset, business and individial background checks, motor vehicle and more. They have access to over 9,000 databases.

Eye Catcher Investigations

PO Box 251
Cumberland Furnace TN 37051

Phone: 615-789-6165

Local Retrieval Area: TN-Dickson, Montgomery.

Normal turnaround time: 48 hours. Projects are generally billed by the number of names searched. The first project may require a prepayment.

Eyewitness Investigations

PO Box 173
East Greenwich RI 02818

Phone: 800-285-9690
401-884-9690
Fax: 401-884-1711

Local Retrieval Area: RI-Bristol, Kent, Newport, Providence, Washington.

Normal turnaround time: 3 days. Expedited service available. Projects are generally billed by the number of names searched. Fees are per name and county and copies are per page. The first project may require a prepayment. Payment due upon receipt of invoice.

They specialize in criminal records; dates, convictions, dispositions, misdemeanors and felonies, civil records, personal injury investigations, asset searches, birth & death records, background searches and workers' compensation.

F

FACFIND Network Inc

PO Box 360262
Decatur GA 30036-0262

Phone: 800-343-6641
770-808-9600
Fax: 770-808-8081

Local Retrieval Area: GA-27 Counties.

Normal turnaround time: 24-48 hours. Projects are generally billed by the number of names searched. Credit accounts are accepted.

Correspondent relationships: the rest of Georgia and all other states. They specialize in criminal research.

Facts Investigative Services

179 Main St
Waterville ME 04901-6672

Phone: 207-872-7505

Local Retrieval Area: ME-Kennebec, Somerset.

Normal turnaround time: 8 to 40 hours. Projects are generally billed by the hour. Projects require prepayment.

They specialize in workers' compensation and criminal searches.

Facts Title Service

PO Box 636
Boaz AL 35957

Phone: 205-593-8308
Fax: 205-593-5140

Local Retrieval Area: AL-11 Counties.

Normal turnaround time: 24-48 hours. Fee basis is per search. The first project may require a prepayment.

Factual Business Information

8300 Executive Center Dr Suite 204
Miami FL 33166

Phone: 305-592-7600
Fax: 305-592-7131

Local Retrieval Area: FL-Broward, Dade, Monroe, Palm Beach.

Normal turnaround time: 24-48 hours. Online computer ordering is also available. Projects are generally billed by the number of names searched. Fees vary by the project. The first project may require a prepayment. Some accounts may require prepayment.

They specialize in all public record retrieval, primarily to end users. These would include; criminal, motor vehicle and workers compensation. Volume work is their speciality.

Fairbanks Courier Service
Phone: 907-452-4292
745 8th Ave   **Fax:** 907-456-5049
Fairbanks AK 99707

Local Retrieval and SOP Area: AK-Fairbanks North Star Borough.

Normal turnaround time: within 24 hours for an oral report. Record copies will be sent following the oral report. Projects are generally billed by the hour. The first project may require a prepayment.

Correspondent relationships: Fairbanks, in the 4th Judicial District of Alaska. They specialize in locating persons, inspecting property occupancy and conditions and court records retrieval.

Fairbanks Process Service
Phone: 907-456-3023
PO Box 73087   **Fax:** 907-456-2084
Fairbanks AK 99707

Local Retrieval and SOP Area: AK-Fairbanks North Star Borough.

Normal turnaround time: 72 hours. Fee basis will vary by the type of search. The first project may require a prepayment. They require prepay from individuals only.

They specialize in process serving and are on-line with state records.

Fairbanks Title Agency
Phone: 907-456-6626
714 3rd Ave   **Fax:** 907-452-5406
Fairbanks AK 99701

Local Retrieval Area: AK-Barrow District, Cape Nome District, Fairbanks North Star Borough, Fort Gibbon District, Kotzebue District, Manley Hot Springs District, Mount McKinley District, Nenana District, Nulato District, Rampart District.

Normal turnaround time: 24 hours. Projects are generally billed by the hour. Projects require prepayment.

They specialize in title insurance searches and escrow closings.

Fairchild Record Search Ltd
Phone: 800-547-7007
PO Box 1368   360-786-8775
Olympia WA 98507   **Fax:** 800-433-3404
     360-943-6656

Local Retrieval Area: OR-Clackamas, Multnomah, Washington; WA-Clark, King, Kitsap, Pierce, Snohomish.

Normal turnaround time: 1-2 days. Online computer ordering is also available. Projects are generally billed by the number of names searched. The first project may require a prepayment. Credit cards are accepted.

Correspondent relationships: nationwide.

Fairview Abstract Co
Phone: 405-227-4524
PO Box 60   **Fax:** 405-227-3607
Fairview OK 73737

Local Retrieval Area: OK-Major.

Normal turnaround time: 1 week. Projects are generally billed by the hour. Credit accounts are accepted.

Faithful Abstract
Phone: 908-351-9398
2 Broad St   **Fax:** 908-654-1847
Elizabeth NJ 07201

Local Retrieval Area: NJ-Union.

Normal turnaround time: 1-5 days. Fee basis will vary by the type of project. The first project may require a prepayment.

They have more than 18 years of abstract and title experience.

Falcon Abstract Co
Phone: 800-828-4081
PO Box 1   814-365-5455
Mayport PA 16240   **Fax:** 814-365-5019

Local Retrieval Area: PA-Armstrong, Clarion, Clearfield, Elk, Forest, Jefferson, Venango.

Normal turnaround time: up to 1 week. Fee basis will vary by the type of project. Credit accounts are accepted.

Correspondent relationships: Erie, Cameron, and Warren counties. They specialize in land research.

Falcon Investigations
Phone: 217-742-5796
30 Market St   **Fax:** 217-742-5796
Winchester IL 62694

Local Retrieval Area: IL-Greene, Morgan, Pike, Scott.

Normal turnaround time: 1-2 days. Projects are generally billed by the hour. The first project may require a prepayment.

Correspondent relationships: Adams, IL county. They specialize in criminal investigations.

Falls County Abstract Co
Phone: 817-883-2051
122 Bridge St   **Fax:** 817-883-6260
Marlin TX 76661

Local Retrieval Area: TX-Falls.

Normal turnaround time: up to 5 days. Fee basis will vary by the type of project. The first project may require a prepayment.

Falls County Title Co Inc
Phone: 817-883-2112
122 Bridge St   **Fax:** 817-883-6260
Marlin TX 76661-2829

Local Retrieval Area: TX-Falls.

Normal turnaround time: 2-3 days. Fee basis will vary by the type of project. Projects require prepayment.

▥ FAR Retriever Bureau
Phone: 616-657-2166
PO Box 377 50794 45th St   **Fax:** 616-657-6566
Paw Paw MI 49079

Local Retrieval and SOP Area: MI-Allegan, Kalamazoo, Van Buren.

Normal turnaround time: 24-48 hours. Projects are generally billed by the number of names searched. The first project may require a prepayment. Monthly billing available.

He has 27 years experience in background checks, loss control, premium audits and delinquent mortgage interviews. Expertise includes fixture filings.

▥ Farmers Title and Abstract Co
Phone: 913-475-2381
106 S Penn PO Box 27   **Fax:** 913-475-2381
Oberlin KS 67749-0027

Local Retrieval Area: KS-Decatur.

Normal turnaround time: 1-3 days. Projects are generally billed by the hour. The first project may require a prepayment.

Correspondent relationships: Rawlins.

Farwell Abstract Co Inc
Phone: 806-481-3361
402 3rd St   **Fax:** 806-481-9060
Farwell TX 79325

Local Retrieval and SOP Area: TX-Bailey, Parmer.

Normal turnaround time: 72 hours. Projects are generally billed by the hour. Credit accounts are accepted.

They specialize in title insurance.

Fax & File Legal Services Inc

Phone: 415-491-0606
Fax: 415-491-0434

24 Professional Ctr Pky Suite 200
San Rafael CA 94903

Local Retrieval and SOP Area: CA-12 Counties.

Normal turnaround time: 3-5 days. Online computer ordering is also available. Projects are generally billed by the hour. The first project may require a prepayment. Credit cards are accepted.

They specialize in filing court documents through offices in Alameda, Contra Costa, Marin, Placer, Sacramento, San Francisco, San Mateo, Santa Clara, Solano, Los Angeles, Orange and Sonoma counties.

Faxalert Network

Phone: 757-850-2870
Fax: 757-850-8035

417 Woodland Rd
Hampton VA 23669

Local Retrieval Area: VA-City of Hampton, Isle of Wight, James City, City of Newport News, City of Poquoson, York.

Normal turnaround time: 24-72 hours. Expedited service available. Projects are generally billed by the number of names searched or records located. Fee basis will vary by type of project. The first project may require a prepayment.

Faxxon Legal Information Svcs

Phone: 800-932-9966
217-522-3280
Fax: 800-229-7028
217-522-3570

Myers Bldg, Suite 805
Springfield IL 62701

Local Retrieval Area: IL-Christian, Logan, Macon, Morgan, Sangamon.

Normal turnaround time: same day if ordered by noon CST. Sangamon County 8-14 hours. Online computer ordering is also available. Projects are generally billed by the number of names searched. The first project may require a prepayment. Credit cards are accepted.

Correspondent relationships: nationwide. The principal of the firm, Bill Stokes, has been in the field of public record searching since 1982. He managed one of the largest national UCC search firms before opening his own shop.

Fayette Professional Services

Phone: 412-439-1450
Fax: 412-439-3460

56 E Main St
Uniontown PA 15401

Local Retrieval Area: PA-Fayette, Greene, Washington, Westmoreland.

Normal turnaround time: the same day. Online computer ordering is also available. Fee basis will vary by type of project. Credit accounts are accepted. Terms are net 30 days when credit has been established.

They specialize in court house research.

FDR Info Centers

Phone: 800-874-4337
202-789-2233
Fax: 202-408-8159

810 1st St NE Suite 700
Washington DC 20002

Local Retrieval Area: DC-District of Columbia; MD-Montgomery, Prince George's; VA-City of Alexandria, Fairfax.

Normal turnaround time: 24 hours. Expedited service available. Online computer ordering is also available. Projects are generally billed by the hour. Charges also include out of pocket expenses. The first project may require a prepayment. Credit cards are accepted. Invoiced after project completion.

Correspondent relationships: nationwide. They specialize in federal, state and local courts, federal, state and local legislation and regulations, municipal bonds, patents, trademarks and copyrights, energy industry, insurance company filings, banking and corporate filings.

FDR Info Centers

Phone: 212-742-1066
Fax: 212-742-0966

83 Maiden Ln 11th Fl
New York NY 10038

Local Retrieval Area: NJ-Hudson; NY-Bronx, Kings, New York, Queens, Richmond, Westchester.

Normal turnaround time: 24 hours. Projects are generally billed by the hour. Charges also include out of pocket expenses. The first project may require a prepayment. Credit cards are accepted. Invoiced after project completion.

Correspondent relationships: Long Island, Westchester, NJ counties and NY State. They specialize in litigation and corporate document retrieval.

Feaster & Associates

Phone: 512-459-1310
Fax: 512-459-1508

PO Box 140543
Austin TX 78714

Local Retrieval and SOP Area: TX-Travis, Williamson.

Normal turnaround time: 24 hours. Projects are generally billed by the number of names searched. The first project may require a prepayment. They often require a deposit in place of a set-up fee.

Correspondent relationships: all other counties in Texas. They specialize in insurance, domestic, skip tracing and asset investigations.

Federal Research Corporation

Phone: 202-783-2700
Fax: 202-783-0145

400 7th NW Suite 101
Washington DC 20004

Local Retrieval Area: MD-Anne Arundel, Baltimore, City of Baltimore, Harford, Howard; VA-City of Alexandria, Arlington, Fairfax, Loudoun, Montgomery, Prince George, Prince William, City of Richmond.

Normal turnaround time: 3-5 days. A 1 to 2 day rush service is also available. Online computer ordering is also available. Fee may be based per index. Federal searches are per hour. The first project may require a prepayment.

Correspondent relationships: nationwide. They specialize in federal agencies in the Washington DC area. They also perform patent, trademark and copyright research.

Angela Feltner
Phone: 606-436-5633
Fax: 606-436-5633
PO Box 262
Jeff KY 41751

Local Retrieval Area: KY-Breathitt, Clay, Knott, Leslie, Letcher, Perry.

Normal turnaround time: 3-4 days. Projects are generally billed by the hour. The first project may require a prepayment.

She specializes in researching surface and mineral titles.

Ferrari
Phone: 716-689-6577
Fax: 716-689-6661
8 Tudor Ct
Getzville NY 14068

Local Retrieval Area: NY-Erie, Niagara.

Normal turnaround time: 3-5 days. Projects are generally billed by the hour. Projects require prepayment. Credit cards are accepted.

Correspondent relationships: nationwide. They specialize in search services.

Ferry County Title & Escrow Co Inc
Phone: 509-775-3119
Fax: 509-775-2492
PO Box 351
Republic WA 99166

Local Retrieval Area: WA-Ferry.

Normal turnaround time: 1 day. Fee basis varies by type of transaction. The first project may require a prepayment.

Fewell Private Investigations
Phone: 803-327-7378
Fax: 803-327-4181
PO Box 10802
Rock Hill SC 29731-0802

Local Retrieval and SOP Area: NC-Gaston, Mecklenburg, Union; SC-Cherokee, Chester, Fairfield, Kershaw, Lancaster, York.

Normal turnaround time: 24-48 hours. No project billing information was given. Credit accounts are accepted.

Correspondent relationships: nationwide. They specialize in asset retrieval and courthouse work.

Fidelifacts
Phone: 800-678-0007
Fax: 800-509-8496
212-248-5619
50 Broadway
New York NY 10004

Local Retrieval Area: NJ-21 Counties; NY-12 Counties.

Normal turnaround time: 2-10 days. Projects are generally billed by the number of names searched. The first project may require a prepayment.

Correspondent relationships: nationwide. They specialize in criminal records checks and credit background investigation nationwide.

Fidelity Abstract & Title Co
Phone: 605-772-5632
Fax: 605-772-5720
PO Box 247 115 N Main
Howard SD 57349

Local Retrieval Area: SD-Miner.

Normal turnaround time: 2 weeks. Projects are generally billed by the hour. Credit accounts are accepted.

Fidelity Home Abstract
Phone: 800-224-5601
717-424-5600
Fax: 717-424-9860
17 S 6th St Suite 101
Stroudsburg PA 18360-2001

Local Retrieval Area: PA-Carbon, Monroe, Northampton, Pike, Wayne.

Normal turnaround time: 10 days. Expedited serice available. Projects are generally billed by the number of records located. Credit accounts are accepted.

Fidelity Legal Investigation Inc
Phone: 205-988-8644
Fax: 205-663-1489
2163 Pelham Pky Suite 218
Pelham AL 35124

Local Retrieval and SOP Area: AL-Autauga, Cullman, Jefferson, Shelby, St. Clair.

Normal turnaround time: 24-48 hours. Expedited service available. Online computer ordering is also available. Projects are generally billed by the number of names searched. If extensive research, they charge per hour. The first project may require a prepayment.

Correspondent relationships: Montgomery and Madison. They specialize in private investigation work, polygraph examinations, interviews and interrogations.

Fidelity Search Inc
Phone: 812-479-8704
Fax: 812-479-8706
1468 Bellemeade Ave
Evansville IN 47714

Local Retrieval Area: IN-Gibson, Posey, Vanderburgh, Warrick; KY-Daviess, Henderson, Ohio.

Normal turnaround time: 48 hours. Projects are generally billed by the hour. The first project may require a prepayment. Terms are net 15 days.

They specialize in investigations, polygraph and pre-employment screening.

Fidelity Title and Guaranty Co
Phone: 407-740-7131
Fax: 407-740-6275
2233 Lee Rd
Winter Park FL 32789

Local Retrieval Area: FL-Brevard, Duval, Flagler, Lake, Marion, Orange, Osceola, Polk, Seminole, Volusia.

Normal turnaround time: 3 working days. Projects are generally billed by the hour. Credit accounts are accepted.

They specialize in serving Central Florida and have a computer database of real estate for Orange, Seminole and Volusia counties.

File Finders
Phone: 619-474-7667
Fax: 619-474-7467
PO Box 846
National City CA 91951

Local Retrieval Area: CA-Kern, Los Angeles, San Diego, Ventura.

Normal turnaround time: 1 to 3 days. Projects are generally billed by the number of names searched or records located. The first project may require a prepayment. Large projects may require a down payment.

Correspondent relationships: nationwide. They are a full service employment verification and screening company specializing in criminal record searches, credit information, credential and education verification, and reference checking.

Fillmore County Abstract Co
Phone: 402-759-3413
PO Box 69
Geneva NE 68361

Local Retrieval Area: NE-Fillmore.

Normal turnaround time: 1 week. Fee basis will vary by the type of project. The first project may require a prepayment.

They specialize in title searches.

🏛 Financial Investigations Inc
Phone: 303-469-3831
Fax: 303-469-5489
PO Box 2023
Broomfield CO 80038-2023

Local Retrieval and SOP Area: CO-Arapahoe, Boulder, Denver, El Paso.

Normal turnaround time: 24 hours. Online computer ordering is also available. Projects are generally billed by the number of records located. The first project may require a prepayment.

Correspondent relationships: Colorado, California and Florida. They specialize in fraud, skips, due diligence, background searches and criminal defense.

Finders Inc
Phone: 810-543-2405
Fax: 810-543-4248
1372 Ann Terrace
Madison Heights MI 48071

Local Retrieval and SOP Area: MI-Macomb, Oakland, Washtenaw, Wayne.

Normal turnaround time: the next day. Projects are generally billed by the hour. The first project may require a prepayment.

Correspondent relationships: all other counties in upper and lower Michigan. They are a full service private detective agency capable of retrieving all public documents from any agency.

Fink Abstract Co
Phone: 316-378-2351
Fax: 316-378-4425
PO Box 418
Fredonia KS 66736

Local Retrieval Area: KS-Wilson.

Normal turnaround time: 2-3 days. Fee basis varies by type of transaction. The first project may require a prepayment.

Finley Abstract & Title Co
Phone: 913-863-2271
Fax: 913-863-2065
309 Jefferson
Oskaloosa KS 66066

Local Retrieval Area: KS-Jefferson.

Normal turnaround time: 2-3 days. Projects are generally billed by the hour. The first project may require a prepayment.

First Abstract and Loan Co
Phone: 712-225-3612
Fax: 712-225-1033
601 W Main
Cherokee IA 51012

Local Retrieval Area: IA-Cherokee.

Normal turnaround time: 2 weeks. Fee basis will vary by type of project. Credit accounts are accepted.

First Abstract Title Co
Phone: 414-684-1261
Fax: 414-684-6581
PO Box 6 807 Jay St
Manitowoc WI 54221

Local Retrieval Area: WI-Manitowoc.

Normal turnaround time: 2-3 days. Projects are generally billed by the number of names searched. The first project may require a prepayment.

First American Title
Phone: 208-354-2771
Fax: 208-354-8825
81 N Main PO Box 42
Driggs ID 83422

Local Retrieval Area: ID-Teton.

Fees vary by project. Credit accounts are accepted.

First American Title & Escrow
Phone: 406-293-3721
Fax: 406-293-3723
PO Box 155
Libby MT 59923

Local Retrieval Area: MT-Lincoln.

Normal turnaround time: the next day. Fee basis varies by type of transaction. Credit accounts are accepted.

First American Title & Escrow
Phone: 800-331-2349
406-883-5258
Fax: 406-883-3056
PO Box 910 402 1st St E
Polson MT 59860

Local Retrieval Area: MT-Lake, Lincoln.

Normal turnaround time: the next day. Fee basis varies by type of transaction. Credit accounts are accepted.

First American Title Co
Phone: 406-822-3391
Fax: 406-822-3396
PO Box 548 305 3rd Ave W
Superior MT 59872

Local Retrieval Area: MT-Mineral.

Normal turnaround time: 48 hours. Fee basis varies by type of transaction. Credit accounts are accepted.

They can only do real estate title information on a written basis. Will pull judgments, UCC, etc. from computer verbally only, and do not charge for this information. Parent company will not allow hard copy for liability reasons.

First American Title Co
Phone: 406-827-3591
Fax: 406-827-3848
Box 850 1211 Main St
Thompson Falls MT 59873

Local Retrieval Area: MT-Sanders.

Normal turnaround time: 2-3 days. Projects are generally billed by the hour. The first project may require a prepayment.

First American Title Co of Montana
Phone: 406-365-5482
Fax: 406-365-5835
114 W Benham St
Glendive MT 59330

Local Retrieval Area: MT-Dawson, McCone.

Normal turnaround time: 1 week or less. Project billed according to amount of mortgage, etc. Credit accounts are accepted.

First American Title Guaranty
Phone: 307-283-1844
Fax: 307-283-1844
PO Box 190
Sundance WY 82729-0190

Local Retrieval Area: WY-Crook.

Normal turnaround time: 3-7 days. Rush service is also available. Projects are generally billed by the hour. The first project may require a prepayment.

They specialize in title insurance, abstracts and certificates of titles.

First American Title Ins of Oregon
Phone: 541-269-0119
Fax: 541-269-0470
454 Commercial St
Coos Bay OR 97420

Local Retrieval Area: OR-Coos.

Normal turnaround time: 1-2 days. Projects are generally billed by the hour. Their hourly rate varies. The first project may require a prepayment.

They specialize in title insurance.

First Coast Investigations Inc

Phone: 904-398-4076
Fax: 904-346-0329

PO Box 10673
Jacksonville FL 32247

Local Retrieval and SOP Area: FL-Clay, Duval, Nassau.

Normal turnaround time: 24-48 for criminal records. Fees are based on a county schedule. Credit accounts are accepted.

Correspondent relationships: Miami and Orlando. They specialize in background investigations and Motor Vehicle Record checks.

First Idaho Title Co

Phone: 208-847-1300
Fax: 208-847-1314

469 Washington
Montpelier ID 83254

Local Retrieval Area: ID-Bear Lake.

Normal turnaround time: 1 week. Fees vary by project. Credit accounts are accepted.

First Insurance Agency of Hoxie

Phone: 913-675-3252
Fax: 913-675-3811

700 Main
Hoxie KS 67740-0108

Local Retrieval Area: KS-Decatur, Gove, Graham, Sheridan, Thomas.

Normal turnaround time: 1 day for Sheridan county and 2 to 3 days for surrounding counties. Projects are generally billed by the number of records located. Credit accounts are accepted. Personal checks are accepted.

They specialize in record searches.

First Mason Title Co

Phone: 915-347-6388
Fax: 915-347-5418

PO Box 1219
Mason TX 76856

Local Retrieval Area: TX-Mason.

Normal turnaround time: 2-3 days. Projects are generally billed by the hour. Projects require prepayment.

First Montana Title Co Great Falls

Phone: 406-727-2600
Fax: 406-727-4404

PO Box 2249
Great Falls MT 59403

Local Retrieval Area: MT-Cascade, Rosebud, Treasure, Yellowstone.

Normal turnaround time: 24 hours. Projects are generally billed by the hour. The first project may require a prepayment.

They specialize in real estate.

First Securities Corp in Aurora

Phone: 402-694-6926

1220 L St
Aurora NE 68818

Local Retrieval Area: NE-Hamilton.

Normal turnaround time: 3-4 days. Fee basis varies by type of transaction. Credit accounts are accepted.

They specialize in title searches.

First Security Service Corp

Phone: 617-568-8845
Fax: 617-568-8815

1 Harborside Dr Suite 302-S
Boston MA 02128

Local Retrieval Area: CT-Hartford; MA-Essex, Middlesex, Norfolk, Suffolk.

Normal turnaround time: 24-48 hours. Online computer ordering is also available. Projects are generally billed by the number of records located. The first project may require a prepayment.

Correspondent relationships: nationwide. They specialize in due diligence, pre-employment screening, insurance fraud, litigation support and general investigations.

First State Abstract

Phone: 501-676-2486
Fax: 501-676-2444

101 E Front St Suite 101
Lonoke AR 72086-3237

Local Retrieval Area: AR-Lonoke.

Normal turnaround time: 3-4 days. Fee basis will vary by type of project. Projects require prepayment.

They specialize in title insurance.

Fisher County Abstract Co

Phone: 915-776-2471
Fax: 915-776-2886

PO Box 428
Roby TX 79543

Local Retrieval Area: TX-Fisher.

Normal turnaround time: 1-2 days. Fee basis will vary by the type of project. The first project may require a prepayment.

Judith A Fitzgerald

Phone: 808-263-2120
Fax: 808-263-5823

421 Manono St
Kailua HI 96734

Local Retrieval Area: HI-Hawaii, Honolulu, Kauai, Maui.

Normal turnaround time: variable depending on project. Projects are generally billed by the hour. The first project may require a prepayment. Terms are net 30 days.

She specializes in real property asset searches and lien searches, and is a Certified Real Estate Appraiser.

FLA Search Company

Phone: 561-969-6594
Fax: 561-641-7516

PO Box 5346
Lake Worth FL 33466

Local Retrieval Area: FL-Broward, Dade, Martin, Palm Beach, St. Lucie.

Normal turnaround time: 24 hours. Projects are generally billed by the number of names searched. Projects require prepayment. Terms are net 30 days.

Correspondent relationships: all other counties in Florida.

Flagler County Abstract Co

Phone: 904-437-4151
Fax: 904-437-1913

PO Box 398
Bunnell FL 32110

Local Retrieval Area: FL-Flagler.

Normal turnaround time: 24 hours. Projects are generally billed by the number of names searched. Projects require prepayment.

They have been established since 1917 and specialize in titles.

Flathead County Title Co

Phone: 406-755-5028
Fax: 406-755-3299

PO Box 188 120 1st Ave W
Mt Kalispell MT 59903

Local Retrieval Area: MT-Flathead.

Normal turnaround time: 1-4 days. Projects are generally billed by the hour. The first project may require a prepayment.

They specialize in title insurance searches.

Fleming Attorney Service

Phone: 800-776-3301
602-253-1155
Fax: 602-253-5841

PO Box 3882
Phoenix AZ 85030

Local Retrieval and SOP Area: AZ-Coconino, Maricopa, Pima, Pinal, Yavapai.

Normal turnaround time: next day for court searches, 2-3 days for UCC, tax, and vital statistic records. Projects are generally billed by the number of names searched. The first project may require a prepayment.

Correspondent relationships: the rest of Arizona. They specialize in process servicing, asset searches, and skip tracing.

Glenn A Fleming

PO Box 772
Belle Chasse LA 70037

Phone: 504-333-4331
Fax: 504-333-9043

Local Retrieval Area: LA-Plaquemines Parish.

Normal turnaround time: 1-3 days. Fee basis varies by type of transaction. The first project may require a prepayment.

He specializes in real estate transfer searches, mortgage searches, tax searches and title abstracts.

Jean R Fletcher

Rt 1 Box 753
Riner VA 24149

Phone: 540-763-2151
Fax: 540-763-2663

Local Retrieval Area: VA-16 Counties.

Normal turnaround time: 2 days. Expedited service available. The fee is usually a flat rate based on name or by a per deed of real estate. Credit accounts are accepted.

She specializes in real estate, tax liens, judgments and UCC searches.

Flink Findzum

505 W Hamilton Ave Suite 201
Linwood NJ 08221

Phone: 800-354-1215
609-653-9400
Fax: 609-653-9577

Local Retrieval and SOP Area: NJ-Atlantic, Burlington, Camden, Cape May, Cumberland, Gloucester, Mercer, Monmouth, Ocean.

Normal turnaround time: 2-3 days. Projects are generally billed by the number of names searched or records located. The first project may require a prepayment.

Correspondent relationships: the rest of New Jersey.

Florence County Abstract

425 Norway St
Florence WI 54121

Phone: 715-528-3272
Fax: 715-528-4707

Local Retrieval Area: WI-Florence.

Normal turnaround time: 24-48 hours. Projects are generally billed by the number of names searched. Credit accounts are accepted.

They have the a complete in-house tract index and judgment index to serve Florence County.

Florida Information Associates

PO Box 11144
Tallahassee FL 32302

Phone: 904-878-0188
Fax: 904-656-2126

Local Retrieval Area: FL-Leon.

Normal turnaround time: 2-3 days. A same day rush service is also available. Projects are generally billed by the number of names searched. They offer flexible charging for large requests. The first project may require a prepayment.

They research and retrieve for state executive, judicial & legislative agencies at the State Capital, including legislative intent, corporations, UCC, motor vehicle records, criminal records, regulatory/licensure agencies and administrative proceedings.

Folks Finders Ltd

PO Box 880 RR 1
Neoga IL 62447

Phone: 800-277-3318
217-895-2524
Fax: 800-476-0782
217-895-2418

Local Retrieval Area: IL-Coles, Cumberland, Effingham, Shelby.

Normal turnaround time: 1-5 days, depending on type of inquiry. No project billing information was given. The first project may require a prepayment. Credit cards are accepted.

Correspondent relationships: nationwide. They specialize in search and locates (NO engative searches such as collections or deadbeat Dads) and death certificate retrieval.

For The Record

9105 Lyon Park Ct
Burke VA 22015

Phone: 703-323-9105
Fax: 703-323-9105

Local Retrieval Area: VA-Fairfax.

Normal turnaround time: daily. Projects are generally billed by the number of names searched. Tax liens are billed monthly. Projects require prepayment.

Correspondent relationships: Alexandria and Arlington, VA and Greenbelt, MD. They specialize in federal/state tax lien information, bankruptcy names filed, business-new listings filed with the court, judgments, background/pre-employment and criminal searches.

Sylvia Forbes

PO Box 522
Fayette MO 65248

Phone: 816-248-3455

Local Retrieval Area: MO-Howard.

Normal turnaround time: 1 week. Charges are varied depending on type of project. The first project may require a prepayment. Credit cards are accepted.

She specializes in searches for ancestor information in the county history books and local history books.

Ford Abstract Corp

221 N Franklin St
Greensburg IN 47240

Phone: 812-663-2190
Fax: 812-663-2190

Local Retrieval Area: IN-Decatur.

Normal turnaround time: 5 days. Projects are generally billed by the number of records located. Credit accounts are accepted.

Forest & Forest

110 Travis Suite 109
Lafayette LA 70503

Phone: 318-237-7651
Fax: 318-233-5860

Local Retrieval Area: LA-Acadia Parish, Lafayette Parish, St. Martin Parish, Vermilion Parish.

Normal turnaround time: 48 hours. Projects are generally billed by the hour. Fees negotiated with volume. Credit accounts are accepted.

Correspondent relationships: all other parishes in Louisiana. They specialize in real estate and commercial transactions.

Janet C Forlenza

PO Box 609
Freehold NJ 07728

Phone: 908-303-1823
Fax: 908-409-0310

Local Retrieval Area: NJ-Monmouth.

Normal turnaround time: 7-10 days. Projects are generally billed by the number of names searched. The first project may require a prepayment. Personal checks are accepted.

Fort Enterprises Process Srv

PO Box 56589
North Pole AK 99705

Phone: 907-488-7766
Fax: 907-451-0132

Local Retrieval and SOP Area: AK-Fairbanks North Star Borough.

Normal turnaround time: 2 days to 2 weeks. Projects are generally billed by the number of names searched. The first project may require a prepayment.

Correspondent relationships: the rest of the state. They specialize in field work and locating persons who are not "in the system".

Foster County Abstract & Title

1005 N 1st St
Carrington ND 58421

Phone: 701-652-3164
Fax: 701-652-3165

Local Retrieval Area: ND-Foster.

Normal turnaround time: 1-2 weeks. Projects are generally billed by the number of records located. Credit accounts are accepted.

Four Corners Abstract

370 East Ave
Rochester NY 14604

Phone: 800-724-3668
716-454-2263
Fax: 716-454-6163

Local Retrieval Area: NY-28 Counties.

Normal turnaround time: 3-5 working days. Fees are calculated on a per year basis. The first project may require a prepayment.

Correspondent relationships: other counties in New York. They specialize in title insurance.

▥ Fourth Corner Network Inc

215 Flora St
Bellingham WA 98225

Phone: 800-321-2455
Fax: 206-734-1286

Local Retrieval and SOP Area: WA-Skagit, Whatcom.

Normal turnaround time: 1-3 days for Whatcom County, and 2-5 days for Skagit County. Projects are generally billed by the number of names searched or records located. Credit accounts are accepted. Terms are net 30 days.

Fowler Abstract & Title Inc

110 N Main
Wakeeney KS 67672

Phone: 913-743-6422
Fax: 913-743-5769

Local Retrieval Area: KS-Trego.

Normal turnaround time: 3-5 days. Projects are generally billed by the hour. Credit accounts are accepted. Personal checks are accepted.

Correspondent relationships: Ness, Gove and Graham counties.

Fox Advertising

199 Main St
White Plains NY 10601

Phone: 914-948-5200
Fax: 914-948-5501

Local Retrieval Area: NY-Dutchess, Putnam, Rockland, Sullivan, Ulster, Westchester.

Normal turnaround time: varied depending on project. Projects are generally billed by the number of records located. Credit accounts are accepted.

Correspondent relationships: New York City, Queens, King, Bronx and Long Island.

Fox Hunt

PO Box 742342
Houston TX 77274

Phone: 713-772-8018
Fax: 713-772-8774

Local Retrieval Area: TX-Brazoria, Fort Bend, Harris, Montgomery.

Projects are generally billed by the number of names searched. The first project may require a prepayment.

Franklin Abstracts & Land Title Inc

Phone: 308-425-3654

RR 1 Box 185
Franklin NE 68939

Local Retrieval Area: NE-Franklin, Harlan, Webster.

Normal turnaround time: 2 days. Projects are generally billed by the hour. Credit accounts are accepted.

They specialize in land titles.

Franklin County Abstract Co

121 1st Ave NW
Hampton IA 50441

Phone: 515-456-4551
Fax: 515-456-2359

Local Retrieval Area: IA-Franklin.

Normal turnaround time: 2-3 days. Fee basis varies by type of transaction. The first project may require a prepayment.

Franklin County Abstract Co

103 Dallas St E
Mt Vernon TX 75457

Phone: 903-537-4223
Fax: 903-537-4223

Local Retrieval Area: TX-Franklin.

Normal turnaround time: 1-2 days. Fee basis will vary by the type of project. The first project may require a prepayment.

▥ Franklin Court Research

23145 Almira
Southfield MI 48034

Phone: 810-356-4666
Fax: 810-356-4666

Local Retrieval Area: MI-Macomb, Oakland, Wayne.

Normal turnaround time: within 5 business days. Expedited service available. Projects are generally billed by the number of names searched. The first project may require a prepayment. Monthly billing for regular clients.

Barbara Fransen

2138 Verdin Ave
Ocheyedan IA 51354

Phone: 515-749-2761

Local Retrieval Area: IA-Clay.

Normal turnaround time: 24-48 hours. Projects are generally billed by the number of names searched. The first project may require a prepayment.

Frazier & Associates

116 S School St
Ukiah CA 95482-4826

Phone: 707-463-1297
Fax: 707-462-8579

Local Retrieval and SOP Area: CA-Mendocino.

Normal turnaround time: 5 days. Rush or next day service is available for an additional charge. Projects are generally billed by the number of names searched. The first project may require a prepayment.

Correspondent relationships: nationwide. They specialize in subpeona preparation, service of process, court record searches and transcription.

Fred Meyers Company

PO Box 792451
San Antonio TX 78279-2451

Phone: 210-349-8119
Fax: 210-341-2679

Local Retrieval Area: TX-Atascosa, Bandera, Bexar, Comal, Guadalupe, Kendall, Medina.

Normal turnaround time: 1 week. Expedited service available. Projects are generally billed by the hour. The first project may require a prepayment.

Correspondent relationships: the rest of Texas. They specialize in missing persons.

Fred Waters Investigations

Phone: 800-506-5060
          916-336-5301

PO Box 654
McArthur CA 96056

Local Retrieval and SOP Area: CA-Butte, Sacramento, Shasta, Sutter, Yolo, Yuba.

Normal turnaround time: 24-72 hours. Projects are generally billed by the hour. Fees vary by county. The first project may require a prepayment. Personal checks are accepted.

Correspondent relationships: Northern half of California. They specialize in skip tracing, background, asset searches, personal interviews, collection, auto recovery, civil and criminal fraud, insurance fraud and restaurant/bar spotting.

June Frederick

Phone: 912-496-2354

105 Park St
Folkston GA 31537

Local Retrieval Area: GA-Charlton.

Normal turnaround time: next day. Rush service is also available. Projects are generally billed by the number of names searched. Credit accounts are accepted. Billed with report.

Fredericksburg Title Inc

Phone: 210-997-3852
Fax: 210-997-0193

112 N Orange St
Fredericksburg TX 78624

Local Retrieval Area: TX-Gillespie.

Normal turnaround time: 1-2 days. Fee basis will vary by the type of project. The first project may require a prepayment.

Freelance Legal Secretary

Phone: 907-278-8855
Fax: 907-276-7817

841 Woodmar Pl
Anchorage AK 99515

Local Retrieval Area: AK-Anchorage Borough, Homer District, Kenai Peninsula Borough, Kodiak Island Borough, Palmer District, Valdez-Cordova.

Normal turnaround time: 1-2 days under normal circumstances. Projects are generally billed by the number of names searched. Fee basis will vary by the type of project. The first project may require a prepayment.

Fremont/Custer County Abstract

Phone: 719-275-4141
Fax: 719-275-5401

PO Box 1890
Canon City CO 81212

Local Retrieval Area: CO-Custer, Fremont.

Normal turnaround time: 1-2 days. Projects are generally billed by the number of names searched. The first project may require a prepayment.

They specialize in real estate and title matters.

Irene Friend

Phone: 606-464-2638
Fax: 606-464-2638

406 Old Hury Rd
Beattyville KY 41311

Local Retrieval Area: KY-Breathitt, Estill, Lee, Owsley, Perry, Powell, Wolfe.

Normal turnaround time: 1-2 days. Fee basis varies by type of transaction. Projects require prepayment.

She specializes in researching coal, oil, and mineral rights.

Fritcher Abstract Co

Phone: 712-732-2732

533 Erie St
Storm Lake IA 50588

Local Retrieval Area: IA-Buena Vista.

Normal turnaround time: up to 4 days. Fee basis is "per search". Credit accounts are accepted.

Frontier Cultural Service

Phone: 605-673-2157
Fax: 605-673-2157

PO Box 6069
Custer SD 57730-6069

Local Retrieval Area: SD-Butte, Custer, Fall River, Jackson, Lawrence, Meade, Pennington; WY-Campbell, Crook, Niobrara, Weston.

Normal turnaround time: 48-72 hours. Projects are generally billed by the hour. They add mileage fees. Credit accounts are accepted. Terms are net 30 days.

They specialize in history of property, mining claims and forest service contract searches.

Ft Lauderdale-Miami Courthouse

Phone: 954-434-6819
Fax: 954-434-5862

4796 SW 110th Ave
Ft Lauderdale FL 33328

Local Retrieval Area: FL-Broward, Dade.

Normal turnaround time: 24-48 hours. Projects are generally billed by the number of names searched. Discounted prices available for volume work. Credit accounts are accepted. Billing is done every 2 weeks.

They search in all courts of the judicial court system in Broward and Dade counties, specializing in docket retrieval and filing documents.

Peg Fuoti

Phone: 609-625-9401

35 English Lane
Egg Harbor Twp NJ 08234

Local Retrieval Area: NJ-Atlantic.

Normal turnaround time: 2-7 days. Fee basis will vary by the type of project. Credit accounts are accepted.

She specializes in credit check searches.

Furnas County Title Co Inc

Phone: 308-268-4005
Fax: 308-268-4005

PO Box 353
Beaver City NE 68926

Local Retrieval Area: NE-Furnas, Harlan.

Normal turnaround time: 3 days. Projects are generally billed by the hour. Payment may vary upon projects. Projects require prepayment. Payment due upon receipt of work.

Correspondent relationships: NE. They specialize in real estate land title searches, abstracting and title insurance.

▥ Future Security Concepts

Phone: 800-398-3051
          913-782-1766
Fax: 913-782-5281

16217 W 144th St
Olathe KS 66062

Local Retrieval Area: KS-Douglas, Johnson, Sedgwick, Shawnee, Wyandotte.

Normal turnaround time: within 24 hours. Expedited service available. Projects are generally billed by the number of names searched. Credit accounts are accepted. Billing at the end of the month.

They specialize in criminal searches and driver's licenses (KS only) by name.

⌂ FYP Inc

14925-A Memorial Dr Suite 200
Houston TX 77079

Phone: 800-569-7143
713-558-4144
Fax: 800-569-7144
713-558-4433

Local Retrieval Area: CA-Alameda, Marin, Sacramento, San Francisco, San Mateo, Santa Clara; TX-Bexar, Comal, Dallas, Fort Bend, Harris, Hays, Montgomery, Tarrant, Travis, Williamson.

Normal turnaround time: 6-48 hours. Projects are generally billed by the number of names searched. Credit accounts are accepted. Credit cards are accepted.

They specialize in criminal searches.

G

G & H Abstract

PO Box 121
Ellsworth KS 67439

Phone: 800-640-7390
913-472-3491
Fax: 913-472-4767

Local Retrieval Area: KS-Ellsworth, Lincoln, Rice, Russell.

Normal turnaround time: 2-3 days. Fee basis varies by type of transaction. The first project may require a prepayment.

⌂ G & L Research Associates

PO Box 11765
Jacksonville FL 32239

Phone: 904-743-4116
Fax: 904-743-0022

Local Retrieval Area: FL-Clay, Duval, Nassau, St. Johns.

Normal turnaround time: 2 days. Online computer ordering is also available. Projects are generally billed by the number of names searched. Credit accounts are accepted. Terms are net 30 days.

Correspondent relationships: Orange, Volusia, Seminole, Brevard and Osceloa, FL counties.

G & O Abstracts Inc

10 E Main St
Freehold NJ 07728

Phone: 908-577-0459
Fax: 908-577-1063

Local Retrieval Area: NJ-Monmouth.

Normal turnaround time: 24-48 hours. Projects are generally billed by the number of names searched or records located. The first project may require a prepayment. Personal checks are accepted.

G T Murphy Abstractor

PO Box 345
New Hampton IA 50659

Phone: 515-394-4291

Local Retrieval Area: IA-Chickasaw.

Normal turnaround time: 1-2 days. Fee basis will vary by the type of project. The first project may require a prepayment.

Norma P Gable

12848 State Rt 664 South
Logan OH 43138

Phone: 614-385-3201
Fax: 614-385-3201

Local Retrieval Area: OH-Athens, Fairfield, Hocking, Perry, Vinton.

Normal turnaround time: 24-48 hours. Charges are varied depending on type of search. Credit accounts are accepted.

Gadsden Abstract Co

120 S Madison St
Quincy FL 32351

Phone: 904-627-6811
Fax: 904-627-6440

Local Retrieval Area: FL-Gadsden.

Normal turnaround time: 1-5 days. Projects are generally billed by the number of names searched. Credit accounts are accepted.

They specialize in real estate.

Gaines County Abstract Co

PO Box 237
Seminole TX 79360

Phone: 915-758-3351
Fax: 915-758-3790

Local Retrieval Area: TX-Gaines.

Normal turnaround time: up to a week. Fee basis will vary by the type of project. The first project may require a prepayment.

Gamma Investigative Research Inc

PO Box 10981
Fairfield NJ 07004-6981

Phone: 800-878-9393
201-785-9393
Fax: 201-785-9002

Local Retrieval and SOP Area: NJ-Bergen, Hudson, Passaic, Sussex, Union, Warren.

Normal turnaround time: 24-48 hours. The on-line is almost immediate. Online computer ordering is also available. Projects are generally billed by the hour. The first project may require a prepayment.

Correspondent relationships: nationwide. They can access many New Jersey courts through an on-line system. They also specialize in field investigations.

Catherine J Garbus

Po Box 504
Tunkhannock PA 18657

Phone: 717-836-6749
Fax: 717-836-8894

Local Retrieval Area: PA-Wyoming.

Normal turnaround time: 24 hours. Projects are generally billed by the number of names searched. Charges are varied depending on type of search. Credit accounts are accepted.

Correspondent relationships: Susquehanna and Lackawannock.

Garland Smith Abstract Co

PO Box 329
Jasper TX 75951

Phone: 409-384-2571
Fax: 409-384-4762

Local Retrieval Area: TX-Jasper, Newton.

Normal turnaround time: 48 hours. Fees vary by project. Credit accounts are accepted.

Garner Abstracting & Land Inc

PO Box 1528 120 W "N" St
Uvalde TX 78802

Phone: 800-443-2065
210-278-9169
Fax: 210-278-3613

Local Retrieval Area: TX-Uvalde.

Fees vary by project. The first project may require a prepayment.

⌂ Francis A Garrett

517 S Haugh Ave
Picayune MS 39466-5343

Phone: 601-798-4992
Fax: 601-798-4992

Local Retrieval Area: MS-Hancock, Harrison, Jackson.

Normal turnaround time: 36-48 hours. Expedited services available. Projects are generally billed by the number of names searched. The first project may require a prepayment. Invoices due upon receipt.

She does an expedited service on a 24 hours notice at double the normal rate.

Garrison Legal Services

400 W 15th
Amarillo TX 79101

Phone: 806-373-6204
Fax: 806-374-6501

Local Retrieval Area: TX-Potter, Randall.

Normal turnaround time: varied depending on project. Projects are generally billed by the number of names searched or records located. Credit accounts are accepted. Personal checks are accepted.

Correspondent relationships: panhandle counties.

Douglas G Garvin

PO Drawer 328
Aiken SC 29802

Phone: 803-649-6281
Fax: 803-641-1216

Local Retrieval Area: SC-Aiken.

Normal turnaround time: 2 days. Fee basis varies by type of transaction. Credit accounts are accepted.

Gates Land Title Corp

PO Box 369 222 W Van Buren St
Columbia City IN 46725

Phone: 219-244-5127
Fax: 219-244-5127

Local Retrieval Area: IN-Whitley.

Normal turnaround time: 1 week. Fee basis varies by type of transaction. Credit accounts are accepted..dd.

Gateway USA

4400 PGA Blvd Suite 304
Palm Beach Gardens FL 33410

Phone: 800-727-7772
561-624-5100
Fax: 561-624-9734

Local Retrieval Area: FL-Palm Beach.

Normal turnaround time: 72 hours. Projects are generally billed by the number of names searched. Projects require prepayment. Credit cards are accepted.

Correspondent relationships: nationwide. They specialize in electronic services and databases retrieval. They are a training center for clients and retrievers.

🏛 Marcia A Gazoorian

PO Box 53
Worcester MA 01613-0053

Phone: 508-754-9503
Fax: 508-754-9503

Local Retrieval Area: MA-Worcester.

Normal turnaround time: 2 days. Expedited service available. Projects are generally billed by the number of names searched. The first project may require a prepayment. Require immediate reimbursement of costs expended.

She specializes in document search and investigation at Worcester Bankruptcy Court.

Gem State Investigations

PO Box 1875 504 Main #424
Lewiston ID 83501

Phone: 208-746-4152
Fax: 208-746-5078

Local Retrieval and SOP Area: ID-Benewah, Clearwater, Idaho, Latah, Lewis, Nez Perce; WA-Asotin, Garfield, Whitman.

Normal turnaround time: varied depending on project. Fee basis varies by type of transaction. The first project may require a prepayment.

Correspondent relationships: Northern Idaho and Eastern Washington. They specialize in insurance fraud.

Genealogically Yours

5275 W Road 450 S
Knightstown IN 46148

Phone: 317-987-8820

Local Retrieval Area: IN-Hancock, Henry, Marion.

Normal turnaround time: 1 week. Projects are generally billed by the hour. The first project may require a prepayment.

They specialize in marriages, divorces, probate, city directories (IN), death certification and obituaries.

General Corporate Investigations

PO Box 2657
Cincinnati OH 45201

Phone: 800-735-7992
606-491-5341
Fax: 606-491-5420

Local Retrieval and SOP Area: KY-Boone, Campbell, Kenton; OH-Butler, Clermont, Cuyahoga, Hamilton, Montgomery, Warren.

Normal turnaround time: 2 days. Projects are generally billed by the hour. The first project may require a prepayment.

Correspondent relationships: Ohio, Kentucky and Indiana. They specialize in surveillance, activity, background and asset checks, financial investigations, subrogation, locations and pre-employment.

General Information Services Inc

PO Box 312080
Jamaica NY 11431-2080

Phone: 800-447-2080
718-221-9100
Fax: 800-463-6649
718-291-8480

Local Retrieval Area: NY-New York.

Normal turnaround time: 48 hours. Projects are generally billed by the number of names searched. The first project may require a prepayment. Credit cards are accepted.

Correspondent relationships: nationwide. They specialize in all types of investigative reports, employment screening, DMV records, tenant reports, locates, criminal history and public record searching.

General Services

1645 S La Cienega Blvd
Los Angeles CA 90035

Phone: 310-859-1122
Fax: 310-859-1123

Local Retrieval Area: CA-Los Angeles, Orange.

Normal turnaround time: 2-3 days. Projects are generally billed by the number of names searched. Credit accounts are accepted.

Geo G Smith & Son Inc

108 E Morrison
Fayette MO 65248

Phone: 816-248-2467
Fax: 816-248-3731

Local Retrieval Area: MO-Howard.

Normal turnaround time: 1-5 days. Projects are generally billed by the number of names searched. Fee may also be based per page. Credit accounts are accepted. Personal checks are accepted.

Correspondent relationships: Cooper, Boone and Randolph, MO counties. They specialize in abstracting and title insurance.

Gietzen & Associates Inc

707 N Franklin St Suite 725
Tampa FL 33602-4430

Phone: 813-254-4383
Fax: 813-254-1174

Local Retrieval and SOP Area: FL-Hillsborough, Pasco, Pinellas, Polk.

Normal turnaround time: 1 day. Projects are generally billed by the hour. The first project may require a prepayment.

Correspondent relationships: all Florida counties. They specialize in financial and general investigations, process and court reporting.

Gilchrist Title Services Inc

PO Box 5
Trenton FL 32693

Phone: 352-463-6403
Fax: 352-463-6908

Local Retrieval Area: FL-Dixie, Gilchrist, Levy.

Normal turnaround time: 24-48 hours. Projects are generally billed by the number of names searched or records located. Credit accounts are accepted. Personal checks are accepted.

Correspondent relationships: Alachua County. They specialize in title insurance, real estate closings and all real property searches.

Joe Gillenwater

PO Box 1545
Texarkana AR 75504-1545

Phone: 800-962-9453
501-772-2923
Fax: 501-773-0108

Local Retrieval and SOP Area: AR-Columbia, Hempstead, Howard, Lafayette, Little River, Miller, Nevada, Sevier; TX-Bowie, Cass.

Normal turnaround time: 12-72 hours. Projects are generally billed by the number of names searched. Fees are plus mileage and copy charge. The first project may require a prepayment. Terms are net 20 days.

Gillette Battey & McAreavey

Box 60
Redfield SD 57469

Phone: 605-472-1210
Fax: 605-472-1280

Local Retrieval Area: SD-Spink.

Normal turnaround time: 48 hours. Projects are generally billed by the hour. The first project may require a prepayment.

They specialize in probate, deeds and real property searches.

Billy J Gilmore

PO Box 629 105 Carrolloton St
Lexington MS 39095

Phone: 601-834-2421
Fax: 601-834-2400

Local Retrieval Area: MS-Holmes.

Normal turnaround time: 1-2 days. Fee basis varies by type of transaction. The first project may require a prepayment.

Gion Law Office

PO Box 101
Regent ND 58650-0101

Phone: 701-563-4354
Fax: 701-563-4497

Local Retrieval Area: ND-Adams, Bowman, Grant, Hettinger, Slope, Stark.

Normal turnaround time: 5 to 7 days. Projects are generally billed by the hour. The first project may require a prepayment.

They specialize in general law practice.

Gladwin County Abstract Co

320 W Cedar
Gladwin MI 48624

Phone: 517-426-7411
Fax: 517-426-2411

Local Retrieval Area: MI-Gladwin.

Normal turnaround time: 1 week. Projects are generally billed by the number of names searched or records located. The first project may require a prepayment. Personal checks are accepted.

They have the only existing complete tract index for Gladwin County.

Gladwin Title Co

247 W Cedar Ave
Gladwin MI 48624

Phone: 517-426-0011
Fax: 517-426-7141

Local Retrieval Area: MI-Gladwin.

Normal turnaround time: 2-3 days. Fee basis may vary by the type of project. The first project may require a prepayment.

Glass & Carson Investigation

1123 Sunday Lane
Jonesboro GA 30236

Phone: 770-603-2887
Fax: 770-477-9779

Local Retrieval and SOP Area: GA-Carroll, Cherokee, Clayton, Cobb, De Kalb, Douglas, Fayette, Fulton, Gwinnett, Muscogee.

Normal turnaround time: 24-48 hours. Projects are generally billed by the number of names searched. Credit accounts are accepted. Payment expected within 15 days of billing.

Correspondent relationships: nationwide.

Howard Glass

1220 Venice Blvd Suite 106
Venise CA 90291

Phone: 310-827-8473
Fax: 310-827-8913

Local Retrieval Area: CA-Los Angeles, Orange, Riverside, San Bernardino, Ventura.

Normal turnaround time: 1-2 days. Projects are generally billed by the number of names searched. The first project may require a prepayment.

Correspondent relationships: Georgia.

Romana Glastetter

PO Box 245 310 s Messmer St
Kelso MO 63758

Phone: 573-264-2887

Local Retrieval Area: MO-Scott.

Normal turnaround time: 1 week. Projects are generally billed by the hour. Projects require prepayment.

She specializes in probate and census records.

Gleem Credit Services

9191 W Florissant Suite 201
St Louis MO 63136

Phone: 314-521-1300
Fax: 314-521-2241

Local Retrieval Area: IL-Madison, St. Clair; MO-St. Louis.

Normal turnaround time: 6-72 hours. Projects are generally billed by the number of names searched. The first project may require a prepayment. Credit cards are accepted. Terms are net 10 & 30 days.

Correspondent relationships: Missouri, Illinois, Minnesota, Maryland, Colorado and Oklahoma. They specialize in credit reports, motor vehicle reports and worker's comp checks.

Global Projects Ltd

520 Washington Blvd Penthouse 500
Marina del Rey CA 90292

Phone: 800-859-8109
310-314-8760
Fax: 310-392-0797

Local Retrieval and SOP Area: CA-Los Angeles, Orange, Riverside, San Bernardino, Ventura.

Normal turnaround time: immediate service up to 2 hours. Online computer ordering is also available. Fee basis will vary by the type of project. The first project may require a prepayment. Credit cards are accepted. Personal checks are accepted.

Correspondent relationships: nationwide and worldwide. The corporation has been in business for over 50 years and is staffed by former law enforcement and intelligence agency personnel. They perform locates and asset searches, and retrieval of foreign court and other records.

Gold Shield Private Investigators

Phone: 914-997-0000
Fax: 914-639-6869

980 Broadway Suite 312
Thornwoods NY 10594

Local Retrieval and SOP Area: NY-Westchester.

Projects are generally billed by the number of names searched. The first project may require a prepayment.

Correspondent relationships: nationwide. They specialize in process service.

Linda Gonzales

Phone: 520-622-1729
Fax: 520-622-1729

334 S 6th Ave
Tucson AZ 85701

Local Retrieval Area: AZ-Pima.

Normal turnaround time: 24 hours. Projects are generally billed by the number of names searched. The first project may require a prepayment.

She specializes in criminal name searches for employment screening, insurance, etc.

Gooding Title Co

Phone: 903-427-3398
Fax: 903-427-2423

228 N Walnut
Clarksville TX 75426

Local Retrieval Area: TX-Red River.

Normal turnaround time: varied depending on project. Fee basis will vary by the type of project. Projects require prepayment.

Goodman & Nichols

Phone: 502-524-9292
Fax: 502-524-9293

PO Box 838 300 N Main
Munfordville KY 42765

Local Retrieval Area: KY-Barren, Hart, Larue.

Normal turnaround time: 3-5 days for title searches (1 1/2 days for Hart County) and 2 days for name checks (1 day for Hart County). Projects are generally billed by the number of records located. Credit accounts are accepted.

Gotcha Legal Process Service

Phone: 516-751-1450
Fax: 516-751-0974

PO Box 1525
Stony Brook NY 11790-0878

Local Retrieval and SOP Area: NY-Nassau, Suffolk.

Normal turnaround time: 4 hours to 2 days. Projects are generally billed by the hour. The first project may require a prepayment.

Government Liaison Services Inc

Phone: 800-642-6564
703-524-8200
Fax: 703-525-8451

3030 Clarendon Blvd Suite 209
Arlington VA 22210

Local Retrieval Area: DC-District of Columbia.

Normal turnaround time: 2 days. Projects are generally billed by the hour. The first project may require a prepayment. Credit cards are accepted.

Graham & Davis Abstracting

Phone: 207-947-6344
Fax: 207-990-3843

50 Columbia St
Bangor ME 04401

Local Retrieval Area: ME-Hancock, Penobscot, Piscataquis, Waldo.

Normal turnaround time: 48 hours. Projects are generally billed by the hour. The first project may require a prepayment.

Graham Abstract Co

Phone: 515-932-7156
Fax: 515-932-3280

202 Washington E
Albia IA 52531

Local Retrieval Area: IA-Monroe.

Normal turnaround time: 2-3 days. Fee basis will vary by the type of project. The first project may require a prepayment.

Graham Abstract Co Inc

Phone: 505-356-8505
Fax: 505-356-8508

107 W 2nd St
Portales NM 88130

Local Retrieval Area: NM-Roosevelt.

Normal turnaround time: 1-5 days. Fee basis will vary by the type of project. The first project may require a prepayment.

They specialize in escrow, title insurance, closings, and mineral searches.

Grand Forks Abstract Co

Phone: 701-772-3484
Fax: 701-772-0701

209 S 3rd St
Grand Forks ND 58201

Local Retrieval Area: MN-Polk; ND-Grand Forks.

Normal turnaround time: 48 hours. Projects are generally billed by the number of names searched. The first project may require a prepayment.

They specialize in title insurance.

Grand Traverse Title Co

Phone: 616-946-5686
Fax: 616-929-5486

116 Boardman Ave
Traverse City MI 49684

Local Retrieval Area: MI-Grand Traverse.

Normal turnaround time: 2-3 days. Fee basis will vary by type of project. The first project may require a prepayment.

They specialize in real estate.

Grant County Abstract & Title Co

Phone: 605-432-5461
Fax: 605-432-5461

210 E 5th Ave
Milbank SD 57252

Local Retrieval Area: SD-Grant.

Normal turnaround time: 1 week to 10 days. Projects are generally billed by the number of records located. Projects require prepayment.

They specialize in real estate titles.

Grant County Abstract Co

Phone: 317-664-7371
Fax: 317-664-0766

PO Box 897
Marion IN 46952

Local Retrieval Area: IN-Grant.

Normal turnaround time: varied depending on project. Projects are generally billed by the number of names searched. Credit accounts are accepted.

They specialize in title insurance.

Grant County Abstract Co

Phone: 701-622-3556

PO Box 228 222 N Main
Carson ND 58529

Local Retrieval Area: ND-Grant.

Normal turnaround time: 1-5 days. Fee basis will vary by type of project. The first project may require a prepayment.

They specialize in title histories.

Grant County Abstract Co
Phone: 405-395-2854
PO Box 25
Medford OK 73759
Local Retrieval Area: OK-Grant.
Normal turnaround time: 1-2 days. Projects are generally billed by the number of records located. The first project may require a prepayment.

Grant County Abstract Co
Phone: 608-723-4192
Fax: 608-723-4228
138 S Madison St
Lancaster WI 53813
Local Retrieval Area: WI-Grant.
Normal turnaround time: 2-3 days. Fee basis varies by type of transaction. The first project may require a prepayment.

Grant County Clerk's Office
Phone: 304-257-4550
Fax: 304-257-2593
5 Highland Ave
Petersburg WV 26847
Local Retrieval Area: WV-Grant.
Normal turnaround time: 1 week. Fee basis varies by type of transaction. Credit accounts are accepted.
She (Alicia) has several associates who work with her and specialize in searching all records in the County Clerk's office.

Gary Grant
Phone: 804-799-3379
PO Box 376
Danville VA 24543
Local Retrieval Area: VA-City of Danville, Halifax, Henry, City of Martinsville, Patrick, Pittsylvania, City of South Boston.
Normal turnaround time: 2-3 days. Projects are generally billed by the number of records located..dd. Credit accounts are accepted.
He specializes in UCC, real estate, tax and simple land searches.

K Maxwell Graves Jr
Phone: 601-384-2733
Fax: 601-384-5568
PO Box 607 Graves Bldg, Walnut St
Meadville MS 39653
Local Retrieval Area: MS-Franklin.
Normal turnaround time: 1 working day. Projects are generally billed by the hour. Credit accounts are accepted. They accept personal checks.

Gray County Abstract Co Inc
Phone: 316-855-3128
215 S Main PO Box 401
Cimarron KS 67835
Local Retrieval Area: KS-Ford, Gray.
Normal turnaround time: 1-7 days. Projects are generally billed by the number of names searched. Credit accounts are accepted. Personal checks are accepted.
Correspondent relationships: Finney, Meade, Haskell and Hodgeman.

Graystone Investigations Inc
Phone: 912-743-5551
Fax: 912-743-5121
2720 Sheriton Dr Bldg D Suite 120
Macon GA 31204
Local Retrieval and SOP Area: GA-Bibb, Crawford, Forsyth, Houston, Jones, Monroe, Peach.
Normal turnaround time: 3 days. Projects are generally billed by the hour. Fees will include mileage when applicable. The first project may require a prepayment.
Correspondent relationships: Kentucky, Indiana, Tennessee, South Carolina, Georgia, Florida, and Alabama. They specialize in background investigation, surveillance, and defense case searches.

Great Lakes Title
Phone: 616-775-0561
Fax: 616-775-4221
PO Box 877
Cadillac MI 49601
Local Retrieval Area: MI-Clare, Lake, Mecosta, Osceola, Wexford.
Normal turnaround time: 3 days. Projects are generally billed by the number of names searched. Projects require prepayment. They request prepay only on the title searches.
Correspondent relationships: Missaukee County. They also offer escrow services.

Great Northern Title & Abstract Inc
Phone: 906-228-6100
Fax: 906-228-4015
309 S 3rd Street Suite 201
Marquette MI 49855
Local Retrieval Area: MI-Marquette.
Normal turnaround time: 1 week. Projects are generally billed by the hour. The first project may require a prepayment.
They specialize in title insurance and abstracts of title.

Greater Tennessee Title Co
Phone: 423-482-1201
Fax: 423-483-4811
231 Jackson Sq
Oak Ridge TN 37830
Local Retrieval Area: TN-Anderson, Blount, Cocke, Knox, Loudon, Morgan, Roane.
Normal turnaround time: 2 days. Fee basis is per search. Credit accounts are accepted.

Green Lake Title & Abstract Co
Phone: 414-294-6070
Fax: 414-294-3630
533 Mill St
Green Lake WI 54941
Local Retrieval Area: WI-Green Lake.
Normal turnaround time: 1-2 days. Fee basis varies by type of transaction. The first project may require a prepayment.

Richard J Green
Phone: 619-770-4702
Fax: 619-770-4702
PO Box 1256
Cathedral City CA 92235-1256
Local Retrieval and SOP Area: CA-Riverside.
Normal turnaround time: 24 hours. Projects are generally billed by the hour. The first project may require a prepayment.
He has over 35 years experience in researching court and other public records.

Greene County Abstract Company
Phone: 515-386-2191
Fax: 515-386-2191
102 S Wilson Ave
Jefferson IA 50129
Local Retrieval Area: IA-Greene.
Normal turnaround time: 1-7 days. Projects are generally billed by the number of names searched or records located. Fee may also be based on a combination of valuation and clerical. Credit accounts are accepted.

🏛 Greenwood Research
Phone: 800-771-0847
817-753-2555
Fax: 817-753-3181
4524 Sanger
Waco TX 76710-4946
Local Retrieval Area: TX-Bell, McLennan.
Normal turnaround time: 24-48 hours. Projects are generally billed by the number of names searched. Credit accounts are accepted. Bill first of month, net 15 days.
Correspondent relationships: all of Texas and San Diego County, CA. They specialize in criminal, civil, UCC, tax lien and property searches.

Greer Guaranty Abstract Co

Phone: 405-782-3121

Drawer C
Mangum OK 73554

Local Retrieval Area: OK-Greer.

Normal turnaround time: 1 to 2 days. Projects are generally billed by the hour. Credit accounts are accepted.

Greet America Public Record Svc

Phone: 214-320-9836
Fax: 214-320-2992

8035 E.R.L. Thornton Fwy Suite 415
Dallas TX 75228

Local Retrieval Area: NC-All Counties; SC-All Counties; TN-All Counties; TX-Dallas, El Paso.

Normal turnaround time: 3 days. Online computer ordering is also available. Projects are generally billed by the number of names searched. The first project may require a prepayment.

Correspondent relationships: nationwide. They specialize in pre-employment screening, background investigations nationwide at all court levels.

🏛 Gregg Investigations Janesville

Phone: 800-866-1976
Fax: 608-755-5853

PO Box 669
Janesville WI 53547-0669

Local Retrieval and SOP Area: IL-Winnebago; WI-Dane, Rock.

Normal turnaround time: the same day. Projects are generally billed by the number of names searched. Credit accounts are accepted. Credit cards are accepted.

Their specialty is "Information Services". They also work with DOT records, boats, city directory library, bartenders and bowlers.

Gregg Investigations Madison

Phone: 800-866-1976
Fax: 608-755-5853

139 W Wilson Suite 104
Madison WI 53701-1641

Local Retrieval and SOP Area: IL-Winnebago; WI-Dane, Rock.

Normal turnaround time: the same day. Projects are generally billed by the number of names searched. Credit accounts are accepted.

Correspondent relationships: Wisconsin. They specialize in "Information Services". They also work with DOT records, boats, city directory library, bartenders and bowlers.

Gregory Abstract and Title Co Inc

Phone: 913-346-5445
Fax: 913-346-5446

124 W Main
Osborne KS 67473

Local Retrieval Area: KS-Osborne.

Normal turnaround time: 12-24 hours. Projects are generally billed by the hour. Credit accounts are accepted.

Gregory County Abstract Co

Phone: 605-775-2943
Fax: 605-775-2943

PO Box 352
Burke SD 57523

Local Retrieval Area: SD-Gregory.

Normal turnaround time: 10 days. Fee basis will vary by the type of project. Projects require prepayment.

They specialize in real estate.

Joe C Griffin

Phone: 601-285-6080
Fax: 601-285-6089

PO Box 237
Ackerman MS 39735

Local Retrieval Area: MS-Choctaw.

Normal turnaround time: 1-2 days. Projects are generally billed by the hour. The first project may require a prepayment.

He specializes in marriage/divorce and property searches.

Charlotte Griffith

Phone: 573-242-3488

Rt 1 Box 228
Clarksville MO 63336

Local Retrieval Area: MO-Lincoln, Pike.

Normal turnaround time: varied depending on job. Projects are generally billed by the hour. The first project may require a pre-payment.

She specializes in genealogy record searches.

🏛 Grissom & Associates

Phone: 800-861-6483
909-881-2646
Fax: 909-883-7076

PO Box 3027
San Bernardino CA 92413

Local Retrieval and SOP Area: CA-San Bernardino.

Normal turnaround time: 24 hours. Longer for criminal archive information. Projects are generally billed by the hour. The first project may require a prepayment.

They can also get records in Guadalajara, Mexico.

Groesbeck Abstract & Title Co

Phone: 817-729-3806
Fax: 817-729-5655

PO Box 127
Groesbeck TX 76642

Local Retrieval Area: TX-Limestone.

Normal turnaround time: 1-2 days. Fee basis will vary by the type of project. The first project may require a prepayment.

🏛 Groves Associates

Phone: 800-447-6837
707-762-9387
Fax: 707-762-0493

PO Box 750159
Petaluma CA 94975-0159

Local Retrieval Area: CA-Marin, Napa, Solano, Sonoma.

Normal turnaround time: 24-72 hours. Projects are generally billed by the number of names searched. The first project may require a prepayment. Credit cards are accepted.

They specialize in pre-employment screening, asset and locate investigations, due diligence and records retrieval.

Grue Abstract Co

Phone: 605-345-3891

PO Box 559
Webster SD 57274

Local Retrieval Area: SD-Day.

Normal turnaround time: 5-10 days. Fee basis will vary by the type of project. Credit accounts are accepted.

They specialize in land title.

Guarantee Abstract

Phone: 512-782-3591
Fax: 512-782-3649

116 W Main PO Box 626
Edna TX 77957

Local Retrieval Area: TX-Jackson.

Normal turnaround time: 24-48 hours. Fees vary by project. Credit accounts are accepted.

Guaranty Abstract & Title Co

Phone: 405-338-3374
Fax: 405-338-3375

Box 319
Guymon OK 73942

Local Retrieval Area: OK-Texas.

Normal turnaround time: 1-3 weeks. Fee basis will vary by the type of project. Credit accounts are accepted.

Guaranty Abstract Co
Phone: 719-336-3261
Fax: 719-336-8106
PO Box 859
Lamar CO 81052
Local Retrieval Area: CO-Prowers.

Normal turnaround time: 1-3 days. Fee basis is determined on "per name/description" or "flat rate". Credit accounts are accepted.

They specialize in real estate and title matters.

Guaranty Abstract Co
Phone: 918-967-8876
Fax: 918-967-2191
PO Box 278
Stigler OK 74462
Local Retrieval Area: OK-Haskell.

Normal turnaround time: 1-2 weeks. Projects are generally billed by the hour. Credit accounts are accepted.

They specialize in land records.

Guaranty Abstract Co
Phone: 806-823-2354
Fax: 806-823-2354
PO Box 718
Silverton TX 79257
Local Retrieval Area: TX-Briscoe.

Normal turnaround time: 2-3 days. Projects are generally billed by the hour. The first project may require a prepayment.

Guaranty Land Title
Phone: 573-636-8388
Fax: 573-636-8835
2013 Williams St Suite B
Jefferson City MO 65109
Local Retrieval Area: MO-Boone, Callaway, Camden, Cole, Cooper, Howard, Miller, Moniteau, Morgan, Osage.

Normal turnaround time: 48-72 hours. There is a next day service on anything needed from the state government. Projects are generally billed by the number of names searched. Credit accounts are accepted.

They specialize in land and abstract, title searches and UCC searches.

Guaranty Title Co
Phone: 501-321-2856
Fax: 501-321-9677
201 Market St
Hot Springs AR 71901
Local Retrieval Area: AR-Garland.

Normal turnaround time: up to 1 week. Fee basis will vary by the type of project. Credit accounts are accepted.

They specialize in real estate titles.

🏛 Guaranty Title Co
Phone: 505-887-3593
Fax: 505-885-5204
108 N Canyon PO Box 430
Carlsbad NM 88221-0430
Local Retrieval Area: NM-Eddy.

Normal turnaround time: 1 week. Fee basis will vary by the type of project. Credit accounts are accepted.

The same family has been in business in Eddy County for over 50 years.

Guaranty Title Co
Phone: 409-873-2250
Fax: 409-873-2056
PO Box 290
Anderson TX 77830
Local Retrieval Area: TX-Grimes.

Normal turnaround time: 2-4 days. Fee basis will vary by the type of project. The first project may require a prepayment.

Guaranty Title Co
Phone: 903-536-2133
Fax: 903-536-7643
PO Box 449
Centerville TX 75833
Local Retrieval Area: TX-Leon.

Normal turnaround time: up to a week. Fee basis will vary by the type of project. The first project may require a prepayment.

Guaranty Title Co
Phone: 409-828-4688
Fax: 409-828-3803
PO Box 481
Franklin TX 77856
Local Retrieval Area: TX-Robertson.

Normal turnaround time: up to a week. Fee basis will vary by the type of project. The first project may require a prepayment.

Guardsmark
Phone: 901-522-7800
Fax: 901-522-7858
PO Box 1181
Memphis TN 38101
Local Retrieval Area: TN-Shelby.

Normal turnaround time: 24-48 hours. Fee basis will vary by the type of project. The first project may require a prepayment.

They specialize in background checks.

Jerry Guffey
Phone: 502-259-4828
Fax: 502-259-8161
62 Public Square
Leitchfield KY 42754
Local Retrieval Area: KY-Grayson.

Normal turnaround time: 3-5 days. Expedited service available. Projects are generally billed by the number of names searched. Credit accounts are accepted. Will mail statement with findings.

Correspondent relationships: Breckinridge, Hart, Sdmonson, Ohio, Butler and Hardin, KY counties. He specializes in real estate searches.

Guier Abstract & Title Co
Phone: 913-985-3562
Fax: 913-985-2322
137 S Main
Troy KS 66087
Local Retrieval Area: KS-Doniphan.

Normal turnaround time: 3 days. Fee basis varies by type of transaction. Credit accounts are accepted.

Gumshoe Investigations Agency
Phone: 800-476-7660
310-396-7507
Fax: 310-396-7507
PO Box 1638
Santa Monica CA 90406-1638
Local Retrieval and SOP Area: CA-Los Angeles, Orange, Riverside, San Bernardino, San Diego, Santa Barbara, Ventura.

Normal turnaround time: as soon as possible, depending upon nature of case. Projects are generally billed by the number of names searched or records located. The first project may require a prepayment.

Correspondent relationships: nationwide. They specialize in asset searches, criminal, insurance defense, skip tracing, witness interview, surveillance, backgrounss, trademark and patent, environmental, full litigation support and process service.

Guthrie County Abstract
Phone: 515-747-3705
Fax: 515-747-8719
110 N 4th St
Guthrie Center IA 50115
Local Retrieval Area: IA-Guthrie.

Normal turnaround time: 1-2 days. Projects are generally billed by the number of names searched or records located. Fee basis varies by type of transaction. The first project may require a prepayment.

🏛 Guzman Enterprises

161 NW Lenoir St
Port Charlotte FL 33948

Phone: 941-743-3690
Fax: 941-743-3313

Local Retrieval Area: FL-Charlotte, De Soto, Lee, Manatee, Sarasota.

Normal turnaround time: 24 hours. Projects are generally billed by the number of names searched. Fees depend on type of service requested. Credit accounts are accepted.

They specialize in real estate title reports, UCC searches, judgments, liens, US tax liens and real estate tax information. The owner has 25 years experience.

H

H S Black

PO Box 717
Childress TX 79201

Phone: 817-937-3681
Fax: 817-937-3682

Local Retrieval Area: TX-Childress.

Normal turnaround time: 1-2 days. Fee basis will vary by the type of project. Credit accounts are accepted.

Haakon County Abstract Co

Box 40
Philip SD 57567-0040

Phone: 605-859-2461

Local Retrieval Area: SD-Haakon.

Normal turnaround time: 1 day except for real estate searches, which averages 7 days. Projects billed by the area searched. Credit accounts are accepted. Personal checks are accepted. Credit accounts not accepted.

Correspondent relationships: Pennington, Jackson and Stanley. They specialize in real estate title searches for abstracts or title insurance.

Haber Investigations

117 Town & Country Village, #523
San Jose CA 95128

Phone: 800-382-6333
408-978-2325
Fax: 408-266-1119

Local Retrieval and SOP Area: CA-Santa Clara.

Projects are generally billed by the hour. Credit accounts are accepted. Terms are net 30 days.

Correspondent relationships: worldwide. He has a law degree and criminal degree.

Lisa Haislip

2315 Hopecrest Dr
Charlotte NC 28210

Phone: 704-553-0974
Fax: 704-552-0609

Local Retrieval Area: NC-Cabarrus, Catawba, Gaston, Mecklenburg, Union; SC-Chester, Fairfield, Lancaster, York.

Projects are generally billed by the number of names searched. The first project may require a prepayment.

Haley Abstract & Title Co

320 S Main St
Ottawa KS 66067

Phone: 913-242-2457
Fax: 913-242-6830

Local Retrieval Area: KS-Franklin.

Normal turnaround time: 1-2 days. Fee basis varies by type of transaction. Credit accounts are accepted.

Halletsville Abstract & Title Co

110 N Texana St
Halletsville TX 77964

Phone: 512-798-3291
Fax: 512-798-2257

Local Retrieval Area: TX-Lavaca.

Normal turnaround time: 2 days. Fee basis will vary by the type of project. The first project may require a prepayment.

Hamilton & Johnson Abstract Inc

PO Box 85
Wahoo NE 68066

Phone: 402-443-3081
Fax: 402-443-4120

Local Retrieval Area: NE-Saunders.

Normal turnaround time: 24 hours. Projects are generally billed by the number of names searched. Credit accounts are accepted.

Sue P Hamm

PO Box 46
Aurora NC 27806

Phone: 919-322-5015
Fax: 919-322-7205

Local Retrieval Area: NC-Beaufort, Craven, Jones, Lenoir, Pamlico, Pitt.

Normal turnaround time: 24-48 hours. Fee basis will vary by the type of project. Credit accounts are accepted.

She specializes in real estate, civil action and lien searches.

Hancock County Abstract Co

130 E 8th St
Garner IA 50438

Phone: 515-923-2454
Fax: 515-923-3381

Local Retrieval Area: IA-Hancock.

Normal turnaround time: 2-3 days. Projects are generally billed by the number of records located. Credit accounts are accepted.

Hand County Abstract & Title Co

PO Box 368 116 E 3rd St
Miller SD 57362

Phone: 605-853-2194
Fax: 605-853-3606

Local Retrieval Area: SD-Hand.

Normal turnaround time: 1 week. Projects are generally billed by the hour. Credit accounts are accepted.

🏛 E J Hanlon

500 4th St
Yreka CA 96097

Phone: 916-842-3588
Fax: 916-842-3566

Local Retrieval and SOP Area: CA-Siskiyou.

Normal turnaround time: 48 hours. Projects are generally billed by the number of names searched. The first project may require a prepayment.

They specialize in filing court documents in the Municipal or Superior Courts.

Hannaford Abstract & Title Co

222 E Main St
Marion KS 66861

Phone: 316-382-2130
Fax: 316-382-3420

Local Retrieval Area: KS-Marion.

Normal turnaround time: 3 days. Fee basis varies by type of transaction. The first project may require a prepayment.

Hanson County Land & Abstract

PO Box 505
Alexandria SD 57311

Phone: 605-239-4559
Fax: 605-239-4559

Local Retrieval Area: SD-Hanson.

Normal turnaround time: 2 weeks. Fee basis will vary by the type of project. The first project may require a prepayment.

Harbor City Research Inc
Phone: 800-445-6029
201 E Baltimore St Suite 630   410-539-0400
Baltimore MD 21202   **Fax:** 800-331-1566
   410-659-0517
Local Retrieval Area: MD-Anne Arundel, Baltimore, City of Baltimore, Harford, Howard, Montgomery, Prince George's.

Normal turnaround time: 1-2 days. Projects are generally billed by the number of names searched or records located. The first project may require a prepayment.

Correspondent relationships: nationwide.

Hardin County Abstract Company
Phone: 618-287-7944
PO Box 158 Courthouse   **Fax:** 618-287-7833
Elizabethtown IL 62931
Local Retrieval Area: IL-Hardin.

Normal turnaround time: 1 week. Projects are generally billed by the number of names searched or records located. The first project may require a prepayment.

Correspondent relationships: Pope County. They are the issuing agents for Chicago Title Insurance Company in Hardin and Pope Counties.

Harding County Abstract Co
Phone: 605-375-3422
PO Box 87
Buffalo SD 57720
Local Retrieval Area: SD-Harding.

Normal turnaround time: 2 weeks. Projects are generally billed by the hour. Credit accounts are accepted.

They specialize in title insurance.

Harmon County Abstract
Phone: 405-688-9255
PO Box 788   **Fax:** 405-688-2287
Hollis OK 73550
Local Retrieval Area: OK-Harmon.

Normal turnaround time: 72 hours. Projects are generally billed by the hour. Credit accounts are accepted.

They specialize in real estate and divorce matters.

Harmon Legal Process Service
Phone: 314-635-6690
PO Box 1794   **Fax:** 314-635-2339
Jefferson City MO 65102
Local Retrieval and SOP Area: MO-Boone, Callaway, Cole, Miller, Morgan, Osage.

Normal turnaround time: 1 day. Projects are generally billed by the number of names searched or records located. Credit accounts are accepted. Billed monthly.

They specialize in statewide criminal searches and public record retrieval.

⌂ Harold Eavenson & Associates
Phone: 972-771-5081
PO Box 1775   **Fax:** 972-771-0133
Rockwall TX 75087-1775
Local Retrieval and SOP Area: TX-Collin, Dallas, Denton, Hunt, Kaufman, Rockwall, Tarrant, Van Zandt.

Normal turnaround time: 5-7 business days, dependent on scope of request. Projects are generally billed by the hour. Fees vary by county, or online if records available. The first project may require a prepayment. Terms are net 30 days.

Correspondent relationships: nationwide. They specialize in investigative research of all types, with 18 years in law enforcement experience with the TX Dept of Public Safety and 10 years in criminal intelligence service. Licensed PI in Texas.

Eileen Harris
Phone: 423-397-7669
PO Box 381
Dandridge TN 37725
Local Retrieval Area: TN-Cocke, Grainger, Greene, Hamblen, Hawkins, Jefferson, Sevier.

Normal turnaround time: 48 hours. Projects are generally billed by the number of names searched. Credit accounts are accepted. Personal checks are accepted.

She specializes in title abstracting and registering of deeds.

Harrison County Abstract Co Inc
Phone: 816-425-3523
1414 Main St PO Box 410   **Fax:** 816-425-6698
Bethany MO 64424
Local Retrieval Area: MO-Harrison.

Normal turnaround time: varied depending on project. Credit accounts are accepted.

They specialize in lien and real estate searches.

Harrison County Title & Guaranty
Phone: 712-644-2703
114 N 2nd Ave   **Fax:** 712-644-2557
Logan IA 51546
Local Retrieval Area: IA-Harrison.

Normal turnaround time: 1 week. Projects are generally billed by the number of records located. Credit accounts are accepted. Payment due upon receipt of billing.

Lawrence Harrison
Phone: 915-446-2317
PO Box 385 401 Main St   **Fax:** 915-446-3319
Junction TX 76849
Local Retrieval Area: TX-Kimble.

Normal turnaround time: 24-48 hours. Projects are generally billed by the hour. Fee basis varies by type of transaction. Credit accounts are accepted.

He does criminal and real estate work.

Harry W Hawley Inc
Phone: 607-746-3860
4 Court St   **Fax:** 607-746-3339
Delhi NY 13753
Local Retrieval Area: NY-Delaware.

Normal turnaround time: 3-10 days. Fee basis will vary by type of project. Credit accounts are accepted. Personal checks and/or cash is accepted. Credit accounts are not accepted.

Correspondent relationships: Otesgo, Scoharie and Chenango Counties.

⌂ Harvey's Research
Phone: 502-378-6452
245 Johnny Harvey Rd   **Fax:** 502-384-2116
Breeding KY 42715
Local Retrieval Area: KY-Adair, Cumberland, Metcalfe.

Normal turnaround time: same day to 3 days. Fee basis will vary by the type of project. The first project may require a prepayment.

She has extensive experience as a deputy clerk at the Circuit and District Court levels.

Haskell Abstract & Title Co
Phone: 817-864-2604
502 S 1st St   **Fax:** 817-864-2840
Haskell TX 79521
Local Retrieval Area: TX-Haskell.

Normal turnaround time: 1-2 days. Fee basis will vary by the type of project. The first project may require a prepayment.

Haskell County Abstract and Title

Phone: 316-675-2322
Fax: 316-675-2322

109 S Inman
Sublette KS 67877

Local Retrieval Area: KS-Haskell.

Normal turnaround time: 2 days. Projects are generally billed by the hour. Credit accounts are accepted.

They specialize in title insurance.

Renee Hastings

Phone: 803-637-5304
Fax: 803-637-6066

PO Box 561
Edgefield SC 29824

Local Retrieval Area: SC-Edgefield.

Normal turnaround time: 1 week. Charges are varied depending on type of search. Credit accounts are accepted.

Attorney John A Hatcher

Phone: 601-728-9444
Fax: 601-728-9440

101 W College St
Booneville MS 38829

Local Retrieval and SOP Area: MS-Alcorn, Itawamba, Lee, Prentiss, Tippah, Tishomingo, Union.

Normal turnaround time: 1-2 days. Projects are generally billed by the hour. The first project may require a prepayment.

He is an attorney in general practice.

Hawkins and Campbell Inc

Phone: 602-254-6147
Fax: 602-271-4517

800 N 4th St
Phoenix AZ 85004

Local Retrieval and SOP Area: AZ-Maricopa.

Normal turnaround time: 24 hours. Projects are generally billed by the hour. The first project may require a prepayment.

Correspondent relationships: all of Arizona.

Hawkins and Campbell Tucson

Phone: 520-628-9737
Fax: 520-624-9965

177 N Chruch Ave
Tucson AZ 85701

Local Retrieval and SOP Area: AZ-Pima.

Normal turnaround time: 24 hours. Projects are generally billed by the hour. Credit accounts are accepted.

Correspondent relationships: all of Arizona.

M M Hawley

Phone: 509-547-6207

PO Box 2247
Pasco WA 99301

Local Retrieval Area: WA-Benton, Franklin.

Normal turnaround time: 2 days. Fee basis will vary by the type of search. Credit accounts are accepted.

Hawthorne & Hawthorne PC

Phone: 804-676-3275
Fax: 804-676-2286

PO Box 603 110 S Broad St
Kenbridge VA 23944

Local Retrieval Area: VA-Brunswick, Charlotte, Lunenburg, Mecklenburg, Prince Edward.

Normal turnaround time: 1-5 days. Projects are generally billed by the hour. Credit accounts are accepted.

They specialize in real estate and commercial searches.

Brenette Haynes

Phone: 601-843-2071

114 Belvedere Ct
Cleveland MS 38732

Local Retrieval Area: MS-Adams, Amite, Bolivar, Franklin, Jefferson.

Normal turnaround time: 1-2 days. Projects are generally billed by the number of names searched. Projects require prepayment.

Brenette specializes in the Cleveland courts. A FAX number is available upon request.

Leta Jo Haynie

Phone: 817-684-1351

Box 322
Crowell TX 79227-0322

Local Retrieval Area: TX-Foard.

Projects are generally billed by the hour. Credit accounts are accepted.

She is a genealogy expert.

Heartland Corporate Services

Phone: 800-327-8806
612-227-7575
Fax: 800-603-0266

200 Minnesota Bldg 46 E 4th St
St Paul MN 55101

Local Retrieval Area: MN-Anoka, Carver, Dakota, Hennepin, Ramsey, Scott, Washington, Wright.

Normal turnaround time: 24-72 hours. Projects are generally billed by the number of names searched. Credit accounts are accepted. Will invoice monthly.

Correspondent relationships: Minnesota, North Dakota, South Dakota and Wisconsin. They specialize in state level filings.

Heartland Information Services

Phone: 800-967-1882
612-371-9255
Fax: 800-695-9531
612-371-9262

PO Box 2918
Minneapolis MN 55402

Local Retrieval Area: MN-Anoka, Carver, Hennepin, Ramsey, Scott, Sherburne, St. Louis, Washington.

Normal turnaround time: 24-72 hours. Projects are generally billed by the number of names searched. Credit accounts are accepted. Credit cards are accepted. Terms are net 15 days.

Correspondent relationships: nationwide. They are a licensed and bonded private investigative agency.

Heartland Investigations

Phone: 618-687-4900
Fax: 618-687-4805

PO Box 1096
Murphysboro IL 62966

Local Retrieval and SOP Area: IL-Franklin, Jackson, Jefferson, Massac, Randolph, Saline, Union, Wayne, White, Williamson.

Normal turnaround time: 48 hours. Projects are generally billed by the hour. The first project may require a prepayment.

Correspondent relationships: Southeast Missouri and Western Kentucky. They are a full service private detective agency specializing in fire cause/origin investigations, workers' compensation and personal injury.

Heartland Title and Abstract Co

Phone: 320-253-8860
Fax: 320-253-5606

18 S 15th Ave
St Cloud MN 56301

Local Retrieval Area: MN-Benton, Sherburne, Stearns.

Normal turnaround time: 10 days. Fee basis will vary by type of project. Projects require prepayment. Credit cards are accepted. They will also invoice.

They specialize in title insurance and real estate closings.

Heartland Title Company
Phone: 915-646-0509
Fax: 915-643-3322
404 N Fisk
Brownwood TX 76801
Local Retrieval Area: TX-Brown.

Normal turnaround time: 3 days. Projects are generally billed by the number of names searched. The first project may require a prepayment.

Their searches are made by attorneys with many years of experience.

Hebert Land Services
Phone: 918-647-9524
Fax: 918-647-9524
PO Box 772
Poteau OK 74953
Local Retrieval Area: AR-Crawford, Franklin, Logan, Pope, Scott, Sebastian, Yell; OK-Haskell, Latimer, Le Flore, Pittsburg, Sequoyah.

Normal turnaround time: 1-2 days. Fee basis is determined "per hour/day". Credit accounts are accepted.

Correspondent relationships: nationwide. They specialize in oil and gas.

Held Abstract Co Inc
Phone: 317-762-2457
Fax: 317-762-2458
10 Railroad St
Williamsport IN 47993-0068
Local Retrieval Area: IN-Warren.

Normal turnaround time: 2 weeks. Fee basis will vary by type of project. Projects require prepayment.

Helena Abstract & Title Co
Phone: 406-442-5080
Fax: 406-442-6179
PO Box 853 6th & Fuller
Helena MT 59624
Local Retrieval Area: MT-Lewis and Clark.

Normal turnaround time: 2-5 days. Fee basis varies by type of transaction. Projects require prepayment.

They specialize in real estate searches.

Helping Hand Services
Phone: 318-463-2528
Fax: 318-463-2528
Hayes Rd
DeRidder LA 70634
Local Retrieval Area: LA-Allen Parish, Beauregard Parish, Calcasieu Parish, Sabine Parish, Vernon Parish.

Normal turnaround time: 6-48 hours. Projects are generally billed by the number of names searched. Credit accounts are accepted.

The specialize in persons using similar name spelling searches.

Hempstead County Abstract & Title
Phone: 501-777-2351
Fax: 501-777-6033
401 S Washington
Hope AR 71801
Local Retrieval Area: AR-Hempstead.

Normal turnaround time: 1 week. Projects are generally billed by the number of records located. Credit accounts are accepted. Credit accounts not accepted.

They specialize in title insurance, land titles and abstracts.

🏛 Barbara K Henritze
Phone: 303-499-3750
825 Waite Dr
Boulder CO 80303-2729
Local Retrieval Area: CO-Adams, Arapahoe, Boulder, Denver, Jefferson.

Normal turnaround time: 3 days. Projects are generally billed by the hour. The first project may require a prepayment.

Henry County Abstract Co
Phone: 319-385-9017
Fax: 319-385-9017
300 S Adams St
Mt Pleasant IA 52641
Local Retrieval Area: IA-Henry.

Normal turnaround time: 2-3 days. Fee basis will vary by the type of project. Credit accounts are accepted.

Henry County Abstract Co
Phone: 317-529-0302
Fax: 317-529-5259
1111 Broad St
New Castle IN 47362
Local Retrieval Area: IN-Henry.

Normal turnaround time: 2-5 days. Projects are generally billed by the number of names searched or records located. Credit accounts are accepted.

Henry County Abstract Co
Phone: 800-748-7985
816-885-6168
Fax: 816-885-3945
101 N Main St
Clinton MO 64735
Local Retrieval Area: MO-Henry.

Normal turnaround time: 2-5 days. Fee basis will vary by the type of project. Credit accounts are accepted.

They specialize in title searches.

Anna Marie Henson
Phone: 573-324-2531
Rt 3 Box 363
Bowling Green MO 63334
Local Retrieval Area: MO-Pike.

Normal turnaround time: 2-3 weeks. Projects are generally billed by the hour. Projects require prepayment.

Heritage Title Inc
Phone: 402-463-6208
Fax: 402-463-6203
PO Box 183 2727 W 2nd St #107
Hastings NE 68902-0183
Local Retrieval Area: NE-Adams.

Normal turnaround time: 48 hours. Projects are generally billed by the hour. Credit accounts are accepted.

They specialize in title insurance searches.

Gilbert S Hetrich
Phone: 908-286-9233
Fax: 609-698-5434
PO Box 743
Manahawkin NJ 08050
Local Retrieval Area: NJ-Monmouth, Ocean.

Normal turnaround time: varied depending on project. Fee basis will vary by the type of project. The first project may require a prepayment.

He has more than 22 years experience in real estate record searches.

Hickman Land Title
Phone: 800-365-7760
801-752-0582
Fax: 801-752-0584
PO Box 386
Logan UT 84323-0386
Local Retrieval Area: UT-Cache, Rich.

Normal turnaround time: 1-2 days. Projects are generally billed by the hour. Credit accounts are accepted.

Attorney John O Hicks III
Phone: 502-273-5749
PO Box 64 105 Main St
Calhoun KY 42327
Local Retrieval Area: KY-Daviess, McLean, Muhlenberg.

Normal turnaround time: 2 days for McLean County and up to 1 week for Muhlenberg and Daviess counties. Fee basis varies by type of transaction. The first project may require a prepayment.

⌂ Hicks Information

PO Box 942
Lawrence KS 66044

Phone: 913-749-1898
Fax: 913-749-7557

Local Retrieval and SOP Area: KS-Douglas, Franklin, Jefferson, Leavenworth, Osage.

Normal turnaround time: 24-72 hours. Expedited service available. Projects are generally billed by the number of names searched. Projects require prepayment.

Correspondent relationships: Johnson, Wyandotte, Shawnee, KS counties and Jackson, Clay, MO counties. They specialize in rent-screening, skip-tracing, general research and document retrieval. They daily update their own specialized regional/local databases. The principal is a former librarian and genealogist.

Hidalgo County Abstract

PO Box 188
Lordsburg NM 88045

Phone: 505-542-9181
Fax: 505-542-9190

Local Retrieval Area: NM-Hidalgo.

Normal turnaround time: 2 days. Projects are generally billed by the number of names searched. Credit accounts are accepted. A deposit is required.

They specialize in land searches.

Hiett Title Co

119 N Grand Ave
Houston MO 65689

Phone: 417-967-3660

Local Retrieval Area: MO-Texas, Wright.

Normal turnaround time: 1 week. Projects are generally billed by the hour. The first project may require a prepayment. Type of payment may vary depending on project.

They specialize in title insurance.

Hiett Title Co

403 W 3rd
Mountain Grove MO 65711

Phone: 417-926-6163
Fax: 417-926-6166

Local Retrieval Area: MO-Douglas, Wright.

Normal turnaround time: 1-2 weeks. Projects are generally billed by the number of names searched. The first project may require a prepayment.

They specialize in real estate records, chains of title and encumbrances.

High-Tech Investigations Inc

1180 S Powerline Rd Suite 201
Pompano Beach FL 33069-4340

Phone: 888-881-7441
954-977-0771
Fax: 954-977-3730

Local Retrieval Area: FL-Broward, Dade, Palm Beach.

Normal turnaround time: 1-5 day. Expedited service available. Projects are generally billed by the number of names searched. Hand searches charged by the hour. Credit accounts are accepted.

Correspondent relationships: nationwide. They have resident agents throughout Florida with access to all counties. They are a full service investigation agency specializing in locates, investigations and surveillance. Nationwide on-line searches are available.

Highlands Abstract and Title Co

126 E Center Ave
Sebring FL 33870

Phone: 941-385-0340
Fax: 941-385-5802

Local Retrieval Area: FL-Highlands.

Normal turnaround time: 7-10 working days. Projects are generally billed by the number of names searched. The first project may require a prepayment.

They specialize in title insurance and abstract updates.

Hilkman Sumners Gozr and Gore

PO Drawer 730 104 N Central Ave
New Albany MS 38652

Phone: 601-534-6326
Fax: 601-534-5205

Local Retrieval Area: MS-Lee, Pontotoc, Tippah, Union.

Normal turnaround time: 1-2 days in Union county, up to 1 week in others. Fee basis varies by type of transaction. The first project may require a prepayment.

Hill County Title Co

PO Box 1688 309 3rd St
Havre MT 59501

Phone: 406-265-7624
Fax: 406-265-8385

Local Retrieval Area: MT-Hill.

Normal turnaround time: 2-3 days. Projects are generally billed by the hour. Credit accounts are accepted.

Hill-N-Dale Abstractors Inc

20 Scotchtown Ave
Goshen NY 10924

Phone: 914-294-5110
Fax: 914-294-9581

Local Retrieval Area: NY-Orange, Sullivan, Ulster.

Normal turnaround time: 2-3 days. Projects are generally billed by the number of names searched. Credit accounts are accepted.

They specialize in foreclosure searches, last owner searches, full searches and title insurance.

Hillam Abstracting & Insurance

PO Box 875
Brigham City UT 84302

Phone: 801-723-5207
Fax: 801-723-5208

Local Retrieval Area: UT-Box Elder, Cache.

Normal turnaround time: 1 day. Fee basis will vary by the type of project. The first project may require a prepayment.

They specialize in real estate.

Hillsdale Title Company

22 N Howell
Hillsdale MI 49242

Phone: 517-437-7345
Fax: 517-439-1659

Local Retrieval Area: MI-Hillsdale.

Normal turnaround time: up to 1 weeks. Fee basis will vary by type of project. Credit accounts are accepted.

They specialize in real estate and title research.

Hines & Hines Lawyers

507 Chief St
Benkelman NE 69021-0607

Phone: 308-423-2611
Fax: 308-423-2628

Local Retrieval Area: NE-Chase, Dundy, Hitchcock, Red Willow.

Normal turnaround time: 2 days. Projects are generally billed by the hour. Credit accounts are accepted. They accept personal checks.

Correspondent relationships: Perkins, Hayes and Keith Counties. They specialize in title insurance, real estate and probate.

Hinsdale County Title Co

PO Box 69
Lake City CO 81235

Phone: 303-944-2614
Fax: 303-944-2277

Local Retrieval Area: CO-Hinsdale.

Normal turnaround time: 3-5 days. Projects are generally billed by the hour. The first project may require a prepayment.

They specialize in real estate.

Hirschfeld Law Office

Phone: 419-586-2323
Fax: 419-586-2154

116 E Market St
Celina OH 45822

Local Retrieval Area: OH-Mercer.

Normal turnaround time: 3 days. Fee basis will vary by type of project. The first project may require a prepayment.

They specialize in real estate record searches.

Hixson Enterprises

Phone: 757-898-9865
Fax: 757-898-9865

800 Dandy Loop Rd
Yorktown VA 23692

Local Retrieval Area: VA-Charles City, Gloucester, James City, King and Queen, Mathews, City of Williamsburg, York.

Normal turnaround time: 2 days. Projects are generally billed by the number of names searched. Charges by the hour are for 60 year searches. Credit accounts are accepted. Payment due upon presentation of statement.

Correspondent relationships: Newport News, Hampton, Norfolk, Isle of Wight and Smithfield, VA counties. They specialize in old land records in York County and do some genealogy research.

Hodgeman County Abstract & Title

Phone: 316-357-8328
Fax: 316-357-6221

112 E Bramley
Jetmore KS 67854

Local Retrieval Area: KS-Hodgeman.

Normal turnaround time: 1-2 days. Fee basis varies by type of transaction. Credit accounts are accepted.

Hogan Information Services

Phone: 405-278-6954
Fax: 405-552-6169

PO Box 26300
Oklahoma City OK 73126

Local Retrieval Area: Counties in Many States.

Normal turnaround time: 2-5 days. Expedited service available. Online computer ordering is also available. Projects are generally billed by the number of names searched. The first project may require a prepayment.

Correspondent relationships: nationwide.

Hogan Land Title Co

Phone: 417-869-6319

921 Boonville St
Springfield MO 65802

Local Retrieval Area: MO-Christian, Dallas, Greene, Stone, Taney.

Normal turnaround time: 3 days. Fee basis varies by type of transaction. Credit accounts are accepted.

David M Holcomb

Phone: 770-388-3712
Fax: 770-476-1719

608 Harmony Grove Rd
Ball Ground GA 30107

Local Retrieval and SOP Area: GA-Bartow, Cherokee, Clayton, Cobb, De Kalb, Douglas, Forsyth, Fulton, Gwinnett, Pickens.

Normal turnaround time: 1 day or same day. Projects are generally billed by the number of names searched. Credit accounts are accepted.

They specialize in UCC, Federal and State tax liens and judgment searches. They are flexible with quick turnaround times and also have access to Federal Archives.

Holden Abstract Co

Phone: 816-726-3417
Fax: 816-726-3487

202 W Wood St
Albany MO 64402

Local Retrieval Area: MO-Gentry.

Normal turnaround time: varied depending on project. Fee basis is per document. Credit accounts are accepted.

They specialize in title searches, abstracts and title insurance.

Hollenbeck Title Co

Phone: 573-422-3633
Fax: 573-422-6190

PO Box 215
Vienna MO 65582

Local Retrieval Area: MO-Maries.

Normal turnaround time: 48 hours. Projects are generally billed by the number of names searched or records located. The first project may require a prepayment.

Hollingsworth Court Reporting

Phone: 504-769-3386
Fax: 504-769-1814

10761 Perkins Rd Suite A
Baton Rouge LA 70810

Local Retrieval Area: All counties in AL, AR, AZ, FL, LA, MS and TN; GA-37 Counties.

Normal turnaround time: 5 days for major metropolitan areas and 15 days for outlying locations. Online computer ordering is also available. Projects are generally billed by the number of names searched. The first project may require a prepayment.

They specialize in derogatory information including tax liens, judgments and bankruptcies. An on-line database for ordering searches is available.

Home Abstract & Title Co

Phone: 601-863-4783
Fax: 601-863-4783

2310 19th St
Gulfport MS 39501

Local Retrieval Area: MS-Hancock, Harrison, Jackson.

Normal turnaround time: 1-2 days. Projects are generally billed by the hour. Projects require prepayment.

Home Abstract Co

Phone: 605-685-6558
Fax: 605-685-6311

PO Box 520
Martin SD 57551

Local Retrieval Area: SD-Bennett.

Normal turnaround time: 2 weeks. Projects are generally billed by the hour. Projects require prepayment.

Home Title

Phone: 303-758-4300
Fax: 303-758-4317

2015 S Pontiac Way Suite 100
Denver CO 80224

Local Retrieval and SOP Area: CO-13 Counties.

Normal turnaround time: 7 days. No project billing information was given. Credit accounts are accepted. Retainer and fee agreement required prior to searches.

They specialize in title underwriting and legal services.

Homestead Title

Phone: 810-227-0140
Fax: 810-227-0145

10327 E Grand River
Brighton MI 48116

Local Retrieval Area: MI-Genesee, Lapeer, Livingston, Oakland, Shiawassee, Washtenaw.

Normal turnaround time: 4-5 days. Fee basis is per search. The first project may require a prepayment.

They specialize in real estate matters.

⌂ Honolulu Information Service

Phone: 808-732-8778
Fax: 808-732-8725

3435 Waialae Ave, Suite 106 PO Box 10447
Honolulu HI 96816

Local Retrieval and SOP Area: HI-Hawaii, Honolulu, Kauai, Maui.

Normal turnaround time: 48 hours. Expedited service available. Projects are generally billed by the number of names searched or records located. The first project may require a prepayment. Terms are net 10 days.

Correspondent relationships: nationwide. They specialize in obtaining government documents, using Hawaii's FOIA if necessary, accessing on-line statewide real estate records and researching all aspects of Hawaii.

Hood & Whalen

Phone: 606-234-4321
Fax: 606-234-4321

43 E Pike St
Cynthiana KY 41031

Local Retrieval Area: KY-Harrison.

Normal turnaround time: 3-4 days. Projects are generally billed by the hour. The first project may require a prepayment.

They are a general practice law firm.

Hooks Title & Abstract

Phone: 409-246-3447
Fax: 409-246-3559

245 Crocker
Kountzer TX 77625

Local Retrieval Area: TX-Hardin.

Normal turnaround time: 2-5 days. Fees vary by project. Credit accounts are accepted.

They have an in-house title plant.

Hoover Professional Investigative

Phone: 206-272-5090

3202 E "M"
Tacoma WA 98404-4027

Local Retrieval and SOP Area: WA-King, Kitsap, Mason, Pierce, Snohomish.

Normal turnaround time: 1-7 days. Projects are generally billed by the hour. The first project may require a prepayment.

They specialize in all phases of investigations.

Horger Barnwell & Reid

Phone: 803-531-3000
Fax: 803-531-3030

PO Drawer 329 1459 Amelia St
Orangeburg SC 29116

Local Retrieval Area: SC-Bamberg, Calhoun, Dorchester, Orangeburg.

Normal turnaround time: 2-3 days. Projects are generally billed by the hour. The first project may require a prepayment.

Correspondent relationships: the rest of the state.

⌂ Hornor-Morris Abstract Co

Phone: 501-338-8306
Fax: 501-338-8307

PO Box 408
Helena AR 72342-0408

Local Retrieval Area: AR-Phillips.

Normal turnaround time: 3-5 days. Projects are generally billed by the hour. The first project may require a prepayment.

Hornthal Riley Ellis & Maland

Phone: 919-335-0871
Fax: 919-335-4223

PO Box 220 301 E Main St (27909)
Elizabeth City NC 27907-0220

Local Retrieval Area: NC-Camden, Chowan, Dare, Gates, Hertford, Pasquotank, Perquimans, Tyrrell, Washington.

Normal turnaround time: 48 hours. Projects are generally billed by the hour. Fee basis varies by type of transaction. Credit accounts are accepted.

They are a full service law firm. They specialize in litigation, real estate, corporate practice and criminal practice.

⌂ Horvath Enterprises

Phone: 320-983-3253
Fax: 320-983-2572

105 Park Ave PO Box 52
Milaca MN 56353

Local Retrieval Area: MN-Becker, Benton, Mille Lacs, Morrison, Stearns.

Normal turnaround time: 1-2 days. Projects are generally billed by the number of names searched. Credit accounts are accepted. Will bill monthly.

Correspondent relationships: Anoka, Hennepin, MN counties.

Hot Spring County Title Services

Phone: 501-332-3770
Fax: 501-337-0729

PO Box 622
Malvern AR 72104

Local Retrieval Area: AR-Garland, Grant, Hot Spring.

Normal turnaround time: 3 days. Fee basis will vary by the type of project. Credit accounts are accepted.

They specialize in real estate records.

Houghton Lake Title & Escrow Co

Phone: 517-366-5551
Fax: 517-366-9702

3225 W Houghton Lake Dr
Prudenville MI 48651

Local Retrieval Area: MI-Clare, Crawford, Gladwin, Missaukee, Ogemaw, Roscommon.

Normal turnaround time: 1 day to 1 week. Fee basis is by rate sheet or per hour. Credit accounts are accepted.

They specialize in abstracting.

⌂ Houston Court Services Inc

Phone: 800-593-2023
713-523-6111
Fax: 713-523-0059

3400 Montrose Blvd Suite 300
Houston TX 77006-4332

Local Retrieval and SOP Area: TX-Brazoria, Brazos, Fort Bend, Harris, Montgomery.

Normal turnaround time: 48-72 hours. Expedited service available. Projects are generally billed by the number of names searched. The first project may require a prepayment. Payment due upon receipt.

Correspondent relationships: the southern states. They specialize in servicing legal documents and court record retrieval on a nationwide basis.

Howard County Abstract & Title Co

Phone: 319-547-4944

219 N Elm St
Cresco IA 52136

Local Retrieval Area: IA-Howard.

Normal turnaround time: 1-2 days. Projects are generally billed by the number of names searched. The first project may require a prepayment.

HR Plus

Phone: 800-332-7587
2902 Evergreen Pky Suite 100   303-670-9877
Evergreen CO 80439   **Fax:** 303-670-8906

Local Retrieval Area: CO-Adams, Arapahoe, Boulder, Denver, El Paso, Jefferson, Larimer.

Normal turnaround time: 1-2 days. Expedited service available. Projects are generally billed by the number of names searched. Credit accounts are accepted. Projects are billed monthly, net 10 days.

Correspondent relationships: nationwide. They specialize in criminal record retrieval.

Hubbard-Kavanaugh Abstract

Phone: 573-378-4411
106 S Fisher St   **Fax:** 573-378-6385
Versailles MO 65084

Local Retrieval Area: MO-Morgan.

Normal turnaround time: 24 hours. Projects are generally billed by the number of records located. Credit accounts are accepted.

They specialize in land titles.

Hubly Adj Inc

Phone: 815-877-3053
2917 N Main St   **Fax:** 815-877-3361
Rockford IL 61103

Local Retrieval and SOP Area: IL-Boone, Stephenson, Winnebago.

Normal turnaround time: 48 hours for criminal and taxes, all others average up to 5 days. Projects are generally billed by the number of names searched. Credit accounts are accepted.

They specialize in criminal record searches.

Huddleston & Huddleston

Phone: 606-567-2818
PO Box 807 309 W Main St   **Fax:** 606-567-2404
Warsaw KY 41095

Local Retrieval Area: KY-Gallatin.

Normal turnaround time: 2-3 days. Projects are generally billed by the hour. Credit accounts are accepted.

He is the prosecuting attorney for the county.

Hudson Research Group Inc

Phone: 914-747-1622
401 Columbus Ave   **Fax:** 914-747-4750
Valhalla NY 10595

Local Retrieval Area: NY-Sullivan, Westchester.

Normal turnaround time: 24-48 hours. Projects are generally billed by the number of names searched. The first project may require a prepayment.

They specialize in UCC, federal and state tax lien, judgment, real property, pending litigation, closed litigation, criminal case searches, UCC filings, land record filings and copying dockets and case files.

Huffmaster Associates Inc

Phone: 800-446-1515
1300 Combermere   810-588-1600
Troy MI 48083   **Fax:** 810-597-7075

Local Retrieval and SOP Area: MI-Genesee, Lapeer, Livingston, Macomb, Monroe, Oakland, St. Clair, Washtenaw, Wayne.

Normal turnaround time: 1 week. Projects are generally billed by the number of names searched. The first project may require a prepayment. Will take a company purchase order number.

They specialize in vehicle/asset tracking, locates, missing persons, business crimes, undercover investigations, legal support services, pre-employment and workers' compensation searches.

Hughes/AMS Attorney Service

Phone: 619-683-2000
PO Box 82125   **Fax:** 619-220-5676
San Diego CA 92138-2125

Local Retrieval and SOP Area: CA-Imperial, San Diego.

Normal turnaround time: up to 24 hours. Rush service is also available. Projects are generally billed by the hour. Driving time is included in fees. The first project may require a prepayment.

Correspondent relationships: Los Angeles, Orange, Riverside, San Bernardino counties. They specialize in messenger service, service of process, public record research and retrieval, private investigations, court filings and photocopying.

Hunter & Oelke

Phone: 806-249-5632
PO Box 792   **Fax:** 806-249-2863
Dalhart TX 79022

Local Retrieval Area: TX-Dallam, Hartley.

Normal turnaround time: 3-4 days. Projects are generally billed by the hour. The first project may require a prepayment.

William Hurley

Phone: 607-734-1743
917 Davis St   **Fax:** 607-734-1743
Elmira NY 14901

Local Retrieval Area: NY-Chemung, Schuyler, Steuben, Tioga, Tompkins, Yates; PA-Bradford, Tioga.

Normal turnaround time: 2-5 days. Projects are generally billed by the number of names searched or records located. Credit accounts are accepted. Terms are net 30 days.

Correspondent relationships: Washington, DC.

Huron Shores Abstract & Title

Phone: 517-734-3344
206 S 3rd Street   **Fax:** 517-734-4920
Rogers City MI 49779

Local Retrieval Area: MI-Alpena, Presque Isle.

Normal turnaround time: 4 days. Fee basis will vary by the type of project. Projects require prepayment.

They specialize in title insurance, oil, gas and mineral research.

Huron Title Co

Phone: 313-987-2141
330 Michigan St   **Fax:** 313-987-1317
Port Huron MI 48060

Local Retrieval Area: MI-St. Clair.

Normal turnaround time: 5 days. Fee basis will vary by type of project. The first project may require a prepayment.

They specialize in real estate and title insurance.

Huron Title Co

Phone: 605-352-6157
PO Box 563   **Fax:** 605-352-7354
Huron SD 57350

Local Retrieval Area: SD-Beadle.

Normal turnaround time: 5-10 days. Fee basis will vary by the type of project. Credit accounts are accepted. Payment due upon completion of order.

They specialize in land title searches.

Hutchinson Title Co

Phone: 316-669-8289
14 W 4th Ave   **Fax:** 316-669-8280
Hutchinson KS 67501-4801

Local Retrieval Area: KS-Harvey, McPherson, Reno.

Normal turnaround time: 5 days. Fee basis varies by type of transaction. The first project may require a prepayment.

Hylind Information Services
307 Dolphin St Suite #1A
Baltimore MD 21217

Phone: 888-449-5463
410-225-0014
Fax: 410-225-0016

Local Retrieval Area: MD-Anne Arundel, Baltimore, City of Baltimore, Howard.

Normal turnaround time: 1-2 days. Projects are generally billed by the number of names searched. Fees are per index searched. The first project may require a prepayment. Terms are net 30 days.

Correspondent relationships: nationwide. The specialize in UCC, corporate and real estate related searches and filing, plus online capability, skip tracing, asset searches and motor vehicle records, all on a national basis.

I

I Information Services
1427 W Douglas
Wichita KS 60213

Phone: 800-658-1688
316-262-1721
Fax: 316-262-3189

Local Retrieval and SOP Area: KS-Butler, Harvey, Kingman, Reno, Sedgwick, Sumner.

Normal turnaround time: 48 hours. Fees are determined case-by-case. The first project may require a prepayment. Credit cards are accepted.

Correspondent relationships: statewide. They specialize in trial preparation, lawyer support, criminal and license checks and asset investigations.

I.G.B. Associates Inc
618 Tropical Breeze Way
Tampa FL 33602

Phone: 813-226-8810
Fax: 813-226-8710

Local Retrieval Area: FL-Hillsborough, Pinellas.

Normal turnaround time: 24-48 hours. Projects are generally billed by the number of names searched. Bankruptcy billed by number of files. Federal, probate and county by the hour. The first project may require a prepayment. Terms are net 10 days.

Correspondent relationships: nationwide. They specialize in bankruptcy, US Federal courts and county courts. They also do comprehensive asset searches.

I.P.S. Inc
7447 Harwin Suite 204
Houston TX 77036

Phone: 713-783-9996
Fax: 713-783-9889

Local Retrieval Area: TX-Harris, Kleberg, Montgomery.

Normal turnaround time: 24-48 hours. Projects are generally billed by the number of names searched. Credit accounts are accepted. Terms are net 30 days, with approved credit.

They specialize in pre-employment screening and third party administrator for drug testing on nationwide level.

ICDI Inc
3826 Edgewater Dr
Orlando FL 32804

Phone: 407-299-6300
Fax: 407-290-2032

Local Retrieval Area: FL-Brevard, Orange, Seminole, Volusia.

Projects are generally billed by the number of names searched. The first project may require a prepayment. Payment due on receipt.

ID-Check Records
4645 Van Nuys Blvd Suite 201
Sherman Oaks CA 91403

Phone: 800-340-4473
818-783-9728
Fax: 818-783-8410

Local Retrieval Area: CA-Imperial, Los Angeles, Orange, San Bernardino, San Diego, Ventura.

Normal turnaround time: 24-48 hours. Projects are generally billed by the number of names searched. Credit accounts are accepted. Terms are net 15 days.

Correspondent relationships: Nevada.

Ida County Abstract Co
217 Main St
Ida Grove IA 51445

Phone: 712-364-2287

Local Retrieval Area: IA-Ida.

Normal turnaround time: 2-3 days. Fee basis will vary by the type of project. Credit accounts are accepted.

Idaho Title & Trust Co
260 W Grand PO Box 802
Arco ID 83213

Phone: 208-527-8517
Fax: 208-527-3930

Local Retrieval Area: ID-Butte.

Fees vary by project..dd. Credit accounts are accepted.

Idealogic
50 Richmond St East Suite 100
Toronto, Ontario, Canada M5C 1N7

Phone: 800-265-0361
416-863-9747
Fax: 800-890-6971
416-367-3405

Local Retrieval and SOP Area: Canada-Ontario.

Normal turnaround time: same or next day. Projects are generally billed by the number of names searched. The first project may require a prepayment. Credit cards are accepted.

Correspondent relationships: all provinces in Canada. They specialize in Canadian corporate information, criminal history, motor vehicle, PPSA and trademark work.

ILS Abstract
991 N Wyoming St
Hazleton PA 18201

Phone: 717-454-5436
Fax: 717-454-5436

Local Retrieval and SOP Area: PA-Carbon, Columbia, Luzerne, Schuylkill.

Normal turnaround time: 4-7 days. Projects are generally billed by the number of names searched or records located. The first project may require a prepayment.

They specialize in real estate searches, 60 year searches, current owner searches and prepare deeds.

Impact Invesigations
2120 W Ina Rd Suite 103
Tucson AZ 85741

Phone: 800-447-3174
520-297-7770
Fax: 520-297-4886

Local Retrieval and SOP Area: AZ-Cochise, Maricopa, Pinal.

Normal turnaround time: depends on project. Online computer ordering is also available. Projects are generally billed by the hour. Projects require prepayment. Credit cards are accepted.

Correspondent relationships: nationwide. They specialize in workers' compensation, insurance fraud, interrogations, retail surveillance, pre-employment screening, locates, civil and criminal investigations and sex crimes.

▥ Incognito Services

Phone: 800-782-7672
415-692-0431
Fax: 415-692-8647

801 Mahler Rd Suite 215
Burlingame CA 94010-1611

Local Retrieval and SOP Area: CA-San Francisco, San Mateo.

Normal turnaround time: 48 hours. Can be done in 24 hours for a rush service fee. Projects are generally billed by the hour. They add mileage and copy costs. The first project may require a prepayment. Credit cards are accepted.

Correspondent relationships: California, West Coast and International. They specialize in investigations, legal process serving, electronic countermeasures equipment and service, including covert video equipment, installations and rentals. They also go to the Federal Archives in San Bruno, CA.

Incorporating Services Ltd

Phone: 800-346-4646
302-678-0855
Fax: 302-678-3150

15 E North St
Dover DE 19903

Local Retrieval Area: DE-Kent, New Castle, Sussex.

Normal turnaround time: 1-5 working days. Projects are generally billed by the number of names searched or records located. The first project may require a prepayment. Credit cards are accepted. Personal checks, certified checks, money orders or cash are accepted.

Correspondent relationships: nationwide and Canada.

Independence County Abstract Co

Phone: 501-793-3333
Fax: 501-793-3343

150 S Broad St
Batesville AR 72501

Local Retrieval Area: AR-Independence.

Normal turnaround time: 5-10 days. Expedited service available. Projects are generally billed by the hour. A minimum charge also applies. Credit accounts are accepted.

They specialize in real estate.

▥ Independent Abstract & Title

Phone: 305-294-5105
Fax: 305-294-5354

600 Whitehead St
Key West FL 33040

Local Retrieval Area: FL-Monroe.

Normal turnaround time: 2 weeks. They charge a flat rate per project. The first project may require a prepayment.

They specialize in title insurance.

Independent Abstracting Service

Phone: 612-789-8440
Fax: 612-789-9294

4111 Central Ave NE
Columbia Heights MN 55421

Local Retrieval Area: MN-11 Counties.

Normal turnaround time: 3-5 days. Fee basis will vary by type of project. Projects require prepayment.

▥ Independent Research Assoc

Phone: 407-277-0076
Fax: 407-277-6786

PO Box 677988 746 Dunhill Dr (32825)
Orlando FL 32867-7988

Local Retrieval Area: FL-Brevard, Orange, Osceola, Seminole, Volusia.

Normal turnaround time: 24 hours. Projects are generally billed by the number of names searched. Credit accounts are accepted.

▥ Independent Research Inc

Phone: 616-429-9873
Fax: 616-429-5693

4318 Hart Dr
St Joseph MI 49085

Local Retrieval Area: MI-15 Counties.

Normal turnaround time: 1 to 3 days. Expedited service available. Projects are generally billed by the number of names searched or records located. Credit accounts are accepted. Credit accounts are payable 30 days net.

Correspondent relationships: nationwide. They specialize in criminal searches and deed and mortgage (title) searches.

Infinity Information Network Inc

Phone: 614-261-1213
Fax: 614-268-3485

4516 Kenny Rd Suite 203
Columbus OH 43220

Local Retrieval Area: OH-All Counties.

Normal turnaround time: 1-3 business days. Projects are generally billed by the number of names searched. Credit accounts are accepted. Invoiced monthly.

Correspondent relationships: nationwide and Canada.

Infinity Infotrac

Phone: 216-291-9696
Fax: 216-291-9694

2635 Noble Rd 102 World Trade Services Bldg
Cleveland Heights OH 44121-2142

Local Retrieval Area: OH-Cuyahoga, Lake, Lorain, Medina, Portage, Summit.

Normal turnaround time: 4-48 hours. Fees are flat rate per project. Credit accounts are accepted. Credit accounts accepted.

▥ Info Quest Inc

Phone: 803-215-3463
Fax: 803-215-4065

PO Box 15521
Surfside Beach SC 29587

Local Retrieval Area: SC-Georgetown, Horry.

Normal turnaround time: 24-48 hours. Online computer ordering is also available. Projects are generally billed by the number of names searched or records located. The first project may require a prepayment. Credit cards are accepted.

They specialize in business research, records retrieval, pre-employment background checks, rental background checks and credit reports.

INFO/DATA

Phone: 800-847-2716
406-468-2716
Fax: 406-468-2716

79 Siebold Ln
Cascade MT 59421

Local Retrieval Area: MT-Cascade, Judith Basin, Lewis and Clark, Meagher, Pondera, Silver Bow, Teton, Toole.

Normal turnaround time: 24 hours to 3 days. Online computer ordering is also available. Projects are generally billed by the number of names searched. Credit accounts are accepted.

Correspondent relationships: the rest of MT, ID, MI and OK. They specialize in private investigation and public records.

▥ InfoCheck

Phone: 520-577-8987
Fax: 520-577-8987

7050 E Sunrise Dr Suite 16204
Tucson AZ 85750

Local Retrieval Area: AZ-Pima.

Normal turnaround time: 24-48 hours. Projects are generally billed by the number of names searched. Credit accounts are accepted.

They specialize in searching USSs, tax liens, judgments, criminal and civil suits as well as searches/document retrieval at District and Bankruptcy courts for Tucson.

Infoforum Inc

Phone: 800-484-1301

1149 E 15th St

718-258-2977

Brooklyn NY 11230-4815   **Fax:** 718-258-3076

Local Retrieval Area: NY-New York.

Normal turnaround time: 24 hours. Online computer ordering is also available. Projects are generally billed by the number of names searched or records located. The first project may require a prepayment.

Correspondent relationships: Kings, Staten Island, Queens, Manhattan, Bronx, Nassau, Westchester, NY counties. They specialize in bankruptcy, federal criminal/civil courts, State supreme courts, civil/criminal, vital records, drivers license, auto registsration, all state/city agencies, hospital records and workman's compensation.

InfoHawks

Phone: 415-666-3914

4644 Geary Blvd Suite 181   **Fax:** 415-221-4966

San Francisco CA 94118

Local Retrieval Area: CA-San Francisco.

Normal turnaround time: 1-5 business days. Online computer ordering is also available. Projects are generally billed by the number of records located. Projects require prepayment. Can pay by online check on website.

Correspondent relationships: nationwide and Canada. They specialize in general public records search and retrieval.

Infomation Retrieval Services

Phone: 302-337-0548

PO Box 268   **Fax:** 302-337-8730

Georgetown DE 19947

Local Retrieval Area: DE-Kent, New Castle, Sussex.

Normal turnaround time: 2-3 days. Projects are generally billed by the number of names searched. Fees vary by depth of search requested (standard search vs. pull and read entire file). Credit accounts are accepted.

Correspondent relationships: MD, PA and NJ. They specialize in complete in-depth criminal searches for attorneys and investigators with subject report and copies of relevant sections of records.

Infonet

Phone: 800-849-6207

6542 Avenida Del Paraiso

619-929-9794

Carlsbad CA 92009   **Fax:** 619-929-9796

Local Retrieval Area: CA-All Counties.

Normal turnaround time: 24-48 hours for criminal searches, 24-72 hours for civil searches. Projects are generally billed by the number of names searched or records located. Credit accounts are accepted. Credit cards are accepted. Projects are billed once a month by number of names searched. Net 15 days from date of invoice.

Correspondent relationships: nationwide.

Informa Alaska Inc

Phone: 907-563-4375

PO Box 190908   **Fax:** 907-345-0793

Anchorage AK 99519-0793

Local Retrieval Area: AK-Anchorage Borough.

Normal turnaround time: 48 hours. Projects are generally billed by the hour. The first project may require a prepayment.

Correspondent relationships: the rest of the state. They specialize in public record retrieval.

Information Direct

Phone: 800-700-0440

PO Box 2508

805-938-3222

Santa Maria CA 93457   **Fax:** 805-938-3225

Local Retrieval Area: CA-Los Angeles, Orange, Riverside, San Bernardino, San Diego, Santa Barbara, Ventura.

Normal turnaround time: 24-72 hours. Flat rate rush service available. 10AM (PST) next day by 4PM (PST) or customer doesn't pay rush fee. Online computer ordering is also available. Fees are flat rate. Volume pricing available. Credit accounts are accepted. Monthly billing, net 30 days.

Correspondent relationships: nationwide. They are a full service criminal and civil records research and retrieval firm. They specialize in providing record research to pre-employment/tenant screening organizations.

Information Highway Inc

Phone: 612-631-8131

PO Box 130002   **Fax:** 612-631-8131

St Paul MN 55113

Local Retrieval Area: MN-Anoka, Carver, Dakota, Hennepin, Nicollet, Ramsey, Scott, Sherburne, Washington, Wright.

Normal turnaround time: 24 hours. Online computer ordering is also available. Projects are generally billed by the number of names searched. The first project may require a prepayment.

Correspondent relationships: nationwide. They specialize in employment background checks, UCC/tax liens at all levels, motor vehicle records, real estate tax and encumberance search, digitizing microfilm and paper documentation.

Information Management Sys

Phone: 860-229-1119

PO Box 2924   **Fax:** 860-225-5524

New Britain CT 06050

Local Retrieval and SOP Area: CT-Fairfield, Hartford, Litchfield, Middlesex, New Haven, New London, Tolland, Windham.

Normal turnaround time: same day. Projects are generally billed by the number of names searched. Fees vary by project volume. Projects require prepayment. Credit cards are accepted.

Correspondent relationships: the Northeast region. They specialize in public and legal record retrieval and bank account locates. They also provide nationwide background investigation services.

Information Reporting Services

Phone: 612-870-8770

2101 Hennepin Ave Suite 201   **Fax:** 612-870-8765

Minneapolis MN 55405

Local Retrieval Area: MN-Anoka, Carver, Dakota, Goodhue, Hennepin, Ramsey, Scott, Washington, Winona, Wright.

Normal turnaround time: 24-48 hours. Projects are generally billed by the number of names searched. The first project may require a prepayment. Monthly billing available.

Correspondent relationships: nationwide. They specialize in background screening for corporations (pre-employment and corporate security) and for law firms. Search capabilities include entire State of MN.

Information Research

251 Florida St Suite 402
Baton Rouge LA 70801

Phone: 504-387-3878
Fax: 504-383-4507

Local Retrieval Area: LA-East Baton Rouge Parish, West Baton Rouge Parish.

Normal turnaround time: 4-5 days. Rush service is also available. Projects are generally billed by the hour. The first project may require a prepayment.

They provide on-line and library research, document delivery and background support for litigation and business development, and court records.

Information Retrieval Service

404 James Robertson Pkwy
Nashville TN 37219-1505

Phone: 615-255-1708

Local Retrieval Area: TN-Davidson.

Normal turnaround time: 2-24 hours. Online computer ordering is also available. Fee basis will vary by the type of project. The first project may require a prepayment.

They specialize in public records search, locate skips and assets.

Information Retrieval Services

110 E 8th St PO Box 863
Junction City KS 66441

Phone: 913-238-8753
Fax: 913-238-1460

Local Retrieval Area: KS-Geary.

Normal turnaround time: 24-48 hours. Projects are generally billed by the number of names searched or records located. The first project may require a prepayment. Accounts billed monthly.

Correspondent relationships: Riley, Dickenson, Saline, Lyon, Shawnee, Chase, Morris, Ottawa, Glen and other areas. They specializes in credit reports and screening services to landlords and employers in Geary and Riley counties. Document retrieval and searches are performed in a number of KS counties for civil, UCC and criminal information.

Information Retrieval Services

12006 22nd St NE
Lake Stevens WA 98258-9148

Phone: 800-769-3051
206-334-2052
Fax: 206-397-6519

Local Retrieval Area: WA-Skagit, Snohomish.

Normal turnaround time: 24-48 hours. Online computer ordering is also available. Projects are generally billed by the number of names searched. Time charged for large files. The first project may require a prepayment.

They have 13 years experience in researching these counties. They will also search files for missing persons information.

Information Search Associates

PO Box 32698
Tucson AZ 85751-2698

Phone: 888-448-4477
520-749-4342
Fax: 520-749-2074

Local Retrieval Area: AZ-Pima.

Normal turnaround time: 2-3 days. Expedited service available. Projects are generally billed by the number of names searched. The first project may require a prepayment.

They specialize in research and document retrieval from county, state and federal agencies. Services include employment screening, asset searches and court records research.

Information Search Inc

2929 Biarritz Dr
Palm Beach FL 33410

Phone: 561-624-5115
Fax: 561-744-1616

Local Retrieval Area: FL-Martin, Palm Beach.

Normal turnaround time: 3-5 days. Projects are generally billed by the number of names searched or records located. Projects require prepayment.

Correspondent relationships: nationwide. They specialize in retrieving or verify information concerning individuals, groups, organizations, companies, industries, business entities or informational topics for our clients.

Information Services of Anchorage

1364 W 23rd Ave
Anchorage AK 99503-1614

Phone: 907-272-4688
Fax: 907-274-6449

Local Retrieval Area: AK-Anchorage Borough.

Normal turnaround time: 2-3 days. Online computer ordering is also available. Projects are generally billed by the hour. Projects require prepayment.

Informed Directions

110 15th St NE
Canton OH 44714

Phone: 800-335-2889
330-471-1577
Fax: 800-882-1274
330-471-1581

Local Retrieval Area: OH-Stark.

Normal turnaround time: 24-48 hours. Projects are generally billed by the number of names searched. Credit accounts are accepted. Terms are net 15 days.

Correspondent relationships: OH. They specialize in criminal searches.

InfoSearch

13300 Bothell Everett Hwy Suite 661
Mill Creek WA 98012

Phone: 206-743-9407
Fax: 206-787-0317

Local Retrieval and SOP Area: WA-King, Snohomish.

Normal turnaround time: 2-4 days. Projects are generally billed by the hour. The first project may require a prepayment.

They specialize in background searches.

Infotrack Information Services

925 N Milwaukee Ave Suite 224
Wheeling IL 60090

Phone: 800-275-5594
708-808-9990
Fax: 800-275-5595
708-808-7773

Local Retrieval Area: IL-Cook, De Kalb, Du Page, Grundy, Kane, Kankakee, Lake, McHenry, Will, Winnebago.

Normal turnaround time: 1-2 days. Projects are generally billed by the number of names searched. Credit accounts are accepted. Credit cards are accepted.

Correspondent relationships: nationwide. They specialize in pre-employment, investigative and litigation support services. Illinois motor vehicle and real estate information is available within 1 hour.

Ingham County Sheriff's Dept-Civil

PO Box 80165
Lansing MI 48908-0165

Phone: 517-393-1200
Fax: 517-393-9330

Local Retrieval and SOP Area: MI-Clinton, Eaton, Ingham.

Normal turnaround time: 2-3 days. Projects are generally billed by the hour. The first project may require a prepayment. Payment due upon receipt of invoice.

They can also visit the Department of Corrections.

▥ INPRO

14870 Granada Ave Suite 323
Apple Valley MN 55124-5514

Phone: 612-891-3617
Fax: 612-891-3618

Local Retrieval and SOP Area: MN-Anoka, Carver, Dakota, Hennepin, Ramsey, Scott, Sherburne, Washington.

Normal turnaround time: 24-48 hours. Fees vary depending on search requested. Credit accounts are accepted. Credit cards are accepted. Terms are net 15 days.

Correspondent relationships: nationwide. They specialize in providing prompt and professional investigative services.

InQuest Inc

PO Box 2549
Lynnwood WA 98036-2549

Phone: 800-827-9182
206-889-0123
Fax: 206-803-9880

Local Retrieval and SOP Area: WA-Snohomish.

Projects are generally billed by the number of names searched. Credit accounts are accepted.

Correspondent relationships: nationwide..

▥ Inquiry Services Inc

Box 144922
Coral Gable FL 33114

Phone: 888-444-4033
305-444-4033
Fax: 888-444-4034
305-442-0960

Local Retrieval and SOP Area: CA-San Francisco, San Mateo; FL-Dade; OR-Marion.

Normal turnaround time: less than 24 hours. Online computer ordering is also available. Projects are generally billed by the number of names searched. The first project may require a prepayment. Net terms upon approval.

Correspondent relationships: nationwide. They specialize in expert service. Special requests available. They provide litigation service of process in Oregon and California.

Instant Information Systems

13345 Copper Ridge Rd
Germantown MD 20874

Phone: 703-281-9312
Fax: 703-281-7669

Local Retrieval Area: DC-District of Columbia; MD-Montgomery, Prince George's; VA-City of Alexandria, Arlington, Fairfax, City of Fairfax, Loudoun, Prince William, Spotsylvania, Stafford.

Normal turnaround time: typically the same day as the order is received. Projects are generally billed by the hour. The first project may require a prepayment.

They specialize in retrieval from federal sources in the Washington DC area. They also do retrieval from the National Library of Medicine.

Insured Titles Inc

PO Box 4706 2501 Catlin #107 (59801)
Missoula MT 59806

Phone: 406-728-7900
Fax: 406-728-5892

Local Retrieval Area: MT-Missoula.

Normal turnaround time: 3-5 days. Projects are generally billed by the number of names searched. Credit accounts are accepted.
They specialize in real estate record searches.

▥ Intellifacts Corporation

13280 NW Frwy, Suite F151
Houston TX 77040

Phone: 800-208-9422
713-469-9422
Fax: 713-469-4685

Local Retrieval Area: TX-Harris.

Normal turnaround time: 24 hours. Projects are generally billed by the number of names searched. Credit accounts are accepted. Invoices twice monthly.

Intelligence Network Inc

PO Box 727
Clearwater FL 34617-0727

Phone: 813-449-0072
Fax: 813-448-0949

Local Retrieval Area: FL-Hillsborough, Pinellas.

Normal turnaround time: 24 hours. Projects are generally billed by the number of names searched or records located. Credit accounts are accepted. Credit cards are accepted. Terms are net 30 days with major credit card.

They can search Dade, Broward and Palm Beach via computer database. Florida records available to them are: property, vehicles, DL's, corporation and UCC.

Intelnet Inc

320 Westcott St Suite 108
Houston TX 77007-7045

Phone: 888-636-3693
713-880-3693
Fax: 888-636-3694
713-880-3694

Local Retrieval Area: TX-Collin, Dallas, Gregg, Harris, McLennan, Nueces, Tarrant, Travis.

Normal turnaround time: 24-48 hours. Projects are generally billed by the number of names searched. Credit accounts are accepted. Terms are net 15 days.

Correspondent relationships: a network of 516 paralegals nationwide. They specialize in pulling physical records as opposed to pulling only index information.

Inter-County Abstract

616 Main St Suite 301
Honesdale PA 18431-1871

Phone: 717-253-4734
Fax: 717-253-1359

Local Retrieval Area: PA-Pike, Wayne.

Normal turnaround time: 1 week. Projects are generally billed by the number of names searched. Charges are also based on title insurance. Projects require prepayment.

Correspondent relationships: Lackawanna. They specialize in information certificates for real estate abstracts.

▥ Intercounty Clearance Corp

105 Chambers St
New York NY 10007

Phone: 800-229-4422
Fax: 212-349-0145

Local Retrieval and SOP Area: NY-Albany, Bronx, Kings, Nassau, New York, Queens, Rensselaer, Saratoga, Suffolk, Westchester.

Normal turnaround time: 2-3 days. Online computer ordering is also available. Projects are generally billed by the number of names searched. Fee may be based on location searched. The first project may require a prepayment. Credit cards are accepted.

Correspondent relationships: nationwide. They have been in business since 1935. They also search pending suits, tax liens and mechanics liens in addition to specializing in UCC searching and filing.

▥ International Investigators Inc

3216 N Pennsylvania St
Indianapolis IN 46205-3414

Phone: 317-925-1496
Fax: 317-926-1177

Local Retrieval and SOP Area: IN-Boone, Hamilton, Hancock, Hendricks, Johnson, Marion, Shelby.

Normal turnaround time: 1-4 days. Projects are generally billed by the hour. The first project may require a prepayment.

Correspondent relationships: international. They specialize in international insurance fraud, corporate request and attorney assistance.

International Research Bur (IRB)

Phone: 800-814-7714
904-942-2500
Fax: 904-656-1738

1331 E Lafayette St Suite A
Tallahassee FL 32301

Local Retrieval Area: FL-Leon.

Normal turnaround time: varied depending on project. Online computer ordering is also available. Projects are generally billed by the number of names searched or records located. The first project may require a prepayment. Credit cards are accepted. Personal checks are accepted.

Correspondent relationships: the western portions of Florida. They specialize in background searches (driving records, criminal histories, workers comp claims), asset searches (vehicles, property, boats, aircraft, corporate, UCC) and nationwide locates.

Internet Investigative Services Inc

Phone: 517-694-2879
Fax: 517-694-3265

5859 W Saginaw Hwy Suite 443
Lansing MI 48917

Local Retrieval and SOP Area: MI-Clinton, Eaton, Ingham.

Normal turnaround time: 1-3 days. Expedited service available. Projects are generally billed by the number of names searched. Credit accounts are accepted. Invoice is due upon receipt.

Correspondent relationships: nationwide. They specialize in public record services, skip tracing services and nationwide asset searches. On-line searches include workers' compensation, criminal records and motor vehicle records.

Interquest Information Services

Phone: 800-455-1655
314-339-1505
Fax: 314-339-7111

PO Box 2082
Cape Girardeau MO 63702

Local Retrieval Area: MO-Bollinger, Cape Girardeau, New Madrid, Perry, Scott, Stoddard.

Normal turnaround time: 24-48 hours. Projects are generally billed by the number of names searched. The first project may require a prepayment. Terms are net 30 days for established accounts.

Correspondent relationships: nationwide. They specialize in employment screening, tenant screening, skip tracing, and general information research for business, industrial and legal use.

Interstate Abstract Inc

Phone: 609-795-4000
Fax: 609-795-2596

413 Rt 70 E
Cherry Hill NJ 08034

Local Retrieval Area: DE-All Counties; NJ-21 Counties; PA-Bucks, Chester, Delaware, Montgomery, Philadelphia.

Normal turnaround time: 24-48 hours. Projects are generally billed by the number of records located. Credit accounts are accepted.

Correspondent relationships: the entire state of Pennsylvania. They specialize in title, real estate, and foreclosure searches.

Interstate Reporting Co Inc (IRC)

Phone: 800-837-6635
414-438-2260
Fax: 414-527-1198

10045 W Lisbon Ave
Milwaukee WI 53222-2446

Local Retrieval Area: WI-Brown, Milwaukee, Ozaukee, Waukesha.

Normal turnaround time: 48 hours. Projects are generally billed by the number of names searched. The first project may require a prepayment.

They specialize in locate/subrogation, pre-employment background reports, insurance fraud and worker's compensation investigations.

Interwest Investigations

Phone: 303-223-2212

PO Box 1773
Ft Collins CO 80522

Local Retrieval Area: CO-Adams, Arapahoe, Boulder, Denver, Jefferson, Larimer, Weld.

Normal turnaround time: 2-3 days. Projects are generally billed by the hour. Projects require prepayment.

They specialize in skip tracing.

Intra-Lex Investigations Inc

Phone: 712-233-1639
Fax: 712-255-1127

505 6th St Suite 502
Sioux City IA 51101

Local Retrieval and SOP Area: IA-12 Counties; NE-13 Counties; SD-Bon Homme, Clay, Lincoln, Minnehaha, Turner, Union, Yankton.

Normal turnaround time: 24 hours. Projects are generally billed by the number of names searched. Mileage charges will be added to the fee. A miminum fee applies. The first project may require a prepayment. Payment in full 30 days from date of service.

Correspondent relationships: Nebraska (Douglas, Sarpy, Cass, counties), Iowa (Cerro, Gordo, Winnebago, Worth, Hancock, Clay, Ida, counties). They are a full line investigation agency, multi-state licensed, bonded and insured.

Intranet Inc

Phone: 903-593-9817
Fax: 903-593-1830

107 E Erwin
Tyler TX 75702

Local Retrieval Area: TX-Bexar, Harris, Jefferson, Smith, Tarrant, Travis.

Normal turnaround time: 24-48 hours. Projects are generally billed by the number of names searched. Credit accounts are accepted. Personal checks are accepted.

Correspondent relationships: Nueces County. They specialize in bankruptcy document retrieval.

▥ Investech Inc

Phone: 800-392-7676
609-748-9370
Fax: 800-392-7676
609-748-9370

PO Box 1361
Absecon NJ 08201

Local Retrieval and SOP Area: NJ-Atlantic, Camden, Cape May, Cumberland, Gloucester, Ocean, Salem.

Normal turnaround time: 3-14 days. Projects are generally billed by the hour. The first project may require a prepayment.

They specialize in commercial industrial investigations and litigation support.

Investigations LLC

Phone: 800-658-1688
316-262-1721
Fax: 316-252-3189

1427 W Douglas
Wichita KS 67213

Local Retrieval and SOP Area: KS-Butler, Harvey, Kingman, Reno, Sedgwick, Sumner.

Normal turnaround time: 48 hours. Charges are case-by-case. The first project may require a prepayment. Credit cards are accepted.

Correspondent relationships: statewide. They specialize in trial preparation, lawyer support, criminal and license checks and asset investigations.

Investigative Consultants Inc

Phone: 202-562-1500
Fax: 301-654-6003

2020 Pennsylvania Ave NW Suite 813
Washington DC 20006

Local Retrieval Area: DC-District of Columbia; MD-Howard, Montgomery, Prince George's; VA-Arlington, Essex, Fairfax, City of Fairfax, Frederick, City of Manassas, City of Manassas Park, Prince William.

Normal turnaround time: 4 hours to 4 days. Online computer ordering is also available. Projects are generally billed by the hour. Retainer of 80% of all fees is required. Projects require prepayment. Wire transfers and firm checks only.

Correspondent relationships: nationwide. They specialize in assisting attorneys who practice in the field of complex federal and state litigation.

Investigative Legal Services Inc

Phone: 407-426-7433
Fax: 407-426-6968

111 N Orange Ave Suite 1230
Orlando FL 32801

Local Retrieval and SOP Area: FL-Orange, Osceola, Seminole.

Normal turnaround time: 5 days. Projects are generally billed by the hour. The first project may require a prepayment. Personal checks are accepted.

Correspondent relationships: the rest of Florida. He was a practicing trial lawyer for 30 years.

Investigative Resources

Phone: 718-317-0043
Fax: 718-967-0688

150 Nassau St
New York NY 10038

Local Retrieval and SOP Area: NY-Bronx, Kings, New York, Queens, Richmond.

Normal turnaround time: as soon as 4 hours. Emergency expedited service available. Projects are generally billed by the number of names searched or records located. The first project may require a prepayment.

Correspondent relationships: the Northeast. They specialize in locating Department of Motor Vehicle records within one hour.

Investigative Resources

Phone: 718-317-0043
Fax: 718-967-0688

558 Main St
Staten Island NY 10307

Local Retrieval Area: NY-Nassau, Suffolk, Westchester.

Normal turnaround time: varies with assignment and county. Projects are generally billed by the number of names searched. The first project may require a prepayment. Credit cards are accepted.

Correspondent relationships: Bergen county, NJ. They specialize in locating hard to finds and old record retrieval.

Investigative Services

Phone: 916-394-1897
Fax: 916-394-1738

9175 Kiefer Blvd Suite 190
Sacramento CA 95826

Local Retrieval Area: CA-Sacramento.

Normal turnaround time: 18-24 hours. Projects are generally billed by the number of names searched. Credit accounts are accepted. Terms are net 30 days.

Correspondent relationships: all Northern California counties. They specialize in criminal background checks for Sacramento county.

Investigative Services Internatnl

Phone: 305-868-7775
Fax: 305-865-5999

PO Box 6731
Miami FL 33154

Local Retrieval and SOP Area: FL-Broward, Dade, Palm Beach.

Normal turnaround time: 24-48 hours. Fees vary with job. Projects require prepayment.

Correspondent relationships: nationwide. They specialize in background checks, litigation support, surveillance and research.

Investigative Solutions

Phone: 330-626-5655
Fax: 330-626-5970

PO Box 2373
Streetsboro OH 44241

Local Retrieval Area: OH-21 Counties.

Normal turnaround time: 1-7 days. Billing is generally based upon the type of search requested. Volume discounts available. The first project may require a prepayment.

Correspondent relationships: nationwide. They specialize in polygraph.

Investigative Solutions of PA

Phone: 717-737-4324
Fax: 717-737-7042

107 April Dr
Camphill PA 17011

Local Retrieval Area: PA-Adams, Cumberland, Dauphin, Lancaster, York.

Normal turnaround time: 1-7 days. Billing is generally based upon the type of search requested. Volume discounts available. The first project may require a prepayment.

Correspondent relationships: nationwide. They specialize in conducting Internet Research, consulting and training.

Iosco County Abstract Office Ltd

Phone: 517-362-3231
Fax: 517-362-7844

432 W Lake St
Tawas City MI 48764-0420

Local Retrieval Area: MI-Iosco.

Normal turnaround time: 5 working days or less. Projects are generally billed by the number of names searched or records located. The first project may require a prepayment. A setup fee is required for abstracts and searches only. Personal checks are accepted.

They specialize in title insurance and closings.

Iowa County Abstract Company

Phone: 319-642-7321
Fax: 319-642-7321

PO Box 226
Marengo IA 52301

Local Retrieval Area: IA-Iowa.

Normal turnaround time: 2-3 days for personal lien searches, and 3-4 days for a full written search. Fee basis is per transaction. Credit accounts are accepted. Personal checks are accepted.

Iowa Title & Guaranty Co

Phone: 319-652-6081

115 S 2nd St
Maquoketa IA 52060

Local Retrieval Area: IA-Jackson.

Normal turnaround time: 1-3 days. Fee basis will vary by the type of project. Credit accounts are accepted.

They also provide credit bureau services.

Iowa Title & Realty Co

203 1/2 N Main St
Charles City IA 50616

Phone: 515-228-1515
Fax: 515-228-7538

Local Retrieval Area: IA-Floyd.

Normal turnaround time: 1-7 days. Fee basis will vary by the type of project. The first project may require a prepayment.

▥ IPSA/Background Plus

201 Center St Suite 200
Anaheim CA 92805

Phone: 800-631-1700
714-518-1000
Fax: 714-518-1012

Local Retrieval and SOP Area: CA-Orange.

Normal turnaround time: 24 hours. Projects are generally billed by the number of names searched. The first project may require a prepayment.

Correspondent relationships: nationwide. They are a full service investigations firm with a concentration in pre-employment screening & business background checks.

Iron Title & Abstract Co

402 Silver St
Hurley WI 54534

Phone: 715-561-3576
Fax: 715-561-5050

Local Retrieval Area: MI-Gogebic; WI-Iron.

Normal turnaround time: 1-2 days. Fee basis varies by type of transaction. Projects require prepayment.

IRS (Insight Research Systems)

21863 Aurora Rd
Bedford Heights OH 44146

Phone: 216-663-5011
Fax: 216-663-5015

Local Retrieval Area: OH-Cuyahoga, Lake, Lorain, Portage, Summit.

Normal turnaround time: 24-48 hours. Expedited service available. Projects are generally billed by the number of names searched. Fees vary by project size. Projects require prepayment. Credit cards are accepted.

Correspondent relationships: nationwide. They specialize in private investigations, pre-employment screening and loss prevention services.

Isabella County Abstract

209 E Broadway
Mt Pleasant MI 48858

Phone: 517-773-3241
Fax: 517-773-6221

Local Retrieval Area: MI-Isabella.

Normal turnaround time: 1 week. Projects are generally billed by the number of records located. Credit accounts are accepted. Personal checks are accepted.

Isador I Lamke PC

PO Box 128 415 Cedar St
Washington MO 63090

Phone: 314-239-7808
Fax: 314-239-4002

Local Retrieval Area: MO-Franklin.

Normal turnaround time: 7 working days. Fee basis will vary by type of project. Fee may be based per tract of land and/or per owner as required. Credit accounts are accepted. Payment due upon receipt.

They specialize in title insurance.

Itasca County Abstract Co

410 2nd Ave NE
Grand Rapids MN 55744

Phone: 218-326-9601
Fax: 218-326-4348

Local Retrieval Area: MN-Itasca.

Normal turnaround time: 24 hours for name and UCC searches. 5 to 10 days for owner's and encumbrance reports and abstracts. Projects are generally billed by the number of names searched or records located. Credit accounts are accepted. Personal checks are accepted.

They specialize in complete title service.

Izard County Abstract Co

PO Box 579
Melbourne AR 72556

Phone: 501-368-4818
Fax: 501-368-5511

Local Retrieval Area: AR-Izard.

Normal turnaround time: 3-5 days. Fee basis will vary by the type of project. Credit accounts are accepted.

They specialize in real estate.

J

J & J Associates

215 W Hoffman Ave
Lindenhurst NY 11757

Phone: 800-850-5568
Fax: 516-226-2298

Local Retrieval and SOP Area: NY-Nassau, New York, Suffolk.

Normal turnaround time: 3-5 days. Projects are generally billed by the number of names searched. The first project may require a prepayment. Credit cards are accepted.

Correspondent relationships: nationwide. They specialize in asset and bank account locations.

J C Humphrey Abstract Co

217 W Broadway
Enid OK 73702

Phone: 405-237-3136
Fax: 405-237-1948

Local Retrieval Area: OK-Garfield.

Normal turnaround time: 1-2 days. Projects are generally billed by the number of records located. The first project may require a prepayment.

Correspondent relationships: Grant County, Oklahoma.

J H L Enterprises

7775 York Rd
Parma OH 44130

Phone: 216-845-2823
Fax: 216-845-2823

Local Retrieval Area: OH-Cuyahoga, Medina, Wayne.

Normal turnaround time: 48 hours. Projects are generally billed by the number of names searched. The first project may require a prepayment. Will invoice monthly.

They specialize in civil, criminal, UCC, tax liens and District and Bankruptcy searches.

J L & A

PO Box 844
Crystal Springs MS 39059

Phone: 800-927-0251
Fax: 601-892-3242

Local Retrieval and SOP Area: LA-All Parishes; MS-All Counties.

Normal turnaround time: 2-3 days. Projects are generally billed by the number of names searched. Credit accounts are accepted.

They specialize in UCC's, tax liens, judgments, motor vehicle records and bankruptcy court searches.

J M Devine & Co Inc

PO Box 1316
Minot ND 58702

Phone: 701-852-6800
Fax: 701-852-6806

Local Retrieval Area: ND-Ward.

Normal turnaround time: 1-2 days. Projects are generally billed by the number of names searched or records located. Abstracting has per item charge. Projects require prepayment. They will also invoice.

They specialize real estate closings, title insurance, title searches, title memorandums and abstracts.

J M White Investigations

PO Box 5404 1322 30th St
Rock Island IL 61204

Phone: 309-794-1499
Fax: 309-794-9952

Local Retrieval and SOP Area: IA-Scott; IL-Henry, Mercer, Peoria, Rock Island, Stark, Tazewell.

Normal turnaround time: 3-4 days. Projects are generally billed by the hour. The first project may require a prepayment.

They specialize in criminal defense.

J Tacchino Agency Private Invest

Phone: 315-344-8828

HC 62 Box 22
Heuvelton NY 13654-9503

Local Retrieval and SOP Area: NY-St. Lawrence.

Normal turnaround time: 7 working days. Projects are generally billed by the hour. The first project may require a prepayment.

J-C Investigations

PO Box 4655
Elkhart IN 46514

Phone: 219-262-2832
Fax: 219-266-5705

Local Retrieval and SOP Area: IN-Allen, Elkhart, Kosciusko, La Porte, LaGrange, Marshall, St. Joseph, Whitley.

Normal turnaround time: 48 hours. Projects are generally billed by the hour. The first project may require a prepayment.

Correspondent relationships: the rest of the state. They specialize in civil, criminal, domestic, workers' compensation, and accident investigation.

J.R. Investigations

313 SW Westlawn Dr
Ankeny IA 50021

Phone: 515-965-2637
Fax: 515-964-0064

Local Retrieval and SOP Area: IA-62 Counties; IL-Rock Island.

Normal turnaround time: 48 hours. Projects are generally billed by the number of names searched. The first project may require a prepayment. Billed at the end of the month.

Jackson Abstract Inc

124 N Main
Berryville AR 72616

Phone: 501-423-2285
Fax: 501-423-3630

Local Retrieval Area: AR-Carroll.

Normal turnaround time: 1 day. Projects are generally billed by the number of records located. Credit accounts are accepted. Personal checks are accepted.

Correspondent relationships: the rest of Arkansas.

Jackson County Abstract Co

PO Box 756
Altus OK 73521

Phone: 405-482-1235
Fax: 405-482-9180

Local Retrieval Area: OK-Jackson.

Normal turnaround time: varied depending on project. Projects are generally billed by the hour. The first project may require a prepayment.

They specialize in real estate records.

Jackson County Title Co

PO Box 544
Kadoka SD 57543

Phone: 605-837-2286

Local Retrieval Area: SD-Jackson.

Normal turnaround time: up to two weeks. Fee basis varies by type of transaction. Credit accounts are accepted.

They specialize in land records.

JAK Abstract

PO Box 416
Belvidere NJ 07823

Phone: 908-475-5007

Local Retrieval Area: NJ-Warren.

Normal turnaround time: 3-10 days. Fee basis will vary by type of project. Credit accounts are accepted.

James F Havill Attorney at Law PC

401 E South St
Washington IN 47501

Phone: 812-254-0050
Fax: 812-254-7633

Local Retrieval Area: IN-Daviess.

Normal turnaround time: 1 week. Projects are generally billed by the number of records located. Credit accounts are accepted. Personal checks are accepted.

Correspondent relationships: Knox, Martin and Pike Counties. They specialize in title opinions, abstracts and title insurance.

Cristina R James

PO Box 5374
Jacksonville AR 72078

Phone: 501-843-5025
Fax: 501-843-5025

Local Retrieval Area: AR-Lonoke, Pulaski.

Normal turnaround time: 24 to 48 hours. Projects are generally billed by the number of names searched. The first project may require a prepayment.

She can be reached at 501-340-1012 (pager) and 501-920-6037 (mobile).

Janke Abstract Co

PO Box 114
St Paul NE 68873

Phone: 308-754-4251
Fax: 308-754-4444

Local Retrieval Area: NE-Greeley, Howard, Merrick, Nance, Sherman.

Normal turnaround time: 2-3 days. Projects are generally billed by the number of names searched. Credit accounts are accepted.

They specialize in real estate.

Jay County Abstract Company Inc

Phone: 219-726-4303

125 W Main St
Portland IN 47371

Local Retrieval Area: IN-Jay.

Normal turnaround time: 5-6 working days. Fee basis will vary by type of project. Projects require prepayment. They will also invoice.

They specialize in real estate searches.

Jay Portland Abstract Inc Co

109 S Commerce St
Portland IN 47371

Phone: 219-726-6466
Fax: 219-726-4222

Local Retrieval Area: IN-Jay.

Normal turnaround time: 5 days. Projects are generally billed by the number of names searched. Projects require prepayment. They will also invoice.

Jayphil Investigations

1005 Pine Oak Dr
Edmond OK 73034

Phone: 405-348-3410
Fax: 405-341-2052

Local Retrieval and SOP Area: OK-Canadian, Cleveland, Kingfisher, Lincoln, Logan, McClain, Oklahoma, Pottawatomie.

Normal turnaround time: 2 working days for county and 4 working days for court searches. Online computer ordering is also available. Projects are generally billed by the hour. The first project may require a prepayment. Credit cards are accepted. Personal checks are accepted.

Correspondent relationships: all of Oklahoma.

Jeff City Filing

222 E Dunklin Suite 102
Jefferson City MO 65101

Phone: 573-634-3894
Fax: 573-634-5159

Local Retrieval Area: MO-Cole.

Normal turnaround time: 1 day. Projects are generally billed by the number of names searched. Credit accounts are accepted.

They specialize in filing & recording legal instruments with local & Missouri Supreme Courts, "walking through" filings with state agencies, UCC searches, tax clearances & recissions, and copying documents. They are a registered agent for corporations.

Jeff Davis County Abstract Co

PO Box 813
Fort Davis TX 79734

Phone: 915-426-3288
Fax: 915-426-3844

Local Retrieval Area: TX-Jeff Davis.

Normal turnaround time: 2 days. Projects are generally billed by the hour. The first project may require a prepayment.

Jefferson County Abstract

PO Box 908
Fairfield IA 52556

Phone: 515-472-5052
Fax: 515-472-5052

Local Retrieval Area: IA-Jefferson.

Normal turnaround time: 1-2 days. Fee basis varies by type of transaction. The first project may require a prepayment.

They specialize in complete land records, updated daily in Jefferson County.

Keith A Jeffries

PO Box 478 East Cross Main
New Castle KY 40050

Phone: 502-845-7603
Fax: 502-845-7536

Local Retrieval Area: KY-Henry, Trimble.

Normal turnaround time: varied depending on project. Projects are generally billed by the hour. Credit accounts are accepted. He will ask for a retainer.

He is an attorney and is very familiar with the local courts.

Jerauld County Abstract Co Inc

Box 341 224 E Main St
Wessington Springs SD 57382

Phone: 605-539-1541

Local Retrieval Area: SD-Jerauld.

Normal turnaround time: varied depending on project. Projects are generally billed by the number of records located. Credit accounts are accepted.

JM Search Services Inc

7787 SW 86th St Suite 102-E
Miami FL 33143

Phone: 800-393-7563
305-273-7766
Fax: 305-273-8855

Local Retrieval Area: FL-Broward, Dade, Palm Beach.

Normal turnaround time: 24-48 hours. Rush service available. Projects are generally billed by the number of names searched. The first project may require a prepayment.

They specialize in asset/lien, civil and criminal, US District Court, bankruptcy and real property searches. They alos perform historical and biographical research for news publications and other organizations.

Joden & Associates Inc

PO Box 842
Bellevue WA 98009

Phone: 206-441-5833
Fax: 206-226-3721

Local Retrieval and SOP Area: WA-King.

Normal turnaround time: 1-3 days in the metro areas, up to 2 weeks in the outlying regions. Online computer ordering is also available. Projects are generally billed by the number of names searched. Credit accounts are accepted. Payment due upon receipt of invoice.

They conduct online computer searchers of SCOMIS & DISCUS databases which cover ALL Superior courts statewide. The DISCIS database covers most Districe and Municipal court dockets statewide.

John Bullock & Co

PO Box 721309
Corpus Christi TX 78472

Phone: 512-992-3060
Fax: 512-851-8899

Local Retrieval Area: TX-Aransas, Kenedy, Kleberg, Nueces, San Patricio.

Normal turnaround time: 1-3 days. Projects are generally billed by the hour. Projects require prepayment.

They specialize in private investigation.

John C Dunaway and Associates

PO Box 202102
Austin TX 78720-2102

Phone: 512-835-5888
Fax: 512-835-2136

Local Retrieval and SOP Area: TX-Bastrop, Hays, Travis, Williamson.

Normal turnaround time: 2-48 hours. Projects are generally billed by the number of names searched. Projects require prepayment. Credit cards are accepted. They bill every 30 days.

Correspondent relationships: nationwide. They specialize in pre-employment services to assist companies in the minimization of risk in the workplace.

John H Rider Abstract & Real Estate

214 S Franklin
Corydon IA 50060

Phone: 515-872-1966
Fax: 515-872-2468

Local Retrieval Area: IA-Wayne.

Normal turnaround time: 2-3 days. Fee basis varies by type of transaction. The first project may require a prepayment.

⊞ John Roberson Investigations

746 Hwy 314
Fayetteville GA 30214

Phone: 800-325-0914
404-461-8958
Fax: 404-461-0119

Local Retrieval and SOP Area: GA-Clayton, Cobb, Coweta, De Kalb, Fayette, Fulton, Gwinnett, Henry, Spalding.

Normal turnaround time: 2 days. Projects are generally billed by the hour. The first project may require a prepayment. Payment due upon receipt.

Correspondent relationships: nationwide. They specialize in skip trace and asset location.

Johnson County Abstract

405 Poplar
Vienna IL 62995

Phone: 618-658-3721
Fax: 618-658-3721

Local Retrieval Area: IL-Johnson.

Normal turnaround time: 2-3 business days. Projects are generally billed by the number of records located. Credit accounts are accepted. Personal checks are accepted.

Correspondent relationships: Williamson, Pope and Union Counties. They specialize in title insurance through Chicago Title Insurance Company.

Lisa R Johnson

17304 Rocky Mount Ln
Dumfries VA 22026

Phone: 703-441-0099
Fax: 540-786-6916

Local Retrieval Area: VA-Caroline, Culpeper, City of Fredericksburg, King George, Louisa, Orange, Spotsylvania, Stafford.

Normal turnaround time: 24-48 hours. Projects are generally billed by the number of names searched. Credit accounts are accepted. Payment due upon receipt of title work.

She is also a licensed title insurance agent in the State of Virginia.

Johnston County Abstract Co

103 N Kemp Ave
Tishomingo OK 73460

Phone: 405-371-9375
Fax: 405-371-2771

Local Retrieval Area: OK-Johnston.

Normal turnaround time: 2-5 days. Projects are generally billed by the hour. They also charge per page or per certificate. Credit accounts are accepted.

John Thomas Johnston

666 Post St Suite 303
San Francisco CA 94109

Phone: 415-885-6211
Fax: 415-885-5901

Local Retrieval Area: CA-Alameda, San Francisco.

Normal turnaround time: same day if received early to 1-2 days. Projects are generally billed by the number of names searched. Credit accounts are accepted. Terms are net 15 days.

Correspondent relationships: nationwide, Canada, Guam and Virgin Islands. They specialize in research/retrieval of legal and financial documents at the federal, state and local levels. They also go to the National Archives at San Brono, CA.

Jones & Associates Inc

1611 S Utica Suite 117
Tulsa OK 74104

Phone: 918-583-4779
Fax: 918-587-8571

Local Retrieval and SOP Area: OK-Creek, Mayes, Okmulgee, Osage, Rogers, Tulsa, Wagoner, Washington.

Normal turnaround time: 24-72 hours. Projects are generally billed by the hour. The first project may require a prepayment.

Correspondent relationships: the rest of Oklahoma. They specialize in private investigation, process service, medical research and interpretation.

Jones & Renfrow Abstract Co

PO Drawer I
Paducah TX 79248

Phone: 806-492-3573
Fax: 806-492-3574

Local Retrieval Area: TX-Cottle, King.

Normal turnaround time: 1-2 days. Fee basis will vary by the type of project. The first project may require a prepayment.

Jones Abstract & Title Co Inc

313 Warren St
Huntington IN 46750

Phone: 219-356-2122
Fax: 219-356-4533

Local Retrieval Area: IN-Huntington.

Normal turnaround time: 3-5 days. Fee basis will vary by the type of project. The first project may require a prepayment.

Correspondent relationships: most of the state through an alliance of title companies. They specialize in title searching.

Jones County Abstract Co

PO Box 485
Murdo SD 57559

Phone: 605-669-2231

Local Retrieval Area: SD-Jones.

Normal turnaround time: 1 week. Projects are generally billed by the hour. Credit accounts are accepted.

They specialize in land titles.

Jones County Abstract Co

1128 W Court Plz
Anson TX 79501

Phone: 915-823-3236
Fax: 915-823-3224

Local Retrieval Area: TX-Jones.

Normal turnaround time: 1-2 days. Fee basis will vary by the type of project. The first project may require a prepayment.

Jordan & McCulloch Abstracters

101 1/2 E Main St
Brady TX 76825

Phone: 915-597-2172
Fax: 915-597-2173

Local Retrieval Area: TX-McCulloch.

Normal turnaround time: 3-4 days. Fee basis will vary by the type of project. The first project may require a prepayment.

Cheryl S Josey

PO Box 394
Pembroke GA 31321

Phone: 912-653-2707

Local Retrieval Area: GA-Bryan, Bulloch, Chatham, Evans, Glynn, Liberty, Long, Tattnall.

Normal turnaround time: 24-48 hours. Fee basis will vary by the type of search. Credit accounts are accepted.

JS Industries

Phone: 717-253-3136

643 R Park St
Honesdale PA 18431-1445

Local Retrieval and SOP Area: PA-Lackawanna, Wayne.

Normal turnaround time: several hours. Charges are varied depending on type of search. Credit accounts are accepted.

They specialize in working with attorneys.

Juab Title & Abstract Co

Phone: 601-623-0387
Fax: 601-623-1000

PO Box 246
Nephi UT 84648

Local Retrieval Area: UT-Juab, Millard, Sanpete.

Normal turnaround time: 1-2 days. Charges vary according to project. Projects require prepayment.

They specialize in real estate.

▥ Judicial Research & Retrieval

Phone: 800-529-6226
305-379-3900
Fax: 305-379-4460

19 W Flagler St 928 Biscayne Bldg
Miami FL 33130

Local Retrieval Area: FL-Broward, Dade, Duval, Escambia, Gadsden, Hillsborough, Leon, Orange, Palm Beach, Pinellas.

Normal turnaround time: 24-48 hours. Projects are generally billed by the number of names searched. The first project may require a prepayment.

Correspondent relationships: nationwide. They specialize in civil litigation, public records and bankruptcy.

Nina F Juncewicz

Phone: 716-873-8315

299 Commonwealth Ave
Buffalo NY 14216

Local Retrieval and SOP Area: NY-Erie.

Normal turnaround time: 2 days or less. Projects are generally billed by the number of names searched. The first project may require a prepayment.

She specializes in criminal record searches.

▥ Justifacts Credential Verification

Phone: 800-356-6885
412-468-5935
Fax: 412-468-3992

PO Box 357
Delmont PA 15626

Local Retrieval Area: CA-Santa Clara; PA-Allegheny, Washington, Westmoreland.

Normal turnaround time: 24-48 hours. Online computer ordering is also available. Projects are generally billed by the number of names searched. Credit accounts are accepted. Credit cards are accepted. Will Invoice monthly.

Correspondent relationships: nationwide. They are a nationwide background information service specializing in comprehensive personnel profiles. They verify employment, credit, driving, education, worker's comp, criminal/civil records and professional licenses.

K

K.R.

Phone: 803-423-3041

PO Box 635
Marion SC 29571

Local Retrieval Area: SC-Marion.

Normal turnaround time: varied depending on search. Projects are generally billed by the hour. Credit accounts are accepted.

▥ Jim Kalyvas

Phone: 614-759-7456
Fax: 614-759-7456

94 Fairway Blvd Suite H
Columbus OH 43213

Local Retrieval Area: OH-Butler, Cuyahoga, Delaware, Fairfield, Franklin, Hamilton, Licking, Lucas, Montgomery, Summit.

Normal turnaround time: 48 hours. Projects are generally billed by the number of names searched. The first project may require a prepayment.

They specialize in rapid results from Ohio Secretary of State, UCC, tax liens, judgments and Federal and Bankruptcy courts.

Kansas Investigative Services Inc

Phone: 316-267-1356
Fax: 316-267-5476

724 N Main St
Wichita KS 67203-3603

Local Retrieval and SOP Area: KS-12 Counties.

Normal turnaround time: the same day. Projects are generally billed by the number of names searched. Charges are by the trip. Projects require prepayment. They will also invoice.

Correspondent relationships: Shawnee County.

Kansas Title Service

Phone: 316-326-8508
Fax: 316-326-8049

209 N Washington
Wellington KS 67152

Local Retrieval Area: KS-Sumner.

Normal turnaround time: up to 48 hours. Fee basis varies by type of transaction. The first project may require a prepayment.

Karnes Land Title Co Inc

Phone: 210-780-2221
Fax: 210-780-2236

108 N Panna Maria St
Karnes City TX 78118

Local Retrieval Area: TX-Karnes.

Normal turnaround time: 1 day. Fee basis will vary by the type of project. The first project may require a prepayment.

Kaufman Information Resources

Phone: 908-438-1967
Fax: 908-438-1971

N7 Quincy Cir
Dayton NJ 08810

Local Retrieval Area: NJ-Mercer, Middlesex, Monmouth, Somerset, Union.

Normal turnaround time: 3 days. Projects are generally billed by the number of names searched. The first project may require a prepayment. Terms are net 30 days.

Correspondent relationships: the rest of New Jersey. They specialize in UCC, corporate records, state and federal tax liens, and federal, state, county and local courts.

KCD Title

Phone: 908-859-6524
Fax: 908-859-1102

9 Greystone Ave
Phillipsburg NJ 08865

Local Retrieval Area: NJ-Warren.

Normal turnaround time: 24 hours. Projects are generally billed by the number of names searched or records located. The first project may require a prepayment. Personal checks are accepted.

Correspondent relationships: state of Pennsylvania. They have 60 years of experience in searches and title insurance.

🏛 Keating & Walker
1 Beekman St Suite 406
New York NY 10038
Phone: 800-797-6444
212-964-6444
Fax: 212-964-5508

Local Retrieval and SOP Area: NY-Kings, Nassau, New York, Queens, Richmond, Westchester.

Normal turnaround time: 24 hours. Projects are generally billed by the number of names searched. The first project may require a prepayment.

Correspondent relationships: nationwide.

Keesee Abstracting Co
785 3rd St
Phillipsburg KS 67661
Phone: 913-543-5115
Fax: 913-543-6832

Local Retrieval Area: KS-Phillips.

Normal turnaround time: 2-3 days. Fee basis varies by type of transaction. Credit accounts are accepted.

Kern Attorney Service Inc
555 N Glendale Blvd
Los Angeles CA 90026
Phone: 213-483-4900
Fax: 213-483-7777

Local Retrieval and SOP Area: CA-Colusa, Los Angeles, Orange, Riverside, San Diego, Ventura.

Normal turnaround time: 1-3 days. Expedited service available. Projects are generally billed by the number of names searched. Projects require prepayment. Credit cards are accepted.

Kern Public Research
221 Comet Ct
Bakersfield CA 93308
Phone: 805-636-6397
Fax: 805-399-4167

Local Retrieval Area: CA-Kern.

Normal turnaround time: 24-48 hours. Projects are generally billed by the number of names searched. Credit accounts are accepted. Monthly billings.

They specialize in criminal, civil, probate, tax lien, judgments, UCC's and document recording (real estate-court).

Ketlett-Landis-Brill Abstr & Land
PO Box 527
West Plains MO 65775
Phone: 417-256-2951
Fax: 417-256-0928

Local Retrieval Area: MO-Howell.

Normal turnaround time: 2-3 days. Projects are generally billed by the number of names searched. Credit accounts are accepted.

They specialize in title insurance.

Key Title
PO Box 59
Roseburg OR 97470
Phone: 541-673-1146
Fax: 541-673-2118

Local Retrieval Area: OR-Douglas.

Normal turnaround time: 2-3 days. The first project may require a prepayment.

They specialize in real estate, title insurance, escrow services, lender insurance and escrow collections.

Kiefer Title Co
21 S Jackson St
Perryville MO 63775-2514
Phone: 314-547-7755
Fax: 314-547-7788

Local Retrieval Area: MO-Perry.

Normal turnaround time: 1-2 weeks. They charge a flat rate per project. Credit accounts are accepted.

King & King
PO Box 249
Pine Knot KY 42635
Phone: 606-354-2153
Fax: 606-354-2005

Local Retrieval Area: KY-McCreary, Pulaski, Wayne, Whitley.

Normal turnaround time: up to 1 week. Fee basis varies by type of transaction. Credit accounts are accepted.

They are a general practice law firm.

Kingman Abstract and Title Co Inc
221 N Main
Kingman KS 67068
Phone: 316-532-2011
Fax: 316-532-5383

Local Retrieval Area: KS-Kingman.

Normal turnaround time: 24-48 hours. Projects are generally billed by the hour. Credit accounts are accepted.

They specialize in title insurance, escrow and closings.

Kings Abstract Company
212 W Washington PO Box 25
Winchester IN 47394
Phone: 800-280-6323
317-584-9882
Fax: 317-584-2302

Local Retrieval Area: IN-Randolph.

Normal turnaround time: 24-48 hours. Projects are generally billed by the number of names searched or records located. The first project may require a prepayment.

They specialize in right of way and railroad research.

Kings Abstract Company Inc
100 S 5th St PO Box 1444
Richmond IN 47374
Phone: 800-757-7762
317-962-6541
Fax: 317-966-3719

Local Retrieval Area: IN-Wayne.

Normal turnaround time: 24-48 hours. Projects are generally billed by the number of names searched or records located. The first project may require a prepayment.

They specialize in right of way and railroad research.

Kings Title & Abstract Co
223 W 9th St
Anderson IN 46016-1366
Phone: 800-317-1515
317-643-3019
Fax: 317-644-0362

Local Retrieval Area: IN-Madison.

Normal turnaround time: 24/48 hours. Projects are generally billed by the number of names searched or records located. The first project may require a prepayment.

They specialize in right of way and railroad research.

Kings Title & Abstract Co
333 W 4th St
Marion IN 46953
Phone: 800-662-1299
317-662-1111
Fax: 317-662-2018

Local Retrieval Area: IN-Grant.

Normal turnaround time: 24-48 hours. Projects are generally billed by the number of names searched or records located. The first project may require a prepayment.

They specialize in right of way and railroad research.

Kings Title & Abstract Co
100 E Washington PO Box 1943
Muncie IN 47305-1725
Phone: 800-288-1642
317-288-1566
Fax: 317-288-1642

Local Retrieval Area: IN-Delaware.

Normal turnaround time: 24-48 hours. Projects are generally billed by the number of names searched or records located. The first project may require a prepayment.

They specialize in right of way and railroad research.

Kings Title & Abstract Co
1111 Broad St
New Castle IN 47362
Phone: 800-860-2990
371-521-2990
Fax: 371-529-0633

Local Retrieval Area: IN-Franklin, Henry.

Normal turnaround time: 24-48 hours. Projects are generally billed by the number of names searched or records located. The first project may require a prepayment.

They specialize in right of way/railroad research.

Kings Title & Abstract Co
125 E 3rd St
Rushville IN 46173-1839
Phone: 317-932-5757
Fax: 317-932-2168

Local Retrieval Area: IN-Rush.

Normal turnaround time: 24-48 hours. Projects are generally billed by the number of names searched or records located. The first project may require a prepayment.

They specialize in right of way and railroad research.

Kings Title & Abstract Co
23 Public Sq
Shelbyville IN 46176
Phone: 800-798-4545
317-398-0424
Fax: 317-392-0174

Local Retrieval Area: IN-Shelby.

Normal turnaround time: 24-48 hours. Projects are generally billed by the number of names searched or records located. The first project may require a prepayment.

They specialize in right of way and railroad research.

Kiowa County Abstract Co
PO Box 128
Eads CO 81036
Phone: 719-438-5811

Local Retrieval Area: CO-Kiowa.

Normal turnaround time: 1-2 weeks. Fee basis will vary by the type of project. Credit accounts are accepted.

They specialize in real estate title.

Kiowa County Abstract Company
108 E 4th St
Hobart OK 73651
Phone: 405-726-5283
Fax: 405-726-3545

Local Retrieval Area: OK-Kiowa.

Normal turnaround time: varied depending on project. Projects are generally billed by the number of names searched or records located. Credit accounts are accepted. They will accept personal checks.

▥ Chris Kirby-Muirhead
PO Box 509
Anguilla MS 38721
Phone: 601-873-6308
Fax: 601-873-2447

Local Retrieval Area: MS-Hinds, Issaquena, Madison, Rankin, Sharkey, Warren, Washington, Yazoo.

Normal turnaround time: 2-3 days. Projects are generally billed by the number of names searched. Credit accounts are accepted.

They cover the SOS/MS for UCC's and corporate documents. At the county level, judgments are covered.

Helen Kirk
RR 1 Box 218
Lewistown PA 17044
Phone: 717-248-4560
Fax: 717-248-3904

Local Retrieval Area: PA-Mifflin.

Normal turnaround time: 48 hours. Charges are varied depending on type of search. Credit accounts are accepted.

She specializes in "current owner" searches and has more than 30 years experience.

KJB Court Search
120 E Tea Rose
McAllen TX 78504
Phone: 210-971-8846
Fax: 210-618-2141

Local Retrieval and SOP Area: TX-Cameron, Hidalgo, Kenedy, Kleberg, Nueces, San Patricio, Starr, Willacy.

Normal turnaround time: 24-48 hours. Projects are generally billed by the number of names searched or records located. Expedited service available. Credit accounts are accepted.

KJK Abstract Co
38 Alpine Wy
Raritan NJ 08869
Phone: 908-725-6336
Fax: 908-253-9228

Local Retrieval Area: NJ-Somerset.

Normal turnaround time: 5-10 days. Fee basis will vary by type of project. Credit accounts are accepted.

They specialize in real estate searches.

Ole Klendshoj
240 E Riverdale Ave
Orange CA 92665
Phone: 714-998-1218
Fax: 714-282-2962

Local Retrieval Area: CA-Orange.

Projects are generally billed by the number of names searched. The first project may require a prepayment.

KOBS Abstracting
PO Box 458
Meade KS 67864
Phone: 316-873-2421
Fax: 316-873-2756

Local Retrieval Area: KS-Meade.

Normal turnaround time: 2-3 days. Fee basis varies by type of transaction. The first project may require a prepayment.

Correspondent relationships: Clark County, KS.

Jeff Kotner
1333 B Locust St
Eldorado IL 62930
Phone: 618-273-7611
Fax: 618-273-7611

Local Retrieval Area: IL-Franklin, Gallatin, Hamilton, Hardin, Jackson, Johnson, Pope, Saline, White, Williamson.

Normal turnaround time: 24 hours. Projects are generally billed by the number of names searched or records located. Credit accounts are accepted.

He specializes in abstracts of title and title insurance. He is a policy issuing agent for First American Title and National Land Title Insurance Companies.

▥ Kroes Detective Agency
7301 E 22nd St
Tucson AZ 85710
Phone: 800-249-0694
520-886-8397
Fax: 520-886-8398

Local Retrieval and SOP Area: AZ-Pima.

Normal turnaround time: 24-48 hours. Online computer ordering is also available. Projects are generally billed by the number of names searched. The first project may require a prepayment.

Correspondent relationships: nationwide. They have 20 years experience, knowledge and equipment in debugging services. They also perform pre-employment screening, all types of investigation and process serving.

🏛 Krotzer Legal Service

319 Elm St Suite 101M
San Diego CA 92101

Phone: 619-232-1291
Fax: 619-232-0910

Local Retrieval and SOP Area: CA-San Diego.

Normal turnaround time: 3-4 days. A same day rush service is also available. Projects are generally billed by the hour. Some cases require fees in advance. The first project may require a prepayment. Terms are net 10 days.

Correspondent relationships: all of California. They also work with the Assessor's office and search fictitious business name. They are a licensed private investigator in California.

🏛 Joan & Kelli Kunkel

Rt 3 Box 117
Carthage MO 64836

Phone: 417-358-6494
Fax: 417-359-5734

Local Retrieval and SOP Area: KS-Cherokee, Crawford, Labette; MO-Barton, Christian, Greene, Jasper, Lawrence, McDonald, Newton, Vernon; OK-Ottawa.

Normal turnaround time: 1-2 days. They charge a flat rate per search. Credit accounts are accepted. Personal checks are accepted.

They have 20 years experience in lost heirs and genealogy, and 10 years experience in other court house searches.

🏛 Kutlus & Company

25 Front St 3rd Fl
Upland PA 19015

Phone: 888-726-5335
610-874-0576
Fax: 610-874-5802

Local Retrieval and SOP Area: DE-All Counties; NJ-All Counties; PA-18 Counties.

Normal turnaround time: 48-72 hours. Projects are generally billed by the number of names searched. The first project may require a prepayment. Credit cards are accepted.

They are a paralegal search firm providing all searches and document retrieval in all jurisdictions and agencies in Pennsylvania, New Jersey and Delaware. All work is negotiable.

🏛 Michelle Kyle

208 Bayless Ave
St Louis MO 63125

Phone: 314-544-3493
Fax: 314-544-6804

Local Retrieval Area: MO-St. Charles, St. Louis, City of St. Louis.

Normal turnaround time: 24-48 hours. Projects are generally billed by the number of records located. Credit accounts are accepted.

L

🏛 L & J Research

263 Dahlia Ave Suite E
Imperial Beach CA 91932

Phone: 619-575-2205
Fax: 619-575-2205

Local Retrieval Area: CA-San Diego.

Normal turnaround time: 24-48 hours. Same day service is available for a fee. Projects are generally billed by the number of names searched. Credit accounts are accepted. Check or money order only accepted. Invoice on the 1st & 15th of each month.

L and L Title Abstract Services

29521 Porpoise Creek Rd
Trappe MD 21673

Phone: 410-820-6566
Fax: 410-476-3956

Local Retrieval Area: MD-Caroline, Dorchester, Talbot.

Normal turnaround time: 1 to 2 days for current owner, 3 days for full title. Projects are generally billed by the number of names searched. The first project may require a prepayment.

They specialize in real estate searches including current owner and 60 year or full title searches.

L Fay Hedden Abstract Office Inc

214 N 7th St
Vincennes IN 47591-2114

Phone: 812-882-5273

Local Retrieval Area: IN-Knox.

Normal turnaround time: 5-10 days. Projects are generally billed by the number of names searched or records located. Credit accounts are accepted.

They specialize in real estate title.

L P Records

98 Avant Rd
Holly Springs MS 38635

Phone: 601-252-8960

Local Retrieval Area: MS-Marshall.

Normal turnaround time: 24 hours. Projects are generally billed by the number of names searched. The first project may require a prepayment. Billed once a month.

La Plata Abstract Co

PO Box 197
Durango CO 81302

Phone: 303-247-5464
Fax: 303-385-4332

Local Retrieval Area: CO-La Plata.

Normal turnaround time: up to 1 week. Fee basis is determined on a "flat rate" (plus costs). Projects require prepayment.

La Prade Services Inc

PO Box 5218
Poughkeepsie NY 12602-5218

Phone: 914-473-0468
Fax: 914-473-1667

Local Retrieval and SOP Area: NY-Dutchess, Orange, Putnam, Ulster.

Normal turnaround time: 2-4 days. Expedited service available. Fee basis will vary by the type of project. Credit accounts are accepted. They may require a retainer.

Correspondent relationships: Westchester, NYC, Long Island, Sullivan and Rockland counties. They have the county contract for social services and handle 200 court papers a week.

Lacey Pioneer Abstract Company

209 W Broadway
Anadarko OK 73005

Phone: 405-247-5152
Fax: 405-247-5777

Local Retrieval Area: OK-Caddo.

Normal turnaround time: 2-3 days. Projects are generally billed by the number of names searched. Credit accounts are accepted. Personal checks are accepted.

They specialize in closings, title insurance and title searches.

LaCrosse Abstract & Title

110 W 8th PO Box 636
La Crosse KS 67548

Phone: 800-256-6911
913-222-2712
Fax: 913-222-3340

Local Retrieval Area: KS-Rush.

Normal turnaround time: up to 1 week. Fee basis varies by type of transaction. The first project may require a prepayment.

Lafayette County Abstract
330 Main St
Darlington WI 53530
Phone: 608-776-3338
Fax: 608-776-4798

Local Retrieval Area: WI-Lafayette.

Normal turnaround time: 1-2 days. Fee basis varies by type of transaction. Credit accounts are accepted.

Lafayette County Land Title Co
1007 Franklin Ave
Lexington MO 64067
Phone: 816-259-4631
Fax: 816-259-3142

Local Retrieval Area: MO-Lafayette.

Normal turnaround time: 2-3 days. Fee basis will vary by type of project. Credit accounts are accepted.

They specialize in real estate title.

LaGrange Title Company
127 W Spring
LaGrange IN 46761
Phone: 219-463-3232
Fax: 219-463-3232

Local Retrieval Area: IN-LaGrange.

Normal turnaround time: 1 week. Projects are generally billed by the number of names searched. Credit accounts are accepted.

Lake County Abstract & Title Co
PO Box 331
Polson MT 59860
Phone: 406-883-6226
Fax: 406-883-2586

Local Retrieval Area: MT-Lake.

Normal turnaround time: 3 days. Projects are generally billed by the hour. Credit accounts are accepted.

Lake County Abstract Co
PO Box 931
Leadville CO 80461
Phone: 719-486-2688
Fax: 719-486-3039

Local Retrieval Area: CO-Lake.

Normal turnaround time: 1 week to 10 days. Fee basis will vary by the type of project. The first project may require a prepayment.

They specialize in real estate title searches.

🏛 Lake County Abstract Co Inc
815 N Michigan Ave
Baldwin MI 49304
Phone: 616-745-3432
Fax: 616-745-7660

Local Retrieval Area: MI-Lake, Osceola.

Normal turnaround time: up to 1 week. Expedited service is available. Fee basis will vary by type of project. The first project may require a prepayment. They will also invoice.

They specialize in real estate.

Lake Michigan Title Co
11 W Main
Hartford MI 49057
Phone: 616-637-8595
Fax: 616-637-1857

Local Retrieval Area: MI-Allegan, Van Buren.

Normal turnaround time: up to 1 week. Fee basis will vary by the type of project. Credit accounts are accepted.

They specialize in title insurance.

Lamancha Search Inc
102 Bayless St
Murphy NC 28906
Phone: 704-837-7580
Fax: 704-837-6416

Local Retrieval Area: NC-Cherokee.

Normal turnaround time: 1 day. They charge by half day and full day. Credit accounts are accepted.

🏛 Lambert Research Services
2601 W Claremont Suite 2041
Phoenix AZ 85017
Phone: 602-433-7677

Local Retrieval Area: AZ-Maricopa, Pima, Pinal.

Normal turnaround time: 24-48 hours. Projects are generally billed by the number of names searched. Fees vary by project, deed searches and title work. The first project may require a prepayment. Terms are net 20 days.

They specialize in real estate, title searches and tax records.

LaMoure County Abstract Co
103 S Main St
LaMoure ND 58458
Phone: 701-883-4246
Fax: 701-883-4425

Local Retrieval Area: ND-La Moure.

Normal turnaround time: 2-5 days. Fee basis will vary by type of project. Projects require prepayment.

Lamparski & Associates
Rd #1721
New Freedom PA 17349
Phone: 717-235-1492
Fax: 717-235-1492

Local Retrieval Area: PA-York.

Normal turnaround time: next day. Projects are generally billed by the number of names searched. Credit accounts are accepted.

Correspondent relationships: Washington, DC; Baltimore, MD and northern VA. They specialize in courthouse searches and obtaining legal and financial documents.

Land Grant Title Group Inc
420 S 2nd St
Elkhart IN 46516
Phone: 219-295-1620
Fax: 219-295-8302

Local Retrieval Area: IN-Elkhart, Lake.

Normal turnaround time: 3 business days. Projects are generally billed by the hour..dd. Credit accounts are accepted. They will also invoice.

Correspondent relationships: LaGrange, IN county. They specialize in title insurance, land record searches and escrow closings.

Land Title & Abstract Inc
247 W Cedar Ave
Gladwin MI 48624
Phone: 517-426-0011
Fax: 517-426-7141

Local Retrieval Area: MI-Clare, Gladwin.

Normal turnaround time: 2-3 days. Fee basis will vary by type of project. Credit accounts are accepted. They require out of town clients to prepay.

They specialize in real estate.

Land Title Co
PO Box 657
Jackson WY 83001
Phone: 800-365-7720
307-733-4713
Fax: 307-733-6186

Local Retrieval Area: WY-Lincoln, Sublette, Teton.

Normal turnaround time: 1-2 days. Projects are generally billed by the hour. Credit accounts are accepted.

Land Title Corp
501 Cedar St
Tipton IA 52772
Phone: 319-886-6915
Fax: 319-886-6466

Local Retrieval Area: IA-Cedar.

Normal turnaround time: up to 3 days. Fee basis will vary by the type of project. The first project may require a prepayment.

Land Title Inc

1900 Silver Lake Rd Suite 200
New Brighton MN 55112

Phone: 612-638-1900
Fax: 612-638-1994

Local Retrieval Area: MN-Anoka, Chisago, Dakota, Hennepin, Ramsey, Washington.

Normal turnaround time: 2-3 days. Projects are generally billed by the number of names searched. Credit accounts are accepted. Personal checks are accepted.

They specialize in distressed property and foreclosure information.

Landmann Abstract & Title Co

119 E 4th
Sedalia MO 65301

Phone: 816-826-0051
Fax: 816-826-1266

Local Retrieval Area: MO-Pettis.

Normal turnaround time: 24 hours. Projects are generally billed by the hour. Fee basis varies by type of transaction. Credit accounts are accepted.

Landmark Title Co of Madison Co

808 S State St
Madisonville TX 77864

Phone: 409-348-5618
Fax: 409-348-5604

Local Retrieval Area: TX-Madison.

Normal turnaround time: 2-4 days. Fee basis will vary by the type of project. The first project may require a prepayment.

Landmark Title Corp

PO Box 666
Oscoda MI 48750

Phone: 517-739-1471
Fax: 517-739-0606

Local Retrieval Area: MI-Alcona, Iosco, Ogemaw.

Normal turnaround time: 3-5 days. Fee basis will vary by the type of project. Credit accounts are accepted. Payment due upon receiving invoice.

They specialize in escrow service.

Landmark Title Service

10315 E Grand River Suite 201
Brighton MI 48116

Phone: 810-227-1733
Fax: 810-227-1570

Local Retrieval Area: MI-Livingston, Oakland, Washtenaw.

Normal turnaround time: 3 days. Fee basis will vary by the type of project. The first project may require a prepayment.

They specialize in title insurance and escrow closings.

Lane County Abstract Co Inc

125 E Long
Dighton KS 67839

Phone: 316-397-5911
Fax: 316-397-5911

Local Retrieval Area: KS-Lane.

Normal turnaround time: 72 hours. Projects are generally billed by the hour. Credit accounts are accepted. Personal checks are accepted.

They specialize in title work.

LaPeer County Abstract & Title Co

303 W Nepessing St
LaPeer MI 48446

Phone: 313-664-9951
Fax: 313-664-8331

Local Retrieval Area: MI-Lapeer.

Normal turnaround time: 1 week. Projects are generally billed by the number of names searched or records located. Credit accounts are accepted.

They specialize in real estate.

Margaret Laratta

935 Indian Hill Rd
Toms River NJ 08753

Phone: 908-349-1301
Fax: 908-341-7224

Local Retrieval Area: NJ-Ocean.

Normal turnaround time: 1-2 days. Projects are generally billed by the number of names searched or records located. Credit accounts are accepted. They will also invoice.

Kris Larock

PO Box 173
Sidney IA 51652

Phone: 712-374-3019
Fax: 712-374-2227

Local Retrieval Area: IA-Fremont.

Normal turnaround time: 24-48 hours. Projects are generally billed by the number of names searched. The first project may require a prepayment.

Correspondent relationships: neighboring counties.

Larry R Dorning PC

111 W Main St
Hohenwald TN 38462-1404

Phone: 615-796-5959
Fax: 615-796-5950

Local Retrieval Area: TN-Hickman, Lawrence, Lewis, Maury, Perry, Wayne.

Normal turnaround time: 48 hours. Charges are varied depending on type of search. Credit accounts are accepted.

He specializes in real estate record searches.

Larson Abstract Co

PO Box 387
Little Falls MN 56345

Phone: 320-632-5667
Fax: 320-632-4583

Local Retrieval Area: MN-Morrison.

Normal turnaround time: 10 days. Fee basis will vary by type of project. Projects require prepayment. They will also invoice.

They specialize in real estate.

Las Vegas Legal Document

1804 N Parkchester Dr
Las Vegas NV 89108

Phone: 702-647-1627
Fax: 702-647-4940

Local Retrieval Area: NV-Clark.

Normal turnaround time: 1 to 4 days. Projects are generally billed by the number of names searched or records located. The first project may require a prepayment.

They are a subsidiary of Shimrak Investigations. They are licensed full-service private investigators.

LaSalle County Abstract Inc

PO Box 486
Cotulla TX 78014

Phone: 210-879-3712
Fax: 210-879-3712

Local Retrieval Area: TX-La Salle.

Normal turnaround time: 2-3 days. Fee basis will vary by the type of project. The first project may require a prepayment.

LaSalle Process Servers

29 S LaSalle St Suite 956
Chicago IL 60603

Phone: 312-263-0620
Fax: 312-263-0622

Local Retrieval and SOP Area: IL-Cook.

Normal turnaround time: the same day to 1 day. If archives need to be searched, the turnaround time averages 1-2 weeks. Projects are generally billed by the hour. Copy expenses will be added to the fee. The first project may require a prepayment.

Correspondent relationships: Will, DuPage, Kane, McHenry and Lake. They specialize in process service.

Brian Laster
Phone: 615-790-8252
PO Box 253
Franklin TN 37065

Local Retrieval Area: TN-Cheatham, Davidson, Maury, Montgomery, Robertson, Rutherford, Sumner, Williamson, Wilson.

Normal turnaround time: 1-3 days. Projects are generally billed by the hour. The first project may require a prepayment.

He specializes in building permit reports.

Latimer County Abstract Co
Phone: 918-465-2131
Fax: 918-465-3545
PO Box 68
Wilburton OK 74578

Local Retrieval Area: OK-Latimer.

Normal turnaround time: up to 2 weeks. Projects are generally billed by the hour. Fee basis is per page. Credit accounts are accepted.

Helen Lattus
Phone: 901-885-0891
PO Box 96
Woodland Mills TN 38271

Local Retrieval Area: KY-Calloway, Fulton, Graves, Hickman, McCracken; TN-Benton, Carroll, Crockett, Dyer, Gibson, Henry, Lake, Madison, Obion, Weakley.

Normal turnaround time: 2-3 days. Projects are generally billed by the number of names searched. Credit accounts are accepted.

Correspondent relationships: Tipton, Lauderdale and Haywood, TN counties. She specializes in real estate title searches.

▥ Law Bulletin Publishing Co
Phone: 312-644-7800
Fax: 312-644-4255
415 N State
Chicago IL 60610

Local Retrieval Area: IL-Cook, De Kalb, Du Page, Kane, Kendall, Lake, McHenry, Will, Winnebago.

Normal turnaround time: 24 hours. Projects are generally billed by the number of names searched. Credit accounts are accepted. Credit cards are accepted.

Correspondent relationships: the rest of Illinois.

Law Office of Roger Gladden
Phone: 404-550-0749
Fax: 404-787-5292
208 W Clarke St
Oxford GA 30267

Local Retrieval and SOP Area: GA-Butts, Newton, Rockdale, Walton.

Normal turnaround time: 1-3 days. Projects are generally billed by the number of names searched or records located. The first project may require a prepayment.

They specialize in record searching at the SE Federal Records Center, and criminal searches only in Newton and Rockdale counties. They are licensed private investigators.

Lawrence County Title
Phone: 618-943-4464
Fax: 618-943-4299
908 Jefferson
Lawrenceville IL 62439

Local Retrieval Area: IL-Crawford, Lawrence, Richland, Wabash.

Normal turnaround time: 24-48 hours for liens and judgment searches, and 1 to 2 weeks for abstracts and title insurance. Projects are generally billed by the hour. A charge per page and length of period (years) searched will be added to the fee. Credit accounts are accepted. Some clients are required to pay a retainer. Personal checks are accepted.

LawServ Inc
Phone: 713-228-1055
Fax: 713-228-1056
412 Main St Suite 450
Houston TX 77002

Local Retrieval and SOP Area: TX-Brazoria, Fort Bend, Galveston, Harris, Jefferson, Montgomery.

Normal turnaround time: 1-3 days. Projects are generally billed by the hour. The first project may require a prepayment.

Correspondent relationships: Travis, Bexar, Nueces, Tarrant and Dallas.

Lawyer Title/Blue Ridge Agency
Phone: 804-295-7196
Fax: 804-979-7208
218 5th St NE
Charlottesville VA 22902

Local Retrieval Area: VA-Albemarle, Augusta, City of Charlottesville, Fluvanna, Greene, Louisa, Nelson, Orange.

Normal turnaround time: 1-2 days in Albemarle and 3-5 days in other counties. Fee basis varies by type of transaction. The first project may require a prepayment.

They specialize in real estate and title searches.

Lawyer's Legal Service
Phone: 800-224-7911
503-224-7911
Fax: 503-224-9611
3301 SW Barbur Blvd Suite 200
Portland OR 97201

Local Retrieval and SOP Area: OR-Clackamas, Clatsop, Columbia, Hood River, Marion, Multnomah, Washington, Yamhill; WA-Clark.

Normal turnaround time: 1-2 days. Projects are generally billed by the number of names searched or records located. The first project may require a prepayment. Terms Re net 30 days.

Correspondent relationships: the rest of Oregon and the Southwest part of Washington. They specialize in process servicing and case file management.

Lawyers Title
Phone: 540-433-8112
Fax: 540-433-5804
66 W Water St
Harrisonburg VA 22801

Local Retrieval Area: VA-City of Harrisonburg, Rockingham.

Normal turnaround time: 5-7 days. Projects are generally billed by the hour. Projects require prepayment.

Lawyers' Abstract Co
Phone: 412-283-3510
Fax: 412-283-2258
220 S Main St Holly Point Suite A
Butler PA 16001

Local Retrieval Area: PA-Armstrong, Butler, Westmoreland.

Normal turnaround time: 2-14 days. Projects are generally billed by the hour. Projects require prepayment. They will also invoice. Personal checks are accepted.

Correspondent relationships: Lawrence, Mercer, Crawford and Clarion Counties. They specialize in title searching and title insurance. The company is owned by Butler County Lawyers and has been in business since 1965. They have the only title plant in Butler County.

Lawyers' Abstract Service Inc
Phone: 941-774-2627
Fax: 941-774-0063
2670 Airport Road S
Naples FL 33962

Local Retrieval Area: FL-Collier.

Normal turnaround time: 5-7 days. Fee basis will vary by the type of project. The first project may require a prepayment.

They specialize in land records.

Attorney David K Layton

Phone: 606-792-4613
Fax: 606-792-4222

13 Public Square
Lancaster KY 40444

Local Retrieval Area: KY-Garrard, Jessamine, Lincoln.

Normal turnaround time: 1-2 days. Projects are generally billed by the hour. Credit accounts are accepted.

Michel B Lecat

Phone: 415-925-9090
Fax: 415-925-9023

62 Lower via Casitas
Greenbrae CA 94904

Local Retrieval Area: CA-Marin, San Francisco, Alameda, Contra Costa, San Mateo, Sonoma, Napa, Santa Clara.

Normal turnaround time: couple of days. Projects are generally billed by the hour. The first project may require a prepayment. Terms are net 30 days.

Lee County Land & Abstract

Phone: 409-542-3636
Fax: 409-542-5604

PO Drawer 1039
Giddings TX 78942

Local Retrieval Area: TX-Lee.

Normal turnaround time: 2-3 days. Fee basis will vary by the type of project. The first project may require a prepayment.

▥ Lee Denney Private Investigatns

Phone: 919-847-3344
Fax: 919-847-3342

PO Box 99802
Raleigh NC 27624

Local Retrieval and SOP Area: NC-Durham, Wake.

Normal turnaround time: 2 days. Projects are generally billed by the hour. Credit accounts are accepted. Payment due upon receipt.

Correspondent relationships: Mecklinburg, NC county.

Leelanau Title Co

Phone: 616-271-6191
Fax: 616-271-3516

PO Box 10
Suttons Bay MI 49682

Local Retrieval Area: MI-Leelanau.

Normal turnaround time: 2-3 days. Fee basis will vary by transactions. The first project may require a prepayment.

They specialize in real estate.

Legal Abstract Co

Phone: 319-263-3171
Fax: 319-263-0829

301 E 2nd St
Muscatine IA 52761

Local Retrieval Area: IA-Muscatine.

Normal turnaround time: up to 1 week. Fee basis will vary by the type of project. Credit accounts are accepted.

Legal Beagles Inc

Phone: 800-743-9897
302-322-9897
Fax: 302-322-8418

PO Box 886
New Castle DE 19720

Local Retrieval and SOP Area: DE-New Castle.

Normal turnaround time: 48 hours or less. Projects are generally billed by the number of names searched. The first project may require a prepayment.

Correspondent relationships: Sussex county and local New Castle County licensed private investigator. They specialize in skip tracing to locate missing and hard-to-find defendants and witnesses and records researching in all local county and state level courts and administrative agencies including Delaware insurance and driving records.

Legal Courier Service

Phone: 612-332-7203
Fax: 612-334-3245

607 Marquette Ave Suite 309
Minneapolis MN 55402

Local Retrieval and SOP Area: MN-Anoka, Carver, Dakota, Hennepin, Ramsey, Scott, Sherburne, Washington, Wright.

Normal turnaround time: 12 hours. Projects are generally billed by the hour. Mileage expenses are added to the hourly fee. Credit accounts are accepted. They will invoice with a deposit.

Correspondent relationships: Beltrami. They specialize in federal litigation document retrieval.

Legal Courier Systems Inc

Phone: 800-869-8586
301-495-0000
Fax: 301-608-9072

PO Box 145
Kensington MD 20895-0145

Local Retrieval and SOP Area: VA-Arlington, Fairfax, Fauquier, Loudoun, Prince William, Stafford.

Normal turnaround time: the same day. A one hour rush service is also available. Projects are generally billed by the hour. Travel expenses will be added to the fee. Credit accounts are accepted.

They specialize in court filings and research, and bankruptcy courts.

Legal Couriers Inc

Phone: 509-453-1134
Fax: 509-575-6680

22 S 3rd Ave
Yakima WA 98902

Local Retrieval and SOP Area: WA-Yakima.

Normal turnaround time: 24 hours. They charge per hour plus costs. The first project may require a prepayment. They will invoice law firms.

Legal Data Resources

Phone: 800-735-9207
773-561-2468
Fax: 773-561-2488

2816 W Summerdale
Chicago IL 60625

Local Retrieval and SOP Area: IL-Cook, Du Page, Lake, Will.

Normal turnaround time: 24 hours. Online computer ordering is also available. Projects are generally billed by the number of names searched or records located. Credit accounts are accepted. Personal checks are accepted.

Correspondent relationships: nationwide. They specialize in legal research including case law, federal and state legislation, property, patent, trademark and copyright searches.

▥ Legal Data Services

Phone: 504-892-5194
Fax: 504-898-0837

PO Box 1119
Covington LA 70434-1119

Local Retrieval Area: LA-St. Tammany Parish, Washington Parish.

Normal turnaround time: 5 working days. Fee basis will vary by type of project. The first project may require a prepayment.

Correspondent relationships: Orleans, Jefferson, St Bernard, St Charles, Tangipahoa and Livingston, LA parishes. They specialize in metes and bounds, lot and block abstracting and property tax research.

Legal Eagles Attorney Services

Phone: 800-929-1285
615-665-1211
Fax: 615-665-1960

729 Magnolia Tr
Nashville TN 37221-3469

Local Retrieval and SOP Area: TN-Davidson.

Normal turnaround time: 1-2 days. Projects are generally billed by the hour. The first project may require a prepayment.

They specialize in federal court case retrieval.

Legal Express

Phone: 719-578-0407

15 S Weber Suite D
Colorado Springs CO 80903

Local Retrieval Area: CO-El Paso, Teller.

Normal turnaround time: 2 working days. Projects are generally billed by the number of names searched. Credit accounts are accepted.

Legal Eye & Legal Judgment

Phone: 800-985-1409
Fax: 805-671-9807

9452 Telephone Rd Suite 230
Ventura CA 93004

Local Retrieval Area: CA-Ventura.

Normal turnaround time: 24-48 hours. Rush service is available. Online computer ordering is also available. Projects are generally billed by the number of names searched. Copy fee is charged with the by name searched fee. Volume discounts available. The first project may require a prepayment. Regular clients invoiced.

Correspondent relationships: All of California, plus Canada and Puerto Rico. They have 15 years in skiptracing, asset searches, background checks, high-profile contacts, family searches, document retrieval and "unusual requests".

Legal Investigations

Phone: 423-584-9700
Fax: 423-584-7001

7113 Stockton Dr
Knoxville TN 37909

Local Retrieval and SOP Area: TN-30 Counties.

Normal turnaround time: 1-3 working days. Projects are generally billed by the hour. The first project may require a prepayment.

Correspondent relationships: other parts of Tennessee. They specialize in personal injury investigation searches and automotive safety. All east Tennessee served on a per case basis.

Legal Net Process Service

Phone: 915-532-7871
Fax: 915-532-7874

1023 E Yandell
El Paso TX 79902

Local Retrieval and SOP Area: NM-Dona Ana; TX-El Paso, Hudspeth.

Normal turnaround time: 1 day in El Paso and 2-3 days in the other counties. Fee basis will vary by the type of project. The first project may require a prepayment.

Legal Recording of Rochester Inc

Phone: 716-232-6710
Fax: 716-232-1475

7 Reynolds Arcade Bldg
Rochester NY 14614-1803

Local Retrieval Area: NY-Monroe.

Normal turnaround time: 24-48 hours. Projects are generally billed by the number of names searched or records located. The first project may require a prepayment.

They specialize in real property tax searches for lenders, criminal searches and real estate DBA searches.

Legal Records Investigations

Phone: 210-675-6258
Fax: 210-675-6258

PO Box 458253
San Antonio TX 78280

Local Retrieval Area: TX-Bandera, Bexar, Medina.

Normal turnaround time: 24-48 hours. The first project may require a prepayment. Terms are net 30 days with account.

Correspondent relationships: Austin, Houston, Dallas, East Texas area and Waco, TX. They specialize in locating hidden assets ie, property, bank accounts. They also do discovery for lawsuits, uncovering fraud through legal document retrieval.

Legal Records Research

Phone: 800-721-0524
305-867-8603
Fax: 305-867-8603

8811 Harding Ave
Surfside FL 33154-3418

Local Retrieval Area: FL-Dade.

Normal turnaround time: 24 hours for individual searches, weekly updates on bulk data retrieved. Online computer ordering is also available. Projects are generally billed by the number of names searched or records located. Projects require prepayment. Weekly data, weekly payment.

Correspondent relationships: Monroe, FL county. They specialize in individual name searches, information verification, bulk data retrieval, judgments and tax liens.

Legal Resources

Phone: 504-542-2199
Fax: 504-543-0058

108 NW Railroad Ave PO Box 992
Hammond LA 70401

Local Retrieval Area: LA-Livingston Parish, St. Helena Parish, St. Tammany Parish, Tangipahoa Parish, Washington Parish.

Normal turnaround time: 1-3 days. Fee basis varies by type of transaction. The first project may require a prepayment.

Correspondent relationships: the other Louisiana parishes. She has been in business for 27 years. She specializes in real estate title searches.

Legal Search

Phone: 907-258-4752
Fax: 907-258-1257

4516 Mountain View Dr
Anchorage AK 99508-1820

Local Retrieval Area: AK-Anchorage Borough, Matanuska-Susitna Borough.

Normal turnaround time: 3-14 days. Projects are generally billed by the hour. Credit accounts are accepted. Payment terms are as negotiated.

Correspondent relationships: the Kenai and Fairbanks regions.

Legal Services

Phone: 810-353-0990
Fax: 810-356-4655

PO Box 267-250
Franklin MI 48025-0267

Local Retrieval and SOP Area: MI-Livingston, Macomb, Monroe, Oakland, Washtenaw, Wayne.

Normal turnaround time: 3-4 days. Projects are generally billed by the hour. Copy expenses will be added to the fee. Credit accounts are accepted. Payment due when invoiced.

Correspondent relationships: nationwide and worldwide. They specialize in obtaining medical records, court records, and information about foreign companies and corporations.

Legal Support Services - II

Phone: 605-642-7146
Fax: 605-642-4760

19 Nickel Pl
Spearfish SD 57783

Local Retrieval Area: SD-Lawrence, Pennington.

Normal turnaround time: 24-48 hours. Projects are generally billed by the number of names searched. Credit accounts are accepted.

Correspondent relationships: all of South Dakota. They specialize in record searches and retrieval of public records from federal, state and county agencies, including state UCC and corporate searches. They also serve as registered agents for corporations.

Legal Wings Inc

Phone: 800-339-1286
609-393-6700
425 Greenwood Ave Suite 300
Trenton NJ 08609   **Fax:** 609-393-8081

Local Retrieval and SOP Area: NJ-14 Counties; PA-Bucks, Chester, Delaware, Philadelphia.

Normal turnaround time: 48 hours for limited partnership, bankruptcy or corporate records. Other records average 24 hours. Projects are generally billed by the number of names searched. The first project may require a prepayment.

Correspondent relationships: nationwide. They are connected by modem to all US District and Bankruptcy docket sheets in New Jersey. They also search foreclosure, matrimonial, DMV records, corporations, partnership, and trade names indexes.

Legal Wings Inc - Newark

Phone: 800-339-1286
201-621-7520
24 Commerce St Suite 1422
Newark NJ 07102   **Fax:** 201-621-8811

Local Retrieval and SOP Area: NJ-Bergen, Essex, Hudson, Morris, Passaic, Union.

Normal turnaround time: 24 hours. Projects are generally billed by the number of names searched or records located. The first project may require a prepayment.

Correspondent relationships: nationwide. They are connected by modem to all US District and Bankruptcy docket sheets in New Jersey. They also retrieve archived records for the NY/NJ Courts from the Federal Records Center in Bayonne, NJ.

LegalEase Inc

Phone: 800-393-1277
212-393-9070
139 Fulton St Suite 1013
New York NY 10038   **Fax:** 212-393-9796

Local Retrieval and SOP Area: NY-Bronx, Kings, Nassau, New York, Putnam, Queens, Richmond, Rockland, Westchester.

Normal turnaround time: 24-72 hours. Rush service available. Projects are generally billed by the number of names searched or records located. Volume searches will be charged by the hour. The first project may require a prepayment.

Correspondent relationships: all areas outside an 85 mile radius of New York City. They specialize in document retrieval (federal and state courts) and on-line information retrieval.

Legalese

Phone: 888-300-3579
916-498-1999
PO Box 1198
Sacramento CA 95812-1198   **Fax:** 916-498-1980

Local Retrieval and SOP Area: CA-El Dorado, Placer, Sacramento, San Joaquin, Sutter, Yolo, Yuba.

Normal turnaround time: 2 days. Projects are generally billed by the number of names searched. The first project may require a prepayment.

They specialize in UCC, corporation and county records.

LegalMedic Services Inc

Phone: 504-347-3408
PO Box 2761
Harvey LA 70059   **Fax:** 504-340-5522

Local Retrieval and SOP Area: LA-Jefferson Parish, Orleans Parish, St. Bernard Parish, St. Tammany Parish.

Normal turnaround time: 24 hours. Projects are generally billed by the number of names searched. Fees are by the job (flat fee). The first project may require a prepayment. Terms are net 10 days.

They specialize in skip trace, assets and liabilities investigations, bankruptcy and civil records.

LegalNet Inc

Phone: 310-530-2200
2510 W 237th Street Suite 110
Torrance CA 90505   **Fax:** 310-530-1014

Local Retrieval Area: CA-Los Angeles, Orange.

Normal turnaround time: 1-3 weeks. Projects are generally billed by the number of records located. Credit accounts are accepted.

Correspondent relationships: Ventura, San Diego, Riverside, and San Bernardino.

LegalTrieve Information Svcs

Phone: 508-238-4227
38 Sharron Dr
South Easton MA 02375   **Fax:** 508-238-4678

Local Retrieval Area: MA-Bristol, Essex, Middlesex, Norfolk, Plymouth, Suffolk.

Normal turnaround time: 1-3 business days. Projects are generally billed by the number of names searched. Credit accounts are accepted. Large projects require prepayment. Payment due upon receipt for smaller projects.

Correspondent relationships: nationwide. They specialize in public record research, document retrieval, asset searches, skip-tracing, employment searches, pre-employment screening and liquid asset searches.

LEGWORK

Phone: 916-944-0581
PO Box 639
Carmichael CA 95609   **Fax:** 916-944-2538

Local Retrieval and SOP Area: CA-Placer, Sacramento, Yolo.

Normal turnaround time: 2 days. Projects are generally billed by the hour. The first project may require a prepayment.

Correspondent relationships: El Dorado, San Francisco, Orange, Riverside, San Bernardino and Central and Bay area counties. They specialize in difficult service of process, high volume legal photocopying and missing persons.

LEGWORK

Phone: 209-577-3053
1829 Ellison Dr
Modesto CA 95355   **Fax:** 209-577-3053

Local Retrieval and SOP Area: CA-Merced, Stanislaus.

Normal turnaround time: 2 days. Projects are generally billed by the hour. The first project may require a prepayment.

They specialize in difficult service of process, high volume legal photocopying and missing persons.

LEGWORK

Phone: 805-965-3908
420 N Voluntario St Suite 6B
Santa Barbara CA 93103   **Fax:** 805-965-0288

Local Retrieval and SOP Area: CA-Santa Barbara, Ventura.

Normal turnaround time: 2 days. Projects are generally billed by the number of names searched. Credit accounts are accepted.

They specialize in meeting tight deadlines, on site legal photocopying, messenger/delivery and missing persons.

Leighton Abstract

Phone: 207-862-3512
210 Kennebec Rd
Hampten ME 04444   **Fax:** 207-862-3512

Local Retrieval Area: ME-Hancock, Penobscot, Piscataquis, Waldo.

Normal turnaround time: 48 hours. Projects are generally billed by the hour. Credit accounts are accepted.

Lemhi Title Co
Phone: 208-756-2977
Fax: 208-756-6286
PO Box J
Salmon ID 83467

Local Retrieval Area: ID-Lemhi.

Normal turnaround time: 3 days. Fee basis varies by type of transaction. Credit accounts are accepted.

Lenow International Inc
Phone: 901-726-0735
Fax: 901-725-4079
PO Box 3092
Memphis TN 38173-0092

Local Retrieval and SOP Area: MS-De Soto; TN-Shelby.

Normal turnaround time: 24 hours. Online computer ordering is also available. Projects are generally billed by the hour. The first project may require a prepayment.

They specialize in locating records when limited information is available.

Bruce Lester
Phone: 609-853-9836
Fax: 609-853-5008
28 Roseberry Ct
Deptford NJ 08096

Local Retrieval Area: NJ-Gloucester.

Normal turnaround time: 24 hours. Fee basis will vary by the type of project. Credit accounts are accepted. Personal checks are accepted.

Lew Davis Investigatons
Phone: 304-523-0055
Fax: 304-529-4552
2022 10th Ave
Huntington WV 25703-2004

Local Retrieval and SOP Area: KY-Boyd; OH-Lawrence; WV-Cabell, Lincoln, Mason, Putnam, Wayne.

Normal turnaround time: 24 hours. No project billing information was given. The first project may require a prepayment.

Lewis County Abstract
Phone: 208-937-2621
Fax: 208-937-2621
PO Box 36
Nezperce ID 83543

Local Retrieval Area: ID-Lewis.

Normal turnaround time: 4-5 days. Fee basis will vary by the type of project. Credit accounts are accepted.

They specialize in providing title insurance.

Lewis County Abstract
Phone: 573-767-5207
Fax: 573-767-5207
200 A E Lafayette
Monticello MO 63457

Local Retrieval Area: MO-Lewis.

Normal turnaround time: the same day. Projects are generally billed by the number of records located. Credit accounts are accepted. Personal checks are accepted.

Lexington Title Corp
Phone: 803-957-1243
Fax: 803-957-9359
301 Gibson Rd
Lexington SC 29072

Local Retrieval Area: SC-Lexington, Saluda.

Normal turnaround time: 24-48 hours. Fee basis varies by type of transaction. Credit accounts are accepted. Terms are net 15 days.

They specialize in title abstracts and title insurance.

Margene Libertino
Phone: 540-785-9930
Fax: 540-785-9933
11609 Bend Bow Dr
Fredericksburg VA 22407-7491

Local Retrieval Area: VA-Caroline, City of Fredericksburg, King George, Spotsylvania, Stafford.

Normal turnaround time: 24-48 hours. Projects are generally billed by the number of names searched. Credit accounts are accepted. Payment due upon receipt of invoice.

Liberty Corporate Services Inc
Phone: 800-334-2735
Fax: 404-986-9326
3998 Ashford Dunwoody Rd
Atlanta GA 30319

Local Retrieval Area: GA-All Counties.

Normal turnaround time: 1-5 days. Online computer ordering is also available. Fee basis is by name and county. Credit accounts are accepted.

Correspondent relationships: nationwide. They specialize in UCC and corporate work. Their personnel visit each county in Georgia on a weekly schedule.

Liberty Record Search Inc
Phone: 304-428-5126
Fax: 304-428-3854
PO Box 3456
Parkersburg WV 26101

Local Retrieval Area: KY-Boyd, Carter, Floyd, Greenup, Johnson, Lawrence, Lewis, Pike, Rowan; OH-Athens, Belmont, Carroll, Columbiana, Gallia, Jefferson, Lawrence, Meigs, Washington; WV-45 Counties.

Normal turnaround time: 24-48 hours depending on county of search. Projects are generally billed by the number of names searched. Credit accounts are accepted. Billed monthly with net due the 15th.

Liberty Record Search of NJ Inc
Phone: 201-887-3854
Fax: 201-887-3854
PO Box 95
Whippany NJ 07981

Local Retrieval Area: NJ-Morris, Passaic, Somerset, Sussex.

Normal turnaround time: 24-48 hours. Projects are generally billed by the number of names searched. Credit accounts are accepted. Billed monthly with net due the 15th of the month.

LIDA Credit Agency Inc
Phone: 516-678-4600
Fax: 516-678-4611
450 Sunrise Hwy
Rockville Centre NY 11570

Local Retrieval and SOP Area: NY-Bronx, Kings, Nassau, New York, Queens, Richmond, Suffolk, Westchester.

Normal turnaround time: 8-48 hours. Projects are generally billed by the number of names searched. The first project may require a prepayment. Credit cards are accepted.

Correspondent relationships: nationwide. They specialize in public record research, background reports, commercial and individual, credit reports and general investigations.

Lightspeed Couriers
Phone: 214-748-3340
Fax: 214-748-9244
1530 Main St Suite 1000
Dallas TX 75201

Local Retrieval and SOP Area: TX-Dallam, Tarrant.

Normal turnaround time: 1 day. Projects are generally billed by the hour. The first project may require a prepayment.

They specialize in locations and background checks.

Lincoln Abstract Co
Phone: 501-628-3144

PO Box 598
Star City AR 71667

Local Retrieval Area: AR-Lincoln.

Normal turnaround time: 5 working days. Projects are generally billed by the hour. Projects require prepayment.

Lincoln County Abstract & Title Co
Phone: 800-635-4692
505-257-5665

PO Drawer 1979
Ruidoso NM 88345
Fax: 505-257-9010

Local Retrieval Area: NM-Lincoln.

Normal turnaround time: varied depending on project. Projects are generally billed by the number of records located. Credit accounts are accepted.

They specialize in title insurance.

Lincoln Trail Title Services Inc
Phone: 502-765-5566
Fax: 502-769-3267

PO Box 111 2935 Dolphin Dr
Elizabethtown KY 42702

Local Retrieval Area: KY-Hardin.

Normal turnaround time: 3-5 days. Projects are generally billed by the hour. Credit accounts are accepted.

Tina Linder
Phone: 419-947-7240
Fax: 419-947-7240

240 W Marion St
Mt Gilead OH 43338

Local Retrieval Area: OH-Morrow.

Normal turnaround time: 12-24 hours. Fee basis is "per job". Credit accounts are accepted.

Linn County Abstract Co
Phone: 888-795-2949
913-795-2949

PO Box 98 106 S 5th St
Mound City KS 66056
Fax: 913-795-2449

Local Retrieval Area: KS-Bourbon, Linn.

Normal turnaround time: 1 day. Fees basis varies by project. Credit accounts are accepted.

Lipscomb County Abstract Co
Phone: 806-658-4525
Fax: 806-658-4524

PO Box L
Booker TX 79005

Local Retrieval Area: TX-Lipscomb.

Normal turnaround time: 2-3 days. Fee basis will vary by the type of project. The first project may require a prepayment.

Litigant Services Inc of Dallas
Phone: 214-880-0070
Fax: 214-880-0071

1 McKinney Plaza 3232 McKinney Ave #1270
Dallas TX 75204

Local Retrieval Area: TX-Dallas.

Normal turnaround time: 1-3 days. Online computer ordering is also available. Projects are generally billed by the number of names searched. Credit accounts are accepted.

Correspondent relationships: Tarrant and Collin. They specialize in accident reconstruction, computer record retrieval, financial/assets, insurance, security/loss prevention and general investigations.

Litigant Services Inc of El Paso
Phone: 915-595-2309
Fax: 915-595-0366

10432 Brian Mooney Ave Suite 100
El Paso TX 79935-2800

Local Retrieval Area: TX-El Paso.

Normal turnaround time: 1-3 days. Online computer ordering is also available. Projects are generally billed by the number of names searched. The first project may require a prepayment.

Correspondent relationships: Dona Ana, New Mexico and Juarez Chihuaha, Mexico. They specialize in accident reconstruction, computer records retrieval, financial/assets, insurance security/loss prevention and general investigations.

Little River Land & Abstract
Phone: 817-697-6962
Fax: 817-697-2592

PO Box 828
Cameron TX 76520

Local Retrieval Area: TX-Milam.

Normal turnaround time: 2-5 days. Fees vary by project. Credit accounts are accepted.

They are familiar with all records maintained at the county courthouse.

Locke-Neosho Abstracts Inc
Phone: 316-244-3641
Fax: 316-244-3234

PO Box 178
Erie KS 66733

Local Retrieval Area: KS-Neosho.

Normal turnaround time: up to 1 week. Fee basis varies by type of transaction. Credit accounts are accepted. They request prepayment from out of area clients, but will invoice established customers.

Logan County Abstract Co
Phone: 701-754-2200

Box C
Napoleon ND 58561

Local Retrieval Area: ND-Logan.

Normal turnaround time: 1-2 days. Projects are generally billed by the number of records located. Credit accounts are accepted.

Logan Registration Service Inc
Phone: 800-524-4111
916-457-5787

PO Box 161644
Sacramento CA 95816
Fax: 916-457-5789

Local Retrieval Area: CA-Sacramento.

Normal turnaround time: 24-48 hours. Online immediately. Projects are generally billed by the number of names searched. Credit accounts are accepted. Terms are net 30 days.

Correspondent relationships: State of California and nationwide DMV records. They specialize in California DMV records by on-line access. They also obtain DMV records from most of the US.

Lone Star Legal
Phone: 415-255-8550
Fax: 415-255-8549

700 7th St Suite 111
San Francisco CA 94107

Local Retrieval Area: CA-Alameda, Contra Costa, Marin, Napa, San Francisco, San Mateo, Santa Clara, Sonoma.

Normal turnaround time: 2 days. Projects are generally billed by the hour. The first project may require a prepayment. Credit cards are accepted.

Correspondent relationships: Sacramento, Santa Cruz and Solono counties. They specialize in complex and routine court research, complete litigation copying and on-site copying.

Gordon B Long
Phone: 606-349-1558
Fax: 606-349-2441
PO Box 531 Maple St
Salyersville KY 41465

Local Retrieval Area: KY-Breathitt, Johnson, Knott, Magoffin, Pike, Wolfe.

Normal turnaround time: up to 1 week. Projects are generally billed by the hour. Projects require prepayment.

Alfred Lopez
Phone: 505-239-6096
Fax: 505-237-1090
PO Box 563
Gallup NM 87305

Local Retrieval and SOP Area: NM-Bernalillo, Cibola, McKinley.

Normal turnaround time: 2 days. Projects are generally billed by the hour. Credit accounts are accepted.

Lora J Musilli & Associates
Phone: 201-383-7763
Fax: 201-875-0650
PO Box 635
Branchville NJ 07826

Local Retrieval Area: NJ-Sussex.

Normal turnaround time: 24 hours. Projects are generally billed by the number of names searched. The first project may require a prepayment. Personal checks are accepted.

They specialize in credit check searches and title searches.

Lorain County Title Co
Phone: 800-624-5507
216-777-4686
Fax: 216-284-5161
424 Middle Ave
Elyria OH 44035

Local Retrieval Area: OH-Cuyahoga, Erie, Lorain.

Normal turnaround time: 3 days. Fee basis varies by type of transaction. Credit accounts are accepted.

Lord and Associates
Phone: 208-939-8258
Fax: 208-939-7244
PO Box 909
Eagle ID 83616

Local Retrieval and SOP Area: ID-Ada, Boise, Canyon, Elmore, Gem, Owyhee, Payette, Valley, Washington.

Normal turnaround time: 72 hours. Online computer ordering is also available. Projects are generally billed by the hour. The first project may require a prepayment. Credit cards are accepted.

They specialize in civil and criminal investigations and security consulting.

Los Angeles Legal Service
Phone: 213-259-9499
Fax: 213-257-0605
PO Box 41411
Los Angeles CA 90041

Local Retrieval and SOP Area: CA-Los Angeles.

Normal turnaround time: 48-72 hours. Bankruptcy may take longer than 48 hours. Fee basis will vary by the type of project. Credit accounts are accepted.

Correspondent relationships: CAPP members in California.

Loss Protection & Investigations
Phone: 800-268-7472
209-268-7472
Fax: 209-268-7459
2882 E Annadale Ave
Fresno CA 93706

Local Retrieval Area: CA-Fresno.

Normal turnaround time: 2 days. Project billing methods vary. The first project may require a prepayment.

Low Country Abstractors
Phone: 803-538-5000
Fax: 803-538-5005
500 Memorial Ave PO Box 21
Walterboro SC 29488

Local Retrieval and SOP Area: SC-Colleton, Dorchester, Hampton.

Normal turnaround time: 2 days. No extra charge for 1 day turnaround. Projects are generally billed by the number of names searched. Credit accounts are accepted. Open invoicing available.

Correspondent relationships: All of South Carolina.

⚏ Rita L Lubey
Phone: 916-722-2568
Fax: 916-722-2568
7800 Sunrise Blvd #2-118
Citrus Heights CA 95610

Local Retrieval and SOP Area: CA-El Dorado, Placer, Sacramento, Solano, Yolo.

Normal turnaround time: same day to 48 hours. Projects are generally billed by the number of names searched. The first project may require a prepayment.

Correspondent relationships: California.

⚏ Patricia O Lueken
Phone: 314-631-5928
Fax: 314-631-5928
9864 Diamond Point Dr
St Louis MO 63123

Local Retrieval Area: MO-St. Louis, City of St. Louis.

Normal turnaround time: the next day. Projects are generally billed by the number of names searched. Credit accounts are accepted.

They specialize in checks for EPA and ERISA liens.

Lufkin Abstract
Phone: 409-634-9611
Fax: 409-634-9714
315 E Frank Ave
Lufkin TX 75901

Local Retrieval Area: TX-Angelina.

Normal turnaround time: 7-10 days. Fees vary by project. The first project may require a prepayment.

⚏ Eleda Luther
Phone: 805-250-8254
Fax: 805-250-8253
15462 Poppyseed Lane
Canyon Country CA 91351-1850

Local Retrieval Area: CA-Los Angeles.

Normal turnaround time: 1-3 days. Projects are generally billed by the number of names searched. Credit accounts are accepted. Will invoice weekly or monthly depending on volume.

She specializes in criminal background checks.

Lyman Title Co
Phone: 605-869-2269
Fax: 605-869-2269
PO Box 187
Kennebec SD 57544

Local Retrieval Area: SD-Lyman.

Normal turnaround time: up to 2 weeks. Fee basis varies by type of transaction. Credit accounts are accepted.

They specialize in land records.

▥ Lynda Harris Document Search

Phone: 800-621-4974
810-569-2882

27690 Shagbark
Southfield MI 48076
Fax: 810-569-7715

Local Retrieval Area: MI-Genesee, Kent, Macomb, Oakland, Washtenaw, Wayne.

Normal turnaround time: 12-48 hours. Projects are generally billed by the number of names searched. Credit accounts are accepted.

Correspondent relationships: all of Michigan. Provide document searches and retrieval for all jurisdictions in Michigan including federal, state, county and local. Services include UCC, tax liens, litigation, criminal background, vital statistics and corporate verification.

Lynn County Abstract Co

Phone: 806-998-4022
Fax: 806-998-4022

PO Box 968
Tahoka TX 79373

Local Retrieval Area: TX-Lynn.

Normal turnaround time: up to a week. Fee basis will vary by the type of project. The first project may require a prepayment.

Lyon Abstract Company

Phone: 501-836-8084
Fax: 501-836-4811

PO Box 216
Camden AR 71701

Local Retrieval and SOP Area: AR-Calhoun, Columbia, Dallas, Lafayette, Ouachita, Union.

Normal turnaround time: varied depending on project. Projects are generally billed by the number of names searched. The first project may require a prepayment.

Correspondent relationships: the rest of Arkansas. They specialize in abstracts of title and judgments, liens, lis pendens and UCC searches.

Lyon County Title

Phone: 712-472-3758

109 S Marshall St
Rock Rapids IA 51246

Local Retrieval Area: IA-Lyon.

Normal turnaround time: 1-3 days. Fee basis will vary by the type of project. The first project may require a prepayment.

M

M & D Records Research

Phone: 419-693-5649
Fax: 419-693-4211

648 Forsythe
Toledo OH 43605

Local Retrieval and SOP Area: OH-Defiance, Fulton, Hancock, Henry, Lucas, Ottawa, Sandusky, Williams, Wood.

Normal turnaround time: 24-48 hours. Projects are generally billed by the number of names searched or records located. Charges are quoted by job. Credit accounts are accepted.

M & M Legal Services

Phone: 503-963-9703
Fax: 503-963-8219

PO Box 364
La Grande OR 97850

Local Retrieval and SOP Area: OR-Baker, Umatilla, Union, Wallowa.

Normal turnaround time: 1 day for Union County, 1-2 days for Baker County, and 4 days for Wallowa and Umatilla Counties. Projects are generally billed by the hour. Credit accounts are accepted. They request prepayment from out of state clients, but will invoice established customers.

M & M Search Service Inc

Phone: 202-393-3144
Fax: 202-393-3242

624 9th St NW Suite 222
Washington DC 20001

Local Retrieval Area: DC-District of Columbia; MD-Baltimore, Charles, Prince George's; VA-Montgomery.

Normal turnaround time: 8 hours for court records and UCC's. Full 60 year real estate searches take 2 to 3 days. They charge by name and address. Credit accounts are accepted. They will accept personal checks.

Correspondent relationships: Howard County, Ann Arundel County and Prince William County. They specialize in real estate and UCC searches.

▥ M L Cozart Copy Service

Phone: 209-334-2171
Fax: 209-333-6254

PO Box 7721
Stockton CA 95267-7721

Local Retrieval Area: CA-Amador, Calaveras, El Dorado, Napa, Placer, Sacramento, San Joaquin, Solano, Stanislaus, Yolo.

Normal turnaround time: 24-48 hours. Projects are generally billed by the number of names searched. Credit accounts are accepted. 30 day billing cycle.

Correspondent relationships: Butte, Colusa, Glenn, Lake, Lassen, Merced, Plumas, Shasta, Siskiyou, Sutter, Tehama, Tuolume, Yuba, Fresno, Tulare, Kings, Madera, Monterrey, Santa Cruz, San Benito, San Luis Obispo, Sonoma, Humboldt, Mariposa, Nevada, San Diego, CA counties & OR. They have over 40 years experience in court record retrieval. They also file UCC's and copy medical records from physicians, hospitals and clinics.

▥ M.J.T. Research

Phone: 800-297-8406
219-326-7637

3902 N US 35
LaPorte IN 46350
Fax: 219-326-1915

Local Retrieval Area: IN-La Porte, Porter, St. Joseph.

Normal turnaround time: 24-48 hours. Projects are generally billed by the number of names searched. Credit accounts are accepted. Billing at the end of the month.

M.R.S. Datascope Inc

Phone: 800-899-3282
713-861-3900

7155 Old Katy Rd Suite 160
Houston TX 77025
Fax: 713-864-0439

Local Retrieval and SOP Area: TX-Fort Bend, Galveston, Harris, Jefferson, Montgomery.

Normal turnaround time: 2-3 days. Project billing methods vary. Projects require prepayment.

Correspondent relationships: Bexar, Dallas, Tarrant and Jefferson. They specialize in record retrieval for pretrial discovery, complete litigation support services, court reporters and legal video.

Mac Abstract & Title Insurance Co

Phone: 501-782-3053
Fax: 501-782-5432

PO Box 2124
Fort Smith AR 72902

Local Retrieval Area: AR-Crawford, Sebastian.

Normal turnaround time: 2 days. Projects are generally billed by the number of names searched. Fee basis will vary by the type of project. The first project may require a prepayment.

They specialize in real estate.

🏛 MacIntire & Associates

531 W Plata Suite 200
Tucson AZ 85705

Phone: 800-641-2737
     520-622-2737
Fax: 888-882-5205
     520-792-2764

Local Retrieval and SOP Area: AZ-Cochise, Graham, Greenlee, Maricopa, Pima, Santa Cruz.

Normal turnaround time: 48 hours maximum. Expedited service available. Online computer ordering is also available. Projects are generally billed by the number of names searched. Prepayment required for volume requests. The first project may require a prepayment. Credit cards are accepted. Payment due upon completion.

Correspondent relationships: nationwide and international. They have extensive background in criminal defense, personal injury, surveillance and employment screening services. Male and female staff speak Spanish and have experience in Mexico.

Mackinac Abstract and Title Co

291 Stockbridge
St Ignace MI 49781

Phone: 906-643-7452
Fax: 906-643-7452

Local Retrieval Area: MI-Chippewa, Luce, Mackinac.

Normal turnaround time: 7-10 business days. Fee basis will vary by type of project. Credit accounts are accepted.

They specialize in real estate and tax record searches, title insurance and abstracts of title.

Madison County Title Co

PO Box 54 106 E Wallace St
Virginia City MT 59755

Phone: 800-570-5337
     406-843-5337
Fax: 406-843-5431

Local Retrieval Area: MT-Madison.

Normal turnaround time: 1-3 days. Projects are generally billed by the hour. Credit accounts are accepted.

Magic P I & Security Inc

529 Northampton Rd
Kalamazoo MI 49006

Phone: 800-362-4388
     616-381-7772
Fax: 616-381-2324

Local Retrieval and SOP Area: MI-Kalamazoo.

Normal turnaround time: 48-72 hours. Projects are generally billed by the hour. The first project may require a prepayment.

They specialize in civil process and private investigations.

Mahaska Title - Johnson Abstract

121 High Ave E
Oskaloosa IA 52577

Phone: 515-673-5666
Fax: 515-673-9224

Local Retrieval Area: IA-Mahaska.

Normal turnaround time: 1-2 days..dd. Projects are generally billed by the number of names searched. Also billed according to accessed value and flat rates. Credit accounts are accepted.

Mahnomen County Abstract Co

PO Box 325 111 E Monroe Ave
Mahnomen MN 56557

Phone: 218-935-5227

Local Retrieval Area: MN-Mahnomen.

Normal turnaround time: the same day. Projects are generally billed by the number of names searched or records located. Credit accounts are accepted. Will send invoice.

They specialize in title searches, owner and encumbrance reports, registered property abstracts and continuation of existing abstracts and preparation of new abstracts.

Main Abstract & Title Co

100 Sherwood Dr
Roscommon MI 48653

Phone: 517-275-5600
Fax: 517-275-8649

Local Retrieval Area: MI-Crawford, Roscommon.

Normal turnaround time: up to 1 week. Fee basis will vary by type of project. Projects require prepayment.

They specialize in real estate transactions.

Main Street Title Corp

118 N Main St
Goshen IN 46526

Phone: 219-533-3774
Fax: 219-534-5445

Local Retrieval Area: IN-Elkhart.

Normal turnaround time: 7-10 days. A 2 day rush service is available for established customers. Projects are generally billed by the number of records located. Credit accounts are accepted.

They specialize in real estate records.

🏛 Maine Public Record Services

PO Box 514
Moody ME 04054

Phone: 207-646-9065
Fax: 207-646-9065

Local Retrieval Area: ME-Cumberland, Knox, Lincoln, Sagadahoc, Waldo, York.

Normal turnaround time: 24-72 hours on variable depending upon county. Per name/per court. Price lists available. The first project may require a prepayment. Terms are net 30 days.

They specialize in asset searches, document retrieval, property report and updates, UCC searches, title chains, state-county-federal court searches, mortgage document retrieval, judgments and lien searches.

Mainline Researchers

PO Box 741 213 S Center St (15931)
Ebensburg PA 15931-0741

Phone: 814-472-7913
Fax: 814-472-7936

Local Retrieval Area: PA-Cambria.

Normal turnaround time: 24 hours. 60 year title searches take longer. Charges are varied depending on type of search. Credit accounts are accepted. Billed monthly, net 10 days.

Correspondent relationships: most counties in western Pennsylvania.

Mainstreet Business Services

Box 674
Miles City MT 59301

Phone: 406-232-6111
Fax: 406-232-0319

Local Retrieval Area: MT-15 Counties.

Normal turnaround time: varied depending on project. Fee basis varies by type of transaction. Credit accounts are accepted.

Correspondent relationships: Garfield and Powder River counties. They specialize in private investigations and bail bonds.

🏛 Major Legal Services Inc

510 Park Plaza 1111 Chester Ave
Cleveland OH 44114

Phone: 216-579-9782
Fax: 216-579-1662

Local Retrieval and SOP Area: OH-Cuyahoga.

Normal turnaround time: 5 days. Expedited service available. Projects are generally billed by the hour. The first project may require a prepayment. Terms are net 30 days.

Correspondent relationships: statewide for process service. They are a temporary paralegal and attorney service, statewide.

Mallard Investigations
Phone: 810-627-6605
Fax: 810-627-6666
PO Box 535
Atlanta MI 49709-0535

Local Retrieval Area: MI-Genesee, Lapeer, Macomb, Oakland, Wayne.

Normal turnaround time: 24-48 hours. Projects are generally billed by the number of records located. Credit accounts are accepted. They require partial prepayment.

Management Information Services
Phone: 216-982-3959
Fax: 216-241-3227
1936 Columbus Rd Suite 8
Cleveland OH 44113

Local Retrieval and SOP Area: OH-Ashtabula, Cuyahoga, Geauga, Lake, Lorain, Medina.

Normal turnaround time: 1-4 days. Online computer ordering is also available. Projects are generally billed by the number of names searched. The first project may require a prepayment.

They specialize in pre-employment screening. Services include: criminal checks, employment verification, OH drivers license and area drug testing.

Manistee Abstract & Title Co
Phone: 616-723-3397
Fax: 616-723-5382
63 Maple St
Manistee MI 49660

Local Retrieval Area: MI-Manistee.

Normal turnaround time: 3-5 days. Fee basis will vary by type of project. Projects require prepayment. They will also invoice.

They specialize in real estate.

Marco & Company
Phone: 707-747-1802
Fax: 707-747-5602
PO Box 302
Benicia CA 94510

Local Retrieval and SOP Area: CA-Alameda, Marin, San Francisco, San Mateo, Santa Clara, Solano.

Normal turnaround time: varies depending on project. Online computer ordering is also available. Fee basis will vary by type of project. Credit accounts are accepted.

Correspondent relationships: nationwide. They specialize in general investigations.

Hannah Marcum
Phone: 606-723-4438
198 Clearview Dr
Irvine KY 40336

Local Retrieval Area: KY-Estill.

Normal turnaround time: up to 1 week. Fee basis varies by type of transaction. Credit accounts are accepted.

Marias Title Company
Phone: 406-434-5156
Fax: 406-434-5157
235 Main St
Shelby MT 59474

Local Retrieval Area: MT-Liberty, Toole.

Normal turnaround time: 5 days. Projects are generally billed by the hour. Projects require prepayment.

Marion County Abstract Co
Phone: 501-449-4218
Fax: 501-449-4220
PO Box 388
Yellville AR 72687

Local Retrieval Area: AR-Miller.

Normal turnaround time: 3 days. Fee basis will vary by type of project. Projects require prepayment.

They have more than 27 years experience in real estate.

Marion County Abstract Co
Phone: 515-842-3518
Fax: 515-842-3528
117 S 3rd St
Knoxville IA 50138

Local Retrieval Area: IA-Marion.

Normal turnaround time: 1-2 days. Fee basis varies by type of transaction. The first project may require a prepayment.

Marion County Abstract Co
Phone: 800-952-5314
573-769-2212
Fax: 573-769-4916
104 E Lafayette
Palmyra MO 63461

Local Retrieval and SOP Area: IL-Adams, Hancock, Pike; MO-Lewis, Marion, Monroe, Ralls, Shelby.

Normal turnaround time: 4-5 days. Fee basis will vary by the type of project. Credit accounts are accepted.

They specialize in title insurance and updating.

Markle Northeast Title Co
Phone: 501-935-7410
Fax: 501-935-6548
2207 Fowler Ave
Jonesboro AR 72401-6132

Local Retrieval Area: AR-Craighead.

Normal turnaround time: 2 days. Fee is based on years searched. Credit accounts are accepted. Prepayment is required before policy is issued.

They specialize in title insurance on land, and title searches on lots and blocks of subdivisions. They also do abstracts and continuations of abstracts.

Marosi & Associates Inc
Phone: 800-858-3668
503-760-2072
Fax: 206-686-3843
510 SW 3rd Ave, Suite 400
Portland OR 97204

Local Retrieval and SOP Area: OR-Clackamas, Multnomah, Washington; WA-Clark, King.

Projects are generally billed by the number of names searched. The first project may require a prepayment.

Correspondent relationships: OR and WA. They specialize in insurance defense matters and internal investigations of employees.

Marquette County Abstract
Phone: 800-388-8485
608-297-2472
Fax: 800-380-8485
608-297-2994
5 E Park St
Montello WI 53949

Local Retrieval Area: WI-Adams, Green Lake, Marquette.

Normal turnaround time: 3-5 days. Fee basis varies by type of transaction. The first project may require a prepayment.

Marshall County Abstract Co
Phone: 405-795-3212
Fax: 405-795-3212
PO Box 50
Madill OK 73446

Local Retrieval Area: OK-Bryan, Carter, Coal, Johnston, Marshall, Murray, Pontotoc.

Normal turnaround time: 2 days. Fee basis will vary by the type of project. Credit accounts are accepted.

Marshall County Abstract Co
Phone: 515-752-5358
Fax: 515-752-5358
30 W Main Room 102
Marshalltown IA 50158

Local Retrieval Area: IA-Marshall.

Normal turnaround time: 2 days. Fee basis will vary by type of project. Credit accounts are accepted.

Marshall Land & Title Co

PO Box 898
Britton SD 57430

Phone: 605-448-5796
Fax: 605-448-2894

Local Retrieval Area: SD-Marshall.

Normal turnaround time: 3-4 days. Fee basis is "by evaluation". Credit accounts are accepted.

MarTech Inc

2255 W Northern Ave Suite A100
Phoenix AZ 85021

Phone: 800-346-0189
602-252-7900
Fax: 602-864-9227

Local Retrieval and SOP Area: AZ-Maricopa, Pima.

Normal turnaround time: 3-5 business days. 24 hour rush available for additional fee. Online computer ordering is also available. Projects are generally billed by the number of names searched or records located. The first project may require a prepayment. Terms are net 10 day after first pre-pay.

Correspondent relationships: Coconino, Yavapai, Pinal, AZ; and Orange, Los Angeles, CA. They specialize in financial investigations, location of liquid assets (bank accounts, CD, money market, etc.), internal investigations, including drug and theft undercovers and embezzlement.

Martin Abstract Co

520 DeQueen St
Mena AR 71953

Phone: 501-394-1963
Fax: 501-394-3091

Local Retrieval Area: AR-Polk.

Normal turnaround time: 2-3 days. Fee basis will vary by the type of project. The first project may require a prepayment.

Martin Abstract Co

PO Box 191
Warren AR 71671

Phone: 501-226-7487
Fax: 501-226-2685

Local Retrieval Area: AR-Bradley, Cleveland.

Normal turnaround time: up to 7 days. Projects are generally billed by the number of names searched. The first project may require a prepayment.

Correspondent relationships: Drew, AR. They specialize in title insurance and record checks.

Maryland Research and Abstract

25 W Chesapeake Ave Suite 214
Baltimore MD 21204-4820

Phone: 410-823-1944
Fax: 410-823-7254

Local Retrieval Area: MD-Baltimore, Harford.

Normal turnaround time: 1 week. Projects are generally billed by the number of names searched. Fee may be charged per property. Credit accounts are accepted.

They specialize in real estate title searches.

Mason County Abstract & Title Inc

111 South Rath Avenue PO Box 547
Ludington MI 49431-0547

Phone: 800-305-6655
616-843-2645
Fax: 616-843-1330

Local Retrieval Area: MI-Mason.

Normal turnaround time: varied depending on project. Projects are generally billed by the number of names searched or records located. Credit accounts are accepted.

They specialize in searches covering real estate in Mason County, MI.

Massey Abstract and Real Estate

307 Washington St
Covington IN 47932

Phone: 317-793-4547
Fax: 317-793-0636

Local Retrieval Area: IN-Fountain, Vermillion, Warren.

Normal turnaround time: 7 working days. Projects are generally billed by the number of names searched. Credit accounts are accepted.

They specialize in title searches.

Stephen Matejik

27 Mistletoe Lane
Levittown PA 19054

Phone: 609-394-9232
Fax: 215-949-2030

Local Retrieval Area: NJ-Mercer.

Normal turnaround time: 1 day to several weeks, depending on the number of years searched. Fee basis will vary by the type of project. Credit accounts are accepted. They require all national inquiries to prepay. Personal checks are accepted.

Maximum Protection Inc

101 Elmwood Dr
Wilkes-Barre PA 18702-7246

Phone: 717-655-3533
Fax: 717-347-7273

Local Retrieval and SOP Area: PA-Lackawanna, Luzerne.

Normal turnaround time: 24 hours. Projects are generally billed by the hour. Credit accounts are accepted. Personal checks are accepted.

Correspondent relationships: Monroe, Wayne, and Pike.

Mayes County Abstract

PO Box 967
Pryor OK 74362

Phone: 918-825-3074
Fax: 918-825-3571

Local Retrieval Area: OK-Mayes.

Normal turnaround time: 1-2 days. Projects are generally billed by the hour. Credit accounts are accepted.

Billy Mayfield

1425 Hillcrest Dr
Canyon TX 79015

Phone: 806-655-3878
Fax: 806-655-3878

Local Retrieval Area: TX-Potter, Randall.

Normal turnaround time: same day if inquiry is in by 9:00 am. Projects are generally billed by the number of names searched. Credit accounts are accepted. Terms are net 30 days or until 1st of month.

🏛 MBK Consulting

60 N Harding Rd
Columbus OH 43209-1524

Phone: 614-239-8977
Fax: 614-239-0599

Local Retrieval Area: OH-Franklin.

Normal turnaround time: 24-48 hours. Online computer ordering is also available. Projects are generally billed by the hour. Project rates available. The first project may require a prepayment.

Correspondent relationships: other counties in Ohio. They specialize in historical and genealogical research as well as general public record retrieval.

McAllister & Associates Inc

Phone: 601-977-0406
Fax: 601-956-4101

1998 Plantation Blvd
Jackson MS 39211

Local Retrieval and SOP Area: MS-Hinds, Lauderdale, Madison, Rankin, Warren, Yazoo.

Normal turnaround time: varied depending on project. Projects are generally billed by the hour. Projects require prepayment. They will also invoice.

Correspondent relationships: the rest of Mississippi. They are a general investigative agency.

McBrayer McDennis Leslie

Phone: 606-473-7303
Fax: 606-473-9003

PO Box 347 Main & Harrison St
Greenup KY 41144

Local Retrieval Area: KY-Boyd, Carter, Fayette, Franklin, Greenup, Lawrence, Lewis.

Normal turnaround time: 2 days. Projects are generally billed by the hour. Credit accounts are accepted.

McCarthy Abstract Co

Phone: 402-336-2860
Fax: 402-336-4489

PO Box 528
O'Neill NE 68763

Local Retrieval Area: NE-Boyd, Holt, Wheeler.

Normal turnaround time: 3 days. Projects are generally billed by the hour. Credit accounts are accepted.

They specialize in real estate records.

Attorney John McCarty

Phone: 502-927-8800
Fax: 502-927-8810

PO Box 189
Hawesville KY 42348

Local Retrieval Area: KY-Breckinridge, Daviess, Hancock, Ohio.

Normal turnaround time: up to 1 week. Projects are generally billed by the hour. Credit accounts are accepted. A "retainer" fee is required.

He specializes in all types of legal work (excluding patent or immigration issues).

McCook Abstract Company

Phone: 308-345-5120
Fax: 308-345-3812

316 Norris Ave, PO Box 338
McCook NE 69001

Local Retrieval Area: NE-Frontier, Hayes, Hitchcock, Red Willow.

Normal turnaround time: 3-8 days. Project billing methods vary. Credit accounts are accepted. Personal checks are accepted.

McCook County Abstract & Title

Phone: 605-425-2612
Fax: 605-425-2722

PO Box 506
Salem SD 57058

Local Retrieval Area: SD-McCook.

Normal turnaround time: 1 week. Fee basis is set by state law. Projects require prepayment.

They specialize in title insurance.

Trisha A & Thomas McCormack

Phone: 941-955-9998
Fax: 941-955-9998

1707 Cunliff Ln
Sarasota FL 34239

Local Retrieval Area: FL-Charlotte, Manatee, Sarasota.

Normal turnaround time: 24 hours to 1 week depending on project. Fees vary by project. The first project may require a prepayment. Terms are net 30 days.

They specialize in real estate searches, current owner property, updates, UCC searches, public record research and retrieval services.

McCormick Detective Agency

Phone: 970-453-6378
Fax: 970-453-6852

PO Box 444
Breckenridge CO 80424

Local Retrieval and SOP Area: CO-Summit.

Normal turnaround time: 1 day. Projects are generally billed by the hour. Credit accounts are accepted. Will bill at the first of the month.

Correspondent relationships: Denver, CO. They specialize in trial preparation for civil and criminal.

McCoy Investigations

Phone: 800-287-6789
916-481-3525
Fax: 916-481-5293

PO Box 174
Carmichael CA 95609

Local Retrieval Area: CA-Placer, Sacramento, Yolo.

Normal turnaround time: 24-72 hours. Projects are generally billed by the number of names searched. The first project may require a prepayment.

Correspondent relationships: nationwide. They specialize in screening services for the business community, nationwide. They use research databases to research public records and government agencies. They provide comprehensive reports on potential candidates.

McGinley Paralegal & Search Svcs

Phone: 317-630-9721
Fax: 317-630-9723

155 E Market St Suite 608
Indianapolis IN 46204

Local Retrieval and SOP Area: IN-39 Counties.

Normal turnaround time: 24-72 hours. Projects are generally billed by the number of names searched. Credit accounts are accepted.

Correspondent relationships: the rest of the state. They specialize in assisting various professionals in filing, searching and retrieval of documents in all local, county, state and district offices.

McGough & Associates

Phone: 800-543-1316
708-343-5600
Fax: 708-343-6940

PO Box 7370
Westchester IL 60154-7370

Local Retrieval and SOP Area: IL-Champaign, Cook, De Kalb, Du Page, Ford, Kane, Kendall, Lake, McHenry, Will.

Normal turnaround time: 72 hours. Projects are generally billed by the hour. The first project may require a prepayment.

Correspondent relationships: Illinois.

McGowan & Clark Investigations
Phone: 206-828-3616
Fax: 206-828-3616

1104 Kirkland Ave Suite 6
Kirkland WA 98033

Local Retrieval Area: WA-Cowlitz, Garfield, Island, King, Pierce, Snohomish, Spokane, Thurston, Yakima.

Normal turnaround time: 24 hours. Expedited service available. Projects are generally billed by the number of names searched. Credit accounts are accepted.

Correspondent relationships: statewide. They specialize in pre-employment searches, covering felonies and misdemeanors.

⛫ McGuire Research Associates
Phone: 401-647-7881
Fax: 401-647-7881

107 Danielson Pike
Scitvate RI 02857

Local Retrieval Area: RI-Bristol, Kent, Newport, Providence, Washington.

Normal turnaround time: 24 hours at State, 24-48 hours at Towns. Projects are generally billed by the number of names searched. Credit accounts are accepted. Terms are net 30 days.

They specialize in filings in Rhode Island, at the state or town level. They cover all thirty-nine (39) towns and need a full address for town level searches.

McHugh Abstract Co
Phone: 701-256-2851
Fax: 701-256-2852

PO Box 151
Langdon ND 58249

Local Retrieval Area: ND-Cavalier.

Normal turnaround time: 2-5 days. Projects are generally billed by the number of names searched. Credit accounts are accepted.

McIver Abstract & Insurance Co
Phone: 501-898-3502
Fax: 501-898-5560

440 W Main St
Ashdown AR 71822

Local Retrieval Area: AR-Little River.

Normal turnaround time: 3-4 days. Fee basis will vary by type of project. The first project may require a prepayment.

They specialize in real estate and title work.

McKerns & McKerns
Phone: 804-580-8225
Fax: 804-580-8626

Rt 360 Box 188
Heathsville VA 22473

Local Retrieval Area: VA-Essex, Lancaster, Northumberland, Richmond, Westmoreland.

Normal turnaround time: 2-3 days. Projects are generally billed by the hour. The first project may require a prepayment. There is a possible retainer fee.

They specialize in criminal and domestic law and litigation.

McKesson Title Corp
Phone: 800-261-8437
219-936-2555
Fax: 219-935-5515

407 N Center St
Plymouth IN 46563

Local Retrieval Area: IN-Elkhart, Fulton, Kosciusko, La Porte, Marshall, Pulaski, St. Joseph, Starke.

Normal turnaround time: 48 hours. Fees vary depending on project. Credit accounts are accepted. Personal or cashier checks are accepted.

They specialize in title insurance and escrow closings.

McKinley Paralegal Services
Phone: 513-662-8106
Fax: 513-662-8106

2616 Gehrum Ln
Cincinnati OH 45238

Local Retrieval Area: KY-Boone, Campbell, Kenton; OH-Butler, Clermont, Greene, Hamilton, Montgomery, Preble, Warren.

Normal turnaround time: 24-48 hours. Projects are generally billed by the number of names searched. Hourly rates apply to general paralegal work. The first project may require a prepayment.

Correspondent relationships: Butler, Franklin and Montgomery counties, OH. They specialize in filings and recordings in all area courts as well as retrievals, background investigations and general paralegal services.

McLain Abstract
Phone: 516-744-0064
Fax: 516-744-0064

Route 25A, Box 1106
Shoreham NY 11786

Local Retrieval Area: NY-Kings, Nassau, Queens, Suffolk.

Normal turnaround time: 2-3 days. Projects are generally billed by the number of names searched. Credit accounts are accepted.

Correspondent relationships: all upstate New York counties. They perform title searches, asset searches, and filing of lawsuits.

McLean County Abstract Inc
Phone: 701-462-3244
Fax: 701-462-8444

PO Box 370
Washburn ND 58577

Local Retrieval Area: ND-McLean.

Normal turnaround time: 2 weeks. Fee basis will vary by type of project. Projects require prepayment. They will also invoice.

McMullen County Title Co
Phone: 512-274-3312
Fax: 512-274-3590

PO Box 395
Tilden TX 78072

Local Retrieval Area: TX-McMullen.

Normal turnaround time: 2-3 days. Fee basis will vary by the type of project. The first project may require a prepayment.

McNeal Investigations
Phone: 601-826-5104
Fax: 601-826-5104

23000 Hwy 57
Ocean Springs MS 39564

Local Retrieval and SOP Area: AL-23 Counties; MS-29 Counties.

Normal turnaround time: varied depending on project. Projects are generally billed by the number of names searched. On-line computer billed by search. The first project may require a prepayment. NAPPS and NALI members have 30 days to pay.

Correspondent relationships: Mississippi-6 most southern counties, Alabama-3 most southern counties. They specialize in investigations, process serving, and pre-employment evaluations.

McPherson County Abstract
Phone: 316-241-1317
Fax: 316-241-3637

211 W Kansas
McPherson KS 67460

Local Retrieval Area: KS-McPherson.

Normal turnaround time: up to 1 week. Fee basis varies by type of transaction. Credit accounts are accepted.

McPherson County Abstract Co
Phone: 605-439-3614
PO Box 440
Leola SD 57456
Local Retrieval Area: SD-McPherson.

Normal turnaround time: 1-5 days. Projects are generally billed by the hour. Credit accounts are accepted. Enclose statement when sending finished work.

They specialize in real estate.

McQueen Abstract Company
Phone: 316-544-2311
Fax: 316-544-8029
PO Box 549 521 S Main
Hugoton KS 67951
Local Retrieval Area: KS-Stevens.

Normal turnaround time: 3-5 days. Projects are generally billed by the hour. Credit accounts are accepted.

▥ MD Abstract & Survey Services
Phone: 410-641-2298
Fax: 410-641-0437
10 Meadow St
Berlin MD 21811
Local Retrieval Area: MD-Somerset, Wicomico, Worcester.

Normal turnaround time: 1-3 days. Prices vary by type of search. The first project may require a prepayment.

Correspondent relationships: Dorchester, MD county. They specialize in property and judgment searches, 60 year title searches, commercial property searches and UCC searches.

Meadowlark Search
Phone: 406-449-5151
Fax: 406-449-3137
3045 Meadowlark Dr
East Helena MT 59635
Local Retrieval Area: MT-Broadwater, Jefferson, Lewis and Clark.

Normal turnaround time: 2 days. Projects are generally billed by the hour. The first project may require a prepayment.

Correspondent relationships: Idaho, Wyoming and Montana. They specialize in mortgages, mining, oil, gas, water right searches and environmental assessment (Phase I audits).

Mellette County Abstract Co
Phone: 605-259-3181
Fax: 605-259-3118
PO Box D
White River SD 57579
Local Retrieval Area: SD-Mellette.

Normal turnaround time: 1 week to 10 days. Projects are generally billed by the number of records located. Credit accounts are accepted. Credit cards are accepted.

Menard Title & Abstract Co Inc
Phone: 501-747-3712
Fax: 501-747-5488
121 Court St
Clarendon AR 72029
Local Retrieval Area: AR-Monroe.

Normal turnaround time: up to 2 weeks. Fee basis will vary by the type of project. Credit accounts are accepted.

They specialize in real estate and title insurance.

Mendo-Lake Paralegals
Phone: 707-263-8755
Fax: 707-263-4319
485 N Main St
Lakeport CA 95453
Local Retrieval and SOP Area: CA-Lake.

Normal turnaround time: 2-3 days. Projects are generally billed by the number of names searched. The first project may require a prepayment.

Correspondent relationships: Mendocino. They specialize in process serving and court filings.

Mercer County Abstract Co Inc
Phone: 701-748-2190
Fax: 701-748-2190
614 4th Ave NE
Hazen ND 58545
Local Retrieval Area: ND-Mercer.

Normal turnaround time: 2 days. Projects are generally billed by the number of names searched. The first project may require a prepayment.

Correspondent relationships: North Dakota.

Mercury Messengers Inc
Phone: 913-357-0078
Fax: 913-357-0078
500 S Kansas Ave
Topeka KS 66603
Local Retrieval and SOP Area: KS-Douglas, Osage, Shawnee.

Normal turnaround time: up to 48 hours. Expedited service available. Projects are generally billed by the hour. Fee basis will vary by the type of search. Credit accounts are accepted.

They specialize in filings for attorneys. They also are process servers.

▥ Mercury Service Inc
Phone: 604-228-9993
Fax: 604-224-8682
PO Box 46196 Station D
Vancouver, BC, Canada V6J 5G5
Local Retrieval Area: Canada-British Columbia.

Normal turnaround time: 4 hours on database searches, 24 hours for "hand" searches. Projects are generally billed by the number of names searched. The first project may require a prepayment.

Correspondent relationships: Alberta, Ontario and Quebec providences. They specialize in business backgrounds (individuals and companies), accident investigation (legal), forensic photography and tracing people.

Merkel Abstract & Title
Phone: 402-254-3547
216 N Broadway
Hartington NE 68739
Local Retrieval Area: NE-Cedar.

Normal turnaround time: 2 days. Project billing methods vary. The first project may require a prepayment.

Correspondent relationships: Dixon.

▥ Merlin Information
Phone: 888-434-6337
407-886-4653
Fax: 407-886-5394
2055 Sawgrass Dr
Apopka FL 32712-2089
Local Retrieval Area: FL-Orange, Osceola, Seminole, Volusia.

Normal turnaround time: 24-48 hours. Projects are generally billed by the number of names searched. The first project may require a prepayment.

Correspondent relationships: nationwide.

▥ Merola Services
Phone: 315-652-5242
Fax: 800-272-7717
315-652-9998
PO Box 2357
Liverpool NY 13089-2357
Local Retrieval Area: NY-Albany, Onondaga.

Normal turnaround time: same day to 2 days. Projects are generally billed by the number of names searched. Credit accounts are accepted. Payment due upon receipt.

Correspondent relationships: FL, OH, NJ, PA, MA and CT. They specialize in retrieval of certified documents at NYS DMV, insurance and police reports.

Charles W Merritt Jr

Phone: 706-342-9668
Fax: 706-342-9843

155 S Main St
Madison GA 30650

Local Retrieval Area: GA-Greene, Jasper, Morgan, Oconee, Putnam, Walton.

Normal turnaround time: varied depending on project. Projects are generally billed by the hour. The first project may require a prepayment. They accept personal checks.

He specializes in real estate searches.

Mesaa Unlimited

Phone: 713-759-7464
Fax: 713-660-8862

2916 Old Spanish Tr Suite 129
Houston TX 77054

Local Retrieval and SOP Area: TX-Brazoria, Fort Bend, Galveston, Harris.

Normal turnaround time: 3 days. Projects are generally billed by the number of names searched. The first project may require a prepayment.

Correspondent relationships: Nevada. They specialize in Real Estate records (50 year chains of title).

Metro Clerking Inc

Phone: 312-263-2977
Fax: 312-263-2985

134 N La Salle Suite 1826
Chicago IL 60602

Local Retrieval Area: IL-Cook, Du Page, Kane, Lake, McHenry, Will.

Normal turnaround time: 24 hours. Projects are generally billed by the number of names searched. The first project may require a prepayment.

They have an attorney on staff to cover court matters in State and Federal Courts. They also do searches in the Federal Records Center.

Metro Legal Services

Phone: 612-332-0202
Fax: 612-332-5215

330 S 2nd Ave Suite 150
Minneapolis MN 55401

Local Retrieval Area: MN-Anoka, Carver, Dakota, Hennepin, Ramsey, Scott, Sherburne, Washington, Wright.

Normal turnaround time: 2-3 days. Expedited service available. Projects are generally billed by the number of names searched. Credit accounts are accepted.

Correspondent relationships: St. Louis, Blue Earth, Winona and Olmsted. They specialize in real estate searches.

Metropolitan Court Services

Phone: 713-616-6971
Fax: 713-983-0231

PO Box 1413
Alief TX 77411-1413

Local Retrieval and SOP Area: TX-Brazoria, Fort Bend, Galveston, Harris, Montgomery.

Normal turnaround time: 3-5 days. Expedited service available. Projects are generally billed by the number of names searched. The first project may require a prepayment. Large projects may require retainer.

Correspondent relationships: nationwide. They specialize in locating hard-to-find witnesses and relevant documents nationwide.

Metropolitan Delivery

Phone: 914-463-0519

3-5 Irwin Ct
Poughkeepsie NY 12603

Local Retrieval Area: NY-Dutchess, Orange, Putnam.

Normal turnaround time: 24-72 hours. Expedited service available. Projects are generally billed by the number of names searched or records located. The first project may require a prepayment. Payment due upon receipt of invoice. Net 15 days.

Metropolitan Title

Phone: 313-234-4554
Fax: 313-232-1476

717 S Grand Traverse Street
Flint MI 48502

Local Retrieval Area: MI-Genesee.

Normal turnaround time: 3-5 days. Fee basis will vary by the type of project. Projects require prepayment.

They specialize in title insurance, escrows and closings.

Metropolitan Title Co

Phone: 616-945-9447
Fax: 616-945-5350

201 E State St
Hastings MI 49058

Local Retrieval Area: MI-Barry.

Normal turnaround time: 3 days. Fee basis will vary by the type of project. Credit accounts are accepted.

They specialize in real estate title work.

Metropolitian Title Co

Phone: 800-466-5263
616-873-2166
Fax: 616-873-2824

117 N State St
Hart MI 49420

Local Retrieval Area: MI-Oceana.

Normal turnaround time: 1 week. They charge a flat rate per project. Credit accounts are accepted.

They specialize in real estate.

George P Metz

Phone: 601-773-5804

PO Box 168
Lousiville MS 39339

Local Retrieval Area: MS-Chickasaw, Clay, Kemper, Lauderdale, Lee, Lowndes, Neshoba, Webster, Winston.

Normal turnaround time: 24 to 48 hours. Projects are generally billed by the hour. Also considers retainer relationships. The first project may require a prepayment.

Correspondent relationships: other counties in Mississippi. He specializes in corporate criminal investigations. Mr. Metz is a retired Mississippi State Department of Audit investigator.

Arthur Metzler

Phone: 201-653-9676
Fax: 201-288-8835

595 Newark Ave Rm 104
Jersey City NJ 07306

Local Retrieval Area: NJ-Hudson.

Normal turnaround time: 48 hours. Projects are generally billed by the number of names searched. The first project may require a prepayment. Personal checks are accepted.

MG Cox Abstract

Phone: 405-238-2600
Fax: 405-238-7553

PO Box 608
Pauls Valley OK 73075

Local Retrieval Area: OK-Garvin.

Normal turnaround time: 1 week. Projects are generally billed by the hour. The first project may require a prepayment.

MGC Courier Inc

1564 Norman Dr
College Park GA 30349

Phone: 800-822-1084
404-991-1084
Fax: 404-991-6928

Local Retrieval Area: GA-Clayton, Cobb, De Kalb, Fulton, Gwinnett, Henry, Rockdale.

Normal turnaround time: the same day. The fee basis is by mileage and time. Credit accounts are accepted.

Correspondent relationships: nationwide.

MGI

24516 Harper Ave
St Clair Shores MI 48080

Phone: 800-929-1758
313-445-3160
Fax: 313-445-3163

Local Retrieval and SOP Area: MI-Macomb, Oakland, Wayne.

Normal turnaround time: 1 week. Online computer ordering is also available. Projects are generally billed by the hour. The first project may require a prepayment.

Correspondent relationships: the remaining 83 counties in Michigan. They specialize in insurance defense investigations, background checks, locates and surveillance.

MHR and Associates

543 E Andy Devine
Kingman AZ 86401

Phone: 520-753-4777
Fax: 520-753-2875

Local Retrieval and SOP Area: AZ-Mohave.

Normal turnaround time: 1-3 days. Projects are generally billed by the number of names searched. Credit accounts are accepted. Payment due upon receipt of invoice.

Michael B Fixman & Associates

72 Hancock St PO Box 83
Everett MA 02149

Phone: 800-434-9626
617-387-1100

Local Retrieval and SOP Area: MA-Middlesex, Suffolk.

Normal turnaround time: 1 day. Projects are generally billed by the hour. The first project may require a prepayment. Personal checks are accepted.

Correspondent relationships: Entire State of MA and other New England state upon request. He is a private detective and process server.

Michael Ramey & Associates Inc

PO Box 744
Danville CA 94526

Phone: 510-820-8900
Fax: 510-820-8082

Local Retrieval Area: CA-Alameda, Marin, San Francisco.

Normal turnaround time: 1-3 weeks. Projects are generally billed by the hour..dd. Credit accounts are accepted.

Michigan Search Company

28741 Florence St
Garden City MI 48135-2787

Phone: 313-427-7224
Fax: 313-427-1218

Local Retrieval Area: MI-Clinton, Ingham, Macomb, Monroe, Oakland, Shiawassee, Washtenaw, Wayne.

Normal turnaround time: 48 hours. Expedited service available. Projects are generally billed by the number of names searched. Credit accounts are accepted.

Correspondent relationships: Allegan, Barry, Bay, Berrien, Branch, Calhoun, Cass, Dickinson, Eaton, Genesee, Grand, Traverse, Hillsdale, Isabella, Jackson, Kalamazoo, Kent, Livingston, Midland, Ottawa, Saginaw, St Joseph, Van Buren, Wesferd. They specialize in UCC & lien searches, criminal record checks, good standings, name reservations and corporate documents.

Mid Michigan Title & Abstract Co

26 E Sanilac Rd
Sandusky MI 48471

Phone: 313-648-4060
Fax: 313-648-9137

Local Retrieval Area: MI-Sanilac.

Normal turnaround time: 2-4 days. Fee basis will vary by type of project. The first project may require a prepayment.

They specialize in real estate.

Mid Montana Title Co

PO Box 2909 16 S Central Ave
Harlowton MT 59036

Phone: 406-632-4145
Fax: 406-632-4145

Local Retrieval Area: MT-Golden Valley, Sweet Grass, Wheatland.

Normal turnaround time: varied depending on project. Fee basis varies by type of transaction. Credit accounts are accepted.

They specialize in title policies governed by the state, lot book reports in company form and real estate searches. They will give verbal replies on "simple searches" but will not send hard copy.

Mid-South Legal Services

PO Box 610008
Birmingham AL 35261

Phone: 205-326-0900
Fax: 205-326-0600

Local Retrieval and SOP Area: AL-Jefferson, Shelby, St. Clair, Talladega, Tuscaloosa, Walker.

Normal turnaround time: 24-48 hours. Projects are generally billed by the number of names searched or records located. May use a combination depending upon request. Credit accounts are accepted.

They specialize in process service, asset searches, and skip tracing.

Mid-West Investigations

5716 S Western Ave
Oklahoma City OK 73109-4527

Phone: 800-359-5410
405-636-1976
Fax: 405-636-1888

Local Retrieval and SOP Area: OK-Canadian, Carter, Cleveland, Grady, Logan, McClain, Oklahoma, Payne, Pottawatomie, Tulsa.

Normal turnaround time: 24-48 hours. Projects are generally billed by the number of names searched. The first project may require a prepayment. Service and application agreement may be required.

Correspondent relationships: OK and TX. They specialize in asset locating, collections, skip-tracing and process serving.

Midland Title Co

5103 Eastman Pl Suite 241
Midland MI 48640

Phone: 517-839-1003
Fax: 517-839-0860

Local Retrieval Area: MI-Isabella, Midland.

Normal turnaround time: 2-3 days. Fee basis will vary on the type of project. Credit accounts are accepted. They require out of town clients to prepay.

They specialize in real estate.

Midstate Legal Support Services

PO Box 7
Utica NY 13503

Phone: 315-797-8609
Fax: 315-733-2292

Local Retrieval and SOP Area: NY-Oneida.

Normal turnaround time: 72 hours. Projects are generally billed by the number of names searched or records located. The first project may require a prepayment. Invoicing is available.

They specialize in judgment enforcement, process service and auto repossessions.

Midwest Abstract Co
Phone: 513-228-2292
Fax: 513-228-0640
4 S Main St Suite 200
Dayton OH 45402

Local Retrieval Area: OH-Hamilton, Montgomery.

Normal turnaround time: 5-7 days. The fee basis is per exam. Credit accounts are accepted.

Correspondent relationships: Miami, Darke, Clark, Preble, Warren, Butler, Clermont and Green counties. They specialize in "ALL" real estate title examinations.

Midwest Applicant Screen Service
Phone: 847-516-3340
Fax: 847-516-9257
62 Oak Valley Dr
Cary IL 60013

Local Retrieval and SOP Area: IL-De Kalb, Du Page, Kane, Kendall, Lake, McHenry.

Normal turnaround time: 24-48 hours. Expedited service available. Projects are generally billed by the number of names searched. The first project may require a prepayment.

Correspondent relationships: Cook, Winnebago, Boone and Ogle, IL counties. They specialize in pre-employment screening and litigation service of process.

Midwest Investigative Services
Phone: 800-227-9740
513-223-3690
Fax: 513-233-4133
130 W 2nd St Suite 1210
Dayton OH 45402-1502

Local Retrieval and SOP Area: OH-Butler, Clark, Clinton, Darke, Greene, Miami, Montgomery, Preble, Warren.

Normal turnaround time: 1-3 days. Expedited service available. Projects are generally billed by the hour. Credit accounts are accepted.

They specialize in pre-employment screening, civil and criminal investigations, process service, corporate investigations, locator service, witness interview and video surveillance.

Elden Mihulka
Phone: 402-352-3053
1322 "C" St
Schuyler NE 68661

Local Retrieval Area: NE-Butler, Colfax.

Normal turnaround time: 2 days. Projects are generally billed by the number of names searched. Credit accounts are accepted.

Mike Moore Private Investigations
Phone: 800-993-3832
209-684-9082
Fax: 209-684-9083
PO Box 2401
Visalia CA 93279

Local Retrieval and SOP Area: CA-Fresno, Kern, Kings, Tulare.

Normal turnaround time: 24 hours. Projects are generally billed by the hour. Credit accounts are accepted. Personal checks are accepted.

They specialize in process serving and investigation.

Miller & Mosley
Phone: 704-264-1125
Fax: 704-262-3544
PO Box 49 766 W Kings St
Boone NC 28607

Local Retrieval Area: NC-Ashe, Avery, Watauga.

Normal turnaround time: 2 days. Projects are generally billed by the hour. Credit accounts are accepted.

They specialize in real estate and foreclosures.

Miller Abstract and Title Co
Phone: 308-832-0969
Fax: 308-832-0969
306 N Colorado, PO Box 107
Minden NE 68959

Local Retrieval Area: NE-Kearney.

Normal turnaround time: 1-4 days. Fee basis is per search. Credit accounts are accepted. Personal checks are accepted.

Correspondent relationships: Phelps, Franklin and Buffalo counties. They specialize in title insurance, abstracting and limited title reports.

Miller Newell Abstract
Phone: 501-523-8976
Fax: 501-523-3969
514 3rd St
Newport AR 72112

Local Retrieval Area: AR-Jackson.

Normal turnaround time: up to 10 days. Projects are generally billed by the hour. Credit accounts are accepted.

They specialize in real estate abstracting and title insurance.

Cynthia H Miller
Phone: 513-474-6408
Fax: 513-624-0858
931 Watch Creek Dr
Cincinnati OH 45230

Local Retrieval Area: OH-Butler, Clermont, Hamilton, Warren.

Normal turnaround time: 2 days. Projects are generally billed by the number of names searched. Credit accounts are accepted. Terms are net 30 days.

She specializes in searches of UCC's, tax liens, suits and judgments, US District court and Bankruptcy court records and filing and retrieving documents.

G Scott Miller
Phone: 614-363-1324
Fax: 614-548-5443
30 Troy Road Shopping Center
Delaware OH 43015

Local Retrieval Area: OH-Delaware, Union.

Normal turnaround time: 24 hours. Fee basis will vary by the type of project. Credit accounts are accepted.

Gail L Miller
Phone: 913-378-3128
Fax: 913-378-3543
208 N Commercial
Mankato KS 66956

Local Retrieval Area: KS-Jewell.

Normal turnaround time: 1-7 days. Projects are generally billed by the hour. Credit accounts are accepted. Personal checks are accepted. Credit accounts are not accepted.

Susan Miller
Phone: 715-478-3932
403 E Jackson
Crandon WI 54520

Local Retrieval Area: WI-Forest.

Normal turnaround time: 24-48 hours. Projects are generally billed by the number of names searched. The first project may require a prepayment.

Mimbres Valley Abstract & Title Co
Phone: 505-546-8896
Fax: 505-546-9697
PO Drawer 2849
Deming NM 88031

Local Retrieval Area: NM-Luna.

Normal turnaround time: 2-5 days. Fee basis is determined per name or "per legal". Credit accounts are accepted.

They specialize in title searches.

Minn*Dak Search Service

Phone: 507-694-1168

PO Box 214

Ivanhoe MN 56142-0214

Local Retrieval Area: MN-21 Counties; SD-22 Counties.

Normal turnaround time: 24-72 hours. Fees depends on number of searches and distance traveled. Credit accounts are accepted. Payment due upon completion of search.

They specialize in UCC's, state and federal tax liens, judgments and litigation. Centrally located offices in both South Dakota and Minnesota assure prompt searches.

Missaukee Title Co

Phone: 616-839-4563

119 Prospect St PO Box 480

Fax: 616-839-4563

Lake City MI 49651

Local Retrieval Area: MI-Missaukee.

Normal turnaround time: within 2 days. Expedited service available. Projects are generally billed by the number of records located. The first project may require a prepayment.

Mississippi County Abstract

Phone: 573-683-4671

105 E Court St

Fax: 573-683-6898

Charleston MO 63834

Local Retrieval Area: MO-Mississippi.

Normal turnaround time: 3-5 days. Fee basis will vary by type of project. Projects require prepayment.

They specialize in title insurance.

Mitchell County Abstract Co

Phone: 515-732-4571

PO Box 328

Fax: 515-432-4918

Osage IA 50461

Local Retrieval Area: IA-Mitchell.

Normal turnaround time: 3-5 days. They charge a flat rate per project. Projects require prepayment.

Mitchell McNutt Threadgill et al

Phone: 601-842-3871

PO Box 7120

Fax: 601-842-8450

Tupelo MS 38802

Local Retrieval Area: MS-Alcorn.

Normal turnaround time: 1-2 days. Projects are generally billed by the hour. Credit accounts are accepted.

They specialize in insurance investigations.

Kent D Mitchener

Phone: 502-422-2611

2075 Bypass Rd

Fax: 502-422-2011

Brandenburg KY 40108-0568

Local Retrieval Area: KY-Breckinridge, Grayson, Meade.

Normal turnaround time: 2 working days. Fee basis varies by type of transaction. The first project may require a prepayment.

He is a lawyer and working in criminal, bankruptcy, divorce, and personal injury cases.

MLQ Attorney Services

Phone: 800-446-8794

3200 Professional Pkwy Bldg 200 Suite 225

770-984-7007

Atlanta GA 30339

Fax: 770-984-7049

Local Retrieval and SOP Area: GA-19 Counties.

Normal turnaround time: 24 hours within Atlanta metropolitan area, and 3 days outside metropolitan area. Expedited service avaliable. Online computer ordering is also available. Projects are generally billed by the number of names searched. Projects require prepayment. Credit cards are accepted.

Correspondent relationships: Rome, Dalton, Athens, Macon, Albany and Savannah. They specialize in small claims court processing.

Mohr Information Services

Phone: 800-799-4363

312 Wood Ave

504-678-8775

Winchester VA 22601-3032

Fax: 800-317-7511

504-678-1696

Local Retrieval Area: DC-District of Columbia; MD-Anne Arundel, Frederick, Montgomery, Prince George's, Washington; VA-12 Counties; WV-Berkeley, Jefferson.

Normal turnaround time: 24 to 48 hours. Projects are generally billed by the number of names searched. The first project may require a prepayment. Will submit an invoice upon completion of research requested and require prompt payment.

They specialize in criminal, civil, UCC, judgments, and property searches.

Monroe County Abstract and Title

Phone: 816-327-4109

229 N Main St

Paris MO 65275

Local Retrieval Area: MO-Monroe.

Normal turnaround time: 3 days. Projects are generally billed by the number of names searched. A fee for the length of the search may also be added to the per name charge. Credit accounts are accepted.

Monroe County Title Co

Phone: 618-939-8292

111 S Main St PO Box 188

Fax: 618-939-3931

Waterloo IL 62298

Local Retrieval Area: IL-Monroe.

Normal turnaround time: 5 days except for US District and Bankruptcy Courts, which take 10 days. Projects are generally billed by the number of names searched. Credit accounts are accepted. Personal checks are accepted.

They specialize in insured real estate title searches.

Monroe Title Insurance Corporation

Phone: 800-966-6763

Albany County Courthouse Room 128A#5

518-462-6566

Albany NY 12207

Fax: 518-462-0625

Local Retrieval Area: NY-Albany, Rensselaer.

Normal turnaround time: 48 hours. Projects are generally billed by the number of names searched or records located. The first project may require a prepayment. Credit cards are accepted.

They have 20 offices statewide. The 800 number is direct to their state customer service administrator.

Monroe Title Insurance Corp

47 W Main St
Rochester NY 14604

Phone: 800-966-6763
716-232-2070
Fax: 716-232-4988

Local Retrieval Area: NY-45 Counties.

Normal turnaround time: 48 hours. Projects are generally billed by the number of names searched or records located. Projects require prepayment. Credit cards are accepted. They will also invoice.

Montana Abstract & Title Co

400 W Granite
Butte MT 59701

Phone: 406-723-6521
Fax: 406-723-6523

Local Retrieval Area: MT-Deer Lodge, Granite, Powell, Silver Bow.

Normal turnaround time: varies with each project. Projects are generally billed by the hour. Credit accounts are accepted.

Montana Abstract Co Inc

PO Box 128
Scobey MT 59263

Phone: 406-487-5961
Fax: 406-487-2242

Local Retrieval Area: MT-Daniels.

Normal turnaround time: 1 week. Project billing methods vary. The first project may require a prepayment.

They specialize in title insurance and abstract updating.

Montezuma-Dolores Title Co

236 W North St
Cortez CO 81321

Phone: 970-565-8491
Fax: 970-565-7050

Local Retrieval Area: CO-Dolores, Montezuma.

Normal turnaround time: 5-7 days. Projects are generally billed by the hour. Credit accounts are accepted. Personal checks are accepted.

They specialize in real estate title searches.

Montgomery County Abstract

106 N Sturgeon St
Montgomery City MO 63361

Phone: 314-564-2298
Fax: 314-564-6158

Local Retrieval Area: MO-Montgomery.

Normal turnaround time: 5-10 days. Fee basis will vary by the type of project. Projects require prepayment. They will also invoice.

They maintain a complete set of in-house record books for Montgomery County.

Montgomery County Abstract Co

PO Box 743
Independence KS 67301-0743

Phone: 316-331-1440
Fax: 316-331-4760

Local Retrieval Area: KS-Montgomery.

Normal turnaround time: 1-2 days. Fee basis varies by type of transaction. The first project may require a prepayment.

Montgomery Investigative Services

12073 Tech Rd
Silver Spring MD 20904

Phone: 301-384-7777
Fax: 301-680-8966

Local Retrieval and SOP Area: MD-Montgomery, Prince George's.

Normal turnaround time: 24-48 hours. Online computer ordering is also available. Projects are generally billed by the number of names searched. Mileage expenses are added to the fee. Credit accounts are accepted. Credit cards are accepted.

Correspondent relationships: DC, VA, PA, FL, NC, NY, WA.

Montmorency Abstract Inc

PO Box 212
Atlanta MI 49709

Phone: 517-785-4889
Fax: 517-785-3689

Local Retrieval Area: MI-Montmorency.

Normal turnaround time: 4-5 days. Projects are generally billed by the number of records located. The first project may require a prepayment.

They specialize in real estate.

Moody Abstract Co

PO Box 325
De Valls Bluff AR 72041

Phone: 501-998-7531
Fax: 501-998-7531

Local Retrieval Area: AR-Prairie.

Normal turnaround time: 3-5 days. Fee basis will vary by the type of project. The first project may require a prepayment.

They have been in business for over 40 years.

Moody County Abstract Co

PO Box 304
Flandreau SD 57028

Phone: 605-997-3723
Fax: 605-997-3722

Local Retrieval Area: SD-Moody.

Normal turnaround time: 1 week. Fee basis will vary by the type or project. The first project may require a prepayment.

They specialize in title insurance and record searches.

Moomaw Abstract Corp

8 E Main St
Bloomfield IN 47424

Phone: 812-384-4702
Fax: 812-384-0561

Local Retrieval Area: IN-Clay, Daviess, Greene, Sullivan.

Normal turnaround time: 1 week. Projects are generally billed by the number of names searched or records located. Credit accounts are accepted. Personal checks are accepted.

Correspondent relationships: Monroe, Owen and Martin Counties.

Moon Abstract Co

421 Commercial St
Emporia KS 66801

Phone: 316-342-1917
Fax: 316-342-6888

Local Retrieval Area: KS-Chase, Coffey, Greenwood, Morris, Osage, Wabaunsee.

Normal turnaround time: "as soon as possible" for Lyon County and up to 1 week for other counties served. Fee basis varies by type of transaction. Statement sent when order completed. Credit accounts are accepted.

They specialize in long term escrow holdings, title insurance, closings and searches.

Attorney Reed Moore Jr

PO Box 235 107 2nd St
Tompkinsville KY 42167

Phone: 502-487-6262
Fax: 502-487-8000

Local Retrieval Area: KY-Barren, Monroe.

Normal turnaround time: 2-3 days. Fee basis varies by type of transaction. The first project may require a prepayment.

Moore Mowdy & Youngblood

PO Box 540
Atoka OK 74525-0540

Phone: 405-889-5656
Fax: 405-889-7149

Local Retrieval Area: OK-Atoka, Bryan, Coal, Johnston, Pushmataha.

Normal turnaround time: 48 hours. Projects are generally billed by the hour. Credit accounts are accepted.

They specialize in probate and real estate record searches.

Conrad Mord

Phone: 601-876-2611
Fax: 601-876-4379

PO Drawer 311
Tylertown MS 39667

Local Retrieval Area: MS-Pike, Walthall.

Normal turnaround time: 1 day in Walthall and 2-3 days in the other counties. Projects are generally billed by the hour. The first project may require a prepayment.

He is an attorney in general practice, including real estate and family law.

Morrilton Abstract Co

Phone: 501-354-2611
Fax: 501-354-4634

110 S Chestnut Suite C
Morrilton AR 72110

Local Retrieval Area: AR-Conway.

Normal turnaround time: 1 week. Fee basis will vary by the type of project. Projects require prepayment. They will also invoice.

They specialize in title and real estate research.

Morris Hills Abstract Co

Phone: 201-267-0450
Fax: 201-267-0981

44 Washington St
Morristown NJ 07960

Local Retrieval Area: NJ-Morris.

Normal turnaround time: up to 2 weeks. Projects are generally billed by the hour. Credit accounts are accepted.

⌂ Melissa F Morris

Phone: 334-222-1986
Fax: 334-222-1986

Rte 7 Box 258-A
Andalusia AL 36420

Local Retrieval Area: AL-Butler, Conecuh, Covington, Crenshaw, Escambia.

Normal turnaround time: 24-48 hours. Projects are generally billed by the number of names searched. The first project may require a prepayment.

Morrissey Morrissey & Dalluge

Phone: 402-335-3344
Fax: 402-335-3345

PO Box 597
Tecumseh NE 68450

Local Retrieval Area: NE-Johnson, Nemaha, Otoe, Pawnee, Richardson.

Normal turnaround time: 1 week. Projects are generally billed by the hour. The first project may require a prepayment. Credit cards are accepted.

They specialize in probate and real estate.

Ralph J Moses

Phone: 618-576-2632
Fax: 618-576-2632

PO Box 326
Hardin IL 62047

Local Retrieval Area: IL-Calhoun.

Normal turnaround time: 12-24 hours. Projects are generally billed by the hour. Credit accounts are accepted..dd.

He specializes in real estate record searches.

Mosley Abstract Co

Phone: 501-782-3053
Fax: 501-782-5432

PO Box 2124
Fort Smith AR 72902-2124

Local Retrieval Area: AR-Sebastian.

Normal turnaround time: 2-3 days. Projects are generally billed by the number of names/properties searched. Projects require prepayment.

Mountain View Abstract Co

Phone: 501-269-8410
Fax: 501-269-8410

PO Box 130
Mountain View AR 72560

Local Retrieval Area: AR-Stone.

Normal turnaround time: 1-2 weeks. Fee basis will vary by the type of project. Projects require prepayment. They will also invoice.

They specialize in real estate and title work.

Mountrail County Abstract & Title

Phone: 701-628-2886

PO Box 519
Stanley ND 58784

Local Retrieval Area: ND-Burke, McKenzie, Mountrail, Ward, Williams.

Normal turnaround time: 1-5 days. Fee basis will vary by type of project. Credit accounts are accepted.

Mt Pleasant Abstract and Title Co

Phone: 517-773-3651
Fax: 517-773-0751

116 Court
Mt Pleasant MI 48858

Local Retrieval Area: MI-Clare, Isabella.

Normal turnaround time: 1 week. Fee basis will vary by type of project. Credit accounts are accepted.

They specialize in real estate and title insurance.

Aaron S Mueller

Phone: 414-821-3405
Fax: 414-821-3405

1400 S Carriage Ln Suite 1
New Berlin WI 53151

Local Retrieval Area: WI-Kenosha, Milwaukee, Ozaukee, Racine, Waukesha.

Normal turnaround time: same day. Projects are generally billed by the number of names searched or records located. Credit accounts are accepted.

He specializes in background searches. Will go to municipal buildings for searches also.

⌂ David Mulberry

Phone: 800-704-1287
407-624-0526
Fax: 407-624-0576

4050 Lakespur Circle S
Palm Beach Gardens FL 33410

Local Retrieval and SOP Area: FL-Palm Beach.

Normal turnaround time: varied depending on project. Projects are generally billed by the number of records located. The first project may require a prepayment.

Correspondent relationships: all of Florida. He is a private investigator and certified process server with over 30 years of investigative experience.

Mullen Abstract Co

Phone: 501-886-2452
Fax: 501-886-5929

119 SW 2nd St
Walnut Ridge AR 72476

Local Retrieval Area: AR-Lawrence.

Normal turnaround time: 3-5 days. Fee basis will vary by the type of project. Credit accounts are accepted.

They specialize in real estate abstracting and title.

Donna Mundwiller

Phone: 573-486-2925
Fax: 573-486-2059

118 E 4th St
Hermann MO 65041

Local Retrieval Area: MO-Gasconade.

Normal turnaround time: varied depending on project. Projects are generally billed by the hour. Projects require prepayment.

She specializes in genealogy searches.

Maxine Munsigner

Phone: 515-858-3585

402 9th Ave
Eldora IA 50627

Local Retrieval Area: IA-Hardin.

Normal turnaround time: normally 24 to 48 hours plus mail time. Expedited service available. Projects are generally billed by the number of names searched or records located. Credit accounts are accepted. She will accept personal checks.

Murray County Abstract Inc

Phone: 405-622-5294
Fax: 405-622-2866

108 W Muskogee
Sulphur OK 73086

Local Retrieval Area: OK-Murray.

Normal turnaround time: 24 hours. Projects are generally billed by the hour. The first project may require a prepayment.

Musselman Abstract Co

Phone: 918-336-6410
Fax: 918-336-4880

PO Box 1072
Bartlesville OK 74005

Local Retrieval Area: OK-Washington.

Normal turnaround time: 24 hours. Fee basis will vary by the type of project. Credit accounts are accepted.

Musselshell County Title Inc

Phone: 406-323-3165
Fax: 406-323-3165

PO Box 838 12 Main St
Roundup MT 59072

Local Retrieval Area: MT-Musselshell.

Normal turnaround time: 3-5 days. Fee basis varies by type of transaction. Credit accounts are accepted.

⬛ Myers Investigations Inc

Phone: 800-788-8018
317-865-1006
Fax: 317-865-1006

PO Box 17457
Indianapolis IN 46217-0457

Local Retrieval and SOP Area: IN-Bartholomew, Hancock, Jackson, Johnson, Marion, Monroe.

Normal turnaround time: 24 hours. Projects are generally billed by the number of names searched. The first project may require a prepayment. Net 10 days after pre-paid case.

Correspondent relationships: all of Indiana, Kentucky and Ohio. They specialize in locates, computer-related cases, background investigations, insurance fraud and witness interviews.

N

N F Field Abstract Co

Phone: 218-736-6844
Fax: 218-739-5331

PO Box 697
Fergus Falls MN 56538

Local Retrieval Area: MN-Otter Tail.

Normal turnaround time: 5-10 days. Projects are generally billed by the number of names searched. Fee may also be based per entry. Projects require prepayment. They will also invoice.

They specialize in title insurance and closings.

N W Legal Support Inc

Phone: 800-729-9426
206-223-9426
Fax: 206-223-9475

703 Columbia St Suite 201
Seattle WA 98104

Local Retrieval and SOP Area: WA-King, Kitsap, Pierce, Snohomish, Thurston.

Normal turnaround time: 48 hours. Projects are generally billed by the hour. Credit accounts are accepted. Terms are net 10 days.

Correspondent relationships: Washington. They do process service only.

⬛ N.M. Factfinders Inc

Phone: 505-869-4829
Fax: 505-869-7721

PO Box 1218
Peralta NM 87042

Local Retrieval and SOP Area: NM-Bernalillo, Cibola, Sandoval, Santa Fe, Socorro, Torrance, Valencia.

Normal turnaround time: 48 to 72 hours. Expedited service available. Projects are generally billed by the number of names searched or records located. Fees vary depending on search. The first project may require a prepayment. Credit cards are accepted. They request prepayment of estimated costs.

Correspondent relationships: Arizona, Colorado and Texas. They specialize in asset searches, background checks and litigation supports.

NACM/Rocky Mountain Affiliate

Phone: 303-837-1280
Fax: 303-830-7808

789 Sherman St Suite 380
Denver CO 80203

Local Retrieval Area: CO-Denver.

Normal turnaround time: 3-4 hours. Projects are generally billed by the number of names searched or records located. Projects require prepayment.

NatCon Searches Inc

Phone: 888-436-5576
307-436-3467
Fax: 888-436-5576

9 S Monkey Box T-1
Glenrock WY 82637

Local Retrieval Area: WY-Converse, Natrona.

Normal turnaround time: 1 week. Projects are generally billed by the number of names searched. Projects require prepayment.

They specialize in land record searches. Independent Landman for petroleum and mineral searches and leases.

National Abstract Corporation

Phone: 800-535-3477
315-376-3911
Fax: 315-376-8305

7659 N State St
Lowville NY 13367

Local Retrieval Area: NY-Lewis.

Normal turnaround time: 24 hours for court records, taxes and UCC's, and 5 working days for real estate searches. Projects are generally billed by the number of names searched or records located. Credit accounts are accepted.

Correspondent relationships: Chenango, Delaware, Jefferson, Madison, Oneida, Ononoaga, Oswego, Otsego and St Lawrence counties.

🏛 National Background Investgtns
Phone: 800-798-0079
410-798-0072
PO Box 156
Mayo MD 21106
Fax: 800-798-7895
410-798-7868

Local Retrieval Area: DE-All Counties; MD-All Counties; NJ-All Counties; VA-City of Alexandria, Arlington, Fairfax, City of Fairfax, City of Falls Church, Prince William.

Normal turnaround time: 24-72 hours. Projects are generally billed by the number of names searched. Credit accounts are accepted. Terms are net 15 days.

Correspondent relationships: Pennsylvania and nationwide. They are a regional firm with collective team experience of over 30 years in public record retrieval.

🏛 National Background Reports
Phone: 800-526-4654
901-526-4654
243 Adams Ave
Memphis TN 38103
Fax: 901-526-4753

Local Retrieval Area: TN-Shelby.

Normal turnaround time: Same day on criminal searches. Online computer ordering is also available. Projects are generally billed by the number of names searched or records located. Credit accounts are accepted. Monthly invoicing available.

Correspondent relationships: the State of Tennessee. They specialize in research in any disignated court or governmental agency nationwide. They also specialize in providing criminal background reports for pre-employment and tenant screening in Shelby, TN county.

🏛 National Business Info Svc
Phone: 303-680-2712
Fax: 303-680-2453
PO Box 461135
Denver CO 80046

Local Retrieval Area: CO-Adams, Arapahoe, Denver, Douglas, Jefferson.

Normal turnaround time: 1-2 days. Projects are generally billed by the number of names searched. The first project may require a prepayment. Payment due upon receipt of invoice.

They specialize in due diligence, asset search and skip tracing. They have 10 years experience in document retrieval.

National Corporate Research Inc
Phone: 800-483-1140
302-734-1450
9 East Loockerman Rd
Dover DE 19901
Fax: 302-734-1476

Local Retrieval Area: DE-Kent.

Normal turnaround time: next day. Projects are generally billed by the number of names searched. Credit accounts are accepted.

Correspondent relationships: all counties in Delaware. They specialize in UCC and corporate searches at the Delaware secretary of state office, to which they are connected on-line.

National Corporate Research Ltd
Phone: 800-828-0938
518-434-0938
211 State St Suite 600
Albany NY 12207
Fax: 518-434-0225

Local Retrieval Area: NY-Albany.

Normal turnaround time: next day. Projects are generally billed by the number of names searched. The first project may require a prepayment. Credit cards are accepted.

Correspondent relationships: all counties in New York State. They specialize in UCC and corporate record searches at the office of the Secretary of State.

National Crime Reporting Systems
Phone: 800-687-0894
214-360-9122
10501 N Central Expy Suite 309
Dallas TX 75248
Fax: 800-600-1408
214-360-0775

Local Retrieval Area: TX-Collin, Dallas, Denton, El Paso, Montgomery, Nueces, Tarrant, Travis, Williamson, Wilson.

Normal turnaround time: 24 hours. Online computer ordering is also available. Projects are generally billed by the number of names searched. Credit accounts are accepted.

Correspondent relationships: nationwide. They specialize in criminal and driving record information for personnel and security managers. They also do all aspects of pre-employment background inquiries.

🏛 National Data Access Corp
Phone: 800-390-2959
919-873-0900
6325-9 Falls of Neuse Rd Suite 339
Raleigh NC 27615
Fax: 800-390-9119
919-873-9144

Local Retrieval Area: NC-45 Counties.

Normal turnaround time: 1-3 days. Projects are generally billed by the number of names searched. Credit accounts are accepted. Terms are net 15 days, 1 1/2% over 30 days.

Correspondent relationships: nationwide. They specialize in lien searches at the County level and corporate and UCC searches at the State level.

🏛 National Data Access Corp
Phone: 800-528-8790
803-699-6130
PO Box 23123
Columbia SC 29224-3123
Fax: 800-542-7499
803-699-6178

Local Retrieval and SOP Area: SC-All Counties.

Normal turnaround time: 1-3 days. Projects are generally billed by the number of names searched. Credit accounts are accepted. Terms are net 15 days.

Correspondent relationships: nationwide. They specialize in lien searching for North and South Carolina.

🏛 National Information Service
Phone: 702-456-4583
Fax: 702-456-4583
3141 Key Largo Dr Suite 203
Las Vegas NV 87120

Local Retrieval Area: NV-Clark.

Normal turnaround time: 24-48 hours. Projects are generally billed by the number of names searched. The first project may require a prepayment.

National Investigative Services Inc
Phone: 417-883-1213
Fax: 417-883-1812
1736 E Sunshine Suite 308
Springfield MO 65804

Local Retrieval Area: MO-23 Counties.

Normal turnaround time: two weeks. Projects are generally billed by the hour. The first project may require a prepayment.

National Legal Process
Phone: 302-429-0652
Fax: 302-429-0656
49 Bancroft Mills Suite 3-H
Wilmington DE 19806

Local Retrieval and SOP Area: DE-All Counties; PA-Chester, Delaware.

Normal turnaround time: 2-5 days. Expedited service available. Projects are generally billed by the number of names searched. Credit accounts are accepted.

They specialize in process service and skip tracing.

National Service Information Inc

Phone: 317-266-0040
Fax: 317-266-8453

320 N Meridian Suite 501
Indianapolis IN 46204

Local Retrieval Area: IN-Marion.

Normal turnaround time: 1-3 days. Fee basis varies by project. Credit accounts are accepted.

Correspondent relationships: IN, OH, KY and nationwide. They are on-line with Ohio and Indiana Secretary of State databases and can provide microfilm copies. They also perform corporate work.

National Service Information Inc

Phone: 800-235-0337
614-387-6806
Fax: 614-382-1256

145 Baker St
Marion OH 43302

Local Retrieval Area: KY-All Counties; OH-All Counties.

Normal turnaround time: 1-3 days. Fee basis will vary by type of project. Credit accounts are accepted.

Correspondent relationships: nationwide. They are on-line with Ohio and Indiana Secretary of State databases and can provide microfilm copies. They also perform corporate work.

▥ Nationwide Court Services Inc

Phone: 516-981-4400
Fax: 516-981-5514

3340 Veterans Hwy
Bohemia NY 11716

Local Retrieval and SOP Area: NY-Bronx, Kings, Nassau, New York, Putnam, Queens, Richmond, Rockland, Suffolk, Westchester.

Normal turnaround time: 2 days. Projects are generally billed by the number of records located. The first project may require a prepayment.

Correspondent relationships: nationwide.

Nationwide Information Services

Phone: 800-227-0575
203-666-3090
Fax: 203-667-2038

1160 Salas Dean Hwy
Wethersfield CT 06109

Local Retrieval and SOP Area: CT-All Counties.

Normal turnaround time: same day for Secretary of State, and 24-48 hours for counties and towns throughout Connecticut. Projects are generally billed by the number of names searched. Projects require prepayment. Terms net 30 days.

Correspondent relationships: nationwide. They specialize in UCC searches, filing and recording, and can do criminal searches. They advise that Superior Courts in Connecticut take up to four weeks to process a request for criminal cases.

Nationwide Information Services

Phone: 800-873-3482
518-449-8429
Fax: 800-234-8522

52 James Street
Albany NY 12207

Local Retrieval Area: NY-Albany.

Normal turnaround time: 24-48 hours. Expedited service available. Projects are generally billed by the number of names searched. The first project may require a prepayment. Credit cards are accepted.

Correspondent relationships: nationwide.

▥ Nationwide Information Services

Phone: 800-443-0824
Fax: 717-238-6522

PO Box 60515
Harrisburg PA 17106-0515

Local Retrieval and SOP Area: PA-Cumberland, Dauphin, Lancaster, Lebanon, York.

Normal turnaround time: 24-48 hours. Projects are generally billed by the number of names searched or records located. Credit accounts are accepted.

Correspondent relationships: the state of Pennsylvania. They specialize in asset searches, state level searches, retrieving driving records and motor vehicle records.

Navarro County Abstract Co

Phone: 903-874-3768
Fax: 903-874-6204

PO Box 685
Corsicana TX 75151

Local Retrieval Area: TX-Navarro.

Normal turnaround time: varied depending on project. Fee basis will vary by type of project. Credit accounts are accepted.

▥ NC Search Inc

Phone: 910-273-4999
Fax: 910-273-5155

620 S Elm St Suite 363
Greensboro NC 27406

Local Retrieval Area: NC-All Counties; SC-Beaufort, Calhoun, Charleston, Fairfield, Kershaw, Lexington, Richland, Spartanburg, York.

Normal turnaround time: 2-3 days. Expedited service available. Projects are generally billed by the number of names searched. Asset searches are done on a per hour basis. Credit accounts are accepted. Terms are net 30 days.

They provide criminal record checks in NC, SC and GA.

NDR (National Document Retrieval)

Phone: 800-829-5578
602-274-5578
Fax: 800-837-5573
602-274-5573

3111 N Central Ave Suite 200
Phoenix AZ 85012

Local Retrieval Area: AZ-Maricopa, Pima, Pinal.

Normal turnaround time: 48 hours. Projects are generally billed by the number of names searched. The first project may require a prepayment.

Correspondent relationships: all of Arizona and nationwide. They are a licensed private investigative agency, and provide due diligence research and investigative services.

NDXR Inc

Phone: 800-687-5080
417-624-8765
Fax: 800-687-5474
417-624-8793

PO Box 1287
Joplin MO 64802

Local Retrieval Area: KS-Cherokee, Crawford; MO-Greene, Jasper, Lawrence, McDonald, Newton, Vernon; OK-Delaware, Ottawa.

Normal turnaround time: 24 hours. Projects are generally billed by the number of names searched. The first project may require a prepayment.

Correspondent relationships: nationwide.

Nebraska Title Company

Phone: 402-228-2233
Fax: 402-228-4543

629 Court St
Beatrice NE 68310

Local Retrieval Area: NE-Gage.

Normal turnaround time: 36 hours. Projects are generally billed by the number of names searched. Credit accounts are accepted.

Ben Neel
Phone: 915-396-2351
PO Box 355
Menard TX 76859
Local Retrieval Area: TX-Menard, Sutton.

Normal turnaround time: 1-2 days. Projects are generally billed by the hour. Projects require prepayment.

Nell Watkins & Assoc
Phone: 972-226-8811
Fax: 972-226-9100
6417 Faircove Circle
Garland TX 75043
Local Retrieval and SOP Area: TX-Collin, Dallas, Hunt, Kaufman, Rockwall.

Normal turnaround time: 24-48 hours. Projects are generally billed by the number of names searched. The first project may require a prepayment.

They specialize in background, asset and locate investigations.

Nemaha County Abstract & Title
Phone: 913-336-2137
Fax: 913-336-2137
402 Main St Suite A
Seneca KS 66538
Local Retrieval Area: KS-Nemaha.

Normal turnaround time: 1-2 days. Fee basis varies by type of transaction. The first project may require a prepayment.

Joe Y Nerio
Phone: 909-824-9358
Fax: 909-824-8012
11750 Mount Vernon Ave Suite C106
Grand Terrace CA 92313
Local Retrieval Area: CA-Los Angeles, Orange, Riverside, San Bernardino.

Normal turnaround time: 1-3 days. Projects are generally billed by the number of names searched. The first project may require a prepayment.

Correspondent relationships: Texas and Arizona. He specializes in criminal record searches.

Tim Neuroth
Phone: 515-832-3156
535 2nd St
Webster City IA 50595-1507
Local Retrieval Area: IA-Hamilton.

Normal turnaround time: 1-2 days. Projects are generally billed by the hour. The first project may require a prepayment. He will accept personal checks.

Nevada Land Services
Phone: 800-233-4999
702-482-5641
Fax: 702-482-8935
PO Box 1169 363 Erie Main St
Tonopah NV 89049
Local Retrieval Area: NV-Churchill, Esmeralda, Eureka, Humboldt, Lander, Lincoln, Mineral, Nye, Pershing, White Pine.

Normal turnaround time: 10 days. Projects are generally billed by the number of names searched. Credit accounts are accepted. Personal checks are accepted.

They specialize in unpatented mining claim reports.

Jean Nevius
Phone: 515-322-3671
604 Terrace Hill Drive
Corning IA 50841
Local Retrieval Area: IA-Adams.

Normal turnaround time: 48 hours. Projects are generally billed by the number of names searched. The first project may require a prepayment.
She publishes the "Corning Service Bulletin" listing Recorder and probate actions.

New England Recovery Inc
Phone: 802-433-6111
Fax: 802-433-6742
PO Box 1025
Barre VT 05641
Local Retrieval Area: VT-14 Counties.

Normal turnaround time: 2 to 4 days. They charge a base fee and per hour. They also charge extra for the copy charges. Credit accounts are accepted.

They specialize in hidden asset searches and location of missing persons.

New Mexico Records Search
Phone: 505-986-0565
Fax: 505-986-0565
36 Santa Barbara Dr
Santa Fe NM 87505
Local Retrieval Area: NM-Santa Fe.

Normal turnaround time: 24 hours for preliminary UCC results. Projects are generally billed by the number of names searched or records located. Credit accounts are accepted.

They specialize in retrieval/filing of state, county and corporate documents.

New Star Enterprises
Phone: 918-567-3241
Fax: 918-567-3573
Rt #1 Box 9050
Talihina OK 74571
Local Retrieval and SOP Area: OK-Haskell, Latimer, Le Flore, McCurtain, Pittsburg, Pushmataha.

Normal turnaround time: 3 business days. Expedited service available. Projects are generally billed by the number of names searched. The first project may require a prepayment.

Correspondent relationships: Coal, Choctaw, Atoka, Bryan and Hughes counties. They have 5 full time investigators that specialize in records retrieval, criminal and civil, asset, workers' compensation, background investigations and missing persons location.

New York Institute of Legal Rsrch
Phone: 914-245-8400
Fax: 914-245-7660
PO Box 398
Yorktown Heights NY 10598-0398
Local Retrieval Area: NY-All Counties.

Normal turnaround time: 24 hours. Projects are generally billed by the number of names searched or records located. The first project may require a prepayment.

Correspondent relationships: nationwide. They specialize in litigation services to attorneys. They have employees in all parts of the state accessible by cellular phone. They also are a unique source of Nassau Supreme Court documents for the period 1941-1965 and other NYC area information.

Newaygo County Abstract & Title
Phone: 800-536-5263
616-924-2000
Fax: 616-924-2111
24 E Main St
Fremont MI 49412
Local Retrieval Area: MI-Newaygo.

Normal turnaround time: 1 week. They charge a flat rate per project. Credit accounts are accepted.

They specialize in real estate.

NEWSI

Phone: 800-517-4636
203-426-5784
Fax: 203-270-9338

PO Box 3008
Newtown CT 06470-3008

Local Retrieval and SOP Area: CT-Fairfield, Hartford, Litchfield, Middlesex, New Haven.

Normal turnaround time: 24 hours. Expedited service available. Projects are generally billed by the hour. Projects require prepayment. Credit cards are accepted.

Correspondent relationships: NY, MA and NJ.

NIA Academy of Public Rec Rsrch

Phone: 561-624-5100
Fax: 561-624-9734

4400 PGA Blvd Suite 304
Palm Beach Gardens FL 33410

Local Retrieval Area: FL-Palm Beach.

Normal turnaround time: 48 hours. Projects are generally billed by the number of names searched. Projects require prepayment. Credit cards are accepted.

Correspondent relationships: 600 affiliates in 44 states. They train public record retrievers in electronic access and provides specialized marketing guidance to expand business opportunities for record retrievers.

Jake Nichols

Phone: 406-765-1651

PO Box 441
Plentywood MT 59254

Local Retrieval Area: MT-Daniels, Roosevelt, Sheridan.

Normal turnaround time: varied depending on project. Projects are generally billed by the hour. The first project may require a prepayment.

He specializes in mineral searches.

Nierman & Nierman Title Co

Phone: 812-358-4766
Fax: 812-358-0895

111 W Walnut St
Brownstown IN 47220

Local Retrieval Area: IN-Jackson.

Normal turnaround time: 10 working days. Projects are generally billed by the number of names searched. Copy charges may be added to the fee. Credit accounts are accepted.

Nodaway County Abstract Co

Phone: 816-582-2332
Fax: 816-582-7173

501 N Market St
Maryville MO 64468-1616

Local Retrieval Area: MO-Nodaway, Worth.

Normal turnaround time: 1 day. Projects are generally billed by the number of names searched. Credit accounts are accepted.

They specialize in complete searches of land records.

Nolan & Associates

Phone: 864-244-6593
Fax: 864-244-6599

117 Bendingwood Cir
Taylors SC 29687

Local Retrieval Area: SC-Anderson, Cherokee, Greenville, Laurens, Pickens, Spartanburg, York.

Normal turnaround time: 1-5 days. Projects are generally billed by the number of names searched. Credit accounts are accepted.

Correspondent relationships: nationwide. They specialize in background checks and skip tracing/missing persons. Court records research is carried out in any county in South Carolina and North Carolina by special request.

🏛 Norcal Public Records Service

Phone: 800-252-0910
Fax: 800-252-0906

2280 Grass Valley Highway #231
Auburn CA 95603

Local Retrieval Area: CA-El Dorado, Fresno, Nevada, Placer, Sacramento, Solano, Sonoma, Sutter, Yolo, Yuba.

Normal turnaround time: 1-2 days. Projects are generally billed by the number of names searched. Credit accounts are accepted. Terms are net 15 days.

Correspondent relationships: Butte, Tehema, Shasta, Amadar, Merced, Napa and Lassen Counties. They specialize in county court, federal court, and County Recorder research. FAX ordering is encouraged.

🏛 North American Investigations

Phone: 800-270-2628
813-882-3411
Fax: 813-882-3325

PO Box 260893
Tampa FL 33685-0893

Local Retrieval and SOP Area: FL-Hillsborough, Pinellas.

Normal turnaround time: 8 hours. Projects are generally billed by the hour. The first project may require a prepayment.

Correspondent relationships: Saracuse, NY. They are certified fraud examiners conducting investigations. Expert reseachers in locating all kinds of information which is invaluable for civil and criminal matters.

🏛 North East Court Services Inc

Phone: 800-235-0794
Fax: 908-322-9098

375 Park Ave 2nd Floor
Scotch Plains NJ 07076

Local Retrieval and SOP Area: CT-Fairfield; NJ-21 Counties; NY-Bronx, Kings, New York, Queens, Richmond.

Normal turnaround time: 24-72 hours. Projects are generally billed by the number of names searched or records located. The first project may require a prepayment.

Correspondent relationships: Western and Southern New York state and Eastern Pennsylvania.

North Florida Abstract & Title Co

Phone: 904-997-2670

PO Box 838
Monticello FL 32344

Local Retrieval Area: FL-Jefferson.

Normal turnaround time: 1 week. Fee basis will vary by the type of project. Credit accounts are accepted.

They specialize in real estate searches.

North Louisiana Title Co Inc

Phone: 800-515-7715
318-323-3836
Fax: 318-325-8357

1101 Royal Ave
Monroe LA 71201

Local Retrieval Area: LA-23 Parishes.

Normal turnaround time: 1-3 days. Fee will vary with the type of search. Projects require prepayment.

They specialize in title searches.

North Pacific Legal

Phone: 541-267-5118
Fax: 541-269-9345

PO Box 1217
Coos Bay OR 97420

Local Retrieval and SOP Area: OR-Coos.

Normal turnaround time: varied depending on project. Projects are generally billed by the hour. Credit accounts are accepted.

They specialize in locating people.

North State Process

Phone: 916-241-2228
Fax: 916-241-6928

1768 West St
Redding CA 96001-1725

Local Retrieval and SOP Area: CA-Butte, Humboldt, Lassen, Shasta, Siskiyou, Tehama, Trinity.

Normal turnaround time: varied depending on project. Projects are generally billed by the number of names searched or records located. The first project may require a prepayment.

Correspondent relationships: all counties in California. Their specialty is process serving, locating and record search.

North Vernon Abstract Co Inc

Phone: 812-346-2259
Fax: 812-346-6056

20 Main St
North Vernon IN 47265

Local Retrieval Area: IN-Jackson, Jefferson, Jennings, Ripley.

Normal turnaround time: varied depending on project. Projects are generally billed by the number of names searched. Credit accounts are accepted. Personal checks are accepted.

North Winds Investigations Inc

Phone: 800-530-4514
501-925-1612
Fax: 501-925-2819

PO Box 1654
Rogers AR 72757

Local Retrieval and SOP Area: AR-Benton, Crawford, Pulaski, Sebastian, Washington.

Normal turnaround time: 2-3 days. Projects are generally billed by the number of names searched or records located. The first project may require a prepayment.

Correspondent relationships: the rest of Arkansas. They specialize in worker's compensation, liability surveillance, skip tracing, fire cause and origin, product liability, background searches and complete asset searches.

North Wisconsin Abstract Co

Phone: 715-682-4234
Fax: 715-682-4234

212 W Main St
Ashland WI 54806

Local Retrieval Area: WI-Ashland, Bayfield.

Normal turnaround time: varied depending on project. Projects are generally billed by the number of names searched. Credit accounts are accepted. Personal checks are accepted.

They specialize in real estate title searches.

Northeast Investigations Inc

Phone: 800-484-5125
315-682-1160
Fax: 315-682-1157

201 W Genesee St Suite 200
Fayetteville NY 13066

Local Retrieval and SOP Area: NY-Cayuga, Herkimer, Jefferson, Madison, Monroe, Oneida, Onondaga, Oswego.

Normal turnaround time: 3-4 days to 1 week. Projects are generally billed by the hour. The first project may require a prepayment.

Correspondent relationships: most of NY State, including Albany and Erie counties.

Northeast Missouri Abstract

Phone: 573-767-5430
Fax: 573-767-5430

106 W Jefferson
Monticello MO 63457

Local Retrieval Area: MO-Lewis.

Normal turnaround time: 4 days. Projects are generally billed by the number of names searched or records located. Fee basis will vary by type of project. The first project may require a prepayment. Personal checks and cash are accepted.

Correspondent relationships: Knox, Scotland, Clark, Marion, Shelby and Adair Counties in Missouri. They have over 25 years experience in legal work.

Northeast Nebraska Title & Escrow

Phone: 800-870-2142
402-371-1221
Fax: 402-439-2145

1105 S 13th St Suite 208
Norfolk NE 68701

Local Retrieval Area: NE-Madison, Pierce.

Normal turnaround time: 1-3 days. Fee basis is a flat rate and per record. Credit accounts are accepted.

They specialize in title insurance.

Northern Arizona Investigations

Phone: 800-657-2747
520-779-2823
Fax: 520-779-1044

PO Box 1326
Flagstaff AZ 86002

Local Retrieval and SOP Area: AZ-Coconino, Navajo.

Normal turnaround time: 1-2 days. Projects are generally billed by the hour. The first project may require a prepayment.

They specialize in skip tracing, surveillance, insurance fraud and background investigations.

Northern Title of Vilas County

Phone: 715-479-6459
Fax: 715-479-7482

Box 877
Eagle River WI 54521

Local Retrieval Area: WI-Vilas.

Normal turnaround time: 2 days. Projects are generally billed by the number of names searched. Standard fees are charged for searches. Credit accounts are accepted.

Northshore Paralegal Services

Phone: 800-883-6020
508-750-6020
Fax: 508-750-8135

130 Centre St
Danvers MA 01923

Local Retrieval Area: MA-Essex, Middlesex, Norfolk, Suffolk.

Normal turnaround time: usually 24-48 hours. Expedited service available. Projects are generally billed by the number of names searched. Credit accounts are accepted. Payment due upon receipt of report/invoice.

Correspondent relationships: Massachusetts and New Hampshire. They specialize in UCC searches at the city and town level. They also perform real estate and litigation searches at the county level and any search or document retrieval needed in Boston.

Northwest Abstract and Title Inc

Phone: 701-774-8829
Fax: 701-774-8944

PO Box 1265
Williston ND 58801

Local Retrieval Area: ND-Dunn, Williams.

Normal turnaround time: 3 days. Projects are generally billed by the hour. The first project may require a prepayment.

They specialize in oil and gas title.

Northwest Corporate Protection

Phone: 630-876-7991
Fax: 708-752-0042

31 W 025 North Ave
West Chicago IL 60185

Local Retrieval and SOP Area: IL-Cook, Du Page, Kane, Kendall, Lake, McHenry, Will.

Normal turnaround time: 1-3 days. Projects are generally billed by the hour. Charges can be case-by-case. The first project may require a prepayment.

Correspondent relationships: nationwide. They specialize in process serving, locations and skip tracing.

Northwestern Illinois Title

116 W Exchange St
Freeport IL 61032

Phone: 815-235-1477
Fax: 815-235-4815

Local Retrieval Area: IL-16 Counties.

Normal turnaround time: 48 hours. Projects are generally billed by the number of records located. Credit accounts are accepted.

They specialize in land title research.

O

O H Vivell Title Co

506 N Court House Square PO Box 31
Carrollton IL 62016-0031

Phone: 217-942-3733
Fax: 217-942-3207

Local Retrieval Area: IL-Greene.

Normal turnaround time: varied depending on project. Projects are generally billed by the number of records located. The first project may require a prepayment.

Correspondent relationships: Calhoun.

Nikki A O'Connell

155 Princess Margaret Dr
Newport News VA 23602

Phone: 757-877-8469
Fax: 757-877-8469

Local Retrieval Area: VA-12 Counties.

Normal turnaround time: 24-48 hours. Projects are generally billed by the number of names searched. Fees also determined by number of catagories. Credit accounts are accepted. Personal checks are accepted.

She specializes in UCC, judgment, tax liens, suits and property/title searches.

Michael J O'Connor

52 N Lehigh Ave
Frackville PA 17931

Phone: 800-518-4529
717-874-3300
Fax: 717-874-4822

Local Retrieval Area: PA-Schuylkill.

Normal turnaround time: 1 week. Projects are generally billed by the number of names searched. Credit accounts are accepted. They accept personal checks.

Correspondent relationships: Columbia and Northumberland.

Oakey and Oakey Abstract Co

108 Chieftain
Osceola WI 54020

Phone: 715-294-2624
Fax: 715-755-3535

Local Retrieval Area: WI-Polk.

Normal turnaround time: 2-7 days. Projects are generally billed by the number of names searched or records located. Credit accounts are accepted.

Correspondent relationships: Burnett and Barron. They specialize in DOT searches for new road set ups, title searches and full abstracting.

Cindy M Oberdier

312 S High St PO Box 0138 (43301-0138)
Marion OH 43302

Phone: 800-273-1858
614-387-4960
Fax: 614-383-4508

Local Retrieval Area: OH-Allen, Clark, Crawford, Franklin, Greene, Hancock, Licking, Marion, Medina, Montgomery.

Normal turnaround time: 24-72 hours. Projects are generally billed by the number of names searched. Credit accounts are accepted. Terms are net 30 days.

Correspondent relationships: State of Ohio. She specializes in UCC's, federal and state tax liens, judgments, bankruptcies, District Court, felony and misdemeanor records, fixture filings, single property searches and delinquent tax information. Filing of UCC's are also available.

Ochiltree County Abstract Co

PO Box 1263
Perryton TX 79070

Phone: 806-435-4572
Fax: 806-435-2239

Local Retrieval Area: TX-Lipscomb, Ochiltree.

Normal turnaround time: 2 days. Projects are generally billed by the hour. Credit accounts are accepted. Personal checks are accepted.

Correspondent relationships: Ochiltree and Lipscomb, TX counties. They specialize in abstracts of title, title insurance, lien searches, abstracts of judgment, copies of filed documents, courtesy filings and search District Court minutes and pending lawsuits.

Office Services of the Keys

133 Palm Ln
Islamorada FL 33036-3016

Phone: 305-853-1155
Fax: 305-853-0036

Local Retrieval Area: FL-Monroe.

Normal turnaround time: 24 hours. Online computer ordering is also available. Projects are generally billed by the number of names searched. The first project may require a prepayment.

Ogeman Title Co

PO Box 384
West Branch MI 48661

Phone: 517-345-7240
Fax: 517-345-4777

Local Retrieval Area: MI-Arenac, Ogemaw.

Normal turnaround time: up to a week. Expedited service available. Fee basis will vary by the type of project. Credit accounts are accepted. They request prepay on out of area transactions.

They specialize in title insurance and closing.

Ogemaw County Abstract Co

111 N 3rd St
West Branch MI 48661

Phone: 517-345-0110
Fax: 517-345-2907

Local Retrieval Area: MI-Ogemaw.

Normal turnaround time: 48 hours. Projects are generally billed by the number of names searched. Credit accounts are accepted.

Ohio Bar Title

250 S Prospect St
Ravenna OH 44266

Phone: 330-297-7003
Fax: 330-296-9644

Local Retrieval Area: OH-Portage.

Normal turnaround time: 24 hours for most searches, and full real estate title searches average 3 working days. Fee basis will vary by type of project. Credit accounts are accepted. Personal checks are accepted.

Ohio Independent Title & Pub Rec

Phone: 419-447-7474
Fax: 419-447-0007

PO Box 593
Tiffin OH 44883

Local Retrieval and SOP Area: OH-12 Counties.

Normal turnaround time: 24-48 hours. Projects are generally billed by the number of names searched or records located. Credit accounts are accepted. Personal checks are accepted.

Correspondent relationships: Putnam, Lucas, Definane, Fulton, Williams, Henry, Richland, Morrow, Ashland, Marion, Delaware and Paulding. They specialize in title searches and felony records.

Ohio Paralegal Services Inc

Phone: 330-759-1430
Fax: 330-759-2068

4628 Middle Dr
Youngstown OH 44505

Local Retrieval Area: OH-All Counties.

Normal turnaround time: 48 to 72 hours. Projects are generally billed by the number of names searched. Credit accounts are accepted.

Correspondent relationships: nationwide. They specialize in the State of Ohio.

Okeechobee Abstract and Title

Phone: 813-763-3710
Fax: 813-763-3787

302 NW 3rd St
Okeechobee FL 34972

Local Retrieval Area: FL-Glades, Martin, Okeechobee.

Normal turnaround time: the same day for name and UCC searches, and 2 to 3 days for real estate commitments. Projects are generally billed by the number of names searched. Credit accounts are accepted.

Correspondent relationships: Palm Beach, Martin, St. Lucie, Broward, Dade and Monroe Counties. They are a family owned company that has been in business for over 50 years at the same location.

Okfusee County Abstract Co

Phone: 918-623-0565
Fax: 918-623-4022

PO Box 66
Okemah OK 74859

Local Retrieval Area: OK-Okfuskee.

Normal turnaround time: 2-3 days. Projects are generally billed by the hour. Credit accounts are accepted.

Olde Reserve Title Inc

Phone: 330-273-3007
Fax: 330-725-7872

677 W Liberty Street
Medina OH 44256

Local Retrieval Area: OH-Medina.

Normal turnaround time: 1-3 days. Credit accounts are accepted.

Oliver County Abstract

Phone: 701-794-3496

Box 105
Center ND 58530

Local Retrieval Area: ND-Oliver.

Normal turnaround time: varied depending on project. Projects are generally billed by the hour. A base rate is charged in addition to the hourly rate. Credit accounts are accepted.

They specialize in title abstracts, lien searches and title memorandums.

Olson Humboldt County Abstract

Phone: 515-332-2353

503 Sumner Ave
Humboldt IA 50548

Local Retrieval Area: IA-Humboldt.

Normal turnaround time: 3-5 days. Projects are generally billed by the number of records located. The first project may require a prepayment.

They specialize in title searches.

On Point Investigations

Phone: 425-646-1143
Fax: 425-454-2611

PO Box 95828
Seattle WA 98145

Local Retrieval and SOP Area: WA-King.

Normal turnaround time: 1 week. Projects are generally billed by the hour. The first project may require a prepayment.

They specialize in criminal defense investigations, civil and insurance investigations, asset searches and witness locations.

One Hour Court Services

Phone: 714-558-1403
Fax: 714-558-0261

PO Box 12194
Santa Ana CA 92712-2194

Local Retrieval Area: CA-Orange.

Normal turnaround time: the same day for federal courts and 1 to 2 days for archives. Fee basis will vary by type of project. Bankruptcy is by case number, indexing is per name. Projects require prepayment.

Oneida Valley Abstract

Phone: 315-363-1444
Fax: 315-363-9547

PO Box 29 Court St
Wampsville NY 13163

Local Retrieval Area: NY-Madison.

Normal turnaround time: 48 hours. Fee basis will vary by years searched. Credit accounts are accepted. Personal checks are accepted.

Onistagrawa Abstracting Corp

Phone: 518-827-8088
Fax: 518-295-7459

PO Box 777
Middleburgh NY 12122-0777

Local Retrieval Area: NY-Columbia, Delaware, Fulton, Greene, Montgomery, Otsego, Schenectady, Schoharie.

Normal turnaround time: 2-4 days for UCC's, judgments, probate, and simple deed searches. Full abstract and title insurance will take 1 to 2 weeks. Projects are generally billed by the number of names searched. The fee basis for real estate is figured on a per parcel basis. Credit accounts are accepted.

Oplinger Abstract & Title Inc

Phone: 605-387-2335

PO Box 133
Olivet SD 57052

Local Retrieval Area: SD-Hutchinson.

Normal turnaround time: 5 days. Projects are generally billed by the hour. Projects require prepayment.

Orange Abstractor Services Co

Phone: 914-294-3331
Fax: 914-294-8748

222 Greenwich Ave
Goshen NY 10924

Local Retrieval and SOP Area: NY-Dutchess, Orange, Putnam, Rockland, Sullivan.

Normal turnaround time: 1-14 days. Fee basis will vary by type of project. Credit accounts are accepted. Terms are net 30 days.

Correspondent relationships: Queens, Nassau, Westchester and Suffolk.

Orange County Abstract and Title
Phone: 812-723-3044
204 E Main St
Paoli IN 47454
Local Retrieval Area: IN-Orange.

Normal turnaround time: 24-72 hours. Projects are generally billed by the number of names searched or records located. Credit accounts are accepted. Personal checks are accepted.

They specialize in title searches and lien searches.

Orange Paper Placers
Phone: 914-294-7810
Fax: 914-294-3511
26 Scotchtown Ave
Goshen NY 10924
Local Retrieval and SOP Area: NY-Dutchess, Orange, Putnam, Rockland, Sullivan, Ulster.

Normal turnaround time: 7 days. Expedited service available. Projects are generally billed by the number of records located. Projects require prepayment.

Oregon Process Service Inc
Phone: 800-599-8133
541-746-3021
Fax: 541-382-7068
PO Box 768
Springfield OR 97477
Local Retrieval and SOP Area: OR-Lane.

Normal turnaround time: 3 days. Expedited service available. Fee basis will vary by type of project. The first project may require a prepayment.

They specialize in process serving.

Orion Protective Services
Phone: 800-705-7353
410-515-7353
Fax: 800-705-7353
410-879-3134
PO Box 579
Churchville MD 21028
Local Retrieval and SOP Area: MD-Harford.

Normal turnaround time: 24 hours. Expedited service available at surcharge. Projects are generally billed by the number of names searched. Volume discounts available. The first project may require a prepayment. All work invoiced upon completion.

Correspondent relationships: worldwide. They specialize in international intelligence services to government, corporate, and private clientele. All Orion field personnel are former government or law enforcement agents.

Orion Research Group
Phone: 908-355-9337
Fax: 908-355-2453
PO Box 789 Townley Station
Union NJ 07083
Local Retrieval Area: NJ-Bergen, Essex, Mercer, Middlesex, Morris, Ocean, Somerset, Union.

Normal turnaround time: 24-48 hours. Projects are generally billed by the hour. Credit accounts are accepted.

They specialize in asset searches and litigation support, and they access the Federal Records Center in Bayonne, NJ.

Dora Orum
Phone: 209-251-5193
Fax: 209-456-3833
4782 E Fountain Way
Fresno CA 93726
Local Retrieval Area: CA-Fresno.

Normal turnaround time: 1-2 days. Fee basis is per search. The first project may require a prepayment.

She specializes in abstracting and public record searching, which includes fictitious business name searches.

Patricia J Osborn
Phone: 214-349-3562
Fax: 214-349-1560
7711 Deer Trail
Dallas TX 75238
Local Retrieval Area: TX-Dallas, Tarrant.

Normal turnaround time: 24 hours. Projects are generally billed by the number of names searched. The first project may require a prepayment. Monthly invoicing available.

She specializes in pre-employment criminal searches.

Oscoda County Abstract Inc
Phone: 517-826-5832
Fax: 517-826-5832
PO Box 127
Mio MI 48647
Local Retrieval Area: MI-Oscoda.

Normal turnaround time: 24 hours. Projects are generally billed by the number of names searched. Projects require prepayment.

OTI Resources
Phone: 800-728-2742
210-822-4684
Fax: 210-822-4663
PO Box 685055
Austin TX 78768-5055
Local Retrieval Area: TX-Bexar, Collin, Dallas, Denton, Fort Bend, Galveston, Harris, Tarrant, Travis.

Normal turnaround time: 48 hours-7 days depending on the project. Projects are generally billed by the number of names searched. The first project may require a prepayment.

Correspondent relationships: Georgia, Mississippi, Virginia, North Carolina, Tennessee, Alabama, Arkansas, Kentucky. They specialize in criminal court research.

Otoe County Abstract Co
Phone: 402-873-5511
Fax: 402-873-7746
PO Box 488
Nebraska City NE 68410
Local Retrieval Area: NE-Cass, Nemaha, Otoe.

Normal turnaround time: 1-2 days. They charge a flat fee per project. The first project may require a prepayment.

They specialize in title records.

Otsego County Abstract Co
Phone: 517-732-5765
Fax: 517-732-7288
120 E Main St
Gaylord MI 49735
Local Retrieval Area: MI-Otsego.

Normal turnaround time: 7-10 days. Expedited service available. Fee basis will vary by type of project. The first project may require a prepayment.

Ouren Title Inc
Phone: 712-755-2174
Fax: 712-755-3865
PO Box 229
Harlan IA 51537-0229
Local Retrieval Area: IA-Shelby.

Normal turnaround time: 24 hours. Projects are generally billed by the number of names searched. Credit accounts are accepted.

They specialize in preparing abstracts, and record ownership and lien reports.

Veda Ousley
Phone: 573-736-5357
Fax: 573-736-2234
20620 Highway DD
Crocker MO 65452
Local Retrieval Area: MO-Pulaski.

Normal turnaround time: varied depending on project. Fee basis will vary with the type of search. Fax costs are extra. The first project may require a prepayment.

Veda specializes in genealogy searches.

Owens & Associates Investigtns
Phone: 800-297-1343
2245 San Diego Ave Suite 225   619-297-1343
San Diego CA 92110-2942   **Fax:** 619-297-7622

Local Retrieval and SOP Area: CA-San Diego.

Normal turnaround time: 24 hours. Projects are generally billed by the hour. The first project may require a prepayment.

Correspondent relationships: nationwide and worldwide. They specialize in on-site criminal and civil searches nationwide. Worldwide full service investigations by former FBI agents and other law enforcement officers.

Ozark Title & Guaranty Co
Phone: 501-743-3333
PO Box 6   **Fax:** 501-743-3333
Harrison AR 72602-0006

Local Retrieval Area: AR-Baxter, Boone, Carroll, Marion, Newton, Searcy.

Normal turnaround time: 7 days. Online computer ordering is also available. Fee basis will vary by the type of project. Projects require prepayment.

He is a licensed attorney in Arkansas and in Missouri.

P

P.I. Services
Phone: 800-553-4842
PO Box 2383   701-235-4842
Fargo ND 58108   **Fax:** 701-232-9368

Local Retrieval and SOP Area: MN-Becker, Clay, Norman, Otter Tail, Wilkin; ND-Barnes, Cass, Richland, Stutsman, Traill.

Normal turnaround time: 48 hours. Projects are generally billed by the number of names searched. Credit accounts are accepted. Payment due upon receipt by client.

Correspondent relationships: Grand Forks. They specialize in civil, criminal, insurance investigation and surveillance.

P.R.I.D.E. Enterprises
Phone: 800-465-7743
1670 S Amphlett Blvd Suite 214   415-571-8488
San Mateo CA 94402   **Fax:** 415-349-4403

Local Retrieval Area: CA-San Francisco, San Mateo, Santa Clara.

Normal turnaround time: 2 days. Projects are generally billed by the number of names searched. The first project may require a prepayment. Will bill monthly.

Correspondent relationships: Southern and Northern California. They specialize in credit reports, criminal records, pre-employment research and DMV records.

Walter J Pace
Phone: 617-389-6730
125 Linden St   **Fax:** 617-389-5936
Everett MA 02149

Local Retrieval Area: MA-Middlesex, Norfolk, Suffolk.

Normal turnaround time: 24-48 hours. Projects are generally billed by the number of names searched. Projects require prepayment.

Pacific Coast Legal Services
Phone: 800-845-8821
849 Almar Ave Suite 210-C   408-471-9168
Santa Cruz CA 95060   **Fax:** 408-471-9169

Local Retrieval and SOP Area: CA-Monterey, Santa Clara, Santa Cruz.

Normal turnaround time: 1-2 days. Same day service available. Projects are generally billed by the number of names searched. Credit accounts are accepted. They bill on the 25th of the month, terms are net 15 days.

They specialize in process serving, legal photo copy, in-house paralegal, in-house investigator, various court services, filings, research, docket sheet preparation for the courts that do not have docket sheets.

Pacific Corporate & Title Services
Phone: 800-266-9469
2317 Boradway Suite 140   415-366-9469
Redwood City CA 94063   **Fax:** 415-366-2703

Local Retrieval Area: CA-21 Counties.

Normal turnaround time: 2-3 days. Projects are generally billed by the number of names searched or records located. The first project may require a prepayment. Credit cards are accepted. Terms are net 30 days for clients.

Correspondent relationships: rural areas. They specialize in UCC, title and litigation searches. They also perform corporate services.

Pacific Corporate & Title Services
Phone: 800-230-4988
1726 11th St   916-558-4988
Sacramento CA 95814   **Fax:** 916-441-2217

Local Retrieval Area: CA-Alameda, Los Angeles, Orange, Riverside, Sacramento, San Bernardino, San Francisco, San Joaquin, San Mateo, Santa Clara.

Normal turnaround time: 1-2 days. Projects are generally billed by the number of names searched. The first project may require a prepayment. Credit cards are accepted.

Correspondent relationships: nationwide. They specialize in UCC, title and publishing and filing services.

Pacific Photocopy & Research
Phone: 305-764-5646
200 N Andrews Ave   **Fax:** 305-764-5447
Ft Lauderdale FL 33301

Local Retrieval Area: FL-Broward.

Normal turnaround time: 1 hour to availability of the file. Fee basis will vary by the type of project. The first project may require a prepayment. Credit cards are accepted.

Correspondent relationships: nationwide. They specialize in bankruptcy court records.

Pacific Photocopy & Research
Phone: 904-355-1062
300 W Adams St Suite 502   **Fax:** 904-355-0958
Jacksonville FL 32202-4304

Local Retrieval Area: FL-15 Counties.

Normal turnaround time: 1 hour to availability of the file. Fee basis will vary by the type of project. The first project may require a prepayment. Credit cards are accepted.

Correspondent relationships: nationwide. They specialize in bankruptcy court records.

Pacific Photocopy & Research

Phone: 305-371-7330
Fax: 305-371-9657

1 NE 1st St #404
Miami FL 33132

Local Retrieval Area: FL-Dade, Highlands, Indian River, Martin, Monroe, Okeechobee, St. Lucie.

Normal turnaround time: 1 hour to availability of the file. Fee basis will vary by the type of project. The first project may require a prepayment. Credit cards are accepted.

Correspondent relationships: nationwide. They specialize in bankruptcy court records.

Pacific Photocopy & Research

Phone: 407-425-7234
Fax: 407-425-7218

35 W Pine St Suite 229
Orlando FL 32801

Local Retrieval Area: FL-Brevard, Lake, Orange, Osceola, Seminole, Volusia.

Normal turnaround time: 1 hour to availability of the file. Fee basis will vary by the type of project. The first project may require a prepayment. Credit cards are accepted.

Correspondent relationships: nationwide. They specialize in bankruptcy court records.

Pacific Photocopy & Research

Phone: 800-934-6999
904-561-8008
Fax: 904-561-1066

227 N Bronough St Suite 7400
Tallahassee FL 32301

Local Retrieval Area: FL-20 Counties.

Normal turnaround time: 1 hour to availability of the file. Fee basis will vary by type of project. The first project may require a prepayment. Credit cards are accepted.

Correspondent relationships: nationwide. They specialize in bankruptcy court records.

Pacific Photocopy & Research

Phone: 813-885-3854
Fax: 813-885-3942

6005 Jarvis St
Tampa FL 33634

Local Retrieval Area: FL-14 Counties.

Normal turnaround time: 1 hour to availability of the file. Fee basis will vary by type of project. The first project may require a prepayment. Credit cards are accepted.

Correspondent relationships: nationwide. They specialize in bankruptcy court records.

Pacific Photocopy & Research

Phone: 561-832-3878
Fax: 561-832-8035

319 Clematis St Suite 209
West Palm Beach FL 33401

Local Retrieval Area: FL-Palm Beach.

Normal turnaround time: 1 hour to availability of the file. Fee basis will vary by type of project. The first project may require a prepayment. Credit cards are accepted.

Correspondent relationships: nationwide. They specialize in bankruptcy court records.

Pacific Photocopy & Research

Phone: 904-435-3183
Fax: 904-435-3185

220 W Garden St Suite 600
Pensacola FL 32501

Local Retrieval Area: FL-Bay, Escambia, Okaloosa, Santa Rosa, Walton, Washington.

Normal turnaround time: 24-48 hours depending on availability of file. Fee basis will vary by type of project. The first project may require a prepayment. Credit cards are accepted.

Correspondent relationships: nationwide. They specialize in bankruptcy court records and Federal court records as well as all County court records, including civil and criminal.

Pacific Process Service

Phone: 509-325-1371
Fax: 509-327-1830

PO Box 9212
Spokane WA 99209

Local Retrieval and SOP Area: WA-Garfield, Pend Oreille, Spokane, Stevens, Whitman.

Normal turnaround time: 1-2 days. Projects are generally billed by the number of names searched or records located. The first project may require a prepayment.

Correspondent relationships: Kootenia County, ID.

PADIC Inc

Phone: 817-665-6130
Fax: 817-665-7486

1609 E Broadway
Gainesville TX 76240

Local Retrieval and SOP Area: TX-Collin, Cooke, Dallas, Denton, Ellis, Grayson, Tarrant.

Normal turnaround time: 48 hours. Projects are generally billed by the number of names searched. Credit accounts are accepted.

Correspondent relationships: nationwide. They specialize in document retrieval, asset searches, environmental investigations, surveillance, witness location and statements, computer database research, polygraphs and insurance defense investigation.

Page County Abstract and Title Co

Phone: 712-542-3613
Fax: 712-542-2629

118 N 16th St
Clarinda IA 51632

Local Retrieval Area: IA-Page.

Normal turnaround time: 48 hours. Fee basis will vary by the type of project. Credit accounts are accepted. Personal checks are accepted.

They specialize in searching county records and abstracting real estate titles.

Pagosa Springs Title Co

Phone: 303-264-4141
Fax: 303-264-4835

PO Box 146
Pagosa Springs CO 81147

Local Retrieval Area: CO-Archuleta.

Normal turnaround time: up to 1 week. Projects are generally billed by the hour. Credit accounts are accepted. Out of town clients are charged a setup fee and must prepay.

They specialize in real estate and title matters.

Paladin Legal Services
13135 Old Glenn Hwy Suite 100-B
Eagel River AK 99577
Phone: 907-694-5222
Fax: 907-276-3306

Local Retrieval and SOP Area: AK-Anchorage Borough, Matanuska-Susitna Borough.

Normal turnaround time: 48 hours. Expedited service available. Projects are generally billed by the hour. Credit accounts are accepted. Set up fee varies. They require prepay for out of state customers and will invoice in state and established customers.

They specialize in private investigations.

Pallorium Inc
PO Box 155
Brooklyn NY 11230
Phone: 212-969-0286
Fax: 800-275-4329

Local Retrieval and SOP Area: NY-Bronx, Kings, Nassau, New York, Queens, Richmond, Suffolk, Westchester.

Normal turnaround time: 1-3 days. Online computer ordering is also available. Project billing methods vary. The first project may require a prepayment. Terms are net 30 days.

Correspondent relationships: San Antonio and Los Angeles. Also Toronto, Canada, Hong Kong and Haifa, Israel. They maintain an on-line investigative support system with criminal, voter, credit, MVR, and other records. They also maintain an on-line network of 700+ investigative agencies.

Palm Title Inc
PO Box 341
LaBelle FL 33935-0341
Phone: 813-675-4545
Fax: 813-675-1418

Local Retrieval Area: FL-Hendry.

Normal turnaround time: 3-5 days. Projects are generally billed by the hour. Credit accounts are accepted.

They specialize in title policy work.

Palmer Abstract Inc
19 1st Ave NW
Waukon IA 52172
Phone: 319-568-3488

Local Retrieval Area: IA-Allamakee.

Normal turnaround time: 48 hours. Projects are generally billed by the number of names searched or records located. Credit accounts are accepted.

Palmer and Murrie Abstract Co Inc
506 N Market St
Marion IL 62959
Phone: 618-993-3866
Fax: 618-993-3015

Local Retrieval Area: IL-Franklin, Johnson, Saline, Williamson.

Normal turnaround time: 5-6 working days. Projects are generally billed by the number of names searched or records located. Credit accounts are accepted. Personal checks are accepted.

Correspondent relationships: Union and Jackson Counties.

▥ Palmer Investigative Services
PO Box 10760
Prescott AZ 86304
Phone: 800-280-2951
602-778-2951
Fax: 800-215-7049
602-445-7204

Local Retrieval and SOP Area: AZ-Yavapai.

Normal turnaround time: 48 hours. Rush service is also available. Document retrieval is charged by the hour, otherwise per name for initial search. Projects require prepayment. Regular clients may arrange for credit.

Correspondent relationships: Coconino and Mohave counties.

Palo Alto County Abstract Co
1009-1011 Broadway St
Emmetsburg IA 50536
Phone: 712-852-4313
Fax: 712-852-4373

Local Retrieval Area: IA-Palo Alto.

Normal turnaround time: varied depending on project. Fee basis will vary by the type of project. Credit accounts are accepted.

Panola County Abstract and Title
105 W Sabine
Carthage TX 75633
Phone: 903-693-3266
Fax: 903-693-2819

Local Retrieval Area: TX-Panola.

Normal turnaround time: varied depending on project. Project billing methods vary. Credit accounts are accepted. Personal checks are accepted.

Paper Chase
2331/690 Larson St
Friday Harbor WA 98250
Phone: 360-378-3345
Fax: 360-378-3345

Local Retrieval and SOP Area: WA-San Juan.

Normal turnaround time: 1-2 days. Projects are generally billed by the hour. Fee basis varies by type of transaction. The first project may require a prepayment.

▥ Paper Chase Research
139 Fulton St
New York NY 10038-2594
Phone: 212-587-7071
Fax: 212-587-7072

Local Retrieval Area: NY-Bronx, Dutchess, Kings, Nassau, New York, Putnam, Queens, Richmond, Suffolk, Westchester.

Normal turnaround time: 24 hours. Projects are generally billed by the number of names searched. The first project may require a prepayment.

Correspondent relationships: nationwide. They specialize in document retrieval, filing and monitoring and custom research.

Paragon Document Research Inc
500 N Robert St Suite 508
St Paul MN 55101
Phone: 800-892-4235
612-222-6844
Fax: 800-847-7369
612-222-2281

Local Retrieval and SOP Area: MN-Dakota, Hennepin, Ramsey, Washington.

Normal turnaround time: 24-48 hours. Expedited service available. Projects are generally billed by the number of names searched. The first project may require a prepayment. Will bill clients on a monthly basis.

Correspondent relationships: Minnesota and all Midwestern state and county levels. They specialize in notification letter processing, federal and state tax lien bulletins and corporate documents.

Paralegal Enterprises Inc
401 W First St Suite 2-D
Greenville NC 27835
Phone: 919-758-6622
Fax: 919-758-6622

Local Retrieval Area: NC-Greene, Pitt.

Normal turnaround time: 48 hours. Projects are generally billed by the number of names searched. Fee basis will vary with portions of tracts of land. The first project may require a prepayment.

They specialize in real estate searches.

Paralegal Field Research Svc

Phone: 800-256-7459

330 Clematis St Suite 209   561-832-7328

West Palm Beach FL 33401   Fax: 561-832-1857

Local Retrieval and SOP Area: FL-Palm Beach.

Normal turnaround time: varied depending on project. Projects are generally billed by the hour. Projects require prepayment.

Correspondent relationships: the rest of Florida. They specialize in criminal investigations and mitigation investigations (Capital cases).

Paralegal Resource Center Inc

Phone: 617-742-1939

4 Faneuil Hall Marketplace   Fax: 617-742-1417

Boston MA 02109

Local Retrieval Area: MA-Essex, Middlesex, Norfolk, Plymouth, Suffolk, Worcester.

Normal turnaround time: 3-5 business days. Expedited service avaliable. Projects are generally billed by the number of names searched. The first project may require a prepayment.

Correspondent relationships: the rest of Massachusetts. They specialize in UCC, corporate records, state and federal tax lien searches and document retrieval of all court records at all Massachusetts courthouses. They also provide permanent and temporary paralegal staffing.

Paralegal Services

Phone: 410-820-8717

26322 Tunis Mills Rd   Fax: 410-820-5147

Easton MD 21601

Local Retrieval Area: MD-Caroline, Dorchester, Talbot.

Normal turnaround time: 48 hours. Projects are generally billed by the number of names searched. The first project may require a prepayment.

They specialize in full title searches and also do bring-to-dates.

Paralegal Services

Phone: 304-258-4287

Rt 2 Box 492   Fax: 304-258-1967

Berkeley Springs WV 25411

Local Retrieval Area: WV-Grant, Hampshire, Hardy, Jefferson, Morgan.

Normal turnaround time: 24-48 hours. Expedited service available. Projects are generally billed by the number of names searched. The first project may require a prepayment.

They specialize in real estate title work, with 10 years of experience. They also assist in civil and criminal litigation, trial preparation and summarize depositions.

Paralegal Services

Phone: 304-675-1997

RR 2 Box 65   Fax: 304-675-2521

Point Pleasant WV 25550-4775

Local Retrieval Area: WV-Mason.

Normal turnaround time: 24-48 hours. Projects are generally billed by the number of names searched. Credit accounts are accepted.

Paralegal Services of Buffalo

Phone: 716-856-3818

947 Ellicott Square Bldg   Fax: 716-852-2028

Buffalo NY 14203

Local Retrieval Area: NY-Erie, Niagara.

Normal turnaround time: 1 day. Projects are generally billed by the number of names searched. The first project may require a prepayment.

Correspondent relationships: Monroe, Chaulaqua, Genesee and Niagara, NY counties. They specialize in motor vehicle searches, amorization schedules, federal and bankruptcy court, and Supreme Court searching.

Paralegal Services of NC

Phone: 919-821-7762

120 Penmarc Dr Suite 118   Fax: 919-832-6378

Raleigh NC 27603

Local Retrieval and SOP Area: NC-Alamance, Chatham, Cumberland, Durham, Franklin, Harnett, Johnston, Orange, Wake, Wayne.

Normal turnaround time: 1-3 days. Projects are generally billed by the number of names searched. Credit accounts are accepted.

Correspondent relationships: the rest of North Carolina. They specialize in real property, asset/lien searches, probate and process service, and Secretary of State information searches. They can cover every county in North Carolina.

Paraprofessional Abstracts

Phone: 800-522-5163

PO Box 48705

Cumberland NC 28331

Local Retrieval Area: NC-Bladen, Cumberland, Harnett, Hoke, Robeson, Sampson, Scotland.

Normal turnaround time: 24 hours or less for Cumberland county, and 48 hours or less for the remaining counties. Projects are generally billed by the number of records located. Charges also by type of searches. Credit accounts are accepted. Payment due within 30 days.

Parasec

Phone: 800-603-5868

1101 "R" St   916-441-1001

Sacramento CA 95814   Fax: 916-447-6091

Local Retrieval Area: CA-Los Angeles, Sacramento, San Diego.

Normal turnaround time: 24-72 hours. Projects are generally billed by the number of names searched or records located. Credit accounts are accepted. Credit cards are accepted. Personal checks are accepted.

They specialize in document filing and retrieval for UCC, corporate, limited partnership, trademark and service marks.

June Park

Phone: 712-523-3490

2566 Newport Way

Bedford IA 50833-8304

Local Retrieval Area: IA-Taylor.

Normal turnaround time: 24 hours. Projects are generally billed by the number of names searched. The first project may require a prepayment. A prepay set up fee is charged for first time customers only. Personal checks are accepted.

🏛 Patrick Investigative Services

PO Box 450250
Sunrise FL 33345

Phone: 800-700-2958
305-749-2311
Fax: 305-749-6202

Local Retrieval Area: FL-Broward, Dade.

Normal turnaround time: 48-72 hours. Projects are generally billed by the number of names searched. Fees based on number of names searched/location. The first project may require a prepayment.

Correspondent relationships: State of Florida. They specialize in complete investigative services.

🏛 Patten Investigations

PO Box 311
Benicia CA 94510

Phone: 800-291-1922
707-745-1922
Fax: 707-746-1337

Local Retrieval and SOP Area: CA-Alameda, Contra Costa, Napa, Solano.

Normal turnaround time: 4 working days or less. Projects are generally billed by the number of names searched. Credit accounts are accepted. Due upon receipt of invoice.

Correspondent relationships: South Alameda, Marin, and Sonoma, CA counties. They are a California licensed private investigator and California registered process servers in Solano County.

Patton Abstract and Title Inc

PO Box 943 110 E 3rd St
Lewisville AR 71845

Phone: 501-921-4263
Fax: 501-921-5262

Local Retrieval Area: AR-Lafayette.

Normal turnaround time: 1 week. Projects are generally billed by the hour. Credit accounts are accepted. They accept personal checks.

🏛 Paul J Ciolino & Associates

900 W Jackson Blvd Suite 4-E
Chicago IL 60607-3024

Phone: 312-226-6300
Fax: 312-432-9300

Local Retrieval and SOP Area: IL-Cook, Du Page, Grundy, Lake, McHenry, Will.

Normal turnaround time: 1 day to 1 week depending on availability of information. Online computer ordering is also available. Projects are generally billed by the hour. The first project may require a prepayment. Credit cards are accepted.

Correspondent relationships: nationwide. They are a licensed experienced chicago investigation firm skilled in background research, criminal and civil cases. National network of skilled, credentialed investigators.

Pawnee County Abstract Co

637 G St
Pawnee City NE 68420

Phone: 402-852-2577
Fax: 402-852-2035

Local Retrieval Area: NE-Pawnee.

Normal turnaround time: varied depending on project. Projects are generally billed by the number of names searched or records located. Credit accounts are accepted.

Nita Payne

1192 Golf Course Rd
Halifax VA 24558

Phone: 804-476-2595

Local Retrieval Area: VA-Halifax, Mecklenburg, City of South Boston.

Normal turnaround time: 1-2 days. Fee basis varies by type of transaction. Credit accounts are accepted.

She specializes in real estate title searches.

PC Fraze Abstract Co

301 N Main
Syracuse KS 67878

Phone: 316-384-7828
Fax: 316-384-7828

Local Retrieval Area: KS-Grant, Hamilton, Kearny, Stanton.

Normal turnaround time: 1 day for Hamilton County, 2 days for Stanton and Grant counties and 3 days for Kearney County. Projects are generally billed by the hour. Credit accounts are accepted. Payment due on receipt of statement.

PCS Inc

9600 G Arapahoe Rd
Englewood CO 80112

Phone: 800-792-2108
303-792-2105
Fax: 303-792-2107

Local Retrieval and SOP Area: CO-Denver.

Normal turnaround time: 3-7 days. Projects are generally billed by the number of names searched. The first project may require a prepayment. Will accept COD, money orders and checks.

Correspondent relationships: Douglas and Arapahoe.

Paul Peduska

74 Court Square
Pocahontas IA 50574

Phone: 712-335-4257

Local Retrieval Area: IA-Pocahontas.

Normal turnaround time: 1-2 days. Projects are generally billed by the hour. Credit accounts are accepted. Personal checks are accepted.

Pelican Land and Abstract Co Inc

PO Box 608
Lake Charles LA 70601

Phone: 318-436-3419
Fax: 318-439-3451

Local Retrieval Area: LA-Acadia Parish, Allen Parish, Beauregard Parish, Calcasieu Parish, Cameron Parish, Jefferson Davis Parish.

Normal turnaround time: varied depending on project. Fee basis will vary by the type of project. The first project may require a prepayment.

Correspondent relationships: the rest of Louisiana. They specialize in oil, gas and leasing research and in residential and commercial abstracts of title and right-of-way research.

Pellish and Pellish Attorneys

809 W Market St
Pottsville PA 17901

Phone: 717-622-2338
Fax: 717-622-2339

Local Retrieval Area: PA-Berks, Carbon, Schuylkill.

Normal turnaround time: 1-14 days. Projects are generally billed by the hour. Credit accounts are accepted. Personal checks are accepted.

Correspondent relationships: Lehigh and Dauphin Counties.

Pemiscot County Abstract

404 Carleton Ave
Caruthersville MO 63830

Phone: 573-333-4666
Fax: 573-333-2641

Local Retrieval Area: MO-Pemiscot.

Normal turnaround time: 1-3 days. Fee basis will vary by the type of project. Credit accounts are accepted.

They specialize in title probate.

Penncorp Service Group Inc

Phone: 800-544-9050
717-234-2300
600 N 2nd St Suite 500
Harrisburg PA 17101   **Fax:** 717-238-8232

Local Retrieval Area: PA-Cumberland, Dauphin, Lancaster, Perry, York.

Normal turnaround time: 24 hours. If certification is needed, allow 3 to 7 days. Projects are generally billed by the number of records located. Credit accounts are accepted. Credit cards are accepted. Personal checks are accepted.

Correspondent relationships: nationwide and Canada. They specialize in LCB transfers and renewals, and in working with the Pennsylvania Department of Transportation.

Pennington County Abstract Co

Phone: 218-681-2527
PO Box 508   **Fax:** 218-681-2528
Thief River Falls MN 56701

Local Retrieval Area: MN-Pennington.

Normal turnaround time: varied depending on project. Fee basis will vary by type of project. Projects require prepayment. They will also invoice.

Penninsula Title and Abstract Corp

Phone: 906-875-6618
15 S 4th St   **Fax:** 906-875-4382
Crystal Falls MI 49920

Local Retrieval Area: MI-Dickinson, Houghton, Iron; WI-Florence.

Normal turnaround time: 1 day. Fee basis will vary by type of project. The first project may require a prepayment.

They specialize in real estate.

Peregrine Investigation & Rsrch

Phone: 303-441-7442
PO Box 3601   **Fax:** 303-499-9834
Boulder CO 80307-3601

Local Retrieval and SOP Area: CO-Adams, Arapahoe, Boulder, Denver, Douglas, Jefferson.

Normal turnaround time: 2 days to 1 week. Online computer ordering is also available. Projects are generally billed by the number of names searched or records located. The first project may require a prepayment.

Correspondent relationships: Larimer, Weld, and El Paso counties. They specialize in finding those who default on consumer and commercial loans, background and asset searches.

Pergerson & Associates

Phone: 209-474-3020
PO Box 690896   **Fax:** 209-474-8952
Stockton CA 95269-0896

Local Retrieval Area: CA-Calaveras, El Dorado, Merced, Placer, Sacramento, San Joaquin, Solano, Stanislaus, Yolo, Yuba.

Normal turnaround time: 24 hours. Projects are generally billed by the number of names searched. The first project may require a prepayment. Terms are net 30 days.

Correspondent relationships: Napa, Amador, Sonora, Sutter, Butte, Tahoma, Shasta, Siskiyou, Colusa, Glenn, Lassen, Plumas, Lake, Trinity, CA and Washoe, NV. They provide a variety of information gathering services that include investigations, on-site record searches and medical record copying services.

Perkins County Abstract Co

Phone: 605-244-5544
PO Box 157   **Fax:** 605-244-5544
Bison SD 57620

Local Retrieval Area: SD-Perkins.

Normal turnaround time: 2 weeks. Projects are generally billed by the hour. Projects require prepayment.

Permian Court Reporters Inc

Phone: 915-683-3032
605 W Texas   **Fax:** 915-683-5324
Midland TX 79701

Local Retrieval Area: TX-Ector, Midland.

Normal turnaround time: 2 days. Projects are generally billed by the hour. Credit accounts are accepted.

Pernell & Sons Investigations

Phone: 510-436-4688
PO Box 9698   **Fax:** 510-436-4688
Oakland CA 94613

Local Retrieval Area: CA-Alameda, Contra Costa, Marin, San Francisco, San Mateo, Santa Clara.

Normal turnaround time: 48 hours. Online computer ordering is also available. Projects are generally billed by the number of names searched. Credit accounts are accepted. Payment due within 30 days of request.

Correspondent relationships: Los Angeles, Fresno, Merced and San Joaquin, CA counties. They specialize in pre-employment background investigations, worker's compensation and surveillances.

Annie Perry

Phone: 615-459-9117
210 Lake Farm Rd   **Fax:** 615-355-8838
Smyrna TN 37167

Local Retrieval Area: TN-Rutherford.

Normal turnaround time: 24 hours. Projects are generally billed by the number of names searched. Charges vary depending on type of search. Credit accounts are accepted. Terms are net 30 days.

They specialize in criminal record searches.

Howard G Perry

Phone: 318-239-7044
109 Allen Ave
Leesville LA 71446

Local Retrieval Area: LA-Vernon Parish.

Normal turnaround time: same day to 72 hours. Projects are generally billed by the number of names searched. Credit accounts are accepted.

They specialize in criminal and civil research.

Marilyn Person

Phone: 605-224-8168
819 W 3rd   **Fax:** 605-945-2440
Pierre SD 57501

Local Retrieval Area: SD-Hughes, Stanley, Sully.

Normal turnaround time: 24-48 hours. Fees based upon project. Credit accounts are accepted.

She acts as registered agent for corporations.

Persona Data Corporation

Phone: 800-735-9555
8700 Crownhill Suite 209
210-829-5505
San Antonio TX 78209   **Fax:** 210-829-5556

Local Retrieval Area: TX-Bexar, Harris.

Normal turnaround time: same day if in by noon central time. Projects are generally billed by the number of names searched. Credit accounts are accepted.

They specialize in pre-employment screening.

▥ Personal Background Investgtns
Phone: 800-949-9982
206-233-1948
PO Box 77308
Seattle WA 98177
Fax: 206-272-9482

Local Retrieval Area: WA-King, Kitsap, Pierce, Snohomish, Thurston.

Normal turnaround time: 24-48 hours for most records. Fee basis varies by type of transaction. The first project may require a prepayment. Will invoice business accounts.

Correspondent relationships: statewide. They have on-line retrieval capabilities for all of Washington. They also specialize in education, Motor Vehicle Records, and credit checks. They also do Washington statewide criminal records.

▥ Personnel Information Plus
Phone: 520-320-0611
2100 E Speedway Blvd PO Box 41441
Fax: 520-321-9593
Tucson AZ 85717-1441

Local Retrieval and SOP Area: AZ-Cochise, Maricopa, Pima.

Normal turnaround time: 36 hours. Online computer ordering is also available. Projects are generally billed by the number of names searched. The first project may require a prepayment. Terms are net 30 days. Volume orders may be discounted.

Correspondent relationships: New York and Northeast and Southeast, SC, NC and FL. They are a public record retrieval and problem solving organization, specializing in pre-employment screening and background checking.

Pete Costanzo Private Investigtns
Phone: 702-868-4043
6055 E Lake Meed Blvd Suite A-120
Fax: 702-459-4723
Las Vegas NV 89115-6909

Local Retrieval Area: NV-Clark.

Normal turnaround time: 1-2 days. Online computer ordering is also available. Projects are generally billed by the number of records located. The first project may require a prepayment.

They specialize in general private investigations.

Peterson Abstract Co
Phone: 612-257-4200
209 N Main Street
Fax: 612-462-7820
Center City MN 55012

Local Retrieval Area: MN-Chisago.

Normal turnaround time: 1 week. Projects are generally billed by the number of names searched or records located. Credit accounts are accepted.

Petroleum Title Service Inc
Phone: 307-235-6237
3603 Hawthorne
Casper WY 82604

Local Retrieval Area: WY-Natrona.

Normal turnaround time: 1 week. Mileage expenses will be added to the fee. All billing is done on per case basis. Credit accounts are accepted.

They prepare abstracts of title, title certificates and any research pertaining to title information on surface, minerals, research for ownership for probates, leasehold checks or any type of title research across the State of Wyoming.

Sandra L Pettengill
Phone: 717-769-6070
RD 2 Box 856
Fax: 717-769-7691
Lock Haven PA 17745

Local Retrieval Area: PA-Clinton, Lycoming.

Normal turnaround time: 24 hours. Charges are varied depending on type of search. The first project may require a prepayment.

She is a paralegal and specializes in current owner breakdowns for titles and research and also does mineral and pipeline record searches.

▥ PFC Information Services
Phone: 510-653-0666
6114 LaSalle Ave Suite 149
Fax: 510-653-0842
Oakland CA 94611

Local Retrieval Area: CA-Alameda, San Francisco.

Normal turnaround time: 24 hours. Projects are generally billed by the number of records located. Credit accounts are accepted. Credit cards are accepted. Personal checks are accepted.

Correspondent relationships: Marin, Santa Clara, Contra Costa and San Mateo. They specialize in asset searches, corporate profiles, skip trace and employment screening.

▥ Phelps & Phelps Investigations
Phone: 800-347-9918
602-807-9799
1235 S Gilbert Rd Suite 3-73
Mesa AZ 85204
Fax: 800-494-7950
602-807-5530

Local Retrieval Area: AZ-Maricopa, Pima.

Normal turnaround time: 24-48 hours. Expedited service available. Projects are generally billed by the number of names searched or records located. Credit accounts are accepted. Credit cards are accepted.

Correspondent relationships: Statewide. They specialize in general investigations, pre-employment screening and retrieving state and county records.

▥ Philip Rosenberger Investigtns
Phone: 800-468-9623
517-789-6005
PO Box 573-0573 One Jackson Square
Jackson MI 49204
Fax: 800-263-0735
517-787-7605

Local Retrieval and SOP Area: MI-Calhoun, Ingham, Jackson.

Normal turnaround time: 48 hours. Expedited service available for a 50% additional charge. Projects are generally billed by the hour. Credit accounts are accepted. Credit cards are accepted.

Correspondent relationships: the southeast quarter of the lower peninsula. They specialize in being a full service detective agency and do background/security investigations and locate missing persons.

Phillips County Abstract Co
Phone: 406-654-1413
PO Box 250 53 S 2nd St E
Fax: 406-654-1413
Malta MT 59538

Local Retrieval Area: MT-Phillips.

Normal turnaround time: 1 week. Projects are generally billed by the hour. Credit accounts are accepted.

Phillips Land Title Company
Phone: 715-339-2230
174 N Avon Ave
Fax: 715-339-4975
Phillips WI 54555

Local Retrieval Area: WI-Price.

Normal turnaround time: 2 days. Fee basis varies by type of transaction. The first project may require a prepayment.

Correspondent relationships: Ashland & Lincoln, WI counties.

Devon L Phillips
Phone: 503-693-8730

1802 NE Thomas St
Hillsboro OR 97123

Local Retrieval Area: OR-Washington.

Normal turnaround time: 2 days. Projects are generally billed by the hour. Projects require prepayment.

Correspondent relationships: Lane, Clackamas, Lincoln, Burton, Linn, OR counties and counties in western Washington.

Phoenix Information Services Inc
Phone: 800-918-8343
512-320-0202
Fax: 512-320-0990

PO Box 1943
Austin TX 78767

Local Retrieval and SOP Area: TX-Bexar, Dallas, El Paso, Harris, Hidalgo, Lubbock, Nueces, Potter, Tarrant, Travis.

Normal turnaround time: 72 hours. Projects are generally billed by the number of names searched. The first project may require a prepayment.

Correspondent relationships: LA, NM, OK, AR and CA. They specialize in worker's compensation, fraud, government, theft, basic investigations and accident reconstructions.

Phoenix Investigations
Phone: 800-999-4701
770-992-4700
Fax: 770-992-4941

1025 Old Roswell Rd Suite 202
Roswell GA 30076

Local Retrieval and SOP Area: GA-Cobb, De Kalb, Fulton, Gwinnett.

Normal turnaround time: 2 days. Projects are generally billed by the number of names searched. The first project may require a prepayment.

Photo Abstract Co
Phone: 918-542-1871
Fax: 918-542-9748

22 E Central Ave
Miami OK 74354

Local Retrieval Area: OK-Ottawa.

Normal turnaround time: 1-3 days. Projects are generally billed by the number of records located. Credit accounts are accepted.

Pickard & Associates Inc
Phone: 508-468-4118
Fax: 508-468-3582

PO Box 473
Wenham MA 01984

Local Retrieval Area: MA-Essex, Middlesex, Suffolk.

Normal turnaround time: 2-10 days. Fees will vary by type of project. The first project may require a prepayment.

Correspondent relationships: nationwide. They are a private investigative firm specializing in asset research and background investigations on a nationwide basis.

Pierce County Abstract
Phone: 701-776-6961
Fax: 701-776-5230

216 2nd St SE
Rugby ND 58368

Local Retrieval Area: ND-Pierce.

Normal turnaround time: 2 weeks. Fee basis will vary by type of project. There is a set fee for abstracting..dd. Credit accounts are accepted.

Pioneer Abstract Co
Phone: 405-257-3351
Fax: 405-257-3329

PO Box 1100
Wewoka OK 74884

Local Retrieval Area: OK-Seminole.

Normal turnaround time: 1-3 days. Fee basis is determined on a per hour or per name plus service charge basis. Credit accounts are accepted.

They specialize in county records.

Pioneer Abstract Co of McAlester
Phone: 918-423-0817
Fax: 918-423-7650

PO Box 926
McAlester OK 74502

Local Retrieval Area: OK-Pittsburg.

Normal turnaround time: 3 days. Projects are generally billed by the hour. The first project may require a prepayment. Credit cards are accepted.

Pioneer-Ward County Abstract Co
Phone: 915-943-5561
Fax: 915-943-3716

PO Box 1639
Monahans TX 79756

Local Retrieval Area: TX-Ward.

Normal turnaround time: 2-3 days. Projects are generally billed by the hour. The first project may require a prepayment.

Pipestone County Abstract Co LLC
Phone: 507-825-5519
Fax: 507-825-5458

PO Box 335
Pipestone MN 56164

Local Retrieval Area: MN-Pipestone.

Normal turnaround time: 2-3 days. Projects are generally billed by the number of names searched or records located. Credit accounts are accepted.

They specialize in real estate recordings.

Julie Pittman
Phone: 515-644-5114

5336 Barnes City Rd
Montezuma IA 50171

Local Retrieval Area: IA-Poweshiek.

Normal turnaround time: up to a week. Fee basis varies by type of transaction. Credit accounts are accepted. All customers outside of the county are asked to prepay.

She specializes in credit research and publishes a monthly bulletin.

Pittsburgh Information and Rsrch
Phone: 412-766-3832
Fax: 412-761-5391

PO Box 99181
Pittsburgh PA 15233

Local Retrieval and SOP Area: PA-66 Counties.

Normal turnaround time: 24-48 hours for a verbal. Fee basis is per index. Credit accounts are accepted.

Correspondent relationships: Pennsylvania. They specialize in all county offices as well as US District and Bankruptcy courts contained within the State of Pennsylvania.

Plains Title and Abstract Inc
Phone: 505-762-4589
Fax: 505-769-1417

1520 Mitchell St Suite 2
Clovis NM 88101-4617

Local Retrieval Area: NM-Curry.

Normal turnaround time: 3-5 days. Projects are generally billed by the number of names searched. Fees depend on complexity of search. The first project may require a prepayment.

They specialize in title insurance.

Platte County Title Co
Phone: 402-563-4519
Fax: 402-564-0588
PO Box 946
Columbus NE 68601
Local Retrieval Area: NE-Platte.

Normal turnaround time: 1 week. Fee basis varies by type of transaction. Credit accounts are accepted.

Correspondent relationships: the counties of Boone, Nance, Butler and Merrick. They specialize in escrow closings.

Plymouth County Abstract
Phone: 712-546-4564
Fax: 712-546-4124
PO Box 1126
Le Mars IA 51031
Local Retrieval Area: IA-Plymouth.

Normal turnaround time: 2-7 days. Fee basis will vary by type of project. Credit accounts are accepted. Personal checks are accepted.

PMDC Associates
Phone: 314-583-1828
Fax: 314-583-1828
PO Box 82
Washington MO 63090
Local Retrieval Area: MO-St. Charles, St. Louis, City of St. Louis.

Normal turnaround time: 48 hours. Projects are generally billed by the number of names searched or records located. Will do projects on a "not to exceed" basis. The first project may require a prepayment. Terms are net 10 days.

Correspondent relationships: New York, Illinois, California, and Texas. They specialize in property searches in all county courts, as well as the full range of public record retrieval and filing services.

Poinsett County Abstract Co
Phone: 501-578-5914
Fax: 501-578-5914
411 Court St
Harrisburg AR 72432
Local Retrieval Area: AR-Poinsett.

Normal turnaround time: 1 week. Fee basis will vary by the type of project. Credit accounts are accepted.

They are a full service title company.

Police Report Acquisition Service
Phone: 972-783-9505
Fax: 972-669-9090
613 Sheffield Dr
Richardson TX 75081
Local Retrieval Area: TX-Collin, Dallas, Denton, Tarrant.

Normal turnaround time: 24 hours. Projects are generally billed by the number of records located. The first project may require a prepayment.

They specialize in police reports and only retrieve from police departments.

Polk Legal Service
Phone: 803-366-9772
Fax: 803-366-9382
619 North Ave
Rock Hill SC 29732
Local Retrieval Area: SC-Chester, Lancaster, York.

Normal turnaround time: 1-3 days. Project billing methods vary. Projects require prepayment.

Pollard & Lott Inc
Phone: 806-495-2989
Fax: 806-495-3876
PO Box 850
Post TX 79356
Local Retrieval Area: TX-Garza.

Normal turnaround time: 1-2 days. Fee basis will vary by the type of project. The first project may require a prepayment.

They specialize in abstract and title searches.

Pondera County Title Co
Phone: 406-278-5823
Fax: 406-278-5820
PO Box 755
Conrad MT 59425
Local Retrieval Area: MT-Pondera.

Normal turnaround time: 2 days. Projects are generally billed by the hour. Projects require prepayment.

Port-o-Wild's Security Services
Phone: 218-751-8200
Fax: 218-751-3132
PO Box 521
Bemidji MN 56619
Local Retrieval and SOP Area: MN-18 Counties.

Normal turnaround time: varied depending on project. Projects are generally billed by the hour. Credit accounts are accepted. Some projects may require prepayment.

Pottawatomie County Abstract Co
Phone: 913-457-3441
Fax: 913-457-3612
108 N 2nd
Westmoreland KS 66549
Local Retrieval Area: KS-Pottawatomie.

Normal turnaround time: 2-3 days. Fee basis varies by type of transaction. The first project may require a prepayment.

Potter & Co
Phone: 406-547-3355
Fax: 406-547-3445
PO Box 650
White Sulphur Springs MT 59645
Local Retrieval Area: MT-Meagher.

Normal turnaround time: 2 weeks. Projects are generally billed by the hour. Credit accounts are accepted.

They specialize in real estate.

Potter County Land & Abstract
Phone: 605-765-2858
Fax: 605-765-2252
PO Box 203
Gettysburg SD 57442
Local Retrieval Area: SD-Potter.

Normal turnaround time: 5 days. Projects are generally billed by the hour. Credit accounts are accepted.

They specialize in real estate.

Powell's Backtracking
Phone: 504-242-7700
Fax: 504-242-7700
4427 Dodt St
New Orleans LA 70126
Local Retrieval and SOP Area: LA-Jefferson Parish, Orleans Parish, St. Bernard Parish, St. Tammany Parish.

Normal turnaround time: 24 hours. Projects are generally billed by the number of names searched. Fees are per court search or per property. Credit accounts are accepted. Payment due upon billing.

They specialize in criminal and civil searches.

Powers Abstract Co Inc
Phone: 405-336-4068
Fax: 405-336-4078
PO Box 707
Perry OK 73077
Local Retrieval Area: OK-Noble.

Normal turnaround time: 5-7 days. Fee basis will vary by the type of project. The first project may require a prepayment.

They specialize in real estate and titles.

Prairie Abstract & Title
Phone: 406-637-5472
Fax: 406-637-5472
PO Box 215
Terry MT 59349
Local Retrieval Area: MT-Prairie.

Normal turnaround time: 2-3 days. Projects are generally billed by the hour. The first project may require a prepayment.

Preferred Land Title

Phone: 573-756-6721
Fax: 573-756-0519

PO Box 708
Farmington MO 63640

Local Retrieval Area: MO-Cape Girardeau, Madison, St. Francois, Ste. Genevieve, Washington.

Normal turnaround time: 3-5 working days. Projects are generally billed by the number of names searched. Fee basis is per chain of title. Projects require prepayment. Personal checks are accepted.

They maintain complete geographical indexed title plants for each county they do business in.

▥ Premier Research

Phone: 330-297-1977
Fax: 330-296-1977

3235 Shawnee Tr
Ravenna OH 44266

Local Retrieval Area: OH-Portage, Summit.

Normal turnaround time: 24-48 hours. Projects are generally billed by the number of names searched. Credit accounts are accepted..dd.

Correspondent relationships: Trumbull, Medina and Stark, OH counties. As an "Investigative Information" specialist they can retrieve a wide variety of information in a timely manner.

▥ PreSearch Background Services

Phone: 800-562-8077
719-533-1880
Fax: 800-562-8071
719-260-7172

PO Box 50134
Colorado Springs CO 80949-0134

Local Retrieval Area: CO-El Paso.

Normal turnaround time: 2-7 days. Projects are generally billed by the number of names searched. The first project may require a prepayment.

Correspondent relationships: Statewide. They have been approved by the State of Colorado, Board of Nursing to run criminal conviction checks on nurse aides prior to certification.

Presidio County Abstract Co

Phone: 915-729-4264
Fax: 915-729-3286

PO Box 1508
Marfa TX 79843

Local Retrieval Area: TX-Presidio.

Normal turnaround time: 1-2 days. Fee basis will vary by the type of project. Projects require prepayment.

Deloris Presley

Phone: 334-867-2968
Fax: 334-867-2968

309 N Pine St
Brewton AL 36426

Local Retrieval Area: AL-Conecuh, Covington, Escambia, Monroe.

Normal turnaround time: 24-48 hours. Bill by type of projects. Credit accounts are accepted. Terms are net 30 days.

She specializes in title searches, UCC, lien & judgments and mineral reports. She has worked for 19 years with the same Title and Abstract Company.

Presque Isle County Abstract

Phone: 517-734-2816
Fax: 517-734-3896

283 N 3rd St
Rogers City MI 49779

Local Retrieval Area: MI-Presque Isle.

Normal turnaround time: 48-72 hours. Fee basis will vary by type of project. Projects require prepayment.

They specialize in real estate.

Preston Land Title Co

Phone: 800-365-7720
208-852-2810
Fax: 208-852-2811

PO Box 148
Preston ID 83263

Local Retrieval Area: ID-Franklin.

Normal turnaround time: 1-2 days. Projects are generally billed by the hour. Credit accounts are accepted.

Prewitt-Rogers Abstract Co

Phone: 501-563-2137
Fax: 501-563-3558

203 E Hale Ave
Osceola AR 72370

Local Retrieval Area: AR-Mississippi.

Normal turnaround time: 2-5 days. Projects are generally billed by the number of names searched or records located. Credit accounts are accepted. Personal checks are accepted.

They specialize in abstracts of title and title insurance.

▥ Prime TEMPUS Inc

Phone: 800-856-5600
512-474-5944
Fax: 512-474-8111

800 Brazos Suite 1030
Austin TX 78701

Local Retrieval Area: TX-Travis, Williamson.

Normal turnaround time: 24-72 hours. Projects are generally billed by the number of names searched or records located. The first project may require a prepayment.

Correspondent relationships: nationwide.

Prime Time Process Service

Phone: 904-457-1021
Fax: 904-456-9211

5806 Margaretta Blvd Suite 142
Pensacola FL 32506

Local Retrieval and SOP Area: FL-Escambia.

Normal turnaround time: 48 hours. Projects are generally billed by the number of names searched. The first project may require a prepayment.

They specialize in process service.

▥ Priority Information Services

Phone: 210-699-9449
Fax: 210-699-6699

5717 Northwest Parkway
San Antonio TX 78249

Local Retrieval and SOP Area: TX-Bexar, Comal, Guadalupe, Kendall.

Projects are generally billed by the number of names searched or records located. The first project may require a prepayment. Monthly billing available.

Correspondent relationships: nationwide.

Priority One Attorney's Service

Phone: 800-444-1365
717-257-1365
Fax: 717-232-6772

99 S Cameron St PO Box 454
Harrisburg PA 17108-0454

Local Retrieval and SOP Area: PA-Cumberland, Dauphin, York.

Normal turnaround time: 48-72 hours. Projects are generally billed by the number of names searched. The first project may require a prepayment.

They specialize in retrieval of UCC, federal and state tax liens and judgments.

Debbie Pritchett

Phone: 505-673-2301
Fax: 505-673-2922

PO Box 1002
Mosquero NM 87733

Local Retrieval Area: NM-Harding.

Normal turnaround time: 2-3 days. Projects are generally billed by the number of names searched. Fee basis may also be per year. Projects require prepayment.

▥ Pro Facto Inc

9300 Batesville Pk	**Phone:** 501-988-5340
Jacksonville AR 72076	**Fax:** 501-988-5874

Local Retrieval Area: AR-Faulkner, Jefferson, Pulaski, Saline.

Normal turnaround time: 1-2 days. Expedited service available. Fee basis will vary by the type of search. The first project may require a prepayment.

Correspondent relationships: statewide, AR. They specialize in getting you the document you need quickly. They also have experience with the Attorney General's office, the Insurance and Securities Departments, etc.

Pro Search Inc

91 Dora St	**Phone:** 203-348-6994
Stamford CT 06902	**Fax:** 203-348-6994

Local Retrieval Area: CT-Fairfield.

Normal turnaround time: 3-5 days. Projects are generally billed by the number of names searched. Credit accounts are accepted.

Correspondent relationships: all counties in Connecticut. They also have a beeper phone number: (203) 977-9035.

Pro Title Inc

3092 Pio Nono Ave	**Phone:** 912-781-9344
Macon GA 31206	**Fax:** 912-781-9682

Local Retrieval Area: GA-27 Counties.

Normal turnaround time: 24-36 hours. Fee basis is per search and per county. The first project may require a prepayment.

They specialize in public record retrieval.

Pro-Serve Investigative Services

2908 Killarney Dr	**Phone:** 970-407-0813
Laporte CO 80535-9339	**Fax:** 970-224-2203

Local Retrieval and SOP Area: CO-Larimer, Weld.

Normal turnaround time: 48 hours for retrieval, 72 hours for process. Expedited service available. Online computer ordering is also available. Projects are generally billed by the hour. The first project may require a prepayment. Terms are net 30 days.

They specialize in skip tracing, financial and asset investigations, background investigations and pre- and post-litigation investigations.

▥ Probus Research

601 Van Ness Ave Suite E	**Phone:** 888-934-3848
	415-553-8068
San Francisco CA 94102	**Fax:** 415-553-8069

Local Retrieval and SOP Area: CA-Alameda, Contra Costa, Marin, Monterey, Napa, San Francisco, San Mateo, Santa Clara, Santa Cruz, Solano.

Normal turnaround time: same day to 2 days. Online computer ordering is also available. Projects are generally billed by the number of names searched. Charge by the hour on special projects. The first project may require a prepayment. Terms are net 30 days for established clients.

Correspondent relationships: most California counties. They specialize in complex litigation case file, regulatory, business and library research. They also provide fax filings and super rush research and document retrievals.

Process Associates

1100 Fleming Bldg	**Phone:** 515-244-2488
Des Moines IA 50309	**Fax:** 515-288-2163

Local Retrieval Area: IA-Polk.

Normal turnaround time: 1-2 days. Projects are generally billed by the hour. Credit accounts are accepted. Personal checks are accepted.

They are also licensed private investigators.

Process Associates/Milwaukee

740 N Plankinton Suite 634	**Phone:** 414-271-9574
Milwaukee WI 53203	**Fax:** 414-271-4018

Local Retrieval and SOP Area: WI-Kenosha, Milwaukee, Ozaukee, Racine, Walworth, Washington, Waukesha.

Normal turnaround time: usually the same day, but maximum 1 day. Projects are generally billed by the hour. Fee may include incurred costs. Credit accounts are accepted.

Correspondent relationships: the state of Wisconsin.

Process Service Unlimited Inc

204 S Main St PO Box 258	**Phone:** 800-726-7068
	301-831-7747
Mount Airy MD 21771	**Fax:** 301-829-1935

Local Retrieval and SOP Area: MD-Baltimore, Carroll, Frederick, Howard, Montgomery, Prince George's, Washington.

Normal turnaround time: 24-72 hours. Projects are generally billed by the hour. The first project may require a prepayment.

Correspondent relationships: all counties in Maryland. They specialize in document retrieval, investigative services, genealogical research and database information research.

Process Serving Unlimited

1832 Gippy Lane	**Phone:** 803-728-2732
Charleston SC 29407	

Local Retrieval and SOP Area: SC-Berkeley, Charleston, Dorchester.

Normal turnaround time: 2 days. Projects are generally billed by the hour. The first project may require a prepayment.

They specialize in process serving.

Professional Civil Process

3008 Bee Cave Rd 2nd Floor	**Phone:** 800-950-7493
	512-329-6644
Austin TX 78746	**Fax:** 512-329-6750

Local Retrieval and SOP Area: TX-Bexar, Cameron, Dallas, Denton, Fort Bend, Harris, Hidalgo, Nueces, Tarrant, Travis.

Normal turnaround time: 2-3 days. Expedited service available. Projects are generally billed by the hour. The first project may require a prepayment.

Correspondent relationships: the rest of Texas.

Professional Civil Process

7417 N 10th St	**Phone:** 800-880-4223
	210-630-4223
McAllen TX 78504	**Fax:** 210-630-4223

Local Retrieval and SOP Area: TX-Cameron, Hidalgo, Starr, Willacy.

Normal turnaround time: 5 working days. Rush service is also available. Projects are generally billed by the hour. Projects require prepayment. Credit cards are accepted. They will invoice to NAPPS members only.

Correspondent relationships: the rest of Texas. They are licensed investigators and their specialties include medical records and process service.

Professional Civil Process

410 S Main Suite 217
San Antonio TX 78204

Phone: 210-225-1239
Fax: 210-225-1243

Local Retrieval and SOP Area: TX-Bexar.

Normal turnaround time: 1 day. Projects are generally billed by the hour. Credit accounts are accepted.

They specialize in process service.

Professional Civil Process

5803 Briargrove
Wichita Falls TX 76310

Phone: 817-692-3011
Fax: 817-692-6918

Local Retrieval and SOP Area: TX-Wichita.

Normal turnaround time: 24-48 hours. Projects are generally billed by the hour. Fees varies by project. The first project may require a prepayment.

They specialize in private investigations and process services.

Professional Courier Service

Waters Bldg 161 Ottowa Suite 305F
Grand Rapids MI 49503

Phone: 616-451-4445
Fax: 616-459-0025

Local Retrieval Area: MI-Kent, Muskegon, Ottawa.

Normal turnaround time: 24-48 hours. Expedited service available. Projects are generally billed by the hour. A flat fee is also charged in addition to the per hour fee. The first project may require a prepayment.

Professional Research Services

7151 Metro Blvd Suite 210
Minneapolis MN 55439

Phone: 612-941-9040
Fax: 612-941-9041

Local Retrieval Area: MN-Anoka, Carver, Dakota, Hennepin, Ramsey, Scott, Washington.

Normal turnaround time: 48 hours for surrounding counties, 1-4 days for the rest of Minnesota and the United States. Projects are generally billed by the number of records located. Credit accounts are accepted.

Correspondent relationships: nationwide. They specialize in background screening.

Professional Service of Process

500 N College St Suite 195
Charlotte NC 28202

Phone: 704-532-6322
Fax: 704-333-0233

Local Retrieval and SOP Area: NC-Cabarrus, Cleveland, Davidson, Gaston, Iredell, Lincoln, Mecklenburg, Rowan, Stanly; SC-Cherokee, Chester, Lexington, Richland, York.

Normal turnaround time: 48 hours. Projects are generally billed by the hour. The first project may require a prepayment.

Correspondent relationships: the entire states of North and South Carolina. They specialize in process serving and location of missing witnesses and defendants, and perform filing and issuance services applicable to state and federal courts.

Professional Services

6816 Kelly Ann NE
Albuquerque NM 87109

Phone: 505-823-2511
Fax: 505-823-4464

Local Retrieval Area: NM-Bernalillo, Sandoval, Santa Fe, Valencia.

Normal turnaround time: 48 hours. Projects are generally billed by the number of names searched. The first project may require a prepayment.

They specialize in search and retrieval of public records.

Professional Services Bureau

10985 N Harrell's Ferry Rd Suite 200
Baton Rouge LA 70816

Phone: 800-864-5154
504-928-3877
Fax: 504-273-8987

Local Retrieval and SOP Area: LA-Lafayette Parish.

Normal turnaround time: 48 hours. A 24 hour rush is also available for extra charge. Projects are generally billed by the number of names searched or records located. Flat rates apply to some services. The first project may require a prepayment. Credit cards are accepted.

Correspondent relationships: the rest of Louisiana and the Mississippi coast. They specialize in research, retrieval, filing, Notary services, abstracting, process service, surveillance, investigations, homicide/suicide, insurance claims adjusting. All services are statewide.

Professional Services Bureau

315 S College Rd Suite 245
Lafayette LA 70503

Phone: 800-960-2214
318-234-9933
Fax: 318-235-5318

Local Retrieval and SOP Area: LA-All Parishes.

Normal turnaround time: 48 hours. A 24 hour rush is also available for an extra charge Projects are generally billed by the number of names searched or records located..dd. Flat rates apply to some services. The first project may require a prepayment. Credit cards are accepted. Personal checks and bank wires are accepted.

Correspondent relationships: Mississippi Coast. They specialize in research, retrieval, filing, Notary services, abstracting, process service, surveillance, investigations, homicide/suicide, insurance claims adjusting. All services are statewide. They have 25 employees who cover the state.

Professional Title & Abstract Co

320 W Main St
Heber Springs AR 72543-3052

Phone: 501-362-3136
Fax: 501-362-2930

Local Retrieval Area: AR-Cleburne.

Normal turnaround time: within 5 days. Fee basis will vary by the type of project. The first project may require a prepayment.

They specialize in real estate and closings.

Professional Title Services

248 E Main
Price UT 84501

Phone: 801-637-2320
Fax: 801-637-2323

Local Retrieval Area: UT-Carbon, Duchesne, Emery.

Normal turnaround time: 24 hours for UCC and name searches; 48 hours for title commitments; 3 days for mineral title memos; and 1 week for abstracts. Projects are generally billed by the number of names searched. The first project may require a prepayment.

They specialize in all services regarding real estate records, abstracts, title insurance, closing and escrow services.

Janie Proffer

416 W Sherman Dr
Aubrey TX 76227

Phone: 817-387-1214
Fax: 817-383-2591

Local Retrieval Area: TX-Denton.

Normal turnaround time: 1-2 days. Projects are generally billed by the number of names searched. The first project may require a prepayment.

Promesa Enterprises
Phone: 800-474-4420
3939 Bee Caves Rd Suite 22
512-328-7230
Austin TX 78746
Fax: 512-328-7066

Local Retrieval Area: TX-Bastrop, Blanco, Burnet, Caldwell, Comal, Fayette, Hays, Llano, Travis, Williamson.

Normal turnaround time: 24-72 hours. Projects are generally billed by the number of names searched. The first project may require a prepayment. Terms are net 30 days.

Correspondent relationships: nationwide. They specialize in litigation support, post lending decision assistance and asset search/verification for individuals nationwide.

Prompt Legal Services
Phone: 310-838-9000
10573 W Pico Blvd Suite 344
Fax: 310-838-0855
Los Angeles CA 90064

Local Retrieval and SOP Area: CA-Los Angeles.

Normal turnaround time: 72 hours. Projects are generally billed by the hour. The first project may require a prepayment.

Correspondent relationships: other counties in Southern California. They specialize in process service, skip tracing, asset searches and court work.

Property Research & Doc Service
Phone: 800-520-7884
5102 Timber Circle
210-520-7884
San Antonio TX 78250
Fax: 210-520-7885

Local Retrieval Area: TX-Atascosa, Bandera, Bexar, Comal, Guadalupe, Hays, Kendall, Kerr, Medina.

Normal turnaround time: up to 2 days. Expedited service is available. Projects are generally billed by the number of names searched. The first project may require a prepayment.

Correspondent relationships: Cameron, Hidalgo, Nueces, Travis, and Williamson counties in Texas. They specialize in subject/adjoiner research for surveyors and engineers; 50 year chains-of titles for environmental site assessments, Phase I; city, county, state & federal abstracting, retrieval & recording services for legal & financial services.

Property Research Associates Inc
Phone: 888-523-1061
5103 Timber Circle
210-523-1061
San Antonio TX 78250
Fax: 888-523-1061
210-523-1061

Local Retrieval Area: TX-Atascosa, Bexar, Caldwell, Comal, Guadalupe, Hays, Kerr, Travis, Williamson, Wilson.

Normal turnaround time: 1-3 business days. Expedited service available within 24 hours of order. Projects are generally billed by the number of names searched or records located. Fee basis varies project to project. Volume discounting available. Credit accounts are accepted. Payment due upon receipt, net 15 days (net 30 days negotiable).

Correspondent relationships: all of Texas, Maryland, California and Ohio. They specialize in 50 year chains of title, surveyor support, asset/lien searches, criminal/background checks, court searches, UCC's, judgments and public records. New service: Child support collections and consulting.

Prospective Renters Ver Svc
Phone: 503-655-0888
PO Box 23713
Fax: 503-655-0900
Portland OR 97281-3713

Local Retrieval Area: OR-Multnomah; WA-Clark.

Normal turnaround time: 1 hour or less. Projects are generally billed by the number of names searched. Credit accounts are accepted. Monthly billing available.

They specialize in tenant and employee screening.

PROTEC Systems Inc
Phone: 800-691-0919
12165 W Center Rd Suite 55
402-691-0919
Omaha NE 68144
Fax: 800-691-9496

Local Retrieval Area: IA-Harrison, Mills, Pottawattamie; NE-Sarpy, Washington.

Normal turnaround time: 24-72 hours. Projects are generally billed by the number of names searched. The first project may require a prepayment.

They specialize in employment services, criminal histories, workers' compensation records, motor vehicle reports, employment confirmation, academic verification and professional license verification.

Prudential Associates Inc
Phone: 301-279-6700
212 N Adams St
Fax: 301-279-2609
Rockville MD 20850

Local Retrieval and SOP Area: MD-Montgomery, Prince George's, Washington.

Normal turnaround time: 7-10 days. Projects are generally billed by the number of names searched. The first project may require a prepayment. Credit cards are accepted.

Correspondent relationships: VA. They specialize in domestic investigations, asset checks and accident investigations.

Public Information Resource
Phone: 800-675-6350
14 Sampson Rd
207-933-3606
Monmouth ME 04259
Fax: 207-933-9064

Local Retrieval Area: ME-Androscoggin, Cumberland, Franklin, Kennebec, Knox, Lincoln, Oxford, Sagadahoc, Somerset.

Normal turnaround time: the same day to 48 hours. Projects are generally billed by the number of names searched. The first project may require a prepayment. Personal checks are accepted.

Correspondent relationships: the state of Maine; New Brunswick, Canada. They perform UCC-11's on a daily basis at the State Department. They file UCC's, articles of incorporation, annual reports and obtain Certificates of Good Standing. (CGS).

Public Record Information Svcs
Phone: 606-879-2141
205 Wooldridge Ln Unit 1
Fax: 606-879-2141
Versailles KY 40383-1337

Local Retrieval Area: KY-Clark, Fayette, Franklin, Scott, Woodford.

Normal turnaround time: same day or by 3 pm next day. Projects are generally billed by the number of names searched or records located. Credit accounts are accepted. Billing is 15th and 30th of each month.

They specialize in felony and misdemeanor searches in Woodford and Fayette counties only. Title searches in Clark, Fayette, Franklin Scott and Woodford counties.

Pulaski County Abstract Company
Phone: 618-748-9233
Fax: 618-748-9233
232 Main St
Mound City IL 62963

Local Retrieval Area: IL-Pulaski.

Normal turnaround time: 2-14 days. Fee basis will vary by complexity and time of the job. Credit accounts are accepted. Personal checks are accepted.

They specialize in real estate transactions and court records.

Pullman Process Service
Phone: 509-332-8310
PO Box 356
Pullman WA 99163

Local Retrieval and SOP Area: ID-Latah; WA-Asotin, Whitman.

Normal turnaround time: 2 days. Projects are generally billed by the hour. The first project may require a prepayment.

They search only in the criminal and civil courts.

Pushmataha County Abstract Co
Phone: 405-298-3189
Fax: 405-298-2322
Box 849
Antlers OK 74523

Local Retrieval Area: OK-Pushmataha.

Normal turnaround time: 3-7 days. Projects are generally billed by the number of names searched or records located. Projects require prepayment.

Putnam County Abstract
Phone: 816-947-3105
PO Box 303
Unionville MO 63565

Local Retrieval Area: MO-Mercer, Putnam, Schuyler.

Normal turnaround time: 1 week. Fee basis varies by type of transaction. Credit accounts are accepted.

Q

Q.S.I. (Quantum Software Inc)
Phone: 614-224-9207
Fax: 614-224-1423
32 W Hoster St Suite 230
Columbus OH 43215

Local Retrieval Area: OH-Delaware, Fairfield, Fayette, Franklin, Hamilton, Licking, Madison, Pickaway, Ross, Union.

Normal turnaround time: 3 days. Expedited service available. Projects are generally billed by the number of names searched or records located. Contract billing available. The first project may require a prepayment.

Correspondent relationships: all counties in Ohio. They specialize in real estate, property taxes, civil courts, domestic relations, and bankruptcy matters.

Quality Abstractors Inc
Phone: 301-695-9329
Fax: 301-695-5016
129 W Patrick St Suite 11
Frederick MD 21701

Local Retrieval Area: MD-Frederick, St Mary's.

Normal turnaround time: 1-14 days. Projects are generally billed by the number of names searched. Credit accounts are accepted. Personal checks are accepted.

Correspondent relationships: Washington County, MD. They have been in the land title abstracting business for more than 25 years.

Quality Business Information
Phone: 916-684-5860
Fax: 916-684-4950
PO Box 2645
Elk Grove CA 95758

Local Retrieval Area: CA-El Dorado, Placer, Sacramento, Yolo.

Normal turnaround time: 48 hours. Projects are generally billed by the number of names searched. Credit accounts are accepted. Terms are net 30-60 days.

Correspondent relationships: San Joaquin.

Queen City Paralegal
Phone: 513-271-2766
Fax: 513-271-2766
3943 Beech St
Cincinnati OH 45227

Local Retrieval Area: OH-Hamilton.

Normal turnaround time: 24-48 hours. Projects are generally billed by the number of names searched. The first project may require a prepayment.

Correspondent relationships: Butler & Warren for real estate, probate and UCC. They specialize in 40 year and current owner real estate searches.

Quest Abstract Inc
Phone: 201-621-6558
Fax: 201-622-6216
291 Willow Ave
Lyndhurst NJ 07071

Local Retrieval Area: NJ-Essex, Union.

Normal turnaround time: 2-3 days. Projects are generally billed by the number of names searched. The first project may require a prepayment.

Correspondent relationships: Bergen.

Quest and Assoc Inc
Phone: 412-563-1007
Fax: 412-563-6869
PO Box 23323
Pittsburgh PA 15222

Local Retrieval Area: PA-Allegheny.

Normal turnaround time: 24-72 hours. Projects are generally billed by the number of names searched. Credit accounts are accepted. Billed last business day of month.

Correspondent relationships: all counties in Pennsylvania. They specialize in criminal and Department of Motor Vehicle records.

Quest Research Inc
Phone: 501-374-4712
Fax: 501-374-3029
101 S Spring St Suite 220
Little Rock AR 72201

Local Retrieval Area: AR-All Counties.

Normal turnaround time: 1-3 days. Projects are generally billed by the number of names searched or records located. Credit accounts are accepted.

They specialize in corporate retrieval and filing service. They do criminal searches in Pulaski county only.

Quick Search
Phone: 214-358-2840
Fax: 214-358-6057
3749 Clover Lane
Dallas TX 75220

Local Retrieval Area: TX-17 Counties.

Normal turnaround time: 6-48 hours. Projects are generally billed by the number of names searched. Credit accounts are accepted. Credit cards are accepted. Terms are net 30 days.

Correspondent relationships: nationwide. They specialize in criminal searches.

Quik Check Records

Phone: 503-373-3543
Fax: 503-585-0502

7503 Skyline Rd S
Salem OR 97306

Local Retrieval Area: OR-Marion.

Normal turnaround time: same day to 24 hours. Projects are generally billed by the number of names searched. Credit accounts are accepted. Terms are net 15 days.

Correspondent relationships: Amador, Calaveras, El Dorado, Napa, Placer, Sacramento, San Joaquin, Solano, Stanislaus, & Yolo, CA counties. They specialize in complete detailed response with a quick turnaround time guarenteed. Copies of records available upon request.

Quirk Associates

Phone: 617-326-1202
Fax: 617-326-0916

368 Washington
Dedham MA 02026

Local Retrieval Area: MA-Middlesex, Norfolk, Suffolk, Worcester.

Normal turnaround time: within one week. The fee basis will vary with the type of search. Credit accounts are accepted.

Correspondent relationships: Plymouth, Essex, and Bristol counties. They specialize in real estate record searches.

R

R A Heales & Associates Ltd

Phone: 303-671-8700
Fax: 303-671-6063

2851 S Parker Rd Suite 550
Aurora CO 80014-2736

Local Retrieval Area: CO-Adams, Arapahoe, Boulder, Denver, Douglas, El Paso, Jefferson.

Normal turnaround time: 2-3 days. Projects are generally billed by the hour. The first project may require a prepayment. Credit cards are accepted. Personal checks are accepted.

R.E.M. Resources Inc

Phone: 800-737-0736
904-997-2959
Fax: 904-997-7406

Rt 5 Box 5430
Monticello FL 32344

Local Retrieval Area: FL-Jefferson, Leon.

Normal turnaround time: 24-48 hours. Expedited service available. No project billing information was given. Credit accounts are accepted. Terms are due on receipt.

Correspondent relationships: the rest of Florida. They specialize in UCC/corporate information, driver's license information, and FDLE criminal history search.

Rafael Jorge Investigations

Phone: 800-344-3754
818-846-5038
Fax: 818-846-5977

2219 W Olive Blvd Suite 295
Burbank CA 91506

Local Retrieval Area: CA-40 Counties.

Normal turnaround time: 1-3 days. Projects are generally billed by the number of names searched. Credit accounts are accepted. Terms are net 30 days.

Correspondent relationships: the rest of California. Thay also have network affiliations with AZ, CO, DC, FL, MD, MI, NM, NV, VA, TX and WA. They specialize in hands on research and record retrieval of criminal, civil, UCC, tax liens and bankruptcy records at the local and federal courts. A full service investigative company.

RAM Services

Phone: 714-441-0230

PO Box 8356
Newport Beach CA 92658-8356

Local Retrieval and SOP Area: CA-Los Angeles, Orange.

Normal turnaround time: 24 hours to 2 weeks. Credit accounts are accepted.

Jean Randall

Phone: 415-897-2361
Fax: 415-897-2305

561 Louis Dr
Novato CA 94945

Local Retrieval and SOP Area: CA-Marin.

Normal turnaround time: 1 day. Projects are generally billed by the number of names searched. The first project may require a prepayment. Personal checks are accepted.

She specializes in voter registration and fictitious business filing searches.

Ranger Recovery

Phone: 914-679-2957
Fax: 914-336-5480

PO Box 1184
Woodstock NY 12498

Local Retrieval and SOP Area: NY-Ulster.

Normal turnaround time: less than 1 week. Projects are generally billed by the number of names searched or records located. Credit accounts are accepted.

Correspondent relationships: Greene, Dutchess, Columbia, DE counties..dd.

Ransom County Title Co

Phone: 701-683-5511
Fax: 701-683-5511

PO Box 511
Lisbon ND 58054

Local Retrieval Area: ND-Ransom.

Normal turnaround time: 12-36 hours. Fee basis will vary by the type of project. The first project may require a prepayment.

Rapid Research

Phone: 510-883-1602
Fax: 510-486-1587

PO Box 1066
Orinda CA 94563

Local Retrieval Area: CA-Alameda, San Francisco, San Mateo.

Normal turnaround time: 1 day. Projects are generally billed by the number of names searched. The first project may require a prepayment.

Correspondent relationships: all of California. They specialize in in-person searches of criminal and civil records.

RASCAL

Phone: 909-693-0165
Fax: 909-695-1912
909-693-4056

41593 Winchester Rd #118-F
Temecula CA 92590

Local Retrieval and SOP Area: CA-Riverside, San Diego.

Normal turnaround time: 1-5 days. Projects are generally billed by the number of names searched. The first project may require a prepayment. They accept personal checks.

Correspondent relationships: Los Angeles, Orange, Ventura, San Bernardino, Riverside and San Diego. They specialize in service of process in those "hard to reach" places. They also specialize in "search and serves".

Raseau-Lake of the Woods Title

Phone: 218-634-2544
Fax: 218-634-1890

PO Box 511
Baudette MN 56623

Local Retrieval Area: MN-Lake of the Woods.

Normal turnaround time: 2-5 days. Fees are billed by the search. Projects require prepayment.

🏛 Raven International Investigtns

Phone: 800-719-1626
305-474-7333

801 S University Dr Suite 138C
Ft Lauderdale FL 33324   **Fax:** 305-475-0087

Local Retrieval Area: FL-Broward, Dade, Monroe, Palm Beach.

Normal turnaround time: 2-3 days. Projects are generally billed by the hour. The first project may require a prepayment. Payment due upon receipt.

Correspondent relationships: nationwide. They specialize in civil/criminal pre-trial prep, overt & covert techical operations (electronic counter surveillance/video security systems), public records & intelligence retrieval, financial & fraud analysis and backgrounds and executive protection.

Rawlins County Abstract and Title

Phone: 913-626-3011

408 Main St PO Box 81
Atwood KS 67730   **Fax:** 913-626-3104

Local Retrieval Area: KS-Rawlins.

Normal turnaround time: 1-3 days. Project billing methods vary. Credit accounts are accepted. Personal checks are accepted.

They specialize in real estate titles and title insurance.

RCC & Associates

Phone: 916-533-7944
Fax: 916-533-7944

PO Box 802
Oroville CA 95965

Local Retrieval and SOP Area: CA-12 Counties.

Normal turnaround time: 24 hours. Projects are generally billed by the number of names searched. The first project may require a prepayment.

Real County Title Co

Phone: 210-232-5303
Fax: 210-232-5399

PO Box 298
Leakey TX 78873

Local Retrieval Area: TX-Real.

Normal turnaround time: 1-2 days. Fee basis will vary by the type of project. Credit accounts are accepted.

Real Data

Phone: 573-893-4898
Fax: 573-893-6282

911 E High #A
Jefferson City MO 65101

Local Retrieval Area: MO-38 Counties.

Normal turnaround time: 48 hours. Fee basis will vary per county. Credit accounts are accepted.

They specialize in real estate and titles, and also do civil court and lien searches. They also have access to the Secretary of State office.

Real Estate Data Inc

Phone: 618-964-1907
Fax: 618-964-1366

Rt 5 Box 334
Marion IL 62959

Local Retrieval Area: IL-Franklin, Jackson, Johnson, Saline, Union, Williamson.

Normal turnaround time: 3 days. Projects are generally billed by the number of names searched. Projects require prepayment.

They specialize in real estate searches.

Real Estate Information Service

Phone: 800-924-1117
703-787-0506

PO Box 5178
Herndon VA 22070   **Fax:** 800-824-8212
703-787-0509

Local Retrieval Area: VA-City of Alexandria, Arlington, Fairfax, Loudoun.

Normal turnaround time: 3 days. Fee basis is per case. Credit accounts are accepted.

Correspondent relationships: Mid-Atlantic. They specialize in real estate title examinations. They also specialize in phase1-grantor/grantee reports in Mid-Atlantic region and multi-site project in all 50 states.

Real Estate Loan Services

Phone: 423-855-0581
Fax: 423-894-3184

Uptain Building Suite 210
Chattanooga TN 37414

Local Retrieval Area: TN-11 Counties.

Normal turnaround time: 24 hours. Projects are generally billed by the number of records located. The first project may require a prepayment.

Correspondent relationships: counties in Georgia and Alabama. They specialize in title openings and closing.

Realty Settlement Inc

Phone: 814-336-1802
Fax: 814-336-5881

915 Liberty St
Meadville PA 16335

Local Retrieval Area: PA-Crawford, Mercer, Venango.

Normal turnaround time: up to 7 days. Fee basis will vary by the type of project. Credit accounts are accepted.

They specialize in title insurance.

Realty Title Co Inc

Phone: 406-538-8176
Fax: 406-538-5184

517 W Janeaux Ave
Lewistown MT 59457

Local Retrieval Area: MT-Fergus, Judith Basin, Petroleum.

Normal turnaround time: 2-3 days. Projects are generally billed by the hour. Credit accounts are accepted.

Record Information Services

Phone: 630-365-6490
Fax: 630-365-6524

PO Box 1183
St Charles IL 60174

Local Retrieval Area: IL-Cook, De Kalb, Du Page, Kane, Kendall, Lake, McHenry, Will, Winnebago.

Normal turnaround time: 24 hours. Online computer ordering is also available. Fees are on project by project basis. Projects require prepayment. Credit cards are accepted.

They specialize in bankruptcies, judgments, foreclosures, new businesses, homeowners lists, criminal, misdemeanors, felonies, foreclosure sales, building permits, state and federal tax liens and DUI's.

🏛 Record Retrieval Services

Phone: 888-311-5001
972-527-5355

PO Box 264
Allen TX 75013   **Fax:** 972-527-5266

Local Retrieval Area: TX-Collin, Dallas, Tarrant.

Normal turnaround time: 24 hours. Projects are generally billed by the number of names searched. Credit accounts are accepted. Invoice sent at the end of each month.

Correspondent relationships: all of TX. They specialize in being fast, accurate and extensive.

Record Search and Info Svcs

2219 N Curtis
Boise ID 83706

Phone: 800-366-1906
208-375-1906
Fax: 208-322-5469

Local Retrieval Area: ID-44 Counties.

Normal turnaround time: 24 hours. Projects are generally billed by the number of names searched. The first project may require a prepayment.

They have a database of specific mortgage lenders. They also do 50 year property & current owner searches. They have a notary public also.

Record-Check Services Inc

1556 W Crestwood Rd
Memphis TN 38119

Phone: 800-530-7226
901-761-9979
Fax: 901-761-3409

Local Retrieval Area: MS-Benton, De Soto, Marshall, Tunica; TN-Fayette, Hardeman, Haywood, Lauderdale, Madison, Shelby, Tipton.

Normal turnaround time: 1-3 days. Expedited services available. Projects are generally billed by the number of names searched. Fees depend on type of search. The first project may require a prepayment.

Correspondent relationships: all counties in Tennessee, Kentucky and Mississippi. They specialize in multi-state and multi-county projects.

Records Deposition Service

500 S Front St Suite 111
Columbus OH 43215

Phone: 614-365-9092
Fax: 614-365-9198

Local Retrieval Area: OH-Cuyahoga, Delaware, Franklin.

Normal turnaround time: 2-3 weeks. A 1 week rush service is also available. Project billing methods vary. They may also charge per page. Credit accounts are accepted.

They specialize in hospital, doctor's offices, clinics and Bureau of Workers Compensation searches.

Records Research

PO Box 10873
Brooksville FL 34601-0873

Phone: 352-544-5997
Fax: 352-544-5008

Local Retrieval Area: FL-Citrus, Hernando, Sumter.

Normal turnaround time: 24-36 hours (FAX). Expedited service available. Billed by type of search plus copies. Projects require prepayment. Individual orders net 30 days.

They specialize in easements and mineral rights in addition to regular 30 year abstract chains of title, and genealogy research in Hernando.

Records Research & Retrieval

15401A LaMacha Dr Suite 1135
Dallas TX 75248

Phone: 800-944-5211
972-661-2969
Fax: 972-661-2969

Local Retrieval Area: AZ-Maricopa.

Projects are generally billed by the hour. The first project may require a prepayment.

They specialize in bankruptcy. They also do creditor representation at 341 meetings of creditors.

Records Research Inc

PO Box 81227
Lincoln NE 68501-1227

Phone: 402-476-3869
Fax: 402-476-0635

Local Retrieval Area: NE-Lancaster.

Normal turnaround time: 24 hours to 2 weeks. Projects are generally billed by the number of names searched. The first project may require a prepayment.

Correspondent relationships: all the counties in the state. They specialize in UCC searches.

Records Research of Knoxville

3305 Knox Ln
Knoxville TN 37917

Phone: 423-524-2630
Fax: 423-524-2177

Local Retrieval Area: TN-Anderson, Blount, Knox.

Normal turnaround time: 24-48 hours. Projects are generally billed by the number of names searched. The first project may require a prepayment. Billing schedule may be applicable.

They specialize in criminal searches and credit bureau reporting.

Records Search

102 S Santa Cruz Ave Suite E
Los Gatos CA 95030-6708

Phone: 408-399-4747
Fax: 408-399-4750

Local Retrieval Area: CA-Alameda, Contra Costa, San Francisco, San Mateo, Santa Clara, Santa Cruz.

Normal turnaround time: same day to 72 hours. Projects are generally billed by the number of names searched. Credit accounts are accepted. Terms are net 30 days.

Correspondent relationships: nationwide.

RecordServe/John Kelley Ent

1315 Ridgeway Suite 104-200
Memphis TN 38119

Phone: 901-853-5320
Fax: 901-853-6372

Local Retrieval Area: AR-Crittenden; MS-De Soto, Marshall; TN-Fayette, Shelby, Tipton.

Normal turnaround time: 2-3 days. Projects are generally billed by the number of names searched. Credit accounts are accepted.

Correspondent relationships: nationwide. They specialize in hard to locate records, i.e. change of address, FAA and expert witness identifications.

Reda's Attorney Service

PO Box 579
Shoreham NY 11786

Phone: 516-821-6060
Fax: 516-744-5314

Local Retrieval Area: NY-Nassau, Suffolk.

Normal turnaround time: 24 hours for Suffolk County and 48 hours for Nassau County. Rush service is also available. Fee basis will vary by the type of search. The first project may require a prepayment.

Redi-Info Information Services

PO Box 12145
Oklahoma City OK 73157

Phone: 800-349-7334
405-946-4636
Fax: 800-410-3299
405-525-2834

Local Retrieval Area: OK-Canadian, Cleveland, Comanche, Garfield, Oklahoma, Payne, Tulsa.

Online computer ordering is also available. Projects are generally billed by the number of names searched. Credit accounts are accepted. Credit cards are accepted.

Correspondent relationships: nationwide.

David Reed

315 W 4th St
Emporium PA 15834

Phone: 814-486-3349
Fax: 814-486-0464

Local Retrieval and SOP Area: PA-Cameron, Elk, McKean, Potter.

Normal turnaround time: 24-48 hours. Fee basis is determined by an established fee schedule. The first project may require a prepayment. They request that individuals prepay, but will invoice attorneys and companies.

He specializes in oil and gas ownership searches.

🏛 Linda V Reed

PO Box 96
Clark Fork ID 83811

Phone: 208-266-1373

Local Retrieval Area: ID-Bonner.

Normal turnaround time: 24 hours. Projects are generally billed by the number of names searched. Credit accounts are accepted. Extensive work will require partial prepayment.

🏛 RefCheck Information Services

3962 Brown Park Dr Suite I
Hilliard OH 43026

Phone: 614-777-8844
Fax: 614-777-8876

Local Retrieval Area: OH-Franklin.

Normal turnaround time: 24-48 hours. Projects are generally billed by the number of names searched. Credit accounts are accepted. Net 30 days with signed agreement.

Correspondent relationships: nationwide. They specialize in pre-employment reference checks and background record checks.

William Ben Regan

225 E Bay St
Magnolia MS 39652

Phone: 601-783-2491
Fax: 601-783-2492

Local Retrieval Area: MS-Pike.

Normal turnaround time: 1 day. Fee basis varies by type of transaction. The first project may require a prepayment.

He is in general practice. He specializes in marriage/divorce searches.

Regier Agency Inc

616 N Main St
Newton KS 67114

Phone: 316-283-2750
Fax: 316-283-5680

Local Retrieval Area: KS-Harvey.

Normal turnaround time: 2-3 days. Fee basis varies by type of transaction. The first project may require a prepayment.

Registry Research

PO Box 448
South Egremont MA 01258

Phone: 413-528-3919
Fax: 413-528-0907

Local Retrieval Area: MA-Berkshire.

Normal turnaround time: 2 weeks. Projects are generally billed by the hour. Credit accounts are accepted. A downpayment is required.

They specialize in title abstracts and historical or genealogical documentation.

Reliable Courier

4300 N Central Suite 108A
Dallas TX 75206

Phone: 214-823-5596
Fax: 214-823-9039

Local Retrieval and SOP Area: TX-Dallas, Ellis, Tarrant.

Normal turnaround time: 2 days. Projects are generally billed by the hour. Credit accounts are accepted.

Reliable Research

2420 NE Dixie Hwy
Jensen Beach FL 34957

Phone: 407-334-5854
Fax: 407-334-8821

Local Retrieval Area: FL-Indian River, Martin, St. Lucie.

Normal turnaround time: 1 week. Expedited service available. Charges are by type of search or by the hour. The first project may require a prepayment.

They specialize in title examination, asset searches, lien searches, ownership information and right of way searches.

Reliance Title Services

725 S Clinton St
Iowa City IA 52244

Phone: 319-354-6505
Fax: 319-354-9705

Local Retrieval Area: IA-Johnson.

Normal turnaround time: 48 hours for court searches, and 3 to 5 working days for real estate. Projects are generally billed by the number of records located. A flat fee charge is also included. Credit accounts are accepted.

🏛 Relyea Services Inc

PO Box 5167
Albany NY 12205-0167

Phone: 800-854-4111
Fax: 800-854-4112

Local Retrieval and SOP Area: NY-Albany, Rensselaer, Saratoga, Schenectady.

Normal turnaround time: same day. Projects are generally billed by the number of names searched. Credit accounts are accepted.

Correspondent relationships: every court in the nation. They specialize in court record retrieval, UCC searching and filing and corporate work.

Reno/Carson Messenger Service

185 Martin St
Reno NV 89509-2827

Phone: 800-222-4249
702-322-2424
Fax: 702-322-3408

Local Retrieval Area: NV-Carson City, Douglas, Washoe.

Normal turnaround time: 24 hours to 3 days. Projects are generally billed by the number of names searched or records located. The first project may require a prepayment.

They specialize in process service.

Renville Abstract Company Inc

PO Box 189
Mohall ND 58761

Phone: 701-756-6487
Fax: 701-756-6186

Local Retrieval Area: ND-Renville.

Normal turnaround time: 10 days. Fee basis will vary by type of project. Credit accounts are accepted.

Renville County Abstract Co

PO Box 86
Olivia MN 56277

Phone: 320-523-5321
Fax: 320-523-5321

Local Retrieval Area: MN-Redwood, Renville.

Normal turnaround time: 2 days. Fee basis will vary by type of project. The first project may require a prepayment.

They specialize in real estate title searches.

📷 Research & Retrieval Services
Phone: 757-463-0030
Fax: 757-463-0040
703 Woodbox Dr
Virginia Beach VA 23462

Local Retrieval and SOP Area: VA-14 Counties.

Normal turnaround time: 24 to 48 hours. Projects are generally billed by the number of names searched. Credit accounts are accepted. Payment due upon receipt of job.

They specialize in knowing the many ideosyncrasies of each individual courthouse.

Research & Revisions Etc
Phone: 303-351-6276
PO Box 1115
Greeley CO 80632

Local Retrieval Area: CO-Weld.

Normal turnaround time: 2-3 days. Projects are generally billed by the hour. Projects require prepayment.

They specialize in abstract judgments.

Research and Investigative Assoc
Phone: 707-444-8767
Fax: 707-444-2164
PO Box 1321
Eureka CA 95502

Local Retrieval and SOP Area: CA-Del Norte, Humboldt, Mendocino, Trinity.

Normal turnaround time: 48 hours for verbal request and 5 days for a written request. Projects are generally billed by the hour. The first project may require a prepayment. A 50% retainer is required. Personal checks are accepted.

Correspondent relationships: Sonoma, Lake, Sacramento, Marin, San Francisco, Alameda and San Mateo. They specialize in investigation and trial preparation.

Research and Retrieval
Phone: 800-707-8771
310-798-8100
Fax: 310-798-9394
111 Pier Ave Suite 111
Hermosa Beach CA 90254

Local Retrieval Area: CA-Los Angeles, Orange, Sacramento, San Diego, San Francisco.

Normal turnaround time: the same day. Projects are generally billed by the number of names searched. Credit accounts are accepted. Terms are net 30 days.

Correspondent relationships: the rest of California and nationwide. They specialize in case files/newspaper monitors, library research, lot book & property information, fictitious business name filing & searches, UCC search & filings, tax lien & judgment searches, and all courts including bankruptcy & document retrieval.

Research Associates
Phone: 216-892-1000
Fax: 216-892-9439
27999 Clemens Rd
Westlake OH 44145

Local Retrieval Area: OH-Sandusky.
Credit accounts are accepted.

📷 Research Express
Phone: 904-421-0387
Fax: 904-421-7944
82 Ann Circle
Crawfordville FL 32327

Local Retrieval Area: FL-22 Counties.

Normal turnaround time: 48 hours. Expedited service available. Projects are generally billed by the number of names searched. Credit accounts are accepted. Terms are net 30 days.

Correspondent relationships: nationwide. They specialize in property searches, state agency public record retrievals and search, filing and retrieval of UCC.

Research Information Services
Phone: 800-766-3320
Fax: 213-680-7813
316 W 2nd St Suite 1210
Los Angeles CA 90012

Local Retrieval Area: CA-24 Counties.

Normal turnaround time: the same or next day. Projects are generally billed by the hour. The first project may require a prepayment..dd.

Correspondent relationships: nationwide. They specialize in obtaining legal and financial docuements from any source in the country.

Research Information Services
Phone: 800-685-3320
Fax: 302-426-9204
902 N Market St Suite 267
Wilmington DE 19801

Local Retrieval Area: DE-All Counties; PA-Berks, Bucks, Lancaster, Philadelphia.

Normal turnaround time: the same or next day. Projects are generally billed by the hour. The first project may require a prepayment.

Correspondent relationships: nationwide. They specialize in obtaining legal and financial documents from any source in the country.

Research Information Services
Phone: 800-447-3320
Fax: 212-349-6048
1 Beekman St Suite 607
New York NY 10038

Local Retrieval Area: NJ-Essex, Hudson; NY-Albany, Bronx, Kings, Nassau, New York, Queens, Richmond, Suffolk, Westchester.

Normal turnaround time: the same or next day. Projects are generally billed by the hour. The first project may require a prepayment.

Correspondent relationships: nationwide. They specialize in obtaining legal and financial documents from any source in the country.

📷 Research Information Services
Phone: 800-522-3884
913-235-6767
Fax: 800-327-6987
913-235-1919
2201 NE Meriden Rd
Topeka KS 66608

Local Retrieval Area: KS-All Counties; SD-All Counties.

Normal turnaround time: 48 hours. Online computer ordering is also available. Projects are generally billed by the number of names searched. Credit accounts are accepted. Terms are 20 day net after billing.

Correspondent relationships: nationwide. They specialize in state parole lists for every county in Kansas, back 20 years.

Research North Inc of Alpena
Phone: 517-356-4500
Fax: 616-354-2106
537 W Chisholm Suite 400
Alpena MI 49707-0637

Local Retrieval and SOP Area: MI-Alcona, Alpena, Montmorency, Oscoda, Presque Isle.

Projects are generally billed by the hour. The first project may require a prepayment.

Correspondent relationships: Chippewa, Ingham, Wayne, Oakland, Macomb and Kent, MI counties. They specialize in investigative services for the insurance industry, legal community and business and industrial groups.

Research North Inc of Alpena

Phone: 616-347-7366
Fax: 517-354-2106

207 Michigan St
Petoskey MI 49770

Local Retrieval Area: MI-Alcona, Alpena, Montmorency, Oscoda, Presque Isle.

Normal turnaround time: varied depending on project. Online computer ordering is also available. Projects are generally billed by the hour. The first project may require a prepayment.

Correspondent relationships: Chippewa, Ingham, Wayne, Oakland, Macomb and Kent. They specialize in insurance defense investigation.

Research North Inc of Lansing

Phone: 517-699-4100
Fax: 517-699-4101

1020 Long Blvd Suite 6
Lansing MI 48911-6859

Local Retrieval and SOP Area: MI-Calhoun, Clinton, Eaton, Ingham, Ionia, Jackson, Livingston, Shiawassee, Washtenaw.

Projects are generally billed by the hour. The first project may require a prepayment.

Correspondent relationships: Chippewa, Wayne, Oakland, Macomb and Kent, MI counties. They specialize in investigative services for the insurance industry, legal community and business and industrial groups.

Research North Inc of Marquette

Phone: 906-225-1200
Fax: 906-225-1201

220 W Washington Suite 320
Marquette MI 49855-4331

Local Retrieval and SOP Area: MI-Baraga, Delta, Dickinson, Marquette, Menominee, Schoolcraft.

Projects are generally billed by the hour. The first project may require a prepayment.

Correspondent relationships: Chippewa, Ingham, Wayne, Oakland, Macomb and Kent, MI counties. They specialize in investigative services for the insurance industry, legal community and business and industrial groups.

Research North Inc of Petoskey

Phone: 616-347-7366
Fax: 616-347-7685

207 Michigan
Petoskey MI 49770-2607

Local Retrieval and SOP Area: MI-Charlevoix, Cheboygan, Emmet, Mackinac, Otsego.

Normal turnaround time: varied depending in project. Online computer ordering is also available. Projects are generally billed by the hour. The first project may require a prepayment.

Correspondent relationships: Chippewa, Ingham, Wayne, Oakland, Macomb and Kent, MI counties. They specialize in insurance defense investigations.

Research North of Traverse City

Phone: 616-947-6300
Fax: 616-947-0706

160 E State St PO Box 930
Traverse City MI 49685-0930

Local Retrieval and SOP Area: MI-Antrim, Benzie, Grand Traverse, Kalkaska, Lenawee, Manistee, Missaukee, Wexford.

Projects are generally billed by the hour. The first project may require a prepayment.

Correspondent relationships: Chippewa, Ingham, Wayne, Oakland, Macomb and Kent, MI counties. They specialize in investigative services for the insurance industry, legal community and business and industrial groups.

Research Specialists Inc

Phone: 214-263-0500
Fax: 214-263-1992

530 S Carrier Pky Suite B-100
Grand Prairie TX 75051

Local Retrieval Area: TX-Dallas, Tarrant.

Normal turnaround time: 1-2 days. Projects are generally billed by the number of names searched. Credit accounts are accepted.

Researchers

Phone: 415-543-9555
Fax: 415-974-6119

130 Townsend St
San Francisco CA 94107

Local Retrieval Area: CA-18 Counties.

Normal turnaround time: 1-3 days. Projects are generally billed by the number of names searched or records located. The first project may require a prepayment.

They provide extensive record retrieval services for state agencies, such as the California Public Utilities Commission, Department of Insurance, Department of Corporations and Department of Real Estate.

Researchers Ltd

Phone: 302-856-7442
Fax: 302-856-7462

105 S Race St
Georgetown DE 19947

Local Retrieval Area: DE-Sussex.

Normal turnaround time: 1-48 hours for document retrieval, 2 to 5 days for title searches and 24-48 hours for current owner property searches. Projects are generally billed by the number of names searched. The first project may require a prepayment.

Correspondent relationships: Kent, New Castle, DE; Worchester, Wicomico and Somerset, MD.

Resume Check/M. King & Assoc

Phone: 800-932-4358
614-885-2333
Fax: 614-885-7744

4770 Indianola Ave Suite 140
Columbus OH 43214

Local Retrieval and SOP Area: OH-Delaware, Fairfield, Franklin, Licking, Pickaway.

Normal turnaround time: 24-48 hours. Online computer ordering is also available. Project billing methods vary. The first project may require a prepayment. Credit cards are accepted. Full payment due within 10 days.

They specialize in pre-employment, background investigations, theft and fraud investigations, criminal investigations, domestic investigations, location and missing persons, process service and document retrieval.

Reveal Inc

Phone: 800-276-4826
703-359-8953
Fax: 703-359-8956

10560 Main St Suite LL15
Fairfax VA 22030

Local Retrieval and SOP Area: DC-District of Columbia; MD-Montgomery, Prince George's; VA-20 Counties.

Normal turnaround time: 24-48 hours. Projects are generally billed by the hour. Fees vary by type of project. Projects require prepayment. Credit cards are accepted. Most projects require a prepayment retainer.

Correspondent relationships: worldwide. They are a full service investigative agency, retrieval of courthouse information, skip tracing, all types of process service (routine or rush), database research, DMV, and UCC.

Rice County Abstract & Title Co
Phone: 507-332-2259
Fax: 507-332-2250
PO Box 97 306 NW 1st Ave
Faribault MN 55021

Local Retrieval Area: MN-Rice.

Normal turnaround time: 1-3 days. Projects are generally billed by the hour. Credit accounts are accepted.

They only go to the County Recorder's office for real estate.

Richardson Abstract Co Inc
Phone: 316-659-2592
Fax: 316-659-2730
521 Marsh
Kinsley KS 67547

Local Retrieval Area: KS-Edwards.

Normal turnaround time: the same day. Projects are generally billed by the hour. Credit accounts are accepted. Personal checks are accepted.

Sharian Richardson
Phone: 601-862-7879
Fax: 601-862-2655
PO Box 506 212 W Main St
Fulton MS 38843

Local Retrieval Area: MS-Itawamba.

Normal turnaround time: 1-2 days. Projects are generally billed by the hour. The first project may require a prepayment.

She is in general practice. She specializes in marriage/divorce searches.

Richland County Abstract Co
Phone: 701-642-3781
Fax: 701-642-3852
123 N 3rd St
Wahpeton ND 58074

Local Retrieval Area: MN-Wilkin; ND-Richland, Sargent.

Normal turnaround time: 1 week or less. Projects are generally billed by the number of names searched or records located. The first project may require a prepayment.

Correspondent relationships: North Dakota and Minnesota. They specialize in real estate records, taxes, judgments and UCC searches.

Ricochet
Phone: 214-855-0303
Fax: 214-855-7877
9115 E R L Thornton
Dallas TX 75228

Local Retrieval and SOP Area: TX-Collin, Dallas, Denton, Ellis, Nueces, Tarrant.

Normal turnaround time: 3 days. Archive records average 10 days. Project billing methods vary. Credit accounts are accepted.

Correspondent relationships: Harris, Bexar and Travis. They specialize in process service and court record searches.

Ringgold County Abstract Co Inc
Phone: 515-464-3902
Fax: 515-464-2265
108 E Madison
Mt Ayr IA 50854

Local Retrieval Area: IA-Ringgold.

Normal turnaround time: 3-5 days. Fee basis will vary by the type of project. The first project may require a prepayment.

Rio Grande Mineral Abstract
Phone: 719-657-3366
Fax: 719-657-2395
PO Box 2-J
Del Norte CO 81132

Local Retrieval Area: CO-Mineral, Rio Grande.

Normal turnaround time: 48 hours. Projects are generally billed by the number of names searched. Credit accounts are accepted.

RJ Research
Phone: 210-824-0037
Fax: 210-824-0037
101 Charles Rd
San Antonio TX 78209

Local Retrieval Area: TX-Bexar, Travis.

Normal turnaround time: 24 hours. Projects are generally billed by the number of names searched. Credit accounts are accepted. Payment due upon receipt.

RLS Inc
Phone: 304-472-5555
Fax: 304-472-5642
PO Box 974
Buckhannon WV 26201

Local Retrieval and SOP Area: WV-17 Counties.

Normal turnaround time: from 3 days to 3 weeks. Projects are generally billed by the hour. Contract prices upon request. The first project may require a prepayment.

Correspondent relationships: the rest of West Virginia. They specialize in real estate, oil, gas and coal records and also serve as private investigators.

Roberts Abstracting Inc
Phone: 912-532-5105
Rt 1 Box 315
Alapaha GA 31622

Local Retrieval Area: GA-Atkinson, Berrien, Cook, Lanier, Lowndes, Tift.

Normal turnaround time: 3-5 days. Expedited service available. Fee basis is determined on "flat rate plus costs". The first project may require a prepayment.

They specialize in real estate matters.

Rocksprings Abstract and Title Co
Phone: 210-683-2185
Fax: 210-683-4185
PO Box 1062
Rocksprings TX 78880

Local Retrieval Area: TX-Edwards.

Normal turnaround time: 1 day. Fee basis will vary by the type of project. The first project may require a prepayment.

Rogers County Abstract Co
Phone: 918-341-0525
Fax: 918-341-0637
PO Box 38
Claremore OK 74018

Local Retrieval Area: OK-Rogers.

Normal turnaround time: 3-4 days. Fee basis will vary by the type of project. Credit accounts are accepted.

They specialize in title insurance and closings.

Rolette County Abstract Inc
Phone: 701-477-3149
PO Box 549
Rolla ND 58367

Local Retrieval Area: ND-Rolette.

Normal turnaround time: 1-2 weeks. Fee basis will vary by the type of project. Credit accounts are accepted.

Jan Rollins
Phone: 806-353-7886
Fax: 806-353-7886
6412 Alpine Lane
Amarillo TX 79109

Local Retrieval Area: TX-11 Counties.

Normal turnaround time: 24 hours for Potter and Randall Counties, and 48 to 72 hours for all other counties. Projects are generally billed by the number of names searched. Credit accounts are accepted.

She specializes in title runs for foreclosures or second liens, UCC and asset searches.

Marvin T Romig
Phone: 308-772-4420
PO Box 467
Oshkosh NE 69154
Local Retrieval Area: NE-Garden.
Normal turnaround time: 3-5 days. Projects are generally billed by the number of records located. Credit accounts are accepted.
They specialize in real estate.

Ronald J Axelrod and Assoc
Phone: 908-658-4606
Fax: 908-722-4606
PO Box 275
Somerville NJ 08876
Local Retrieval Area: NJ-Somerset.
Normal turnaround time: varied. Contact office to discuss your time frame. Projects are generally billed by the number of names searched. Credit accounts are accepted. Terms are net 30 days.
Correspondent relationships: Hunderdon and Union counties. They specialize in title searches and title abstracts.

Roosevelt County Abstract Co Inc
Phone: 406-653-2800
Fax: 406-653-2803
PO Box 176
Wolf Point MT 59201
Local Retrieval Area: MT-Roosevelt.
Normal turnaround time: 4 days. Projects are generally billed by the hour. Credit accounts are accepted.
They specialize in title insurance.

Roseau-Lake of the Woods Title
Phone: 218-463-3313
Fax: 218-463-1174
PO Box 297
Roseau MN 56751
Local Retrieval Area: MN-Roseau.
Normal turnaround time: 2-5 days. Fee basis is per search. Projects require prepayment.

Ross Legal Services
Phone: 415-485-0736
PO Box 9107
San Rafael CA 94912
Local Retrieval Area: CA-Alameda, Contra Costa, Marin, San Francisco, San Mateo, Sonoma.
Normal turnaround time: unknown. Projects are generally billed by the hour. The first project may require a prepayment.
Correspondent relationships: Napa, Santa Clara, and Solano counties. They are a family owned business. Larry Ross has experience as an investigative journalist and photographer.

Betty M Rowell
Phone: 912-449-0849
Fax: 912-449-0849
6672 College Ave
Blackshear GA 31516
Local Retrieval Area: GA-Appling, Bacon, Brantley, Charlton, Pierce, Ware, Wayne.
Normal turnaround time: 24-48 hours. Projects are generally billed by the hour. Credit accounts are accepted.
She specializes in real estate matters.

Royal Title Services
Phone: 800-773-7279
317-482-2270
Fax: 317-483-3549
108 N Lebanon St
Lebanon IN 46052
Local Retrieval Area: IN-Boone.
Normal turnaround time: 3-5 days. Projects are generally billed by the number of names searched. Credit accounts are accepted.
Correspondent relationships: the rest of Indiana. They specialize in title searching and closings.

Pat Royce
Phone: 918-465-3425
936 Henry St
Wilburton OK 74578
Local Retrieval Area: OK-Latimer.
Normal turnaround time: varied depending on search. Pat charges on a per day basis. Credit accounts are accepted.
Pat specializes in mineral interest searches.

RSI
Phone: 800-881-5993
954-989-9965
Fax: 888-800-8543
6365 Taft St
Hollywood FL 33024
Local Retrieval Area: FL-Alachua, Broward, Dade, Duval, Hillsborough, Leon, Orange, Palm Beach, Pinellas, Volusia.
Online computer ordering is also available. Projects are generally billed by the number of names searched. Credit accounts are accepted. Credit cards are accepted.
Correspondent relationships: nationwide, Canada, Europe and Asia. They have over 2,600 field agents with coverage in Europe, Asia and Canada.

RSI
Phone: 800-633-6125
816-471-1414
Fax: 816-472-7155
1828 Walnut 6th Floor
Kansas City MO 64108
Local Retrieval Area: KS-Johnson, Wyandotte; MO-Clay, Jackson, Platte.
Normal turnaround time: 24 hours. Projects are generally billed by the number of names searched or records located. The first project may require a prepayment.
They specialize in document retrieval from Kansas City Federal Records Center and Archives as well as in UCC, tax lien, property, civil and criminal records from ann the counties in the KC metro area.

David M Rumancik
Phone: 330-837-7737
1681 Cadbury St NW
Massillon OH 44646
Local Retrieval Area: OH-Carroll, Holmes, Stark, Summit, Trumbull, Tuscarawas, Wayne; PA-Crawford, Mercer, Venango.
Normal turnaround time: 24 hours and up depending on the service requested. Credit accounts are accepted.
He specializes in real estate titles, oil & gas titles, oil & gas research, easement & right of way research for utility companies, criminal & misdemeanor background checks on individuals for employment purposes and lien searches.

Joyce Rupert
Phone: 717-248-4649
Rd 2 Box 235K
Lewistown PA 17044
Local Retrieval Area: PA-Juniata, Mifflin.
Normal turnaround time: 48 hours. Projects are generally billed by the number of names searched. Credit accounts are accepted.
She specializes in real estate record searches.

Rus B Robison & Associates Inc
Phone: 800-827-7623
405-721-2295
Fax: 405-722-2422
5909 NW Expressway Suite 500
Oklahoma City OK 73132
Local Retrieval and SOP Area: OK-Canadian, Cleveland, Creek, Oklahoma, Rogers, Tulsa.
Normal turnaround time: 2 business days. Projects are generally billed by the hour. The first project may require a prepayment.
They have numerous legal proprietary databases for added access.

Russel Abstract
Phone: 417-637-2414
Fax: 417-637-2214
PO Box 6
Greenfield MO 65661
Local Retrieval Area: MO-Dade.
Normal turnaround time: 2-5 days. Fee basis will vary by type of project. Credit accounts are accepted.
They specialize in title searches.

Russell Abstracting & Title
Phone: 308-872-5938
Fax: 308-872-5938
420 S 10th
Broken Bow NE 68822
Local Retrieval Area: NE-Blaine, Custer, Loup, Thomas.
Normal turnaround time: 1 week. Fee basis varies by type of transaction. Credit accounts are accepted.

Russell-Surles Title Inc
Phone: 915-854-1115
Fax: 915-854-1459
337 Market St
Baird TX 79504
Local Retrieval Area: TX-Callahan, Taylor.
Normal turnaround time: varied depending on project. Projects are generally billed by the number of names searched. Credit accounts are accepted. Personal checks are accepted.

Ryco Information Services Inc
Phone: 315-461-8308
Fax: 315-461-8395
7591 Morgan Rd Suite 1
Liverpool NY 13090
Local Retrieval Area: NY-13 Counties.
Normal turnaround time: 24-48 hours. Projects are generally billed by the number of names searched. Credit accounts are accepted.
They specialize in property searches from last owners to full searches including tax searches.

S

S & J Attorney Service
Phone: 310-558-8088
Fax: 310-838-8551
Box 1612
Beverly Hills CA 90213
Local Retrieval and SOP Area: CA-Los Angeles, Orange, Ventura.
Normal turnaround time: 3-5 days. Projects are generally billed by the hour. Credit accounts are accepted.
Correspondent relationships: the remaining counties in California. They specialize in process serving.

S.A.F.E.
Phone: 717-286-9831
Fax: 717-286-8774
250 Market St
Sunbury PA 17801
Local Retrieval Area: PA-Montour, Northumberland, Snyder, Union.
Normal turnaround time: 24-48 hours. Projects are generally billed by the number of names searched. Charges are varied depending on type of search. Credit accounts are accepted.
Correspondent relationships: the rest of Pennsylvania. They specialize in title insurance. All searches are insured against errors and omissions.

Sac County Abstract Co
Phone: 712-662-7317
Fax: 712-662-4090
420 Main
Sac City IA 50583
Local Retrieval Area: IA-Sac.
Normal turnaround time: 2-3 days. Fee basis will vary by the type of project. The first project may require a prepayment.

Sacandaga Abstract Corp
Phone: 518-773-2828
Fax: 518-725-9875
6-8 Fremont St
Gloversville NY 12078
Local Retrieval Area: NY-Fulton, Montgomery.
Normal turnaround time: 1-7 days. Projects are generally billed by the number of names searched or records located. Credit accounts are accepted. Personal checks are accepted.

Saguache County Abstract
Phone: 719-655-2611
Fax: 719-655-2326
309 4th St
Saguache CO 81149
Local Retrieval Area: CO-Saguache.
Normal turnaround time: 2-5 days. Projects are generally billed by the number of records located. Credit accounts are accepted. Out of state clients prepay, in-state terms are net 30 days.
They specialize in all related title insurance company searches.

Salem Title Corporation
Phone: 812-883-5806
Fax: 812-883-5229
54 Courthouse Sq
Salem IN 47167
Local Retrieval Area: IN-Clark, Crawford, Floyd, Harrison, Jackson, Lawrence, Orange, Scott, Washington.
Normal turnaround time: 1 day for judgement or UCC searches, and 3 to 5 days for complete title searches. Fee basis will vary by the type of project. Credit accounts are accepted. Personal checks are accepted.
They maintain a title plant in their office.

Saline County Abstract
Phone: 501-778-2471
Fax: 501-778-4128
316 N Main St
Benton AR 72015
Local Retrieval Area: AR-Saline.
Normal turnaround time: 1 week. Projects are generally billed by the hour. Credit accounts are accepted.
They specialize in real estate and title insurance.

Saline County Abstract
Phone: 402-826-3312
Fax: 402-826-4797
PO Box 627
Wilber NE 68465
Local Retrieval Area: NE-Saline.
Normal turnaround time: 1-2 days. Projects are generally billed by the number of records located. Credit accounts are accepted.

San Diego Attorney Service Inc
Phone: 619-236-9585
Fax: 619-236-9136
2330 1st Ave Suite 203
San Diego CA 92101
Local Retrieval Area: CA-San Diego.
Normal turnaround time: the same day, if requested. Project billing methods vary. The first project may require a prepayment.
Correspondent relationships: all of California.

San Juan County Abstract & Title
Phone: 505-325-2808
Fax: 505-327-7485
111 N Orchard Ave
Farmington NM 87401
Local Retrieval Area: NM-San Juan.
Normal turnaround time: 1-3 days. Fee basis will vary by the type of project. A minimum fee is involved. Credit accounts are accepted. Payment due upon delivery of order.

San Juan County Title Co
Phone: 360-376-4939
Fax: 360-376-4951
104 Fern St
Eastsound WA 98245
Local Retrieval Area: WA-San Juan.

Normal turnaround time: 1 day. Projects are generally billed by the hour. The first project may require a prepayment.

Sanborn County Realty & Title
Phone: 605-796-4417
Fax: 605-796-4248
PO Box 127 207 S Dumont Ave
Woonsocket SD 57385-0127
Local Retrieval Area: SD-Sanborn.

Normal turnaround time: 1-2 weeks. The fee basis is a flat fee. Credit accounts are accepted. Personal checks and cash are accepted.

They specialize in abstracts and title insurance. They also search liens and real estate taxes.

Sandhills Abstracting
Phone: 308-282-0715
Fax: 308-282-0715
218 N Main St
Gordon NE 69343
Local Retrieval Area: NE-Sheridan.

Normal turnaround time: 1 week. Projects are generally billed by the number of names searched or records located. Credit accounts are accepted. Personal checks are accepted.

They specialize in real estate sales.

Sandhills Title & Abstracting
Phone: 402-376-2639
Fax: 402-376-2639
PO Box 181
Valentine NE 69201
Local Retrieval Area: NE-Brown, Cherry, Keya Paha, Thomas.

Normal turnaround time: 1 week. Projects are generally billed by the hour. Credit accounts are accepted.

They specialize in record searches.

Sargents Abstract & Title Co
Phone: 313-767-2355
Fax: 313-767-2430
625 S Grand Traverse St
Flint MI 48502
Local Retrieval Area: MI-Genesee.

Normal turnaround time: 5 days. Projects are generally billed by the hour. Projects require prepayment.

They specialize in title insurance.

Michelle Sarkisian
Phone: 201-342-7541
Fax: 201-342-5750
898D Boulevard
New Milford NJ 07646
Local Retrieval Area: NJ-Bergen.

Normal turnaround time: 24 hours. Projects are generally billed by the number of names searched. The first project may require a prepayment.

Correspondent relationships: Passaic, Hudson, Essex, NJ counties. She specializes in title, lien and judgment searches of every nature in county courthouses.

Sathre Abstractors Inc
Phone: 218-751-4565
Fax: 218-751-7991
720 Beltrami Ave NW
Bemidji MN 56601
Local Retrieval Area: MN-Beltrami.

Normal turnaround time: varied depending on project. Fee basis will vary by type of project. Credit accounts are accepted.

They specialize in real estate and property reports.

Sawyer County Abstract
Phone: 715-266-2312
Fax: 715-266-2312
PO Box 100
Winter WI 54896
Local Retrieval Area: WI-Rusk, Sawyer.

Normal turnaround time: 48 hours. Projects are generally billed by the number of names searched or records located. Credit accounts are accepted. Personal checks are accepted.

SCC Information Services
Phone: 803-957-1243
Fax: 803-957-9359
301 Gibson Rd
Lexington SC 29072
Local Retrieval Area: SC-Lexington, Saluda.

Normal turnaround time: 24 hours. Projects are generally billed by the number of names searched. Credit accounts are accepted. Terms are net 30 days.

They specialize in a full range of title insurance and loan closing services.

Schaeffer Papers
Phone: 800-848-6119
901-725-9555
Fax: 901-458-8438
423 Dickinson St
Memphis TN 38112
Local Retrieval and SOP Area: AR-Crittenden; MS-De Soto; TN-Fayette, Haywood, Shelby, Tipton.

Normal turnaround time: 24-72 hours. Projects are generally billed by the hour. Incurred expenses will be added to the fee. Projects require prepayment. Personal checks are accepted.

They specialize in civil court matters and process service.

Schillinger & Keith Abstracting Inc
Phone: 800-275-2959
412-465-9520
Fax: 412-465-9583
840 Philadelphia St
Indiana PA 15701
Local Retrieval Area: PA-Allegheny, Armstrong, Cambria, Indiana, Jefferson, Westmoreland.

Normal turnaround time: 24 hours. Charges are varied depending on type of search. They do monthly invoicing. Credit accounts are accepted.

Correspondent relationships: East Central Pennsylvania.

Kathleen Schloesser
Phone: 717-253-5368
RR 3 Box 630
Honesdale PA 18431
Local Retrieval Area: PA-Wayne.

Normal turnaround time: 24 hours. Projects are generally billed by the number of names searched. Credit accounts are accepted.

She specializes in real estate searches, current owner, 60 year and real estate closings.

Tomma J Schneider
Phone: 216-357-0280
Fax: 216-357-0280
179 Clairmont Dr
Painesville OH 44077
Local Retrieval Area: OH-Lake.

Normal turnaround time: within 24 hours. Projects are generally billed by the number of names searched or records located. Projects require prepayment. Payment due within 30 days of completion.

Correspondent relationships: Geauga, OH county.

Scholtes Investigation & Atty Svcs
Phone: 407-683-4174
PO Box 1262
Fax: 407-683-4174
West Palm Beach FL 33402
Local Retrieval and SOP Area: FL-Palm Beach.

Normal turnaround time: varied depending on project. Projects are generally billed by the number of names searched. Projects require prepayment.

Correspondent relationships: Broward, Dade, Martin and St. Lucie. They specialize in private investigating.

Susan Bailey Schramm
Phone: 304-876-2750
PO Box 308
Fax: 304-876-0584
Shepherdstown WV 25443
Local Retrieval Area: WV-Berkeley, Jefferson, Morgan.

Normal turnaround time: 48 hours. Fee basis will vary by name or index. Credit accounts are accepted.

She has 19 years experience and specializes in record searching and real estate.

Sharon Schroeder
Phone: 717-296-6604
RR 4 Box 7146
Milford PA 18337
Local Retrieval Area: PA-Pike.

Normal turnaround time: 24 hours for last owner. Other search time is varied. Projects are generally billed by the number of names searched. The first project may require a prepayment.

Scotland County Abstract Inc
Phone: 816-465-7052
205 E Monroe St
Fax: 816-465-7052
Memphis MO 63555
Local Retrieval Area: MO-Scotland.

Normal turnaround time: 3 days. Projects are generally billed by the number of records located. Projects require prepayment.

They specialize in title insurance.

Scott Abstract
Phone: 308-532-8535
PO Box 929
Fax: 308-532-6559
North Platte NE 69103
Local Retrieval Area: NE-Frontier, Hayes, Hooker, Lincoln, Logan, McPherson, Thomas.

Normal turnaround time: 3 days for Lincoln County. Longer for other counties. Fee basis varies by type of transaction. Credit accounts are accepted.

Scott County Abstract and Title
Phone: 316-872-3470
310 Court St
Fax: 316-872-7105
Scott City KS 67871
Local Retrieval Area: KS-Scott, Wichita.

Normal turnaround time: 24-48 hours. Projects are generally billed by the number of names searched or records located. The first project may require a prepayment. Personal checks are accepted.

Scrivelsby
Phone: 800-484-2462
PO Box 219052
503-297-5402
Portland OR 97225
Local Retrieval Area: OR-12 Counties.

Normal turnaround time: varies. Online computer ordering is also available. Projects are generally billed by the number of records located. Projects require prepayment.

Correspondent relationships: ID. They specialize in mortgage and tax lien leads and locations.

Scurry County Abstract Co
Phone: 915-573-6339
1816 26th St
Fax: 915-573-8112
Snyder TX 79549
Local Retrieval Area: TX-Scurry.

Normal turnaround time: 2-3 days. Fee basis will vary by the type of project. The first project may require a prepayment.

Search Associates
Phone: 414-325-9330
3100 W Layton
Fax: 414-325-9334
Greenfield WI 53221
Local Retrieval Area: WI-All Counties.

Normal turnaround time: 24-48 hours. Projects are generally billed by the number of names searched. Fee depends on type of search. The first project may require a prepayment.

They specialize in real estate title searches and all types of record searching and loan closings.

Search Company International
Phone: 800-727-2120
1535 Grant St Suite 140
303-863-1800
Denver CO 80203-1843
Fax: 303-863-7767
Local Retrieval Area: CO-12 Counties.

Normal turnaround time: 24-48 hours. Online computer ordering is also available. Projects are generally billed by the number of names searched. The first project may require a prepayment. Credit cards are accepted. Personal checks are accepted.

Correspondent relationships: the rest of Colorado. They are experienced and on-line with Colorado's new Central Indexing System. They also have the Secretary of State microfilm library. They specialize in UCC, lien, property and litigations (state and federal).

Search Company of ND
Phone: 701-258-5375
1008 E Capitol Ave
Fax: 701-258-5375
Bismarck ND 58501
Local Retrieval and SOP Area: ND-Burleigh, Cass, Morton.

Normal turnaround time: 24-72 hours. Projects are generally billed by the number of names searched. Credit accounts are accepted.

Correspondent relationships: all counties in North Dakota. They have 9 years of public record experience in North Dakota at the city, county, state and federal levels. They also provide registered agent services.

Search Enterprises
Phone: 817-752-2057
PO Box 1613
Fax: 817-752-8201
Waco TX 76703
Local Retrieval Area: TX-16 Counties.

Normal turnaround time: 48-72 hours. Projects are generally billed by the number of names searched or records located. The first project may require a prepayment.

They specialize in real estate, environmental, and other public record research.

Search International Inc
Phone: 606-342-0456
PO Box 426
Fax: 606-342-0457
Independence KY 41051
Local Retrieval Area: KY-Kenton; OH-Hamilton.

Normal turnaround time: 24-48 hours. Projects are generally billed by the number of names searched. Credit accounts are accepted. Invoices monthly by statement.

They specialize in felony, misdemeanor, UCC searches, civil, tax liens. They also cover federal courts in Southwest Ohio. They are court research specialists.

Search Network Ltd

Phone: 800-383-5050
515-223-1153
Fax: 800-383-5060
515-223-2814

2 Corporate Pl, Suite 210 1501 42nd St
West Des Moines IA 50266

Local Retrieval Area: IA-Polk.

Normal turnaround time: State UCC - same day, County 2-4 days. Online computer ordering is also available. Projects are generally billed by the number of names searched. The first project may require a prepayment. Credit cards are accepted. Terms are net 30 days.

Correspondent relationships: nationwide and Ontario, Canada. They specialize in UCC and lien searches, and national document filing.

Search Network Ltd

Phone: 800-338-3618
913-235-5777
Fax: 913-235-5788

700 SW Jackson Suite 100
Topeka KS 66603

Local Retrieval Area: KS-Shawnee.

Normal turnaround time: for State UCC; same day, County; 4 days. Projects are generally billed by the number of names searched. The first project may require a prepayment. Credit cards are accepted. Terms are net 30 days.

Correspondent relationships: nationwide. They are on-line with Kansas for UCC records.

Search NY

Phone: 718-854-1492
Fax: 718-854-1492

161 Prospect Pk SW
Brooklyn NY 11218

Local Retrieval Area: NY-Bronx, Kings, Nassau, New York, Queens, Richmond, Westchester.

Normal turnaround time: 24-72 hours. Projects are generally billed by the number of names searched. Credit accounts are accepted.

They specialize in all public record searches.

Search Plus

Phone: 800-465-1525
210-496-7186
Fax: 800-333-5184

16608 San Pedro Suite 315
San Antonio TX 78232

Local Retrieval Area: TX-Atascosa, Bexar, Caldwell, Comal, Gonzales, Guadalupe, Hays, Victoria, Wilson.

Normal turnaround time: 24-48 hours. Projects are generally billed by the number of names searched. Credit accounts are accepted. Terms are net 30 days.

Correspondent relationships: Missouri and Oklahoma. They specialize in pre-employment screening with a quick turnaruond time in most searches.

Search/America

Phone: 800-572-8815
813-636-8887
Fax: 813-636-9006

PO Box 20193
Tampa FL 33622-2193

Local Retrieval Area: FL-Broward, Collier, Dade, Hillsborough, Lee, Manatee, Palm Beach, Pasco, Pinellas, Sarasota.

Normal turnaround time: 72 hours. Projects are generally billed by the number of names searched. Credit accounts are accepted. Terms are net 10 days.

Correspondent relationships: nationwide.

Searcher Girls Search & Abstr

Phone: 800-292-2757
Fax: 800-292-2858

160 Lawr-Penn Rd Suite 16-114
Lawrenceville NJ 08648

Local Retrieval Area: NJ-21 Counties.

Normal turnaround time: 24-48 hours. Projects are generally billed by the number of names searched. Credit accounts are accepted. Credit cards are accepted.

Correspondent relationships: nationwide. They have a nationwide forwarding and retrieval department.

Searching Registration Service

Phone: 800-488-0238
916-452-8231
Fax: 800-488-0231
916-451-2322

PO Box 15824
Sacramento CA 95852

Local Retrieval Area: CA-Sacramento.

Online computer ordering is also available. Projects are generally billed by the number of names searched. The first project may require a prepayment. Terms are net 10 days.

They also do driver/license and vehicle registration searches.

Searchtec

Phone: 800-762-5018
Fax: 215-851-8775

211 N 13th St Suite 703
Philadelphia PA 19107

Local Retrieval Area: PA-Bucks, Chester, Delaware, Montgomery, Philadelphia.

Normal turnaround time: 24-48 hours. Online computer ordering is also available. Projects are generally billed by the number of names searched. The first project may require a prepayment.

Correspondent relationships: all of New Jersey and Delaware. They specialize in record searches, title insurance and appraisal services.

Seattle Process Service Inc

Phone: 800-842-8913
206-233-9454
Fax: 206-233-9475

157 Yesler Suite 505
Seattle WA 98104

Local Retrieval Area: WA-King, Pierce, Snohomish.

Normal turnaround time: approximately 5 business days. Projects are generally billed by the hour. The first project may require a prepayment.

Secrest Legal Services

Phone: 214-696-3959
Fax: 214-696-5377

4515 Prentice St Suite 102
Dallas TX 75206

Local Retrieval and SOP Area: TX-Collin, Dallas.

Normal turnaround time: 24 hours. Projects are generally billed by the number of names searched. The first project may require a prepayment.

Correspondent relationships: nationwide and Canada. They specialize in UCC, county and Federal court searches. Individual attention given to all orders. Owner operated and managed.

Secretarial Outsource Services

Phone: 309-347-3736
Fax: 309-347-1144

1303 Catherine St
Pekin IL 61554

Local Retrieval Area: IL-Tazewell.

Normal turnaround time: 24 hours. Projects are generally billed by the number of names searched. The first project may require a prepayment.

Security Abstract & Title Co

Phone: 406-232-3415
Fax: 406-232-3447

PO Box 1588 510 Main St
Miles City MT 59301

Local Retrieval Area: MT-Carter, Custer, Garfield.

Normal turnaround time: as much as two weeks. Projects are generally billed by the hour. Credit accounts are accepted.

Security Abstract and Title Inc

Phone: 515-462-1691
Fax: 515-462-3927

114 N 1st Ave
Winterset IA 50273

Local Retrieval Area: IA-Madison.

Normal turnaround time: 2-5 days. Projects are generally billed by the number of names searched..dd. Credit accounts are accepted.

Security Abstract Co

Phone: 501-234-5990
501-234-1291

112 E Calhoun St
Magnolia AR 71753

Local Retrieval Area: AR-Columbia.

Normal turnaround time: 2-3 days for civil, criminal and UCC searches, 5-7 days for real estate and probate. Fee basis will vary by the type of project. Credit accounts are accepted.

They specialize in title insurance.

Security Abstract Co

Phone: 573-748-2372
Fax: 573-748-2372

305 Main
New Madrid MO 63869

Local Retrieval Area: MO-New Madrid.

Normal turnaround time: 1 week or less. Projects are generally billed by the number of names searched. Credit accounts are accepted. Personal checks are accepted.

Security Abstract Co

Phone: 406-482-1010
Fax: 406-482-8245

106 2nd St SW
Sidney MT 59270

Local Retrieval Area: MT-Richland.

Normal turnaround time: 3-4 days. Projects are generally billed by the hour. Credit accounts are accepted.

They specialize in title insurance.

Security Abstract Co of Clarendon

Phone: 806-874-3511
Fax: 806-874-3160

PO Box 673
Clarendon TX 79226

Local Retrieval Area: TX-Armstrong, Donley, Hall.

Normal turnaround time: 1-2 days. Projects are generally billed by the hour. The first project may require a prepayment.

Security Abstract Co of Claude

Phone: 806-226-3621
Fax: 806-874-3160

PO Box 527
Claude TX 79019

Local Retrieval Area: TX-Armstrong, Donley, Hall.

Normal turnaround time: 1-2 days. Projects are generally billed by the hour. The first project may require a prepayment.

Security Abstract Co of Memphis

Phone: 806-259-2931
Fax: 806-874-3160

205 S 6th St
Memphis TX 79245

Local Retrieval Area: TX-Armstrong, Donley, Hall.

Normal turnaround time: 1-2 days. Projects are generally billed by the hour. The first project may require a prepayment.

Security Abstract Company

Phone: 913-877-2141
Fax: 913-877-2141

PO Box 444
Norton KS 67654-0444

Local Retrieval Area: KS-Norton.

Normal turnaround time: 24 hours. Projects are generally billed by the hour. The first project may require a prepayment. Payment due on completion of project.

Correspondent relationships: Phillips County. They specialize in title insurance.

Security Consultants Inc

Phone: 202-686-3953
Fax: 202-686-0264

5020 45th St NW
Washington DC 20016-4043

Local Retrieval and SOP Area: DC-District of Columbia; MD-Anne Arundel, Baltimore, Frederick, Howard, Montgomery, Prince George's; VA-City of Alexandria, Arlington, Fairfax, City of Fairfax, City of Falls Church, Loudoun, Prince William.

Normal turnaround time: 24-48 hours. Expedited services available. Projects are generally billed by the number of names searched. Credit accounts are accepted. Terms are net 30 days.

Correspondent relationships: nationwide. They specialize in county, state and federal searches and retrieval of documents from any source. The SCI President had a career of excellence as a Chief of Station with the CIA, and 8 years experience in the private sector as a information provider.

Security Enforcement Inc

Phone: 800-924-2896
516-678-0344
Fax: 516-678-7134

2463 Long Beach Rd PO Box 279
Oceanside NY 11572

Local Retrieval and SOP Area: NY-Nassau, Suffolk.

Normal turnaround time: varied depending on project. Projects are generally billed by the number of names searched or records located. Projects require prepayment. Personal checks are accepted.

Correspondent relationships: Westchester, Kings, Queens, Richmond, New York City, Nassau and Suffolk.

Security Information Service Inc

Phone: 800-525-5747
214-637-4055
Fax: 214-637-1443

8585 N Stemmons Fwy Suite M-28
Dallas TX 75247

Local Retrieval and SOP Area: TX-Collin, Dallas, Denton, Ellis, Hunt, Johnson, Kaufman, Rockwall, Tarrant.

Normal turnaround time: 1-3 days. Online computer ordering is also available. Projects are generally billed by the number of names searched or records located. The first project may require a prepayment.

Correspondent relationships: nationwide and international. They specialize in security consulting, investigations and loss prevention. They also have experience in theft by fraud/embezzlement, due diligence/financial risk analysis, litigation/legal support, conflict of interest/bribery, kickbacks, etc.

Security Land & Abstract Co

Phone: 605-347-3443
Fax: 605-347-4817

PO Box 718
Sturgis SD 57785

Local Retrieval Area: SD-Meade.

Normal turnaround time: 1-4 days. Projects are generally billed by the hour. Credit accounts are accepted.

They specialize in title insurance.

Security Land Title Co

Phone: 712-262-1074
Fax: 712-262-1082

607 1st Ave Box 113
Spencer IA 51301

Local Retrieval Area: IA-Clay.

Normal turnaround time: varied depending on project. They charge a flat fee. Credit accounts are accepted.

Security Services Inc (SSI)

Phone: 800-383-4312
309-674-4321
Fax: 309-674-9357

1009 N Sheridan Rd
Peoria IL 61606

Local Retrieval and SOP Area: IL-Fulton, Knox, Marshall, McLean, Peoria, Stark, Tazewell, Woodford.

Normal turnaround time: 1-3 working days. Established clients are billed by the hour plus expenses. The first project may require a prepayment.

Security Source Nationwide

Phone: 303-628-3973
Fax: 303-443-7324

PO Box 7971
Boulder CO 80306-7971

Local Retrieval and SOP Area: AZ-Maricopa; CO-Adams, Arapahoe, Boulder, Denver, Jefferson; IL-Cook; NV-Clark.

Normal turnaround time: 12-72 hours. Projects are generally billed by the number of names searched. Credit accounts are accepted.

Correspondent relationships: nationwide and Canada.

Security Title Co of Garfield Co

Phone: 801-676-8808
Fax: 801-676-2421

15 N Main St
Panguitch UT 84759

Local Retrieval Area: UT-Garfield, Piute.

Normal turnaround time: 3-5 days. Projects are generally billed by the hour. Credit accounts are accepted.

They specialize in recreational properties.

Security Title of Beaver County

Phone: 801-438-2354
Fax: 801-438-5805

PO Box 819
Beaver UT 84713

Local Retrieval Area: UT-Beaver.

Normal turnaround time: 24 hours. Projects are generally billed by the number of names searched. Projects require prepayment.

Security Title of Park County Inc

Phone: 406-222-0362
Fax: 406-222-8764

PO Box 928 219 S Main St
Livingston MT 59047

Local Retrieval Area: MT-Park.

Normal turnaround time: 24 hours. Fee basis varies by type of transaction. Credit accounts are accepted.

Mark T Segars

Phone: 601-423-1006
Fax: 601-423-1091

915 Battleground Dr
Iuka MS 38852

Local Retrieval Area: MS-Tishomingo.

Normal turnaround time: 1-2 days. Fee basis will vary by the type of project. The first project may require a prepayment.

He is an attorney in general and real estate practice.

Service Abstract Company

Phone: 501-892-4538
Fax: 501-892-9808

208 E Everett
Pocahontas AR 72455

Local Retrieval and SOP Area: AR-Randolph.

Normal turnaround time: varied depending on project. Fee basis will vary by the type of project. Credit accounts are accepted. Personal checks accepted.

Correspondent relationships: various counties within the state. They specialize in title insurance, abstracts and loan closings.

Services for Attorneys

Phone: 805-564-4107
Fax: 805-564-8755

1032 Santa Barbara St
Santa Barbara CA 93101

Local Retrieval and SOP Area: CA-Santa Barbara.

Normal turnaround time: varied depending on project. Fee basis will vary by type of project. The first project may require a prepayment. Personal checks are accepted.

Correspondent relationships: nationwide. They specialize in litigation/trial support, legal research, drafting, registered process serving and licensed private investigations.

Services Rendered

Phone: 315-853-6327
Fax: 315-853-1933

PO Box 435
Clinton NY 13323-0435

Local Retrieval and SOP Area: NY-Madison, Oneida.

Normal turnaround time: 24 hours. Projects are generally billed by the number of names searched. The first project may require a prepayment.

Seyfried Support Services

Phone: 916-366-9136
Fax: 916-369-0615

9878 Burline St
Sacramento CA 95827

Local Retrieval Area: CA-Sacramento.

Normal turnaround time: 24 hours. Projects are generally billed by the number of names searched. Credit accounts are accepted. Bill monthly.

They personally review records in the Sacramento area. They have great familarity with the records to accurately find what you want.

Shannon County Abstract Co

Phone: 573-226-3331

PO Box 334
Eminence MO 65466

Local Retrieval Area: MO-Shannon.

Normal turnaround time: 1-2 weeks. Fee basis will vary by the type of project. Credit accounts are accepted.

They specialize in real estate.

Sharon K Hannaman Abstracter

Phone: 507-526-5144

PO Box 246
Blue Earth MN 56013

Local Retrieval Area: MN-Faribault.

Normal turnaround time: 1-2 weeks. Projects are generally billed by the number of names searched. The first project may require a prepayment.

Sharp County Abstract Co Inc
PO Box 81
Ash Flat AR 72513
Phone: 501-994-7314
Fax: 501-994-2880

Local Retrieval Area: AR-Sharp.

Normal turnaround time: 10 days. Expedited service available. Fee basis will vary by the type of project. Credit accounts are accepted. A down payment is required.

They specialize in title insurance, escrow and closings.

W Allan Sharrett
314 S Main St
Emporia VA 23847
Phone: 804-634-2167
Fax: 804-634-3798

Local Retrieval Area: VA-Brunswick, City of Emporia, Greensville.

Normal turnaround time: 2 days. Projects are generally billed by the hour. The first project may require a prepayment.

He is a trial lawyer.

John Shaw
PO Box 744 241 N Madison St
Kosciusko MS 39090
Phone: 601-289-3110
Fax: 601-289-2048

Local Retrieval Area: MS-Attala, Choctaw, Holmes, Leake.

Normal turnaround time: 1-2 days. Fee basis varies by type of transaction. Projects require prepayment.

He is a country lawyer.

Shawver and Associates
PO Box 1592
Corpus Christi TX 78403
Phone: 800-364-2333
512-991-5055
Fax: 512-993-3135

Local Retrieval and SOP Area: TX-14 Counties.

Normal turnaround time: 2 days for areas within a 50 mile radius. Projects are generally billed by the hour. The first project may require a prepayment.

Correspondent relationships: all of Texas. They specialize in third party liability identification, personal injury claims and insurance defense.

Shelby County Land Title Corp
PO Box 473
Shelbyville IL 62565
Phone: 217-774-2623
Fax: 217-774-3702

Local Retrieval Area: IL-Shelby.

Normal turnaround time: 2 days. Projects are generally billed by the number of records located. Credit accounts are accepted. Payment due after work is completed.

Shenandoah Title Services Inc
31 S Braddock St Suite 3
Winchester VA 22601-4121
Phone: 540-667-1393
Fax: 540-667-0464

Local Retrieval Area: VA-Clarke, Frederick, Loudoun, Page, Shenandoah, Warren, City of Winchester.

Normal turnaround time: 3-5 days. Expedited service available. Fee basis will vary by type of project. Projects require prepayment.

They specialize in real estate searches.

Sheridan County Abstract Co
Box 428
McClusky ND 58463
Phone: 701-363-2285

Local Retrieval Area: ND-Sheridan.

Normal turnaround time: 3-4 days. Fee basis will vary by type of project. Credit accounts are accepted.

They specialize in title and land ownership.

▥ Sherlock and Company
5960-204 Jake Sears Circle
Virginia Beach VA 23464
Phone: 757-366-5142
Fax: 757-366-0832

Local Retrieval Area: VA-City of Chesapeake, City of Hampton, City of Newport News, City of Norfolk, City of Portsmouth, City of Virginia Beach.

Normal turnaround time: 24-48 hours. Projects are generally billed by the number of names searched or records located. Credit accounts are accepted. Billed monthly.

Victoria Sherrill
323 E 20th St
Kannapolis NC 28083
Phone: 704-938-9529
Fax: 704-938-9529

Local Retrieval Area: NC-Cabarrus, Davidson, Iredell, Rowan, Stanly.

Normal turnaround time: 48 hours. Projects are generally billed by the number of names searched. The first project may require a prepayment.

Correspondent relationships: Wake, Randolph, Orange, Union, Johnston, Durham, Alamance and Chatham and Gulford. She has 25 years of legal experience. She specializes in real estate title searches.

Valerie Shickel
42 Book Hill Rd
Essex CT 06426
Phone: 860-767-2269
Fax: 860-767-7621

Local Retrieval Area: CT-Middlesex, New Haven, New London.

Normal turnaround time: 2-3 days. Fees are based on a per search basis. Credit accounts are accepted.

Valerie specializes in 40 or 60 year land and probate record searches.

▥ SI Services Inc
PO Box 438
Swartz Creek MI 48473
Phone: 800-258-7604
810-635-9754
Fax: 810-635-4009

Local Retrieval and SOP Area: MI-Genesee, Ingham, Lapeer, Livingston, Oakland, Saginaw, Shiawassee, Tuscola.

Normal turnaround time: 1-3 days. Online computer ordering is also available. Projects are generally billed by the number of names searched. The first project may require a prepayment.

They specialize in obtaining hard-to-find information.

SIC Inc
986 NE 84th St
Miami FL 33138
Phone: 305-751-0015
Fax: 305-758-3341

Local Retrieval and SOP Area: FL-Alachua, Broward, Collier, Dade, Duval, Monroe, Orange, Palm Beach, Pinellas, Volusia.

Normal turnaround time: varied depending on project. Online computer ordering is also available. Projects are generally billed by the number of names searched. The first project may require a prepayment.

Correspondent relationships: the state of Florida.

Sierra Attorney Service
PO Box 1193
Bishop CA 93515
Phone: 619-872-1208
Fax: 619-872-1208

Local Retrieval and SOP Area: CA-Inyo.

Normal turnaround time: 1-2 days. Expedited service available. Projects are generally billed by the hour. The first project may require a prepayment.

Correspondent relationships: Mono, Kern. They specialize in process serving and photocopying documents.

Sierra Legal Services

Phone: 916-878-2203
Fax: 916-878-2203

3037 Grass Valley Hwy
Auburn CA 95602-2595

Local Retrieval and SOP Area: CA-El Dorado, Nevada, Placer, Sacramento.

Normal turnaround time: 3-4 business days. Expedited service available. Projects are generally billed by the number of names searched. Fee may also be based per trip. The first project may require a prepayment. Personal checks are accepted.

Correspondent relationships: Sacramento, Placer, El Dorado, CA counties and Nevada. They specialize in Superior Municipal Court searches and difficult-to-locate process serving.

Sikoral & Associates Investigtns

Phone: 908-257-2550
Fax: 908-257-9266

12 Salem Rd
East Brunswick NJ 08816

Local Retrieval and SOP Area: NJ-Mercer, Middlesex, Monmouth, Morris, Somerset, Union.

Normal turnaround time: 3-4 working days. Expedited service available. Projects are generally billed by the hour. Credit accounts are accepted. Terms are net 45 days after work performed.

They specialize in background investigations, environmental investigations and health care fraud.

Silk Attorney Service

Phone: 913-432-2755

5301 W 50th St
Shawnee Mission KS 66205-1219

Local Retrieval Area: KS-Johnson, Leavenworth, Wyandotte; MO-Clay, Jackson, Platte.

Normal turnaround time: 24-36 hours. Projects are generally billed by the hour. Mileage and copy expenses are added to the fee. Credit accounts are accepted. They request prepayment for process serving.

They specialize in Northeast Kansas and Northwest Missouri. They will also go to Federal Records Center in Kansas City, Missouri.

Silver Eagle Services

Phone: 212-922-0223
Fax: 212-922-0223

305 Madison Ave Suite 1166
New York NY 10165-0099

Local Retrieval and SOP Area: NJ-Hudson; NY-Bronx, Kings, Nassau, New York, Queens, Richmond, Rockland, Suffolk, Westchester.

Normal turnaround time: 48 hours. Projects are generally billed by the number of names searched or records located. Credit accounts are accepted.

Correspondent relationships: all of New York, Pennsylvania and New Jersey.

Teresa Simerly

Phone: 423-725-3901
Fax: 423-743-3924

Rt 1 Box 613
Hampton TN 37658

Local Retrieval Area: TN-Carter, Johnson, Sullivan, Unicoi, Washington.

Normal turnaround time: 24-48 hours. Projects are generally billed by the number of records located. Credit accounts are accepted.

Correspondent relationships: Mitchell and Madison, NC and Washington, VA. She is a certified legal assistant. She specializes in real estate.

Simmons & Grillo

Phone: 614-596-5291

114 W Main
McArthur OH 45651

Local Retrieval Area: OH-Jackson, Vinton.

Normal turnaround time: varied depending on search. Charges are varied depending on the type of search. Credit accounts are accepted.

They are attorneys and specialize in real estate record searches.

🏛 Simmons Agency Inc

Phone: 800-237-8230
617-523-2289
Fax: 617-695-1815

200 Lincoln St
Boston MA 02111

Local Retrieval Area: MA-Barnstable, Middlesex, Norfolk, Suffolk.

Normal turnaround time: 3-5 business days. Rush of 1-2 days available. Projects are generally billed by the hour. The first project may require a prepayment.

Correspondent relationships: Essex, MA county. They specialize in location of documents with ability to follow through on addtional searches. They also locate assets, missing people and skip tracing.

🏛 SingleSource Services Corp

Phone: 800-713-3412
904-241-1821
Fax: 904-241-0601

PO Box 49149
Jacksonville Beach FL 32240

Local Retrieval Area: FL-56 Counties; NC-98 Counties; SC-41 Counties; VA-121 Counties.

Normal turnaround time: 48 hours requested, most results suplies in 24 hours or less. Online computer ordering is also available. Projects are generally billed by the number of names searched. The first project may require a prepayment. Terms are net 30 days.

Correspondent relationships: North Carolina, South Carolina, Virginia, Tennessee, Kentucky. They specialize in accurate and timely service. "The customer is always right".

Singleton & Deeds

Phone: 540-839-5009
Fax: 540-839-2986

PO Box 116 Courthouse Rd
Warm Springs VA 24484

Local Retrieval Area: VA-Alleghany, Bath, City of Clifton Forge, City of Covington, Highland, Rockbridge.

Normal turnaround time: 24 hours. Projects are generally billed by the hour. Credit accounts are accepted.

🏛 Six County Search

Phone: 614-962-3995
Fax: 614-962-4074

961 W Glenn Cordray Rd
McConnelsville OH 43756-9365

Local Retrieval and SOP Area: OH-Fairfield, Fayette, Guernsey, Muskingum, Perry, Pickaway.

Normal turnaround time: 1-3 days. Projects are generally billed by the number of names searched. The first project may require a prepayment.

Skimerhorn Investigations

Phone: 815-933-0843
Fax: 815-933-0843

444 N Jackson Ave
Bradley IL 60915

Local Retrieval and SOP Area: IL-Iroquois, Kankakee, Will.

Normal turnaround time: 1-2 days. Expedited service available. Projects are generally billed by the hour. Fees are per name searched, per class of record. The first project may require a prepayment. May be billed monthly.

They specialize in skip tracing, asset searches and conduct missing person checks.

Skyline Consulting

Phone: 507-359-1131
Fax: 507-359-1131

PO Box 582
New Elm MN 56073

Local Retrieval Area: MN-Brown.

Normal turnaround time: a few days. Fee basis is per project. Projects require prepayment.

They specialize in pre trial civil and criminal investigations. Video and photographic services also available.

Slamal & Swayden Inc

Phone: 316-886-5141

105 E Kansas
Medicine Lodge KS 67104

Local Retrieval Area: KS-Barber.

Normal turnaround time: 1 week. Projects are generally billed by the hour. Credit accounts are accepted.

They specialize in title and abstract work.

Slover Investigations

Phone: 602-917-3708
Fax: 602-917-2603

PO Box 6515
Chandler AZ 85246-6515

Local Retrieval Area: AZ-Maricopa.

Normal turnaround time: 1-2 days. Online computer ordering is also available. Projects are generally billed by the number of names searched. The first project may require a prepayment.

They specialize in criminal records checks, motor vehicle, watercraft and aircraft searches, skip tracing, personal injury, asset, background and pre-employment investigations.

Slueth Research

Phone: 404-288-4598
Fax: 404-289-0621

4213 Northstrand Dr
Decatur GA 30035

Local Retrieval Area: GA-Clayton, Cobb, De Kalb, Douglas, Fulton, Gwinnett, Henry, Newton, Rockdale.

Normal turnaround time: 24-48 hours. Projects are generally billed by the number of names searched. Credit accounts are accepted.

They specialize in criminal background retrieval.

Smith Abstract Co Inc

Phone: 501-222-5001
Fax: 501-222-6159

PO Box 261
McGehee AR 71654

Local Retrieval Area: AR-Desha.

Normal turnaround time: 1-2 weeks. Projects are generally billed by the hour. The first project may require a prepayment.

They specialize in real estate, civil judgments and probate.

Smith County Abstract Co

Phone: 903-597-7711
Fax: 903-595-6738

200 W Erwin
Tyler TX 75702

Local Retrieval Area: TX-Smith.

Normal turnaround time: 1-3 days. Projects are generally billed by the number of names searched. Credit accounts are accepted. Personal checks are accepted.

Susan Smith Hicks

Phone: 518-537-4103
Fax: 518-537-4103

119 Main St
Germantown NY 12526

Local Retrieval Area: NY-Albany, Columbia, Dutchess, Greene, Ulster.

Normal turnaround time: 2 weeks or less. Projects are generally billed by the hour. Credit accounts are accepted.

They specialize in real property title searches and closings.

Cheryl Smith

Phone: 919-633-3890
Fax: 919-633-3890

692 New Liberty Rd
New Bern NC 28562

Local Retrieval Area: NC-Craven, Jones, Pamlico.

Normal turnaround time: 1-3 days. Projects are generally billed by the hour. Credit accounts are accepted. Personal checks are accepted.

She specializes in title examinations.

Pat Smith

Phone: 317-447-1684

3837 Harper Dr
Lafayette IN 47905

Local Retrieval Area: IN-Tippecanoe.

Normal turnaround time: 24 hours. No project billing information was given. Credit accounts are accepted. Billing is sent out at the end of each month.

SMS/Strategic Mortgage Services

Phone: 800-475-2334
615-367-2300
Fax: 615-367-2521

1100 Kermit Dr Suite 204
Nashville TN 37217

Local Retrieval Area: TN-32 Counties.

Normal turnaround time: 24 hours. Projects are generally billed by the number of records located. Fees are based on the number of property addresses searches. Projects require prepayment.

Correspondent relationships: Kentucky and Alabama. They specialize in appraisals, property reports, commitments for title insurance, closing documents (prepared, closing, escrow service, foreclosure sales) and other courthouse related services.

Solomon Abstract Co Inc

Phone: 405-375-4151
Fax: 405-375-5023

PO Box 449
Kingfisher OK 73750-0449

Local Retrieval Area: OK-Kingfisher.

Normal turnaround time: 3-7 days. Fee basis will vary by the type of project. The first project may require a prepayment.

Solons Legal Documents Svc

Phone: 800-732-0175
Fax: 205-547-9593

PO Box 664
Gadsden AL 35902

Local Retrieval Area: AL-Jefferson, Montgomery, Tuscaloosa.

Normal turnaround time: 48 hours. Projects are generally billed by the number of names searched. The first project may require a prepayment.

They specialize in nationwide searches.

Somerset Abstract Co Ltd

Phone: 814-445-9525

124 N Center Ave
Somerset PA 15501

Local Retrieval Area: PA-Cambria, Somerset.

Normal turnaround time: up to 1 week. Fee basis is per transaction. Credit accounts are accepted.

They specialize in real estate.

Sooner Abstract & Title Co

Phone: 918-647-3202
Fax: 918-647-8784

PO Box 772
Poteau OK 74953

Local Retrieval Area: OK-Le Flore.

Normal turnaround time: 1-2 days. Fee is determined on a "per hour/day" basis. Credit accounts are accepted.

Source

PO Box 88
Cookeville TN 38503

Phone: 800-678-8774
Fax: 800-537-3297

Local Retrieval and SOP Area: TN-Cumberland, De Kalb, Jackson, Macon, Overton, Putnam, Roane, Smith, White.

Normal turnaround time: 1-7 working days. Online computer ordering is also available. Projects are generally billed by the number of names searched. Projects require prepayment. Credit cards are accepted.

Correspondent relationships: nationwide. They specialize in extended court filings and searches for New Jersey, Pennsylvania and New York. They also search public record information on individuals and businesses.

South Georgia Title

PO Box 938
Cordele GA 31015

Phone: 912-273-1977

Local Retrieval Area: GA-Crisp.

Normal turnaround time: 2 days. Projects are generally billed by the hour. The first project may require a prepayment. A minimum fee is required.

They specialize in real estate.

South Plain Abstract Co

PO Box 418
LaMesa TX 79331

Phone: 806-872-3023
Fax: 806-872-2904

Local Retrieval Area: TX-Dawson.

Normal turnaround time: 2 days. Fee basis will vary by the type of project. Projects require prepayment.

South Ridge Abstract and Title Co

229 S Commerce
Sebring FL 33870

Phone: 941-385-2521
Fax: 941-382-6438

Local Retrieval Area: FL-Highlands.

Normal turnaround time: 7-10 working days. Projects are generally billed by the number of names searched. The first project may require a prepayment. Invoice sent with client's search results.

They maintain an in-house title plant.

Southeast Nebraska Abstract

1524 Stone St
Falls City NE 68355

Phone: 402-245-4222
Fax: 402-245-3859

Local Retrieval Area: NE-Richardson.

Normal turnaround time: 24-48 hours. Fee basis will vary by the type of project. Credit accounts are accepted.

They specialize in real estate transactions, probate and family practice.

Southeastern Utah Title

PO Box 855
Price UT 84501

Phone: 801-637-4455
Fax: 801-637-4459

Local Retrieval Area: UT-Carbon, Emery, Grand, San Juan.

Normal turnaround time: 24 hours. Fee basis will vary by the type of project. The first project may require a prepayment.

Southern Abstract & Title Co

PO Box 507
Idabel OK 74745

Phone: 405-286-2288
Fax: 405-286-7885

Local Retrieval Area: OK-McCurtain.

Normal turnaround time: 2-3 weeks. Projects are generally billed by the hour. Fee basis is also determined "per abstract". Credit accounts are accepted. Clients pay before searches are released.

Southern Colorado Title Co

100 E Main St Suite 311
Trinidad CO 81082

Phone: 719-846-4944
Fax: 719-846-4944

Local Retrieval Area: CO-Las Animas.

Normal turnaround time: 3-5 days. Projects are generally billed by the hour. Credit accounts are accepted.

They specialize in real estate matters.

Southern Indiana Abstract & Title

411 W 1st
New Albany IN 47150

Phone: 812-944-4931
Fax: 812-948-9329

Local Retrieval Area: IN-Clark, Floyd, Harrison.

Normal turnaround time: 2-10 days. Projects are generally billed by the number of names searched. Credit accounts are accepted.

Correspondent relationships: Kentucky. They specialize in title searches.

Southern Mountain Abstract & Title

PO Box 390
Dillon MT 59725

Phone: 406-683-4445
Fax: 406-683-4393

Local Retrieval Area: MT-Beaverhead.

Normal turnaround time: 5 days. Fee basis varies by type of transaction. Credit accounts are accepted.

🏛 Southern Research Company

2850 Centenary Blvd
Shreveport LA 71104

Phone: 888-772-6952
318-227-9700
Fax: 318-424-1801

Local Retrieval and SOP Area: LA-Bossier Parish, Caddo Parish.

Normal turnaround time: 48 hours. Projects are generally billed by the number of names searched. The first project may require a prepayment. Credit cards are accepted.

Correspondent relationships: the remainder of state. They specialize in employment screening, localized court documents & field investigation searches. Since inception the firm has focused on providing premium general investigative and fact finding assignments for diverse clientele throughout the US.

Southern Utah Title Co

44 N Main
Kanab UT 84741

Phone: 801-644-5891
Fax: 801-644-8136

Local Retrieval Area: UT-Kane.

Normal turnaround time: 1-2 weeks. Fee basis will vary by the type of project. Projects require prepayment.

Southwest Abstract & Title Co

PO Box 13
Rankin TX 79778

Phone: 915-693-2242
Fax: 915-693-2249

Local Retrieval Area: TX-Upton.

Normal turnaround time: 2-3 days. Fee basis will vary by the type of project. Credit accounts are accepted.

Southwest Abstract Co

PO Box 1149
Lawton OK 73502

Phone: 405-355-3680
Fax: 405-248-1849

Local Retrieval Area: OK-Comanche.

Normal turnaround time: 2-4 days. Fee basis will vary by the type of project. Credit accounts are accepted.

They specialize in title insurance.

Southwest Abstract Co Inc

Phone: 210-775-8508
Fax: 210-775-9183

PO Box 1175
Del Rio TX 78841

Local Retrieval Area: TX-Val Verde.

Normal turnaround time: 2 days. Fee basis will vary by the type of project. Projects require prepayment.

Southwest Patrol & Investigations

Phone: 713-697-1577
Fax: 713-697-1580

607 Sunnyside
Houston TX 77076

Local Retrieval Area: TX-Fort Bend, Harris, Montgomery.

Normal turnaround time: varied depending on project. Fee basis will vary by type of project. Projects require prepayment.

They specialize in family law, asset and child recovery.

Tony Spadachene

Phone: 409-826-8610

1345 13th
Hempstead TX 77445

Local Retrieval Area: TX-Waller.

Normal turnaround time: 24-48 hours..dd. Projects are generally billed by the number of names searched. Credit accounts are accepted.

▥ Special Private Investigations

Phone: 800-577-3783
616-887-8574
Fax: 616-887-8775

PO Box 2174
Grand Rapids MI 49501-2174

Local Retrieval and SOP Area: MI-Allegan, Barry, Ionia, Kent, Muskegon, Ottawa.

Normal turnaround time: 3-10 days for UCC, tax, real estate, and vital stats. 2 days for civil cases and probate. Projects are generally billed by the hour. The first project may require a prepayment.

They specialize in vehicle and driver license registrations for the State of Michigan.

Special Service Investigations

Phone: 970-490-5200
Fax: 888-303-5200
970-484-6897

PO Box 1015
Fort Collins CO 80522-1015

Local Retrieval and SOP Area: CO-Boulder, Larimer, Weld.

Normal turnaround time: 24-48 hours. Projects are generally billed by the number of names searched or records located. The first project may require a prepayment. Terms are net 30 days.

Correspondent relationships: Vail, Jefferson, Denver and Adams counties. They specialize in courthouse and record searches. They also do pretrial work, background checks, person and asset locations.

▥ Specialized Investigations

Phone: 800-714-3728
818-909-9607
Fax: 818-782-3012

14530 Delano St 1st Floor
Van Nuys CA 91411

Local Retrieval and SOP Area: CA-Los Angeles, Orange, Riverside, San Bernardino, San Diego, Santa Barbara.

Normal turnaround time: 1-7 working days. Online computer ordering is also available. Projects are generally billed by the hour. The first project may require a prepayment. Terms are net 30 days.

They specialize in insurance fraud, surveillance, background checks, asset searches, trial preparation, skip tracing and medical audits.

▥ Specialty Services

Phone: 770-942-8264
Fax: 770-942-5355

8491 Hospital Dr Suite 151
Douglasville GA 30134

Local Retrieval and SOP Area: GA-57 Counties.

Normal turnaround time: from same day to 72 hours. Projects are generally billed by the number of names searched. The first project may require a prepayment. Billed monthly, due upon receipt (late fees after 30 days).

Correspondent relationships: nationwide. They specialize in record retrieval from county, state and federal courts. Criminal and civil backgrounds for pre-employment screening, litigation support, insurance fraud investigation assistance, asset reports, UCC searches, title work, etc.

R Scott Spidel

Phone: 502-782-8471

444 Moats Lane
Bowling Green KY 42103

Local Retrieval Area: KY-Warren.

Normal turnaround time: up to 1 week. Projects are generally billed by the hour. The first project may require a prepayment.

They specialize in mineral ownership and deed plotting.

Spiller Abstract

Phone: 817-567-2271
Fax: 817-567-2271

122 E Belknap PO Box I
Jacksboro TX 76458

Local Retrieval Area: TX-Jack.

Fees vary by project. Credit accounts are accepted.

They only search real estate records.

▥ Sharry N Sprague

Phone: 540-743-4874
Fax: 540-743-3229

421 Beylor's Ferry Rd
Rileyville VA 22650

Local Retrieval Area: VA-Page, Rockingham, Shenandoah, Warren.

Normal turnaround time: 24-48 hours. Projects are generally billed by the hour. The first project may require a prepayment.

She specializes in accurate information and efficient service guarantied.

▥ Spyglass Pre-Employment Spec

Phone: 800-555-4018
312-581-0180
Fax: 312-581-5727

5935 S Pulaski Rd #2
Chicago IL 60629

Local Retrieval and SOP Area: IL-Cook, Du Page, Kane, Lake, Will.

Normal turnaround time: 24-48 hours. Projects are generally billed by the number of names searched. Credit accounts are accepted.

Correspondent relationships: Florida, Texas, Oregon, Washington and California.

SRS Private Investigations Inc

Phone: 707-537-1091
Fax: 707-537-1095

100 Brush Creek Rd Suite 106
Santa Rosa CA 95409

Local Retrieval and SOP Area: CA-Sonoma.

Normal turnaround time: 3 days. Expedited service available. Projects are generally billed by the hour. The first project may require a prepayment.

They specialize in full range investigative services that include backgrounds, locates, asset searches, security surveys, witness statements and much more.

SRT Investigations

PO Box 35403
Tulsa OK 74153

Phone: 800-800-7119
918-481-6045
Fax: 918-491-9774

Local Retrieval Area: OK-Creek, Muskogee, Oklahoma, Tulsa, Wagoner.

Normal turnaround time: 24 hours. Projects are generally billed by the number of names searched or records located. The first project may require a prepayment.

Correspondent relationships: a network for the rest of Oklahoma. They specialize in marriage/divorce searches.

St Croix Valley Title Services Inc

219 N Main St PO Box 138
River Falls WI 54022

Phone: 715-425-1519
Fax: 715-425-7586

Local Retrieval Area: WI-Pierce, St. Croix.

Normal turnaround time: 1-2 days. Fee basis varies by type of transaction. The first project may require a prepayment.

St Ives

1124 2nd St
Old Sacramento CA 95814

Phone: 800-995-9443
916-446-5900
Fax: 916-446-7459

Local Retrieval and SOP Area: CA-14 Counties.

Normal turnaround time: 2 days within California and 3-5 days outside California. Projects are generally billed by the number of names searched. The first project may require a prepayment.

Correspondent relationships: nationwide, Canada and Philipines. They specialize in pre-employment background searches and asset searches.

St Joseph County Abstract Office

PO Box 217
Centreville MI 49032

Phone: 616-467-6075
Fax: 616-467-4314

Local Retrieval Area: MI-Cass, St. Joseph.

Normal turnaround time: 3 days. Projects are generally billed by the hour. Credit accounts are accepted.

They specialize in title and real estate.

St Vrain Resources

Jenkins Bldg 699 W Woodbine
St Louis MO 63122

Phone: 314-821-9029
Fax: 314-821-9035

Local Retrieval and SOP Area: IL-Madison, St. Clair; MO-St. Charles, City of St. Louis.

Normal turnaround time: 24-72 hours. Projects are generally billed by the hour. Charge by the mile also. The first project may require a prepayment.

Correspondent relationships: Northwest Missouri in the Kansas City area and Northeast Illinois in the Chicago area. They specialize in conducting investigation, research and documentation.

Stafford County Abstract & Title

PO Box 265
St John KS 67576

Phone: 316-549-3579
Fax: 316-549-6594

Local Retrieval Area: KS-Stafford.

Normal turnaround time: up to 1 week. Projects are generally billed by the hour. Projects require prepayment.

Stanton Co Abstract

PO Box 86
Stanton NE 68779

Phone: 402-439-2142
Fax: 402-439-2145

Local Retrieval Area: NE-Colfax, Cuming, Platte, Stanton.

Normal turnaround time: 1-3 days. Fee basis is flat rate and per record. Credit accounts are accepted. Payment due upon invoicing after services.

They specialize in title insurance, title searches, abstracts, closings and escrows.

Starke County Abstract Title

14 E Washington St
Knox IN 46534

Phone: 219-772-3733
Fax: 219-772-7603

Local Retrieval Area: IN-Starke.

Normal turnaround time: 3-5 days. Fee basis will vary by type of project. Credit accounts are accepted.

They specialize in record searching.

⏗ Starr Investigations & Security

1848 43rd St NE
Cedar Rapids IA 52402-3008

Phone: 319-393-1007
Fax: 319-393-1007

Local Retrieval and SOP Area: IA-Benton, Cedar, Iowa, Johnson, Jones, Linn.

Normal turnaround time: 2 business days. Projects are generally billed by the number of names searched or records located. Credit accounts are accepted. Can invoice if requested.

They specialize in process serving, court research and divorce matters.

State Court Retrievers

2535 Kettner Blvd Suite 1A2
San Diego CA 92101

Phone: 619-687-3897
Fax: 619-696-5360

Local Retrieval Area: CA-San Diego.

Normal turnaround time: 2-3 days. The first project may require a prepayment.

Correspondent relationships: nationwide. They specialize in land records and state court records.

⏗ State Information Bureau

842 E Park Ave
Tallahassee FL 32301

Phone: 800-881-1742
904-561-3990
Fax: 904-561-3995

Local Retrieval Area: FL-Gadsden, Jefferson, Leon, Wakulla.

Normal turnaround time: 24-48 hours for Leon County. Fee basis will vary by type of project. The first project may require a prepayment.

Correspondent relationships: major counties in Florida. They are a licensed private investigative agency that specializes in background checks, asset checks and locating witnesses. They specialize in obtaining information from state records.

Staton Abstract & Title Co

PO Box 168
Chillicothe MO 64601

Phone: 816-646-1421
Fax: 816-646-1441

Local Retrieval Area: MO-Livingston.

Normal turnaround time: 2 days. Fee basis varies by type of transaction. Credit accounts are accepted.

Steele County Abstract Co

PO Box 413
Owatonna MN 55060

Phone: 507-451-6487
Fax: 507-451-6487

Local Retrieval Area: MN-Steele.

Normal turnaround time: 4 days. Projects are generally billed by the number of names searched. The first project may require a prepayment.

Steele Investigation Agency

1507 Flamingo Blvd
Bradenton FL 34207

Phone: 813-758-5890
Fax: 813-755-1100

Local Retrieval and SOP Area: FL-Manatee, Sarasota.

Normal turnaround time: 3 days. Expedited service available. Projects are generally billed by the hour. The first project may require a prepayment.

Correspondent relationships: nationwide. They specialize in on-line Florida records, and are a full service investigative agency including, but not limited to asset location, criminal, civil, background, video, photograph, missing persons and surveillance.

Steele Investigations & Info Svcs

226 S 7th
Louisville KY 40202

Phone: 800-587-0965
502-587-0965
Fax: 502-587-6468

Local Retrieval and SOP Area: KY-Jefferson.

Normal turnaround time: 24-48 hours. Projects are generally billed by the hour. Credit accounts are accepted.

They specialize in dead beat dads. Locating done on no hit/no fee. They have instant access to online information. They do physical & electronic surveillance.

Steelman Abstracting Co

PO Box 544
Salem MO 65560

Phone: 573-729-6183
Fax: 573-729-6183

Local Retrieval Area: MO-Dent.

Normal turnaround time: 2 weeks. Projects are generally billed by the number of records located. Credit accounts are accepted.

They specialize in title insurance.

Stehlik Law Office

653 G St
Pawnee City NE 68420

Phone: 402-852-2973
Fax: 402-852-2940

Local Retrieval Area: NE-Pawnee.

Normal turnaround time: 24 hours. Projects are generally billed by the hour. Credit accounts are accepted. Personal checks are accepted.

They specialize in general law and abstracting.

Stephen's Research

PO Box 277
Owensboro KY 42302-0277

Phone: 502-687-7329

Local Retrieval Area: KY-Daviess.

Normal turnaround time: the same day, if the client has a toll free number. Projects are generally billed by the number of names searched. Projects require prepayment.

Stephens County Abstract

100 N Baylor
Breckenridge TX 76424

Phone: 817-559-9089
Fax: 817-559-8935

Local Retrieval Area: TX-Stephens.

Normal turnaround time: 2 days. Fee basis will vary by the type of project. Projects require prepayment.

Stephens County Abstract Co

PO Box 220
Duncan OK 73534

Phone: 405-255-2525
Fax: 405-255-3844

Local Retrieval Area: OK-Stephens.

Normal turnaround time: 4-5 days. Fee basis is per page and time. Credit accounts are accepted. Payment due when service is delivered.

Pat Stephens

605 Agnew
Bonham TX 75418

Phone: 903-583-5215

Local Retrieval and SOP Area: TX-Collin, Fannin, Grayson, Hunt, Lamar.

Normal turnaround time: 2-3 days. Online computer ordering is also available. Projects are generally billed by the number of names searched or records located. Credit accounts are accepted.

Correspondent relationships: OK, TX. She specializes in genealogy research, especially descendant searching and abstracting deeds.

Sarah Sterne

Rt 1 Box 67
Clarksville MO 63336

Phone: 573-242-3240

Local Retrieval Area: MO-Pike.

Normal turnaround time: varied depending on job. Projects are generally billed by the hour. Credit accounts are accepted.

She specializes in genealogy record searches.

Steve Knight Services

PO Box 1282
Jeffersonville IN 47131

Phone: 812-288-8528

Local Retrieval and SOP Area: IN-Clark, Floyd; KY-Jefferson.

Normal turnaround time: 24 hours or sooner. Projects are generally billed by the number of names searched. Projects require prepayment.

They specialize in public record research, skip trace, missing heirs, unclaimed property and service of process.

Stevens County Title

PO Box 349 280 S Oak St
Colville WA 99114

Phone: 509-684-4589
Fax: 509-684-5448

Local Retrieval Area: WA-Stevens.

Normal turnaround time: 24-48 hours. Projects are generally billed by the hour. The first project may require a prepayment.

They specialize in title searches.

Stewart and Associates Inc

50 W Douglas St Suite 1001
Freeport IL 61032-4136

Phone: 815-235-3807
Fax: 815-235-1290

Local Retrieval and SOP Area: IL-Boone, Carroll, De Kalb, Jo Daviess, Lee, Ogle, Stephenson, Whiteside, Winnebago.

Normal turnaround time: 24-48 hours for Winnebago and Stephenson, other counties average 1-5 business days. Projects are generally billed by the number of names searched. The first project may require a prepayment.

Correspondent relationships: Dubuque and Iowa. They are a licensed private detective agency that specializes in professional investigative services.

Stillwater Abstract

PO Box 806
Columbus MT 59019

Phone: 406-322-5216
Fax: 406-322-4465

Local Retrieval Area: MT-Stillwater.

Normal turnaround time: 2-3 days. Fee basis depends on the project. Credit accounts are accepted.

⊞ Donna Stovall

28 Solitaire Rd
Rocky Point NY 11778

Phone: 516-744-5834
Fax: 516-744-9379

Local Retrieval and SOP Area: NY-Suffolk.

Normal turnaround time: 48 hours. Fee basis will vary by type of project. The first project may require a prepayment. Jobs are billed monthly.

Strander Abstract Inc

PO Box 622
Crookston MN 56716

Phone: 218-281-1191
Fax: 218-281-1191

Local Retrieval Area: MN-Polk.

Normal turnaround time: 1 week. Projects are generally billed by the number of names searched. Projects require prepayment.

Strauss & Associates

529 Court St Suite 510
Reading PA 19606

Phone: 610-378-9020
Fax: 610-378-9020

Local Retrieval Area: PA-Berks.

Normal turnaround time: 24-48 hours. Projects are generally billed by the number of names searched. Credit accounts are accepted.

Correspondent relationships: New York City, NY and Philadelphia, PA. They specialize in heir/probate research. They are also accredited genealogists.

Street Abstract Co

PO Box 306
Yates Center KS 66783

Phone: 316-625-2421
Fax: 316-625-3631

Local Retrieval Area: KS-Allen, Coffey, Woodson.

Normal turnaround time: 48 hours. Fee basis varies by type of transaction. The first project may require a prepayment.

Keith Street

325 Franklin
Wapello IA 52653-1515

Phone: 319-523-8164

Local Retrieval Area: IA-Louisa.

Normal turnaround time: 1-7 days. Projects are generally billed by the number of names searched. Credit accounts are accepted.

He specializes in genealogy searches.

Marg M Strein

PO Box 132
Taylor PA 18517

Phone: 717-457-3939
Fax: 717-457-3939

Local Retrieval Area: PA-Lackawanna.

Normal turnaround time: 24 hours. Projects are generally billed by the number of names searched. Miscellaneous research charged by the hour. Projects require prepayment.

She specializes in civil/criminal for state/county and Federal records. Miscellanous research would include a state statute/law or county matter.

Joan Strickland

32 Windmill Hill Rd
Branford CT 06405

Phone: 203-488-6251
Fax: 203-483-7136

Local Retrieval Area: CT-New Haven.

Normal turnaround time: 1 week. Projects are generally billed by the number of names searched. Charges can also be based on a per address fee. Credit accounts are accepted.

Strother-Wilbourn Land Title Co

308 E Market Ave
Searcy AR 72143

Phone: 501-268-8273
Fax: 501-268-3275

Local Retrieval Area: AR-White.

Normal turnaround time: 5-10 days. Fee basis will vary by the type of project. Credit accounts are accepted.

They specialize in title insurance.

Stutsman County Abstract

113 3rd St SW
Jamestown ND 58401

Phone: 701-252-4870
Fax: 701-252-4960

Local Retrieval Area: ND-La Moure, Stutsman.

Normal turnaround time: 2-5 days. Fee basis will vary by type of project. The first project may require a prepayment.

Correspondent relationships: the rest of North Dakota.

⊞ Suburban Record Research

12 Main St
Dover MA 02030

Phone: 617-536-3486
Fax: 508-785-2852

Local Retrieval Area: MA-Essex, Middlesex, Norfolk, Suffolk, Worcester.

Normal turnaround time: 24-48 hours. A same day rush service is also available. Projects are generally billed by the number of names searched. Credit accounts are accepted.

They specialize in UCC, court record searches and real estate record searches.

Suit McCartney Price

207 Court Square
Flemingsburg KY 41041

Phone: 606-849-2338
Fax: 606-845-8701

Local Retrieval Area: KY-Fleming.

Normal turnaround time: up to 1 week. Projects are generally billed by the hour. The first project may require a prepayment.

Sullivan County Abstract Co

217 E 3rd St
Milan MO 63556

Phone: 816-265-3744
Fax: 816-265-4908

Local Retrieval Area: MO-Sullivan.

Normal turnaround time: 2 days. Fee basis will vary by the type of project. Credit accounts are accepted.

They specialize in title insurance.

Sullivan County Abstract Inc

PO Box 430
Sullivan IN 47882

Phone: 812-268-4242
Fax: 812-268-0564

Local Retrieval Area: IN-Sullivan.

Normal turnaround time: 3 weeks. Fee basis will vary by type of project. The first project may require a prepayment.

🏛 Summit Documents

PO Box 1603
Owensboro KY 42301

Phone: 502-281-5406
Fax: 502-281-5406

Local Retrieval Area: IN-Perry, Spencer, Vanderburgh, Warrick; KY-Daviess, Hancock, Henderson, Ohio, Union, Webster.

Normal turnaround time: 24-48 hours. Projects are generally billed by the number of names searched. Credit accounts are accepted.

Sunrise Title Co

193 N State #73-13
Roosevelt UT 84066

Phone: 800-244-1644
801-722-2257
Fax: 801-722-2258

Local Retrieval Area: UT-Carbon, Daggett, Duchesne, Emery, Uintah.

Normal turnaround time: 1 week to 10 days for mineral searches and 3 days for others. Projects are generally billed by the hour. Credit accounts are accepted.

They specialize in real estate.

Sunshine State Abstract & Title

5606 US 27 N
Sebring FL 33870

Phone: 941-382-9797
Fax: 941-382-8513

Local Retrieval Area: FL-Highlands.

Normal turnaround time: 1 week. Fee basis will vary by the type of project. Credit accounts are accepted.

Sunstate Research Associates Inc

143 Whetherbine Way W
Tallahassee FL 32301

Phone: 800-621-7234
904-656-5454

Local Retrieval Area: FL-Calhoun, Gadsden, Holmes, Jackson, Jefferson, Leon, Liberty, Madison, Wakulla, Washington; GA-Brooks, Colquitt, Cook, Decatur, Grady, Lowndes, Miller, Mitchell, Seminole, Thomas.

Normal turnaround time: the same or next day for Secretary of State, and 1 to 3 days for the remainder of their service area. Projects are generally billed by the number of names searched. The first project may require a prepayment. Personal checks are accepted.

Correspondent relationships: Pinellas and Hillsborough counties. They specialize in filing and retrieval of UCC and corporate documents from the Florida Secretary of State. They also search federal and state tax liens.

🏛 Super Search

PO Box 770 1021 Knights Circle
Hurst TX 76053

Phone: 800-589-7029
817-589-7029
Fax: 800-687-9369
817-590-9369

Local Retrieval Area: TX-Collin, Dallas, Denton, Ellis, Hood, Johnson, Parker, Somervell, Tarrant, Wise.

Normal turnaround time: 1-2 days. Projects are generally billed by the number of names searched. Credit accounts are accepted.

Correspondent relationships: other counties in Texas. They specialize in court research, including retrieval from the Federal Records Center serving Texas, Oklahoma, Arkansas and Louisiana.

🏛 SuperBureau Inc

2600 Garden Rd 224 West
Monterey CA 93942

Phone: 800-541-6821
408-655-7700
Fax: 800-423-8915
408-372-7166

Local Retrieval Area: CA-Monterey.

Normal turnaround time: varied depending on project. Online computer ordering is also available. Fee basis will vary by the type of project. Credit accounts are accepted. Credit cards are accepted.

Correspondent relationships: nationwide. They specialize in on-line searches for corporate, UCC, licensed occupations and skip tracing.

Superior Subpoena Service

214 1st Ave
Linden NJ 07036

Phone: 908-862-5660

Local Retrieval Area: NJ-Union.

Normal turnaround time: varied depending on project. Projects are generally billed by the hour. Credit accounts are accepted.

Correspondent relationships: the rest of New Jersey. They also go to the Federal Archives in Bayonne NJ.

Superior Title and Abstract

PO Box 766
Iron Mountain MI 49801-0766

Phone: 906-774-9010
Fax: 906-774-8994

Local Retrieval Area: MI-Dickinson.

Normal turnaround time: 2 days. Projects are generally billed by the hour. Credit accounts are accepted.

Correspondent relationships: all counties in the upper penisula of Michigan.

Surety Abstract & Title Company

174 N Avon Ave
Phillips WI 54555

Phone: 715-339-2110
Fax: 715-339-4975

Local Retrieval Area: WI-Ashland.

Normal turnaround time: 48 hours. Fee basis varies by type of transaction. The first project may require a prepayment.

Surety Title Co

PO Box 551
New Rockford ND 58356

Phone: 701-947-2446
Fax: 701-947-2443

Local Retrieval Area: ND-Benson, Eddy, Griggs.

Normal turnaround time: 5 days. Fee basis will vary by the type of project. Credit accounts are accepted.

Surety Title Co of Ballenger

803 Hutchings
Ballinger TX 76821

Phone: 915-365-5713
Fax: 915-365-3897

Local Retrieval Area: TX-Runnels.

Normal turnaround time: 1-2 days. Fee basis will vary by the type of project. The first project may require a prepayment.

Surety Title Co of Eden

19 Market
Eden TX 76837

Phone: 915-869-7081
Fax: 915-869-5426

Local Retrieval Area: TX-Concho.

Normal turnaround time: 1-2 days. Fee basis will vary by the type of project. The first project may require a prepayment.

Surety Title Co of San Angelo
Phone: 915-658-7588
Fax: 915-655-3743
136 W Twohig Ave
San Angelo TX 76903
Local Retrieval Area: TX-Tom Green.

Normal turnaround time: 1-2 days. Fee basis will vary by the type of project. The first project may require a prepayment.

Suwanne Title and Abstract Inc
Phone: 352-493-2564
Fax: 352-493-2111
PO Box 889
Chiefland FL 32626
Local Retrieval Area: FL-Dixie, Gilchrist, Levy.

Normal turnaround time: 5-10 working days. Projects are generally billed by the number of names searched. Fee basis may per parcel for real estate searches. Credit accounts are accepted. They require a non refundable deposit. Payment is deducted from closing proceeds, if they handle the closing.

They specialize in title searches and real estate closings.

_T_

T D Disheroone Land Surveyor
Phone: 800-645-0665
Fax: 817-732-2014
6717 Calmont Ave
Fort Worth TX 76116
Local Retrieval Area: TX-Denton, Hood, Johnson, Parker, Tarrant, Wise.

Normal turnaround time: 5 working days. Credit accounts are accepted.

They specialize in boundary searches.

T D Title Services
Phone: 804-633-6868
Fax: 804-633-9436
PO Box 1072
Bowling Green VA 22427
Local Retrieval Area: VA-Caroline, King George, King and Queen.

Normal turnaround time: 1-2 days. Fee basis varies by type of transaction. The first project may require a prepayment.

T L Dearth Records Research
Phone: 813-671-2140
11425 Rustic Pine Ct
Riverview FL 33569
Local Retrieval Area: FL-Hillsborough, Pasco, Pinellas, Polk.

Normal turnaround time: 12-24 hours. Projects are generally billed by the number of records located. Credit accounts are accepted. Projects must be paid within 2 weeks of completion.

They specialize in bankruptcy, federal court, criminal, tax liens and judgments, UCC's, and county and civil court records.

T.G.I.F.
Phone: 217-223-4186
PO Box 5032
Quincy IL 62305
Local Retrieval Area: IL-Adams.

Normal turnaround time: 24 hours. Credit accounts are accepted. Will send billing statements.

TABB Inc
Phone: 800-887-8222
908-879-2323
Fax: 908-879-8675
PO Box 10
Chester NJ 07930
Local Retrieval Area: NJ-Middlesex, Morris, Somerset.

Normal turnaround time: 2 days. Projects are generally billed by the number of names searched. The first project may require a prepayment.

Talone and Associates
Phone: 800-553-5189
215-546-6080
Fax: 215-546-2412
423 S 15th St
Philadelphia PA 19146
Local Retrieval Area: NJ-Burlington, Camden, Gloucester; PA-Bucks, Chester, Delaware, Montgomery, Philadelphia.

Normal turnaround time: varied depending on project. Projects are generally billed by the hour. Credit accounts are accepted.

Tama County Abstract
Phone: 515-484-4386
Fax: 515-484-5449
PO Box 2
Toledo IA 52342
Local Retrieval Area: IA-Tama.

Normal turnaround time: 3-5 days. Fee basis varies by type of transaction. Projects require prepayment.

Tappan Abstract
Phone: 501-338-3311
Fax: 501-338-8221
430 Ohio St
Helena AR 72342
Local Retrieval Area: AR-Phillips.

Normal turnaround time: 2-3 days. Projects are generally billed by the hour. Projects require prepayment.

They specialize in title insurance.

Tarheel Paralegal Services
Phone: 910-455-3178
5 Laran Rd
Jacksonville NC 28540-5723
Local Retrieval Area: NC-Onslow.

Normal turnaround time: 24 hours, except for real estate. Projects are generally billed by the number of names searched. Flat rate for real estate title searches. Credit accounts are accepted. Payment due upon receipt of invoice.

Correspondent relationships: All of North Carolina less Onslow. They specialize in criminal record checks, UCC filing/searches, document retrieval and real estate title searches/filings.

Taurus Data Search
Phone: 308-436-3173
Fax: 308-436-7535
PO Box 327
Gering NE 69341
Local Retrieval Area: NE-Banner, Box Butte, Cheyenne, Morrill, Scotts Bluff.

Credit accounts are accepted. Credit cards are accepted..dd.

Taylor Abstract Co
Phone: 316-285-2026
Fax: 316-285-2753
114 W 5th St
Larned KS 67550
Local Retrieval Area: KS-Pawnee.

Normal turnaround time: 3 days. Fee basis varies by type of transaction. The first project may require a prepayment.

Taylor Title Inc
Phone: 318-741-1373
Fax: 318-741-1821
PO Box 5377 3018 Old Minden Rd #1208
Bossier City LA 71171-5377
Local Retrieval Area: LA-Bossier Parish, Caddo Parish.

Normal turnaround time: 1 week. Projects are generally billed by the hour. Credit accounts are accepted.

Correspondent relationships: Webster, Red River, DeSoto and Natchitoches. They specialize in title searches and real estate.

Team Eagle

10675 110th St
Cologne MN 55322

Phone:	800-251-2540
	612-466-4778
Fax:	800-321-4135
	612-466-2600

Local Retrieval Area: MN-16 Counties; ND-Cass.

Normal turnaround time: 24-48 hours for criminal, UCC's. Vary somewhat by location. Online computer ordering is also available. Projects are generally billed by the number of names searched. Credit accounts are accepted.

Correspondent relationships: nationwide. They specialize in criminal record searches and UCC's.

Teeters Abstract and Title Co

1200 Main St
Goodland KS 67735

| Phone: | 913-899-7138 |
| Fax: | 913-899-6644 |

Local Retrieval Area: KS-Sherman, Wallace.

Normal turnaround time: 2 days. Projects are generally billed by the hour. The first project may require a prepayment.

Correspondent relationships: Greeley and Cheyenne Counties. They specialize in real estate searches.

Tenant Registry Inc

212 Saxon Dr
Springfield IL 62704

| Phone: | 217-793-8146 |
| Fax: | 217-793-8175 |

Local Retrieval Area: IL-Sangamon.

Normal turnaround time: 24 hours. Projects are generally billed by the number of names searched. Credit accounts are accepted. Will do monthly billing.

Teresa D Havens & Associates

PO Box 95
Yampa CO 80483-0095

| Phone: | 970-638-0455 |
| Fax: | 970-638-0477 |

Local Retrieval and SOP Area: CO-Routt.

Normal turnaround time: varies with the service requested. Projects are generally billed by the hour. The first project may require a prepayment.

They specialize in financial investigations and litigation support services. Other services include local document retrieval and research, civil process service and skip tracing.

Territorial Title

PO Box 987
Las Vegas NM 87701

| Phone: | 505-425-3563 |
| Fax: | 505-425-9637 |

Local Retrieval Area: NM-Guadalupe, Mora, San Miguel; OK-Alfalfa.

Normal turnaround time: 1 week for San Miguel, 4 weeks for Mora and 2 weeks for Guadelupe. Projects are generally billed by the hour. Credit accounts are accepted.

They specialize in title insurance and closings.

Terry Sharp Law Office

PO Box 906
Mt Vernon IL 62864

| Phone: | 618-242-0246 |
| Fax: | 618-242-1170 |

Local Retrieval Area: IL-Franklin, Jefferson, Marion, Williamson.

Normal turnaround time: 3-5 days. Projects are generally billed by the hour. Credit accounts are accepted.

They specialize in real estate searches.

Texas Abstract Services

412 Main St Suite 250
Houston TX 77002

Phone:	800-484-5690
	713-221-1757
Fax:	713-221-1756

Local Retrieval Area: TX-Bexar, Brazoria, Dallas, Fort Bend, Galveston, Harris, Montgomery, Nueces, Travis, Wharton.

Normal turnaround time: 1-3 days. Flat fee per order, quoted in advance. The first project may require a prepayment.

Correspondent relationships: nationwide. They are a full service abstract company that specializes in historical deed searches (environmental) and abstractor's certificates. They also do oil and gas title research.

Texas Civil Process

1731 S Staples
Corpus Christi TX 78463-3785

Phone:	800-976-9595
	512-887-9595
Fax:	512-887-9597

Local Retrieval and SOP Area: TX-11 Counties.

Normal turnaround time: 1 day. Projects are generally billed by the number of names searched or records located. The first project may require a prepayment. Invoiced payment net 30 days.

Correspondent relationships: Bexar, Travis, Harris, Tarrant, Dallas, McMillian, Cameron, Hidalgo, Williamson and Taylor. They specialize in process service, record research and skip tracing. Licensed Private Investigator on staff.

Texas Industrial Security Inc

1140 Empire Central Suite 635
Dallas TX 75247

| Phone: | 214-634-2791 |

Local Retrieval Area: TX-Bexar, Dallas, Tarrant.

Normal turnaround time: 2-5 days. Project billing methods vary. Projects require prepayment.

They specialize in asset locations.

Texas Legal Support Service

PO Box 331623
Corpus Christi TX 78463-1623

| Phone: | 512-883-2247 |
| Fax: | 512-883-4515 |

Local Retrieval Area: TX-Aransas, Jim Wells, Kleberg, Nueces, San Patricio.

Normal turnaround time: the same day for Nueces County. Other counties are 24 to 48 hours. Projects are generally billed by the number of names searched. Credit accounts are accepted.

They specialize in bankruptcy and lien searches.

Texas Records Search

2223 Mangum Suite 210
Houston TX 77092

Phone:	800-869-1405
	713-862-2698
Fax:	713-862-2798

Local Retrieval and SOP Area: TX-Brazoria, Chambers, Fort Bend, Galveston, Harris, Jefferson, Liberty, Montgomery, Orange.

Normal turnaround time: 24 hours. Projects are generally billed by the number of names searched or records located. The first project may require a prepayment. Personal checks are accepted.

They specialize in courthouse research in Southeast Texas.

Thalken Abstract & Title Co

PO Box 307 520 N Spruce
Ogallala NE 69153

| Phone: | 308-284-3972 |
| Fax: | 308-284-6802 |

Local Retrieval Area: NE-Arthur, Banner, Chase, Deuel, Garden, Grant, Keith, Perkins.

Normal turnaround time: 1 day. Fee basis varies by type of transaction. Credit accounts are accepted.

They specialize in title insurance searches.

Thayer County Abstract Office Inc

Phone: 402-768-6324
Fax: 402-768-7274

PO Box 207
Hebron NE 68370

Local Retrieval Area: NE-Thayer.

Normal turnaround time: 3-5 days. They charge a flat rate per project. Credit accounts are accepted.

They specialize in title insurance.

The Abstract & Title Co

Phone: 701-872-4531
Fax: 701-872-4241

PO Box 369
Beach ND 58621

Local Retrieval Area: ND-Golden Valley.

Normal turnaround time: 3-5 days. Projects are generally billed by the number of names searched. The first project may require a prepayment.

The Amherst Group

Phone: 800-521-0237
909-785-5777
Fax: 909-785-5888

4804 Arlington Ave Suite A
Riverside CA 92506

Local Retrieval Area: CA-16 Counties.

Normal turnaround time: 24-48 hours. Projects are generally billed by the number of names searched. Credit accounts are accepted. Credit cards are accepted. Terms are net 20 days.

Correspondent relationships: nationwide. They specialize in national criminal, credit and motor vehicle records.

The August Professional Group

Phone: 415-441-9627
Fax: 415-749-3887

880 Bush St Suite 208
San Francisco CA 94108

Local Retrieval and SOP Area: CA-Alameda, Contra Costa, Marin, San Francisco, San Mateo.

Normal turnaround time: 24-48 hours. Projects are generally billed by the number of names searched. The first project may require a prepayment.

Correspondent relationships: Santa Clara, Monterey, Santa Cruz, Sonoma and Sacramento counties. They specialize in criminal background checks for pre-employment screening. They also offer a full range of attorney support services for service of process, photocopying and court filings.

The Bister Agency

Phone: 800-247-8375
803-838-2307
Fax: 803-838-7089

PO Box 1172
Beaufort SC 29901

Local Retrieval and SOP Area: SC-Beaufort.

Normal turnaround time: 4 business days. Expedited service available. Projects are generally billed by the hour. Mileage and expenses are added to the hourly fee. Credit accounts are accepted.

Correspondent relationships: the state of South Carolina and Savannah, Georgia. They specialize in investigation, surveillance and process service.

The Cole Group

Phone: 713-880-9494
Fax: 713-880-9595

5225 Katy Fwy Suite 490
Houston TX 77007

Local Retrieval Area: TX-Bexar, Dallas, Harris, Montgomery, Tarrant.

Normal turnaround time: 1 day. Projects are generally billed by the number of names searched. Credit accounts are accepted. Terms are net 30 days.

Correspondent relationships: nationwide. They specialize in applicant screening.

The Copy Store & More - Reno

Phone: 702-329-0999
Fax: 702-329-3402

333 Flint St
Reno NV 89501

Local Retrieval Area: NV-Washoe.

Normal turnaround time: the same day. Fee basis varies by type of transaction. The first project may require a prepayment.

Correspondent relationships: the rest of Nevada. They specialize in legal support services.

The Court System Inc

Phone: 800-856-0585
214-744-0585
Fax: 214-744-0586

1700 Commerce Suite 1050
Dallas TX 75201

Local Retrieval Area: TX-16 Counties.

Normal turnaround time: 1-2 days in Dallas, and 1 to 3 days in most areas outside of Dallas. Expedited service available. Projects are generally billed by the number of names searched. The first project may require a prepayment. Terms are net 10 and COD.

Correspondent relationships: nationwide. They specialize in bankruptcy, Federal local court research and retrieval, all public records and corporate services.

▥ The Coynes

Phone: 215-945-6227
Fax: 215-945-9470

29 Graceful Ln
Levittown PA 19055

Local Retrieval and SOP Area: NJ-Burlington, Camden, Mercer; PA-Bucks, Chester, Delaware, Montgomery, Philadelphia.

Normal turnaround time: 24 hours. They charge per name and per index. Credit accounts are accepted.

They retrieve records from the US Coast Guard-Philadelphia, Federal Records Center and the New Jersey Superior Court Record Center.

▥ The Croson Agency

Phone: 304-343-1564
Fax: 304-727-1353

241 Peoples Building 179 Summers St
Charleston WV 25301

Local Retrieval Area: WV-All Counties.

Normal turnaround time: often the same day. A search may take 24 to 48 hours. Projects are generally billed by the number of names searched or records located. The first project may require a prepayment. Terms are net 30 days.

Correspondent relationships: Kentucky, Virginia, Ohio, Tennessee and Indiana. They have been serving the legal profession since 1958.

The Daily Report

Phone: 805-322-3226
Fax: 805-322-9084

1705 K St
Bakersfield CA 93301

Local Retrieval Area: CA-Kern.

Normal turnaround time: 2 days. Projects are generally billed by the hour. Credit accounts are accepted. Credit cards are accepted.

They specialize in legal advertising. They also search at the municipal court level.

The Dataprompt Corporation

4902 Colleyville Blvd Suite 108
Colleyville TX 76034

Phone: 800-577-8157
817-577-8157
Fax: 800-340-3854
817-498-3282

Local Retrieval Area: IN-Marion; TX-Bexar, Collin, Dallas, Denton, Harris, Hunt, Tarrant, Travis.

Normal turnaround time: next day. Projects are generally billed by the number of names searched. Credit accounts are accepted. Terms are net 30 days.

Correspondent relationships: nationwide including Puerto Rico. They specialize in criminal and eviction record data on a per report basis or in a full database format.

The Electronic Detective

5309 Walzem Rd Suite 105
San Antonio TX 78218

Phone: 210-653-2110
Fax: 210-653-4097

Local Retrieval Area: TX-Bexar.

Normal turnaround time: same day up to 24 hours. Online computer ordering is also available. Projects are generally billed by the number of records located. The first project may require a prepayment.

They have dial-in computer service at 1-210-656-6757 (8-N-1). They specialize in criminal history, missing persons, asset discovery and background investigations.

The Fatman Intl Private Detective

194 N Union St
Battle Creek MI 49017

Phone: 616-964-2445
Fax: 616-949-4800

Local Retrieval and SOP Area: MI-Barry, Calhoun, Kent.

Normal turnaround time: 1-2 days. Fee basis varies by type of transaction. Credit accounts are accepted. They ask for a retainer.

Correspondent relationships: worldwide. They specialize in investigations.

The Gordon Company of Colby

450 N Franklin
Colby KS 67701-0489

Phone: 913-462-7555
Fax: 913-462-2099

Local Retrieval Area: KS-Logan, Sheridan, Sherman, Thomas.

Normal turnaround time: 24 hours. Online computer ordering is also available. Projects are generally billed by the number of names searched or records located. Credit accounts are accepted. Credit cards are accepted. Personal checks are accepted.

They specialize in title insurance searches.

The H O Smith Company

104 E 7th
Lexington NE 68850

Phone: 308-324-2216
Fax: 308-324-6443

Local Retrieval Area: NE-Dawson.

Normal turnaround time: 2-7 days. Projects are generally billed by the number of names searched or records located. Credit accounts are accepted.

Correspondent relationships: Frontier and Gosper Counties. They specialize in title insurance and abstracting.

The Home Abstract Co

2380 Washington Suite 200
Ogden UT 84401

Phone: 800-669-7861
801-621-7861
Fax: 801-621-7850

Local Retrieval Area: UT-Box Elder, Cache, Davis, Morgan, Summit, Weber.

Normal turnaround time: 24 hours. The first project may require a prepayment. Credit cards are accepted. Terms are net 30 days. Personal checks are accepted.

Correspondent relationships: all counties in Utah. They specialize in title insurance.

The Information Bank of Texas

111 W 14th St
Houston TX 77008

Phone: 713-864-9122
Fax: 713-862-6237

Local Retrieval and SOP Area: TX-Brazoria, Dallas, Fort Bend, Galveston, Harris, Montgomery, Tarrant, Travis.

Normal turnaround time: 5-7 working days. Projects are generally billed by the number of names searched. The first project may require a prepayment. Credit cards are accepted. Personal checks are accepted. Billing after each assignment.

Correspondent relationships: most Texas counties and many counties nationwide. They specialize in asset investigations and public record searches. They also have nationwide capabilities for multitude of information databanks.

The Information Super Store

PO Box 5992
Scottsdale AZ 85261-5992

Phone: 800-774-6585
602-661-7964
Fax: 800-774-6586

Local Retrieval Area: AZ-Coconino, Maricopa, Mohave, Pima.

Normal turnaround time: 1-3 days. Online computer ordering is also available. Projects are generally billed by the number of names searched. The first project may require a prepayment. Credit cards are accepted.

Correspondent relationships: nationwide and Canada. They specialize in pre-employment screening, property management (tenant), asset searches, pre-trial preparation and locates.

The Knowledge Bank

23679 Calabasas Rd Suite 274
Calabasas CA 91302-3306

Phone: 818-224-5235
Fax: 818-224-4827

Local Retrieval Area: CA-Los Angeles, Ventura.

Normal turnaround time: 2-5 days. Expedited service available. Projects are generally billed by the hour. Fees are plus expenses and charges for faxing and express delivery. The first project may require a prepayment. Credit cards are accepted.

They speciailze in public records searching--in particular--on-line & traditional legal research-to attorneys. Court record retrieval, review and analysis are also provided. Pre-Employement screening/tenant screening are also offered.

The Legal Source

PO Box 1542
Chico CA 95927

Phone: 800-786-8163
916-895-8163
Fax: 916-891-6616

Local Retrieval Area: CA-Butte, Colusa, Glenn, Lassen, Nevada, Plumas, Shasta, Sutter, Tehama, Yuba.

Normal turnaround time: up to 5 days for remote counties. Rush service is also available. Projects are generally billed by the number of records located. Charge is by location and by the page. The first project may require a prepayment. Terms are net 30 days.

Correspondent relationships: all of California, Nevada and Oregon. They also prepare subpoenas to retrieve and photocopy records.

The Marston Agency Inc

PO Box 29940
Richmond VA 23242

Phone: 800-308-7790
804-784-0111
Fax: 804-784-4807

Local Retrieval and SOP Area: VA-Chesterfield, Goochland, Hanover, Henrico, City of Petersburg, City of Richmond.

Normal turnaround time: 24-72 hours. Projects are generally billed by the hour. The first project may require a prepayment.

Correspondent relationships: nationwide.

The Niles Agency

350 Ward Ave Suite 106
Honolulu HI 96814

Phone: 808-591-7707
Fax: 808-596-0940

Local Retrieval and SOP Area: HI-Honolulu.

Normal turnaround time: 48 hours. Online computer ordering is also available. Projects are generally billed by the hour. The first project may require a prepayment. Personal checks are accepted.

They specialize in fraud investigations.

The North Dakota Guaranty & Title

400 E Broadway Ave Suite 409
Bismarck ND 58501

Phone: 701-223-6835
Fax: 701-224-1571

Local Retrieval Area: ND-Burleigh.

Normal turnaround time: 2-3 days. Projects are generally billed by the number of names searched. They charge a minimum charge; however, the fee basis will vary by type of project. Credit accounts are accepted.

They specialize in title and UCC searches.

The Pettit Company

1744 Theresa Ln
Powhatan VA 23139

Phone: 800-752-6158
804-379-2462
Fax: 800-236-2859
804-379-3217

Local Retrieval Area: VA-11 Counties.

Normal turnaround time: 1-2 days. Projects are generally billed by the number of names searched. Credit accounts are accepted. Terms are net 30 days.

Correspondent relationships: nationwide. They specialize in providing quick, accurate and inexpensive personal service. They also offer filing services nationwide. Call to discuss special needs.

The Pre-Check Company

14701 Detroit Ave Suite 370
Lakewood OH 44107-4109

Phone: 216-226-7700
Fax: 216-226-0777

Local Retrieval Area: OH-Cuyahoga, Franklin, Lake, Lorain, Summit.

Normal turnaround time: 3 days. Projects are generally billed by the number of names searched. The first project may require a prepayment.

Correspondent relationships: nationwide. They specialize in national pre-employment background checks. Services include criminal, credit, motor vehicle reports, drug tests, workers' compensation and employment histories.

The R M Jaqua Abstract Co

Box 665
St Francis KS 67756

Phone: 913-332-3041

Local Retrieval Area: KS-Cheyenne.

Normal turnaround time: within 48 hours. Projects are generally billed by the number of names searched. Credit accounts are accepted. Personal checks are accepted.

The Records Reviewer Inc

PO Box 600577
North Miami Beach FL 33160

Phone: 954-947-1186
Fax: 954-962-3764

Local Retrieval Area: FL-Broward, Dade, Palm Beach.

Normal turnaround time: 48 hours or less. Expedited service available. They bill by the 1/4 hour. The first project may require a prepayment.

Correspondent relationships: Palm Beach, Hillsborough, Pinellas and Orange counties. They specialize in bankruptcy, environmental searches and criminal searches.

The Research Staff Inc

5718 Hewitt St
Houston TX 77092-5125

Phone: 800-822-3584
713-688-3584
Fax: 713-688-1121

Local Retrieval Area: TX-22 Counties.

Normal turnaround time: 24-48 hours. Rush service is available. Projects are generally billed by the number of names searched. The first project may require a prepayment.

Correspondent relationships: the entire state of Texas. They specialize in property reports (all kinds), specific name searches, UCC, T/L, A/J, business closings, asset searches and courts (all levels). Will design reports for special projects.

The Search Is On

1912 Hays St
Nashville TN 37203

Phone: 800-324-2050
615-321-2050
Fax: 800-788-0835
615-329-3343

Local Retrieval Area: TN-Davidson, Sumner, Williamson, Wilson.

Normal turnaround time: 1-3 days. Online computer ordering is also available. Projects are generally billed by the number of names searched. Credit accounts are accepted.

Correspondent relationships: TN and KY. They specialize in UCC, tax liens, judgments and current owner searches.

The Seto Company

2000 "L" St NW Suite 200
Washington DC 20036

Phone: 202-416-1898
Fax: 202-466-8865

Local Retrieval Area: DC-District of Columbia; MD-Montgomery, Prince George's; VA-City of Alexandria, Arlington, Fairfax.

Normal turnaround time: 1-2 days. Projects are generally billed by the number of names searched. The first project may require a prepayment.

Correspondent relationships: nationwide. They specialize in complex commercial investigations and asset searches.

The Title Co Inc

317 9th St
Sibley IA 51249

Phone: 712-754-2284
Fax: 712-754-3195

Local Retrieval Area: IA-Osceola.

Normal turnaround time: 1-3 days. Fee basis will vary by the type of project. The first project may require a prepayment.

The Title Co Inc

618 S Barstow St
Eau Claire WI 54701

Phone: 715-838-2800
Fax: 715-726-9507

Local Retrieval Area: WI-Chippewa, Dunn, Eau Claire.

Normal turnaround time: varied depending on project. Title insurance search fees are preset by insurance. Credit accounts are accepted.

They specialize in title insurance, abstracting and judgment searches.

The Todd Wiegele Research Co

Phone: 800-754-7800

1345 16th Ave #6   414-276-3393

Grafton WI 53024   **Fax:** 414-276-3395

Local Retrieval Area: WI-Milwaukee, Ozaukee, Washington, Waukesha.

Normal turnaround time: 24 hours. No project billing information was given. The first project may require a prepayment. Terms are net 15 days.

They specialize in real estate, civil, criminal, on-line database searches, marketing and asset investigations. They are covered by error and ommissions policy. They are located in the Milwaukee County Counthouse.

Donna Thomas

Phone: 402-339-7291

1019 Tekamah Ln   **Fax:** 402-339-0051

Papillion NE 68128-6245

Local Retrieval Area: IA-Harrison, Mills, Pottawattamie; NE-Cass, Douglas, Sarpy, Washington.

Normal turnaround time: 24-48 hours. Expedited service available. Projects are generally billed by the number of names searched. The first project may require a prepayment. Personal checks are accepted.

Correspondent relationships: Iowa, Audubon, Cass, Crawford, Shelby, Page, Union, Adair, Muscatine, Mills, IA counties. Dodge and Sanders, NE counties. She specializes in genealogy. She is compiling a book on Audubon county, IA cemetery inscriptions. She also performs research for maiden and other married names for indexing the book.

Julie L Thomas

Phone: 815-234-2261

7645 N Crestview Rd   **Fax:** 815-234-2261

Stillman Valley IL 61084

Local Retrieval and SOP Area: IL-Boone, Ogle, Stephenson, Winnebago.

Normal turnaround time: same day if requested before 8:30AM. Projects are generally billed by the number of names searched. Credit accounts are accepted. Will send bill at the end of the month.

Correspondent relationships: McHenry, Kane, DeKalb and Dupage, IL counties; Dane, WI county.

Thompson & Hollingsworth PA

Phone: 601-469-3411

PO Drawer 119   **Fax:** 601-469-3411

Forest MS 39074

Local Retrieval Area: MS-Scott.

Normal turnaround time: 1 day. Projects are generally billed by the hour. The first project may require a prepayment.

They are in general practice. They specialize in marriage/divorce searches.

Three Rivers Title Co

Phone: 219-424-2929

727 Clinton St Suite 100   **Fax:** 219-424-0037

Fort Wayne IN 46802-1801

Local Retrieval Area: IN-11 Counties.

Normal turnaround time: 2-3 days. Fee basis varies by type of transaction. Credit accounts are accepted.

Thurman Investigative Services Inc

Phone: 912-759-1700

110 Starksville St   **Fax:** 912-759-9652

Leesburg GA 31763

Local Retrieval Area: GA-12 Counties.

Normal turnaround time: 24-48 hours. Projects are generally billed by the hour. Credit accounts are accepted.

They specialize in criminal and civil matters as well as insurance fraud investigation.

Nellie Tilton

Phone: 513-839-1176

48 W 3rd St   **Fax:** 513-839-1176

West Alexandria OH 45381

Local Retrieval Area: OH-Butler, Darke, Miami, Montgomery, Preble.

Normal turnaround time: 48-72 hours for real estate records and 72 hours for all other. Fee basis will vary by the type of project. Credit accounts are accepted. Bill month following project.

They specialize in title work.

Tinnon Beshear Abstract Co

Phone: 501-325-6832

PO Box 487   **Fax:** 501-325-6265

Rison AR 71665

Local Retrieval Area: AR-Cleveland.

Normal turnaround time: 3-5 days. Fee basis will vary by the type of project. The first project may require a prepayment.

They specialize in title insurance, searches, and reports.

Tippecanoe Title Services Inc

Phone: 317-423-2457

133 N 4th St Suite 32   **Fax:** 317-742-0194

Lafayette IN 47901

Local Retrieval Area: IN-Benton, Carroll, Cass, Clinton, Fountain, Jasper, Montgomery, Tippecanoe, Warren, White.

Normal turnaround time: 3-7 days. Projects are generally billed by the number of records located. Credit accounts are accepted.

Title Abstract Co

Phone: 913-364-2040

120 W 5th Courthouse Square   **Fax:** 913-364-3420

Holton KS 66436

Local Retrieval Area: KS-Jackson.

Normal turnaround time: 2 days for name searches, 1 week for title insurance and 2 weeks for abstracting. Projects are generally billed by the number of names searched. Credit accounts are accepted. Personal checks are accepted.

Title Abstract Co

Phone: 918-273-0225

119 N Maple St   **Fax:** 918-273-0259

Nowata OK 74048

Local Retrieval Area: OK-Nowata.

Normal turnaround time: 24-36 hours. Projects are generally billed by the hour. Projects require prepayment.

They are the county's only source of complete records (the court house burned down in 1911), and the only company in the county with computerized records.

Title Abstract Services

Phone: 410-228-1188
Fax: 410-228-1572

501 Poplar St
Cambridge MD 21613

Local Retrieval Area: MD-Caroline, Dorchester, Talbot.

Normal turnaround time: 24-48 hours. Fee basis will vary with type of search. Credit accounts are accepted. Payment due upon completion/settlement.

Correspondent relationships: Eastern Shore counties. She specializes in title searches and P and J's.

⛁ Title Express Inc

Phone: 423-587-9886
Fax: 423-587-5682

4940 Davy Crockett Pky
Morristown TN 37813

Local Retrieval Area: TN-Claiborne, Cocke, Grainger, Greene, Hamblen, Hancock, Hawkins, Jefferson, Sevier.

Normal turnaround time: 48 hours. Projects are generally billed by the number of names searched. The first project may require a prepayment.

Correspondent relationships: Washington. They specialize in real estate title examinations and UCC searches.

Title Guaranty & Trust

Phone: 615-266-5751
Fax: 615-265-8855

617 Walnut St
Chattanooga TN 37402

Local Retrieval Area: AL-Cherokee, De Kalb, Houston; GA-Catoosa, Chattooga, Dade, Fannin, Gilmer, Gordon, Murray, Walker, Whitfield; TN-15 Counties.

Normal turnaround time: 2 days. Projects are generally billed by the hour. The first project may require a prepayment.

Correspondent relationships: nationwide. They specialize in title insurance.

⛁ Title Runners

Phone: 805-685-5576
Fax: 805-685-2099

PO Box 92247
Santa Barbara CA 93190

Local Retrieval Area: CA-Santa Barbara, Ventura.

Normal turnaround time: 24-48 hours. Expedited service available. Projects are generally billed by the number of names searched. Fees depend on the type of search. Credit accounts are accepted. Projects estimates over $300.00 require 50% prepayment of estimated final cost, otherwise payment is net 30 days of invoice date.

Correspondent relationships: San Luis Obispo, Kern and Fresno, CA counties. They specialize in title searches for 50 year environmental chains, parcel validity studies, book reports, lien searches and court research.

⛁ Title Search Services Inc

Phone: 757-490-7009
Fax: 757-456-0069

804 Newtown Rd Suite 104
Virginia Beach VA 23462

Local Retrieval Area: VA-City of Chesapeake, City of Norfolk, City of Portsmouth, City of Suffolk, City of Virginia Beach.

Normal turnaround time: 1-2 days. Projects are generally billed by the number of names searched or records located. Credit accounts are accepted.

They specialize in foreclosure searches and updates and "P & J" searches.

Title Services Inc

Phone: 800-736-9331
601-264-3500
Fax: 601-264-6622

130 Westover Dr
Hattiesburg MS 39402

Local Retrieval Area: MS-14 Counties.

Normal turnaround time: 1 day in Forrest county, 2 days all others. Fee basis varies by type of transaction. The first project may require a prepayment.

Title Services Unlimited

Phone: 803-527-6326
Fax: 803-546-2144

PO Box 611
Georgetown SC 29442

Local Retrieval Area: SC-Georgetown.

Normal turnaround time: varied depending on project. Fee basis is per project. Credit accounts are accepted.

TitleInfo

Phone: 817-244-7757
Fax: 817-244-7455

4614 Ridge North Rd
Fort Worth TX 76126

Local Retrieval Area: TX-Bexar, Collin, Dallas, Denton, Harris, Johnson, Parker, Tarrant, Travis.

Normal turnaround time: 1 week or less. Projects are generally billed by the number of names searched. Credit accounts are accepted. Terms are net 30 days.

Correspondent relationships: most of TX. They specialize in title and property searches and 50 year environmental chains for ESA SiteI assessments.

Titles of Dakota Inc

Phone: 605-365-5247
Fax: 605-365-5248

PO Box 100
Dupree SD 57623-0100

Local Retrieval Area: SD-Ziebach.

Normal turnaround time: 1 week. Fee basis will vary by the type of project. Credit accounts are accepted.

Titles of Dakota Inc

Phone: 800-794-2725
605-223-2727
Fax: 605-223-9237

PO Box 278
Fort Pierre SD 57532-0278

Local Retrieval Area: SD-Stanley.

Normal turnaround time: 1 week. Fee basis will vary by the type of project. Credit accounts are accepted.

Titles of Dakota Inc

Phone: 605-258-2291
Fax: 605-223-9237

PO Box 167
Onida SD 57564-0167

Local Retrieval Area: SD-Sully.

Normal turnaround time: 1 week. Fee basis will vary by the type of project. Credit accounts are accepted.

Correspondent relationships: Stanley, Dewey and Ziebach counties in South Dakota. They specialize in loan closings, escrow services, abstracts, and title insurance.

Titles of Dakota Inc

Phone: 605-365-5247
Fax: 605-365-5248

PO Box 402
Timber Lake SD 57656-0402

Local Retrieval Area: SD-Dewey.

Normal turnaround time: 1 week. Fee basis will vary by the type of project. Credit accounts are accepted.

Correspondent relationships: Ziebach, Selby and Stanley, SD.

Titus County Title Company

Phone: 903-577-0333
Fax: 903-577-1666

103 N Madison
Mt Pleasant TX 75455

Local Retrieval Area: TX-Titus.

Normal turnaround time: 2-3 days. Fee basis will vary by the type of project. The first project may require a prepayment.

TJM & Associates

Phone: 800-749-4254
203-227-8360
Fax: 203-221-0852

65 Norfield Rd
Weston CT 06883

Local Retrieval Area: CT-Fairfield, Hartford, Middlesex, New Haven.

Normal turnaround time: 48 hours. Expedited service available. Projects are generally billed by the number of names searched or records located. Project fees available for large projects. The first project may require a prepayment.

Toma Abstract Inc

Phone: 717-454-7899
Fax: 717-454-5999

55 N Laurel St
Hazleton PA 18201-5951

Local Retrieval Area: PA-Carbon, Columbia, Luzerne, Monroe, Montour, Northumberland, Schuylkill.

Normal turnaround time: 2 weeks or less. Projects are generally billed by the number of names searched. Credit accounts are accepted.

They specialize in title searching and title insurance.

Vicki Tomich

Phone: 304-845-7315
Fax: 304-845-7315

210 9th St
Glen Dale WV 26038

Local Retrieval Area: OH-Belmont, Guernsey, Harrison, Jefferson, Monroe, Noble; WV-Brooke, Hancock, Marshall, Ohio, Wetzel.

Normal turnaround time: 24-48 hours. Projects are generally billed by the number of names searched. Fee basis varies by type of transaction. Pick-up for out of county filings and listing changes. Credit accounts are accepted.

She specializes in non commercial property searches.

Tompkins and Watkins Abstract

Phone: 607-273-0884
Fax: 607-277-5584

215 N Cayuga St Suite 6-B, DeWitt Bldg
Ithaca NY 14850-4315

Local Retrieval Area: NY-Tompkins.

Normal turnaround time: 5-7 days. Projects are generally billed by the number of names searched. Credit accounts are accepted.

Toni Rose Associates

Phone: 800-848-0055
216-946-8681
Fax: 216-975-9808

560 Howells Ct
Eastlake OH 44095

Local Retrieval Area: OH-Cuyahoga, Erie, Geauga, Lake, Lorain, Mahoning, Portage, Trumbull.

Normal turnaround time: 4 days. Expedited service available. Projects are generally billed by the number of names searched or records located. The first project may require a prepayment.

Correspondent relationships: Florida, New York, New Jersey.

Tooele Title Company

Phone: 801-882-1120
Fax: 801-882-1111

123 W Vine
Tooele UT 84074

Local Retrieval Area: UT-Tooele.

Normal turnaround time: 2-3 days for all areas within county, 3 to 5 days for mining searches. Fee basis will vary by the type of project. Credit accounts are accepted. A setup fee and prepayment is required for individuals.

They specialize in tax sales, mining, special county searches, foreclosure reports, plating problems, escrow services and any title service.

Torri's Legal Services

Phone: 800-990-7378
202-296-0222
Fax: 202-296-4584

PO Box 18647
Washington DC 20036

Local Retrieval and SOP Area: DC-District of Columbia.

Normal turnaround time: 1 day. Expedited service available. Projects are generally billed by the number of names searched or records located. The first project may require a prepayment.

They specialize in skip tracing, process serving, asset searches, filing and court house record research.

Town & Country Abstract Co

Phone: 501-738-2055
Fax: 501-738-2075

Hwy 412W
Huntsville AR 72740

Local Retrieval Area: AR-Madison.

Normal turnaround time: 1-2 days. Fee basis will vary by the type of project. The first project may require a prepayment.

They specialize in title insurance.

Town and Country Abstract Co

Phone: 816-277-3467
Fax: 816-277-3939

101 S Main
Huntsville MO 65259

Local Retrieval Area: MO-Randolph.

Normal turnaround time: 24-48 hours. Projects are generally billed by the number of names searched or records located. Credit accounts are accepted. Personal checks are accepted.

Correspondent relationships: nationwide.

Towner County Abstract Co

Phone: 701-968-3651

PO Box 668
Cando ND 58324

Local Retrieval Area: ND-Towner.

Normal turnaround time: 2 weeks. Fee basis is per entry. The first project may require a prepayment.

Townsend Detective & Security

Phone: 414-327-0221
Fax: 414-327-0221

4900 W Norwich Ct
Milwaukee WI 53220

Local Retrieval and SOP Area: WI-Milwaukee.

Normal turnaround time: 24 hours. Projects are generally billed by the hour. The first project may require a prepayment.

They specialize in surveillance, business ijntelligence, domestic, security guard and process service.

🏛 Trace Investigations

PO Box 2603
Bloomington IN 47402

Phone: 800-310-8857
812-334-8857
Fax: 812-334-2274

Local Retrieval and SOP Area: IN-Brown, Monroe, Morgan.

Normal turnaround time: 24-48 hours. Projects are generally billed by the number of names searched. Type of search determines billing. The first project may require a prepayment. Terms are net 30 days.

Correspondent relationships: throughout Indiana for legal investigations and service of process. They specialize in legal investigations, service of process, public record retrieval and skip tracing.

🏛 Trace Unlimited

5501 N Swan Rd Suite 225
Tucson AZ 85718-5445

Phone: 520-299-0015
Fax: 520-299-0524

Local Retrieval and SOP Area: AZ-Pima.

Normal turnaround time: 2 days. Tucson municipal averages 5 days. Projects are generally billed by the hour. The first project may require a prepayment.

Correspondent relationships: Maricopa. They specialize in skip tracing and locating individuals.

🏛 Tracers International

146-148 Barrett St
Schenectady NY 12305

Phone: 800-872-2377
518-370-3463
Fax: 518-374-0335

Local Retrieval and SOP Area: NY-Albany, Rensselaer, Saratoga, Schenectady, Schoharie.

Normal turnaround time: 3-5 days. Online computer ordering is also available. Projects are generally billed by the number of records located. The first project may require a prepayment. Credit cards are accepted.

Correspondent relationships: Orange, Dutchess, Rockland, Bronx, New York, Queens, Nassau, Suffolk and Ulster. They specialize in elusive information worldwide. They also specialize in assets discovery and skip tracing.

Track Down Inc

115 W McDowell Rd Suite 2
Phoenix AZ 85003

Phone: 888-252-8521
602-252-8521
Fax: 602-252-8682

Local Retrieval and SOP Area: AZ-Maricopa.

Normal turnaround time: 24 hours. Projects are generally billed by the hour. The first project may require a prepayment.

Correspondent relationships: the rest of Arizona. They specialize in service of process and special investigations/research.

Traill County Abstract Co

PO Box 69
Hillsboro ND 58045

Phone: 701-436-4880

Local Retrieval Area: ND-Traill.

Normal turnaround time: 2-3 weeks. Fees are based according to state law. The first project may require a prepayment.

Trax

17 Joy St
Barrington RI 02806

Phone: 401-245-3004
Fax: 401-245-9443

Local Retrieval and SOP Area: MA-Bristol, Plymouth; RI-Bristol, Kent, Newport, Providence, Washington.

Normal turnaround time: 24 hours. Expedited service available. Projects are generally billed by the number of names searched. The first project may require a prepayment. Terms are net 30 days.

Correspondent relationships: MA, CT, NH, VT, ME, and FL. They specialize in asset search, title search, skip tracing, insurance carrier search, divorce records, Locus (accident location diagrams), corporate ownership, annual reports and news articles search.

Treasure Coast Abstract & Title Ins

401-B S Indian River Dr
Fort Pierce FL 34950

Phone: 561-461-7190
Fax: 561-468-8461

Local Retrieval Area: FL-Indian River, Martin, Okeechobee, St. Lucie.

Normal turnaround time: 7 days. Fee basis will vary by the type of project. Credit accounts are accepted.

They specialize in residential and commercial title searches.

Treasure State Title

409 N Center
Hardin MT 59034

Phone: 406-665-3797
Fax: 406-665-1099

Local Retrieval Area: MT-Big Horn.

Normal turnaround time: up to 10 days. Projects are generally billed by the hour. Credit accounts are accepted.

Tri County Process Service

PO Box 3527
Salinas CA 93912

Phone: 800-757-7623
408-757-2580
Fax: 408-424-7334

Local Retrieval and SOP Area: CA-Monterey, San Benito, Santa Cruz.

Normal turnaround time: 1 week. Projects are generally billed by the hour. Credit accounts are accepted.

Correspondent relationships: all of California. They specialize in process service, only. They do not do record retrieval.

Tri-County Abstract and Title Guar

921 1st St N
St Cloud MN 56303

Phone: 800-892-2399
320-253-2096
Fax: 320-253-4536

Local Retrieval Area: MN-Benton, Cass, Kanabec, McLeod, Meeker, Mille Lacs, Morrison, Sherburne, Stearns, Wright.

Normal turnaround time: 1-10 business days. Projects are generally billed by the number of names searched or records located. Credit accounts are accepted. Personal checks are accepted.

They do abstracting in ten counties, have 3 licensed abstractors, and store records for 5 counties.

Tri-County Land Title

PO Box 303 110 S Jefferson St
Berne IN 46711

Phone: 219-589-3139
Fax: 219-589-3130

Local Retrieval Area: IN-Adams, Blackford, Jay, Wells.

Normal turnaround time: 1-5 days. Projects are generally billed by the number of records located. Projects require prepayment.

Tri-County Process Serving

417 W Fort St
Boise ID 83702

Phone: 800-473-3454
208-344-4132
Fax: 208-338-1530

Local Retrieval and SOP Area: ID-Ada, Boise, Canyon, Elmore, Gem, Payette, Valley.

Normal turnaround time: varied depending on project. Projects are generally billed by the number of names searched. Credit accounts are accepted.

Correspondent relationships: Twin Falls, Gooding, Jerome, Bonneville, Madison, Jefferson, Power, and most counties in northern Idaho. They specialize in process service and skip tracing.

Tri-County Title Services

411 N Hernando St
Lake City FL 32055

Phone: 904-755-5566
Fax: 904-755-5799

Local Retrieval Area: FL-Baker, Columbia, Dixie, Gilchrist, Hamilton, Lafayette, Suwannee, Union.

Normal turnaround time: 3-5 days. Fee basis will vary by the type of project. Credit accounts are accepted.

They specialize in ownership and encumbrance searches and title insurance.

🏛 Triad Consultants Ltd

7025 Mission St Suite 301
Daly City CA 94014

Phone: 415-994-6600
Fax: 415-994-5364

Local Retrieval and SOP Area: CA-San Francisco, San Mateo.

Normal turnaround time: 48 hours. Projects are generally billed by the number of names searched. The first project may require a prepayment. Credit cards are accepted. Billing payable upon receipt.

Correspondent relationships: nationwide and international. They specialize in pre-employment screening, background investigations, asset and pre-marital, adoptee and birth mother searches and polygraph.

Trident Investigative Service

PO Box 1725
Renton WA 98057-1725

Phone: 888-277-3238
206-277-3238
Fax: 206-277-6143

Local Retrieval and SOP Area: WA-King.

Normal turnaround time: 1-2 days. Online computer ordering is also available. Projects are generally billed by the number of names searched or records located. Fee varies depending on type of search. The first project may require a prepayment.

They specialize in investigative research.

Trinity County Abstract

PO Box 249
Groveton TX 75845

Phone: 409-642-1698
Fax: 409-642-1697

Local Retrieval Area: TX-Trinity.

Normal turnaround time: 5-10 working days. Commitments and land searches take 15 working days. Projects are generally billed by the number of names searched or records located. The first project may require a prepayment. Personal checks are accepted.

They specialize in land title searches and title insurance.

Tripp & Todd Title Company

PO Box 1831
Winner SD 57580

Phone: 605-842-0334
Fax: 605-842-3088

Local Retrieval Area: SD-Todd, Tripp.

Normal turnaround time: 5 business days. Fee basis will vary by the type of project. The first project may require a prepayment.

Troy Title Co

115 N Lincoln Dr
Troy MO 63379

Phone: 314-528-2220
Fax: 314-528-2220

Local Retrieval Area: MO-Lincoln.

Normal turnaround time: 2-3 days. Projects are generally billed by the number of names searched. Credit accounts are accepted. Personal checks are accepted.

They specialize in real estate title searches.

Trumbull County Abstract Co

174 N Park Ave PO Box 1268 (44482)
Warren OH 44481

Phone: 330-399-1891
Fax: 330-399-1892

Local Retrieval Area: OH-Ashtabula, Columbiana, Geauga, Mahoning, Portage, Trumbull.

Normal turnaround time: 3 days. Projects are generally billed by the hour. Credit accounts are accepted.

Tucker Abstract Co

202 E Central
Bentonville AR 72712

Phone: 501-273-2111
Fax: 501-273-9247

Local Retrieval Area: AR-Benton.

Normal turnaround time: 3 days for UCC and taxes and 5 days for real estate. Projects are generally billed by the hour. Flat fee for closing. Projects require prepayment.

Taylor Tucker

PO Box 7
Louisville MS 39339

Phone: 601-773-9254
Fax: 601-773-9255

Local Retrieval Area: MS-Winston.

Normal turnaround time: 2 days. Projects are generally billed by the hour. The first project may require a prepayment.

He is an attorney in general practice.

Helen Turner

931 Marshall Ave
New Castle PA 16101

Phone: 412-652-5402

Local Retrieval Area: PA-Lawrence.

Normal turnaround time: 24-48 hours. Fee basis will vary by the type of project. The first project may require a prepayment. Out of state clients are charged a setup fee.

🏛 Turning Wheels Inc

PO Box 13002
Greensboro NC 27415

Phone: 910-621-9064
Fax: 910-621-8202

Local Retrieval Area: NC-Forsyth, Guilford.

Normal turnaround time: 24-48 hours. Fee basis varies by type of transaction. Credit accounts are accepted. Terms are net 30 days.

Correspondent relationships: Orange, Durham. They specialize in litigation support, document preparation, foreclosure searches and residential title searches.

Barbara Tweedle

PO Box 9
Rosedale MS 38769

Phone: 601-759-3762

Local Retrieval Area: MS-Bolivar.

Normal turnaround time: 1-2 days. Projects are generally billed by the number of names searched. Projects require prepayment.

She specializes in records at the Rosedale courts. A FAX number is available upon request.

Twin City Abstract Corp

200 University Ave W Suite 225
St Paul MN 55103

Phone: 612-224-7072
Fax: 612-223-5819

Local Retrieval Area: MN-Anoka, Carver, Dakota, Hennepin, Ramsey, Scott, Washington.

Normal turnaround time: 3 days. Projects are generally billed by the number of names searched. Fee basis can also be per entry for abstracts. Credit accounts are accepted.

Twin City Title Co Inc

PO Box 2791
Texarkana TX 75504

Phone: 903-793-7671
Fax: 903-792-2847

Local Retrieval Area: TX-Bowie.

Normal turnaround time: 1-2 days. Projects are generally billed by the hour. Projects require prepayment.

TWT Title

PO Box 380 100 S Main
Wolcottville IN 46795

Phone: 800-742-9362
Fax: 800-824-2563

Local Retrieval Area: IN-DeKalb, LaGrange, Noble, Steuben.

Normal turnaround time: 2 days for all counties directly served, and approximately 1 week for all others. Projects are generally billed by the hour. Credit accounts are accepted. Personal checks are accepted.

Correspondent relationships: all counties in Indiana. They have an on-staff attorney who specializes in real estate law including quiet title actions, zoning, title insurance and insured closings.

🏛 Tyler-McLennon Inc

707 W 7th St
Austin TX 78701

Phone: 512-482-0808
Fax: 512-482-0912

Local Retrieval Area: TX-32 Counties.

Normal turnaround time: 24-72 hours. Online computer ordering is also available. Projects are generally billed by the number of names searched. The first project may require a prepayment. Terms are net 30 days.

Correspondent relationships: Texas, Maryland, Virginia, California, Oklahoma, Louisiana and Illinois. They specialize in all types of county courthouse, Federal courthouse, criminal and Secretary of State searches.

🏛 Tyler-McLennon Inc-Illinois

3166 River Rd Suite 14
Des Plaines IL 60018-2898

Phone: 847-297-4460
Fax: 847-297-1024

Local Retrieval Area: IL-11 Counties; MO-Jefferson, St. Charles, St. Louis, City of St. Louis.

Normal turnaround time: 24 to 72 hours. Expedited service available. Projects are generally billed by the number of names searched. The first project may require a prepayment. Terms are net 30 days.

Correspondent relationships: All of Illinois. They specialize in UCC's, liens, civil and real estate. They will also do criminal and Secretary of State searches.

U

UCC Filing & Search Services

526 E Park Ave
Tallahassee FL 32301-2551

Phone: 800-822-5436
904-681-6528
Fax: 904-681-6011

Local Retrieval Area: FL-Calhoun, Gadsden, Jackson, Jefferson, Leon, Liberty, Madison, Taylor, Wakulla.

Normal turnaround time: next day. Projects are generally billed by the number of names searched. Credit accounts are accepted. Credit cards are accepted.

Correspondent relationships: nationwide. They specialize in corporate, UCC, tax lien, suits and judgment reporting as well as nationwide registered agent services.

UCC Retrievals

7288-A Hanover Green Dr
Mechanicsville VA 23111

Phone: 804-559-5919
Fax: 804-559-5920

Local Retrieval Area: VA-49 Counties.

Normal turnaround time: 3 days. They offer same or next day service at the Secretary of State's office for searches and corporate filings. Projects are generally billed by the number of names searched. Credit accounts are accepted.

Correspondent relationships: Buchanan, Dickenson, Wise, Lee, Washington, Frederick, Winchester City, Loudoun, Warren, Clarke, Fauquier, Prince William, Arlington and Alexandria.

UCC Search Inc

104 S Capitol #8 PO Box 9315 (87504-9315)
Santa Fe NM 87501

Phone: 800-453-9404
505-983-4228
Fax: 800-642-6382
505-983-1169

Local Retrieval Area: NM-Bernalillo, Los Alamos, Mora, Rio Arriba, San Miguel, Sandoval, Santa Fe, Taos, Torrance, Valencia.

Normal turnaround time: 2 days. Projects are generally billed by the number of names searched. Credit accounts are accepted. Terms are net 30 days. 1% interest for late payment.

Correspondent relationships: the rest of the state of New Mexico.

Union Abstract Co

200 N Jeffersn Ave Suite 214
El Dorado AR 71730

Phone: 501-863-6053
Fax: 501-864-0094

Local Retrieval Area: AR-Union.

Normal turnaround time: 1 day. Projects are generally billed by the hour. Projects require prepayment.

Union County Abstract and Title

104 W Main St
Elk Point SD 57025

Phone: 605-356-3180
Fax: 605-356-3112

Local Retrieval Area: SD-Union.

Normal turnaround time: 24-48 hours. Projects are generally billed by the hour. Credit accounts are accepted.

They specialize in title searches, lien searches, abstracting and title insurance. They are a licensed abstractor for Union County, South Dakota.

Union-Speer Abstract Co

PO Box 710
Sapulpa OK 74067

Phone: 918-224-4540
Fax: 918-224-4549

Local Retrieval Area: OK-Creek.

Normal turnaround time: varied depending on project. Fee basis is per page. Credit accounts are accepted.

Unisearch Inc

1130 K St Suite LL21
Sacramento CA 95814

Phone: 800-769-1864
Fax: 800-769-1868

Local Retrieval Area: CA-Sacramento.

Normal turnaround time: 1-2 days. Projects are generally billed by the number of names searched or records located. Credit accounts are accepted.

Correspondent relationships: nationwide..dd.

Unisearch Inc

311 S Wacker Suite 4550
Chicago IL 60606

Phone: 800-215-5168
Fax: 800-261-1814

Local Retrieval Area: IL-Cook, Du Page.

Normal turnaround time: 1-2 days. Projects are generally billed by the number of names searched or records located. Credit accounts are accepted.

Correspondent relationships: nationwide.

Unisearch Inc

1295 Bandana Blvd N Suite 300
St Paul MN 55108

Phone: 800-227-1256
Fax: 800-227-1263

Local Retrieval Area: MN-Hennepin.

Normal turnaround time: 1-2 days. Projects are generally billed by the number of names searched or records located. Credit accounts are accepted.

Correspondent relationships: nationwide.

Unisearch Inc

605 Center St Suite 201
Salem OR 97301

Phone: 800-554-3113
Fax: 800-554-3114

Local Retrieval Area: OR-Marion.

Normal turnaround time: 1-2 days. Projects are generally billed by the number of names searched or records located. Credit accounts are accepted.

Correspondent relationships: nationwide.

Unisearch Inc

101 Capitol Way N Suite 202
Olympia WA 98501-1077

Phone: 800-722-0708
Fax: 800-531-1717

Local Retrieval Area: WA-King, Mason, Pierce, Skagit, Snohomish, Thurston.

Normal turnaround time: 24-48 hours. Projects are generally billed by the number of names searched or records located. Copy costs and disbursements are added to the search charge. Credit accounts are accepted.

Correspondent relationships: nationwide. They have on-line access to 30 states' records.

Unisource Screening & Info

937 Via Lata Suite 200
Colton CA 92324

Phone: 909-783-0909
Fax: 909-783-0923

Local Retrieval and SOP Area: CA-11 Counties.

Normal turnaround time: 24-72 hours. Projects are generally billed by the number of names searched. The first project may require a prepayment.

Correspondent relationships: nationwide. They conduct drug testing and background screening nationally. With over 10 years investigative experience, they are dedicated to "providing safe environments" for employers and employees nationally.

United Attorneys' Services

601 University Ave Suite 134
Sacramento CA 95825

Phone: 916-457-3000

Local Retrieval Area: CA-Placer, Sacramento, San Joaquin, Yolo.

Normal turnaround time: 4 days. Projects are generally billed by the number of names searched. Credit accounts are accepted. Personal checks are accepted.

Correspondent relationships: Solano, El Dorado and Nevada counties.

United Legal Services

217 N Harvey Suite 102
Oklahoma City OK 73102

Phone: 888-232-8432
405-232-8432
Fax: 405-232-8442

Local Retrieval and SOP Area: OK-Canadian, Cleveland, Grady, Lincoln, Logan, McClain, Oklahoma, Pottawatomie.

Normal turnaround time: 48 hours for close in counties. Contract areas average 3-4 days. Projects are generally billed by the hour. The first project may require a prepayment. Personal checks are accepted.

Correspondent relationships: all of Oklahoma.

United Title Services Inc

312 1st St SE
Cedar Rapids IA 52401

Phone: 319-365-1478
Fax: 319-364-3217

Local Retrieval Area: IA-Linn.

Normal turnaround time: 24-48 hours. Fee basis varies by type of transaction. Credit accounts are accepted. They request prepayment from individuals, but will invoice companies.

University Process Service

PO Box 2114
Silver Spring MD 20915-2114

Phone: 301-681-7206
Fax: 301-593-1583

Local Retrieval and SOP Area: DC-District of Columbia; MD-Anne Arundel, Baltimore, City of Baltimore, Carroll, Charles, Frederick, Howard, Montgomery, Prince George's, Washington; VA-City of Alexandria, Arlington, Fairfax.

Normal turnaround time: 1-2 days. Projects are generally billed by the number of names searched. Washington, DC searches are charged by the hour. Credit accounts are accepted. Terms are net 15 days.

Upper Penninsula Title and Abstr

810 Ludington St
Escanaba MI 49829

Phone: 800-743-2091
906-786-3821
Fax: 906-786-7910

Local Retrieval Area: MI-Alger, Delta, Marquette, Menominee, Schoolcraft.

Normal turnaround time: 1-5 days. Fee basis will vary by type of project. Credit accounts are accepted. Payment due upon receipt of invoice.

They specialize in full title service.

Upper State Title Corp

PO Box 2205
Anderson SC 29625-2205

Phone: 864-260-4649
Fax: 864-231-8419

Local Retrieval Area: SC-Abbeville, Anderson, Greenville, Greenwood, Laurens, McCormick, Oconee, Pickens, Spartanburg.

Normal turnaround time: 1 day. Projects are generally billed by the hour. Credit accounts are accepted.

Urban Title Search Services
410 Broad St
Ashland OH 44805

Phone: 419-289-0437
Fax: 419-289-0437

Local Retrieval Area: OH-Ashland, Holmes, Richland, Wayne.

Normal turnaround time: 24-48 hours. Projects are generally billed by the number of names searched or records located. The first project may require a prepayment. Payment due upon billing.

🏛 US Document Services Inc
PO Box 50486
Columbia SC 29250

Phone: 800-796-0698
803-254-9193
Fax: 803-771-9905

Local Retrieval Area: SC-42 Counties.

Normal turnaround time: 24-48 hours. Online computer ordering is also available. Projects are generally billed by the number of names searched. Credit accounts are accepted. Terms are net 30 days.

Correspondent relationships: nationwide. They specialize in all aspects of public record research. Their staff has over 15 years experience in the public record field. They have on-line services with the Secretary of State (SC) and have their own Secretary of State UCC microfilm library.

US Legal Support
PO Box 1053
Amarillo TX 79105

Phone: 806-374-2900
Fax: 806-358-4272

Local Retrieval and SOP Area: TX-Potter, Randall.

Normal turnaround time: 24 hours. Projects are generally billed by the number of names searched or records located. The first project may require a prepayment.

They specialize in process service.

US Legal Support of Lubbock
PO Box 11564 1202 Ave "O"
Lubbock TX 79408

Phone: 806-747-8500
Fax: 806-741-0947

Local Retrieval Area: TX-Lubbock.

Normal turnaround time: 2 days. Fee basis varies by type of transaction. The first project may require a prepayment.

Correspondent relationships: a network for the panhandle of Texas. They specialize in marriage/divorce searches.

USA Inc - Private Investigators
5660 Emerson Way
Indianapolis IN 46220-5377

Phone: 317-254-8721
Fax: 317-251-7355

Local Retrieval and SOP Area: IN-Boone, Brown, Hamilton, Hendricks, Johnson, Marion, Monroe, Morgan.

Normal turnaround time: 24-48 hours for county courts and 48-72 hours for US courts. Projects are generally billed by the number of names searched. The first project may require a prepayment. Credit cards are accepted.

They specialize in legal investigations, i.e. investigations for plaintiff attorney in personal injury and negligence civil actions, investigations for criminal defense, service of process and skip tracing.

Utah Title & Abstract
PO Box 337
Richfield UT 84754

Phone: 801-896-5429
Fax: 801-896-4084

Local Retrieval Area: UT-Millard, Piute, Sevier, Wayne.

Normal turnaround time: as long as 2-3 weeks. Projects are generally billed by the hour. Projects require prepayment.

V

🏛 V & A Research Etc
Rt 1 Box 653
Ozark AL 36360

Phone: 334-774-7092
Fax: 334-774-7092

Local Retrieval Area: AL-Barbour, Coffee, Dale, Geneva, Henry, Houston, Pike.

Normal turnaround time: 24-48 hours. If takes longer, will notify client. Credit accounts are accepted.

They research probate, tax, real estate, marriage and estate records, specializing in title searches, UCC/lien searches, updates and document recordings.

Valley Copy Service Inc
PO Box 3449
Modesto CA 95353

Phone: 209-524-0223
Fax: 209-524-1505

Local Retrieval and SOP Area: CA-Amador, Fresno, Merced, Sacramento, San Joaquin, Stanislaus, Tehama, Tulare.

Normal turnaround time: 5-10 days. Projects are generally billed by the number of names searched or records located. Credit accounts are accepted. Terms are net 30 days.

Correspondent relationships: all of California. They are an attorney service. They prepare subpoenas, serve and copy medical employment and other records for many hospitals in the valley.

Valley County Abstract Company
218 5th St South
Glasgow MT 59230

Phone: 406-228-2350
Fax: 406-228-2350

Local Retrieval Area: MT-Valley.

Normal turnaround time: varied depending on project. Projects are generally billed by the hour. Credit accounts are accepted.

They specialize in mineral searches and title insurance.

🏛 Valley Court Services
1314 Maple Ct
Harlingen TX 78550

Phone: 210-412-2306
Fax: 210-412-8121

Local Retrieval Area: TX-Cameron, Hidalgo, Willacy.

Normal turnaround time: 24-48 hours. Expedited service available Projects are generally billed by the number of names searched. Fees vary by type of search. Credit accounts are accepted.

They specialize in current property and lien searches, 50 year chain of title searches, lien searches, STL's, FTL's, AJ's, UCC's (real & personal) and civil litigation.

Valley Land Title Co
100 N Oak St
Sallisaw OK 74955

Phone: 918-775-4872
Fax: 918-775-4812

Local Retrieval Area: OK-Sequoyah.

Normal turnaround time: 12-24 hours. Projects are generally billed by the number of records located. Projects require prepayment.

They specialize in real estate.

Van Buren Abstract Association
PO Box 310
Keosauqua IA 52565

Phone: 319-293-3783
Fax: 319-293-3956

Local Retrieval Area: IA-Van Buren.

Normal turnaround time: 2-3 days. Fee basis will vary by the type of project. The first project may require a prepayment.

▥ Melissa Vanagas

Phone: 815-338-9234
Fax: 815-338-0379

1026 Tappan St
Woodstock IL 60098

Local Retrieval Area: IL-McHenry.

Normal turnaround time: 24 hours. Projects are generally billed by the number of names searched. Projects require prepayment.

Correspondent relationships: Boone, Winnebago, Ogle counties in Illinois. She specializes in local court civil and criminal cases, UCC liens and recordings, and real property liens.

VanBuren County Abstract Office

Phone: 616-657-4250
Fax: 616-657-3207

207 Paw Paw St
Paw Paw MI 49079

Local Retrieval Area: MI-Van Buren.

Normal turnaround time: 2-3 days. Expedited service available. Fee basis will vary by type of project. Projects require prepayment. They specialize in real estate matters.

Linda Vanderhoof

Phone: 804-430-1316
Fax: 804-430-0423

3152 Winterberry Ln
Virginia Beach VA 23456

Local Retrieval Area: VA-City of Chesapeake, City of Hampton, City of Newport News, City of Norfolk, City of Portsmouth, City of Suffolk, City of Virginia Beach, City of Williamsburg.

Normal turnaround time: 24-48 hours. Projects are generally billed by the number of names searched. Credit accounts are accepted. Personal checks are accepted.

Correspondent relationships: Virginia Beach.

Jeffrey A Varas

Phone: 601-452-0360

PO Box 157
Pass Christian MS 39571-0157

Local Retrieval Area: MS-Copiah, Hinds, Lincoln.

Normal turnaround time: 1-2 days. Projects are generally billed by the hour. The first project may require a prepayment.

He is an attorney and specializes in criminal law and domestic relations.

Verbatim Investigative Services

Phone: 800-750-4231
954-389-6485
Fax: 954-349-0635

2400 E Las Olas Blvd Suite 253
Ft Lauderdale FL 33301

Local Retrieval and SOP Area: FL-Broward, Dade, Palm Beach.

Normal turnaround time: 1-3 days. Online computer ordering is also available. Projects are generally billed by the number of names searched. The first project may require a prepayment.

Correspondent relationships: nationwide. They specialize in information brokerage, unlisted phone numbers, asset retrieval, translation services (English, Spanish, Italian, French and Portugese) and bank account searches.

▥ Verified Credentials

Phone: 612-431-1811
Fax: 612-431-6235

1020 E 146th St
Burnsville MN 55337

Local Retrieval Area: MN-Anoka, Carver, Dakota, Hennepin, Ramsey, Scott, Washington.

Normal turnaround time: 1-3 days. Online computer ordering is also available. Projects are generally billed by the number of names searched. Credit accounts are accepted.

Correspondent relationships: all of Minnesota and other states. They specialize in background screening.

Vigil Enterprises

Phone: 800-541-3220
916-927-3282
Fax: 916-927-3389

1804 Tribute Rd Suite 210
Sacramento CA 95815

Local Retrieval and SOP Area: CA-Amador, El Dorado, Nevada, Placer, Sacramento, Yolo.

Normal turnaround time: 24 hours unless files need to be ordered. Projects are generally billed by the hour. Credit accounts are accepted. They will accept personal checks.

They specialize in the investigation and structuring of white collar crime cases and the location of hidden assets.

Vinita Title Co

Phone: 918-256-2617
Fax: 918-256-3412

PO Box 306
Vinita OK 74301

Local Retrieval Area: OK-Craig.

Normal turnaround time: 48 hours. Projects are generally billed by the number of names searched. The first project may require a prepayment.

Vinson Detective Agency

Phone: 800-441-7899
Fax: 504-529-4393

955 Howard
New Orleans LA 70113

Local Retrieval and SOP Area: LA-Jefferson Parish, Orleans Parish, St. Bernard Parish.

Normal turnaround time: 1-2 days. Projects are generally billed by the hour. The first project may require a prepayment.

▥ VISTA Inc

Phone: 810-559-3500
Fax: 810-559-4757

29524 Southfield Rd
Southfield MI 48076-2004

Local Retrieval Area: MI-Macomb, Monroe, Oakland, Washtenaw, Wayne.

Normal turnaround time: 1-2 weeks depending on the county. Projects are generally billed by the number of names searched. The first project may require a prepayment. May require retainer if not affiliated with national PI organization.

Correspondent relationships: the rest of Michigan. They specialize in surveillance and defense sub rosa. Licensed in Michigan, California and Florida

▥ Fred & Margaret Vogel

Phone: 201-539-5093
Fax: 609-397-3562

46 Ferry St
Lambertville NJ 08530

Local Retrieval Area: NJ-Morris.

Normal turnaround time: 24-48 hours. Projects are generally billed by the number of names searched. They charge by name for civil and criminal searches and by the type of search for real estate. The first project may require a prepayment. They require all out of state client to prepay. Personal checks are accepted.

Robert Vollrath

Phone: 305-829-5559
Fax: 305-829-5559

2895 Biscayne Blvd, Suite 528
Miami FL 33137

Local Retrieval and SOP Area: FL-Dade.

Normal turnaround time: 1 week. Projects are generally billed by the hour. Projects require prepayment.

Correspondent relationships: nationwide. He is a licensed private investigator who specializes in process service.

Volusia Legal Services

Phone: 904-822-9067

10 Lake Ruby Dr
Deland FL 32724

Local Retrieval and SOP Area: FL-Volusia.

Normal turnaround time: 24 hours. Some same day service is available. Projects are generally billed by the number of names searched. The first project may require a prepayment.

They specialize in criminal/misdemeanor records and process serving.

VTS Inc

Phone: 800-538-4464
847-888-4464
Fax: 847-888-8588

PO Box 971
Elgin IL 60121-0971

Local Retrieval and SOP Area: IL-Cook, De Kalb, Du Page, Kane, Kendall, Lake, McHenry.

Normal turnaround time: 24-48 hours. Online computer ordering is also available. Projects are generally billed by the number of names searched or records located. The first project may require a prepayment. Personal checks are accepted.

A licensed investigative agency that specializes in paralegal service, computerized information and foreign language translation. Routine clerking and filing fees for Chicago Metro area.

VW Abstract

Phone: 817-552-7712
Fax: 817-552-9648

PO Box 2038
Vernon TX 76385

Local Retrieval Area: TX-Wilbarger.

Normal turnaround time: 2-5 days. Fees vary by project. The first project may require a prepayment.

They specialize in real estate and title records.

W

W A Haag & Associates Inc

Phone: 703-765-2138
Fax: 703-765-1264

PO Box 7065
Alexandria VA 22307

Local Retrieval and SOP Area: DC-District of Columbia; MD-Baltimore, City of Baltimore, Calvert, Charles, Montgomery, Prince George's, St. Mary's; VA-City of Alexandria, Arlington, Fairfax, City of Fairfax, Loudoun, Prince William, Spotsylvania, Stafford.

Normal turnaround time: 1-3 days. Projects are generally billed by the hour. The first project may require a prepayment.

Correspondent relationships: Virginia, Maryland and District of Columbia.

W T Butcher & Associates

Phone: 701-224-1541
Fax: 701-224-1097

311 E Theyer Ave Suite 119
Bismarck ND 58501

Local Retrieval and SOP Area: ND-Burleigh, Cass, McLean, Morton, Ward.

Normal turnaround time: 24-48 hours. Projects are generally billed by the number of names searched. Fee basis varies by type of transaction. The first project may require a prepayment. Credit cards are accepted.

Correspondent relationships: all of the state and nationwide. They specialize in asset locations, skip tracing, private investigations and computer information services.

Wabash Valley Abstract Co Inc

Phone: 317-472-4351
Fax: 317-472-4352

PO Box 1350 National City Bank Bldg #203
Peru IN 46970

Local Retrieval Area: IN-Miami.

Normal turnaround time: 5-7 days. Projects are generally billed by the number of records located. Payments are also based on the premium and search time. Credit accounts are accepted.

Wabasha County Abstract Co

Phone: 612-565-3391
Fax: 612-565-4558

100 W Main St
Wabasha MN 55981

Local Retrieval Area: MN-Wabasha.

Normal turnaround time: 1 week. Projects are generally billed by the number of names searched. Credit accounts are accepted. Payment upon receipt of invoice.

They specialize in posting abstract of title, preparing Owner's & Encumbrance reports, name searches, real estate tax searches, preparation of new abstracts and research of real estate records.

Wagoner County Abstract Co

Phone: 918-485-2215
Fax: 918-485-9162

PO Box 188 219 E Cherokee (74467)
Wagoner OK 74477

Local Retrieval Area: OK-Wagoner.

Normal turnaround time: 2-3 days. Projects billed on per case basis. Credit accounts are accepted. Personal checks and cash are accepted.

They have serviced Wagoner County since 1907.

Diane K Wakelin

Phone: 712-243-2189

1505 Roosevelt Dr
Atlantic IA 50022

Local Retrieval Area: IA-Audubon, Cass.

Normal turnaround time: 24-48 hours. Projects are generally billed by the number of names searched. The first project may require a prepayment.

She specializes in civil, criminal, probate, UCC, real estate, vital records, tax liens and voter registration.

Wakeman Microfilm Service

Phone: 510-886-7667
Fax: 510-886-1523

22283 Main Street
Hayward CA 94541

Local Retrieval Area: CA-Alameda, Contra Costa, Marin, San Francisco, San Mateo, Santa Clara, Solano.

Normal turnaround time: 3-5 business days depending on size of job. Projects are generally billed by the number of names searched or records located. The first project may require a prepayment.

All records copied on microfilm copier and reproduced according to request. Also offer subpoena preparation and service.

Walla Walla Title Co

Phone: 509-525-8660
Fax: 509-529-4713

102 W Main Suite 100
Walla Walla WA 99362

Local Retrieval Area: WA-Walla Walla.

Normal turnaround time: 1-2 days. Fee basis is determined on "per job". Credit accounts are accepted. Out of area clients are asked to prepay.

They specialize in real estate matters.

Wallace Document Retrieval
Phone: 520-726-5055
10120 Ave F
Yuma AZ 85364
Local Retrieval Area: AZ-Yuma.

Normal turnaround time: 12-24 hours. Projects are generally billed by the number of names searched. The first project may require a prepayment. Terms are net 15-30 days.

They specialize in Recorder's office searches, UCC,s, federal and state liens, judgments and fictitious names.

🏛 Walsh Process & Legal Services
Phone: 888-438-9757
124 Old Glenham Rd
Fishkill NY 12524   **Fax:** 914-838-2398
914-838-2213
Local Retrieval and SOP Area: NY-Dutchess, Orange, Putnam, Rockland, Ulster, Westchester.

Normal turnaround time: 2-4 days. Expedited service available. Projects are generally billed by the number of names searched. Credit accounts are accepted.

Correspondent relationships: New York County, Long Island and Albany.

Walters & Associates
Phone: 281-242-2243
PO Box 2248   **Fax:** 281-242-2253
Sugarland TX 77487-2248
Local Retrieval and SOP Area: TX-Brazoria, Fort Bend, Galveston, Harris, Waller, Wharton.

Normal turnaround time: 3 days. Online computer ordering is also available. Projects are generally billed by the number of names searched or records located. The first project may require a prepayment. Personal checks are accepted.

Correspondent relationships: Bexar, Comal and Kendall. They specialize in background, asset and liability, and legal investigations.

Walworth County Abstract & Title
Phone: 605-649-7772
PO Box 418
Selby SD 57472-0418
Local Retrieval Area: SD-Walworth.

Normal turnaround time: 1 week. Projects are generally billed by the hour. Credit accounts are accepted.

Larry M Warner
Phone: 615-484-1611
PO Box 601   **Fax:** 615-484-4509
Crossville TN 38557
Local Retrieval Area: TN-Cumberland.

Normal turnaround time: 1-2 days. Fee basis will vary with type of search. Credit accounts are accepted.

He is an attorney who specializes in real estate record searches.

Warren County Abstract Company
Phone: 515-961-7479
210 W Ashland   **Fax:** 515-961-7470
Indianola IA 50047
Local Retrieval Area: IA-Warren.

Normal turnaround time: 24 hours for most abstract continuations and 1 week for title abstracts. Projects are generally billed by the number of names searched or records located. Credit accounts are accepted. Personal checks are accepted.

Washington County Title Co
Phone: 800-576-6770
90 E 100 S Suite 201   801-628-6717
St George UT 84770   **Fax:** 801-628-6874
Local Retrieval Area: UT-Iron, Washington.

Normal turnaround time: 24-48 hours. Fees are determined on a "variable per name" basis. Credit accounts are accepted.

They specialize in title examination.

Washington County Title Company
Phone: 303-345-2256
158 Main St   **Fax:** 303-345-2953
Akron CO 80720
Local Retrieval Area: CO-Washington.

Normal turnaround time: 3 days for abstracting and title memos, and 3 to 7 days for title insurance commitment. Projects are generally billed by the hour. The first project may require a prepayment.

They provide title memos for oil companies.

Washington Document Service
Phone: 800-728-5201
400 7th St NW 3rd Floor   202-628-5200
Washington DC 20004   **Fax:** 800-385-3823
202-626-7628
Local Retrieval Area: DC-District of Columbia; MD-Montgomery; VA-Arlington, Fairfax, City of Richmond.

Normal turnaround time: same day. Projects are generally billed by the hour. The first project may require a prepayment. Credit cards are accepted.

Correspondent relationships: nationwide and Canada. They specialize in court research and obtaining documents nationwide including the Supreme Court and all state, federal and bankrkuptcy courts. They also search public agencies including the Securities and Exchange Commission. Case monitoring available.

Washington Document Services
Phone: 800-422-2776
299 Broadway Suite 805   212-267-9600
New York NY 10007   **Fax:** 800-537-1711
212-267-9665
Local Retrieval Area: NY-Bronx, Dutchess, Kings, Nassau, Queens, Richmond, Suffolk, Westchester.

Normal turnaround time: same day or requested deadline. Projects are generally billed by the hour. The first project may require a prepayment. Credit cards are accepted.

Correspondent relationships: nationwide. They specialize in complex research and retrieval of all aspects of court documents. They deal directly with county and federal courts and archives in New York and New Jersey. Case monitoring available.

Washita Valley Abstract Co
Phone: 405-224-6111
PO Box 458   **Fax:** 405-222-4429
Chickasha OK 73023
Local Retrieval Area: OK-Grady.

Normal turnaround time: 4-5 days. Fee basis is per page and time. Credit accounts are accepted.

Watertown Title & Escrow Co
Phone: 605-886-8406
PO Box 1444 20 E Maple St   **Fax:** 605-882-3473
Watertown SD 57201
Local Retrieval Area: SD-Codington.

Normal turnaround time: 2-5 days. Fee basis varies by type of transaction. Credit accounts are accepted.

Watonga Abstract Co
Phone: 405-623-7248
Fax: 405-623-7268
PO Box 610 101 N Noble St
Watonga OK 73772
Local Retrieval Area: OK-Blaine.
Normal turnaround time: 1 week. Projects billed by rate schedules. Credit accounts are accepted. Personal checks are accepted.

Kathi Watson
Phone: 704-648-5830
19 Mears Ave
Canton NC 28716
Local Retrieval Area: NC-Buncombe, Haywood, Jackson, Macon, Madison, Swain.
Normal turnaround time: 1 day. Projects are generally billed by the number of names searched. Projects require prepayment.
She specializes in real estate and title searches.

Wayne County Title Co
Phone: 216-262-2916
Fax: 216-263-1738
141 E Liberty St
Wooster OH 44691
Local Retrieval Area: OH-Ashland, Holmes, Wayne.
Normal turnaround time: 1-5 days. Projects are generally billed by the hour. Projects require prepayment.

Wayne Professional Services
Phone: 201-696-7229
Fax: 201-696-3438
PO Box 355
Wayne NJ 07479-0355
Local Retrieval and SOP Area: NJ-Passaic.
Normal turnaround time: 48 hours. Projects are generally billed by the number of names searched. The first project may require a prepayment. They require a retainer fee of $50.00. They will invoice after that.
Correspondent relationships: other parts of New Jersey. They are state licensed and bonded private investigators.

WE Investigate Inc
Phone: 619-672-1664
Fax: 619-672-0676
PO Box 500128
San Diego CA 92150-0128
Local Retrieval and SOP Area: CA-San Diego.
Normal turnaround time: 2-3 days. Projects are generally billed by the hour. Projects require prepayment.
Correspondent relationships: Southern California. They specialize in asset searches, interviews, skip tracing, investigation, sub rosa, insurance defense and trial preparation.

Weatherford-Parker County Abstr
Phone: 817-594-4435
Fax: 817-594-0861
PO Box 278
Weatherford TX 76086
Local Retrieval Area: TX-Parker.
Normal turnaround time: 2-3 days. Fee basis will vary by the type of project. The first project may require a prepayment.

Weatherly Law Office
Phone: 606-878-9661
Fax: 606-878-6948
309 S Broad St
London KY 40741
Local Retrieval Area: KY-Bell, Clay, Knox, Laurel, Pulaski, Rockcastle, Whitley.
Normal turnaround time: 2-3 days. Projects are generally billed by the hour. Credit accounts are accepted. They will ask for out of area or first time clients to prepay.
They are a small town law office that works closely with the County Attorney's office.

Weber Abstract Co
Phone: 605-256-4640
PO Box 263
Madison SD 57042
Local Retrieval Area: SD-Lake.
Normal turnaround time: 1 day to 2 weeks. Fee basis is set by law. The first project may require a prepayment.
They specialize in real estate.

Attorney David V Weber
Phone: 706-860-8160
Fax: 706-860-1568
PO Box 211149
Augusta GA 30917-1149
Local Retrieval Area: GA-Burke, Columbia, Richmond.
Normal turnaround time: usually up to 3 days. Fee basis will vary by the type of project. Credit accounts are accepted.
He specializes in real estate, criminal, and domestic matters.

Webster County-Butler & Rhodes
Phone: 515-573-3341
Fax: 515-573-8806
805 Central Ave
Fort Dodge IA 50501
Local Retrieval Area: IA-Webster.
Normal turnaround time: 1-2 days. Fee basis will vary by the type of project. The first project may require a prepayment.

Welch & Ekman PC
Phone: 701-284-7833
Fax: 701-284-7832
PO Box 198
Park River ND 58270
Local Retrieval Area: ND-Cavalier, Walsh.
Normal turnaround time: 1 day. Projects are generally billed by the hour. Credit accounts are accepted.

Wells Abstract Company
Phone: 573-221-0644
Fax: 573-221-7303
109 Virginia Suite 174
Hannibal MO 63401
Local Retrieval Area: MO-Marion, Ralls.
Normal turnaround time: 2 days. Projects are generally billed by the number of records located. Credit accounts are accepted. Personal checks are accepted.

Wells County Abstract Co
Phone: 701-547-3433
PO Box 597
Fessenden ND 58438
Local Retrieval Area: ND-Wells.
Normal turnaround time: 2 days. Projects are generally billed by the number of records located. Credit accounts are accepted.
They specialize in real estate.

Weltmer Law Office
Phone: 913-378-3172
Fax: 913-378-3203
Box 303
Mankato KS 66956
Local Retrieval Area: KS-Jewell.
Normal turnaround time: 24 hours. Projects are generally billed by the hour. The first project may require a prepayment. They accept personal checks.
Correspondent relationships: Mitchell, Republic and Smith, KS counties..dd. They also operate Weltmer Abstract and Title Insurance Company, which specializes in title searches, abstracts and title insurance. The company has been in business for 57 years.

Charles Jr Wessinger

Phone: 601-873-6258
Fax: 601-873-6903

PO Box 215
Rolling Fork MS 39159

Local Retrieval Area: MS-Issaquena, Sharkey.

Normal turnaround time: 2 days. Projects are generally billed by the hour. The first project may require a prepayment..dd.

West Central Abstracting Co

Phone: 218-736-5685
Fax: 218-739-4610

128 W Junius Ave
Fergus Falls MN 56537-2529

Local Retrieval Area: MN-Otter Tail.

Normal turnaround time: 3-5 days. Fee basis is per entry. Credit accounts are accepted.

West Coast MCI

Phone: 510-372-8909
Fax: 510-372-9093

PO Box 627
Martinez CA 94553

Local Retrieval and SOP Area: CA-Contra Costa, Solano.

Normal turnaround time: 24-48 hours. Projects are generally billed by the hour. The first project may require a prepayment.

Correspondent relationships: the bay area of Northern California. They specialize in hands-on searching and investigation.

Thomas West

Phone: 614-373-6688
Fax: 614-373-7442

PO Box 5557
Athens OH 45701

Local Retrieval Area: OH-Athens, Hocking, Meigs, Morgan, Muskingum, Noble, Washington; WV-Ritchie, Tyler, Wetzel, Wood.

Normal turnaround time: up to one week. Fee basis will vary by the type of project. Credit accounts are accepted.

He specializes in current owner searches and oil and gas records.

Westchester Court Service

Phone: 914-948-5200
Fax: 914-948-5501

199 Main St
White Plains NY 10601

Local Retrieval and SOP Area: NY-Dutchess, Orange, Putnam, Rockland, Sullivan, Ulster, Westchester.

Normal turnaround time: 1-2 days. Projects are generally billed by the number of records located. The first project may require a prepayment.

They specialize in process serving.

Western Attorney Services

Phone: 415-487-4140
Fax: 415-864-6238

75 Columbia Square
San Francisco CA 94103-4099

Local Retrieval Area: CA-Alameda, Contra Costa, Marin, Monterey, San Francisco, San Mateo, Santa Clara, Solano, Sonoma.

Normal turnaround time: the same day. Fee basis is per hour and a distance charge. The first project may require a prepayment.

Correspondent relationships: nationwide. They specialize in civil case record searches.

Western Title Insurance Agency

Phone: 303-874-8286
Fax: 303-874-4762

PO Box 528
Delta CO 81416

Local Retrieval Area: CO-Delta.

Normal turnaround time: 1 week to 10 days. Fee basis will vary by the type of project. Credit accounts are accepted.

They specialize in title insurance.

Western Title Insurance Agency

Phone: 303-249-7944
Fax: 303-249-5341

PO Box 579
Montrose CO 81401

Local Retrieval Area: CO-Montrose, Ouray.

Normal turnaround time: 1 week to 10 days. Fee basis will vary by the type of project. Credit accounts are accepted. Terms are net 30 days.

Correspondent relationships: Delta, Montrose, Ogray, Gannison, San Miguel. They specialize in title insurance and full closing services.

Westwood Research

Phone: 803-635-3716
Fax: 803-635-3716

Rt 1 Box 210-B
Winnsboro SC 29180

Local Retrieval Area: SC-All Counties.

Normal turnaround time: 24-48 hours. Projects are generally billed by the number of names searched. The first project may require a prepayment.

Correspondent relationships: North Carolina. They also have access to the State Law Enforcement Division records for South Carolina.

Richard Wetherill

Phone: 812-649-2221
Fax: 812-649-2222

215 Main St
Rockport IN 47635

Local Retrieval Area: IN-Spencer.

Normal turnaround time: varied depending on search. Charges vary with the type of record. Credit accounts are accepted.

White Abstract Co

Phone: 816-385-2515
Fax: 816-385-5516

PO Box 85
Macon MO 63552

Local Retrieval Area: MO-Macon.

Normal turnaround time: 1 week to 10 days. Projects are generally billed by the number of names searched. Credit accounts are accepted.

They specialize in title insurance.

Whiteside Abstract and Title Ins

Phone: 906-643-9292
Fax: 906-643-7157

132 N State St
St Ignace MI 49781

Local Retrieval Area: MI-Mackinac.

Normal turnaround time: up to 1 week. Fee basis will vary by type of project. The first project may require a prepayment.

They specialize in real estate and title insurance.

Nancy Wiley

Phone: 615-226-0792
Fax: 615-227-7064

629 Poplar Pl
Nashville TN 37115

Local Retrieval Area: TN-Davidson.

Normal turnaround time: 1-3 days. Projects are generally billed by the hour. The first project may require a prepayment. Cashiers check or money order first time.

She specializes in personal injury defense. She is a paralegal.

Shirley Wilhelm

Phone: 614-374-8444

909 Phillips St
Marietta OH 45750

Local Retrieval Area: OH-Morgan, Noble, Washington.

Normal turnaround time: 48 hours. Projects are generally billed by the number of names searched. Credit accounts are accepted.

Wilkes Law Office

PO Box 876
Kenmare ND 58746

Phone: 701-385-4082
Fax: 701-385-4083

Local Retrieval Area: ND-Burke, Ward.

Normal turnaround time: varied depending on project. Fee basis will vary by type of project. Credit accounts are accepted.

Wilkin County Abstract

PO Box 200
Breckenridge MN 56520

Phone: 218-643-4002
Fax: 701-642-2631

Local Retrieval Area: MN-Wilkin.

Normal turnaround time: 2-4 weeks. Projects are generally billed by the number of names searched. Credit accounts are accepted.

They are escrow agents and title insurance agents representing Old Republic and Stuart Title Insurance Company.

William C Brown and Co

629 Walnut St
Reading PA 19601

Phone: 610-373-1516
Fax: 610-373-7360

Local Retrieval Area: PA-Berks.

Normal turnaround time: 1-2 days. Fee basis will vary by the type of project. The first project may require a prepayment.

They specialize in title searches.

William Olmsted Investigations

455 University Ave Suite 230
Sacramento CA 95825

Phone: 916-646-3443

Local Retrieval Area: CA-El Dorado, Placer, Sacramento, San Joaquin, Sutter, Yolo, Yuba.

Normal turnaround time: varied depending on project. Same day service is available. Projects are generally billed by the hour. Mileage and expenses will be added to the hourly charge. The first project may require a prepayment.

Correspondent relationships: the rest of California. They specialize in investigations including civil, criminal, background, assets and fraud.

George Williams

PO Box 63 113 A Main St
Quitman MS 39355

Phone: 601-776-2111
Fax: 601-776-2112

Local Retrieval Area: MS-Clarke.

Normal turnaround time: 2-3 days. Projects are generally billed by the hour. The first project may require a prepayment.

He is a lawyer.

Nancy Williams

2703 Barton Court
Elon College NC 27244

Phone: 910-584-0450
Fax: 910-584-1679

Local Retrieval Area: NC-Alamance, Caswell, Guilford, Rockingham.

Normal turnaround time: 12 hours. Projects are generally billed by the number of names searched. Credit accounts are accepted.

She specializes in title searches.

Williamson Abstract Co

Box 43
Greenfield IA 50849

Phone: 515-743-2175
Fax: 515-743-6201

Local Retrieval Area: IA-Adair.

Normal turnaround time: 2-5 days. Fee basis will vary by the type of search. Credit accounts are accepted. They require a retainer and will accept personal checks.

They specialize in abstract and real estate searches.

Jeanette Willingham

PO Box 670
Geneva AL 36340

Phone: 334-898-7625

Local Retrieval Area: AL-Geneva.

Normal turnaround time: 1-3 days. Fee basis varies by type of transaction. Credit accounts are accepted.

She has over 30 years experience as an attorney paralegal.

Sally Wilmot

PO Box 68
Athens GA 30603

Phone: 800-282-2686
     706-546-7411
Fax: 706-354-4177

Local Retrieval Area: GA-11 Counties.

Normal turnaround time: 24-48 hours. Projects are generally billed by the number of names searched. Credit accounts are accepted.

Correspondent relationships: Clayton, Cobb, DeKalb, Fulton, Jivinnett, Cherokee, Douglas, Fayette, Henry, Rockdale, Muscogee, plus all Georgia counties.

▥ Wilsearch Information Network

20 Gilbert Ave Suite 102
Smithtown NY 11787

Phone: 800-391-5502
     516-979-1290
Fax: 516-979-1325

Local Retrieval Area: NY-Bronx, Kings, Nassau, New York, Queens, Richmond, Suffolk.

Normal turnaround time: 5 business days. Project billing methods vary. Credit accounts are accepted. Credit cards are accepted. Terms are net 30 days.

Correspondent relationships: nationwide. They specialize in off-line information retrieval, such as building, tax and fire information.

Wilson & Associates

425 W Capital Suite 1500
Little Rock AR 72201

Phone: 501-375-1820
Fax: 501-375-8609

Local Retrieval Area: AR-56 Counties.

Normal turnaround time: varied depending on search. Fee basis will vary with type of search. Credit accounts are accepted.

Correspondent relationships: all counties in Arkansas through their three offices. They have four locations in Arkansas with 10 searchers who cover the entire state under existing statewide contracts with customers.

Wilson & Associates

123 Pine St
Pine Bluff AR 71601

Phone: 501-534-1200

Local Retrieval Area: AR-12 Counties.

Normal turnaround time: variable depending upon search requirements. Fee basis varies by project. Credit accounts are accepted.

See Little Rock offices description.

▥ Wilson & Associates

2031 N 36th St PO Box 8222 (64508)
St Joseph MO 64506

Phone: 816-233-6334
Fax: 816-233-6934

Local Retrieval and SOP Area: MO-Andrew, Buchanan.

Normal turnaround time: 1-4 days depending on county. Projects are generally billed by the number of names searched. Fee basis will vary by the type and location (distance) of project. The first project may require a prepayment.

Correspondent relationships: Clay, MO; Jackson, Johnson, and Wyandotto, KS counties. They specialize in process service, surveillance and missing persons.

Wilson Abstract Co

Phone: 309-833-2049
Fax: 309-833-5311

215 W Washington
Macomb IL 61455

Local Retrieval Area: IL-Fulton, Hancock, Henderson, McDonough, Schuyler, Warren.

Normal turnaround time: 2 days for a judgment search, 4 days for title work. Projects are generally billed by the hour. Travel expenses will be included in the fee. Projects require prepayment. They have been in business for 46 years.

Wilson Enterprises

Phone: 209-437-9602
Fax: 209-437-9604

PO Box 9189
Fresno CA 93791-9189

Local Retrieval Area: CA-Fresno.

Normal turnaround time: 1-2 days. Fee basis will vary by the type of project. Projects require prepayment.

They specialize in workers' compensation and other private investigation.

Win With Information (WWI Assoc)

Phone: 602-661-9628
Fax: 602-661-4923

13793 E Lupine Ave
Scottsdale AZ 85259-3717

Local Retrieval Area: AZ-Maricopa.

Projects are generally billed by the hour. Credit accounts are accepted. Payment due upon completion.

They specialize in general research, including science and technology, business, industry, medicine, law, social science and the arts.

Wendell D Winkler

Phone: 913-294-2339
Fax: 913-294-5702

133 S Pearl
Paola KS 66071

Local Retrieval Area: KS-Miami.

Normal turnaround time: 2-5 days. Projects are generally billed by the number of names searched. Credit accounts are accepted.

Winnebago County Abstract

Phone: 515-582-3101
Fax: 515-582-3446

133 E J St
Forest City IA 50436

Local Retrieval Area: IA-Winnebago.

Normal turnaround time: 2-3 days. Fee basis varies by type of transaction. The first project may require a prepayment.

Wisconsin Title of Fond Du Lac

Phone: 414-922-2200
Fax: 414-922-3867

113 S Main St
Fond Du Lac WI 54935

Local Retrieval Area: WI-Fond du Lac.

Normal turnaround time: 2 days. Fee basis varies by type of transaction. The first project may require a prepayment.

Wisconsin Title of Richland Center

Phone: 800-236-4596
608-647-4596
Fax: 608-647-8033

PO Box 436 133 N Central Ave
Richland Center WI 53581

Local Retrieval Area: WI-Richland.

Normal turnaround time: 1-2 days. Fee basis varies by type of transaction. The first project may require a prepayment.

Wisconsin Title of Shawano Inc

Phone: 715-524-2413
Fax: 715-526-9110

218 N Washington St PO Box 330
Shawano WI 54166

Local Retrieval Area: WI-Menominee, Shawano.

Normal turnaround time: 1-2 days. Fee basis varies by type of transaction. The first project may require a prepayment.

Wood & Tait Inc

Phone: 800-774-8585
808-885-5090
Fax: 808-885-5622

P O Box 1650
Kamuela HI 96743

Local Retrieval Area: HI-Hawaii, Honolulu, Kauai, Maui.

Normal turnaround time: 7 days. Projects are generally billed by the number of names searched. The first project may require a prepayment. Credit cards are accepted.

They specialize in finding property tax records, business registrations, professional and occupational licenses and bankruptcies.

Woodard and Bohse Law Office

Phone: 330-343-8848
Fax: 330-343-3496

121 W 3rd St
Dover OH 44622

Local Retrieval Area: OH-Carroll, Coshocton, Harrison, Holmes, Tuscarawas.

Normal turnaround time: 1 week. Projects are generally billed by the hour. Credit accounts are accepted. They will accept personal checks.

Correspondent relationships: Tuscarawas, Coshocton, Carroll, Holmes and Harrison Counties.

Woods County Abstract Corp

Phone: 405-327-1746
Fax: 405-327-1780

PO Box 686
Alva OK 73717

Local Retrieval Area: OK-Woods.

Normal turnaround time: 1-5 days. Fee basis will vary by the type of project. Credit accounts are accepted.

They specialize in title work and special certificates.

Woodward County Abstract Co

Phone: 405-256-3344
Fax: 405-256-4530

1513 Main
Woodward OK 73802

Local Retrieval Area: OK-Ellis, Harper, Woodward.

Normal turnaround time: 2-3 days. Credit accounts are sometimes accepted. Credit accounts are accepted.

They specialize in abstracts of title and title insurance.

🏛 Worcester Record Search

Phone: 508-842-7282
Fax: 508-842-2236

4 Jill Circle
Shrewsbury MA 01545

Local Retrieval and SOP Area: MA-Worcester.

Normal turnaround time: 24 hours. Projects are generally billed by the number of names searched. Credit accounts are accepted.

World Class Investigations

Phone: 407-728-0641
Fax: 407-728-0818

PO Box 510549
Melbourne Beach FL 32951-0549

Local Retrieval and SOP Area: FL-Brevard, Indian River.

Normal turnaround time: 2-3 days. Projects are generally billed by the number of records located. Credit accounts are accepted.

Correspondent relationships: the rest of Florida.

Worldwide Insurance Group

Phone: 314-878-1800
Fax: 314-878-2760

11975 Westline Dr
St Louis MO 63177

Local Retrieval Area: MO-St. Louis.

Credit accounts are accepted.

Retriever Profiles

Worth County Abstract Co Inc
Phone: 515-324-1761
736 Central Ave
Northwood IA 50459
Local Retrieval Area: IA-Worth.

Normal turnaround time: 1-3 days. Projects are generally billed by the hour. The first project may require a prepayment.

Cheri Wortmann
Phone: 215-736-0486
Fax: 215-736-3545
5093 Grace Dr
Morrisville PA 19067-5172
Local Retrieval Area: NJ-All Counties.

Normal turnaround time: 2 weeks. Projects are generally billed by the number of records located. Credit accounts are accepted. She will invoice if the charges are under $50.00
She specializes in New Jersey vital records and probate.

Wright County Land Title Co
Phone: 800-532-2259
515-532-2259
112 Central Ave E PO Box 307
Fax: 515-532-2259
Clarion IA 50525
Local Retrieval Area: IA-Wright.

Normal turnaround time: up to 1 week. Fee basis will vary by the type of project. Credit accounts are accepted.

Wyatt Land Title Services Inc
Phone: 913-263-7722
PO Box 503
Abilene KS 67410
Local Retrieval Area: KS-Dickinson.

Normal turnaround time: 2 days. Fee basis varies by type of transaction. Credit accounts are accepted.

X,Y,Z

Edna M Yerks
Phone: 908-349-9747
103 Brand Rd
Toms River NJ 08753
Local Retrieval Area: NJ-Ocean.

Normal turnaround time: 24-48 hours. Projects are generally billed by the number of names searched. Credit accounts are accepted.

Yoakum County Abstract Co
Phone: 806-456-2615
Fax: 806-456-2625
PO Box 457
Plains TX 79355
Local Retrieval Area: TX-Yoakum.

Normal turnaround time: 2-3 days. Fee basis will vary by the type of project. The first project may require a prepayment.

York County Title Co
Phone: 402-362-4405
Fax: 402-362-4421
608 Grant Ave PO Box 572
York NE 68467
Local Retrieval Area: NE-York.

Normal turnaround time: 24 hours. Fee basis varies by type of transaction. The first project may require a prepayment.

▥ Beth Young
Phone: 712-767-2510
Fax: 712-767-2510
610 5th St
Elliott IA 51532
Local Retrieval Area: IA-Montgomery, Page.

Normal turnaround time: 24 hours. Projects are generally billed by the number of names searched. The first project may require a prepayment.

Youngblood Process Service
Phone: 813-743-4952
Fax: 813-637-4663
97 Robina St
Port Charlotte FL 33954
Local Retrieval and SOP Area: FL-Charlotte.

Normal turnaround time: 1-3 days. Projects are generally billed by the hour. Credit accounts are accepted.

They specialize in civil process service.

Zap! Courier Service
Phone: 518-449-3361
Fax: 518-449-1332
90 S Swan St
Albany NY 12210
Local Retrieval Area: NY-Albany, Greene, Rensselaer, Saratoga, Schenectady.

Normal turnaround time: 24 hours depending on court turnaround. Projects are generally billed by the number of names searched. Credit accounts are accepted.

Correspondent relationships: New York City. They work closely with the Public Service Commission, Department of State, Insurance Department and New York State Legislature.

John A Zapf II
Phone: 610-868-5101
Fax: 610-691-1216
PO Box 1006
Bethlehem PA 18016
Local Retrieval Area: PA-Lehigh, Northampton.

Normal turnaround time: 1 week. Projects are generally billed by the number of names searched or records located. Credit accounts are accepted.

They specialize in real estate title searches and abstracts.

Zavala County Abstract Co Inc
Phone: 210-374-3218
Fax: 210-374-3947
PO Drawer F
Crystal City TX 78839
Local Retrieval Area: TX-Zavala.

Normal turnaround time: up to a week. Fee basis will vary by the type of project. The first project may require a prepayment.

▥ Ziegler & Associates Inc
Phone: 609-538-0508
Fax: 609-637-9403
PO Box 214
Titusville NJ 08560-0214
Local Retrieval Area: NJ-Mercer.

Normal turnaround time: 2 weeks for statewide criminal records; other records 2 days. Projects are generally billed by the number of names searched. The first project may require a prepayment.

They specialize in polygraph, training, fire/arson/explosion investigations, backgrounds and asset locations.

Zumwalt Enterprises LLC
Phone: 972-554-6968
Fax: 972-554-6970
1817 E Grauwyler Rd Suite 158
Irving TX 75061-3021
Local Retrieval Area: TX-Dallas, Denton, Tarrant.

Normal turnaround time: 3 days. Projects are generally billed by the number of names searched. The first project may require a prepayment.

They specialize in asset, liability searches and real estate searches.

Public Record Research Library

Sources, Retrieval & Unique Searching Aids

At The State

At The Court And County Level

At The State~

The Sourcebook of State Public Records 3rd Edition~ The definitive guide to searching all the major state public record databases and licensing boards.
[ISBN# 1-879792-32-X • PUB 1/97 • PAGES 416 • $35]

The 1997 Mvr Book The national reference, detailing -in practical terms- the privacy restrictions, access procedures, and regulations of all state held driver and vehicle records.
[ISBN# 1-879792-35-4 • PUB 2/97 • PAGES 272 • $19]

The 1997 Decoder Digest The companion to The MVR Book, translating the codes and abbreviations of violations and licensing categories that appear on motor vehicle records for all states.
[ISBN# 1-879792-35-4 • PUB 2/97 • PAGES 304 • $19]

At The Court and County Level~

The Sourcebook of Federal Courts–US & Bankruptcy 2nd Edition~ The definitive guide to searching for case information at the local level within the federal court system. [ISBN# 1-879792 • PUB 1/96 • PAGES 420 • $36]

The Sourcebook of County Court Records A national guide to civil criminal, and probate records at the county and municipal levels within the state court systems. [ISBN# 1-879792-33-8 • PUB 1/97 • PAGES 656 • $35]

The Sourcebook of County Asset/Lien Records A national guide to all county/city agencies where real estate transactions, UCC financing statements, and federal/state tax liens are recorded.
[ISBN# 1-879792-17-6 • PUB 1/95 • PAGES 464 • $29]

Sources, Retrieval and Unique Searching Aids~

The Sourcebook of Online Public Record Experts The national directory to ONLINE proprietary databases, gateways, and national and regional public record search firms. Includes CD-ROM providers, also.
[ISBN# 1-879792-31-1 • PUB 4/96 • PAGES 360 • $29]

The Sourcebook of Local Court & County Record Retrievers 2nd Edition~ The National directory to information retrievers who pull files and documents from the US, state, and local courts and from county agencies.
[ISBN# 1-879792-37-0 • PUB 1/97 • PAGES 544 • $45]

The County Locator The ultimate place, name and zip code locator that shows over 95,000 places and indicates the 10,000 zip codes that cross county lines. [ISBN# 1-879792-39-7 • PUB 1/97 • PAGES 640 • $25]

The Sourcebook of College & University Records A national guide to records of student attendance, degrees, and transcripts at accredited post-secondary schools. [ISBN# 1-879792-24-9 • PUB 9/95 • PAGES 464 • $19]

The Librarian's Guide to Public Records
The national sourcebook to find public records fast at over 11,500 major federal, state, and county public record locations.
[ISBN# 1-879792-38-9 • PUB 1/97 • PAGES 556 • $39]

THE PUBLIC RECORD RESEARCH LIBRARY
Published by BRB Publications, Inc.
4653 S. Lakeshore #3 • Tempe, Arizona 85282
FAX (800) 929-3810 • Phone (800) 929-3811
http://www.brbpub.com

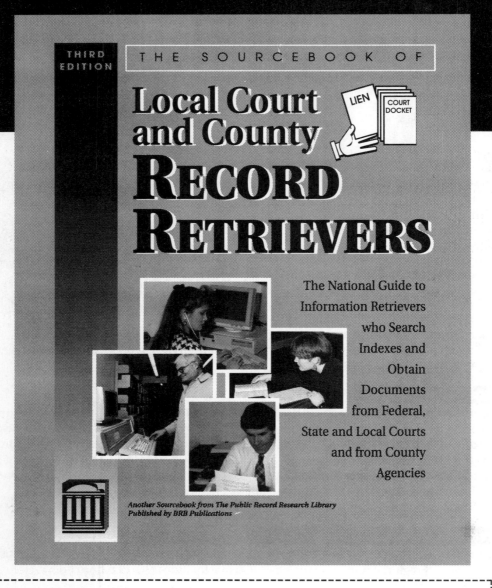

LEONARD BERNSTEIN AT WORK

LEONARD BERNSTEIN AT WORK

HIS FINAL YEARS, 1984–1990

PHOTOGRAPHS BY
STEVE J. SHERMAN

ARTIST INTERVIEWS BY ROBERT SHERMAN

*To Joshua Smith
with all warmest wishes
Steve J Sherman
Nov 2000*

Published in 2010 by Amadeus Press
An Imprint of Hal Leonard Corporation
7777 West Bluemound Road
Milwaukee, WI 53213

Trade Book Division Editorial Offices
33 Plymouth Street, Montclair, NJ 07042

Artist interviews by Robert Sherman
Book design by Mary Belibasakis
Front jacket design by Susanna Ronner Graphic Design
Printed in the United States of America

Library of Congress Cataloging-in-Publication Data

Sherman, Steve J.
  Leonard Bernstein at work : his final years, 1984/1990 / photographs by Steve J. Sherman.
      p. cm.
  Includes bibliographical references and index.
  ISBN 978-1-57467-190-2
  1. Bernstein, Leonard, 1918-1990—Pictorial works. 2. Composers—United States—Biography. I. Title.
  ML410.B566S47 2010
  780.92—dc22
  [B]
                                                    2010026837

www.amadeuspress.com

To my beautiful children, Fiona and Jesse, with total love forever.
You are my greatest heroes.

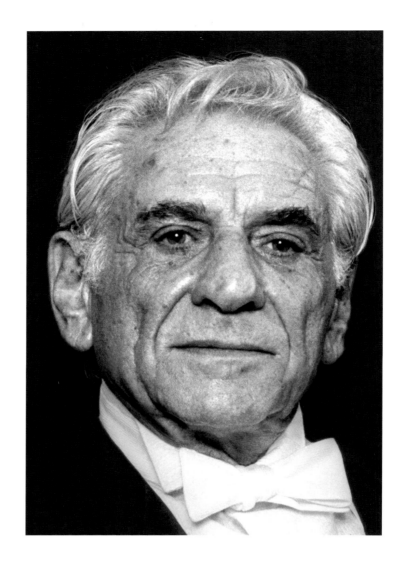

And so I have lived my long and varied life
Happily housed in music (work and play)
And in close-held, heart-bound family
(Including my most precious, long-loved wife),
And teaching (which is learning) and in countless
Loving friends. I have no grave complaints.
I feel that I have lived five lives or so
Already. By the grace of God. Although
I am not quite content to die just yet:
There still remains so much to be composed.
But if I did indeed cease life today
I would not beat my fists against my Fates.
For I am the luckiest, and most blesséd, and
Most grateful person I have ever met.

—LEONARD BERNSTEIN, 1988
"Beauty and Truth Revisited," Part II

CONTENTS

FOREWORD

Lauren Bacall backstage at Carnegie Hall, March 7, 1990.

It was at the home of Lee and Ira Gershwin, the great house of music filled with the sounds of Harold Arlen, Vincent Youmans, Richard Rodgers, Roger Edwins, Johnny Mercer, Oscar Levant, who was always at the piano reliving with Ira, the work, the excitement, the brilliance of those days with brother, George Gershwin, when creativity was overflowing and the unforgettable Gershwin music was played and heard on Broadway and everywhere, giving life to one hit show after another, in addition *Rhapsody in Blue* concerto in F for piano and orchestra, *Porgy and Bess*, and an endless assortment of piano pieces.

On this one night there was someone new at the piano, unknown to me, his name— Leonard Bernstein. He took over the room with his exuberance, thrilling playing of his music, and more. That personality, lighting up the room. We clicked immediately; he forced (well not exactly) me to sit next to him on the piano bench.

I had always been a music lover; show tunes, and some classical music. Though my knowledge was limited, I was hooked, transformed, living my girlhood dream of sitting on a piano or at a piano, singing songs (there was always singing at the Gershwins', even not-so-hot singing). When Lena Horne or Judy Garland arrived the not-so-hot singing quieted down. Except for Lenny, who sang loud and clear, not great, but would not stop. That was okay with me as long as he kept playing. Even Bogie was drawn in, which pleased Lenny no end. From that night on our friendship blossomed. I was completely mesmerized by Lenny, he knew it, and Bogie, the smartest, most intuitive man I've ever known, knew what a romantic I was. Still in my early twenties, finding myself in the company of all this brilliance and creativity, I entered Lenny's world.

When he came to California the excitement began. He came to our house often, lunch around the pool, tennis on our court. In those days we had a court. He took over as usual, talking about his work, music. When Bogie knew Lenny was coming to town, he also knew he'd be at our piano. Betty Comden and Adolph Green would be with us. I'd be at his feet probably. Bogie's reaction to that picture, including staying up to all hours, was, "Lenny's coming, great, I'm going to the boat." Bogie knew it was the talent, the music, the newness, the fun, and the flirtation. Lenny was not a threat. Bogie was right; nevertheless it was a crush, me for him and him for me.

I remember one weekend Lenny, with his portfolio in hand as always, was explaining to us how he was progressing on *Candide*. It was to open soon; he was still working on it. It was afternoon and Lenny had to leave to continue his enormous undertaking, to go home to his beloved family in New York. After he left, Bogie knew I was sad. He said, "He's a man with a mission. He'd be great for a weekend, but that's all." He had a lot to do; he was consumed by music, at the piano, his composing, his conducting. Watching him overseeing the playing of his work at the Hollywood Bowl, with me sitting four rows behind him, with his black cape over his shoulders, totally focused on what was happening onstage, every note of his, perfect.

There are endless memories: Lenny driving me to Malibu to a fish restaurant, me on a trip to New York with Lenny playing his song "Maria" from *West Side Story*, before the show had opened. The visions remain, the vivid, electrifying Lenny, conducting, his body in motion with every note, never still. He was a powerhouse all right. Not always easy, never easy. He loved being loved by everyone at all times, and he was. He put both feet into the occasional blunt remark that came from nowhere.

In his pursuit of composing and perfection, from the first moment to the end of Lenny's life, through Christmas carols sung around his piano, the fun we had, his enthusiasm with friends and family. Through giving up smoking (he never could). Through laughter and tears, loss, strong feelings for each other remained. He introduced me to Brahms and Mahler. He shook up his world and everybody else's. He enhanced my life; he brought to my life the music that was his life. He shared his talent. He was infectious and infuriating. We were Virgos together, a solid bond. I recently came upon a note from him. He never forgot my birthday. The note read, "Ah love, what did we Virgos do to deserve this? But as long as there's love, and there is, xxx Lenny."

— LAUREN BACALL
December 2008

Lauren Bacall (right, foreground) with Betty Comden (center) backstage at Carnegie Hall, March 7, 1990.

PREFACE

WHEN I WAS YOUNG, MY FATHER SEEMED LIKE A KNOWN QUANTITY TO ME. IN EARLY childhood, he was the Daddy with the big laugh, the massive hugs: the one who took me on roller coasters, the one who could eat more corn on the cob than anyone else. As I entered adolescence, he was my co-delighter in the Beatles, my go-to guy for questions about literature, history, Latin. By college age, I'd begun to comprehend that Leonard Bernstein was a deeply complex person: a rare emulsion of elements, some of which I might never understand.

By the time I was married with children, my father had become older, moodier, even cantankerous, as is sometimes the case with older people. But to the end of his life, he was still able to whip up that inner turbine that made his conducting performances so extraordinary. Steve Sherman was there with his camera for this final chapter in my father's professional life.

Studying these pictures, I found myself feeling that I was learning about a part of my father that I hadn't grasped at the time. Steve's images illustrate not only the focus and drive of an explosively gifted musician, but also what it cost the man to generate that energy within himself. What we can see in my father's face, in addition to the sheer intensity of music-making, is the struggle, the exhaustion, the grinding determination to keep going in spite of the increasing physical limitations. (Leonard Bernstein, as everyone knows, was not a kindly caretaker of his body.)

Steve asked me to take a close look at his shots of my father taking his bow after what turned out to be the last concert he conducted at Carnegie Hall—the very spot from which he'd catapulted to fame forty-seven years earlier. Usually during his bows, my father would look tired but gratified by his experience of having shared music with the audience. In this series of photographs, he looks as if part of him has already moved on somewhere else. In the last shot of the series, he looks directly into Steve's camera with a bleak, quiet expression. Looking at this image, I had the sensation that I was eavesdropping on my father's most private discourse with himself—the one he refrained from sharing even with his loved ones:

Thousands applaud me. It means nothing. I am almost gone.

Leonard Bernstein was not very good at handling his diminished physical capacity. It made him furious, fearful, frantic with impatience. The only solution for him was to keep working, to become as absorbed in music as he possibly could, so that he'd have as little time as possible to dwell on what was coming. In his final years, Leonard Bernstein was a man whose brain and spirit burned as fiercely as ever with the fire of the music he loved and shared, but whose body could barely sustain those searing, foundry-level temperatures. All this is poignantly evident in Steve J. Sherman's photographs.

—JAMIE BERNSTEIN
April 2010

INTRODUCTION

James M. Keller, January 26, 2007.

For I am hid away, and there
Is no one else to tell me where.
I mean to hunt myself, and find
Myself, and, finding, be defined,
And, in defining, reexpress
The nature of my singleness.

SO WROTE LEONARD BERNSTEIN IN *Letter to Myself*, A "LONG AUDEN-ESQUE POEM" (as he described it) begun in 1948 and published thirty-four years later, at which time he explained, "I find enough personal declaration here to retrieve it from the flames, or the eternal Bank Vault." When he embarked on his poem, he had already earned accolades as a conductor and a composer. In the ensuing decades, his achievements in both fields would increase exponentially, and he would attain parallel renown as a "broadcast educator," as an ardent voice for progressive social causes and as an all-round celebrity who summed up the bravest aspirations of his era. As it turned out, his "personal declaration" from 1948 would serve as a precept for his life. His path would be both exhilarating and exhausting, fulfilling and frustrating, choreographed and chaotic, and all of it served to find, define, and re-express the nature of his singleness.

His poem referred to an inner quest, to be sure. To the outer world, Bernstein seemed anything but "hid away," and when, through the course of six years, Steve Sherman aimed his camera in the maestro's direction, concealment was out of the question. Rather than rehearse familiar memories of the dashing, youthful Bernstein of the 1950s and '60s—the "Let's Put on a Show" dynamo of *West Side Story*, the charismatic host of the Young People's Concerts, the magnetic music director of the New York Philharmonic— Steve's photographs provide a glimpse into the twilight of this extraordinary life. Although this archive came into being click by click with no sense of overarching design, its existence was nonetheless inevitable. For nearly three decades, Steve has been wherever great music resounds in New York City. His pony-tailed, camera-swathed figure is so familiar to veteran concertgoers that none of them is surprised to see him dash down the aisle once the final notes have sounded, crouching into a duck-waddle as he nears the stage lest he should block the sight lines of paying customers. During the late 1980s and on until 2000, he was on call seven nights a week to document concerts for the *New York Times*. For several years, he chronicled the activities of the New York Philharmonic, and from 1984 through 2001, he served as the official house photographer for Carnegie Hall, where he continues to work frequently to this day. It was therefore inescapable that his lens should have focused often on Leonard Bernstein during the maestro's final half dozen years.

On a January afternoon, I walk out of the stage door of Carnegie Hall and three minutes later am ascending in an elevator to Steve's studio, situated little more than a block away. He has made that walk thousands of times, grateful for his proximity to the vortex of musical New York. "Back in the day" he would have returned to a studio that was buzzing with activity. When his business was at its height, five employees kept the place humming through day and night shifts, and his two darkrooms operated ceaselessly. That was in the pre-digital days. Photojournalism underwent a sea change with the advent of digital photography, which a shrinking newspaper industry has deemed adequate in light of belt-tightened resources. Steve's darkrooms are now given over to storage, their sinks and trays idle since 2004. Not a whiff of acetic acid perfumes the studio on this day—nor, indeed, on any day. Framed photos crowd the walls, jockeying for space with drawings by Steve's two children and posters proclaiming liberal political causes. The phone still rings and the e-mails ping, but on the whole this is a nostalgic place, a digital-age remnant from a darkroom era that photojournalism has left behind.

"With the digital techniques available today," Steve says, "I could easily manipulate a photo to create the image I wish had existed rather than the one that actually did. Let's say I have a really fine shot from an ideal angle of a conductor in front of an orchestra, attacking some dramatic moment; and then I have another shot in which he doesn't look so good, but a percussionist has just let loose a huge crash on the cymbals and is holding them up to resonate—a view everybody would love. Today a client might say to me, 'Let's combine those pictures so the conductor looks great *and* the cymbal player looks great.' If it's for something like a marketing brochure, we actually might end up doing that if it supports the goal of the project. But in a book documenting Leonard Bernstein? Absolutely not. A picture combined in that way is really not a true picture. What's more, it's likely that I'm not the only person who would know it's falsified, because somebody is going to notice that in this doctored photo another percussionist is striking the triangle two people down from the cymbal player, and in fact the triangle and the cymbals never sound together in this particular symphony. So, no: I would never consider doing this in a situation where a photograph is presented as a historical record, which is the case here. If there's not enough drama to begin with, then I simply don't use the photo."

Such an attitude may strike some people as overly fastidious, but to Steve it seems obvious. He respects music deeply and knows the repertoire intimately. Born into a family of professional music makers, he studied the clarinet seriously while a young man, until he veered toward other disciplines as an undergraduate at Oberlin. He understands from firsthand what's happening onstage as a concert unrolls. He knows where the action is from moment to moment, where to train his lens to best follow the flow of the score. "For photos of an orchestra, newspaper editors like the 'last moment' shot," he says, "taken the split second when the string players have just lifted their bows from their instruments. But this is not a very interesting shot from a *musical* point of view. I want the viewer to hear the music through the photograph."

Then there is the question that no photographer can escape: black-and-white or color? This collection makes clear where Steve's sympathies lie. "The knowledge of light vs. shadow: that's what black-and-white photography is," he explains. "Color photography: that's the depiction of reality. If we remove color from the equation, the image becomes about form and direction. And yet, it is a curious paradox that black-and-white photography can trigger emotions so quickly. We're used to seeing in color, and that very fact lends a 'differentness' to black-and-white photography. It seems to engage the emotions differently from color. I often used to shoot both black-and-white film and color slides during the same job, as one or the other, or both, might be required by a client; but I always found the black-and-white images more interesting. When I photographed in color, I captured a scene as it was. When I photographed in black-and-white, I made a scene happen."

He continues: "Leonard Bernstein was a superb subject for black-and-white photography during the period covered in this book. Very often he would be wearing a black suit with a white shirt. By that time his hair was white, and often I was shooting him against a background that was essentially black. Of course, between shooting a frame and completing a developed picture, a photographer can exercise a lot of control over a black-and-white photo. You can lighten the darks or darken the lights ('burning and dodging,' we call it), you can crop the images. But I like my photographs to look natural, and I like to keep the photographic process as invisible as possible. Most of the photos in this book aren't cropped at all. These are the images I experienced as they happened."

In 1984, when Steve's beat began to include Bernstein, the conductor was embarking on his senior phase—he turned sixty-six that year—and his "finding and defining" increasingly turned to questions of summation and posterity. Composing had been a struggle through much of his career, and, apart from a couple of pieces that were basically arrangements of earlier works, his last six years gave rise to only three new compositions: Concerto for Orchestra (1986–'89), *Arias and Barcarolles* for two singers and piano four-hands (1988), and *Dance Suite* for brass quintet (1989). He continued to maintain a demanding schedule as a conductor, mostly leading orchestras with which he had developed close relationships over the years. "Since collecting these images was an afterthought," says Steve, "I never set out to document those years in a systematic way. It was just out of luck that I intersected with him when he was engaging with most of the orchestras that were closest to him. I therefore got to photograph him repeatedly working with the Vienna Philharmonic, the New York Philharmonic, the Israel Philharmonic. I was there to witness a tremendous performance of Shostakovich's Seventh with the Chicago Symphony at Lincoln Center. Back then I was one of the Boston Symphony's regular photographers, and though I shot them often, in both Boston and New York, I never happened to overlap with Bernstein's engagements there—a regret, since that orchestra was central to his musical career." Also absent is the Amsterdam Concertgebouw Orchestra; much though Bernstein was attached to that ensemble during the 1980s, he never conducted it in New York. Nonetheless, this archive seems close to comprehensive in its coverage of Bernstein's final years on the podium, seen from a New Yorker's perspective, and it achieves closure by documenting his last concert in that city.

Bernstein had long since been granted a throne among the royals of high culture, and he had nothing left to prove by this time in his career. People who spend time illuminated by the performing-arts spotlight tend to be picky about how they look; and although Bernstein was certainly attentive to his appearance (even to the point of being positively dapper when he was so moved), he was comfortable in his skin. "He never mugged or acted for photos," Steve recalls. "If he reacted at all, it would be to deflate a situation he felt was pretentious. He could play havoc with ceremonial occasions. But he never struck a pose to make himself look different strictly for the camera. He was a very unaffected person: he was who he was. In commercial photography, sometimes one needs to effect subtle alterations, to downplay a double chin, to clean up things in general. There's none of that in this book. He was never worried about that aspect of a photo. What he would comment about when reviewing photos was the sense of energy. That's what was most important to him."

Bernstein's quest for self continued to the end, even as he grew increasingly intractable, gasping from emphysema while dragging on a cigarette, a glass of scotch rarely far from his reach. He was living hard in these final laps, but he was hurting. In this collection, we often glimpse him in his grandeur, but we also follow him offstage into a more personal realm. It stands to Steve Sherman's great credit that he was admitted to Bernstein's private world as well as his public one, and that his unintrusiveness enabled him to document such moments in their unvarnished authenticity. These remarkable photographs bring us very close to their subject as he hunts himself, finds himself, defines himself. Through the power of their medium they do much to re-express the nature of his singleness. They ensure that Bernstein will be "hid away" a little less.

—JAMES M. KELLER
April 2010

PREAMBLE

Nadia Reisenberg and Leonard Bernstein at Tanglewood, summer of 1948. Photograph by Robert Sherman.

I GUESS ONE COULD SAY THAT THIS PHOTOGRAPH OF LEONARD BERNSTEIN WITH MY grandmother, the great pianist Nadia Reisenberg, taken by my dad back in 1948, proves that I knew Lenny at least eleven years longer than I've been alive. I certainly feel that way—as a child, my friend Andrew Litton (now a world-class conductor, and still a dear friend) took me to see a few of the Young People's Concerts at New York's Philharmonic Hall (now Avery Fisher Hall), and I remember distinctly being enthralled by this intense man and his wild energy and huge enthusiasm.

I actually met Mr. Bernstein for the first time on an unusually hot and steamy July 4th in 1974 at the Danbury (CT) State Fair Grounds. He was standing with two other men in the blazing noon-day sun on the podium of an outdoor stage, otherwise empty except for the chairs and music stands strewn about. All three men were shirtless and glistening with sweat, animatedly discussing the evening's Charles Ives Centennial Concert. My dad introduced me to Leonard Bernstein, Aaron Copland, and Michael Tilson Thomas, and I dutifully got their autographs, as well as samples of their DNA in the drops of sweat that also anointed my concert program.

The next time I met Bernstein was exactly ten years later, and also with my dad, who was to interview him on the final day of his controversial *West Side Story* recording session. I was just a year back from Jerusalem, where I had worked for a few years as a news and archeological photographer, and in NYC was trying to break into the music biz, so when dad called, I grabbed my cameras and happily went along. Little did I know that this would be the first of many amazing opportunities to photograph the great maestro.

Photographing Lenny was always an event. There was always a buzz in the air, an excitement, an anticipation. When Lenny was in the house, something was going to happen.

You could feel it. Lenny would walk out onstage to begin a rehearsal, and everyone would stop talking or tuning and focus on him. There were always detours on his way to the podium, saying hi to old friends or new ones, with a warm smile, a reminiscence, and if not a hug, then a hand on an arm or a one-handed one-squeeze shoulder massage—he was a very tactile person. But once he hit the podium, he made it clear that he expected 100 percent from each and every musician on the stage. He didn't have to say it—he simply led by example.

He gave all of himself, and allowed his love, his extreme passion, his raw charisma, his powerful convictions, to guide his heart and mind. His fresh and sincere exhilaration for the music, and his insatiable lust for and curiosity about life, infected everyone in the room. As a result we gave him 150 percent back . . . and the results are legendary.

I say we, as if I were one of the musicians. But I was also onstage (or hovering close by), and I found myself equally compelled to rise above my limits, and break through my upper expectations.

And that was good. I was never able to let my guard down for a second—my concentration had to be complete if I wanted to follow where he was going—his energy could burst forth suddenly, and then recede just as quickly. He could conduct with only his shoulders, or his eyebrows, or his feet as he gently bounced his otherwise still body. . . . Whatever it was, it was total immersion.

I think my photos of Lenny are just a bit better than most everything else in my archive. And I wish I could claim credit for that. But I can't—it was simply the way things had to be when photographing Lenny.

· · ·

In 2006, when Judith Clurman, another great friend and fantastic conductor, co-directed the prestigious Leonard Bernstein, Boston to Broadway concerts and symposia at Harvard University, she invited me to create a photo exhibition for this event. Never before had I looked at my complete collection of Bernstein images or tried to put them together into a narrative. The experience was utterly fascinating and exhilarating, and became the genesis for this book.

Any photographic essay is a result of rigorous editing processes, influenced not only by content, emotion, flow, and artistic integrity but practical considerations of time, space, and budget. Only one editing decision was easy: to bypass all my color images in favor of black-and-white, a much more emotionally direct and powerful medium. The other decisions were much more complex, and while I ache for all the wonderful shots that did not make the final cut, I am very happy with my selection. I even managed to include a number of "outtakes."

Normally in concert photography, one "action" photograph is published as the representative or definitive image of a particular event, while most, if not all, others remain unseen. However, the photos taken just seconds before and/or after that primary image, "outtakes," can often place that main image in its wider context and reveal the full arc of the movement and momentum in a way that a single photo cannot. In this book I am excited to show you the "outtakes" surrounding my most iconic images.

I am also delighted that I am able to spice my photo essay with the insightful and learned voices of Lenny's colleagues, friends, and family—in the hope that it helps bring Lenny closer to you and you closer to Lenny. Nothing would have pleased him more.

—STEVE J. SHERMAN
May 2010

TECHNICAL INFORMATION: For the photographically inclined, these photographs were all taken with Canon F1 camera bodies and Canon FD fixed lenses of various focal lengths up to 300 mm F 2.8. They were photographed on Kodak B/W negative films: Tri-X 400 (up to 1986) and T-Max 400 (from 1987 on) and processed in my darkroom with Kodak D-76 developer diluted 1:1. For this book, I scanned all the images from the original negatives on a Nikon Super Coolscan 5000 and prepared them on my Mac G5 computer using Adobe Photoshop; however, they are mostly full frame and unretouched.

ACKNOWLEDGMENTS

Of course, I could never have completed this work without the extraordinary help and support of family, friends, colleagues, and so many others…my thank-you list only scratches the surface.

My most deeply felt thanks…

To Lenny.

To Jamie, Nina, and Alexander Bernstein for your constant support, encouragement, and friendship, and to the people at the Bernstein Office: Craig Urquhart, Marie Carter, Eleonor Sandresky, and Paul Epstein, without whom this could never have happened.

To John Cerullo, my publisher and stalwart guide, who believed in this project from the start—and to Carol Flannery, Godwin Chu, Mary Belibasakis, Diane Levinson, Clare Cerullo, and everyone at Amadeus Press who helped make this book a reality.

To my dad, Robert Sherman, whose brilliant interviews for this book provided much of the text from Lenny's colleagues, and who first introduced me to Lenny, and then did it again.

To all the musicians, friends, and colleagues, who contributed thoughts, stories, remembrances, and anecdotes about Lenny.

To Lauren Bacall, Jamie Bernstein, and James Keller, who graciously gave me such amazing and insightful essays.

To Susanna Ronner of Susanna Ronner Graphic Design, who selflessly offered her services before I even had a publisher, and then designed my most beautiful cover.

To Véronique Firkušný for her unwavering support, invaluable research assistance, and expert language translations from German, Italian, and French.

To Barbara Haws and the New York Philharmonic Archives for their gracious permission to quote from interviews conducted by Robert Sherman and collected for their "Bernstein Live" Special Edition 2000.

To Mark Eden Horowitz and the staff at the Library of Congress Music Division, who so ably helped me through my research inside the Leonard Bernstein Archives.

To Ruth Greenstein and Irene Reichbach of Greenline Publishing Consultants, who took my early idea and worked hard to make it a reality.

To Judith Clurman, who conceived of my first all-Bernstein photography exhibition at Harvard University's 2006 Bernstein Symposium, and who made it all happen. And to Carol J. Oja, Jack Megan, Thomas Lee, and Yoav Liberman of Harvard University for that opportunity, and for their trust and support.

Last but not least, to my children, Fiona and Jesse, my mom, Ruth, my dad, Robert, and their spouses, my brother, Peter, and his family, my former wife, Dorothy Lawson, and to all the rest of my incredible family, past and present, with all my love . . .

And to the following people, with my heartfelt and grateful appreciation and thanks for your inspiration, support, and friendship:

Myril Adler	Ken Heyman
Richard and Barbara Debs	Laura Kaminsky
Mary Lou Falcone	Lawrence Perelman
Gino Francesconi	Robert Perlstein
Meir (Miro) Gal	Charles Prince

And to the following people for helping me locate specific texts for the book, helping me organize the interviews, and/or helping me secure permissions and rights to reproduce these marvelous texts:

Marlene Adler	James Johnson
Renate Anderle	Julia Kadar
Herbert Breslin	Ron Konecky and
Humphrey Burton	Mark Merriman
Ted, Henry, Sam, and	David McGill
Miles Chapin	Lee Musiker
Stephanie Challener	Phyllis Newman
Joanna Chaundy	Charles Pignone
Michael Feinstein	Johnny Planco
Jennifer Freeman	Stephen Plotkin
Byron Gustafson	Ned Rorem
Ruth Henderson	Bill Smith
Ken Hunt	Claire Speciner

—STEVE J. SHERMAN

THE PHOTOGRAPHS

Carnegie Hall, November 6, 1988.

PROLOGUE

"Lenny was the most alive person I've ever worked with."

—Gidon Kremer

"He was a determined humanist, believing in the absolute necessity of decency."

—Isaac Stern

"He left me believing in music, like a religion, and I keep it in my heart, still now."

—Peter Wächter
Vienna Philharmonic Orchestra

Avery Fisher Hall, June 24, 1988.

"He just could not help being totally involved in everything he was doing....
Lenny's emotional commitment was so extreme that he seemed to inject the flow,
the shape of a piece into every single measure."

—JON DEAK
New York Philharmonic

"I saw him do everything at either extreme and everything in between.
He just stayed in the moment, and was so in the present that he could figure out what was right when."

—MICHAEL BARRETT

"I can't stop talking about him. Lenny was unique; he inspired me more than I can ever say.
He was Number One in my book, and always will be. I'll never forget him."

—JOHN WARE
New York Philharmonic

"Nobody can replace that man. I think he influenced everybody who touched him;
he was that kind of amazing personality—you couldn't help but be changed by him."

—GLENN DICTEROW
New York Philharmonic

Central Park (New York), August 4, 1986.

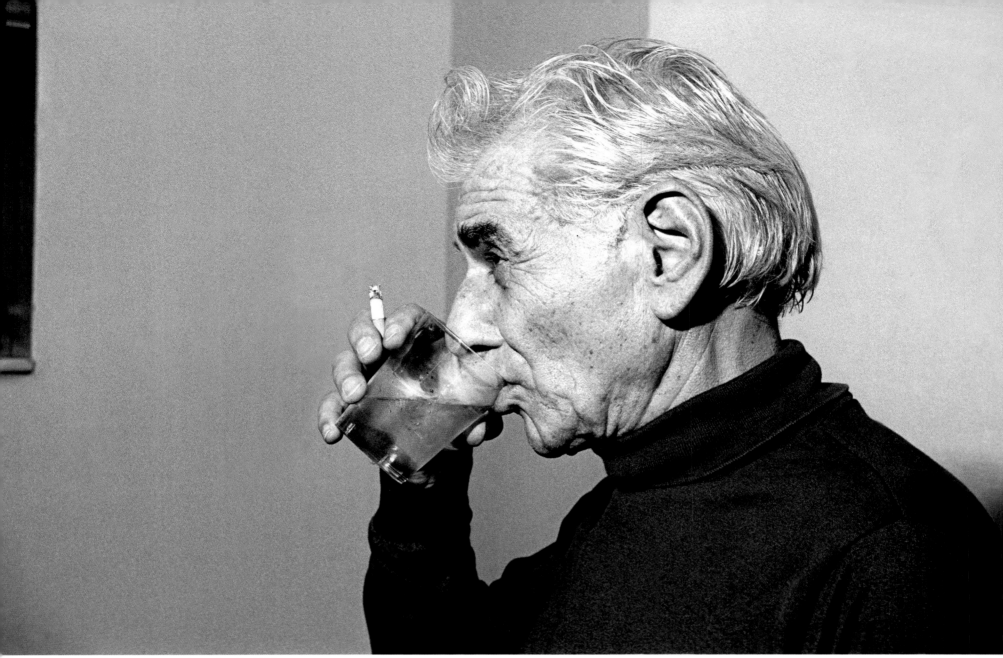

Carnegie Hall dressing room, November 17, 1985.

"He was a great influence, a great teacher, a wonderful collaborator.
He was also nuts—Lenny had his demons."

—MARILYN HORNE

"Despite all the flamboyance, he was very generous of spirit. He was a mensch."
—NED ROREM

Equitable Center (New York), November 8, 1987.

"To me, Lenny was always young, and then he died."
—STANLEY DRUCKER, New York Philharmonic

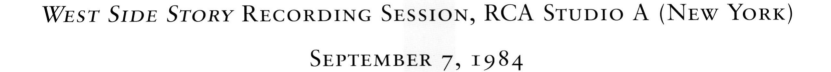

West Side Story Recording Session, RCA Studio A (New York)

September 7, 1984

"In my opinion his artistry and integrity on the podium were much greater than all his idiosyncrasies. He tore down, in one giant stroke, the invisible wall between the classical and popular schools with the score of *West Side Story*."
—Skitch Henderson

"In one recording session, the timpanist didn't enter on time. Lenny made many takes, but not one went the way he wanted. Finally, he stopped the orchestra and asked the timpanist, 'What do you want me to do? Would you like me to shine your shoes?' The next take was successful."
—Avraham Leventhal, Israel Philharmonic Orchestra

INTERVIEW WITH ROBERT SHERMAN

·

During the final day of recording, Robert Sherman of radio station WQXR
sits down with Leonard Bernstein for an exclusive interview.

"It's wonderful. I'd never conducted this piece [*West Side Story*] in my life and I love it. I'm amazed at how fresh it seems, so hot off the press, and it took a lot of doing, a lot of study, because I'd never really studied the score. I've never seen the score, actually. I've seen only the symphonic dances, which I made with a whole new orchestration, and that I've played a lot. I actually never studied *West Side Story* from beginning to end—I was too busy writing it and rehearsing it, and re-composing it."

— LEONARD BERNSTEIN, from the WQXR interview

"With *West Side Story* [recording session in 1984]…the casting was a problem from the get-go…and I got to deal with all these awful headaches that arose…. The sparks were flying—there was so much pressure and so much tension during the whole thing."

—ALISON AMES

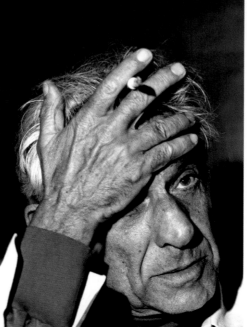

"It was a perfect illustration of Leonard Bernstein, the yin and yang of Leonard Bernstein, his whole life was like that. The flamboyance versus this deep intellectuality, this tremendous emotionality versus the superficial flibbertigibbet joke-telling. He really was a pretty amazing and complicated person. So I was at one time very repelled and very attracted to the whole business, the empire that was Leonard Bernstein."
— ALISON AMES

ISRAEL PHILHARMONIC ORCHESTRA, CARNEGIE HALL

SEPTEMBER 21, 1985

CONCERT

Mahler's Symphony No. 9

•

"The sea of music in which Bernstein bathed…had no shores."

—GIDON KREMER

"He felt himself being somehow the orchestra's godfather.
When he found the players too noisy, he lectured them about the
institution they represented, and the meaning of
being in a world-class orchestra. Each time was a revelation,
and I always longed for his next visit.... We were amazed by
his personality; his aura was quite sweeping.
We miss him so much."

— Jacob Aviram
Israel Philharmonic Orchestra

"He introduced our orchestra to the symphonies of Gustav Mahler.
He was so expressive in explaining this music:
'You have to exaggerate this…' Suddenly *fortepiano*—
pow—'You take the whole bow'—pow—'and off.'
'Only the idea of the sound has to stay—not the tone itself.'
He seemed to *be* Gustav Mahler."

  —Peter Wächter
    Vienna Philharmonic Orchestra

"The first time I wasn't too clear on what his beating technique was — 'You'll get used to it,' he told me later,
'I'm not a beater, I'm an inspirer' — but the orchestral sound was totally transformed the first few moments,
with him conducting. It was electrifying. I just couldn't believe what I heard around me."
— GLENN DICTEROW, New York Philharmonic

"In his last years he found himself even more involved with the indefinable magic of music. He would exclaim,
with a sense of wonder in his voice, how, in going back to perform once again a Brahms symphony — or one
by Tchaikovsky or Mahler — he had to take a clean score, unmarked by his analyses of previous years, in order
to look at the music with fresh eyes, discovering still greater beauties hidden within those lines and dots on
white paper. He found renewed delight in those small spaces between the notes where music truly is made."
— ISAAC STERN

Left to right: Leonard Bernstein conferring with Leonard Stein (ICM artist manager) and Harry Kraut
(Bernstein's manager) prior to the start of the concert. Behind Mr. Stein, in the background, is flutist Ransom Wilson.

3

ISRAEL PHILHARMONIC ORCHESTRA, CARNEGIE HALL

SEPTEMBER 22, 1985

BACKSTAGE

Before the Concert

•

"Lenny was an incredible talent, but he wasn't a businessman.... He needed somebody who was actually as careful as Harry, as shrewd as Harry, and as cultured as Harry was to work with him."
— CRAIG URQUHART

"As Daddy's own father was the first to point out, his son was hopeless at business. With the exponential growth of his career, someone very capable had to oversee all the aspects of his multi-faceted life. Enter Harry.... He could make popes, presidents and queens appear; he could make deranged stalkers go away. He turned Leonard Bernstein into a superstar."
— NINA BERNSTEIN SIMMONS

CONCERT

Bernstein's Halil *and* Symphonic Dances from "West Side Story"

•

"Lenny could become angry, but only for a few moments at rehearsals, especially if someone made a mistake at a place where he had made corrections already. Then he felt frustration at having to repeat such a passage again. He would yell a short 'damn it!'…and that was it. In concert, I never saw him express any anger whatsoever. If something went wrong—a bad entrance, or a missed note, he would simply give a little wink to let you know that he was aware of the 'goof.' It was very much like a father who acknowledged your mistake, but forgave you because he realized that we are all human and these things happen. On the other hand, whenever he was particularly pleased by a musical effort on the part of a performer, he would smile and let you know of his satisfaction, and these smiles were treasured by those who received them!"

—RAY PARNES, Israel Philharmonic Orchestra

CONCERT

Brahms's Symphony No. 1

•

"What influenced me most about Lenny was his ability to persuade the people you're working
with to do something that matches your conviction. A conductor has to be persuasive in the sense that his
musical vision, or conception, communicates in every possible way to the people who are playing.
Lenny's musicianship and communicative gifts let him accomplish that."
—JAMES LEVINE

BACKSTAGE

After the Concert

●

"No matter what he was doing, because he was living five lives at a time, he always had time for his friends. He always wrote thank-you notes, always did little poems for friends for their birthdays, these kind of loving gestures that a man of his stature didn't need to do, but it was his nature to be that way."
— CRAIG URQUHART

With Zubin Mehta. Inside the dressing room, former Bernstein assistant Charlie Harmon (with mustache) behind Bernstein, and ICM president Lee Lamont partially visible behind the door.

With Betty Comden, Adolph Green, and Nancy Walker.

Leonard Bernstein to Betty Comden — "Beddim"

B *lush ye gods, for justice gone awry!*

E *xamine your Wotan callousness, and cry!*

D *ivine you may have been, once, but no more.*

D *own down you go, beneath Walhalla's floor.*

I *nstead, let there be joy, and songs to sing!*

M *y Betty, dearest friend, I cling, I cling . . .*

Betty Comden to Leonard Bernstein — "Lenushka"

What I feel for, with, about and/or by you

L *ove*

E *mpathy*

N *aches*

U *m-beschrie-en*

S *lobbering*

H *appiness*

K *nocked out*

A *ugmented*

Love my flowers
Love my poem
Love you,
Betty

With Isaac Stern.

"[Lenny was] a man whose greatest talent was his mind. He had the most amazing sponge for a brain—
he thought more about more things than anybody I've ever known…and he remembered everything….
Lenny was as close to the over-used word 'genius' as I've known in my time."

—ISAAC STERN

With Isaac Stern and Itzhak Perlman.

"When you play with a conductor who has a strong attitude towards the music, it's infectious, and he was a very warm and effusive personality.... Bernstein was very outgoing, very expressive, very dramatic. He was a dramatic person, even offstage. He would talk about things with great panache. I think he wanted to be Mahler."

—Itzhak Perlman

With Isaac Stern, Itzhak Perlman, and Zubin Mehta.

"Why? They ask me. Why at your advanced age, and with an inevitable sacrifice of precious composing time—why do you do it? Indeed, I repeat inwardly; why? Then the answer comes, twofold: 1) because of deep commitments to certain orchestras and their audiences (Israel, Vienna, New York, Boston, for example), but more important 2) because at least half of this activity involves teaching."

—LEONARD BERNSTEIN (on conducting)

AMERICAN COMPOSER'S ORCHESTRA, CARNEGIE HALL

NOVEMBER 17, 1985

CONCERT

World Premiere of David Diamond's Symphony No. 9 — David Arnold, Baritone

•

"We had a lot of fun doing contemporary music…. The main thing is that he was
convinced about the music, so he convinced us, and when things worked, they worked wonderfully well."

—NEWTON MANSFIELD, New York Philharmonic

Applauding the composer, with baritone David Arnold.

"Especially with contemporary music,
he would take the piece apart in front of
you until you not only played it better,
you understood it better. And eventually,
he made you love it."

— ORIN O'BRIEN
New York Philharmonic

Carnegie Café reception, left to right: Nicolas Roussakis, David Diamond, Francis Thorne,
Paul Lustig Dunkel, Leonard Bernstein, and Erick Friedman.

BACKSTAGE

After the Concert

•

November 18, 1985

Dear Maestro:

I think what you did with the Diamond Symphony was a miracle. No other conductor could
have pulled it off. I studied the piece again today and although there is great beauty in each section
there seem to be tremendous problems in the construction. Yet in the performance one was not
aware of these difficulties.

I was also glad that the orchestra, who are more my friends than my employees, had the
opportunity to play under you. For many it was the first time. For all it was a labor of love.

Very sincerely,
Paul Dunkel

In his dressing room, with Morton Gould and Claire Speciner.

"I myself was touched and moved by your words, and couldn't help being aware of the many hills and valleys traveled from the bittersweet past years to the present. Thanks for sharing yourself with us."

— MORTON GOULD

"Seeing Lenny that day, I had such a warm feeling towards him. I know Lenny is for Lenny, basically—he's not particularly sympathetic to me or my music. My colleagues are basically egos; you have to live around them. However, in Lenny's case, he has every reason to be egotistical."

— MORTON GOULD (diary entry)

"I have been so lucky and blessed, for everything that's happened, and all the privileges that
I've had in my working life, quite apart from the privileges of my personal life. I don't think there's
anything in the world to be more grateful for than the possibility of spending your time
doing what you love, and being with works of art that consume you."

— LEONARD BERNSTEIN

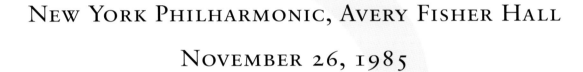

NEW YORK PHILHARMONIC, AVERY FISHER HALL

NOVEMBER 26, 1985

REHEARSAL

Mahler's Symphony No. 7

•

"Bernstein was genuinely enthusiastic at rehearsals. He didn't suddenly turn it on for concerts,
although he certainly had a sense of the dramatic, and what the concert meant. He had a way of absolutely
insisting that a certain passage be a certain way, and he would stay with those few bars until he got it right....
There was so much going on, so much intensity, such nit-picking, that it almost created a crisis
in everybody's life. You couldn't just play a solo according to the legal letter of the notes; he wanted something
special on an emotional level. He wanted you to give, he wanted you to sweat with him. By the
time the concert came, everybody was high-strung, and it would be a great moment."

— JOHN CERMINARO, New York Philharmonic

"Bernstein loved to talk but that's because he loved to teach; he needed to share his ideas about the music and his concepts of what made something tick, what made it interesting or different. He wanted to tell you every last detail, and that's why rehearsals were never long enough with him: he often wanted to go overtime, because he just had one more thing to explain that he couldn't stand for you not to know. His love of the music overcame every other aspect of his personality."

—ORIN O'BRIEN, New York Philharmonic

"He liked to talk, but he rehearsed intensively.... I found him to be my kind of conductor, somebody who choreographs his feelings about the music. Beating time, I find, is a secondary thing. Everybody beats time, but he really showed, in his movements, in his face, what he feels about the music.... He showed the members of the orchestra what he felt. The other thing...was the most amazing way he paced, the inner rhythm.... You can be rhythmic but not feel it. But throughout his body he felt everything."

—ITZHAK PERLMAN

"Lenny loved everybody and he wanted to be loved by everybody, but music came first. He pushed the orchestra, and while we'd gripe about the long rehearsals, we really played for him.... He was a real mensch."

— WALTER BOTTI, New York Philharmonic

"When we had a rehearsal break, most conductors would go down to their dressing room, but Bernstein stayed onstage and talked to us. He liked people—he needed people around him—and we'd have long conversations.... He would ask you questions, listen to your opinions. I found that a very warm, human quality."

— MICHAEL HENOCH, Chicago Symphony Orchestra

"There was always some commotion.
I remember once he got angry.
He stopped the rehearsal and said,
'What the hell is going on here?
The only thing you guys want to do is talk
and talk. There's an incredible amount
of noise; we're here to work.'
Well, he was absolutely right, so we shut up.
And we went on working for ten or
fifteen minutes, and he stopped again, and said,
'What the hell is this, a morgue?'"

—NEWTON MANSFIELD
New York Philharmonic

Left to right: Wolf-Dieter Karwatky (DG recording engineer) and Elisabeth Karwatky greet Leonard Bernstein and Alison Ames (Bernstein's DG senior producer). Background, Harry Kraut is partially visible behind Bernstein, in the center, and Hanno Rinke (DG senior producer) is on the extreme right.

PRESS CONFERENCE AND CONTRACT SIGNING

NEW YORK PHILHARMONIC AND DEUTSCHE GRAMMOPHON

AVERY FISHER HALL

NOVEMBER 26, 1985

"I had to deal with Lenny eye to eye, and it was both scary and really thrilling at the same time, to think that I was in a position to do that, and what an incredible privilege it was."

—ALISON AMES

Left to right: Leonard Bernstein with Hans Fantel, Margaret Carson, and Jennie Williams.

"A complicated and complex man was Leonard Bernstein…on many levels. But he was the *supreme* musician.… He was perhaps happiest when he was passing along knowledge, wisdom, whether in rehearsal…or in a press conference."
— MARTIN BOOKSPAN

"Margaret Carson was Leonard Bernstein's press agent for decades. Tough, classy and good-looking, she could easily have been the template for the original Career Gal. She had a sixth sense for what would work and what was right."
— JAMIE BERNSTEIN

Leonard Bernstein greets members of the press. Left to right: Bernstein with Margaret Carson (Leonard Bernstein's press representative), Martin Bookspan, Israel Horowitz, and Alison Ames.

New York Times reporter Gerald Gold (foreground, facing the camera) taking notes for his article, quoted below. Seated at left, Margaret Carson. Standing, Alison Ames. Seated at the table, left to right: Hanno Rinke, Leonard Bernstein, Christoph Schmökel (DG vice president), and Albert K. Webster (New York Philharmonic general manager).

"Record Notes: New Series Tapes Bernstein Live" by Gerald Gold, *The New York Times*, Dec. 8, 1985:

Leonard Bernstein arrived elated at the reception room atop Avery Fisher Hall after a morning rehearsal the other day, on the eve of a performance with the New York Philharmonic of Mahler's Seventh Symphony.

"I was moved by the rehearsal," he said. "That final movement—the one that's not supposed to work—we got it to work. The orchestra was able to capture the sense of parody." That and many other felicities were duly noted later in the week, when such terms as "gusto" and "triumph" were used in the course of a glowing review by Donal Henahan.

There was another reason for elation—the formal signing of a new, long-term contract between Mr. Bernstein and Deutsche Grammophon, extending an exclusive commitment that, among other things, reunites Mr. Bernstein with the Philharmonic—"my family," he calls it—for a series of recordings taped at live performances....

At the news conference/contract-signing reception, Mr. Bernstein declared his preference for live recordings over studio performances. "Live recordings have a certain spirit," he said. "There's always an extra measure of subtlety, depth, and excitement from the 'improvisatory' nature of performance."

Touching his cufflinks for good luck, Bernstein climbs the stairs to the stage.

NEW YORK PHILHARMONIC, CENTRAL PARK

AUGUST 4, 1986

CONCERT

Bernstein's Serenade — *Glenn Dicterow, Violin*

•

"Lenny would go to a concert 125% prepared, so that he could give 150% — that's the way it was."

— CRAIG URQUHART

"The *Serenade* is incredibly great, one of the great masterpieces certainly from the 20th century.
We played it on tour at least ten times, each one got freer and more expressive.... He sort of let me go on my
way. Certainly he took off when the tuttis arrived—he wasn't in the background, jumping all over the
podium—but I came in with my own concept, and he allowed me to express it."
—GLENN DICTEROW, New York Philharmonic

"In the last years, he looked more tired at the beginning of a rehearsal or performance, but when the music took over, he was his old wonderful self."

—THOMAS STACY
New York Philharmonic

"Lenny was unique—his abilities and his opinions and his
personality simply don't match any other conductor I've worked with."

—LEONARD DAVIS, New York Philharmonic

Bowing, with Glenn Dicterow.

"He had learned to live with his emphysema and his other physical conditions. Once he was onstage, thirty, forty years were erased, and he was like a youth again. When he mounted that podium he was transformed, and he transformed me. He was able to do that—his love of music was infectious; that's what made him so special."

—GLENN DICTEROW, New York Philharmonic

CONCERT

Tchaikovsky's Symphony No. 6, "Pathétique"

Leonard Bernstein being escorted to the stage.

"I think Lenny was a student all his life. I'll never forget his coming in with the Tchaikovsky Sixth Symphony, thrilled like a kid with a new toy, because he'd discovered that the whole first movement was based on appoggiaturas, and he changed our interpretation to emphasize that.... For me it's made that piece work every time I hear it. It's no longer a routine warhorse, because I continue to remember Lenny's enthusiasm about it. The way he made music seem organic, his insights, the way he understood it and the way he would talk about it, have always stayed with me."

—EVANGELINE BENEDETTI
New York Philharmonic

"What he did in concert was totally convincing; to me it just felt magical."

—DANIEL DRUCKMAN
New York Philharmonic

"He was so incredible with certain pieces—the Shostakovich Fifth, for instance, or the [Tchaikovsky] 'Pathétique,' or any Mahler—he opened a whole world to me. He kept growing and changing through the years as well…he seemed to get deeper and deeper into the works we were playing, his concentration was less on Lenny himself, and more about what this thing of music is all about. Everything he did seemed real, it came from someplace very deep within him."

—EVANGELINE BENEDETTI
New York Philharmonic

"Life without music is unthinkable. Music without life is academic.
That is why my contact with music is a total embrace."

—Leonard Bernstein

Greeting audience members following the concert. Craig Urquhart, Bernstein's assistant, is at extreme right.

BACKSTAGE

After the Concert

•

"He loved his fans and he knew how important they were to him because it takes them to make music too.…
One of my jobs was to create space…keep people moving, not let them linger too long with Lenny…
although he knew who he wanted to see."

—CRAIG URQUHART

Left to right: Craig Urquhart and Margaret Carson escort Leonard Bernstein to the stage.

"Three Protégés"

Coaching and Photo Op

Avery Fisher Hall

September 3, 1986

"He was extremely grateful to everybody that worked with him and helped him create, because he was very much aware that he could not do this all on his own."

—Craig Urquhart

Photos op: The maestro and his protégés, affectionately known as the Three Michaels. Left to right: Michael Barrett, Michael Morgan, Leonard Bernstein, and Michael Stern.

"He was the most significant musical influence in my life.... He was very patient, yet very demanding.... He would do things that would continually challenge me.... He was one of the most intuitive human beings.... He knew when to show a little temper, or displeasure, or when to say, 'Okay, come on, baby, that's going to be okay. Just take a big breath. We're going to get through this phrase.'—to be a loving coach or a friend instead of a demanding maestro."

— MICHAEL BARRETT

Leonard Bernstein never could take these photo ops seriously.

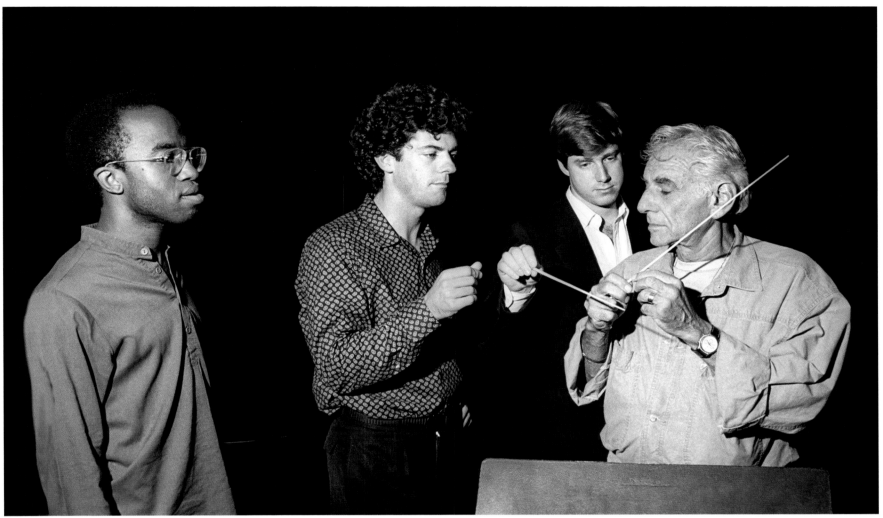

Getting down to real work, Leonard Bernstein coaches (left to right) Michael Morgan, Michael Barrett, and Michael Stern
in preparation for their upcoming New York Philharmonic concert, in which each would conduct one piece.

"You should have learned, with any luck, to love learning. Loving (yourselves, one another, your teachers,
Keats, Euclid, Bach, Beatles) is the only way to genuine learning—that is, learning that will always be part of
you, always animating your mere existence. There is no other way."

—Leonard Bernstein

"There are more young composers per square inch than ever before, but there's a paradox
about the whole thing because there is less and less of an outlet for them: big orchestras don't
want them and big recording companies don't want them, and big publishers don't want them.
And so you say, what's to become of them? Does God want all of these young people?
I mentioned this to Lenny Bernstein once, and he said, 'Well, God wants cockroaches too.'"

—NED ROREM

Filming often involves long periods of waiting…

New York Philharmonic, Carnegie Hall Reopening Gala

December 15, 1986

FILMING THE DRESS REHEARSAL

…or maybe a chance to visit with friends. With Thomas Stacy.

"I found him to be very warm and personable, and a master psychologist, making performers
feel good and wanting to play at 100 percent of their creativity.... He was certainly inspirational to me,
because of his genius as a performer, at transforming the printed page into music. He once said,
'If you hear the beat, it ruins the music.' I use that still as a pedagogue: the beat has to be there, but as the
underpinning of which the listener is unaware.... Once we were rehearsing Copland's *Music for the
Theatre* and I asked Lenny if I should make the English horn solo sound more jazzy. And he said,
'Just make it sound more Tom Stacy.' So, of course, that makes you go beyond what you can do."

—Thomas Stacy
New York Philharmonic

"The orchestra really was like a family for him; he made the atmosphere warm and welcoming, and made me feel like a friend, not just a flute player. He treated everybody that way."

—JULIUS BAKER
New York Philharmonic

With Lorne Monroe and Nathan Stutch.

With Zubin Mehta.

With Isaac Stern.

"I always considered myself extremely fortunate
having Lenny as my guest conductor
every season both in New York and Israel.
Which music director could wish for more?
[We] thoroughly miss him to this day, not only
for his human spirit but for the great
educational impulses he was giving in every
rehearsal and concert he conducted."

—ZUBIN MEHTA

"To make music with him was always
an adventure; nothing was taken for granted.
Together we shared the quest for a deeper
subtlety, a sharper contrast, a sudden
burst of energy, or a sustained quiet, long line.
Most of all, it was so alive; and
nothing was ever done casually."

—ISAAC STERN

"People reacted to him, they were moved by his presence; you just couldn't ignore his intensity as a person."
—STANLEY DRUCKER, New York Philharmonic

CONCERT

World Premiere of Bernstein's Opening Prayer, *Carnegie Hall's First Commission*

•

"Lenny spoke several languages fluently, including New York. He created a tremendous amount of electricity; he came across to us with such emotion and love that he was able to draw out of us more than we thought we had to give.... His whole spirit was such that he really didn't have to do more than walk out on the stage and things happened. We couldn't help responding to him; his concerts were events, not just performances."
—Stanley Drucker, New York Philharmonic

"He gathered energy from the audience, and he just didn't give concerts—they were events...
and part of that event was the energy coming from the audience, the excitement, the anticipation."
—Craig Urquhart

VIENNA PHILHARMONIC ORCHESTRA, CARNEGIE HALL

SEPTEMBER 24, 1987

CONCERT

Mozart's Symphony No. 29 and Sibelius's Symphony No. 5

•

"The orchestra was nervous because he was not an easy person—his was not a calm life. I never had the feeling
that Lenny ever calculated a day… his music making was this way too. The concert time was exciting but
produced the same nervous tension—what can we expect now? What kind of surprise will he give us now?
Is it the same as it was in rehearsal? We all had to get into Lenny's mind—so he got all our attention."

—ERNST OTTENSAMER, Vienna Philharmonic Orchestra

"He had unbelievable rhythm in his body language.
Whenever you had an after-beat or
something else that was tricky, he would give you
the rhythm with the flick of an eyebrow,
or a smile, or just a look."

— Orin O'Brien
New York Philharmonic

"He needed to come as close as he could to the spirit of a
composer, and then he did everything with that kind of intense conviction."
— LEONARD DAVIS, New York Philharmonic

"I'm not interested in having an orchestra sound like itself. I want it to sound like the composer."
— LEONARD BERNSTEIN

"When Vienna came to Carnegie Hall, his style changed not in the making the music but in the circumstances. He was at home."

—Ernst Ottensamer
Vienna Philharmonic Orchestra

BACKSTAGE

After the Concert

•

"When your Mahler started to fill—(but that is the wrong word—because it was more sensitive trembling) the Cathedral today—I thought it the most beautiful music I had ever heard—your music was everything in my heart, of peace and pain and such drowning beauty—you could just close your eyes and be lost in it forever."

—JACQUELINE KENNEDY

Jacqueline Kennedy going backstage to visit the maestro after the concert.

With Leontyne Price.

"Music for Life" AIDS Benefit, Carnegie Hall

November 8, 1987

THE CONCERT

•

*Leonard Bernstein and James Levine conducted a "pickup" orchestra
of New York's finest musicians—members of the New York Philharmonic,
Met Opera Orchestra, New York City Ballet Orchestra, and freelancers—
with a star-studded cast of soloists and celebrities.*

"The music community put together its first benefit after the AIDS epidemic became clear—and they asked Lenny and me to program it. We had a really great time. We met often; the whole point was for us to exchange ideas and come towards each other, and that's exactly what happened. We both felt very strongly about this project and we arrived at solutions very easily, dividing the program up in a really convincing way, so that Lenny did some things he was famous for, but also some he didn't always do. It would have been more typical for me to conduct for Luciano [Pavarotti], for instance, but he did. And I conducted his *Candide* Overture."

—JAMES LEVINE

"Un forte abbraccio con tutto il mio affetto e la più profonda stima di uomo e d'artista."
[A big hug with all my affection and deepest esteem for man and artist.]

—LUCIANO PAVAROTTI

With Luciano Pavarotti.

With Marilyn Horne.

"He was not dictatorial, but I also must say that
when I was working with somebody like Bernstein,
I was really deferring to him a lot. I wasn't going to
throw down a gauntlet much of the time....
One of the most wonderful experiences I had with
him...I thought I knew [this piece] pretty well,
but when I brought it to him, he gave me more
insight into special things—it gave me a
whole other world of knowledge of the piece."

—MARILYN HORNE

With James Levine—as conductors.

"We worked out a way of doing Ives's *Unanswered Question* with Lenny in front of the stage, conducting the strings, and me standing against the back wall facing him, cueing the trumpet and the four flutes in front of me. Acoustically and dramatically, it was the best realization of the piece I ever was in."
—JAMES LEVINE

With James Levine—as pianists.

"It was unusual, but the only really convincing way to end the program was not with some razzle-dazzle finale, but with the slow movement of the Mozart Two-Piano Sonata, especially since this piece has no distracting technical features, so you can concentrate on the music. So many people commented that this focused everyone's feelings, which I had hoped it would."

—JAMES LEVINE

Left to right: Murray Perahia, Marilyn Horne, Leonard Bernstein, Leontyne Price, James Levine, and Samuel Ramey.

BACKSTAGE
Intermission Photo Op

Left to right: Yo-Yo Ma, Charles Wadsworth, James Levine, Leontyne Price, Leonard Bernstein, Marilyn Horne, Luciano Pavarotti, Samuel Ramey, Edgar Bronfman Jr., and Joanne Woodward.

Left to right: Paula Robison, James Levine, Leontyne Price, Luciano Pavarotti, Leonard Bernstein, Samuel Ramey, and Joanne Woodward.

Left to right: James Levine, Leontyne Price, Luciano Pavarotti, Leonard Bernstein, and Joanne Woodward.

Left to right: Betty Comden, Shirley Bernstein, James Levine, and Leonard Bernstein.

POST-CONCERT DINNER
RECEPTION IN THE EQUITABLE CENTER

•

"Every time we were together…he was enormously erudite, perceptive, fun, serious…
the whole spectrum of his personality. He had a capacity for this entire range, all the time."
—JAMES LEVINE

Left to right: Shirley Bernstein, James Levine, and Leonard Bernstein.

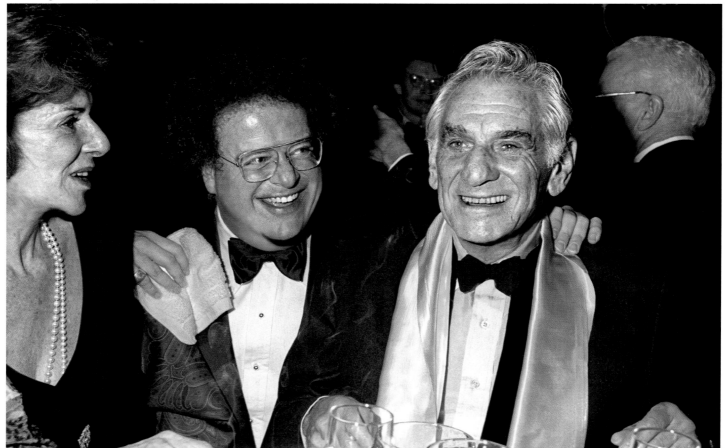

Leonard Bernstein, Rosamond Bernier, and Adolph Green.

"How happy your friendship makes me. It fills me with the simple and complicated joy of knowing there can be a meaning to life—that our haphazard and rambling walk is filled with endless connections into the past and the future. What I'm saying is—I'm not writing—I'm only looking for a way to say I love you, my friend."

—ADOLPH GREEN

Left to right: Shirley Bernstein, Gunter Hensler (standing),
Leonard Bernstein, Alison Ames, Adolph Green, and Nina Bernstein.

When it came time for Leonard Bernstein to rehearse, he appeared onstage draped in Nell Carter's purple boa and wearing shades, to the surprise and delight of everyone present.

12

IRVING BERLIN'S

ONE HUNDREDTH BIRTHDAY GALA REHEARSAL, CARNEGIE HALL

MAY 11, 1988

"My father never grew up, entirely. He was very much a child, with that kind of curiosity, that kind of energy, and that kind of lack of boundaries. That had everything to do with his genius and with his accomplishments."
—ALEXANDER BERNSTEIN

"He was very perverse, absolutely a perverse child in many ways. He was a jokester, absolutely, but I think as with so many jokesters, it was the smiley mask that fit over, that covered the deep tragedy."
—ALISON AMES

"I liked his piano playing very much. His touch was smooth...like a massage for the soul."

—Peter Wächter
Vienna Philharmonic Orchestra

With Rosemary Clooney.

"Lenny was always communicating with people.... It was so natural for LB to not only communicate, but to connect with people.... He had an uncanny sense about what interested you and he made you feel that he knew you better than you imagined he did."

—LEONARD HINDELL
New York Philharmonic

13

IRVING BERLIN'S

ONE HUNDREDTH BIRTHDAY GALA CONCERT, CARNEGIE HALL

MAY 11, 1988

"Lenny's playing was amazing—I've never heard the piano part with such
personality and creativity, it was so poetic, so interesting."

—GLENN DICTEROW
New York Philharmonic

August 25, 1988

Dear Genius,

You are one of the few who deserves everything warm and wonderful that will be said about you on this marvelous occasion of reaching what Abe Lincoln would have called three score and ten.... Be assured, Lenny, that between songs here in Reno, where I am performing tonight, I raise a toast in your honor in gratitude for all you have done for the musical world, which bows towards you in appreciation this day and for all you have done for the personal world I alone inhabit and which is a far better place because of your friendship, which I will always cherish. Happy Birthday, young man. I can hardly wait for your next seventy.

Warmest hugs,
Francis Albert
[Frank Sinatra]

Grand finale, with all singing. Left to right: Madeline Kahn, Rosemary Clooney, Frank Sinatra, Leonard Bernstein, Shirley MacLaine, Walter Cronkite, Isaac Stern, Marilyn Horne, and Tony Bennett, with the U.S. Army Chorus.

LEONARD BERNSTEIN GALA

CULMINATION OF THE AMERICAN SYMPHONY ORCHESTRA LEAGUE'S

ANNUAL CONFERENCE

CHICAGO'S MUSEUM OF SCIENCE AND INDUSTRY

JUNE 18, 1988

"Lenny, Dear…Those Chicago reviews! How rhapsodical can they be?…Love, love—lot's of it, M."
—MARGARET CARSON

"With Lenny, the bombast that accompanied practically everything he did, the way he spoke and dressed
and the rest of his personal habits, in a sense were all a cover-up for a basic shyness.… I don't ever remember
hearing him say, 'I'm the greatest' or 'I'm the authority'; he always left room for a little insecurity."
—LEONARD DAVIS, New York Philharmonic

With Irma Lazarus.

With Skitch Henderson and Schuyler Chapin.

"Dearest LB, You are the biggest problem: how to write about someone you love without making it maudlin, sentimental, vapid and dull. But this very morning I awoke with the problem at least philosophically oriented. The 'thrust' of what I am going to say will be based on a line of your own about Beethoven: accessible without being ordinary. That's you, baby. And away we go!"

—SCHUYLER CHAPIN

"Your thoughts, your friendship, the years, the mountains and the valleys....
Somehow I don't feel that Father Time is an enemy."

—SKITCH HENDERSON

"Austere, outspoken, domineering, elegant, witty and a total professional...it was Maggie's extraordinary skill and charm that opened doors and brought people together."

—CRAIG URQUHART

With Margaret Carson.

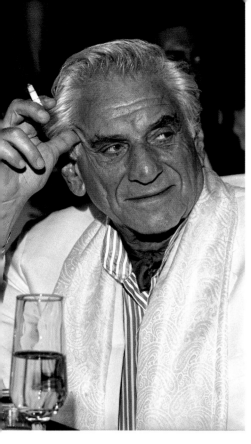

"You couldn't sit down and have a meal with Lenny without learning—
the man's mind was unbelievable. They called him a Renaissance man and there's no
question that he was."

—MARILYN HORNE

Trying to eat dinner . . . (on the right, Morton Gould).

"Everyone wanted a piece of Lenny.... There was this orbit around Lenny...and he was always so gracious."

—CRAIG URQUHART

"Stars...always complain about not ever having a private moment.... Lenny loved it
and hated it at the same time...like one of those scenes where you see all those people looking over
him at the table, where he would have an earnest ten-second chat with you that could be very,
very meaningful to the recipient but probably not so much to him."

—ALISON AMES

With Kenneth Kiesler.

"He was utterly present in that moment; completely and thrillingly 'there.' As soon as
Morton Gould said, 'Lenny, Kenny; Kenny, Lenny. Kenny conducted Lukas's *Renaissance Concerto*
this afternoon,' he took my hands and connected. I could see the piece playing in his memory; he was
so intent, he could have been conducting it himself that day—asking about this bowing and
that chord, a tempo and a phrase.... When I mentioned how his being who he was as a human being
and artist had influenced me and offered my deepest gratitude, he thanked me for my 'sweet words.'
His eyes were moist and he squeezed my hands in his."

—Kenneth Kiesler

"He had this enormous brain, this enormous intellectual ability, and he really *had* read everything—
the fact that he didn't sleep a lot meant that he read a lot."

—ALISON AMES

CHICAGO SYMPHONY ORCHESTRA
AVERY FISHER HALL
JUNE 24, 1988

CONCERT

Shostakovich's Symphony No. 7, "Leningrad"

•

"When he came to us [June 1988], you could tell just by looking at him that his health was failing,
his breathing was difficult, but you'd never know from the music.... He was very outgoing, very emotional,
he generated a lot of electricity.... There was something extremely personal in his approach...
he inspired us, he made us want to give out more, to do something together."

— CHARLES PIKLER
Chicago Symphony Orchestra

"How would I describe Lenny? Uncontrolled Vesuvius!"
—ISAAC STERN

"Lenny was unequivocally a Dionysos."
—GIDON KREMER

"Despite all his aberrations, he is such a unique genius. I have no idea how he survives."
—MORTON GOULD

"Yes, some people complained about his jumping around, but it seemed natural to me.... It was Lenny's totality as a musician, his true collaboration in art, that was unique."

—STANLEY DRUCKER, New York Philharmonic

"Critics often complained that Lenny moved around too much, but I never thought so. What he did was always in the service of the music. And his style went over great with audiences...jumping or no jumping, they went wild for Lenny."

—WALTER BOTTI, New York Philharmonic

"Lenny would trace fast arcs with his hands, he would go from here to there with a bang, and that tends to make you react differently. Working with him was really incredible."

—JON DEAK, New York Philharmonic

"Onstage, Lenny had absolute faith that, for himself as well as for all the musicians in front of him, the greatest thing in life at that moment was playing that particular piece with full wonderment and abandon. None of this was ever contrived—what Lenny felt about music came from deep inside."

—ISAAC STERN

"Playing music on a certain
level is tough, it's hard work,
but in the end it should bring
joy to the players as well as the
audience. Lenny was able to
satisfy both in the same way."

—CLEMENS HELLSBERG
Vienna Philharmonic Orchestra

"I remember him working with
me on the oboe solo in the
Shostakovich *Leningrad* Symphony,
and when I play that piece now,
I can still hear Lenny. No matter
who's conducting, I see him."

— MICHAEL HENOCH
Chicago Symphony Orchestra

"Most audiences
don't know, never realize
what an important
role they play in a concert."

—CLEMENS HELLSBERG
Vienna Philharmonic
Orchestra

"The Shostakovich [Seventh Symphony] is very long, and when we came offstage,
he [Bernstein] said to me, 'Wow, we really got through this.'"
—CHARLES PIKLER, Chicago Symphony Orchestra

"After a performance...Lenny walked off, erect and in full control, but as he left the stage, he seemed to
crumple into a bent figure. He was so emotionally drained that he could barely regain his composure.
He began to tremble, took a drink and a puff from a cigarette that was held for him; remained bent over
for several minutes, then straightened up and went onstage for a bow. This process was repeated again and again—
the audience refused to let him leave. Finally he sent the orchestra off and remained for a long solo bow.
I will never forget this unbelievable transformation which he underwent time and time again."
—RAY PARNES, Israel Philharmonic Orchestra

"His smoking was incessant. I remember…he had a bad spell with his lungs,
and as he came offstage, he had to use a Nebulizer to clear his passages,
but he was smoking at the same time."
—MARILYN HORNE

"I said, 'When are you going to quit smoking? You're a smart guy, you know it's bad for you.'
You know what he answered? 'Why don't you spank me? I'm a bad boy.'"
—JOHN WARE, New York Philharmonic

"I was diagnosed as having
emphysema in my mid-20s,
and to be dead by the age of 35.
Then they said I'd be dead
by the age of 45. And 55.
Well, I beat the rap. I smoke.
I drink. I stay up all night.
I screw around. I'm
overcommitted on all fronts."

—LEONARD BERNSTEIN

Teasing long-time CBS photographer Don Hunstein by fixing his hair before the shoot.

BACKSTAGE

After the Concert, Receiving the CBS Laureate Medal

•

"I can never forget the first time I was introduced to Lenny…as the new head of CBS Masterworks
(and therefore the 'custodian' of his huge recording legacy). Without any further ado, he clamps my cheek
between his two hands, and proceeds to kiss me squarely on the lips. I did not flinch! Harry
[Kraut] told me that I had passed the acid test with Lenny, and from that day forward he considered me to be
his friend and someone he could trust with his catalog. Now, is that spontaneity?"

—JOSEPH DASH

VIENNA PHILHARMONIC ORCHESTRA, CARNEGIE HALL

NOVEMBER 6, 1988

CONCERT

Beethoven's Leonore *Overture No. 3*

•

"They [Vienna Philharmonic Orchestra] are so proud to have this great tradition,
they are so loving of what they do and of who they are. This is something I catch like a disease—
it's so contagious for me because I operate in terms of love."

—LEONARD BERNSTEIN

"Lenny was unique.... His ability to understand
all types of music and convey that understanding to us was pretty
phenomenal.... He wasn't really a taskmaster, either. He cajoled,
he cried, he pleaded, he did whatever it took to get the
results he wanted."

—ALBERT GOLTZER
New York Philharmonic

"He was always dancing with that music—always dancing on the podium.... He was able to put
his energy to the musicians and get his energy back—like ping-pong. For Lenny, the orchestra likes to play."

—PETER WÄCHTER
Vienna Philharmonic Orchestra

"Two years before he died, I saw him jump four feet high and he probably
wouldn't have known that he did it. He was so spontaneous, just so into the music."

—MICHAEL BARRETT

"It was the authenticity. It was always him—he was never a hypocrite.
He was always honest. This was a person who always expressed his own soul,
ready to share his feelings, the good as well as the bad."

—CLEMENS HELLSBERG
Vienna Philharmonic Orchestra

NEW YORK PHILHARMONIC
COMMEMORATION OF THE FORTY-FIFTH ANNIVERSARY
OF LEONARD BERNSTEIN'S CONDUCTING DEBUT
AND HIS SEVENTIETH BIRTH YEAR, CARNEGIE HALL
NOVEMBER 14, 1988

CONCERT

Bernstein's Chichester Psalms

•

הִנֵּה מַה טּוֹב וּמַה נָּעִים שֶׁבֶת אָחִים גַּם יַחַד.

Hine ma tov u'manayim, shevet achim gam yachad.
[How good and pleasant it is for people to dwell together in unity.]

—PSALM 133
(and the ending of Chichester Psalms)

"When he took his stick from one hand to the other, it produced quite a different sound. One of the miracles of the great conductors—he could explain more with the fingers of his hands. The greatest conductors give their expressions of sound with the fingers…with the moving of the hands. With Lenny, also his face."
—PETER WÄCHTER, Vienna Philharmonic Orchestra

"I think he had a much wider range of emotion to express than most other conductors. Yes, it welled out of the music, but it had to be something that he could feel himself, as a person, and therefore relate to in the music."
—PHILIP MYERS, New York Philharmonic

CONCERT

Bernstein's Serenade — *Gidon Kremer, Violin*

•

"In 1986, we were rehearsing his *Serenade* in London [with the London Symphony]. I had already played it many times, also with Bernstein.... I still loved the *Serenade* and strove the get the maximum out of it. Although it was only a rehearsal, I was completely in it. While I was floating so absent-mindedly in the high strains of the violin's sound, Lenny, looking at me awestruck, suddenly, and out loud in front of the entire orchestra, said: 'You play so beautifully! You are so wonderful! Can I marry you?'"

— GIDON KREMER

With Gidon Kremer.

"You had always to be ready for surprises. When we played
the same piece—be it the Brahms Concerto or his own
Serenade—several days in a row, today was never the same as
yesterday, tomorrow never the same as today.... Indeed, one
never knew what to expect on any given evening.... He sought
out risks and was also prepared to put up with the defeats....
It was precisely this creativity that made a performance with
Bernstein so thrilling."

—GIDON KREMER

"With his sound...he succeeded in captivating me
irresistibly.... It was as if secretly I longed to find myself in
him.... It was specifically through Bernstein and his art
that I felt myself encouraged to open up."

—GIDON KREMER

BACKSTAGE AT INTERMISSION

Carnegie Hall Gift Presentation

•

"I found in Lenny a person who allowed me to be myself."

—GIDON KREMER

With Gidon Kremer backstage at intermission.

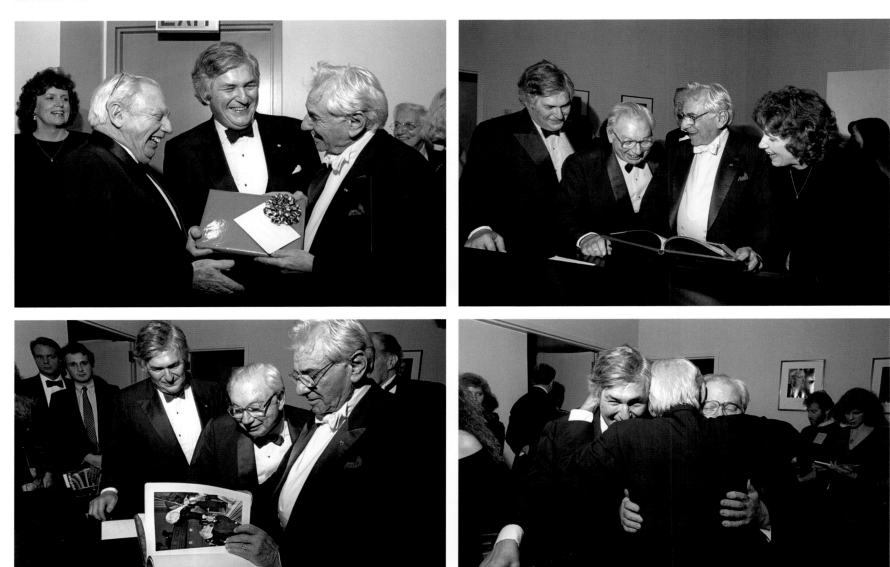

Carnegie Hall's President Isaac Stern, Board Chairman James D. Wolfensohn, and Executive Director Judith Arron
present Leonard Bernstein with a commemorative photo album of his forty-five-year career at Carnegie Hall.

"Leonard Bernstein was for me and my family both an inspiration and…a unique presence
in our lives. His passion, his understanding, and his insight into music helped all of us to reach a new level of
enjoyment and of participation. I shall always remember his personal kindnesses to us, and I shall
treasure the time we were able to have with him."
—JAMES D. WOLFENSOHN

"He was a wonderful, loyal friend."
—ISAAC STERN

ONSTAGE

New York Philharmonic Gift Presentation

•

"Here's the box story, which my father told when he accepted that award you have the
picture of: "My father explained that when he was very young, his mother took him to meet Santa Claus
at Filene's department store in Boston. Why his very Jewish mother thought this was a good idea
I'm not sure, but anyway, off they went, and they stood in line for a very long time. Finally it was my father's
turn to sit in Santa's lap. Santa had been doing this for many hours, and he was clearly tired, plus
he reeked of alcohol. 'So,' he said wearily, 'what would *you* like for Christmas, little boy?' My father became
tongue-tied. What should he say? A bicycle? A ball? Finally, he gathered the courage to speak, and said:
'A b-... a b-... a—*box*!'
"'And now,' my father said at the ceremony, waving his award, 'I got one!'"

—JAMIE BERNSTEIN

Leonard Bernstein is presented with a commemorative gift box
by New York Philharmonic Chairman Stephen Stamas (left) and
members of the New York Philharmonic board.

CONCERT

Bernstein's Symphony No. 2, "The Age of Anxiety"—Krystian Zimerman, Piano

•

"Lenny was all encompassing…sometimes he'd love us and sometimes he'd hate us, but we responded no matter what."
—NEWTON MANSFIELD, New York Philharmonic

"In his last years, I noticed him trying to go even deeper into the music, and of course he was starting from an already pretty deep place.... He would try to milk things, to extract more heat or more juice, or more pathos out of the music. That seemed to be what he cared most about, he was striving towards something deeper."

—MICHAEL BARRETT

"Lenny always transferred some of his energy and power to his soloists.
Here they are to be found, the vibrations of inspiration, which are so difficult to describe
in words and which make the performer float above the music."

—GIDON KREMER

With Krystian Zimerman following their performance.

"I probably played under a couple of hundred conductors during my forty years in the New York Philharmonic, but Lenny was Number One, the finest all-around music director we ever had.... Lenny inspired us to make music from the heart, to play above and beyond what we thought we could do.... I give Lenny all the credit. I may have pushed the buttons and blown through the horn, but the whole inspiration came from him.... Lenny made things happen emotionally."

—JOHN WARE
New York Philharmonic

With concertmasters Glenn Dicterow and Charles Rex (left) at the end of the concert.

PHOTO SESSION — DOUBLE PORTRAIT
WITH DENNIS RUSSELL DAVIES
AVERY FISHER HALL GREENROOM
NOVEMBER 29, 1988

"I treasure the memories that…[he] inspired. I have come to admire and
revere a man who, with all of his other achievements, must be acknowledged as a great composer.
His voice is clearly heard today through his music."

—DENNIS RUSSELL DAVIES

During the session, Ned Rorem and Gidon Kremer stopped in to say hi after rehearsing
Rorem's violin concerto with the New York Philharmonic.

"Basically, Lenny's personality didn't change over the years. He was always full of himself,
and full of music, and full of talent, and he was able to put all of that energy to good use."

—Ned Rorem

Leonard Bernstein on piano, with his children, left to right: Alexander Bernstein, David Thomas (Jamie's former husband), Jamie Bernstein, and Nina Bernstein. Turning pages for Bernstein is Mark Stringer.

"CHILDREN WILL LISTEN"

BENEFIT FOR CHILDREN WITH AIDS

CARNEGIE HALL

JANUARY 30, 1989

CONCERT

World Premiere of Close Together,
Co-Written by Jamie and Leonard Bernstein and Performed by the Bernstein Family

•

"My father, at one point in his last years, said to me, 'I'm so sick of *LEONARD BERNSTEIN*.' He felt that he'd become something of an industry, something over which he no longer had much control. Family became even more important to him in many ways because of it."
—ALEXANDER BERNSTEIN

"He loved his kids, hugely, and I was always tremendously envious of his kids but also proud of him for the relationship they had with him. They knew they were loved."
—ALISON AMES

VIENNA PHILHARMONIC ORCHESTRA

CARNEGIE HALL

MARCH 7, 1990

*These concerts would become Bernstein's last performances
at Carnegie Hall, and indeed his last in New York.*

"I think the rehearsal period [March 1990] was a kind of farewell, not consciously but in his heart."
—CLEMENS HELLSBERG, Vienna Philharmonic Orchestra

"There's no doubt in the last years, he had to deal with some illness—what human being doesn't?—
but there was so much talent, so much vitality in the man, so much going on in his mind....
I just loved him so much, because of the way it was all there, and after he died I missed him a lot.
His was a singular personality that we will not see again."
—JAMES LEVINE

"I can tell you exactly the last contact I had with him. The Vienna Philharmonic was in town...1990.
I had sung the Mahler Third with Jimmy [James Levine] the night before, and on the program
this time was Lenny conducting Bruckner Nine. He didn't conduct much Bruckner, you know,
and I really wanted to hear it...I went because of Lenny."
—MARILYN HORNE

CONCERT

Bruckner's Symphony No. 9

•

"He was larger than life, just an amazing force of nature,
and his heart was on his sleeve at all times."

—GLENN DICTEROW
New York Philharmonic

"With extraordinary intelligence, Lenny attempted, through music and words,
to make sadness and joy audible, perceptible and tangible to humankind."

—GIDON KREMER

"You somehow felt that you were playing just for Lenny at that moment. As a conductor, in other words, he had the ability to inspire us individually as well as collectively. I felt that he wanted each person to really do his utmost, and for all of us to put in our personalities as well as being part of the group. I've not experienced that kind of oneness on a collective emotional level with any other conductor."
—EVANGELINE BENEDETTI, New York Philharmonic

"I don't think there's a musician alive who was in contact with Lenny who didn't find an incredible change in his own personality. You just couldn't help having some of that brilliant personality rub off on you."

—GLENN DICTEROW
New York Philharmonic

"I miss him, of course…. Lenny always breathed very naturally and he knew such a lot about music.
He was not a man who needed a lot of words to explain it—he could show it, and that for me
is the greater genius…. We need somebody who loves the music, not to make it from the
brain and think of their bank account. Lenny was like that."

—Peter Wächter
Vienna Philharmonic Orchestra

"Leonard Bernstein as an artist penetrated into the collective consciousness….
His talent, his cosmopolitan ambitions, his emotional generosity: all spoke to people as a matter of course….
He himself with all his contradictions was one of the few truly creative figures of our century."

—Gidon Kremer

HIS FINAL BOWS

•

"Everybody who loved him or loved to play with him was a bit worried about the way he lived,
but it wouldn't have made any sense if he would have lived differently. He died at the age of seventy-two, but
he lived a life so full of music, so full of humanity, so full of interest in philosophy, religion,
culture, and music, as well as in human beings, all together was of such an intensity that a normal average man
would have needed at least 120 years.... So I refuse to say that he died at the age of seventy-two—
just as I refuse to say that Mozart died at the age of less than thirty-six years."

—CLEMENS HELLSBERG
Vienna Philharmonic Orchestra

LEONARD BERNSTEIN'S FINAL PERFORMANCES IN NEW YORK WERE VINTAGE BERNSTEIN; on the podium, he was as powerful and vital as ever. After the last notes had sounded and the audience erupted in a surging ovation, he bowed with the orchestra and walked off the stage, exhausted. Backstage, I imagine as was his custom, he toweled off, knocked down a scotch, and dragged on a waiting cigarette before heading out for more bows. He loved his audiences, and took great energy from their extraordinary level of adoration, yet on this night with the ovation reaching the decibel level of those rare, fabled, and never forgotten "Carnegie roars," Bernstein did not face them with his characteristic smile, grace, or gratified delight. On the contrary, I saw a gentle but profound sadness in his eyes as he slowly gazed out across the hall, starting on his left and turning to his right as if in slow motion, as if oblivious to the wild ovation around him, as if to take in every possible gold-leafed detail of his magnificent hall, and to look into each and every face of his people, to reach out and touch each beating heart…

Exhaustion? The after-effect of Bruckner? I sensed a melancholy much deeper; I stood transfixed, strangely moved as I watched this long, quiet journey. These were the last photos I would ever take of Leonard Bernstein.

Years later, as I looked at these photos, I e-mailed his daughter Jamie and asked if he knew at that time that he was dying. She e-mailed back: "I don't know the answer to the question. But he knew 'something wasn't right' as far back as that January. I think maybe he had a feeling."

— STEVE J. SHERMAN

EPILOGUE

"And so ended the last chapter in the life of one of the most remarkable and flamboyant artists and towering musical presences of the twentieth century. In his music he had expressed the spirit of a restless, yearning, anxious age. Through his teaching, conducting, and cultural leadership he had given inspiration to entire generations of musicians and music lovers. Early in his life he became America's best-known classical musician; by the time of his death, he truly belonged to the world."

—Humphrey Burton

"It's the artists of the world, the feelers and the thinkers, who will ultimately save us, who can articulate, educate, defy, insist, sing and shout the big dreams. Only the artists can turn the 'Not-Yet' into reality.... And there's no time to lose.... You've got to work fast, but not be in a hurry. You've got to be patient, but not passive. You've got to recognize the hope that exists in you, but not let impatience turn it into despair.... And out of this paradox you have to produce the brilliant synthesis...it is you who must produce it, with your new atomic minds, your flaming, angry hope, and your secret weapon of art."

—Leonard Bernstein

NOTES

Epigraph

vi "And so I have lived": Leonard Bernstein, "Beauty and Truth Revisited," part II, August 8, 1988, Library of Congress Music Division—Leonard Bernstein Archive, Box 101.

Prologue

3 "Lenny was the most": Gidon Kremer, interview with Robert Sherman, January 11, 2010.

3 "He was a determined": Isaac Stern, preface to *Bernstein Remembered* (New York: Carol & Graf, 1991), 7.

3 "He left me believing": Peter Wächter, interview with the author, January 14, 2010.

4 "He just could not": Jon Deak, interview with Robert Sherman, July 8, 2000, *Bernstein Live Program Notes*, New York Philharmonic CD booklet, 136.

4 "I saw him do": Michael Barrett, interview with Robert Sherman, November 11, 2009.

5 "I can't stop talking": John Ware, interview with Robert Sherman, July 8, 2000, *Bernstein Live at the New York Philharmonic*, New York Philharmonic CD booklet, 72.

5 "Nobody can replace": Glenn Dicterow, interview with Robert Sherman, September 28, 2009.

6 "He was a great": Marilyn Horne, interview with Robert Sherman, November 15, 2009.

7 "Despite all the flamboyance": Ned Rorem, interview with Robert Sherman, October 22, 2009.

7 "To me, Lenny was": Stanley Drucker, interview with Robert Sherman, summer 1999.

Chapter 1

9 "In my opinion his artistry": Skitch Henderson, program notes to *Berlin to Bernstein: A Celebration of Their Music*, Carnegie Hall, November 8, 1991.

9 "In one recording session": Avraham Leventhal, interview with Robert Sherman, October 30, 2009.

10 "It's wonderful": Leonard Bernstein, interview with Robert Sherman for WQXR Radio, September 7, 1984.

10 "With *West Side Story*": Alison Ames, interview with the author, January 25, 2010.

11 "It was a perfect": Alison Ames, interview with the author, January 25, 2010.

Chapter 2

13 "The sea of music": Gidon Kremer, *Obertöne [Harmonics]* (Salzburg: Residenz Verlag, 1998), 140.

14 "He felt himself being": Jacob Aviram, interview with Robert Sherman, December 19, 2009.

16 "He introduced our orchestra": Peter Wächter, interview with the author, January 14, 2010.

17 "The first time I": Glenn Dicterow, interview with Robert Sherman, September 28, 2009.

17 "In his last years": Isaac Stern, preface to *Bernstein Remembered* (New York: Carol & Graf, 1991), 7.

Chapter 3

19 "Lenny was an incredible": Craig Urquhart, interview with the author, January 28, 2010.

19 "As Daddy's own father": Nina Bernstein Simmons, "Harry J. Kraut: April 11, 1933–December 11, 2007," *Prelude, Fugue & Riffs*, Spring/Summer 2008, 6.

20 "Lenny could become angry": Ray Parnes, interview with Robert Sherman, October 31, 2009.

21 "What influenced me most": James Levine, interview with Robert Sherman, January 30, 2010.

22 "No matter what he": Craig Urquhart, interview with Edward Seckerson, *The Independent*, January 21, 2010.

22 "B lush ye gods": Leonard Bernstein, personal letter—acrostic poem written for Betty Comden, Yom Kippur, September 1985, Library of Congress Music Division—Leonard Bernstein Archive, Box 98.

22 "What I feel for": Betty Comden, personal letter, May 5, 1988, Library of Congress Music Division—Leonard Bernstein Archive, Box 16.

23 "[Lenny was] a man": Isaac Stern, interview with Robert Sherman, July 8, 2000, *Bernstein Live Program Notes*, New York Philharmonic CD booklet, 172.

24 "When you play with": Itzhak Perlman, interview with Robert Sherman, September 30, 2009.

25 "Why? They ask me": Leonard Bernstein, "An Aging Maestro Reports," July 28, 1988, Library of Congress Music Division—Leonard Bernstein Archive, Box 101.

Chapter 4

27 "We had a lot": Newton Mansfield, interview with Robert Sherman, July 18, 2000, *Bernstein Live at the New York Philharmonic*, New York Philharmonic CD booklet, 61.

28 "Especially with contemporary": Orin O'Brien, interview with Robert Sherman, c. 1999, *Bernstein Live at the New York Philharmonic*, New York Philharmonic CD booklet, 79.

29 "Dear Maestro": Paul Lustig Dunkel, personal letter, November 18, 1985, Library of Congress Music Division—Leonard Bernstein Archive, Box 19.

30 "I myself was touched": Morton Gould, personal letter, May 5, 1988, Library of Congress Music Division—Leonard Bernstein Archive, Box 25.

30 "Seeing Lenny that day": Morton Gould, diary entry in *Morton Gould: American Salute*, by Peter Goodman (New York: Amadeus Press, 2000), 325.

31 "I have been so": Leonard Bernstein, interview with Arnold Michaelis for WQXR Radio, 1968.

Chapter 5

33 "Bernstein was genuinely enthusiastic": John Cerminaro, interview with Robert Sherman, Aspen Music Festival, 1993, *New York Philharmonic—The Historic Broadcasts 1923 to 1987* CD booklet, 89.

34 "Bernstein loved to talk": Orin O'Brien, interview with Robert Sherman, c. 1999, *Bernstein Live at the New York Philharmonic*, New York Philharmonic CD booklet, 77.

34 "He liked to talk": Itzhak Perlman, interview with Robert Sherman, September 30, 2009.

35 "Lenny loved everybody": Walter Botti, interview with Robert Sherman, July 12, 2000, *Bernstein Live at the New York Philharmonic*, New York Philharmonic CD booklet, 64.

35 "When we had a rehearsal": Michael Henoch, interview with Robert Sherman, December 16, 2009.

36 "There was always some": Newton Mansfield, interview with Robert Sherman, July 18, 2000, *Bernstein Live at the New York Philharmonic*, New York Philharmonic CD booklet, 59–61.

Chapter 6

39 "I had to deal": Alison Ames, interview with the author, January 25, 2010.

40 "A complicated and complex": Martin Bookspan, interview with Robert Sherman, April 2, 2010.

40 "Margaret Carson was": Jamie Bernstein, "Diminished Ranks," *Prelude, Fugue & Riffs*, Spring/Summer 2008, 6.

41 "Leonard Bernstein arrived elated": Gerald Gold, "Record Notes; New Series Tapes Bernstein," *The New York Times*, December 8, 1985.

Chapter 7

43 "Lenny would go": Craig Urquhart, interview with the author, January 28, 2010.

44 "The *Serenade* is incredibly": Glenn Dicterow, interview with Robert Sherman, September 28, 2009.

45 "In the last years": Thomas Stacy, interview with Robert Sherman, November 11, 2009.

46 "Lenny was unique": Leonard Davis, interview with Robert Sherman, July 21, 2000, *Bernstein Live at the New York Philharmonic*, New York Philharmonic CD booklet, 75.

47 "He had learned to live": Glenn Dicterow, interview with Robert Sherman, September 28, 2009.

49 "I think Lenny was": Evangeline Benedetti, interview with Robert Sherman, July 23, 2000, *Bernstein Live at the New York Philharmonic*, New York Philharmonic CD booklet, 58.

50 "What he did in concert": Daniel Druckman, interview with Robert Sherman, July 28, 2000, for *Bernstein Live Program Notes*, New York Philharmonic CD booklet, 197.

50 "He was so incredible": Evangeline Benedetti, interview with Robert Sherman, July 23, 2000, *Bernstein Live at the New York Philharmonic*, New York Philharmonic CD booklet, 56.

51 "Life without music": Leonard Bernstein, "A Total Embrace," November 10, 1967.

53 "He loved his fans": Craig Urquhart, interview with the author, January 28, 2010.

Chapter 8

55 "He was extremely grateful": Craig Urquhart, interview with Edward Seckerson, *The Independent*, January 21, 2010.

56 "He was the most": Michael Barrett, interview with Robert Sherman, November 11, 2009.

57 "You should have learned": Leonard Bernstein, letter to junior high school students, March 2, 1988, Library of Congress Music Division—Leonard Bernstein Archive, Box 101.

58 "There are more young": Ned Rorem, interview with Robert Sherman for WQXR Radio, October 9, 1993.

Chapter 9

62 "I found him to be": Thomas Stacy, interview with Robert Sherman, November 11, 2009.

63 "The orchestra really was": Julius Baker, interview with Robert Sherman, July 12, 2000, *Bernstein Live at the New York Philharmonic*, New York Philharmonic CD booklet, 73.

64 "I always considered myself": Zubin Mehta, e-mail to the author, April 22, 2008.

64 "To make music with": Isaac Stern, preface to *Bernstein Remembered* (New York: Carol & Graf, 1991), 7.

65 "People reacted to him": Stanley Drucker, interview with Robert Sherman, c. 2000.

67 "Lenny spoke several": Stanley Drucker, interview with Robert Sherman, c. 1997.

67 "He gathered energy from": Craig Urquhart, interview with the author, January 28, 2010.

Chapter 10

69 "The orchestra was nervous": Ernst Ottensamer, interview with the author, January 14, 2010.

70 "He had unbelievable rhythm": Orin O'Brien, interview with Robert Sherman, c. 1999, *Bernstein Live at the New York Philharmonic*, New York Philharmonic CD booklet, 79.

71 "He needed to come": Leonard Davis, interview with Robert Sherman, July 21, 2000, *Bernstein Live at the New York Philharmonic*, New York Philharmonic CD booklet, 77.

71 "I'm not interested": Leonard Bernstein, in *Musical Events—A Chronicle 1983–1986, by* Andrew Porter (New York: Summit Books, 1987).

72 "When Vienna came": Ernst Ottensamer, interview with the author, January 14, 2010.

74 "When your Mahler started": Jacqueline Kennedy Onassis, personal letter, June 8, 1968, Library of Congress Music Division—Leonard Bernstein Archive, Box 32.

Chapter 11

78 "The music community put": James Levine, interview with Robert Sherman, January 30, 2010.

79 "Un forte abbraccio": Luciano Pavarotti, personal telegram, August 25, 1988, Library of Congress Music Division—Leonard Bernstein Archive, Box 43.

80 "He was not dictatorial": Marilyn Horne, interview with Robert Sherman, November 15, 2009.

81 "We worked out a way": James Levine, interview with Robert Sherman, January 30, 2010.

82 "It was unusual": James Levine, interview with Robert Sherman, January 30, 2010.

86 "Every time we were": James Levine, interview with Robert Sherman, January 30, 2010.

87 "How happy your friendship": Adolph Green, personal letter, c. 1968, Library of Congress Music Division—Leonard Bernstein Archive, Box 25.

Chapter 12

89 "My father never grew up": Alexander Bernstein, from *Leonard Bernstein: A Total Embrace* (film), by Nina Bernstein Simmons, 2005.

89 "He was very perverse": Alison Ames, interview with the author, January 25, 2010.

90 "I liked his piano": Peter Wächter, interview with the author, January 14, 2010.

91 "Lenny was always communicating": Leonard Hindell, interview with Robert Sherman, December 15, 2009.

Chapter 13

93 "Lenny's playing was": Glenn Dicterow, interview with Robert Sherman, C. 1999, *Bernstein Live Program Notes*, New York Philharmonic CD booklet, 154.

94 "Dear Genius": Frank Sinatra, personal letter, August 25, 1988, Library of Congress Music Division—Leonard Bernstein Archive, Box 51.

Chapter 14

97 "Lenny, Dear": Margaret Carson, personal letter, June 23, 1988, Library of Congress Music Division—Leonard Bernstein Archive, Box 11.

97 "With Lenny, the bombast": Leonard Davis, interview with Robert Sherman, July 21, 2000, *Bernstein Live at the New York Philharmonic*, New York Philharmonic CD booklet, 75.

98 "Dearest LB": Schuyler Chapin, personal letter, August 19, 1976, Library of Congress Music Division—Leonard Bernstein Archive, Box 12.

98 "Your thoughts": Skitch Henderson, personal letter, January 1988, Library of Congress Music Division—Leonard Bernstein Archive, Box 28.

98 "Austere, outspoken": Craig Urquhart, "Remembering Maggie," *MusicalAmerica.com*, October 17, 2007.

99 "You couldn't sit down": Marilyn Horne, interview with Robert Sherman, November 15, 2009.

100 "Everyone wanted a piece": Craig Urquhart, interview with the author, January 28, 2010.

100 "Stars . . . always complain": Alison Ames, interview with the author, January 25, 2010.

101 "He was utterly present": Kenneth Kiesler, e-mail to the author, April 8, 2010.

102 "He had this enormous": Alison Ames, interview with the author, January 25, 2010.

Chapter 15

105 "When he came to us": Charles Pikler, interview with Robert Sherman, December 16, 2009.

106 "How would I describe Lenny?" Isaac Stern, interview with Robert Sherman, 2000, *Bernstein Live Program Notes*, New York Philharmonic CD booklet, 172.

106 "Lenny was unequivocally": Gidon Kremer, *Obertöne [Harmonics]* (Salzburg: Residenz Verlag, 1998), 140.

106 "Despite all his aberrations": Morton Gould, in *Morton Gould: American Salute,* by Peter Goodman (New York: Amadeus Press, 2000), 325.

108 "Yes, some people complained": Stanley Drucker, interview with Robert Sherman, c. 2000.

108 "Critics often complained": Walter Botti, interview with Robert Sherman, July 12, 2000, *Bernstein Live at the New York Philharmonic*, New York Philharmonic CD booklet, 64.

108 "Lenny would trace": Jon Deak, interview with Robert Sherman, July 8, 2000, *Bernstein Live Program Notes*, New York Philharmonic CD booklet, 137.

109 "Onstage, Lenny": Isaac Stern, interview with Robert Sherman, c. 2000, *Bernstein Live Program Notes*, New York Philharmonic CD booklet, 172.

110 "Playing music on": Clemens Hellsberg, interview with the author, January 14, 2010.

110 "I remember him working": Michael Henoch, interview with Robert Sherman, December 16, 2009.

113 "Most audiences don't know": Clemens Hellsberg, interview with the author, January 14, 2010.

114 "The Shostakovich": Charles Pikler, interview with Robert Sherman, December 16, 2009.

114 "After a performance": Ray Parnes, interview with Robert Sherman, October 31, 2009.

115 "His smoking was incessant": Marilyn Horne, interview with Robert Sherman, November 15, 2009.

115 "I said, 'when are you . . .'": John Ware, interview with Robert Sherman, July 8, 2000.

116 "I was diagnosed": Leonard Bernstein, written for *USA Today*, August 1986, in *Leonard Bernstein, by* Humphrey Burton (New York: Anchor Books, 1994), 484.

117 "I can never forget": Joseph Dash, CBS Masterworks general manager, e-mail to Robert Sherman, 15 September 2009.

Chapter 16

119 "They [Vienna Philharmonic Orchestra] are so proud": Leonard Bernstein, 1984, in *Leonard Bernstein*, by Humphrey Burton (New York: Anchor Books, 1994), 478.

120 "Lenny was unique": Albert Goltzer, interview with Robert Sherman, July 19, 2000, *Bernstein Live at the New York Philharmonic*, New York Philharmonic CD booklet, 52.

122 "He was always dancing": Peter Wächter, interview with the author, January 14, 2010.

122 "Two years before": Michael Barrett, interview with Robert Sherman, November 11, 2009.

123 "It was the authenticity": Clemens Hellsberg, interview with the author, January 14, 2010.

Chapter 17

127 "When he took his stick": Peter Wächter, interview with the author, January 14, 2010.

127 "I think he had": Philip Myers, interview with Robert Sherman, July 12, 2000, *Bernstein Live Program Notes*, New York Philharmonic CD booklet, 175.

129 "In 1986, we were": Gidon Kremer, *Obertöne [Harmonics]* (Salzburg: Residenz Verlag, 1998), 144.

130 "You had always to be ready": Gidon Kremer, interview with Robert Sherman, January 11, 2010.

130 "With his sound": Gidon Kremer, *Obertöne [Harmonics]* (Salzburg: Residenz Verlag, 1998), 142.

131 "I found in Lenny": Gidon Kremer, interview with Robert Sherman, January 11, 2010.

132 "Leonard Bernstein was for me": James D. Wolfensohn, letter to the author, April 21, 2008.

132 "He was a wonderful": Isaac Stern, preface to *Bernstein Remembered* (New York: Carol & Graf, 1991), 7.

133 "Here's the box story": Jamie Bernstein, e-mail to the author, February 3, 2010.

134 "Lenny was all encompassing": Newton Mansfield, interview with Robert Sherman, July 18, 2000, *Bernstein Live at the New York Philharmonic*, New York Philharmonic CD booklet, 59.

135 "In his last years": Michael Barrett, interview with Robert Sherman, November 11, 2009.

136 "Lenny always transferred": Gidon Kremer, *Obertöne [Harmonics]* (Salzburg: Residenz Verlag, 1998), 144.

137 "I probably played under": John Ware, interview with Robert Sherman, July 8, 2000, *Bernstein Live at the New York Philharmonic*, New York Philharmonic CD booklet, 70.

Chapter 18

140 "I treasure the memories": Dennis Russell Davies, fax to the author, April 10, 2008.

141 "Basically, Lenny's personality": Ned Rorem, interview with Robert Sherman, October 22, 2009.

Chapter 19

143 "My father, at one point": Alexander Bernstein, e-mail to the author, April 14, 2010.

143 "He loved his kids": Alison Ames, interview with the author, January 25, 2010.

Chapter 20

145 "I think the rehearsal": Clemens Hellsberg, interview with the author, January 14, 2010.

145 "There's no doubt": James Levine, interview with Robert Sherman, January 30, 2010.

145 "I can tell you exactly": Marilyn Horne, interview with Robert Sherman, November 15, 2009.

146 "He was larger than life": Glenn Dicterow, interview with Robert Sherman, September 28, 2009.

147 "With extraordinary intelligence": Gidon Kremer, *Obertöne [Harmonics]* (Salzburg: Residenz Verlag, 1998), 140.

148 "You somehow felt": Evangeline Benedetti, interview with Robert Sherman, July 23, 2000, *Bernstein Live at the New York Philharmonic CD*, New York Philharmonic booklet, 56–58.

149 "I don't think": Glenn Dicterow, interview with Robert Sherman, summer 1999, *New York Philharmonic—An American Celebration Vol. 2* CD booklet, 49.

151 "I miss him, of course": Peter Wächter, interview with the author, January 14, 2010.

151 "Leonard Bernstein as an artist": Gidon Kremer, *Obertöne [Harmonics]* (Salzburg: Residenz Verlag, 1998), 141–146.

His Final Bows

153 "Everybody who loved him": Clemens Hellsberg, interview with the author, January 14, 2010.

156 "I don't know the answer": Jamie Bernstein, e-mail to the author, 2006.

Epilogue

159 "And so ended": prologue to *Leonard Bernstein*, by Humphrey Burton (New York: Anchor Books, 1994), xx.

159 "It's the artists of the world": Leonard Bernstein, speaking to Tanglewood students, July 8. 1970, in *Leonard Bernstein*, by Humphrey Burton (New York: Anchor Books, 1994), 398–399.

VOICES

ESSAYISTS

Lauren Bacall is an internationally renowned actress, Hollywood legend, and Broadway star. She was married to Humphrey Bogart and was Leonard Bernstein's longtime neighbor and close friend.

Jamie Bernstein, the eldest child of Leonard Bernstein and Felicia Montealegre, is an acclaimed narrator, writer, performer, and broadcaster, who has transformed a lifetime of loving music into a career of sharing her knowledge and enthusiasm with others.

James M. Keller is program annotator of the New York Philharmonic and the San Francisco Symphony. During the 2008–'09 season, he served as Leonard Bernstein Scholar in Residence at the New York Philharmonic. From 1990 to 2000, he wrote about music, recordings, and the concert scene on staff at *The New Yorker*.

Robert Sherman, who conducted most of the artist interviews in this book, is a multi-award-winning broadcaster; creator and host of *The Listening Room* and The McGraw-Hill Companies' *Young Artists Showcase* on WQXR, and since 1969, *Woody's Children*, now on WFUV. A former *New York Times* critic and columnist, he is an author, concert narrator, and faculty member of The Juilliard School. *[Author's note: For me, the most famous thing about Robert Sherman is that he's my dad. What an absolute pleasure and delight (and how lucky I am) to finally work together with Dad on such a project.]*

TEXT CONTRIBUTORS

Alison Ames, Bernstein's senior producer—Deutsche Grammophon Records

Jacob Avriham, recording engineer—Israel Philharmonic Orchestra

Julius Baker, flutist—New York Philharmonic

Michael Barrett, pianist/conductor/Bernstein's conducting assistant

Evangeline Benedetti, cellist—New York Philharmonic

ALEXANDER BERNSTEIN, second child of Leonard Bernstein and Felicia Montealegre/president of the Bernstein Family Foundation/Chairman of the Leonard Bernstein Center for Learning

JAMIE BERNSTEIN, first child of Leonard Bernstein and Felicia Montealegre/narrator/writer/performer/broadcaster

NINA BERNSTEIN SIMMONS, third child of Leonard Bernstein and Felicia Montealegre/actress/journalist/film maker

LEONARD BERNSTEIN

MARTIN BOOKSPAN, broadcaster/writer/voice of the New York Philharmonic

WALTER BOTTI, double bassist—New York Philharmonic

HUMPHREY BURTON, TV director/producer/Bernstein biographer

MARGARET CARSON, Bernstein's longtime publicist

JOHN CERMINARO, French hornist—New York Philharmonic

Schuyler Chapin, general manager— Metropolitan Opera/Bernstein's close personal friend

BETTY COMDEN, composer/librettist/Bernstein's close personal friend

JOSEPH DASH, CBS Masterworks general manager

DENNIS RUSSELL DAVIES, conductor—American Composer's Orchestra

LEONARD DAVIS, violist—New York Philharmonic

JON DEAK, double bassist—New York Philharmonic

GLENN DICTEROW, violinist/concertmaster—New York Philharmonic

STANLEY DRUCKER, clarinetist—New York Philharmonic

DANIEL DRUCKMAN, percussionist—New York Philharmonic

PAUL LUSTIG DUNKEL, flutist/conductor—American Composer's Orchestra/Westchester Philharmonic

GERALD GOLD, journalist—*The New York Times*

ALBERT GOLTZER, oboist—New York Philharmonic

MORTON GOULD, composer/conductor

ADOLPH GREEN, composer/Bernstein's close personal friend

CLEMENS HELLSBERG, violinist—Vienna Philharmonic Orchestra

SKITCH HENDERSON, pianist/bandleader/conductor—New York Pops

MICHAEL HENOCH, oboist—Chicago Symphony Orchestra

LEONARD HINDELL, bassoonist—New York Philharmonic

MARILYN HORNE, mezzo-soprano

JACQUELINE KENNEDY (Jacqueline Kennedy Onassis), former First Lady

KENNETH KIESLER, conductor

GIDON KREMER, violinist

AVRAHAM LEVENTHAL, violist—Israel Philharmonic Orchestra

JAMES LEVINE, conductor—Metropolitan Opera/Boston Symphony Orchestra

NEWTON MANSFIELD, violinist—New York Philharmonic

ZUBIN MEHTA, conductor—New York Philharmonic

PHILIP MYERS, French hornist—New York Philharmonic

ORIN O'BRIEN, double bassist—New York Philharmonic

ERNST OTTENSAMER, clarinetist—Vienna Philharmonic Orchestra

RAY PARNES, trombonist—Israel Philharmonic Orchestra

LUCIANO PAVAROTTI, tenor

ITZHAK PERLMAN, violinist

CHARLES PIKLER, violist—Chicago Symphony Orchestra

NED ROREM, composer/Bernstein's close personal friend

STEVE J. SHERMAN, photographer and author of this book

FRANK SINATRA—vocalist/entertainer/American icon

THOMAS STACY, English hornist—New York Philharmonic

ISAAC STERN, violinist/president of Carnegie Hall

CRAIG URQUHART, Bernstein's last personal assistant/senior consultant of the Leonard Bernstein Office

PETER WÄCHTER, violinist—Vienna Philharmonic Orchestra

JOHN WARE, trumpeter—New York Philharmonic

JAMES D. WOLFENSOHN, chairman emeritus of Carnegie Hall/former president of the World Bank

INDEX

ABOUT THE AUTHOR

Steve J. Sherman is one of New York City's premier performing arts photographers, widely recognized for his close, long-term associations with Carnegie Hall and the *New York Times*. His photos have been featured in countless books and magazines, on CD and DVD covers worldwide, in television documentaries on most major networks, and have been exhibited at many museums, including the International Center of Photography and the Metropolitan Museum of Art.

Sherman is also a peace and justice activist. He lives in New York City with his children. Readers can visit his website at www.stevejsherman.com.